W9-CNR-869

Teacher Wraparound Edition

Glencoe Spanish 1

¡Buen viaje!

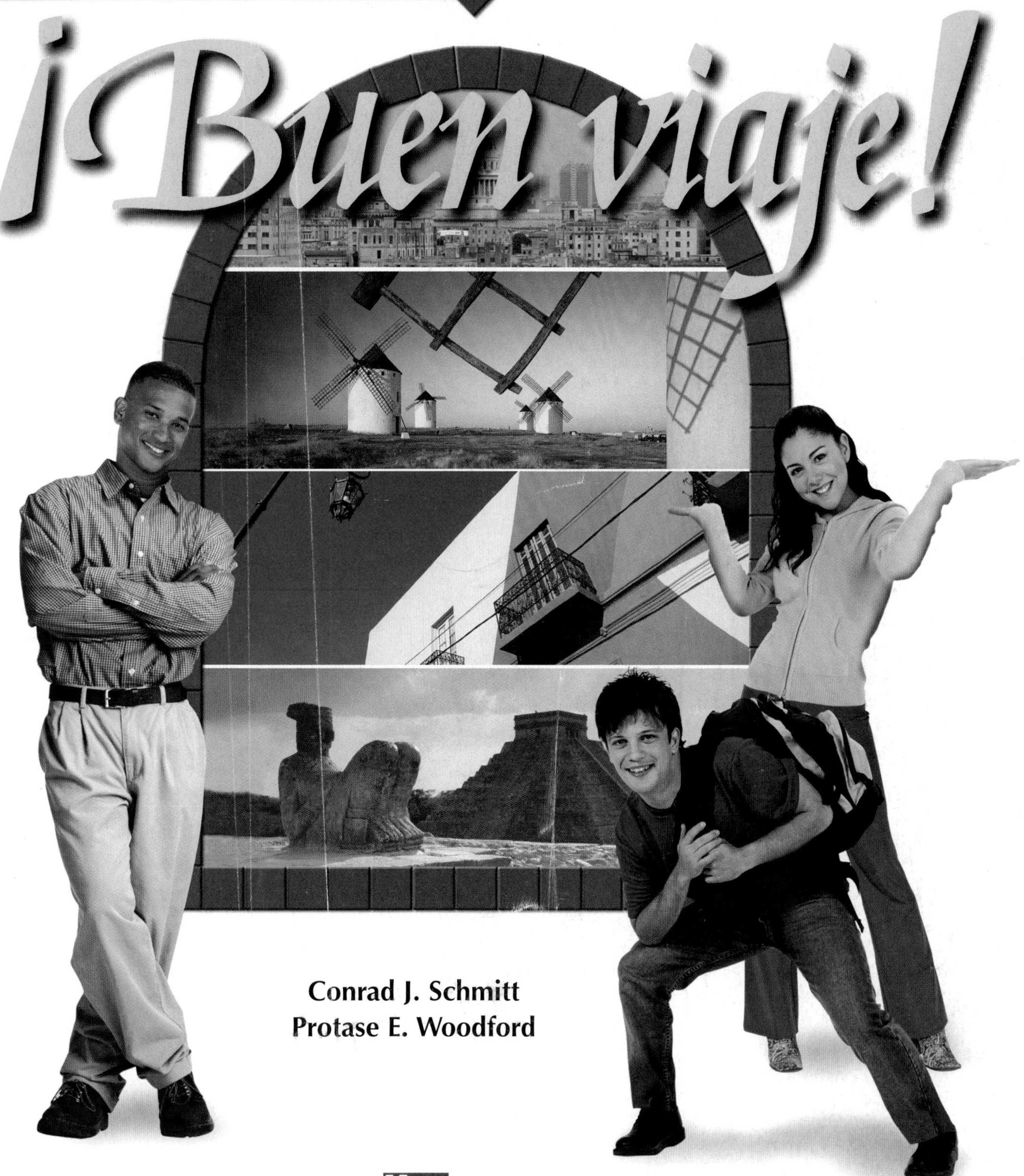

Conrad J. Schmitt
Protase E. Woodford

McGraw Hill Glencoe

New York, New York   Columbus, Ohio   Chicago, Illinois   Peoria, Illinois   Woodland Hills, California

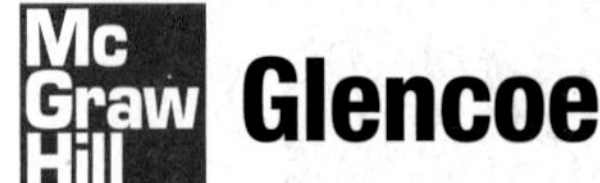

The McGraw-Hill Companies

Send all inquiries to:
Glencoe/McGraw-Hill
8787 Orion Place
Columbus, Ohio 43240-4027

ISBN 0-07-846570-2 *(Student Edition)*
ISBN 0-07-861951-3 *(Teacher Wraparound Edition)*

Printed in the United States of America

2 3 4 5 6 7 8 9 10 055/071 10 09 08 07 06 05 04

From the Authors

Itinerary for Success

- ✓ Exposure to Hispanic culture
- ✓ Clear expectations and goals
- ✓ Thematic, contextualized vocabulary
- ✓ Useful and thematically linked structure
- ✓ Progressive practice
- ✓ Real-life conversation
- ✓ Cultural readings in the target language
- ✓ Connections to other disciplines . . . in Spanish!
- ✓ Recycling and review
- ✓ High-interest articles from **People en español**

Dear Spanish Teacher,

Welcome to Glencoe's **¡Buen viaje!** Spanish program. We hope you will find that the way in which we have organized the presentation of the Spanish language and Hispanic cultures will make the Spanish language more teachable for you and more learnable for your students.

Upon completion of each chapter of **¡Buen viaje!** your students will be able to communicate in Spanish in a real-life situation. The high-frequency, productive vocabulary presented at the beginning of the chapter focuses on a specific communicative topic and covers key situations where students would have to use Spanish to survive. The structure point that follows the vocabulary presentation will enable students to put their new words together to communicate coherently.

After students acquire the essential vocabulary and structure needed to function in a given situation, we present a realistic conversation that uses natural, colloquial Spanish and, most importantly, Spanish that students can readily understand. To introduce students to the culture of the Hispanic world, the chapter topic is subsequently presented in a cultural milieu in narrative form. The **Lecturas culturales** recombine known language and enable students to read and learn—in Spanish—about the fascinating cultures of the people who speak Spanish.

Any one of us who has taught Spanish realizes the importance of giving students the opportunity to practice, a factor so often overlooked in many textbooks today. Throughout **¡Buen viaje!** we provide students with many opportunities to use their Spanish in activities with interesting and varied, but realistic, formats. The activities within each chapter progress from simple, guided practice to more open-ended activities that may use all forms of the particular structure in question. Finally, activities that encourage completely free communication enable students to recall and reincorporate all the Spanish they have learned up to that point.

We are aware that your students have varied learning styles and abilities. For this reason we have provided a great deal of optional material in **¡Buen viaje!** to permit you to pick and choose material appropriate for the needs of your classes. In this Teacher Wraparound Edition we have clearly outlined the material that is required, recommended, or optional in each chapter.

Many resources accompany **¡Buen viaje!** to help you vary and enliven your instruction. We hope you will find these materials not only useful but an integral part of the program. However, we trust you will agree that the Student Text is the lifeline of any program; the supporting materials can be used to reinforce and expand upon the themes of the main text.

Again, we hope that your yearlong journey with each of your classes will indeed be a **¡Buen viaje!**

Atentamente,

Conrad J. Schmitt • Protase E. Woodford

Teacher Edition

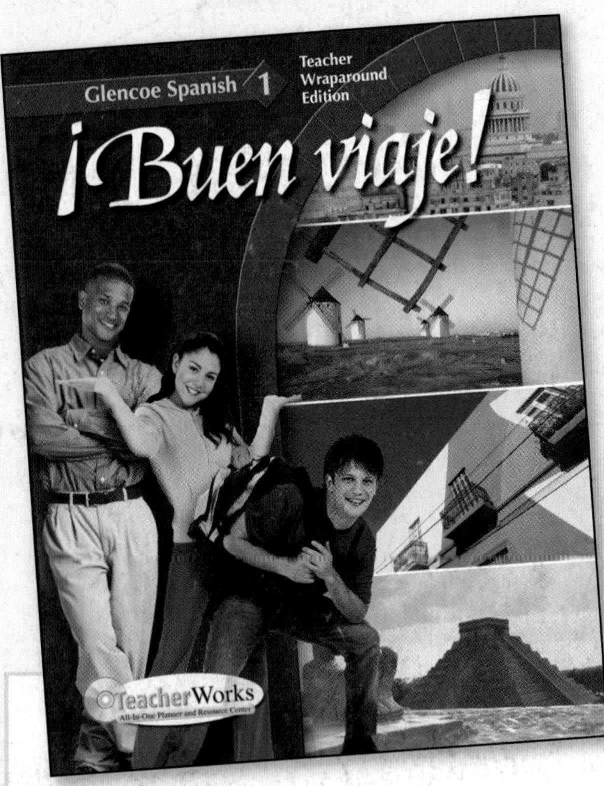

Student Edition

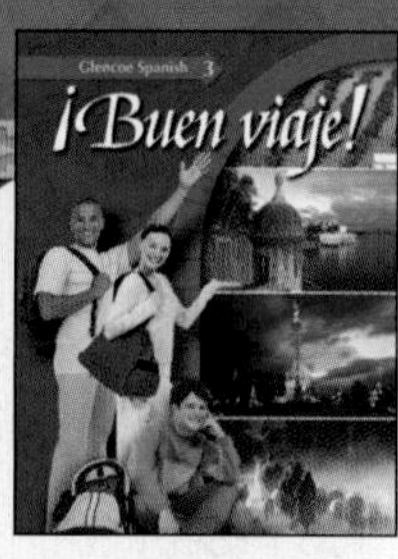

Glencoe's **¡Buen viaje!** is a carefully articulated program written by experienced authors. The Scope and Sequence of **¡Buen viaje!** ensures that students are presented with material in a way that enables them to build the skills they need to become proficient in Spanish. To allow you flexibility in moving through the program there is a review section at the beginning of **¡Buen viaje!** Level 2. In addition Chapters 13 and 14 of Level 1 are repeated as Chapters 1 and 2 of Level 2. The subjunctive is presented in Chapter 12 of **¡Buen viaje!** Level 2 but is presented as brand new material in **¡Buen viaje!** Level 3

LEVEL 1

Preliminary Lessons

Topics
- Greeting people
- Saying good-bye
- Being courteous
- Ordering food
- Days of the week
- Asking the day
- Months of the year
- Asking the date
- Numbers 0–30
- Seasons

Culture
- Calendario maya
- Puerto Vallarta, México
- El besito, dar la mano, el abrazo
- Formality
- Salamanca, España
- Guanajuato, México
- Buenos Aires, Argentina
- El Cinco de Mayo

Functions
- How to greet people
- How to say good-bye to people
- How to express simple courtesies
- How to find out and tell the days of the week
- How to find out and tell the months of the year
- How to count from 0–30
- How to find out and tell the seasons of the year

Capítulo 1

Topics
- Describing people
- Describing places
- Numbers 0–30

Culture
- Francisco de Goya, *Muchachos trepando a un árbol*
- *El Quijote,* the novel
- Miguel de Cervantes Saavedra
- Map of Spain (featuring La Mancha)
- Pablo Picasso, *Don Quijote*
- Alicia Bustelo, student from Venezuela
- Map of Venezuela
- Two Latin American heroes: Simón Bolívar and José de San Martín
- Connections—Geographical terms in Spanish

Functions
- How to ask or tell who someone is
- How to ask or tell what something is
- How to describe yourself or someone else
- How to ask or tell where someone is from
- How to ask or tell what someone is like

Structure
- Singular forms of definite and indefinite articles—**el, la, un, una**
- Singular forms of adjectives
- Present singular forms of the verb **ser**

Capítulo 2

Topics
- School
- Class subjects
- Numbers 31–99
- Telling time
- Nationalities

Culture
- Juan Carlos Liberti, *Concierto barroco*
- Alejandro Chávez and Guadalupe Garza, two Mexican Americans
- Raúl Ugarte and Marta Dávila, two Cuban Americans
- San Antonio, a bilingual city
- The Alamo, San Antonio, Texas
- Coyoacán, México
- The Frida Kahlo museum
- Connections—Latin American ethnicities
- Diego Rivera, *La almendra del cacao*

Functions
- How to describe people and things
- How to talk about more than one person or thing
- How to discuss classes in school
- How to express opinions about classes
- How to tell time
- How to tell at what time an event takes place

Structure
- Plural forms of nouns, articles, and adjectives
- Present plural forms of **ser**
- Telling time

LEVEL 1

Capítulo 3

Topics
- School supplies
- Shopping
- Clothing, sizes
- Color
- Numbers 100–1999

Culture
- Joaquín Torres-García, *Art in Five Tones and Complimentaries*
- Julio Torres, a student from Madrid
- Discussing differences between school in the United States and in Spanish-speaking countries
- El Retiro, Madrid, España
- Indigenous clothing in Central and South America
- A famous clothing designer: Oscar de la Renta
- Connections—Computers and technology

Functions
- How to identify and describe school supplies
- How to describe articles of clothing
- How to ask questions while shopping
- How to state color and size preference
- How to speak to people formally and informally

Structure
- Singular forms of **-ar** verbs (present tense)
- **Tú** versus **usted**

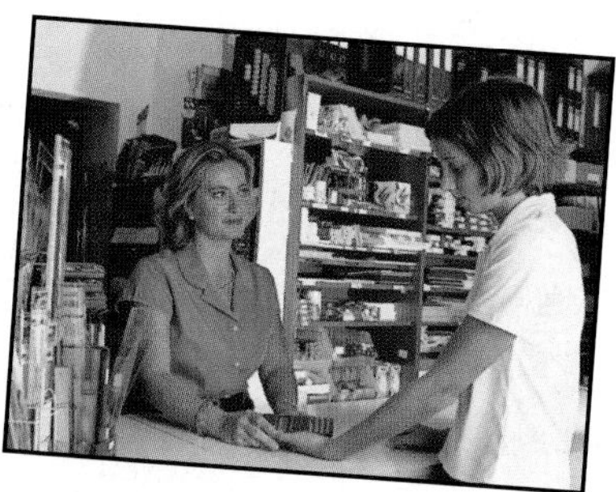

Capítulo 4

Topics
- Going to school
- The school day
- Activities at school
- Numbers 1,000–999,999,999

Culture
- Diego Rivera, *Alfabetización*
- Paula and Armando, two students from Miraflores, Perú
- Differences between schools in the United States and in Spanish-speaking countries
- Miraflores, Perú
- La Universidad de Santo Domingo
- Chilean poet, Gabriela Mistral
- Connections—Biology terms in Spanish

Functions
- How to discuss going to school
- How to talk about school activities
- How to greet people and ask how they feel
- How to tell how you feel
- How to describe where you and others go
- How to describe where you and others are

Structure
- Plural forms of **-ar** verbs (present tense)
- Present of **ir, dar,** and **estar**
- Contractions **al** and **del**

Capítulo 5

Topics
- Eating at a café
- Foods and beverages
- Shopping for food

Culture
- Bernardita Zegers, *Don Diego y doña Patricia*
- A café in Madrid, España
- Meal times in Spanish-speaking countries
- Buenos Aires, Argentina
- Open-air markets and supermarkets in Spanish-speaking countries
- Connections—Math terms in Spanish

Functions
- How to order food or a beverage at a café
- How to identify some food
- How to shop for food
- How to talk about activities

Structure
- Forms of **-er** and **-ir** verbs (present tense)

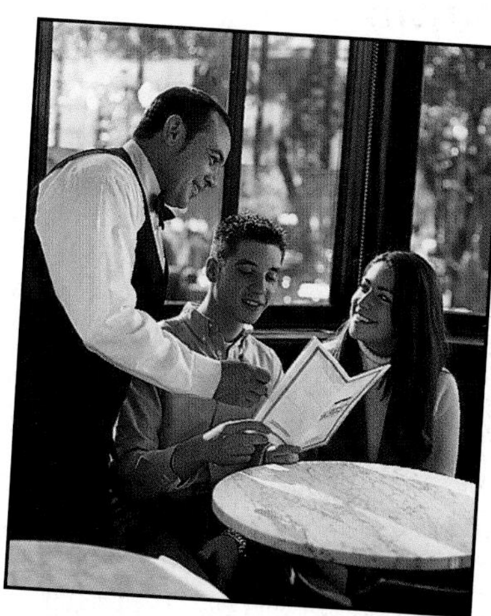

LEVEL 1

Capítulo 6

Topics
- Family relationships
- Houses and apartments
- Rooms in houses and apartments
- Telling your age, birthdays

Culture
- María Izquierdo, *Mis sobrinos*
- The Hispanic family
- La Sagrada Familia, Barcelona, España
- La quinceañera
- Diego Velázquez, *Las Meninas*
- Connections—Great artists from Spain and Latin America
- Frida Kahlo, *Autorretrato*
- Francisco de Goya, *El tres de mayo*
- José Clemente Orozco, *Zapatistas*
- El Greco, *El entierro del Conde de Orgaz*

Functions
- How to talk about your family
- How to describe your home
- How to tell your age and find out someone else's age
- How to tell what you have to do
- How to tell what you are going to do
- How to tell what belongs to you and to others

Structure
- Present of **tener**
- **Tener que, ir a**
- Possessive adjectives

Capítulo 7

Topics
- El fútbol
- Parts of the body
- Baseball
- Basketball

Culture
- Ángel Zarraga, *Futbolistas en el llano*
- El fútbol in Spain
- The World Cup
- Baseball
- Jai alai
- Connections—Archeological terms in Spanish
- Copán, Honduras
- Chichén Itzá, México
- Ponce, Puerto Rico

Functions
- How to talk about team sports and other physical activities
- How to tell what you want to, begin to, and prefer to do
- How to talk about people's activities
- How to express what interests, bores, or pleases you

Structure
- Stem-changing verbs in the present e → ie
- Stem-changing verbs in the present o → ue
- **Interesar, aburrir,** and **gustar**

Capítulo 8

Topics
- Minor illness
- Emotions
- The doctor's office
- More parts of the body
- The pharmacy

Culture
- Pablo Picasso, *Head of a Medical Student*
- Visiting the doctor's office
- Differences between pharmacies in the United States and in Spanish-speaking countries
- Cuban American doctor Antonio Gassett
- Connections—Information about nutrition in Spanish

Functions
- How to explain a minor illness to a doctor
- How to describe some feelings
- How to have a prescription filled at a pharmacy
- How to describe characteristics and conditions
- How to tell where things are and where they're from
- How to tell where someone or something is now
- How to tell what happens to you or someone else

Structure
- **Ser** and **estar**
- **Me, te, nos**

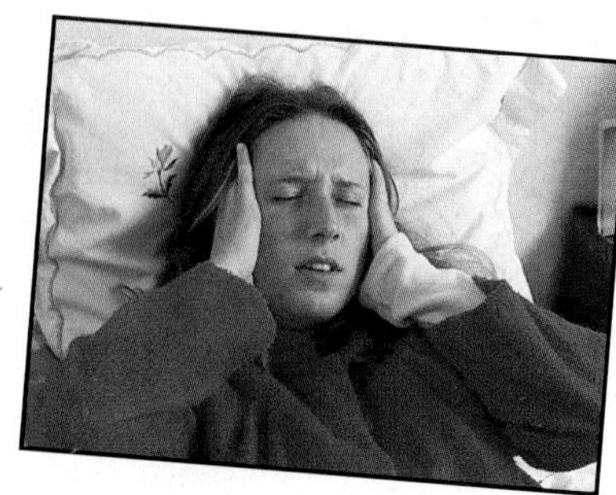

LEVEL 1

Capítulo 9

Topics
- Summer weather and activities
- Winter weather and activities

Culture
- Daniel Hernández, *A Breath of Fresh Air*
- World-class beaches and resorts in Spanish-speaking countries
- Marbella, España
- Cancún, México
- La playa de Varadero, Cuba
- Playa de Guajataca, Puerto Rico
- Pocitos, Uruguay
- Opposite seasons in the northern and southern hemispheres
- Snowboarding in Chile and Argentina
- Connections—Weather and climate in Spanish-speaking countries

Functions
- How to describe summer and winter weather
- How to talk about summer activities and sports
- How to talk about winter sports
- How to discuss past actions and events
- How to refer to people and things already mentioned

Structure
- Preterite tense of **-ar** verbs
- Pronouns—**lo, la, los, las**
- **Ir** and **ser** in the preterite

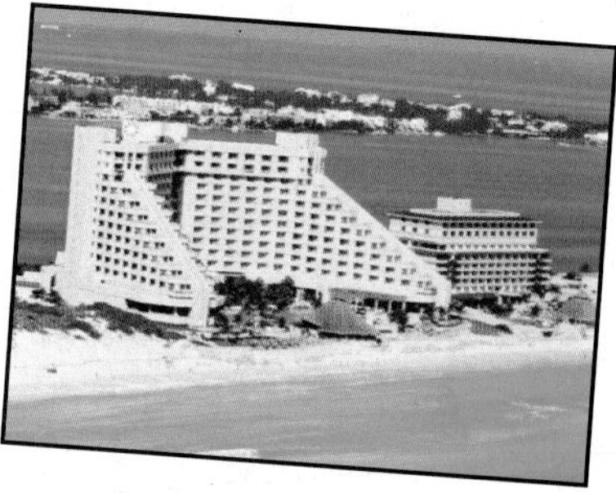

Capítulo 10

Topics
- Attending cultural events
- Taking the bus, subway

Culture
- Rufino Tamayo, *Músicos*
- Dating in Spanish-speaking countries
- Teatro Colón, Lima, Perú
- La Zarzuela
- El Ballet Folklórico de México
- Connections—Fine Arts in the Spanish-speaking world

Functions
- How to discuss movies, museums, and theater
- How to discuss cultural events
- How to relate more past actions or events
- How to tell for whom something is done

Structure
- Preterite of **-er** and **-ir** verbs
- Indirect object pronouns—**le, les**

Capítulo 11

Topics
- Air travel

Culture
- Alexander Aramburo Maldonado, *San Francisco to New York in One Hour*
- The importance of air travel in South America
- The Andes mountains
- The Amazon river
- Comparing the flight time from New York to Madrid and the flight time from Caracas to Buenos Aires
- The Nazca lines in Perú
- Connections—Everyday finances in the Spanish-speaking world

Functions
- How to check in for a flight
- How to talk about some services on board the plane
- How to get through the airport after deplaning
- How to tell what you or others are currently doing
- How to tell what you know and whom you know

Structure
- Present tense of **hacer, poner, traer,** and **salir**
- Present progressive
- Present tense of **saber** and **conocer**

LEVEL 1

Capítulo 12

Topics
- Daily routines
- Grooming habits
- Having breakfast
- Camping

Culture
- Susana González-Pagliere, *Southern Lake*
- Iván Orama describes a backpacking trip in northern Spain
- El lago Enol en el Parque Nacional de Covadonga, España
- San Sebastián, España
- El Camino de Santiago
- The cathedral in Santiago de Compostela, España
- Galicia, España
- Hostal de los Reyes Católicos, Santiago de Compostela
- Connections—Ecology in the Spanish-speaking world

Functions
- How to describe your personal grooming habits
- How to talk about your daily routine
- How to tell some things you do for yourself

Structure
- Reflexive verbs
- Stem-changing reflexive verbs

Capítulo 13

Topics
- The train station
- Traveling by train

Culture
- Casimiro Castro, *Álbum del ferrocarril mexicano*
- Taking the AVE from Madrid to Sevilla
- Plaza de España, Sevilla
- Torre del Oro, Sevilla
- Taking a train from Cuzco to Machu Picchu
- La Plaza de Armas, Cuzco
- El valle del Urubamba, Perú
- Machu Picchu
- Connections—The 24-hour clock and the metric system

Functions
- How to use expressions related to train travel
- How to purchase a train ticket and request information about arrival, departure, etc.
- How to talk about more past events or activities
- How to tell what people say

Structure
- Preterite of **hacer**, **querer**, and **venir**
- Irregular verbs in the preterite
- Present and preterite of **decir**

Capítulo 14

Topics
- Restaurants
- Eating utensils
- Types of food

Culture
- Hernán Miranda, *Interiores con mesa*
- Typical Mexican cuisine
- Diego Rivera, *El cultivo del maíz*
- Typical Spanish cuisine
- Typical Caribbean cuisine
- Connections—Regional variations of pronunciation and vocabulary in the Spanish-speaking world

Functions
- How to order food or a beverage at a restaurant
- How to identify eating utensils and dishes
- How to identify more foods
- How to make a reservation at a restaurant
- How to talk about present and past events

Structure
- Stem-changing verbs in the present e → i
- Stem-changing verbs in the preterite e → i, o → u

LEVEL 2

Repaso

The **Repaso** section reviews the material taught in **¡Buen viaje!** Level 1. In addition Chapters 13 and 14 in **¡Buen viaje!** Level 1 are the same as Chapters 1 and 2 in **¡Buen viaje!** Level 2. The **Repaso** section provides the opportunity to review the following functions and structures.

Functions
- How to describe the school day
- How to purchase school supplies
- How to describe clothing while shopping
- How to describe another person
- How to talk about family
- How to describe the inside of a house or apartment
- How to shop for food at the market
- How to talk about sports
- How to talk about air travel
- How to talk about daily routines
- How to talk about minor illness
- How to talk about the doctor's office
- How to talk about winter and summer activities

Structure
- Present tense -**ar** verbs
- **ir, dar, estar**
- Present tense of **ser**
- Agreement of nouns, articles, and adjectives
- Present tense of -**er** and -**ir** verbs
- **Tener**
- Possessive adjectives
- Stem-changing verbs
- Verbs like **aburrir, interesar,** and **gustar**
- Present of irregular verbs
- **Ser** and **estar**
- Reflexive verbs
- The preterite
- Direct object pronouns

Capítulo 1

Topics
- The train station
- Traveling by train

Culture
- Casimiro Castro, *Álbum del ferrocarril mexicano*
- Taking the AVE from Madrid to Sevilla
- Plaza de España, Sevilla
- Torre del Oro, Sevilla
- Taking a train from Cuzco to Machu Picchu
- La Plaza de Armas, Cuzco
- El valle del Urubamba, Perú
- Machu Picchu
- Connections—The 24-hour clock and the metric system

Functions
- How to use expressions related to train travel
- How to purchase a train ticket and request information about arrival, departure, etc.
- How to talk about more past events or activities
- How to tell what people say

Structure
- Preterite of **hacer, querer,** and **venir**
- Irregular verbs in the preterite
- Present and preterite of **decir**

Capítulo 2

Topics
- Restaurants
- Eating utensils
- Types of food

Culture
- Hernán Miranda, *Interiores con mesa*
- Typical Mexican cuisine
- Diego Rivera, *El cultivo del maíz*
- Typical Spanish cuisine
- Typical Caribbean cuisine
- Connections—Regional variations of pronunciation and vocabulary in the Spanish-speaking world

Functions
- How to order food or a beverage at a restaurant
- How to identify eating utensils and dishes
- How to identify more foods
- How to make a reservation at a restaurant
- How to talk about present and past events

Structure
- Stem-changing verbs in the present e → i
- Stem-changing verbs in the preterite e → i, o → u

LEVEL 2

Capítulo 3

Topics
- Describing the parts of a computer
- Telling how to use a computer
- Telling how to use a fax
- Telephones
- Answering the telephone

Culture
- Ernesto Bertani, *Nueva visión*
- Carmen Tordesillas, engineering student in Madrid
- Madrid, España
- Phone cards in Spain and in the United States
- The use of cell phones in Spanish-speaking countries and in the United States
- Connections—Computers and technology

Functions
- How to talk about computers, e-mail, the Internet, faxes, and telephones
- How to talk about past habitual and routine actions
- How to describe people and events in the past
- How to make and receive telephone calls in Spanish

Structure
- Imperfect of **-ar** verbs
- Imperfect of **-er** and **-ir** verbs
- Imperfect of **ser** and **ir**
- Uses of the imperfect

Capítulo 4

Topics
- Men's clothing
- Women's clothing
- Shoes
- Jewelry
- Shopping for food

Culture
- Pedro de Vega Muñoz, *Market Day, Seville*
- Open-air markets and supermarkets in the Spanish-speaking world
- The market in Chichicastenango, Guatemala
- Indigenous clothing in Guatemala
- Connections—Commerce and marketing

Functions
- How to shop for apparel and food in Spanish-speaking countries
- How to ask for the quantities and sizes you want
- How to find out prices
- How to talk about different types of past actions
- How to talk in general terms about what is done

Structure
- The preterite and the imperfect
- Narrating sequence of events
- Expressing feelings in the past
- Passive voice with **se**

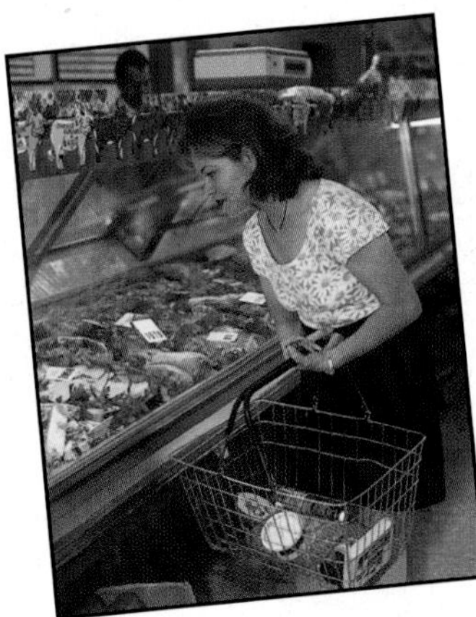

Capítulo 5

Topics
- Pastimes and hobbies
- The park
- Amusement parks

Culture
- Gonzalo Cienfuegos, *The Enchanted Crystal*
- Sunday in the park
- Parque de Chapultepec, Ciudad de México
- Palermo, Buenos Aires, Argentina
- Sevilla, España
- Video arcades in Spanish speaking countries
- Dominoes
- Connections—Literature

Functions
- How to talk about popular hobbies and games
- How to talk about activities in the park
- How to give details about location
- How to talk about what will happen in the future
- How to compare objects and people
- How to describe your favorite pastime

Structure
- Future tense of regular verbs
- Comparatives and superlatives

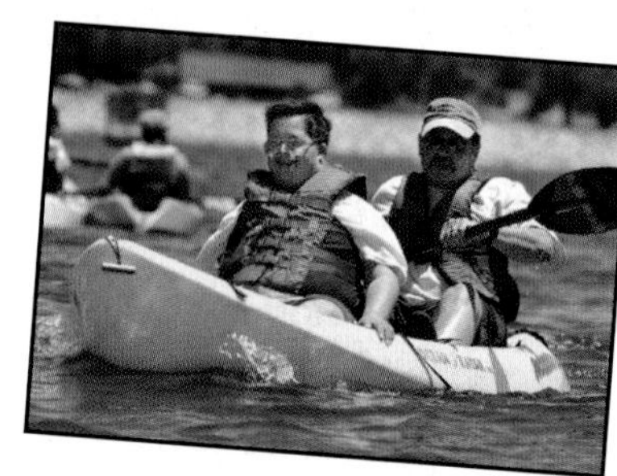

LEVEL 2

Capítulo 6

Topics
- Staying in a hotel
- Hotel rooms

Culture
- José Agustín Arrieta, *View of the Patio*
- Los paradores
- Youth hostels in Spanish-speaking countries
- Hotels
- Connections—Exercise

Functions
- How to check into and out of a hotel
- How to ask for things you may need while at a hotel
- How to talk about future events
- How to refer to previously mentioned people

Structure
- Future tense of irregular verbs
- Using direct and indirect objects in a sentence

Capítulo 7

Topics
- Inside an airplane
- At the airport
- Geographic terminology

Culture
- Susana González-Pagliere, *Village with Volcano*
- The airport in La Paz, Bolivia
- Areas surrounding La Paz
- Latin American aviation hero, Emilio Carranza
- Connections—Geography of Spain

Functions
- How to talk about air travel
- How to discuss the influence of geography on travel in Latin America
- How to talk about things that would happen under certain conditions

Structure
- The conditional of regular verbs
- The conditional of irregular verbs
- Changing **le, les** to **se** before direct object pronouns

Capítulo 8

Topics
- Parts of the body
- Minor medical problems
- The emergency room
- In the hospital

Culture
- Manuel Jiménez Prieto, *Hospital Visit*
- Practicantes in rural, Spanish-speaking countries
- The Buena Vista hospital
- Medical problems
- Connections—Medical terminology

Functions
- How to talk about accidents and medical problems
- How to talk about hospital stays
- How to discuss things that you and others have done recently
- How to compare things with like characteristics

Structure
- Present perfect
- Irregular past participles
- Comparison of like things

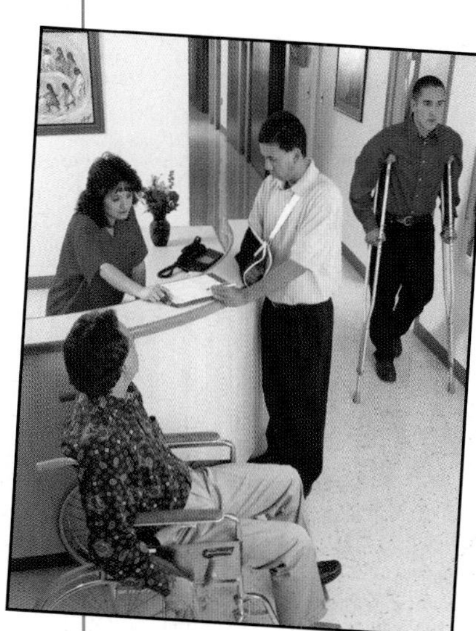

LEVEL 2

Capítulo 9

Topics
- The city
- Transportation in the city
- The country
- Farm animals

Culture
- María Eugenia Terrazas, *Inmensidad cordillerana*
- Buenos Aires, Argentina
- Raising cattle in Argentina
- Lima, Perú
- Santa Fe, New Mexico, United States
- Connections—Demography of Latin America

Functions
- How to talk about life in the city
- How to talk about life in the country
- How to describe things that were happening
- How to refer to things already mentioned
- How to indicate where things are located

Structure
- Imperfect progressive
- Placement of direct and indirect object pronouns
- Adjectives and demonstrative pronouns

Capítulo 10

Topics
- The kitchen
- Cooking
- Types of food
- Using a recipe

Culture
- Manuel Serrano, *A Mexican Kitchen in 1885*
- Recipe for paella
- Valencia, España
- History of the tomato in Spanish-speaking countries and in the United States
- History of corn and potatoes, foods indigenous to Latin America
- Connections—Nutrition and diet

Functions
- How to talk about foods and food preparation
- How to give commands
- How to refer to people and things previously mentioned
- How to prepare some regional specialties

Structure
- Commands (regular forms)
- Commands (irregular forms)
- Placement of direct object pronouns with a command

Capítulo 11

Topics
- Cars
- Gas stations
- Driving on the highway
- Driving in the city

Culture
- Norberto Russo, *De mi Buenos Aires*
- The Pan American highway
- Parking in Spanish-speaking countries
- International traffic signs
- Connections—Ecology and pollution

Functions
- How to check in for a flight
- How to talk about some services on board the plane
- How to get through the airport after deplaning
- How to tell what you or others are currently doing
- How to tell what you know and whom you know

Structure
- **Tú** commands (regular forms)
- **Tú** commands (irregular forms)
- Negative **tú** commands

LEVEL 2

Capítulo 12

Topics
- The hair salon
- Washing clothes
- Mailing letters and packages
- The bank

Culture
- Hernán Miranda, *Metro*
- Students from Madrid visit Andalucía
- Palacio de la Moneda, Santiago de Chile
- Hairstyles in the Spanish-speaking world
- Connections—Finance

Functions
- How to talk about going to the hair salon
- How to talk about having your clothes cleaned
- How to talk about using the services of the post office and bank
- How to talk about things that may or may not happen

Structure
- The subjunctive
- Expressing wishes and orders with the subjunctive
- Expressing opinions with the subjunctive

Capítulo 13

Topics
- Birthdays
- Weddings
- Christmas
- The New Year
- Three Kings Day
- Hanukkah

Culture
- Alfredo Ramos Martínez, *Casamiento indio*
- New Year's Eve in Madrid
- Engagement and marriage in Spanish-speaking countries
- A wedding announcement
- Connections—Spanish painting

Functions
- How to describe and talk about parties and weddings
- How to talk about some holidays
- How to give advice and make recommendations
- How to express doubt, uncertainty, or disbelief
- How to express emotional reactions to what others do

Structure
- Subjunctive of stem-changing verbs
- Subjunctive of verbs like **pedir** and **aconsejar**
- Expressing doubt with the subjunctive
- Expressing emotion with the subjunctive

Capítulo 14

Topics
- Professions
- Trades
- Looking for a job
- Job applications and interviews

Culture
- Antonio Gattorno, *Agricultores*
- Story of an ambassador to Latin America
- The importance of learning foreign languages
- Advertisements for jobs
- Connections—Economics

Functions
- How to talk about professions and occupations
- How to interview for a job
- How to state work qualifications
- How to talk about future events
- How to talk about probable events

Structure
- Infinitive versus subjunctive
- Subjunctive with **ojalá** and **quizá(s)**
- Subjunctive in relative clauses

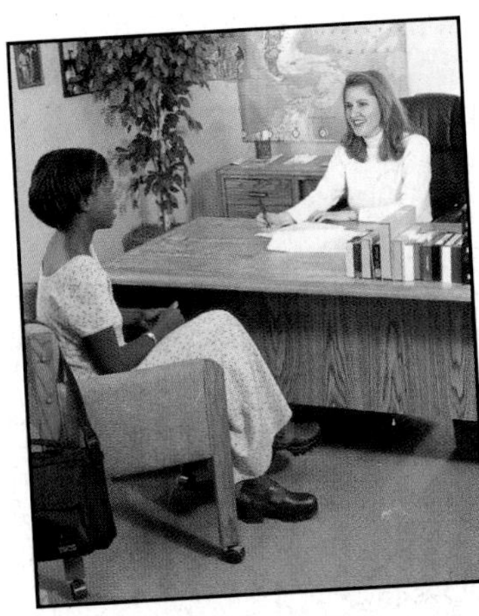

LEVEL 3

Capítulo 1

Topics
- The geography of Spain
- The history of Spain
- Spanish culture

Culture
- Trains of the future
- Immigrants in Tarifa

Functions
- How to express past actions
- How to refer to specific things
- How to express ownership

Structure
- The preterite of regular verbs
- The preterite of stem-changing verbs
- The preterite of irregular verbs
- Nouns that begin with **a-** and **ha-**
- Irregular nouns that end in **-a**
- Demonstrative pronouns
- Possessive pronouns

Capítulo 2

Topics
- The geography of Ecuador, Peru, and Bolivia
- The history of Ecuador, Peru and Bolivia
- The culture of Ecuador, Peru, and Bolivia

Culture
- Tungurahua volcano
- Peruvian woman who celebrates her 110th birthday

Functions
- How to describe habitual past actions
- How to talk about past events
- How to express what may or may not take place
- How to express necessity and possibility
- How to express wishes, preferences, and demands

Structure
- The imperfect
- The imperfect versus the preterite
- Expressing two past actions in the same sentence
- The subjunctive
- Expressing necessity and possibility with the subjunctive
- Expressing wishes, preferences, and demands with the subjunctive

Capítulo 3

Topics
- The geography of Chile, Argentina, Paraguay, and Uruguay
- The history of Chile, Argentina, Paraguay, and Uruguay
- The culture of Chile, Argentina, Paraguay, and Uruguay

Culture
- Summer fashion
- Leaving home to go to college

Functions
- How to state location and origin
- How to state characteristics and conditions
- How to express surprise, interest, and annoyance
- How to express likes, dislikes, and needs
- How to express affirmative and negative ideas
- How to express emotions, doubt, or uncertainty

Structure
- **Ser** versus **estar** with location and origin
- **Ser** versus **estar** with characteristics and conditions
- Special uses of **ser** and **estar**
- Using verbs with indirect objects to express surprise, interest, and annoyance
- Expressing likes and needs with **gustar** and **faltar**
- Affirmative and negative words
- Using the subjunctive to express emotion
- Using the subjunctive to express doubt or uncertainty
- Using the subjunctive in adverbial clauses

LEVEL 3

Capítulo 4

Topics
- The geography of Central American countries
- The history of Central American countries
- The culture of Central American countries

Culture
- Public announcements in the newspaper
- Microchip implants in pets for identification

Functions
- How to express future events
- How to refer to people and things already mentioned
- How to express emotions and possibilities about past events
- How to use time expressions such as **en cuanto** and **hasta que**

Structure
- The future tense
- The conditional tense
- Direct and indirect object pronouns
- The imperfect subjunctive
- The subjunctive with conjunctions of time

Capítulo 5

Topics
- The geography of Mexico
- The history of Mexico
- The culture of Mexico

Culture
- Windsurfing
- Mexican families

Functions
- How to express what you have done recently
- How to give commands
- How to describe actions in progress
- How to refer to people and things already mentioned
- How to describe actions completed prior to other actions
- How to express what you would have done and will have done
- How to express indefinite ideas and the known and unknown

Structure
- The present perfect
- Commands
- The progressive tenses
- Placement of direct and indirect object pronouns
- Direct and indirect object pronouns with commands
- The pluperfect
- The conditional perfect
- The future perfect
- Using the subjunctive with indefinite ideas
- Using the subjunctive in relative clauses

Capítulo 6

Topics
- The geography of Cuba, Puerto Rico, and the Dominican Republic
- The history of Cuba, Puerto Rico, and the Dominican Republic
- The culture of Cuba, Puerto Rico, and the Dominican Republic

Culture
- Synchronized swimming
- Educational programs in prisons in the Dominican Republic

Functions
- How to express what people do for themselves
- How to express reciprocal actions
- How to make comparisons
- How to express *although* and *perhaps*
- How to express opinions and feelings about what has or had happened
- How to discuss contrary-to-fact situations

Structure
- Reflexive verbs
- Reciprocal verbs
- Regular forms of comparatives and superlatives
- Irregular forms of comparatives and superlatives
- Stating like qualities
- The subjunctive with **aunque**
- The subjunctive with **quizás** and **tal vez**
- The present perfect subjunctive
- **Si** clauses

LEVEL 3

Capítulo 7

Topics
- The geography of Venezuela and Colombia
- The history of Venezuela and Colombia
- The culture of Venezuela and Colombia

Culture
- Different kinds of teachers
- Gasoline in Colombia

Functions
- How to use shortened forms of adjectives
- How to use articles
- How to use prepositional pronouns
- How to use **por** and **para**
- How to express duration of time using **hace** and **hacía**

Structure
- Shortened forms of adjectives
- Special uses of definite and indefinite articles
- Addressing and referring to people with the definite article
- The definite article with days of the week
- The definite article with clothing and parts of the body
- The indefinite article when telling one's profession
- Pronouns after prepositions
- **Por** versus **para**
- **Por** and **para** with expressions of time
- **Por** and **para** with the infinitive
- Other uses of **por** and **para**
- Expressing duration of time with **hace** and **hacía**

Capítulo 8

Topics
- The geography of the United States
- The history of the United States
- The culture of the United States

Culture
- Growth of the Hispanic population in the United States
- A storm and mudslides in California

Functions
- How to tell how actions are carried out
- How to express more activities in the present and past
- How to tell what was done or what is done in general

Structure
- Adverbs ending in **-mente**
- **-uir** verbs in the past and present
- Passive voice
- Passive voice with **se**

Pacing and Leveling

Each chapter of **¡Buen viaje!** contains required, recommended, and optional material. **Vocabulario, Estructura,** and **Conversación** sections are always required. The recommended sections include the first cultural reading in **Lecturas culturales, ¡Te toca a ti!,** and **Assessment. Lectura opcional, Conexiones,** and **Tecnotur** are optional. The following chart provides you with a guide to the number of required, recommended, and optional pages in each of the fourteen chapters.

Chapter Planning in the Student Edition

	required number of pages	recommended number of pages	optional number of pages
Chapter 1	15	7	8
Chapter 2	17	7	8
Chapter 3	13	7	8
Chapter 4	17	7	8
Chapter 5	13	7	8
Chapter 6	17	7	8
Chapter 7	17	7	8
Chapter 8	17	7	8
Chapter 9	17	7	8
Chapter 10	15	7	8
Chapter 11	15	7	8
Chapter 12	15	7	8
Chapter 13	15	7	8
Chapter 14	13	7	8
Total:	216 required	98 recommended	112 optional

Note: Chapters 13 and 14 of **¡Buen viaje! Level 1** are repeated as Chapters 1 and 2 of **¡Buen viaje! Level 2** for additional flexibility.

Watch for the "little green man." This icon indicates that you have finished the new material in the chapter.

LEVELING

The activities, conversations, and reading within each chapter are marked according to level of difficulty. E indicates easy. A indicates average. C indicates challenging. Some activities cover a range of difficulty. In some activities, for example, advanced students will be able to produce more extensive responses while students who learn at a different rate may give less detailed responses. The leveling indicators will help you individualize instruction to best meet your students' needs.

Analytic Scoring Guide for Rating Speaking Products

VOCABULARY

4. Vocabulary is generally accurate and appropriate to the task; minor errors, hesitations, and circumlocutions may occur.

3. Vocabulary is usually accurate; errors, hesitations, and circumlocutions may be frequent.

2. Vocabulary is not extensive enough for the task; inaccuracies or repetition may be frequent; may use English words.

1. Vocabulary inadequate for most basic aspects of the task.

0. No response.

GRAMMAR

4. Grammar may contain some inaccuracies, but these do not negatively affect comprehensibility.

3. Some grammatical inaccuracies may affect comprehensibility; some control of major patterns.

2. Many grammatical inaccuracies may affect comprehensibility; little control of major patterns.

1. Almost all grammatical patterns inaccurate, except for a few memorized patterns

0. No response.

PRONUNCIATION

4. Completely or almost completely comprehensible; pronunciation errors, rhythm and/or intonation problems do not create misunderstandings.

3. Generally comprehensible, but pronunciation errors, rhythm and/or intonation problems may create misunderstandings.

2. Difficult to comprehend because of numerous pronunciation errors, rhythm, and intonation problems.

1. Practically incomprehensible.

0. No response.

MESSAGE CONTENT

4. Relevant, informative response to the task. Adequate level of detail and creativity.

3. Response to the task is generally informative; may lack some detail and/or creativity.

2. Response incomplete; lacks some important information.

1. Response not informative; provides little or no information.

0. No response.

Luis Delgado

Owen Franken/CORBIS

Analytic Scoring Guide for Rating Writing Products

VOCABULARY

4. Vocabulary is generally accurate and appropriate to the task; minor errors may occur.

3. Vocabulary is usually accurate; occasional inaccuracies may occur.

2. Vocabulary is not extensive enough for the task; inaccuracies may be frequent; may use English words.

1. Vocabulary inadequate for most basic aspects of the task.

0. No response.

GRAMMAR

4. Grammar may contain some inaccuracies, but these do not negatively affect comprehensibility.

3. Some grammatical inaccuracies may affect comprehensibility; some control of major patterns.

2. Many grammatical inaccuracies may affect comprehensibility; little control of major patterns.

1. Almost all grammatical patterns inaccurate, except for a few memorized patterns.

0. No response.

SPELLING

4. Good control of the mechanics of Spanish; may contain occasional errors in spelling, diacritics, or punctuation, but these do not affect comprehensibility.

3. Some control of the mechanics of Spanish; contains errors in spelling, diacritics, or punctuation that sometimes affect comprehensibility.

2. Weak control of the mechanics of Spanish; contains numerous errors in spelling, diacritics, or punctuation that seriously affect comprehensibility.

1. Almost no control of the mechanics of Spanish.

0. No response.

MESSAGE CONTENT

4. Relevant, informative response to the task. Adequate level of detail and creativity.

3. Response to the task is generally informative; may lack some detail and/or creativity.

2. Response incomplete; lacks some important information.

1. Response not informative; provides little or no information.

0. No response.

en Franken/CORBIS

How Can I Use the Internet to Teach Foreign Language?

From the Internet to round-the-clock live newscasts, teachers and students have never before had so much information at their fingertips. Yet never before has it been so confusing to determine where to turn for reliable content and what to do with it once you have found it. In today's world, foreign language teachers must not only use the Internet as a source of up-to-the-minute information for students; they must teach students how to find and evaluate sources on their own.

What's available On the Internet?

✔ **Teacher-Focused Web Sites**
These Web sites provide teaching tips, detailed lesson plans, and links to other sites of interest to teachers and students.

✔ **Cultural Information**
Sites on the Web provide information to help students explore both "Big C" and "Little C" culture. Information about museums, stores, restaurants, schools, holiday celebrations, and customs can be found on Web sites that allow the student to virtually immerse into the culture.

✔ **Geographical Information**
The Web holds a variety of geographical resources, from historical, physical, and political maps; to interactive mapping programs; to information about people and places around the world.

✔ **Statistics**
Government Web sites are rich depositories for statistics of all kinds, including census data and information about climate, education, the economy, and political processes and patterns.

✔ **Reference Sources**
Students can access full-text versions of encyclopedias, dictionaries, atlases, and other reference books. Students have easy access to newspapers written in the target language.

✔ **News**
Traditional media sources, including television, radio, newspapers, and news magazines, sponsor Web sites that provide updates, as well as in-depth news coverage and analysis.

✔ **Topical Information**
Among the most numerous Web sites are those organized around a particular topic or issue. These Internet pages may contain essays, analyses, and other commentaries, as well as primary source documents, maps, photographs, video and audio clips, bibliographies, and links to related online resources.

✔ **Organizations**
Many organizations such as museums post Web pages that provide online exhibits, archives, and other information.

Glencoe Online

Glencoe provides engaging **Student Web Activities** plus **Self-Check Quizzes** for each chapter that let you and your students assess their knowledge. There are games in each chapter to afford students extra practice. You can also access additional resources,

including enrichment links.

Finding Things on the Internet

The greatest asset of the Internet—its vast array of materials—is also its greatest deterrent. Many excellent foreign language-specific sites provide links to relevant content. Using Internet search engines can also help you find what you need.

- ✔ A search engine is an Internet search tool. You type in a keyword, name, or phrase, and the search engine lists the URLs for Web sites that match your search. However, a search engine may find things that are not at all related or may miss sites that you would consider of interest. The key is to find ways to define your search.
- ✔ Not all search engines are the same. Each seeks out information a little bit differently. Different search engines use different criteria to determine what constitutes a "match" for your search topic. The Internet holds numerous articles that compare search engines and offer guidelines for choosing those that best meet your needs.
- ✔ An advanced search allows you to refine the search by using a phrase or a combination of words. The way to conduct an advanced search varies from search engine to search engine; check the search engine's *Help* feature for information. Encourage students to review this information regularly for each of the search engines they use.

How do I teach students to evaluate Web sites?

Anyone can put up a Web site. Web content is easy to change, too, so Webmasters constantly update their Web sites by adding, modifying, and removing content. These characteristics make evaluating Web sites both more challenging and more important than traditional print resources. Teach students to critically evaluate Web resources, using the questions and criteria below.

1. ***Purpose:*** *What is the purpose of the Web site or Web page? Is it an informational Web page, a news site, a business site, an advocacy site, or a personal Web page? Many sites serve more than one purpose. For instance, a news site may provide current events accompanied by banner ads that market the products advertisers think readers might want.*

2. ***URL:*** *What is the URL, or Web address? Where does the site originate? That can sometimes tell you about the group or business behind the Web page. For example, URLs with .edu and .gov domain names indicate that the site is connected to an educational institution or a government agency, respectively. A .com suffix usually means that a commercial or business interest hosts the Web site, but may also indicate a personal Web page. A nonprofit organization's Web address may end with .org.*

3. ***Authority:*** *Who wrote the material or created the Web site? What qualifications does this person or group have? Who has ultimate responsibility for the site? If the site is sponsored by an organization, are the organization's goals clearly stated?*

4. ***Accuracy:*** *How reliable is the information? Are sources listed so that they can be verified? Is the Web page free from surface errors in spelling and grammar? How does it compare with other sources you've found on the Web and in print?*

5. ***Objectivity:*** *If the site presents itself as an informational site, is the material free from bias? If there is advertising, is it easy to tell the difference between the ads and other features? If the site mixes factual information with opinion, can you spot the difference between the ads and other features? If the site advocates an opinion or viewpoint, is the opinion clearly stated and logically defended?*

6. ***Currency:*** *When was the information first placed on the Web? Is the site updated on a regular basis? When was the last revision? If the information is time-sensitive, are the updates frequent enough?*

7. ***Coverage:*** *What topics are covered on the Web site? What is the depth of coverage? Are all sides of an issue presented? How does the coverage compare with other Web and print sources?*

Addressing the Needs of Special Students

How can I help ALL my students learn foreign language?

Today's classroom contains students from a variety of backgrounds and with a variety of learning styles, strengths, and challenges. With careful planning, you can address the needs of all students in the foreign language classroom. The following tips for instruction can assist your efforts to help all students reach their maximum potential.

- ✔ Survey students to discover their individual differences. Use interest inventories of their unique talents so you can encourage contributions in the classroom.
- ✔ Model respect of others. Adolescents crave social acceptance. The student with learning differences is especially sensitive to correction and criticism—particularly when it comes from a teacher. Your behavior will set the tone for how students treat one another.
- ✔ Expand opportunities for success. Provide a variety of instructional activities that reinforce skills and concepts.
- ✔ Establish measurable objectives and decide how you can best help students meet them.
- ✔ Celebrate successes and praise "work in progress".
- ✔ Keep it simple. Point out problem areas—if doing so can help a student affect change. Avoid overwhelming students with too many goals at one time.
- ✔ Assign cooperative group projects that challenge all students to contribute to solving a problem or creating a product.

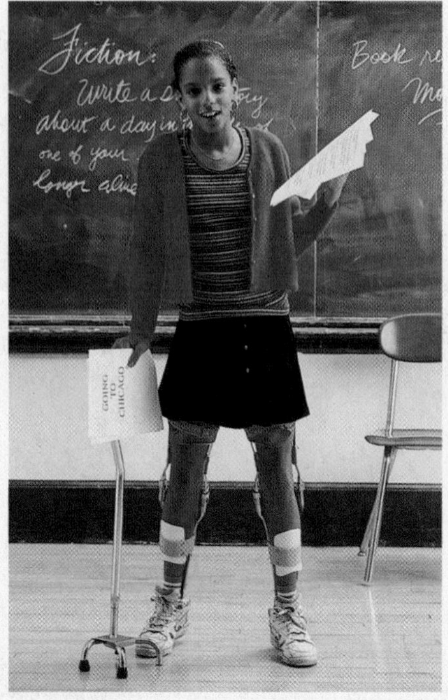

How do I reach students with learning disabilities?

- ✔ Provide support and structure. Clearly specify rules, assignments, and responsibilities.
- ✔ Practice skills frequently. Use games and drills to help maintain student interest.
- ✔ Incorporate many modalities into the learning process. Provide opportunities to say, hear, write, read, and act out important concepts and information.
- ✔ Link new skills and concepts to those already mastered.
- ✔ Allow students to record answers on audiotape.
- ✔ Allow extra time to complete tests and assignments.
- ✔ Let students demonstrate proficiency with alternative presentations, including oral reports, role plays, art projects, and with music.
- ✔ Provide outlines, notes, or recordings of readings.
- ✔ Pair students with peer helpers, and provide class time for pair interaction.

How do I reach students with behavioral disorders?

- ✔ Provide a structured environment with clear-cut schedules, rules, seat assignments, and safety procedures.
- ✔ Reinforce appropriate behavior and model it for students.
- ✔ Cue distracted students back to the task through verbal signals and teacher proximity.
- ✔ Set very small goals that can be achieved in the short term. Work for long term improvement in the big areas.

How do I reach students with physical challenges?

- ✔ Openly discuss with the student any uncertainties you have about when to offer aid.
- ✔ Ask parents or therapists and students what special devices or procedures are needed, and whether any special safety precautions need to be taken.
- ✔ Welcome students with physical challenges into all activities, including field trips, special events, and projects.
- ✔ Provide information to help able-bodied students and adults understand other students' physical challenges.

How do I reach students with visual impairments?

- ✔ Facilitate independence. Modify assignments as needed.
- ✔ Teach classmates how and when to serve as guides.
- ✔ Limit unnecessary noise in the classroom if it distracts the student with visual impairments.
- ✔ Provide tactile models whenever possible.
- ✔ Foster a spirit of inclusion.

Describe people and events as they occur in the classroom. Remind classmates that the student with visual impairments cannot interpret gestures and other forms of nonverbal communication.
- ✔ Provide taped lectures and reading assignments.
- ✔ Team the student with a sighted peer for written work.

How do I reach students with hearing impairments?

- ✔ Seat students where they can see your lip movements easily and where they can avoid visual distractions.
- ✔ Avoid standing with your back to the window or light source.
- ✔ Use an overhead projector to maintain eye contact while writing.
- ✔ Seat students where they can see speakers.
- ✔ Write out all assignments on the board, or hand out written instructions.
- ✔ If the student has a manual interpreter, allow both student and interpreter to select the most favorable seating arrangements.
- ✔ Teach students to look directly at each other when they speak.

How do I reach English language learners?

- ✔ Remember, students' ability to speak English does not reflect their academic abilities.
- ✔ Try to incorporate the students' cultural experience into your instruction. The help of a bilingual aide may be effective.
- ✔ Avoid cultural stereotypes.
- ✔ Pre-teach important vocabulary and concepts.
- ✔ Be cognizant of difficulties that may arise from learning a new written notation.
- ✔ Encourage students to make comparisons between their heritage culture and language and the target culture and language.
- ✔ Encourage students to preview text before they begin reading, noting headings, graphic organizers, photographs, and maps.

How do I reach gifted students?

- ✔ Make arrangements for students to take selected subjects early and to work on independent projects.
- ✔ Ask "what if" questions to develop high-level thinking skills. Establish an environment safe for risk taking.
- ✔ Call on gifted students to provide more open-ended responses. Use the material as optional for enrichment.
- ✔ Emphasize concepts, theories, ideas, relationships, and generalizations.
- ✔ Promote interest in the past by inviting students to make connections to the present.
- ✔ Let students express themselves in alternate ways, such as creative writing, acting, debate, simulations, drawing, or music.
- ✔ Provide students with a catalog of helpful resources, listing such things as agencies that provide free and inexpensive materials, appropriate community services and programs.
- ✔ Assign extension projects that allow students to solve real-life problems related to their communities.

Hints for Inclusion Classes

Advice from Diane Russell
Delaware City Schools
Delaware, Ohio

In an inclusion setting, all students can respond to and get immediate feedback when using a set of dry-erase boards (cut at the local hardware store from a 4′ by 8′ laminated panel). For vocabulary review, students can write dictated words or sketch their meanings on the boards. Students can also be asked to draw what they hear from a story read aloud by the teacher to check listening comprehension. When students take turns illustrating different pages of a story, the pictures can be displayed on the chalk ledge as cues for retelling or writing a summary.

The What, Why, and How of Reading

Reading is a learned process. You have been reading in your first language for a long time and noe your challenge is to transfer what you know to enable you to read fluently in Spanish. Reading will help you improve your vocabulary, cultural knowledge, and productive skills in Spanish. The strategies in the chart are reading strategies you are probably familiar with. Review them and apply them as you continue to improve your spanish reading skills.

Skill/Strategy

What is it?	Why It's Important	How To Do It
Preview Previewing is looking over a selection before you read.	Previewing lets you begin to see what you already know and what you'll need to know. It helps you set a purpose for reading.	Look at the title, illustrations, headings, captions, and graphics. Look at how ideas are organized. Ask questions about the text.
Skim Skimming is looking over an entire selection quickly to get a general idea of what the piece is about.	Skimming will tell you what a selection is about. If the selection you skim isn't what you're looking for, you won't need to read the entire piece.	Read the title of the selection and quickly look over the entire piece. Read headings and captions and maybe part of the first paragraph to get a general idea of the selection's content.
Scan Scanning is glancing quickly over a selection in order to find specific information.	Scanning helps you pinpoint information quickly. It saves you time when you have a number of selections to look at.	As you move your eyes quickly over the lines of text, look for key words or phrases that will help you locate the information you're looking for.
Predict Predicting is taking an educated guess about what will happen in a selection.	Predicting gives you a reason to read. You want to find out if your prediction and the selection events match, don't you? As you read, adjust or change your prediction if it doesn't fit what you learn.	Combine what you already know about an author or subject with what you learned in your preview to guess at what will be included in the text.
Summarize Summarizing is stating the main ideas of a selection in your own words and in a logical sequence.	Summarizing shows whether you've understood something. It teaches you to rethink what you've read and to separate main ideas from supporting information.	Ask yourself: What is this selection about? Answer who, what, where, when, why, and how? Put that information in a logical order.

What is it?	Why It's Important	How To Do It
Clarify Clarifying is looking at difficult sections of text in order to clear up what is confusing.	Authors will often build ideas one on another. If you don't clear up a confusing passage, you may not understand main ideas or information that comes later.	Go back and reread a confusing section more slowly. Look up words you don't know. Ask questions about what you don't understand. Sometimes you may want to read on to see if further information helps you.
Question Questioning is asking yourself whether information in a selection is important. Questioning is also regularly asking yourself whether you've understood what you've read.	When you ask questions as you read, you're reading strategically. As you answer your questions, you're making sure that you'll get the gist of a text.	Have a running conversation with yourself as you read. Keep asking yourself, Is this idea important? Why? Do I understand what this is about? Might this information be on a test later?
Visualize Visualizing is picturing a writer's ideas or descriptions in your mind's eye.	Visualizing is one of the best ways to understand and remember information in fiction, nonfiction, and informational text.	Carefully read how a writer describes a person, place, or thing. Then ask yourself, What would this look like? Can I see how the steps in this process would work?
Monitor Comprehension Monitoring your comprehension means thinking about whether you're understanding what you're reading.	The whole point of reading is to understand a piece of text. When you don't understand a selection, you're not really reading it.	Keep asking yourself questions about main ideas, characters, and events. When you can't answer a question, review, read more slowly, or ask someone to help you.

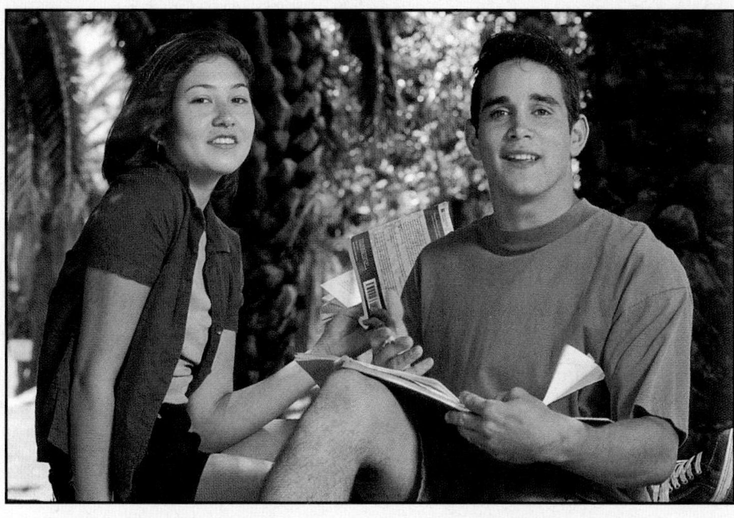

What is it?	Why It's Important	How To Do It
Identify Sequence Identifying sequence is finding the logical order of ideas or events.	In a work of fiction, events usually happen in chronological order. With nonfiction, understanding the logical sequence of ideas in a piece helps you follow a writer's train of thought. You'll remember ideas better when you know the logical order a writer uses.	Think about what the author is trying to do. Tell a story? Explain how something works? Present how something works? Present information? Look for clues or signal words that might point to time order, steps in a process, or order of importance.
Determine the Main Idea Determining an author's main idea is finding the most important thought in a paragraph or selection.	Finding main ideas gets you ready to summarize. You also discover an author's purpose for writing when you find the main ideas in a selection.	Think about what you know about the author and the topic. Look for how the author organizes ideas. Then look for the one idea that all of the sentences in a paragraph or all the paragraphs in a selection are about.
Respond Responding is telling what you like, dislike, find surprising or interesting in a selection.	When you react in a personal way to what you read, you'll enjoy a selection more and remember it better.	As you read, think about how you feel about story elements or ideas in a selection. What's your reaction to the characters in a story? What grabs your attention as you read?
Connect Connecting means linking what you read to events in your own life or to other selections you've read.	You'll "get into" your reading and recall information and ideas better by connecting events, emotions, and characters to your own life.	Ask yourself: Do I know someone like this? Have I ever felt this way? What else have I read that is like this selection?
Review Reviewing is going back over what you've read to remember what's important and to organize ideas so you'll recall them later.	Reviewing is especially important when you have new ideas and a lot of information to remember.	Filling in a graphic organizer, such as a chart or diagram, as you read helps you organize information. These study aids will help you review later.
Interpret Interpreting is using your own understanding of the world to decide what the events or ideas in a selection mean.	Every reader constructs meaning on the basis of what he or she understands about the world. Finding meaning as you read is all about interacting with the text.	Think about what you already know about yourself and the world. Ask yourself: What is the author really trying to say here? What larger idea might these events be about?

What is it?	Why It's Important	How To Do It
Infer Inferring is using your reason and experience to guess at what an author does not come right out and say.	Making inferences is a large part of finding meaning in a selection. Inferring helps you look more deeply at characters and points you toward the theme or message in a selection.	Look for clues the author provides. Notice descriptions, dialogue, events, and relationships that might tell you something the author wants you to know.
Draw Conclusions Drawing conclusions is using a number of pieces of information to make a general statement about people, places, events, and ideas.	Drawing conclusions helps you find connections between ideas and events. It's another tool to help you see the larger picture.	Notice details about characters, ideas, and events. Then make a general statement on the basis of these details. For example, a character's actions might lead you to conclude that he is kind.
Analyze Analyzing is looking at separate parts of a selection in order to understand the entire selection.	Analyzing helps you look critically at a piece of writing. When you analyze a selection, you'll discover its theme or message, and you'll learn the author's purpose for writing.	To analyze a story, think about what the author is saying through the characters, setting, and plot. To analyze nonfiction, look at the organization and main ideas. What do they suggest?
Synthesize Synthesizing is combining ideas to create something new. You may synthesize to reach a new understanding or you may actually create a new ending to a story.	Synthesizing helps you move to a higher level of thinking. Creating something new of your own goes beyond remembering what you learned from someone else.	Think about the ideas or information you've learned in a selection. Ask yourself: Do I understand something more than the main ideas here? Can I create something else from what I now know?
Evaluate Evaluating is making a judgment or forming an opinion about something you read. You can evaluate a character, an author's craft, or the value of the information in a text.	Evaluating helps you become a wise reader. For example, when you judge whether an author is qualified to speak about a topic or whether the author's points make sense, you can avoid being misled by what you read.	As you read, ask yourself questions such as: Is this character realistic and believable? Is this author qualified to write on this subject? Is this author biased? Does this author present opinions as facts?

Expand your students' view of the Spanish-speaking world

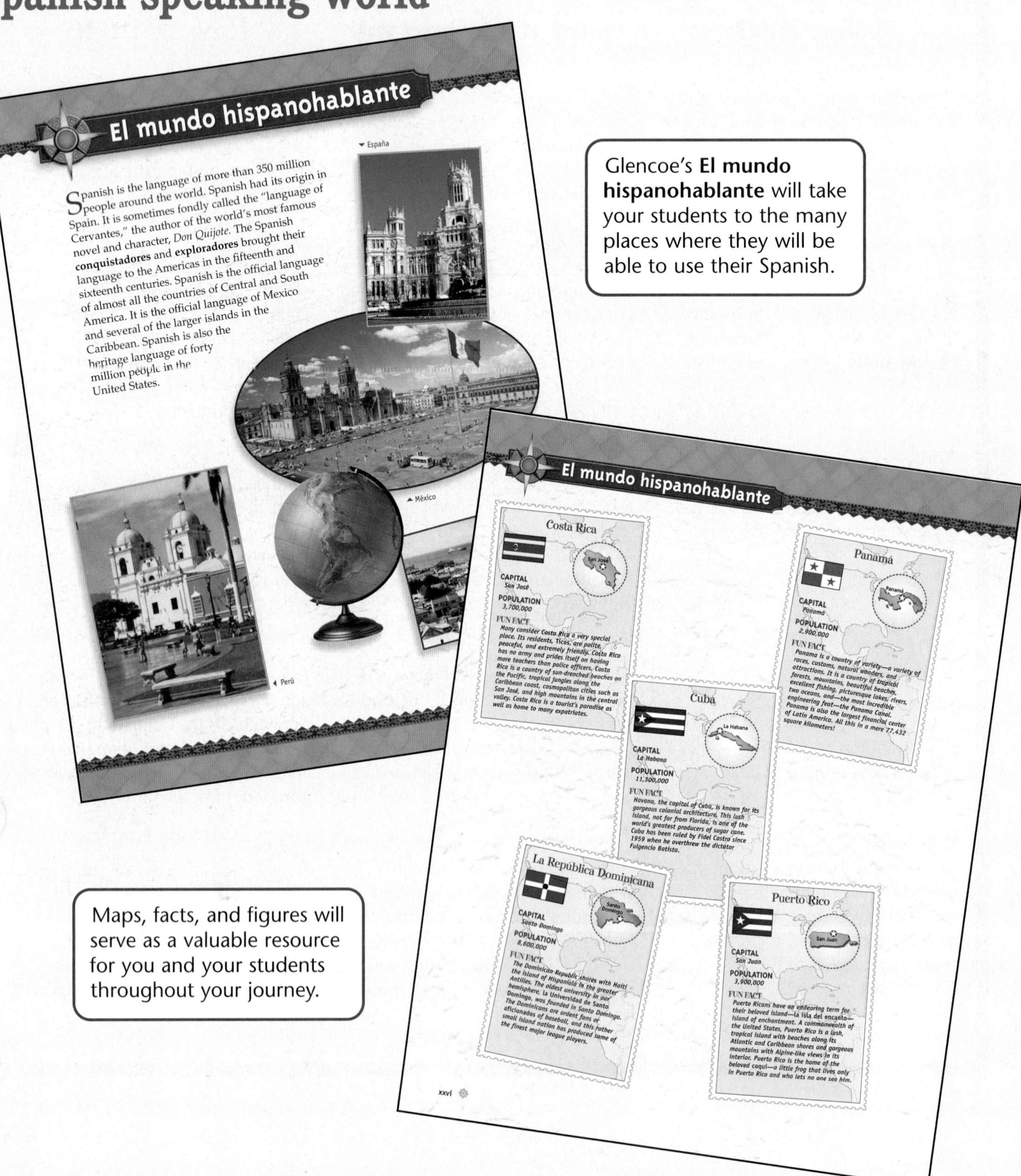
El mundo hispanohablante

Spanish is the language of more than 350 million people around the world. Spanish had its origin in Spain. It is sometimes fondly called the "language of Cervantes," the author of the world's most famous novel and character, *Don Quijote*. The Spanish **conquistadores** and **exploradores** brought their language to the Americas in the fifteenth and sixteenth centuries. Spanish is the official language of almost all the countries of Central and South America. It is the official language of Mexico and several of the larger islands in the Caribbean. Spanish is also the heritage language of forty million people in the United States.

España

México

Perú

El mundo hispanohablante

Costa Rica
CAPITAL San José
POPULATION 3,700,000
FUN FACT *Many consider Costa Rica a very special place. Its residents, Ticos, are polite, peaceful, and extremely friendly. Costa Rica has no army and prides itself on having more teachers than police officers. Costa Rica is a country of sun-drenched beaches on the Pacific, tropical jungles along the Caribbean coast, cosmopolitan cities such as San José, and high mountains in the central valley. Costa Rica is a tourist's paradise as well as home to many expatriates.*

Panamá
CAPITAL Panamá
POPULATION 2,900,000
FUN FACT *Panama is a country of variety—a variety of races, customs, natural wonders, and attractions. It is a country of tropical forests, mountains, beautiful beaches, excellent fishing, picturesque lakes, rivers, two oceans, and—the most incredible engineering feat—the Panama Canal. Panama is also the largest financial center of Latin America. All this in a mere 77,432 square kilometers!*

Cuba
CAPITAL La Habana
POPULATION 11,300,000
FUN FACT *Havana, the capital of Cuba, is known for its gorgeous colonial architecture. This lush island, not far from Florida, is one of the world's greatest producers of sugar cane. Cuba has been ruled by Fidel Castro since 1959 when he overthrew the dictator Fulgencio Batista.*

La República Dominicana
CAPITAL Santo Domingo
POPULATION 8,600,000
FUN FACT *The Dominican Republic shares with Haiti the island of Hispaniola in the greater Antilles. The oldest university in our hemisphere, la Universidad de Santo Domingo, was founded in Santo Domingo. The Dominicans are ardent fans or aficionados of baseball, and this rather small island nation has produced some of the finest major league players.*

Puerto Rico
CAPITAL San Juan
POPULATION 3,900,000
FUN FACT *Puerto Ricans have an endearing term for their beloved island—la isla del encanto—island of enchantment. A commonwealth of the United States, Puerto Rico is a lush, tropical island with beaches along its Atlantic and Caribbean shores and gorgeous mountains with Alpine-like views in its interior. Puerto Rico is the home of the beloved coquí—a little frog that lives only in Puerto Rico and who lets no one see him.*

xxvi

Glencoe's **El mundo hispanohablante** will take your students to the many places where they will be able to use their Spanish.

Maps, facts, and figures will serve as a valuable resource for you and your students throughout your journey.

Awaken your students' interest with an introduction to the chapter theme in a cultural context

Itinerary for Success

- ✓ Exposure to Hispanic culture
- ✓ Clear expectations and goals
- ✓ Thematic, contextualized vocabulary
- ✓ Useful and thematically linked structure
- ✓ Progressive practice
- ✓ Real-life conversation
- ✓ Cultural readings in the target language
- ✓ Connections to other disciplines . . . in Spanish!
- ✓ Recycling and review
- ✓ High-interest articles from **People en español**

Objectives let students know what they will be able to do at the end of the chapter.

Capítulo 9

El verano y el invierno

Objetivos

In this chapter you will learn to:

- describe summer and winter weather
- talk about summer activities and sports
- talk about winter sports
- discuss past actions and events
- refer to people and things already mentioned
- talk about resorts in the Hispanic world

Daniel Hernández *A Breath of Fresh Air*

272 doscientos setenta y dos

Fine Art related to the chapter enriches students' cultural knowledge. The Fine Art pieces are also available on transparencies.

Opening photo provides a cultural backdrop for the chapter.

Give students something to talk about with thematic, contextualized vocabulary

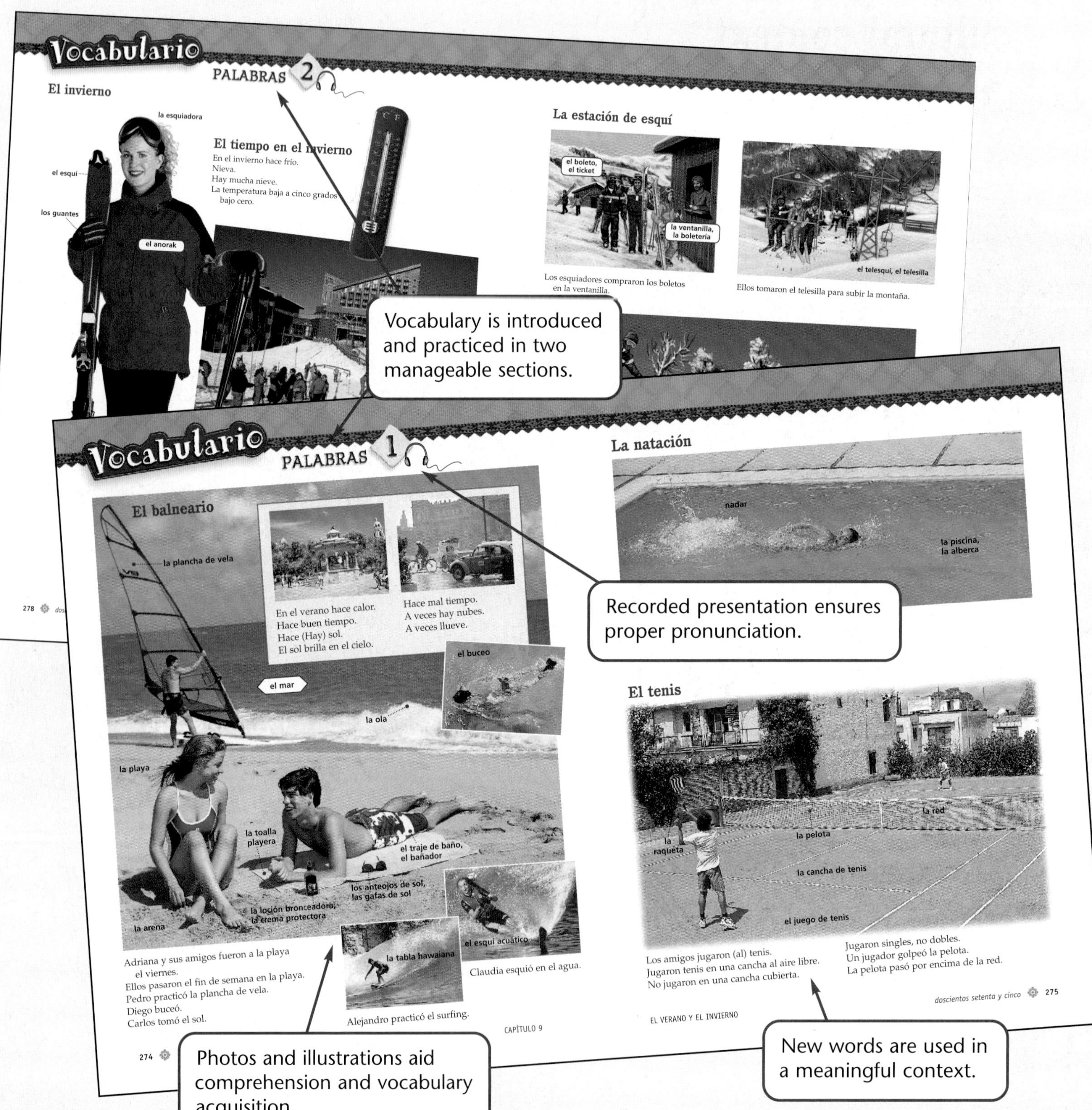

Provide practice for the mastery of new vocabulary

Itinerary for Success

- ✓ Exposure to Hispanic culture
- ✓ Clear expectations and goals
- ✓ Thematic, contextualized vocabulary
- ✓ Useful and thematically linked structure
- ✓ Progressive practice
- ✓ Real-life conversation
- ✓ Cultural readings in the target language
- ✓ Connections to other disciplines . . . in Spanish!
- ✓ Recycling and review
- ✓ High-interest articles from **People en español**

Historieta enables students to tell and retell a story, using their new words.

Vocabulario

¿Qué palabra necesito?

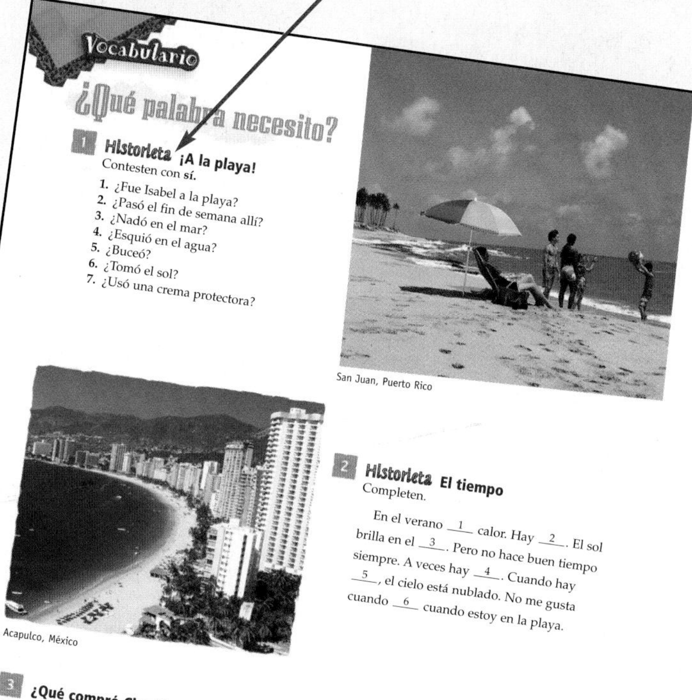

1 Historieta ¡A la playa!
Contesten con **sí.**

1. ¿Fue Isabel a la playa?
2. ¿Pasó el fin de semana allí?
3. ¿Nadó en el mar?
4. ¿Esquió en el agua?
5. ¿Buceó?
6. ¿Tomó el sol?
7. ¿Usó una crema protectora?

San Juan, Puerto Rico

Acapulco, México

2 Historieta El tiempo
Completen.

En el verano __1__ calor. Hay __2__. El sol brilla en el __3__. Pero no hace buen tiempo siempre. A veces hay __4__. Cuando hay __5__, el cielo está nublado. No me gusta cuando __6__ cuando estoy en la playa.

3 ¿Qué compró Claudia? Contesten según las fotografías.
Claudia fue a la tienda. ¿Qué compró?

1. 2. 3. 4.

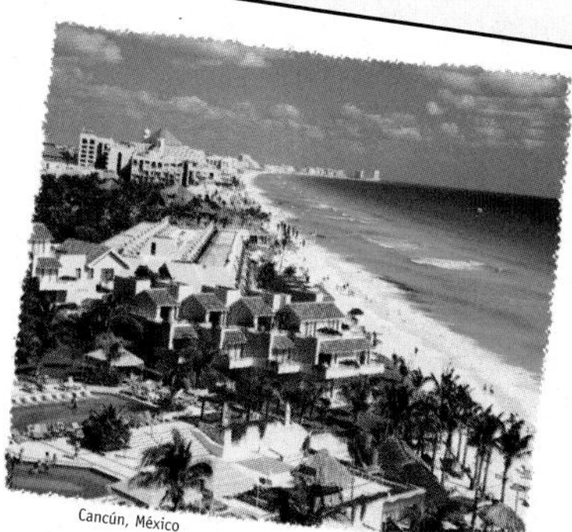

Cancún, México

Vocabulario

4 Historieta El balneario
Completen.

1. Un balneario tiene ___.
2. El Mediterráneo es un ___ y el Caribe es un ___.
3. En un mar o en un océano hay ___.
4. En la playa la gente ___ y ___ el sol.
5. ___ da protección contra el sol.
6. Una persona lleva ___ y ___ cuando va a la playa.
7. Me gusta mucho ir a la playa en el ___ cuando hace ___ y hay mucho ___.
8. Si uno no vive cerca de la costa y no puede ir a la playa, puede nadar en ___.

5 Historieta Un juego de tenis
Contesten.

1. ¿Dónde jugaron los tenistas al tenis?
2. ¿Jugaron singles o dobles?
3. ¿Cuántas personas hay en la cancha cuando juegan dobles?
4. ¿Golpearon los tenistas la pelota?
5. ¿La pelota tiene que pasar por encima de la red?

Estepona, España

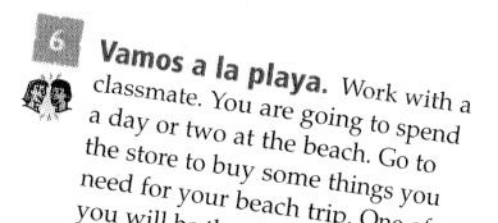

6 Vamos a la playa. Work with a classmate. You are going to spend a day or two at the beach. Go to the store to buy some things you need for your beach trip. One of you will be the clerk and the other will be the shopper. Take turns.

7 ¿Dónde vamos a jugar tenis? Call some friends (your classmates) to try to arrange a game of doubles. Decide where you're going to play, when, and with whom.

SPANISH Online
For more information about the popularity of tennis in the Spanish-speaking world, go to the Glencoe Spanish Web site: spanish.glencoe.com

Paired and small-group activities allow students to communicate about the chapter topic.

Glencoe's Web site, **spanish.glencoe.com**, takes students on virtual field trips to learn more about the chapter theme.

Build communicative competence with thematically linked structure

Immediate reinforcement shows students how structure works to build meaning.

New structures are presented in simple terms with familiar vocabulary.

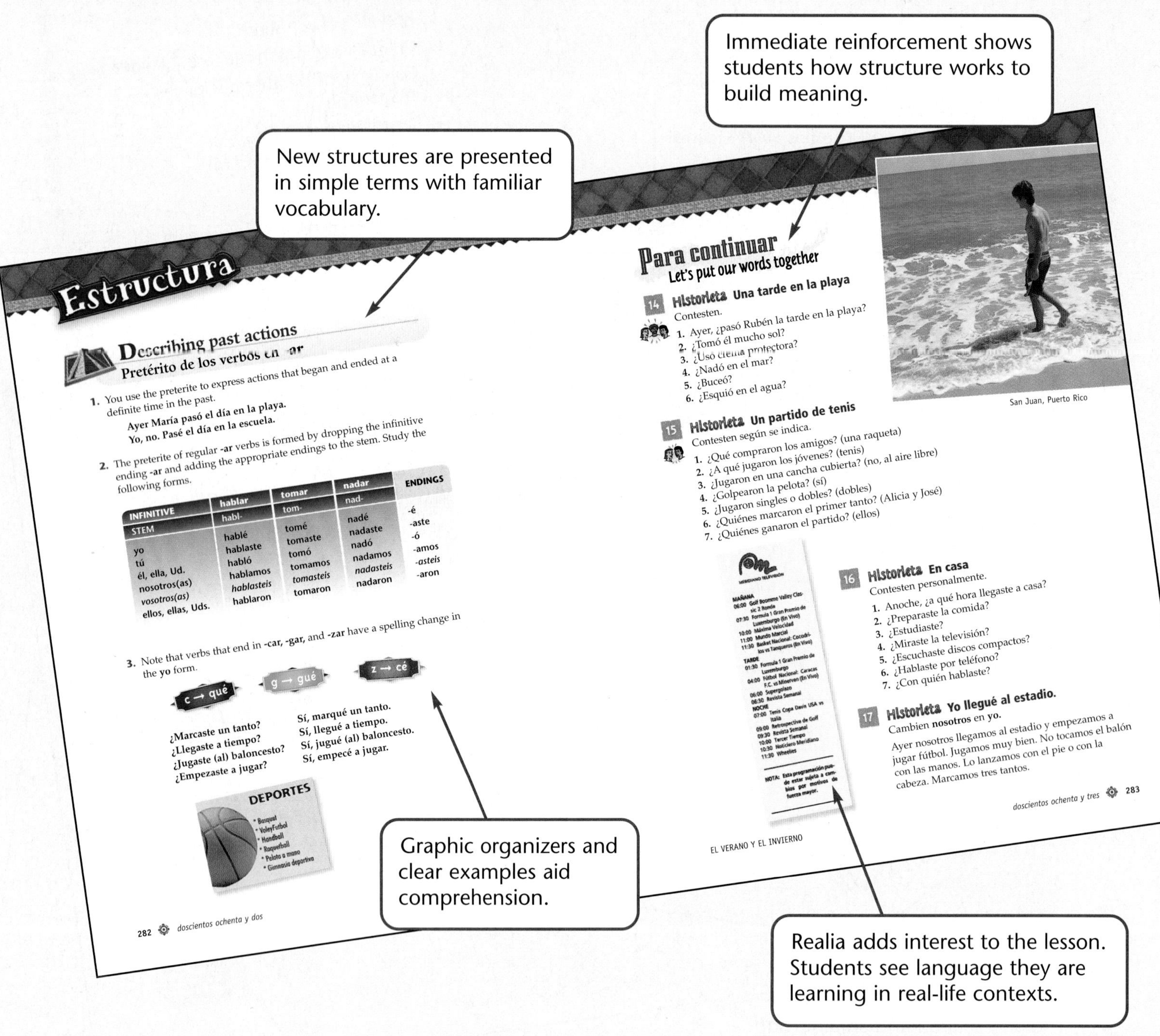

Estructura

Describing past actions
Pretérito de los verbos en -ar

1. You use the preterite to express actions that began and ended at a definite time in the past.

   Ayer María pasó el día en la playa.
   Yo, no. Pasé el día en la escuela.

2. The preterite of regular **-ar** verbs is formed by dropping the infinitive ending **-ar** and adding the appropriate endings to the stem. Study the following forms.

INFINITIVE	hablar	tomar	nadar	ENDINGS
STEM	habl-	tom-	nad-	
yo	hablé	tomé	nadé	-é
tú	hablaste	tomaste	nadaste	-aste
él, ella, Ud.	habló	tomó	nadó	-ó
nosotros(as)	hablamos	tomamos	nadamos	-amos
vosotros(as)	*hablasteis*	*tomasteis*	*nadasteis*	*-asteis*
ellos, ellas, Uds.	hablaron	tomaron	nadaron	-aron

3. Note that verbs that end in **-car**, **-gar**, and **-zar** have a spelling change in the **yo** form.

c → qué   g → gué   z → cé

¿Marcaste un tanto? — **Sí, marqué un tanto.**
¿Llegaste a tiempo? — **Sí, llegué a tiempo.**
¿Jugaste (al) baloncesto? — **Sí, jugué (al) baloncesto.**
¿Empezaste a jugar? — **Sí, empecé a jugar.**

DEPORTES
* Basquet
* VoleyFutbol
* Handball
* Raquetball
* Pelota a mano
* Gimnasio deportivo

282 doscientos ochenta y dos

Para continuar
Let's put our words together

14 Historieta Una tarde en la playa
Contesten.
1. Ayer, ¿pasó Rubén la tarde en la playa?
2. ¿Tomó él mucho sol?
3. ¿Usó crema protectora?
4. ¿Nadó en el mar?
5. ¿Buceó?
6. ¿Esquió en el agua?

San Juan, Puerto Rico

15 Historieta Un partido de tenis
Contesten según se indica.
1. ¿Qué compraron los amigos? (una raqueta)
2. ¿A qué jugaron los jóvenes? (tenis)
3. ¿Jugaron en una cancha cubierta? (no, al aire libre)
4. ¿Golpearon la pelota? (sí)
5. ¿Jugaron singles o dobles? (dobles)
6. ¿Quiénes marcaron el primer tanto? (Alicia y José)
7. ¿Quiénes ganaron el partido? (ellos)

16 Historieta En casa
Contesten personalmente.
1. Anoche, ¿a qué hora llegaste a casa?
2. ¿Preparaste la comida?
3. ¿Estudiaste?
4. ¿Miraste la televisión?
5. ¿Escuchaste discos compactos?
6. ¿Hablaste por teléfono?
7. ¿Con quién hablaste?

17 Historieta Yo llegué al estadio.
Cambien **nosotros** en **yo**.
Ayer nosotros llegamos al estadio y empezamos a jugar fútbol. Jugamos muy bien. No tocamos el balón con las manos. Lo lanzamos con el pie o con la cabeza. Marcamos tres tantos.

EL VERANO Y EL INVIERNO   doscientos ochenta y tres 283

Graphic organizers and clear examples aid comprehension.

Realia adds interest to the lesson. Students see language they are learning in real-life contexts.

Strengthen proficiency with continuous reinforcement and reentry

Itinerary for Success

- ✓ Exposure to Hispanic culture
- ✓ Clear expectations and goals
- ✓ Thematic, contextualized vocabulary
- ✓ Useful and thematically linked structure
- ✓ Progressive practice
- ✓ Real-life conversation
- ✓ Cultural readings in the target language
- ✓ Connections to other disciplines . . . in Spanish!
- ✓ Recycling and review
- ✓ High-interest articles from **People en español**

Students build confidence as they complete activities that progress from easy to more challenging.

18 El baloncesto
Formen preguntas según el modelo.

—¿Jugó Pablo?
—A ver, Pablo, ¿jugaste?

1. ¿Jugó Pablo al baloncesto?
2. ¿Dribló con el balón?
3. ¿Pasó el balón a un amigo?
4. ¿Tiró el balón?
5. ¿Encestó?
6. ¿Marcó un tanto?

19 Historieta Una fiesta
Sigan el modelo.

hablar →
Mis amigos y yo hablamos durante la fiesta.

1. bailar
2. cantar
3. tomar un refresco
4. tomar fotos
5. escuchar música

Valdesquí, España

20 Historieta En una estación de esquí
Completen.

El fin de semana pasado José, algunos amigos y yo __1__ (esquiar). __2__ (Llegar) a la estación de esquí el viernes por la noche. Luego nosotros __3__ (pasar) dos días en las pistas.

José __4__ (comprar) un pase para el telesquí. Todos nosotros __5__ (tomar) el telesquí para subir la montaña. Pero todos nosotros __6__ (bajar) una pista diferente. José __7__ (bajar) la pista para expertos porque él esquía muy bien. Pero yo, no. Yo __8__ (tomar) la pista para principiantes. Y yo __9__ (bajar) con mucho cuidado.

284 doscientos ochenta y cuatro

CAPÍTULO 9

21 Pasaron el fin de semana en la playa. Look at the illustration. Work with a classmate, asking and answering questions about what these friends did at the beach in Acapulco.

Continuous reentry occurs as the chapter vocabulary and topic are used to practice the new structure points.

22 Pasé un día en una estación de esquí. You went on a skiing trip in the Sierra Nevada, Granada, Spain. You had a great time. Call your friend (a classmate) to tell him or her about your trip. Your friend has never been skiing so he or she will have a few questions for you.

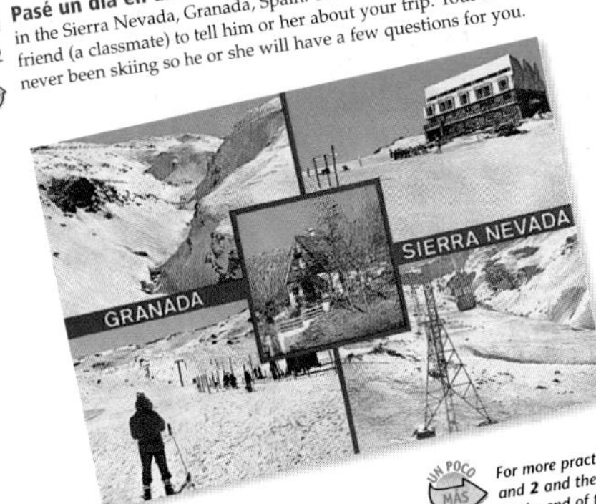

UN POCO MÁS *For more practice using words from **Palabras 1** and **2** and the preterite, do Activity 9 on page H10 at the end of this book.*

EL VERANO Y EL INVIERNO

doscientos ochenta y cinco 285

Un poco más points students to InfoGap activities. Pairs of students do these activities for additional practice.

Engage students in real conversation

Students can watch and participate in the interactive conversation on CD-ROM.

Students apply newly learned vocabulary and structures to real-life situations.

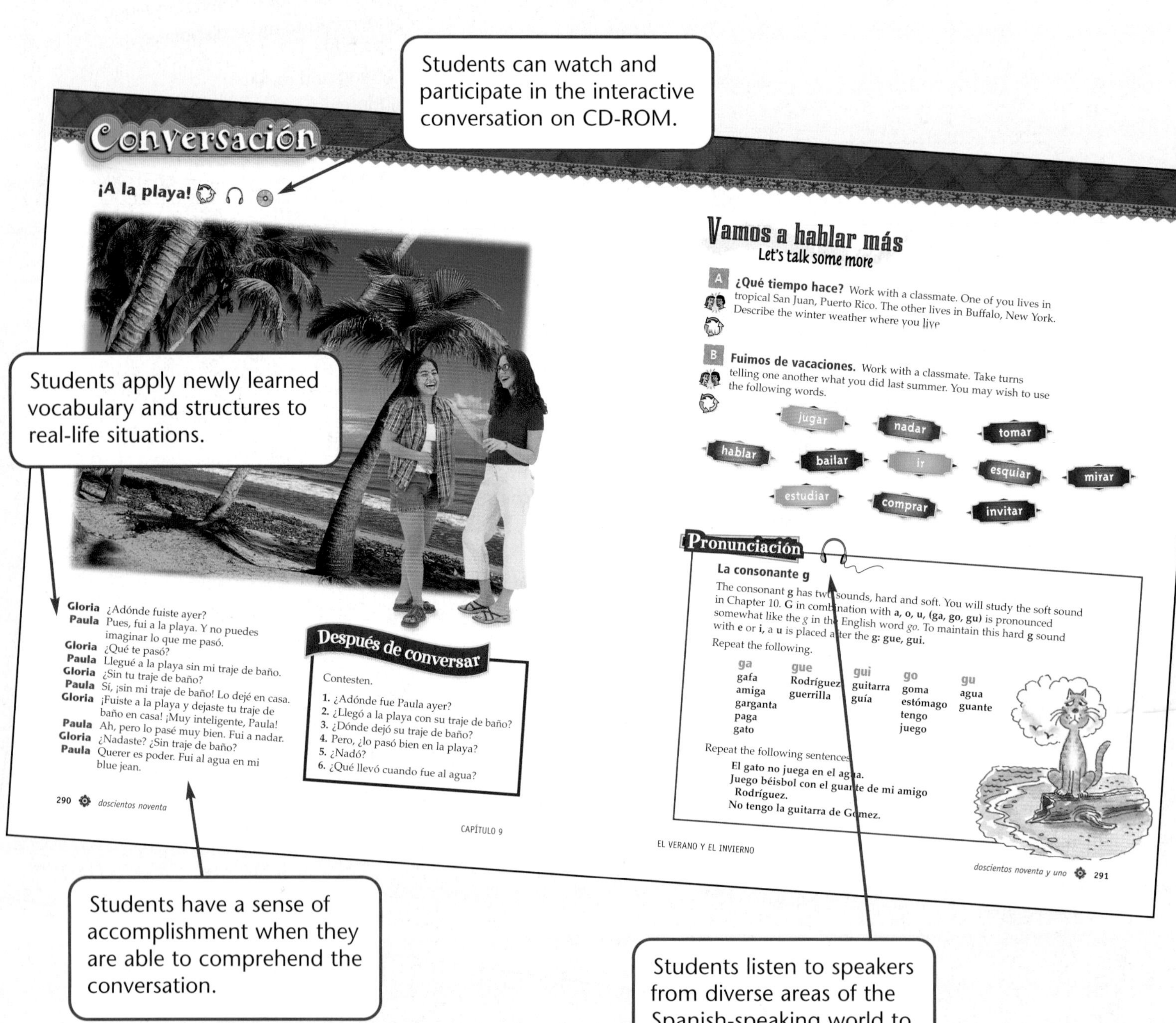

Conversación

¡A la playa!

Gloria ¿Adónde fuiste ayer?
Paula Pues, fui a la playa. Y no puedes imaginar lo que me pasó.
Gloria ¿Qué te pasó?
Paula Llegué a la playa sin mi traje de baño.
Gloria ¿Sin tu traje de baño?
Paula Sí, ¡sin mi traje de baño! Lo dejé en casa.
Gloria ¡Fuiste a la playa y dejaste tu traje de baño en casa! ¡Muy inteligente, Paula!
Paula Ah, pero lo pasé muy bien. Fui a nadar.
Gloria ¿Nadaste? ¿Sin traje de baño?
Paula Querer es poder. Fui al agua en mi blue jean.

Después de conversar

Contesten.

1. ¿Adónde fue Paula ayer?
2. ¿Llegó a la playa con su traje de baño?
3. ¿Dónde dejó su traje de baño?
4. Pero, ¿lo pasó bien en la playa?
5. ¿Nadó?
6. ¿Qué llevó cuando fue al agua?

290 dosdientos noventa — CAPÍTULO 9

Vamos a hablar más
Let's talk some more

A ¿Qué tiempo hace? Work with a classmate. One of you lives in tropical San Juan, Puerto Rico. The other lives in Buffalo, New York. Describe the winter weather where you live.

B Fuimos de vacaciones. Work with a classmate. Take turns telling one another what you did last summer. You may wish to use the following words.

jugar, nadar, tomar, hablar, bailar, ir, esquiar, mirar, estudiar, comprar, invitar

Pronunciación

La consonante g

The consonant **g** has two sounds, hard and soft. You will study the soft sound in Chapter 10. **G** in combination with **a, o, u, (ga, go, gu)** is pronounced somewhat like the *g* in the English word *go*. To maintain this hard **g** sound with **e** or **i**, a **u** is placed after the **g: gue, gui.**

Repeat the following.

ga	gue	gui	go	gu
gafa	Rodríguez	guitarra	goma	agua
amiga	guerrilla	guía	estómago	guante
garganta			tengo	
paga			juego	
gato				

Repeat the following sentences.

El gato no juega en el agua.
Juego béisbol con el guante de mi amigo Rodríguez.
No tengo la guitarra de Gómez.

EL VERANO Y EL INVIERNO — dosdientos noventa y uno 291

Students have a sense of accomplishment when they are able to comprehend the conversation.

Students listen to speakers from diverse areas of the Spanish-speaking world to improve pronunciation.

Heighten students' cultural awareness

Itinerary for Success

- ✓ Exposure to Hispanic culture
- ✓ Clear expectations and goals
- ✓ Thematic, contextualized vocabulary
- ✓ Useful and thematically linked structure
- ✓ Progressive practice
- ✓ Real-life conversation
- ✓ Cultural readings in the target language
- ✓ Connections to other disciplines . . . in Spanish!
- ✓ Recycling and review
- ✓ High-interest articles from **People en español**

Recorded reading on CD provides options for addressing various skills and learning styles.

Reading Strategies help students develop reading skills.

Lecturas culturales

Paraísos del mundo hispano

¿Viajar[1] por el mundo hispano y no pasar unos días en un balneario? ¡Qué lástima[2]! En los países de habla española hay playas fantásticas. España, Puerto Rico, Cuba, México, Uruguay—todos son países famosos por sus playas.

En el verano cuando hace calor y un sol bonito brilla en el cielo, ¡qué estupendo es pasar un día en la playa! Y en lugares (sitios) como México, Puerto Rico y Venezuela, el verano es eterno. Podemos ir a la playa durante todos los meses del año.

Muchas personas toman sus vacaciones en una playa donde pueden disfrutar de[3] su tiempo libre. En la playa nadan o toman el sol. Vuelven a casa muy tostaditos o bronceados. Pero, ¡cuidado! Es necesario usar una crema protectora porque el sol es muy fuerte[4] en las playas tropicales.

[1]Viajar *To travel* [2]lástima *pity* [3]disfrutar de *enjoy* [4]fuerte *strong*

Reading Strategy

Summarizing When reading an informative passage, we try to remember what we read. Summarizing helps us to do this. The easiest way to begin to summarize is to begin to read for the general sense and take notes on what you are reading. It is best to write a summarizing statement for each paragraph and then one for the entire passage.

Marbella, España

Cancún, México

La playa de Varadero, Cuba

Playa de Guajataca, Puerto Rico

Pocitos, Uruguay

¿Comprendes?

A La palabra, por favor. Den la palabra apropiada.

1. un lugar que tiene playas donde la gente puede nadar
2. una cosa triste y desagradable
3. maravillosas, estupendas
4. célebres
5. lindo, hermoso
6. de y para siempre
7. regresan a casa

B En la playa Contesten.

1. ¿Qué hay en los países de habla española?
2. ¿Cuándo es estupendo pasar un día en la playa?
3. ¿Cómo disfruta de su tiempo la gente que va a la playa?
4. ¿Cómo es el sol en las playas tropicales?

CAPÍTULO 9 EL VERANO Y EL INVIERNO

doscientos noventa y tres 293

Cultural reading uses learned language to reinforce chapter theme.

Many visuals help students comprehend what they read.

Activities reinforce vocabulary skills and comprehension.

Enrich students' cultural knowledge

Optional cultural readings reinforce the chapter theme.

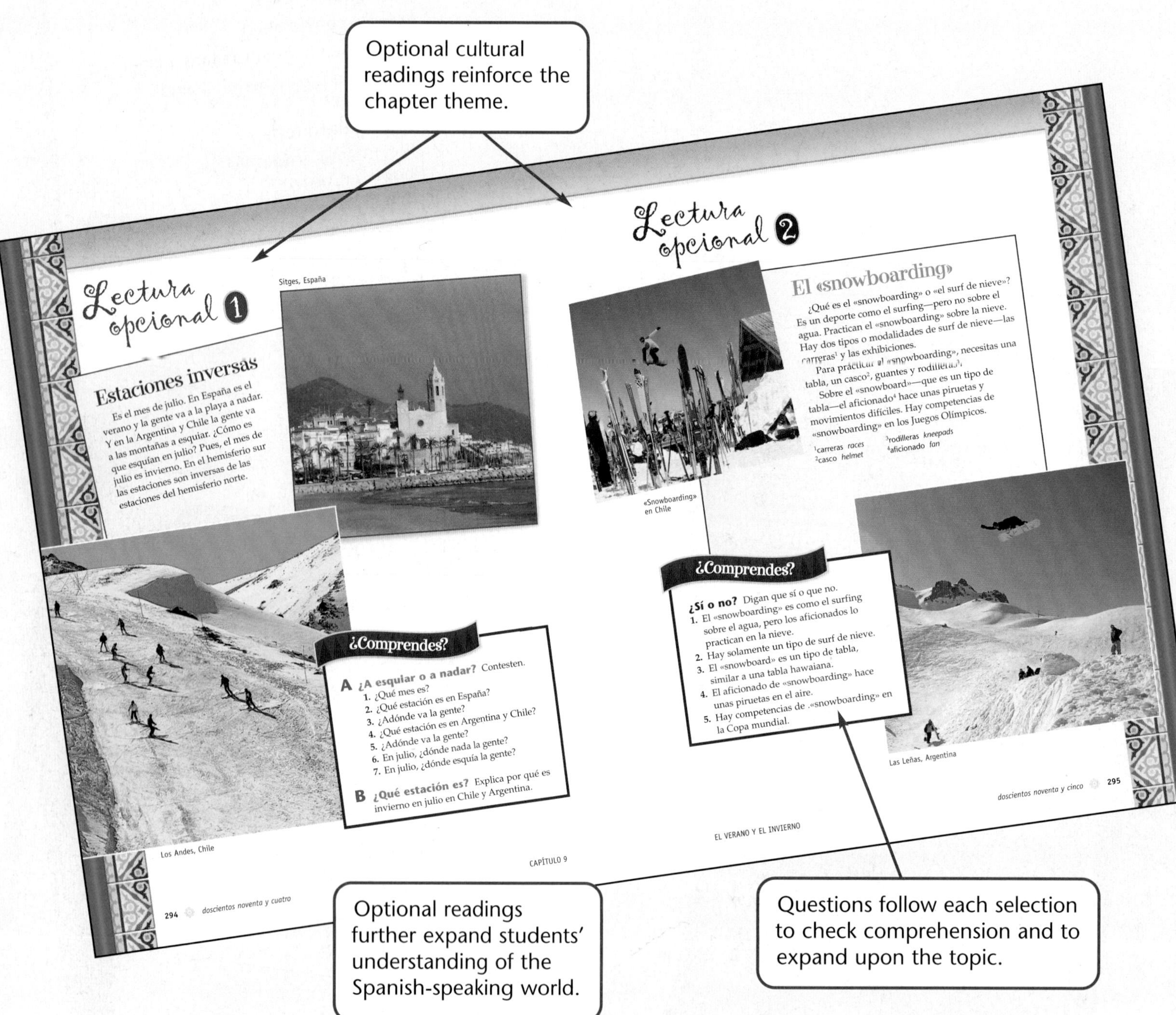

Lectura opcional 1

Sitges, España

Estaciones inversas

Es el mes de julio. En España es el verano y la gente va a la playa a nadar. Y en la Argentina y Chile la gente va a las montañas a esquiar. ¿Cómo es que esquían en julio? Pues, el mes de julio es invierno. En el hemisferio sur las estaciones son inversas de las estaciones del hemisferio norte.

¿Comprendes?

A ¿A esquiar o a nadar? Contesten.

1. ¿Qué mes es?
2. ¿Qué estación es en España?
3. ¿Adónde va la gente?
4. ¿Qué estación es en Argentina y Chile?
5. ¿Adónde va la gente?
6. En julio, ¿dónde nada la gente?
7. En julio, ¿dónde esquía la gente?

B ¿Qué estación es? Explica por qué es invierno en julio en Chile y Argentina.

Los Andes, Chile

294 doscientos noventa y cuatro — CAPÍTULO 9

Lectura opcional 2

El «snowboarding»

¿Qué es el «snowboarding» o «el surf de nieve»? Es un deporte como el surfing—pero no sobre el agua. Practican el «snowboarding» sobre la nieve. Hay dos tipos o modalidades de surf de nieve—las carreras[1] y las exhibiciones.

Para practicar el «snowboarding», necesitas una tabla, un casco[2], guantes y rodilleras[3].

Sobre el «snowboard»—que es un tipo de tabla—el aficionado[4] hace unas piruetas y movimientos difíciles. Hay competencias de «snowboarding» en los Juegos Olímpicos.

[1]carreras *races*
[2]casco *helmet*
[3]rodilleras *kneepads*
[4]aficionado *fan*

«Snowboarding» en Chile

¿Comprendes?

¿Sí o no? Digan que sí o que no.

1. El «snowboarding» es como el surfing sobre el agua, pero los aficionados lo practican en la nieve.
2. Hay solamente un tipo de surf de nieve.
3. El «snowboard» es un tipo de tabla, similar a una tabla hawaiana.
4. El aficionado de «snowboarding» hace unas piruetas en el aire.
5. Hay competencias de «snowboarding» en la Copa mundial.

Las Leñas, Argentina

EL VERANO Y EL INVIERNO — doscientos noventa y cinco 295

Optional readings further expand students' understanding of the Spanish-speaking world.

Questions follow each selection to check comprehension and to expand upon the topic.

Connect with other disciplines

Itinerary for Success

- ✓ Exposure to Hispanic culture
- ✓ Clear expectations and goals
- ✓ Thematic, contextualized vocabulary
- ✓ Useful and thematically linked structure
- ✓ Progressive practice
- ✓ Real-life conversation
- ✓ Cultural readings in the target language
- ✓ Connections to other disciplines . . . in Spanish!
- ✓ Recycling and review
- ✓ High-interest articles from **People en español**

Introduction to the **Conexiones** provides the background for students to understand the reading.

Conexiones

Las ciencias sociales

El clima

We often talk about the weather, especially when on vacation. When planning a vacation trip, it's a good idea to take into account the climate of the area we are going to visit. When we talk about weather or climate, we must remember, however, that there is a difference between the two. Weather is the condition of the atmosphere for a short period of time. Climate is the term used for the weather that prevails in a region over a long period of time. Let's read about weather and climate throughout the vast area of the Spanish-speaking world.

El Parque Nacional de los Glaciares, Argentina

El clima y el tiempo

El clima y el tiempo son dos cosas muy diferentes. El tiempo es la condición de la atmósfera durante un período breve o corto. El tiempo puede cambiar[1] frecuentemente. Puede cambiar varias veces en un solo día.

El clima es el término que usamos para el tiempo que prevalece[2] en una zona por un período largo. El clima es el tiempo que hace cada año en el mismo lugar.

Zonas climáticas

En el mundo de habla española hay muchas zonas climáticas. Mucha gente cree que toda la América Latina tiene un clima tropical, pero es erróneo. El clima de Latinoamérica varía de una región a otra.

[1]cambiar *change*
[2]prevalece *prevails*

La vegetación tropical, Costa Rica

296 *doscientos noventa y seis*

CAPÍTULO 9

El Amazonas

Toda la zona o cuenca amazónica es una región tropical. Hace mucho calor y llueve mucho durante todo el año.

El río Santiago Cayapas, Ecuador

Los Andes

En los Andes, aún en las regiones cerca de la línea ecuatorial, el clima no es tropical. En las zonas montañosas el clima depende de la elevación. En los picos andinos, por ejemplo, hace frío.

Clima templado

Algunas partes de Argentina, Uruguay y Chile tienen un clima templado. España también tiene un clima templado. En una región de clima templado hay cuatro estaciones: el verano, el otoño, el invierno y la primavera. Y el tiempo cambia con cada estación. ¡Y una cosa importante! Las estaciones en la América del Sur son inversas de las de la América del Norte.

Los picos andinos cerca de Cuzco, Perú

Una aldea en las montañas, Ecuador

¿Comprendes?

¿Sabes? Contesten en inglés.

1. What's the difference between weather and climate?
2. What is an erroneous idea that many people have about Latin America?
3. How can it be cold in some areas that are actually on the equator?
4. What is a characteristic of a tropical area?
5. What is a characteristic of a region with a temperate climate?

doscientos noventa y siete 297

Students further their knowledge of other disciplines—in Spanish!

Encourage students to apply what they have learned

Students use their newly acquired skills to communicate in meaningful, open-ended activities.

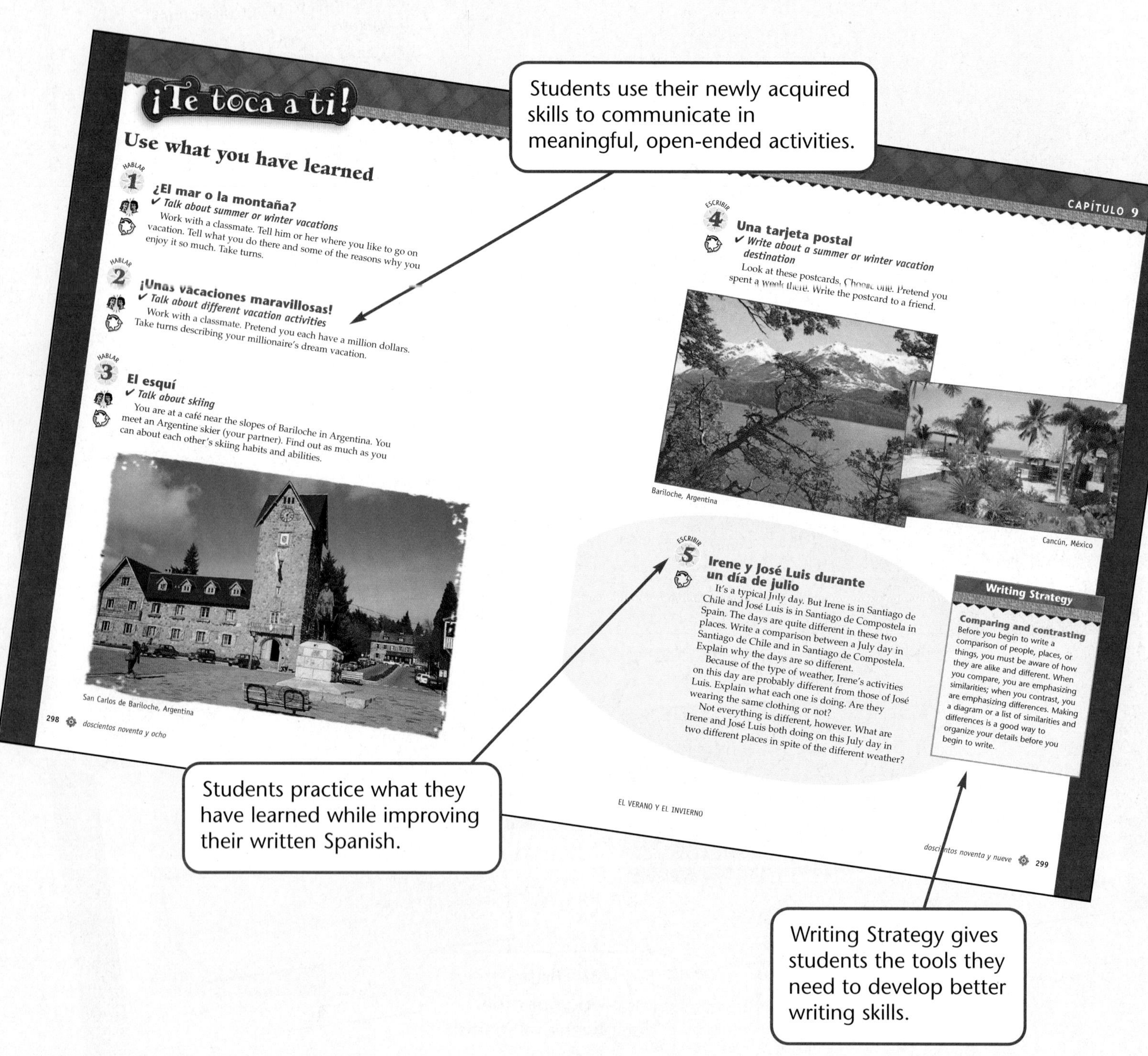

¡Te toca a ti!

Use what you have learned

HABLAR **1** **¿El mar o la montaña?**

✔ *Talk about summer or winter vacations*

Work with a classmate. Tell him or her where you like to go on vacation. Tell what you do there and some of the reasons why you enjoy it so much. Take turns.

HABLAR **2** **¡Unas vacaciones maravillosas!**

✔ *Talk about different vacation activities*

Work with a classmate. Pretend you each have a million dollars. Take turns describing your millionaire's dream vacation.

HABLAR **3** **El esquí**

✔ *Talk about skiing*

You are at a café near the slopes of Bariloche in Argentina. You meet an Argentine skier (your partner). Find out as much as you can about each other's skiing habits and abilities.

San Carlos de Bariloche, Argentina

298 doscientos noventa y ocho

CAPÍTULO 9

ESCRIBIR **4** **Una tarjeta postal**

✔ *Write about a summer or winter vacation destination*

Look at these postcards. Choose one. Pretend you spent a week there. Write the postcard to a friend.

Bariloche, Argentina

Cancún, México

ESCRIBIR **5** **Irene y José Luis durante un día de julio**

It's a typical July day. But Irene is in Santiago de Chile and José Luis is in Santiago de Compostela in Spain. The days are quite different in these two places. Write a comparison between a July day in Santiago de Chile and in Santiago de Compostela. Explain why the days are so different.

Because of the type of weather, Irene's activities on this day are probably different from those of José Luis. Explain what each one is doing. Are they wearing the same clothing or not?

Not everything is different, however. What are Irene and José Luis both doing on this July day in two different places in spite of the different weather?

Writing Strategy

Comparing and contrasting Before you begin to write a comparison of people, places, or things, you must be aware of how they are alike and different. When you compare, you are emphasizing similarities; when you contrast, you are emphasizing differences. Making a diagram or a list of similarities and differences is a good way to organize your details before you begin to write.

EL VERANO Y EL INVIERNO

doscientos noventa y nueve 299

Students practice what they have learned while improving their written Spanish.

Writing Strategy gives students the tools they need to develop better writing skills.

Check students' progress

Itinerary for Success

- ✓ Exposure to Hispanic culture
- ✓ Clear expectations and goals
- ✓ Thematic, contextualized vocabulary
- ✓ Useful and thematically linked structure
- ✓ Progressive practice
- ✓ Real-life conversation
- ✓ Cultural readings in the target language
- ✓ Connections to other disciplines . . . in Spanish!
- ✓ Recycling and review
- ✓ High-interest articles from **People en español**

Assessment activities give students a chance to evaluate what they have really learned.

"Sticky" notes direct students to the correct pages for review.

Assessment

Vocabulario

1 Identifiquen.

1. 2. 3. 4. 5.

To review **Palabras 1**, turn to pages 274–275.

...mpo hace en el verano?

To review **Palabras 2**, turn to pages 278–279.

3 Completen.

7. La esquiadora lleva un ___ cuando hace frío y nieva mucho.
8. Para esquiar es necesario tener (uno necesita) ___ y bastones.
9. Los esquiadores tomaron el ___ para subir la montaña.
10. Los esquiadores que no esquían bien bajan la ___ para principiantes.

Estru...

4 Completen con ...

11. Él ___ en el mar. (nadar)
12. Sus amigos ___ en la piscina. (nadar)
13. Y tú, ¿___ en el agua? (esquiar)
14. No. Yo ___ el sol. (tomar)
15. Nosotros ___ toda la tarde en la playa. (pasar)
16. Y Uds., ¿___ a la playa también? (ir)

To review the pret..., turn to pages 282 and 288.

5 Escriban en el pretérito.

17. Juego al fútbol.
18. Sí, empiezo a jugar.

To review direct object pronouns, turn to page 286.

6 Escriban con un pronombre.

19. No tengo *mis anteojos de sol.*
20. Compré *la loción bronceadora* en la farmacia.
21. Tomás tomó *las fotografías.* Yo, no.
22. Invitamos *a José* a ir a la playa.
23. Ella compró *el bañador* en El Corte Inglés.

Cultura

To review this cultural information, turn to page 292.

7 ¿Sí o no?

24. Un balneario es una estación de esquí.
25. Muchos países de habla española tienen playas fabulosas.

300 trescientos — CAPÍTULO 9 — EL VERANO Y EL INVIERNO — trescientos uno 301

Take students beyond the text to learn more about culture and language
Give students opportunities to review and use their vocabulary in creative ways

The illustration provided at the end of each chapter recombines material students have learned to remind them of what they know how to say in Spanish. Use this illustration as a prompt to allow your students to demonstrate all they know how to say or write.

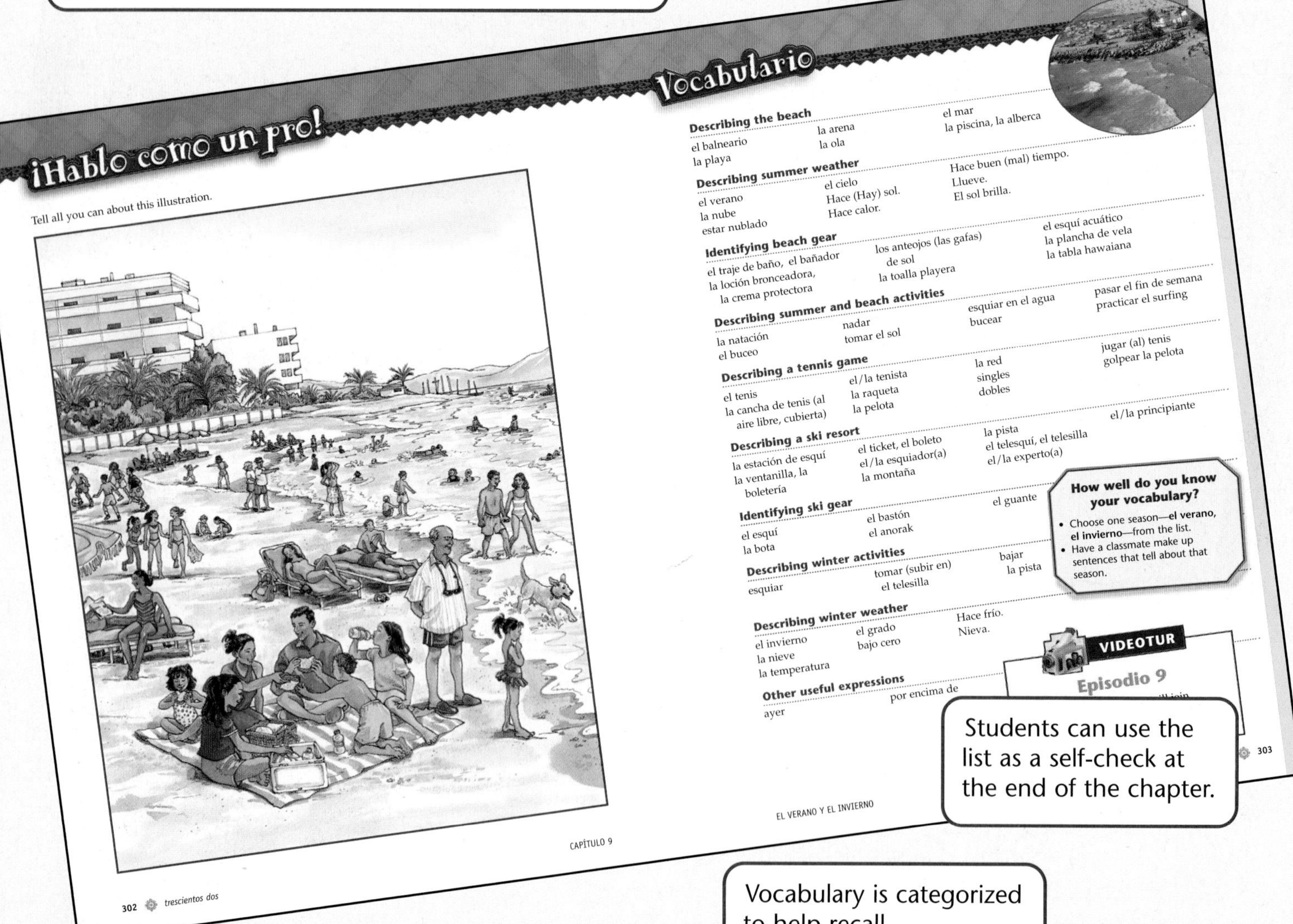

¡Hablo como un pro!

Tell all you can about this illustration.

302 trescientos dos — CAPÍTULO 9

Vocabulario

Describing the beach
el balneario, la playa, la arena, la ola, el mar, la piscina, la alberca

Describing summer weather
el verano, la nube, estar nublado, el cielo, Hace (Hay) sol., Hace calor., Hace buen (mal) tiempo., Llueve., El sol brilla.

Identifying beach gear
el traje de baño, el bañador, la loción bronceadora, la crema protectora, los anteojos (las gafas) de sol, la toalla playera, el esquí acuático, la plancha de vela, la tabla hawaiana

Describing summer and beach activities
la natación, el buceo, nadar, tomar el sol, esquiar en el agua, bucear, pasar el fin de semana, practicar el surfing

Describing a tennis game
el tenis, la cancha de tenis (al aire libre, cubierta), el/la tenista, la raqueta, la pelota, la red, singles, dobles, jugar (al) tenis, golpear la pelota

Describing a ski resort
la estación de esquí, la ventanilla, la boletería, el ticket, el boleto, el/la esquiador(a), la montaña, la pista, el telesquí, el telesilla, el/la experto(a), el/la principiante

Identifying ski gear
el esquí, la bota, el bastón, el anorak, el guante

Describing winter activities
esquiar, tomar (subir en) el telesilla, bajar la pista

Describing winter weather
el invierno, la nieve, la temperatura, el grado, bajo cero, Hace frío., Nieva.

Other useful expressions
ayer, por encima de

How well do you know your vocabulary?
- Choose one season—**el verano, el invierno**—from the list.
- Have a classmate make up sentences that tell about that season.

VIDEOTUR
Episodio 9

EL VERANO Y EL INVIERNO — 303

Students can use the list as a self-check at the end of the chapter.

Vocabulary is categorized to help recall.

People en español motivates students to read and learn about the diverse cultures of the Spanish-speaking world

Itinerary for Success

- ✓ Exposure to Hispanic culture
- ✓ Clear expectations and goals
- ✓ Thematic, contextualized vocabulary
- ✓ Useful and thematically linked structure
- ✓ Progressive practice
- ✓ Real-life conversation
- ✓ Cultural readings in the target language
- ✓ Connections to other disciplines . . . in Spanish!
- ✓ Recycling and review
- ✓ High-interest articles from **People en español**

People en español articles throughout **¡Buen viaje!** take students to different regions in the world where Spanish is spoken.

People Entérate Región andina

Una expedición a los países andinos

Bolivia es un país sudamericano. ¿De dónde o de qué origen es el nombre Bolivia? Antes de[1] llegar los conquistadores españoles, ¿qué país es el centro de la civilización de los famosos incas? Y, ¿de qué origen es el nombre de otro país de los Andes, Ecuador? ¿Cómo contestas?

- **"Bolivia" es del nombre del gran héroe y libertador latinoamericano, Simón Bolívar. Es la contestación correcta.**
- **Perú es el centro de la civilización incaica—de los incas. Una vez más, una respuesta correcta.**
- **Ecuador recibe su nombre de la línea del ecuador, de la línea ecuatorial que divide el mundo en dos hemisferios: el hemisferio norte y el hemisferio sur.**

Hay otros datos de la región andina que son muy interesantes. La UNESCO de las Naciones Unidas declara los siguientes sitios Patrimonio Mundial de la Humanidad.

Entérate Perú

Machu Picchu Las famosas ruinas de los incas están en un pico estrecho[2] de los majestuosos Andes. En Machu Picchu hay torres de vigilancia, acueductos, casas, observatorios y un reloj solar[3]. El reloj solar marca las estaciones del año. En quechua, la lengua de los incas, Machu Picchu significa "montaña vieja". En la época en que llegan los españoles, los incas no tienen una forma escrita[4] de su lengua. Interpretan mensajes[5] y números con cuerdas de muchos colores con nudos[6].

Muchos aspectos de la historia de Machu Picchu son un misterio. Pero algo está muy claro; en la época en que construyen los incas la fabulosa ciudad no tienen cemento, no tienen ruedas y no tienen caballos ni bestias de carga ni carritos.

Cuzco Por mucho tiempo Cuzco es la capital de los incas y es el centro de un sistema de caminos que une Sudamérica. Cuando llega Francisco Pizarra a Cuzco y conquista la ciudad, los españoles transforman los templos y palacios de los incas en iglesias y magníficas casas.

Arequipa Arequipa es "la Ciudad Blanca." Es una ciudad blanca porque construyen las casas y los otros edificios de una piedra volcánica que hay en Arequipa. La piedra tiene un color blanco brillante.

Machu Picchu

[1]antes de: *before*
[2]estrecho: *narrow*
[3]reloj solar: *solar clock*
[4]escrita: *written*
[5]mensajes: *messages*
[6]cuerdas... con nudos: *cords... with knots*

Entérate Bolivia

Potosí Durante una parte de la época colonial Potosí es la ciudad más grande de las Américas a causa de la explotación de plata[1] en la región. Hoy Potosí es la ciudad más alta[2] del mundo.

Sucre La ciudad colonial de Sucre es muy importante porque es en Sucre donde acuñan monedas[3] de plata. Los españoles envían[4] las monedas a España. El dinero que envían a España tiene mucha importancia en la economía de España y Europa en el siglo XVII.

[1]plata: *silver*
[2]más alta: *highest*
[3]acuñan monedas: *they mint coins*
[4]envían: *send*

Potosí

368

Las Islas Galápagos

Entérate Ecuador

Parque Nacional Sangay En el parque hay tres volcanes. El parque lleva el nombre de uno de los volcanes—el volcán Sangay. De todos los volcanes del mundo el Sangay es activo durante más tiempo que cualquier otro[1]. Varias comunidades indígenas viven en el parque que está en la lista de Patrimonios en Peligro[2]. ¿Por qué está en peligro? A causa de la construcción de una carretera moderna y la caza[3] ilegal.

Quito Cerca del volcán Pichincha, la bella ciudad de Quito tiene iglesias coloniales decoradas de pan de oro[4]. El barrio antiguo de la ciudad con sus calles estrechas de piedra y casas con balcones y patios refleja la influencia española.

Las Islas Galápagos Galápagos son las tortugas[5] gigantes que habitan el archipiélago de las Galápagos a unos mil kilómetros de la costa ecuatoriana. En el pasado naturalistas como Charles Darwin estudian las especies de flora y fauna del archipiélago. Algunas son únicas en el mundo.

[1]cualquier otro: *any other*
[2]peligro: *danger*
[3]caza: *hunting*
[4]pan de oro: *gold leaf*
[5]tortugas: *turtles*

Calendario de fiestas

Carnaval, Oruro, Bolivia, febrero
Declarado Obra Maestra por la UNESCO el carnaval de Oruro, Bolivia, es una fiesta muy alegre. Hay danzantes en las calles que llevan trajes y máscaras vistosas[1] de muchos colores.

Pachamama Raymi, todo el país, Perú, 1° de agosto
Pachamama es la diosa de la Tierra de los indígenas peruanos. El 1° de agosto marca el comienzo del año andino y los indígenas hacen tributo[2] a su diosa con una ceremonia de ofrenda[3] que llaman[4] "Pago de la Tierra".

Carnaval, Oruro, Bolivia

Tradiciones ancestrales, Amazonia, Ecuador
En la comunidad indichuris y la comunidad de los quechuas—poblaciones indígenas—habitan shamanes que practican sus tradiciones ancestrales. A veces dejan a los visitantes participar en los rituales.

[1]vistosas: *colorful*
[3]ofrenda: *offering*
[4]llaman: *they call*

música

El sonido andino

En todo el mundo goza de cierta popularidad la música andina. Pero hay muchos que no son familiares con los instrumentos musicales de los Andes. Unos son de origen puro andino y datan de miles de años. Otros son de origen europeo pero adaptados a los distintos ritmos y tonos andinos. ¡A tocar la zampoña!

La zampoña

La zampoña Es un instrumento de tubos de caña de tamaños diferentes. La nota musical varía según el tamaño del tubo.

La quena Es un instrumento de viento. Es de caña, madera[1] o hueso[2]. El tamaño del instrumento varía de una región a otra.

El charango

El charango Es como la guitarra, pero el instrumento es más pequeño que la guitarra y tiene catorce cuerdas[3].

[1]madera: *wood*
[2]hueso: *bone*
[3]cuerdas: *strings*

369

Students learn about topics that interest them—holidays, foods, entertainment, and famous people—in Spanish they can read!

Enhance appreciation of literature and culture

Literary Companion affords students yet another opportunity to apply their reading skills in Spanish.

Literary selections present another view of Hispanic culture.

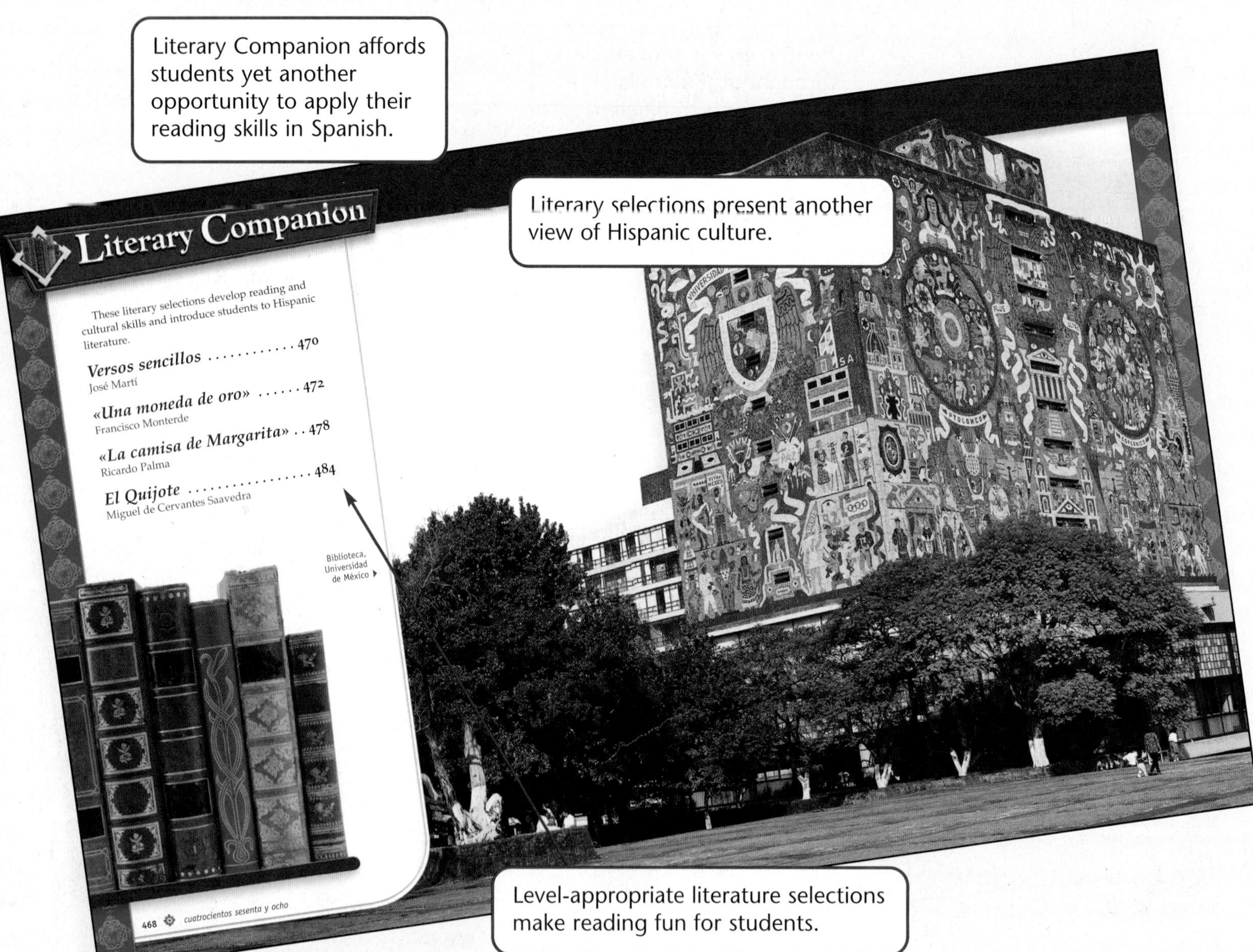

Level-appropriate literature selections make reading fun for students.

Take your students on a tour of the Spanish-speaking world with ¡Viva el mundo hispano!

Itinerary for Success

- ✓ Exposure to Hispanic culture
- ✓ Clear expectations and goals
- ✓ Thematic, contextualized vocabulary
- ✓ Useful and thematically linked structure
- ✓ Progressive practice
- ✓ Real-life conversation
- ✓ Cultural readings in the target language
- ✓ Connections to other disciplines . . . in Spanish!
- ✓ Recycling and review
- ✓ High-interest articles from **People en español**

¡Viva el mundo hispano!, filmed in eight Spanish-speaking countries, lets your students experience the diversity of the Spanish-speaking world while reinforcing the language they have learned and improving their listening and viewing skills.

Video Companion

Using video in the classroom

The use of video in the classroom can be a w… a most beneficial learning tool for the langu… whatever it is they are learning in their text… are able to take a vicarious field trip. They see peo… etc., in an authentic milieu. Students sitting in a cla… life in real places. They may experience the target c… limitless.

Developing listening and viewing skills

In addition to its tremendous cultural value, vide… needed practice in developing good listening and vi… numerous clues that are evident in a tone of voice, f… students can see and hear the diversity of the target c… compare and contrast the Spanish-speaking cultures to each other and to their own culture. Video introduces a dimension into classroom instruction that no other medium—teachers, overhead, text, audio CDs—can provide.

Reinforcing learned language

Video that is properly developed for classroom use has speakers reincorporate the language students have learned in a given lesson. In keeping with reality, however, speakers introduce some new words, expressions, and structures because students functioning in a real-life situation would not know every word native speakers use with them in a live conversation. The lively and interactive nature of video allows students to use their listening and viewing skills to comprehend new language in addition to seeing and hearing the language they have learned come to life.

Getting the most out of video

The intrinsic benefit of video is often lost when students are allowed to read the scripted material before viewing. In many cases, students will have come to understand language used by the speakers in the video by means of reading comprehension, thus negating the inherent benefits of video as a tool to develop listening and viewing skills. Because today's students are so accustomed to the medium of video as a tool for entertainment and learning, a well-written and well-produced video program will help them develop real-life language skills and confidence in those skills in an enjoyable way.

490 cuatrocientos noventa

Your students will love seeing the adventures and mishaps of the teen characters in **¡Viva el mundo hispano!**

On Location

Soy Alberto. Soy colombiano. Soy de Bogota, Colombia.
Soy Alejandra. Soy mexicana. Soy de la Ciudad de México.
Soy Francisco. Soy español. Soy de Madrid, España.
Soy Vicky. Soy argentina. Soy de Buenos Aires.
Soy Claudia. Soy argentina. Soy de Buenos Aires, Argentina.
Soy Julián. Soy venezolano. Soy de Caracas, Venezuela.

Students will visit places where they will hear different accents, dialects, and languages spoken. **¡Viva el mundo hispano!** will take you and your students on an exciting tour of the Spanish-speaking world.

Preview and objectives let you know what to plan for

Spotlight on Culture gives you facts and information about the art and photographs on the page. Your students will think you know everything.

References to the National Standards are made for you.

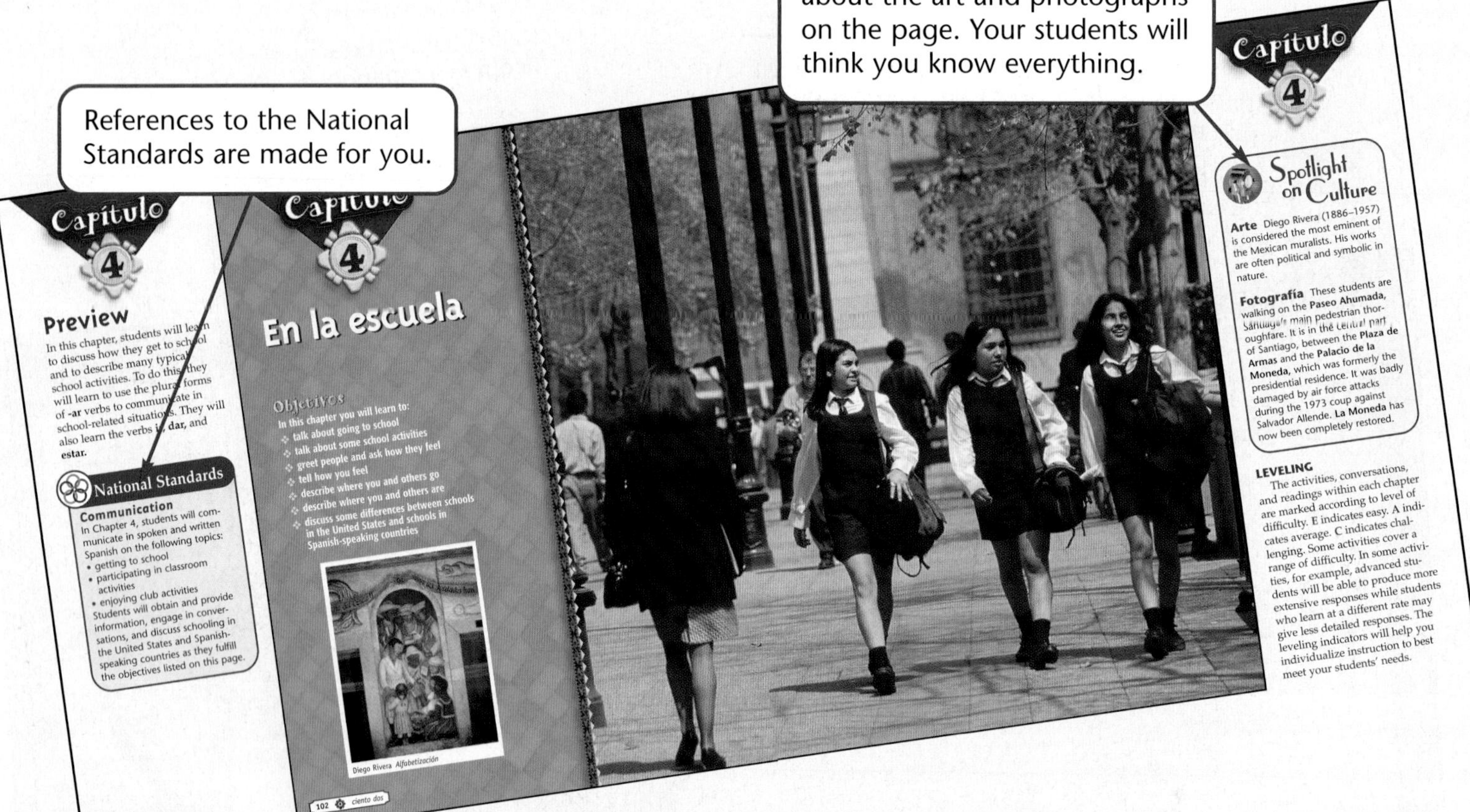

Capítulo 4

Preview

In this chapter, students will learn to discuss how they get to school and to describe many typical school activities. To do this, they will learn to use the plural forms of **-ar** verbs to communicate in school-related situations. They will also learn the verbs **ir, dar,** and **estar.**

National Standards

Communication
In Chapter 4, students will communicate in spoken and written Spanish on the following topics:

- getting to school
- participating in classroom activities
- enjoying club activities

Students will obtain and provide information, engage in conversations, and discuss schooling in the United States and Spanish-speaking countries as they fulfill the objectives listed on this page.

Capítulo 4

En la escuela

Objetivos

In this chapter you will learn to:

- talk about going to school
- talk about some school activities
- greet people and ask how they feel
- tell how you feel
- describe where you and others go
- describe where you and others are
- discuss some differences between schools in the United States and schools in Spanish-speaking countries

Diego Rivera *Alfabetización*

102 ciento dos

Capítulo 4

Spotlight on Culture

Arte Diego Rivera (1886–1957) is considered the most eminent of the Mexican muralists. His works are often political and symbolic in nature.

Fotografía These students are walking on the **Paseo Ahumada,** Santiago's main pedestrian thoroughfare. It is in the central part of Santiago, between the **Plaza de Armas** and the **Palacio de la Moneda,** which was formerly the presidential residence. It was badly damaged by air force attacks during the 1973 coup against Salvador Allende. **La Moneda** has now been completely restored.

LEVELING

The activities, conversations, and readings within each chapter are marked according to level of difficulty. E indicates easy. A indicates average. C indicates challenging. Some activities cover a range of difficulty. In some activities, for example, advanced students will be able to produce more extensive responses while students who learn at a different rate may give less detailed responses. The leveling indicators will help you individualize instruction to best meet your students' needs.

Get some great ideas for fun activities from **Chapter Projects.**

Spanish Online gives you ideas for expanding your lesson—virtually.

¡Buen viaje! is written to address learners with different ability levels. The activities, conversations, and readings throughout the text are marked to indicate their level of difficulty to help you individualize instruction.

Step-by-step hints help you through the chapter

Resource Manager lets you know which resources you will need for each part of the chapter.

Bellringer Reviews (also available in the Transparency Binder) provide quick checks of previously taught material.

Clear, step-by-step instruction guides your presentation of the lesson.

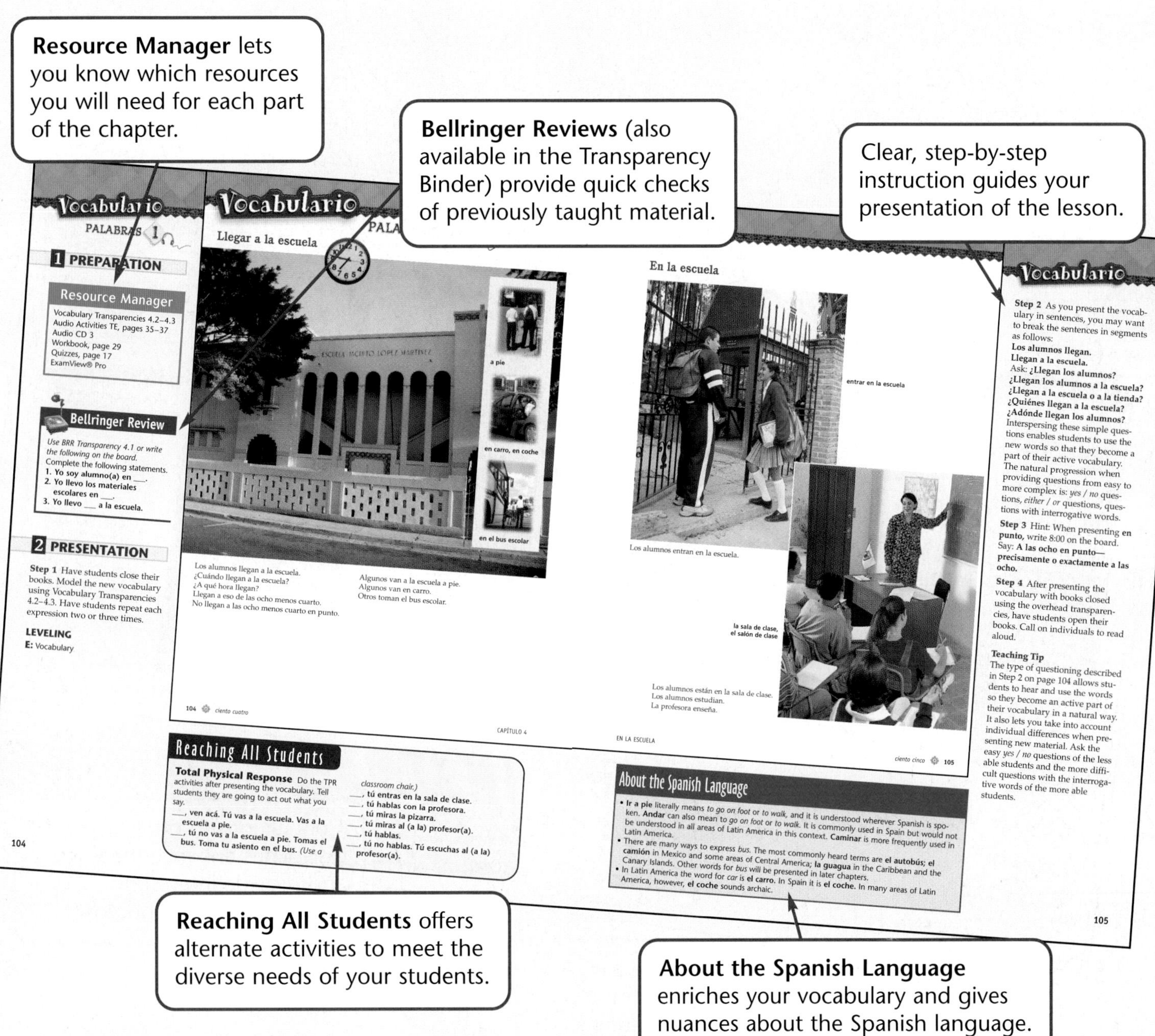

Vocabulario

PALABRAS 1

1 PREPARATION

Resource Manager

Vocabulary Transparencies 4.2–4.3
Audio Activities TE, pages 35–37
Audio CD 3
Workbook, page 29
Quizzes, page 17
ExamView® Pro

Bellringer Review

Use BRR Transparency 4.1 or write the following on the board.
Complete the following statements.
1. **Yo soy alumno(a) en ___.**
2. **Yo llevo los materiales escolares en ___.**
3. **Yo llevo ___ a la escuela.**

2 PRESENTATION

Step 1 Have students close their books. Model the new vocabulary using Vocabulary Transparencies 4.2–4.3. Have students repeat each expression two or three times.

LEVELING
E: Vocabulary

Vocabulario

Llegar a la escuela

Los alumnos llegan a la escuela.
¿Cuándo llegan a la escuela?
¿A qué hora llegan?
Llegan a eso de las ocho menos cuarto.
No llegan a las ocho menos cuarto en punto.

Algunos van a la escuela a pie.
Algunos van en carro.
Otros toman el bus escolar.

104 ciento cuatro — CAPÍTULO 4

En la escuela

Los alumnos entran en la escuela.

Los alumnos están en la sala de clase.
Los alumnos estudian.
La profesora enseña.

EN LA ESCUELA — ciento cinco 105

Vocabulario

Step 2 As you present the vocabulary in sentences, you may want to break the sentences in segments as follows:
Los alumnos llegan.
Llegan a la escuela.
Ask: **¿Llegan los alumnos?**
¿Llegan los alumnos a la escuela?
¿Llegan a la escuela o a la tienda?
¿Quiénes llegan a la escuela?
¿Adónde llegan los alumnos?
Interspersing these simple questions enables students to use the new words so that they become a part of their active vocabulary. The natural progression when providing questions from easy to more complex is: *yes / no* questions, *either / or* questions, questions with interrogative words.

Step 3 Hint: When presenting **en punto**, write 8:00 on the board. Say: **A las ocho en punto—precisamente o exactamente a las ocho.**

Step 4 After presenting the vocabulary with books closed using the overhead transparencies, have students open their books. Call on individuals to read aloud.

Teaching Tip
The type of questioning described in Step 2 on page 104 allows students to hear and use the words so they become an active part of their vocabulary in a natural way. It also lets you take into account individual differences when presenting new material. Ask the easy *yes / no* questions of the less able students and the more difficult questions with the interrogative words of the more able students.

Reaching All Students

Total Physical Response Do the TPR activities after presenting the vocabulary. Tell students they are going to act out what you say.
___, **ven acá. Tú vas a la escuela. Vas a la escuela a pie.**
___, **tú no vas a la escuela a pie. Tomas el bus. Toma tu asiento en el bus.** *(Use a classroom chair.)*
___, **tú entras en la sala de clase.**
___, **tú hablas con la profesora.**
___, **tú miras la pizarra.**
___, **tú miras al (a la) profesor(a).**
___, **tú hablas.**
___, **tú no hablas. Tú escuchas al (a la) profesor(a).**

104

About the Spanish Language

- **Ir a pie** literally means *to go on foot* or *to walk*, and it is understood wherever Spanish is spoken. **Andar** can also mean *to go on foot* or *to walk*. It is commonly used in Spain but would not be understood in all areas of Latin America in this context. **Caminar** is more frequently used in Latin America.
- There are many ways to express *bus*. The most commonly heard terms are **el autobús; el camión** in Mexico and some areas of Central America; **la guagua** in the Caribbean and the Canary Islands. Other words for *bus* will be presented in later chapters.
- In Latin America the word for *car* is **el carro**. In Spain it is **el coche**. In many areas of Latin America, however, **el coche** sounds archaic.

105

Reaching All Students offers alternate activities to meet the diverse needs of your students.

About the Spanish Language enriches your vocabulary and gives nuances about the Spanish language.

Painless presentation of structure makes it easier for you to reach your students

¡Ojo! points out potential problems and gives you tips for avoiding them.

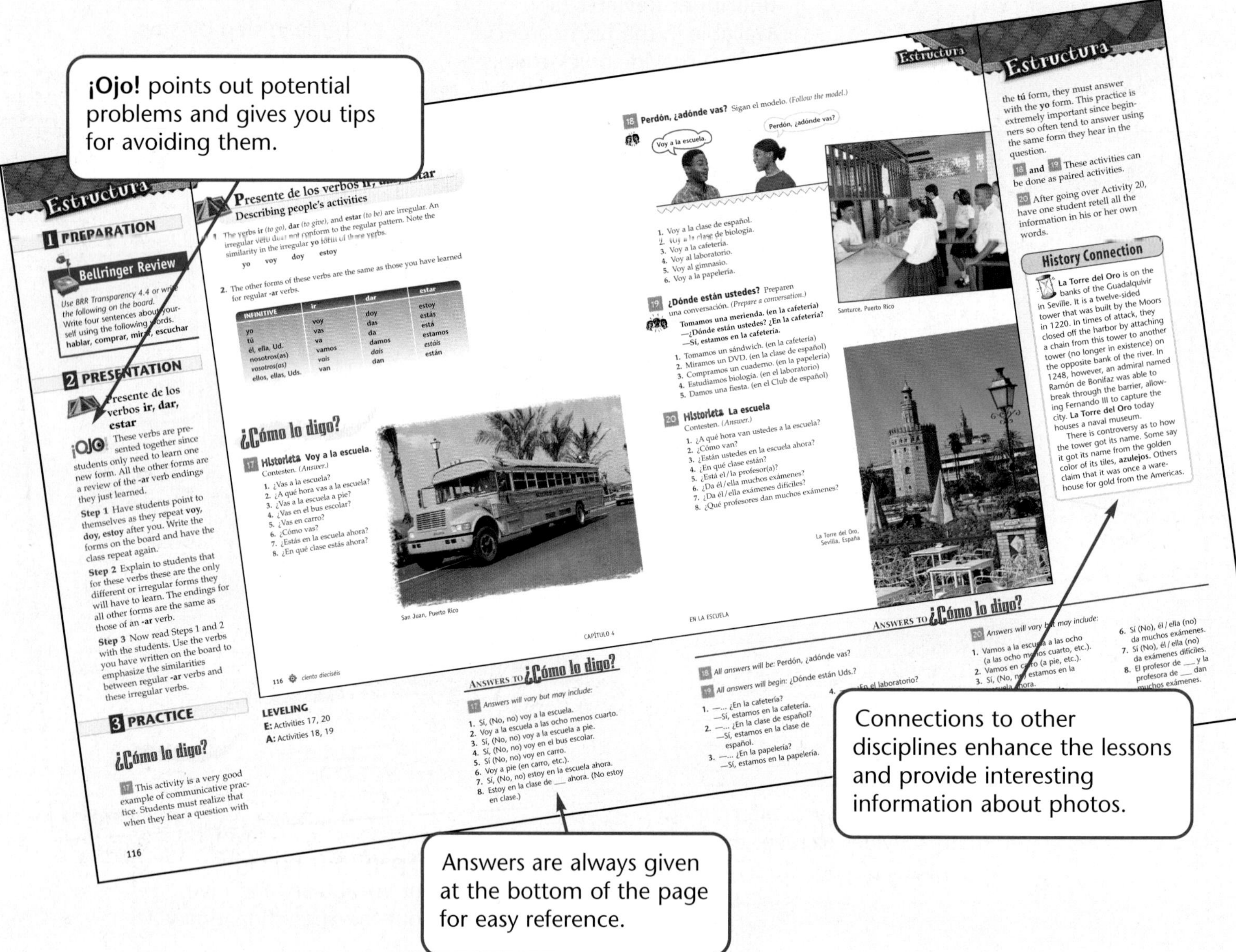
Estructura

PREPARATION

Bellringer Review

Use BRR Transparency 4.4 or write the following on the board. Write four sentences about yourself using the following words. hablar, comprar, mirar, escuchar

PRESENTATION

Presente de los verbos ir, dar, estar

¡Ojo! These verbs are presented together since students only need to learn one new form. All the other forms are a review of the -ar verb endings they just learned.

Step 1 Have students point to themselves as they repeat voy, doy, estoy after you. Write the forms on the board and have the class repeat again.

Step 2 Explain to students that for these verbs these are the only different or irregular forms they will have to learn. The endings for all other forms are the same as those of an -ar verb.

Step 3 Now read Steps 1 and 2 with the students. Use the verbs you have written on the board to emphasize the similarities between regular -ar verbs and these irregular verbs.

PRACTICE

¿Cómo lo digo?

17 This activity is a very good example of communicative practice. Students must realize that when they hear a question with

116

Presente de los verbos ir, dar, estar
Describing people's activities

1. The verbs ir (to go), dar (to give), and estar (to be) are irregular. An irregular verb does not conform to the regular pattern. Note the similarity in the irregular yo form of these verbs.

yo voy doy estoy

2. The other forms of these verbs are the same as those you have learned for regular -ar verbs.

INFINITIVE	ir	dar	estar
yo	voy	doy	estoy
tú	vas	das	estás
él, ella, Ud.	va	da	está
nosotros(as)	vamos	damos	estamos
vosotros(as)	vais	dais	estáis
ellos, ellas, Uds.	van	dan	están

¿Cómo lo digo?

17 Historieta Voy a la escuela.
Contesten. (Answer.)
1. ¿Vas a la escuela?
2. ¿A qué hora vas a la escuela?
3. ¿Vas a la escuela a pie?
4. ¿Vas en el bus escolar?
5. ¿Vas en carro?
6. ¿Cómo vas?
7. ¿Estás en la escuela ahora?
8. ¿En qué clase estás ahora?

San Juan, Puerto Rico

116 ciento dieciséis

CAPÍTULO 4

18 Perdón, ¿adónde vas? Sigan el modelo. (Follow the model.)

Voy a la escuela.
Perdón, ¿adónde vas?

1. Voy a la clase de español.
2. Voy a la clase de biología.
3. Voy a la cafetería.
4. Voy al laboratorio.
5. Voy al gimnasio.
6. Voy a la papelería.

Santurce, Puerto Rico

19 ¿Dónde están ustedes? Preparen una conversación. (Prepare a conversation.)
Tomamos una merienda. (en la cafetería)
—¿Dónde están ustedes? ¿En la cafetería?
—Sí, estamos en la cafetería.
1. Tomamos un sándwich. (en la cafetería)
2. Miramos un DVD. (en la clase de español)
3. Compramos un cuaderno. (en la papelería)
4. Estudiamos biología. (en el laboratorio)
5. Damos una fiesta. (en el Club de español)

20 Historieta La escuela
Contesten. (Answer.)
1. ¿A qué hora van ustedes a la escuela?
2. ¿Cómo van?
3. ¿Están ustedes en la escuela ahora?
4. ¿En qué clase están?
5. ¿Está el/la profesor(a)?
6. ¿Da él/ella muchos exámenes?
7. ¿Da él/ella exámenes difíciles?
8. ¿Qué profesores dan muchos exámenes?

La Torre del Oro, Sevilla, España

EN LA ESCUELA

Estructura

the tú form, they must answer with the yo form. This practice is extremely important since beginners so often tend to answer using the same form they hear in the question.

18 and 19 These activities can be done as paired activities.

20 After going over Activity 20, have one student retell all the information in his or her own words.

History Connection

La Torre del Oro is on the banks of the Guadalquivir in Seville. It is a twelve-sided tower that was built by the Moors in 1220. In times of attack, they closed off the harbor by attaching a chain from this tower to another tower (no longer in existence) on the opposite bank of the river. In 1248, however, an admiral named Ramón de Bonifaz was able to break through the barrier, allowing Fernando III to capture the city. La Torre del Oro today houses a naval museum.

There is controversy as to how the tower got its name. Some say it got its name from the golden color of its tiles, azulejos. Others claim that it was once a warehouse for gold from the Americas.

LEVELING
E: Activities 17, 20
A: Activities 18, 19

Answers to ¿Cómo lo digo?

17 Answers will vary but may include:
1. Sí, (No, no) voy a la escuela.
2. Voy a la escuela a las ocho menos cuarto.
3. Sí, (No, no) voy a la escuela a pie.
4. Sí, (No, no) voy en el bus escolar.
5. Sí, (No, no) voy en carro.
6. Voy a pie (en carro, etc.).
7. Sí, (No, no) estoy en la escuela ahora.
8. Estoy en la clase de ___ ahora. (No estoy en clase.)

18 All answers will be: Perdón, ¿adónde vas?

19 All answers will begin: ¿Dónde están Uds.?
1. —... ¿En la cafetería? —Sí, estamos en la cafetería.
2. —... ¿En la clase de español? —Sí, estamos en la clase de español.
3. —... ¿En la papelería? —Sí, estamos en la papelería.
4. ... ¿En el laboratorio?

20 Answers will vary but may include:
1. Vamos a la escuela a las ocho (a las ocho menos cuarto, etc.).
2. Vamos en carro (a pie, etc.).
3. Sí, (No, no) estamos en la escuela ahora.
6. Sí (No), él/ella (no) da muchos exámenes.
7. Sí (No), él/ella (no) da exámenes difíciles.
8. El profesor de ___ y la profesora de ___ dan muchos exámenes.

Connections to other disciplines enhance the lessons and provide interesting information about photos.

Answers are always given at the bottom of the page for easy reference.

Help your students feel confident about their speaking skills

¡Buen viaje! CD-ROM presents the conversation in an interactive format. Students are able to converse with native speakers with this interactive technology.

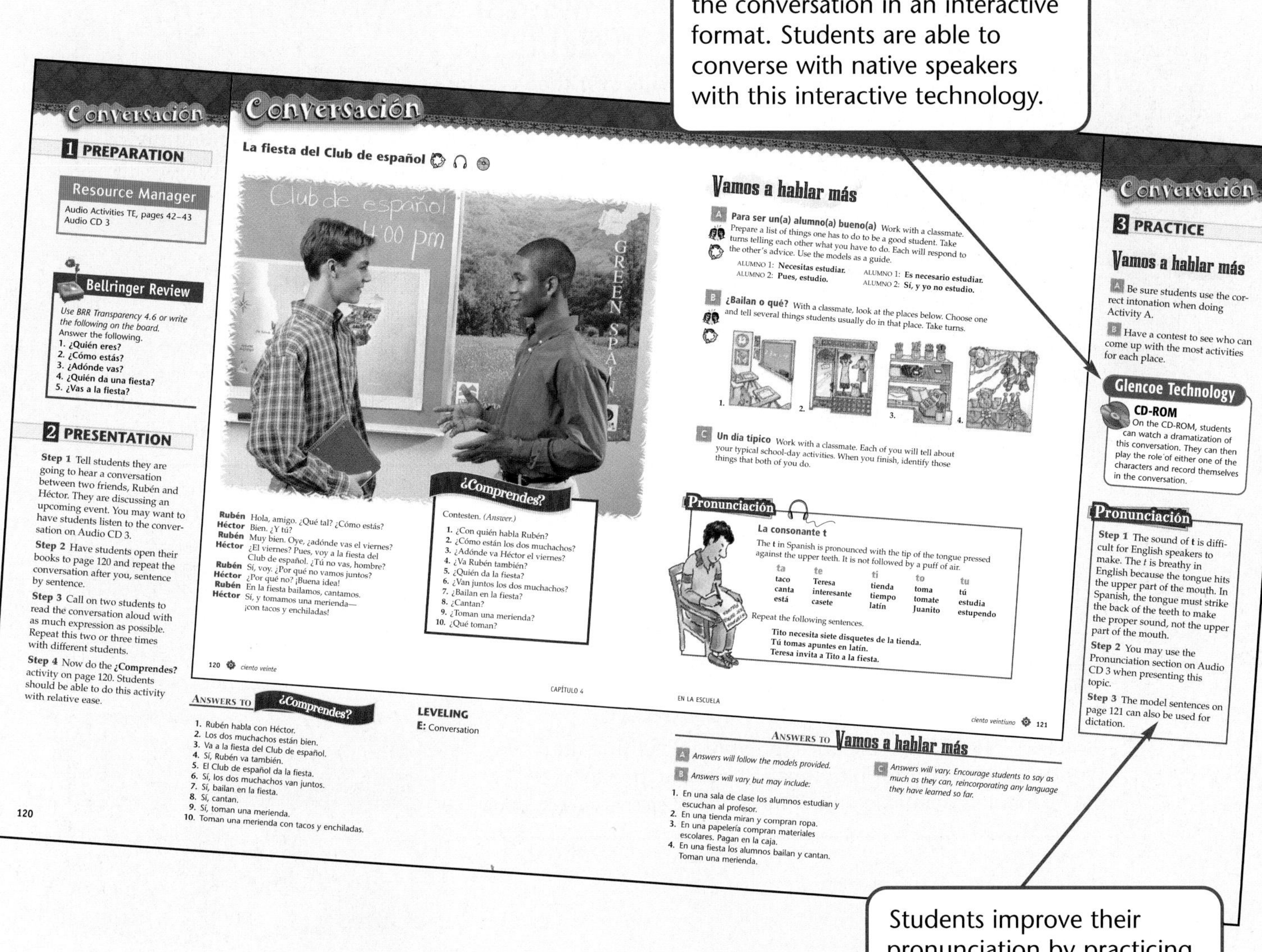

Conversación

1 PREPARATION

Resource Manager

Audio Activities TE, pages 42–43
Audio CD 3

Bellringer Review

Use BRR Transparency 4.6 or write the following on the board. Answer the following.

1. **¿Quién eres?**
2. **¿Cómo estás?**
3. **¿Adónde vas?**
4. **¿Quién da una fiesta?**
5. **¿Vas a la fiesta?**

2 PRESENTATION

Step 1 Tell students they are going to hear a conversation between two friends, Rubén and Héctor. They are discussing an upcoming event. You may want to have students listen to the conversation on Audio CD 3.

Step 2 Have students open their books to page 120 and repeat the conversation after you, sentence by sentence.

Step 3 Call on two students to read the conversation aloud with as much expression as possible. Repeat this two or three times with different students.

Step 4 Now do the **¿Comprendes?** activity on page 120. Students should be able to do this activity with relative ease.

Conversación

La fiesta del Club de español

Rubén Hola, amigo. ¿Qué tal? ¿Cómo estás?
Héctor Bien. ¿Y tú?
Rubén Muy bien. Oye, ¿adónde vas el viernes?
Héctor ¿El viernes? Pues, voy a la fiesta del Club de español. ¿Tú no vas, hombre?
Rubén Sí, voy. ¿Por qué no vamos juntos?
Héctor ¿Por qué no? ¡Buena idea!
Rubén En la fiesta bailamos, cantamos.
Héctor Sí, y tomamos una merienda—¡con tacos y enchiladas!

¿Comprendes?

Contesten. (*Answer.*)

1. ¿Con quién habla Rubén?
2. ¿Cómo están los dos muchachos?
3. ¿Adónde va Héctor el viernes?
4. ¿Va Rubén también?
5. ¿Quién da la fiesta?
6. ¿Van juntos los dos muchachos?
7. ¿Bailan en la fiesta?
8. ¿Cantan?
9. ¿Toman una merienda?
10. ¿Qué toman?

120 ciento veinte — CAPÍTULO 4

Vamos a hablar más

A Para ser un(a) alumno(a) bueno(a) Work with a classmate. Prepare a list of things one has to do to be a good student. Take turns telling each other what you have to do. Each will respond to the other's advice. Use the models as a guide.

ALUMNO 1: **Necesitas estudiar.**
ALUMNO 2: **Pues, estudio.**
ALUMNO 1: **Es necesario estudiar.**
ALUMNO 2: **Sí, y yo no estudio.**

B ¿Bailan o qué? With a classmate, look at the places below. Choose one and tell several things students usually do in that place. Take turns.

1. 2. 3. 4.

C Un día típico Work with a classmate. Each of you will tell about your typical school-day activities. When you finish, identify those things that both of you do.

Pronunciación

La consonante t

The **t** in Spanish is pronounced with the tip of the tongue pressed against the upper teeth. It is not followed by a puff of air.

ta	te	ti	to	tu
taco canta está	Teresa interesante casete	tienda tiempo latín	toma tomate Juanito	tú estudia estupendo

Repeat the following sentences.

Tito necesita siete disquetes de la tienda.
Tú tomas apuntes en latín.
Teresa invita a Tito a la fiesta.

EN LA ESCUELA — ciento veintiuno 121

Conversación

3 PRACTICE

Vamos a hablar más

A Be sure students use the correct intonation when doing Activity A.

B Have a contest to see who can come up with the most activities for each place.

Glencoe Technology

CD-ROM

On the CD-ROM, students can watch a dramatization of this conversation. They can then play the role of either one of the characters and record themselves in the conversation.

Pronunciación

Step 1 The sound of **t** is difficult for English speakers to make. The *t* is breathy in English because the tongue hits the upper part of the mouth. In Spanish, the tongue must strike the back of the teeth to make the proper sound, not the upper part of the mouth.

Step 2 You may use the Pronunciation section on Audio CD 3 when presenting this topic.

Step 3 The model sentences on page 121 can also be used for dictation.

ANSWERS TO **¿Comprendes?**

1. Rubén habla con Héctor.
2. Los dos muchachos están bien.
3. Va a la fiesta del Club de español.
4. Sí, Rubén va también.
5. El Club de español da la fiesta.
6. Sí, los dos muchachos van juntos.
7. Sí, bailan en la fiesta.
8. Sí, cantan.
9. Sí, toman una merienda.
10. Toman una merienda con tacos y enchiladas.

LEVELING
E: Conversation

120

ANSWERS TO **Vamos a hablar más**

A *Answers will follow the models provided.*

B *Answers will vary but may include:*

1. En una sala de clase los alumnos estudian y escuchan al profesor.
2. En una tienda miran y compran ropa.
3. En una papelería compran materiales escolares. Pagan en la caja.
4. En una fiesta los alumnos bailan y cantan. Toman una merienda.

C *Answers will vary. Encourage students to say as much as they can, reincorporating any language they have learned so far.*

Students improve their pronunciation by practicing with the CD-ROM or audio program.

Build proficiency in all language skills

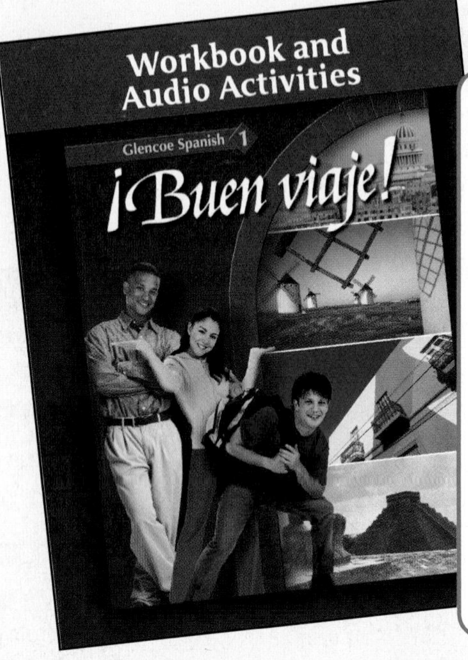

Provide Meaningful and Varied Practice for Your Students!

The **¡Buen viaje! Workbook** includes numerous activities to reinforce every concept presented in the Student Edition. Varied activities provide several ways for students to practice and apply the material you have presented in class. **Un poco más** provides additional opportunity to have students practice with realia. **Mi autobiografía** provides a tool for portfolio assessment.

Improve Listening and Speaking Skills!

The **Audio CDs** provide recordings of the vocabulary words and some of the activities from the Student Edition as well as new activities to reinforce and expand upon what students have learned. The cultural readings are also recorded. Students may use the Audio Activities sheets to guide them through the **Audio Activities.**

StudentWorks Plus™ Helps Lighten the Load!

StudentWorks Plus™ includes the **Student Edition** and **Workbook and Audio Activities**. This alternative to the textbook is available on CD or online at spanish.glencoe.com.

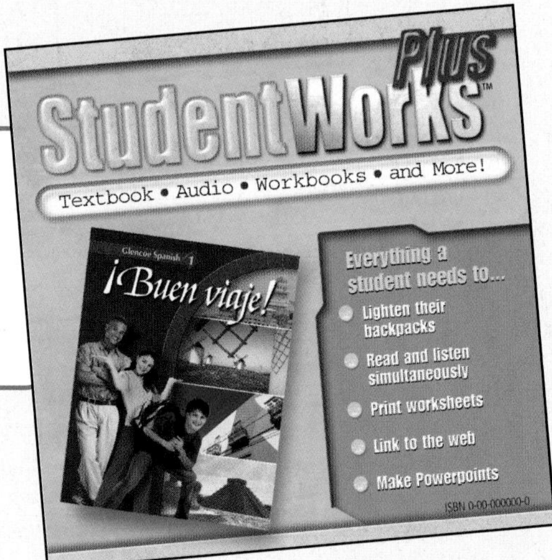

Glencoe Spanish Online gives students many opportunities to review, practice, and explore. There are chapter-related activities, online quizzes, and many links to Web sites throughout the vast Hispanic world. Go to spanish.glencoe.com.

Have students learn by interacting in Spanish!

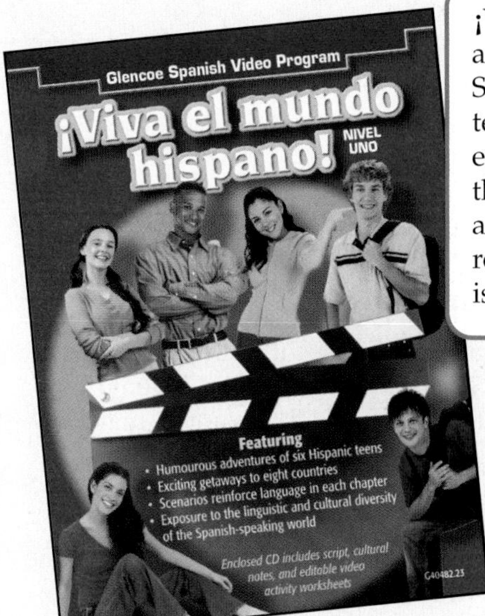

¡Viva el mundo hispano! takes students on many adventures through the Spanish-speaking world. Students become involved with the escapades of six teens and travel to eight different countries. Each episode is related to a chapter of the textbook by its theme. The language provides comprehensible input and gives the students opportunities to hear many regionalisms and dialects. **¡Viva el mundo hispano!** is available on VHS and DVD.

With the **Interactive Conversations CD-ROM** students have an opportunity to interact with a native speaker by participating in the chapter conversation. Students first watch a video of the conversation. They then choose to play the role of one of the characters in the conversation, record their own voice into the conversation and compare their pronunciation and fluency to that of the native speaker.

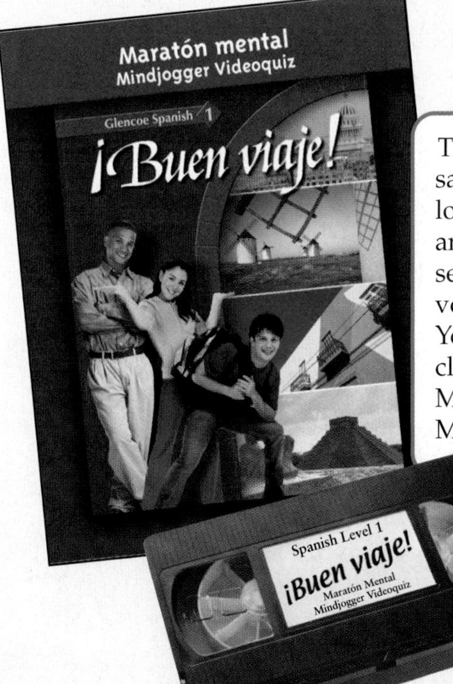

The **MindJogger** is a video review game that saves teachers precious time and that students love to play. Each chapter of the text (Levels 1 and 2) has an accompanying MindJogger segment in which students are quizzed about the vocabulary, structure, and culture of the chapter. You may form teams and play MindJogger as a class activity or students may play the MindJogger DVD individually on a computer. MindJogger is available on VHS and DVD.

¡Buen viaje! Resources

Save planning time with ancillaries organized and filed by chapter!

We make your life easier by organizing your written resources by chapter in convenient **FastFile Booklets**. The FastFile booklets include several essential resources

- **Letter to Parents** Explains goals and suggests activities to do at home.
- **Workbook Teacher Edition** In your version of the student workbook answers are provided for all activities.
- **Audio Program Teacher Edition** The Audio Program TE includes the scripts to the audio activities and the answers to the students' activities. The audio activities found on these pages are recorded on the ¡Buen viaje! Audio Program CDs.
- **TPR Storytelling** We have written a story for each chapter and provided the illustrations to allow you to implement TPR Storytelling in your classroom. The stories are written using the vocabulary and structure for each chapter.
- **Situation Cards** Provide your students with topics they can talk about with the Situation Cards. Several scenarios are provided for each chapter. There are blank cards provided as well should you or your students want to make up new situations.
- **Quizzes** Quizzes are provided to cover every concept taught in each chapter. These quizzes give you immediate feedback about your students' progress.
- **Tests** There are four kinds of tests with each chapter: Reading and Writing, Listening, Speaking, and Proficiency. The Listening Tests are available on CD. You can be sure that you are assessing your students' proficiency in each of the skill areas. In addition, the Reading and Writing Tests are leveled, meaning that there is a separate test for average students and another more challenging test for more able students.
- **Performance Assessment** The Performance Assessment Tasks allow your students to show you what they can do with their language skills at the end of each chapter. Rubrics are provided to help you evaluate your students' performances.

Multimedia resources help you diversify your instruction!

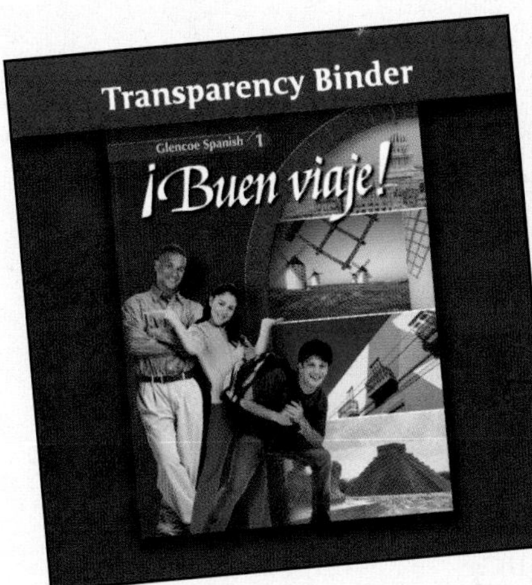

Enhance Your Lessons Visually!

The **Transparency Binder** gives you all the visual support you need to enhance your presentation.

- **Vocabulary** transparencies include the photos and art you see on the Student Edition pages, overlays with the Spanish words, and Spanish/English vocabulary lists for chapter vocabulary.
- **Maps** help you present the Hispanic world.
- **Bellringer Review** transparencies provide a quick review activity to begin each class.
- **Pronunciation** transparencies provide a visual for pronunciation practice.
- **Communication** transparencies illustrate the chapter theme. These can be used for communicative practice or for assessment.
- **Assessment** transparencies replicate the Assessment pages of the student text. Assessment Answer transparencies allow you to easily review the answers with your students in class.

Fine Art transparencies are full-color reproductions of the fine art from the text. These transparencies can be used to reinforce the cultural topics introduced in the text and improve your students' awareness of Hispanic Fine Art.

The **Vocabulary PuzzleMaker** allows you to create four kinds of puzzles at the touch of a key. The Vocabulary PuzzleMaker includes all the vocabulary introduced in your **¡Buen viaje!** It is also easy to add your own words to the vocabulary banks.

The **Audio CDs** provide additional practice to reinforce the material presented in **¡Buen viaje!** Students benefit from hearing a variety of voices from around the entire Spanish-speaking world.

The **Test Program CD** includes the recorded portion for the Listening Tests.

Interactive Chalkboard provides ready-made, customizable PowerPoint presentations with sound, interactive graphics and video. This presentation tool will help you vary your lessons and reach all students in your classroom.

ExamView®Pro helps you make a test in a matter of minutes by choosing from existing banks of questions, editing them, or creating your own test questions. You can also print several versions of the same test. The clip art bank allows you to create a test using visuals from the text.

TeacherWorks is your all-in-one planner and resource center. This convenient tool will help you reduce the time you spend planning for classes. Simply populate your school year calendar with customizable lesson plans. TeacherWorks will also allow you to easily view your resources without carrying around a heavy bag of books. TeacherWorks provides correlations to standards.

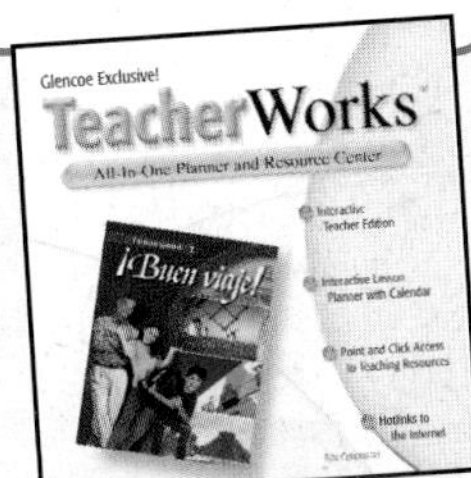

Spanish Names

The following are some Spanish boys' and girls' names that you may wish to give to your students.

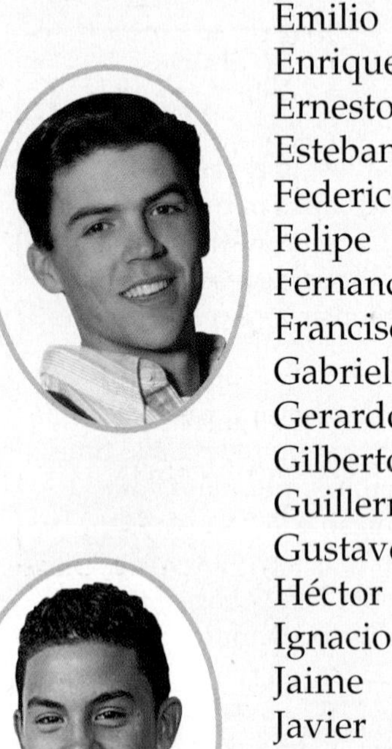

Chicos

Adán
Alberto
Alejandro
Alfonso
Álvaro
Andrés
Antonio
Arnulfo
Arturo
Benjamín
Benito
Camilo
Carlos
César
Cristóbal
Daniel
David
Diego
Eduardo
Efraím
Emilio
Enrique
Ernesto
Esteban
Federico
Felipe
Fernando
Francisco
Gabriel
Gerardo
Gilberto
Guillermo
Gustavo
Héctor
Ignacio
Jaime
Javier
Jorge
José
Juan

Julio
Justo
Leonardo
Luis
Manuel
Marcos
Mateo
Miguel
Nicolás
Octavio
Omar
Óscar
Pablo
Paco
Patricio
Pedro
Rafael
Ramón
Raúl
Ricardo
Rigoberto
Roberto
Rubén
Santiago
Teodoro
Timoteo
Tomás
Víctor
Wilfredo

Chicas

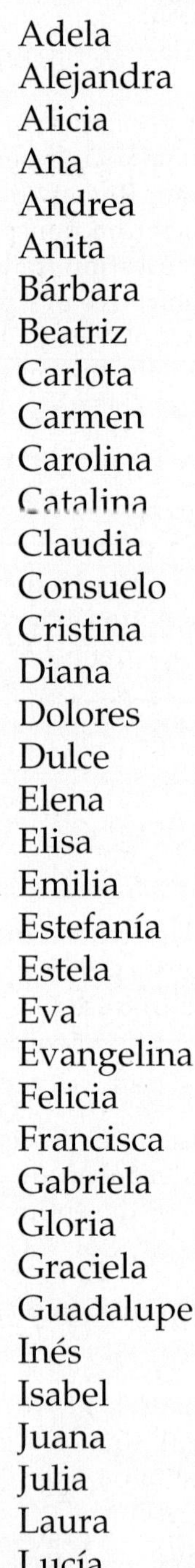

Adela
Alejandra
Alicia
Ana
Andrea
Anita
Bárbara
Beatriz
Carlota
Carmen
Carolina
Catalina
Claudia
Consuelo
Cristina
Diana
Dolores
Dulce
Elena
Elisa
Emilia
Estefanía
Estela
Eva
Evangelina
Felicia
Francisca
Gabriela
Gloria
Graciela
Guadalupe
Inés
Isabel
Juana
Julia
Laura
Lucía
Luisa
Lupe
Luz

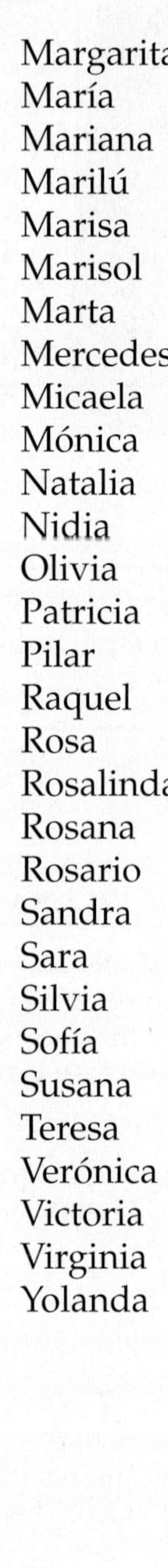

Margarita
María
Mariana
Marilú
Marisa
Marisol
Marta
Mercedes
Micaela
Mónica
Natalia
Nidia
Olivia
Patricia
Pilar
Raquel
Rosa
Rosalinda
Rosana
Rosario
Sandra
Sara
Silvia
Sofía
Susana
Teresa
Verónica
Victoria
Virginia
Yolanda

Classroom Expressions

Below is a list of words and expressions frequently used when conducting a Spanish class.

el papel	paper
la hoja de papel	sheet of paper
el cuaderno	notebook, workbook
el libro	book
el diccionario	dictionary
la regla	ruler
la cinta	tape
el bolígrafo, la pluma	ballpoint pen
el lápiz	pencil
el sacapuntas	pencil sharpener
la goma	eraser
la tiza	chalk
la pizarra, el pizarrón	chalkboard
el borrador	chalkboard eraser
el escritorio	desk
la silla	chair
la fila	row
el CD	CD
la computadora, el ordenador	computer
el DVD	DVD
la pantalla	the screen
el video	video

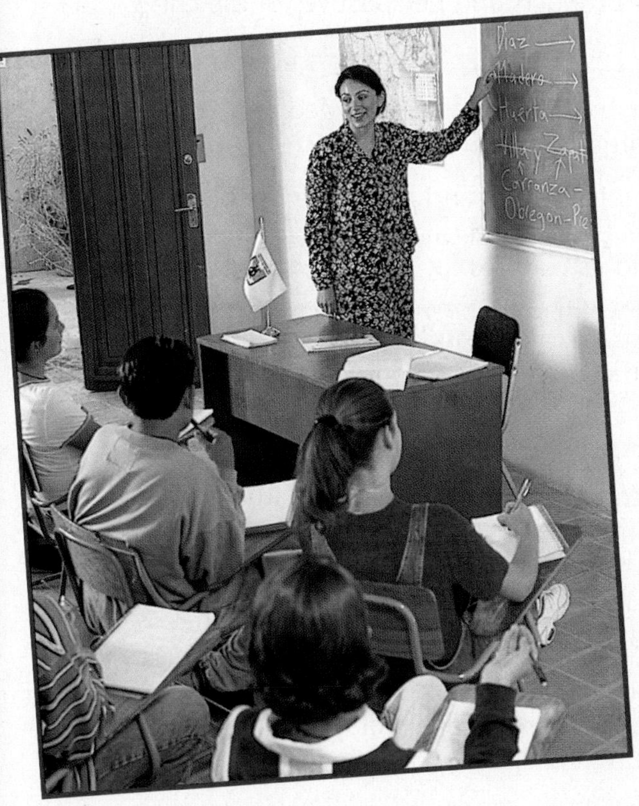

Ven.	**Vengan.**	Come.
Ve.	**Vayan.**	Go.
Entra.	**Entren.**	Enter.
Sal.	**Salgan.**	Leave.
Espera.	**Esperen.**	Wait.
Pon.	**Pongan.**	Put.
Dame.	**Denme.**	Give me.
Dime.	**Díganme.**	Tell me.
Repite.	**Repitan.**	Repeat.
Practica.	**Practiquen.**	Practice.
Estudia.	**Estudien.**	Study.
Contesta.	**Contesten.**	Answer.
Aprende.	**Aprendan.**	Learn.
Escoge.	**Escojan.**	Choose.
Prepara.	**Preparen.**	Prepare.
Mira.	**Miren.**	Look at.
Describe.	**Describan.**	Describe.
Empieza.	**Empiecen.**	Begin.
Pronuncia.	**Pronuncien.**	Pronounce.
Escucha.	**Escuchen.**	Listen.
Habla.	**Hablen.**	Speak.
Lee.	**Lean.**	Read.
Escribe.	**Escriban.**	Write.
Pregunta.	**Pregunten.**	Ask.
Sigue el modelo.	**Sigan el modelo.**	Follow the model.
Abre.	**Abran.**	Open.
Cierra.	**Cierren.**	Close.
Continúa.	**Continúen.**	Continue.
Siéntate.	**Siéntense.**	Sit down.
Levántate.	**Levántense.**	Get up.
Cállate.	**Cállense.**	Be quiet.
Presta atención.	**Presten atención.**	Pay attention.

Atención, por favor.	Your attention, please.
Silencio.	Quiet.
Otra vez.	Again.
Todos juntos.	All together.
En voz alta.	Out loud.
Más alto, por favor.	Louder, please.
En español, por favor.	In Spanish, please.
En inglés, por favor.	In English, please.

Standards for Foreign Language Learning

¡Buen viaje! has been written to help you meet the Standards for Foreign Language Learning as set forth by ACTFL. The focus of the text is to provide students with the skills they need to create language for communication. Culture is integrated throughout the text, from the basic introduction of vocabulary to the photographic contributions of the National Geographic Society. Special attention has been given to meeting the standard of Connections with a reading in Spanish in each chapter about another discipline. Linguistic and cultural comparisons are made throughout the text. Suggestions are made for activities that encourage students to use their language skills in their immediate community and more distant ones. Students who complete the **¡Buen viaje!** series are prepared to participate in the Spanish-speaking world.

Specific correlations to each chapter are provided on the teacher pages preceeding each chapter.

Communication

Communicate in Languages Other than English	**Standard 1.1**	Students engage in conversations, provide and obtain information, express feelings and emotions, and exchange opinions.
	Standard 1.2	Students understand and interpret written and spoken language on a variety of topics.
	Standard 1.3	Students present information, concepts, and ideas to an audience of listeners or readers on a variety of topics.

Cultures

Gain Knowledge and Understanding of Other Cultures	**Standard 2.1**	Students demonstrate an understanding of the relationship between the practices and perspectives of the culture studied.
	Standard 2.2	Students demonstrate an understanding of the relationship between the products and perspectives of the culture studied.

Connections

Connect with Other Disciplines and Acquire Information	**Standard 3.1**	Students reinforce and further their knowledge of other disciplines through the foreign language.
	Standard 3.2	Students acquire information and recognize the distinctive viewpoints that are only available through the foreign language and its cultures.

Comparisons

Develop Insight into the Nature of Language and Culture	**Standard 4.1**	Students demonstrate understanding of the nature of language through comparisons of language studied and their own.
	Standard 4.2	Students demonstrate understanding of the concept of culture through comparisons of the cultures studied and their own.

Communities

Participate in Multilingual Communities at Home and Around the World	**Standard 5.1**	Students use the language both within and beyond the school setting.
	Standard 5.2	Students show evidence of becoming life-long learners by using the language for personal enjoyment and enrichment.

Glencoe Spanish 1

¡Buen viaje!

Conrad J. Schmitt
Protase E. Woodford

New York, New York   Columbus, Ohio   Chicago, Illinois   Peoria, Illinois   Woodland Hills, California

The McGraw·Hill Companies

Send all inquiries to:
Glencoe/McGraw-Hill
8787 Orion Place
Columbus, OH 43240-4027

ISBN: 0-07-846570-2 *(Student Edition)*
ISBN: 0-07-861951-3 *(Teacher Wraparound Edition)*

Printed in the United States of America.

2 3 4 5 6 7 8 9 10 071/055 10 09 08 07 06 05 04

About the Authors

Conrad J. Schmitt

Conrad J. Schmitt received his B.A. degree magna cum laude from Montclair State College, Upper Montclair, NJ. He received his M.A. from Middlebury College, Middlebury, VT. He did additional graduate work at Seton Hall University and New York University. Mr. Schmitt has taught Spanish and French at the elementary, junior, and senior high school levels, as well as at the undergraduate and graduate levels. In addition, he has traveled extensively throughout Spain, Central and South America, and the Caribbean.

Protase E. Woodford

Protase "Woody" Woodford has taught Spanish at all levels from elementary through graduate school. At Educational Testing Service in Princeton, NJ, he was Director of Test Development, Director of Language Programs, Director of International Testing Programs and Director of the Puerto Rico Office. He has served as a consultant to the United Nations Secretariat, UNESCO, the Organization of American States, the U.S. Office of Education, and many ministries of education in Asia, Latin America, and the Middle East.

For the Parent or Guardian

We are excited that your child has decided to study Spanish. Foreign language study provides many benefits for students in addition to the ability to communicate in another language. Students who study another language improve their first language skills. They become more aware of the world around them and they learn to appreciate diversity.

You can help your child be successful in his or her study of Spanish even if you are not familiar with that language. Encourage your child to talk to you about the places where Spanish is spoken. Engage in conversations about current events in those places. The section of their Glencoe Spanish book called **El mundo hispanohablante** on pages xxi–xxxiii may serve as a reference for you and your child. In addition, you will find information about the geography of the Spanish-speaking world and links to foreign newspapers at **spanish.glencoe.com**.

The methodology employed in the Glencoe Spanish books is logical and leads students step by step through their study of the language. Consistent instruction and practice are essential for learning a foreign language. You can help by encouraging your child to review vocabulary each day. As he or she progresses through the text, you will want to use the Study Tips on pages H16–H29 to help your child learn Spanish. If you have Internet access, encourage your child to practice using the activities, games, and practice quizzes at **spanish.glencoe.com**.

¡Buen viaje!

Contenido

Lecciones preliminares

Objetivos

In these preliminary lessons you will learn to:

- greet people
- say good-bye to people
- express simple courtesies
- find out and tell the days of the week
- find out and tell the months of the year
- count from 1 to 30
- find out and tell the seasons

Capítulo 1

Objetivos

In this chapter you will learn to:

- **ask or tell who someone is**
- **ask or tell what something is**
- **ask or tell where someone is from**
- **ask or tell what someone is like**
- **describe yourself or someone else**
- **talk about a famous Spanish novel and some Latin American heroes**

Un amigo o una amiga

Capítulo 2

Alumnos y cursos

Objetivos

In this chapter you will learn to:

- **describe people and things**
- **talk about more than one person or thing**
- **tell what subjects you take in school and express some opinions about them**
- **tell time**
- **tell at what time an event takes place**
- **talk about Spanish speakers in the United States**

Capítulo 3 Las compras para la escuela

Objetivos

In this chapter you will learn to:

- identify and describe school supplies
- identify and describe articles of clothing
- shop for school supplies and clothing
- state color and size preferences
- speak to people formally and informally
- discuss differences between schools in the United States and in Spanish-speaking countries

Contenido

Capítulo 4 En la escuela

Objetivos

In this chapter you will learn to:

- **talk about going to school**
- **talk about some school activities**
- **greet people and ask how they feel**
- **tell how you feel**
- **describe where you and others go**
- **describe where you and others are**
- **discuss some differences between schools in the United States and schools in Spanish-speaking countries**

Capítulo 5

Objetivos

In this chapter you will learn to:

- **order food or a beverage at a café**
- **identify some food**
- **shop for food**
- **talk about activities**
- **talk about differences between eating habits in the United States and in the Spanish-speaking world**

En el café

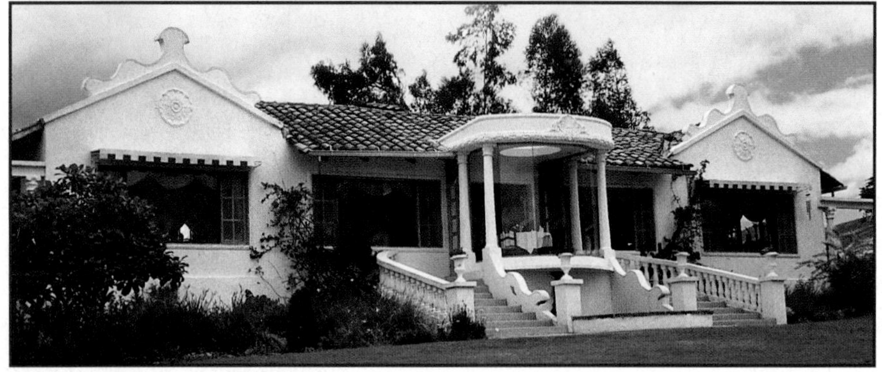

Capítulo 6

Objetivos

In this chapter you will learn to:

- **talk about your family**
- **describe your home**
- **tell your age and find out someone else's age**
- **tell what you have to do**
- **tell what you are going to do**
- **tell what belongs to you and to others**
- **talk about families in Spanish-speaking countries**

La familia y su casa

Capítulo 7

Deportes de equipo

Objetivos

In this chapter you will learn to:

- talk about team sports and other physical activities
- tell what you want to, begin to, and prefer to do
- talk about people's activities
- express what interests, bores, or pleases you
- discuss the role of sports in the Hispanic world

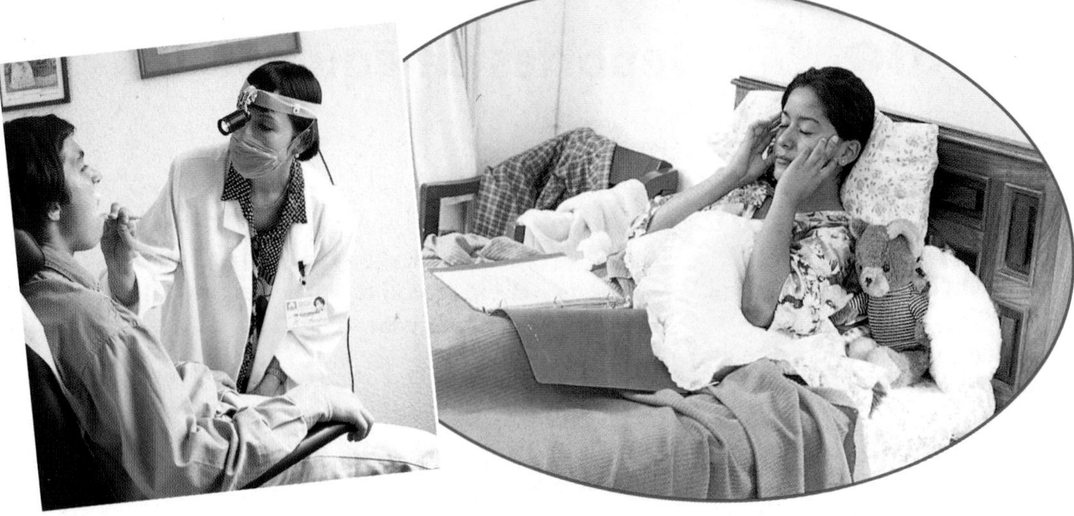

Capítulo 8 

La salud y el médico

Objetivos

In this chapter you will learn to:

- explain a minor illness to a doctor
- describe some feelings
- have a prescription filled at a pharmacy
- describe characteristics and conditions
- tell where things are and where they're from
- tell where someone or something is now
- tell what happens to you or someone else

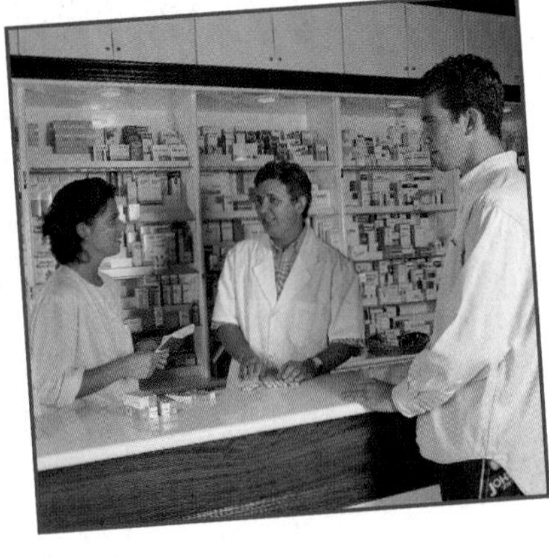

Capítulo 9

El verano y el invierno

Objetivos

In this chapter you will learn to:

- **describe summer and winter weather**
- **talk about summer activities and sports**
- **talk about winter sports**
- **discuss past actions and events**
- **refer to people and things already mentioned**
- **talk about resorts in the Hispanic world**

Capítulo 10 Diversiones culturales

Objetivos

In this chapter you will learn to:

- **discuss movies, museums, and theater**
- **discuss cultural events**
- **relate more past actions or events**
- **tell for whom something is done**
- **discuss some dating customs in the United States and compare them with those in Spanish-speaking countries**
- **talk about cultural activities that are popular in the Spanish-speaking world**

Capítulo 11 Un viaje en avión

Objetivos

In this chapter you will learn to:

- check in for a flight
- talk about some services on board the plane
- get through the airport after deplaning
- tell what you or others are currently doing
- tell what you know and whom you know
- discuss the importance of air travel in South America

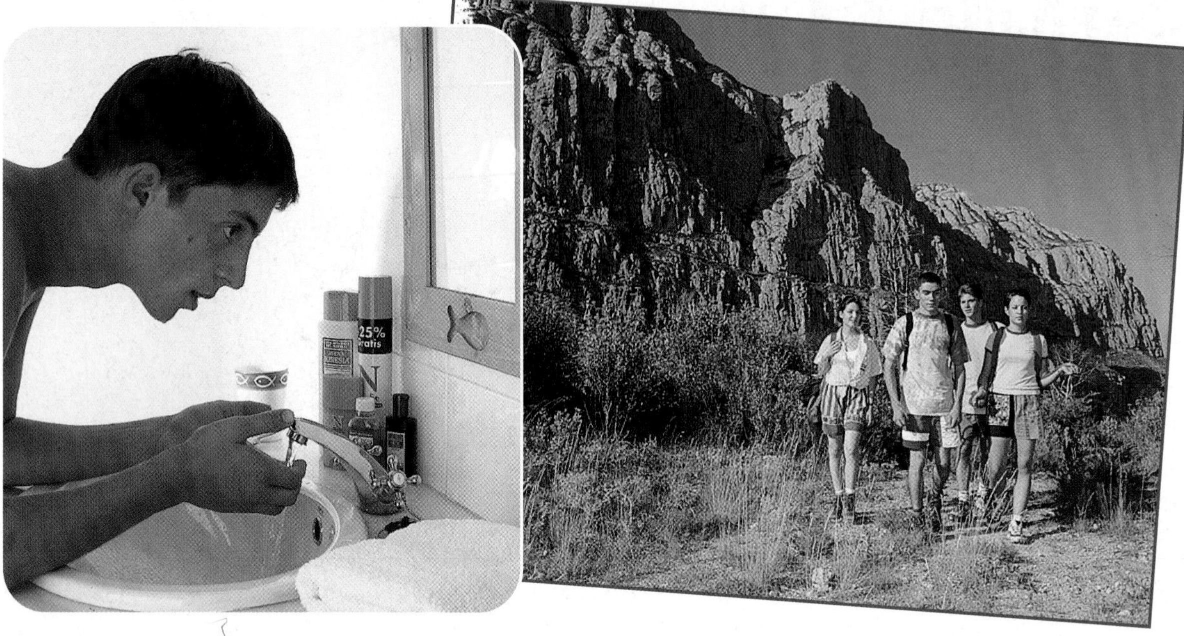

Capítulo 12 Una gira

Objetivos

In this chapter you will learn to:

- **describe your personal grooming habits**
- **talk about your daily routine**
- **tell some things you do for yourself**
- **talk about a backpacking trip**

Capítulo 13 Un viaje en tren

Objetivos

In this chapter you will learn to:

- use expressions related to train travel
- purchase a train ticket and request information about arrival, departure, etc.
- talk about more past events or activities
- tell what people say
- discuss an interesting train trip in Spain and Peru

Contenido

Capítulo 14 En el restaurante

Objetivos

In this chapter you will learn to:

- **order food or a beverage at a restaurant**
- **identify eating utensils and dishes**
- **identify more foods**
- **make a reservation at a restaurant**
- **talk about present and past events**
- **describe some cuisines of the Hispanic world**

Literary Companion

Video Companion

Handbook

Guide to Symbols

Throughout **¡Buen viaje!** you will see these symbols, or icons. They will tell you how to best use the particular part of the chapter or activity they accompany. Following is a key to help you understand these symbols.

Audio link This icon indicates material in the chapter that is recorded on compact disk.

Recycling This icon indicates sections that review previously introduced material.

Paired Activity This icon indicates sections that you can practice orally with a partner.

Group Activity This icon indicates sections that you can practice together in groups.

Un poco más This icon indicates additional practice activities that review knowledge from each chapter.

¡Adelante! This icon indicates the end of new material in each chapter. All remaining material is recombination and review.

Literary Companion This icon appears in the review lessons to let you know that you are prepared to read the literature selection indicated if you wish.

Interactive CD-ROM This icon indicates that the material is also on the Interactive CD-ROM.

El mundo hispanohablante

Spanish is the language of more than 350 million people around the world. Spanish had its origin in Spain. It is sometimes fondly called the "language of Cervantes," the author of the world's most famous novel and character, *Don Quijote.* The Spanish **conquistadores** and **exploradores** brought their language to the Americas in the fifteenth and sixteenth centuries. Spanish is the official language of almost all the countries of Central and South America. It is the official language of Mexico and several of the larger islands in the Caribbean. Spanish is also the heritage language of forty million people in the United States.

▼ España

▲ México

◀ Perú

▲ Chile

El mundo

OCÉANO ÁRTICO
Mar de Beaufort
Bahía de Baffin
Mar de Bering
Golfo de Alaska
CANADÁ
Bahía de Hudson
Mar del Labrador
AMÉRICA DEL NORTE
ESTADOS UNIDOS
OCÉANO ATLÁNTICO
MÉXICO
Golfo de México
MAR CARIBE
OCÉANO PACÍFICO
VENEZUELA
GUYANA
SURINAM
GUAYANA FRANCESA
COLOMBIA
ECUADOR
AMÉRICA DEL SUR
PERÚ
BRASIL
SAMOA
POLINESIA FRANCESA
TONGA
BOLIVIA
PARAGUAY
URUGUAY
CHILE
ARGENTINA

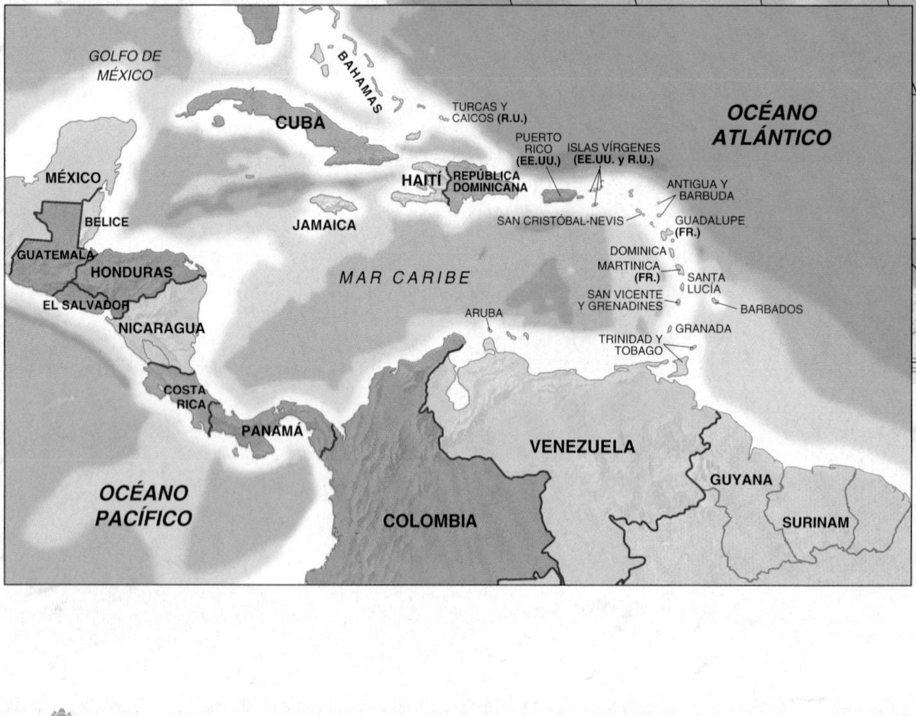

GOLFO DE MÉXICO
BAHAMAS
TURCAS Y CAICOS (R.U.)
OCÉANO ATLÁNTICO
CUBA
PUERTO RICO (EE.UU.)
ISLAS VÍRGENES (EE.UU. y R.U.)
MÉXICO
HAITÍ
REPÚBLICA DOMINICANA
ANTIGUA Y BARBUDA
BELICE
JAMAICA
SAN CRISTÓBAL-NEVIS
GUADALUPE (FR.)
GUATEMALA
HONDURAS
DOMINICA
MARTINICA (FR.)
MAR CARIBE
SANTA LUCÍA
SAN VICENTE Y GRENADINES
BARBADOS
EL SALVADOR
ARUBA
NICARAGUA
GRANADA
TRINIDAD Y TOBAGO
COSTA RICA
PANAMÁ
VENEZUELA
OCÉANO PACÍFICO
GUYANA
COLOMBIA
SURINAM

xxii

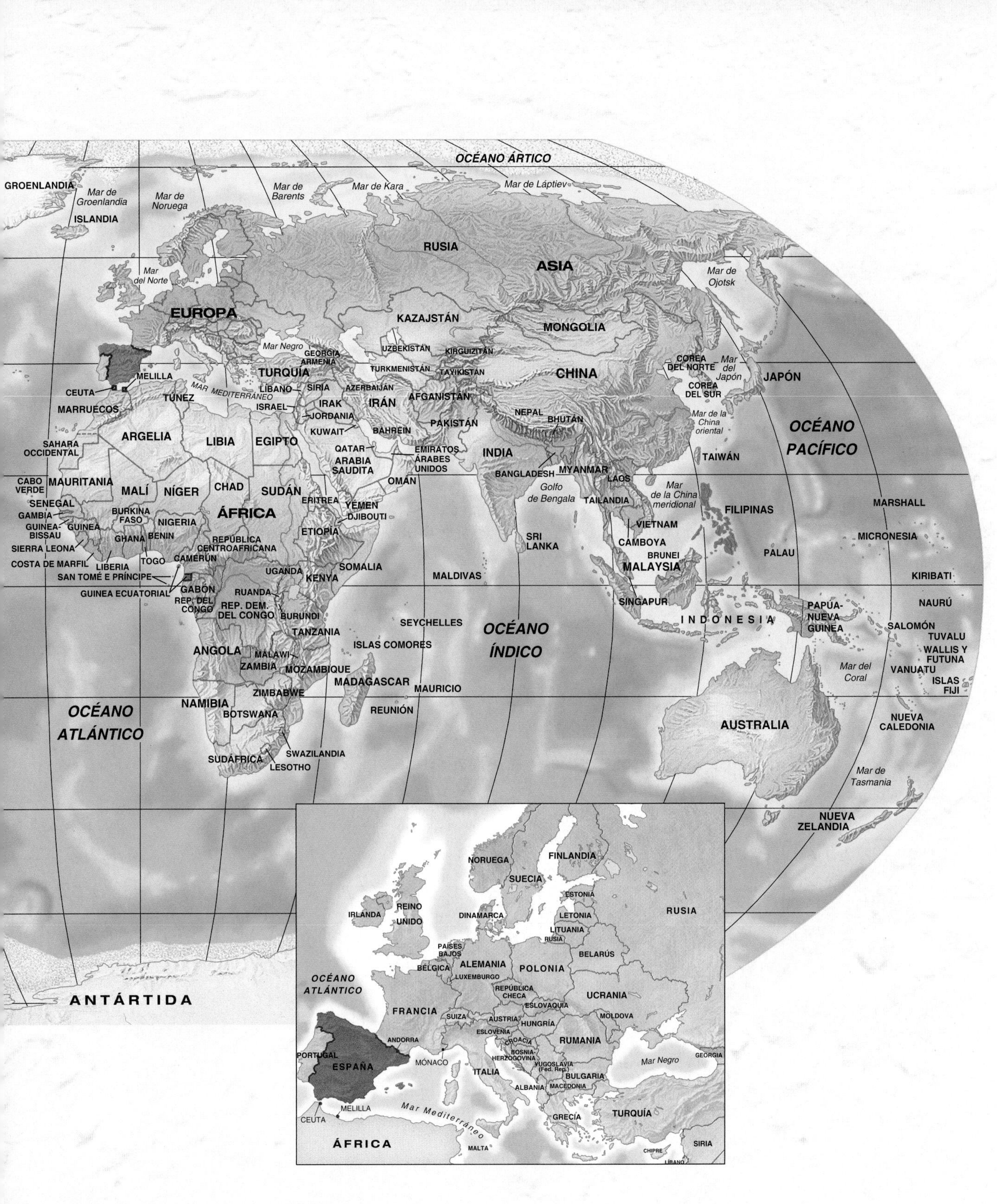

OCÉANO ÁRTICO
GROENLANDIA
Mar de Groenlandia
ISLANDIA
Mar de Noruega
Mar de Barents
Mar de Kara
Mar de Láptiev
RUSIA
ASIA
Mar del Norte
Mar de Ojotsk
EUROPA
KAZAJSTÁN
MONGOLIA
Mar Negro
GEORGIA
ARMENIA
UZBEKISTÁN
KIRGUIZITÁN
TURKMENISTÁN
TAYIKISTÁN
TURQUÍA
CHINA
COREA DEL NORTE
Mar del Japón
JAPÓN
COREA DEL SUR
MELILLA
CEUTA
MAR MEDITERRÁNEO
LÍBANO
SIRIA
AZERBAIJÁN
AFGANISTÁN
TÚNEZ
ISRAEL
IRAK
IRÁN
MARRUECOS
JORDANIA
NEPAL
BHUTÁN
Mar de la China oriental
KUWAIT
BAHREIN
PAKISTÁN
OCÉANO PACÍFICO
ARGELIA
LIBIA
EGIPTO
SAHARA OCCIDENTAL
QATAR
EMIRATOS ÁRABES UNIDOS
INDIA
TAIWÁN
ARABIA SAUDITA
BANGLADESH
MYANMAR
LAOS
CABO VERDE
MAURITANIA
OMÁN
Mar de la China meridional
MALÍ
NÍGER
CHAD
SUDÁN
Golfo de Bengala
TAILANDIA
SENEGAL
ERITREA
YEMEN
FILIPINAS
MARSHALL
GAMBIA
BURKINA FASO
ÁFRICA
DJIBOUTI
VIETNAM
GUINEA-BISSAU
GUINEA
NIGERIA
GHANA
BENIN
ETIOPÍA
SRI LANKA
CAMBOYA
MICRONESIA
SIERRA LEONA
REPÚBLICA CENTROAFRICANA
PALAU
COSTA DE MARFIL
LIBERIA
TOGO
CAMERÚN
BRUNEI
SOMALIA
MALAYSIA
SAN TOMÉ E PRÍNCIPE
UGANDA
KENYA
MALDIVAS
KIRIBATI
GUINEA ECUATORIAL
GABÓN
RUANDA
REP. DEL CONGO
REP. DEM. DEL CONGO
BURUNDI
SINGAPUR
NAURÚ
SEYCHELLES
INDONESIA
PAPÚA-NUEVA GUINEA
TANZANIA
OCÉANO ÍNDICO
SALOMÓN
TUVALU
ANGOLA
ISLAS COMORES
MALAWI
WALLIS Y FUTUNA
ZAMBIA
MOZAMBIQUE
Mar del Coral
VANUATU
MADAGASCAR
ISLAS FIJI
MAURICIO
ZIMBABWE
NAMIBIA
OCÉANO ATLÁNTICO
BOTSWANA
REUNIÓN
NUEVA CALEDONIA
AUSTRALIA
SWAZILANDIA
SUDÁFRICA
LESOTHO
Mar de Tasmania
NUEVA ZELANDIA
ANTÁRTIDA
NORUEGA
FINLANDIA
SUECIA
ESTONIA
RUSIA
IRLANDA
REINO UNIDO
DINAMARCA
LETONIA
LITUANIA
RUSIA
PAÍSES BAJOS
BELARÚS
ALEMANIA
POLONIA
BÉLGICA
OCÉANO ATLÁNTICO
LUXEMBURGO
REPÚBLICA CHECA
UCRANIA
ESLOVAQUIA
FRANCIA
SUIZA
AUSTRIA
HUNGRÍA
MOLDOVA
ESLOVENIA
CROACIA
RUMANIA
ANDORRA
BOSNIA-HERZEGOVINA
PORTUGAL
ESPAÑA
MÓNACO
YUGOSLAVIA (Fed. Rep.)
Mar Negro
GEORGIA
ITALIA
BULGARIA
ALBANIA
MACEDONIA
MELILLA
CEUTA
Mar Mediterráneo
GRECIA
TURQUÍA
ÁFRICA
MALTA
CHIPRE
LÍBANO
SIRIA

xxiii

España

CAPITAL
Madrid

POPULATION
39,800,000

FUN FACT
The verdant hills of Galicia, the golden fields of Castilla, and the white villages of Andalucía as well as the industrial areas of Cataluña and the Basque Country are all a part of beautiful Spain. Once home to Iberians, Carthaginians, Romans, Celts, and Moors, Spain is the birthplace of Spanish—the language of many nations scattered on five continents of the globe. Madrid, in the exact center of the country, is considered a major cultural center of Europe.

México

CAPITAL
Ciudad de México

POPULATION
99,600,000

FUN FACT
Beautiful Mexico shares a border with the United States. This magnificent nation of Aztec, Mayan, and Spanish heritage is a country of contrasts: cosmopolitan cities such as Mexico City; industrial centers such as Monterrey; quaint towns such as Taxco and San Miguel de Allende; world-famous beaches like Acapulco and Cancún; as well as magnificent vestiges of pre-Columbian civilization in Chichén Itzá and Tulum.

Estados Unidos

CAPITAL
Washington, D.C.

POPULATION
284,500,000

FUN FACT
The influence of Spanish and Mexican heritage has been evident in Texas and in the Southwest of the United States for generations. More recent is the proliferation of Hispanic or Latin cultures in all areas of the United States. New arrivals from the Caribbean, Central America, and South America bring their language, customs, music, and foods, adding to the rich cultural diversity of this "melting pot" country. Today Spanish is heard in New York, Chicago, Minneapolis, Denver, and Miami as well as El Paso, Phoenix, and Los Angeles.

xxiv

Guatemala

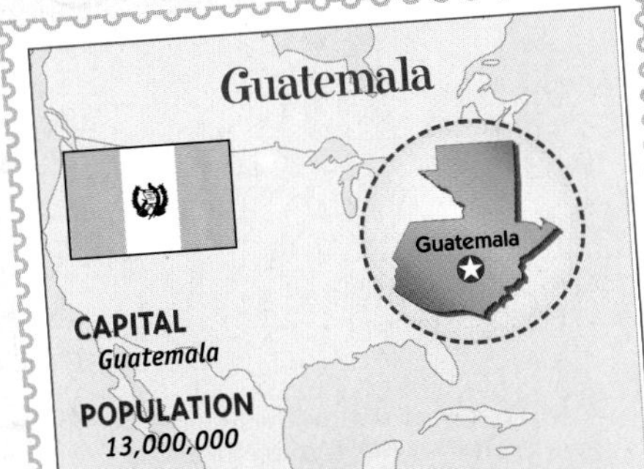

CAPITAL
Guatemala

POPULATION
13,000,000

FUN FACT

Guatemala is a verdant country with a large indigenous population—descendants of the Mayans. Incredible ruined cities overgrown by jungle tell of a civilization that lasted for two thousand years and whose decline has never been definitively explained. Guatemala is considered by many to be one of the most beautiful countries in the world, with its volcanoes, mountains, jungles, and scenic cities and villages, such as Antigua, Panajachel, and Chichicastenango.

El Salvador

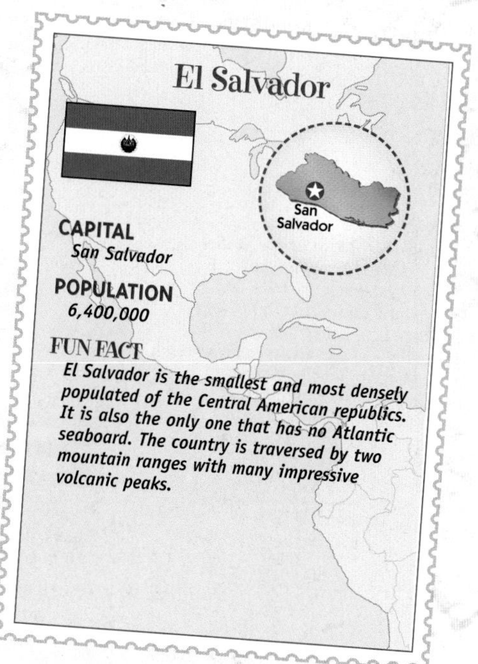

CAPITAL
San Salvador

POPULATION
6,400,000

FUN FACT

El Salvador is the smallest and most densely populated of the Central American republics. It is also the only one that has no Atlantic seaboard. The country is traversed by two mountain ranges with many impressive volcanic peaks.

Honduras

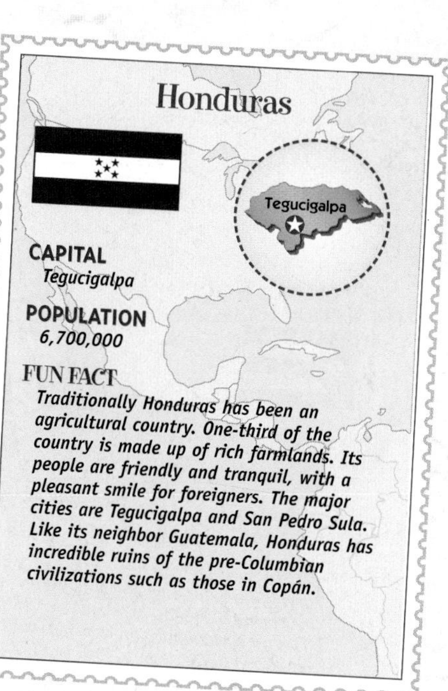

CAPITAL
Tegucigalpa

POPULATION
6,700,000

FUN FACT

Traditionally Honduras has been an agricultural country. One-third of the country is made up of rich farmlands. Its people are friendly and tranquil, with a pleasant smile for foreigners. The major cities are Tegucigalpa and San Pedro Sula. Like its neighbor Guatemala, Honduras has incredible ruins of the pre-Columbian civilizations such as those in Copán.

Nicaragua

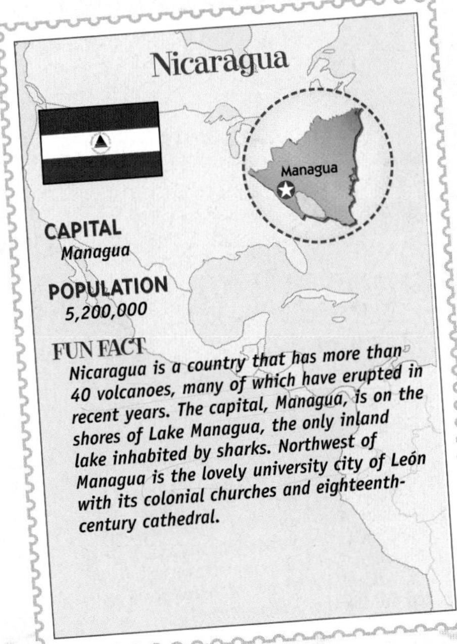

CAPITAL
Managua

POPULATION
5,200,000

FUN FACT

Nicaragua is a country that has more than 40 volcanoes, many of which have erupted in recent years. The capital, Managua, is on the shores of Lake Managua, the only inland lake inhabited by sharks. Northwest of Managua is the lovely university city of León with its colonial churches and eighteenth-century cathedral.

XXV

Costa Rica

CAPITAL
San José

POPULATION
3,700,000

FUN FACT
Many consider Costa Rica a very special place. Its residents, Ticos, are polite, peaceful, and extremely friendly. Costa Rica has no army and prides itself on having more teachers than police officers. Costa Rica is a country of sun-drenched beaches on the Pacific, tropical jungles along the Caribbean coast, cosmopolitan cities such as San José, and high mountains in the central valley. Costa Rica is a tourist's paradise as well as home to many expatriates.

Panamá

CAPITAL
Panamá

POPULATION
2,900,000

FUN FACT
Panama is a country of variety—a variety of races, customs, natural wonders, and attractions. It is a country of tropical forests, mountains, beautiful beaches, excellent fishing, picturesque lakes, rivers, two oceans, and—the most incredible engineering feat—the Panama Canal. Panama is also the largest financial center of Latin America. All this in a mere 77,432 square kilometers!

Cuba

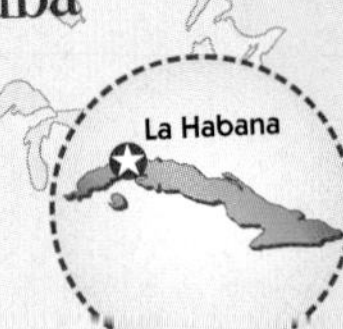

CAPITAL
La Habana

POPULATION
11,300,000

FUN FACT
Havana, the capital of Cuba, is known for its gorgeous colonial architecture. This lush island, not far from Florida, is one of the world's greatest producers of sugar cane. Cuba has been ruled by Fidel Castro since 1959 when he overthrew the dictator Fulgencio Batista.

La República Dominicana

CAPITAL
Santo Domingo

POPULATION
8,600,000

FUN FACT
The Dominican Republic shares with Haiti the island of Hispaniola in the greater Antilles. The oldest university in our hemisphere, la Universidad de Santo Domingo, was founded in Santo Domingo. The Dominicans are ardent fans or aficionados of baseball, and this rather small island nation has produced some of the finest major league players.

Puerto Rico

CAPITAL
San Juan

POPULATION
3,900,000

FUN FACT
Puerto Ricans have an endearing term for their beloved island—la isla del encanto—island of enchantment. A commonwealth of the United States, Puerto Rico is a lush, tropical island with beaches along its Atlantic and Caribbean shores and gorgeous mountains with Alpine-like views in its interior. Puerto Rico is the home of the beloved coquí—a little frog that lives only in Puerto Rico and who lets no one see him.

Venezuela

CAPITAL
Caracas

POPULATION
24,600,000

FUN FACT
Venezuela was the name given to this country by Spanish explorers in 1499, when they came across indigenous villages where people lived on the water and where all commerce was conducted by dugout canoes. The waterways reminded them of Venice, Italy. Caracas is a teeming cosmopolitan city of high-rises surrounded by mountains and tucked in a narrow nine-mile valley. Angel Falls in southern Venezuela is the highest waterfall in the world, reaching a height of 3,212 feet with an unbroken fall of 2,648 feet.

Colombia

CAPITAL
Bogotá

POPULATION
43,100,000

FUN FACT
Colombia covers over 440,000 square miles of tropical and mountainous terrain. Bogotá is situated in the center of the country in an Andean valley 8,640 feet above sea level. The Caribbean coast in the North boasts many beautiful beaches; the South is covered by jungle, and the southern port of Leticia is on the Amazon River.

Ecuador

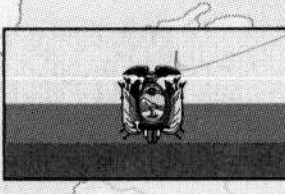

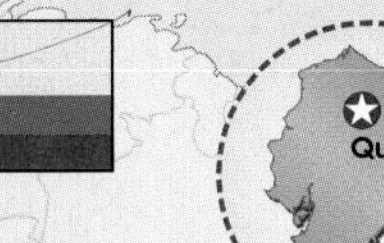

CAPITAL
Quito

POPULATION
12,900,000

FUN FACT
Ecuador takes its name from the equator, which cuts right across the country. Ecuador is the meeting place of the high Andean sierra in the center, the tropical coastal plain to the west, and the Amazon Basin jungle to the east. Snowcapped volcanoes stretch some 400 miles from north to south. The beautiful colonial section of the capital, Quito, is sometimes called "the Florence of the Americas."

Perú

CAPITAL
Lima

POPULATION
26,100,000

FUN FACT
Peru, like Ecuador, is divided into three geographical areas—a narrow coastal strip of desert along the Pacific, the Andean highlands where nearly half the population lives, and the Amazon jungle to the east. Lima is on the coast, and for almost nine months out of the year it is enshrouded in a fog called la garúa. Peru is famous for its Incan heritage. Nothing can prepare visitors for the awe-inspiring view of the Incan city of Machu Picchu, an imposing architectural complex high in the Andes.

Bolivia

CAPITAL
La Paz

POPULATION
8,500,000

FUN FACT
Bolivia is one of two landlocked countries in South America. Mountains dominate the Bolivian landscape. La Paz is the highest city in the world at an altitude of 12,500 feet. Bolivia also has the world's highest navigable lake, Lake Titicaca, which is surrounded by the picturesque villages of the Aymara Indians.

Chile

CAPITAL
Santiago

POPULATION
15,400,000

FUN FACT
Chile, a "string bean" country never more than 111 miles wide, stretches 2,666 miles from north to south along the Pacific Coast. The imposing Andes isolate it from Bolivia and Argentina. The northern part of the country is characterized by the super-arid Atacama desert, the South by the spectacular wind-swept glaciers and fjords of Patagonia. Over one-third of the country's population lives in the Santiago area.

Argentina

CAPITAL
Buenos Aires

POPULATION
37,500,000

FUN FACT
Argentina is often considered the most European country of South America. Buenos Aires is a beautiful city of parks, boutiques, restaurants, and wide boulevards. Argentina is famous for its beef from the cattle that graze on the huge estancias of the grassy Pampas. Farther south on the Chilean border is the gorgeous lake area with Swiss-like villages around Bariloche. To the south is Patagonia with its rocky countryside where the Welsh still graze sheep.

Paraguay

CAPITAL
Asunción

POPULATION
5,700,000

FUN FACT
Paraguay, like Bolivia, is landlocked. Asunción, situated on seven small hills on the east bank of the río Paraguay, is home to one-fifth of the country's total population. Located in the center of South America, this somewhat quaint city is nearly equidistant from the Atlantic and the Andes. The area to the west of the río Paraguay is called the Chaco—a very dry, hot, windy area of grasslands and scrubby forests.

Uruguay

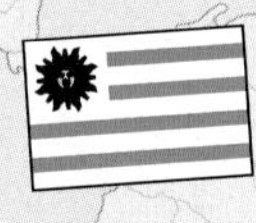

CAPITAL
Montevideo

POPULATION
3,400,000

FUN FACT
Uruguay is the smallest country in South America. Most of the country's terrain is grazing land for sheep and cattle. Montevideo, situated where the río de la Plata empties into the Atlantic, is a rather peaceful city whose suburbs look more like beautiful resorts. The beaches of Uruguay's Atlantic coastline, particularly Punta del Este, attract many people from Brazil and Argentina.

Ceuta and Melilla
Ceuta
Melilla
POPULATION
72,200
FUN FACT
Ceuta and Melilla, located on the north coast of Africa, comprise an autonomous community of Spain. Both of these modern cities are free ports and offer a beautiful blend of many cultures: Christian, Moslem, Hebrew, and Hindu.

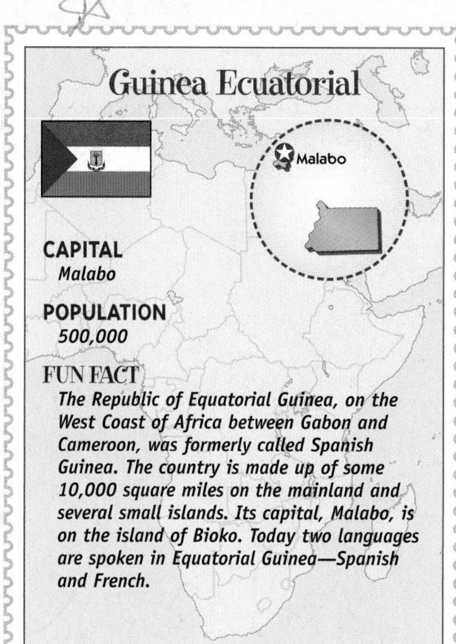
Guinea Ecuatorial
Malabo
CAPITAL
Malabo
POPULATION
500,000
FUN FACT
The Republic of Equatorial Guinea, on the West Coast of Africa between Gabon and Cameroon, was formerly called Spanish Guinea. The country is made up of some 10,000 square miles on the mainland and several small islands. Its capital, Malabo, is on the island of Bioko. Today two languages are spoken in Equatorial Guinea—Spanish and French.

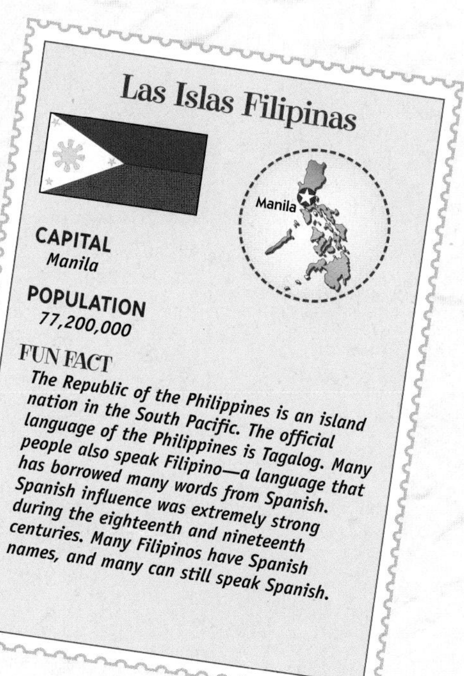
Las Islas Filipinas
Manila
CAPITAL
Manila
POPULATION
77,200,000
FUN FACT
The Republic of the Philippines is an island nation in the South Pacific. The official language of the Philippines is Tagalog. Many people also speak Filipino—a language that has borrowed many words from Spanish. Spanish influence was extremely strong during the eighteenth and nineteenth centuries. Many Filipinos have Spanish names, and many can still speak Spanish.

xxix

España

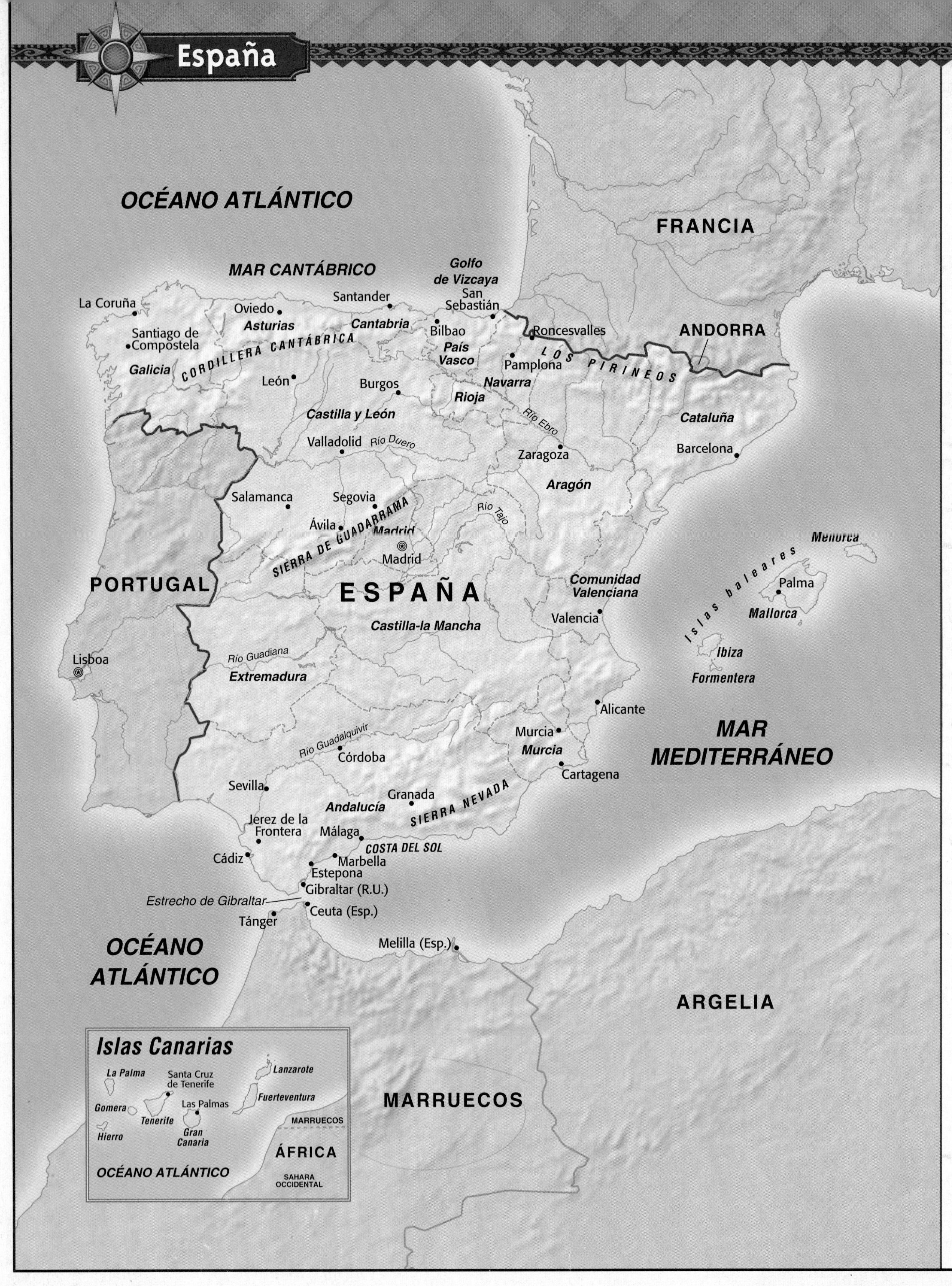

OCÉANO ATLÁNTICO
FRANCIA
MAR CANTÁBRICO
Golfo de Vizcaya
La Coruña
Oviedo
Santander
San Sebastián
Santiago de Compostela
Asturias
Cantabria
Bilbao
Roncesvalles
ANDORRA
CORDILLERA CANTÁBRICA
País Vasco
Pamplona
LOS PIRINEOS
Galicia
León
Burgos
Navarra
Rioja
Castilla y León
Río Ebro
Cataluña
Valladolid
Río Duero
Zaragoza
Barcelona
Aragón
Salamanca
Segovia
Río Tajo
Ávila
SIERRA DE GUADARRAMA
Madrid
Menorca
Madrid
Islas baleares
PORTUGAL
Comunidad Valenciana
Palma
ESPAÑA
Valencia
Mallorca
Castilla-la Mancha
Ibiza
Lisboa
Río Guadiana
Formentera
Extremadura
Alicante
MAR MEDITERRÁNEO
Murcia
Murcia
Río Guadalquivir
Córdoba
Cartagena
Sevilla
Granada
Andalucía
SIERRA NEVADA
Jerez de la Frontera
Málaga
COSTA DEL SOL
Cádiz
Marbella
Estepona
Gibraltar (R.U.)
Estrecho de Gibraltar
Ceuta (Esp.)
Tánger
Melilla (Esp.)
OCÉANO ATLÁNTICO
ARGELIA
MARRUECOS
Islas Canarias
La Palma
Santa Cruz de Tenerife
Lanzarote
Fuerteventura
Gomera
Tenerife
Las Palmas
Hierro
Gran Canaria
MARRUECOS
ÁFRICA
OCÉANO ATLÁNTICO
SAHARA OCCIDENTAL

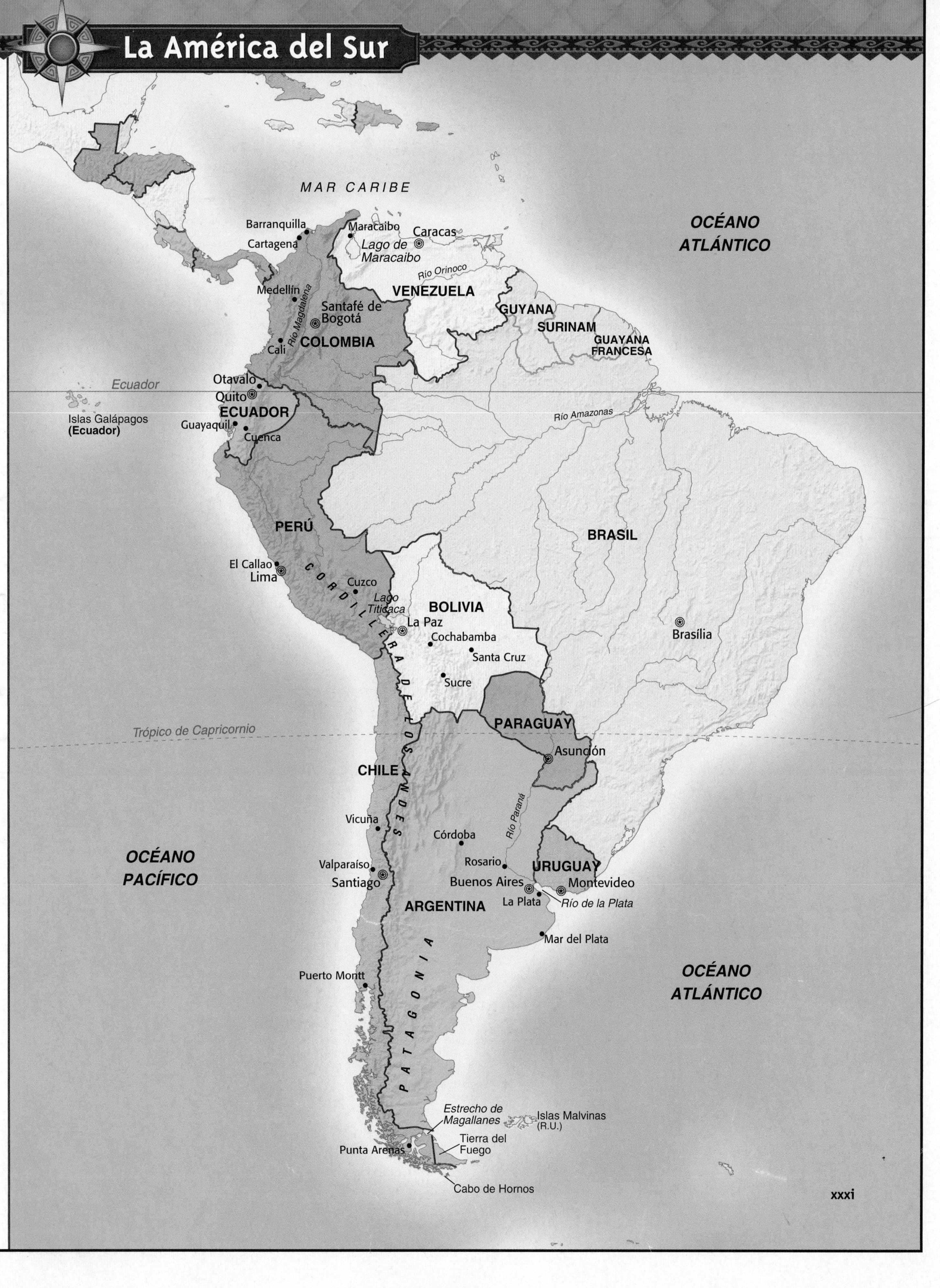
MAR CARIBE
OCÉANO ATLÁNTICO
Barranquilla
Cartagena
Maracaibo
Caracas
Lago de Maracaibo
Río Orinoco
VENEZUELA
Medellín
Río Magdalena
Santafé de Bogotá
Cali
COLOMBIA
GUYANA
SURINAM
GUAYANA FRANCESA
Ecuador
Otavalo
Quito
ECUADOR
Islas Galápagos (Ecuador)
Guayaquil
Cuenca
Río Amazonas
PERÚ
BRASIL
El Callao
Lima
CORDILLERA DE LOS ANDES
Cuzco
Lago Titicaca
BOLIVIA
La Paz
Cochabamba
Santa Cruz
Sucre
Brasília
PARAGUAY
Trópico de Capricornio
Asunción
CHILE
Río Paraná
Vicuña
Córdoba
OCÉANO PACÍFICO
Valparaíso
Santiago
Rosario
URUGUAY
Buenos Aires
Montevideo
La Plata
Río de la Plata
ARGENTINA
Mar del Plata
OCÉANO ATLÁNTICO
Puerto Montt
PATAGONIA
Estrecho de Magallanes
Islas Malvinas (R.U.)
Tierra del Fuego
Punta Arenas
Cabo de Hornos
xxxi

México, la América Central y el Caribe

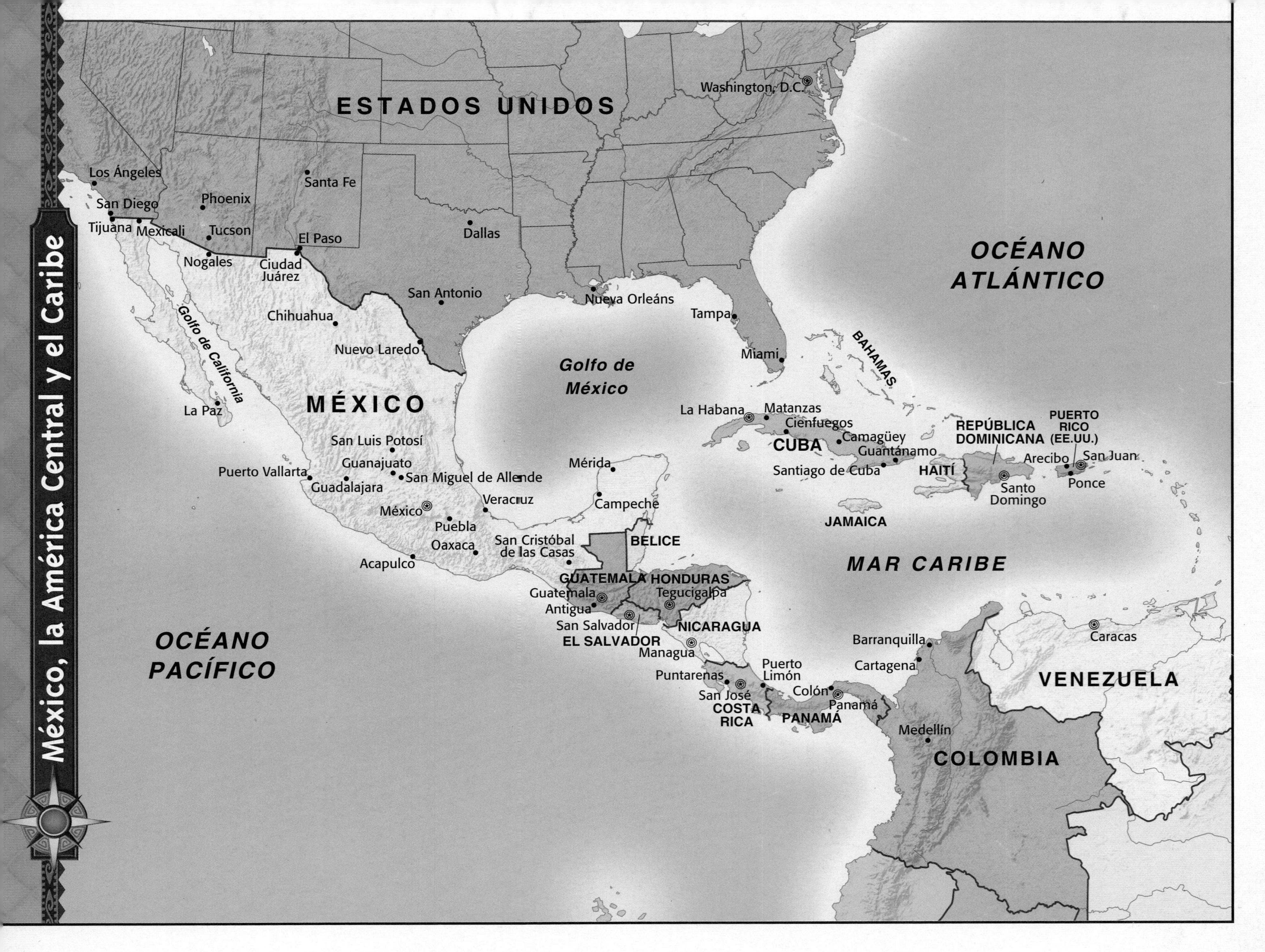

Estados Unidos

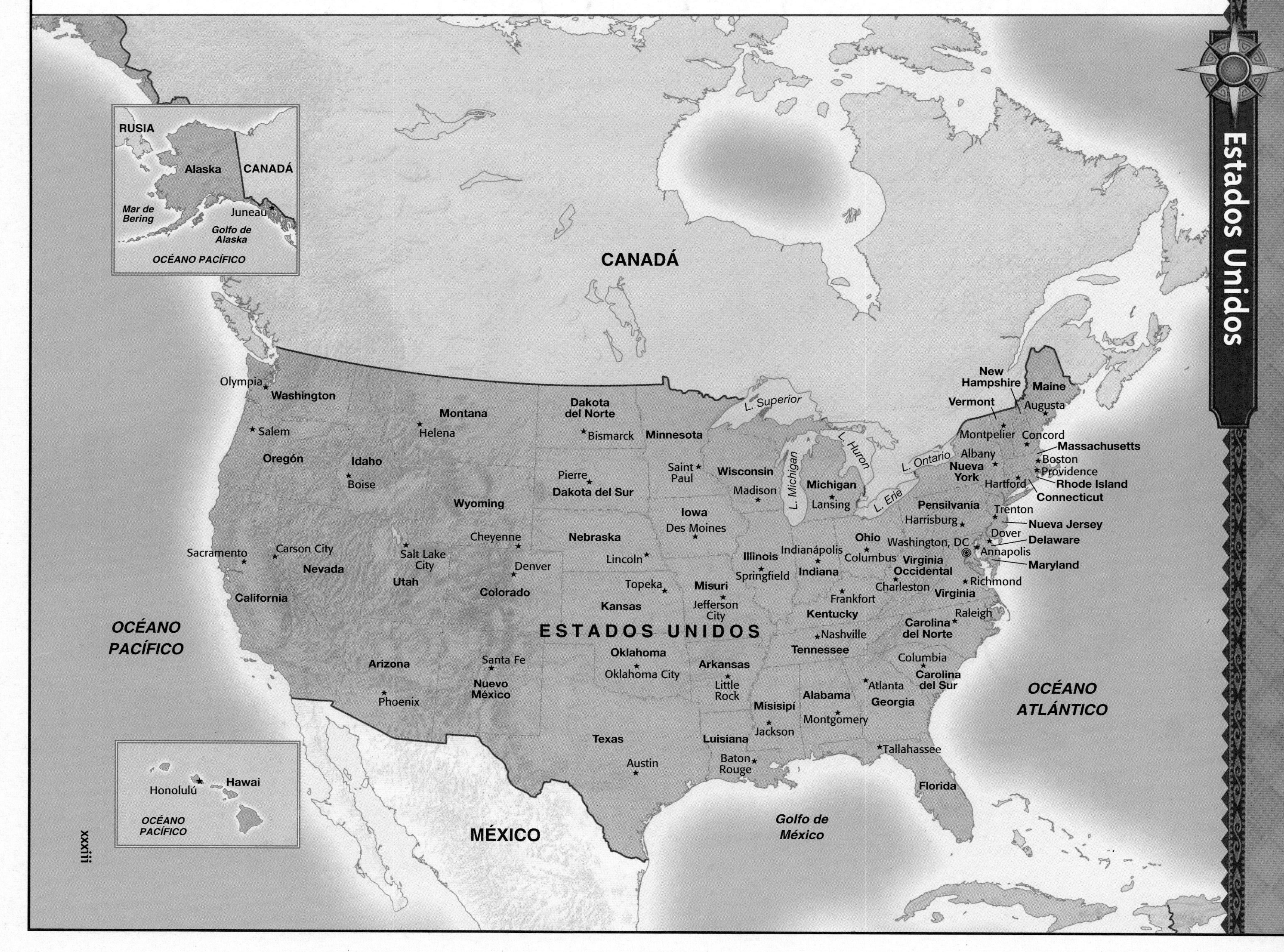

Why Learn Spanish?

The Spanish-Speaking World

Culture Knowing Spanish will open doors to you around the world. As you study the language, you will come to understand and appreciate the way of life, customs, values, and cultures of people from many different areas of the world. Look at the map on pages xxii–xxiii to see where Spanish is spoken, either as a first or second language.

Learning Spanish can be fun and will bring you a sense of accomplishment. You'll be really pleased when you are able to carry on a conversation in Spanish. You will be able to read the literature of Spain and Latin America, keep up with current events in magazines and newspapers from Spain and Latin America, and understand Spanish language films without relying on subtitles.

The Spanish language will be a source of enrichment for the rest of your life—and you don't have to leave home to enjoy it. In all areas of the United States there are Hispanic radio and television stations, Latin musicians, Spanish-language magazines and newspapers, and a great diversity of restaurants serving foods from all areas of the Spanish-speaking world. The Latin or Hispanic population of the United States today totals forty million people and is the fastest growing segment of the population.

xxxiv

Career Opportunities

Business Your knowledge of Spanish will also be an asset to you in a wide variety of careers. Many companies from Spain and Latin America are multinational and have branches around the world, including the United States. Many U.S. corporations have great exposure in the Spanish-speaking countries. With the growth of the Hispanic population in the U.S., bilingualism is becoming an important asset in many fields including retail, fashion, cosmetics, pharmaceutical, agriculture, automotive, tourism, airlines, technology, finance, and accounting.

You can use your Spanish in all these fields, not only abroad but also in the United States. On the national scene there are innumerable possibilities in medical and hospital services, banking and finance, law, social work, and law enforcement. The opportunities are limitless.

Language Link

Another benefit to learning Spanish is that it will improve your English. Once you know another language, you can make comparisons between the two and gain a greater understanding of how languages function. You'll also come across a number of Spanish words that are used in English. Just a few examples are: **adobe, corral, meseta, rodeo, poncho, canyon, llama, alpaca.** Spanish will also be helpful if you decide to learn yet another language. Once you learn a second language, the learning process for acquiring other languages becomes much easier.

Spanish is a beautiful, rich language spoken on many continents. Whatever your motivation is for choosing to study it, Spanish will expand your horizons and increase your job opportunities. **¡Viva el español! Y ¡buen viaje!**

El alfabeto español

a

***a**vión*

b

***b**ebé*

c

***c**esta*

d

***d**edo*

e

***e**lefante*

f

***f**oto*

g

***g**emelos*

h

***h**amaca*

i

***i**glesia*

j

***j**abón*

k

***k**ilo*

l

***l**ago*

m

***m**ono*

n

***n**ariz*

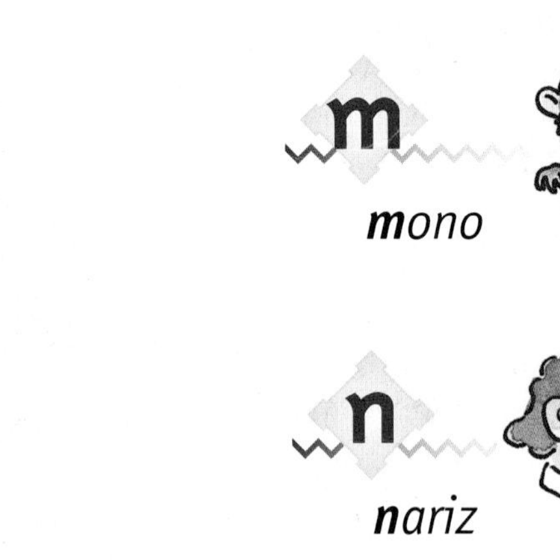

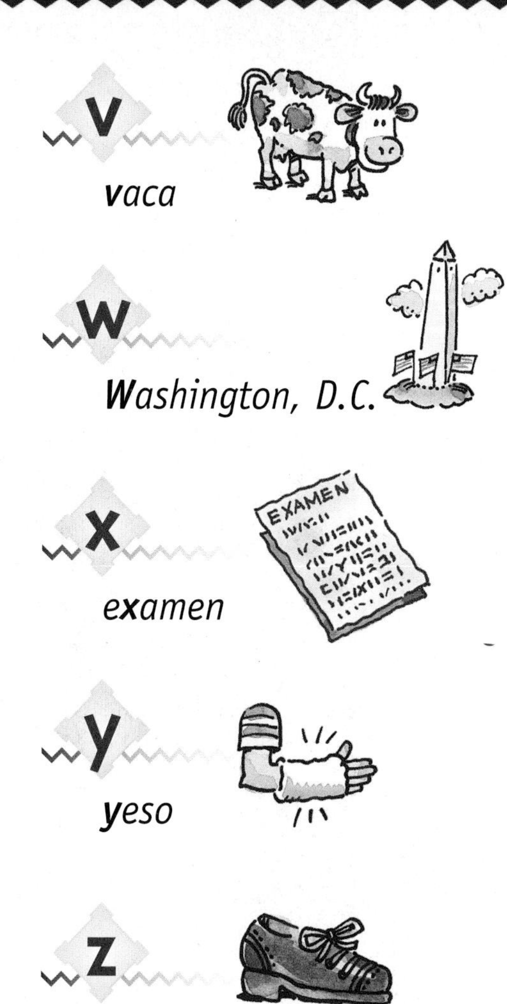

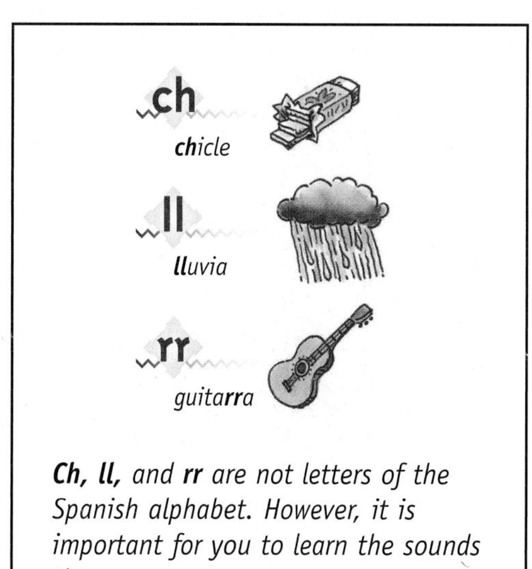

Ch, ll, *and* ***rr*** *are not letters of the Spanish alphabet. However, it is important for you to learn the sounds they represent.*

Resource Manager

Vocabulary Transparencies BV.1–BV.6

Preview

In the **Bienvenidos** section, students will begin their study by communicating immediately in Spanish. In this preliminary section they will learn to greet one another, take leave of one another, use some expressions of courtesy, and give the date and season.

National Standards

Communication

In this preliminary section students will communicate in spoken Spanish on the following topics:

- saying hello
- saying good-bye
- being polite
- dates and seasons

Students will obtain and provide information and engage in short conversations dealing with these introductory topics and situations.

¡OJO! In the short lessons in this preliminary section, students only learn expressions that do not require any grammatical or structural manipulation. For example, **¿Qué tal?** is presented rather than **¿Cómo estás?** and **¿Cómo está Ud.?**

Lecciones preliminares

Bienvenidos

Objetivos

In these preliminary lessons you will learn to:

- greet people
- say good-bye to people
- express simple courtesies
- find out and tell the days of the week
- find out and tell the months of the year
- count from 1 to 30
- find out and tell the seasons

Calendario maya

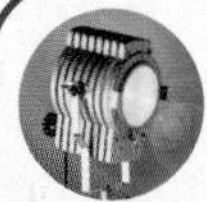

Spotlight on Culture

Arte The Maya used two calendars, a 365-day calendar based on the sun, and a 260-day sacred almanac. Each calendar was thought of as a wheel. The two wheels connected at a single point, and each one moved one step every day. Days were named by putting together the names on both calendars for that day. The Maya were very advanced in abstract mathematics and astronomy, and Maya astronomers could make very complex calculations and measurements.

Fotografía The students in this photo are arriving at a house in Cádiz, Spain.

Preview

In this short lesson, which should take less than one class period, students will learn to greet their peers and older people.

¡OJO! It is suggested that you present these preliminary lessons for oral work only. Writing begins in Chapter 1.

PRESENTATION

Greeting people

Step 1 Have students repeat **¡Hola!**

Step 2 Use a gesture to convey **¿Qué tal?**

Step 3 Smile as you say and have the class repeat **Bien, gracias.**

Step 4 Point directly to a student as you say and have them repeat **¿Y tú?**

Step 5 Have students repeat the entire miniconversation after you with books closed. You may also wish to use Vocabulary Transparency BV.2 for this activity.

Step 6 Have students open their books and read the conversation aloud in pairs.

PRACTICE

1 and 2 Students can move around the room or stay at their desks as they do these activities.

2 When doing Activity 2, have students change partners after each conversation so that each practices three or four conversations.

Saludos

Greeting people

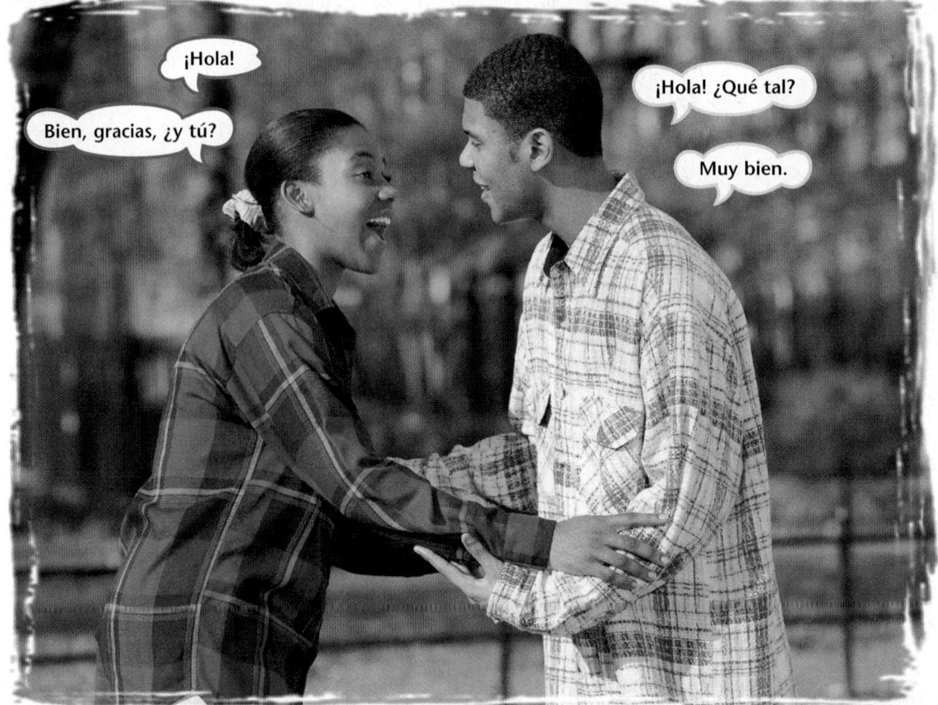

¡Hola!
Bien, gracias, ¿y tú?
¡Hola! ¿Qué tal?
Muy bien.

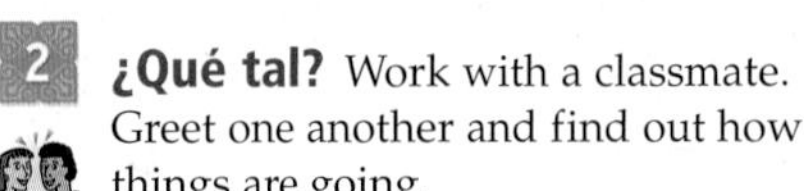

1 **¡Hola!** Get up from your desk. Walk around the classroom. Say hello to each classmate you meet.

2 **¿Qué tal?** Work with a classmate. Greet one another and find out how things are going.

Puerto Vallarta, México

Answers

1 *Students will either say* ¡Hola! *or* ¡Hola! ¿Qué tal?

2 *Students will use the greetings presented in the text on this page. Dialogues may include* ¡Hola! ¿Qué tal? / Muy bien, gracias. ¿Y tú? / Bien, gracias.

PRESENTATION

Greeting people throughout the day

1. Some greetings are more formal than ¡**Hola!** When you greet an older person, you may use one of the following expressions.

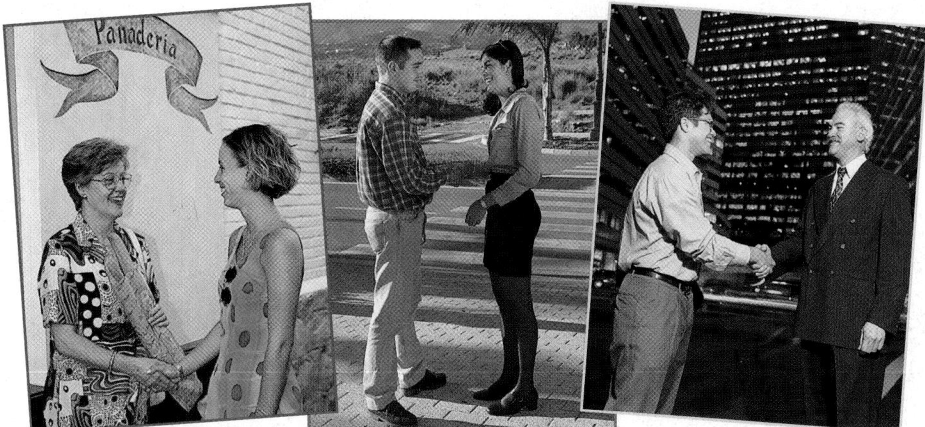

Buenos días, señora. **Buenas tardes, señorita.** **Buenas noches, señor.**

2. The titles **señor, señora,** and **señorita** are often used without the last name of the person.

Buenos días, señor.
Buenas tardes, señora.
Buenas noches, señorita.

3 Buenos días Draw some figures on the board. Some will represent friends your own age and others will represent older people. Greet each of the figures on the board with the proper expression.

4 Saludos Look at these photographs of young people in Spain and Mexico. As they greet one another, they do some things that are different from what we do when we greet each other. What do you notice in the photographs?

Greeting people throughout the day

Step 1 Have students repeat each greeting. You may also wish to write an appropriate time of day on the board. Students do not have to give the time.

Step 2 Explain that the use of the title without a name is common when we do not know the name of the person. We can use the title with a last name when we know the person: **Buenos días, Señora Romero.**

National Standards

Comparisons
Indicate to students how the information above concerning titles is not the same when speaking English. In English, *Hello, Mr.* or *Hello, Mrs.* would not be said. The title would not be used without the person's name.

Learning from Photos

(page 3) Have students look at the people in the photo giving each other the **besito**, which is exchanged both when greeting and taking leave of someone. Note that the **besito** is merely touching cheek to cheek.
(page 3) Also have students look at the people shaking hands in these photos. The handshake is much more common in Spanish-speaking countries, even among young people, than it is in the United States.
(page 3 bottom right) Two men who know one another will tend to give one another a "bear hug" with a slap on the back.

Reaching All Students

Additional Practice Practice greeting the following people.
1. your history teacher
2. a young saleswoman at the department store
3. your parents' friend, Mrs. Brown
4. your neighbor, Mr. Roberts
5. the principal of your school

ANSWERS

3 *Students will use the appropriate greetings taught on page 3.*

4 *Women typically give each other a light kiss on the cheek when greeting one another. Men frequently shake hands, then give each other* un abrazo, *a "bear hug."*

Preview

In this lesson students will learn farewell expressions. **Preliminar A** and **B** together should take about one class period.

PRESENTATION

Saying good-bye

Step 1 Have students look at the photos as they repeat the expressions for leave-taking.

Step 2 Have them read Items 1, 2, and 3 aloud or read them to the students. Have the class repeat each word or expression in unison.

Step 3 You may wish to use Vocabulary Transparency BV.3 to review the expressions.

PRACTICE

1, 2, and 3 Students can circulate around the room as they do these activities.

Recycling

You are walking down the street in Buenos Aires, Argentina, when you run into one of your Hispanic friends (your partner). Greet each other and ask how he or she is.

Preliminar B Adiós

Saying good-bye

Adiós, José.
Adiós, Gloria.

Chao, Patricia.
Chao, Roberto. ¡Hasta luego!

1. The common expression to use when saying good-bye to someone is **¡Adiós!**
2. If you plan to see the person again soon, you can say **¡Hasta pronto!** or **¡Hasta luego!** If you plan to see the person the next day, you can say **¡Hasta mañana!**
3. An informal expression you often hear, particularly in Spain and in Argentina, is **¡Chao!**

1 **¡Chao!** Go over to a classmate and say good-bye to him or her.

2 **¡Hasta luego!** Work with a classmate. Say **¡Chao!** to one another and let each other know that you will be getting together again soon.

3 **¡Adiós!** Say good-bye to your Spanish teacher. Then say good-bye to a friend. Use a different expression with each person.

Answers

1 *Students will either say* Adiós *or* Chao *(followed by the person's name) or* ¡Hasta luego!

2 *Students will say* Chao *followed by either* ¡Hasta luego!, ¡Hasta pronto!, *or* ¡Hasta mañana!

3 *Students will use two of the expressions taught on page 4—one for the Spanish teacher, another for their friend.*

Conversando más

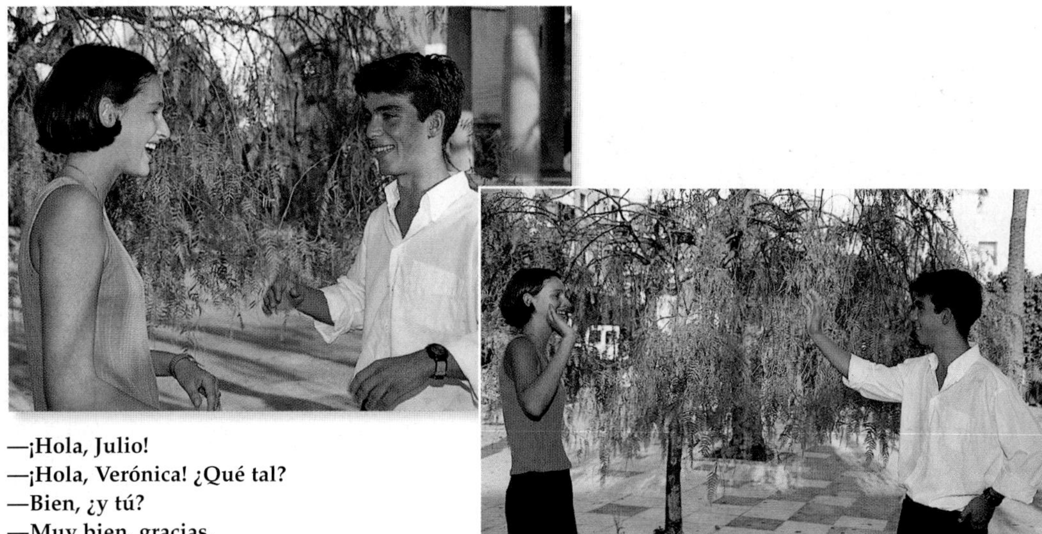

—¡Hola, Julio!
—¡Hola, Verónica! ¿Qué tal?
—Bien, ¿y tú?
—Muy bien, gracias.

—Chao, Julio
—Chao, Verónica. ¡Hasta luego!

4 **¡Hola, amigo(a)!** Work with a classmate. Have a conversation in Spanish. Say as much as you can to one another.

Salamanca, España

PRESENTATION

Conversando más

Step 1 This conversation recombines the greetings and farewells presented in Preliminary Lessons A and B.

Step 2 Have pairs of students present the conversation to the class. They can read it if necessary, but many will probably be able to do it on their own. If they make any changes that make sense, that's fine.

Step 3 Encourage students to use as much expression and as many gestures as possible when presenting the conversation.

Geography Connection

Salamanca is situated on the banks of the río Tormes about 205 kilometers northwest of Madrid. The **Plaza Mayor**, shown here, is one of the most elegant squares in Spain. Salamanca remains one of the richest Spanish cities architecturally and is especially known for its buildings dating from the Spanish Renaissance.

History Connection

Salamanca was an important settlement even in Iberian times. The later importance of the town was due mainly to its famous university, which grew out of a college founded by Alfonso IV in about 1220. Isabel la Católica was a great supporter of the university, and she had it rebuilt during her reign. The university today is one of the most prestigious in Europe.

Reaching All Students

Additional Practice

- Say the following to a classmate. He or she will answer.
  ¡Hola! **¡Adiós!**
  ¿Qué tal? **¡Chao!**
- Say good-bye to your Spanish teacher.
- Say good-bye to a friend. Say that you'll see him or her later in the day.

Answers

4 *Answers will vary. Encourage students to use as many of the expressions for saying hello and good-bye as they have learned to date.*

Preview

In this lesson students will learn to order a few simple food items. They will also learn the polite expressions one needs to know when dealing with people.

PRESENTATION

Ordering food politely

Step 1 The expressions in this conversation should be very easy to present, since most students are probably already familiar with them, with the exception of **No hay de qué.** You may wish to use Vocabulary Transparency BV.4 to present the conversation.

Step 2 Have students read the information about *You're welcome* and repeat the expressions aloud several times.

Step 3 Now have students do the activities.

Preliminar C La cortesía

Ordering food politely

There are several ways to express *you're welcome.*

No hay de qué.
De nada.
Por nada.

CAFE HAITI GALERIAS NACIONALES LTDA.
CAFETERIA, TE, HELADERIA Y SIMILARES
San Antonio 53- Fono: 633 15 36
SANTIAGO CENTRO- R.U.T.89.560.800-9

CAFÉ Haití
Fecha:
1 CORTADO GRANDE
$ 360 (IVA Incluido)
496969
BOLETA VENTA Cliente
Impresos T.G Fono 6396150

La cortesía With a classmate, practice reading the conversation above. Be as animated and polite as you can.

Answers

Students will practice the conversation aloud.

2 **Una cola, por favor.** You are at a café in Manzanillo, Mexico. Order the following things from the waiter or waitress (your partner). Be polite when you order.

1. un sándwich
2. una cola
3. una limonada

4. un café
5. una pizza

3 **Tacos, enchiladas, tamales** You are in a Mexican restaurant. Order the following foods from the waiter or waitress (your partner). Be polite to each other.

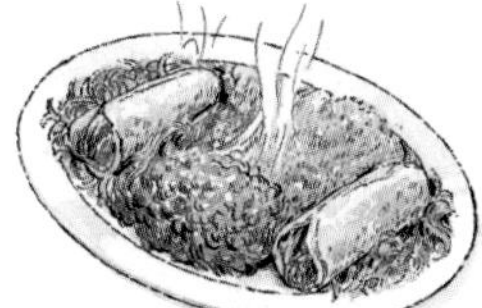

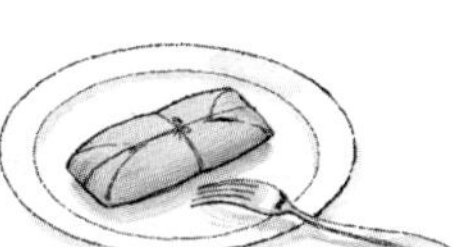

1. un taco
2. una enchilada
3. un tamal

Guanajuato, México

FUN-FACTS

Un taco is a tortilla that has been fried, folded, and stuffed with chicken, shredded beef, beans and/or cheese. **Una enchilada** is a soft tortilla that is rolled and stuffed with the same ingredients as a taco and then baked. **Un tamal** is made of ground corn meal. It is stuffed with some type of meat, wrapped in a leaf, and steamed.

Geography Connection

Guanajuato, Mexico, was once an important silver mining city. It is a stunning city with beautiful colonial architecture and lovely narrow cobblestoned streets. Guanajuato also has a very good university.

Answers

2 and **3** *Answers will vary, but students should follow the model conversation on page 6 when doing these activities.*

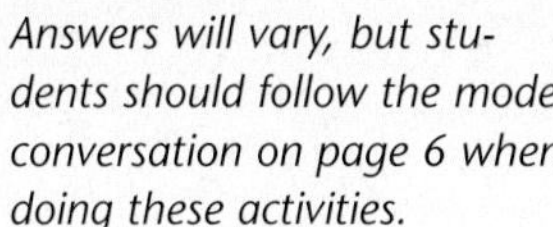

Preview

In this lesson students learn the days of the week, the months, the seasons, and the numbers from 1 to 30. These topics will be reinforced and recycled in later chapters.

PRESENTATION

Telling the days of the week and the months

Step 1 Have students repeat the days of the week and months of the year. You may wish to use Vocabulary Transparency BV.5 for this activity.

Step 2 Have them give different days of the week and months at random rather than in a fixed order. Many students know the days of the week when they recite them in a row but don't know the difference between **martes** and **jueves,** for example. Having them give the days of the week in other than a set order helps avoid this problem.

Step 3 Although we will concern ourselves with writing starting in Chapter 1, you may wish to point out to students that days and months are not always capitalized in Spanish.

Preliminar D La fecha

Telling the days of the week

lunes	martes	miércoles	jueves	viernes	sábado	domingo
1	2	3	4	5	6	7
8	9	10	11	12	13	14

To find out and give the day of the week, you say:

—¿Qué día es hoy?
—Hoy es lunes.

1 ¿Qué día es? Answer in Spanish.

1. ¿Qué día es hoy?
2. ¿Qué día es mañana?
3. ¿Cuáles son los días del fin de semana o del *weekend?*

Telling the months

Answers

1. Hoy es ___.
2. Mañana es ___.
3. Sábado y domingo son los días del fin de semana.

Finding out and giving the date

¿Cuál es la fecha de hoy?
Hoy es el doce de septiembre.
SEPTIEMBRE
12

When giving the date, you use **primero** for the first day of the month. For other days you use **dos, tres, cuatro,** etc.

Nota

1 uno	**11** once	**21** veintiuno
2 dos	**12** doce	**22** veintidós
3 tres	**13** trece	**23** veintitrés
4 cuatro	**14** catorce	**24** veinticuatro
5 cinco	**15** quince	**25** veinticinco
6 seis	**16** dieciséis	**26** veintiséis
7 siete	**17** diecisiete	**27** veintisiete
8 ocho	**18** dieciocho	**28** veintiocho
9 nueve	**19** diecinueve	**29** veintinueve
10 diez	**20** veinte	**30** treinta

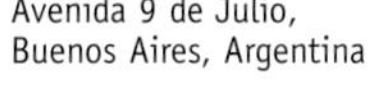

Avenida 9 de Julio, Buenos Aires, Argentina

Celebración del Cinco de Mayo

PRESENTATION

Finding out and giving the date

In this lesson we have presented the numbers from 1 to 30 so students can say the date. At this point, students should not be expected to know these numbers perfectly. They will be reintroduced in Chapters 1, 2 and 3. It is suggested that you not make students write the numbers.

Geography Connection

The **Avenida 9 de Julio** in Buenos Aires, Argentina, is 425 feet across. **Los porteños,** residents of Buenos Aires, claim it is the world's widest street. It is also 26 blocks long. It is an ideal street for strolling and people-watching from one of the many **confiterías**—Argentine tearooms or cafés. The obelisk reminds some people of the Washington Monument. It marks the intersection of **Avenida 9 de Julio** and **Corrientes,** a main thoroughfare in Buenos Aires.

History Connection

Many people erroneously think that **el Cinco de Mayo** is Mexican Independence Day, but it is not. **El Cinco de Mayo** marks the anniversary of a French defeat by Mexican troops in Puebla in 1862. **El día de la Independencia** is September 15–16.

PRESENTATION

Telling the seasons

Step 1 Have students look at Vocabulary Transparency BV.6 as they repeat the name of each season.

Step 2 Then have them open their books and read for additional reinforcement.

Preliminar D

Telling the seasons

2 **¿Cuántos?** Answer in Spanish.

1. ¿Cuántos días hay en una semana, siete o cuatro?
2. ¿Cuántos meses hay en un año, siete o doce?
3. ¿Cuántas estaciones hay en un año, cuatro o doce?

3 **¿En qué mes?** Each of you will stand up in class and give your birthday **(cumpleaños)** in Spanish. Listen carefully and keep a record of how many classmates were born in the same month. Then tell, in Spanish, in which month the greatest number of students were born. In which month were the fewest born?

4 **La estación, por favor.** Tell in which season the following months are. Answer in Spanish.

1. ¿En qué estación es mayo?
2. ¿En qué estación es enero?
3. ¿En qué estación es julio?
4. ¿En qué estación es octubre?

Answers

2

1. Hay siete días en una semana.
2. Hay doce meses en un año.
3. Hay cuatro estaciones en un año.

3

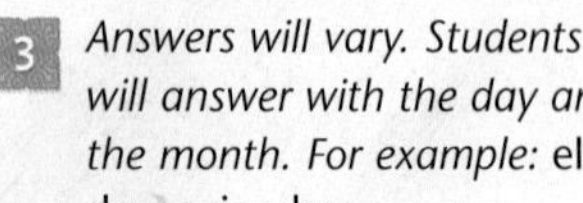

Answers will vary. Students will answer with the day and the month. For example: el 4 de noviembre.

4

1. Mayo es en la primavera.
2. Enero es en el invierno.
3. Julio es en el verano.
4. Octubre es en el otoño.

Greeting people

¡Hola!
Buenos días.
Buenas tardes.
Buenas noches.
¿Qué tal?
Muy bien.

Identifying titles

señor
señora
señorita

Saying good-bye

¡Adiós!
¡Chao!
¡Hasta luego!
¡Hasta pronto!
¡Hasta mañana!

Being courteous

Por favor.
Gracias.
De (Por) nada.
No hay de qué.

How well do you know your vocabulary?

- Choose an expression from the list to begin a conversation.
- Have a classmate respond.
- Take turns.

Identifying the days of the week

lunes
martes
miércoles
jueves
viernes
sábado
domingo
hoy
mañana
el fin de semana

Identifying the months of the year

enero
febrero
marzo
abril
mayo
junio
julio
agosto
septiembre
octubre
noviembre
diciembre

Identifying the seasons

la primavera
el verano
el otoño
el invierno

Other useful expressions

¿Qué día es hoy?
¿Cuál es la fecha?

Vocabulary Review

The words and phrases in the **Vocabulario** have been taught for productive use in these preliminary lessons. They are summarized here as a resource for both student and teacher.

¡OJO! You will notice that the vocabulary list here is not translated. This has been done intentionally, since we feel that by the time students have finished the material in the lessons they should be familiar with the meanings of all the words. If there are several words they still do not know, we recommend that they refer to the preliminary lessons or go to the dictionaries at the end of this book to find the meanings. However, if you prefer that your students have the English translations, please refer to Vocabulary Transparency BV.1, where you will find all these words with their translations.

Planning for Chapter 1

SCOPE AND SEQUENCE, PAGES 12–41

Topics

- Describing people and places
- Nationalities
- Numbers: 0–30

Culture

- *El Quijote*, the novel
- Miguel de Cervantes Saavedra
- Map of Spain **(La Mancha)**
- Alicia Bustelo, a student from Venezuela
- Plaza Simón Bolívar, Caracas
- Two Latin American heroes: Simón Bolívar and San Martín
- Geographical terms in Spanish

Functions

- How to ask who someone is
- How to state where someone is from
- How to describe a person or thing
- How to identify people or things
- How to count from 0 to 30

Structure

- Singular forms of definite and indefinite articles—**el, la, un, una**
- Singular forms of adjectives
- Singular forms of **ser**

National Standards

- Communication Standard 1.1 pages 16, 17, 20, 21, 22, 24, 26, 27, 29, 36, 37
- Communication Standard 1.2 pages 17, 21, 23, 24, 27, 28, 29, 31, 32, 33, 36, 37
- Communication Standard 1.3 pages 21, 37
- Cultures Standard 2.1 pages 22, 28, 30–31, 32, 33
- Cultures Standard 2.2 page 30
- Connections Standard 3.1 pages 34–35
- Comparisons Standard 4.1 pages 22, 33
- Communities Standard 5.1 page 36

PACING AND PRIORITIES

The chapter content is color coded below to assist you in planning.

■ required ■ recommended ■ optional

Vocabulario *(required)* *Days 1–4*

- ■ Palabras 1
  - ¿Quién es?
  - ¿Qué es?
  - ¿Cómo es el muchacho?
  - ¿Cómo es la muchacha?
- ■ Palabras 2
  - ¿Quién soy yo y de dónde soy?
  - ¿Quién es y cómo es?
  - Los números

Estructura *(required)* *Days 5–7*

- ■ Artículos—**el, la, un, una**
- ■ Adjetivos en el singular
- ■ Presente del verbo **ser** en el singular

Conversación *(required)*

- ■ ¿De dónde eres?

Pronunciación *(recommended)*

- ■ Las vocales **a, o, u**

Lecturas culturales

- ■ *El Quijote (recommended)*
- ■ Una alumna *(optional)*
- ■ Simón Bolívar y José de San Martín *(optional)*

Conexiones

- ■ La geografía *(optional)*

■ **¡Te toca a ti!** *(recommended)*

■ **Assessment** *(recommended)*

■ **¡Hablo como un pro!** *(optional)*

RESOURCE GUIDE

Section	Pages	Section Resources
Vocabulario PALABRAS 1		
¿Quién es? ¿Qué es? ¿Cómo es el muchacho? ¿Cómo es la muchacha?	14, 16–17 14, 16–17 15, 16–17 15, 16–17	Vocabulary Transparencies 1.2–1.3 Audio CD 2 Audio Activities TE, pages 1–2 Workbook, pages 1–2 Quiz 1, page 1 ExamView® Pro
Vocabulario PALABRAS 2		
¿Quién soy yo y de dónde soy? ¿Quién es y cómo es? Los números	18, 20–21 19, 20–21 19, 20–21	Vocabulary Transparencies 1.4–1.5 Audio CD 2 Audio Activities TE, pages 2–4 Workbook, pages 3–4 Quiz 2, page 2 ExamView® Pro
Estructura		
Artículos—**el, la, un, una** Adjetivos en el singular Presente del verbo **ser** en el singular	22–23 23–24 25–27	Audio CD 2 Audio Activities TE, pages 5–6 Workbook, pages 5–8 Quizzes 3–5, pages 3–5 ExamView® Pro
Conversación		
¿De dónde eres?	28	Audio CD 2 Audio Activities TE, page 7 Interactive CD-ROM
Pronunciación		
Las vocales **a, o, u**	29	Pronunciation Transparency P 1 Audio CD 2 Audio Activities TE, page 8
Lecturas culturales		
El Quijote Una alumna Simón Bolívar y José de San Martín	30–31 32 33	Audio CD 2 Audio Activities TE, page 8 Tests, pages 4, 6
Conexiones		
La geografía	34–35	Tests, page 7
¡Te toca a ti!		
	36–37	**¡Viva el mundo hispano!** Video, Episode 1 Video Activities, Chapter 1 Spanish Online Activities spanish.glencoe.com
Assessment		
	38–39	Communication Transparency C 1 Quizzes 1–5, pages 1–5 Performance Assessment, Task 1 Tests, pages 1–12 Situation Cards, Chapter 1 ExamView® Pro **Maratón mental** Videoquiz

Using Your Resources for Chapter 1

Transparencies

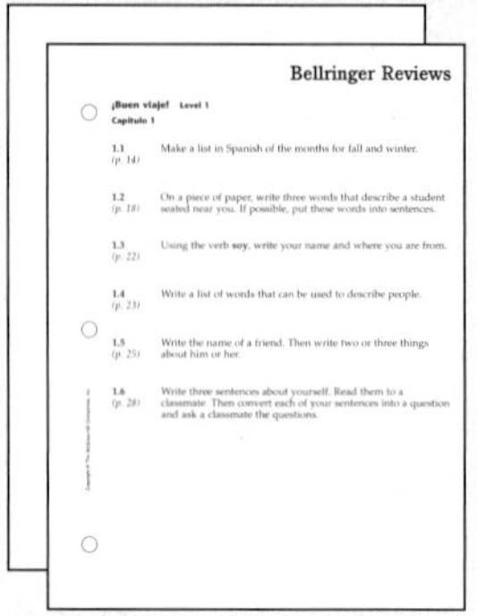

Bellringer 1.1–1.6

Vocabulary 1.1–1.5

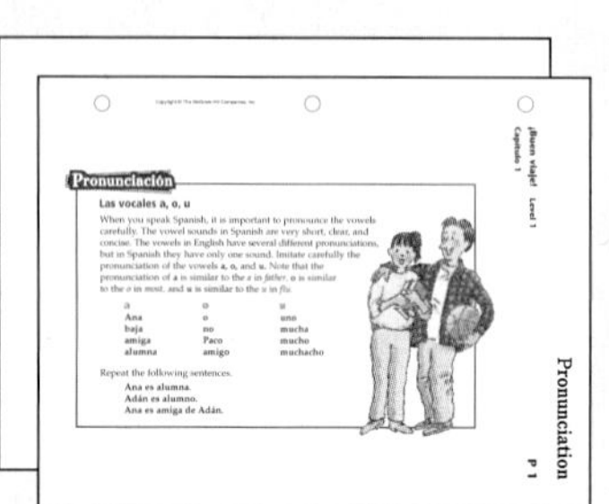
Pronunciation P 1

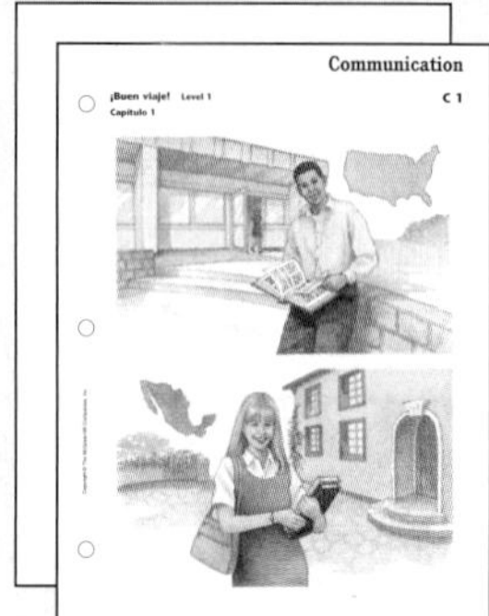
Communication C 1

Workbook

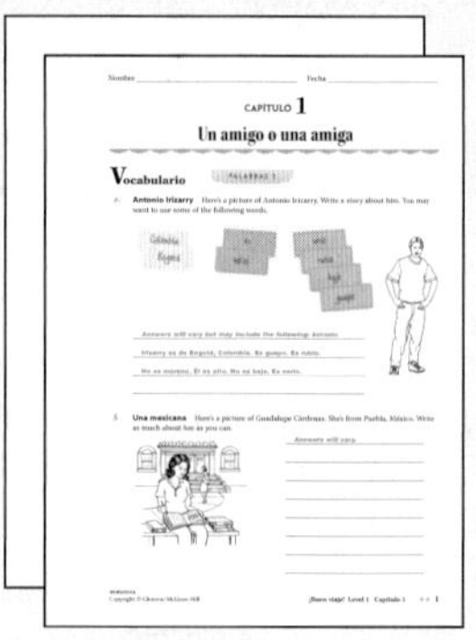
Vocabulary, pages 1–4

Structure, pages 5–8

Enrichment, pages 9–10

Audio Activities

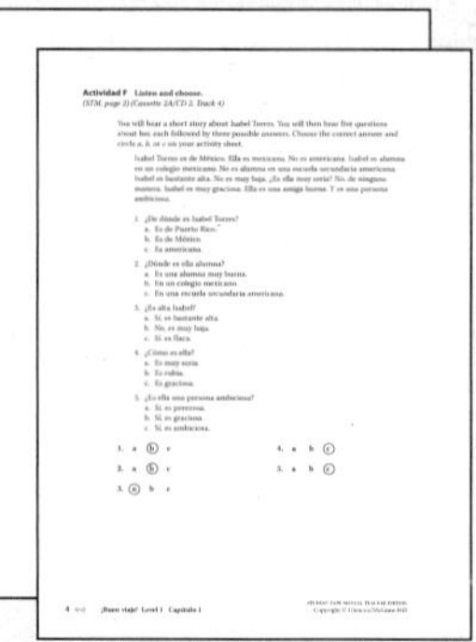
Vocabulary, pages 1–4

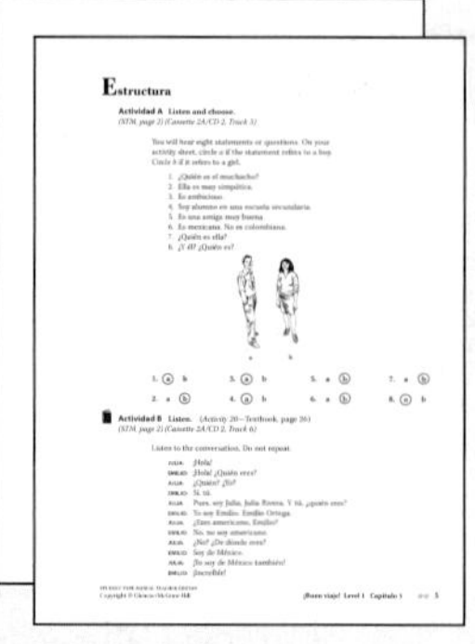
Structure, pages 5–6

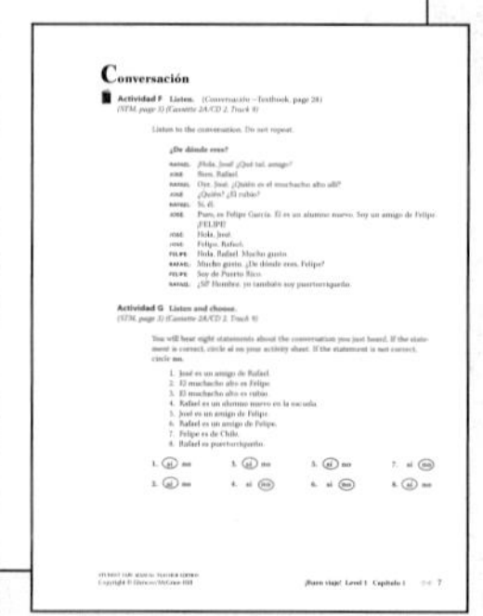
Conversation, Pronunciation, pages 7–8

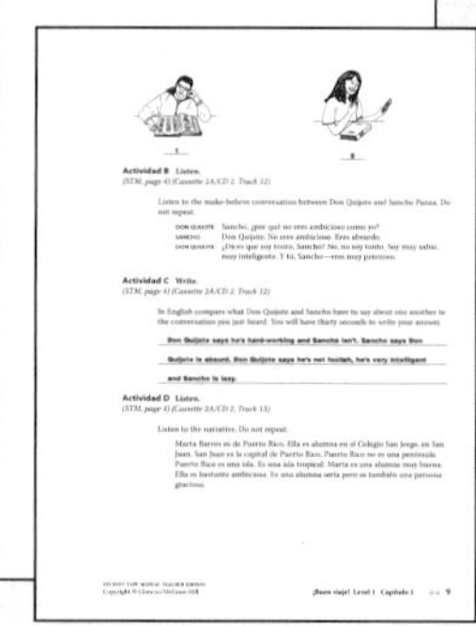
Additional Practice, pages 9–10

Assessment

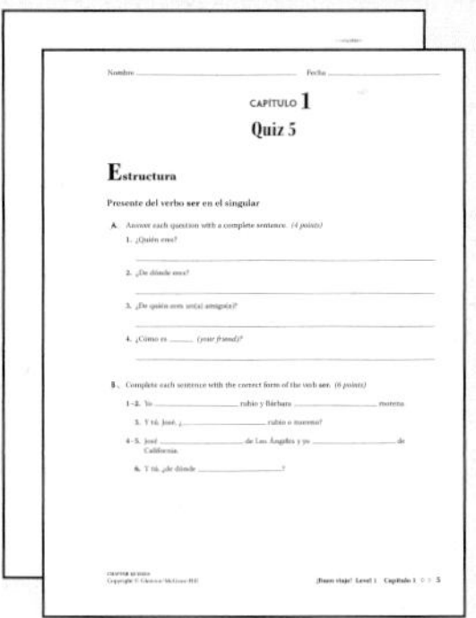
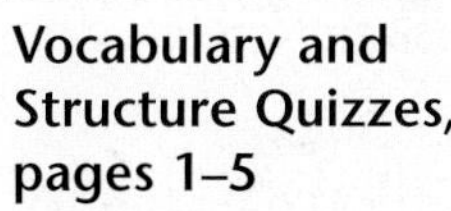

Vocabulary and Structure Quizzes, pages 1–5

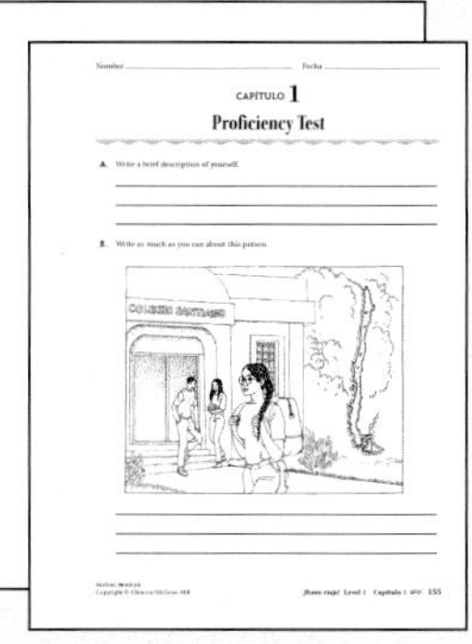

Chapter Tests, pages 1–12

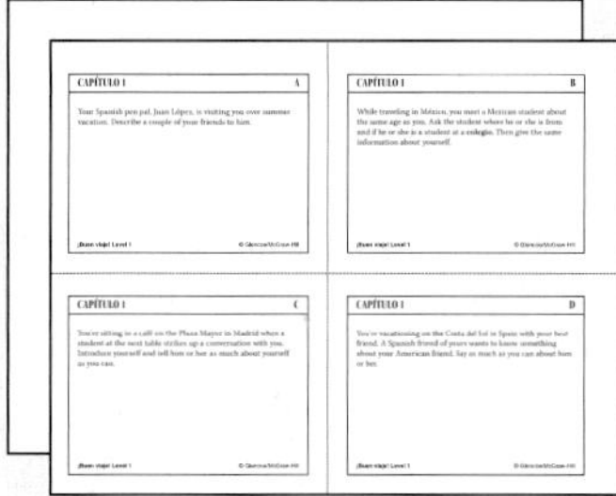

Situation Cards, Chapter 1

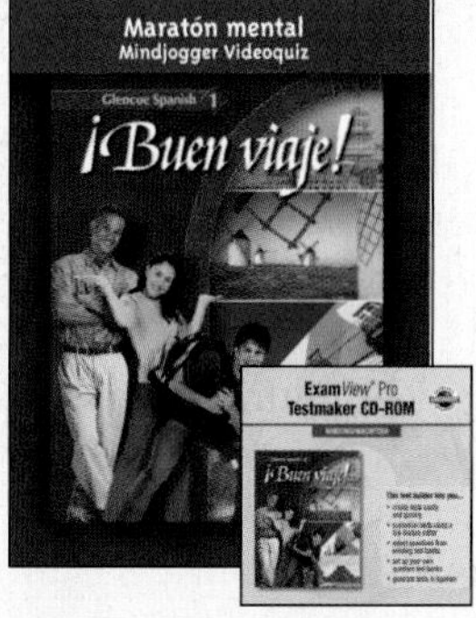

MindJogger Videoquiz, ExamView® Pro, Chapter 1

Timesaving Teacher Tools

TeacherWorks™ is your all-in-one teacher resource center. Personalize lesson plans, access resources from the Teacher Wraparound Edition, connect to the Internet, or make a to-do list. These are only a few of the many features that can assist you in the planning and organizing of your lessons.

Includes:

- A calendar feature
- Access to all program blackline masters
- Standards correlations and more

ExamView® Pro

Test Bank software for Macintosh and Windows makes creating, editing, customizing, and printing tests quick and easy.

Technology Resources

In the Chapter 1 Internet Activity, you will have a chance to learn more about the Spanish-speaking world. Visit spanish.glencoe.com

On the interactive CD-ROM, students can listen to and take part in a recorded version of the conversation in Chapter 1.

¡Viva el mundo hispano! Video and Video Activities, Chapter 1. Available on VHS and DVD.

Help your students prepare for the chapter test by playing the **Maratón mental** Videoquiz game show. Teams will compete against each other to review chapter vocabulary and structure and sharpen listening comprehension skills. Available on VHS and DVD.

¡Buen viaje! is also available on CD or Online.

Capítulo 1

Preview

In this chapter students will learn to describe themselves as well as a friend, using the singular forms of the verb **ser** and high-frequency descriptive adjectives. The plural forms of the verb **ser** will be presented in Chapter 2 to avoid introducing an overwhelming number of forms in this initial chapter.

National Standards

Communication

In Chapter 1, students will communicate in spoken and written Spanish to:

- identify and describe themselves and others
- find out where people are from and say their nationality

Students will engage in conversations, provide and obtain information, and exchange opinions as they fulfill the chapter objectives listed on this page.

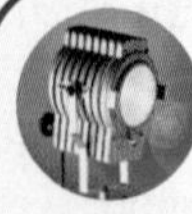

Spotlight on Culture

Arte Francisco de Goya (1746–1828) is one of the great Spanish masters. His early frescoes, innovative tapestry cartoons, and later lithographs, as well as his paintings which range from elegant to satirical and pessimistic, left a great influence on later artists.

Fotografía The students in this photograph are standing in the **Plaza de Armas,** the oldest plaza in Santiago, the capital of Chile.

Capítulo 1

Un amigo o una amiga

Objetivos

In this chapter you will learn to:

- ask or tell who someone is
- ask or tell what something is
- ask or tell where someone is from
- ask or tell what someone is like
- describe yourself or someone else
- talk about a famous Spanish novel and some Latin American heroes

Francisco de Goya *Muchachos trepando a un árbol*

Capítulo 1

¡OJO! It is extremely important that students be able to use and respond correctly to interrogative expressions in the very early stages of language acquisition. In this chapter, the interrogative words **¿quién?, ¿qué?, ¿cómo?,** and **¿de dónde?** are introduced.

The most common interrogative wording throughout **¡Buen viaje!** is inverted order. **¿Es Juan americano? ¿De dónde es el muchacho?** However, students will sometimes encounter the upward intonation pattern: **¿Juan es americano? ¿Él es de qué nacionalidad?,** since it is so frequently used in many areas of the Spanish-speaking world, particularly when speaking.

LEVELING

The activities, conversations, and readings within each chapter are marked according to level of difficulty. **E** indicates easy. **A** indicates average. **C** indicates challenging. Some activities cover a range of difficulty. In some activities, for example, advanced students will be able to produce more extensive responses while students who learn at a different rate may give less detailed responses. The leveling indicators will help you individualize instruction to best meet your students' needs.

Music Connection

Canta con Justo
The song **Pamplona,** found on Track 5 of the **Canta con Justo** music CD, will be easy for learners of all ability levels. It will help students practice some numbers and months of the year introduced in the **Lecciones preliminares** of **¡Buen viaje!**

1 PREPARATION

Resource Manager

Vocabulary Transparencies 1.2–1.3
Audio Activities TE, pages 1–2
Audio CD 2
Workbook, pages 1–2
Quizzes, page 1
ExamView® Pro

Bellringer Review

Use BRR Transparency 1.1 or write the following on the board.
Make a list in Spanish of the months for fall and winter.

2 PRESENTATION

Step 1 Present the vocabulary first with books closed using Vocabulary Transparencies 1.2–1.3. You may also wish to use students as "models" as you present many of the descriptive adjectives.

Step 2 Present one word or phrase at a time and build to a complete sentence. For example, point to Guadalupe as the class says **Guadalupe.** Point to the map of Mexico as you and the class say **mexicana.** Then have the class say the entire sentence: **Guadalupe es mexicana.**

Step 3 After the initial presentation with the overhead transparencies, have students open their books and look at the new vocabulary words as they repeat either after you or Audio CD 2.

Vocabulario
PALABRAS 1

¿Quién es?

¿Qué es?

¿Qué es un colegio?
Un colegio es una escuela secundaria.
Es una escuela secundaria en Latinoamérica.

Guadalupe es mexicana.
Guadalupe es de San Miguel de Allende.
Ella es alumna en un colegio.
Es alumna en el Colegio Juárez.
Guadalupe es una amiga de José Antonio.

Reaching All Students

Total Physical Response The expressions **levántate, anda, párate,** and **señala** are new to the students. You can convey their meanings by doing the activity yourself the first time and having a student imitate you while the others look on.
(Student 1), **levántate.**
Anda por la sala de clase. Párate.
Señala o indica a un muchacho.
Señala a un muchacho alto.
Señala a un muchacho moreno.
Señala a un muchacho alto y rubio.
Señala a una muchacha.
Señala a una muchacha rubia.
Señala a una muchacha alta.
Señala a una muchacha alta y morena.

¿Cómo es el muchacho?

alto bajo

guapo

feo

rubio

moreno

pelirrojo

gracioso, cómico

serio

ambicioso

perezoso

¿Cómo es la muchacha?

alta baja

bonita, linda

fea

rubia

morena

pelirroja

graciosa, cómica

seria

ambiciosa

perezosa

Anita es alta. No es baja.
Ella es muy bonita, muy linda.

José es rubio.
Él es guapo. No es feo.

Nota There are many ways to express *good-looking, handsome,* or *pretty* in Spanish. The word **guapo(a)** can be used to describe a boy or a girl. The words **bonito, lindo, hermoso,** and **bello** all mean *pretty.* They can describe a pretty girl or a pretty item. The word **feo** in Spanish is not as strong as the word *ugly* in English. To get a friend's attention, you could even say jokingly, **¡Oye, feo!**

The following words are used to express degrees.

Él es guapo.	**Ella es bonita.**
Es bastante guapo.	**Es bastante bonita.**
Es muy guapo.	**Es muy bonita.**

Vocabulario

Step 4 You may wish to ask the following types of questions during the oral presentation of the vocabulary or as the students are reading from their books: **¿Es Guadalupe? ¿Es Guadalupe o María? ¿Es mexicana Guadalupe? ¿Quién es mexicana? ¿De qué nacionalidad es Guadalupe?** These questions that build from very easy to more complex permit you to take into account the varying abilities of your students. Gear the questions to the skill level of each student.

Step 5 Use the overhead transparencies to check comprehension. Ask **¿Cómo es el muchacho (la muchacha)?** as you point to the illustrations randomly.

Teaching Tips

- Use gestures to help convey the meaning of words such as: **gracioso, cómico, serio, ambicioso, perezoso, alto, bajo,** or call on students who like to perform and have them pantomime the meaning of each word.
- Use intonation and expression to illustrate the difference between **Es bastante guapo** and **Es muy guapo.**

About the Spanish Language

- In many areas of the Spanish-speaking world, the terms **el chico** and **la chica** are heard as frequently as **el muchacho** and **la muchacha.**
- The word **moreno** refers to hair coloring and complexion. A dark-haired person is **moreno.** In some areas of the Caribbean, **moreno** can refer to a person of color.
- **El alumno** and **la alumna** are used for both elementary and secondary school students. **El / La estudiante** usually refers to a university student but can sometimes be used to refer to a secondary school student.

Vocabulary Expansion

When students ask for additional related vocabulary in the early chapters, it is strongly recommended that you not give them more words at this point. This will complicate or confuse the language concepts being presented. For example, in this chapter do not introduce students to adjectives that have irregular forms.

LEVELING

E: Vocabulary

3 PRACTICE

¿Qué palabra necesito?

¡OJO! When students are doing the **¿Qué palabra necesito?** activities, accept any answer that makes sense. The purpose of these activities is to have students use the new vocabulary. They are not factual recall activities. Thus, it is not necessary for students to remember specific factual information from the vocabulary presentation when answering. If you wish, have students use the photos on this page as a stimulus, when possible.

Historieta Each time **Historieta** appears, it means that the answers to the activity form a short story. Encourage students to look at the title of the **Historieta,** since it can help them do the activity.

1 and 2 Have students close their books. Model the cognates that appear in Activities 1 and 2 on page 16, and have students repeat them: **mexicano, colombiano, americana, secundaria, seria.** Now ask the questions and call on a different student to answer each one. Then have students open their books and do the activities again.

3 and 4 These activities can be done first with books closed and then with books open. Note that Activity 3 reinforces the interrogative word **quién,** and Activity 4 reinforces **cómo.**

Writing Development

Have students write the answers to Activity 3 in a paragraph to illustrate how all the items tell a story.

¿Qué palabra necesito?

San Miguel de Allende, México

1 Historieta Un muchacho mexicano

Contesten. *(Answer.)*

1. ¿Es Manolo mexicano o colombiano?
2. ¿Es de San Miguel de Allende o de Bogotá?
3. ¿Es alumno en el Colegio Juárez?
4. ¿Es el Colegio Juárez un colegio mexicano?
5. ¿Es Manolo un amigo de Alicia Gómez?

2 Historieta Una muchacha americana

Contesten. *(Answer.)*

1. ¿Es Debbi una muchacha americana?
2. ¿Es ella de Miami?
3. ¿Es ella alumna en una escuela secundaria de Miami?
4. ¿Es ella una alumna seria?
5. ¿Es Debbi una amiga de Bárbara Jones?

3 ¿Quién? ¿Manolo o Debbi?

Contesten. *(Answer.)*

1. ¿Quién es de San Miguel de Allende?
2. ¿Quién es de Miami?
3. ¿Quién es alumno en el Colegio Juárez?
4. ¿Quién es alumna en una escuela secundaria de Miami?

Miami, la Florida

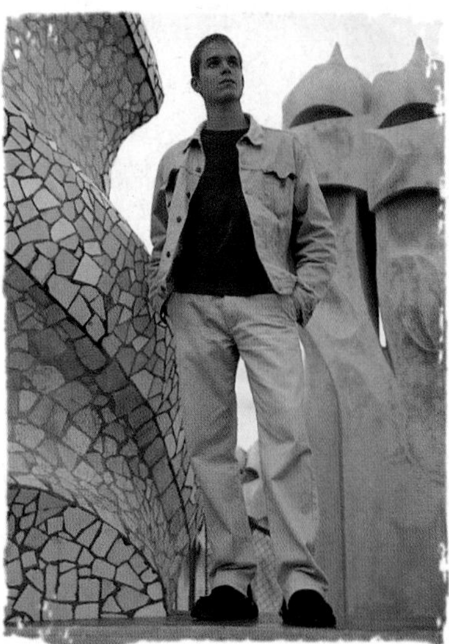

Barcelona, España

4 Historieta ¿Cómo es Fernando?

Contesten según la foto. *(Answer according to the photo.)*

1. ¿Cómo es Fernando? ¿Es alto o bajo?
2. ¿Cómo es Fernando? ¿Es gracioso o serio?
3. ¿Cómo es Fernando? ¿Es guapo o feo?
4. ¿Cómo es Fernando? ¿Es rubio o moreno?

ANSWERS TO ¿Qué palabra necesito?

1. Manolo es mexicano.
2. Es de San Miguel de Allende.
3. Sí, (No, no) es alumno en el Colegio Juárez.
4. Sí, es un colegio mexicano.
5. Sí, (No, no) es un amigo de Alicia Gómez.

1. Sí, Debbi es una muchacha americana.
2. Sí, ella es de Miami.
3. Sí, ella es alumna en una escuela secundaria de Miami.
4. Sí (No), ella (no) es una alumna seria.
5. Sí, (No, no) es una amiga de Bárbara Jones.

1. Manolo es de San Miguel de Allende.
2. Debbi es de Miami.
3. Manolo es alumno en el Colegio Juárez.
4. Debbi es alumna en una escuela secundaria de Miami.

1. Es alto.
2. Es serio.
3. Es guapo.
4. Es moreno.

5 **Todo lo contrario** Contesten según el modelo.
(Answer according to the model.)

¿Es alta Teresa?

No, de ninguna manera.
Es bastante baja.

1. ¿Es muy seria Teresa?
2. ¿Es pelirroja Teresa?
3. ¿Es baja Teresa?
4. ¿Es muy ambiciosa Teresa?

Málaga, España

6 **¿Quién es?** Work with a classmate. Choose one of the photographs below, but don't tell which one. Describe the student in the photo. Your partner has to guess which person you are describing. Take turns.

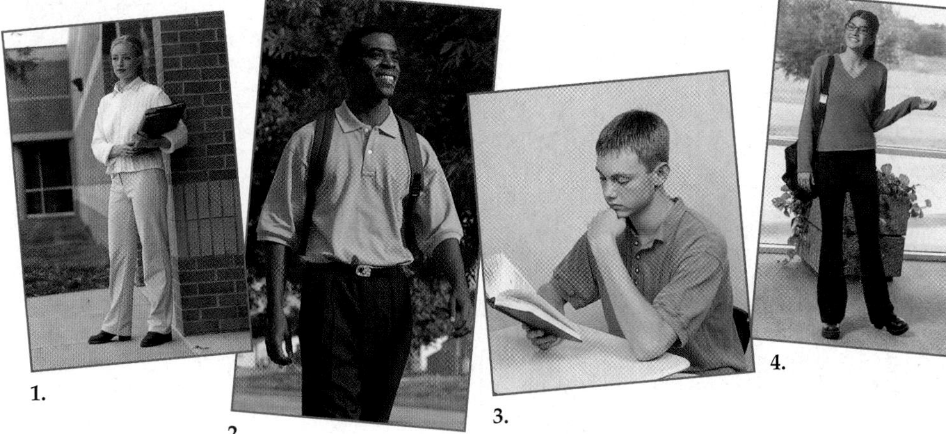

1. 2. 3. 4.

7 Juego **¿Es un muchacho o una muchacha?**

Work with a classmate. Describe someone in the class. First your partner will tell whether you're describing a boy or a girl and will then guess who it is. Take turns.

UN POCO MÁS *For more practice using words from **Palabras 1**, do Activity 1 on page H2 at the end of this book.*

Vocabulario

5 This activity can be done as a miniconversation. You may have students work in pairs.

¡OJO! Note that the activities are color-coded. All the activities in the text are communicative. However, the ones with blue titles are guided communication. The red titles indicate that the answers to the activity are more open-ended and can vary more. You may wish to correct students' mistakes more so in the guided activities than in the activities with a red title, which lend themselves to a freer response.

Paired Activities

- Have students work in pairs to write sentences describing two other students in the class—one male and one female.
- Have students compare two other students. For example: **Roberto es moreno. Tadeo es moreno también. Roberto es de México. Es mexicano. Tadeo no es de México. Él es de Los Ángeles. Tadeo es americano.**

UN POCO MÁS This *InfoGap* Activity will allow students to practice in pairs. The activity should be very manageable for them, since all vocabulary and structures are familiar to them.

LEVELING

E: Activities 1, 2
A: Activities 3, 5, 7
C: Activity 6

ANSWERS TO ¿Qué palabra necesito?

5

1. No, de ninguna manera. Es bastante graciosa.
2. No, de ninguna manera. Es bastante rubia.
3. No, de ninguna manera. Es bastante baja.
4. No, de ninguna manera. Es bastante perezosa.

6

1. Es rubia, guapa, baja, bonita, linda.
2. Es alto, guapo, moreno, gracioso.
3. Es serio, rubio, guapo, ambicioso.
4. Es alta, graciosa, cómica, morena.

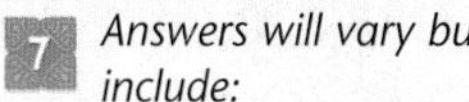

7 *Answers will vary but may include:*

Ella es rubia. Es cómica. Ella es bonita.
Él es alto. Es guapo y serio. Él es mexicano.

1 PREPARATION

Resource Manager

Vocabulary Transparencies 1.4–1.5
Audio Activities TE, pages 2–4
Audio CD 2
Workbook, pages 3–4
Quizzes, page 2
ExamView® Pro

Bellringer Review

Use BRR Transparency 1.2 or write the following on the board.
On a piece of paper, write three words that describe a student seated near you. If possible, put these words into sentences.

2 PRESENTATION

¡OJO! In this lesson we have students identify themselves and give their names using **soy.** This is done to avoid the perennial **me llamo (es)** problem. The verb **llamarse** is presented in Chapter 12, which introduces reflexive verbs. It is recommended that the students not be given this form at this point.

Step 1 Have students close their books. Present the vocabulary, using Vocabulary Transparencies 1.4–1.5 or student models.

Step 2 Model each new word or phrase. Have students repeat each word or phrase after you or Audio CD 2.

Step 3 If you have a male student whose pronunciation is quite good, call him to the front of the room. Say to the class: **Él es Roberto Davidson.** Tell the students in English that Roberto is going to tell them something about himself.

¿Quién soy yo y de dónde soy?

¡Hola!
Yo soy Roberto. Roberto Davidson.
Soy de California.
Soy un alumno serio.
Soy un amigo de Carmen.

Carmen es una amiga muy buena.
Ella es una persona muy simpática.

Reaching All Students

Total Physical Response
Dramatize the meaning of **gestos.** You may also dramatize or give the meaning of **haz, compórtate,** and **indica.**
(Student 1), **ven acá. Vas a hacer gestos.**
Compórtate de una manera tímida.
Haz algo cómico.
Haz una expresión seria.
Indica que eres alto(a).
Compórtate de una manera perezosa.

¿Quién es y cómo es?

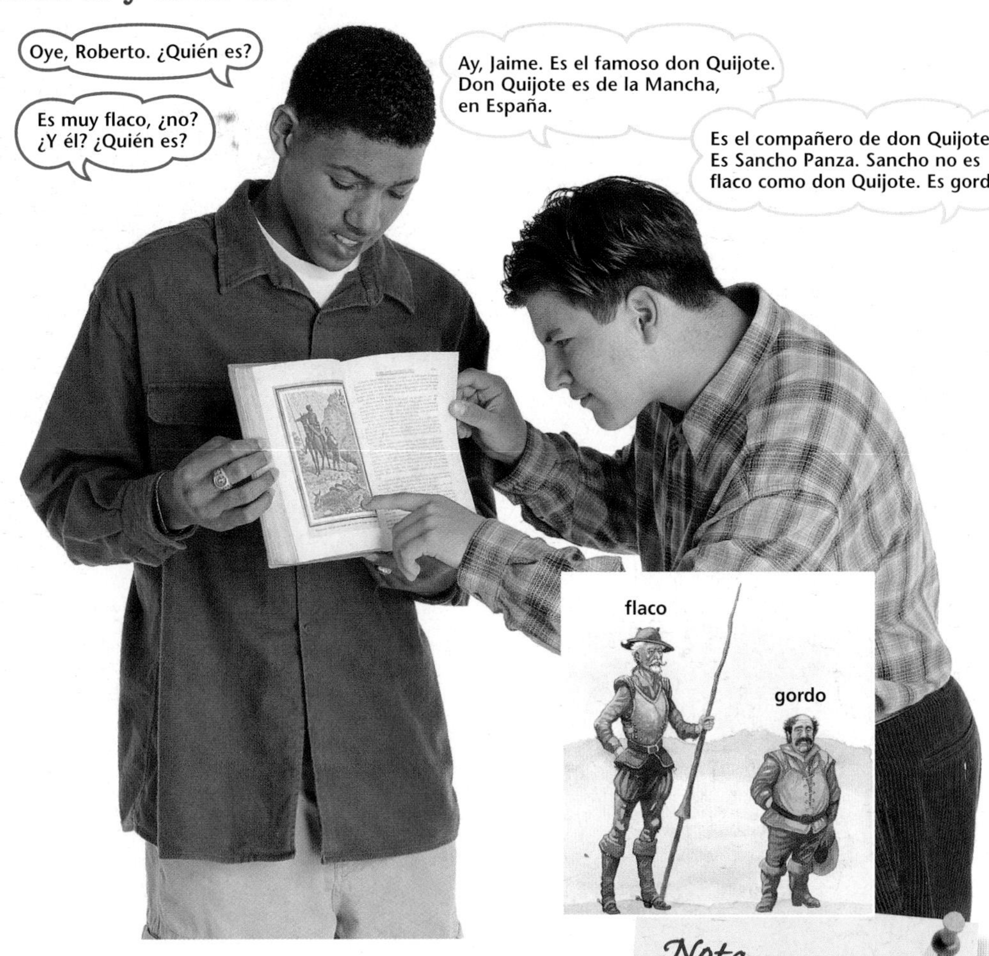

Oye, Roberto. ¿Quién es?
Es muy flaco, ¿no? ¿Y él? ¿Quién es?
Ay, Jaime. Es el famoso don Quijote. Don Quijote es de la Mancha, en España.
Es el compañero de don Quijote. Es Sancho Panza. Sancho no es flaco como don Quijote. Es gordo.
flaco
gordo

Los números

0	cero	11	once	21	veintiuno
1	uno	12	doce	22	veintidós
2	dos	13	trece	23	veintitrés
3	tres	14	catorce	24	veinticuatro
4	cuatro	15	quince	25	veinticinco
5	cinco	16	dieciséis	26	veintiséis
6	seis	17	diecisiete	27	veintisiete
7	siete	18	dieciocho	28	veintiocho
8	ocho	19	diecinueve	29	veintinueve
9	nueve	20	veinte	30	treinta
10	diez				

Nota Words that look alike and have similar meanings in Spanish and English are called "cognates." It is very easy to guess the meaning of cognates. But, **¡Cuidado!** *(Watch out!)* because even though they look alike and mean the same thing, they are pronounced differently. Here are some cognates. Take care to pronounce them correctly.

fantástico **honesto**
tímido **generoso**
sincero

Then have the student taking the role of Roberto read Roberto's lines on page 18 to the class.

Step 4 In addition to having students look at the illustrations, you can use gestures when describing don Quijote and Sancho Panza.

Step 5 Ask the following questions as you present the vocabulary on page 19: **¿Quién es alto? ¿Don Quijote o Sancho Panza? ¿Quién es flaco? ¿Don Quijote o Sancho Panza? ¿Quién es gordo? ¿Don Quijote o Sancho Panza? ¿De dónde es don Quijote? ¿Es la Mancha una región de España?**

¡OJO! The numbers 1–30 were also presented in the **Bienvenidos** section to allow students to give the date. Note that in this lesson we reintroduce these same numbers. To avoid teaching too many numbers at once, we present the remaining numbers in Chapter 2, page 49, and Chapter 3, page 81. It is suggested that you not stress the spelling of numbers, since students will very seldom, if ever, have to spell them out in real-life situations.

- Have students repeat the numbers after you.
- Write some numbers from 1–30 in random order on the board and call on individuals to give the number in Spanish.

Assessment

As an informal assessment, ask *yes/no* and *either/or* questions. Call on the entire class as well as individuals to respond. For example:

¿Es Roberto Davidson o Pablo González?
¿Es Roberto americano o colombiano?
¿Es él alumno en un colegio o en una escuela secundaria?

Chapter Projects

Un(a) amigo(a) Have students get a pen pal in a Spanish-speaking country. Have them request a photograph of their pen pal. Students can prepare a bulletin board with the photographs they receive. They can also write a short paragraph about their pen pal to accompany the photograph. Tell students to use only Spanish they know when writing their description. At this very early level, we do not want to encourage students to try to say and write things that are beyond their knowledge.

3 PRACTICE

¿Qué palabra necesito?

8 and 9 Go over these activities once in class before assigning them as homework.

8 This activity reinforces the interrogative word **¿dónde?** This activity can be done with books closed or open.
Expansion: After students complete this activity, have a student summarize all the information about Jim in his or her own words.

9 Have students look at the illustrations as they give the description of each girl.

Reaching All Students

Additional Practice Ask students the following questions about one of their female classmates:

¿Es ___ americana o colombiana?
¿Es alumna?
¿Es una alumna seria?
¿Es ___ alumna en una escuela secundaria americana o en un colegio colombiano?
¿Ella es alumna en qué escuela?

¿Qué palabra necesito?

8 Historieta Jim Collins, un muchacho americano Contesten. *(Answer.)*

1. ¿Quién es americano, Jim Collins o Eduardo Dávila?
2. ¿De dónde es Jim? ¿Es de San Francisco, California o es de Guadalajara, México?
3. ¿De qué nacionalidad es Jim? ¿Es americano o mexicano?
4. ¿Dónde es alumno Jim? ¿En un colegio mexicano o en una escuela secundaria de California?
5. ¿Cómo es Jim? ¿ Es serio o gracioso?

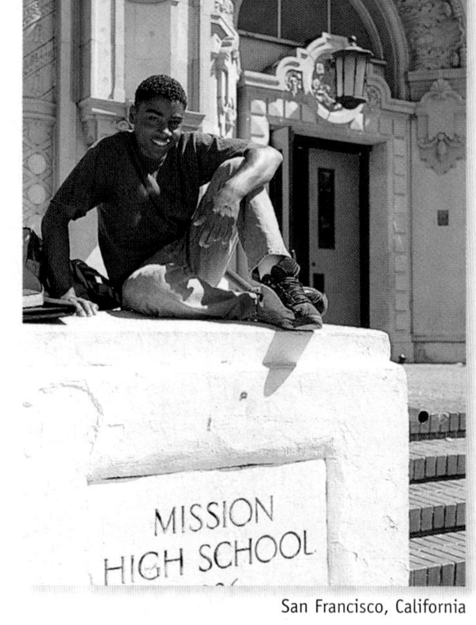

San Francisco, California

9 ¿Cómo es la muchacha?
Describan a cada muchacha. *(Describe each girl.)*

1. Ana

2. Alicia

3. Isabel

4. Victoria

5. Beatriz

6. Juanita

Answers to ¿Qué palabra necesito?

8

1. Jim Collins es americano.
2. Es de San Francisco, California.
3. Es americano.
4. Es alumno en una escuela secundaria de California.
5. Es serio (gracioso).

9 *Answers will vary but may include:*

1. Es cómica (graciosa).
2. Es bonita (linda, morena).
3. Es seria (morena).
4. Es generosa (simpática).
5. Es rubia (linda, bonita).
6. Es alta (ambiciosa).

Una alumna mexicana

10 Historieta Gabriela Torres, la graciosa
Completen. *(Complete.)*

Gabriela Torres es de México. Ella es __1__. No es americana. Gabriela es alumna en un __2__ mexicano. No es alumna en una __3__ secundaria americana. Gabriela no es baja. Ella es bastante __4__. ¿Es ella muy seria? No, de ninguna manera. Gabriela es muy __5__. Ella es una amiga __6__.

11 ¿Quién es? Think of a student in the class. A classmate will ask you questions about the person and try to guess who it is. Take turns.

12 Un(a) amigo(a) ideal What are some of the qualities an ideal friend should have? With a classmate, discuss what you think an ideal friend is like.

El Zócalo, Ciudad de México

Vocabulario

10 Activity 10 must be done with books open. You may wish to go over it a second time and have one student read the entire activity.

11 and 12 These activities provide an opportunity for students to recycle and combine all the vocabulary they have learned to this point to describe people.

Note: Activities 11 and 12 encourage students to use the chapter vocabulary in open-ended situations. It is not necessary to have students do all the activities. Let students choose the ones they wish to do. Encourage them to write or tell as much as they can.

Reteaching

Bring to class a magazine photo of a well-known personality all the students will recognize. Have them describe the person, using vocabulary they know.

Learning from Photos

(page 21 bottom) The photograph is of **El Zócalo, Ciudad de México.** The formal name of **el Zócalo** is **la Plaza de la Constitución.** It is the main square of Mexico City and was built by the Spaniards on the site of the main temple of Tenochtitlán, the capital of the Aztecs. **La Catedral metropolitana,** seen in this photo, is the oldest and largest cathedral in Latin America. Construction began in 1573. Over the centuries the cathedral has been sinking in the subsoil.

Answers to ¿Qué palabra necesito?

10

1. mexicana
2. colegio
3. escuela
4. alta
5. cómica (graciosa)
6. buena (sincera)

11 *Answers will vary, but students should use the vocabulary from* Palabras 1 *and* 2.

12 *Answers will vary, but may include:*

Un(a) amigo(a) ideal es simpático(a), sincero(a), generoso(a), cómico(a), etc.

LEVELING

E: Activities 9, 11
A: Activities 8, 10
C: Activity 12

1 PREPARATION

Resource Manager

Audio Activities TE, pages 5–6
Audio CD 2
Workbook, pages 5–8
Quizzes, pages 3–5
ExamView® Pro

Bellringer Review

Use BRR Transparency 1.3 or write the following on the board.
Using the verb **soy,** write your name and where you are from.

2 PRESENTATION

Artículos—el, la, un, una

Step 1 Read Items 1–3 aloud.

Step 2 Have students repeat the examples in Item 3 as you write them on the board. Underline the article and the **o** or **a** ending.

Step 3 Contrast the use of a definite article to refer to a specific person with the indefinite article to refer to any person. Say **el muchacho** and have students point to a specific boy in the class. Say **un muchacho** and have students look around the class and say **¿Quién? ¿Roberto o José?** Do the same thing with **la muchacha/una muchacha.**

3 PRACTICE

¿Cómo lo digo?

13 You can do Activity 13 with books closed and then with books open.

Artículos—el, la, un, una
Describing one person or thing

1. The name of a person, place, or thing is a noun. In Spanish, every noun has a gender, either masculine or feminine. Many Spanish nouns end in either **o** or **a**. Almost all nouns that end in **o** are masculine, and almost all nouns that end in **a** are feminine.

2. There are two types of articles. The English word *the* is called a definite article because it is used to refer to a definite or specific person or thing—the girl, the school. The word *a (an)* is called an indefinite article because it refers to any person or thing, not a specific one—a girl, a school.

3. The definite articles in Spanish are **el** and **la. El** is used with a masculine noun and **la** is used with a feminine noun. The indefinite articles are **un** and **una. Un** is used with a masculine noun and **una** is used with a feminine noun.

el muchacho	**la muchacha**	**un muchacho**	**una muchacha**
el colegio	**la escuela**	**un colegio**	**una escuela**

¿Cómo lo digo?

Historieta El muchacho y la muchacha

Contesten con **sí.** *(Answer with* sí.*)*

1. ¿Es americano el muchacho?
2. ¿Y la muchacha? ¿Es ella americana?
3. ¿Es bastante guapo el muchacho?
4. ¿Es muy bonita la muchacha?

Una amiga y un amigo, California

LEVELING

E: Activity 13
A: Activities 14, 15

Answers to ¿Cómo lo digo?

13

1. Sí, el muchacho es americano.
2. Sí, ella es americana.
3. Sí, el muchacho es bastante guapo.
4. Sí, la muchacha es muy bonita.

14 Historieta El muchacho mexicano y la muchacha americana

Completen con **el** o **la.** *(Complete with* el *or* la.*)*

_1_ muchacho es mexicano. _2_ muchacha es americana. _3_ muchacho mexicano es Paco y _4_ muchacha americana es Linda. _5_ muchacha es morena y _6_ muchacho es moreno. _7_ muchacha es alumna en _8_ Escuela Belair en Houston. _9_ muchacho es alumno en _10_ Colegio Hidalgo en Guanajuato.

Guanajuato, México

15 Historieta Un muchacho y una muchacha

Completen con **un** o **una.** *(Complete with* un *or* una.*)*

Roberto es _1_ muchacho americano y Maricarmen es _2_ muchacha chilena. Roberto es _3_ alumno muy serio. Pero es _4_ muchacho muy gracioso. Él es alumno en _5_ escuela secundaria en Nueva York. Maricarmen es _6_ alumna muy seria también. Ella es alumna en _7_ colegio chileno en Santiago.

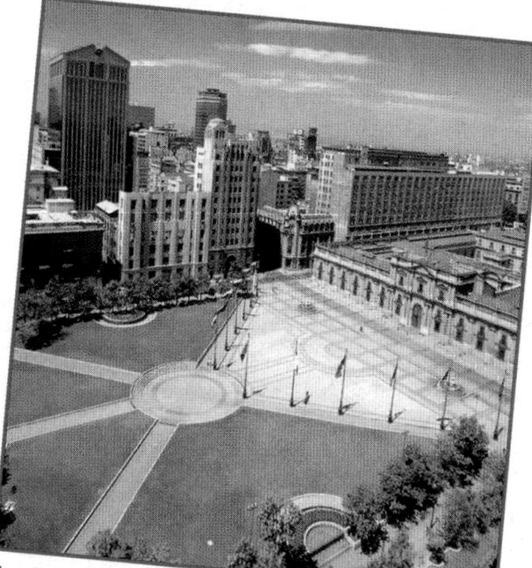

Santiago, Chile

Adjetivos en el singular
Describing a person or thing

1. A word that describes a noun is an adjective. The highlighted words in the following sentences are adjectives.

   El muchacho pelirrojo es muy guapo.
   La muchacha morena es una alumna muy buena.

2. In Spanish, an adjective must agree with the noun it describes or modifies. If the noun is masculine, then the adjective must be in the masculine form. If the noun is feminine, the adjective must be in the feminine form. Many singular masculine adjectives end in **o**, and many singular feminine adjectives end in **a**.

un muchacho gracioso	**una muchacha graciosa**
un alumno serio	**una alumna seria**

SPANISH Online

For more information about Santiago and other cities in the Spanish-speaking world, go to the Glencoe Spanish Web site: spanish.glencoe.com

Answers to ¿Cómo lo digo?

14

1. El
2. La
3. El
4. la
5. La
6. el
7. La
8. la
9. El
10. el

15

1. un
2. una
3. un
4. un
5. una
6. una
7. un

Estructura

14 and 15 These activities must be done with books open. Have one student complete two or three sentences before calling on the next student. If a student makes an error, call on another to get the correct response. Return to the student who made the error and see if he or she can now give the correct response.

Expansion: After calling on several individuals to complete Activities 14 and 15, have one student do each of the activities in its entirety. Call on other students in the class to ask questions about the information in the activities. This allows them to use the interrogative words on their own. You can answer the questions or have students answer them.

1 PREPARATION

Bellringer Review

Use BRR Transparency 1.4 or write the following on the board.
Write a list of words that can be used to describe people.

2 PRESENTATION

Adjetivos en el singular

Step 1 Draw two stick figures on the board. Name them Paco and Elena. Point to Paco as you say **alto, cómico, cubano,** etc. Point to Elena as you say **alta, cómica, cubana,** etc. Ask students what sound they hear repeated when describing a boy. Ask what sound they hear when describing a girl.

Step 2 Model the sentences and phrases given in Items 1 and 2 and have the students repeat them after you.

Estructura

3 PRACTICE

¿Cómo lo digo?

16 You can do Activity 16 with books closed and then with books open.

Expansion:

- Have one student read all of Activity 16. Then have another student retell the story in the activity in his or her own words.
- Have students substitute the names of students in the class for the names in the activity and then have them ask the new questions.
- Have students give a description of Elena and another description of Eduardo in their own words.

17 Encourage students to use both affirmative and negative sentences in their answers.

Expansion: You can also make a game out of Activity 17. Students can work in pairs or groups and guess who is being described.

18 and **19** Allow students to choose which activity they would like to do.

Learning from Photos

(page 25 bottom) Much of the city of Bogotá contains modern high-rise towers such as those seen in this photo.

Estructura

¿Cómo lo digo?

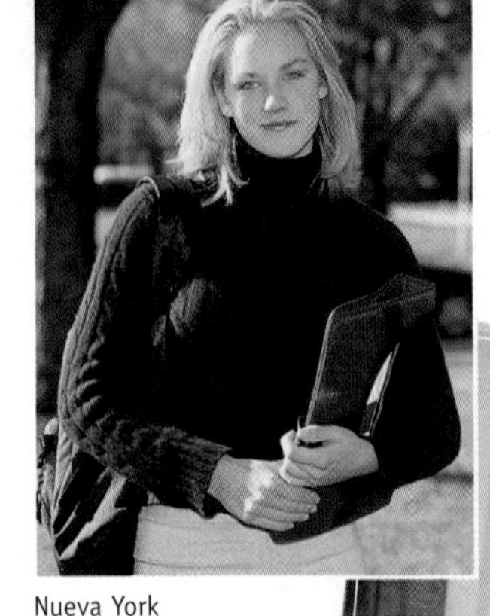

Nueva York

Caracas, Venezuela

16 **Historieta Elena y Eduardo**

Contesten. *(Answer.)*

1. ¿Es Elena americana o venezolana?
2. Y Eduardo, ¿es él americano o venezolano?
3. ¿Es moreno o rubio el muchacho?
4. Y la muchacha, ¿es ella rubia o morena?
5. ¿Es Elena una alumna seria?
6. ¿Es ella alumna en una escuela americana?
7. Y Eduardo, ¿es él un alumno serio también?
8. ¿Es él alumno en un colegio venezolano?

17 **¿Quién es gracioso?** Describan. *(Here are some adjectives that describe people. Choose a classmate and an adjective that describes that person. Then make up a sentence about him or her.)*

tímido

San Miguel de Allende, México

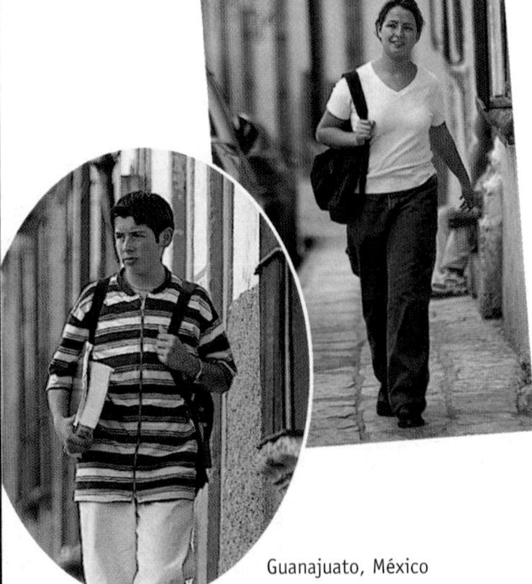

Guanajuato, México

18 **¿Quién es y cómo es?** Show a classmate this photo of Isabel García, a new friend you made in San Miguel de Allende, Mexico. One of your classmates wants to know all about Isabel. Answer his or her questions.

19 **¿Quién es y cómo es?** Here's a photo of Pablo Gómez, another friend you met on your trip. He's from Guanajuato. Answer your classmate's questions about him.

ANSWERS TO ¿Cómo lo digo?

16

1. Es americana.
2. Es venezolano.
3. Es moreno.
4. Es rubia.
5. Sí, es una alumna seria.
6. Sí, es alumna en una escuela americana.
7. Sí, es un alumno serio también. (No, no es un alumno serio.)
8. Sí, es alumno en un colegio venezolano.

17 *Answers will vary, but students will use the adjectives in the colored boxes in the appropriate masculine or feminine form.*

18 *Answers will vary but may include:*

Es de San Miguel de Allende. Es mexicana. Es morena y muy simpática.

19 *Answers will vary but may include:*

Es de Guanajuato. Es mexicano. Es moreno, bajo y serio.

Presente del verbo **ser** en el singular

Identifying a person or thing

1. The verb *to be* in Spanish is **ser.** Study the following forms of this verb.

SER	
yo	soy
tú	eres
él	es
ella	es

2.

Yo soy Eugenio.
Tú eres Juan.

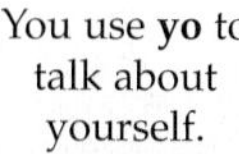

Él es Alejandro.

Ella es una alumna seria.

You use **yo** to talk about yourself.	You use **tú** to address a friend.	You use **él** or the person's name to talk about a boy or a man.	You use **ella** or the person's name to talk about a girl or a woman.

Note that the form of the verb changes with each person.

3. Since the form of the verb changes with each person, the subjects **yo, tú, él,** and **ella** can be omitted.

   Soy Paco.
   Eres mexicano, ¿no?
   Es alumna.

4. To make a sentence negative, you simply put **no** in front of the verb.

   Antonio es mexicano. Él no es colombiano.
   Yo soy de Bogotá. No soy de Cali.

Bogotá, Colombia

Reaching All Students

For the Heritage Speakers Because of interference from English, students may use the indefinite article incorrectly with nationalities and professions. Provide them with a list of professions such as:

abogado(a)	**ingeniero(a)**	**enfermero(a)**
dentista	**médico(a)**	**vendedor(a)**
policía	**agricultor(a)**	

Ask: **¿A quién conoces que es abogado(a)/médico(a),** etc.? If they use the article, correct them, but first provide examples such as: **Tom Cruise es actor.** Do the same with a list of adjectives of nationality such as **alemán(a), español(a), mexicano(a), argentino(a), americano(a), ruso(a),** etc. For this activity, you can use pictures of famous people like Napoleon Bonaparte: **¿Es mexicano?**

Estructura

1 PREPARATION

Bellringer Review

Use BRR Transparency 1.5 or write the following on the board.
Write the name of a friend. Then write two or three things about him or her.

2 PRESENTATION

Presente del verbo ser en el singular

Step 1 Before presenting the verb **ser,** go over the meaning of the personal pronouns **yo, tú, él, ella.**

Have students do the following:
- point to themselves as they say **yo**
- look at a neighbor as they say **tú**
- point to a boy as they say **él**
- point to a girl as they say **ella**

Step 2 Have students look at the photos as they read the sentences in Item 2 aloud.

Step 3 Read the explanatory material in Item 3 to the students and have them read the sentences in unison.

Step 4 Write the affirmative and negative examples in Item 4 on the board and have students read them aloud.

Assessment

As an informal assessment, you may wish to ask students questions that require naming appropriate male and female students. For example: **¿Quién es rubio? ¿Quién es rubia?**

LEVELING
E: Activity 16
A: Activities 17, 18, 19

3 PRACTICE

¿Cómo lo digo?

20 Have students work in pairs and read the conversation in Activity 20 aloud. Insist that they use the best intonation and expression possible. Call on a pair of students to present the conversation to the class.

21 Before having students do Activity 21, you may wish to ask questions such as:
¿Es Julia de California?
¿De dónde es Julia?
¿De qué nacionalidad es?, etc.
Ask similar questions about Emilio; then have students do the activity.

22 Do this activity first with books closed and then with books open.
Expansion: Once you have elicited all the answers to this activity from various students, have one student give the same information about himself or herself.

Paired Activities

- You may have students work in pairs and interview one another using Activity 22 as a guide.
- You may wish to do Activities 23 and 24 a second time as paired activities. One student asks the questions and another answers.

LEVELING

E: Activities 20, 22, 27
A: Activities 21, 23, 24, 26
C: Activity 25

¿Cómo lo digo?

20 **¡Qué coincidencia!** Practiquen la conversación. *(Practice the conversation.)*

—¡Hola!
—¡Hola! ¿Quién eres?
—¿Quién? ¿Yo?
—Sí, tú.
—Pues, soy Julia. Julia Rivera. Y tú, ¿quién eres?
—Yo soy Emilio. Emilio Ortega.
—¿Eres americano, Emilio?
—No, no soy americano.
—¿No? ¿De dónde eres?
—Soy de México.
—¡Yo soy de México también!
—¡Increíble!

21 **Julia Rivera y Emilio Ortega** Hablen de Julia y Emilio. *(Based on the conversation, tell what you know about Julia and Emilio.)*

22 **Yo soy...** Contesten personalmente. *(Answer about yourself.)*

1. ¿Eres americano(a) o cubano(a)?
2. ¿Eres alumno(a)?
3. ¿Eres alumno(a) en una escuela secundaria?
4. ¿De dónde eres?
5. ¿Cómo eres? ¿Eres alto(a) o bajo(a)?
6. ¿Eres muy serio(a) o bastante gracioso(a)?

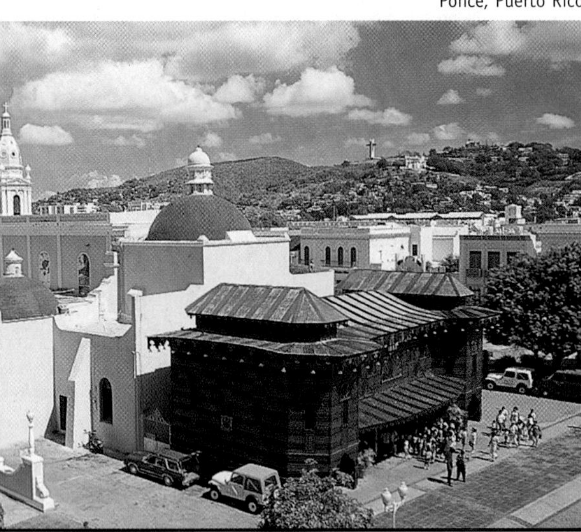
Ponce, Puerto Rico

23 **Historieta** **José, ¿eres... ?** Pregúntenle a José Fuentes si es... *(Ask José Fuentes if he is . . .)*

1. puertorriqueño
2. de Ponce
3. alumno en un colegio de Ponce
4. un amigo de Inés García

Answers to ¿Cómo lo digo?

21 *Answers will vary but may include:*

Julia es simpática. Es morena. Es mexicana. Emilio es de México también. Es simpático y moreno también.

22 *Answers will vary but may include:*

1. Soy americano(a). (Soy cubano[a].)
2. Sí, soy alumno(a).
3. Sí, soy alumno(a) en una escuela secundaria.
4. Soy de ___.
5. Soy alto(a). (Soy bajo[a].)
6. Soy muy serio(a). (Soy bastante gracioso[a].)

1. ¿Eres puertorriqueño?
2. ¿Eres de Ponce?
3. ¿Eres alumno en un colegio de Ponce?
4. ¿Eres un amigo de Inés García?

24 **Historieta** **Inés, ¿eres...?**
Pregúntenle a Inés García si es...
(Ask Inés García if she is . . .)

1. de Chile
2. de Santiago
3. alumna en un colegio
4. una amiga de José Fuentes

Santiago, Chile

San Miguel de Allende, México

25 **En un café** You've just met a student your own age at a café in San Miguel de Allende, Mexico. Have a conversation to get to know one another better.

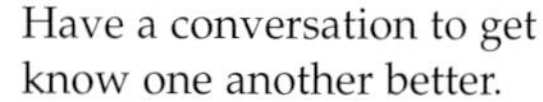

26 **Un(a) amigo(a) nuevo(a)**
A classmate will think of someone in class you both know and pretend that that person is his or her new boyfriend or girlfriend. Ask as many questions as you can to try to find out who the new boyfriend or girlfriend is.

27 **Juego** **¡Soy una persona fantástica!** Have a contest with a classmate to see which one of you can boast the most. Say something good about yourself and then your partner will "one-up" you.

ALUMNA 1: **Yo soy simpática.**
ALUMNA 2: **Yo soy simpática. Y soy generosa también.**

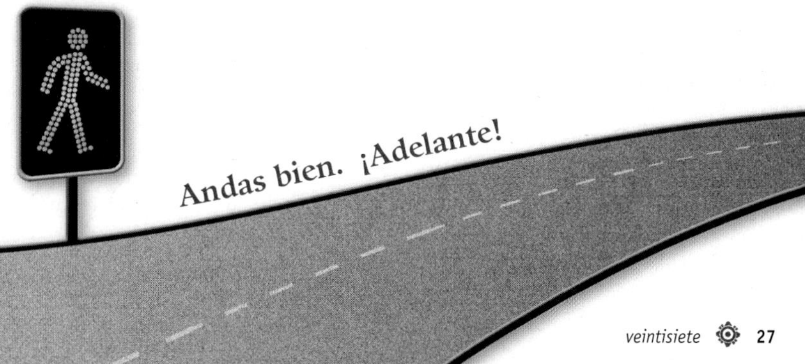

Answers to ¿Cómo lo digo?

24
1. ¿Eres de Chile?
2. ¿Eres de Santiago?
3. ¿Eres alumna en un colegio?
4. ¿Eres una amiga de José Fuentes?

25 *Answers will vary. The conversations will encourage students to be as creative as possible and say as much as they can.*

26 *Questions will vary but may include:*
¿Es rubio(a)?
¿Es alto(a)?
¿Es serio(a) o gracioso(a)?

27 *Answers will vary, but students will use as many adjectives as possible to describe themselves.*

Estructura

Learning from Photos

(page 26 bottom) The cathedral and square are located in Ponce, the second largest city in Puerto Rico after the capital, San Juan. Ponce is in the southern part of the island on the Caribbean Sea. The firehouse in the photo, **el Parque de bomberos,** is very colorful and attracts thousands of visitors annually.
(page 27 top) Santiago, the capital of Chile, is located at the foot of the Andes and stretches 40 miles north to south and 20 miles east to west. Santiago is situated in a valley with some of the most productive farmland in the nation. The city is about a one-hour drive from the thriving port of Valparaíso and the beautiful resort of Viña del Mar.
(page 27 middle) These teenagers are seated at a café called La Terraza in San Miguel de Allende, México.

¡Adelante!
At this point in the chapter, students have learned all the vocabulary and structure necessary to complete the chapter. The conversation and cultural readings that follow recycle all the material learned up to this point.

Reaching All Students

Additional Practice
- **Soy yo** Ask students to bring photos of themselves to class and have them describe the photos to their classmates.
- **¿De dónde eres?** To reinforce the singular forms of the verb **ser,** ask individual students:
¿Eres ___? ¿Eres de ___?
¿Eres un(a) amigo(a) de ___?
¿Es simpático(a)?
¿De dónde es él/ella?
¿Dónde es alumno(a)?

1 PREPARATION

Resource Manager

Audio Activities TE, page 7
Audio CD 2

Bellringer Review

Use BRR Transparency 1.6 or write the following on the board.
Write three sentences about yourself. Read them to a classmate. Then convert each of your sentences into a question and ask a classmate the questions.

2 PRESENTATION

Step 1 Tell students that they are going to hear a conversation among three boys, Rafael, José, and Felipe. Rafael wants to know who someone is. It turns out they have something in common.

Step 2 Ask students to open their books to page 28. Have them follow along as you read the conversation or play the recorded version on Audio CD 2.

Step 3 Have students work in groups of three to practice the conversation. Then have several groups present it to the class.

Step 4 After presenting the conversation, go over the **¿Comprendes?** activity. If students can answer the questions with relative ease, move on. Students should not be expected to memorize the conversation.

LEVELING

E: Conversation

¿De dónde eres?

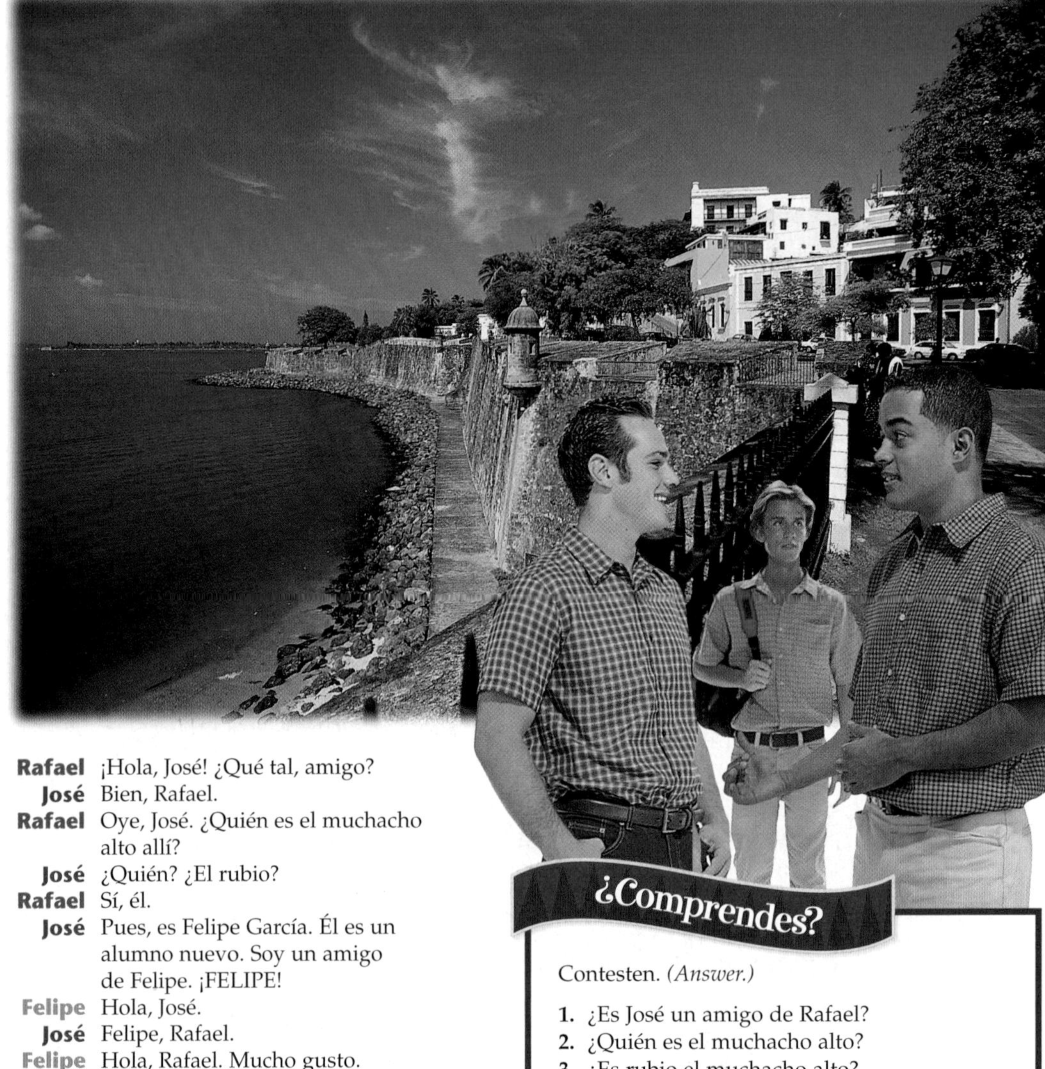

Rafael ¡Hola, José! ¿Qué tal, amigo?
José Bien, Rafael.
Rafael Oye, José. ¿Quién es el muchacho alto allí?
José ¿Quién? ¿El rubio?
Rafael Sí, él.
José Pues, es Felipe García. Él es un alumno nuevo. Soy un amigo de Felipe. ¡FELIPE!
Felipe Hola, José.
José Felipe, Rafael.
Felipe Hola, Rafael. Mucho gusto.
Rafael Mucho gusto. ¿De dónde eres, Felipe?
Felipe Soy de Puerto Rico.
Rafael ¿Sí? Hombre, yo también soy puertorriqueño.

¿Comprendes?

Contesten. *(Answer.)*

1. ¿Es José un amigo de Rafael?
2. ¿Quién es el muchacho alto?
3. ¿Es rubio el muchacho alto?
4. ¿Quién es un alumno nuevo en la escuela?
5. ¿Es José un amigo de Felipe?
6. ¿Es Rafael un amigo de Felipe?
7. ¿De dónde es Felipe?
8. Y Rafael, ¿de qué nacionalidad es?

Answers to ¿Comprendes?

1. Sí, José es un amigo de Rafael.
2. El muchacho alto es Felipe García.
3. Sí, el muchacho alto es rubio.
4. Felipe García es un alumno nuevo en la escuela.
5. Sí, José es un amigo de Felipe.
6. No, Rafael no es un amigo de Felipe.
7. Felipe es de Puerto Rico.
8. Rafael es puertorriqueño también.

Learning from Photos

(page 28) The beautiful scene in this photo is a part of the wall that encircles much of the old colonial section of San Juan, Puerto Rico.

Vamos a hablar más

A **¿Quién es?** Think of someone in the class, but don't tell who it is. Say just one thing about the person and let your partner take a guess. If he or she guesses incorrectly, give another hint. Continue until your partner guesses correctly. Take turns.

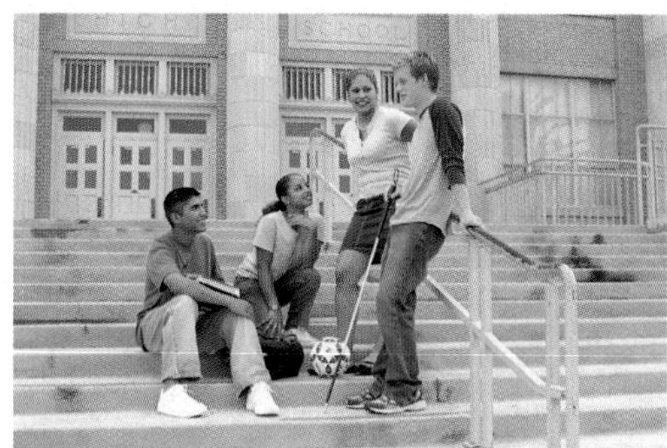

B *Juego* **¿Quién soy yo?** Play a guessing game. Think of someone in the class. Pretend you're that person and describe yourself. A classmate has to guess who you are.

Pronunciación

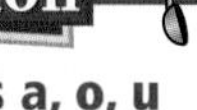

Las vocales a, o, u

When you speak Spanish, it is important to pronounce the vowels carefully. The vowel sounds in Spanish are very short, clear, and concise. The vowels in English have several different pronunciations, but in Spanish they have only one sound. Imitate carefully the pronunciation of the vowels **a, o,** and **u.** Note that the pronunciation of **a** is similar to the *a* in *father,* **o** is similar to the *o* in *most,* and **u** is similar to the *u* in *flu.*

a	o	u
Ana	**o**	**uno**
baja	**no**	**mucha**
amiga	**Paco**	**mucho**
alumna	**amigo**	**muchacho**

Repeat the following sentences.

Ana es alumna.
Adán es alumno.
Ana es amiga de Adán.

3 PRACTICE

Vamos a hablar más

A Have students work in pairs. You may wish to choose a pair of students to do this activity for the class.

B *Juego* This recycling activity is fun for students to play either with a partner or in teams.

Glencoe Technology

CD-ROM

On the CD-ROM, students can watch a dramatization of this conversation. They can then play the role of either one of the characters and record themselves in the conversation.

Pronunciación

Step 1 Have students repeat the vowels after you or Audio CD 2. Have them imitate very carefully.

Step 2 Now have students repeat the words after you or Audio CD 2.

Step 3 Have students open their books to page 29. Call on individuals to read the sentences carefully.

Step 4 All model sentences on page 29 can be used for dictation.

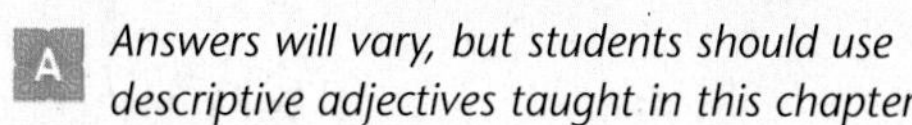

Answers to Vamos a hablar más

A *Answers will vary, but students should use descriptive adjectives taught in this chapter.*

B *Answers will vary but may include:*

—Yo soy rubia y alta.
—¿Tú eres Elena?
—No, yo no soy Elena. Yo soy de Nueva York y soy amiga de Roberto.
—¿Tú eres Ana?
—Sí, yo soy Ana.

Chapter Projects

Héroes hispanos Have one or more students do a research project on an important hero from Spain, Mexico, or Latin America and prepare a brief biography of the person. Some possibilities include: Simón Bolívar, José de San Martín, and Benito Juárez.

Lecturas culturales

Resource Manager

Audio Activities TE, page 8
Audio CD 2

National Standards

Cultures
This short, simple reading exposes students to the two main characters of the famous Spanish novel, ***El Quijote.***

Communication
Students will say as much as they can in their own words about don Quijote and Sancho Panza.

PRESENTATION

Pre-reading

Step 1 Have students locate La Mancha on the map of Spain, page xxx, or use Map Transparency M 2.

Step 2 Ask students the names of the two characters from a famous Spanish novel that they learned about in the Vocabulary section of this chapter (see page 19).

Reading

Step 1 Lead students through the **Lectura** on page 30 by reading it aloud. Have students repeat each sentence after you.

Step 2 After every two or three sentences, ask questions such as: **¿Es *El Quijote* una novela famosa? ¿Es una novela mexicana o española? ¿Quién es el autor de la novela?**

Step 3 Call on some students to read aloud individually. After a student has read about three sentences, ask questions of other students to check comprehension.

Post-reading

Have students do the **¿Comprendes?** activity on page 31.

Lecturas culturales

Reading Strategy

Cognates Words that look alike and have similar meanings in Spanish and English (**famoso**, *famous*) are called "cognates." Look for cognates whenever you read in Spanish. Recognizing cognates can help you figure out the meaning of many words in Spanish and will thus help you understand what you read.

El Quijote

El Quijote es una novela famosa de la literatura española. El autor de *El Quijote* es Miguel de Cervantes Saavedra.

El Quijote es la historia del famoso caballero andante[1], don Quijote de la Mancha. La Mancha es una región de España.

Don Quijote es alto y flaco. Sancho Panza es el compañero o escudero[2] de don Quijote. ¿Es alto y flaco como don Quijote? No, de ninguna manera. Sancho es bajo y gordo. Sancho Panza es una persona muy graciosa. Es muy cómico. ¿Y don Quijote? De ninguna manera. No es cómico. Él es muy serio y es muy honesto y generoso. Pero según[3] Sancho Panza, don Quijote es muy tonto[4]. Y según don Quijote, Sancho es perezoso.

[1]caballero andante *knight errant*
[2]escudero *knight's attendant*
[3]según *according to*
[4]tonto *foolish*

Sancho Panza y don Quijote

FUN FACTS

It is claimed that ***El Quijote*** is the most widely read book in the world with the exception of the Bible. Ask how many students have seen the Broadway musical *Man of La Mancha.* Show a clip of the movie version to the class and encourage them to see the play or the movie on their own.

La Mancha, España

Don Quijote
de Pablo Picasso

¿Comprendes?

A ¿Es don Quijote o Sancho Panza? Decidan. *(Decide whether each sentence describes Don Quijote or Sancho Panza.)*

1. Es bajo.
2. Es alto.
3. Es muy gracioso.
4. Es gordo.
5. Es flaco.
6. Es muy serio.
7. Es un caballero andante.
8. Es honesto y generoso.
9. Es un escudero.

B Palabras afines Busquen cinco palabras afines en la lectura. *(Find five cognates in the reading.)*

Lecturas culturales

Writing Development

Have students write as much as they can in their own words about don Quijote and Sancho Panza.

Geography Connection

La Mancha is located in Central Spain. This area is very arid and has few trees. The delicious, well-known **queso manchego** comes from this area. See the map of Spain on page 30.

Art Connection

You may wish to project the Fine Art Transparency and have students do the corresponding activities.

LEVELING

E: Activity A
A: Reading
C: Activity B

Answers to ¿Comprendes?

A

1. Sancho Panza
2. don Quijote
3. Sancho Panza
4. Sancho Panza
5. don Quijote
6. don Quijote
7. don Quijote
8. don Quijote
9. Sancho Panza

B *Answers will vary but may include:*

novela, famosa, literatura, autor, región, compañero, persona, cómico, serio, honesto, generoso

Lectura opcional 1

National Standards

Cultures
The reading selections on pages 32–33 familiarize students with Venezuela and two important historical figures—Simón Bolívar and José de San Martín.

PRESENTATION

Step 1 Have students read the selection quickly as they look at the photos that accompany it.

Step 2 Ask students to say as much about Alicia as they can.

¿Comprendes?

Have students scan the reading for the answers to this activity.

History Connection

Simón Bolívar was born in Venezuela in 1783. Although he came from a wealthy family, he was always interested in the welfare of the less fortunate. He spent time in France, Spain, and the United States. In 1810, he returned to Venezuela to take part in the rebellion against the Spaniards.

Assessment

You may want to give the following quiz to those students who read this selection.
Answer.

1. **¿De dónde es Alicia Bustelo?**
2. **¿Cuál es la capital de Venezuela?**
3. **¿Cómo es Alicia?**
4. **¿Dónde es ella alumna?**
5. **¿Quién es un héroe latinoamericano?**

Lectura opcional 1

Una alumna venezolana

Alicia Bustelo es una muchacha venezolana. Ella es de Caracas, la capital de Venezuela. Alicia es alta y es una muchacha bastante bonita. Es muy graciosa. Pero es también una alumna muy seria. Es alumna en el Colegio Simón Bolívar. En Latinoamérica un colegio es una escuela secundaria. El Colegio Simón Bolívar es una escuela muy buena.

VENEZUELA
Caracas
AMÉRICA DEL SUR

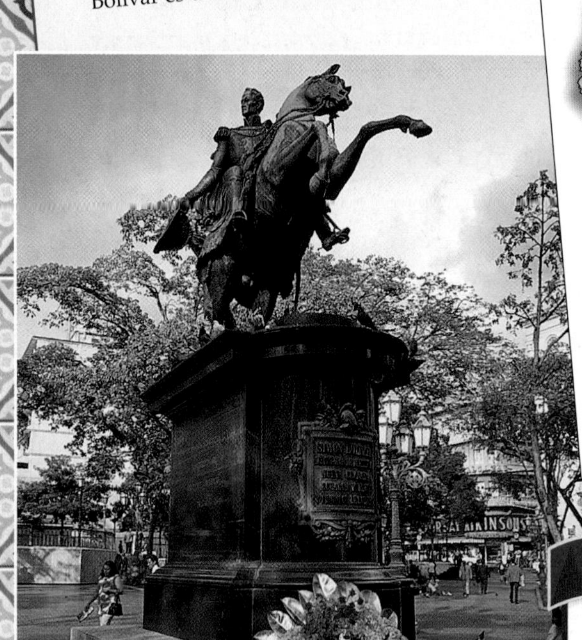

Plaza Simón Bolívar, Caracas

¿Comprendes?

Latinoamérica Busquen la información en la lectura. *(Find the information in the reading.)*

1. the name of a Latin American country
2. the name of a Latin American capital
3. the name of a Latin American hero
4. the term for the Spanish-speaking countries of the Americas

Answers to ¿Comprendes?

1. Venezuela
2. Caracas
3. Simón Bolívar
4. Latinoamérica

Geography Connection

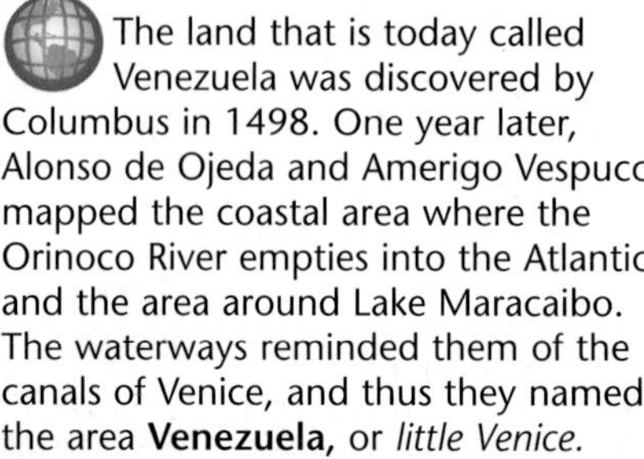

The land that is today called Venezuela was discovered by Columbus in 1498. One year later, Alonso de Ojeda and Amerigo Vespucci mapped the coastal area where the Orinoco River empties into the Atlantic and the area around Lake Maracaibo. The waterways reminded them of the canals of Venice, and thus they named the area **Venezuela,** or *little Venice.*

Lectura opcional 2

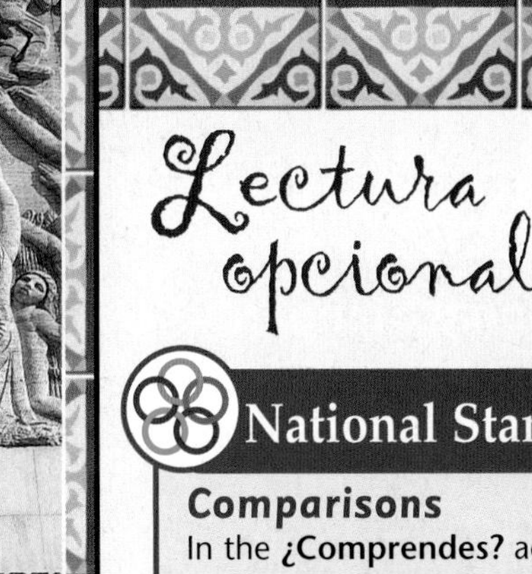

Simón Bolívar y José de San Martín

María Iglesias es una muchacha venezolana. Ella es de Caracas, la capital. Es alumna en el Colegio Simón Bolívar. Y la plaza principal de Caracas es la Plaza Simón Bolívar. Simón Bolívar es un héroe famoso de la América del Sur.

José Ayerbe no es venezolano. Él es peruano. Es de Lima, la capital de Perú. Es alumno en el Colegio San Martín. Y la plaza principal de Lima es la Plaza San Martín. San Martín es otro héroe famoso de la América del Sur.

Simón Bolívar y José de San Martín luchan contra[1] España por la independencia de los países[2] de la América del Sur. Simón Bolívar es el gran[3] «libertador» de los países del norte del continente sudamericano y San Martín es el libertador de los países del sur.

[1]luchan contra *fight against* [2]países *countries* [3]gran *great*

Simón Bolívar

José de San Martín

¿Comprendes?

A Héroes Den ejemplos. *(Give examples.)*
Many schools in Spain and in Latin America are named after heroes. Is the same true in the United States? Give some examples.

B El libertador Expliquen. *(Explain.)*
What is the meaning of the word **libertador** or *liberator* in English? What does a liberator do?

C Historia de Estados Unidos
Contesten. *(Answer.)*
Who is considered the liberator of the United States? What did he fight for?

Lectura opcional 2

National Standards

Comparisons
In the **¿Comprendes?** activities, students are encouraged to compare Spanish and English and to make comparisons between Hispanic and American cultures.

¡OJO! The readings on pages 32–33 are optional. You may skip them completely, have the entire class read them, have only several students read them and report to the class, or assign either of them for extra credit.

PRESENTATION

Step 1 Have students locate Caracas and Lima on the map of South America on page xxxi, or use Map Transparency M 3. Point out that both cities are close to the sea. This is the case with most of the major cities in South America.

Step 2 Have students read the selection to themselves.

Step 3 Now have students do the **¿Comprendes?** activities.

Answers to ¿Comprendes?

A
Many American schools are named after presidents or other famous political and historical figures such as John F. Kennedy, Martin Luther King, and George Washington.

B
A liberator is a person who frees a country from a foreign power.

C
George Washington fought to free the colonies from British rule in order to gain religious and political freedom and freedom from unfair taxation.

LEVELING
E: Reading 1
C: Reading 2

Conexiones

National Standards

Connections
This reading establishes a connection with another discipline—geography. Knowledge students already have from previous study will enable them to read this selection with ease as they increase their vocabulary in Spanish and learn more about the geography of Spain and Latin America.

¡OJO! The readings in the **Conexiones** section are optional. They focus on some of the major disciplines taught in schools and universities. The vocabulary is useful for discussing such topics as history, literature, art, economics, business, science, etc. You may choose any of the following ways to do the readings in the **Conexiones** sections.

Independent reading Have students read the selections and do the post-reading activities as homework, which you collect. This option is least intrusive on class time and requires a minimum of teacher involvement.

Homework with in-class follow-up Assign the readings and post-reading activities as homework. Review and discuss the material in class the next day.

Intensive in-class activity This option includes a pre-reading vocabulary presentation, in-class reading and discussion, assignment of the activities for homework, and a discussion of the assignment in class the following day.

Conexiones

Las ciencias sociales

La geografía

Geography is the scientific study of the Earth's surface. It deals with all of Earth's features, particularly the natural forces that create these features and cause them to change. It is also the study of where people, animals, and plants live and how rivers, deserts, and other of Earth's features affect their lives. It is a subject that has interested human beings since earliest times.

Look at the map of South America. Notice how many geographical terms you will be able to recognize in Spanish. Now find out how easy it is to read about geography in Spanish.

El río Tajo, España

El desierto Atacama, Chile

Class Motivator

¿Sí o no? Have students play the following **sí o no** game after they complete the reading.

1. **Puerto Rico es una península.**
2. **El norte es uno de los cuatro puntos cardinales.**
3. **Hay cinco puntos cardinales.**
4. **La América del Norte es un continente.**
5. **Australia es una isla.**
6. **Puerto Rico es una isla.**
7. **España es parte de una isla.**
8. **El Atlántico es un océano.**
9. **El Pacífico es un río.**

La geografía

Hay cuatro puntos cardinales: el norte, el sur, el este y el oeste.

Hay siete continentes: la América del Norte, la América del Sur, Europa, África, Asia, Australia y la Antártida.

El océano Atlántico es muy grande. Es inmenso. El océano Pacífico es muy grande también.

España es parte de una península. Puerto Rico es una isla. El español es la lengua[1] de España. Es la lengua de Puerto Rico también. El español es una lengua muy importante. Es la lengua de países[2] en la América del Sur, en la América Central, en el Caribe, en la América del Norte y en Europa.

[1]lengua *language* [2]países *countries*

Montevideo, Uruguay

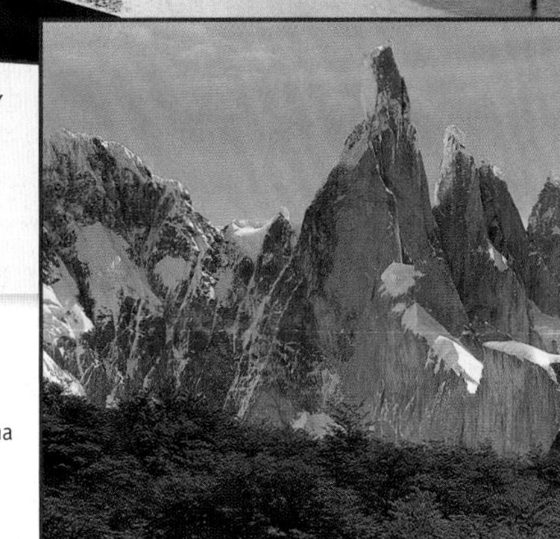

Los Andes, Argentina

¿Comprendes?

A Un poco de geografía Escojan la palabra. *(Choose the correct word to complete each sentence. You may use a word more than once.)*

1. Europa es un ____.
2. España no es una isla. España es parte de una ____.
3. Puerto Rico es una ____.
4. Cuba es otra ____.
5. El Sahara es un ____ de África y el Atacama es un ____ de la América del Sur.

B Estrategias Adivinen. *(Guess the meaning of the following words.)* Often you can guess the meaning of words because of other knowledge you have. You may not know the meaning of **el río** but when you see **el río Misisipí** or **el río Hudson,** you can probably figure out what **río** means.

1. el **río** Hudson
2. la **bahía** Chesapeake
3. el **lago** Superior, el **lago** Erie
4. el **golfo** de México
5. el **mar** Mediterráneo

Conexiones

PRESENTATION

Las ciencias sociales
La geografía

Step 1 Have students read the introduction in English on page 34.

Step 2 Have them quickly skim the terms on the map of South America on page 34. You may also have them repeat the terms after you.

Step 3 Have students read the selection quickly or have them skim it.

Step 4 You may wish to have them find and repeat all the cognates in the reading selection. Explain to them that there are two important strategies to use when reading unfamiliar material—they should learn to recognize cognates and derive meaning from context.

¿Comprendes?

A Have students do this activity. Call on one student to read all the answers as the others listen.

B Explain to students that the strategy outlined in this activity is very important. Quite often previous knowledge will help their comprehension.

Assessment

You may wish to give the following quiz to students who have done the **Conexiones** section. Find the following information.

1. **los cuatro puntos cardinales**
2. **los nombres de cuatro continentes**
3. **un país que forma parte de una península**
4. **la lengua de Puerto Rico**
5. **el número de países donde el español es la lengua oficial**

Answers to ¿Comprendes?

A

1. continente
2. península
3. isla
4. isla
5. desierto, desierto

B

1. river
2. bay
3. lake
4. gulf
5. sea

LEVELING

A: Connections

Use what you have learned

Recycling

These activities allow students to use the vocabulary and structure from this chapter in completely open-ended, real-life situations.

PRESENTATION

Encourage students to say as much as possible when they do these activities. Tell them not to be afraid to make mistakes, since the goal of the activities is real-life communication. If someone in the group makes an error, allow the others to politely correct him or her. Let students choose the activities they would like to do.

You may wish to divide students into pairs or groups. Encourage students to elaborate on the basic theme and to be creative. They may use props, pictures, or posters if they wish.

Writing Development

Have students keep a notebook or portfolio containing their best written work from each chapter. These selected writings can be based on assignments from the Student Textbook and the Workbook. The two activities on page 37 are examples of writing assignments that may be included in each student's portfolio.
On page 10 in the Workbook, students will begin to develop an organized autobiography **(Mi autobiografía).** These workbook pages may also become a part of their portfolio.

¡Te toca a ti!

Use what you have learned

HABLAR 1

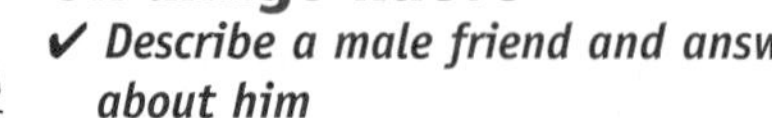

Un amigo nuevo

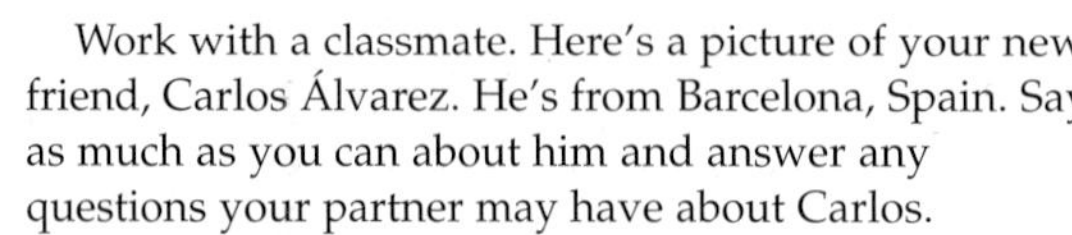

✔ ***Describe a male friend and answer questions about him***

Work with a classmate. Here's a picture of your new friend, Carlos Álvarez. He's from Barcelona, Spain. Say as much as you can about him and answer any questions your partner may have about Carlos.

Barcelona, España

HABLAR 2

Una alumna nueva

✔ ***Ask a female friend questions and tell her about yourself***

Inés Figueroa (a classmate) is a new girl in your school. You want to get to know her better and help her feel at home. Find out as much as you can about her. Tell Inés about yourself, too.

HABLAR 3

Oye, ¿quién es?

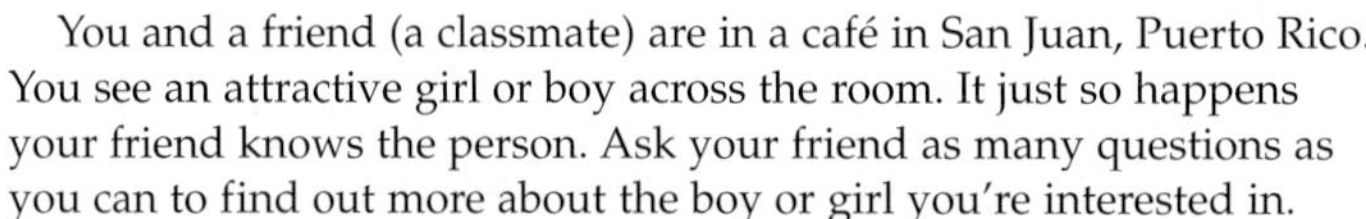

✔ ***Ask someone questions about another person***

You and a friend (a classmate) are in a café in San Juan, Puerto Rico. You see an attractive girl or boy across the room. It just so happens your friend knows the person. Ask your friend as many questions as you can to find out more about the boy or girl you're interested in.

San Juan, Puerto Rico

Answers to ¡Te toca a ti!

1 *Answers will vary but may include:*
Es Carlos Álvarez. Es bajo y moreno. Carlos es de Barcelona, España. Es alumno en una escuela secundaria de Barcelona.

2 *Answers will vary, but students can use the conversation on page 28 as a model.*

3 *Answers will vary, but students can use the conversation on page 28 as a model.*

4 Un amigo español

✓ Write a postcard telling about yourself

The following is a postcard you just received from a new pen pal. First read the postcard. Then answer it. Give Jorge similar information about yourself.

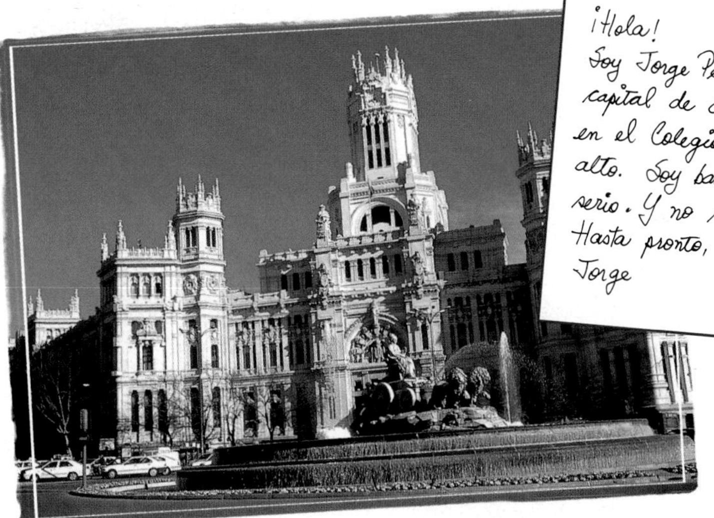

¡Hola!
Soy Jorge Pérez Navarro. Soy de Madrid, la capital de España. Soy español. Soy alumno en el Colegio Sorolla. Soy rubio y bastante alto. Soy bastante gracioso. No soy muy serio. Y no soy tímido. De ninguna manera.
Hasta pronto,
Jorge

Plaza de Cibeles, Madrid, España

Writing Strategy

Freewriting One of the easiest ways to begin any kind of personal writing is simply to begin—to let your thoughts flow and write the first thing that comes to mind. Sometimes as you think of one word, another word will come to mind. If you get stuck, take several minutes to think of another word or phrase. Such brainstorming and freewriting are sometimes the best sources when doing any type of writing about yourself.

5 ¿Quién soy yo?

On a piece of paper, write down as much as you can about yourself in Spanish. Your teacher will collect the descriptions and choose students to read them to the class. You will all try to guess who's being described.

¡Te toca a ti!

PRACTICE

4 Students can write this letter on a sheet of paper.

Writing Strategy

Freewriting Have students read the Writing Strategy on page 37. If students have difficulty thinking of words to describe themselves, have them use the vocabulary list on page 41.

LEVELING

These activities encompass all three levels. All students will be able to do them at a sophistication level commensurate with their ability in Spanish. Some students will be able to speak for several minutes, and others may be able to give just a few sentences. This is to be expected when students are functioning completely on their own generating their own language to the best of their ability.

Answers to ¡Te toca a ti!

4 *Answers will vary but may include:*

Soy *(nombre)*. Soy de *(ciudad)*. Soy *(nacionalidad)*. Soy alumno en *(nombre de la escuela)*. Soy alto(a), moreno(a).

5 *Answers will vary. Students should describe themselves, using as many adjectives and words as possible from the chapter vocabulary.*

Resource Manager

Communication Transparency C 1
Quizzes, pages 1–5
Performance Assessment, Task 1
Tests, pages 1–12
Situation Cards, Chapter 1
ExamView® Pro, Chapter 1
Maratón mental Videoquiz, Chapter 1

Assessment

This is a pre-test for students to take before you administer the chapter test. Note that each section is cross-referenced so students can easily find the material they have to review in case they made errors. You may use Assessment Answers Transparency A 1 to do the assessment in class, or you may assign this assessment for homework. You can correct the assessment yourself, or you may prefer to project the answers on the overhead in class.

Glencoe Technology

MINDJOGGER VHS/DVD

You may wish to help your students prepare for the chapter test by playing the MindJogger game show. Teams will compete against each other to review chapter vocabulary and structure and sharpen listening comprehension skills.

Vocabulario

To review **Palabras 1**, turn to pages 14–15.

1 Escojan. *(Choose.)*

1. 
   a. serio
   b. gracioso

2. 
   a. guapo
   b. feo

3. 
   a. morena
   b. rubia

4. 
   a. ambiciosa
   b. perezosa

5. 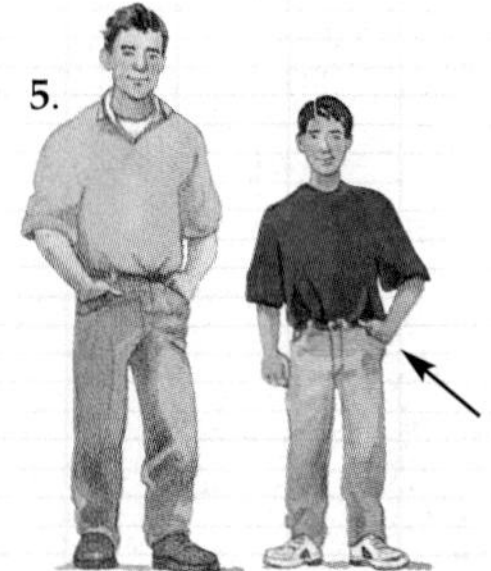
   a. alto
   b. bajo

To review **Palabras 2**, turn to pages 18–19.

2 Completen. *(Complete.)*

6. Roberto es ____ en una escuela secundaria.
7. Roberto no es ____. Él es bastante serio.
8. Carmen es una ____ de Roberto. Ella es una ____ muy simpática.
9. Sancho Panza es ____. No es flaco.

Estructura

To review definite and indefinite articles, turn to page 22.

3 Completen con el o la. *(Complete with* el *or* la.*)*

10–11. ____ muchacho es americano y ____ muchacha es mexicana.
12. Ella es alumna en ____ Colegio de Santa Teresa.

4 Completen con un o una. *(Complete with* un *or* una.*)*

13–14. ____ colegio es ____ escuela secundaria.

Answers to Assessment

1
1. a
2. b
3. a
4. b
5. b

2
6. alumno
7. gracioso (cómico)
8. amiga, amiga (muchacha)
9. gordo

3
10. El
11. la
12. el

4
13. Un
14. una

Music Connection

Canta con Justo

You may wish to have students listen to **Eres tú** found on Track 10 of the **Canta con Justo** music CD. Some students will probably recognize this song. It is particularly appropriate as students learn the verb **ser**.

5 Completen. *(Complete.)*

15. El muchacho es ____. (pelirrojo)
16. La muchacha es ____ también. (pelirrojo)
17. Ella es muy ____. (gracioso)
18. Pero él es bastante ____. (serio)

To review adjectives, turn to page 23.

6 Completen con ser. *(Complete with* ser.*)*

19. El muchacho ____ cubano.
20. Yo ____ americano(a).
21. Y tú, ¿de dónde ____?

To review ser in the singular, turn to page 25.

7 Contesten con no. *(Answer with* no.*)*

22. ¿Es muy tímida la muchacha?
23. ¿Eres argentino(a)?

To review negative sentences, turn to page 25.

Cultura

8 Escojan. *(Choose the correct completion.)*

24. Don Quijote es ____.
    a. escudero b. alto y flaco c. bajo y gordo
25. El autor de *El Quijote* es ____.
    a. Shakespeare b. Sancho Panza c. Cervantes

To review this cultural information, turn to pages 30–31.

Assessment

SPANISH Online

The **Glencoe Spanish Web site** (spanish.glencoe.com) offers options that enable you and your students to experience the Spanish-speaking world via the Internet. For each **Capítulo,** there are activities, games, and quizzes. In addition, an **Enrichment** section offers students an opportunity to visit Web sites related to the theme of the chapter.

Chapter Projects

Los países hispanohablantes Have one or more students do a research project on a Spanish-speaking country or region. Some possibilities are: Argentina, Peru, Madrid, Mexico, or any others they choose from pages xxiv–xxix.

FOLDABLES™ Study Organizer **Dinah Zike's Study Guides**

Your students may wish to use Foldable 3 to organize, display, and arrange data as they learn about the vast Spanish-speaking world. You may wish to encourage them to add information from each chapter as they continue to gather facts and make observations about all the different countries they will be studying.

A *pocket book foldable* is also ideal for having students differentiate between masculine and feminine forms.

Answers to Assessment

5

15. pelirrojo
16. pelirroja
17. graciosa
18. serio

6

19. es
20. soy
21. eres

7

22. No, la muchacha no es muy tímida.
23. No, yo no soy argentino(a).

8

24. b
25. c

¡Hablo como un pro!

This unique page gives students the opportunity to speak freely and say whatever they can, using the vocabulary and structures they have learned in the chapter. The illustration serves to remind students of precisely what they know how to say in Spanish. There are no activities that students do not have the ability to describe or talk about in Spanish. The art not only depicts the vocabulary and content of this chapter, but also reinforces what they learned in previous chapters.

You may wish to use this page in many ways. Some possibilities are to have students do the following:

1. Look at the illustration and identify items by giving the correct Spanish words.
2. Make up sentences about what they see in the illustration.
3. Make up questions about the illustration. They can call on another class member to respond if you do this as a class activity, or you may prefer to allow students to work in small groups. This activity is extremely beneficial because it enables students to actively use interrogative words.
4. Answer questions you ask them about the illustration.
5. Work in pairs and make up a conversation based on the illustration.
6. Look at the illustration and give a complete oral review of what they see.
7. Look at the illustration and write a paragraph (or essay) about it.

You can also use this page as an assessment or testing tool, taking into account individual differences by having students go from simple to quite complicated tasks.

¡Hablo como un pro!

Tell all you can about this illustration.

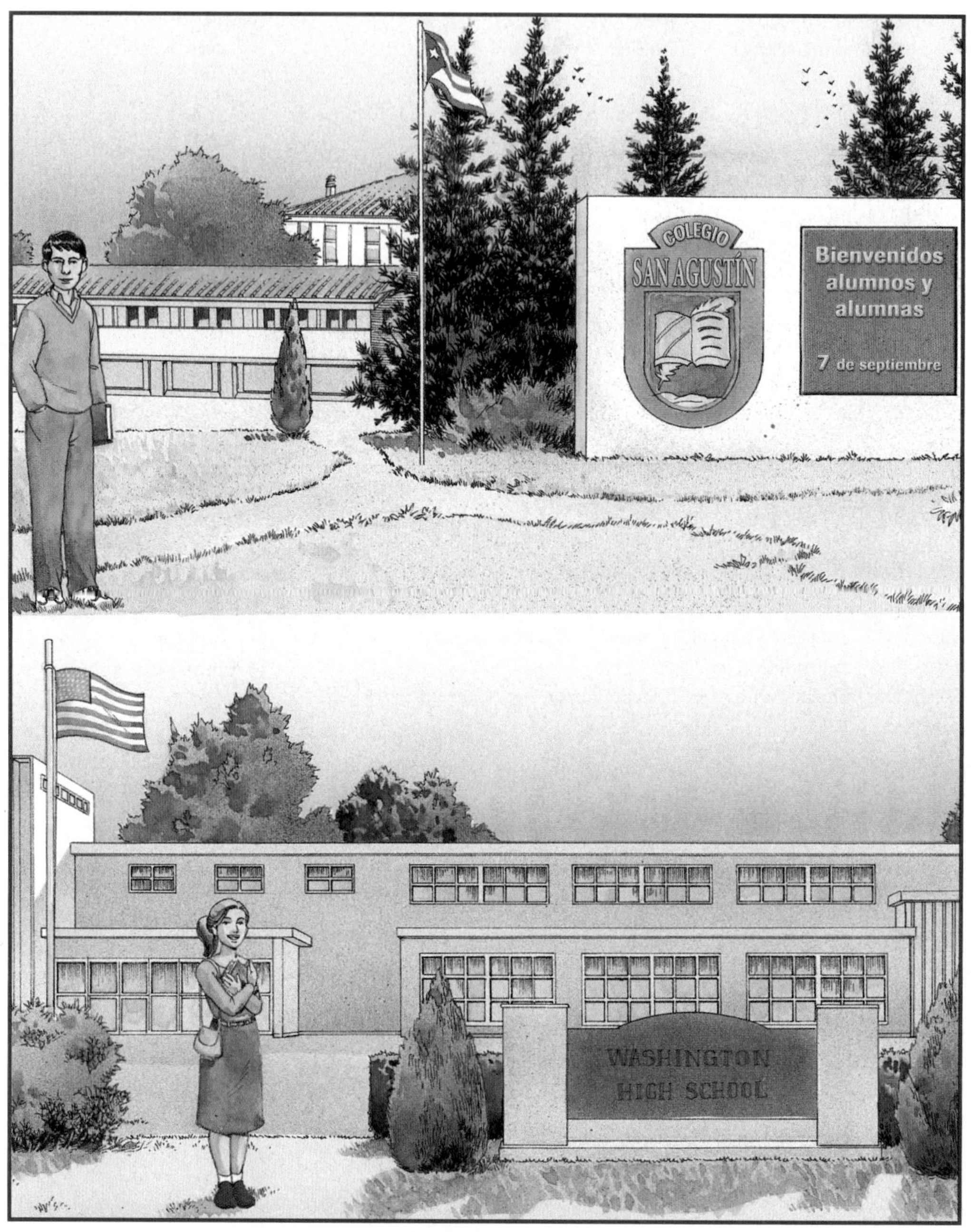

The assessment can be either oral or written. You may wish to use the rubrics provided on pages T20–T21 as you give students the following directions.

1. Identify the topic or situation of the illustration.
2. Give the Spanish words for as many items as you can.
3. Think of as many sentences as you can to describe the illustration.
4. Go over your sentences and put them in the best sequencing to give a coherent story based on the illustration.

Vocabulario

Identifying a person or thing

el muchacho
la muchacha
el amigo
la amiga
el alumno
la alumna
la persona
el colegio
la escuela

Describing a person

alto(a)
bajo(a)
guapo(a)
bonito(a)
lindo(a)
feo(a)
moreno(a)
rubio(a)
pelirrojo(a)
flaco(a)
gordo(a)
gracioso(a)
cómico(a)
serio(a)
ambicioso(a)
perezoso(a)
bueno(a)
fantástico(a)
tímido(a)
sincero(a)
honesto(a)
generoso(a)
simpático(a)
ser

Stating nationality

americano(a)
chileno(a)
colombiano(a)
cubano(a)
mexicano(a)
puertorriqueño(a)
venezolano(a)

Finding out information

¿quién?
¿qué?
¿cómo?
¿de dónde?
¿de qué nacionalidad?
¿no?

How well do you know your vocabulary?

- Choose five words that describe a good friend.
- Use these words to write several sentences about him or her.

Expressing degrees

bastante
muy
no, de ninguna manera

Other useful expressions

secundario(a)

VIDEOTUR

Episodio 1

In this video episode, you will meet six friends from different Spanish-speaking countries. Get to know Alejandra, Julián, Claudia, Alberto, Vicky, and Fernando as they themselves become acquainted. See page 492 for more about the adventures of our new friends.

Vocabulario

Vocabulary Review

The words and phrases in the **Vocabulario** have been taught for productive use in this chapter. They are summarized here as a resource for both student and teacher. This list also serves as a convenient resource for the **¡Te toca a ti!** activities on pages 36 and 37. There are approximately twenty cognates in this vocabulary list. Have students find them.

VIDEO VHS/DVD

The Video Program allows students to see how the chapter vocabulary and structures are used by native speakers within an engaging story line. For maximum reinforcement, show the video episode as a final activity for Chapter 1.

Reaching All Students

For the Younger Students Have students draw a series of faces that illustrate the meaning of adjectives presented in this chapter. Have them label each drawing with the appropriate Spanish word. Select the most attractive ones and put them on a bulletin board entitled **Características.**

¡OJO! You will notice that the vocabulary list here is not translated. This has been done intentionally, since we feel that by the time students have finished the material in the chapter they should be familiar with the meanings of all the words. If there are several words they still do not know, we recommend that they refer to the **Palabras 1** and **2** sections in the chapter or go to the dictionaries at the end of this book to find the meanings. However, if you prefer that your students have the English translations, please refer to Vocabulary Transparency 1.1, where you will find all these words with their translations.

Planning for Chapter 2

SCOPE AND SEQUENCE, PAGES 42–73

Topics

- School subjects and courses
- Telling time
- Nationalities
- Numbers: 31–90

Culture

- Alejandro Chávez and Guadalupe Garza, two Mexican Americans
- Raúl Ugarte and Marta Dávila, two Cuban Americans
- San Antonio, a bilingual city
- The Alamo, San Antonio, Texas
- Coyoacán, a suburb of Mexico City
- The Frida Kahlo Museum

Functions

- How to describe people and things
- How to talk about more than one person or thing
- How to discuss classes in school
- How to express opinions about classes
- How to tell time
- How to tell at what time an event takes place
- How to count from 31 to 90

Structure

- Plural forms of nouns, articles, and adjectives
- Plural forms of **ser**
- Telling time

National Standards

- Communication Standard 1.1 pages 42, 46, 47, 50, 51, 53, 55, 56, 57, 61, 68
- Communication Standard 1.2 pages 47, 51, 53, 55, 59, 60, 61, 63, 64, 65, 67
- Communication Standard 1.3 pages 68, 69
- Cultures Standard 2.1 pages 56, 60, 62–63, 64–65
- Cultures Standard 2.2 page 62
- Connections Standard 3.1 pages 57, 66–67
- Connections Standard 3.2 page 68
- Comparisons Standard 4.2 page 63
- Communities Standard 5.2 page 73

PACING AND PRIORITIES

The chapter content is color coded below to assist you in planning.

■ required ■ recommended ■ optional

Vocabulario *(required)* *Days 1–4*

- ■ Palabras 1
  - ¿Quiénes son?
  - ¿Qué son?
  - ¿Cómo son las clases?
- ■ Palabras 2
  - Los cursos escolares
  - ¿Qué son?
  - Más números

Estructura *(required)* *Days 5–7*

- ■ Sustantivos, artículos y adjetivos en el plural
- ■ Presente de **ser** en el plural
- ■ La hora

Conversación *(required)*

- ■ ¿De qué nacionalidad son Uds.?

Pronunciación *(recommended)*

- ■ Las vocales **e, i**

Lecturas culturales

- ■ El español en los Estados Unidos *(recommended)*
- ■ San Antonio *(optional)*
- ■ Coyoacán *(optional)*

Conexiones

- ■ La sociología *(optional)*

■ **¡Te toca a ti!** *(recommended)*

■ **Assessment** *(recommended)*

■ **¡Hablo como un pro!** *(optional)*

RESOURCE GUIDE

SECTION	PAGES	SECTION RESOURCES
Vocabulario PALABRAS 1		
¿Quiénes son? ¿Qué son? ¿Cómo son las clases?	44, 46–47 44, 46–47 45, 46–47	Vocabulary Transparencies 2.2–2.3 Audio CD 2 Audio Activities TE, pages 11–12 Workbook, pages 11–12 Quiz 1, page 6 ExamView® Pro
Vocabulario PALABRAS 2		
Los cursos escolares ¿Qué son? Más números	48, 50–51 49, 50–51 49, 50–51	Vocabulary Transparencies 2.4–2.5 Audio CD 2 Audio Activities TE, pages 13–15 Workbook, page 13 Quiz 2, page 7 ExamView® Pro
Estructura		
Sustantivos, artículos y adjetivos en el plural Presente de **ser** en el plural La hora	52–53 54–57 58–59	Audio CD 2 Audio Activities TE, pages 15–19 Workbook, pages 14–16 Quizzes 3–5, pages 8–10 ExamView® Pro
Conversación		
¿De qué nacionalidad son Uds.?	60	Audio CD 2 Audio Activities TE, pages 19–20 Interactive CD-ROM
Pronunciación		
Las vocales **e, i**	61	Pronunciation Transparency P 2 Audio CD 2 Audio Activities TE, page 20
Lecturas culturales		
El español en los Estados Unidos San Antonio Coyoacán	62–63 64 65	Audio CD 2 Audio Activities TE, page 21 Tests, pages 18, 20–21
Conexiones		
La sociología	66–67	Tests, page 22
¡Te toca a ti!		
	68–69	**¡Viva el mundo hispano!** Video, Episode 2 Video Activities, Chapter 2 Spanish Online Activities spanish.glencoe.com
Assessment		
	70–71	Communication Transparency C 2 Quizzes 1–5, pages 6–10 Performance Assessment, Task 2 Tests, pages 15–26 Situation Cards, Chapter 2 ExamView® Pro **Maratón mental** Videoquiz

Using Your Resources for Chapter 2

Transparencies

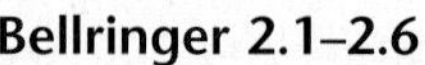
Bellringer 2.1–2.6

Vocabulary 2.1–2.5

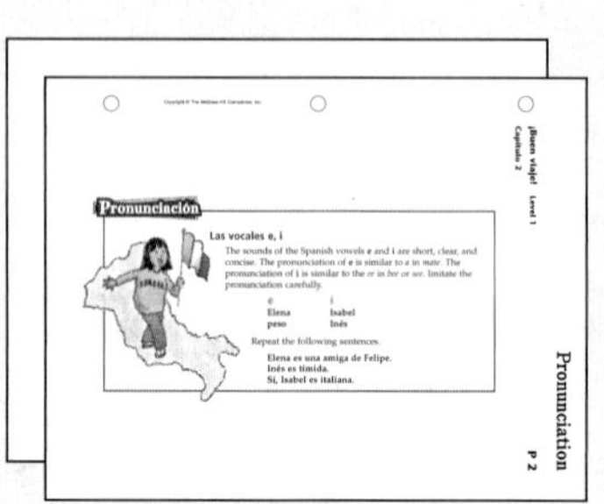

Pronunciation P 2

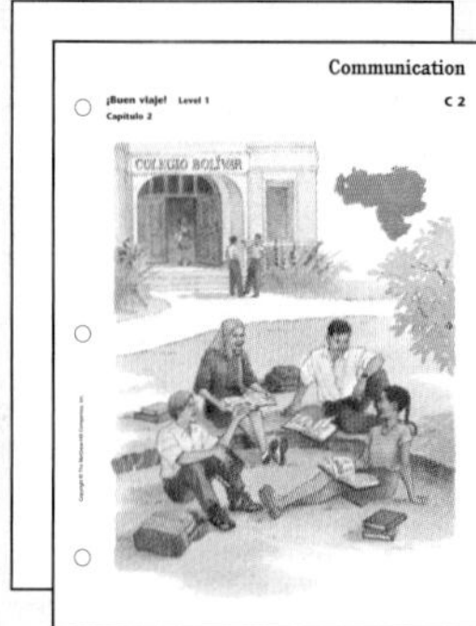

Communication C 2

Workbook

Vocabulary, pages 11–13

Structure, pages 14–16

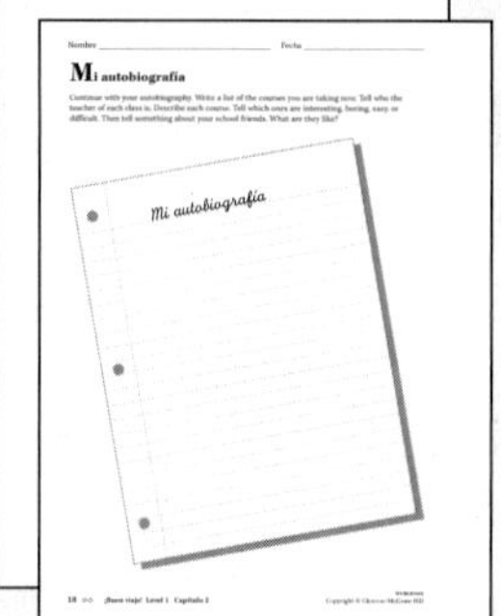

Enrichment, pages 17–18

Audio Activities

Vocabulary, pages 11–15

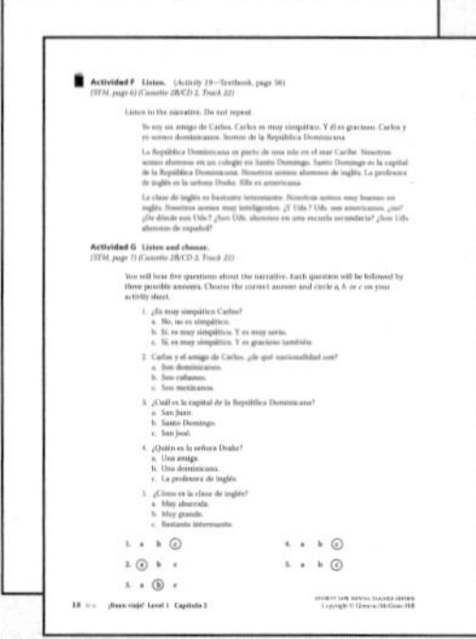

Structure, pages 15–19

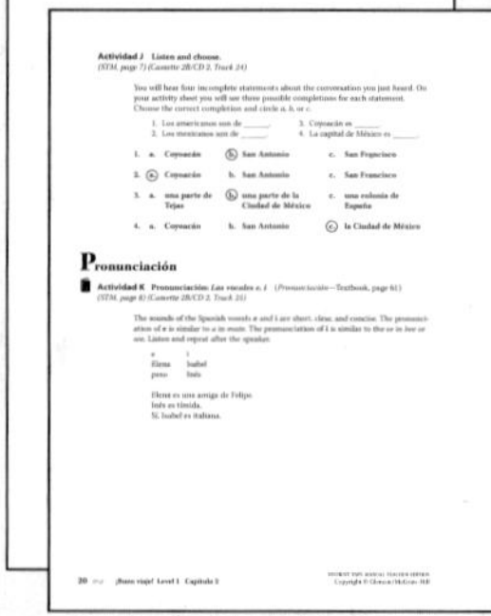

Conversation, Pronunciation, pages 19–20

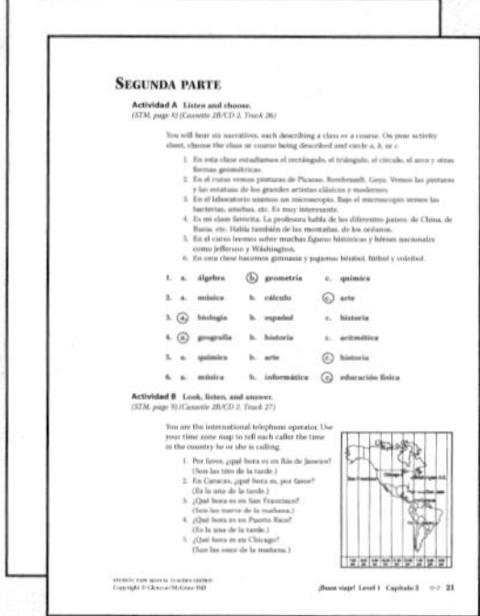

Additional Practice, pages 21–23

Assessment

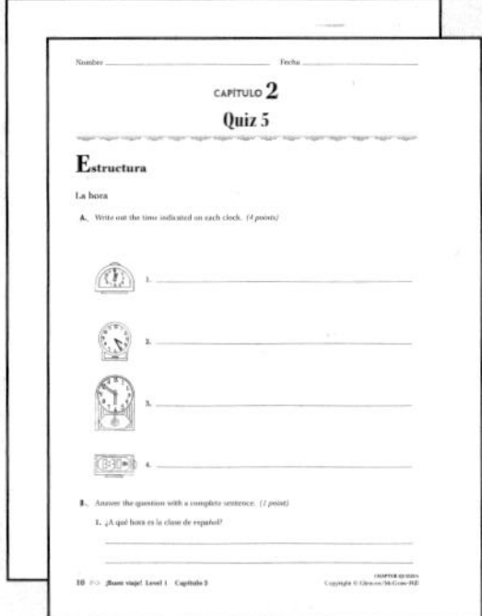
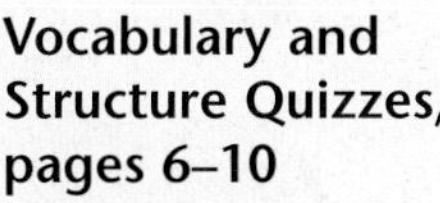

Vocabulary and Structure Quizzes, pages 6–10

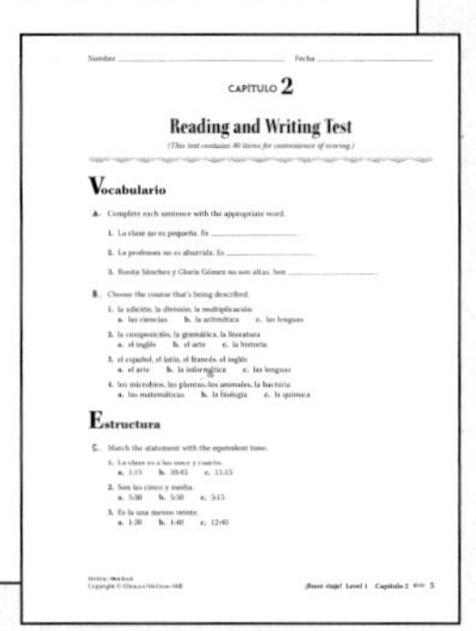

Chapter Tests, pages 15–26

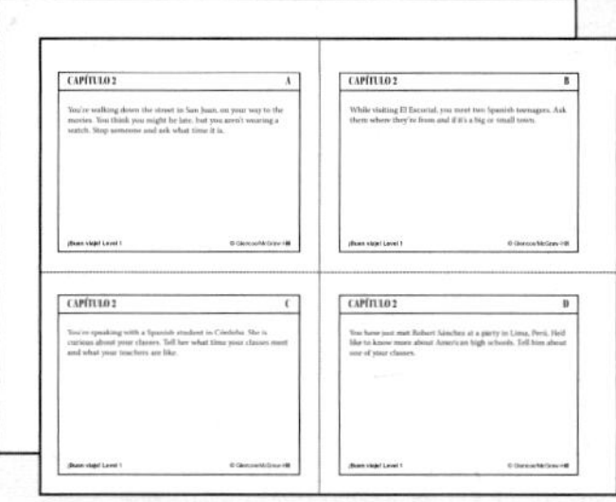

Situation Cards, Chapter 2

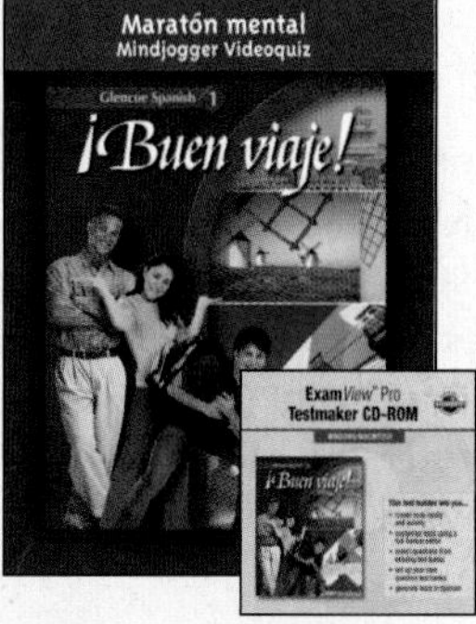

MindJogger Videoquiz, ExamView® Pro, Chapter 2

Timesaving Teacher Tools

TeacherWorks™ is your all-in-one teacher resource center. Personalize lesson plans, access resources from the Teacher Wraparound Edition, connect to the Internet, or make a to-do list. These are only a few of the many features that can assist you in the planning and organizing of your lessons.

Includes:

- A calendar feature
- Access to all program blackline masters
- Standards correlations and more

ExamView® Pro

Test Bank software for Macintosh and Windows makes creating, editing, customizing, and printing tests quick and easy.

Technology Resources

In the Chapter 2 Internet Activity, you will have a chance to learn more about the Spanish-speaking world. Visit spanish.glencoe.com

On the interactive CD-ROM, students can listen to and take part in a recorded version of the conversation in Chapter 2.

¡Viva el mundo hispano! Video and Video Activities, Chapter 2. Available on VHS and DVD.

Help your students prepare for the chapter test by playing the **Maratón mental** Videoquiz game show. Teams will compete against each other to review chapter vocabulary and structure and sharpen listening comprehension skills. Available on VHS and DVD.

¡Buen viaje! is also available on CD or Online.

Capítulo 2

Preview

In this chapter students will learn to describe people and things, using the plural forms of articles, adjectives, and the verb **ser.** (The singular forms were taught in Chapter 1.) Active vocabulary from Chapter 1 is recycled in this chapter as new descriptive adjectives and school-related terms are presented.

National Standards

Communication

In Chapter 2, students will communicate in spoken and written Spanish on the following topics:

- obtaining and providing information about their friends and courses
- talking about themselves

Students will engage in conversations, provide and obtain information, and exchange opinions as they fulfill the chapter objectives listed on this page.

¡OJO! Since the vocabulary in this chapter has to do with school and school subjects, there are many cognates. The large number of cognates will help students learn the new words quickly. However, cognates often present a pronunciation problem. Since they are so similar to the English words, students will often anglicize the pronunciation. Take care to model the pronunciation of cognates very carefully. However, the cognates do give students the feeling that they are progressing rapidly in their language acquisition.

Capítulo 2

Alumnos y cursos

Objetivos

In this chapter you will learn to:

- describe people and things
- talk about more than one person or thing
- tell what subjects you take in school and express some opinions about them
- tell time
- tell at what time an event takes place
- talk about Spanish speakers in the United States

Juan Carlos Liberti *Concierto barroco*

Capítulo 2

Spotlight on Culture

Arte Juan Carlos Liberti was born in Buenos Aires in 1930. He is also famous for his paintings of people doing the tango.

Fotografía This photo shows some friends who are students in Madrid. They are at one of the entrances to Retiro Park in Madrid.

LEVELING

The activities, conversations, and readings within each chapter are marked according to level of difficulty. **E** indicates easy. **A** indicates average. **C** indicates challenging. Some activities cover a range of difficulty. In some activities, for example, advanced students will be able to produce more extensive responses while students who learn at a different rate may give less detailed responses. The leveling indicators will help you individualize instruction to best meet your students' needs.

1 PREPARATION

Resource Manager

Vocabulary Transparencies 2.2–2.3
Audio Activities TE, pages 11–12
Audio CD 2
Workbook, pages 11–12
Quizzes, page 6
ExamView® Pro

Bellringer Review

Use BRR Transparency 2.1 or write the following on the board.
Use the following words in a sentence: **serio, cómico, alto, mexicano, guapo.**

2 PRESENTATION

Step 1 Have students close their books. Present the vocabulary, using Vocabulary Transparencies 2.2–2.3. Point to the girls as you have students repeat **las alumnas** after you. Point to the girls and the books to help convey the meaning of **alumnas.** Then do the same with the boys. Now indicate that both girls are together, and then that both boys are together, as the class repeats: **las amigas, los amigos.**

Step 2 Have the class repeat their names: **Marta, Adela, Juan, Ricardo.** Ask questions:
¿Son alumnas Marta y Adela?
¿Quiénes son alumnas?
¿Son amigas también?
¿Son las dos muchachas amigas?
Then do the same with the boys.

Step 3 Point to the map of Puerto Rico as students repeat **Puerto Rico. Los amigos son de Puerto Rico. Son puertorriqueños. Son inteligentes.** Ask questions such as: **¿De dónde son los alumnos?**

¿Quiénes son?

¿Qué son?

Marta y Adela son puertorriqueñas.
Juan y Ricardo son puertorriqueños también.
Los cuatro amigos son de Ponce.
Ellos son alumnos en la misma escuela.
Son muy inteligentes.

Reaching All Students

Total Physical Response Before doing this activity, make sure students understand each of the following verbs by acting them out: **levántate, ven acá, toma, señala, dame, siéntate.** You will need a ruler in order to do this activity.

(Student 1), **levántate.**
Ven acá.
Toma. *(Hand him or her the ruler.)*
Con la regla, señala a un muchacho moreno.
Señala a dos muchachos rubios.
Señala a una muchacha.
Señala a una muchacha rubia.
Señala a dos muchachas morenas.
Muy bien. Dame la regla.
Gracias, *(Student 1).* **Siéntate.**

¿Cómo son las clases?

Es una clase pequeña.
¿Cuántos alumnos hay en la clase?
Hay pocos alumnos en la clase.
Es una clase aburrida.

Es una clase grande.
Hay muchos alumnos en la clase.
Es una clase interesante.

El curso de español no es difícil. Es fácil.

El curso de matemáticas es bastante difícil (duro).

Nota Once again you will see how many Spanish words you already know because they are cognates. You should have no trouble guessing the meaning of these words.

el curso	inteligente	dominicano
la clase	interesante	ecuatoriano
el profesor, la profesora	popular	panameño

Vocabulario

¿Son amigos?
¿Son puertorriqueños los cuatro amigos?
¿De qué nacionalidad son los amigos?
¿Son alumnos en la misma escuela o en escuelas diferentes?

Step 4 Have students repeat words in isolation first and build to complete sentences. For example: **la clase, pequeña, aburrida (no interesante). Es una clase pequeña. Es una clase aburrida. No es una clase interesante.** Then ask questions using the new words.

Step 5 You can use a gesture to help convey the meaning of **difícil**—wipe your brow or make a hand motion. Then say **difícil, no fácil.**

Step 6 After presenting the vocabulary orally, have students open their books and read the words and sentences as they repeat either after you or Audio CD 2. Intersperse questions throughout the reading to continue to elicit oral responses.

Vocabulary Expansion

To have some fun you may wish to present the opposite of **fantástico** or **fabuloso—horrible.**
You may also present:
estupendo
sensacional
genial
Genial is a rather "in" expression in some areas. It is used for anything that is great or "awesome."

About the Spanish Language

- You may wish to give students the word **el / la maestro(a)** and explain to them that this is the term most frequently used when referring to an elementary school teacher.
- The most frequently heard term for an elementary school used to be **la escuela primaria.** However, it is very common these days to hear **la escuela elemental.**

LEVELING
E: Vocabulary

3 PRACTICE

¿Qué palabra necesito?

¡OJO! When students are doing the **¿Qué palabra necesito?** activities, accept any answer that makes sense. The purpose of these activities is to have students use the new vocabulary. They are not factual recall activities. Thus, it is not necessary for students to remember specific factual information from the vocabulary presentation when answering. If you wish, have students use the photos on this page as a stimulus, when possible.

Historieta Each time **Historieta** appears, it means that the answers to the activity form a short story. Encourage students to look at the title of the **Historieta,** since it can help them do the activity.

1 Do Activity 1 orally with books closed; then have students read it for additional reinforcement.
Expansion: Call on one student to answer all the questions. Then have another student retell the **Historieta** in his or her own words.

2 Go over Activity 2 once orally, asking questions of individual students. Have them open their books and read it for additional reinforcement. Now reverse the process. Have students close their books and give them the response. Have them ask you the question.

Writing Development

Have students write the answers to Activity 2 in a paragraph. Answers will give them a unified story.

¿Qué palabra necesito?

1 Historieta Los cuatro amigos argentinos

Contesten. *(Answer.)*

1. ¿Son amigas Sara y Julia?
2. ¿Son amigos David y Alejandro?
3. ¿Son argentinos o mexicanos los cuatro amigos?
4. ¿Son de Buenos Aires o de Puebla?
5. ¿Son ellos alumnos muy buenos?

Plaza San Martín, Buenos Aires, Argentina

2 Historieta La clase de español

Contesten. *(Answer based on your own experience.)*

1. ¿Es grande o pequeña la clase de español?
2. ¿Hay muchos o pocos alumnos en la clase de español?
3. ¿Quién es el profesor o la profesora de español?
4. ¿De qué nacionalidad es él o ella?
5. ¿Cómo es el curso de español? ¿Es un curso interesante o aburrido?
6. ¿Es fácil o difícil el curso de español?
7. ¿Son muy inteligentes los alumnos en la clase de español?
8. ¿Son ellos alumnos serios?
9. ¿Cuántos alumnos hay en la clase de español?

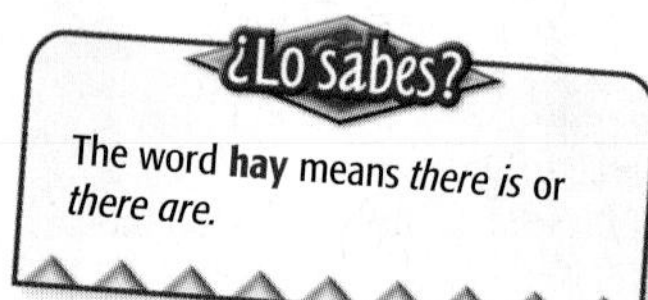

¿Lo sabes?
The word **hay** means *there is* or *there are.*

Una clase de español

Answers to ¿Qué palabra necesito?

1

1. Sí, son amigas.
2. Sí, son amigos.
3. Los cuatro amigos son argentinos.
4. Son de Buenos Aires.
5. Sí, son alumnos muy buenos.

2 *Answers will vary but may include:*

1. La clase de español es grande (pequeña).
2. Hay muchos (pocos) alumnos en la clase de español.
3. El/La profesor(a) de español es ___.
4. Es ___.
5. El curso de español es interesante (aburrido).
6. El curso de español es fácil (difícil).
7. Sí, los alumnos en la clase de español son muy inteligentes.
8. Sí, (No, no) son alumnos serios.
9. Hay ___ alumnos en la clase de español.

3 **De ninguna manera**
Sigan el modelo. *(Follow the model.)*

Son interesantes, ¿no?
No, de ninguna manera.
Entonces, ¿cómo son?
Son aburridos.

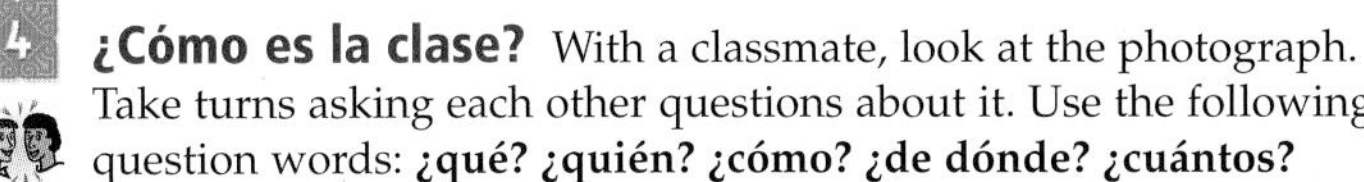

1. Son pequeños, ¿no?
2. Son aburridos, ¿no?
3. Son fáciles, ¿no?
4. Son altos, ¿no?
5. Son bonitos, ¿no?

4 **¿Cómo es la clase?** With a classmate, look at the photograph. Take turns asking each other questions about it. Use the following question words: **¿qué? ¿quién? ¿cómo? ¿de dónde? ¿cuántos?**

5 **La escuela ideal** Get together with a classmate. Describe what for each of you is an ideal school. Say as much as you can about the teachers, classes, and students. Determine whether you agree.

3 Have students do Activity 3 as a miniconversation. Encourage them to use as much expression as possible.

4 Encourage students to make up as many questions as they can. It is important to get the students actively using the question words on their own.

5 You can help less able students do Activity 5 by asking: **¿Cómo son los alumnos de una escuela ideal? Y las clases, ¿cómo son? ¿Grandes, pequeñas, interesantes, aburridas? ¿Y los profesores?**

Learning from Photos

(page 46 top) The students in the photo are standing in front of the statue of San Martín, in the Plaza San Martín, a favorite downtown gathering place in Buenos Aires. Children play on the swings, and people read newspapers on the benches under the many trees in the plaza.

LEVELING

E: Activity 1
A: Activities 2, 4
C: Activities 3, 5

Answers to ¿Qué palabra necesito?

3 *Students will follow the model.*

4 *Answers will vary but may include:*

¿Cómo son los alumnos?
¿Cómo es el profesor?
¿Quién es el profesor?
¿De dónde es el profesor?
¿Cuantos alumnos hay en la clase?

5 *Answers will vary but may include:*

—En una escuela ideal, las clases son interesantes.
—En una escuela ideal, las clases son fáciles.

Vocabulario

PALABRAS 2

1 PREPARATION

Resource Manager

Vocabulary Transparencies 2.4–2.5
Audio Activities TE, pages 13–15
Audio CD 2
Workbook, page 13
Quizzes, page 7
ExamView® Pro

Bellringer Review

Use BBR Transparency 2.2 or write the following on the board.
Write some information about your Spanish class using the following words.
la clase de español
interesante / aburrida
grande / pequeña
el / la profesor(a)

2 PRESENTATION

Step 1 Have students imitate the pronunciation of these words as carefully as they can. Since these words are almost all cognates, students will have a tendency to mispronounce them.

Step 2 Point to Germany on a map as students say **el alemán,** or say: **el alemán, una lengua germánica.**

PALABRAS 2

Los cursos escolares

Las ciencias
la biología
la química
la física

Las matemáticas
la aritmética
el álgebra
la geometría
el cálculo

Las lenguas
el español
el inglés
el francés
el alemán
el latín

Las ciencias sociales
la historia
la geografía

Otras asignaturas o disciplinas
la educación física
la música
el arte
la economía doméstica
la informática

Reaching All Students

Total Physical Response Before doing this activity, make sure students understand each of the following commands by acting them out: **levántate, levanta la mano.** Hold up a book that represents the subject mentioned and point to a student as you say:
Si tomas un curso de historia, levanta la mano.
Si tomas un curso de música, levanta la mano.
Si tomas un curso de química, levanta la mano.
Si tomas un curso de educación física, levanta la mano.
Si tomas un curso de arte, levanta la mano.
Si tomas un curso de latín, levanta la mano, etc.

¿Qué son?

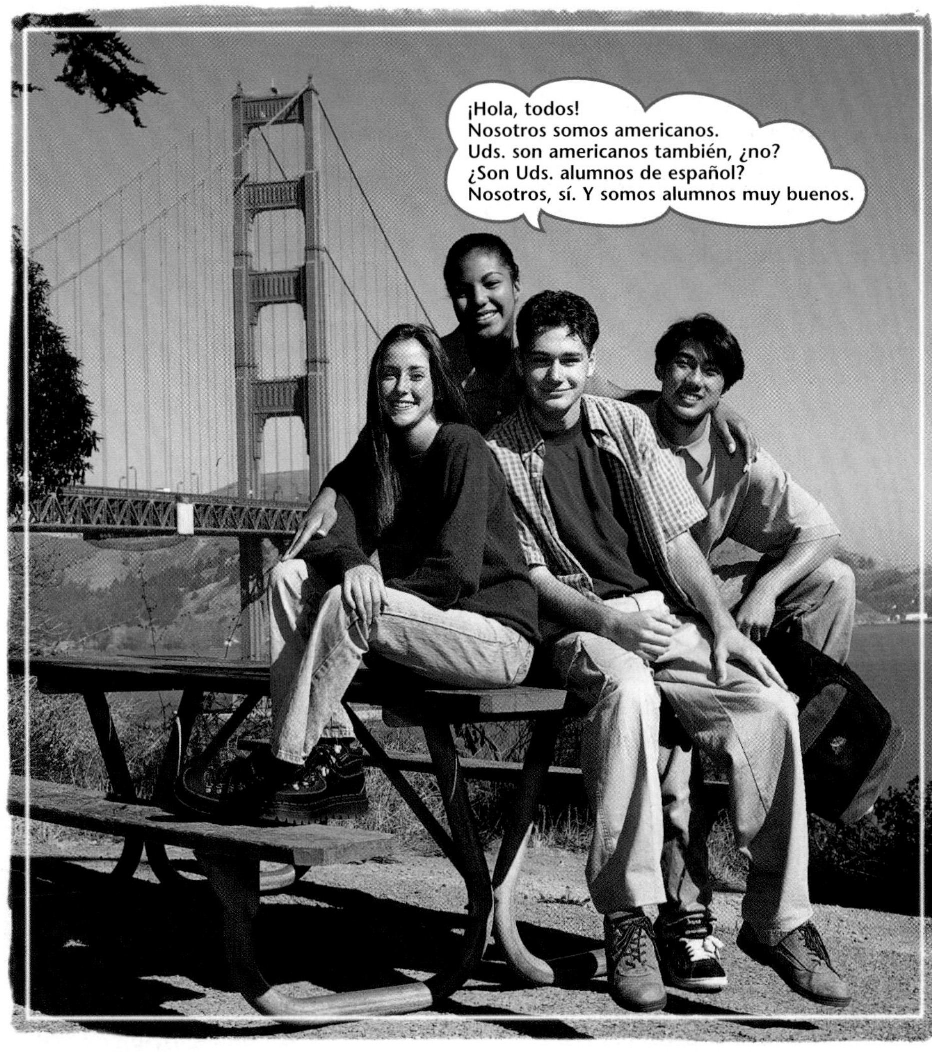

¡Hola, todos!
Nosotros somos americanos.
Uds. son americanos también, ¿no?
¿Son Uds. alumnos de español?
Nosotros, sí. Y somos alumnos muy buenos.

Más números

31	treinta y uno	**36**	treinta y seis	**50**	cincuenta
32	treinta y dos	**37**	treinta y siete	**60**	sesenta
33	treinta y tres	**38**	treinta y ocho	**70**	setenta
34	treinta y cuatro	**39**	treinta y nueve	**80**	ochenta
35	treinta y cinco	**40**	cuarenta	**90**	noventa

Step 3 Call two students to the front of the room. Select two who have fairly good pronunciation. Have them open their books to page 49 and read the words in the speech bubble to the class as if they were the people in the photo. This procedure helps students grasp the meaning of **nosotros(as).**

Step 4 Go around the room pointing to two students at a time and say **Uds.** Have someone point to himself or herself and someone else and say **nosotros(as).**

Step 5 Más números Have students repeat the numbers. Then write numbers on the board in random order and have students say them aloud.

Vocabulary Expansion

You may want to give the following additional vocabulary if there are students in the class who are taking these subjects.

la trigonometría
el japonés
el ruso
la mecánica
la psicología
las artes manuales

FUN-FACTS

In the public schools of Spain and some Latin American countries, students must buy their textbooks. Textbooks are selected and approved by the Ministry of Education and sold in bookstores and supermarkets.

Reaching All Students

Additional Practice Have students make a list of their courses and indicate whether they consider each one **fácil** or **difícil.** They can then tell about the class using **interesante** or **aburrida.**

FOLDABLES™ Study Organizer — Dinah Zike's Study Guides

Your students may wish to use Foldable 1 to organize, display, and arrange data as they expand their Spanish vocabulary. You may wish to encourage them to add information from each chapter as they continue to learn new words related to the different topics they will be studying.

A *vocabulary book* foldable is an ideal reference, especially as students begin to make word associations and write simple passages in Spanish.

3 PRACTICE

¿Qué palabra necesito?

6 Activity 6 can be done with books open. Note that it serves as an introduction to the plural, since it contrasts **es** and **son** as well as singular and plural forms of nouns and adjectives.

7 Ask questions from Activity 7 and have students answer orally with books closed.

8 Have students refer to the photograph as they answer the questions in Activity 8.

9 Students should be able to recognize the cognates used in Activity 9 but should not be expected to learn or produce this receptive vocabulary.

¿Qué palabra necesito?

6 Ciencias, lenguas o matemáticas

Contesten con **sí** o **no.** *(Answer with* sí *or* no.*)*

1. La biología es una ciencia.
2. La historia y la geografía son matemáticas.
3. El cálculo es una lengua.
4. El latín y el francés son lenguas.
5. El arte y la música son cursos obligatorios.

7 Cursos fáciles y difíciles

Contesten. *(Answer based on your own experience.)*

1. ¿Es el español un curso difícil o fácil?
2. ¿Es grande o pequeña la clase de español?
3. ¿Qué cursos son fáciles?
4. ¿Cuántos cursos son fáciles?
5. ¿Qué cursos son difíciles?
6. ¿Cuántos cursos son difíciles?
7. ¿Qué cursos son interesantes?
8. ¿Qué cursos son aburridos?

8 Historieta Alumnos americanos

Contesten. *(Answer.)*

1. ¿De qué nacionalidad son los alumnos?
2. ¿Son alumnos en una escuela secundaria?
3. ¿Son alumnos de química?
4. ¿Son alumnos buenos o malos en la química?

Una clase de ciencias

9 ¿Qué curso o asignatura es?

Identifiquen el curso. *(Identify the course.)*

1. el problema, la ecuación, la solución, la multiplicación, la división
2. la literatura, la composición, la gramática
3. un microbio, un animal, una planta, el microscopio, el laboratorio
4. el círculo, el arco, el rectángulo, el triángulo
5. el piano, el violín, la guitarra, el concierto, la ópera, el coro
6. las montañas, los océanos, las capitales, los recursos naturales
7. la pintura, la estatua, la escultura
8. el fútbol, el básquetbol, el béisbol, el voleibol, el tenis

Answers to ¿Qué palabra necesito?

6

1. Sí, la biología es una ciencia.
2. No, la historia y la geografía no son matemáticas.
3. No, el cálculo no es una lengua.
4. Sí, el latín y el francés son lenguas.
5. No, el arte y la música no son cursos obligatorios.

7 *Answers will vary but may include:*

1. El español es un curso fácil (difícil).
2. La clase de español es grande (pequeña).
3. Las lenguas (Las ciencias, etc.) son fáciles.
4. Dos (Tres) cursos son fáciles. (Un curso es fácil.)
5. Las lenguas (Las ciencias, etc.) son difíciles.
6. Dos (Tres) cursos son difíciles. (Un curso es difícil.)
7. El español, el inglés, etc. son interesantes.
8. Las matemáticas, la biología, etc. son aburridas.

8

1. Los alumnos son americanos.
2. Sí, son alumnos en una escuela secundaria.
3. Sí, son alumnos de química.
4. Son alumnos buenos (malos) en la química.

9

1. el álgebra (las matemáticas)
2. el inglés
3. la biología
4. la geometría
5. la música
6. la geografía
7. el arte
8. la educación física

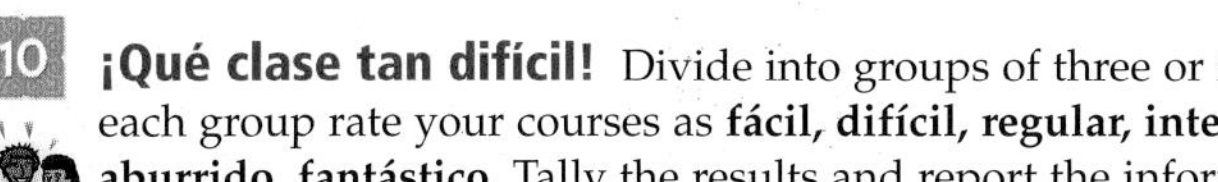

10 ¡Qué clase tan difícil! Divide into groups of three or four. In each group rate your courses as **fácil, difícil, regular, interesante, aburrido, fantástico.** Tally the results and report the information to the class.

SPANISH Online

For more information about Córdoba and other cities in the Spanish-speaking world, go to the Glencoe Spanish Web site: spanish.glencoe.com

11 En España You are spending the summer with a family in Córdoba in southern Spain. Tell your Spanish "brother" or "sister" (your partner) all you can about your Spanish class and your Spanish teacher. Answer any questions he or she may have.

Córdoba, España

12 Juego Un número secreto Think of a number between 1 and 99. Your partner will try to guess the number you have in mind. Use a hand gesture to indicate whether the number you are thinking of is higher or lower. Continue until your partner guesses the correct number. Take turns.

Answers to ¿Qué palabra necesito?

10 *Answers will vary.*

11 *Answers will vary. Students should use adjectives that can describe a class:* interesante, aburrido, fácil, difícil, *etc.*

12 *Answers will vary.*

LEVELING

E: Activities 6, 7, 8, 12

A: Activities 9, 10

C: Activity 11

¡OJO! Note that the activities are color-coded. All the activities in the text are communicative. However, the ones with blue titles are guided communication. The red titles indicate that the answers to the activity are more open-ended and can vary more. You may wish to correct students' mistakes more so in the guided activities than in the activities with a red title, which lend themselves to a freer response.

Recycling

The activities on this page recycle the singular forms of nouns, adjectives, and the verb **ser** from Chapter 1.

12 **Juego** This is a good end-of-class activity. **Hint:** You may want to change the number span if your time is limited.

Learning from Photos

(page 51) This photo shows the city of Córdoba, Spain. The **puente romano,** which dates from the time of the Romans, is still in use. It crosses the **río Guadalquivir.** From the bridge we see **la Mezquita de Córdoba,** one of the earliest and most beautiful examples of Muslim architecture in Spain.

History Connection

The Great Mosque, **la Mezquita de Córdoba,** was built between the eighth and tenth centuries. The Moors crossed the Straits of Gilbraltar in 711 and conquered most of Spain. They remained there until 1492 when Ferdinand and Isabel conquered Granada, the last Moorish territory in Spain.

1 PREPARATION

Resource Manager

Audio Activities TE, pages 15–19
Audio CD 2
Workbook, pages 14–16
Quizzes, pages 8–10
ExamView® Pro

Bellringer Review

Use BRR Transparency 2.3 or write the following on the board.
Quickly write down in Spanish the names of the subjects you are taking this semester.

2 PRESENTATION

Sustantivos, artículos y adjetivos en el plural

Step 1 If you wish to present the grammar point deductively, have students close their books. On the board write the singular forms of the nouns from Item 1 on page 52. Now ask students to supply the plural forms. (They know the plural forms of the articles from the vocabulary presentation in **Palabras 1.**) Then have students open their books and read Items 1 and 2.

Step 2 Have students read the model sentences aloud in Items 3 and 4.

Estructura

Sustantivos, artículos y adjetivos en el plural
Describing more than one

1. Plural means *more than one.* In Spanish, the plural of most nouns is formed by adding an **s**.

SINGULAR	PLURAL
el muchacho	**los muchachos**
el colegio	**los colegios**
la amiga	**las amigas**
la escuela	**las escuelas**

2. The plural forms of the definite articles **el** and **la** are **los** and **las.** The plural forms of the indefinite articles **un** and **una** are **unos** and **unas.**

SINGULAR	PLURAL
el curso	**los cursos**
la alumna	**las alumnas**
un amigo	**unos amigos**
una amiga	**unas amigas**

3. To form the plural of adjectives that end in **o, a,** or **e,** you add **s** to the singular form.

El alumno es serio. — **Los alumnos son serios.**
La alumna es seria. — **Las alumnas son serias.**
La lengua es interesante. — **Las lenguas son interesantes.**

4. To form the plural of adjectives that end in a consonant, you add **es.**

El curso es fácil. — **Los cursos son fáciles.**
La lengua es fácil. — **Las lenguas son fáciles.**

COLEGIO EXTERNADO DE SAN JOSE
SAN SALVADOR.

EXAMEN DE 2a. QUINCENA III TRIMESTRE
I N G L E S.
TURNO VESPERTINO.

NOMBRE: Diana Aída Martínez Cortez # 22 SECC: B 10

I PARTE: Tranlate into English.

- La casa esta limpia. — The house is clean
- El policia es fuerte. — The policeman is strong
- El doctor es guapo. — The doctor is handsome
- Rose es gorda. — Rose is fat
- El carro es caro. — The car is expensive

Class Motivator

¿Singular o plural? Give students a word orally. Have them raise one hand if it is singular, two hands if it is plural. Example: **la clase, los libros.**

¿Cómo lo digo?

13 **Historieta Amigos nuevos**
Contesten con **sí.** *(Answer with* sí.*)*

1. ¿Son amigos nuevos los dos muchachos?
2. ¿Son chilenos los dos muchachos?
3. ¿Son ellos alumnos en un colegio en Santiago, Chile?
4. ¿Son alumnos serios?
5. ¿Son ellos muchachos populares?

Santiago, Chile

14 **¿Cómo son?**
Describan a las personas. *(Describe the people.)*

1. David, Domingo

2. Inés, Susana

3. Paco, Eduardo

4. Isabel, Carmen

15 **Historieta La señora Ortiz** Completen.
(Complete with an appropriate word.)

La señora Ortiz es una profesora muy __1__. Las clases de la señora Ortiz son __2__. Las clases de la señora Ortiz no son __3__. Los alumnos de la señora Ortiz son __4__. No son __5__.

Estructura

3 PRACTICE

¿Cómo lo digo?

13 This activity can be done with books closed or open.

14 Have students look at the photographs of the students and make up any sentences that describe them accurately.

15 Do Activity 15 with books open. Note that it reinforces both the singular and plural forms.
Expansion: After going over Activity 15, you can call on one student to read the entire activity as a story.

Reaching All Students

Additional Practice
Have students make up original sentences about one or more persons.

Learning from Photos

(page 53) Santiago is a beautiful city with many high-rise buildings and magnificent views of the Andes.

LEVELING
E: Activities 13, 14
A: Activity 15

Answers to ¿Cómo lo digo?

13

1. Sí, los dos muchachos son amigos nuevos.
2. Sí, los dos muchachos son chilenos.
3. Sí, son alumnos en un colegio en Santiago, Chile.
4. Sí, son alumnos serios.
5. Sí, son muchachos populares.

14 *Answers will vary but may include:*

David y Domingo son rubios.
Inés y Susana son graciosas.
Paco y Eduardo son cómicos.
Isabel y Carmen son inteligentes.

15 *Answers will vary but may include:*

1. buena (interesante, aburrida)
2. interesantes (aburridas)
3. difíciles (interesantes, fáciles)
4. buenos (malos, americanos, serios)
5. malos (buenos, mexicanos, perezosos)

1 PREPARATION

Bellringer Review

Use BRR Transparency 2.4 or write the following on the board.
On a piece of paper, write four sentences using the verb **ser** and the following subjects: **yo, tú, él, ella.**

2 PRESENTATION

Presente de ser en el plural

Step 1 Have students keep their books closed as you write **yo, tú, él / ella** on the board with the appropriate forms of the verb **ser.** Use the standard conjugation format shown in the chart on page 54. Remind students that they learned the singular forms of the verb **ser** in Chapter 1.

Step 2 Now write in **ellos / ellas** and ask students if they remember the corresponding verb form (from the **Palabras 1** section). Do the same with **nosotros** and then introduce the **Uds.** form. (The difference between **tú** and **Ud.** will be presented in Chapter 3, page 87.)

Step 3 Have students open their books and read the information in Item 3 aloud. It is important that students understand to whom they are referring when they use a verb form.

Step 4 Have students read the sentences in the speech bubbles with correct intonation.

Presente de ser en el plural

Talking about more than one

1. You have already learned the singular forms of the verb **ser.** Review the following.

SER	
yo	soy
tú	eres
él	es
ella	es

2. Now study the plural forms of the verb **ser.**

SER	
nosotros(as)	somos
ellos	son
ellas	son
Uds.	son

3.

Nosotros somos amigos.

When you talk about yourself and another person or other people, you use the **nosotros(as)** form.

Ellos son americanos.

You use **ellos** when talking about two or more males or a mixed group of males and females.

Ellas son simpáticas.

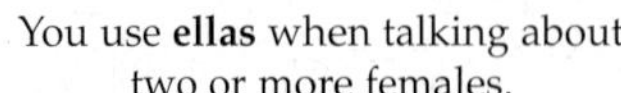

You use **ellas** when talking about two or more females.

¿Uds. son amigos?
Sí, somos amigos.

When talking to more than one person, you use **ustedes,** the plural form for **tú. Ustedes** is commonly abbreviated as **Uds.**

Reaching All Students

Kinesthetic Learners Some students learn by moving and doing. Have individuals and various groups made up of two, three, or four students stand in different locations in the room. Some groups should be all one sex, some mixed. Choose one base sentence such as **Él es cómico.** Have different students apply this sentence to various groups or individuals to whom they point, changing subject pronoun, verb, and adjective as necessary. For example: **Ellos son cómicos. Ella es cómica. Nosotros somos cómicos.**

¿Cómo lo digo?

16 **Somos alumnos americanos.**

Practiquen la conversación. *(Practice the conversation.)*

—¿Son ustedes americanos?
—Sí, somos americanos.
—¿Son ustedes alumnos?
—Sí, somos alumnos. Y somos alumnos serios.
—¿En qué escuela son ustedes alumnos?
—Somos alumnos en la Escuela Jorge Wáshington. Y ustedes, ¿son alumnas?
—Sí, somos alumnas en la Escuela Martin Luther King.

Completen según la conversación. *(Complete based on the conversation.)*

Los muchachos __1__ americanos. Ellos __2__ alumnos. __3__ alumnos muy serios. __4__ alumnos buenos. __5__ alumnos en la Escuela Jorge Wáshington. Las muchachas __6__ americanas también. __7__ alumnas en la Escuela Martin Luther King.

17 **Él, ella y yo** Contesten. *(Answer.)*

1. ¿Son ustedes amigos?
2. ¿Son ustedes alumnos serios?
3. ¿Son ustedes graciosos?
4. ¿En qué escuela son ustedes alumnos?
5. ¿Son ustedes alumnos en la misma clase de español o en clases diferentes?
6. ¿Son ustedes alumnos buenos en español?

Estructura

3 PRACTICE

¿Cómo lo digo?

16 Have students work in pairs and dramatize this conversation. Have them read with as much expression as possible. Note that the conversation acquaints students with the **somos** response to **son Uds.** questions. After a few pairs of students have read the conversation aloud, call on individuals to complete the narrative that follows.

17 Have students close their books and ask them the questions yourself. This activity has students supply answers to questions with **Uds.** They hear **son** and must answer with **somos.**

LEVELING

E: Activity 16

A: Activity 17

Chapter Projects

Amigos hispanos

Have students begin a correspondence with a Spanish or Latin American pen pal. By the end of this chapter they will be able to say something about themselves and about the courses they are taking in school.

Answers to ¿Cómo lo digo?

16

1. son
2. son
3. Son
4. Son
5. Son
6. son
7. Son

17

1. Sí, (No, no) somos amigos.
2. Sí, (No, no) somos alumnos serios.
3. Sí, (No, no) somos graciosos.
4. Somos alumnos en la Escuela ___.
5. Somos alumnos en la misma clase de español. (Somos alumnos en clases diferentes.)
6. Sí, (No, no) somos alumnos buenos en español.

Estructura

18 Have students do Activity 18 as a group activity.

19 Call on an individual to supply the responses to about three sentences in Activity 19 before going on to another student. Note that this activity makes students use all forms of **ser.**

Writing Development

After going over Activity 19, have students read it silently. Then have them close their books and rewrite it in their own words.

Learning from Photos

(page 56) The Dominican Republic occupies the eastern two-thirds of the island of Hispaniola. The western section is Haiti.

18 **¿Qué son ustedes?** Formen preguntas según el modelo. *(Form questions based on the model.)*

cubanos

—María y José, ¿son ustedes americanos o cubanos?
—Somos cubanos.

1. chilenos / mexicanos
2. bajos / altos
3. morenos / rubios

19 **Historieta El amigo de Carlos**
Completen con **ser.** *(Complete with* ser.*)*

Yo __1__ un amigo de Carlos. Carlos __2__ muy simpático. Y él __3__ gracioso. Carlos y yo __4__ dominicanos. __5__ de la República Dominicana.

La República Dominicana __6__ parte de una isla en el mar Caribe. Nosotros __7__ alumnos en un colegio en Santo Domingo. Santo Domingo __8__ la capital de la República Dominicana. Nosotros __9__ alumnos de inglés. La profesora de inglés __10__ la señora Drake. Ella __11__ americana.

La clase de inglés __12__ bastante interesante. Nosotros __13__ muy buenos en inglés. Nosotros __14__ muy inteligentes.

¿Y ustedes? Ustedes __15__ americanos, ¿no? ¿De dónde __16__ ustedes? ¿__17__ ustedes alumnos en una escuela secundaria? ¿__18__ ustedes alumnos de español?

La República Dominicana

Answers to ¿Cómo lo digo?

18 *Answers will vary but may include:*

1. Sara y Ángel, ¿son Uds. americanos o mexicanos? Somos americanos.
2. María y Andrés, ¿son Uds. bajos o altos? Somos altos.
3. Juan y José, ¿son Uds. morenos o rubios? Somos rubios.

19

1. soy
2. es
3. es
4. somos
5. Somos
6. es
7. somos
8. es
9. somos
10. es
11. es
12. es
13. somos
14. somos
15. son
16. son
17. Son
18. Son

20 **¿De qué nacionalidad son?** Work in groups of four. Two of you get together and choose a city from the map below. The other two will guess where you are from. Take turns. Follow the model.

Estructura

20 Since students may not be very familiar with the geography of the Spanish-speaking world, it is suggested that you point out these cities and countries on a larger map, or have them open their books to the maps on pages xxxi–xxxii. Another option is to use Map Transparencies M 3 and M 4 as students do the activity.

LEVELING

A: Activities 18, 20

C: Activity 19

Answers to ¿Cómo lo digo?

20 *Answers will vary but may include:*

—¿Son Uds. argentinos?
—Sí, somos de Buenos Aires.

—¿Son Uds. colombianos?
—Sí, somos de Santafé de Bogotá.

—¿Son Uds. cubanos?
—Sí, somos de La Habana.

—¿Son Uds. venezolanos?
—Sí, somos de Caracas.

—¿Son Uds. puertorriqueños?
—Sí, somos de San Juan.

—¿Son Uds. americanos?
—Sí, somos de Miami.

—¿Son Uds. chilenos?
—Sí, somos de Santiago.

—¿Son Uds. mexicanos?
—Sí, somos de la Ciudad de México.

Estructura

1 PREPARATION

Bellringer Review

Use BRR Transparency 2.5 or write the following on the board.
Write the following in the plural.
1. **El muchacho es mexicano.**
2. **Yo soy alumno.**
3. **Ella es morena.**

2 PRESENTATION

La hora

¡OJO! It is recommended that you teach a few of these time expressions each day rather than present them all at once. A possible plan is:
Day 1: **Es la una. Son las dos,** etc. (hours)
Day 2: **Es la una y cinco. Son las dos y diez,** etc. (after the hour)
Day 3: **Es la una menos cinco. Son las dos menos diez,** etc. (before the hour)
Day 4: **Son las dos y media, y cuarto,** etc.
Day 5: **¿A qué hora es… ? Es a las…**

Step 1 Have students open their books to page 58. Have them repeat the time shown on each clock after you.

Step 2 Introduce the question **¿Qué hora es?** Then ask the time for each clock.

Step 3 Introduce the concept **¿A qué hora?** to indicate at what time an event takes place. Contrast this concept with simply asking what time it is.

La hora
Telling time

1. To find out the time, you ask:
¿Qué hora es?

2. To tell time, you say:

Es la una.

Son las dos.

Son las diez.

Son las doce.

Es el mediodía.

Es la medianoche.

Es la una y diez.

Son las tres y cinco.

Son las cuatro y veinticinco.

Son las cinco menos veinte.

Son las seis menos diez.

Son las diez menos cinco.

Son las dos y cuarto.

Son las siete menos cuarto.

Son las seis y media.

Reaching All Students

For the Younger Students
Have students draw pictures of themselves doing their various daily activities. Have them label the drawings with the time of day that they do each activity.

3. To indicate A.M. and P.M. in Spanish, you use the following expressions.

Son las ocho de la mañana.

Son las tres de la tarde.

Son las once de la noche.

4. To ask and tell at what time something (such as a party) takes place you say:

—¿A qué hora es la fiesta?
—La fiesta es a las nueve.

¿Cómo lo digo?

21 **¿Qué hora es?** Digan la hora. *(Tell the time on each clock.)*

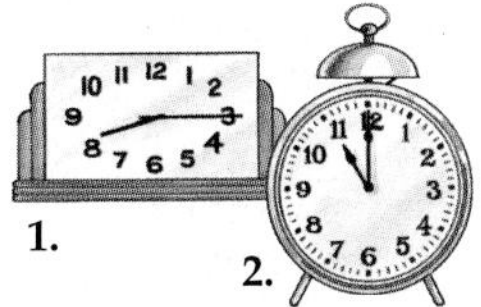
1. 2.

3.

4. 5. 6.

22 **El horario escolar** Digan la hora de la clase. *(Tell the time of each class.)*

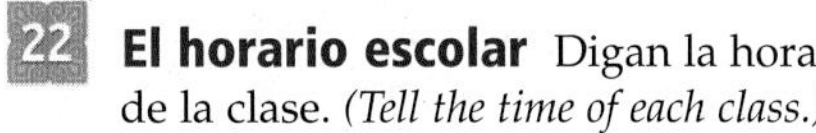

Nombre: Diana A. Martínez Tel.: 284-1519
Centro de Estudios: "Externado San Jose"
Materia: Lenguaje y literatura

	Lunes	Martes	Miércoles	Jueves	Viernes	Sábado
1:00	ed. Fisica	C.S.M.A	Matematica	Sociales	For. Cristiana	
1:45	C.S.M.A	Leng. Lit	Leng. Lit	Leng. Lit	Leng. Lit.	
2:30	Recreo	Recreo	Recreo	Recreo	Recreo	
2:45	Ingles	For. Cristiana	Ingles	Ingles.	Matematicas	
3:30	Sociales	ed. Fisica	Sociales	Matematica	Mecanografia	
4:15	Recreo	Recreo	Recreo	Recreo	Recreo	
4:45	Matematica	Sociales	Mecanografia	C.S.M.A	Sociales	
5:30	Leng. Lit	Matematica	C.S.M.A	Mecanografia	C.S.M.A	

23 **¿A qué hora** Find out from a partner what time he or she has a particular class. He or she will respond with the time. Take turns.

For more practice telling time, do Activity 2 on page H3 at the end of this book.

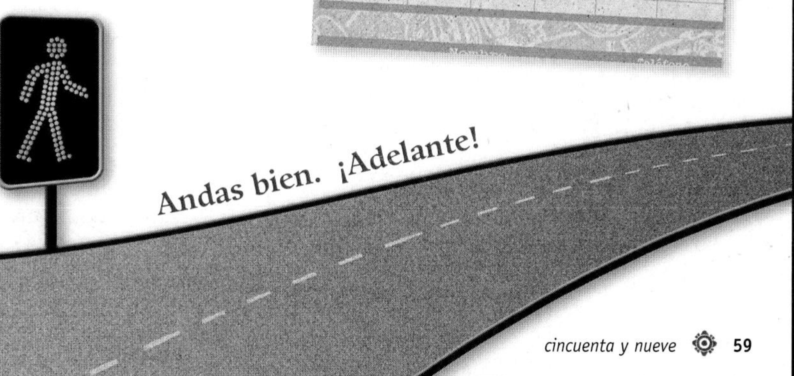

Estructura

3 PRACTICE

¿Cómo lo digo?

Teaching Tip
Use a toy clock or make your own cardboard clock with movable hands. Using the clock, ask **¿Qué hora es?** Repeat the question as many times as you can and monitor student responses. Then have a student ask the question and have another respond.

21 and 22 Students can do these activities in pairs. In Activity 21, Student 1 will ask: **¿Qué hora es?** while pointing to each clock. In Activity 22, Student 1 will ask: **¿A qué hora es la clase de... ?** In both cases, Student 2 will respond accordingly. Have students reverse roles and repeat the activities.

UN POCO MÁS This *InfoGap* Activity will allow students to practice in pairs. The activity should be very manageable for them, since all vocabulary and structures are familiar to them.

¡Adelante!
At this point in the chapter, students have learned all the vocabulary and structure necessary to complete the chapter. The conversation and cultural readings that follow recycle all the material learned up to this point.

ANSWERS TO ¿Cómo lo digo?

21

1. Son las ocho y cuarto.
2. Son las once.
3. Son las cinco y media.
4. Es la una menos cuarto.
5. Son las dos y veinticinco.
6. Son las cuatro menos diez.

22 *Answers will vary according to the day students choose. One possibility could be the following:*

La clase de educación física es a la una.
La clase de C.S.M.A. es a las dos menos cuarto.
El recreo es a las dos y media.
La clase de inglés es a las tres menos cuarto.
La clase de (ciencias) sociales es a las tres y media.
El recreo es a las cuatro y cuarto.
La clase de matemáticas es a las cinco menos cuarto.
La clase de lengua y literatura es a las cinco y media.
La clase de mecanografía es a las cinco menos cuarto.

Conversación

1 PREPARATION

Resource Manager

Audio Activities TE, pages 19–20
Audio CD 2

Bellringer Review

Use BRR Transparency 2.6 or write the following on the board.
Write down the times of your classes. Follow the model.
La clase de ___ es a las ___.

2 PRESENTATION

Step 1 Tell students they are going to hear a conversation between Patricio and Manuel. Have students repeat the conversation after you once or twice, or have them listen to Audio CD 2. Begin with the whole class and then have individual students repeat.

Step 2 Call on pairs of students to present the conversation to the class.

FUN-FACTS

Once upon a time, Coyoacán was a suburb of Mexico City. It has now been incorporated into the city proper.

Conversación

¿De qué nacionalidad son ustedes?

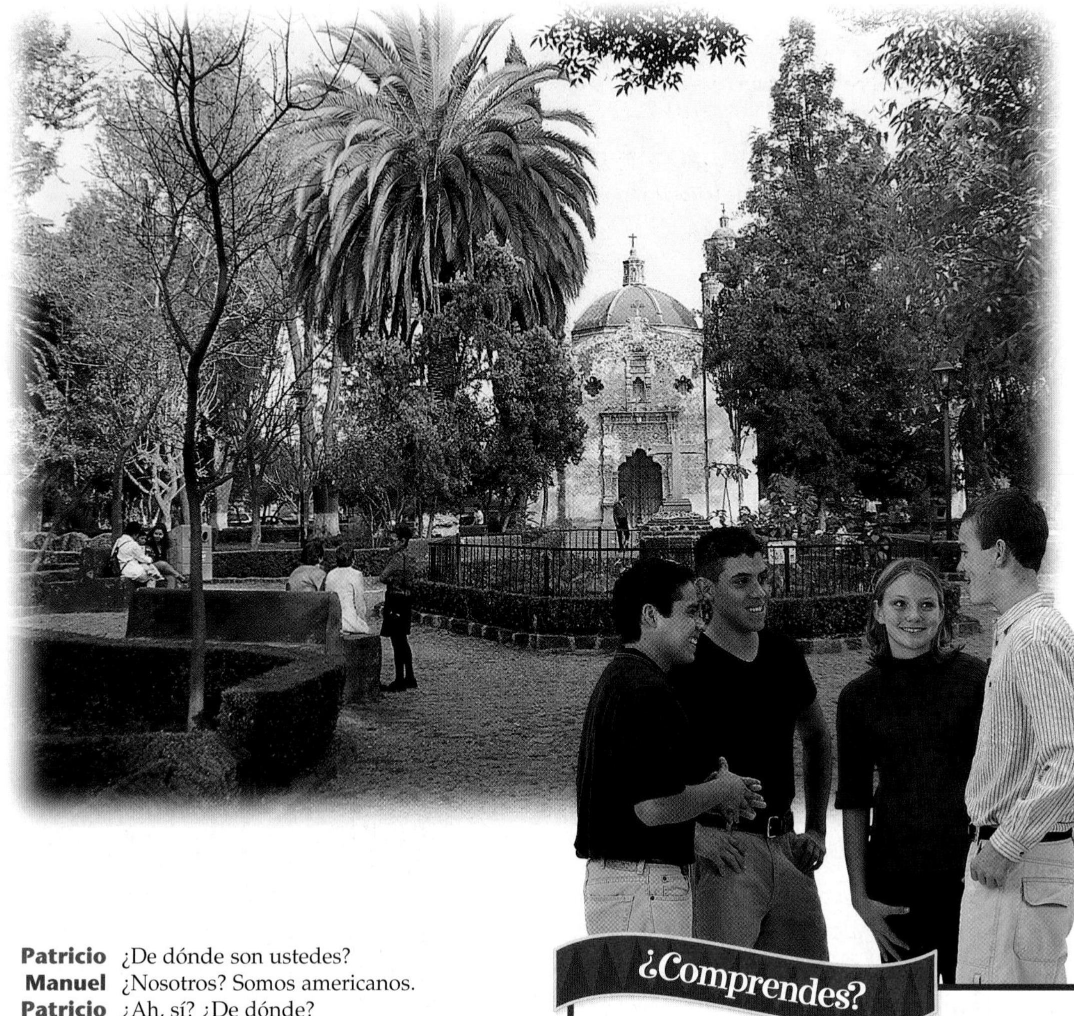

Patricio ¿De dónde son ustedes?
Manuel ¿Nosotros? Somos americanos.
Patricio ¿Ah, sí? ¿De dónde?
Manuel Somos de Tejas, de San Antonio. ¿De qué nacionalidad son ustedes?
Patricio Somos mexicanos. Somos de Coyoacán.
Manuel ¿Coyoacán?
Patricio Sí, es una colonia de la Ciudad de México, la capital.

¿Comprendes?

Contesten. *(Answer.)*

1. ¿De dónde son los muchachos americanos?
2. ¿De dónde son los muchachos mexicanos?
3. ¿Cuál es la capital de México?
4. ¿Cuál es una ciudad en el estado de Tejas?
5. ¿Cuál es una parte de la Ciudad de México?

ANSWERS TO ¿Comprendes?

1. Los muchachos americanos son de Tejas (de San Antonio).
2. Los muchachos mexicanos son de Coyoacán.
3. La capital de México es la Ciudad de México.
4. San Antonio es una ciudad en Tejas.
5. Coyoacán es una parte de la Ciudad de México.

About the Spanish Language

The word **colonia** is used in Mexico City to refer to a section of the city—**Colonia de Chapultepec, Colonia de Coyoacán.**

Vamos a hablar más

A **En México** Work in groups of four. Two of you are visiting Mexico and you meet two Mexican students in a café. Find out as much about each other and your schools as you can.

Guanajuato, México

B *Juego* **¿Qué clase es?** Work with a classmate. He or she gives you a one-sentence description of a class. Guess what class it is. If you're wrong, your partner will give you another hint. Continue until you guess the class being described. Take turns.

Pronunciación

Las vocales e, i

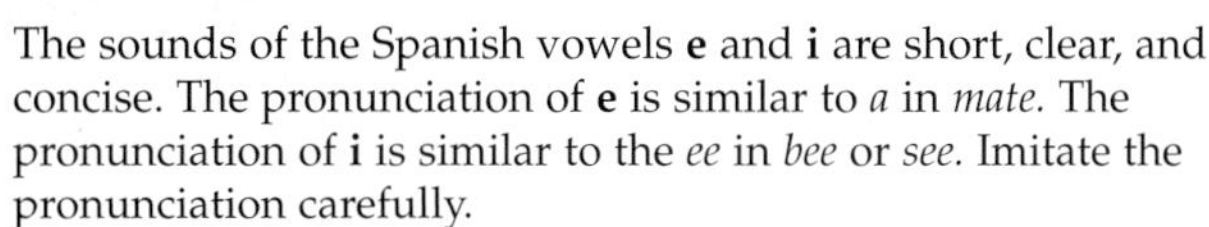

The sounds of the Spanish vowels **e** and **i** are short, clear, and concise. The pronunciation of **e** is similar to *a* in *mate*. The pronunciation of **i** is similar to the *ee* in *bee* or *see*. Imitate the pronunciation carefully.

e	i
Elena	**Isabel**
peso	**Inés**

Repeat the following sentences.

Elena es una amiga de Felipe.
Inés es tímida.
Sí, Isabel es italiana.

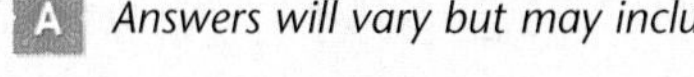

Answers to Vamos a hablar más

A *Answers will vary but may include:*

—¿De dónde son Uds.?
—Somos de Los Ángeles.
—¿De qué nacionalidad son Uds.?
—Nosotros somos mexicanos. Somos de Guanajuato.
—¿En qué escuela son Uds. alumnos?
—Somos alumnos en la Escuela ___, en Guanajuato.

B *Answers will vary but may include:*

—Es una clase difícil.
—Es la clase de álgebra.
—No. La profesora es muy interesante.
—Ah, ¡es la clase de español!

Conversación

3 PRACTICE

Vamos a hablar más

A and **B** You may have students do one or both of these activities. Allow them to select the activity they wish to take part in.

Pronunciación

Step 1 Have students repeat the vowels **e** and **i** very carefully. English speakers tend to make them into a diphthong or to produce the "shwa" sound.

Step 2 Using Pronunciation Transparency P 2, model the word **Italia.** Have students say it in unison and individually.

Step 3 Now lead students through the presentation on page 61, modeling the words and phrases.

Step 4 For additional pronunciation practice, you may wish to play the Pronunciation section on Audio CD 2.

Step 5 The sentences on page 61 can also be used for dictation.

Glencoe Technology

CD-ROM

On the CD-ROM, students can watch a dramatization of this conversation. They can then play the role of either one of the characters and record themselves in the conversation.

LEVELING

E: Conversation

Lecturas culturales

Resource Manager

Audio Activities TE, page 21
Audio CD 2

National Standards

Cultures
This reading and the related activities on pages 62–63 about the Hispanic population in the United States give students an understanding of the importance of learning Spanish.

Communities
This selection familiarizes students with Hispanic influence in communities in the United States.

Geography Connection

Due to both Spanish and Mexican influences, there are many places in the United States with Spanish names. This is particularly true in many parts of the Southwest, but it is not limited to this area. Some examples are: Arizona, Colorado, New Mexico, Albuquerque, Pueblo, El Paso, Laredo, Los Angeles, San Francisco, Nevada, Sierra Nevada, Florida, San Agustín.

PRESENTATION

Pre-reading

Step 1 Have students locate Pueblo, Colorado, on a map.

Step 2 Show students a map of the United States. Have them point out places with Spanish names.

Step 3 Read and discuss the Reading Strategy on page 62.

Step 4 Have students scan the reading quickly and silently.

Lecturas culturales

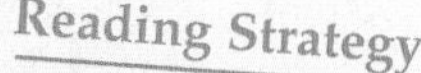

Reading Strategy

Using titles and subtitles Look at titles and subtitles before you begin to read. They will usually help you know what a reading selection will be about. Having an idea of what a reading will be about will help you understand better as you read.

El español en Estados Unidos

Mexicanoamericanos

¡Hola! Somos Alejandro Chávez y Guadalupe Garza. Somos alumnos en una escuela secundaria de Pueblo, Colorado. Somos alumnos en una escuela secundaria americana. Pero para nosotros el español no es una lengua extranjera[1]. ¿Por qué[2]? Porque nosotros somos de ascendencia[3] mexicana. Somos mexicanoamericanos.

[1]extranjera *foreign*
[2]¿Por qué? *Why?*
[3]ascendencia *background, descent*

Jóvenes de ascendencia mexicana

Learning from Photos

(page 62) Have students look at this photo and describe the boy and girl in their own words.

Miami, la Florida

Jóvenes de ascendencia cubana

Cubanoamericanos

Nosotros somos Raúl Ugarte y Marta Dávila. Somos de Miami, en la Florida. Como muchas personas en Miami, somos de ascendencia cubana. Somos cubanoamericanos.

En Estados Unidos hay unos cuarenta millones de hispanohablantes[4]. El español es una lengua muy importante en Estados Unidos.

[4]hispanohablantes *Spanish speakers*

¿Comprendes?

A Alejandro Chávez y Guadalupe Garza

Contesten. *(Answer.)*

1. ¿Quiénes son Alejandro Chávez y Guadalupe Garza?
2. ¿Dónde son alumnos?
3. ¿De dónde son ellos?
4. Para Alejandro y Guadalupe, ¿es el español una lengua extranjera?
5. ¿Por qué no? ¿Qué son ellos?

B Raúl Ugarte y Marta Dávila

Corrijan. *(Correct the false statements.)*

1. Raúl Ugarte y Marta Dávila son de ascendencia mexicana.
2. Ellos son mexicanoamericanos.
3. Ellos son de San Antonio, Tejas.
4. Hay unos cuarenta millones de hispanohablantes en Cuba.

Lecturas culturales

Reading

Step 1 Have students close their books as you read the selection for them. Then have them listen as they follow along in their books.

Step 2 Ask questions from Activity A as you read the selection. Call on a student to read several sentences. Ask questions after every three sentences.

Post-reading

Have students do the activities in the **¿Comprendes?** section. Call on several students to give, in their own words, some information about Spanish speakers in the United States.

LEVELING

E: Reading, Activity A

A: Activity B

Answers to ¿Comprendes?

A

1. Alejandro Chávez y Guadalupe Garza son alumnos.
2. Son alumnos en una escuela secundaria americana.
3. Son de Pueblo, Colorado.
4. El español no es una lengua extranjera para ellos.
5. No es una lengua extranjera porque son de ascendencia mexicana. Son mexicanoamericanos.

B

1. Raúl Ugarte y Marta Dávila son de ascendencia cubana.
2. Ellos son cubanoamericanos.
3. Ellos son de Miami, en la Florida.
4. Hay unos cuarenta millones de hispanohablantes en Estados Unidos.

Lectura opcional 1

National Standards

Communities
This selection familiarizes students with the importance of the Spanish-speaking population in the United States.

PRESENTATION

¡OJO! This reading on San Antonio is optional. You may skip it completely, have the entire class read it, have only several students read it, or assign it for extra credit.

Step 1 Have students read the short selection quickly and then respond to the **sí / no** questions in Activity A.

History Connection

Domingo Terán de los Ríos arrived in what is now San Antonio in 1691. He called it San Antonio because he arrived on Saint Anthony's Day. In 1718 a Franciscan priest established a mission called San Antonio de Valero. In order to boost the non-Indian population, Spain allowed fifty-five colonists from the Canary Islands to emigrate to San Antonio. San Antonio grew and became the capital of Spanish Texas. The Misión San Antonio became a military garrison. After the Mexican Revolution of 1821, San Antonio became a part of the Republic of Mexico. When López de Santa Ana seized the Mexican presidency and abolished the constitution, many Texans, both Anglo and Hispanic, refused to recognize his dictatorship. That led to the famous Battle of the Alamo and the declaration of Texas' independence from Mexico.

Lectura opcional 1

San Antonio

San Antonio es una ciudad[1] muy bonita de Tejas. Es una ciudad muy histórica. Es la ciudad favorita de muchos turistas. San Antonio es una ciudad bilingüe. Hay mucha gente[2] de ascendencia mexicana en San Antonio. Hay muchos mexicanoamericanos.

[1]ciudad *city*
[2]gente *people*

El Álamo, San Antonio

El río, San Antonio

¿Comprendes?

A ¿Cómo es San Antonio?
Contesten con **sí** o **no**.
(Answer with sí *or* no.*)*

1. San Antonio es una ciudad bastante fea.
2. Hay monumentos históricos en San Antonio.
3. San Antonio es una ciudad de México.
4. Hay muchos hispanohablantes en San Antonio.
5. Hay muchos mexicanoamericanos en San Antonio.

B En español, por favor.
Busquen las palabras afines en la lectura.
(Find the following cognates in the reading.)

1. favorite
2. historic
3. bilingual
4. tourists

Answers to ¿Comprendes?

A

1. No, San Antonio es una ciudad muy bonita.
2. Sí, hay monumentos históricos en San Antonio.
3. No, San Antonio es una ciudad de Tejas.
4. Sí, hay muchos hispanohablantes en San Antonio.
5. Sí, hay muchos mexicanoamericanos en San Antonio.

B

1. favorita
2. histórica
3. bilingüe
4. turistas

Lectura opcional 2

Coyoacán, México

Coyoacán

La Ciudad de México es hoy día[1] la ciudad más grande del mundo[2]. Coyoacán es una colonia en la zona sur de la ciudad. Es una colonia bonita y tranquila. Es elegante también. Muchos residentes o habitantes de Coyoacán son personas famosas.

[1]hoy día *these days*
[2]mundo *world*

¿Comprendes?

A La Ciudad de México

Completen. *(Complete.)*

1. ____ es la ciudad más grande del mundo.
2. ____ es una colonia de la Ciudad de México.
3. Coyoacán es una colonia en la zona ____ de la ciudad.
4. Hay muchas personas ____ en Coyoacán.

B En español, por favor. Busquen las palabras afines en la lectura. *(Find the following cognates in the reading.)*

1. zone
2. tranquil, calm
3. elegant
4. residents
5. inhabitants

El Museo de Frida Kahlo, Coyoacán

Lectura opcional 2

PRESENTATION

¡OJO! This reading on Coyoacán is optional. You may skip it completely, have the entire class read it, have only several students read it, or assign it for extra credit.

Step 1 Have students read the short selection quickly; then have them do the **¿Comprendes?** activities.

FUN-FACTS

Coyoacán is in the southern part of Mexico City. It was originally settled by the Toltecas in the tenth century. Bernal Díaz del Castillo said that at the time of the conquest there were six thousand homes in Coyoacán. It was here that Cortés set up headquarters during his siege of Tenochtitlán.

Contemporary Coyoacán is a charming area with buildings of traditional colonial architecture and an animated street life. Some of its famous inhabitants have been:

- Miguel de la Madrid, president of Mexico
- José Clemente Orozco, muralist
- Dolores del Río, film star
- Frida Kahlo, artist
- Elena Poniatowska, writer

ANSWERS TO ¿Comprendes?

A

1. La Ciudad de México
2. Coyoacán
3. sur
4. famosas

B

1. zona
2. tranquila
3. elegante
4. residentes
5. habitantes

LEVELING

A: Readings 1, 2

Conexiones

National Standards

Connections
This reading about the different ethnic groups in the Spanish-speaking world establishes a connection with another discipline—social sciences. It allows students to draw from material they have most probably learned in their social studies classes. At the same time it increases their knowledge by presenting the specific ethnicities of Latin America.

¡OJO! The readings in the **Conexiones** section are optional. They focus on the major disciplines taught in schools and universities. The vocabulary is useful for discussing such topics as history, literature, art, economics, business, science, etc. You may choose any of the following ways to do the readings in the **Conexiones** sections.

Independent reading Have students read the selections and do the post-reading activities as homework, which you collect. This option is least intrusive on class time and requires a minimum of teacher involvement.

Homework with in-class follow-up Assign the readings and post-reading activities as homework. Review and discuss the material in class the next day.

Intensive in-class activity This option includes a pre-reading vocabulary presentation, in-class reading and discussion, assignment of the activities for homework, and a discussion of the assignment in class the following day.

Conexiones

Las ciencias sociales

La sociología

Sociology is the study of society in all its aspects. A society is composed of many groups. All of us belong to a number of groups. We belong to a family group, a language group, and an ethnic or racial group.

The large Spanish-speaking world is one of great diversity. There are many ethnic groups living in Spain and in Latin America. Let's take a look at some of these groups.

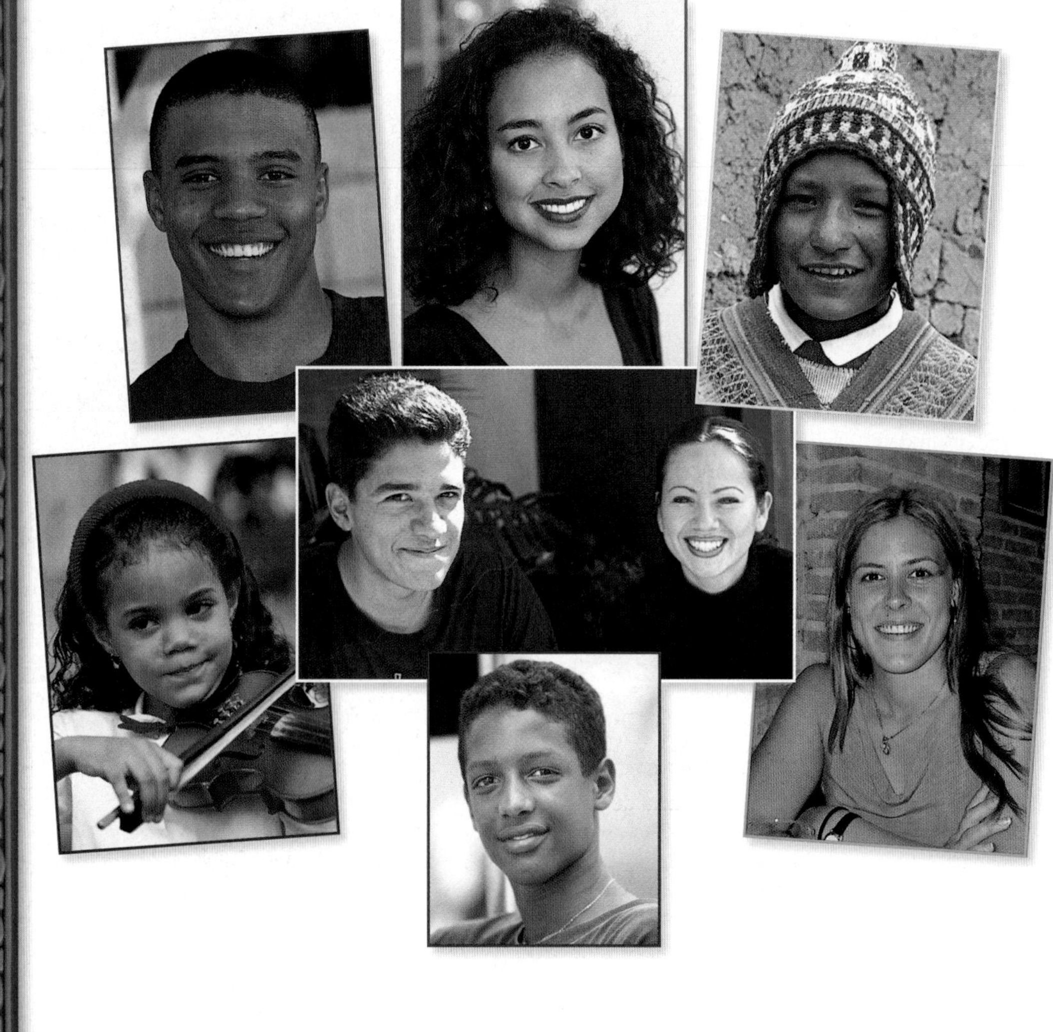

LEVELING
A: Reading

Grupos étnicos de Latinoamérica

En Latinoamérica hay muchos grupos étnicos. ¿Cuáles son los grupos étnicos de Latinoamérica?

Influencia africana

En la región del Caribe hay mucha influencia africana. En Puerto Rico, Cuba, la República Dominicana, Panamá y en la costa norte de la América del Sur, la influencia negra es notable. Hay mucha gente[1] de ascendencia africana. Hay también mucha gente de raza mixta—de sangre[2] blanca y negra.

Influencia india o indígena

En México, Guatemala y la región andina—de los Andes—hay muchos indios. En Ecuador, Perú y Bolivia, hay muchos descendientes de los incas. En México y Guatemala hay muchos descendientes de los mayas. Hay también muchos mestizos, personas con una mezcla[3] de sangre india y blanca.

Criollos

¿Y quiénes son los criollos? Los criollos son los blancos nacidos[4] en las colonias—los españoles nacidos en América.

[1]gente *people* [2]sangre *blood* [3]mezcla *mixture* [4]nacidos *born*

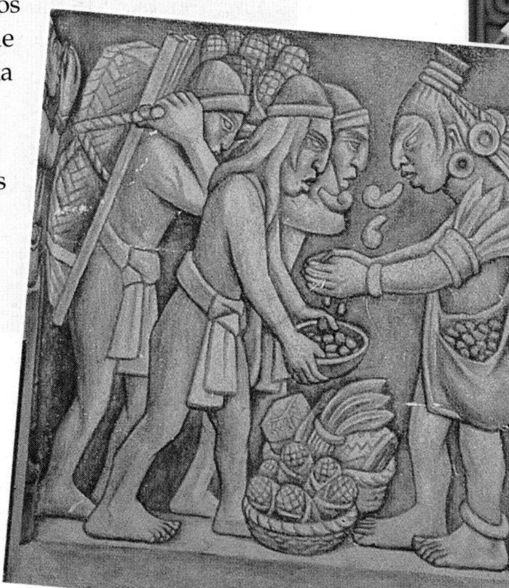

La almendra del cacao de Diego Rivera

¿Comprendes?

A En español Busquen las palabras afines en la lectura. *(Find the cognates in the reading.)*

B La palabra, por favor. Pareen. *(Match.)*

1. área de las Américas donde el español es la lengua oficial
2. una persona de África
3. la región de los Andes
4. los indios del Perú, Ecuador y Bolivia
5. los indios de México y Guatemala
6. una persona con una mezcla de sangre india y blanca

a. mestizo
b. Latinoamérica
c. africano
d. andina
e. descendientes de los incas
f. descendientes de los mayas

Conexiones

PRESENTATION

Las ciencias sociales
La sociología

Step 1 Have students look at the photographs on page 66 of the many types of people that make up the population of Latin America. You may wish to give the information in the introduction in Spanish. See if students can understand.

La sociología es el estudio de la sociedad en todos sus aspectos. En una sociedad hay muchos grupos. Todos somos miembros de varios grupos—un grupo familiar, un grupo lingüístico, un grupo étnico o racial.

En España y Latinoamérica hay muchos grupos étnicos.

Step 2 Have students read the selection silently on their own.

Step 3 Then have them go over the **¿Comprendes?** activities very quickly. Students should be able to recognize the cognates and easily understand the reading selection. However, they should not be expected to learn the vocabulary or produce it, since it is receptive vocabulary only.

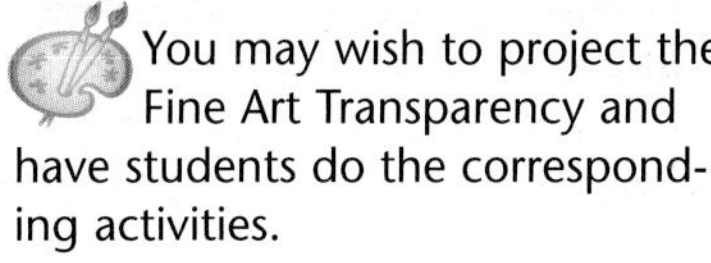

Art Connection

You may wish to project the Fine Art Transparency and have students do the corresponding activities.

Answers to ¿Comprendes?

A *Answers will vary but may include:*

grupos, étnicos, región, influencia, africana, notable, descendientes, colonias

B

1. b
2. c
3. d
4. e
5. f
6. a

¡Te toca a ti!

Use what you have learned

Recycling

These activities allow students to use the vocabulary and structure from this chapter in completely open-ended, real-life situations. They also give students the opportunity to reuse the vocabulary and structure from Chapter 1.

PRESENTATION

Encourage students to say as much as possible when they do these activities. Tell them not to be afraid to make mistakes, since the goal of the activities is real-life communication. If someone in the group makes an error, allow the others to politely correct him or her. Let students choose the activities they would like to do.

LEVELING

These activities encompass all three levels. All students will be able to do them at a sophistication level commensurate with their ability in Spanish. Some students will be able to speak for several minutes, and others may be able to give just a few sentences. This is to be expected when students are functioning completely on their own generating their own language to the best of their ability.

¡Te toca a ti!

Use what you have learned

1 Nosotros(as)

✔ *Describe yourself and someone else*

Work with a classmate. Together prepare a speech that you are going to present to the class. To help you organize your presentation, use the following as a guide.

- tell who you are
- tell where you're from
- give the name of your school
- describe one of your classes

2 La escuela ideal

✔ *Talk about school*

Work with a classmate. Describe what for each of you is an ideal school. Say as much as you can about the teachers, classes, and students.

Salón de clase, San Miguel de Allende, México

*** LICEO SALVADORENO ***

INFORME DE NOTAS

22 - MANUEL ERNESTO MARTINEZ CORTEZ

PROF. RODRIGO RAMIREZ SANTOS

TERCERA AREA

Nombre materia	1ra. Area	2da. Area	Act 10%	Activ. 40%	P.O. 50%	Nota	30%	3ra. Area	Nota Acum.	Obs.
EDUCACION EN LA FE	0.9	1.3	10	34	44	88	26.4	2.6	4.8	
LENGUAJE	1.2	1.3	9	31	46	86	25.8	2.6	5.1	
ESTUDIOS SOCIALES	1.0	1.2	8	33	46	87	26.1	2.6	4.8	
INGLES	1.4	1.2	10	38	49	97	29.1	2.9	5.5	
MATEMATICAS	1.2	1.4	10	37	40	87	26.1	2.6	5.2	
CIENCIA,SALUD Y MEDIO A	1.3	1.4	9	38	36	83	24.9	2.5	5.2	
EDUCACION ESTETICA	1.2	1.2	9	36	50	95	28.5	2.9	5.3	
EDUCACION FISICA	1.4	1.4	10	40	50	100	30.0	3.0	5.8	
MECANOGRAFIA	1.2	1.3	10	31	45	86	25.8	2.6	5.1	
COMPUTACION	1.3	1.3	9	36	50	95	28.5	2.9	5.5	

FIRMA ENCARGADO

ANSWERS TO ¡Te toca a ti!

1 *Answers will include the following:*

Soy *(nombre).*
Soy de *(ciudad).*
Soy alumno en la Escuela ____.
La clase de ____ es ____.

2 *Answers will vary. Allow students to say as much as they can. They will use several forms of the verb* ser *and adjectives that describe their courses.*

¡Te toca a ti!

3 Un correo electrónico

✔ Write about your classes and friends

Answer an e-mail message from a student in Colombia who wants to know about your life in the United States. Give him or her as many details as possible about school, classes, and friends.

San Andrés, Colombia

4 Clases y profesores

You've been in school for about a month. You've had a chance to get to know what your courses are like and to become familiar with your teachers. Create a journal entry in which you write about your classes and your teachers. Try to write about your classes—the days and times of each, whether there are many or few students, whether the class is big or small, what the class is like, who the teacher is, and what he or she is like. When you have finished, reread your journal entry. Did you discover anything about your courses or your teachers that you hadn't thought of before?

Writing Strategy

Keeping a journal There are many kinds of journals you can keep, each having a different purpose. One type of journal is the kind in which you write about daily events and record your thoughts and impressions about these events. It's almost like "thinking out loud." By keeping such a journal, you may find that you discover something new that you were not aware of.

Writing Development

Have students keep a notebook or portfolio containing their best written work from each chapter. These selected writings can be based on assignments from the Student Textbook and the Workbook. The two activities on page 69 are examples of writing assignments that may be included in each student's portfolio. On page 18 in the Workbook, students will begin to develop an organized autobiography **(Mi autobiografía).** These workbook pages may also become a part of their portfolio.

Writing Strategy

Keeping a journal Have students read the Writing Strategy on page 69. If they need help getting started, have them use the vocabulary list on page 73.

Career Connection

Teaching is an excellent way to use one's knowledge of a foreign language and culture. Have your students interview you about the education and training that was necessary for you to obtain your position. Be sure to mention your travel and study abroad experiences or any specialized workshops that you attended. At this level, the interview will be in English.

Answers to ¡Te toca a ti!

3 *Answers will vary but may include:*

Las clases son interesantes. Los amigos son buenos. La clase de biología es difícil. La clase de español es fácil. La profesora de español es muy seria. Pero el profesor de álgebra es muy cómico.

Resource Manager

Communication Transparency C 2
Quizzes, pages 6–10
Performance Assessment, Task 2
Tests, pages 15–26
Situation Cards, Chapter 2
ExamView® Pro, Chapter 2
Maratón mental Videoquiz, Chapter 2

Assessment

This is a pre-test for students to take before you administer the chapter test. Note that each section is cross-referenced so students can easily find the material they have to review in case they made errors. You may use Assessment Answers Transparency A 2 to do the assessment in class, or you may assign this for homework. You can correct the assessment yourself, or you may prefer to project the answers on the overhead in class.

Glencoe Technology

MINDJOGGER VHS/DVD

You may wish to help your students prepare for the chapter test by playing the MindJogger game show. Teams will compete against each other to review chapter vocabulary and structure and sharpen listening comprehension skills.

Assessment

Vocabulario

To review **Palabras 1**, turn to pages 44–45.

1 ¿Sí o no? *(True or false?)*

1. Hay muchos alumnos en una clase pequeña.
2. Una clase aburrida es muy interesante.
3. Marta y Tomás son alumnos en el Colegio Rubén Torres. Son alumnos en la misma escuela.

2 Den lo contrario. *(Give the opposite.)*

4. difícil
5. interesante
6. pequeño

3 Identifiquen. *(Identify.)*

¿Qué curso es?

To review **Palabras 2**, turn to pages 48–49.

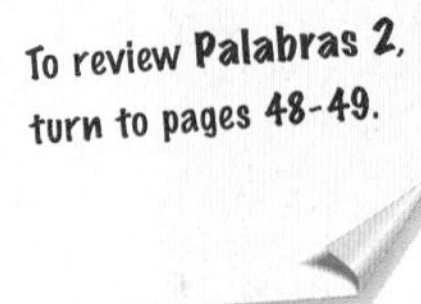
7.

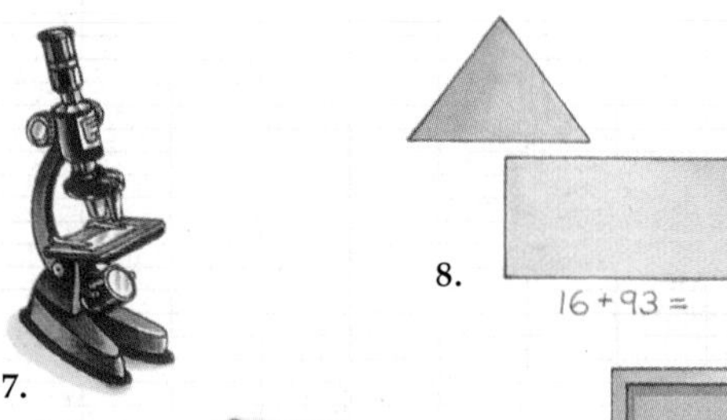

8.

9.

10.

Estructura

To review plurals, turn to page 52.

4 Completen con el plural. *(Complete with the plural.)*

11. El alumno es muy inteligente.
    ____ alumno__ ____ muy inteligente__.
12. La amiga de Carlos es puertorriqueña.
    ____ amiga__ de Carlos ____ puertorriqueña__.
13. El curso de matemáticas es fácil.
    ____ curso__ de matemáticas ____ fácil__.
14. La muchacha rubia es chilena.
    ____ muchacha__ rubia__ ____ chilena__.

Answers to Assessment

1
1. No
2. No
3. Sí

2
4. fácil
5. aburrido
6. grande

3
7. la química
8. las matemáticas
9. la geografía
10. el español

4
11. Los alumnos son muy inteligentes.
12. Las amigas de Carlos son puertorriqueñas.
13. Los cursos de matemáticas son fáciles.
14. Las muchachas rubias son chilenas.

5 **Completen con ser.** *(Complete with* ser.*)*

15. ¿De qué nacionalidad ____ ustedes?
16. Ustedes ____ alumnos en la misma escuela, ¿no?
17. Sí, (nosotros) ____ alumnos en el Colegio Hidalgo.
18. Nosotros ____ mexicanos.

To review **ser**, turn to page 54.

Cultura

6 **Completen.** *(Complete.)*

19–20. Hay muchos mexicanoamericanos y cubanoamericanos en Estados Unidos. Los mexicanoamericanos son de ascendencia ____ y los cubanoamericanos son de ascendencia ____.

To review this cultural information, turn to pages 62–63.

Assessment

Learning from Photos

(page 71) **Charreadas,** or Mexican rodeos, are very popular in the El Paso area of Texas. **Charreadas** are held almost every Sunday from April to October. In this photo, we see the cowboys, or **charros,** at the opening parade of a **charreada.**

SPANISH Online

The **Glencoe Spanish Web** site (**spanish.glencoe.com**) offers options that enable you and your students to experience the Spanish-speaking world via the Internet. For each **Capítulo,** there are activities, games, and quizzes. In addition, an *Enrichment* section offers students an opportunity to visit Web sites related to the theme of the chapter.

Answers to 

5

15. son
16. son
17. somos
18. somos

6

19. mexicana
20. cubana

¡Hablo como un pro!

This unique page gives students the opportunity to speak freely and say whatever they can, using the vocabulary and structures they have learned in the chapter. The illustration serves to remind students of precisely what they know how to say in Spanish. There are no activities that students do not have the ability to describe or talk about in Spanish. The art not only depicts the vocabulary and content of this chapter, but also reinforces what they learned in previous chapters.

You may wish to use this page in many ways. Some possibilities are to have students do the following:

1. Look at the illustration and identify items by giving the correct Spanish words.
2. Make up sentences about what they see in the illustration.
3. Make up questions about the illustration. They can call on another class member to respond if you do this as a class activity, or you may prefer to allow students to work in small groups. This activity is extremely beneficial because it enables students to actively use interrogative words.
4. Answer questions you ask them about the illustration.
5. Work in pairs and make up a conversation based on the illustration.
6. Look at the illustration and give a complete oral review of what they see.
7. Look at the illustration and write a paragraph (or essay) about it.

You can also use this page as an assessment or testing tool, taking into account individual differences by having students go from simple to quite complicated tasks. The assessment can be either oral or written. You may wish to use the rubrics provided on pages T20–T21 as you give students the following directions.

1. Identify the topic or situation of the illustration.
2. Give the Spanish words for as many items as you can.
3. Think of as many sentences as you can to describe the illustration.
4. Go over your sentences and put them in the best sequencing to give a coherent story based on the illustration.

¡Hablo como un pro!

Tell all you can about this illustration.

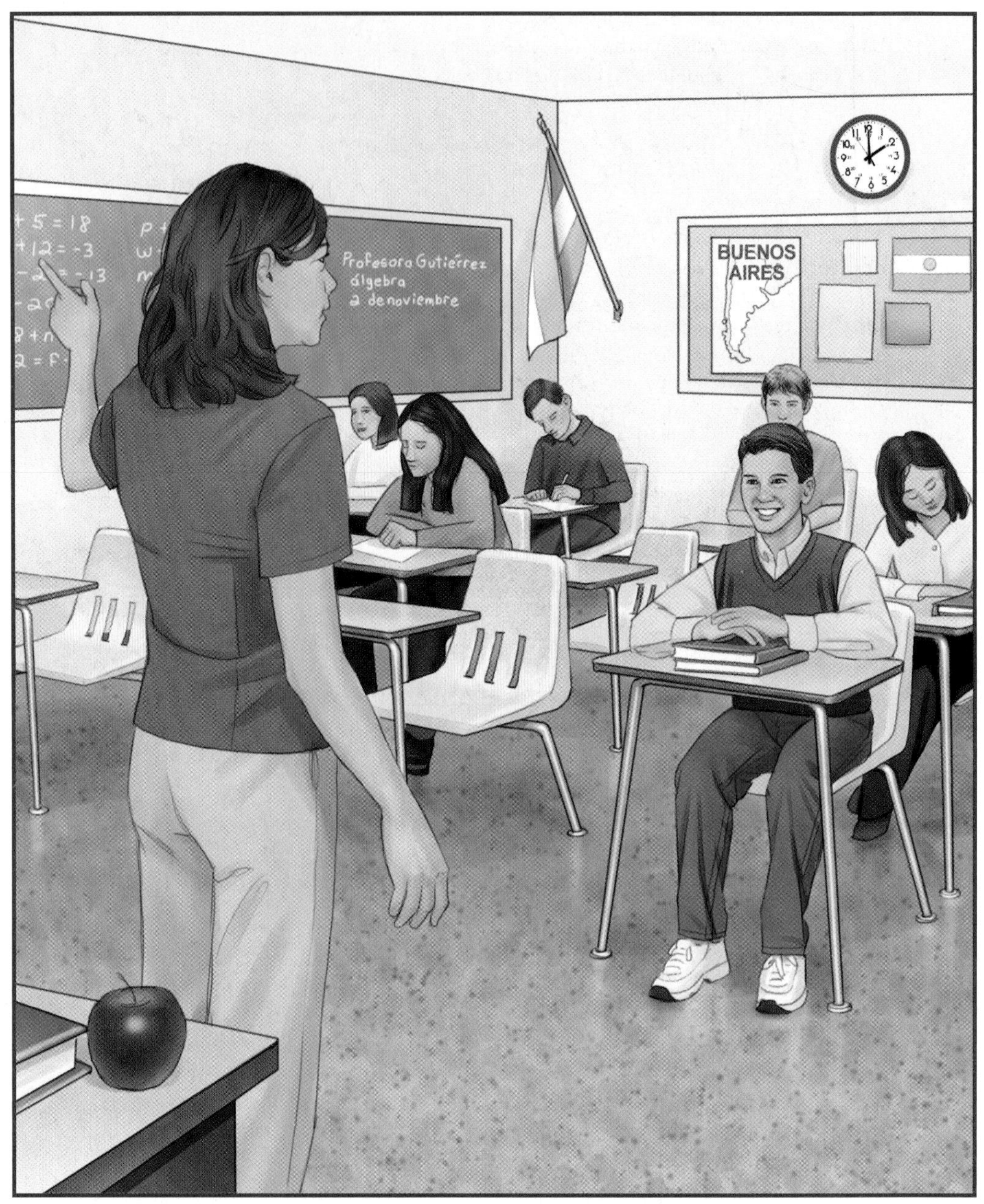

Vocabulario

Identifying a person or thing

el profesor
la profesora
la clase
el curso

Identifying school subjects

las ciencias
- la biología
- la química
- la física

las matemáticas
- la aritmética
- el álgebra
- la geometría
- el cálculo

las ciencias sociales
- la historia
- la geografía

las lenguas
- el inglés
- el español
- el francés
- el alemán
- el latín

otras asignaturas o disciplinas
- la educación física
- la música
- el arte
- la economía doméstica
- la informática

VIDEOTUR

Episodio 2

In this video episode, you will join Alberto and Claudia in time for class. See page 493 for more information.

Describing teachers and courses

inteligente
interesante
aburrido(a)
pequeño(a)
grande
fácil
difícil, duro(a)
popular
obligatorio(a)

How well do you know your vocabulary?

- Choose your favorite school subject. Choose words to describe this subject.
- Use these words to describe the subject and your teacher.

Identifying other nationalities

argentino(a)
dominicano(a)
ecuatoriano(a)
panameño(a)

Finding out information

¿quiénes?
¿cuántos(as)?

Agreeing and disagreeing

sí, también
no, de ninguna manera

Other useful expressions

hay
mucho
poco
mismo(a)
todos(as)

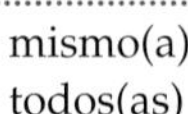

Vocabulario

Vocabulary Review

The words and phrases in the **Vocabulario** have been taught for productive use in this chapter. They are summarized here as a resource for both students and teacher. This list also serves as a convenient resource for the **¡Te toca a ti!** activities on pages 68 and 69. There are approximately thirty cognates in this vocabulary list. Have students find them.

VIDEO VHS/DVD

The Video Program allows students to see how the chapter vocabulary and structures are used by native speakers within an engaging story line. For maximum reinforcement, show the video episode as a final activity for Chapter 2.

¡OJO! You will notice that the vocabulary list here is not translated. This has been done intentionally, since we feel that by the time students have finished the material in the chapter they should be familiar with the meanings of all the words. If there are several words they still do not know, we recommend that they refer to the **Palabras 1** and **2** sections in the chapter or go to the dictionaries at the end of this book to find the meanings. However, if you prefer that your students have the English translations, please refer to Vocabulary Transparency 2.1, where you will find all these words with their translations.

Planning for Chapter 3

SCOPE AND SEQUENCE, PAGES 74–101

Topics

- ❖ School supplies
- ❖ Clothing
- ❖ Colors, sizes
- ❖ Shopping
- ❖ Numbers: 100–1,000

Culture

- ❖ Julio Torres, a student from Madrid
- ❖ Discussing differences between school in the United States and in Spanish-speaking countries
- ❖ El Retiro, Madrid
- ❖ Indigenous clothing in Central and South America
- ❖ A famous clothing designer: Oscar de la Renta

Functions

- ❖ How to identify and describe school supplies
- ❖ How to describe articles of clothing
- ❖ How to state color and sizes
- ❖ How to count from 100 to 1,000
- ❖ How to talk formally and informally

Structure

- ❖ Singular forms of **-ar** verbs
- ❖ **Tú** versus **usted**

National Standards

- ❖ Communication Standard 1.1 pages 74, 78, 79, 82, 83, 85, 86, 87, 89, 96, 97
- ❖ Communication Standard 1.2 pages 79, 83, 85, 86, 88, 89, 91, 92, 93, 95, 96, 97
- ❖ Communication Standard 1.3 page 97
- ❖ Cultures Standard 2.1 pages 81, 88, 89, 90, 92
- ❖ Cultures Standard 2.2 pages 77, 91, 93
- ❖ Connections Standard 3.1 page 94
- ❖ Connections Standard 3.2 page 95
- ❖ Comparisons Standard 4.2 pages 81, 90, 92, 96
- ❖ Communities Standard 5.1 pages 97, 101

PACING AND PRIORITIES

The chapter content is color coded below to assist you in planning.

■ required ■ recommended ■ optional

Vocabulario *(required)* *Days 1–4*

- ■ Palabras 1
  - Los materiales escolares
  - En la papelería
- ■ Palabras 2
  - La ropa
  - Los colores
  - Más números

Estructura *(required)* *Days 5–7*

- ■ Presente de los verbos en **-ar** en el singular
- ■ **Tú** o **Ud.**

Conversación *(required)*

- ■ En la tienda de ropa

Pronunciación *(recommended)*

- ■ Las consonantes **l, f, p, m, n**

Lecturas culturales

- ■ Un alumno madrileño *(recommended)*
- ■ La ropa indígena *(optional)*
- ■ Un diseñador famoso *(optional)*

Conexiones

- ■ La computadora *(optional)*

■ **¡Te toca a ti!** *(recommended)*

■ **Assessment** *(recommended)*

■ **¡Hablo como un pro!** *(optional)*

RESOURCE GUIDE

SECTION	PAGES	SECTION RESOURCES
Vocabulario PALABRAS 1		
Los materiales escolares En la papelería	76, 78–79 77, 78–79	Vocabulary Transparencies 3.2–3.3 Audio CD 3 Audio Activities TE, pages 25–26 Workbook, pages 19–20 Quiz 1, pages 11–12 ExamView® Pro
Vocabulario PALABRAS 2		
La ropa Los colores Más números	80, 82–83 81, 82–83 81, 82–83	Vocabulary Transparencies 3.4–3.5 Audio CD 3 Audio Activities TE, pages 27–28 Workbook, pages 21–22 Quiz 2, pages 13–14 ExamView® Pro
Estructura		
Presente de los verbos en **-ar** en el singular **Tú** o **Ud.**	84–86 87	Audio CD 3 Audio Activities TE, pages 29–32 Workbook, pages 23–24 Quizzes 3–4, pages 15–16 ExamView® Pro
Conversación		
En la tienda de ropa	88	Audio CD 3 Audio Activities TE, page 32 Interactive CD-ROM
Pronunciación		
Las consonantes **l, f, p, m, n**	89	Pronunciation Transparency P 3 Audio CD 3 Audio Activities TE, page 33
Lecturas culturales		
Un alumno madrileño La ropa indígena Un diseñador famoso	90–91 92 93	Audio CD 3 Audio Activities TE, page 33 Tests, pages 30, 33
Conexiones		
La computadora	94–95	Tests, page 34
¡Te toca a ti!		
	96–97	**¡Viva el mundo hispano!** Video, Episode 3 Video Activities, Chapter 3 Spanish Online Activities spanish.glencoe.com
Assessment		
	98–99	Communication Transparency C 3 Quizzes 1–4, pages 11–16 Performance Assessment, Task 3 Tests, pages 27–40 Situation Cards, Chapter 3 ExamView® Pro **Maratón mental** Videoquiz

Using Your Resources for Chapter 3

Transparencies

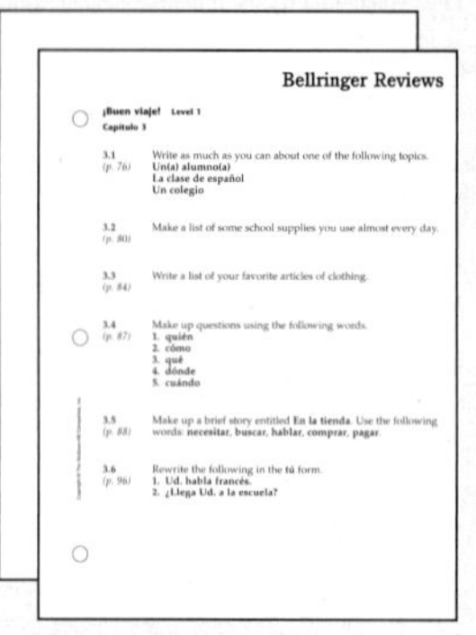

Bellringer 3.1–3.6

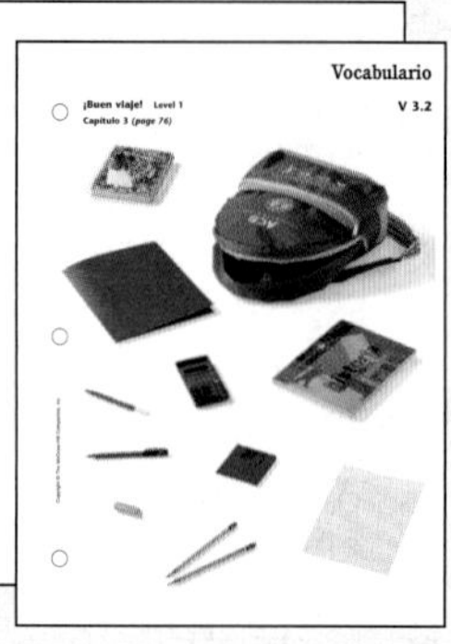
Vocabulary 3.1–3.5

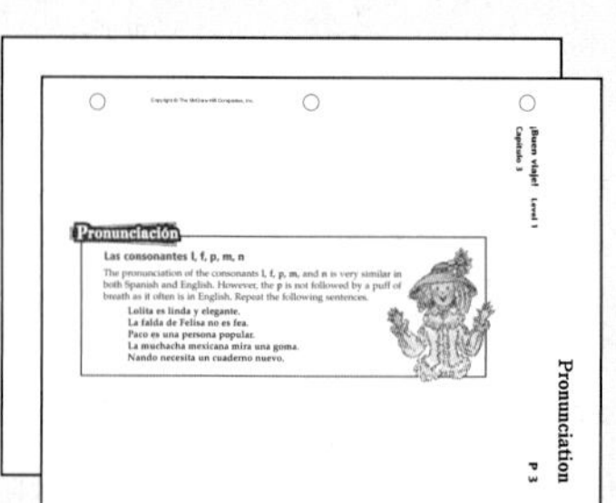
Pronunciation P 3

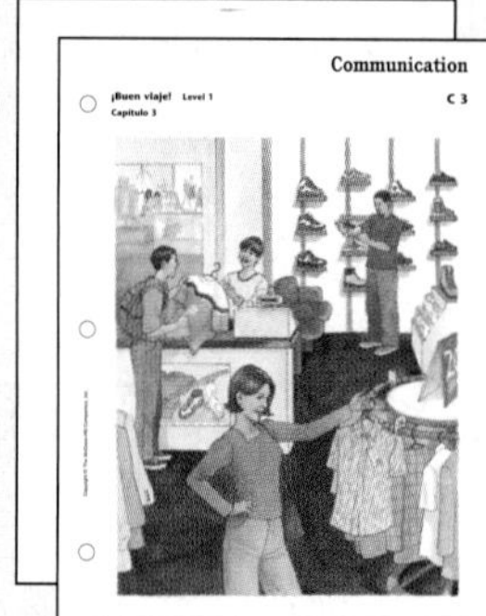
Communication C 3

Workbook

Vocabulary, pages 19–22

Structure, pages 23–24

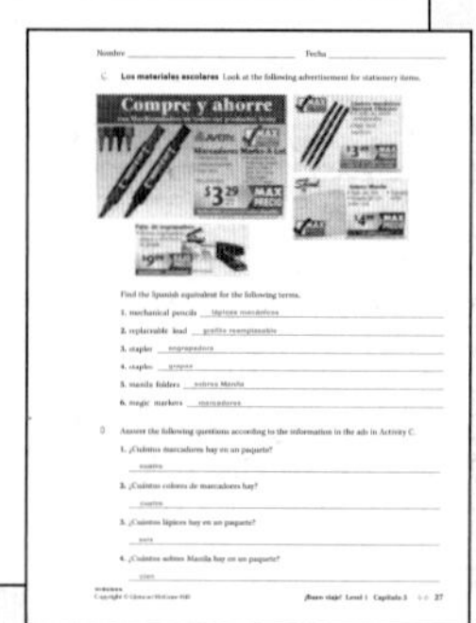
Enrichment, pages 25–28

Audio Activities

Vocabulary, pages 25–28

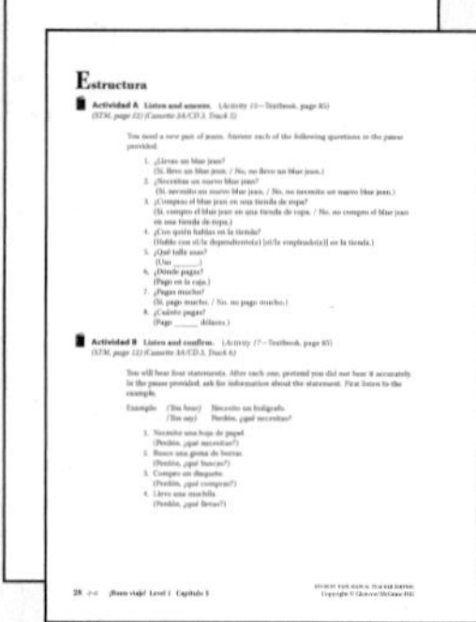
Structure, pages 29–32

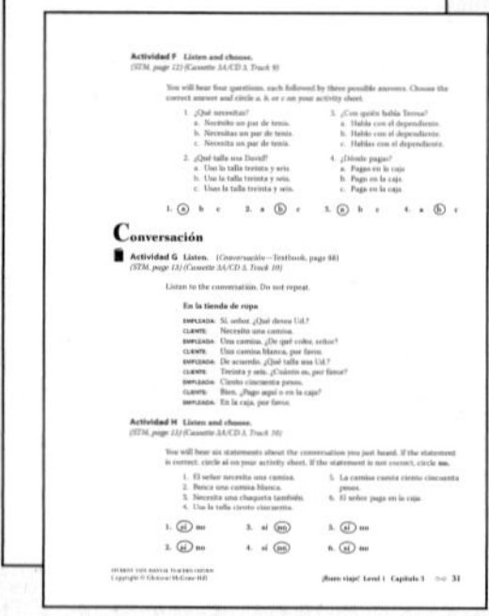
Conversation, Pronunciation, pages 32–33

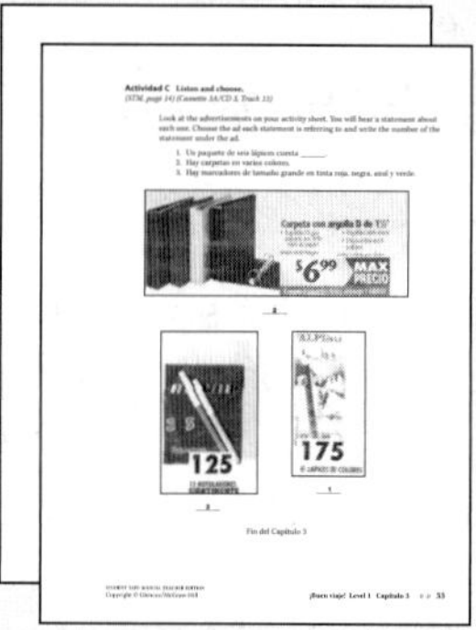
Additional Practice, pages 33–34

Assessment

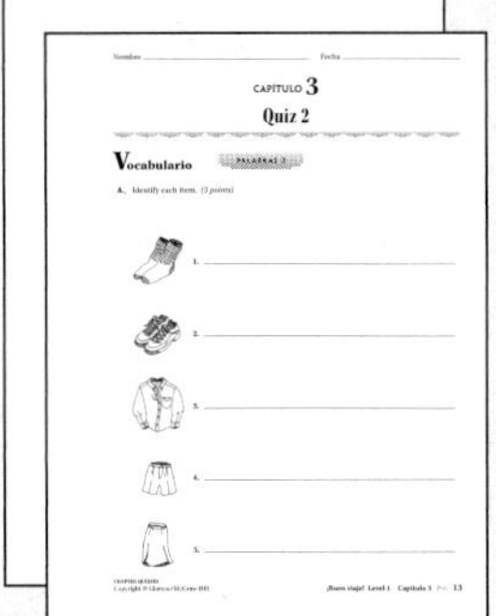

Vocabulary and Structure Quizzes, pages 11–16

Chapter Tests, pages 27–40

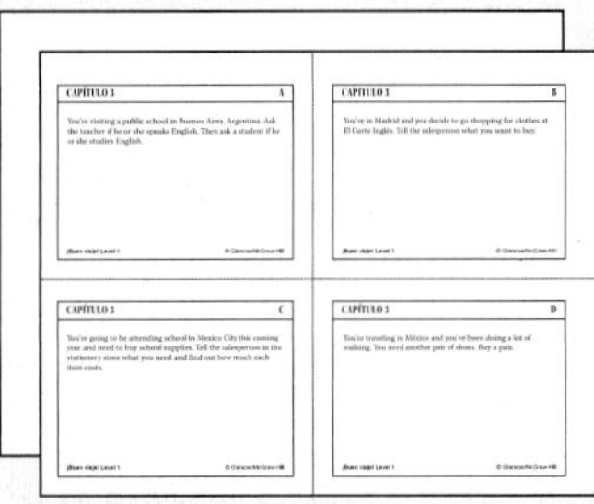

Situation Cards, Chapter 3

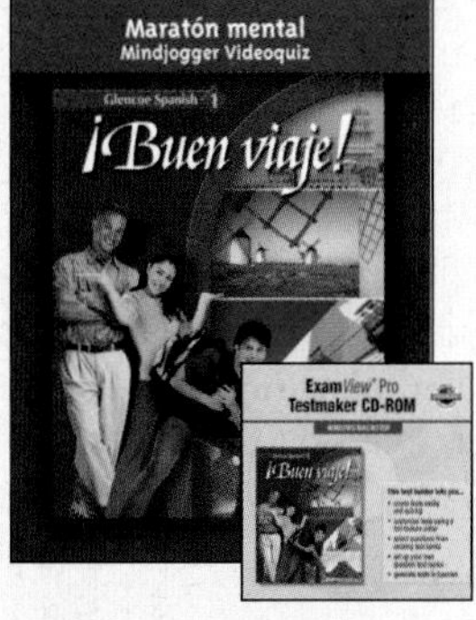

MindJogger Videoquiz, ExamView® Pro, Chapter 3

Timesaving Teacher Tools

TeacherWorks™ is your all-in-one teacher resource center. Personalize lesson plans, access resources from the Teacher Wraparound Edition, connect to the Internet, or make a to-do list. These are only a few of the many features that can assist you in the planning and organizing of your lessons.

Includes:

- A calendar feature
- Access to all program blackline masters
- Standards correlations and more

ExamView® Pro

Test Bank software for Macintosh and Windows makes creating, editing, customizing, and printing tests quick and easy.

Technology Resources

In the Chapter 3 Internet Activity, you will have a chance to learn more about the Spanish-speaking world. Visit spanish.glencoe.com

On the interactive CD-ROM, students can listen to and take part in a recorded version of the conversation in Chapter 3.

¡Viva el mundo hispano! Video and Video Activities, Chapter 3. Available on VHS and DVD.

Help your students prepare for the chapter test by playing the **Maratón mental** Videoquiz game show. Teams will compete against each other to review chapter vocabulary and structure and sharpen listening comprehension skills. Available on VHS and DVD.

¡Buen viaje! is also available on CD or Online.

Capítulo 3

Preview

In this chapter, students will learn to identify, describe, and shop for school supplies and clothing. They will also learn to use singular forms of **-ar** verbs to communicate in various situations that arise when shopping. Plural forms will be presented in Chapter 4.

National Standards

Communication

In Chapter 3, students will communicate in spoken and written Spanish on the following topics:

- clothing
- school supplies and related subjects

Students will engage in conversations, provide and obtain information, and exchange opinions as they fulfill the chapter objectives listed on this page.

LEVELING

The activities, conversations, and readings within each chapter are marked according to level of difficulty. **E** indicates easy. **A** indicates average. **C** indicates challenging. Some activities cover a range of difficulty. In some activities, for example, advanced students will be able to produce more extensive responses while students who learn at a different rate may give less detailed responses. The leveling indicators will help you individualize instruction to best meet your students' needs.

Capítulo 3

Las compras para la escuela

Objetivos

In this chapter you will learn to:

- identify and describe school supplies
- identify and describe articles of clothing
- shop for school supplies and clothing
- state color and size preferences
- speak to people formally and informally
- discuss differences between schools in the United States and in Spanish-speaking countries

Joaquín Torres-García *Abstract Art in Five Tones and Complementaries*

Capítulo 3

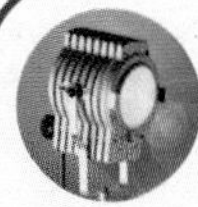

Spotlight on Culture

Arte Joaquín Torres-Garcia (1874–1949) was born in Montevideo, Uruguay and studied art in Barcelona, Spain. He developed the style of Constructive Universalism. Known as a pioneer of modernism, abstraction, and American art, he founded the **Taller Torres-García,** a workshop school where students explored ideas about constructivism and abstraction and experimented with materials and techniques.

Fotografía The photo is of the **Galerías Pacífico** shopping mall on **Calle Florida** in Buenos Aires, Argentina.

Construction began in 1889 on the building, which was supposed to house a department store in the style of the famous Galeries Lafayette in Paris. Economic difficulties, however, changed the course of events and the building was sold. The new buyer was the now defunct **Ferrocarril de Buenos Aires al Pacífico.**

Two famous Argentine architects, Aslan and Ezcurra, completed construction of the building.

Galerías Pacífico opened as a retail outlet in 1946 and was refurbished in 1992. It has an eating area that is famous for people-watching.

Vocabulario

PALABRAS 1

1 PREPARATION

Resource Manager

Vocabulary Transparencies 3.2–3.3
Audio Activities TE, pages 25–26
Audio CD 3
Workbook, pages 19–20
Quizzes, pages 11–12
ExamView® Pro

Bellringer Review

Use BRR Transparency 3.1 or write the following on the board.
Write as much as you can about one of the following topics.
Un(a) alumno(a)
La clase de español
Un colegio

2 PRESENTATION

¡OJO! Note that all the verbs in the vocabulary presentation are in the **él / ella** form so that you can immediately ask questions. Students can answer and practice the new words without having to make pronoun and ending changes. Students will learn how to manipulate the **-ar** verbs in the structure section of this chapter.

Step 1 Have students close their books. Model the new vocabulary on pages 76–77 using Vocabulary Transparencies 3.2–3.3. Have them repeat each word or expression two or three times.

Step 2 Identify the school supplies your students are actually using. Have the class repeat each item after you once or twice. Ask **¿Qué es?** and have a student respond.

Vocabulario

PALABRAS 1

Los materiales escolares

la mochila

un cuaderno, un bloc

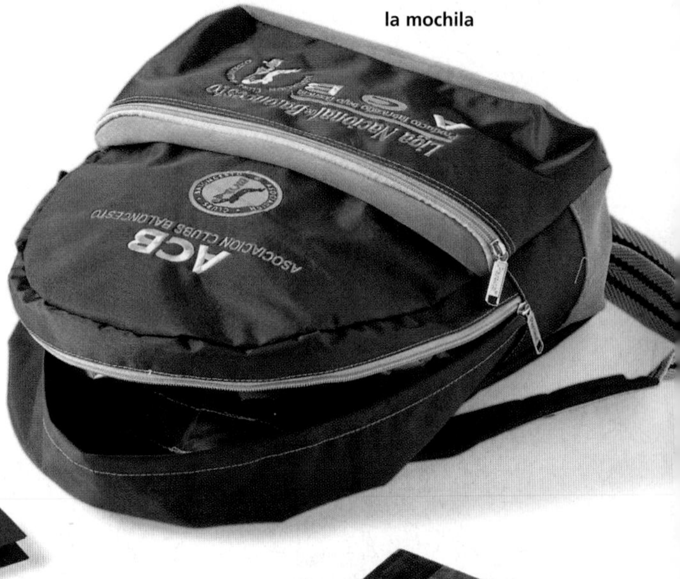

una carpeta

un libro

una calculadora

un marcador

una hoja de papel

un bolígrafo, una pluma

un disquete

una goma de borrar

un lápiz, dos lápices

Reaching All Students

Total Physical Response If students don't already know the meaning of **levántate, ven acá,** and **siéntate,** teach these expressions by using the appropriate gestures as you say each expression.
(Student 1), **levántate y ven acá, por favor.**
Busca un libro. Mira el libro. Dame el libro.
(Gesture to convey the meaning of dame.*)*
Ahora, busca una goma. Dame la goma.
Busca una hoja de papel. Dame la hoja de papel.
Busca un lápiz. Dame el lápiz.
Gracias, *(Student 1).* **Siéntate.**

Now call on another student to do the following:
(Student 2), **levántate y ven acá, por favor.**
Busca un cuaderno. Mira el cuaderno. Dame el cuaderno.
Gracias, *(Student 2).* **Siéntate.**

En la papelería

Alejandro necesita materiales escolares.
Busca un cuaderno en la papelería.

Alejandro mira un cuaderno.
Mira un bolígrafo también.

¿El cuaderno?
¿Cuánto es, por favor?
Noventa pesos.
la dependienta,
la empleada

Alejandro habla con la dependienta.

90
la caja

Alejandro compra el cuaderno.
El cuaderno cuesta noventa pesos.
Alejandro paga noventa pesos.
Paga en la caja.

Alejandro lleva los materiales escolares en una mochila.

Vocabulario

Step 3 Pantomime **busca** and **mira** to help convey their meaning.

Step 4 Have students repeat the short conversation with the clerk in the photo on page 77.

Step 5 Have students repeat the sentences under the two illustrations at the bottom of page 77. As they do, intersperse with questions such as the following, building from simple to more complex sentences:

¿Compra Alejandro el cuaderno?
¿Qué compra Alejandro?
¿Quién compra el cuaderno?
¿Compra el cuaderno en la papelería?
¿Dónde compra Alejandro el cuaderno?

Have students answer with the complete sentence or sometimes have them use just the specific word or expression that responds to the question word.

Step 6 After presenting the vocabulary orally, have students open their books and read the new vocabulary aloud. You can have the class read in chorus or call on individuals to read. Intersperse with questions such as those outlined above.

About the Spanish Language

- The words **el cuaderno, la libreta,** and **el bloc** are all commonly used to refer to a notebook. **Una carpeta** is more like a folder.
- Some Spanish speakers use **el bolígrafo** when referring to a ballpoint pen; others use **la pluma,** which also means a fountain pen. In some countries, **la pluma** is used for both a ballpoint pen and a fountain pen.

Class Motivator

¿Qué hay en la mochila? Bring an empty backpack to class. Pass the backpack around the room. As each person gets the backpack, he or she puts a school supply in it, names it, and tells what else is in the pack: **En la mochila hay un cuaderno, una goma,** etc. If someone has already put an item in the pack, the others can still put in the same item. However, the other students now have to say how many notebooks, pens, etc., are in the backpack. The last student has to name everything in the pack. (Hint: You may allow students to look in the pack if they need help remembering.)

LEVELING

E: Vocabulary

Vocabulario

3 PRACTICE

¿Qué palabra necesito?

¡OJO! When students are doing the **¿Qué palabra necesito?** activities, accept any answer that makes sense. The purpose of these activities is to have students use the new vocabulary. They are not factual recall activities. Thus, it is not necessary for students to remember specific factual information from the vocabulary presentation when answering. If you wish, have students use the photos on this page as a stimulus, when possible.

Historieta Each time **Historieta** appears, it means that the answers to the activity form a short story. Encourage students to look at the title of the **Historieta,** since it can help them do the activity.

1 Have a contest to see who has written the most words for Activity 1.

2 Do Activity 2 with books closed first. Then have a student retell it in his or her own words.

3 Have individual students read the entire sentence, including the correct completion word. **Expansion:** Ask the more able students to make up original sentences using the word choices that do not fit in the blanks. In Item 1, for example, they could say: **Diego paga los materiales escolares en la caja. Diego habla con el dependiente.**

Writing Development

To illustrate how all the items tell a story, have students write the answers to Activity 3 in a paragraph.

Vocabulario

¿Qué palabra necesito?

1 Los materiales escolares

Preparen una lista de materiales escolares importantes. *(Make a list of important school supplies.)*

2 Historieta En la papelería

Contesten. *(Answer.)*

1. ¿Necesita la muchacha materiales escolares?
2. ¿Busca los materiales escolares en la papelería?
3. ¿Mira ella un bolígrafo?
4. ¿Habla con el dependiente?
5. ¿Compra el bolígrafo?
6. ¿Paga en la caja?

Una papelería, Santiago, Chile

grafoplas
3 CARPETAS
Blíster de 3 carpetas con gomas y solapa TECNIGRAF,
€2,85

3 Historieta De compras

Escojan. *(Choose.)*

1. Diego ____ materiales escolares.
   a. paga **b.** habla **c.** necesita
2. Él ____ un bolígrafo y un cuaderno.
   a. mira **b.** cuesta **c.** habla
3. Diego ____ con el empleado.
   a. paga **b.** habla **c.** mira
4. Él necesita ____ para la computadora.
   a. un disquete **b.** un bloc **c.** un lápiz
5. Diego ____ en la caja.
   a. paga **b.** compra **c.** lleva
6. Él ____ los materiales escolares en una mochila.
   a. compra **b.** mira **c.** lleva

Answers to ¿Qué palabra necesito?

1 *Answers will vary but may include:*

unos lápices, unos bolígrafos (unas plumas), unos marcadores, unos cuadernos (unos blocs), unas carpetas, unos libros, unas hojas de papel, una calculadora, unos disquetes, una(s) goma(s), una mochila.

2

1. Sí, la muchacha necesita materiales escolares.
2. Sí, busca los materiales escolares en la papelería.
3. Sí, ella mira un bolígrafo.
4. Sí, habla con el dependiente.
5. Sí, compra el bolígrafo.
6. Sí, paga en la caja.

3

1. c
2. a
3. b
4. a
5. a
6. c

4 Historieta Una calculadora, por favor.

Contesten. *(Answer.)*

Una papelería, Málaga, España

1. ¿Con quién habla Casandra en la papelería?
2. ¿Qué necesita ella?
3. ¿Qué busca?
4. ¿Compra la calculadora?
5. ¿Cuánto cuesta la calculadora?
6. ¿Dónde paga Casandra?

5 En la papelería

Work with a classmate. You're buying the school supplies below. Take turns being the customer and the salesperson.

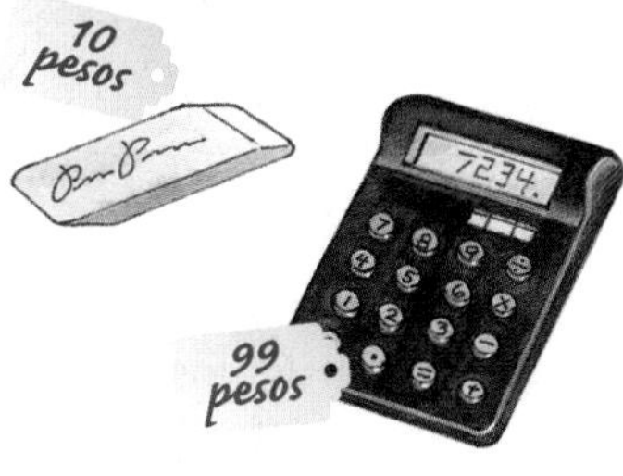

6 Juego ¿Qué es?

Play a guessing game. Your partner will hide a school supply behind his or her back. Guess what he or she is hiding. Take turns.

4 Do Activity 4 with books closed first. Then have a student retell the information given in Items 1–6 in his or her own words.

5 Have students work in pairs. The first student will ask the price of the item, and the second student will respond with the price given. Make sure each student has the opportunity to role-play both the customer and the salesperson. Have students volunteer to role-play this activity for the class.

6 Juego This is a good activity to use at the beginning or the end of the class period.

Learning from Realia

(page 78) Have students look at the ad. Ask them to figure out what is being advertised by using the vocabulary of the chapter. **Blíster** refers to the term **Blíster Pack,** which means *vacuum-packed.* In this context, **solapa** means *the flap of an envelope.* You may wish to point out the symbol for the euro.

LEVELING

E: Activities 1, 3, 6
A: Activities 2, 4
C: Activity 5

Answers to ¿Qué palabra necesito?

4

1. Casandra habla con la dependienta en la papelería.
2. Necesita una calculadora.
3. Busca una calculadora.
4. Sí, (No, no) compra la calculadora.
5. La calculadora cuesta ___ pesos.
6. Casandra paga en la caja.

5 *Students can make up their own conversations. They may use words such as:* necesitar, buscar, ¿cuánto cuesta?, pagar.

6 *Answers will vary. Students will use items taught in* Palabras 1.

Vocabulario

PALABRAS 2

1 PREPARATION

Resource Manager

Vocabulary Transparencies 3.4–3.5
Audio Activities TE, pages 27–28
Audio CD 3
Workbook, pages 21–22
Quizzes, pages 13–14
ExamView® Pro

Bellringer Review

Use BRR Transparency 3.2 or write the following on the board.
Make a list of some school supplies you use almost every day.

2 PRESENTATION

Step 1 Have students close their books. Then model the new vocabulary on pages 80–81 using Vocabulary Transparencies 3.4–3.5. Have students repeat each word or expression two or three times.

Step 2 Identify articles of clothing students are wearing. Have the class repeat each item after you once or twice. Ask **¿Qué es?** and have a student respond.

Step 3 Ask: **¿Lleva la muchacha un blue jean? ¿Lleva una chaqueta? ¿Qué lleva? ¿Lleva una falda? ¿Lleva zapatos o un par de tenis?**

Step 4 Have students read the two conversations on page 81 aloud with as much expression as possible.

Vocabulario

PALABRAS 2

La ropa

una gorra
una blusa
un traje
un pantalón corto
una chaqueta
un T-shirt, una camiseta
un pantalón largo
una camisa
una falda
36
la talla, el tamaño
los zapatos
38
el número
una corbata
un blue jean
los calcetines
un par de tenis

La muchacha lleva un T-shirt y un blue jean.
Lleva un par de tenis.
Lleva una chaqueta.
No lleva una falda.

Reaching All Students

Total Physical Response Teach the words **anda** and **indica** by acting them out in front of the class. Point to individual students as you say the word **indica.**

(Student 1), **ven acá. Anda por la sala de clase.**
Indica una camisa blanca.
Contesta: ¿Quién lleva una camisa blanca?
Indica una falda azul.
¿Quién lleva una falda azul?
Indica un pantalón.
Contesta: ¿Es un pantalón largo o corto?
Gracias, *(Student 1).*

Now repeat the above with another student. Change the articles of clothing.

¿Qué desea Ud.?
Una blusa, por favor.
Sí, señorita. ¿Qué talla usa Ud.?
Treinta y cuatro.

Gloria habla con la dependienta.
La dependienta trabaja en la tienda de ropa.

¿Qué número usa (calza) Ud.?

Treinta y ocho.

Rubén compra un par de zapatos.
Él habla con el dependiente.

La camisa cuesta mucho.
Es muy cara.

La gorra no cuesta mucho.
Cuesta poco.
Es bastante barata.

¿Lo sabes?

Ciento is shortened to **cien** before any word that is not a number: **cien pesos, ciento ochenta pesos.**

Los colores

¿De qué color es?

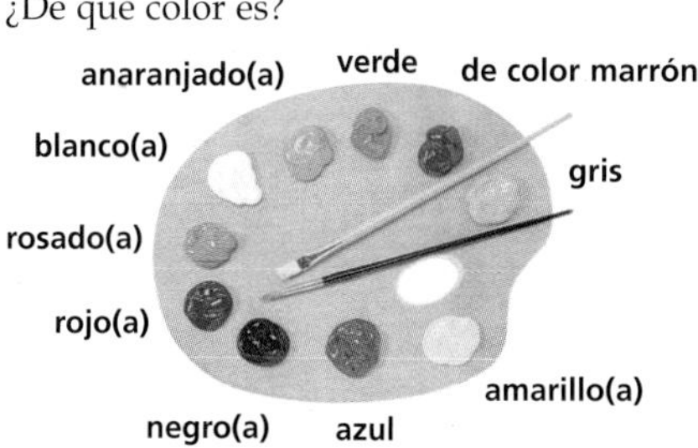

Más números

100	ciento, cien	600	seiscientos
200	doscientos	700	setecientos
300	trescientos	800	ochocientos
400	cuatrocientos	900	novecientos
500	quinientos	1000	mil

150	ciento cincuenta
790	setecientos noventa
1800	mil ochocientos

Vocabulario

Step 5 As you present the sentences on page 81, ask questions such as **¿Con quién habla Gloria? ¿Habla con la dependienta en la tienda? ¿Dónde trabaja la dependienta? ¿En qué tipo de tienda trabaja?**

Step 6 After you present the colors on page 81, have students identify the colors of the clothes on page 80.

Step 7 Más números Model and have students repeat the numbers. Write random numbers on the board and call on students to say them.

Vocabulary Expansion

You may wish to give students a few extra words that are useful when shopping for clothing.

a rayas	*striped*
a cuadros	*checked*
de lana	*wool*
de algodón	*cotton*
de nilón	*nylon*

National Standards

Comparisons

Students learn on page 81 that clothing sizes are not the same in Spain or in many areas of Latin America as the sizes used in the United States. Ask students what size shoe the young man in the illustration is trying on (38) and what the equivalent size would be in the United States. Ask them what size shoe they would ask for in a Spanish shoe store. (See chart on page 85.)

About the Spanish Language

- **El saco** is used for both a man's and a woman's jacket. In Spain, **la chaqueta** or **la americana** are common terms. In Mexico, the word **chamarra** is used. Other kinds of outer jackets are **la cazadora, el blusón, el chaquetón.** One will also hear **el gabán** used for *jacket.*
- In many areas of Latin America, **medias** is used for women's stockings and men's socks. In other areas, **medias** are women's stockings only, and socks are **calcetines.**
- **El pantalón** is often used in the plural: **los pantalones.** *Blue jeans* are called **blue jeans** or **blujins, vaqueros,** and **pantalones de mezclilla.** In Puerto Rico, the word **mahones** is used.
- **Zapatería** can mean *a shoe store (department)* or *factory.* Another term is **tienda (departamento) de calzado.**
- Other words for *sweater* are **la chompa** and **el pulóver.**

Vocabulario

3 PRACTICE

¿Qué palabra necesito?

7 Before doing this activity, review the colors on page 81. Now have students identify each item by saying what the article of clothing is and what color it is.

8 Students should answer in complete sentences. For example: **Eugenio habla con la dependienta.**

9 Have individual students answer each of the items. Then have one student answer Items 1–3 and a second student answer 4–6.

Chapter Projects

El catálogo Have students prepare a catalogue containing the articles of clothing taught in this chapter. Tell students to label each item of clothing in Spanish and make sure the clothing colors can be described by their classmates.

LEVELING

E: Activities 7, 8, 9, 11

A: Activities 10, 13

C: Activity 12

¿Qué palabra necesito?

7 ¿Qué es? Identifiquen. *(Identify.)*

1. 2. 3. 4. 5. 6.

Madrid, España

8 Historieta En la tienda de ropa

Contesten según se indica. *(Answer according to the cues.)*

1. ¿Con quién habla Eugenio? (con la dependiente)
2. ¿Dónde trabaja la dependiente? (en la tienda de ropa)
3. ¿Qué necesita Eugenio? (un T-shirt)
4. ¿Qué talla usa? (treinta y ocho)
5. ¿De qué color es el T-shirt? (blanco)
6. ¿Cuánto es? (cinco pesos)
7. ¿Cuesta mucho? (no, poco)
8. ¿Es caro? (no, barato)
9. ¿Compra Eugenio el T-shirt? (sí)
10. ¿Dónde paga? (en la caja)

9 ¿De qué color es? Completen con el color. *(Complete with the color.)*

1. Tomás compra un pantalón ____.
2. Ana compra una blusa ____.
3. Emilio compra una camisa ____.

4. Paco compra una gorra ____.
5. Adriana compra una falda ____.
6. César compra zapatos de color ____.

ANSWERS TO ¿Qué palabra necesito?

1. Es una camisa.
2. Es una gorra.
3. Es una falda.
4. Es un blue jean.
5. Es una mochila.
6. Es un par de tenis.

1. Eugenio habla con la dependienta.
2. La dependienta trabaja en la tienda de ropa.
3. Eugenio necesita un T-shirt.
4. Usa la talla (el tamaño) treinta y ocho.
5. El T-shirt es blanco.
6. Es cinco pesos.
7. No, (cuesta) poco.
8. No, (es) barato.
9. Sí, Eugenio compra el T-shirt.
10. Paga en la caja.

10 **¿Qué es?** With a classmate, take turns asking each other what each of the following items is. Then ask questions about each one. Find out how much it costs and tell what you think about the price. Is it a real bargain—**¿una ganga?**

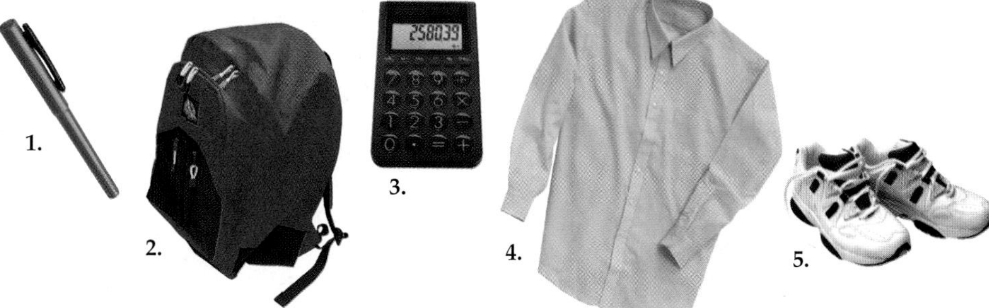

11 **¿Quién es?** Work in small groups. One person tells what someone in the class is wearing. The others have to guess who it is. If several people are wearing the same thing, you will have to give more details.

12 **En la tienda de ropa** With a classmate, look at the photograph. Ask one another questions about it. Answer each other's questions. Then work together to make up sentences about the photograph. Put the sentences in logical order to form a paragraph.

13 **Juego ¿Cuál es el número?** Give some numbers in a mathematical pattern but leave one out. Your partner will try to figure out what the missing number is. Take turns. You can use the model as a guide.

Vocabulario

¡OJO! Note that the activities are color-coded. All the activities in the text are communicative. However, the ones with blue titles are guided communication. The red titles indicate that the answers to the activity are more open-ended and can vary more. You may wish to correct students' mistakes more so in the guided activities than in the activities with a red title, which lend themselves to a freer response.

10 Have students work in pairs. Student 1 begins by asking, **¿Qué es?** Student 2 then identifies the object. Student 1 then asks the price, **¿Cuánto cuesta?** Students can use **dólares** instead of **pesos,** since they will need to make up the price of each object.

11 As students work in their groups, you may wish to circulate to make sure they are on task.

Recycling

If students need to give additional details about the person they are describing in Activity 11, they can use words they learned in Chapter 1, such as **alto, bajo, rubio,** etc.

12 Have students work in pairs to come up with at least six questions about the photo on page 83.

13 **Juego** This is a good activity to use when students need a "break" during the class period or as an opening or closing activity.

Writing Development

Activity 12 works well as a written activity. When students have finished their paragraphs, ask volunteers to read them to the class.

Answers to ¿Qué palabra necesito?

9

1. negro
2. roja
3. blanca
4. azul y blanca (a rayas)
5. verde
6. marrón

10 *Answers will vary.*

11 *Answers will vary, but students should use the verb* llevar, *articles of clothing, and colors.*

12 *Answers will vary. Students can use any articles of clothing and verbs such as* necesitar, buscar, mirar, hablar, comprar, pagar. *They may also ask questions such as* ¿Cuánto cuesta?

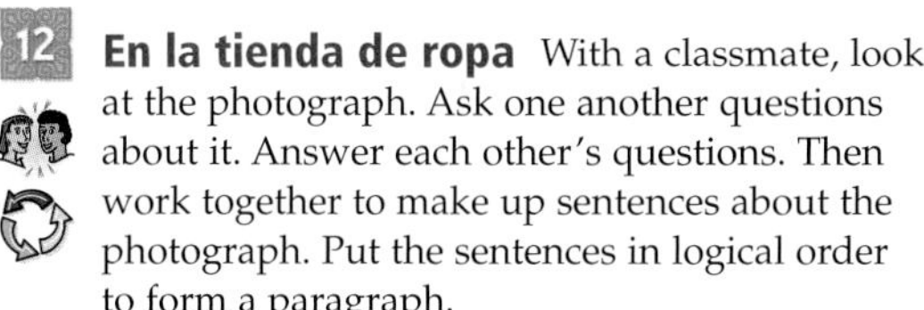

Estructura

1 PREPARATION

Resource Manager

Audio Activities TE, pages 29–32
Audio CD 3
Workbook, pages 23–24
Quizzes, pages 15–16
ExamView® Pro

Bellringer Review

Use BRR Transparency 3.3 or write the following on the board.
Write a list of your favorite articles of clothing.

2 PRESENTATION

Presente de los verbos en -ar en el singular

Step 1 Draw two stick figures on the board. Give them the names Paco and Julia. Write the verbs **hablar, comprar,** and **mirar**. Have students make up sentences about either Paco or Julia. They can do this because they know the **él / ella** verb form from the vocabulary presentation.

Step 2 Ask students what they say when they talk about themselves **(yo).** Write **yo** on the board and explain that the ending changes to **-o** with **yo.** Write **yo hablo** on the board and have students give you the **yo** form of the other verbs. Follow the same procedures for the **tú** form.

Step 3 Write the verb forms on the board, underline the endings, and have students repeat again.

Estructura

Presente de los verbos en -ar en el singular

Telling what people do

1. All verbs, or action words, in Spanish belong to a family, or conjugation. Verbs whose infinitive ends in **-ar** (**hablar:** *to speak,* **comprar:** *to buy*) are called first conjugation verbs.

necesitar	**comprar**
buscar	**hablar**
mirar	**pagar**

2. Spanish verbs change their endings according to the subject. Study the following forms.

INFINITIVE	hablar	comprar	mirar	ENDINGS
STEM	habl-	compr-	mir-	
yo	hablo	compro	miro	-o
tú	hablas	compras	miras	-as
él	habla	compra	mira	-a
ella	habla	compra	mira	-a

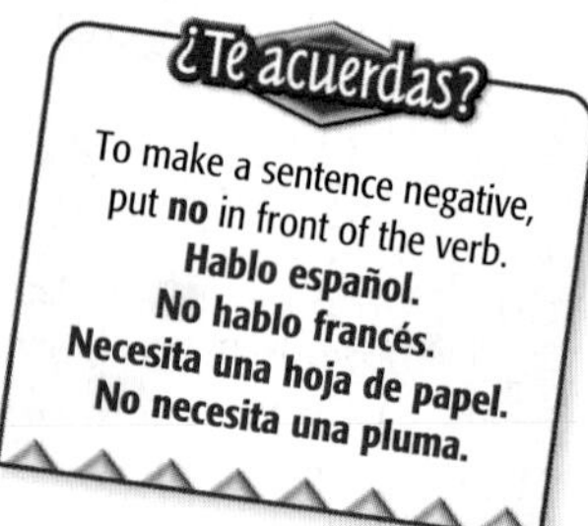

3. Since the ending of the verb in Spanish indicates who performs the action, the subjects **(yo, tú, él, ella)** are often omitted.

Use **-o** when you talk about yourself.

Use **-as** when you talk to a friend.

Use **-a** when you talk about someone.

LEVELING
E: Activities 14, 15
A: Activities 16, 17

ANSWERS TO ¿Cómo lo digo?

14

1. Sí, Andrea necesita materiales escolares.
2. Sí (No), ella (no) busca un bolígrafo.
3. Sí, (No, no) compra un bolígrafo en la papelería.
4. Sí, (No, no) habla con la empleada.
5. Sí, paga en la caja.
6. Sí, lleva los materiales escolares en una mochila.

¿Qué palabra necesito?

Una papelería, Caracas, Venezuela

14 Historieta En la papelería

Contesten. *(Answer.)*

1. ¿Necesita Andrea materiales escolares?
2. ¿Busca ella un bolígrafo?
3. ¿Compra un bolígrafo en la papelería?
4. ¿Habla ella con la empleada?
5. ¿Paga ella en la caja?
6. ¿Lleva los materiales escolares en una mochila?

15 Historieta Llevo un blue jean.

Contesten personalmente. *(Answer about yourself.)*

1. ¿Llevas un blue jean?
2. ¿Necesitas un nuevo blue jean?
3. ¿Compras el blue jean en una tienda de ropa?
4. ¿Con quién hablas en la tienda?
5. ¿Qué talla usas?
6. ¿Dónde pagas?
7. ¿Pagas mucho?
8. ¿Cuánto pagas?

CONVERSION DE TALLAS

Ropa de señora – Vestidos y abrigos						
Estados Unidos	6	8	10	12	14	16
España	36	38	40	42	44	46
Sudamérica	34	36	38	40	42	44
Ropa de señora – Blusas y jersey						
Estados Unidos	30	32	34	36	38	40
España	38	40	42	44	46	48
Sudamérica	38	40	42	44	46	48
Ropa de caballeros – Trajes						
Estados Unidos	34	36	38	40	42	44
España	44	46	48	50	52	54
Sudamérica	44	46	48	50	52	54
Calzado – señoras						
Estados Unidos	4	5	6	7	8	9
España	34/35	35/36	36/37	38/39	39/40	41/42
Sudamérica	2	3	4	5	6	7
Calzado – caballeros						
Estados Unidos	8	8½	9	9½	10	10½
España	41	42	43	43	44	45
Sudamérica	6	6½	7	7½	8	8½

16 Historieta Necesito un par de tenis, por favor.

Contesten según se indica. *(Answer according to the cues.)*

1. ¿Qué necesitas? (un par de tenis)
2. ¿Dónde buscas los tenis? (en la zapatería)
3. ¿Qué número usas? (treinta y seis)
4. ¿Miras un par de tenis? (sí)
5. ¿Compras los tenis? (sí)
6. ¿Cuánto pagas? (quinientos pesos)
7. ¿Dónde pagas? (en la caja)

17 Perdón, ¿qué necesitas?

Sigan el modelo. *(Follow the model.)*

Necesito un bolígrafo.
Perdón, ¿qué necesitas?

1. Necesito una hoja de papel.
2. Busco una goma de borrar.
3. Compro un disquete.
4. Llevo una mochila.

Answers to ¿Cómo lo digo?

15 *Answers will vary but may include:*

1. Sí, (No, no) llevo un blue jean.
2. Sí, (No, no) necesito un nuevo blue jean.
3. Sí, compro el blue jean en una tienda de ropa.
4. Hablo con el / la dependiente(a) (el / la empleado[a]) en la tienda.
5. Uso la talla (el tamaño) ___.
6. Pago en la caja.
7. Sí, (No, no) pago mucho.
8. Pago ___ dólares.

16

1. Necesito un par de tenis.
2. Busco los tenis en la tienda González.
3. Uso treinta y seis.
4. Sí, miro un par de tenis.
5. Sí, compro los tenis.
6. Pago quinientos pesos.
7. Pago en la caja.

17

1. Perdón, ¿qué necesitas?
2. Perdón, ¿qué buscas?
3. Perdón, ¿qué compras?
4. Perdón, ¿qué llevas?

Estructura

Note: Have students point to themselves as they say **yo** or when they use the **-o** ending. Have them look directly at a friend as they say **tú** or use the **-as** ending. It is important that they always realize to whom they are referring when they use a specific verb ending.

3 PRACTICE

¿Cómo lo digo?

¡OJO! The activities on pages 85–86 give students guided practice on **-ar** verb forms in the singular. These activities build from simple to more complex: Activity 14 uses the **-a** ending only. Activities 15 and 16 enable students to hear **-as** as they answer with **-o.** Activity 17 makes students use both **-as** and **-o** endings. Activity 18, the most difficult activity, has them use all forms.

14, **15**, and **16** These activities can be done first with books closed and then with books open.

14 For visual learners, the photo on page 85 provides cues to the answers.

15 This is a good activity for students to do in pairs because they are communicating information about themselves. Have students look at one another as they answer the questions.

16 This activity, like those above, tells a story. You can call on a student to retell the story in his or her own words.

17 Have two students role-play the dialogue. Ask volunteers to come up with additional items. For example: **Necesito una camisa; Busco la tienda de ropa,** etc.

3 PRACTICE *(continued)*

18 This activity recombines all singular forms of **-ar** verbs. Call on three students to read Activity 18 aloud. One reads the narration; the other two role-play the conversation.

19 Have students do this activity in pairs. This activity makes students use all singular forms of the verb on their own.

20 Encourage students to say as much as possible. Follow up by having students report to the class what their friend said he or she needs for the beginning of the school year.

About the Spanish Language

In some areas children still refer to their parents as **usted.** In other areas people use **tú** even with strangers. Ask students with whom they use **tú** and with whom they use **usted.** Ask whether they think it is simpler to have only one form as in English. Encourage them to discuss the subtleties in usage of **tú** and **usted.**

LEVELING

E: Activity 21

A: Activities 19, 22

C: Activities 18, 20

18 Historieta En la tienda de ropa Completen. *(Complete.)*

Casandra __1__ (necesitar) una blusa. Ella __2__ (buscar) una blusa verde. En la tienda de ropa Casandra __3__ (hablar) con una amiga.

—Casandra, ¿qué __4__ (buscar)?

—Yo __5__ (buscar) una blusa.

—¿__6__ (Necesitar) un color especial?

—Sí, verde.

—¿Qué talla __7__ (usar)?

—Treinta y seis.

—¿Por qué no __8__ (hablar) con la dependienta?

—¡Buena idea!

Casandra __9__ (hablar) con la dependienta. Ella __10__ (mirar) varias blusas verdes. Casandra __11__ (comprar) una blusa que es muy bonita. Ella __12__ (pagar) en la caja.

Marbella, España

19 ¿Trabajas o no? Find out from a classmate whether he or she works. Try to find out where and when. Tell the class about your friend's work.

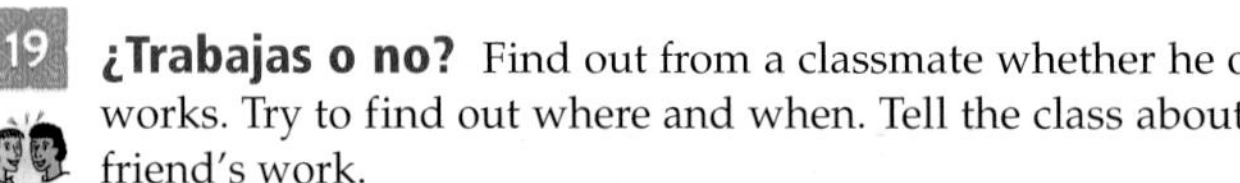

20 ¿Qué necesitas? You're talking on the phone with a good friend. The new school year **(la apertura de clases)** is about to begin. You need lots of things. Have a conversation with your friend. You may want to use some of the following words and expressions.

*For more practice using words from **Palabras 1** and **2** and **-ar** verbs, do Activity 3 on page H4 at the end of this book.*

ANSWERS TO ¿Cómo lo digo?

18

1. necesita
2. busca
3. habla
4. buscas
5. busco
6. Necesitas
7. usas
8. hablas
9. habla
10. mira
11. compra
12. paga

19 *Answers will vary; however, students should use the correct form of* trabajar, *as well as the question words* dónde *and* cuándo (¿a qué hora?).

20 *Answers will vary; however, students should use the verb* necesitar *and the cues in the colored boxes on this page.*

21

1. ¿Qué necesitas tú y qué buscas tú?
2. ¿Qué necesitas tú y qué buscas tú?
3. ¿Qué necesitas Ud. y qué busca Ud.?
4. ¿Qué necesita Ud. y qué busca Ud.?
5. ¿Qué necesitas tú y qué buscas tú?

Tú o usted
Talking formally and informally

1. In Spanish, there are two ways to say *you*. You can use **tú** when talking to a friend, to a person your own age, or to a family member. **Tú** is called the informal or familiar form of address.

   José, ¿hablas español? **Carolina, ¿qué necesitas?**

2. You use **usted** when talking to an older person, a person you do not know very well, or anyone to whom you wish to show respect. The **usted** form of address is polite, or formal. **Usted** is usually abbreviated **Ud. Usted** takes the same verb ending as **él** or **ella.**

   Señor, ¿habla usted inglés?
   Señora, usted trabaja en la papelería, ¿no?

¿Qué palabra necesito?

21 **¿Tú o usted?** Pregunten. *(Ask the following people what they need and what they are looking for. Use* tú *or* usted *as appropriate.)*

1.

2.

3.

4.

5.

22 **Claudia y el señor** Sigan el modelo. *(Follow the model.)*

Necesito una hoja de papel. →
—Y tú, Claudia, ¿qué necesitas?
—¿Y qué necesita usted, señor?

1. Necesito un cuaderno.
2. Busco una goma de borrar.
3. Compro una camisa.
4. Hablo español.

Andas bien. ¡Adelante!

Answers to ¿Cómo lo digo?

22

1. Y tú, Claudia, ¿qué necesitas? ¿Y qué necesita Ud., señor?
2. Y tú, Claudia, ¿qué buscas? ¿Y qué busca Ud., señor?
3. Y tú, Claudia, ¿qué compras? ¿Y qué compra Ud., señor?
4. Y tú, Claudia, ¿hablas español? ¿Y habla Ud. español, señor?

UN POCO MÁS

This *InfoGap* Activity will allow students to practice in pairs. The activity should be very manageable for them, since all vocabulary and structures are familiar to them.

Estructura

1 PREPARATION

Bellringer Review

Use BRR Transparency 3.4 or write the following on the board.
Make up questions using the following words.

1. **quién**
2. **cómo**
3. **qué**
4. **dónde**
5. **cuándo**

2 PRESENTATION

Tú o Ud.

Step 1 Have students open their books to page 87. Explain how the two forms of *you* are used, leading students through the examples on this page. Explain that **tú** is also used when talking to a pet.

Step 2 You may present **usted** and **tú** using magazine photos. Show a photo of a child when using **tú** and a photo of an adult when using **usted.** Show both photos when teaching **ustedes.**

Step 3 Use additional photos of pets, children, and adults, each labeled with a name, and ask students to respond in unison with either **usted** or **tú.**

Step 4 Give the photos to various students. Each student takes the role of the person whose photo he or she is holding. Now ask the person questions. For example: **Sra. Martínez, ¿es usted inteligente?**

3 PRACTICE

¿Cómo lo digo?

21 Have students make up a name for each person. For example, Item 1: **Luis, ¿qué necesitas tú?** Item 2: **Sra. García, ¿qué busca usted?**

Conversación

1 PREPARATION

Resource Manager

Audio Activities TE, page 32
Audio CD 3

Bellringer Review

Use BRR Transparency 3.5 or write the following on the board.
Make up a brief story entitled **En la tienda.** Use the following words: **necesitar, buscar, hablar, comprar, pagar.**

2 PRESENTATION

Step 1 Have students open their books to page 88. Before reading the conversation, have them look at the photo and guess what the conversation is about.

Step 2 Now have students listen to the conversation on Audio CD 3. Then have them repeat the conversation after you.

Step 3 Call on two individuals to read the conversation in its entirety with as much expression as possible.

Step 4 Do the **¿Comprendes?** activity.

Conversación

En la tienda de ropa

Empleada Sí, señor. ¿Qué desea usted?
Cliente Necesito una camisa.
Empleada Una camisa. ¿De qué color, señor?
Cliente Una camisa blanca.
Empleada De acuerdo. ¿Qué talla usa usted?
Cliente Treinta y seis.
(After looking at some shirts)
Cliente ¿Cuánto es, por favor?
Empleada Ciento cincuenta pesos.
Cliente Bien. ¿Pago aquí o en la caja?
Empleada En la caja, por favor.

¿Comprendes?

Contesten. *(Answer.)*

1. ¿Con quién habla el cliente?
2. ¿Qué necesita?
3. ¿Qué talla usa?
4. ¿Mira el señor una camisa?
5. ¿Cuánto es la camisa?
6. ¿Compra el señor la camisa?
7. ¿Dónde paga?

Glencoe Technology

CD-ROM
On the CD-ROM, students can watch a dramatization of this conversation. They can then play the role of either one of the characters and record themselves in the conversation.

Answers to ¿Comprendes?

1. El cliente habla con la dependienta (la empleada).
2. Necesita una camisa.
3. Usa la talla treinta y seis.
4. Sí, el señor mira una camisa.
5. La camisa es (cuesta) ciento cincuenta pesos.
6. Sí, el señor compra la camisa.
7. Paga en la caja.

Vamos a hablar más

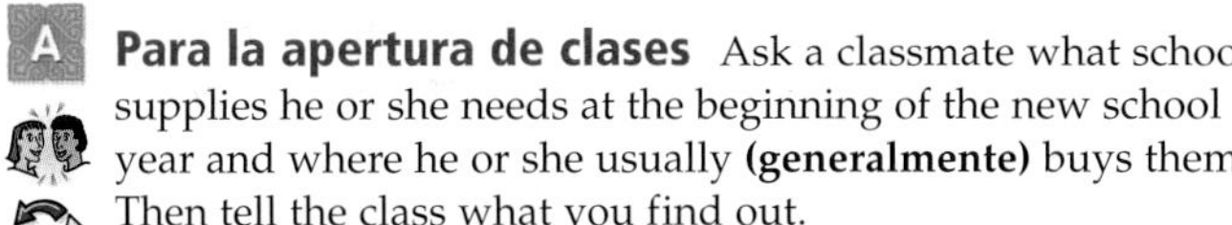

For more information about schools in the Spanish-speaking world, go to the Glencoe Spanish Web site: spanish.glencoe.com

A **Para la apertura de clases** Ask a classmate what school supplies he or she needs at the beginning of the new school year and where he or she usually **(generalmente)** buys them. Then tell the class what you find out.

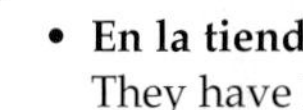

B **En las tiendas** Work with a classmate. Take turns playing the roles of the salesperson and the customer in the following situations.

- **En la papelería** You want to buy two pens—preferably red ones—, a notebook, and a calculator.
- **En la tienda de ropa** You want to buy a blue shirt for your friend. They have his size, but only in white.
- **En la zapatería** You need a pair of brown shoes. The ones the salesperson shows you are expensive.

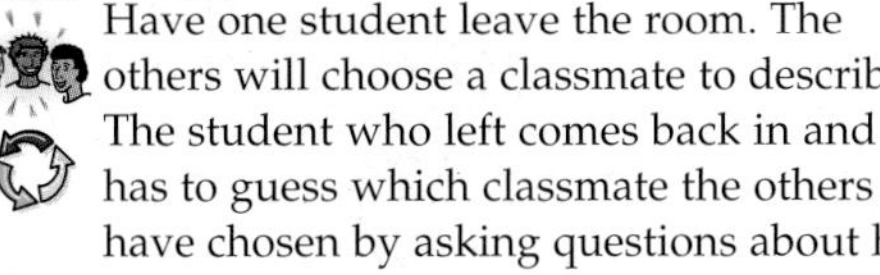

C *Juego* **¿Qué lleva?**
Have one student leave the room. The others will choose a classmate to describe. The student who left comes back in and has to guess which classmate the others have chosen by asking questions about his or her clothes. Use the model as a guide.

¿Lleva un blue jean azul y una camiseta roja?
No.
¿Lleva un par de tenis negros?
Sí.
¡Es Tomás!

Pronunciación

Las consonantes l, f, p, m, n

The pronunciation of the consonants **l, f, p, m,** and **n** is very similar in both Spanish and English. However, the **p** is not followed by a puff of breath as it often is in English. Repeat the following sentences.

Lolita es linda y elegante.
La falda de Felisa no es fea.
Paco es una persona popular.
La muchacha mexicana mira una goma.
Nando necesita un cuaderno nuevo.

Answers to Vamos a hablar más

A *Answers will vary but may include:*
¿Qué materiales escolares necesitas?
Generalmente, ¿dónde compras... ? *Student responses should begin with* Necesito... *and* Generalmente compro...

B *Answers will vary, but students can use the* Conversación *dialogue, page 88, as a model for these activities.*

Conversación

3 PRACTICE

Vamos a hablar más

A To enable students to report to the class, have them write down the school supplies their partners mention. Model the activity with one of your more able students.

B Have each pair of students choose one of the three situations in Activity B. As a follow-up, have different pairs role-play each situation for the class.

C *Juego* This is a good end-of-class activity.

Pronunciación

¡OJO! The consonant-vowel combinations presented in this chapter should not create problems for students. These sounds are rather easy for English speakers to pronounce properly.

Step 1 Write the following on the board and have students pronounce each sound after you.

la le li lo lu
fa fe fi fo fu
pa pe pi po pu
ma me mi mo mu

Step 2 You may wish to have students repeat the following:

La sala de Lolita
Felipe es profesor de física.
El amigo de Manolo Malo
El papá de Pepe Pinto

Step 3 Now have students open their books and repeat the sentences on page 89 after you or Audio CD 3.

Step 4 These sentences can also be used for dictation.

LEVELING
E: Conversation

Lecturas culturales

Resource Manager

Audio Activities TE, page 33
Audio CD 3

National Standards

Cultures
The reading on page 90 gives students insights into some aspects of the school life of their counterparts in Spain.

Comparisons
The reading on this page makes some comparisons between schools in Latin America and Spain and those in the United States.

PRESENTATION

Pre-reading

Step 1 You may wish to present one paragraph of the story per day, or you may choose to present the reading in its entirety.

Step 2 Have students open their books to page 90. Tell them they are going to read a story about a student in Madrid.

Step 3 Go over the Reading Strategy on page 90. Then have students look at the photos on this page. Tell them that as they read, they are going to learn about a difference between the schools in Madrid and their own school. The photo may help them guess what this difference is.

Step 4 Have students scan the reading quickly and silently.

Step 5 Ask them to locate Madrid on the map on page xxx.

Reading

Step 1 Have students open their books and ask the entire class to repeat two or three sentences after you. Ask some of the **¿Comprendes?** questions on page 91 to check for comprehension. Then continue reading.

Lecturas culturales

Reading Strategy

Using pictures and photographs Before you begin to read, look at pictures, photographs, or any other visuals that accompany a reading. By doing this, you can often tell what the reading selection is about before you actually read it.

Un alumno madrileño

Julio Torres es de Madrid. Él es alumno en el Liceo Joaquín Turina en Madrid. Un liceo o colegio es una escuela secundaria en España. En Madrid, la apertura de clases[1] es a fines de[2] septiembre. Julio necesita muchas cosas para la apertura de clases. Necesita materiales escolares. En una papelería compra un libro, un bolígrafo, tres lápices y varios cuadernos. Compra también un disquete para la computadora.

Pero Julio no necesita ropa nueva para la escuela. ¿Por qué? Porque Julio no lleva un blue jean o una camiseta a la escuela. Él lleva un uniforme. Es obligatorio llevar uniforme a la escuela. Un muchacho lleva un pantalón negro y una camisa blanca. En algunas[3] escuelas es necesario llevar chaqueta y corbata también. Una muchacha lleva una falda y una blusa. Y a veces[4] es necesario llevar una chaqueta. ¿Qué opinas? ¿Es una buena idea llevar uniforme a la escuela?

[1]apertura de clases *opening of school*
[2]a fines de *at the end of*
[3]algunas *some*
[4]a veces *sometimes*

FUN-FACTS

Explain to students that wearing a uniform to school is very common in Spain and throughout Latin America. In some elementary schools, the uniform is simply a smock. In some secondary schools, the uniform can be quite formal.

Learning from Photos

(page 91 top) Give students the following information about the photo of the Colegio de Nuestra Señora de la Consolación in Madrid: **Muchas escuelas en España son religiosas. Hay muchas escuelas católicas en España.**

¿Comprendes?

A Un alumno madrileño
Contesten. *(Answer.)*

1. ¿De dónde es Julio Torres?
2. ¿En qué escuela es alumno?
3. ¿Cuándo es la apertura de clases en Madrid?
4. ¿Qué necesita Julio para la apertura de clases?
5. ¿Dónde compra las cosas que necesita?
6. ¿Necesita Julio ropa nueva para la escuela?
7. ¿Qué lleva él a la escuela?
8. ¿Qué lleva una muchacha a la escuela?

B Julio Torres Busquen la información en la lectura. *(Find the information in the reading.)*

1. de dónde es Julio Torres
2. la escuela de Julio
3. cuándo es la apertura de clases en Madrid
4. las cosas que compra Julio
5. lo que es obligatorio llevar a la escuela
6. lo que Julio no lleva a la escuela
7. el uniforme típico de un muchacho
8. el uniforme típico de una muchacha

C Discusión ¿Qué opinas? *(What is your opinion?)*
¿Es una buena idea llevar uniforme a la escuela?

Colegio de Nuestra Señora de la Consolación, Madrid

El Retiro, Madrid

Lecturas culturales

Step 2 Now go over the reading again, calling on individual students to read aloud.

Post-reading

Have students do the **¿Comprendes?** activities on page 91 orally after reading the selection in class. Then assign these activities to be written at home. Go over them again the following day.

¿Comprendes?

A Allow students to refer to the story to look up the answers, or you may use this activity as a testing device for factual recall.

B Have individual students read the appropriate phrase or sentence aloud. Make sure all students find the information in the **Lectura.**

C The **Discusión** on page 91 can be done in English. Students should enjoy discussing this topic. Ask them how they would react if they were required to wear uniforms to school beginning the next semester. How would their lives be different?

LEVELING
E: Reading

Answers to ¿Comprendes?

A

1. Es de Madrid.
2. Es alumno en el Liceo Joaquín Turina.
3. La apertura de clases es a fines de septiembre.
4. Necesita materiales escolares.
5. Compra las cosas que necesita en una papelería.
6. Julio no necesita ropa nueva para la escuela.
7. Julio lleva un uniforme.
8. Una muchacha lleva un uniforme también. Lleva una falda y una blusa.

B

1. de Madrid
2. Liceo Joaquín Turina
3. a fines de septiembre
4. un libro, un bolígrafo, tres lápices, varios cuadernos y un disquete
5. un uniforme
6. un blue jean o una camisa
7. un pantalón negro y una camisa blanca
8. una falda y una blusa

Lectura opcional 1

National Standards

Cultures
This selection familiarizes students with the dress of several different indigenous groups that live in various regions of Latin America.

¡OJO! This reading is optional. You may skip it completely, have the entire class read it, have only several students read it and report to the class, or assign it for extra credit.

PRESENTATION

Step 1 Have students read the passage quickly as they look at the photos that accompany it. The photos will increase comprehension because students can visualize what they are reading.

Step 2 Have students discuss the information they find interesting.

Step 3 Ask students to think of at least one article of clothing that they know of with a Spanish name.

History Connection

A very large percentage of Guatemalans are descendants of the Mayans. As in other areas of South and Central America, the Indians were severely oppressed by their Spanish conquerors. However, the native people of Guatemala remained defiantly apart from the culture of their conquerors. The highland Mayans of Guatemala retained their own cultural identity, which continues to be very strong.

LEVELING
A: Reading 1
C: Reading 2

Lectura opcional 1

La ropa indígena

La ropa que lleva la población india o indígena de Latinoamérica es muy interesante y muy bonita.

En Guatemala, por ejemplo, la ropa cambia o varía de un pueblo[1] a otro. El traje que lleva una señora de Santiago de Atitlán no es el mismo traje que lleva una señora de Chichicastenango.

La india de Guatemala no lleva sombrero. Pero la india del Perú, sí. Ella lleva sombrero.

La india del famoso pueblo de Otavalo en el Ecuador lleva dos faldas de lana[2] oscura con una blusa muy brillante. El señor otavaleño lleva un pantalón blanco, una camisa blanca y un poncho azul.

[1]pueblo *town* [2]lana *wool*

¿Comprendes?

La ropa indígena
Identifiquen. *(Identify.)*
Some articles of clothing retain their Spanish names in English. Look at the photographs to find out what they are.

huaraches

sarape

poncho

Learning from Photos

(page 92) The woman pictured at the top left of the page is from Chichicastenango, Guatemala. The woman in the top right photo is from Santiago de Atitlán, one of the twelve villages on Lake Atitlán named after the apostles. The woman in the middle is from Ecuador. The hat she is wearing is the same as or very similar to those worn by women in Perú and Bolivia. The photos below are of **otavaleños,** from the famous market town of Otavalo, north of Quito. They are famous around the world for their weavings.
Although it is not evident in these photos, the men of Otavalo wear their hair in a long braid.

Lectura opcional 2

Un diseñador famoso

El famoso diseñador de ropa Oscar de la Renta es de Santo Domingo, la capital de la República Dominicana. Los estilos de de la Renta son muy elegantes y lujosos. Los trajes de gala de de la Renta son muy caros. La fama de Oscar de la Renta es mundial[1].

Oscar de la Renta es también una persona muy buena y muy humana. En la República Dominicana, de la Renta funda un orfanato[2] y un tipo de «Boys' Town». El «Boys' Town» es para niños desamparados[3]. Funda también una escuela especial para sordos[4].

[1]mundial *worldwide*
[2]orfanato *orphanage*
[3]niños desamparados *homeless children*
[4]sordos *deaf people*

¿Comprendes?

A En español, por favor. Busquen las palabras afines en la lectura. *(Find the cognates in the reading.)*

B Oscar de la Renta Contesten. *(Answer.)*

1. ¿De dónde es Oscar de la Renta?
2. ¿Por qué es él un hombre (señor) muy famoso?

Lectura opcional 2

¡OJO! This reading is optional. You may skip it completely, have the entire class read it, have only several students read it and report to the class, or assign it for extra credit.

PRESENTATION

Step 1 Have students read the selection to themselves.

Step 2 Now have students do the **¿Comprendes?** activities.

Step 3 You may wish to ask students to bring to class any articles of clothing they may have that were made in a Spanish-speaking country. These could be clothing items mentioned in the reading or other items.

Assessment

You may wish to give the following quiz to those students who read this selection.
Answer.

1. **¿De dónde es Oscar de la Renta?**
2. **¿Cuál es la capital de la República Dominicana?**
3. **¿Qué es Oscar de la Renta? ¿Cuál es la profesión de de la Renta?**
4. **¿Cómo son los estilos de de la Renta?**
5. **¿Qué tipo de persona es de la Renta?**
6. **¿Qué funda él?**
7. **¿Para quiénes es el «Boy's Town»?**

Answers to ¿Comprendes?

A

famoso, la capital, elegantes, la fama, una persona, humana, un tipo, especial

B

1. Es de Santo Domingo en la República Dominicana.
2. Es un diseñador de ropa muy elegante y lujosa.

Chapter Projects

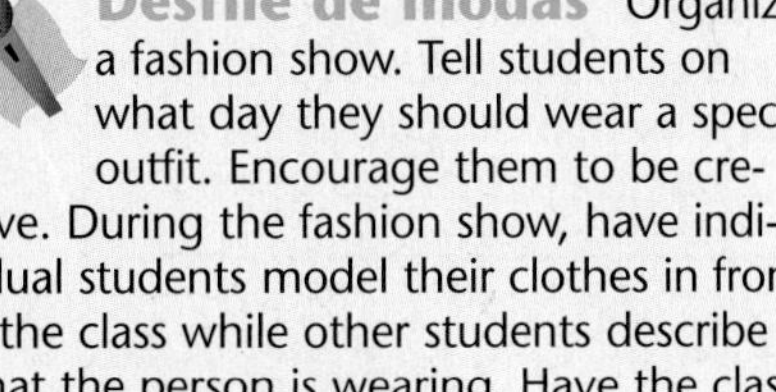

Desfile de modas Organize a fashion show. Tell students on what day they should wear a special outfit. Encourage them to be creative. During the fashion show, have individual students model their clothes in front of the class while other students describe what the person is wearing. Have the class vote on their favorite outfit.

Conexiones

National Standards

Connections
This reading establishes a connection with computer science. Since most students today are familiar with computers they should find it very easy to use computer terms in Spanish and thus increase their Spanish vocabulary.

This introduction to computer vocabulary in Spanish is very useful for reading advertisements or instructions concerning the use of computers.

¡OJO! The readings in the **Conexiones** section are optional. They focus on some of the major disciplines taught in schools and universities. The vocabulary is useful for discussing such topics as history, literature, art, economics, business, science, etc. You may choose any of the following ways to do the readings in the **Conexiones** sections.

Independent reading Have students read the selections and do the post-reading activities as homework, which you collect. This option is least intrusive on class time and requires a minimum of teacher involvement.

Homework with in-class follow-up Assign the readings and post-reading activities as homework. Review and discuss the material in class the next day.

Intensive in-class activity This option includes a pre-reading vocabulary presentation, in-class reading and discussion, assignment of the activities for homework, and a discussion of the assignment in class the following day.

LEVELING
E: Reading

Conexiones
La tecnología

La computadora

Some years ago computers began to revolutionize the way people conduct their lives. They have changed the way we view the world and, in reality, they've changed the world. Computers have a place in our homes, in our schools, and in our world of business. If you are interested in computers, you may want to familiarize yourself with some basic computer vocabulary in Spanish. Then read the information about computers on the next page.

About the Spanish Language

In Spain, **el ordenador** is used instead of **la computadora.** The latter is used in all countries in Latin America.

Critical Thinking Activity

Drawing conclusions, making inferences Ask students why so many computer-related terms come from English. Point out that languages constantly borrow words from other languages. For example, on page 92 of this chapter, students were shown several articles of clothing that have retained their Spanish names in English.

Conecta la computadora y ¡a trabajar!

Una computadora procesa datos. El hardware es la computadora y todo el equipo[1] conectado con la computadora. El software son los programas de la computadora. Un programa es un grupo o conjunto de instrucciones.

La computadora almacena[2] datos. Envía o transmite los datos a un disco. La computadora calcula, compara y copia datos. Pero la computadora no piensa[3]. El operador o la operadora de la computadora entra las instrucciones y la computadora procesa la información.

[1]equipo *equipment* [2]almacena *stores* [3]piensa *think*

El Internet—¡Conecta al mundo!

Con el Internet hay acceso al mundo[4] entero. Hay información sobre la historia, la economía, el arte, la música y muchas otras áreas de interés. Cuando navegas por la red[5], es posible conectar con los centros de noticias. Es posible enviar correo[6] electrónico y conversar con amigos en otras partes del mundo. Cuando estamos conectados a la red por cable or por satélite nuestras comunicaciones son casi instantáneas. Los satélites llevan los mensajes hasta 20 veces más rápido que el modem. Y las conexiones DSL llevan los mensajes de 50 a 150 veces más rápido que el modem. Cada día los avances tecnológicos resultan en comunicaciones más fáciles y más rápidas. Y hay la posibilidad de crear una página Web. Sí, ¡el mundo entero en una pantalla!

[4]mundo *world* [5]red *Net* [6]correo *mail*

¿Comprendes?

A En español, por favor.
Busquen las palabras en la lectura.
(Find the following words in the reading.)

1. hardware
2. software
3. program
4. data
5. satelite
6. surf the Net
7. Web page
8. e-mail (electronic mail)
9. to process information
10. access
11. computer operator

B Una página Web Look at the monitor on page 94. If you have access to the Internet either at home or at school, go to **spanish.glencoe.com ¡a practicar el español!**

Los alumnos navegan por la red.

Conexiones

PRESENTATION

La tecnología
La computadora

Step 1 Most students will be familiar with these computer terms in English. Model the terms in Spanish and have students repeat after you.

Step 2 If there is a computer in your classroom, have students name the equipment in Spanish.

Step 3 Explain to students that there are some basic strategies to use when reading unfamiliar material. They should learn to (1) recognize cognates and (2) derive meaning from context.

Step 4 Ask students to scan the reading on page 95 and make a list of words they do not know the meaning of.

Step 5 As a whole-class activity, go over the words students have listed, asking other students to guess their meaning based on the context.

Después de leer

A This is a skimming activity designed to provide practice in reading for specific information. Do this activity orally.

Answers to ¿Comprendes?

A

1. el hardware
2. el software
3. el programa
4. los datos
5. el satélite
6. navegar por la red
7. una página Web
8. el correo electrónico
9. procesar la información
10. el acceso
11. el / la operador(a) de la computadora

Career Connection

Explain to students that knowledge of computer vocabulary in Spanish could be a tremendous asset in careers in business and finance. Have them do some research to find out which North American companies have offices in Spanish-speaking countries.

¡Te toca a ti!

Use what you have learned

Bellringer Review

Use BRR Transparency 3.6 or write the following on the board.
Rewrite the following in the **tú** form.
1. **Ud. habla francés.**
2. **¿Llega Ud. a la escuela?**

Recycling

These activities allow students to use the vocabulary and structure from this chapter in completely open-ended, real-life situations.

PRESENTATION

Encourage students to say as much as possible when they do these activities. Tell them not to be afraid to make mistakes, since the goal of the activities is real-life communication. If someone in the group makes an error, allow the others to politely correct him or her. Let students choose the activities they would like to do.

You may wish to divide students into pairs or groups. Encourage students to elaborate on the basic theme and to be creative. They may use props, pictures, or posters if they wish.

¡Te toca a ti!

Use what you have learned

HABLAR **1**

En la papelería

✔ ***Identify and shop for school supplies***

With a classmate, take turns playing the parts of a student shopping and a salesperson in a stationery store. Tell some supplies you need and find out how much each item costs. The salesperson will give you the information.

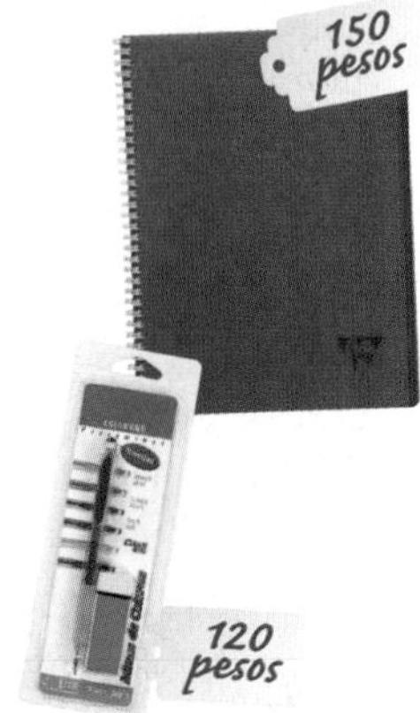

HABLAR **2**

Lo que llevo yo

✔ ***Identify and describe articles of clothing***

Work with a classmate. Each of you will describe what you typically wear to school.

Madrid, España

HABLAR **3** ESCRIBIR

Regalos

✔ ***Shop for clothing***

You have just spent a few weeks in Spain and want to buy some articles of clothing as gifts for several friends. Make a list of what you want to buy. Go to the different stores to buy the items you want. With a classmate, take turns being the customer and salesperson at the stores where you are purchasing the items on your list.

Answers to ¡Te toca a ti!

1 *Answers will vary but may include:*
—Necesito una goma. ¿Cuánto cuesta?
—Una goma cuesta 12 pesos.

2 *Answers will vary, but students should use vocabulary from the chapter to describe what they wear to school.*

3 *Answers will vary but may include:*
—¿Qué desea Ud.?
—Necesito una mochila.
—¿De qué color?
—Una mochila roja. ¿Cuánto es, por favor?
—80 pesos.
—¿Pago aquí o en la caja?
—En la caja, por favor.

¡Te toca a ti!

ESCRIBIR

4 Necesito ropa

✔ *Order clothing from a catalogue and give the size and color you need*

You want to order from the catalogue. Write a letter stating which items, what color, and what size.

B - MOCASINES planos con forma de zuecos y pequeño talón de 1.5 cm. Empeine pespunteado de color crudo por el exterior. Exterior y plantilla en piel de serraje acabado ante.
malva 580.1030 negro 580.3374
beige 580.3036
35, 36, 37 **3.795 pesos**
38, 39, 40, 41 **4.195 pesos**

Camisa manga corta varios diseños.
€9,59

Pantalón corto de vestir, en varios colores.
€11,99

C - BLUSA. 100% algodón.
MANGA CORTA CON VUELTA.
blanco 810.0638
38, 40 **1.995 pesos**
42, 44, 46 **2.195 pesos**
48, 50, 52 **2.395 pesos**
54 **2.595 pesos**

E - BERMUDAS. Largo desde el tiro 20 cm, boquilla 30 cm aprox.
1. malva 280.1116 4. marino 280.4409
2. beige 280.0118 5. negro 280.3468
3. caqui 280.2528
36, 38, 40 **2.495 pesos**
42, 44, 46 **2.695 pesos**

Writing Strategy

Preparing for an interview
An interview is one way to gather information for a story or a report. A good interviewer should prepare questions ahead of time. In preparing the questions, think about what you hope to learn from the interview. The best interview questions are open-ended. Open-ended questions cannot be answered with *yes* or *no*. They give the person being interviewed more opportunity to "open up" and speak freely.

HABLAR ESCRIBIR

5 Guadalupe Álvaro

It is the beginning of a new school year. Your first assignment for the school newspaper is to write an article about a new exchange student, Guadalupe Álvaro. Guadalupe is from Salamanca, Spain.

You decide to interview Guadalupe before writing your article. To prepare for the interview, write down as many questions as you can. Ask her about her personal life, school life in her country, her friends, etc. After you have prepared your questions, conduct the interview with a partner who plays the role of Guadalupe. Write down your partner's answers to your questions. Then organize your notes and write your article.

Answers to ¡Te toca a ti!

4 *Answers will vary, but students will use the ads to choose and describe items they wish to purchase.*

5 *Answers will vary, depending on the questions students prepare for the interview.*

¡Te toca a ti!

Writing Development

Have students keep a notebook or portfolio containing their best written work from each chapter. These selected writings can be based on assignments from the Student Textbook and the Workbook. The two activities on page 97 are examples of writing assignments that may be included in each student's portfolio. On page 28 in the Workbook, students will begin to develop an organized autobiography **(Mi autobiografía).** These workbook pages may also become a part of their portfolio.

Writing Strategy

Preparing for an interview
Have students read the Writing Strategy on page 97. Now give students the following pairs of questions and have them decide which are open-ended.

¿Necesitas un bolígrafo?
¿Qué necesitas?

¿Es cara la camisa?
¿Cuánto cuesta la camisa?

National Standards

Communities
If possible, have students conduct the interview they have prepared on page 97 with a Spanish-speaking student in their school.

LEVELING

These activities encompass all three levels. All students will be able to do them at a sophistication level commensurate with their ability in Spanish. Some students will be able to speak for several minutes, and others may be able to give just a few sentences. This is to be expected when students are functioning completely on their own generating their own language to the best of their ability.

Assessment

Resource Manager

Communication Transparency C 3
Quizzes, pages 11–16
Performance Assessment, Task 3
Tests, pages 27–40
Situation Cards, Chapter 3
ExamView® Pro, Chapter 3
Maratón mental Videoquiz, Chapter 3

Assessment

This is a pre-test for students to take before you administer the chapter test. Note that each section is cross-referenced so students can easily find the material they have to review in case they made errors. You may use Assessment Answers Transparency A 1 to do the assessment in class, or you may assign this assessment for homework. You can correct the assessment yourself, or you may prefer to project the answers on the overhead in class.

Glencoe Technology

MINDJOGGER VHS/DVD

You may wish to help your students prepare for the chapter test by playing the MindJogger game show. Teams will compete against each other to review chapter vocabulary and structure and sharpen listening comprehension skills.

Reaching All Students

For the Heritage Speakers Some Spanish-speaking countries use U.S. sizes; others use metric or European sizes. If there are students in the class from different Hispanic countries, ask them to tell what sizes they use in those countries: **¿Qué número (tamaño) usan para los zapatos, etc.?**

Assessment

Vocabulario

To review **Palabras 1**, turn to pages 76–77.

1 Identifiquen. *(Identify.)*

¿Qué es?

2 Completen. *(Complete.)*

4. Alejandro ____ con la dependienta en la papelería.
5. El cuaderno ____ noventa pesos.
6. Alejandro paga en la ____.

To review **Palabras 2**, turn to pages 80–81.

3 Identifiquen. *(Identify.)*

ANSWERS TO

1
1. un libro
2. una hoja de papel
3. una calculadora

2
4. habla
5. es (cuesta)
6. caja

3
7. una camisa
8. una falda
9. los zapatos

Chapter Projects

En la tienda de ropa Have pairs of students prepare a skit that takes place at a clothing store. One student is the customer, the other is the store clerk. Students should use some articles of clothing and price tags with prices in **pesos** as props.

4 **Completen.** *(Complete.)*

10. La muchacha ____ un blue jean y un T-shirt.
11. La camisa no cuesta mucho. Es bastante ____.
12. Rubén compra un par de ____, número 38.

Estructura

To review -ar verbs in the singular, turn to page 84.

5 **Completen.** *(Complete.)*

13. ¿Cuánto ____ (tú)? (pagar)
14. Yo ____ un nuevo blue jean. (necesitar)
15. ¿Dónde ____ tú el blue jean? (comprar)
16. La dependienta ____ en la tienda de ropa. (trabajar)

To review tú and usted, turn to page 87.

6 **Escojan.** *(Choose.)*

17. ¿Dónde ____, señor?
 a. trabajas **b.** trabaja usted
18. Amigo, ¿qué ____?
 a. buscas **b.** busca usted

Cultura

To review this cultural information, turn to page 90.

7 **Contesten.** *(Answer)*

19. ¿Qué es un colegio o un liceo en España?
20. En España, ¿qué lleva un alumno o una alumna a la escuela?

La Ciudad de México

Assessment

SPANISH Online

The **Glencoe Spanish Web** site (**spanish.glencoe.com**) offers options that enable you and your students to experience the Spanish-speaking world via the Internet. For each **Capítulo,** there are activities, games, and quizzes. In addition, an *Enrichment* section offers students an opportunity to visit Web sites related to the theme of the chapter.

FOLDABLES™ Study Organizer **Dinah Zike's Study Guides**

Your students may wish to use Foldable 5 to organize, display, and arrange data as they practice interrogative words. You may wish to encourage them to add information from each chapter as they continue to ask and answer questions in Spanish.

Encourage students to keep this *tab book* foldable in a safe place so they can refer to it and add content as they acquire more knowledge.

Answers to Assessment

4

10. lleva
11. barata
12. zapatos

5

13. pagas
14. necesito
15. compras
16. trabaja

6

17. b
18. a

7

19. Es una escuela secundaria.
20. Lleva un uniforme.

¡Hablo como un pro!

This unique page gives students the opportunity to speak freely and say whatever they can, using the vocabulary and structures they have learned in the chapter. The illustration serves to remind students of precisely what they know how to say in Spanish. There are no activities that students do not have the ability to describe or talk about in Spanish. The art not only depicts the vocabulary and content of this chapter, but also reinforces what they learned in previous chapters.

You may wish to use this page in many ways. Some possibilities are to have students do the following:

1. Look at the illustration and identify items by giving the correct Spanish words.
2. Make up sentences about what they see in the illustration.
3. Make up questions about the illustration. They can call on another class member to respond if you do this as a class activity, or you may prefer to allow students to work in small groups. This activity is extremely beneficial because it enables students to actively use interrogative words.
4. Answer questions you ask them about the illustration.
5. Work in pairs and make up a conversation based on the illustration.
6. Look at the illustration and give a complete oral review of what they see.
7. Look at the illustration and write a paragraph (or essay) about it.

You can also use this page as an assessment or testing tool, taking into account individual differences by having students go from simple to quite complicated tasks. The assessment can be either oral or written. You may wish to use the rubrics provided on pages T20–T21 as you give students the following directions.

1. Identify the topic or situation of the illustration.
2. Give the Spanish words for as many items as you can.
3. Think of as many sentences as you can to describe the illustration.
4. Go over your sentences and put them in the best sequencing to give a coherent story based on the illustration.

¡Hablo como un pro!

Tell all you can about this illustration.

Vocabulario

Identifying school supplies

los materiales escolares
la mochila
el lápiz, los lápices
el bolígrafo, la pluma
el marcador
la goma de borrar
el cuaderno, el bloc
la carpeta
el libro
la hoja de papel
la calculadora
el disquete

Identifying articles of clothing

la ropa
el pantalón
la camisa
la corbata
el T-shirt, la camiseta
el blue jean, los blue jeans
la falda
la blusa
la chaqueta
el traje
la gorra
los calcetines
los zapatos
los tenis, un par de tenis

Describing clothes

largo(a)
corto(a)

Identifying colors

¿De qué color es?
blanco(a)
negro(a)
gris
azul
amarillo(a)
anaranjado(a)
rojo(a)
rosado(a)
verde
de color marrón

How well do you know your vocabulary?

- Identify the words and expressions that describe what you do to get ready for a new school year.
- Use as many words as you can from your list to write a story to tell about your preparation for going back to school.

Identifying some types of stores

la papelería
la tienda de ropa

Shopping

el/la dependiente(a)
el/la empleado(a)
la caja
la talla, el tamaño
el número
barato(a)
caro(a)
mucho
poco
necesitar
buscar
mirar
comprar
pagar
usar, calzar
llevar
hablar
trabajar

VIDEOTUR

Episodio 3

In this video episode, you will accompany Vicky and Julián on a shopping expedition. See page 494 for more information.

Other useful expressions

¿Qué desea usted?
¿Cuánto es?, ¿Cuánto cuesta?

¡OJO! You will notice that the vocabulary list here is not translated. This has been done intentionally, since we feel that by the time students have finished the material in the chapter they should be familiar with the meanings of all the words. If there are several words they still do not know, we recommend that they refer to the **Palabras 1** and **2** sections in the chapter or go to the dictionaries at the end of this book to find the meanings. However, if you prefer that your students have the English translations, please refer to Vocabulary Transparency 3.1, where you will find all these words with their translations.

Vocabulario

Vocabulary Review

The words and phrases in the **Vocabulario** have been taught for productive use in this chapter. They are summarized here as a resource for both student and teacher. This list also serves as a convenient resource for the **¡Te toca a ti!** activities on pages 96 and 97. There are approximately six cognates in this vocabulary list. Have students find them.

VIDEO VHS/DVD

The Video Program allows students to see how the chapter vocabulary and structures are used by native speakers within an engaging storyline. For maximum reinforcement, show the video episode as a final activity for Chapter 3.

Reaching All Students

For the Younger Students Have students draw a picture with colored markers or crayons of a boy or a girl wearing an outfit they like. Ask students to label the clothes and their colors in Spanish.

Planning for Chapter 4

SCOPE AND SEQUENCE, PAGES 102–133

Topics

- Going to school
- School activities
- Afterschool activities
- Numbers: 1,000–2,000,000

Culture

- Paula and Armando, two students from Peru
- Differences between schools in the United States and schools in Spanish-speaking countries
- Miraflores, a suburb of Lima, Peru
- A famous Chilean poet: Gabriela Mistral
- Punta Arenas, Chile
- Biology terms in Spanish
- **Vistas de México**

Functions

- How to talk about going to school
- How to talk about classes and school events
- How to greet people and ask how they feel
- How to count from 1,000 to 2,000,000

Structure

- Plural forms of **-ar** verbs
- **Ir, dar,** and **estar**
- The contractions **al** and **del**

National Standards

- Communication Standard 1.1 pages 102, 106, 107, 110, 111, 113, 114, 115, 117, 119, 121, 129
- Communication Standard 1.2 pages 107, 111, 115, 120, 121, 123, 124, 125, 127, 129
- Communication Standard 1.3 pages 107, 129
- Cultures Standard 2.1 pages 107, 120, 122–123, 124–125
- Connections Standard 3.1 pages 126–127
- Connections Standard 3.2 page 129
- Comparisons Standard 4.2 pages 122, 125
- Communities Standard 5.2 page 133

PACING AND PRIORITIES

The chapter content is color coded below to assist you in planning.

■ **required** ■ **recommended** ■ **optional**

Vocabulario *(required)* *Days 1–4*

- ■ Palabras 1
  - Llegar a la escuela
  - En la escuela
- ■ Palabras 2
  - En la clase
  - La fiesta del Club de español
  - Más números

Estructura *(required)* *Days 5–7*

- ■ Presente de los verbos en **-ar** en el plural
- ■ Presente de los verbos **ir, dar, estar**
- ■ Las contracciones **al** y **del**

Conversación *(required)*

- ■ La fiesta del Club de español

Pronunciación *(recommended)*

- ■ La consonante **t**

Lecturas culturales

- ■ Escuelas del mundo hispano *(recommended)*
- ■ Una conferencia universitaria *(optional)*
- ■ Gabriela Mistral *(optional)*

Conexiones

- ■ La biología *(optional)*

■ **¡Te toca a ti!** *(recommended)*

■ **Assessment** *(recommended)*

■ **¡Hablo como un pro!** *(optional)*

RESOURCE GUIDE

Section	Pages	Section Resources
Vocabulario PALABRAS 1		
Llegar a la escuela En la escuela	104, 106–107 105, 106–107	Vocabulary Transparencies 4.2–4.3 Audio CD 3 Audio Activities TE, pages 35–37 Workbook, page 29 Quiz 1, page 17 ExamView® Pro
Vocabulario PALABRAS 2		
En la clase La fiesta del Club de español Más números	108, 110–111 109, 110–111 109, 110–111	Vocabulary Transparencies 4.4–4.5 Audio CD 3 Audio Activities TE, pages 38–39 Workbook, pages 30–31 Quiz 2, page 18 ExamView® Pro
Estructura		
Presente de los verbos en **-ar** en el plural Presente de los verbos **ir, dar, estar** Las contracciones **al** y **del**	112–115 116–117 118–119	Audio CD 3 Audio Activities TE, pages 40–42 Workbook, pages 32–37 Quizzes 3–5, pages 19–21 ExamView® Pro
Conversación		
La fiesta del Club de español	120	Audio CD 3 Audio Activities TE, pages 42–43 Interactive CD-ROM
Pronunciación		
La consonante **t**	121	Pronunciation Transparency P 4 Audio CD 3 Audio Activities TE, page 43
Lecturas culturales		
Escuelas del mundo hispano Una conferencia universitaria Gabriela Mistral	122–123 124 125	Audio CD 3 Audio Activities TE, page 44 Tests, pages 44, 47
Conexiones		
La biología	126–127	Tests, page 48
¡Te toca a ti!		
	128–129	**¡Viva el mundo hispano!** Video, Episode 4 Video Activities, Chapter 4 Spanish Online Activities spanish.glencoe.com
Assessment		
	130–131	Communication Transparency C 4 Quizzes 1–5, pages 17–21 Performance Assessment, Task 4 Tests, pages 41–56 Situation Cards, Chapter 4 ExamView® Pro **Maratón mental** Videoquiz

Using Your Resources for Chapter 4

Transparencies

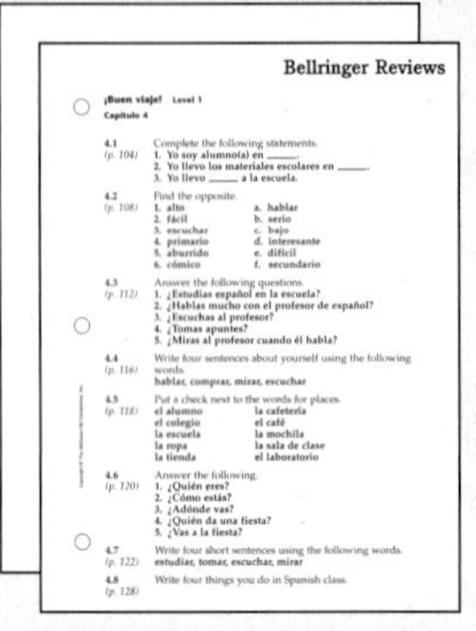
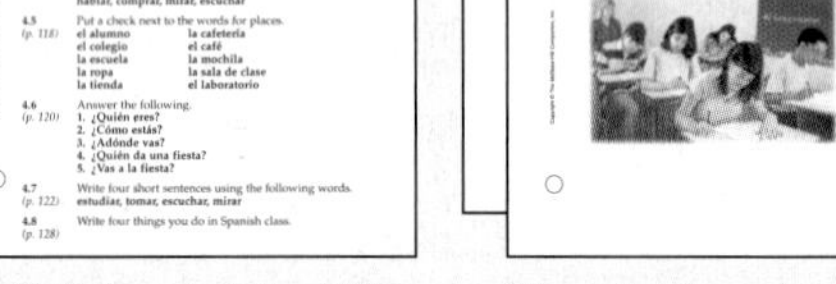
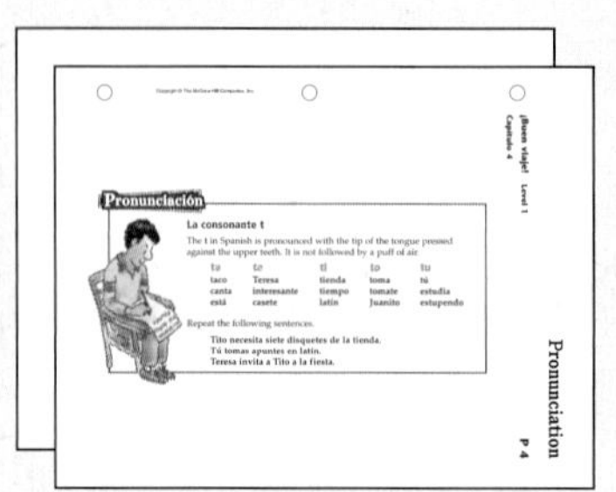

Bellringer 4.1–4.8

Vocabulary 4.1–4.5

Pronunciation P 4

Communication C 4

Workbook

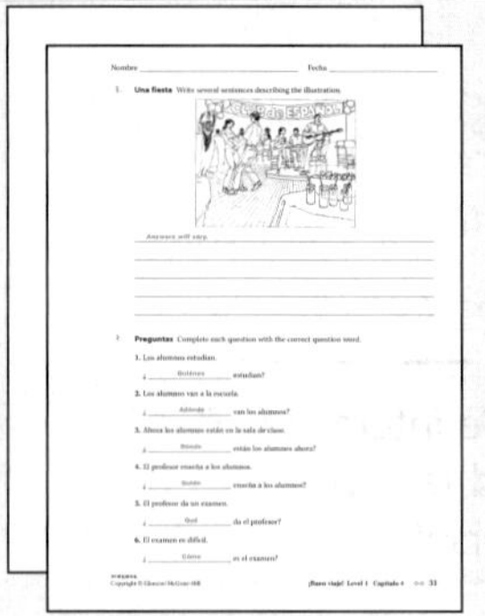

Vocabulary, pages 29–31

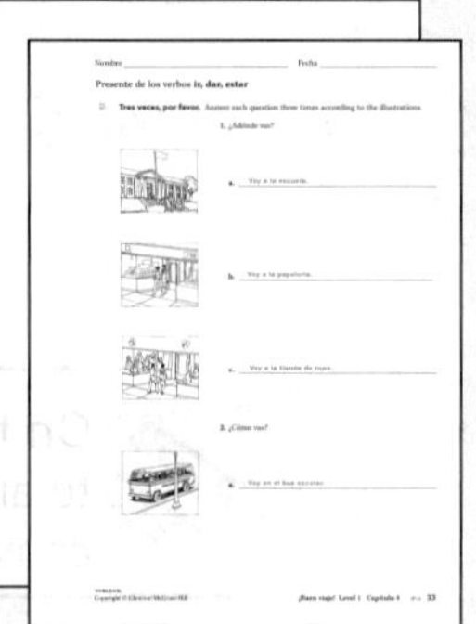

Structure, pages 32–37

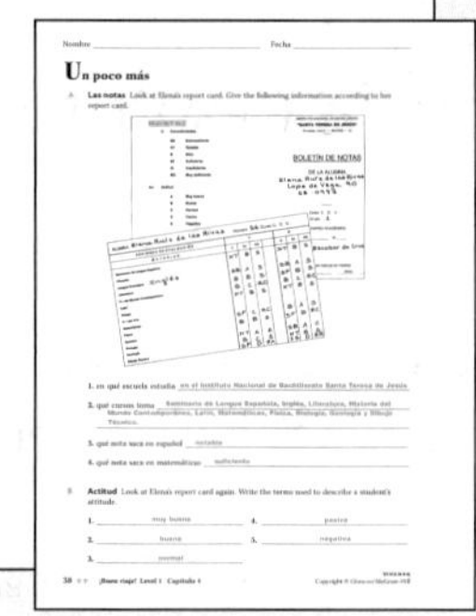

Enrichment, pages 38–40

Audio Activities

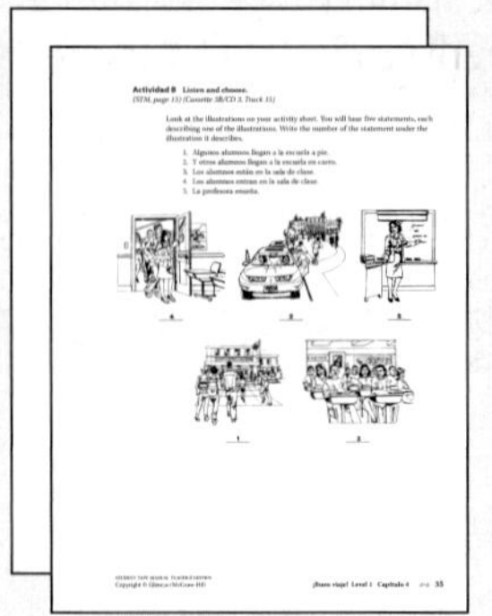

Vocabulary, pages 35–39

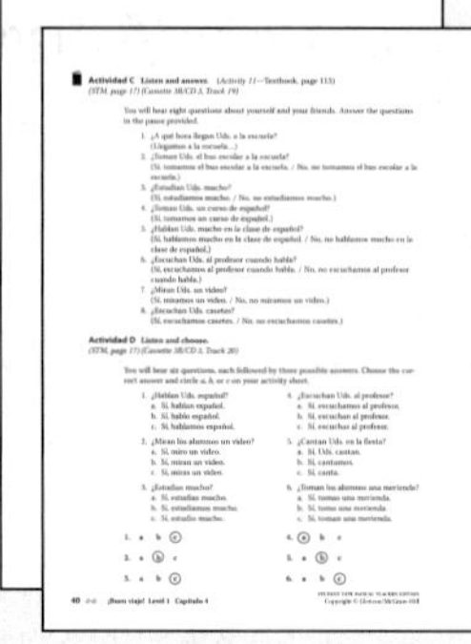

Structure, pages 40–42

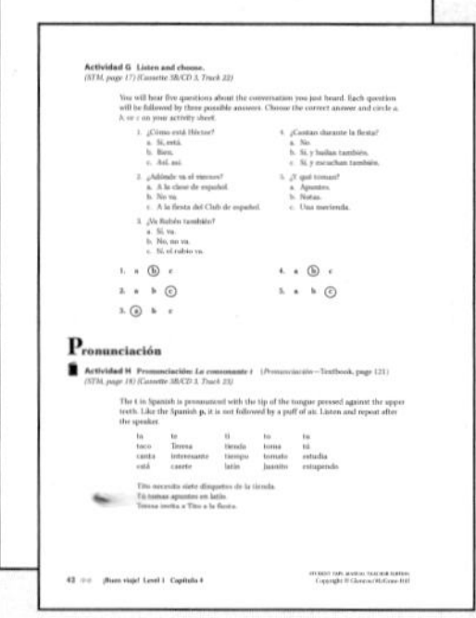

Conversation, Pronunciation, pages 42–43

Additional Practice, pages 44–48

Assessment

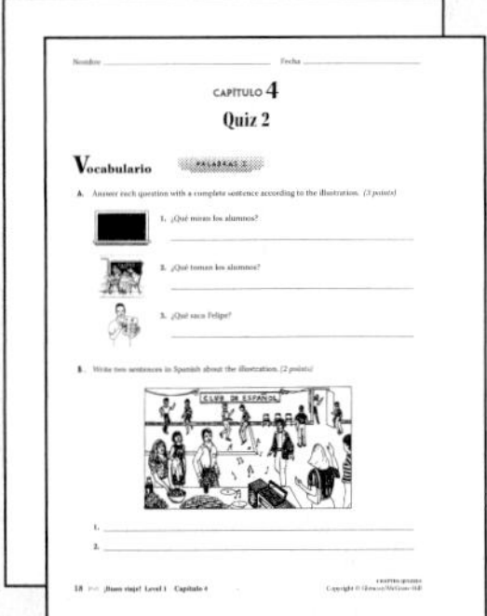

Vocabulary and Structure Quizzes, pages 17–21

Chapter Tests, pages 41–56

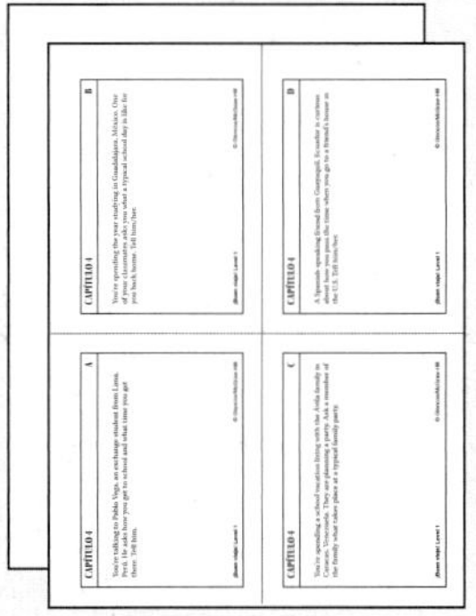

Situation Cards, Chapter 4

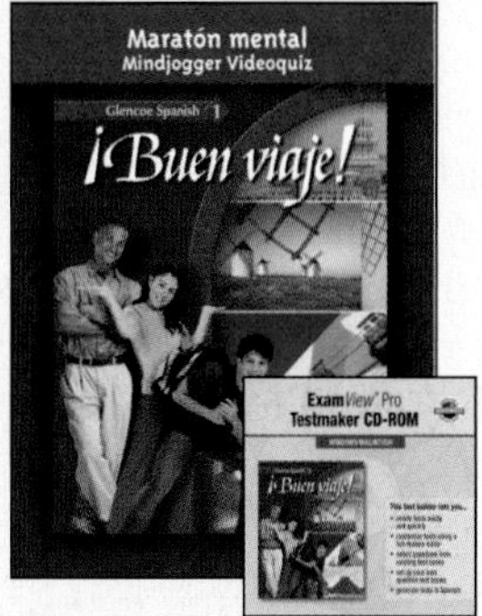

MindJogger Videoquiz, ExamView® Pro, Chapter 4

Timesaving Teacher Tools

TeacherWorks™ is your all-in-one teacher resource center. Personalize lesson plans, access resources from the Teacher Wraparound Edition, connect to the Internet, or make a to-do list. These are only a few of the many features that can assist you in the planning and organizing of your lessons.

Includes:

- A calendar feature
- Access to all program blackline masters
- Standards correlations and more

ExamView® Pro

Test Bank software for Macintosh and Windows makes creating, editing, customizing, and printing tests quick and easy.

Technology Resources

In the Chapter 4 Internet Activity, you will have a chance to learn more about the Spanish-speaking world. Visit spanish.glencoe.com

On the interactive CD-ROM, students can listen to and take part in a recorded version of the conversation in Chapter 4.

¡Viva el mundo hispano! Video and Video Activities, Chapter 4. Available on VHS and DVD.

Help your students prepare for the chapter test by playing the **Maratón mental** Videoquiz game show. Teams will compete against each other to review chapter vocabulary and structure and sharpen listening comprehension skills. Available on VHS and DVD.

¡Buen viaje! is also available on CD or Online.

Capítulo 4

Preview

In this chapter, students will learn to discuss how they get to school and to describe many typical school activities. To do this, they will learn to use the plural forms of **-ar** verbs to communicate in school-related situations. They will also learn the verbs **ir, dar,** and **estar.**

National Standards

Communication

In Chapter 4, students will communicate in spoken and written Spanish on the following topics:

- getting to school
- participating in classroom activities
- enjoying club activities

Students will obtain and provide information, engage in conversations, and discuss schooling in the United States and Spanish-speaking countries as they fulfill the objectives listed on this page.

Capítulo 4

En la escuela

Objetivos

In this chapter you will learn to:

- talk about going to school
- talk about some school activities
- greet people and ask how they feel
- tell how you feel
- describe where you and others go
- describe where you and others are
- discuss some differences between schools in the United States and schools in Spanish-speaking countries

Diego Rivera *Alfabetización*

Spotlight on Culture

Arte Diego Rivera (1886–1957) is considered the most eminent of the Mexican muralists. His works are often political and symbolic in nature.

Fotografía These students are walking on the **Paseo Ahumada,** Santiago's main pedestrian thoroughfare. It is in the central part of Santiago, between the **Plaza de Armas** and the **Palacio de la Moneda,** which was formerly the presidential residence. It was badly damaged by air force attacks during the 1973 coup against Salvador Allende. **La Moneda** has now been completely restored.

LEVELING

The activities, conversations, and readings within each chapter are marked according to level of difficulty. **E** indicates easy. **A** indicates average. **C** indicates challenging. Some activities cover a range of difficulty. In some activities, for example, advanced students will be able to produce more extensive responses while students who learn at a different rate may give less detailed responses. The leveling indicators will help you individualize instruction to best meet your students' needs.

Vocabulario

PALABRAS 1

1 PREPARATION

Resource Manager

Vocabulary Transparencies 4.2–4.3
Audio Activities TE, pages 35–37
Audio CD 3
Workbook, page 29
Quizzes, page 17
ExamView® Pro

Bellringer Review

Use BRR Transparency 4.1 or write the following on the board.
Complete the following statements.

1. **Yo soy alumno(a) en ___.**
2. **Yo llevo los materiales escolares en ___.**
3. **Yo llevo ___ a la escuela.**

2 PRESENTATION

Step 1 Have students close their books. Model the new vocabulary using Vocabulary Transparencies 4.2–4.3. Have students repeat each expression two or three times.

LEVELING
E: Vocabulary

Vocabulario

PALABRAS 1

Llegar a la escuela

a pie

en carro, en coche

en el bus escolar

Los alumnos llegan a la escuela.
¿Cuándo llegan a la escuela?
¿A qué hora llegan?
Llegan a eso de las ocho menos cuarto.
No llegan a las ocho menos cuarto en punto.

Algunos van a la escuela a pie.
Algunos van en carro.
Otros toman el bus escolar.

Reaching All Students

Total Physical Response Do the TPR activities after presenting the vocabulary. Tell students they are going to act out what you say.

___, ven acá. Tú vas a la escuela. Vas a la escuela a pie.
___, tú no vas a la escuela a pie. Tomas el bus. Toma tu asiento en el bus. *(Use a classroom chair.)*
___, tú entras en la sala de clase.
___, tú hablas con la profesora.
___, tú miras la pizarra.
___, tú miras al (a la) profesor(a).
___, tú hablas.
___, tú no hablas. Tú escuchas al (a la) profesor(a).

En la escuela

entrar en la escuela

Los alumnos entran en la escuela.

la sala de clase,
el salón de clase

Los alumnos están en la sala de clase.
Los alumnos estudian.
La profesora enseña.

Vocabulario

Step 2 As you present the vocabulary in sentences, you may want to break the sentences in segments as follows:
Los alumnos llegan.
Llegan a la escuela.
Ask: **¿Llegan los alumnos?**
¿Llegan los alumnos a la escuela?
¿Llegan a la escuela o a la tienda?
¿Quiénes llegan a la escuela?
¿Adónde llegan los alumnos?
Interspersing these simple questions enables students to use the new words so that they become a part of their active vocabulary. The natural progression when providing questions from easy to more complex is: *yes / no* questions, *either / or* questions, questions with interrogative words.

Step 3 Hint: When presenting **en punto,** write 8:00 on the board. Say: **A las ocho en punto—precisamente o exactamente a las ocho.**

Step 4 After presenting the vocabulary with books closed using the overhead transparencies, have students open their books. Call on individuals to read aloud.

Teaching Tip
The type of questioning described in Step 2 on page 104 allows students to hear and use the words so they become an active part of their vocabulary in a natural way. It also lets you take into account individual differences when presenting new material. Ask the easy *yes / no* questions of the less able students and the more difficult questions with the interrogative words of the more able students.

About the Spanish Language

- **Ir a pie** literally means *to go on foot* or *to walk,* and it is understood wherever Spanish is spoken. **Andar** can also mean to *go on foot* or *to walk.* It is commonly used in Spain but would not be understood in all areas of Latin America in this context. **Caminar** is more frequently used in Latin America.
- There are many ways to express *bus.* The most commonly heard terms are **el autobús; el camión** in Mexico and some areas of Central America; **la guagua** in the Caribbean and the Canary Islands. Other words for *bus* will be presented in later chapters.
- In Latin America the word for *car* is **el carro.** In Spain it is **el coche.** In many areas of Latin America, however, **el coche** sounds archaic.

3 PRACTICE

¿Qué palabra necesito?

¡OJO! When students are doing the **¿Qué palabra necesito?** activities, accept any answer that makes sense. The purpose of these activities is to have students use the new vocabulary. They are not factual recall activities. Thus, it is not necessary for students to remember specific factual information from the vocabulary presentation when answering. If you wish, have students use the photos on this page as a stimulus, when possible.

Historieta Each time **Historieta** appears, it means that the answers to the activity form a short story. Encourage students to look at the title of the **Historieta,** since it can help them do the activity.

1 and 2 Do these activities orally, and then have students open their books and read them for reinforcement. For Activity 1, have students answer first with complete sentences and then with just the word or phrase that responds to the interrogative word.

Writing Development

Have students write the answers to Activity 2 in a paragraph to illustrate how all items are connected in meaning.

UN POCO MÁS This *InfoGap* Activity will allow students to practice in pairs. The activity should be very manageable for them, since all vocabulary and structures are familiar to them.

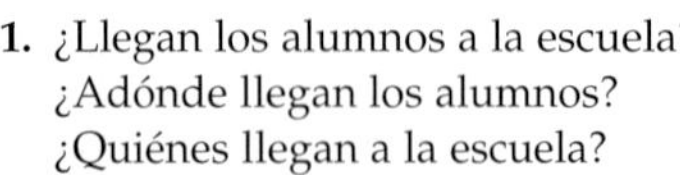

¿Qué palabra necesito?

1 Historieta ¡A la escuela!

Contesten. *(Answer.)*

1. ¿Llegan los alumnos a la escuela?
   ¿Adónde llegan los alumnos?
   ¿Quiénes llegan a la escuela?
2. ¿Llegan a la escuela a eso de las ocho menos cuarto?
   ¿Cuándo llegan a la escuela?
   ¿A qué hora llegan a la escuela?
3. ¿Van algunos alumnos a la escuela a pie?
   ¿Cómo van a la escuela?
   ¿Adónde van a pie?
4. ¿Toman otros alumnos el bus escolar?
   ¿Qué toman?
   ¿Adónde toman el bus escolar?
   ¿Cómo llegan ellos a la escuela?

Colegio San José, Estepona, España

Autobuses escolares, Málaga, España

2 Historieta En la escuela

Contesten según se indica.
(Answer according to the cues.)

1. ¿Dónde están los alumnos? (en clase)
2. ¿Quiénes estudian? (los alumnos)
3. ¿Estudian mucho? (sí)
4. ¿Quién no estudia? (la profesora)
5. ¿Quién enseña? (la profesora)

UN POCO MÁS *For more practice using words from* ***Palabras 1****, do Activity 4 on page H5.*

ANSWERS TO ¿Qué palabra necesito?

1

1. Sí, los alumnos llegan a la escuela.
   A la escuela.
   Los alumnos.
2. Sí, llegan a la escuela a eso de las ocho menos cuarto.
   A las ocho menos cuarto.
   A las ocho menos cuarto.
3. Sí, algunos alumnos van a la escuela a pie.
   A pie.
   A la escuela.
4. Sí, otros alumnos toman el bus escolar.
   Toman el bus escolar.
   A la escuela.
   En el bus.

2

1. Los alumnos están en clase.
2. Los alumnos estudian.
3. Sí, estudian mucho.
4. La profesora no estudia.
5. La profesora enseña.

3 Historieta ¡A la escuela, todos!

Completen. *(Complete.)*

Los alumnos __1__ a la escuela. Llegan a eso de las __2__ menos cuarto—a las ocho menos veinte o a las ocho menos trece. No __3__ a las ocho menos cuarto en punto. Algunos van a la escuela a __4__. Algunos __5__ en carro. Y otros __6__ el bus escolar.

Los alumnos entran en la __7__ de clase a eso de las ocho. Cuando entran en la clase, hablan con el __8__. Los alumnos __9__ mucho en la escuela. Pero el profesor no __10__; él __11__.

Toman el bus escolar, Quito, Ecuador

4 Entrevista

Work with a classmate. Pretend you are on the staff of your school newspaper and have been assigned to interview a Mexican exchange student about a school day in his or her hometown. Interview him or her.

Tec de Monterrey, Ciudad de México

3 Have a student retell the information in Activity 3 in his or her own words.

Note: Go over all the activities in class before assigning them for homework.

Learning from Photos

(page 106 top) This is a photo of the Colegio San José in Estepona, Spain. Ask the following questions: **¿Es el Colegio San José una escuela moderna? ¿Qué llevan los alumnos a la escuela? ¿Es una escuela mixta para muchachos y muchachas?**

(page 106 bottom and page 107 top) Ask the following questions about the **autobuses escolares,** in Málaga, Spain: **Los autobuses escolares, ¿cómo son? ¿Son grandes o pequeños? ¿Son modernos?** Then you can ask the same questions about Quito, Ecuador.

(page 107 bottom) Monterrey is Mexico's third largest city, located some 242 kilometers south of Nuevo Larredo on the U.S. border. Monterrey is a very important industrial center and is home to more than 3 million people.

LEVELING

E: Activities 1, 2

A: Activities 1, 4

C: Activity 3

Answers to ¿Qué palabra necesito?

3

1. llegan
2. ocho
3. llegan
4. pie
5. van
6. toman
7. sala
8. profesor
9. estudian
10. estudia
11. enseña

4 *Answers will vary but may include:*

—¿A qué hora llegas a la escuela?
—A eso de las siete y treinta.
—¿Cómo vas a la escuela? ¿Tomas el bus?
—No, voy a pie a la escuela.
—¿A qué hora entran los alumnos en la sala de clase?
—A eso de las ocho menos diez.

Vocabulario

PALABRAS 2

1 PREPARATION

Resource Manager

Vocabulary Transparencies 4.4–4.5
Audio Activities TE, pages 38–39
Audio CD 3
Workbook, pages 30–31
Quizzes, page 18
ExamView® Pro

Bellringer Review

Use BRR Transparency 4.2 or write the following on the board.
Find the opposite.

1. **alto**	a. **hablar**
2. **fácil**	b. **serio**
3. **escuchar**	c. **bajo**
4. **primario**	d. **interesante**
5. **aburrido**	e. **difícil**
6. **cómico**	f. **secundario**

2 PRESENTATION

Step 1 You may wish to refer to the teaching suggestions on page 104.

Step 2 Use gestures to help convey meaning and to assist in eliciting responses.
mirar (point to eyes)
hablar (point to mouth)
escuchar (point to ears)
tomar apuntes (make a writing motion with hand)

Step 3 Note that vocabulary is presented in the third person so students can immediately use the new words and respond to questions without having to make ending changes. Students will learn how to manipulate these verbs in the **Estructura** section of this chapter.

Vocabulario

PALABRAS 2

En la clase

un examen

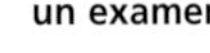

una nota buena,
una nota alta

una nota mala,
una nota baja

la pizarra, el pizarrón

Los alumnos miran la pizarra.
Miran al profesor también.

El profesor habla.
El profesor explica la lección.
Los alumnos escuchan al profesor.
Prestan atención.
Cuando el profesor habla, los alumnos escuchan.

Los alumnos toman apuntes.

Ahora la profesora da un examen.
Los alumnos toman el examen.

Elena saca una nota buena.

Reaching All Students

Total Physical Response Before doing these activities, make sure students understand the meaning of **levántate, ven acá,** and **anda por la sala de clase.** Now call on individual students to do the following.
(Student 1), **levántate.**
Ven acá.
Anda por la sala de clase.
Indica a un muchacho alto.
Indica a una muchacha alta.
Mira al / a la profesor(a).
Habla con el / la profesor(a).
Toma una hoja de papel.
Toma un lápiz.
Pon unos apuntes en el papel.
Escucha al / a la profesor(a).
Gracias, *(Student 1).*

La fiesta del Club de español

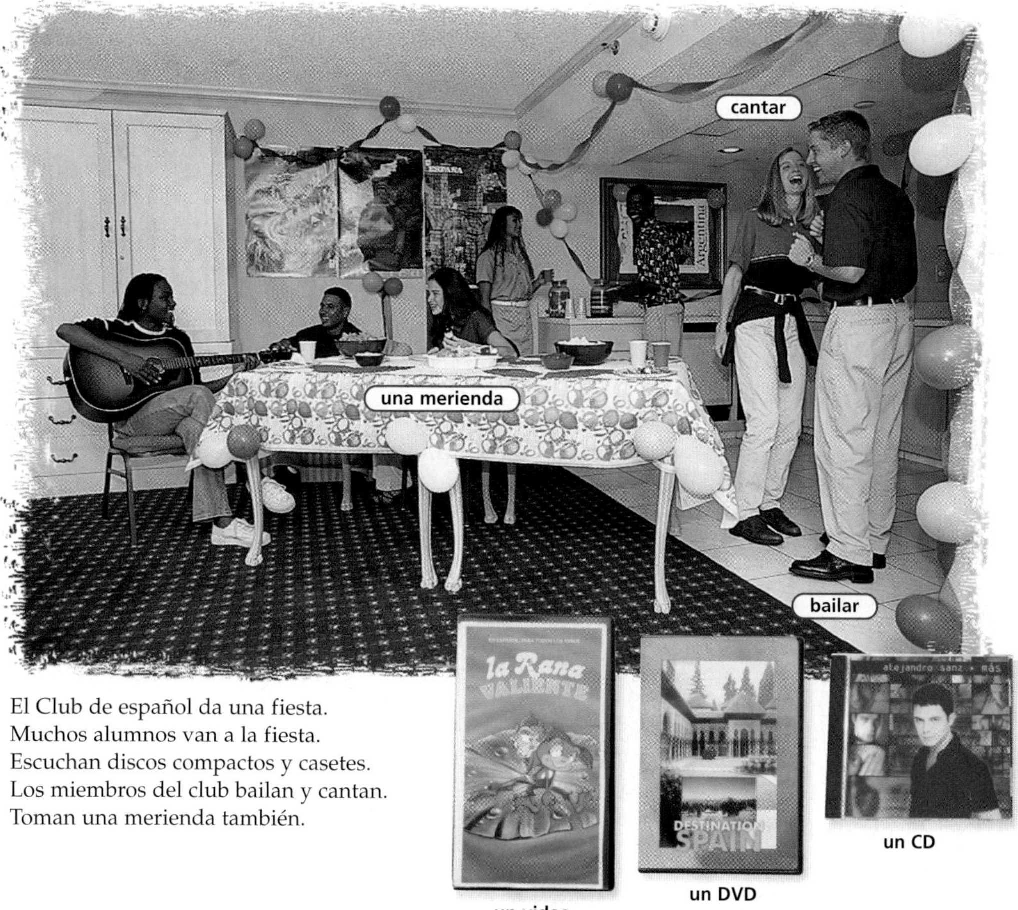

El Club de español da una fiesta.
Muchos alumnos van a la fiesta.
Escuchan discos compactos y casetes.
Los miembros del club bailan y cantan.
Toman una merienda también.

un video

un DVD

un CD

Más números

1000	mil	1200	mil doscientos
2000	dos mil	1492	mil cuatrocientos noventa y dos
2002	dos mil dos	1814	mil ochocientos catorce
2500	dos mil quinientos	1898	mil ochocientos noventa y ocho
3000	tres mil	1,000,000	un millón
3015	tres mil quince	2,000,000	dos millones
3650	tres mil seiscientos cincuenta		

Vocabulario

Step 4 Más números Write additional numbers on the board and have students say them. It is suggested that you not make students spell the numbers. If you wish to check comprehension of numbers on paper, give a number orally and have students write the number using numerals.

National Standards

Communication
After learning the vocabulary presented on pages 108–109, students will be able to communicate with others about their school activities.

About the Spanish Language

- The word **pizarrón** is used in many areas of Latin America. **Pizarra** is used in Spain and in some areas of Latin America.
- The expression **sacar una nota buena** is more commonly heard in Spain. **Recibir una nota buena** will be presented when students learn **-er** and **-ir** verbs.
- Another commonly used word for a student's grade in school is **calificación.**
- **Tomar un curso** is the most commonly used term, but in Spain you will hear **seguir un curso.**
- **El / La profesor(a)** refers to a secondary school teacher or a college professor. **El / La catedrático(a)** is also used for a college professor. **El / La maestro(a)** refers to an elementary school teacher.

Learning from Photos

(page 108 top) This photo was taken at the Colegio San José in Estepona, Spain. Have students compare this photo of El Colegio San José to the photo of the classroom on page 110. For each photo, ask them: **¿Qué clase es?** Point out to students that this is the same room in both photos and that the teachers, not the students, have changed rooms. (This point is also discussed in the **Lectura,** page 122.)

Vocabulary Expansion

You may wish to present these additional useful terms.

la tarea para mañana
la tiza
el borrador
la prueba

Note: Many teachers use **la prueba** for a quiz and **el examen** for a test.

Vocabulario

3 PRACTICE

¿Qué palabra necesito?

5, 6, and 7 After completing Activities 5, 6, and 7 with the class, call on individual students to retell the story in each activity in their own words.

Paired Activities
Students can work in pairs and ask one another their own questions about the stories in the **¿Qué palabra necesito?** activities.

Writing Development
Have students write the answers to Activities 5, 6, and 7 in paragraph form. Have students close their books and rewrite the information from Activity 6 in their own words.

Assessment
As an informal assessment, you may wish to show Vocabulary Transparencies 4.2–4.5 again and call on students to say whatever they can about any of the illustrations or photographs.

LEVELING
E: Activity 5
A: Activities 8, 9
C: Activity 6

¿Qué palabra necesito?

5 Historieta En clase Contesten. *(Answer.)*

1. ¿Miran los alumnos la pizarra?
2. ¿Habla la profesora?
3. ¿Escuchan los alumnos?
4. ¿Prestan atención cuando la profesora habla?
5. ¿Toman los alumnos apuntes en un cuaderno?
6. ¿Estudian mucho los alumnos?
7. ¿Trabajan ellos mucho?
8. ¿Da la profesora un examen?
9. ¿Toman los alumnos el examen?
10. ¿Sacan notas buenas o malas en el examen?

Colegio San José, Estepona, España

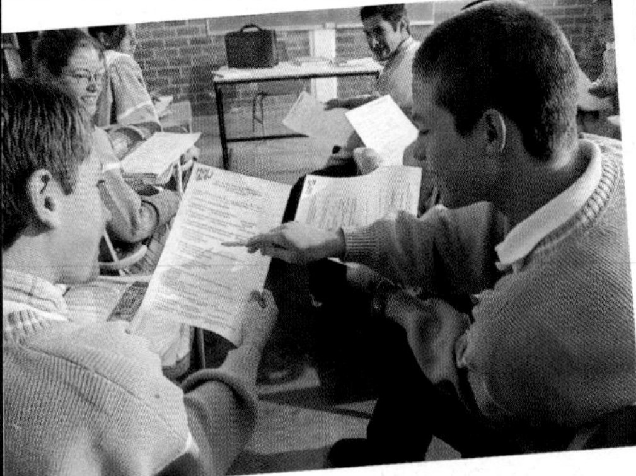

6 Historieta La escuela Completen. *(Complete.)*

Los alumnos llegan a la escuela y luego van a __1__. Los alumnos __2__ mucho en la escuela y los profesores __3__. Los alumnos toman __4__ en un cuaderno. Cuando el profesor habla, los alumnos __5__ atención. El profesor da un __6__ y los alumnos toman el __7__. Algunos alumnos sacan notas __8__ y otros sacan notas __9__. Una nota buena es una nota __10__ y una nota mala es una nota __11__.

7 Historieta El Club de español Contesten con **sí** o **no.** *(Answer with* sí *or* no.*)*

1. ¿Da una fiesta el Club de español?
2. ¿Van muchos alumnos a la fiesta?
3. ¿Bailan en la fiesta?
4. ¿Cantan también?
5. ¿Preparan los miembros del club una merienda?
6. ¿Toman una merienda?

ANSWERS TO ¿Qué palabra necesito?

5

1. No, los alumnos no miran la pizarra.
2. Sí, la profesora habla.
3. Sí, los alumnos escuchan.
4. Sí, prestan atención cuando la profesora habla.
5. Sí, los alumnos toman apuntes en un cuaderno. (No, los alumnos no toman apuntes en un cuaderno.)
6. Sí (No), los alumnos (no) estudian mucho.
7. Sí (No), ellos (no) trabajan mucho.
8. Sí (No), la profesora (no) da un examen.
9. Sí (No), los alumnos (no) toman el examen.
10. Sacan notas buenas (malas) en el examen.

6

1. la sala de clase
2. estudian
3. enseñan
4. apuntes
5. prestan
6. examen
7. examen
8. buenas (malas)
9. malas (buenas)
10. alta
11. baja

8 En clase
With a classmate, look at the photograph. Take turns saying as much as you can about it.

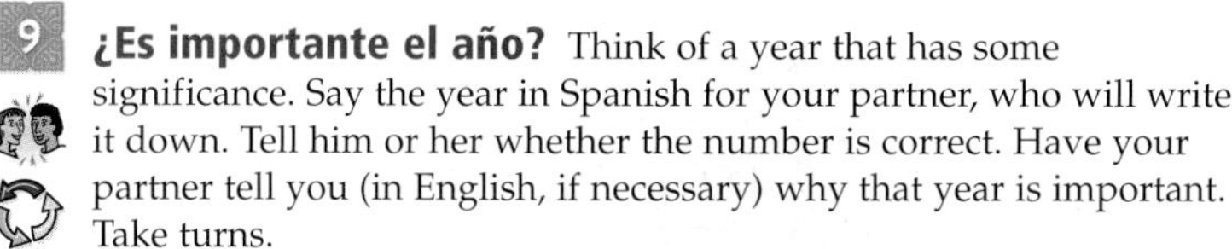

9 ¿Es importante el año? Think of a year that has some significance. Say the year in Spanish for your partner, who will write it down. Tell him or her whether the number is correct. Have your partner tell you (in English, if necessary) why that year is important. Take turns.

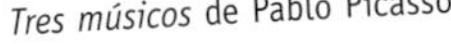
Tres músicos de Pablo Picasso

SPANISH Online

For more information about Pablo Picasso and other Hispanic artists, go to the Glencoe Spanish Web site: spanish.glencoe.com

8 and 9 It is suggested that you let students select the activity they want to participate in. Let students say as much as they can. When doing these open-ended activities, as per the ACTFL Guidelines, it is recommended that you not correct all errors.

8 Variation: Students love to ask the teacher questions. Have students look at the photo and ask you questions about it.

Art Connection

Picasso is one of the most famous of modern Spanish painters. He was born on October 25, 1881, in Málaga. Both his parents were Andalusian. His father was an artist and taught in La Coruña. He did not like the cold, damp weather of Galicia, and shortly after their arrival, Picasso's sister Concepción died of diphtheria. His father decided to leave La Coruña immediately to return to Málaga. On the way, they stopped in Madrid, and the young Picasso was enthralled by the works of the Spanish painters he saw in the Prado. Shortly thereafter, his father was appointed to teach at the famous Escuela de Bellas Artes in Barcelona. The young Picasso passed the entrance exam immediately, and the jury was stupefied by the talent of this young boy. You may wish to use this Fine Art Transparency for activities related to this painting.

Answers to ¿Qué palabra necesito?

7 *Students may also answer with* no.

1. Sí, el Club de español da una fiesta.
2. Sí, muchos alumnos van a la fiesta.
3. Sí, bailan en la fiesta.
4. Sí, cantan también.
5. Sí, los miembros del club preparan una merienda.
6. Sí, toman una merienda.

8 *Answers will vary. Students will probably use the verbs* escuchar, prestar, hablar, mirar, *and the classroom vocabulary presented in this chapter.*

9 *Answers will vary but may include:*

Mil novecientos ______ y ______. *(I was born in ______.)*

Mil cuatrocientos noventa y dos. *(Columbus sailed to the Americas.)*

Estructura

1 PREPARATION

Resource Manager

Audio Activities TE, pages 40–42
Audio CD 3
Workbook, pages 32–37
Quizzes, pages 19–21
ExamView® Pro

Bellringer Review

Use BRR Transparency 4.3 or write the following on the board.
Answer the following questions.

1. **¿Estudias español en la escuela?**
2. **¿Hablas mucho con el profesor de español?**
3. **¿Escuchas al profesor?**
4. **¿Tomas apuntes?**
5. **¿Miras al profesor cuando él habla?**

2 PRESENTATION

Presente de los verbos en -ar en el plural

Step 1 Write the verbs **hablar, estudiar,** and **tomar** on the board. Ask students what endings they use with **los alumnos** or **los amigos.** They can respond because they know the ending from the vocabulary presentation. Write **hablan, estudian,** and **toman** on the board.

Step 2 Tell students they have a new form to learn when talking about themselves and someone else. Then have them repeat **nosotros** and write **hablamos** on the board. Since they have just used **hablamos** with the verb **hablar,** ask students what they think the verb form is with **estudiar.** Have them volunteer **estudiamos** and **tomamos.**

Estructura

Presente de los verbos en -ar en el plural

Talking about things people do

1. You have already learned the singular forms of regular **-ar** verbs. Now study the plural forms.

INFINITIVE	hablar	estudiar	tomar	ENDINGS
STEM	habl-	estudi-	tom-	
nosotros(as)	hablamos	estudiamos	tomamos	-amos
ellos, ellas, Uds.	hablan	estudian	toman	-an

2.

Hablamos español.
José y Casandra estudian mucho.

When you talk about yourself and someone else, you use **-amos.**

When you talk about two or more people, you use **-an.**

3. In most parts of the Spanish-speaking world, except for some regions of Spain, there is no difference between formal and informal address in the plural.

Uds. toman muchos apuntes.

When speaking to more than one person, you use the **ustedes** form of the verb. Note that **Uds.** is an abbreviation of **ustedes.**

¿Lo sabes?

Vosotros(as) is a familiar plural form used in much of Spain. **¿Cantáis y bailáis en la fiesta?**

LEVELING
E: Activities 10, 11
A: Activity 11

About the Spanish Language

Students learned the difference between the **tú** and **usted** forms in Chapter 3. Explain to students that **ustedes (Uds.)** is the plural form of both **tú** and **usted** throughout Latin America. **Ustedes** is used for both formal and familiar address in all countries of Latin America. In many parts of Spain, however, **vosotros** is the plural of **tú.** When speaking to two or more friends or family members, you would use the **vosotros** form: **habláis, estudiáis, tomáis.** Throughout **¡Buen viaje!,** the **vosotros** form is included in all explanations, but students are not required to use the **vosotros** form actively.

4. Now review all the forms of the present tense of the regular **-ar** verbs.

INFINITIVE	hablar	estudiar	tomar	ENDINGS
STEM	habl-	estudi-	tom-	
yo	hablo	estudio	tomo	-o
tú	hablas	estudias	tomas	-as
él, ella, Ud.	habla	estudia	toma	-a
nosotros(as)	hablamos	estudiamos	tomamos	-amos
vosotros(as)	*habláis*	*estudiáis*	*tomáis*	*-áis*
ellos, ellas, Uds.	hablan	estudian	toman	-an

¿Cómo lo digo?

10 Historieta En la escuela

Sigan el modelo.
(Follow the model.)

llegar →
Los alumnos llegan.

1. llegar a la escuela a las ocho
2. llevar los materiales escolares en una mochila
3. entrar en la sala de clase
4. hablar con el profesor
5. prestar atención
6. tomar apuntes
7. estudiar mucho
8. sacar notas buenas

Colegio San José, Estepona, España

11 Historieta ¿Y ustedes? Contesten personalmente.

(Answer about yourself and a friend.)

1. ¿A qué hora llegan ustedes a la escuela?
2. ¿Toman ustedes el bus escolar a la escuela?
3. ¿Estudian ustedes mucho?
4. ¿Toman ustedes un curso de español?
5. ¿Hablan ustedes mucho en la clase de español?
6. ¿Escuchan ustedes al profesor cuando habla?
7. ¿Miran ustedes un video?
8. ¿Escuchan ustedes CDs?

Step 3 Go over Item 3 to explain **Uds.** Then have students give the **Uds.** form of some other verbs.

3 PRACTICE

¿Cómo lo digo?

¡OJO! Note that the **¿Cómo lo digo?** activities build from simple to more complex. In Activities 10, 11, and 12, students concentrate on only one subject and verb form in each activity. In Activity 13 students use all forms.

10 and 11 Do Activities 10 and 11 first with books closed for strictly oral practice. Then have students read the material for additional reinforcement. You may ask the questions from Activity 11, or students can do it as a paired activity.

Answers to ¿Cómo lo digo?

10

1. Los alumnos llegan a la escuela a las ocho.
2. Los alumnos llevan los materiales escolares en una mochila.
3. Los alumnos entran en la sala de clase.
4. Los alumnos hablan con el profesor.
5. Los alumnos prestan atención.
6. Los alumnos toman apuntes.
7. Los alumnos estudian mucho.
8. Los alumnos sacan notas buenas.

11 *Answers will vary but may include:*

1. Llegamos a la escuela a las ocho menos cuarto.
2. Sí, (No, no) tomamos el bus escolar a la escuela.
3. Sí, (No, no) estudiamos mucho.
4. Sí, tomamos un curso de español.
5. Sí, hablamos mucho en la clase de español.
6. Sí, escuchamos al profesor (a la profesora) cuando habla.
7. Sí, miramos un video.
8. Sí, escuchamos CDs.

3 PRACTICE *(continued)*

12 You may wish to have students do this activity in small groups.

13 After going over Activity 13, have students work in groups. Ask each group to think of as many questions as possible about the story in Activity 13. Now have the groups ask other groups their questions. They can then tell the story in their own words.

LEVELING

E: Activity 15
A: Activities 12, 15, 16
C: Activities 13, 14

About the Spanish Language

El voseo The pronoun **vos** is used in many areas of Latin America instead of **tú.** This phenomenon is referred to as **el voseo.** In some areas, **el voseo** is used by speakers from all social and educational levels in both oral and written form. In other areas it is considered popular. The ending for **vos** is **-ás: hablás, estudiás, tomás. Vos** is widely used throughout the Southern Cone—Argentina, Uruguay, Paraguay, and Chile. It is also used in varying degrees in the following areas: Bolivia, parts of Peru, Ecuador, Colombia (excluding the northern coast), parts of Venezuela and Panama, Costa Rica, Nicaragua, El Salvador, Honduras, Guatemala, the state of Chiapas in Mexico, and in a very small area of Cuba. (Note: You may wish to explain **el voseo** to students at a later time.)

Estructura

12 **Historieta Sí, estudiamos.** Sigan el modelo. *(Follow the model.)*

Uds. necesitan estudiar.
Pero, estudiamos.

1. Ustedes necesitan estudiar mucho.
2. Ustedes necesitan mirar el video.
3. Ustedes necesitan escuchar los casetes.
4. Ustedes necesitan trabajar.
5. Ustedes necesitan prestar atención.
6. Ustedes necesitan escuchar al profesor cuando habla.

13 **Historieta En un colegio de Perú** Completen. *(Complete.)*

Emilio __1__ (ser) un muchacho peruano. Él __2__ (estudiar) en un colegio en Trujillo. Los amigos de Emilio __3__ (llevar) uniforme a la escuela. Uno de los amigos de Emilio __4__ (hablar):

—Sí, todos nosotros __5__ (llevar) uniforme a la escuela. __6__ (Llevar) un pantalón negro, una camisa blanca yuna corbata negra. ¿__7__ (Llevar) ustedes uniforme a la escuela en Estados Unidos?

Los amigos de Emilio __8__ (tomar) muchos cursos. Y Emilio también __9__ (tomar) muchos cursos. Algunos cursos __10__ (ser) fáciles y otros __11__ (ser) difíciles. Los amigos de Emilio __12__ (hablar):

—Nosotros __13__ (tomar) nueve cursos. En algunos cursos nosotros __14__ (sacar) notas muy buenas y en otros __15__ (sacar) notas bajas.

Un amigo __16__ (preguntar):

—¡Oye, Emilio! ¿En qué cursos __17__ (sacar) tú notas buenas y en qué cursos __18__ (sacar) tú notas malas?

Emilio __19__ (contestar):

—Cuando yo __20__ (trabajar) y __21__ (estudiar) yo __22__ (sacar) notas buenas en todos los cursos.

Plaza de Armas, Trujillo, Perú

ANSWERS TO ¿Cómo lo digo?

12

1. Pero, estudiamos mucho.
2. Pero, miramos el video.
3. Pero, escuchamos los casetes.
4. Pero, trabajamos.
5. Pero, prestamos atención.
6. Pero, escuchamos al profesor cuando habla.

13

1. es
2. estudia
3. llevan
4. habla
5. llevamos
6. Llevamos
7. Llevan
8. toman
9. toma
10. son
11. son
12. hablan
13. tomamos
14. sacamos
15. sacamos
16. pregunta
17. sacas
18. sacas
19. contesta
20. trabajo
21. estudio
22. saco

14 Una clase Ask a classmate about one of his or her classes. Then he or she will ask you about one of your classes. The following are some words or expressions you may want to use.

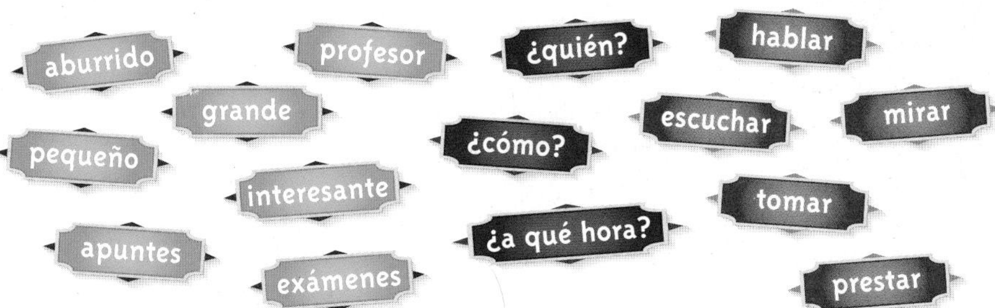

15 Un día típico With a classmate look at the illustrations. Take turns talking about them.

1.

2.

3.

4.

16 ¿Cuándo? ¿En clase, después de las clases o en una fiesta? Work with a classmate. He or she will suggest an activity. You will tell where or when you and your friends typically take part in the activity. Take turns.

Estructura

14, 15, and 16 Allow students to select the activity or activities they want to take part in. Different groups can be doing different activities at the same time. Circulate from group to group to ensure that students are focusing on the task at hand.

14 The cued words in Activity 14 deter students from becoming frustrated by trying to use words and structures they do not know.

15 You may wish to assign only one or two illustrations to each group or pair to work on.

Recycling

Have students say what time the activity in each illustration in Activity 15 is taking place.

16 Encourage students to think of as many activities as possible; see who comes up with the longest list.

Chapter Projects

Actividades escolares Have students prepare a list of things they do in school. Have them include only those activities they learned to discuss in Spanish. Use their lists for a bulletin board display.

Answers to ¿Cómo lo digo?

14 *Answers will vary but may include:*

—¿A qué hora es la clase de español?
—A las ocho.
—¿Es aburrida o interesante la clase de español?
—La clase de español es interesante y es fácil.
—¿Cómo es el profesor?
—El profesor es interesante.
—¿Sacas notas buenas o malas en los exámenes?
—Yo saco notas buenas.

15 *Answers will vary but may include:*

Illustration 1
—Los alumnos llegan a la escuela por la mañana.
—Algunos alumnos van a la escuela a pie.
Illustration 2
—Los alumnos van a clase.
—Los alumnos no llevan uniforme.
Illustration 3
—La profesora enseña.
—Los alumnos escuchan.
Illustration 4
—El profesor habla.
—Es una clase de geografía.

16 *Answers will vary. Students should use the* nosotros *form of the verbs they have learned up to now.*

1 PREPARATION

Bellringer Review

Use BRR Transparency 4.4 or write the following on the board.
Write four sentences about yourself using the following words.
hablar, comprar, mirar, escuchar

2 PRESENTATION

Presente de los verbos **ir, dar, estar**

¡OJO! These verbs are presented together since students only need to learn one new form. All the other forms are a review of the **-ar** verb endings they just learned.

Step 1 Have students point to themselves as they repeat **voy, doy, estoy** after you. Write the forms on the board and have the class repeat again.

Step 2 Explain to students that for these verbs these are the only different or irregular forms they will have to learn. The endings for all other forms are the same as those of an **-ar** verb.

Step 3 Now read Steps 1 and 2 with the students. Use the verbs you have written on the board to emphasize the similarities between regular **-ar** verbs and these irregular verbs.

3 PRACTICE

¿Cómo lo digo?

17 This activity is a very good example of communicative practice. Students must realize that when they hear a question with

Presente de los verbos **ir, dar, estar**
Describing people's activities

1. The verbs **ir** *(to go)*, **dar** *(to give)*, and **estar** *(to be)* are irregular. An irregular verb does not conform to the regular pattern. Note the similarity in the irregular **yo** form of these verbs.

   yo voy doy estoy

2. The other forms of these verbs are the same as those you have learned for regular **-ar** verbs.

INFINITIVE	ir	dar	estar
yo	voy	doy	estoy
tú	vas	das	estás
él, ella, Ud.	va	da	está
nosotros(as)	vamos	damos	estamos
vosotros(as)	*vais*	*dais*	*estáis*
ellos, ellas, Uds.	van	dan	están

¿Cómo lo digo?

17 Historieta Voy a la escuela.
Contesten. *(Answer.)*

1. ¿Vas a la escuela?
2. ¿A qué hora vas a la escuela?
3. ¿Vas a la escuela a pie?
4. ¿Vas en el bus escolar?
5. ¿Vas en carro?
6. ¿Cómo vas?
7. ¿Estás en la escuela ahora?
8. ¿En qué clase estás ahora?

San Juan, Puerto Rico

LEVELING
E: Activities 17, 20
A: Activities 18, 19

ANSWERS TO ¿Cómo lo digo?

17 *Answers will vary but may include:*

1. Sí, (No, no) voy a la escuela.
2. Voy a la escuela a las ocho menos cuarto.
3. Sí, (No, no) voy a la escuela a pie.
4. Sí, (No, no) voy en el bus escolar.
5. Sí (No, no) voy en carro.
6. Voy a pie (en carro, etc.).
7. Sí, (No, no) estoy en la escuela ahora.
8. Estoy en la clase de ___ ahora. (No estoy en clase.)

Estructura

 **Perdón, ¿adónde vas?** Sigan el modelo. *(Follow the model.)*

1. Voy a la clase de español.
2. Voy a la clase de biología.
3. Voy a la cafetería.
4. Voy al laboratorio.
5. Voy al gimnasio.
6. Voy a la papelería.

Santurce, Puerto Rico

 **¿Dónde están ustedes?** Preparen una conversación. *(Prepare a conversation.)*

Tomamos una merienda. (en la cafetería)
—¿Dónde están ustedes? ¿En la cafetería?
—Sí, estamos en la cafetería.

1. Tomamos un sándwich. (en la cafetería)
2. Miramos un DVD. (en la clase de español)
3. Compramos un cuaderno. (en la papelería)
4. Estudiamos biología. (en el laboratorio)
5. Damos una fiesta. (en el Club de español)

20 **Historieta La escuela**

Contesten. *(Answer.)*

1. ¿A qué hora van ustedes a la escuela?
2. ¿Cómo van?
3. ¿Están ustedes en la escuela ahora?
4. ¿En qué clase están?
5. ¿Está el/la profesor(a)?
6. ¿Da él/ella muchos exámenes?
7. ¿Da él/ella exámenes difíciles?
8. ¿Qué profesores dan muchos exámenes?

La Torre del Oro, Sevilla, España

the **tú** form, they must answer with the **yo** form. This practice is extremely important since beginners so often tend to answer using the same form they hear in the question.

18 **and** 19 These activities can be done as paired activities.

20 After going over Activity 20, have one student retell all the information in his or her own words.

History Connection

La Torre del Oro is on the banks of the Guadalquivir in Seville. It is a twelve-sided tower that was built by the Moors in 1220. In times of attack, they closed off the harbor by attaching a chain from this tower to another tower (no longer in existence) on the opposite bank of the river. In 1248, however, an admiral named Ramón de Bonifaz was able to break through the barrier, allowing Fernando III to capture the city. **La Torre del Oro** today houses a naval museum.

There is controversy as to how the tower got its name. Some say it got its name from the golden color of its tiles, **azulejos.** Others claim that it was once a warehouse for gold from the Americas.

Answers to ¿Cómo lo digo?

18 *All answers will be:* Perdón, ¿adónde vas?

19 *All answers will begin:* ¿Dónde están Uds.?

1. —... ¿En la cafetería?
   —Sí, estamos en la cafetería.
2. —... ¿En la clase de español?
   —Sí, estamos en la clase de español.
3. —... ¿En la papelería?
   —Sí, estamos en la papelería.
4. —... ¿En el laboratorio?
   —Sí, estamos en el laboratorio.
5. —... ¿En el Club de español?
   —Sí, estamos en el Club de español.

20 *Answers will vary but may include:*

1. Vamos a la escuela a las ocho (a las ocho menos cuarto, etc.).
2. Vamos en carro (a pie, etc.).
3. Sí, (No, no) estamos en la escuela ahora.
4. Estamos en la clase de __. (No estamos en clase.)
5. Sí (No), el / la profesor(a) (no) está.
6. Sí (No), él / ella (no) da muchos exámenes.
7. Sí (No), él / ella (no) da exámenes difíciles.
8. El profesor de ___ y la profesora de ___ dan muchos exámenes.

1 PREPARATION

Bellringer Review

Use BRR Transparency 4.5 or write the following on the board.
Put a check next to the words for places.

el alumno	la cafetería
el colegio	el café
la escuela	la mochila
la ropa	la sala de clase
la tienda	el laboratorio

2 PRESENTATION

Las contracciones al y del

Step 1 Ask students to open their books to page 118. Have students follow along as you read Items 1–4 aloud to the class.

Step 2 Have students repeat all the model sentences after you in unison.

Step 3 You may wish to explain to students that these contractions are very logical. Indicate to them how difficult it would be, when speaking, to separate the sounds of **a el** and **de el,** particularly in rapid speech.

3 PRACTICE

¿Cómo lo digo?

21 Before doing this activity, give students the following words orally. Tell them to raise their hands when the word they hear refers to a person.

el bolígrafo
la alumna
el muchacho
la caja
el dependiente

Las contracciones al y del

Expressing direction and possession

1. The preposition **a** means *to* or *toward.* **A** contracts with the article **el** to form one word: **al.** The preposition **a** does not change when used with the other articles **la, las,** and **los.**

   a + el = al

   En la escuela voy al laboratorio.
   Después voy a la cafetería.
   Y después voy a las tiendas.

2. The preposition **a** is also used before a direct object that refers to a specific person or persons. It is called the "personal **a**" and has no equivalent in English.

Miro la televisión.	**Miro al profesor.**
Escucho el CD.	**Escucho a los amigos.**

3. The preposition **de** can mean *of, from,* or *about.* Like **a,** the preposition **de** contracts with the article **el** to form one word: **del.** The preposition **de** does not change when used with the other articles **la, las,** and **los.**

   de + el = del

   Él habla del profesor de español.
   Es de la ciudad de Nueva York.
   Él es de Estados Unidos.

4. You also use the preposition **de** to indicate possession.

   Es la calculadora del profesor.
   Son los bolígrafos de Teresa y Sofía.
   Son los cuadernos de Juan y Fernando.
   Son los exámenes de los alumnos de la clase de español.

La alumna usa una máquina de braille.

¿Cómo lo digo?

21 **Historieta ¿Qué o a quién?** Contesten con **sí.** *(Answer with* sí.*)*

1. ¿Miras el video?
2. ¿Miras la pizarra?
3. ¿Miras al muchacho?
4. ¿Miras a la muchacha?
5. ¿Escuchas el CD?
6. ¿Escuchas la música?
7. ¿Escuchas al profesor?
8. ¿Escuchas a las profesoras?

Answers to ¿Cómo lo digo?

1. Sí, miro el video.
2. Sí, miro la pizarra.
3. Sí, miro al muchacho.
4. Sí, miro a la muchacha.
5. Sí, escucho el CD.
6. Sí, escucho la música.
7. Sí, escucho al profesor.
8. Sí, escucho a las profesoras.

LEVELING

E: Activities 21, 23
A: Activity 22

Historieta ¿Adónde vas? Preparen una conversación.

(Prepare a conversation based on each illustration.)

—¿Adónde vas?
—¿Quién? ¿Yo?
—Sí, tú.
—Pues, voy a la escuela.

1.

2.

3.

4.

5.

Historieta Roberta Smith

Contesten. *(Answer.)*

1. ¿Es Roberta de la ciudad de Nueva York?
2. ¿Es Roberta de Estados Unidos?
3. ¿Habla Roberta del curso de biología?
4. ¿Habla del profesor de biología?
5. Y después de las clases, ¿habla Roberta con los amigos?
6. ¿Hablan de la escuela?
7. ¿Hablan de los cursos que toman?
8. ¿Hablan de la fiesta del Club de español?

Estructura

22 You may have students work in pairs as they do Activity 22. Have each pair present their mini-conversation to the class.

Learning from Photos

(page 119) Ask the following questions about the photo:
¿Dónde están los alumnos?
¿Son americanos?
¿Cuántos alumnos hay?
¿En qué clase están los alumnos?
¿Están en el laboratorio?
¿Qué estudian?

Una invitación a una fiesta Have students prepare an invitation for a Spanish Club party.

¡Adelante!

At this point in the chapter, students have learned all the vocabulary and structure necessary to complete the chapter. The conversation and cultural readings that follow recycle all the material learned up to this point.

Answers to ¿Cómo lo digo?

22

1. —¿Adónde vas?
   —¿Quién? ¿Yo?
   —Sí, tú.
   —Pues, voy a la escuela.
2. —... Pues, voy a la tienda.
3. —... Pues, voy al Café Sol.
4. —... Pues, voy a la sala de clase.
5. —... Pues, voy a la papelería.

23

1. Sí, Roberta es de la Ciudad de Nueva York.
2. Sí, Roberta es de Estados Unidos.
3. Sí, Roberta habla del curso de biología.
4. Sí, habla del profesor de biología.
5. Sí, después de las clases Roberta habla con los amigos.
6. Sí, hablan de la escuela.
7. Sí, hablan de los cursos que toman.
8. Sí, hablan de la fiesta del Club de español.

Conversación

1 PREPARATION

Resource Manager

Audio Activities TE, pages 42–43
Audio CD 3

Bellringer Review

Use BRR Transparency 4.6 or write the following on the board.
Answer the following.

1. **¿Quién eres?**
2. **¿Cómo estás?**
3. **¿Adónde vas?**
4. **¿Quién da una fiesta?**
5. **¿Vas a la fiesta?**

2 PRESENTATION

Step 1 Tell students they are going to hear a conversation between two friends, Rubén and Héctor. They are discussing an upcoming event. You may want to have students listen to the conversation on Audio CD 3.

Step 2 Have students open their books to page 120 and repeat the conversation after you, sentence by sentence.

Step 3 Call on two students to read the conversation aloud with as much expression as possible. Repeat this two or three times with different students.

Step 4 Now do the **¿Comprendes?** activity on page 120. Students should be able to do this activity with relative ease.

Conversación

La fiesta del Club de español

Rubén Hola, amigo. ¿Qué tal? ¿Cómo estás?
Héctor Bien. ¿Y tú?
Rubén Muy bien. Oye, ¿adónde vas el viernes?
Héctor ¿El viernes? Pues, voy a la fiesta del Club de español. ¿Tú no vas, hombre?
Rubén Sí, voy. ¿Por qué no vamos juntos?
Héctor ¿Por qué no? ¡Buena idea!
Rubén En la fiesta bailamos, cantamos.
Héctor Sí, y tomamos una merienda—¡con tacos y enchiladas!

¿Comprendes?

Contesten. *(Answer.)*

1. ¿Con quién habla Rubén?
2. ¿Cómo están los dos muchachos?
3. ¿Adónde va Héctor el viernes?
4. ¿Va Rubén también?
5. ¿Quién da la fiesta?
6. ¿Van juntos los dos muchachos?
7. ¿Bailan en la fiesta?
8. ¿Cantan?
9. ¿Toman una merienda?
10. ¿Qué toman?

Answers to ¿Comprendes?

1. Rubén habla con Héctor.
2. Los dos muchachos están bien.
3. Va a la fiesta del Club de español.
4. Sí, Rubén va también.
5. El Club de español da la fiesta.
6. Sí, los dos muchachos van juntos.
7. Sí, bailan en la fiesta.
8. Sí, cantan.
9. Sí, toman una merienda.
10. Toman una merienda con tacos y enchiladas.

LEVELING

E: Conversation

Vamos a hablar más

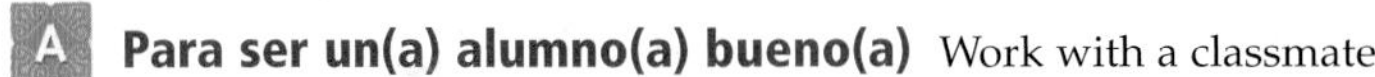
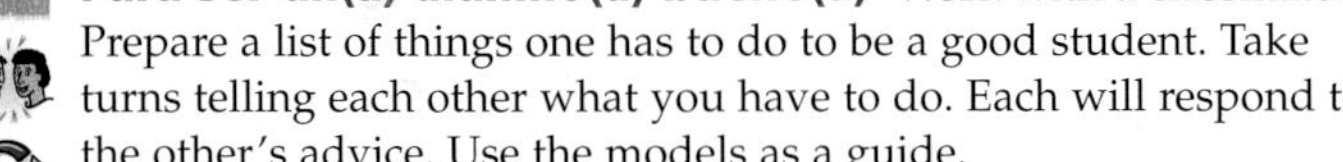

A **Para ser un(a) alumno(a) bueno(a)** Work with a classmate. Prepare a list of things one has to do to be a good student. Take turns telling each other what you have to do. Each will respond to the other's advice. Use the models as a guide.

ALUMNO 1: **Necesitas estudiar.**	ALUMNO 1: **Es necesario estudiar.**
ALUMNO 2: **Pues, estudio.**	ALUMNO 2: **Sí, y yo no estudio.**

B **¿Bailan o qué?** With a classmate, look at the places below. Choose one and tell several things students usually do in that place. Take turns.

1.

2.

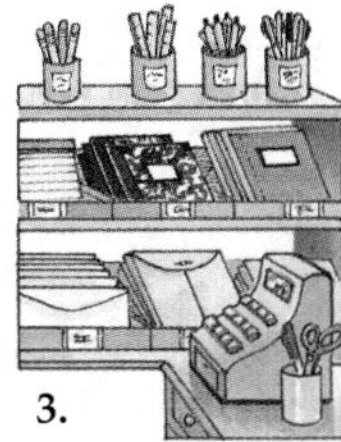
3.

4.

C **Un día típico** Work with a classmate. Each of you will tell about your typical school-day activities. When you finish, identify those things that both of you do.

Pronunciación

La consonante t

The **t** in Spanish is pronounced with the tip of the tongue pressed against the upper teeth. It is not followed by a puff of air.

ta	te	ti	to	tu
taco	**Teresa**	**tienda**	**toma**	**tú**
canta	**interesante**	**tiempo**	**tomate**	**estudia**
está	**casete**	**latín**	**Juanito**	**estupendo**

Repeat the following sentences.

Tito necesita siete disquetes de la tienda.
Tú tomas apuntes en latín.
Teresa invita a Tito a la fiesta.

ANSWERS TO Vamos a hablar más

A *Answers will follow the models provided.*

B *Answers will vary but may include:*

1. En una sala de clase los alumnos estudian y escuchan al profesor.
2. En una tienda miran y compran ropa.
3. En una papelería compran materiales escolares. Pagan en la caja.
4. En una fiesta los alumnos bailan y cantan. Toman una merienda.

C *Answers will vary. Encourage students to say as much as they can, reincorporating any language they have learned so far.*

3 PRACTICE

Vamos a hablar más

A Be sure students use the correct intonation when doing Activity A.

B Have a contest to see who can come up with the most activities for each place.

Glencoe Technology

CD-ROM
On the CD-ROM, students can watch a dramatization of this conversation. They can then play the role of either one of the characters and record themselves in the conversation.

Pronunciación

Step 1 The sound of **t** is difficult for English speakers to make. The *t* is breathy in English because the tongue hits the upper part of the mouth. In Spanish, the tongue must strike the back of the teeth to make the proper sound, not the upper part of the mouth.

Step 2 You may use the Pronunciation section on Audio CD 3 when presenting this topic.

Step 3 The model sentences on page 121 can also be used for dictation.

Lecturas culturales

Resource Manager

Audio Activities TE, page 44
Audio CD 3

National Standards

Cultures
The reading about public and private schools in Latin America and the related activities give students insight into some aspects of Hispanic culture.

Comparisons
Students learn some differences between schools in the United States and those in Spain and Latin America.

Bellringer Review

Use BRR Transparency 4.7 or write the following on the board.
Write four short sentences using the following words.
estudiar, tomar, escuchar, mirar

PRESENTATION

Pre-reading

Step 1 Tell students they are going to read about a school in Peru.

Step 2 Have them scan the selection quickly. Tell them to look for at least one difference between their school and this school in Peru.

Lecturas culturales

Reading Strategy

Making comparisons while reading If you read a passage that discusses a topic from different points of view, you can make comparisons while reading. Noting such similarities and differences will help make the ideas clearer and you will probably remember more of what you read. You can make these comparisons in your head or write them down as you read.

Escuelas del mundo hispano

Paula y Armando son dos amigos peruanos. Son de Miraflores. Miraflores es un suburbio bonito de Lima.

Paula y Armando no van a la misma escuela. Paula va a una academia privada y Armando va a un colegio privado. Muchas escuelas privadas en España y Latinoamérica no son para muchachos y muchachas. No son mixtas. Pero la mayoría[1] de las escuelas públicas son mixtas.

Hay otra diferencia interesante entre una escuela norteamericana y una escuela hispana. Aquí los alumnos van de un salón a otro. El profesor o la profesora de álgebra enseña en un salón y el profesor o la profesora de español enseña en otro. En España y Latinoamérica, no. Los alumnos no van de un salón a otro. Pasan la mayor parte[2] del día en el mismo salón. Son los profesores que «viajan[3]» o van de una clase a otra.

[1]mayoría *majority*
[2]mayor parte *greater part*
[3]viajan *travel*

Colegio de Nuestra Señora del Carmen, Miraflores, Perú

Miraflores, Perú

Learning from Photos

(page 122) You may wish to ask the following questions about the photos.
¿Es el colegio de Nuestra Señora del Carmen una escuela moderna? ¿Es una escuela mixta o no? ¿Llevan uniforme a la escuela los alumnos? ¿Son de Miraflores los dos amigos? ¿Son guapos? ¿Son simpáticos? ¿Son rubios o morenos? ¿Lleva el muchacho una mochila?

LEVELING
E: Reading

Una vista de Miraflores

¿Comprendes?

A ¿En Latinoamérica o en Estados Unidos?

Decidan. *(Decide whether each statement describes more accurately a school in Latin America or one in the United States.)*

1. Los muchachos y las muchachas van a la misma escuela.
2. Los alumnos van de un salón a otro.
3. Los profesores van de un salón a otro.

B Las escuelas de Paula y Armando

Contesten. *(Answer.)*

1. ¿De dónde son Paula y Armando?
2. ¿Van a la misma escuela?
3. ¿Va Paula a una escuela pública o privada?
4. ¿Y Armando? ¿Va él a una escuela pública o privada?
5. ¿Son mixtas la mayoría de las escuelas privadas en Latinoamérica?
6. ¿Dónde pasan la mayor parte del día los alumnos hispanos?
7. ¿Quiénes «viajan» de una clase a otra?

C En español, por favor.

Busquen las palabras afines. *(Find the cognates in the reading.)*

Lecturas culturales

Reading

Step 1 Have students open their books. Ask the entire class to repeat two or three sentences.

Step 2 Ask questions about the sentences they just read. For example:

¿Quiénes son dos amigos peruanos?
¿De dónde son?
¿Qué es Miraflores?

Step 3 Vary the procedure in Step 1 and call on a student to read several sentences aloud. Then ask questions about what the student read.

Post-reading

Assign the reading selection, as well as the **¿Comprendes?** activities that follow, for homework.

Geography Connection

Miraflores is a lovely section of Lima. It is a small and elegant suburb along the Pacific. The beachfront road is called **el malecón.** It is lined with expensive apartment buildings and grand, colonial mansions. Many of the mansions, however, have been torn down to make room for the more profitable high-rises. There are several pretty little parks in Miraflores. Miraflores also has many commercial areas with banks, restaurants, and stores. San Isidro is the most elegant residential area in greater Lima. San Isidro is between downtown central Lima and Miraflores.

Answers to ¿Comprendes?

A

1. en Estados Unidos
2. en Estados Unidos
3. en Latinoamérica

B

1. Paula y Armando son de Miraflores.
2. No, no van a la misma escuela.
3. Paula va a una escuela privada.
4. Armando va a una escuela privada.
5. La mayoría de las escuelas privadas en Latinoamérica no son mixtas.
6. Los alumnos hispanos pasan la mayor parte del día en el mismo salón.
7. Los profesores «viajan» de una clase a otra.

C *Answers will vary but may include:*
suburbio, academia, privada, Latinoamérica, mixtas, públicas, diferencia, interesante, norteamericana, hispana, otro, profesor(a), álgebra, parte, clase.

Lectura opcional 1

National Standards

Cultures
This selection familiarizes students with the oldest university in the Americas.

¡OJO! The reading selections on pages 124–125 are optional. You may skip them completely, have the entire class read them, have only several students read them and report to the class, or assign either of them for extra credit.

PRESENTATION

Step 1 Have students read the passage quickly as they look at the photos that accompany it. The photos will increase comprehension because students can visualize what they are reading.

Step 2 Have students discuss the information they find interesting.

LEVELING

A: Reading 1
C: Readings 1, 2

Geography Connection

Have students locate the Dominican Republic on the map on page xxxii, or use Map Transparency M 4. The Dominican Republic occupies the eastern two-thirds of the island of Hispaniola, in the West Indies. Haiti occupies the western third. The Mona Passage separates the Dominican Republic from Puerto Rico. Hispaniola was explored by Columbus during his first voyage in 1492.

Lectura opcional 1

Harvard University, Massachusetts

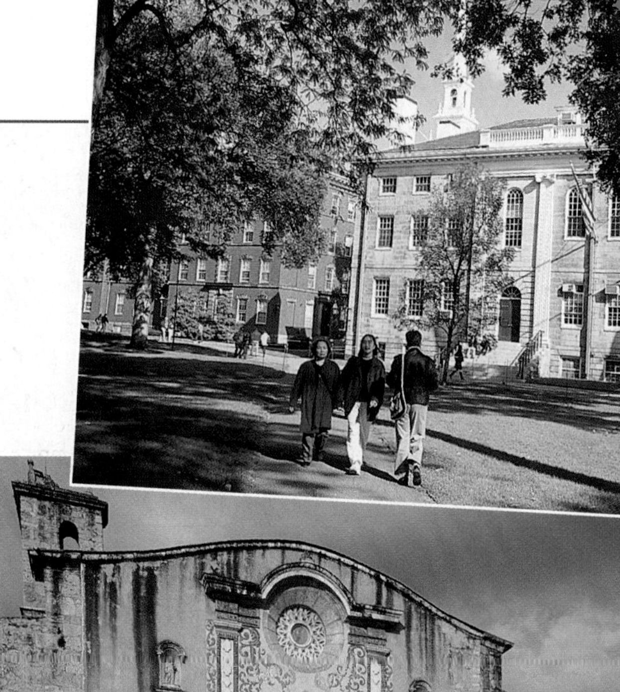

Una conferencia universitaria

En la universidad los profesores dan conferencias a los estudiantes. Hay una conferencia universitaria muy histórica y famosa. Es famosa porque es la primera[1] conferencia universitaria de las Américas. Y la primera conferencia que da un profesor en una universidad de América es una conferencia en español.

¿Por qué en español? Es en español porque el profesor da la conferencia en la Universidad de Santo Domingo. La universidad más antigua[2] de las Américas es la Universidad de Santo Domingo (1538). La universidad más antigua de Estados Unidos es Harvard (1636).

[1]primera *first* [2]más antigua *oldest*

Antigua Universidad de Santo Domingo

¿Comprendes?

En inglés, por favor. Expliquen.
(Explain the significance of the information presented in the reading.)

¿Lo sabes?

The Spanish word **conferencia** is a false cognate. It looks like the English word *conference*, but it actually means *lecture*.

Answers to ¿Comprendes?

Answers will vary but may include:
The first lecture given by a professor in the Americas was in Spanish at the University of Santo Domingo, the oldest university in the Americas (1538).

Lectura opcional 2

Gabriela Mistral (1889-1957)

Punta Arenas, Chile

Gabriela Mistral es una poeta famosa. Es de Vicuña. Vicuña es un pequeño pueblo rural de Chile. De joven[1], Gabriela Mistral enseña en varias escuelas primarias en áreas rurales de Chile. Ella pasa unos años[2] como directora de una escuela en Punta Arenas, en el extremo sur de la Patagonia chilena. Hoy la escuela lleva el nombre[3] de la maestra y poeta—el Liceo Gabriela Mistral. Es una maestra excelente y es también una poeta excelente. Como poeta, Gabriela Mistral recibe un gran honor. Gana[4] el Premio Nóbel de Literatura.

[1]De joven *As a young woman*
[2]años *years*
[3]nombre *name*
[4]Gana *She wins*

Liceo Gabriela Mistral, Punta Arenas

¿Comprendes?

A Gabriela Mistral ¿Sí o no? *(True or false?)*

1. Gabriela Mistral es novelista.
2. Gabriela Mistral es venezolana.
3. Ella es de Santiago, Chile.
4. Ella enseña en muchas áreas urbanas de Chile.
5. Ella enseña en varias escuelas secundarias.

B No es así. Corrijan. *(Correct the statements in Activity A that are not correct.)*

C Un poco de geografía Busquen en el mapa. *(On the map of South America on page xxxi, locate* Punta Arenas *and* la Patagonia. *Patagonia is in two countries. What countries are they?)*

Answers to ¿Comprendes?

A

1. No
2. No
3. No
4. No
5. No

B

1. Gabriela Mistral es poeta.
2. Es chilena.
3. Es de Vicuña.
4. Enseña en áreas rurales de Chile.
5. Enseña en varias escuelas primarias.

C

Patagonia está en la Argentina y Chile.

Lectura opcional 2

National Standards

Cultures
This selection familiarizes students with one of the world's most important literary figures.

PRESENTATION

Step 1 Have students read the passage quickly as they look at the photos that accompany it. The photos will increase comprehension because students can visualize what they are reading.

Step 2 Have students discuss the information they find interesting.

Step 3 Ask students to think of other literary figures with whom they are familiar.

Geography Connection

Have students locate Punta Arenas on the map of South America on page xxxi, or use Map Transparency M 3. The only city of the Americas that is farther south than Punta Arenas is Ushuaia, Argentina. Punta Arenas is a stark little port on the Straits of Magellan in Patagonia. This is a gray land where the sun seldom shines. Most days are drizzly and hazy. Even in the summer, cold biting winds howl between 70 and 85 miles per hour. In winter, the daylight hours are from 9 A.M. to 4 P.M., in summer from 4 A.M. to 11 P.M.

Conexiones

National Standards

Connections
This reading on biology establishes a connection with another discipline. It enables students to draw from previous knowledge and to talk about a scientific topic in Spanish.

¡OJO! The readings in the **Conexiones** section are optional. They focus on some of the major disciplines taught in schools and universities. The vocabulary is useful for discussing such topics as history, literature, art, economics, business, science, etc. You may choose any of the following ways to do the readings in the **Conexiones** sections.

Independent reading Have students read the selections and do the post-reading activities as homework, which you collect. This option is least intrusive on class time and requires a minimum of teacher involvement.

Homework with in-class follow-up Assign the readings and post-reading activities as homework. Review and discuss the material in class the next day.

Intensive in-class activity This option includes a pre-reading vocabulary presentation, in-class reading and discussion, assignment of the activities for homework, and a discussion of the assignment in class the following day.

Conexiones

Las ciencias naturales

La biología

Sciences are an important part of the school curriculum. If you like science, it would be fun to be able to read some scientific material in Spanish. You will see how easy it is. It's easy because you already have some scientific background and knowledge. The knowledge you already have helps you understand what you are reading. In addition, many scientific terms are cognates. The following is a short selection in Spanish about biology.

Plantas, Puerto Montt, Chile

La biología

La biología es la ciencia que estudia los animales y las plantas. Es el estudio de la estructura de los organismos vivos. El/La biólogo(a) es el/la científico(a) que estudia la biología.

El microscopio

Los biólogos trabajan en un laboratorio. Un instrumento importante para los biólogos es el microscopio. El microscopio permite a los biólogos observar objetos muy pequeños, muy diminutos. Con el microscopio los biólogos observan y analizan células, microbios y bacterias.

Una clase de biología, Buenos Aires

Llamas, Puerto Montt, Chile

La célula

¿Qué es una célula? La célula es el elemento básico y más importante de los seres vivientes[1]. Generalmente una célula es microscópica. Consiste en una masa llamada[2] «protoplasma» envuelta[3] en una membrana. Un microbio es un ser monocelular vegetal o animal. El microbio es solamente visible con el microscopio.

[1]seres vivientes *living creatures*
[2]llamada *called*
[3]envuelta *wrapped, encased*

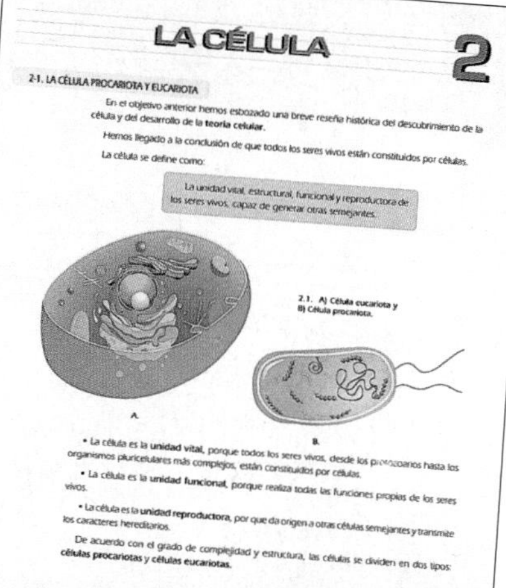

LA CÉLULA 2

2-1. LA CÉLULA PROCARIOTA Y EUCARIOTA

En el objetivo anterior hemos esbozado una breve reseña histórica del descubrimiento de la célula y del desarrollo de la **teoría celular.**

Hemos llegado a la conclusión de que todos los seres vivos están constituidos por células.

La célula se define como:

La unidad vital, estructural, funcional y reproductora de los seres vivos, capaz de generar otras semejantes.

2.1. A) Célula eucariota y B) Célula procariota.

A.

B.

• La célula es la **unidad vital**, porque todos los seres vivos, desde los protozoarios hasta los organismos pluricelulares más complejos, están constituidos por células.

• La célula es la **unidad funcional**, porque realiza todas las funciones propias de los seres vivos.

• La célula es la **unidad reproductora**, por que da origen a otras células semejantes y transmite los caracteres hereditarios.

De acuerdo con el grado de complejidad y estructura, las células se dividen en dos tipos: **células procariotas** y **células eucariotas.**

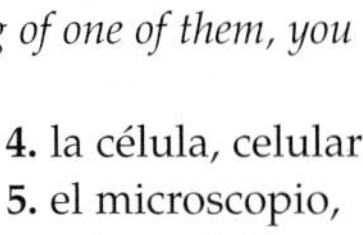

Una clase de biología, Buenos Aires

¿Comprendes?

A Palabras científicas

Hagan una lista. *(Make a list of science terms you recognize.)*

B La biología ¿Sí o no? *(True or false?)*

1. La biología es la ciencia que estudia los elementos químicos.
2. Los biólogos estudian los animales y las plantas.
3. Un vegetal es un animal.
4. Los biólogos trabajan en un laboratorio.
5. Los biólogos usan un telescopio.
6. Hay muchas cosas que son visibles solamente con el microscopio.
7. Una célula es bastante grande.
8. Un microbio es un ser de una sola célula—es monocelular.

C Estudio de palabras Adivinen. *(Note that the following words are all related to one another. If you know the meaning of one of them, you can guess the meaning of the others.)*

1. la biología, el biólogo, biológico
2. observar, la observación, el observador
3. analizar, el análisis, analítico
4. la célula, celular
5. el microscopio, microscópico

Conexiones

PRESENTATION

Las ciencias naturales
La biología

Step 1 Most students will be familiar with the biological terms in this selection from their study of science.

Step 2 You may wish to have only those students who are interested in science read this selection.

Step 3 You may ask the following comprehension questions:
¿Qué estudia la biología?
¿Dónde trabajan los biólogos?
¿Cuál es un instrumento que usan?
¿Qué observan los biólogos con el microscopio?
¿Qué es una célula?
¿Es grande o pequeña una célula?
¿Qué es un microbio?

LEVELING

E: Reading

ANSWERS TO ¿Comprendes?

A *Answers will vary but may include:* animales, plantas, estructura, organismos, microscopio, laboratorio, instrumento, observar, objetos, analizan, células, bacteria, elemento, básico, microscópica, masa, protoplasma, membrana, monocelular, vegetal, visible.

B

1. No
2. Sí
3. No
4. Sí
5. No
6. Sí
7. No
8. Sí

C

1. biology, biologist, biological
2. to observe, observation, observer
3. to analyze, analysis, analytic
4. cell, cellular
5. microscope, microscopic

¡Te toca a ti!

Use what you have learned

1 PREPARATION

Bellringer Review

Use BRR Transparency 4.8 or write the following on the board.
Write four things you do in Spanish class.

Recycling

These activities allow students to use the vocabulary and structure from this chapter in completely open-ended, real-life situations.

2 PRESENTATION

Encourage students to say as much as possible when they do these activities. Tell them not to be afraid to make mistakes, since the goal of the activities is real-life communication. If someone in the group makes an error, allow the others to politely correct him or her. Let students choose the activities they would like to do.

You may wish to divide students into pairs or groups. Encourage students to elaborate on the basic theme and to be creative. They may use props, pictures, or posters if they wish.

¡Te toca a ti!

Use what you have learned

HABLAR **1** **En el café**

✔ *Talk about school life in the United States*

You're seated at a café in Barcelona. You're chatting with a friend (your partner). He or she has some questions about school life in the United States. Have a conversation. Be sure to answer his or her questions.

Barcelona, España

HABLAR **2** **Diferencias**

✔ *Talk about differences between schools in the United States and the Spanish-speaking world*

Your school is going to have an exchange student from Spain. Based on what you have learned about schools in the Spanish-speaking world, tell some things the exchange student will find that are different. Tell also what he or she will find that is similar.

Tec de Monterrey, Ciudad de México

ESCRIBIR **3** **La rutina típica**

✔ *Write about a typical school day*

You can now go back to the e-mail you sent your new friend on page 69 and add more details about what a typical school day is like in the United States.

Answers to ¡Te toca a ti!

1 *Answers will vary. Students should use vocabulary from the chapter, incorporating interrogative words with verbs and vocabulary words related to school.*

2 *Answers will vary but may include:*

En Estados Unidos los alumnos viajan de un salón a otro. En Latinoamérica y en España los alumnos no viajan de un salón a otro. En Estados Unidos las escuelas son mixtas. En Latinoamérica y en España las escuelas no son mixtas.

3 *Answers will vary but may include:*

Los alumnos llegan a la escuela a las ocho. Algunos toman el bus escolar y otros van a pie. Los alumnos entran en la sala de clase. El profesor enseña. Los alumnos escuchan al profesor y toman muchos apuntes. Los alumnos van de un salón a otro.

¡Te toca a ti!

4 Una fiesta del Club de español

✔ *Write about some typical party activities*

Write a brief letter to a friend of yours who is also studying Spanish. Tell him or her that you're a member of your school's Spanish Club. Describe to your friend a typical Spanish Club party.

Writing Strategy

Ordering ideas You can order ideas in a variety of ways when writing. Therefore, you must be aware of the purpose of your writing in order to choose the best way to organize your material. When describing an event, it is logical to put the events in the order in which they happen. Using a sensible and logical approach helps readers develop a picture in their minds.

5 Una fiesta

In the most recent letter from your Spanish pen pal, Gloria Velázquez, she described a party she had for her best friend. She told you what she had to do to prepare for the party and what her friends did at the party. She wants to know whether the types of parties she has are similar to the ones teenagers give here in the United States. Write her a letter explaining what you do to prepare for a party and what the parties are like. Include as many details as you can. These words may be helpful to you: **dar, invitar, necesitar, preparar, llegar, estar, hablar, tomar, escuchar, bailar, cantar.**

Madrid, España

Answers to ¡Te toca a ti!

4 *Answers will vary but may include:*

El Club de español da una fiesta. Los alumnos cantan y bailan. Toman una merienda también.

5 *Answers will vary, but students will use vocabulary associated with parties.*

Writing Development

Have students keep a notebook or portfolio containing their best written work from each chapter. These selected writings can be based on assignments from the Student Textbook and the Workbook. The two activities on page 129 are examples of writing assignments that may be included in each student's portfolio. On page 40 in the Workbook, students will begin to develop an organized autobiography **(Mi autobiografía).** These workbook pages may also become a part of their portfolio.

3 PRACTICE

5 Have students edit each other's letters.

National Standards

Communities

If possible, have students speak with a student in your school who comes from a Spanish-speaking country. Have them find out as much as they can about schools and schooling in that person's country.

LEVELING

These activities encompass all three levels. All students will be able to do them at a sophistication level commensurate with their ability in Spanish. Some students will be able to speak for several minutes, and others may be able to give just a few sentences. This is to be expected when students are functioning completely on their own generating their own language to the best of their ability.

Assessment

Resource Manager

Communication Transparency C 4
Quizzes, pages 17–21
Performance Assessment, Task 4
Tests, pages 41–56
Situation Cards, Chapter 4
ExamView® Pro, Chapter 4
Maratón mental Videoquiz, Chapter 4

Assessment

This is a pre-test for students to take before you administer the chapter test. Note that each section is cross-referenced so students can easily find the material they have to review in case they made errors. You may use Assessment Answers Transparency A 4 to do the assessment in class, or you may assign this assessment for homework. You can correct the assessment yourself, or you may prefer to project the answers on the overhead in class.

Glencoe Technology

MINDJOGGER VHS/DVD

You may wish to help your students prepare for the chapter test by playing the MindJogger game show. Teams will compete against each other to review chapter vocabulary and structure and sharpen listening comprehension skills.

Assessment

Vocabulario

To review **Palabras 1**, turn to pages 104–105.

1 Completen. *(Complete.)*

1. Los alumnos no van a la escuela a pie. Toman el ____.
2. ¿____ llegan los alumnos a la escuela? Llegan a las ocho en punto.

3–4. En la escuela los alumnos ____ y la profesora ____.

To review **Palabras 2**, turn to pages 108–109.

2 Contesten. *(Answer.)*

5. ¿Quién habla en la sala de clase?
6. ¿Quiénes escuchan y prestan atención?
7. ¿Qué miran los alumnos?

3 Completen. *(Complete.)*

8–9. La profesora ____ un examen y los alumnos ____ el examen.

10. El Club de español da una ____.
11. Los miembros del club bailan y ____ durante la fiesta.

Estructura

To review the plural of **-ar** verbs, turn to pages 112–113.

4 Completen. *(Complete.)*

12–13. Los alumnos ____ atención cuando el profesor ____. (prestar, hablar)

14–15. Nosotros ____ mucho y ____ notas buenas. (estudiar, sacar)

16. ¿En qué ____ ustedes los materiales escolares? (llevar)

To review **ir** and **estar**, turn to page 116.

5 Contesten. *(Answer.)*

17. ¿Vas a la escuela a pie o en carro?
18. ¿Estás en la escuela ahora?

ANSWERS TO Assessment

1

1. bus escolar
2. Cuándo (A qué hora)
3. escuchan
4. enseña

2

5. El / La profesor(a) habla.
6. Los alumnos escuchan y prestan atención.
7. Los alumnos miran la pizarra.

3

8. da
9. toman
10. fiesta
11. cantan

4

12. prestan
13. habla
14. estudiamos
15. sacamos
16. llevan

5

17. Voy a la escuela a pie / en carro / en el bus escolar.
18. Sí, (No, no) estoy en la escuela ahora.

6 **Escojan.** *(Choose.)*

19. Ahora nosotros ____ en la cafetería.
    a. estás b. están c. estamos
20. Pero en cinco minutos (nosotros) ____ a la clase de biología.
    a. va b. vamos c. van
21. Los miembros del Club de español ____ una fiesta el viernes.
    a. da b. dan c. damos

To review **ir, dar,** and **estar,** turn to page 116.

7 **Completen.** *(Complete.)*

22. No es la calculadora ____ profesor. Es la calculadora de los alumnos.
23. Ellos van ____ colegio en el bus escolar.

To review the contractions with **a** and **de,** turn to page 118.

Cultura

8 **¿Sí o no?** *(True or false?)*

24. En una escuela mixta hay muchachos y muchachas. Muchas escuelas públicas en España y Latinoamérica son mixtas.
25. En las escuelas de España y Latinoamérica los alumnos van de un salón de clase a otro como aquí en Estados Unidos.

To review this cultural information, turn to page 122.

Alumnos en San Juan, Puerto Rico

Assessment

SPANISH Online

The **Glencoe Spanish Web** site (**spanish.glencoe.com**) offers options that enable you and your students to experience the Spanish-speaking world via the Internet. For each **Capítulo,** there are activities, games, and quizzes. In addition, an *Enrichment* section offers students an opportunity to visit Web sites related to the theme of the chapter.

FOLDABLES™ Study Organizer — Dinah Zike's Study Guides

Your students may wish to use Foldable 6 to organize, display, and arrange data as they develop communication skills in Spanish. You may wish to encourage them to add information from each chapter as they continue to expand their ability to describe, explain, and discuss all the different topics they will be studying.

A *miniature matchbook* foldable is ideal in helping students to give more complex descriptions about topics they have studied in Spanish.

Answers to Assessment

6	7	8
19. c	22. del	24. Sí
20. b	23. al	25. No
21. b		

¡Hablo como un pro!

This unique page gives students the opportunity to speak freely and say whatever they can, using the vocabulary and structures they have learned in the chapter. The illustration serves to remind students of precisely what they know how to say in Spanish. There are no activities that students do not have the ability to describe or talk about in Spanish. The art not only depicts the vocabulary and content of this chapter, but also reinforces what they learned in previous chapters.

You may wish to use this page in many ways. Some possibilities are to have students do the following:

1. Look at the illustration and identify items by giving the correct Spanish words.
2. Make up sentences about what they see in the illustration.
3. Make up questions about the illustration. They can call on another class member to respond if you do this as a class activity, or you may prefer to allow students to work in small groups. This activity is extremely beneficial because it enables students to actively use interrogative words.
4. Answer questions you ask them about the illustration.
5. Work in pairs and make up a conversation based on the illustration.
6. Look at the illustration and give a complete oral review of what they see.
7. Look at the illustration and write a paragraph (or essay) about it.

¡Hablo como un pro!

Tell all you can about this illustration.

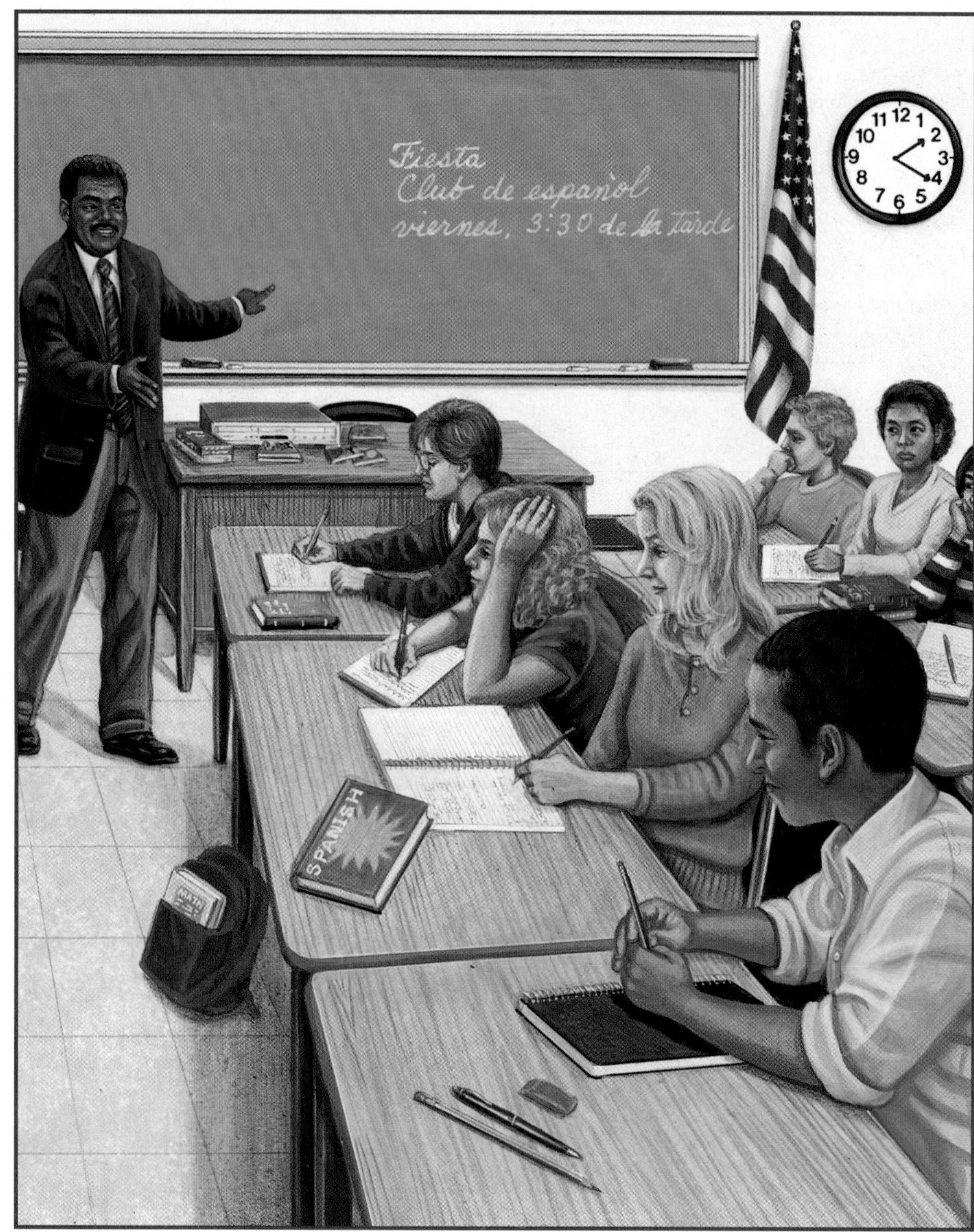

You can also use this page as an assessment or testing tool, taking into account individual differences by having students go from simple to quite complicated tasks. The assessment can be either oral or written. You may wish to use the rubrics provided on pages T20–T21 as you give students the following directions.

1. Identify the topic or situation of the illustration.
2. Give the Spanish words for as many items as you can.
3. Think of as many sentences as you can to describe the illustration.
4. Go over your sentences and put them in the best sequencing to give a coherent story based on the illustration.

Vocabulario

Getting to school

llegar
ir a pie
en el bus escolar
en carro, en coche
entrar en la escuela

Identifying classroom objects

la sala (el salón) de clase
la pizarra, el pizarrón

Discussing classroom activities

estar en clase
estudiar
enseñar
mirar
escuchar

prestar atención
tomar apuntes
dar un examen
sacar notas buenas (altas)
sacar notas malas (bajas)

Discussing the Spanish Club

el Club de español
el miembro
la fiesta
la música
un CD
un video

un DVD
la merienda
bailar
cantar
preparar
dar una fiesta

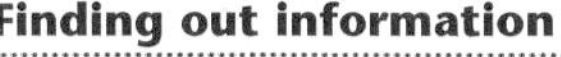

How well do you know your vocabulary?

- Choose words from the list that describe a typical school day.
- Use these words to write about or tell what you do at school.

Finding out information

¿a qué hora?
¿cuándo?
¿adónde?

Other useful expressions

a eso de
en punto
otros(as)

algunos(as)
ahora
también

VIDEOTUR

Episodio 4

In this video episode, you will spend an interesting math class with Vicky and Fernando. See page 495 for more information.

Vocabulario

Vocabulary Review

The words and phrases in the **Vocabulario** have been taught for productive use in this chapter. They are summarized here as a resource for both student and teacher. This list also serves as a convenient resource for the **¡Te toca a ti!** activities on pages 128 and 129. There are approximately ten cognates in this chapter. Have students find them.

VIDEO VHS/DVD

The Video Program allows students to see how the chapter vocabulary and structures are used by native speakers within an engaging story line. For maximum reinforcement, show the video episode as a final activity for Chapter 4.

Reaching All Students

For the Younger Students

- **Una fiesta** Have students draw a picture of a party. Have them write several sentences to describe their picture.
- **El Club de español** Have students prepare an invitation for the next meeting of the Spanish Club.

¡OJO! You will notice that the vocabulary list here is not translated. This has been done intentionally, since we feel that by the time students have finished the material in the chapter they should be familiar with the meanings of all the words. If there are several words they still do not know, we recommend that they refer to the **Palabras 1** and **2** sections in the chapter or go to the dictionaries at the end of this book to find the meanings. However, if you prefer that your students have the English translations, please refer to Vocabulary Transparency 4.1, where you will find all these words with their translations.

Repaso

Preview

This section reviews the salient points from Chapters 1–4. In the **Conversación,** students will review school vocabulary, regular **-ar** verbs, and the irregular verbs **ser, ir,** and **estar** in context. In the **Estructura** section, students will study the conjugations of these verbs and review articles, nouns, and adjective agreement. They will practice these structures as they talk about some Spanish friends.

Resource Manager

Workbook, Check-up 1, pages 41–44
Tests, pages 57–65
Performance Assessment, Tasks 1–4

PRESENTATION

Conversación

Step 1 Have students open their books to page 134. Call on two students to read this short conversation aloud.

Step 2 Go over the activities in the **¿Comprendes?** section.

Repaso

Conversación

La apertura de clases

Julio Anamari, ¿cómo estás?
Anamari Muy bien, Julio. ¿Y tú?
Julio Bien. ¿Adónde vas?
Anamari Voy a la papelería. Necesito comprar algunas cosas para la apertura de clases.
Julio ¡Ay, septiembre, una vez más y la apertura de clases! ¡Es increíble!

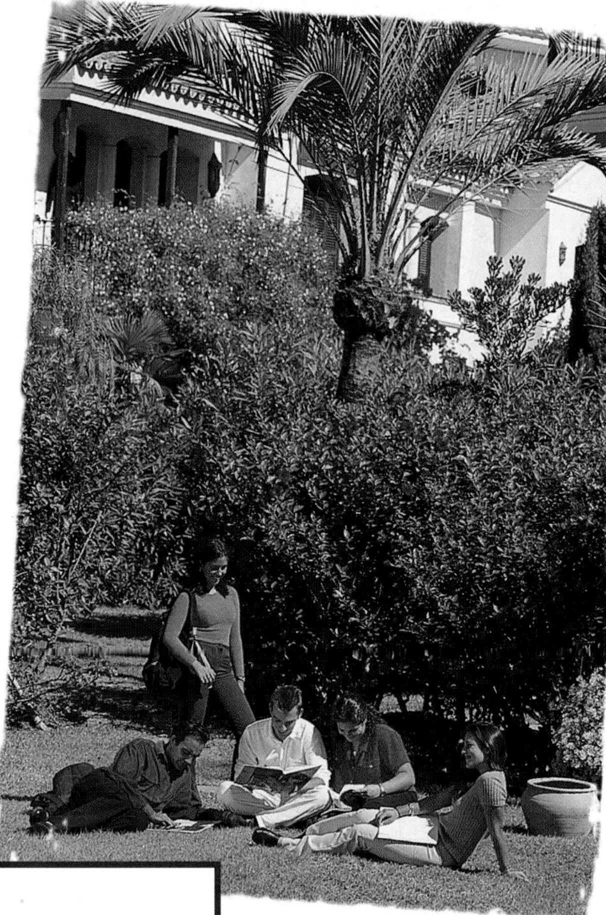

Estepona, España

¿Comprendes?

A Anamari y Julio Contesten. *(Answer.)*

1. ¿Con quién habla Anamari?
2. ¿Cómo está Julio?
3. ¿Son amigos Julio y Anamari?
4. ¿Son alumnos?
5. ¿Adónde va Anamari? ¿Qué necesita?
6. ¿De qué hablan los dos amigos?

B ¿Qué compra Anamari? Preparen una lista de los materiales escolares que Anamari compra para la apertura de clases. *(Prepare a list of school supplies that Anamari buys for the beginning of school.)*

Answers to ¿Comprendes?

A

1. Anamari habla con Julio.
2. Julio está bien.
3. Sí, son amigos.
4. Sí, son alumnos.
5. Anamari va a la papelería. Necesita comprar algunas cosas para la apertura de clases.
6. Hablan de la apertura de clases.

B *Answers will vary; however, the list should include the school supplies that students learned in Chapter 3.*

Estructura

Verbos, sustantivos, artículos y adjetivos

1. Review the forms of regular **-ar** verbs.

HABLAR	**hablo**	**hablas**	**habla**	**hablamos**	*habláis*	**hablan**
LLEVAR	**llevo**	**llevas**	**lleva**	**llevamos**	*lleváis*	**llevan**

2. Review the irregular verbs you have learned so far.

SER	**soy**	**eres**	**es**	**somos**	*sois*	**son**
IR	**voy**	**vas**	**va**	**vamos**	*vais*	**van**
ESTAR	**estoy**	**estás**	**está**	**estamos**	*estáis*	**están**
DAR	**doy**	**das**	**da**	**damos**	*dais*	**dan**

3. An adjective must agree with the noun it describes. Remember that adjectives that end in **o** have four forms. Adjectives that end in a consonant have two forms.

el amigo sincero	los amigos sinceros	la amiga sincera	las amigas sinceras
el curso difícil	los cursos difíciles	la clase difícil	las clases difíciles

1 Entrevista Contesten personalmente.
(Answer about yourself.)

1. ¿Vas a una escuela secundaria?
2. ¿Estás en la escuela ahora?
3. ¿Cuántos cursos tomas?
4. ¿Habla mucho la profesora?
5. ¿Son buenos los alumnos de español?
6. ¿Escuchan ustedes cuando la profesora habla?
7. ¿Sacan ustedes notas buenas?
8. ¿Dan los profesores muchos exámenes?

2 Julio y Anamari Work with a classmate. Look at the photo of Julio and Anamari. They are from Málaga, Spain. Say as much as you can about Julio. Then say as much as you can about Anamari. Take turns.

3 Los amigos Look at the photo of a group of friends from Estepona, Spain, on page 134. With a classmate, talk about the group. Ask one another questions about some of the people in the photo.

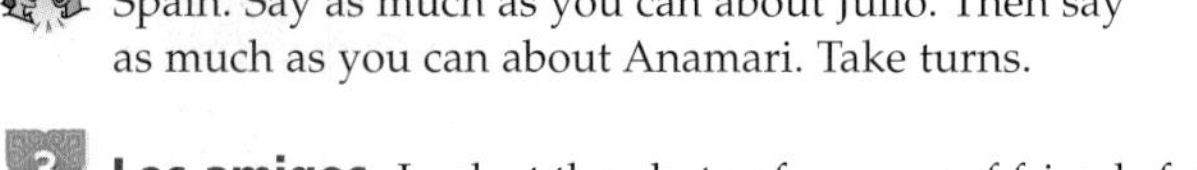

Literary Companion

You may wish to read the poem from *Versos sencillos* by José Martí. This literary selection is found on pages 470–471.

ANSWERS TO Repaso

1

1. Sí, voy a una escuela secundaria.
2. Sí, (No, no) estoy en la escuela ahora.
3. Tomo ___ cursos.
4. Sí (No), la profesora (no) habla mucho.
5. Sí (No), los alumnos de español (no) son buenos.
6. Sí, (No, no) escuchamos cuando la profesora habla.
7. Sí, (No, no) sacamos notas buenas.
8. Sí, (No,) los profesores (no) dan muchos exámenes.

2 and 3 *Answers will vary. Remind students that they should try to use as much of the vocabulary and as many of the structures as they can from* Capítulos 1–4.

CAPÍTULOS 1–4

PRESENTATION

Verbos, sustantivos, artículos y adjetivos

Step 1 Quickly go over the verb paradigms that appear here.

Step 2 You may also write the verbs on the board and underline the endings.

Step 3 Point out to students that except for the verb **ser,** all forms of these verbs are the same as those of an **-ar** verb with the exception of the **yo** form.

Step 4 When going over Item 3, draw some stick figures on the board and have students make up sentences.

PRACTICE

1 Have students refer to the photo on page 135 as they do Activity 2.

Literary Companion

When you finish this chapter, if you wish, have students read the poem from *Versos sencillos* by José Martí on pages 470–471.

Entérate México

This section was prepared by Time Learning Ventures of Time Incorporated. Its purpose is to give students greater insight, through visual images and fun articles, into the culture and people of Mexico. Using a map, you may wish to review the geographic regions of Mexico before the students begin reading.

Have students look at the photographs and read the articles. Encourage the students to talk about what they've seen and read. Let them say anything they can, using the vocabulary they have learned to this point.

Mexico, the fifth largest country in the Western Hemisphere, has an extrordinarily rich cultural and historical heritage. Since the Spanish conquest of the Aztec empire in the sixteenth century, the people of Mexico have fostered a unique blend of European and indigenous traditions. Today Mexico is increasingly regarded as a formidable international force despite a long history of political and economic challenges.

People en Español Entérate México

Los secretos precolombinos

Hay misterios sobre dos ciudades en ruinas, declaradas Patrimonio Mundial de la Humanidad[1] por la UNESCO.

La Pirámide del Sol

Teotihuacán

■ El nombre original de la ciudad es un misterio. Es un misterio también la lengua de los habitantes de la ciudad—igual que la escritura[2].

■ Sus monumentos principales datan de 200 después de Cristo.

■ Los aztecas dan el nombre de Teotihuacán a la ciudad. Teotihuacán significa "Ciudad de los Dioses". Antes de la llegada de los aztecas la ciudad está abandonada por unos 700 años.

■ En la ciudad hay dos pirámides famosas—la Pirámide del Sol[3] y la Pirámide de la Luna[4]. La Pirámide del Sol es muy grande. Es de una altura de 66 metros y una base de 225 metros. La pirámide tiene[5] dos millones de ladrillos[6].

■ En la ciudad hay estatuas de cabezas[7] grandes. Una es del dios Quetzalcóatl.

Chichén Itzá

■ La antigua ciudad de Chichén Itzá es una ciudad importante entre 300 y 900 antes de Cristo. Los habitantes de Chichen Itzá son los mayas. Ellos levantan las grandes construcciones de la ciudad sin usar bestias de carga (animales) ni rueda[8].

La pirámide maya Castillo

■ ¡Una cosa muy interesante! La pirámide Castillo de Kukulcán tiene una escalinata[9] de 365 peldaños[10]—un peldaño para cada día del año. La antigua civilización maya domina las matemáticas y ellos inventan un calendario muy exacto, muy preciso.

■ En los equinoccios[11] una sombra[12] forma una serpiente en la escalinata. Según[13] una leyenda la serpiente es el dios maya Kukulcán. El nombre que los aztecas dan a Kukulcán es Quetzalcóatl.

Chichén Itzá

[1]Patrimonio Mundial de la Humanidad: *World Heritage Sites*
[2]escritura: *writing*
[3]sol: *sun*
[4]luna: *moon*
[5]tiene: *has*
[6]ladrillos: *bricks*
[7]cabezas: *heads*
[8]rueda: *wheel*
[9]escalinata: *staircase*
[10]peldaños: *stairs*
[11]equinoccios: *the Equinoxes*
[12]sombra: *shadow*
[13]según: *according to*

Autorretrato
Una obra del pintor

Un vistazo a Diego Rivera

Los últimos detalles sobre la vida del pintor y muralista que a los tres años sabe dibujar[1].

■ Diego Rivera nace en 1892. Su nombre completo es Diego María Concepción Juan Nepomuceno Estanislao de la Rivera y Barrientos Acosta y Rodríguez.

■ Arriba he su autorretrato[2].

■ En las pinturas o murales de Rivera, él pinta escenas del pasado precolombino, la historia mexicana y la vida del campesino[3].

■ Se casa con[4] Frida Kahlo. Se divorcian y pronto se casan de nuevo. Frida Kahlo es una artista famosa también. Durante un tiempo ellos tienen un estudio uno al lado del otro. Diego Rivera muere[5] en 1957.

El estudio de Rivera
Rivera y Kahlo

[1]dibujar: *sketch*
[2]autorretrato: *self-portrait*
[3]vida del campesino: *life of a peasant*
[4]se casa con: *he marries*
[5]muere: *dies*

Calendario de fiestas

Muchas fiestas tradicionales varían según[1] el lugar donde se celebran.

Las Posadas—del 16 al 24 de diciembre

Durante las Posadas hay desfiles[2]. La gente va de una casa a otra como María y José cuando buscan alojamiento[3] en Belén. Los participantes en los desfiles llevan el mismo tipo de ropa que María, José y los pastores. El desfile termina en una casa donde todos celebran una fiesta con una piñata.

El Día de la Independencia—el 16 de septiembre

Los mexicanos celebran el Día de la Independencia para conmemorar el día que comienza la lucha por la independencia de México, el 16 de septiembre de 1810. Hay desfiles, fuegos artificiales[4], fiestas con comida típica, bailes folklóricos y música de mariachi.

El Día de los Muertos[5]—el 2 de noviembre

Las familias mexicanas van a las tumbas en el cementerio para honrar a sus parientes muertos. Tocan música y llevan flores[6] y comida tradicional. Llevan esqueletos de azúcar[7] y pan[8] de muertos. Pero no es un tiempo de luto[9]. Es un tiempo de alegría[10].

[1]según: *according to*
[2]desfiles: *parades*
[3]alojamiento: *lodging*
[4]fuegos artificiales: *fireworks*
[5]muertos: *dead*
[6]flores: *flowers*
[7]azúcar: *sugar*
[8]pan: *bread*
[9]luto: *mourning*
[10]alegría: *joy*

SUCESOS

Maná

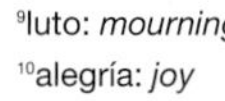

Anthony Quinn

■ **Maná,** la banda de rock, tiene[1] mucho interés en la ecología. El grupo trabaja para proteger millas y millas de la costa del Pacífico de México. Trabajan para proteger la población de tortugas[2] amenazadas[3] por cazadores[4] de huevos[5].

■ El legendario actor **Anthony Quinn** interpreta muchos roles étnicos como Zorba el griego[6]. Es de Chihuahua, México. Su madre mexicana es de ascendencia indígena y su padre es mexicanoirlandés.

[1]tiene: *has*
[2]tortugas: *turtles*
[3]amenazadas: *threatened*
[4]cazadores: *hunters*
[5]huevos: *eggs*
[6]griego: *Greek*

Una receta sana

micocina

Croquetas de avena[1]

Ingredientes

4 huevos
2 tazas[2] de avena
1 cebolla
2 ramitos de perejil[3]
3–4 chiles, sin semillas[4] (opcional)
sal y pimienta al gusto[5]
aceite de oliva para freír

Preparación

Batir[6] los huevos, añadir[7] la avena y mezclar[8]. Picar[9] la cebolla y el perejil finamente. Incorporarlos a la mezcla de avena y huevo. Añadir sal, pimienta y los chiles. En una sartén[10], calentar el aceite de oliva. Formar pequeñas tortas[11] y aplastarlas[12] hasta lograr un disco de 1½ o 2 pulgadas de diámetro. Freírlas, secarlas[13] en un papel de cocina[14] y luego servirlas.

[1]avena: *oat*
[2]tazas: *cups*
[3]ramitos de perejil: *sprigs of parsley*
[4]sin semillas: *without seeds*
[5]al gusto: *to taste*
[6]batir: *beat*
[7]añadir: *add*
[8]mezclar: *mix*
[9]picar: *chop up*
[10]sartén: *frying pan*
[11]tortas: *cakes*
[12]aplastarlas: *squash them*
[13]secarlas: *dry them*
[14]papel de cocina: *paper towel*

137

People EN ESPAÑOL

A Los secretos precolombinos
¿Verdadero o falso? Escojan.

1. Teotihaucán significa "Ciudad de los Dioses".
2. Según una leyenda, el perro es el dios maya Kukulcán.
3. Los habitantes de Chichén Itzá son los mayas.

B Un vistazo a Diego Rivera
Escojan.

1. Se casa con Frida Kahlo ___ veces.
   a. tres
   b. cinco
   c. dos
2. Diego Rivera pinta ___.
   a. los objetos abstractos
   b. la vida francesa
   c. el pasado precolombino
3. Nace en ___ y muere en ___.
   a. 1899, 1945
   b. 1892, 1957
   c. 1928, 1975

C Calendario de fiestas
Contesten.

1. Durante las Posadas, ¿por qué la gente va de una casa a otra?
2. ¿Cuándo comienza la lucha por la independencia de México?
3. ¿Qué hacen las familias cuando van a las tumbas?
4. ¿A quiénes honran las familias cuando van a las tumbas en el cementario?

D Sucesos Contesten.

1. ¿Qué tipo de banda es Maná?
2. ¿Para qué trabaja el grupo?
3. ¿De dónde es Anthony Quinn?

LEVELING

E: Activity A
A: Activity B
C: Activity C

ANSWERS

A

1. verdadero
2. falso
3. verdadero

B

1. c
2. c
3. b

C

1. La gente va como María y José, cuando buscan alojamiento en Belén.
2. La lucha comienza el 16 de septiembre de 1810.
3. Las familias tocan música y llevan flores y comida tradicional.
4. Honran a sus parientes muertos.

D

1. Es una banda de rock.
2. Trabaja para proteger millas y millas de la costa del Pacífico de México.
3. Es de Chihuahua, México.

People EN ESPAÑOL

Mexico has always had a strong artistic tradition but in recent years Mexican filmmakers, actors, musicians, and T.V. personalities are increasingly recognized at the international level. Mexican artists, once largely unknown beyond their borders, are becoming familiar faces and household names worldwide. Globalization—particularly the blurring boundary between the creative industries in the U.S. and Mexico—is spawning a new, hybrid Mexican American artistic movement.

People

¡Acción!

Salma Hayek

Salma Hayek nace con estrella[1]

De pequeña, el sueño[2] de Salma Hayek es de ser actriz. Nace en Coatzacoalcos de madre mexicana y padre libanés. Durante su adolescencia pasa unos años en Houston, Texas con su tía pero regresa a México para ir a la universidad. En contra de la voluntad y los deseos de su familia deja[3] sus estudios para ser actriz. En muy poco tiempo es una actriz famosa con un papel (o rol) importante en una telenovela[4] mexicana. Pero Salma deja todo para ir a Hollywood.

Ella estudia inglés, toma clases de interpretación[5], va a audiciones y por fin tiene un papel secundario en un filme. Pero no es muy famosa en EE.UU. hasta tener un papel importante en el filme *Desesperado* con Antonio Banderas. Luego Hayek aparece en numerosos filmes incluyendo *El coronel no tiene quien le escriba* basado en la novela del famoso autor colombiano Gabriel García Márquez.

Desde 1999 Hayek produce varios filmes con su propia compañía. Uno es *Frida*. Ella misma juega un papel[6] importante en el filme que trata de[7] la vida de la pintora mexicana Frida Kahlo. Por su interpretación en el filme Hayek fue[8] nominada al Óscar. Y, es ella la primera latina inmortalizada con una estatua de cera[9] en el Museo de Cera de Madame Tussaud en Nueva York.

[1]nace con estrella: *was born with luck*
[2]sueño: *dream*
[3]deja: *she gives up*
[4]telenovela: *soap opera*
[5]interpretación: *acting*
[6]juega un papel: *plays a part*
[7]trata de: *deals with*
[8]fue: *was*
[9]cera: *wax*

138

Cuarón

Alfonso Cuarón, director
Alfonso Cuarón es director de películas hollywoodenses (filmes) como *A Little Princess* y *Great Expectations*. Además rodea[1] películas en México. Pero Cuarón hace[2] historia cuando es seleccionado para ser director de *Harry Potter and the Prisoner of Azkaban*. Es la tercera parte de la famosa serie de películas basadas en las aventuras de Harry Potter. Es quizás la primera (1ª) vez en la historia del cine que un latino tenga[3] la oportunidad y responsabilidad de ser director de un filme tan espectacular—un filme cuyo éxito de taquilla[4] fue[5] garantizado antes de comenzar la producción.

García Bernal

Gael García Bernal, actor
Es nativo de Guadalajara. Varias veces trabaja en películas que tienen el honor de ser candidatas al Óscar.

Luna

Diego Luna, actor
Desde la infancia él es amigo de Gael García Bernal. En la película *Frida*, con Salma Hayek, él interpreta el papel del primer novio[6] de Frida Kahlo.

[1]rodea: *he films*
[2]hace: *makes*
[3]tenga: *has*
[4]filme cuyo éxito de taquilla: *film whose box office success*
[5]fue: *was*
[6]novio: *boyfriend*

En la tele y la radio

Ana María Canseco

Ana María Canseco da su mejor sonrisa[1] como copresentadora del show *Despierta América* (Univisión). Si da una interviú a un cantante, prueba algún plato[2] o habla de la moda o algo política, siempre es encantadora, muy simpática.

María Hinojosa es autora, corresponsal de CNN, y presentadora de programas de National Public Radio. De su nuevo libro *Raising Raúl* dice[3] "Habla de encontrar nuestras voces[4] como mujeres[5] y encontrar cosas en común que van más lejos de[6] la raza y la cultura."

[1]su mejor sonrisa: *her best smile*
[2]prueba algún plato: *trying a dish*
[3]dice: *she says*
[4]encontrar nuestras voces: *finding our voices*
[5]mujeres: *women*
[6]van más lejos de: *go further than*

María Hinojosa

música

Café Tacuba

Lo mejor del año

La firma[1] de autógrafos de **Café Tacuba**, siempre es "un desmadre," lo que en el argot[2] es un "caos[3]." Nada extraño[4] para el grupo que cruza fronteras con un sonido original, producto de la fusión de ritmos mexicanos con rock, punk, ska, reggae y balada.

Los Tucanes de Tijuana

Los Tucanes[5] de Tijuana no son tucanes y no son de Tijuana. Pero su nombre refleja el carácter imaginativo de este grupo importante de la música regional mexicana. Tienen muchos aficionados y seguidores[6] que compran millones de sus discos.

En el CD *Shaman* del famoso músico **Carlos Santana**, figura la valiosa colaboración de **Michelle Branch** con la canción "The Game of Love." Además de Branch, Plácido Domingo, entre varios otros, colabora en este CD del guitarrista y cantante mexicano.

Santana y Branch

[1]firma: *signing*
[2]argot: *slang*
[3]caos: *chaos*
[4]nada extraño: *nothing unusual*
[5]tucanes: *a type of bird*
[6]aficionados y seguidores: *fans and followers*

Nuestros Hits

Bajo el azul de tu misterio / Jaguares.
Este super álbum doble de rock contiene 10 temas grabados[1] y 11 en concierto. Con un trabajo de guitarras excelente y el timbre agridulce[2] de las interpretaciones es el grupo uno de los más universales y mexicanos de todos los tiempos.

El más grande homenaje a los Tigres del Norte / varios.
Si en el pasado medio mundo[3] respeta y escucha a los Tigres del Norte, después de este homenaje[4] el otro medio mundo va a adorar a los Tigres del Norte. Los Lobos y Café Tacuba, entre otros grupos, presentan la música y las letras[5] de los Tigres del Norte—y la realidad del México de la frontera[6].

[1]grabados: *recorded*
[2]timbre agridulce: *bittersweet ring*
[3]mundo: *world*
[4]homenaje: *tribute*
[5]letras: *lyrics*
[6]frontera: *border*

A Salma Hayek y En el set
¿Quién es?
1. Desde 1999 produce varios filmes con su propia compañía.
2. Interpreta el papel del primer novio de Frida Kahlo.
3. Es director de *Harry Potter and the Prisoner of Azkaban.*

B En la tele y la radio Corrijan.
1. Ana María Canseco es copresentadora de CNN.
2. María Hinojosa es cantante.
3. *Despierta América* es un programa de National Public Radio.

C Lo mejor del año Contesten.
1. ¿Qué grupo emplea una fusión de ritmos mexicanos, rock, punk, ska, reggae y balada?
2. ¿Quiénes hacen el CD *Shaman* en colaboración con Carlos Santana?
3. ¿Los Tucanes de Tijuana realmente son de Tijuana?

LEVELING
E: Activity A
A: Activity B
C: Activity C

Answers

A
1. Salma Hayek
2. Diego Luna
3. Alfonso Cuarón

B
1. Es copresentadora de *Despierta América.*
2. Es autora, corresponsal de CNN, y presentadora de National Public Radio.
3. Es un programa de Univisión.

C
1. una banda de rock
2. para proteger la costa del Pacífico de México/ para proteger la población de tortugas
3. es de Chihuahua, México

Planning for Chapter 5

SCOPE AND SEQUENCE, PAGES 140–167

Topics

- ❖ Foods and beverages
- ❖ Eating at a café
- ❖ Shopping for food

Culture

- ❖ Differences between eating habits in the United States and in the Spanish-speaking world
- ❖ Eating times in the Spanish-speaking world compared to the United States
- ❖ Paseo de la Castellana, Madrid
- ❖ Buenos Aires, Argentina
- ❖ Open-air markets and supermarkets in Spain and Latin America
- ❖ Math terms in Spanish

Functions

- ❖ How to find a table at a café
- ❖ How to order in a café
- ❖ How to pay the bill in a café
- ❖ How to identify food
- ❖ How to shop for food
- ❖ How to describe breakfast, lunch, and dinner

Structure

- ❖ **-er** and **-ir** verbs in the present

National Standards

- ❖ Communication Standard 1.1 pages 140, 144, 145, 148, 149, 151, 152, 153, 155, 162
- ❖ Communication Standard 1.2 pages 145, 149, 151, 153, 154, 155, 157, 158, 159, 161, 162, 163
- ❖ Communication Standard 1.3 page 163
- ❖ Cultures Standard 2.1 pages 151, 154, 156–157, 158
- ❖ Cultures Standard 2.2 pages 147, 159, 163
- ❖ Connections Standard 3.1 pages 160–161
- ❖ Connections Standard 3.2 page 162
- ❖ Comparisons Standard 4.1 page 160
- ❖ Comparisons Standard 4.2 pages 157, 158, 159
- ❖ Communities Standard 5.1 pages 149, 163

PACING AND PRIORITIES

The chapter content is color coded below to assist you in planning.

■ **required** ■ **recommended** ■ **optional**

Vocabulario *(required)* *Days 1–4*

- ■ Palabras 1
  - En el café
  - Para beber / Para comer
  - Antes de comer / Después de comer
- ■ Palabras 2
  - En el mercado
  - En el supermercado
  - Las comidas

Estructura *(required)* *Days 5–7*

- ■ Presente de los verbos en **-er** e **-ir**

Conversación *(required)*

- ■ En la terraza de un café

Pronunciación *(recommended)*

- ■ La consonante **d**

Lecturas culturales

- ■ En un café en Madrid *(recommended)*
- ■ Las horas para comer *(optional)*
- ■ ¿Mercado o supermercado? *(optional)*

Conexiones

- ■ La aritmética *(optional)*

■ **¡Te toca a ti!** *(recommended)*

■ **Assessment** *(recommended)*

■ **¡Hablo como un pro!** *(optional)*

RESOURCE GUIDE

Section	Pages	Section Resources
Vocabulario PALABRAS 1		
En el café Para beber / Para comer Antes de comer / Después de comer	142, 144–145 143, 144–145 143, 144–145	Vocabulary Transparencies 5.2–5.3 Audio CD 4 Audio Activities TE, pages 49–52 Workbook, pages 45–46 Quiz 1, pages 22–23 ExamView® Pro
Vocabulario PALABRAS 2		
En el mercado En el supermercado Las comidas	146, 148–149 147, 148–149 147, 148–149	Vocabulary Transparencies 5.4–5.5 Audio CD 4 Audio Activities TE, pages 52–54 Workbook, pages 47–48 Quiz 2, page 24 ExamView® Pro
Estructura		
Presente de los verbos en **-er** e **-ir**	150–153	Audio CD 4 Audio Activities TE, pages 55–56 Workbook, pages 49–52 Quiz 3, page 25 ExamView® Pro
Conversación		
En la terraza de un café	154	Audio CD 4 Audio Activities TE, page 57 Interactive CD-ROM
Pronunciación		
La consonante **d**	155	Pronunciation Transparency P 5 Audio CD 4 Audio Activities TE, page 58
Lecturas culturales		
En un café en Madrid Las horas para comer ¿Mercado o supermercado?	156–157 158 159	Audio CD 4 Audio Activities TE, page 59 Tests, pages 70, 73
Conexiones		
La aritmética	160–161	Tests, page 74
¡Te toca a ti!		
	162–163	**¡Viva el mundo hispano!** Video, Episode 5 Video Activities, Chapter 5 Spanish Online Activities spanish.glencoe.com
Assessment		
	164–165	Communication Transparency C 5 Quizzes 1–3, pages 22–25 Performance Assessment, Task 5 Tests, pages 67–80 Situation Cards, Chapter 5 ExamView® Pro **Maratón mental** Videoquiz

Using Your Resources for Chapter 5

Transparencies

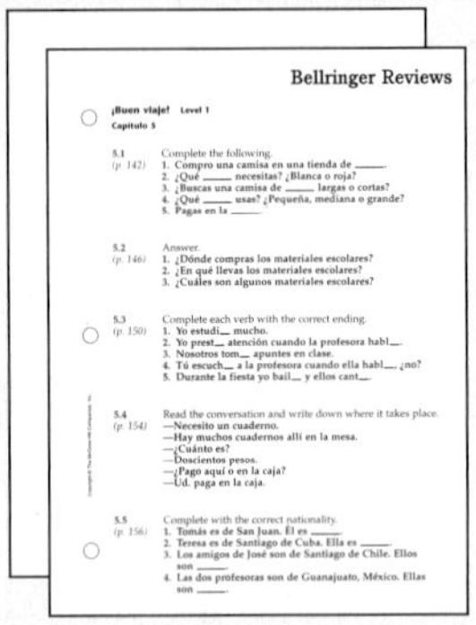

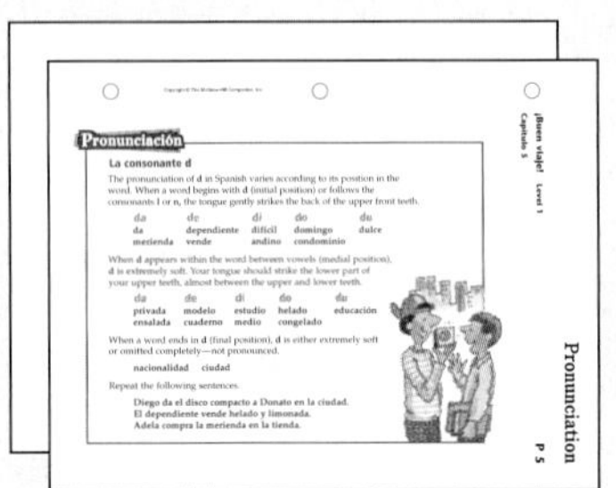
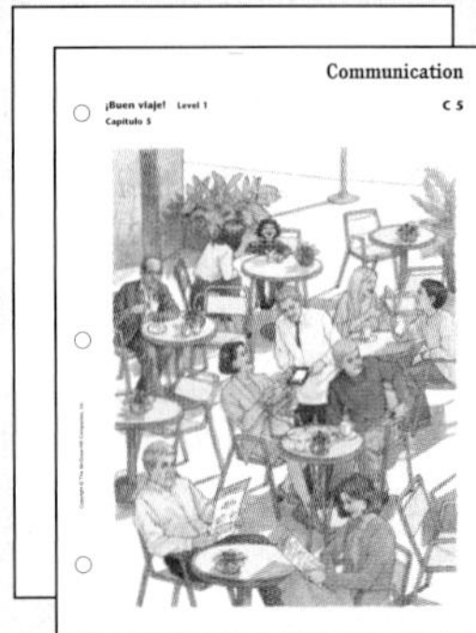

Bellringer 5.1–5.5

Vocabulary 5.1–5.5

Pronunciation P 5

Communication C 5

Workbook

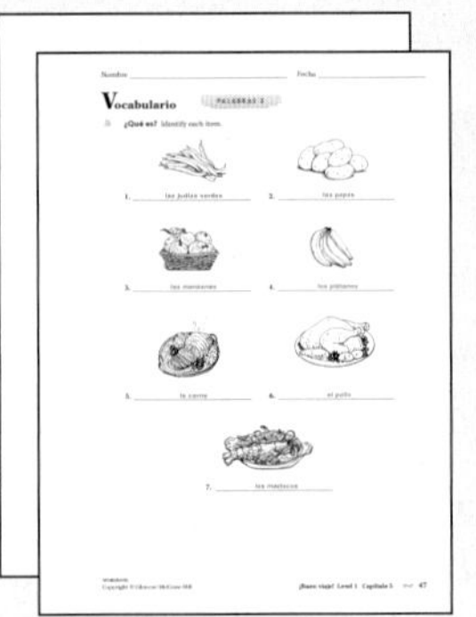

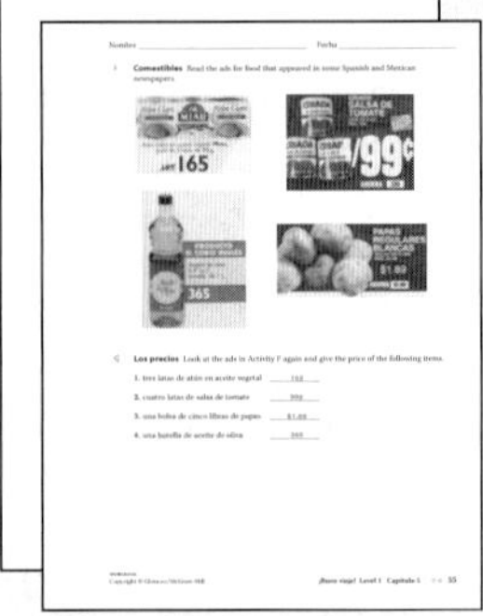

Vocabulary, pages 45–48

Structure, pages 49–52

Enrichment, pages 53–56

Audio Activities

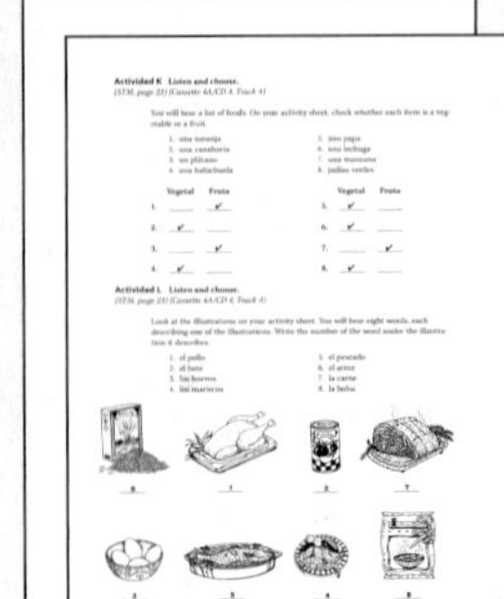

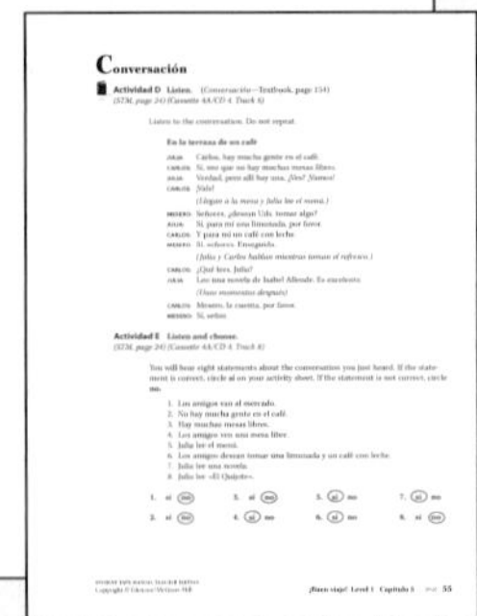

Vocabulary, pages 49–54

Structure, pages 55–56

Conversation, Pronunciation, pages 57–58

Additional Practice, pages 60–62

Assessment

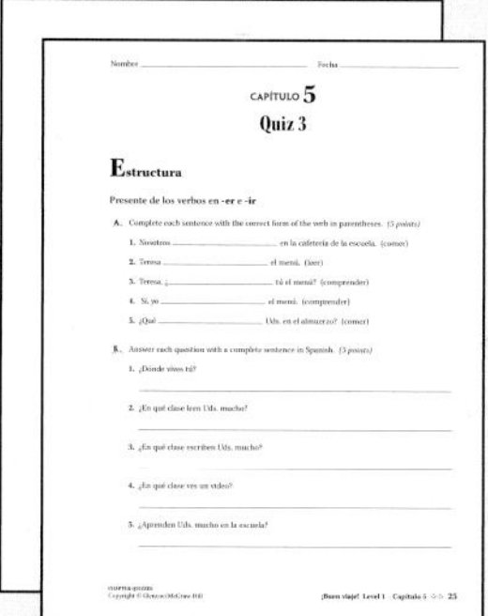

Vocabulary and Structure Quizzes, pages 22–25

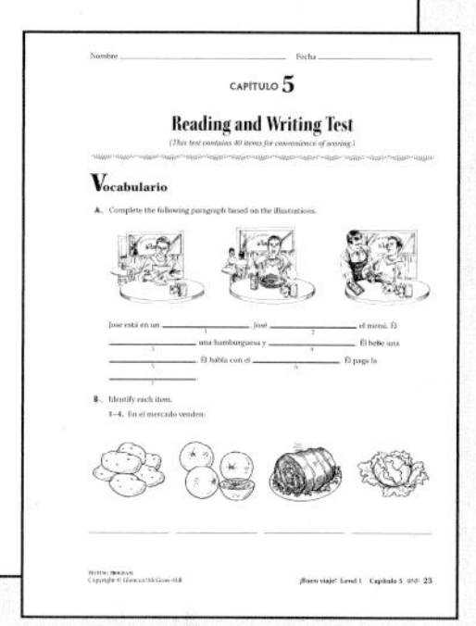

Chapter Tests, pages 67–80

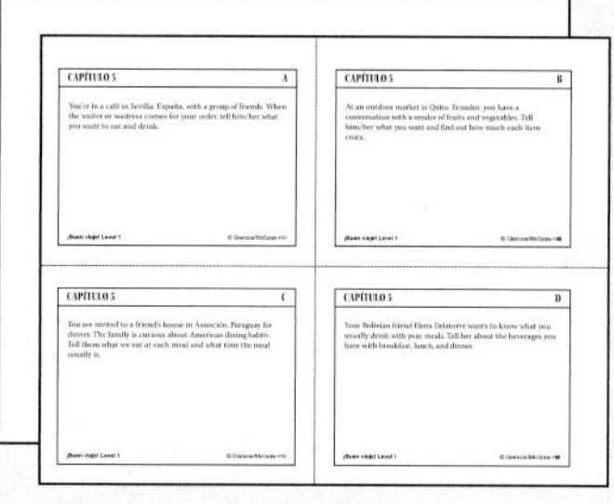

Situation Cards, Chapter 5

MindJogger Videoquiz, ExamView® Pro, Chapter 5

Timesaving Teacher Tools

TeacherWorks™ is your all-in-one teacher resource center. Personalize lesson plans, access resources from the Teacher Wraparound Edition, connect to the Internet, or make a to-do list. These are only a few of the many features that can assist you in the planning and organizing of your lessons.

Includes:

- A calendar feature
- Access to all program blackline masters
- Standards correlations and more

ExamView® Pro

Test Bank software for Macintosh and Windows makes creating, editing, customizing, and printing tests quick and easy.

Technology Resources

In the Chapter 5 Internet Activity, you will have a chance to learn more about the Spanish-speaking world. Visit spanish.glencoe.com

On the interactive CD-ROM, students can listen to and take part in a recorded version of the conversation in Chapter 5.

¡Viva el mundo hispano! Video and Video Activities, Chapter 5. Available on VHS and DVD.

Help your students prepare for the chapter test by playing the **Maratón mental** Videoquiz game show. Teams will compete against each other to review chapter vocabulary and structure and sharpen listening comprehension skills. Available on VHS and DVD.

¡Buen viaje! is also available on CD or Online.

Capítulo 5

Preview

In this chapter, students will learn how to order food at a café and shop for food at a store or market. To do this they will learn to identify some food items, to use expressions needed for ordering food, and to use the **-er** and **-ir** verbs. They will also learn some differences between eating customs in the United States and Spanish-speaking countries.

National Standards

Communication

In Chapter 5, students will communicate in spoken and written Spanish on the following topics:

- ordering food at a café
- shopping for food at a market or supermarket
- eating habits

Students will obtain and provide information and engage in conversations in a café or market setting as they fulfill the objectives listed on this page.

LEVELING

The activities, conversations, and readings within each chapter are marked according to level of difficulty. **E** indicates easy. **A** indicates average. **C** indicates challenging. Some activities cover a range of difficulty. In some activities, for example, advanced students will be able to produce more extensive responses while students who learn at a different rate may give less detailed responses. The leveling indicators will help you individualize instruction to best meet your students' needs.

Capítulo 5

En el café

Objetivos

In this chapter you will learn to:

- order food or a beverage at a café
- identify some food
- shop for food
- talk about activities
- talk about differences between eating habits in the United States and in the Spanish-speaking world

Bernardita Zegers *Don Diego y doña Patricia*

Capítulo 5

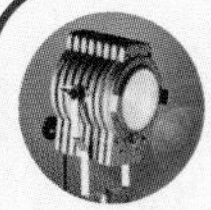

Spotlight on Culture

Fotografía This photo was taken on the **Plaza Mayor** in Madrid. This historic seventeenth-century plaza has been superbly restored. The square is closed to traffic and is a pleasant spot to have a coffee or refreshment at one of the many cafés. The **Plaza Mayor** is one of the largest squares in Europe. It was designed by the architect of Felipe II, but construction on it was completed in 1620 during the reign of Fernando III.

Vocabulario
PALABRAS 1

1 PREPARATION

Resource Manager

Vocabulary Transparencies 5.2–5.3
Audio Activities TE, pages 49–52
Audio CD 4
Workbook, pages 45–46
Quizzes, pages 22–23
ExamView® Pro

Bellringer Review

Use BRR Transparency 5.1 or write the following on the board.
Complete the following.

1. **Compro una camisa en una tienda de ___.**
2. **¿Qué ___ necesitas? ¿Blanca o roja?**
3. **¿Buscas una camisa de ___ largas o cortas?**
4. **¿Qué ___ usas? ¿Pequeña, mediana o grande?**
5. **Pagas en la ___.**

2 PRESENTATION

Step 1 Have students close their books. Point to each new vocabulary item using Vocabulary Transparencies 5.2–5.3. Have students repeat each word several times. Intersperse questions such as: **¿Qué es?, ¿Quién es?**

Step 2 When you present sentences, ask questions building from simple to more complex. For example:
¿Va Rafael al café?
¿Quién va al café?
¿Adónde va Rafael?
¿Va al café con Catalina?
¿Con quién va?

Vocabulario
PALABRAS 1

En el café

el mesero, el camarero

una mesa libre

el menú

una mesa ocupada

la mesa

Rafael va al café.
Él va al café con Catalina.
Ellos van juntos.
Buscan una mesa.
Ven una mesa libre.

Catalina lee el menú.

Reaching All Students

Total Physical Response If students don't already know the meaning of **levántate, ven acá,** and **siéntate,** teach these expressions by using the appropriate gestures as you say each expression. Call on individual students to do the following.
(Student 1), **levántate. Ven acá.**
Es el café. Busca una mesa libre.
Siéntate en el café.
(Student 2), **ven acá. Tú vas a ser el / la mesero(a).**
Ve a la mesa donde está ___. Habla con ___.
(Student 1), **habla con el / la mesero(a).**
(Student 2), **dale el menú a** *(Student 1).*
(Student 1), **lee el menú.**
Da la orden al / a la mesero(a).
(Student 2), **toma el lápiz. Escribe la orden.**
Gracias, *(Student 1).* **Siéntate.**

Para beber

un café solo

un café con leche

los refrescos

una cola

un té helado

una limonada

Para comer

una sopa

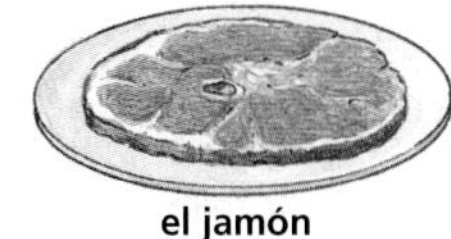
el jamón

el queso

una ensalada

una tortilla

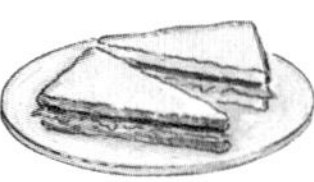
un bocadillo, un sándwich

papas fritas

una hamburguesa

un pan dulce

el postre

un helado de vainilla

un helado de chocolate

Antes de comer

Sí, señores, ¿qué desean Uds.?
Para mí, un café con leche, por favor.
Y para mí, una cola.

Los clientes hablan con el mesero.
El mesero escribe la orden.

Después de comer

La cuenta, por favor.
Sí, señor. Enseguida.
¿Está incluido el servicio?
Sí, señor.
el Café
la cuenta

Nota When learning a language, try to guess the meaning of unfamiliar words. The other words in the sentence provide the context and will help you understand words you do not know.
Elena estudia español en la escuela. *Aprende* el español en la escuela. Elena lee un menú en español. Ella *comprende* el menú. *Comprende* porque *aprende* el español en la escuela. Elena *comprende*, habla, lee y escribe el español. Es una alumna buena. *Recibe* notas muy buenas.

Vocabulario

Step 3 Have students dramatize the miniconversations using as much expression as possible.

Step 4 After the initial presentation of the vocabulary with the overhead transparencies, have students open their books and read the new material for additional reinforcement.

Step 5 Read the **Nota** aloud to the class. Emphasize the new words they are learning from context. You may add the following to give further clarification.
Elena aprende porque es una alumna buena y estudia.
Point to your ears as you say:
Ella comprende el español. El mesero habla español y Elena comprende al mesero.

About the Spanish Language

- The word **el mesero** is used throughout Latin America. **El camarero** is used in Spain.
- The tortilla shown here is a Spanish tortilla which is similar to an omelette. **Una tortilla a la española** is an omelette with potatoes and onions.
- The two most common words for *sandwich* are **el sándwich** and **el bocadillo. Bocadillo** is more common in Spain. In Spain you will also hear **el bocata. El emparedado** is also used in Spain and in some areas of Latin America.
- **Papas** is used throughout Latin America. **Patatas** is used in Spain.
- **Helado** is the most commonly used word for *ice cream.* **Mantecado,** however, is often used for *vanilla ice cream.*
- Among friends **la cuenta** is sometimes referred to as **la dolorosa.**

Chapter Projects

Una fiesta Have students plan a menu for a Spanish Club party. They should plan who will bring the beverages and various food items.

LEVELING
E: Vocabulary

3 PRACTICE

¿Qué palabra necesito?

¡OJO! When students are doing the **¿Qué palabra necesito?** activities, accept any answer that makes sense. The purpose of these activities is to have students use the new vocabulary. They are not factual recall activities. Thus, it is not necessary for students to remember specific factual information from the vocabulary presentation when answering. If you wish, have students use the photo on this page as a stimulus, when possible.

Historieta Each time **Historieta** appears, it means that the answers to the activity form a short story. Encourage students to look at the title of the **Historieta,** since it can help them do the activity.

1 and 4 Have students close their books. Do these activities orally first, then reinforce by calling on individuals to read. It is suggested that you go over all the activities in class before assigning them for homework.

Expansion: Have students retell the stories in Activities 1, 2, and 4 in their own words.

¿Qué palabra necesito?

1 Historieta Al café Contesten. *(Answer.)*

1. ¿Adónde van los amigos?
2. ¿Qué buscan?
3. ¿Están ocupadas todas las mesas?
4. ¿Ven una mesa libre?
5. ¿Toman la mesa?
6. ¿Lee Gabriela el menú?
7. ¿Con quién hablan los amigos?
8. ¿Quién escribe la orden?
9. ¿Qué bebe Gabriela?
10. ¿Qué bebe Tomás?
11. ¿Toman un refresco los amigos?

Caracas, Venezuela

2 Historieta En el café Contesten. *(Answer.)*

1. Los amigos van ____.
   a. al café **b.** a la cafetería de la escuela
2. Buscan ____.
   a. una mesa ocupada **b.** una mesa libre
3. Los amigos leen ____.
   a. el menú **b.** la orden
4. El mesero ____ la orden.
   a. lee **b.** escribe
5. Para ____ hay café, té y cola.
   a. comer **b.** beber
6. El cliente paga ____.
   a. el menú **b.** la cuenta

3 ¿Qué toma José? Sigan el modelo. *(Follow the model.)*

José bebe una cola.

José come un bocadillo de jamón y queso.

1. 

2.  

3. 

4. 

5.

Answers to ¿Qué palabra necesito?

1

1. Los amigos van al café.
2. Buscan una mesa.
3. No, todas las mesas no están ocupadas.
4. Sí, (No, no) ven una mesa libre.
5. Sí, (No, no) toman la mesa.
6. Sí (No), Gabriela (no) lee el menú.
7. Los amigos hablan con el / la mesero(a) (camarero[a]).
8. El / La mesero(a) (camarero[a]) escribe la orden.
9. Gabriela bebe ___.
10. Tomás bebe ___.
11. Sí, los amigos toman un refresco.

2

1. a
2. b
3. a
4. b
5. b
6. b

3

1. José come una hamburguesa.
2. José come papas fritas.
3. José come una ensalada.
4. José come un helado.
5. José bebe una limonada.

4 Historieta Una experiencia buena

Contesten. *(Answer.)*

1. ¿Va Linda a un café?
2. ¿Va a un café en Jerez?
3. ¿Va con un grupo de alumnos americanos?
4. ¿Habla Linda con el camarero?
5. ¿Lee Linda el menú?
6. ¿Es en español el menú?
7. ¿Comprende Linda el menú?
8. ¿Y comprende Linda al camarero cuando él habla?
9. ¿Por qué comprende Linda? ¿Aprende ella el español en la escuela?
10. ¿Habla, lee y comprende Linda el español?

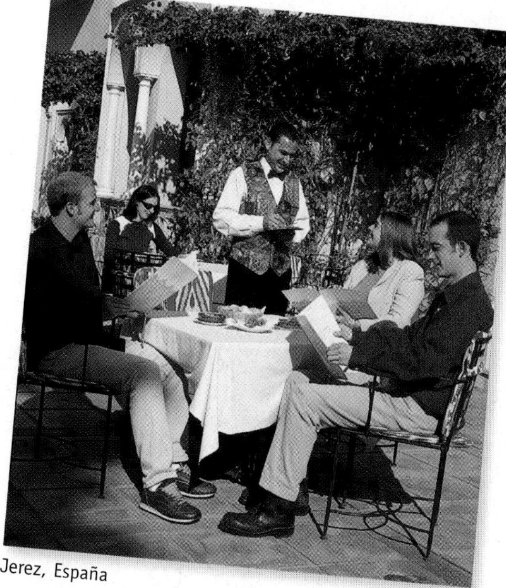

Jerez, España

5 Al café

Work in small groups. You're in a café in Mexico City. One of you will be the server. Have a conversation from the time you enter the café until you leave. You will get a table, order, get the check, and pay.

6 ¿Qué toman los amigos?

Look at the photographs below. With a classmate, take turns telling one another what's happening in each one.

Madrid, España

Vocabulario

5 Expansion: If you have access to a video camera, you may wish to have students prepare this conversation/skit, practice it, and then record it on a "set" (in another location, perhaps the school cafeteria). Then have a "movie" day complete with popcorn where the whole class watches the videotape of the different skits.

6 Have students ask you questions about the photos that accompany Activity 6. This encourages students to use the interrogative words.

Learning from Photos

(page 144) Ask the following questions about the photo of Caracas, Venezuela:
¿Están en Caracas los amigos? ¿Van a un café? ¿Entran en el café? ¿Quién indica dónde hay una mesa libre, Tomás o Gabriela?
(page 145 top) Have students tell a story by describing the photo of Jerez. They can use Activity 4 as a guide.

For review, have students tell what each person is wearing. They know all the necessary vocabulary with the exception of *vest,* **el chaleco,** and *bow tie,* **la corbata de lazo.**

LEVELING

E: Activities 2, 3, 4, 6
A: Activities 1, 6
C: Activity 5

Answers to ¿Qué palabra necesito?

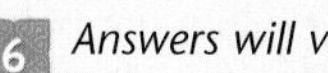

4

1. Sí, Linda va a un café.
2. Sí, va a un café en Jerez.
3. Sí, va con un grupo de alumnos americanos.
4. Sí, Linda habla con el camarero.
5. Sí, Linda lee el menú.
6. Sí, el menú es en español.
7. Sí, Linda comprende el menú.
8. Sí, Linda comprende al camarero cuando él habla.
9. Linda comprende porque aprende el español en la escuela.
10. Sí, Linda habla, lee y comprende el español.

5 *Answers will vary but may include:*

—¿Qué desean Uds.?
—Un café con leche, por favor.
—Para mí, una limonada.
—Sí, señor(a).
—La cuenta, por favor.
—Sí, señor(a). Enseguida.

6 *Answers will vary.*

Vocabulario

PALABRAS 2 

1 PREPARATION

Resource Manager

Vocabulary Transparencies 5.4–5.5
Audio Activities TE, pages 52–54
Audio CD 4
Workbook, pages 47–48
Quizzes, page 24
ExamView® Pro

Bellringer Review

Use BRR Transparency 5.2 or write the following on the board.
Answer.

1. **¿Dónde compras los materiales escolares?**
2. **¿En qué llevas los materiales escolares?**
3. **¿Cuáles son algunos materiales escolares?**

2 PRESENTATION

Step 1 Have students close their books. Present the vocabulary, using Vocabulary Transparencies 5.4–5.5. Have students repeat each word several times.

Step 2 Have students dramatize the miniconversations on page 147, using as much expression as possible.

Step 3 When you present the sentences on page 147, ask questions building from simple to more complex. For example: **¿Va de compras la señora? ¿Quién va de compras? ¿Va de compras en México? ¿Adónde va la señora? ¿Dónde vive la señora?**

Step 4 After presenting the vocabulary with the transparencies, have students open their books and read the new material.

Vocabulario

PALABRAS 2

En el mercado

las manzanas
las naranjas
la lechuga
los plátanos
los tomates
las papas
las judías verdes
las frutas
las zanahorias
los guisantes
las habichuelas, los frijoles
los vegetales
los mariscos
la carne
los huevos
el pollo
el pescado

Reaching All Students

Total Physical Response If students don't already know the meaning of **levántate, ven acá, siéntate,** and **hacer unos gestos,** teach these expressions by using the appropriate gestures as you say each expression. Call on individual students to pantomime the following.

(Student 1), **ven acá, por favor.**
Vas a hacer unos gestos.
Come la manzana.
Come el tomate.
Bebe la cola.
Bebe el café.
Toma el paquete. Abre el paquete.
Come las papas fritas.
Toma la lata. Mira la lata. Abre la lata.
Prepara una ensalada de atún.
Gracias, *(Student 1).* **Siéntate.**

¿A cuánto están los guisantes hoy?

A cincuenta el kilo.

Medio kilo, por favor.

¿Algo más, señora?

No, nada más, gracias.

La señora va de compras.
Va de compras en México.
La señora vive en México.

En el supermercado

Venden:

un bote (una lata) de atún

productos congelados

un paquete de arroz

una bolsa de papas fritas

Las comidas

el desayuno

el almuerzo

la cena

About the Spanish Language

- There are many different words for *beans:* **las habichuelas, los frijoles, los frejoles, las judías,** and **los porotos.** The most commonly used term for *green beans* is **las judías verdes,** but you will also hear **los ejotes, las vainitas, las chauchas, los porotos verdes,** and **las verduras.**
- **El tomate** in Mexico is **el jitomate.**
- In areas of the Caribbean, **la naranja** is **la china.**
- *Vegetables* can be **los vegetales, las legumbres,** or **las verduras.**
- Another common expression for **¿A cuánto están?** is **¿A cómo son?** (It is recommended that you do not confuse students by introducing this expression.)
- The word **la bolsa** can be problematic. A bag is sometimes **el bolso,** but **la bolsa** is quite universal for a paper bag or a bag or package of potato chips, for example. **La bolsa** can also be a woman's purse.
- In almost all countries, **huevos** can have a vulgar meaning, but it is safe to use the word in the proper context. In Mexico and Guatemala, people will sometimes avoid it and use **blanquillos.**
- The official names for the meals are: **el desayuno, el almuerzo, la cena. La comida** is the general term for *meal,* but it is often associated with the main meal of the day. In some countries **la comida** is the midday meal or **el almuerzo,** and in others, it is the evening meal or **la cena.**

Chapter Projects

La cocina hispana Prepare a dish from a Spanish-speaking country or have students bring some Spanish or Latin American foods to class. Students should be prepared to say something about the food they bring, such as where it comes from and what the main ingredients are.

3 PRACTICE

¿Qué palabra necesito?

7 Have students close their books. Ask them the questions from Activity 7 orally. Call on individuals to respond. Then ask a student to retell all the information in his or her own words.

Writing Development

Have students write out Activity 8 in paragraph form.

Learning from Photos

(page 148 top) This photo shows a market in Málaga, España. Have students identify the products they recognize in the market.
(page 148 middle) Ask the following questions about the photo taken in San Miguel de Allende, México:
¿Qué vende la señora?
¿A cuánto están los huevos ahora?
¿Compra la señora los huevos?
¿Paga ella?
¿Da el dinero a la empleada?

9 Have students open their books and do Activity 9. In more able groups you may have students correct the false statements.

¿Qué palabra necesito?

Málaga, España

7 Historieta Al mercado
Contesten. *(Answer.)*

1. ¿Van ustedes al mercado?
2. ¿Compran ustedes comida en el mercado?
3. En el mercado, ¿venden vegetales y frutas?
4. ¿Venden carne y pescado también?
5. ¿Quiénes venden, los clientes o los empleados?
6. ¿Van ustedes al supermercado también?
7. En el supermercado, ¿venden productos en botes, paquetes y bolsas?
8. ¿Venden también muchos productos congelados?

San Miguel de Allende, México

8 Historieta De compras Completen según la foto. *(Complete according to the photo.)*

La señora está en el mercado. La señora va a un mercado en México porque ella __1__ en México. Habla con la empleada. Compra una docena de __2__. Hoy los huevos están a __3__ pesos la docena. La señora compra los huevos pero no necesita __4__ más.

9 ¿El desayuno, el almuerzo o la cena? Contesten con **sí** o **no**. *(Answer with* sí *or* no.*)*

1. En el desayuno comemos cereales, huevos, pan dulce, yogur y pan tostado con mermelada.
2. En la cena comemos un biftec.
3. En el desayuno comemos un bocadillo de pollo con papas fritas y una ensalada de lechuga y tomate.
4. En la cena comemos carne o pescado, papas o arroz, un vegetal y un postre.

ANSWERS TO ¿Qué palabra necesito?

7

1. Sí, vamos al mercado.
2. Sí, compramos comida en el mercado.
3. Sí, en el mercado venden vegetales y frutas.
4. Sí, venden carne y pescado también.
5. Los empleados venden.
6. Sí, vamos al supermercado también.
7. Sí, en el supermercado venden productos en botes, paquetes y bolsas.
8. Sí, venden también muchos productos congelados.

8

1. vive
2. huevos
3. diez
4. nada

9

1. Sí
2. Sí
3. No
4. Sí

10 Lo contrario

Escojan lo contrario. *(Choose the opposite.)*

1. algo	a. escribir
2. ocupado	b. aprender
3. para beber	c. nada
4. leer	d. libre
5. comprar	e. vender
6. enseñar	f. para comer

Málaga, España

11 Al mercado Visit a Hispanic market in your community with your classmates. If you don't know the names of some foods that appeal to you, ask the vendor. Choose a few items and find out how much you owe. Be sure to speak Spanish. If there isn't a Latin American market in your community, set one up in your classroom. Bring in photos of food items. Take turns pretending to be the vendor and the customers.

12 Las comidas para mañana Work with a classmate. Prepare a menu for tomorrow's meals—**el desayuno, el almuerzo y la cena.** Based on your menus, prepare a shopping list.

13 ¿Qué compras en el mercado? You're at an open-air food market in Ecuador. Make a list of the items you want to buy. With a classmate, take turns being the vendor and the customer as you shop for the items on your lists.

Un mercado del altiplano, Ecuador

10 You may wish to have more able students use each word in Activity 10 in an original sentence.

11, 12, and 13 These activities enable students to use the language creatively on their own as if they were communicating in real-life, survival situations. They are an excellent follow-up to the more controlled communicative activities presented on these pages.

Let students choose the activities they wish to do. It is to be expected that students will make some errors as they communicate on their own.

National Standards

Communities

You may wish to organize your students' visit to a Hispanic market in your community (Activity 11, page 149) as a class field trip. This would give students an opportunity to practice the vocabulary and structures of the chapter in a real-life setting.

Learning from Photos

(page 149 top) This photo shows a market in Málaga, España. Have students identify the products they recognize in the market.

(page 149 bottom) Each village of the Ecuadorian highlands has market days, most often twice a week. At the market there are many stalls selling food products, clothing, housewares, animals, etc. Markets start at sunrise, and almost all activity ceases at about 1 P.M.

Answers to ¿Qué palabra necesito?

10

1. c
2. d
3. f
4. a
5. e
6. b

11 *Answers will vary. Students should use the vocabulary from* Palabras 2. *Their conversations should be similar to those on page 147.*

12 and 13 *Answers will vary. Students should use the vocabulary from* Palabras 1 *and* 2.

LEVELING

E: Activities 9, 10, 12

A: Activities 7, 8, 11

C: Activity 13

Estructura

1 PREPARATION

Resource Manager

Audio Activities TE, pages 55–56
Audio CD 4
Workbook, pages 49–52
Quizzes, page 25
ExamView® Pro

Bellringer Review

Use BRR Transparency 5.3 or write the following on the board.
Complete each verb with the correct ending.

1. **Yo estudi__ mucho.**
2. **Yo prest__ atención cuando la profesora habl__.**
3. **Nosotros tom__ apuntes en clase.**
4. **Tú escuch__ a la profesora cuando ella habl__, ¿no?**
5. **Durante la fiesta yo bail__ y ellos cant__.**

2 PRESENTATION

Presente de los verbos en -er e -ir

Step 1 Read the introductory paragraph on page 150 to the class.

Step 2 Now have them take a look at the verb paradigms.

Step 3 Put the verbs **comer** and **vivir** on the board. Ask students what to say when:

- talking about someone or talking to a stranger: **Juan / Ud.**
- talking about two people or to two or more people: **Juan y Sandra / Uds.**
- talking about yourself: **yo**
- talking to a friend: **tú**

Write the forms on the board as you elicit responses from the class. Point out that the endings are the same for both **-er** and **-ir** verbs.

Estructura

Presente de los verbos en -er e -ir
Describing people's activities

You have already learned that many Spanish verbs end in **-ar.** These verbs are referred to as first conjugation verbs. Most regular Spanish verbs belong to the **-ar** group. The other two groups of regular verbs in Spanish end in **-er** and **-ir.** Verbs whose infinitive ends in **-er (comer, beber, leer, vender, aprender, comprender)** are second conjugation verbs. Verbs whose infinitive ends in **-ir (vivir, escribir, recibir)** are third conjugation verbs. Study the following forms. Note that the endings of **-er** and **-ir** verbs are the same except for the **nosotros** and **vosotros** forms.

-ER VERBS			
INFINITIVE	**comer**	**leer**	**ENDINGS**
STEM	com-	le-	
yo	como	leo	-o
tú	comes	lees	-es
él, ella, Ud.	come	lee	-e
nosotros(as)	comemos	leemos	-emos
vosotros(as)	*coméis*	*leéis*	*-éis*
ellos, ellas, Uds.	comen	leen	-en

-IR VERBS			
INFINITIVE	**vivir**	**escribir**	**ENDINGS**
STEM	viv-	escrib-	
yo	vivo	escribo	-o
tú	vives	escribes	-es
él, ella, Ud.	vive	escribe	-e
nosotros(as)	vivimos	escribimos	-imos
vosotros(as)	*vivís*	*escribís*	*-ís*
ellos, ellas, Uds.	viven	escriben	-en

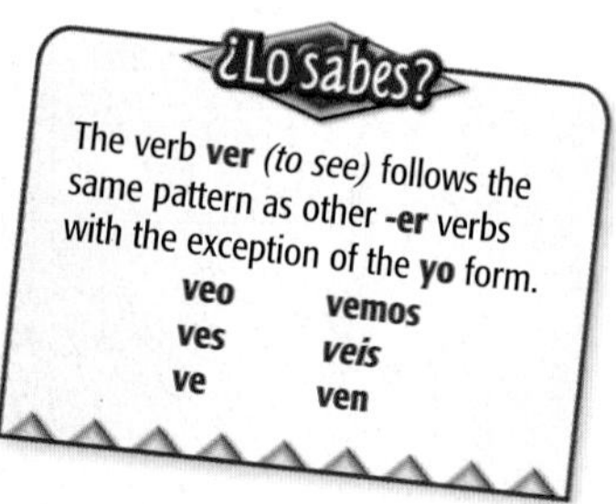

¿Lo sabes?

The verb **ver** *(to see)* follows the same pattern as other **-er** verbs with the exception of the **yo** form.

veo	**vemos**
ves	***veis***
ve	**ven**

Learning from Realia

(page 151) Ask the following questions about the business card: **¿Cuál es el nombre del restaurante? ¿Dónde está? ¿Cuál es el número de teléfono?** Now find the following expressions on the card: *air conditioning, fine cuisine.*

Ask the following about the menu: **¿Es caro o barato un menú económico? ¿Lleva un plato combinado varias cosas?**

¿Cómo lo digo?

14 Historieta Un menú español

Lean y contesten. *(Read and answer.)*

PABLO Linda, ¿lees el menú en español?
LINDA ¡Sí, claro!
PABLO Pero, ¿comprendes un menú en español?
LINDA Sí, comprendo. ¿Por qué preguntas?
PABLO Pero no eres española. Y no vives aquí en Madrid. ¿Lees el español? ¿Cómo es posible?
LINDA Pues, aprendo el español en la escuela en Nueva York. En clase hablamos mucho. Leemos y escribimos también.
PABLO Pues, yo aprendo el inglés aquí en Madrid. Hablo un poco, pero cuando leo no comprendo casi nada. Comprendo muy poco.

1. ¿Qué lee Linda?
2. ¿En qué lengua lee el menú?
3. ¿Comprende el menú?
4. ¿Es de España Linda?
5. ¿Vive ella en Madrid?
6. ¿Por qué comprende? ¿Dónde aprende ella el español?
7. En la clase de español, ¿hablan mucho los alumnos?
8. ¿Leen y escriben también?
9. ¿Qué lengua aprende Pablo en Madrid?
10. ¿Comprende él cuando lee algo en inglés?

Madrid, España

MESON RESTAURANTE
EL TABIÓN
PATIO ANDALUZ
AIRE ACONDICIONADO
AMPLIOS SALONES
COMIDA SELECTA
Y GARANTIZADA
Cardenal González, 69
Teléfono 47 60 61 - Fax 48 62 40
14003 CORDOBA

PLATOS COMBINADOS
1 - CHULETA, HUEVO, TOMATE Y PATATAS 7,50 €
2 - FLAMENQUIN, CALAMARES, PAELLA Y TOMATE 7,50 €
3 - PAELLA, PESCADO, ENSALADA Y TOMATE 7,50 €
4 - HAMBURGUESA, FLAMENQUIN, TOMATE Y PATATAS 7,50 €

MENUS ECONOMICOS
MENU 1.° PAELLA
PESCADO O CARNE
PAN, VINO Y FRUTA 12,50 €
MENU 2.° SOPA DE PICADILLO
PESCADO O CARNE
PAN, VINO Y FRUTA 12,50 €
MENU 3.° GAZPACHO CON GUARNICION
PESCADO O CARNE
PAN, VINO Y FRUTA 12,50 €

ENTRADAS
GAZPACHO CON GUARNICION
REVUELTO DE ESPARRAGOS
JAMON Y QUESO
SOPAS DE PICADILLO O MARISCO
ENSALADAS MIXTA O DE LA CASA
MENESTRA DE VERDURAS CASERA
TORTILLAS A ELEGIR • PINCHITOS MORUNOS
HUEVOS CON JAMON • PAELLA MIXTA
SETAS A LA CORDOBESA

CARNES
POLLO EN SALSA CORDOBESA • SAN JACOBO
FILETE DE TERNERA • CHULETON DE TERNERA
CHULETAS DE CORDERO • CHULETAS DE CERDO
CHURRASCO • FLAMENQUIN CASERO
RABO DE TORO • COCHIFRITO

PESCADOS
MERO EMPANADO • PEZ ESPADA PLANCHA
LENGUADOS FRITOS O PLANCHA
CALAMARES FRITOS • PIJOTAS FRITAS
PESCADA FRITA • BOQUERONES
CHIPIRONES • JAPUTA EN ADOBO
ROSADA PLANCHA • PEZ A LA MILANESA

Step 4 Teach the **nosotros** form separately from the others since it has a different ending depending on whether it is an **-er** or **-ir** verb. Put more verbs on the board and have students repeat the **nosotros** forms: **comemos, leemos, aprendemos, comprendemos, vivimos, escribimos, recibimos.**

3 PRACTICE

¿Cómo lo digo?

14 Have students open their books to page 151 and repeat the conversation in Activity 14 after you. Call on two individuals with good pronunciation to read the conversation aloud with as much expression as possible. Ask the class in English why Pablo is so surprised. Then ask the questions that follow the conversation. **Expansion:** Have a student retell the information in the conversation in his or her own words in narrative form.

Recycling

Have students give a complete description of the couple seated at the café in the photo. Have them describe their clothes as well as their physical characteristics and personalities. This activity recycles vocabulary and structures from Chapters 1, 2, and 3.

LEVELING

E: Activity 14

Answers to ¿Cómo lo digo?

14

1. Linda lee el menú.
2. Lee el menú en español.
3. Sí, comprende el menú.
4. No, Linda no es de España.
5. No, no vive en Madrid.
6. Comprende porque aprende el español en la escuela en Nueva York.
7. Sí, los alumnos hablan mucho.
8. Sí, leen y escriben también.
9. Pablo aprende el inglés en Madrid.
10. No, no comprende nada cuando lee algo en inglés.

3 PRACTICE *(continued)*

¡OJO! All these activities can be done with books closed or open. It is recommended that you go over the activities in class before assigning them for homework.

Writing Development

Students can write Activities 15, 16, and 18 in paragraph form.

Learning from Photos

(page 152) Ask the following questions about the photo taken in Cádiz, España:

¿Qué lleva el muchacho?
Y la muchacha, ¿qué lleva ella?
¿Cómo es el muchacho?
¿Cómo es la muchacha?
¿Lee el muchacho el periódico?
¿Toman ellos un refresco?
¿Es un café al aire libre?
¿Es el verano o el invierno?

UN POCO MÁS This *InfoGap* Activity will allow students to practice in pairs. The activity should be very manageable for them, since all vocabulary and structures are familiar to them.

15 Historieta En un café Completen. *(Complete.)*

En el café los clientes __1__ (ver) al mesero. Ellos __2__ (hablar) con el mesero. Los clientes __3__ (leer) el menú y __4__ (decidir) lo que van a comer o beber. Los meseros __5__ (tomar) la orden y __6__ (escribir) la orden en una hoja de papel o en un bloc pequeño. Los meseros no __7__ (leer) el menú. Los clientes __8__ (leer) el menú. Y los clientes no __9__ (escribir) la orden. Los meseros __10__ (escribir) la orden.

Aji Verde
LO MEJOR EN COCINA FINA CHILENA

16 Yo Contesten personalmente. *(Answer about yourself.)*

1. ¿Dónde vives?
2. En casa, ¿hablas inglés o español?
3. ¿Aprendes el español en la escuela?
4. En la clase de español, ¿hablas mucho?
5. ¿Lees mucho?
6. ¿Escribes mucho?
7. ¿Comprendes al profesor o a la profesora cuando él o ella habla?
8. ¿Comprendes cuando lees?

17 ¿Qué comen todos? Sigan el modelo. *(Follow the model.)*

carne →
—Teresa come carne.
—Yo como carne también. / Yo no como carne.
Y tú, ¿comes carne o no?

1. vegetales
2. pescado
3. mariscos
4. ensalada
5. postre
6. pollo
7. huevos

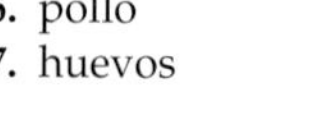

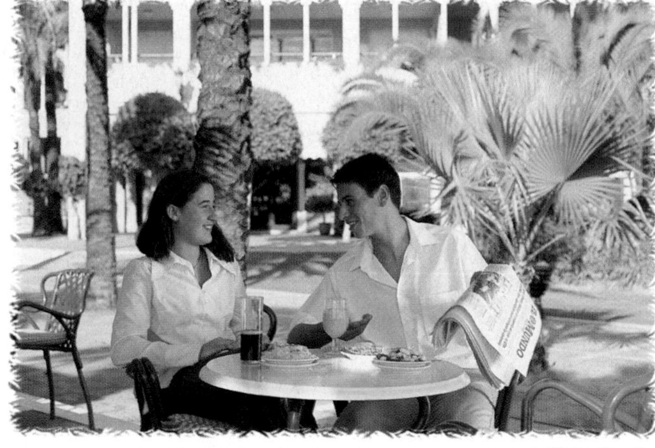

Cádiz, España

*For more practice using words from **Palabras 1** and **2** and **-er** verbs, do Activity 5 on page H6 at the end of this book.*

ANSWERS TO ¿Cómo lo digo?

15

1. ven
2. hablan
3. leen
4. deciden
5. toman
6. escriben
7. leen
8. leen
9. escriben
10. escriben

16

1. Vivo en ___.
2. Hablo inglés (español) en casa.
3. Sí, aprendo el español en la escuela.
4. Sí, (No, no) hablo mucho en la clase de español.
5. Sí, (No, no) leo mucho.
6. Sí, (No, no) escribo mucho.
7. Sí, (No, no) comprendo al profesor (a la profesora) cuando él (ella) habla.
8. Sí, (No, no) comprendo cuando leo.

17 *Answers will follow the model.*

18 **Nosotros** Contesten personalmente.
(Answer about yourself and a friend.)

1. ¿Dónde viven ustedes?
2. ¿A qué escuela asisten ustedes. (van ustedes)?
3. ¿Escriben ustedes mucho en la clase de español?
4. ¿Escriben ustedes mucho en la clase de inglés?
5. ¿Leen ustedes mucho en la clase de español?
6. ¿En qué clase leen ustedes novelas y poemas?
7. ¿Aprenden ustedes mucho en la clase de español?
8. ¿Comprenden ustedes cuando el profesor o la profesora habla?
9. ¿Ven ustedes un video en la clase de español?
10. Recibimos notas buenas en español. ¿Reciben ustedes notas buenas también?

¿Lo sabes?

The verb **asistir** is a false cognate. It means *to attend.*

19 **¿Toman ustedes un refresco?** Sigan el modelo. *(Follow the model.)*

una cola →
—Nosotros bebemos una cola. / No bebemos una cola.
¿Y ustedes? ¿Beben una cola o no?

1. café solo
2. café con leche
3. leche
4. limonada
5. té

20 **¿Qué comes?** With a classmate, take turns finding out what each of you eats for breakfast, lunch, and dinner.

21 **¿Cuánto es, por favor?** You are at a little café in South America. Your classmate is the waiter or waitress. Order something you want to eat and drink. Then find out how much it is. The waiter or waitress can refer to the menu to tell you how much you owe.

Café Luna

sándwich	14 pesos
tamal	10 pesos
enchilada	11 pesos
café	2 pesos
limonada	3 pesos

22 **El curso de inglés** Have a discussion with a classmate about your English class. Tell as much as you can about what you do and learn in class. You may want to use some of the following words: **aprender, leer, recibir, escribir, comprender.**

Andas bien. ¡Adelante!

Estructura

18 **and** **19** You may wish to have students do these activities in small groups.

21 Students doing Activity 21 can also present their skit to the class.

22 Students doing Activity 22 can put their information together as a report and present it to the class.

LEVELING

E: Activities 15, 16, 20, 22
A: Activities 16, 17, 18, 19, 21, 22
C: Activities 18, 19

¡Adelante!
At this point in the chapter, students have learned all the vocabulary and structure necessary to complete the chapter. The conversation and cultural readings that follow recycle all the material learned up to this point.

Answers to ¿Cómo lo digo?

18

1. Vivimos en ___.
2. Asistimos a la Escuela ___.
3. Sí, (No, no) escribimos mucho en la clase de español.
4. Sí, (No, no) escribimos mucho en la clase de inglés.
5. Sí, (No, no) leemos mucho en la clase de español.
6. Leemos novelas y poemas en la clase de inglés (en la clase de español).
7. Sí, (No, no) aprendemos mucho en la clase de español.
8. Sí, (No, no) comprendemos mucho cuando el / la profesor(a) habla.
9. Sí, (No, no) vemos un video en la clase de español.
10. Sí, (No, no) recibimos notas buenas en español.

19 *Answers will follow the model.*

20 and **21** *Answers will vary. Students should use the vocabulary from* Palabras 1 *and* 2.

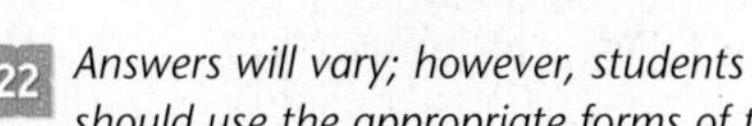

22 *Answers will vary; however, students should use the appropriate forms of the verbs listed.*

Conversación

1 PREPARATION

Resource Manager

Audio Activities TE, page 57
Audio CD 4

Bellringer Review

Use BRR Transparency 5.4 or write the following on the board.
Read the conversation and write down where it takes place.
—**Necesito un cuaderno.**
—**Hay muchos cuadernos allí en la mesa.**
—**¿Cuánto es?**
—**Doscientos pesos.**
—**¿Pago aquí o en la caja?**
—**Ud. paga en la caja.**

2 PRESENTATION

Step 1 To vary the presentation, tell students nothing at all about the conversation. Have them listen to it as you play Audio CD 4.

Step 2 Play the recording once again and have students look at the photo as they listen.

Step 3 Have three students play the roles of Julia, Carlos, and the **mesero** and read the conversation aloud using as much expression as possible.

Step 4 Ask the questions in the **¿Comprendes?** section.

Step 5 Have students make up a similar conversation on their own.

Step 6 After presenting the conversation, go over the **¿Comprendes?** activity. If students can answer the questions with relative ease, move on. Students should not be expected to memorize the conversation.

Conversación

En la terraza de un café

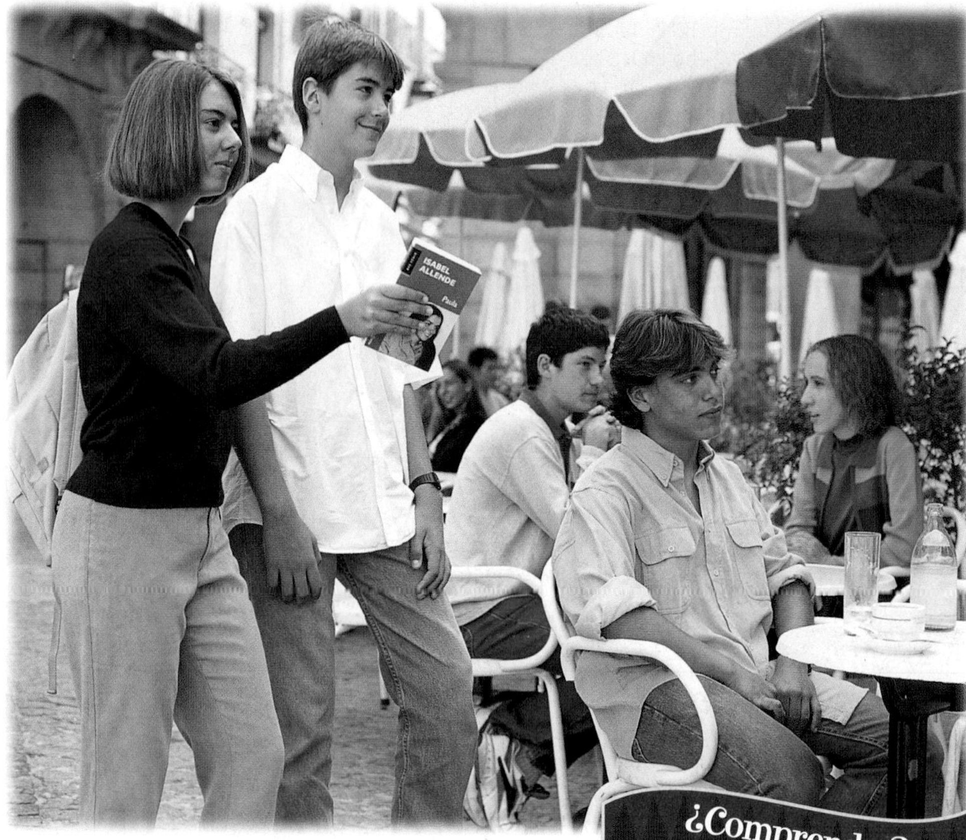

Julia Carlos, hay mucha gente en el café.
Carlos Sí, veo que no hay muchas mesas libres.
Julia Verdad, pero allí hay una. ¿Ves? ¡Vamos!
Carlos ¡Vale!
(Llegan a la mesa y Julia lee el menú.)
Mesero Señores, ¿desean ustedes tomar algo?
Julia Sí, para mí una limonada, por favor.
Carlos Y para mí un café con leche.
Mesero Sí, señores. Enseguida.
(Julia y Carlos hablan mientras toman el refresco.)
Carlos ¿Qué lees, Julia?
Julia Leo una novela de Isabel Allende. Es excelente.
(Unos momentos después)
Carlos Mesero, la cuenta, por favor.
Mesero Sí, señor.

¿Comprendes?

Contesten. *(Answer.)*

1. ¿Dónde están Julia y Carlos?
2. ¿Hay mucha gente en el café?
3. ¿Qué ve Julia?
4. ¿Qué lee Julia?
5. ¿Con quién hablan Carlos y Julia?
6. ¿Qué desea Julia?
7. ¿Y Carlos?
8. ¿Qué novela lee Julia?
9. ¿Cómo es la novela?

Answers to ¿Comprendes?

1. Julia y Carlos están en (la terraza de) un café.
2. Sí, hay mucha gente en el café.
3. Julia ve una mesa libre.
4. Lee el menú.
5. Carlos y Julia hablan con el mesero.
6. Julia desea una limonada.
7. Carlos desea un café con leche.
8. Julia lee una novela de Isabel Allende.
9. La novela es excelente.

About the Spanish Language

The expression **¡Vale!** is used a great deal in Spain. It's similar to the English expression *OK*.

LEVELING

A: Conversation

Vamos a hablar más

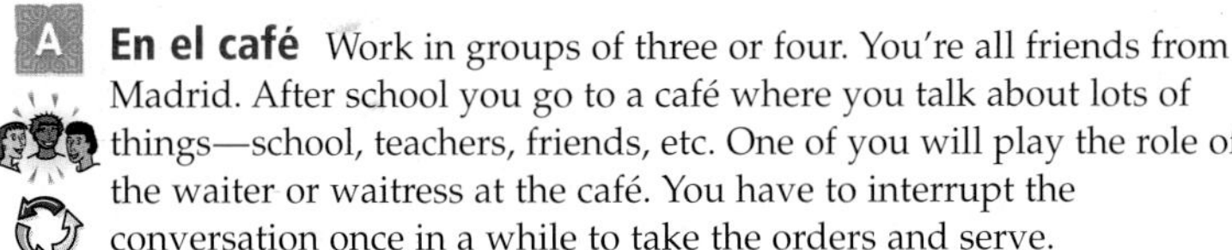

A **En el café** Work in groups of three or four. You're all friends from Madrid. After school you go to a café where you talk about lots of things—school, teachers, friends, etc. One of you will play the role of the waiter or waitress at the café. You have to interrupt the conversation once in a while to take the orders and serve.

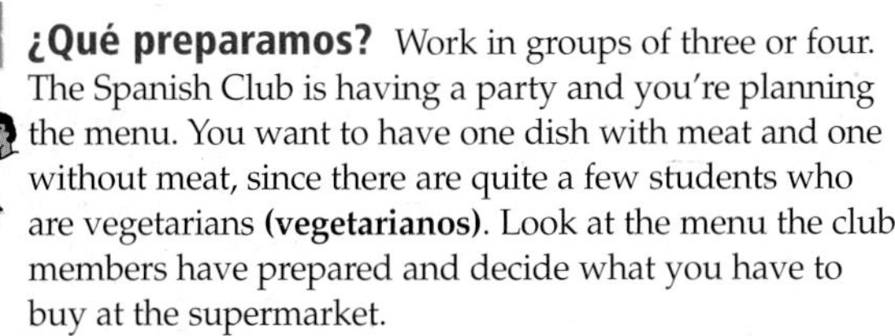

B **¿Qué preparamos?** Work in groups of three or four. The Spanish Club is having a party and you're planning the menu. You want to have one dish with meat and one without meat, since there are quite a few students who are vegetarians **(vegetarianos)**. Look at the menu the club members have prepared and decide what you have to buy at the supermarket.

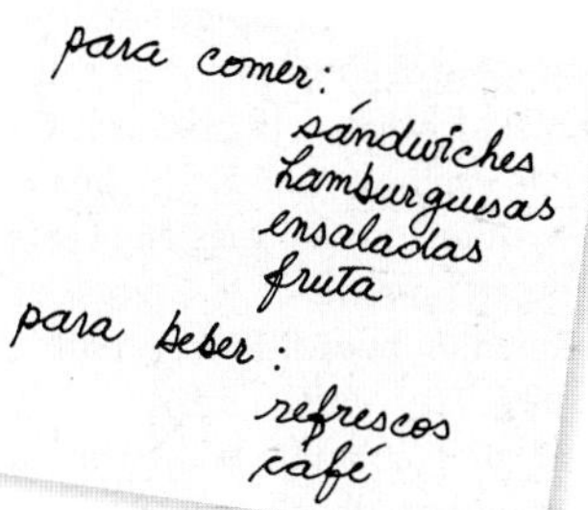

Pronunciación

La consonante d

The pronunciation of **d** in Spanish varies according to its position in the word. When a word begins with **d** (initial position) or follows the consonants **l** or **n,** the tongue gently strikes the back of the upper front teeth.

da	de	di	do	du
da	**dependiente**	**difícil**	**domingo**	**dulce**
merienda	**vende**	**andino**	**condominio**	

When **d** appears within the word between vowels (medial position), **d** is extremely soft. Your tongue should strike the lower part of your upper teeth, almost between the upper and lower teeth.

da	de	di	do	du
privada	**modelo**	**estudio**	**helado**	**educación**
ensalada	**cuaderno**	**medio**	**congelado**	

When a word ends in **d** (final position), **d** is either extremely soft or omitted completely—not pronounced.

nacionalidad **ciudad**

Repeat the following sentences.

Diego da el disco compacto a Donato en la ciudad.
El dependiente vende helado y limonada.
Adela compra la merienda en la tienda.

Answers to Vamos a hablar más

A *Answers will vary. Students may wish to use the conversation on page 154 as a model.*

B *Answers will vary but should include the food items from* Palabras 1 *and* 2.

3 PRACTICE

Vamos a hablar más

A **and** **B** Allow students to choose the activities they would like to do.

Glencoe Technology

CD-ROM

On the CD-ROM, students can watch a dramatization of this conversation. They can then play the role of either one of the characters and record themselves in the conversation.

Pronunciación

Step 1 This is a very difficult sound for most English speakers to produce correctly. Have students imitate the sounds carefully, paying particular attention to the position of the tongue, as explained in the presentation. You may also wish to use Audio CD 4 to present this material.

Step 2 The model words and sentences on page 155 can also be used for dictation to determine the accuracy of students' spelling.

Lecturas culturales

Resource Manager

Audio Activities TE, page 59
Audio CD 4

PREPARATION

Bellringer Review

Use BRR Transparency 5.5 or write the following on the board.
Complete with the correct nationality.

1. **Tomás es de San Juan. Él es ___.**
2. **Teresa es de Santiago de Cuba. Ella es ___.**
3. **Los amigos de José son de Santiago de Chile. Ellos son ___.**
4. **Las dos profesoras son de Guanajuato, México. Ellas son ___.**

National Standards

Cultures
The reading about cafés in Madrid and mealtimes in Spain gives students insight into daily life in Spain.

PRESENTATION

Pre-reading

Step 1 Give students about two minutes to scan the first paragraph on page 156. In English, have them tell in one sentence what it's about.

Step 2 Do the same with the second paragraph on page 157.

Lecturas culturales

Reading Strategy

Guessing meaning from context It's easy to understand words you have already studied. There are also ways to understand words you are not familiar with. One way is to use the context—the way these words are used in the sentence or reading—to help you guess the meaning of those words you do not know.

En un café en Madrid

José Luis vive en Madrid. Después de las clases, los amigos de José Luis van juntos, en grupo, a un café. En el otoño y en la primavera, ellos van a un café al aire libre[1]. Pasan una hora o más en el café. Toman un refresco y a veces comen un bocadillo o un pan dulce. En el café, hablan y hablan. Hablan de la escuela, de los amigos, de la familia. Y a veces miran a la gente que pasa.

[1]al aire libre *outdoor*

Paseo de la Castellana, Madrid

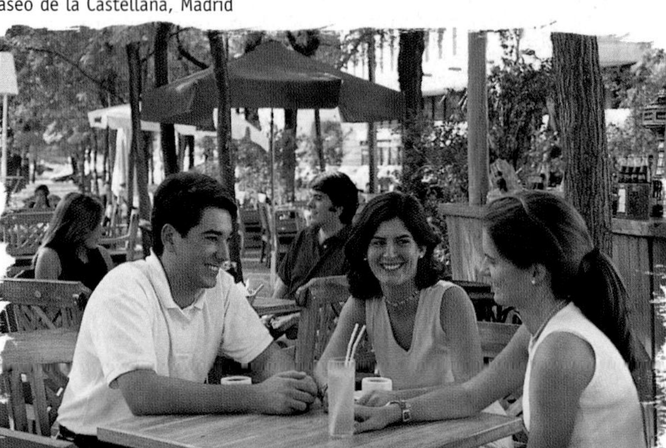

Madrid, España

Learning from Photos

(page 156 top) **Paseo de la Castellana** is a lovely, wide boulevard in Madrid that runs for several kilometers. It is lined with beautiful old mansions and elegant apartment buildings.
(page 156 bottom) This photo was taken just off the **Puerta del Sol,** Madrid's busy city center. The bronze statue in the background of **el oso y el madroño** is Madrid's official symbol—a bear sniffing a strawberry tree.

LEVELING

E: Reading

Después de una hora o más, van a casa. Cuando llegan a casa, ¿comen o cenan enseguida, inmediatamente? No, no comen inmediatamente. En España, no cenan hasta las diez o las diez y media de la noche. Pero en España y en algunos países latinoamericanos la comida principal es la comida del mediodía.

Estepona, España

¿Comprendes?

A José Luis Contesten con **sí** o **no.** *(Answer with* sí *or* no.*)*

1. José Luis es un muchacho de la Ciudad de México.
2. José Luis va solo al café.
3. En el invierno, José Luis y un grupo de amigos van a un café al aire libre.
4. En el café, toman un refresco.
5. Hablan de muchas cosas diferentes.
6. Pasan solamente unos minutos en el café.
7. Cuando llegan a casa, los muchachos comen enseguida con la familia.
8. La comida principal es la cena.

B La verdad, por favor. Corrijan las oraciones falsas de la Actividad A. *(Correct the false statements from Activity A.)*

Lecturas culturales

Reading

Step 1 Call on individual students to read aloud.

Step 2 Intersperse comprehension questions such as:
¿Dónde vive José Luis?
¿Adónde van los amigos de José Luis?
¿Cuándo van?
¿Cómo van al café?

These questions have a dual objective. They check comprehension, and they also allow students to use the language so that upon completion of the reading, they can discuss the information on their own.

Post-reading

Step 1 Go over the **¿Comprendes?** activities on this page.

Step 2 Call on a student to summarize the **Lectura** in his or her own words.

Writing Development

You may wish to have some students write a summary of the **Lectura.**

Answers to ¿Comprendes?

A

1. No, José Luis no es un muchacho de la Ciudad de México.
2. No, José Luis no va solo al café.
3. No, José Luis y un grupo de amigos no van a un café al aire libre en el invierno.
4. Sí, toman un refresco en el café.
5. Sí, hablan de muchas cosas diferentes.
6. No, no pasan solamente unos minutos en el café.
7. No, cuando llegan a casa, los muchachos no comen enseguida.
8. No, la comida principal no es la cena.

B

1. José Luis es un muchacho de Madrid.
2. José Luis y un grupo de amigos van juntos al café.
3. En el otoño y en la primavera, José Luis y un grupo de amigos van a un café al aire libre.
4. Pasan una hora o más en el café.
5. Cuando llegan a casa, los muchachos no comen hasta las diez o las diez y media de la noche.
6. La comida principal es la comida del mediodía.

Lectura opcional 1

National Standards

Cultures
The reading about dining hours and meals in the Spanish-speaking world and the related activities give students an understanding of daily life in Spain and Latin America.

Comparisons
This reading selection compares dining hours and eating habits in the Spanish-speaking world with those in the United States.

¡OJO! This reading is optional. You may skip it completely, have the entire class read it, have only several students read it and report to the class, or assign it for extra credit.

Learning from Photos

(page 158) Have students take a look at the colorful buses in Buenos Aires. There are many different terms for *bus,* and in Argentina a municipal bus is usually called **un colectivo.**

Fun-Facts

Churros are fried in olive oil and coated with sugar. Ideally they are served hot. People dunk them in either **café con leche** or **chocolate.**

Lectura opcional 1

Las horas para comer

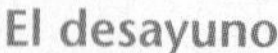

El desayuno

En España y en los países de Latinoamérica, la gente suele[1] comer más tarde que aquí en Estados Unidos. Como nosotros, toman el desayuno a eso de las siete o las ocho de la mañana. A eso de las diez van a un café o a una cafetería donde toman otro café con leche y un churro o pan dulce.

El almuerzo

El almuerzo es a la una o, en el caso de España, a eso de las dos de la tarde. Hoy día la mayoría[2] de la gente no va a casa a tomar el almuerzo. Toman el almuerzo en la cafetería de la escuela o en la cafetería donde trabajan. Si no, comen en un café o en un restaurante. Muchos no van a casa a tomar el almuerzo porque hay mucho tráfico. Tarda (toma) demasiado tiempo[3].

La cena

En la mayoría de los países latinoamericanos la gente suele cenar a las ocho y media o a las nueve de la noche. Pero, en España, no. En España la cena es a las diez o a las diez y media.

Buenos Aires, Argentina

[1]suele *tend to*
[2]mayoría *majority*
[3]demasiado tiempo *too much time*

¿Comprendes?

¡A comer en el mundo hispano! Contesten. *(Answer.)*

1. ¿Dónde suele comer la gente más tarde, en Estados Unidos o en los países hispanos?
2. ¿A qué hora toman el desayuno en los países hispanos?
3. ¿A qué hora toman ustedes el desayuno?
4. ¿A qué hora es el almuerzo?
5. ¿Dónde toma la gente el almuerzo?
6. ¿Van muchos a casa?
7. ¿Por qué no van a casa?
8. ¿A qué hora cenan en Latinoamérica?
9. Y en España, ¿a qué hora cenan?
10. ¿A qué hora cenan ustedes?

Answers to ¿Comprendes?

1. La gente suele comer más tarde en los países hispanos.
2. Toman el desayuno a eso de las siete o las ocho de la mañana en los países hispanos.
3. Tomamos el desayuno a eso de las ___.
4. El almuerzo es a la una o, en el caso de España, a eso de las dos de la tarde.
5. La gente toma el almuerzo en la cafetería de la escuela o en la cafetería donde trabajan.
6. No, muchos no van a casa.
7. No van a casa porque hay mucho tráfico. Tarda demasiado tiempo.
8. Cenan a las ocho y media o a las nueve.
9. En España cenan a las diez o a las diez y media.
10. Cenamos a eso de las ___.

Lectura opcional 2

Málaga, España

¿Mercado o supermercado?

En los países hispanos hay muchos mercados. Algunos son mercados al aire libre. En el mercado la gente compra los alimentos o comestibles[1] que necesitan para las tres comidas. Los productos que venden en los mercados están muy frescos[2]. ¡Qué deliciosos!

Hay también supermercados—sobre todo (particularmente) en las grandes ciudades y en los alrededores[3] de las grandes ciudades. En los supermercados venden muchos productos en lata, en paquete o en bolsa. En los supermercados hay un gran surtido[4] de productos congelados.

[1]comestibles *foods*
[2]frescos *fresh*
[3]alrededores *outskirts*
[4]surtido *assortment*

Estepona, España

¿Comprendes?

A De compras para la comida Completen. *(Complete.)*

1. En los países hispanos hay ____.
2. En los mercados la gente compra ____.
3. Los productos del mercado están ____.
4. Hay supermercados en ____.
5. En los supermercados venden ____.

B Otra expresión Busquen una expresión equivalente en la lectura. *(Find an equivalent expression in the reading for the italicized words.)*

1. En *las naciones* hispanas hay muchos mercados al aire libre.
2. La gente compra *los alimentos* que necesitan.
3. Están muy frescos. ¡Y qué ricos y *sabrosos!*
4. Venden productos *enlatados.*
5. Hay *una gran selección.*

Answers to ¿Comprendes?

A

1. muchos mercados
2. los alimentos o comestibles que necesitan para las tres comidas
3. muy frescos
4. las grandes ciudades y en los alrededores de las grandes ciudades
5. muchos productos en lata, en paquete o en bolsa y productos congelados

B

1. los países
2. los comestibles
3. deliciosos
4. en lata
5. un gran surtido

Lectura opcional 2

National Standards

Cultures
The reading and the related activities on this page introduce students to the types of food stores that exist in the Spanish-speaking world.

¡OJO! This reading is optional. You may skip it completely, have the entire class read it, have only several students read it and report to the class, or assign it for extra credit.

PRESENTATION

Step 1 Have students read the two paragraphs quickly on their own.

Step 2 Now do the **¿Comprendes?** activities with them orally.

Assessment

You may want to give the following quiz to those students who read this selection.
Answer.

1. **¿Qué hay en los países hispanos?**
2. **¿Están al aire libre algunos de los mercados?**
3. **¿Qué compra la gente en el mercado?**
4. **¿Cómo están los productos que venden en el mercado?**
5. **¿Hay supermercados?**
6. **¿Dónde hay supermercados?**
7. **¿Qué venden en los supermercados?**

LEVELING

A: Readings 1,2

Conexiones

National Standards

Connections
This reading about arithmetic establishes a connection with another discipline, allowing students to reinforce and further their knowledge of mathematics through the study of Spanish.

Comparisons
Students are introduced to the different way some numbers are handwritten and the different use of the decimal point.

¡OJO! The readings in the **Conexiones** section are optional. They focus on some of the major disciplines taught in schools and universities. The vocabulary is useful for discussing such topics as history, literature, art, economics, business, science, etc. You may choose any of the following ways to do the readings in the **Conexiones** sections.

Independent reading Have students read the selections and do the post-reading activities as homework, which you collect. This option is least intrusive on class time and requires a minimum of teacher involvement.

Homework with in-class follow-up Assign the readings and post-reading activities as homework. Review and discuss the material in class the next day.

Intensive in-class activity This option includes a pre-reading vocabulary presentation, in-class reading and discussion, assignment of the activities for homework, and a discussion of the assignment in class the following day.

Conexiones

Las matemáticas

La aritmética

When we go shopping or out to eat, it is often necessary to do some arithmetic. We either have to add up the bill ourselves or check the figures someone else has done for us. In a café or restaurant we want to figure out how much tip we should leave. In order to do this we have to do some arithmetic.

We seldom do a great deal of arithmetic in a foreign language. We normally do arithmetic in the language in which we learned it. It is fun, however, to know some basic arithmetical terms in case we have to discuss a bill or a problem with a Spanish-speaking person.

Before we learn some of these terms in Spanish, let's look at some differences in numbers. Note how the numbers 1 and 7 are written in some areas of the Spanish-speaking world.

1 7

Also note the difference in the use of the decimal point in some countries.

1,000 1.000 1,07 1.07

La aritmética

sumar +
restar −
multiplicar x
dividir ÷

Para resolver un problema oralmente

Suma dos y dos.
Dos y dos son cuatro. $2 + 2 = 4$
Resta dos de cinco.
Cinco menos dos son tres. $5 - 2 = 3$
Multiplica dos por cinco.
Dos por cinco son diez. $2 \times 5 = 10$
Divide quince entre tres.
Quince entre tres son cinco. $15 \div 3 = 5$

El diez por ciento de ciento cincuenta pesos son quince pesos.

Nº 002246 B
Restaurante Del Valle
Humilladero, 4 · Teléf. 366 90 25 · Madrid
MESA Núm. 1

2	Cartas	5,50
1	Espinacas	5,50
1	Pastel verduras	18,00
1	Lenguado	12,00
1	Callos	
1	Ribera Duero	9,50
1	Sorbete	5,00
1	Sorbete champán	7,00
	TOTAL	62,50

I.V.A. incluido

¿Comprendes?

A ¿Cuánto es? Resuelvan los problemas aritméticos en voz alta. *(Solve the following problems aloud.)*

1. $2 + 2 = 4$
2. $14 + 6 = 20$
3. $30 - 8 = 22$
4. $20 - 4 = 16$
5. $4 \times 4 = 16$
6. $8 \times 3 = 24$
7. $27 \div 9 = 3$
8. $80 \div 4 = 20$

B La respuesta, por favor. Contesten en español. *(Do the following problems in Spanish.)*

1. Suma 5 y 2.
2. Suma 20 y 3.
3. Resta 3 de 10.
4. Resta 8 de 25.
5. Multiplica 5 por 3.
6. Multiplica 9 por 4.
7. Divide 9 entre 3.
8. Divide 16 entre 2.

C La cuenta, por favor. Sumen. *(Add the bill in Spanish.)*

Conexiones

PRESENTATION

Las matemáticas
La aritmética

¡OJO! As the introduction states, one rarely does arithmetic in a foreign language. The purpose of this section is to introduce students to only the most basic and important arithmetical terms.

Step 1 Go over the reading with the students. Before beginning the **¿Comprendes?** activities, call on students to do the math problems orally from the blackboard on page 160.

Learning from Realia

(page 161) Have students look at the way the numbers 1 and 7 are written on this bill. Then ask students what country the bill is from.

LEVELING

E: Reading

Answers to ¿Comprendes?

A

1. Dos y dos son cuatro.
2. Catorce y seis son veinte.
3. Treinta menos ocho son veintidós.
4. Veinte menos cuatro son dieciséis.
5. Cuatro por cuatro son dieciséis.
6. Ocho por tres son veinticuatro.
7. Veintisiete entre nueve son tres.
8. Ochenta entre cuatro son veinte.

B

1. Cinco y dos son siete.
2. Veinte y tres son veintitrés.
3. Diez menos tres son siete.
4. Veinticinco menos ocho son diecisiete.
5. Cinco por tres son quince.
6. Nueve por cuatro son treinta y seis.
7. Nueve entre tres son tres.
8. Dieciséis entre dos son ocho.

C *Students should say all the amounts in Spanish and then give the total:* Sesenta y dos cincuenta (euros).

¡Te toca a ti!

Use what you have learned

Recycling

These activities allow students to use the vocabulary and structure from this chapter in completely open-ended, real-life situations.

PRESENTATION

Encourage students to say as much as possible when they do these activities. Tell them not to be afraid to make mistakes, since the goal of the activities is real-life communication. If someone in the group makes an error, allow the others to politely correct him or her. Let students choose the activities they would like to do.

You may wish to divide students into pairs or groups. Encourage students to elaborate on the basic theme and to be creative. They may use props, pictures, or posters if they wish.

Writing Development

Have students keep a notebook or portfolio containing their best written work from each chapter. These selected writings can be based on assignments from the Student Textbook and the Workbook. The activities on page 163 are examples of writing assignments that may be included in each student's portfolio. On page 56 in the Workbook, students will begin to develop an organized autobiography **(Mi autobiografía).** These workbook pages may also become a part of their portfolio.

¡Te toca a ti!

Use what you have learned

HABLAR 1

En el café

✔ ***Order something to eat and drink at a café***

Work with a classmate. You're in a café on the Gran Vía in Madrid. One of you is the customer. The other is the waiter or waitress. Have a conversation. Say as much as you can to each other.

SPANISH Online

For more information about the Gran Vía and other interesting parts of Madrid, go to the Glencoe Spanish Web site: spanish.glencoe.com

HABLAR 2

En el mercado

✔ ***Buy food from a vendor at a market***

You are spending a semester studying in Spain. You are going to prepare a dinner for your "Spanish family." Decide what you need to buy at the market. Then have a conversation with a classmate who will be the clerk at the food store.

HABLAR 3

Juego Una competición

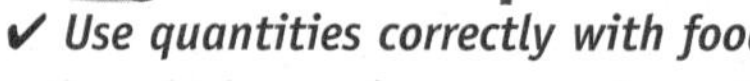

✔ ***Use quantities correctly with food***

See which one of you can make up the most expressions using the following words.

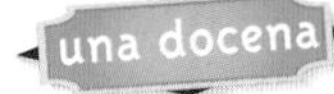

un kilo

ANSWERS TO ¡Te toca a ti!

1 *Answers will vary, but students can use the conversation on page 154 as a model.*

2 *Answers will vary. Students should write their grocery lists before beginning their conversations. Answers may include:*

—¿A cuánto están las papas hoy?
—A cuarenta el kilo.
—Medio kilo, por favor.
—¿Algo más, señor(a)?

3 *Answers will vary but should include foods from the chapter combined with the words given.*

4 El menú

✔ ***Plan a meal***

Write a menu in Spanish for your school cafeteria.

Estepona, España

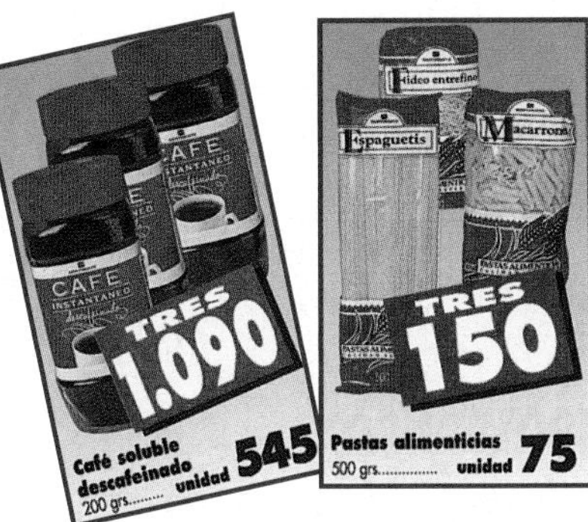

5 Un anuncio

✔ ***Write an advertisement for a supermarket***

Using these supermarket ads as a guide, write similar food advertisements in Spanish for your local supermarket. Choose any three foods you would like to feature.

Writing Strategy

Visualizing Many writers have a mental picture of what they want to write before they actually begin to write. The mental picture helps organize what they want to say. It also helps them visualize what they want to describe in their writing. Closing your eyes and visualizing what you want to write can make the writing experience more pleasant. When writing in a foreign language, you must limit your mental picture to what you know how to say.

6 Un café

You have been asked to write a short article about a visit to a café. Look at this photo. Pretend this is the mental picture you have of the restaurant you are going to write about. Look at it for several minutes and then write a paragraph about it.

¡Te toca a ti!

4 You may ask students to write the school cafeteria menu in Spanish for a given day or for the whole week.

Writing Strategy

Visualizing Have students read the Writing Strategy on page 163 and identify the main ideas before they begin to write.

National Standards

Communities

To do the Writing Strategy activity on page 163, students should go, if possible, to a Spanish restaurant in their community. You may wish to organize this as a field trip with your class so that the students can practice their Spanish in a real-life setting.

Chapter Projects

Al supermercado

Have students check their local supermarket to find out what kinds of Hispanic foods they sell. Have them report back to the class about their findings.

Answers to ¡Te toca a ti!

4 *Answers will vary but should include the various food items taught in this chapter.*

5 *Answers will vary, but students will use the ads as a model.*

6 *Answers will vary but should include vocabulary from the chapter.*

LEVELING

These activities encompass all three levels. All students will be able to do them at a sophistication level commensurate with their ability in Spanish. Some students will be able to speak for several minutes, and others may be able to give just a few sentences. This is to be expected when students are functioning completely on their own generating their own language to the best of their ability.

Assessment

Resource Manager

Communication Transparency C 5
Quizzes, pages 22–25
Performance Assessment, Task 5
Tests, pages 67–80
Situation Cards, Chapter 5
ExamView® Pro, Chapter 5
Maratón mental Videoquiz, Chapter 5

Assessment

This is a pre-test for students to take before you administer the chapter test. Note that each section is cross-referenced so students can easily find the material they have to review in case they made errors. You may use Assessment Answers Transparency A 5 to do the assessment in class, or you may assign this assessment for homework. You can correct the assessment yourself, or you may prefer to project the answers on the overhead in class.

Glencoe Technology

MINDJOGGER VHS/DVD

You may wish to help your students prepare for the chapter test by playing the MindJogger game show. Teams will compete against each other to review chapter vocabulary and structure and sharpen listening comprehension skills.

Music Connection

Canta con Justo
The song **Te toca a ti, me toca a mí** will be easy for learners of all ability levels. It will help students practice food vocabulary introduced in this chapter. You can find this song on Track 3 of the music CD. You may wish to have students act out this song as they listen.

Assessment

Vocabulario

To review **Palabras 1**, turn to pages 142–143.

1 Identifiquen. *(Identify.)*

1. 
2. 
3. 
4.
5. 

2 Completen la conversación. *(Complete the conversation.)*

En el café

6. **Mesero** Sí, señores. ¿Qué ____ ustedes?
Cliente Un café con leche y una limonada, por favor.
(Después)
7. **Cliente** Mesero, la ____, por favor.
Mesero Sí, señor. Enseguida.
8. **Cliente** ¿Está incluido el ____?
Mesero Sí, señor.

To review **Palabras 2**, turn to pages 146–147.

3 Identifiquen. *(Identify.)*

9. 
10. 
11. 
12. 

4 Completen. *(Complete.)*

13–14. Las tres comidas del día son el ____, el almuerzo y la ____.

Answers to Assessment

1
1. la ensalada
2. el helado (de chocolate)
3. las papas fritas
4. el bocadillo / el sándwich
5. la tortilla (española)

2
6. desean
7. cuenta
8. servicio

3
9. las naranjas
10. la lechuga
11. las papas
12. la carne

4
13. desayuno
14. cena

Assessment

Estructura

5 Completen. *(Complete.)*

15–16. Nosotros ____ soda y ustedes ____ limonada. (beber)
17–18. Yo ____ muchos vegetales y mi amigo ____ muchas frutas. (comer)
19. Nosotros ____ en Estepona pero el profesor ____ en Málaga. (vivir)

To review -er and -ir verbs, turn to page 150.

6 Completen. *(Complete.)*

20–21. Nosotros aprend____ mucho en la escuela y recib____ notas muy buenas.
22–23. Nosotros le____ novelas pero no escrib____ novelas.

Cultura

7 ¿Sí o no? *(True or false?)*

24. Los cafés son muy populares en España.
25. En España la gente cena a las seis. Cuando llegan a casa comen enseguida.

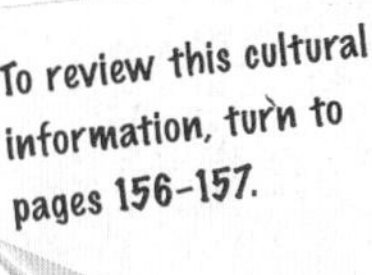
To review this cultural information, turn to pages 156–157.

Valldemossa, España

Learning from Photos

(page 165) Valldemossa is on the island of Mallorca, about 18 kilometers north of Palma. It is famous for its Carthusian monastery. After the expulsion of the monks in 1835, the cells became lodgings for travelers and continue to be leased as summer apartments. Many famous people have stayed there, including Frédéric Chopin and the famous French novelist George Sand.

SPANISH Online

The **Glencoe Spanish Web** site (**spanish.glencoe.com**) offers options that enable you and your students to experience the Spanish-speaking world via the Internet. For each **Capítulo,** there are activities, games, and quizzes. In addition, an *Enrichment* section offers students an opportunity to visit Web sites related to the theme of the chapter.

FOLDABLES™ Study Organizer — Dinah Zike's Study Guides

Your students may wish to use Foldable 7 to organize, display, and arrange data as they learn to write more extensively in Spanish. You may wish to encourage them to add information from each chapter as they continue to write about and illustrate all the different topics they will be studying.

A *single picture frame* foldable will help different types of learners organize. When it comes to writing, it may help students begin to gather their thoughts to depict what it is they want to write about.

Answers to Assessment

5

15. bebemos
16. beben
17. como
18. come
19. vivimos, vive

6

20. aprendemos
21. recibimos
22. leemos
23. escribimos

7

24. Sí
25. No

¡Hablo como un pro!

This unique page gives students the opportunity to speak freely and say whatever they can, using the vocabulary and structures they have learned in the chapter. The illustration serves to remind students of precisely what they know how to say in Spanish. There are no activities that students do not have the ability to describe or talk about in Spanish. The art not only depicts the vocabulary and content of this chapter, but also reinforces what they learned in previous chapters.

You may wish to use this page in many ways. Some possibilities are to have students do the following:

1. Look at the illustration and identify items by giving the correct Spanish words.
2. Make up sentences about what they see in the illustration.
3. Make up questions about the illustration. They can call on another class member to respond if you do this as a class activity, or you may prefer to allow students to work in small groups. This activity is extremely beneficial because it enables students to actively use interrogative words.
4. Answer questions you ask them about the illustration.
5. Work in pairs and make up a conversation based on the illustration.
6. Look at the illustration and give a complete oral review of what they see.
7. Look at the illustration and write a paragraph (or essay) about it.

You can also use this page as an assessment or testing tool, taking into account individual differences by having students go from simple to quite complicated tasks. The assessment can be either oral or written. You may wish to use the rubrics provided on pages T20–T21 as you give students the following directions.

1. Identify the topic or situation of the illustration.
2. Give the Spanish words for as many items as you can.
3. Think of as many sentences as you can to describe the illustration.
4. Go over your sentences and put them in the best sequencing to give a coherent story based on the illustration.

¡Hablo como un pro!

Tell all you can about this illustration.

Vocabulario

Getting along in a cafe

el café
la mesa
el/la mesero(a),
el/la camarero(a)
el menú
la orden
la cuenta
libre
ocupado(a)
ver
leer
comer
beber
¿Qué desean ustedes?
¿Está incluido el servicio?

Identifying snacks and beverages

los refrescos
una cola
un café solo, con leche
un té helado
una limonada
el cereal
el pan tostado
un yogur
una sopa
un bocadillo, un sándwich
el jamón
el queso
una hamburguesa
papas fritas
una tortilla
una ensalada
el postre
un helado de vainilla,
de chocolate
un pan dulce

Shopping for food

el mercado
el supermercado
un bote, una lata
un paquete
una bolsa
un kilo
congelado(a)
vender
¿A cuánto está(n)?
algo más
nada más

Identifying foods and meals

los vegetales
los guisantes
las habichuelas,
los frijoles
las judías verdes
las zanahorias
las papas
la lechuga
las frutas
las naranjas
las manzanas
los plátanos
los tomates
la carne
el biftec
los mariscos
el pescado
el pollo
el huevo
el atún
el arroz
las comidas
el desayuno
el almuerzo
la cena

How well do you know your vocabulary?

- Choose words for specific foods you enjoy.
- Create a menu using these words.

Other useful expressions

juntos(as)
antes de
después de
enseguida
comprender
aprender
escribir
recibir
vivir

VIDEOTUR

Episodio 5

In this video episode, you will join Alejandra and Julián at a café. See page 496 for more information.

Vocabulario

Vocabulary Review

The words and phrases in the **Vocabulario** have been taught for productive use in this chapter. They are summarized here as a resource for both student and teacher. This list also serves as a convenient resource for the **¡Te toca a ti!** activities on pages 162 and 163. More foods will be presented in Chapter 14. There are approximately twenty cognates in this chapter. Have students find them.

VIDEO VHS/DVD

The Video Program allows students to see how the chapter vocabulary and structures are used by native speakers within an engaging story line. For maximum reinforcement, show the video episode as a final activity for Chapter 1.

Reaching All Students

For the Younger Students

El mercado Have students set up a marketplace in class. You can use boxes or desks and chairs and plastic foods. Have them go to the "market" when they do the activities in the chapter that are related to shopping for food.

¡OJO! You will notice that the vocabulary list here is not translated. This has been done intentionally, since we feel that by the time students have finished the material in the chapter they should be familiar with the meanings of all the words. If there are several words they still do not know, we recommend that they refer to the **Palabras 1** and **2** sections in the chapter or go to the dictionaries at the end of this book to find the meanings. However, if you prefer that your students have the English translations, please refer to Vocabulary Transparency 5.1, where you will find all these words with their translations.

Planning for Chapter 6

SCOPE AND SEQUENCE, PAGES 168–199

Topics

- Family relationships
- Rooms in a house or apartment
- Telling your age

Culture

- The importance of family
- Godparents
- An invitation to a baptism
- **La quinceañera**
- *Las Meninas* by Diego Velázquez
- Great artists from Spain and Latin America

Functions

- How to talk about your family
- How to describe your home
- How to talk about birthdays
- How to tell what you have to do
- How to discuss what you are going to do
- How to talk about what belongs to you and others

Structure

- The verb **tener**
- **Tener que; Ir a**
- Possessive adjectives

National Standards

- Communication Standard 1.1 pages 168, 172, 173, 176, 177, 178, 179, 180, 181, 182, 184, 194
- Communication Standard 1.2 pages 171, 173, 177, 179, 180, 182, 185, 186, 187, 189, 190, 191, 193, 195
- Communication Standard 1.3 page 195
- Cultures Standard 2.1 pages 186, 187, 188–189, 190, 191
- Connections Standard 3.1 pages 191, 192–193
- Comparisons Standard 4.2 pages 188, 190
- Communities Standard 5.2 page 199

PACING AND PRIORITIES

The chapter content is color coded below to assist you in planning.

■ required ■ recommended ■ optional

Vocabulario *(required)* *Days 1–4*

- ■ Palabras 1
  La familia
- ■ Palabras 2
  La casa
  Una casa de apartamentos (departamentos)

Estructura *(required)* *Days 5–7*

- ■ Presente de **tener**
- ■ **Tener que; Ir a**
- ■ Adjetivos posesivos

Conversación *(required)*

- ■ ¿Vas a la fiesta?

Pronunciación *(recommended)*

- ■ Las consonantes **b, v**

Lecturas culturales

- ■ La familia hispana *(recommended)*
- ■ La quinceañera *(optional)*
- ■ *Las Meninas (optional)*

Conexiones

- ■ El arte *(optional)*

■ **¡Te toca a ti!** *(recommended)*

■ **Assessment** *(recommended)*

■ **¡Hablo como un pro!** *(optional)*

RESOURCE GUIDE

SECTION	PAGES	SECTION RESOURCES
Vocabulario PALABRAS 1		
La familia	170–173	Vocabulary Transparencies 6.2–6.3 Audio CD 4 Audio Activities TE, pages 63–66 Workbook, pages 57–58 Quiz 1, pages 26–27 ExamView® Pro
Vocabulario PALABRAS 2		
La casa Una casa de apartamentos (departamentos)	174, 176–177 175, 176–177	Vocabulary Transparencies 6.4–6.5 Audio CD 4 Audio Activities TE, pages 67–70 Workbook, pages 58–60 Quiz 2, page 28 ExamView® Pro
Estructura		
Presente de **tener** **Tener que; Ir a** Adjetivos posesivos	178–180 181–182 183–185	Audio CD 4 Audio Activities TE, pages 70–73 Workbook, pages 61–64 Quizzes 3–5, pages 29–31 ExamView® Pro
Conversación		
¿Vas a la fiesta?	186	Audio CD 4 Audio Activities TE, page 74 Interactive CD-ROM
Pronunciación		
Las consonantes **b, v**	187	Pronunciation Transparency P 6 Audio CD 4 Audio Activities TE, page 75
Lecturas culturales		
La familia hispana La quinceañera *Las Meninas*	188–189 190 191	Audio CD 4 Audio Activities TE, page 75 Tests, pages 86, 89
Conexiones		
El arte	192–193	Tests, page 91
¡Te toca a ti!		
	194–195	**¡Viva el mundo hispano!** Video, Episode 6 Video Activities, Chapter 6 Spanish Online Activities spanish.glencoe.com
Assessment		
	196–197	Communication Transparency C 6 Quizzes 1–5, pages 26–31 Performance Assessment, Task 6 Tests, pages 81–98 Situation Cards, Chapter 6 ExamView® Pro **Maratón mental** Videoquiz

Using Your Resources for Chapter 6

Transparencies

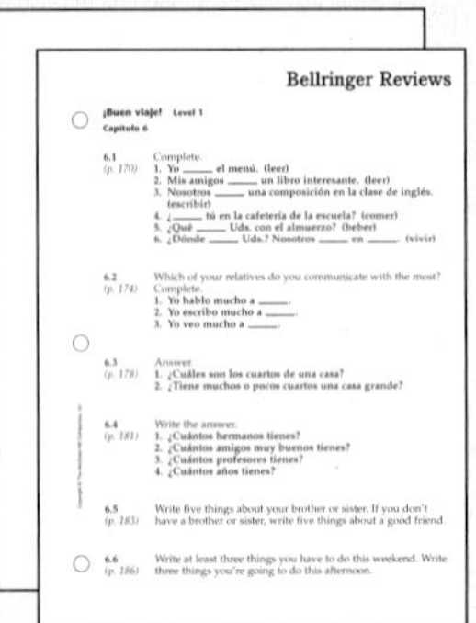

Bellringer 6.1–6.6

Vocabulary 6.1–6.5

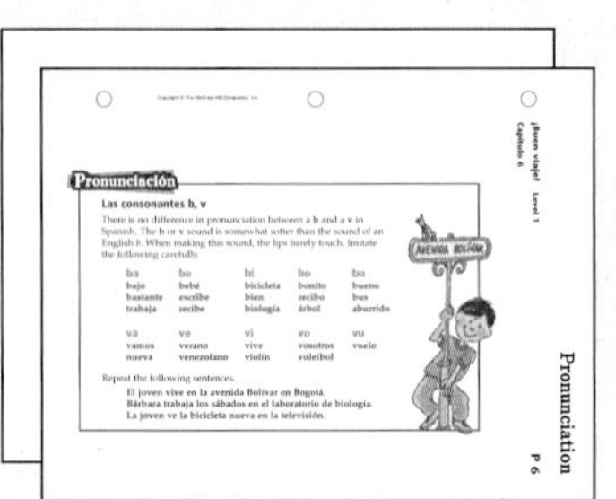

Pronunciation P 6

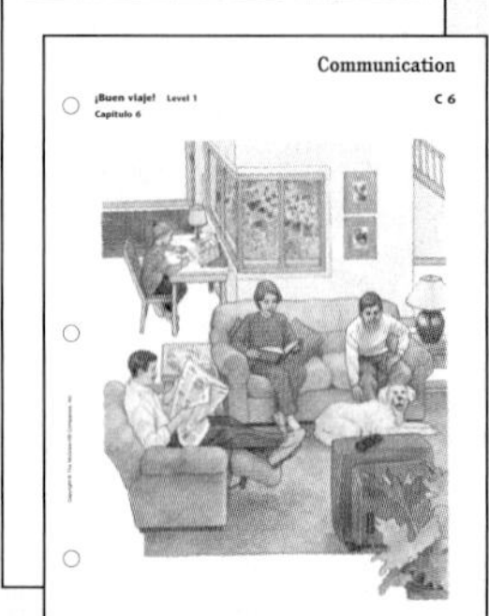

Communication C 6

Workbook

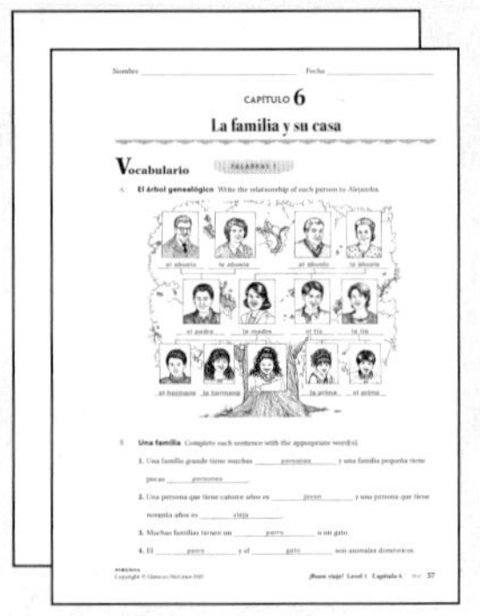

Vocabulary, pages 57–60

Structure, pages 61–64

Enrichment, pages 65–70

Audio Activities

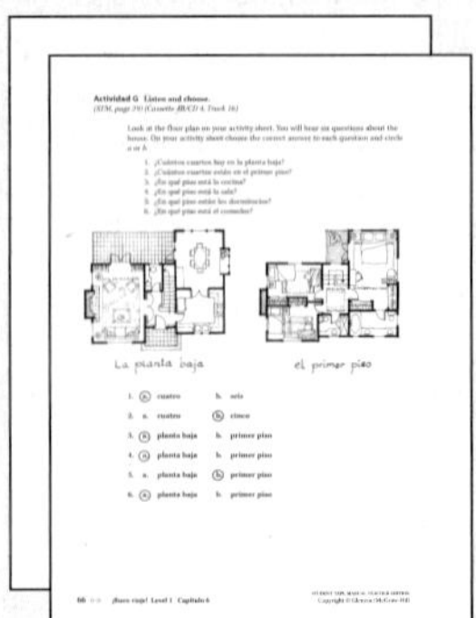

Vocabulary, pages 63–70

Structure, pages 70–73

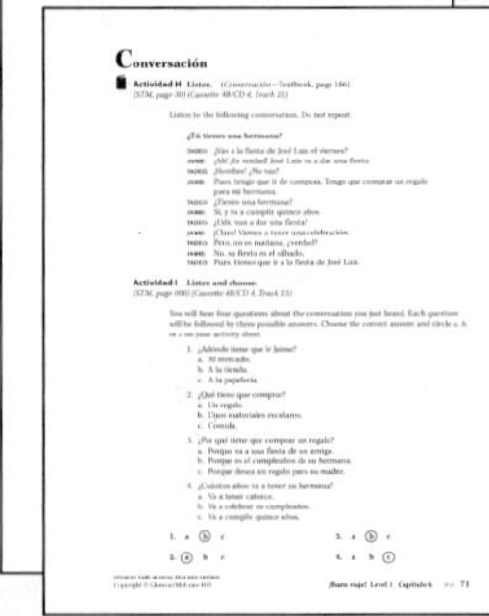

Conversation, Pronunciation, pages 74–75

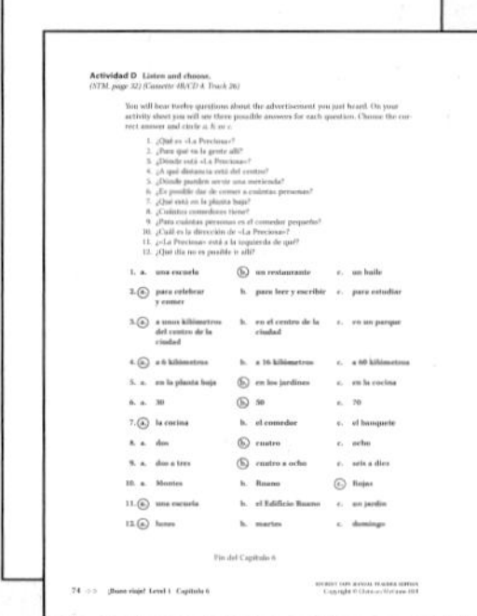

Additional Practice, pages 76–78

Assessment

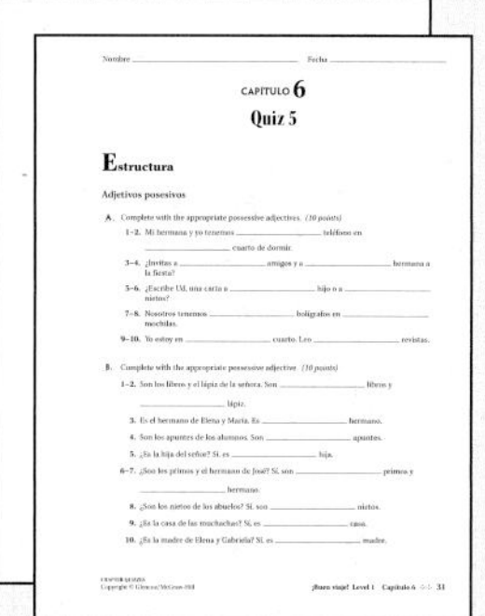
Vocabulary and Structure Quizzes, pages 26–31

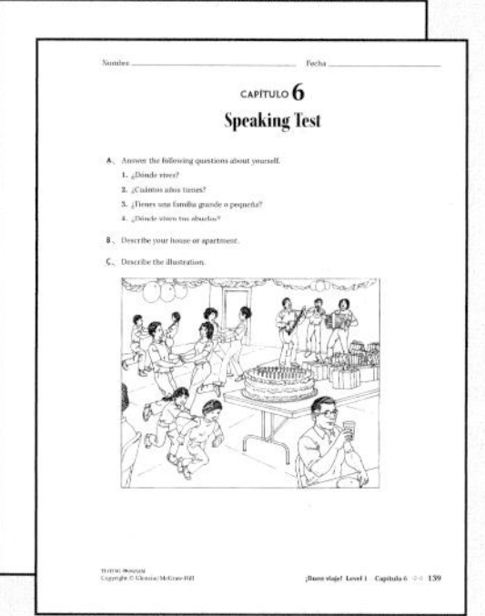
Chapter Tests, pages 81–98

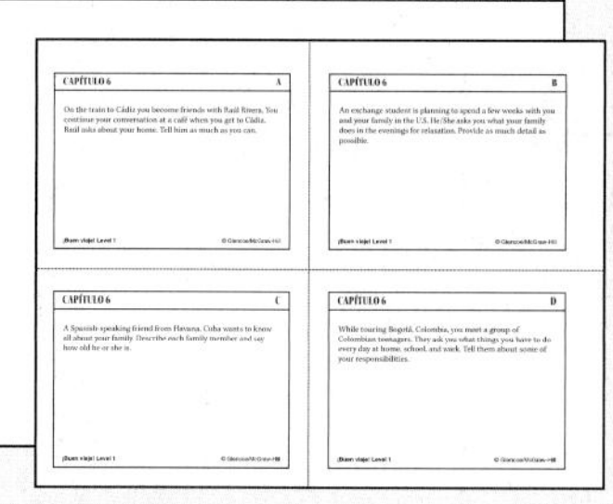
Situation Cards, Chapter 6

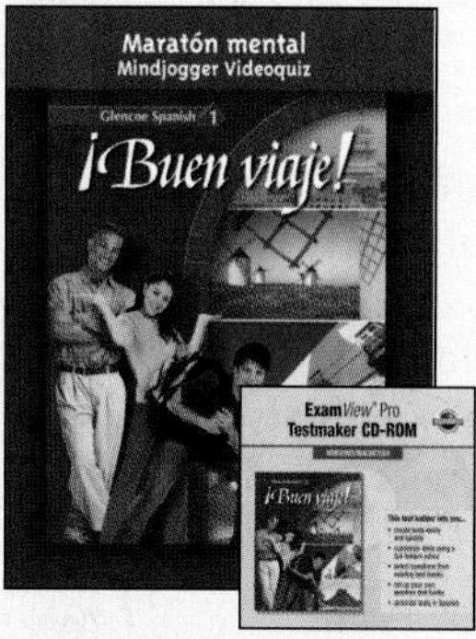

MindJogger Videoquiz, ExamView® Pro, Chapter 6

Timesaving Teacher Tools

TeacherWorks™ is your all-in-one teacher resource center. Personalize lesson plans, access resources from the Teacher Wraparound Edition, connect to the Internet, or make a to-do list. These are only a few of the many features that can assist you in the planning and organizing of your lessons.

Includes:

- A calendar feature
- Access to all program blackline masters
- Standards correlations and more

ExamView® Pro

Test Bank software for Macintosh and Windows makes creating, editing, customizing, and printing tests quick and easy.

Technology Resources

In the Chapter 6 Internet Activity, you will have a chance to learn more about the Spanish-speaking world. Visit spanish.glencoe.com

On the interactive CD-ROM, students can listen to and take part in a recorded version of the conversation in Chapter 6.

¡Viva el mundo hispano! Video and Video Activities, Chapter 6. Available on VHS and DVD.

Help your students prepare for the chapter test by playing the **Maratón mental** Videoquiz game show. Teams will compete against each other to review chapter vocabulary and structure and sharpen listening comprehension skills. Available on VHS and DVD.

¡Buen viaje! is also available on CD or Online.

Capítulo 6

Preview

In this chapter, students will learn to describe their family and home. To do this they will learn vocabulary associated with family members and housing. They will also learn to use the verb **tener** to describe what kind of family and house they have. They will also learn the possessive adjectives. The cultural focus of the chapter is the importance of the family in Hispanic cultures.

National Standards

Communication

In Chapter 6, students will communicate in spoken and written Spanish on the following topics:

- describing their family
- describing some family functions
- describing their house

Students will obtain and provide information about these topics and engage in conversations concerning their own family and families throughout the Spanish-speaking world.

LEVELING

The activities, conversations, and readings within each chapter are marked according to level of difficulty. **E** indicates easy. **A** indicates average. **C** indicates challenging. Some activities cover a range of difficulty. In some activities, for example, advanced students will be able to produce more extensive responses while students who learn at a different rate may give less detailed responses. The leveling indicators will help you individualize instruction to best meet your students' needs.

Capítulo 6

La familia y su casa

Objetivos

In this chapter you will learn to:

- talk about your family
- describe your home
- tell your age and find out someone else's age
- tell what you have to do
- tell what you are going to do
- tell what belongs to you and to others
- talk about families in Spanish-speaking countries

María Izquierdo *Mis sobrinos*

Capítulo 6

Spotlight on Culture

Arte María Izquierdo (1902–1955) was a Mexican painter whose style was lively and spontaneous. Her works depict Mexican popular subjects as well as more universal themes.

Fotografía This family feeding the pigeons is in the **Plaza de Mayo** in Buenos Aires, Argentina.

Learning from Photos

(pages 168–169) Point to the pigeons and give students the word **las palomas.** Explain to students: **La familia da de comer a las palomas.**

You may wish to have students describe each family member and describe what they are wearing.

Ask the following questions about the photo after presenting the new vocabulary on pages 170–171.

¿Está la familia en el parque?
¿Cómo es la madre de la familia?
¿Cómo es el padre?
¿Cuántos hijos tienen?

Vocabulario

PALABRAS 1

1 PREPARATION

Resource Manager

Vocabulary Transparencies 6.2–6.3
Audio Activities TE, pages 63–66
Audio CD 4
Workbook, pages 57–58
Quizzes, pages 26–27
ExamView® Pro

Bellringer Review

Use BRR Transparency 6.1 or write the following on the board.
Complete.

1. **Yo ___ el menú. (leer)**
2. **Mis amigos ___ un libro interesante. (leer)**
3. **Nosotros ___ una composición en la clase de inglés. (escribir)**
4. **¿ ___ tú en la cafetería de la escuela? (comer)**
5. **¿Qué ___ Uds. con el almuerzo? (beber)**
6. **¿Dónde ___ Uds.? Nosotros ___ en ___ . (vivir)**

2 PRESENTATION

Step 1 Have students close their books. Present the vocabulary using Vocabulary Transparencies 6.2–6.3. Have students repeat the names of the Moliner family after you or Audio CD 4. Be sure that they pronounce the words as carefully as possible.

Vocabulario

PALABRAS 1

La familia

Reaching All Students

Total Physical Response Dramatize the meaning of **escribe**.

Si tienen un hermano, levántense.
Y ahora siéntense.
Si tienen una hermana, levanten la mano.
(Student 1), **¿tú tienes una hermana, no?**
Levántate, por favor.
Ven acá.
Ve a la pizarra.
Toma la tiza.
Escribe el nombre de tu hermana en la pizarra.
¿Cuántos años tiene? Escribe su edad.
¿Ella va a qué escuela? Escribe el nombre de su escuela.
Gracias, *(Student 1).* **Pon la tiza aquí, por favor.**
Y ahora, regresa a tu asiento y siéntate.

Es la familia Moliner. Son de Quito.
El señor y la señora Moliner tienen dos hijos.
Tienen un hijo, Felipe, y una hija, Verónica.
Los Moliner tienen un gato, Tico.
La familia no tiene un perro.

¿Cuántos años tienen los hijos?
Felipe, el hijo, tiene dieciséis años.
Verónica, la hija, tiene catorce años.
Son jóvenes. No son viejos (ancianos).

el regalo

Hoy es el 28 de noviembre.
Es el cumpleaños de Verónica.
Los Moliner van a dar una fiesta para Verónica.
Van a invitar a todos sus parientes (los tíos, los abuelos) a la fiesta.
Los amigos van a llevar regalos para Verónica.

LEVELING
A: Vocabulary

Vocabulario

Step 2 Ask the following questions as students look at the transparencies:
¿Es la familia Moliner? ¿Es la familia Moliner o Marechal? ¿Qué familia es? ¿Tienen el señor y la señora Moliner dos hijos? ¿Tienen un hijo? ¿Tienen una hija? ¿Tienen dos o tres hijos? ¿Cuántos hijos tienen los Moliner? ¿Tienen un perro? ¿Tienen un gato? ¿Qué animalito tienen?

Step 3 Now have students open their books to pages 170–171 and read the words and sentences for additional reinforcement.

Vocabulary Expansion

You may wish to give students the following additional words:

una mascota	*pet*
un cachorro	*puppy*
hijo único	*only child (m.)*
hija única	*only child (f.)*
gemelos	*twins*

About the Spanish Language

- Explain to students that in Spanish when you want to refer to a whole family, you do not add **-s** to the family name as you do in English. Instead you use **los** before the family name: **los García, los Álvarez.**
- To express relationships such as stepfather, stepmother, etc., you use the suffix **-astro(a): el padrastro, la madrastra, el hijastro, la hijastra.** In many areas its meaning is almost pejorative, and it is not used. Depending on the degree of intimacy and whether the biological parent is deceased, one may say **mi madre** for a stepmother. If the biological mother is alive, one would say, **la esposa de mi padre.** Instead of **hermanastro(a)** one would say **hermano(a)** or **el / la hijo(a) de la esposa de mi padre.**

3 PRACTICE

¿Qué palabra necesito?

¡OJO! When students are doing the **¿Qué palabra necesito?** activities, accept any answer that makes sense. The purpose of these activities is to have students use the new vocabulary. They are not factual recall activities. Thus, it is not necessary for students to remember specific factual information from the vocabulary presentation when answering. If you wish, have students use the photos on this page as a stimulus, when possible.

Historieta Each time **Historieta** appears, it means that the answers to the activity form a short story. Encourage students to look at the title of the **Historieta**, since it can help them do the activity.

1 You can have students refer to the photo as they respond to Activity 1, or they can respond freely about any family named **Rodríguez.** You may want to point out to students that **Rodríguez** is one of the most common names in the Spanish language. It is like the name *Smith* in English.

2 When doing Activity 2, you may wish to have younger students make their own dictionary page. For example, **Abuelo: el padre de mi padre.**

Writing Development

Have students write the answers to Activity 1 in a paragraph to illustrate how the answers to all the items tell a story.

¿Qué palabra necesito?

1 Historieta La familia Rodríguez de España

Contesten. *(Answer.)*

1. ¿Vive la familia Rodríguez en España?
2. ¿Tienen dos hijos los señores Rodríguez?
3. ¿Es grande o pequeña la familia Rodríguez?
4. ¿Cuántos años tiene Antonio?
5. ¿Cuántos años tiene Maricarmen?
6. ¿Tienen los Rodríguez un gato o un perro?

Madrid, España

2 Los parientes Completen. *(Complete.)*

1. El hermano de mi padre es mi ____.
2. La hermana de mi padre es mi ____.
3. El hermano de mi madre es mi ____.
4. La hermana de mi madre es mi ____.
5. El hijo de mi tío o de mi tía es mi ____.
6. La hija de mis tíos es mi ____.
7. Los hijos de mis tíos son mis ____.
8. Los padres de mis padres son mis ____.

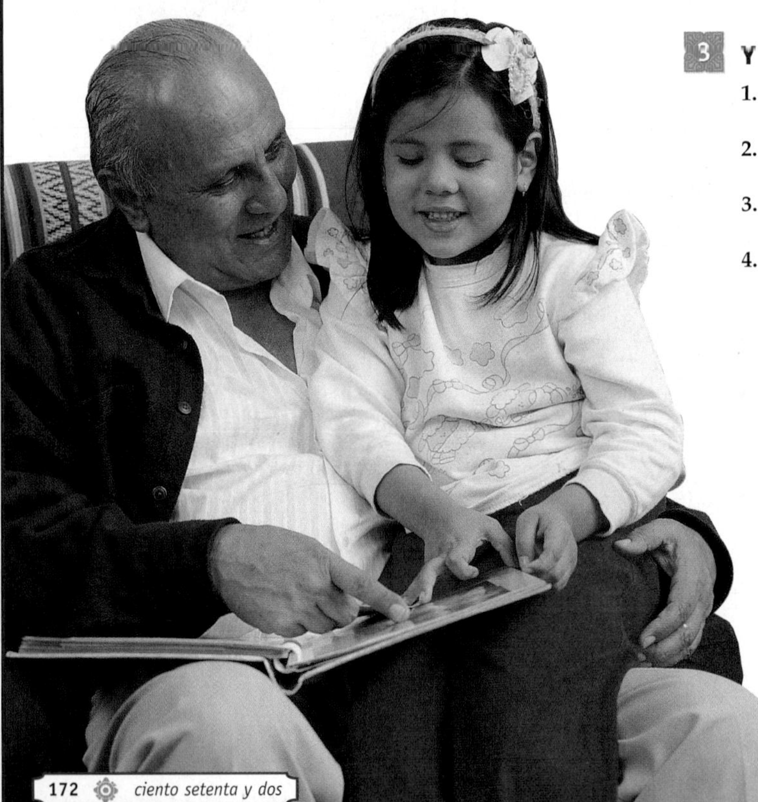

Lima, Perú

3 Y yo Escojan. *(Choose.)*

1. Yo soy ____ de mis abuelos.
   a. el nieto **b.** la nieta
2. Yo soy ____ de mis padres.
   a. el hijo **b.** la hija
3. Yo soy ____ de mis tíos.
   a. el sobrino **b.** la sobrina
4. Yo soy ____ de mis primos.
   a. el primo **b.** la prima

ANSWERS TO ¿Qué palabra necesito?

1

1. Sí, la familia Rodríguez vive en España.
2. Sí, los señores Rodríguez tienen dos hijos.
3. La familia Rodríguez es pequeña.
4. Antonio tiene ___ años.
5. Maricarmen tiene ___ años.
6. Los Rodríguez tienen un perro (gato).

2

1. tío
2. tía
3. tío
4. tía
5. primo
6. prima
7. primos
8. abuelos

3 *Answers will vary according to the gender of the student.*

4 Historieta El cumpleaños de Luisa

Contesten según se indica. *(Answer according to the cues.)*

1. ¿Qué es hoy? (el cumpleaños de Luisa)
2. ¿Cuántos años tiene hoy? ¿Cuántos años cumple? (quince)
3. ¿Qué dan sus padres en su honor? (una fiesta)
4. ¿A quiénes invitan a la fiesta? (a sus amigos y a sus parientes)
5. ¿Qué va a recibir Luisa? (muchos regalos)

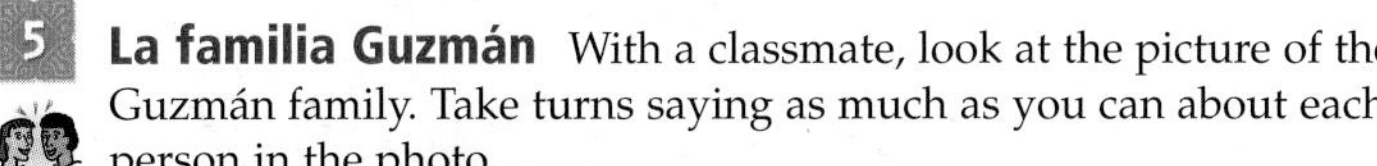

5 La familia Guzmán

With a classmate, look at the picture of the Guzmán family. Take turns saying as much as you can about each person in the photo.

6 Juego ¿Cúal de los parientes es?

Give a definition in Spanish of a relative. Your partner will then tell which relative you're referring to. Take turns.

Vocabulario

¡OJO! Note that the activities are color-coded. All the activities in the text are communicative. However, the ones with blue titles are guided communication. The red titles indicate that the answers to the activity are more open-ended and can vary more. You may wish to correct students' mistakes more so in the guided activities than in the activities with a red title, which lend themselves to a freer response.

5 Students can discuss each person in relationship to the other members of the **familia.** They can also give a description of each person and tell what they are wearing.

LEVELING

E: Activities 1, 3, 6

A: Activities 2, 4, 5

Answers to ¿Qué palabra necesito?

 **4**

1. Hoy es el cumpleaños de Luisa.
2. Tiene (cumple) quince años hoy.
3. Sus padres dan una fiesta en su honor.
4. Invitan a sus amigos y a sus parientes a la fiesta.
5. Luisa va a recibir muchos regalos.

5 *Answers will vary but may include:*

Es la familia Guzmán.
El señor y la señora Guzmán tienen dos hijos.
Tienen tres hijos: Pedro, Carlos y Luis.
La familia Guzmán tiene un perro.
Pedro tiene ___ años.
Carlos tiene ___ años.
Luis teine ___ años.

6 *Answers will vary, but students can use the phrases from Activity 2 as a model.*

Vocabulario

PALABRAS 2

1 PREPARATION

Resource Manager

Vocabulary Transparencies 6.4–6.5
Audio Activities TE, pages 67–70
Audio CD 4
Workbook, pages 58–60
Quizzes, page 28
ExamView® Pro

Bellringer Review

Use BRR Transparency 6.2 or write the following on the board.
Which of your relatives do you communicate with the most? Complete.

1. **Yo hablo mucho a ___.**
2. **Yo escribo mucho a ___.**
3. **Yo veo mucho a ___.**

2 PRESENTATION

Step 1 Using Vocabulary Transparencies 6.4–6.5, have students repeat each word after you two or three times.

Step 2 Ask the question **¿Qué es?** as you point to various objects on the transparencies.

Step 3 When presenting the sentences, intersperse them with questions to allow students to use the new words. For example: **¿Es la casa de la familia Moliner? ¿Tiene la casa un jardín? ¿Hay un jardín alrededor de la casa? ¿Dónde está el jardín?**

Step 4 When teaching **alrededor de,** with your hand, make a circle around the house as you show the transparency.

Step 5 Stand close to the classroom door and say: **Estoy cerca de la puerta.** Go to the far corner

Vocabulario

PALABRAS 2

La casa

Es la casa de la familia Moliner.
Alrededor de la casa hay un jardín.
El garaje está cerca de la casa.
Los Moliner viven en una casa privada (particular).
Tienen un carro.
El carro está en el garaje.
La casa está en la calle Juan Elcano.

La casa de los Moliner tiene siete cuartos.

Reaching All Students

Total Physical Response

(Student 1), **ven acá.**
Aquí hay un libro. Toma el libro.
Abre el libro.
Lee el libro.
(Student 2), **ven acá.**
Toma el periódico.
Abre el periódico.
Lee el periódico.
(Student 3), **ven acá.**
Es la televisión. Pon la televisión.
(Pantomime turning on the T.V.)
¡Qué aburrido! Cambia el canal.
Gracias, *(Student 3).* **Siéntate.**

Después de la cena, la familia va a la sala.
En la sala ellos leen.
Y ven la televisión.

una emisión deportiva

una película

Una casa de apartamentos (departamentos)

Los García tienen un apartamento en el quinto piso.
Suben al apartamento en el ascensor.
No toman la escalera.
Toman el ascensor.

away from the door and say: **No estoy cerca de la puerta; estoy lejos de la puerta.** Ask: **¿Está** *(name of your town)* **cerca de Nueva York? ¿___ está cerca de qué ciudad?**

About the Spanish Language

- **El garaje** has two spellings: **el garaje, el garage.**
- The word **apartamento** is the most universally used word for *apartment.* It would be understood anywhere in the Spanish-speaking world. However, in many areas of the Caribbean the term used is **apartamiento.** In many countries of South America the word is **departamento. El piso** is used in Spain.
- The word for *bedroom* varies. **Habitación** usually means *bedroom,* but it can sometimes mean *room.* In Mexico the words **recámara** and **dormitorio** are both used for *bedroom.* In the Río de la Plata area of Argentina, **el cuarto** is *bedroom,* and **habitación** or **pieza** is *room.* In most areas **el cuarto** by itself means *room,* not specifically a *bedroom.*
- The term **el living** is often used to refer to a living room. **La sala** and **el salón** are also used.

Reaching All Students

Additional Practice Mi casa Have students work in pairs. Each student draws and labels a floor plan of his or her own house or apartment. Then, without showing the drawing to his or her partner, the student will describe the house or apartment. Each student draws the floor plan according to the description provided by the partner. When finished, student pairs compare the two plans and discuss any differences.

History Connection

Juan Elcano or Juan Sebastián El Cano was a famous navigator and explorer who accompanied Magellan on his voyage around the world. Magellan died during the voyage, and Elcano completed the circumnavigation in 1512.

Fun Facts

In Spain and in most areas of Latin America, the ground floor of a building is called **la planta baja.** What is referred to as **el primer piso** is what we call the second floor.

Vocabulario

3 PRACTICE

¿Qué palabra necesito?

7 and 8 Do Activities 7 and 8 orally first. Then have students open their books and do the activities again.

Writing Development

Students can write the information in Activities 7 and 8 in paragraph form.

Learning from Photos

(page 176 top) Have students describe the photograph of Málaga, Spain, in their own words.

About the Spanish Language

- You will hear both **mirar la televisión** and **ver la televisión.** There is a tendency to shorten many words. **La televisión** is often referred to as **la tele.**
- In addition to **el ascensor,** you will hear **el elevador** in many areas.
- You may wish to explain briefly to the students that **primero** and **tercero** are shortened to **primer** and **tercer** before a masculine singular noun.

¿Qué palabra necesito?

7 Historieta La casa de los Baeza

Contesten. *(Answer. Make up a story.)*

1. ¿Tienen los Baeza una casa bonita?
2. ¿Está en la calle Silva la casa?
3. ¿Cuántos cuartos tiene la casa?
4. ¿Tiene dos pisos la casa?
5. ¿Qué cuartos están en la planta baja?
6. ¿Qué cuartos están en el primer piso?
7. ¿Tienen los Baeza un carro?
8. ¿Está en el garaje el carro?
9. ¿Está el garaje cerca de la casa?
10. ¿Hay un jardín alrededor de la casa?

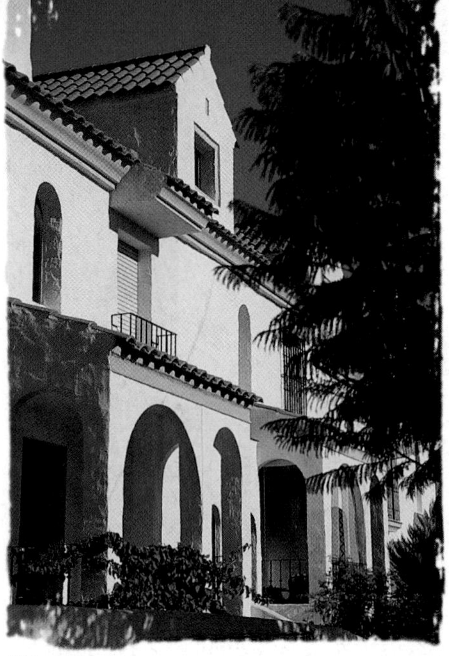

Málaga, España

8 Historieta Actividades en casa

Completen. *(Complete.)*

1. La familia prepara la comida en la ____.
2. La familia come en ____ o ____. A veces comen en ____ y a veces comen en ____.
3. Después de la cena, la familia va o pasa a ____.
4. En la sala leen ____, ____ o ____. No escriben cartas.
5. En la sala ven ____.
6. Ven ____, ____ o ____ en la televisión.

Madrid, España

ANSWERS TO ¿Qué palabra necesito?

7

1. Sí, (No, no) los Baeza (no) tienen una casa bonita.
2. La casa está en la calle ___.
3. La casa tiene ___ cuartos.
4. Sí, la casa tiene dos pisos.
5. ___ están en la planta baja.
6. ___ están en el primer piso.
7. Sí (No), los Baeza (no) tienen un carro.
8. Sí (No), el carro (no) está en el garaje.
9. Sí (No), el garaje (no) está cerca de la casa.
10. Sí, (No, no) hay un jardín alrededor de la casa.

9 **Historieta ¿Es verdad o no?** Contesten con **sí** o **no.**
(Answer with sí *or* no.*)*

1. Una casa pequeña tiene sólo dos cuartos.
2. Un apartamento grande tiene dos cuartos.
3. La casa de apartamentos es alta.
4. Una casa privada o particular tiene sólo uno o dos pisos y una casa de apartamentos tiene muchos pisos.
5. En una casa privada la familia sube de un piso a otro en el ascensor.
6. La familia toma la escalera para subir de un piso a otro en una casa particular.

Santiago, Chile

Málaga, España

El Viejo San Juan, Puerto Rico

10 **Mi casa** Work with a classmate. One of you lives in a private house and the other lives in an apartment building. Ask each other as many questions as you can about your homes. Answer each other's questions, too.

11 **La rutina de mi familia** Get together with a classmate and discuss the routine your family follows after school or after work. You may want to use some of the following words.

Answers to ¿Qué palabra necesito?

8

1. cocina
2. el comedor, la cocina; el comedor, la cocina (la cocina, el comedor)
3. la sala
4. periódicos, revistas, libros
5. la televisión
6. una película, una emisión deportiva, las noticias

9

1. Sí
2. No
3. Sí
4. Sí
5. No
6. Sí

10 *Answers will vary, but students should use the vocabulary from* Palabras 1 *and* 2.

11 *Answers will vary. Encourage students to use the vocabulary in the colored boxes.*

Vocabulario

9 Have students do Activity 9 with books open. Students can also correct the false statements.

10 and **11** These activities encourage students to use the chapter vocabulary and structures in open-ended situations. It is not necessary to have them do both activities. Choose the one you consider most appropriate.

Learning from Photos

(page 177) Have students listen to the following short descriptions of the dwellings in the photos and ask them to tell you which one is being described by telling where it's located.

1. **Hay un jardín alrededor de la casa. (Es la casa en Santiago.)**
2. **No hay carros en la calle. (Es la casa en el Viejo San Juan.)**
3. **Tiene muchos pisos. (Son las casas de apartamentos en Málaga.)**
4. **Es una casa grande y blanca. (Es la casa en Santiago.)**

LEVELING

E: Activities 7, 8, 9
A: Activity 11
C: Activity 10

Chapter Projects

Mi casa Have students make floor plans of their house or apartment and give a "tour" to their classmates.

Estructura

1 PREPARATION

Resource Manager

Audio Activities TE, pages 70–73
Audio CD 4
Workbook, pages 61–64
Quizzes, pages 29–31
ExamView® Pro

Bellringer Review

Use BRR Transparency 6.3 or write the following on the board.
Answer.

1. **¿Cuáles son los cuartos de una casa?**
2. **¿Tiene muchos o pocos cuartos una casa grande?**

2 PRESENTATION

Presente de tener

Step 1 Review the forms **tiene** and **tienen** that students already know from the **Vocabulario** section of this chapter.

Step 2 Draw a stick figure on the board. Label it **Roberto.** Have students make up sentences with **Roberto tiene.** Do the same with **Carolina y Juana tienen.**

Step 3 Have students repeat **yo tengo** after you as they point to themselves. Then have them tell some things they have.

Step 4 Have students open their books to page 178 and read the verb paradigm. You may also want to write the verb forms on the board.

Step 5 Go over the information about expressing age in Item 2.

Estructura

Presente de tener

Telling what you and others have

1. The verb **tener** *(to have)* is irregular. Study the following forms.

INFINITIVE	tener
yo	tengo
tú	tienes
él, ella, Ud.	tiene
nosotros(as)	tenemos
vosotros(as)	*tenéis*
ellos, ellas, Uds.	tienen

2. You also use the verb **tener** to express age in Spanish.

¿Cuántos años tienes?
Tengo dieciséis años.
¿Cuántos años tiene usted?

¿Cómo lo digo?

 **¿Cómo es tu familia?** Contesten personalmente.
(Answer about yourself.)

1. ¿Tienes un hermano?
2. ¿Cuántos hermanos tienes?
3. ¿Tienes una hermana?
4. ¿Cuántas hermanas tienes?
5. ¿Tienes un perro?
6. ¿Tienes un gato?
7. ¿Tienes muchos amigos?
8. ¿Tienes una familia grande o pequeña?

Los Ángeles, California

Answers to ¿Cómo lo digo?

1. Sí, (No, no) tengo un hermano.
2. Tengo ___ hermano(s). (No tengo hermanos.)
3. Sí, (No, no) tengo una hermana.
4. Tengo ___ hermana(s). (No tengo hermanas.)
5. Sí, (No, no) tengo un perro.
6. Sí, (No, no) tengo un gato.
7. Sí, (No, no) tengo muchos amigos.
8. Tengo una familia grande (pequeña).

 *Answers will vary but may include:*

Ernesto no tiene un hermano. Tiene una hermana. La hermana de Ernesto tiene 14 años. Ernesto tiene 16 años. La familia de Ernesto no tiene un perro, pero tiene una gata adorable.

13 **¿Tienes un hermano?** Practiquen la conversación.
(Practice the conversation.)

Ernesto, ¿tienes un hermano?

No, no tengo un hermano. Tengo una hermana.

¿Cuántos años tiene ella?
Tiene catorce años.
Y tú, ¿cuántos años tienes?
Yo tengo dieciséis.

¿Uds. tienen un perro?
No, perrito no tenemos. Pero tenemos una gata adorable.

14 **Ernesto y Teresa** Hablen de Ernesto y Teresa.
(In your own words, tell all about Ernesto and Teresa.)

15 **¿Qué tienes?** Formen preguntas con **tienes.**
(Form questions with tienes.*)*

1. un hermano
2. una hermana
3. primos
4. un perro
5. un gato
6. muchos amigos

16 **¿Qué tienen ustedes?** Sigan el modelo.
(Follow the model.)

una casa o un apartamento →
—Marcos y Adela, ¿ustedes tienen una casa o un apartamento?
—Tenemos una casa. / Tenemos un apartamento.

1. un perro o un gato
2. un hermano o una hermana
3. un sobrino o una sobrina
4. una familia grande o pequeña
5. una bicicleta o un carro
6. CDs o videos

Santiago, Chile

*For more practice using **tener**, do Activity 6 on page H7 at the end of this book.*

Estructura

3 PRACTICE

¿Cómo lo digo?

12 Note that Activity 12 on page 178 focuses attention on the **yo tengo** form. Students get practice hearing **tienes** and then responding with **tengo.**

13 Have students present Activity 13 as a real conversation. They can dramatize it in front of the class. Have students retell it in narrative form. The conversation reinforces the **tú** and **yo** forms and then students use the third person in their narration.

15 You can also do Activity 15 as a paired activity and have the second student provide the answer to each question.

LEVELING

E: Activities 12, 13, 14
A: Activity 15
C: Activity 16

Answers to ¿Cómo lo digo?

15

1. ¿Tienes un hermano?
2. ¿Tienes una hermana?
3. ¿Tienes primos?
4. ¿Tienes un perro?
5. ¿Tienes un gato?
6. ¿Tienes muchos amigos?

16

1. Marcos y Adela, ¿Uds. tienen un perro o un gato? Tenemos un perro. / Tenemos un gato.
2. Marcos y Adela, ¿Uds. tienen un hermano o una hermana? Tenemos un hermano. / Tenemos una hermana.
3. Marcos y Adela, ¿Uds. tienen un sobrino o una sobrina? Tenemos un sobrino. / Tenemos una sobrina.
4. Marcos y Adela, ¿Uds. tienen una familia grande o pequeña? Tenemos una familia grande. / Tenemos una familia pequeña.
5. Marcos y Adela, ¿Uds. tienen una bicicleta o un carro? Tenemos una bicicleta. / Tenemos un carro.
6. Marcos y Adela, ¿Uds. tienen CDs o videos? Tenemos CDs. / Tenemos videos.

3 PRACTICE *(continued)*

Writing Development

Have students write a paragraph about the Sánchez family based on their answers to Activity 17.

18 This is a very natural, communicative situation, since students usually enjoy talking about themselves and their families.

Learning from Photos

(page 180 bottom) Chinchón is a lovely town just 54 kilometers southeast of Madrid. This photo is of its famous **Plaza Mayor.** The plaza is surrounded by ancient three- and four-story houses with wooden balconies. From time to time the plaza is still converted into a bullring.

Vocabulary Expansion

You may wish to teach students:

¿De qué raza es el perro?
Es un dálmata.

Some other dog breeds are:

un perro cruzado	*mutt*
un pastor alemán	*German shepherd*
un labrador	*labrador*
un caniche	*poodle*
un dóberman	*doberman*
un rotweiler	*rottweiler*

17 Historieta La familia Sánchez
Completen con **tener.** *(Complete with* tener.*)*

Aquí __1__ (nosotros) una foto de la familia Sánchez. La familia Sánchez __2__ un piso (apartamento) muy bonito en Madrid. El piso __3__ seis cuartos y está en Salamanca, una zona bastante elegante de Madrid. Los Sánchez __4__ una casa de campo en Chinchón también. La casa de campo en Chinchón es un pequeño chalé donde los Sánchez pasan los fines de semana o los *weekend* y sus vacaciones. La casa de campo __5__ cinco cuartos.

Hay cuatro personas en la familia Sánchez. Carolina __6__ nueve años y su hermano Gerardo __7__ once años. Gerardo y Carolina __8__ un perrito encantador, Chispa. Adoran a su Chispa.

¿Tú __9__ un perro? ¿Tú __10__ un gato? ¿Tu familia __11__ un apartamento o una casa? ¿Ustedes también __12__ una casa de campo donde pasan los fines de semana como los Sánchez?

La Plaza, Chinchón, España

For more information about the Salamanca quarter of Madrid and Chinchón, go to the Glencoe Spanish Web site: spanish.glencoe.com

18 Tengo tres hermanos. With a classmate, take turns telling one another some things about your family. Tell whether you have a large or small family; tell the numbers of brothers and sisters you have and their ages, etc.

ANSWERS TO ¿Cómo lo digo?

17

1. tenemos
2. tiene
3. tiene
4. tienen
5. tiene
6. tiene
7. tiene
8. tienen
9. tienes
10. tienes
11. tiene
12. tienen

18 *Answers will vary, but students should use the appropriate forms of the verb* tener *when describing their family members and giving their ages.*

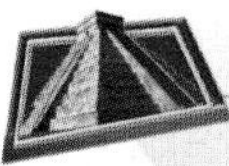

Tener que; Ir a
Telling what you have to and are going to do

1. **Tener que** + *infinitive* (**-ar, -er,** or **-ir** form of the verb) means *to have to.*

   Tengo que comprar un regalo.

2. **Ir a** + *infinitive* means *to be going to.* It is used to express what is going to happen in the near future.

   Vamos a llegar mañana.
   Ella va a cumplir quince años.

¿Cómo lo digo?

19 **Historieta ¡Cuánto tengo que trabajar!**
Contesten personalmente. *(Answer about yourself.)*

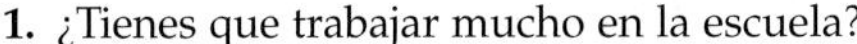

1. ¿Tienes que trabajar mucho en la escuela?
2. Antes de la apertura de clases, ¿tienes que comprar materiales escolares?
3. ¿Tienes que comprar ropa también?
4. ¿Tienes que estudiar mucho?
5. ¿Tienes que leer muchos libros?
6. ¿Tienes que tomar apuntes?
7. ¿Tienes que escribir mucho?

Answers to ¿Cómo lo digo?

19

1. Sí, (No, no) tengo que trabajar mucho en la escuela.
2. Sí, antes de la apertura de clases, tengo que comprar materiales escolares.
3. Sí, tengo que comprar ropa también.
4. Sí, (No, no) tengo que estudiar mucho.
5. Sí, (No, no) tengo que leer muchos libros.
6. Sí, (No, no) tengo que tomar apuntes.
7. Sí, (No, no) tengo que escribir mucho.

Estructura

1 PREPARATION

Bellringer Review

Use BRR Transparency 6.4 or write the following on the board.
Write the answer.
1. **¿Cuántos hermanos tienes?**
2. **¿Cuántos amigos muy buenos tienes?**
3. **¿Cuántos profesores tienes?**
4. **¿Cuántos años tienes?**

2 PRESENTATION

Tener que; Ir a

Step 1 Ask students to open their books to page 181. Read Items 1 and 2 to them.

Step 2 Have students name as many verbs as they can. Then have them make up simple sentences using these verbs with **tengo que** or **no tengo que; voy a** or **no voy a.** This is an easy way to practice using the infinitive form of the verb along with another verb. The first time students do this, it is rather tricky for them.

3 PRACTICE

¿Cómo lo digo?

19 After going over Activity 19, have students tell anything else they have to do.

LEVELING
E: Activity 19
A: Activity 18
C: Activity 17

3 PRACTICE *(continued)*

Writing Development

After doing Activity 20, have students write a short note to a friend. The note starts with: **Voy a dar una fiesta para...**

21 Note how Activity 21 combines **tener que** with **ir a** in a very natural, communicative context.

22 **and** 23 These activities bring about very real communication. We frequently tell people what we have to do or explain why we are not going to do something.

LEVELING

E: Activity 20

A: Activities 20, 21, 22, 23

C: Activity 23

20 Historieta Voy a dar una fiesta.

Contesten con **sí.** *(Answer with* sí.)

1. ¿Vas a dar una fiesta?
2. ¿Vas a dar la fiesta para Ángel?
3. ¿Ángel va a cumplir diecisiete años?
4. ¿Vas a invitar a sus amigos?
5. ¿Van ustedes a bailar durante la fiesta?
6. ¿Van a comer?

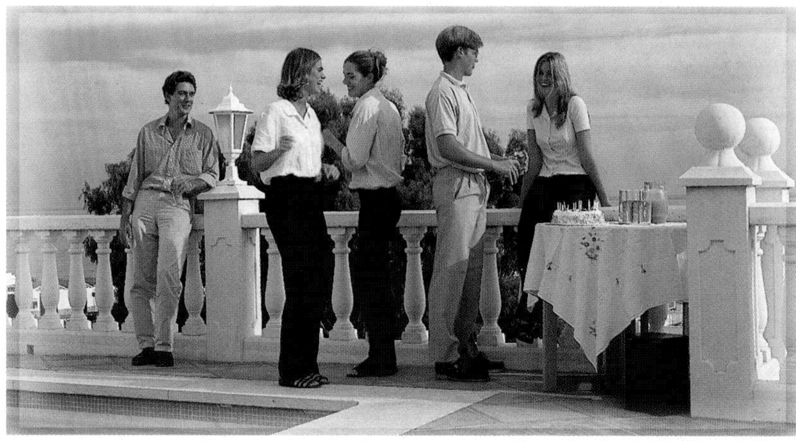

Estepona, España

21 Historieta ¡Tenemos tanto que hacer!

Sigan el modelo. *(Follow the model.)*

ver la televisión / preparar la comida →
No vamos a ver la televisión porque tenemos que preparar la comida.

1. escuchar discos compactos / estudiar
2. hablar por teléfono / escribir una composición
3. tomar seis cursos / sacar notas buenas
4. tomar apuntes / escuchar al profesor
5. ir a la fiesta / trabajar

22 Tengo que...

Tell a classmate some things you have to do tomorrow. Then find out if he or she has to do the same things. Report your findings to the class.

23 No voy a...

Tell a classmate some things you're not going to do tomorrow because you have to do something else. Tell what you have to do. Your classmate will let you know if he or she is in the same situation.

ANSWERS TO ¿Cómo lo digo?

20

1. Sí, voy a dar una fiesta.
2. Sí, voy a dar la fiesta para Ángel.
3. Sí, Ángel va a cumplir diecisiete años.
4. Sí, voy a invitar a sus amigos.
5. Sí, vamos a bailar durante la fiesta.
6. Sí, vamos a comer.

21

1. No vamos a escuchar discos compactos porque tenemos que estudiar.
2. No vamos a hablar por teléfono porque tenemos que escribir una composición.
3. No vamos a tomar seis cursos porque tenemos que sacar notas buenas.
4. No vamos a tomar apuntes porque tenemos que escuchar al profesor.
5. No vamos a ir a la fiesta porque tenemos que trabajar.

22 *Answers will vary, but students should use the appropriate forms of* tener.

23 *Answers will vary, but students should use the expressions* ir a *and* tener que.

Adjetivos posesivos
Telling what belongs to whom

1. You use possessive adjectives to show possession or ownership. Like other adjectives, the possessive adjective must agree with the noun it modifies. The possessive adjectives **mi, tu,** and **su** have only two forms: singular and plural.

mi libro y mi revista	**mis libros y mis revistas**
tu libro y tu revista	**tus libros y tus revistas**
su libro y su revista	**sus libros y sus revistas**

2. The possessive adjective **su** can mean *his, her, their,* or *your.* Its meaning is usually obvious from the way it is used in the sentence. However, if it is not clear, **su** can be replaced by a prepositional phrase.

el libro { **de él** / **de ella** / **de Ud.** } **el libro** { **de ellos** / **de ellas** / **de Uds.** }

3. The possessive adjective **nuestro** *(our)* has four forms.

nuestro apartamento	**nuestros libros**
nuestra casa	**nuestras revistas**

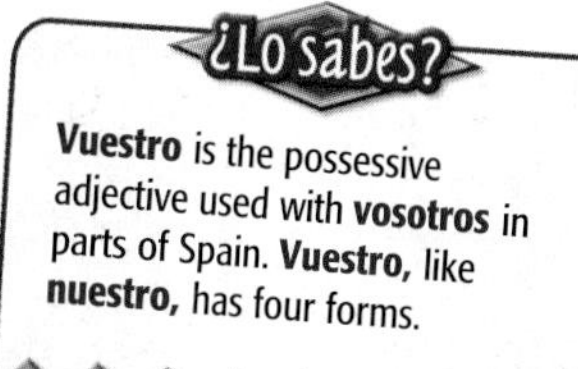

Vuestro is the possessive adjective used with **vosotros** in parts of Spain. **Vuestro,** like **nuestro,** has four forms.

Marbella, España

Estructura

1 PREPARATION

Bellringer Review

Use BRR Transparency 6.5 or write the following on the board.
Write five things about your brother or sister. If you don't have a brother or sister, write five things about a good friend.

2 PRESENTATION

Adjetivos posesivos

Step 1 Have students point to themselves as they say **mi,** to a neighbor as they say **tu,** to themselves and someone else as they say **nuestro,** and to two neighbors as they say **su.**

Step 2 Call on a student to read the examples in Item 1.

Step 3 Write **su libro** on the board. Then have students read or repeat aloud all the phrases in Item 2 as you point to **su** to show students that it does, in fact, have several meanings.

Step 4 Indicate to students that **nuestro** has four forms, the same as any other adjective ending in **o.**

Step 5 It is your decision regarding how thoroughly you teach the **vuestro** forms.

About the Spanish Language

The possessive adjective **tu** is used with the subject **vos.**

Chapter Projects

Dos personas famosas Have students think of at least two famous people. Students will pretend they are working for a magazine such as *¡Hola!* and describe the people, explain where they live, and tell something about their homes. Have them present the information as if it were an article for the magazine. Encourage them to include some photographs in the article.

3 PRACTICE

¿Cómo lo digo?

24 Do Activity 24 first with books closed. Call on individual students to answer one item each. Do the activity a second time, having one student respond to several consecutive items before calling on the next student.

Writing Development
Have students write a paragraph about their family and home based on their responses to Activity 24.

25 Have students look at a neighbor as they make up questions. Have them use the name of the neighbor, rather than **Lupita.**

26 Have students work in pairs to prepare a miniconversation. **Note:** This activity has students use a possessive adjective that is different from the subject. Students sometimes get the erroneous idea that they should always use the possessive adjective that corresponds to the subject of the sentence. For this reason, the type of material presented in this activity is quite important.

27 You can do Activity 27 with books closed or open.

¿Cómo lo digo?

24 Historieta Mi familia y mi casa

Contesten personalmente. *(Answer about yourself.)*

1. ¿Dónde está tu casa o tu apartamento?
2. ¿Cuántos cuartos tiene tu casa o tu apartamento?
3. Tu apartamento o tu casa, ¿es grande o pequeño(a)?
4. ¿Cuántas personas hay en tu familia?
5. ¿Dónde viven tus abuelos?
6. Y tus primos, ¿dónde viven?

25 Tengo una pregunta para ti.
Sigan el modelo. *(Follow the model.)*

la casa →
Lupita, ¿dónde está tu casa?

1. el hermano
2. la hermana
3. los primos
4. los libros
5. la escuela
6. el/la profesor(a) de español

26 La verdad es que...
Preparen una conversación. *(Make up a conversation.)*

—¿Tienes tú mi libro? →
—No. De ninguna manera. No tengo tu libro. La verdad es que tú tienes tu libro.

1.

2.

3.

4.

27 ¿Cómo son sus parientes?
Sigan el modelo. *(Follow the model.)*

el hermano de Susana →
Su hermano es muy simpático.

1. el hermano de Pablo
2. la amiga de Pablo
3. el primo de Carlos y José
4. la tía de Teresa y José
5. los tíos de Teresa y José
6. los padres de usted

Answers to ¿Cómo lo digo?

24

1. Mi casa (apartamento) está en la calle ___.
2. Mi casa (apartamento) tiene ___ cuartos.
3. Mi apartamento (casa) es grande (pequeño[a]).
4. Hay ___ personas en mi familia.
5. Mis abuelos viven en ___.
6. Mis primos viven en ___.

25

1. Lupita, ¿dónde está tu hermano?
2. Lupita, ¿dónde está tu hermana?
3. Lupita, ¿dónde están tus primos?
4. Lupita, ¿dónde están tus libros?
5. Lupita, ¿dónde está tu escuela?
6. Lupita, ¿dónde está tu profesor(a) de español?

26

1. —¿Tienes mis revistas?
   —No. De ninguna manera. No tengo tus revistas. La verdad es que tú tienes tus revistas.
2. —¿Tienes mi calculadora?
   —No. De ninguna manera. No tengo tu calculadora. La verdad es que tú tienes tu calculadora.
3. —¿Tienes mi CD?
   —No. De ninguna manera. No tengo tu CD. La verdad es que tú tienes tu CD.

(continued)

28 **Historieta Nuestra casa y nuestra escuela**
Contesten personalmente. *(Answer about yourself.)*

1. Su casa (la casa de ustedes), ¿es grande o pequeña?
2. ¿Cuántos cuartos tiene su casa?
3. ¿Su casa está en la ciudad o en el campo?
4. ¿En qué calle está su escuela?
5. Su escuela, ¿es una escuela intermedia o una escuela superior?
6. En general, ¿sus profesores son simpáticos?
7. ¿Son interesantes sus cursos?
8. ¿Son grandes o pequeñas sus clases?

Lima, Perú

29 **Mi hermano y yo...** Work with a classmate. Tell him or her about yourself and a sibling, or your friend if you don't have a sibling. Then ask your classmate questions about his or her family. Here are some words you may want to use.

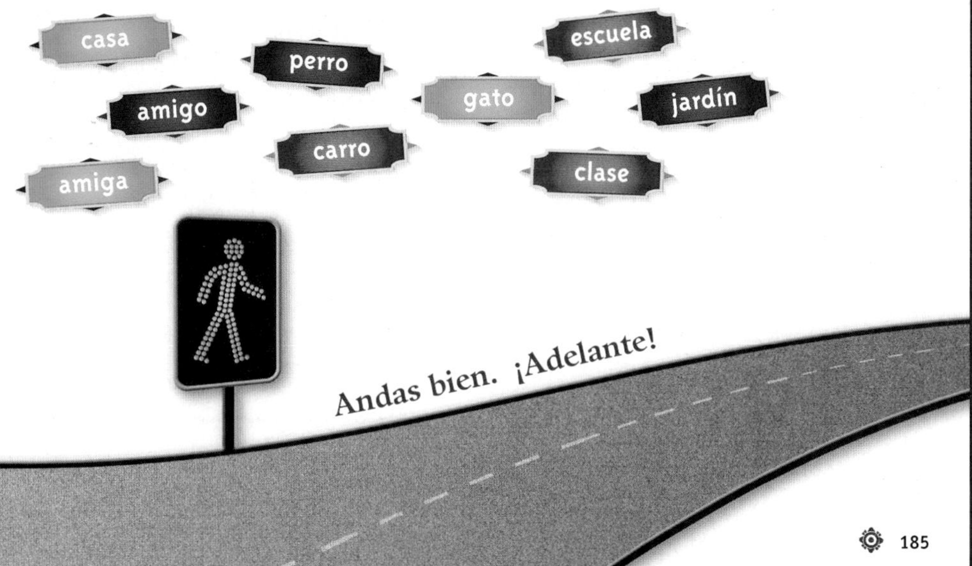

28 It is recommended that you go over Activity 28 first with books closed and have students answer with the correct form of **nuestro.** Do the activity a second time with students reading in pairs. One reads the questions, and the other responds. You can do this as a paired activity or as a round-robin class activity.

Reaching All Students

Additional Practice
¿Dónde está... ? Have students do the following: Think of a place in your house or apartment where your family pet is hiding. Your partner will try to guess where the pet is. For example:
—¿Tu perro está en el jardín?
—No, no está en el jardín. (Sí está en el jardín.)

LEVELING
E: Activities 24, 25
A: Activities 26, 27, 28, 29

Answers to ¿Cómo lo digo?

4. —¿Tienes mis cuadernos?
—No. De ninguna manera. No tengo tus cuadernos. La verdad es que tú tienes tus cuadernos.

27

1. Su hermano es muy simpático.
2. Su amiga es muy simpática.
3. Su primo es muy simpático.
4. Su tía es muy simpática.
5. Sus tíos son muy simpáticos.
6. Mis padres son muy simpáticos.

28

1. Nuestra casa es grande (pequeña).
2. Nuestra casa tiene ___ cuartos.
3. Nuestra casa está en la ciudad (el campo).
4. Nuestra escuela está en la calle ___.
5. Nuestra escuela es una escuela ___.
6. Sí (No), en general, nuestros profesores (no) son simpáticos.
7. Sí (No), nuestros cursos (no) son interesantes.
8. Nuestras clases son grandes (pequeñas).

29 *Answers will vary. Encourage students to use possessive adjectives and the words in the colored boxes.*

Conversación

1 PREPARATION

Resource Manager

Audio Activities TE, page 74
Audio CD 4

Bellringer Review

Use BRR Transparency 6.6 or write the following on the board.
Write at least three things you have to do this weekend. Write three things you're going to do this afternoon.

2 PRESENTATION

Step 1 Tell students they are going to hear a conversation between two friends. One of them has to go somewhere. Have them listen for the place where he has to go and the reason why.

Step 2 Have students close their books and listen to the conversation on Audio CD 4.

Step 3 Now have students open their books to page 186 and repeat the conversation after you line by line.

Step 4 Call on pairs of students to read the conversation aloud with as much expression as possible.

Step 5 After presenting the conversation, go over the **¿Comprendes?** activity. If students can answer the questions with relative ease, move on. Students should not be expected to memorize the conversation.

Glencoe Technology

CD-ROM

On the CD-ROM, students can watch a dramatization of this conversation. They can then play the role of either one of the characters and record themselves in the conversation.

Conversación

¿Vas a la fiesta?   

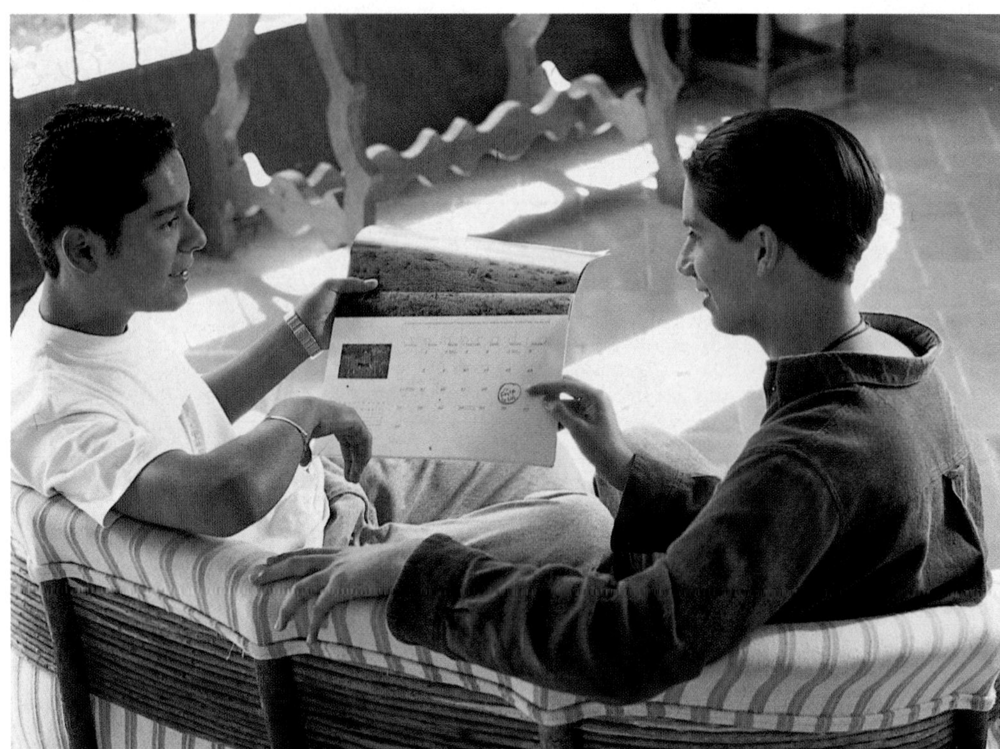

Tadeo ¿Vas a la fiesta de José Luis el viernes?
Jaime ¡Ah! ¡Es verdad! José Luis va a dar una fiesta.
Tadeo ¡Hombre! ¿No vas?
Jaime Pues, tengo que ir de compras. Tengo que comprar un regalo para mi hermana.
Tadeo ¿Tienes una hermana?
Jaime Sí, y va a cumplir quince años.
Tadeo ¿Ustedes van a dar una fiesta?
Jaime ¡Claro! Vamos a tener una celebración.
Tadeo Pero, no es mañana, ¿verdad?
Jaime No. Su fiesta es el sábado.
Tadeo Pues, tienes que ir a la fiesta de José Luis.

¿Comprendes?

Contesten. *(Answer.)*

1. ¿Con quién habla Tadeo?
2. ¿Adónde tiene que ir Jaime?
3. ¿Qué tiene que comprar?
4. ¿Por qué tiene que comprar un regalo para su hermana?
5. ¿Cuántos años tiene su hermana?
6. ¿Cuántos años va a cumplir el sábado?
7. ¿Van a dar una fiesta?
8. ¿Cuándo es la fiesta de su hermana?
9. ¿Cuándo es la fiesta de José Luis?

Answers to ¿Comprendes?

1. Tadeo habla con Jaime.
2. Tiene que ir de compras.
3. Tiene que comprar un regalo.
4. Tiene que comprar un regalo para su hermana porque su hermana va a cumplir quince años.
5. Su hermana tiene catorce años.
6. Va a cumplir quince años el sábado.
7. Sí, van a dar una fiesta.
8. La fiesta de su hermana es el sábado.
9. La fiesta de José Luis es el viernes.

Vamos a hablar más

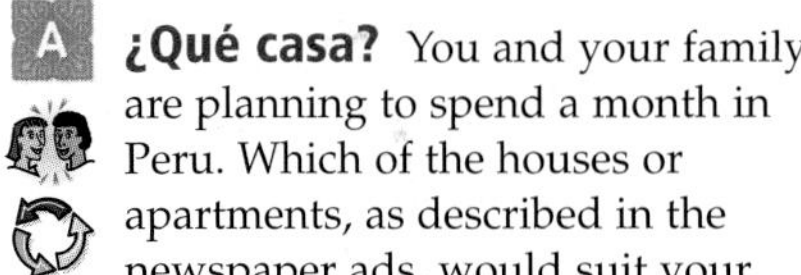

A **¿Qué casa?** You and your family are planning to spend a month in Peru. Which of the houses or apartments, as described in the newspaper ads, would suit your family best? Explain why.

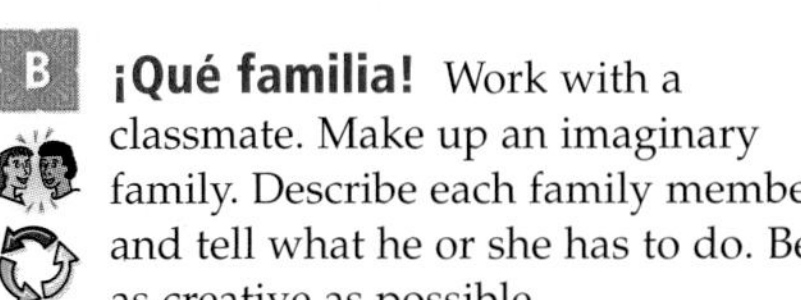

B **¡Qué familia!** Work with a classmate. Make up an imaginary family. Describe each family member and tell what he or she has to do. Be as creative as possible.

1
RENTA
ALQUILER DE CASAS
DEPARTAMENTOS
Y RESIDENCIAS
En Lima, Callao
y balnearios

1A.- CASAS

01 $ 1,500 2 chalets 21 Benavides colegio Humboldt Juana Larco Dammert 4 dorm. escritorio 9780150 o 9435188

01 CHACARILLA Maravillosa residencia 1 planta piscina 4 dormitorios 4 baños ideal diplomaticos funcionarios $ 2200 telefono 4613661.

ALQUILO casa 5 baños 3 salas comedor cocina 3 cocheras piscina 2 bares amoblada area de servicio lavanderia preferencia extranjeros Tf. 4469062 - 9940537

CHALET 2 plantas $ 300 Pueblo Libre 3 dormitorios sala comedor 2 baños lavanderia Telef. 4443394.

1B.- DEPARTAMENTOS

07 ALOJAMIENTO Temporal suite Los Pinos Pardo Miraflores departamentos full equipo 1 2 dormitorios cochera directo con departamentos cable VHS limpieza seguridad privacidad excelente ubicacion desde $ 45 diarios reservas 2421354 - 2421503 - 4477745

04 ALOJAMIENTO temporal San Isidro departamento independiente completamente equipado Tv cable limpieza diaria mínimo 1 semana T. 421-8092

02 VISTA AL MAR departamento nuevo 3 dormitorios 2 cocheras piscina jacuzzi c/s muebles $ 2,000 T. 445-8748

Pronunciación

Las consonantes b, v

There is no difference in pronunciation between a **b** and a **v** in Spanish. The **b** or **v** sound is somewhat softer than the sound of an English *b*. When making this sound, the lips barely touch. Imitate the following carefully.

ba	be	bi	bo	bu
bajo	bebé	bicicleta	bonito	bueno
bastante	escribe	bien	recibo	bus
trabaja	recibe	biología	árbol	aburrido

va	ve	vi	vo	vu
vamos	verano	vive	vosotros	vuelo
nueva	venezolano	violín	voleibol	

Repeat the following sentences.

El joven vive en la avenida Bolívar en Bogotá.
Bárbara trabaja los sábados en el laboratorio de biología.
La joven ve la bicicleta nueva en la televisión.

Answers to Vamos a hablar más

A *Answers will vary, but students should be encouraged to use* tener, tener que, ir a, *and possessive adjectives.*

B *Answers will vary. Encourage students to use the descriptive adjectives they have learned, as well as the expression* tener que.

About the Spanish Language

According to Spanish phonetics there is no difference between the sounds of **b** and **v.** The phonetic symbol for each one is the same. In some areas, however, there is a very slight English sound given to **v.** The **b** and **v** cause quite a spelling problem for many people.

3 PRACTICE

Vamos a hablar más

A and **B** These activities enable students to use the language on their own as if they were communicating in real-life situations.

Pronunciación

Step 1 Using Pronunciation Transparency P 6, model the first sentence in the Pronunciation section.

Step 2 Now have students repeat the sounds and words after you or the recording on Audio CD 4.

Step 3 Have students open their books to page 187. Call on individuals to read the sentences carefully.

Step 4 The words and sentences on page 187 can also be used for dictation.

LEVELING

E: Conversation

Learning from Realia

(page 187) Have students look at the ads. Ask them what word is used for *apartment* in Peru **(departamento).**

Explain that Callao is a port city near Lima. **Balnearios** refers to those areas on the outskirts of Lima on the Pacific coast. Bordering Miraflores there is a group of beaches known as the **Costa Verde.**

Lecturas culturales

Resource Manager

Audio Activities TE, page 75
Audio CD 4

National Standards

Cultures
In the reading on page 188, students will learn about the importance of the family in Hispanic cultures. They will also learn about the role of godparents in the family.

PRESENTATION

Pre-reading

Step 1 Have students open their books to page 188. Have them read the Reading Strategy and look at the photos, as the strategy suggests.

Step 2 Have students scan the reading.

Reading

Step 1 Call on individuals to read aloud. After every two or three sentences ask questions from the **¿Comprendes?** section.

Step 2 After completing the reading, call on students to give some information about Hispanic families.

Post-reading

Have students do the **¿Comprendes?** activity on page 189.

Lecturas culturales

La familia hispana

Reading Strategy

Using background knowledge When you are first assigned a reading, quickly look at the accompanying visuals to determine what the reading is about. Once you know what the topic is, spend a short time thinking about what you already know about it. If you do this, the reading will be easier to understand.

Cuando un joven hispano habla de su familia, no habla solamente de sus padres y de sus hermanos. Habla de toda su familia—sus abuelos, tíos, primos, etc. Incluye también a sus padrinos—a su padrino y a su madrina.

¿Quiénes son los padrinos? Los padrinos son los que asisten al bebé durante el bautizo[1]. En la sociedad hispana, los padrinos forman una parte íntegra de la familia. Y la familia es una unidad muy importante en la sociedad hispana. Cuando hay una celebración familiar como un bautizo, una boda[2] o un cumpleaños, todos los parientes van a la fiesta. Y los padrinos también van a la fiesta.

[1]bautizo *baptism* [2]boda *wedding*

Estepona, España

San Juan, Puerto Rico

FUN FACTS

Apellidos You may wish to explain to students the system used for Hispanic names.

			Last name of father	Last name of mother
	Man	Julio	Guzmán	Echeverría
	Woman	Ana	Blanco	Robles
Julio and Ana marry:	**Man**	Julio Guzmán Echeverría		
	Woman	Ana Blanco de Guzmán		
Julio and Ana have children:	**Son**	José Guzmán Blanco		
	Daughter	Teresa Guzmán Blanco		

Expansion: Have students write their names using this system.

La Sagrada Familia, Barcelona, España

¿Comprendes?

La familia hispana Contesten. *(Answer.)*

1. Cuando una persona hispana habla de su familia, ¿de quiénes habla?
2. ¿Quiénes son los padrinos?
3. ¿Son una parte importante de la familia los padrinos?
4. ¿Cuáles son algunas celebraciones familiares?
5. ¿Quiénes asisten a una celebración familiar?

Lecturas culturales

Learning from Photos

(page 189) The complete Catalán name of this famous church in Barcelona is **Temple Expiatori de la Sagrada Familia.** Done by the famous Catalán architect Antoni Gaudí, the cathedral was not completed before Gaudí's untimely death in 1926, and it is still under construction. Tragically, Gaudí was run over by a tram. He was not identified and died in a pauper's ward.

Chapter Projects

Tarjetas Have students find out if the local card store, stationery store, or supermarket has greeting cards in Spanish. If they are not too expensive, have each student buy one and prepare a bulletin board of Spanish-language greeting cards. If your students can't buy cards in your town, have them draw their own greeting cards.

LEVELING

E: Reading

Answers to ¿Comprendes?

1. Habla de toda su familia—sus abuelos, tíos, primos, etc.
2. Los padrinos son los que asisten al bebé durante el bautizo.
3. Sí, los padrinos forman una parte íntegra de la familia.
4. Algunas celebraciones familiares son el bautizo, la boda y el cumpleaños.
5. Todos los parientes asisten a una celebración familiar.

Lectura opcional 1

National Standards

Comparisons

The reading and the related activity on this page about **la quinceañera** give students the opportunity to compare customs and celebrations in Hispanic cultures to their own.

If there are any Hispanic students in your class, ask them to describe any **quinceañera** celebrations they have attended.

¡OJO! The readings on pages 190–191 are optional. You may skip them completely, have the entire class read them, have only several students read them and report to the class, or assign either of them for extra credit.

Learning from Photos

(page 190) Have students look at the photograph. Note that **la quinceañera** is frequently dressed like a bride.

Lectura opcional 1

En Tus Quince Años

La quinceañera

En Estados Unidos celebramos la *Sweet Sixteen.* La *Sweet Sixteen* es una fiesta en honor de la muchacha que cumple dieciséis años.

En una familia hispana hay una gran celebración en honor de la quinceañera. ¿Quién es la quinceañera? La quinceañera es la muchacha que cumple quince años. La familia siempre da una gran fiesta en su honor. Todos los parientes y amigos asisten a la fiesta.

La quinceañera recibe muchos regalos. A veces los regalos son extraordinarios—como un viaje[1] a Europa o a Estados Unidos, por ejemplo. Y si la quinceañera vive en Estados Unidos es a veces un viaje a Latinoamérica o a España.

[1]viaje *trip*

Una quinceañera, México

¿Comprendes?

¿Una costumbre hispana o estadounidense? Lean las frases. *(Read the statements and tell whether each more accurately describes a Hispanic or an American custom. In some cases, it may describe a custom of both cultures.)*

1. Dan una fiesta en honor de una muchacha que cumple quince años.
2. Dan una fiesta en honor de la muchacha que cumple dieciséis años.
3. La muchacha recibe regalos para su cumpleaños.
4. La fiesta es principalmente para los amigos jóvenes de la muchacha.
5. Toda la familia asiste a la fiesta—los abuelos, los tíos, los padrinos.

Answers to ¿Comprendes?

1. Es una costumbre hispana.
2. Es una costumbre estadounidense.
3. Es una costumbre de las dos culturas.
4. Es una costumbre estadounidense.
5. Es una costumbre hispana.

Lectura opcional 2

Las Meninas de Diego Velázquez

Las Meninas

Todos tenemos fotos de nuestra familia, ¿no? Muchos tenemos todo un álbum. No hay nada más adorable que la foto de un bebé—sobre todo (especialmente) si el bebé es un hijo, sobrino o nieto, ¿verdad?

Muchas familias tienen retratos[1] de su familia—sobre todo, las familias nobles. Aquí tenemos el famoso cuadro *Las Meninas*[2]. El cuadro *Las Meninas* es del famoso artista español del siglo XVII, el pintor Diego Velázquez.

En su cuadro, *Las Meninas,* vemos a la hija del Rey[3] con sus damas y su perro. Vemos al pintor mismo de pie delante de su caballete[4]. Y en el cuadro hay algo maravilloso. Más atrás en el espejo[5] vemos el reflejo del Rey y la Reina. En el cuadro vemos a toda la familia real[6]: al padre, el Rey; a la madre, la Reina; a la hija, la princesa.

[1]retratos *portraits*
[2]Las Meninas *The ladies-in-waiting*
[3]Rey *King*
[4]caballete *easel*
[5]espejo *mirror*
[6]real *royal*

¿Comprendes?

A Una familia real Contesten. *(Answer.)*

1. ¿Qué tienen muchas familias?
2. ¿Qué es una colección de fotos?
3. ¿Son adorables las fotos de un bebé?
4. ¿Tienen muchas familias retratos familiares también?
5. ¿Quién es el pintor de *Las Meninas?*
6. ¿Es español o latinoamericano Velázquez?
7. La muchacha en el cuadro, ¿es hija de quién?
8. ¿Dónde está el pintor en el cuadro?
9. ¿De quiénes hay un reflejo en el espejo?
10. ¿A quiénes vemos en el cuadro?

B *Las Meninas* Busquen a las personas en el cuadro. *(Find the following people in the painting.)*

1. el artista
2. la hija del Rey
3. las meninas o damas de la princesa
4. el Rey
5. el perro de la princesa
6. la madre de la princesa, la Reina

Lectura opcional 2

PRESENTATION

Step 1 You may wish to use the Fine Art Transparency with this reading. In the Transparency Binder, you will find additional background information about the painting, as well as related student activities.

Step 2 Have students read the selection to themselves. Then have them do the **¿Comprendes?** activities.

Step 3 If you decide to do the **Conexiones** section on pages 192–193 with the entire class, you may wish to include this reading as a part of it.

LEVELING

E: Reading 1

C: Reading 2

Answers to ¿Comprendes?

A

1. Muchas familias tienen fotos.
2. Una colección de fotos es un álbum.
3. Sí, las fotos de un bebé son adorables.
4. Sí, muchas familias tienen retratos familiares.
5. Diego Velázquez es el pintor de *Las Meninas.*
6. Es español.
7. La muchacha en el cuadro es la hija del Rey.
8. El pintor está de pie delante de su caballete.
9. Hay un reflejo del Rey y de la Reina en el espejo.
10. Vemos a toda la familia real.

B *Have students point to each individual in the painting and describe each one. You may wish to project Fine Art Transparency F 0 so that everyone can see more clearly.*

Conexiones

National Standards

Connections

This reading about painting and the photos of the famous works of art by Spanish and Latin American artists establish a connection with another discipline, allowing students to reinforce and further their knowledge of fine art through the study of Spanish.

PRESENTATION

Las bellas artes

El arte

Step 1 Have students read the introduction in English on page 192.

Step 2 Give the students any information you like about the artists listed on page 192.

Step 3 Model the new vocabulary words presented on page 192. Then have students read the information on page 193.

Step 4 You may wish to project the Fine Art transparencies as you do the reading. Students can also do the related activities that accompany the transparencies.

LEVELING

C: Reading

Conexiones

Las bellas artes

El arte

One may know a great deal or just a little about art. But almost everyone has at least some interest in art. How often have we heard, "I may not know anything about art, but I certainly know what I like"?

There is no doubt that many of the world's great artists have come from Spain and Latin America. Do you recognize any of the following names?

El Greco, Velázquez, Murillo, Goya, Zurbarán, Sorolla, Picasso, Dalí, Miró, Rivera, Orozco, Siqueiros, Kahlo, Tamayo, Botero.

Let's first read some information about art and then enjoy some famous works of Spanish and Latin American artists.

Autorretrato de Frida Kahlo

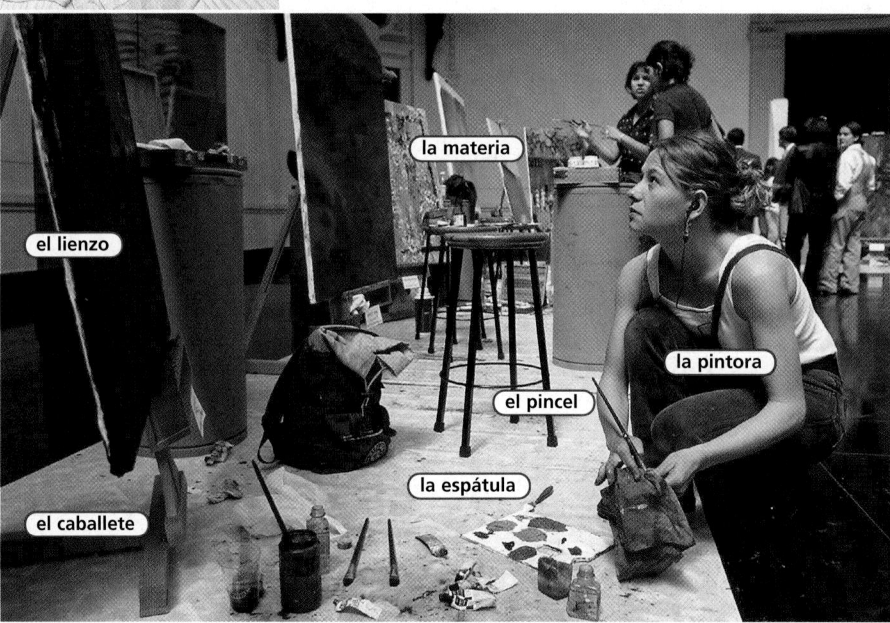

Art Connection

El Greco (1541–1614) was born in Greece but painted in Spain. He made his paintings of saints and martyrs look supernatural.
Velázquez (1599–1660), born to a rich family in Seville, went to Madrid and became the painter of the court of Felipe IV.
Murillo (1617–1682) was born to a poor family in Seville. He was deeply religious and did many paintings for monasteries and convents.
Goya (1746–1828) was born in Aragón, Spain. During his lifetime he witnessed the brutality and suffering of war, which greatly influenced his works.
Zurbarán (1598–1664) was born in Badajoz, Spain. Many of his paintings have religious themes.
Sorolla (1863–1923) was born in Valencia. He did many portraits and scenes of the Spain of his time. *(continued on page 193)*

La pintura

El pintor

Antes de pintar, el pintor o artista tiene que preparar su lienzo. Tiene que colocar el lienzo en el caballete. El pintor escoge o selecciona el medio en que va a pintar. Los medios más populares son la acuarela[1], el óleo y el acrílico. El artista aplica los colores al lienzo con un pincel o una espátula.

El tres de mayo de Francisco de Goya

El motivo o tema

Para el observador, el individuo que mira el cuadro, el motivo o tema de una obra de arte es el principal elemento de interés. Es la materia que pinta el artista—una persona, un santo, una escena, una batalla, un paisaje[2].

El estilo

El estilo es el modo de expresión del artista. En términos generales, clasificamos el estilo en figurativo o abstracto. Una obra figurativa presenta una interpretación literal o realista de la materia. El observador sabe[3] enseguida lo que ve en el cuadro.

Una obra de arte abstracto enfatiza o da énfasis al diseño más que a la materia. El artista no pinta la escena misma. Pinta algo que representa la escena o materia.

Aquí vemos unas obras famosas de algunos maestros de España y Latinoamérica.

Zapatistas de José Clemente Orozco

[1]acuarela *watercolor* [2]paisaje *landscape* [3]sabe *knows*

El entierro del Conde de Orgaz de El Greco

¿Comprendes?

El cuadro favorito Identifiquen su favorito. *(Identify your favorite.)*

Look at the paintings and tell which one is your favorite. Explain why it's your favorite.

Conexiones

Art Connection

Dalí (1904–1989) was born in Cataluña. Many of his images are so bizarre that some have called him a madman.
Miró (1893–1983) was also born in Cataluña. He painted the world of dreams and the subconscious.
Rivera (1886–1957) was born in Mexico. He is one of the world's most famous muralists. His murals, often of revolutionary character, deal with the history and social problems of Mexico.
Orozco (1883–1949) was also born in Mexico. Along with Diego Rivera and David Alfaro Siqueiros, he is one of the famed Mexican muralists. He used art to express his anger against all types of tyranny.
Siqueiros (1896–1974) was another Mexican muralist who was very involved in politics. He was imprisoned and driven into exile on several occasions.
Kahlo (1907–1954), wife of Diego Rivera, was born in Mexico. Her works have received worldwide acclaim in recent years. Kahlo, who had polio at age 6, was left a partial invalid for life after surviving a bus crash in her teens. She suffered constant pain and represented her pain by adding such things as thorn necklaces to her paintings. She painted numerous self-portraits.
Picasso (1881–1973) was born in Málaga. Few artists have achieved as much fame during their lifetimes, or produced such a variety of artworks.

Art Connection

Zapatistas In this painting we see the followers of Emiliano Zapata on their way to war. The plodding of the sad-faced peons and the rhythm created by their bodies leaning forward give the impression of a slow, steady march. The repeating hats, swords, and **sarapes** add to this feeling of movement. These peons are joined together to overcome their oppressors, the wealthy, powerful landowners.
El entierro del Conde de Orgaz El Greco called this his most famous painting. It is divided into two parts, heaven and earth. Note the realistic portrayal of the people attending the burial in comparison to the elongated, mystical figures of heaven. Many think that the young boy on the lower right is El Greco's son. The paper sticking out of the boy's pocket has his son's birth date on it. Some think that the thin man a bit left of center, just above the fingers of an upturned hand, is El Greco himself. Note that these are the only two people looking out toward the viewer.

¡Te toca a ti!

Use what you have learned

Recycling

These activities allow students to use the vocabulary and structure from this chapter in completely open-ended, real-life situations.

PRESENTATION

Encourage students to say as much as possible when they do these activities. Tell them not to be afraid to make mistakes, since the goal of the activities is real-life communication. If someone in the group makes an error, allow the others to politely correct him or her. Let students choose the activities they would like to do.

You may wish to divide students into pairs or groups. Encourage students to elaborate on the basic theme and to be creative. They may use props, pictures, or posters if they wish.

PRACTICE

2 Students can become extremely creative when doing Activity 2. You may wish to have some groups present their comments about each family to the entire class.

¡Te toca a ti!

Use what you have learned

1 Una residencia bonita

✔ ***Describe a home or an apartment***

You are trying to sell one of the apartments or houses listed in the ads. Say as much as you can to convince your client (your classmate) to buy one.

TETELA DEL MONTE. Excelente, colonial mexicano. Arq. Sánchez. 1,500 m2 terreno, 500 m2 construcción, 4 rec., 3.5 baños, alberca, palapa

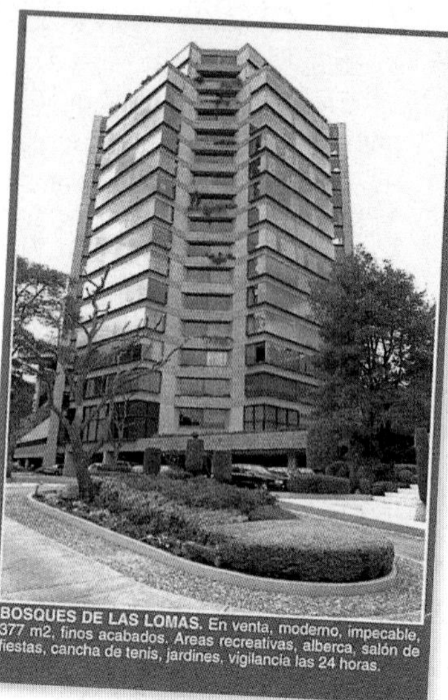

BOSQUES DE LAS LOMAS. En venta, moderno, impecable, 377 m2, finos acabados. Areas recreativas, alberca, salón de fiestas, cancha de tenis, jardines, vigilancia las 24 horas.

2 Una casa de apartamentos

✔ ***Talk about families and where they live***

With a classmate, look at this plan of the fourth floor of an apartment building. A different family lives in each apartment. Give each family a name. Then say as much as you can about the families and their activities. Don't forget to describe their apartment. Give as many details as possible.

Answers to ¡Te toca a ti!

1 *Answers will vary but should include words from* Palabras 2. *Encourage students to use as much detail as possible.*

2 *Answers will vary but should include words from* Palabras 1 *and* 2. *Encourage students to be as creative as possible.*

Learning from Photos

(page 195) Fuengirola is a resort town on the **Costa del Sol,** just west of Málaga.

3 La quinceañera

✔ *Invite a friend to a birthday party*

Your best friend Anita will soon be fifteen years old. Write out an invitation to her birthday party.

4 Mi familia y yo

✔ *Describe yourself and your family*

You plan to spend next year as an exchange student in Argentina. You have to write a letter about yourself and your family to the agency in your community that selects the exchange students. Make your description as complete as possible.

Writing Strategy

Ordering details There are several ways to order details when writing. The one you choose depends on your purpose for writing. When describing a physical place, sometimes it is best to use spatial ordering. This means describing things as they actually appear—from left to right, from back to front, from top to bottom, or any other combination of logical order that works.

5 La casa de mis sueños

Write a description of your dream house. Be as complete as you can.

Fuengirola, España

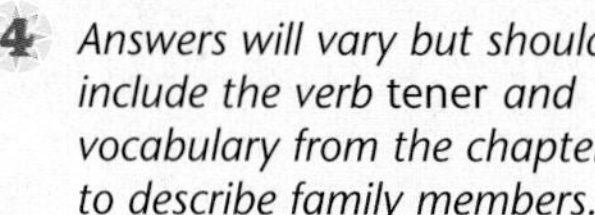

Answers to ¡Te toca a ti!

3 *Answers should include the person's name, as well as when and where the party will take place.*

4 *Answers will vary but should include the verb* tener *and vocabulary from the chapter to describe family members.*

5 *Answers will vary but should include the verb* tener *and vocabulary from the chapter to describe a dream house.*

¡Te toca a ti!

Writing Development

Have students keep a notebook or portfolio containing their best written work from each chapter. These selected writings can be based on assignments from the Student Textbook and the Workbook. The activities on page 195 are examples of writing assignments that may be included in each student's portfolio. On page 70 in the Workbook, students will begin to develop an organized autobiography **(Mi autobiografía).** These workbook pages may also become a part of their portfolio.

3 Have students read the **Conversación** on page 186 before they write their invitation.

4 Have students review **Palabras 1** and **2** and the structures presented in this chapter before they begin to write.

Writing Strategy

Ordering details Have students read the Writing Strategy on page 195. Have students review the vocabulary presentation on pages 174–175, then have them do the writing activity.

LEVELING

These activities encompass all three levels. All students will be able to do them at a sophistication level commensurate with their ability in Spanish. Some students will be able to speak for several minutes, and others may be able to give just a few sentences. This is to be expected when students are functioning completely on their own generating their own language to the best of their ability.

Resource Manager

Communication Transparency C 6
Quizzes, pages 26–31
Performance Assessment, Task 6
Tests, pages 81–98
Situation Cards, Chapter 6
ExamView® Pro, Chapter 6
Maratón mental Videoquiz, Chapter 6

Assessment

This is a pre-test for students to take before you administer the chapter test. Note that each section is cross-referenced so students can easily find the material they have to review in case they made errors. You may use Assessment Answers Transparency A 6 to do the assessment in class, or you may assign this assessment for homework. You can correct the assessment yourself, or you may prefer to project the answers on the overhead in class.

Glencoe Technology

MINDJOGGER VHS/DVD

You may wish to help your students prepare for the chapter test by playing the MindJogger game show. Teams will compete against each other to review chapter vocabulary and structure and sharpen listening comprehension skills.

Career Connection

Students who pursue careers in the humanities often need to have a reading knowledge of at least one foreign language in order to do research. This is particularly true for students of art history, history, and literature.

Vocabulario

1 Identifiquen. *(Identify.)*

1. la madre de mi madre
2. el hermano de mi madre
3. el hijo de mi tío
4. la hija de mis padres
5. la esposa de mi padre

To review **Palabras 1**, turn to pages 170–171.

2 Completen. *(Complete.)*

6. Hoy es el ____ de Verónica. Hoy tiene quince años.
7. Los amigos tienen ____ para Verónica.

3 Identifiquen. *(Identify.)*

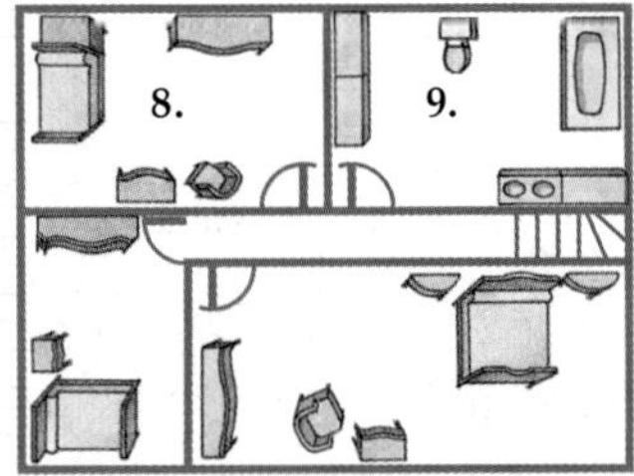

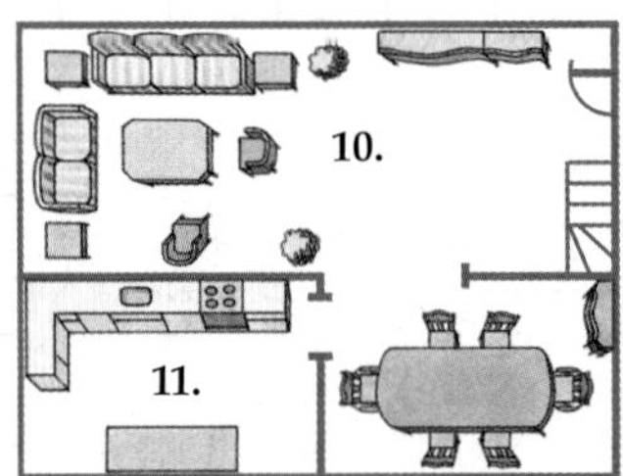

To review **Palabras 2**, turn to pages 174–175.

4 Escojan. *(Choose.)*

12. Después de la cena, papá lee ____.
    a. la televisión **b.** el periódico **c.** una emisión
13. Ellos ____ al quinto piso en el ascensor.
    a. toman **b.** ven **c.** suben

ANSWERS TO 

1
1. mi abuela
2. mi tío
3. mi primo
4. mi hermana
5. mi madre

2
6. cumpleaños
7. regalos

3
8. el dormitorio (la recámara, el cuarto)
9. el cuarto de baño
10. la sala
11. la cocina

4
12. b
13. c

Estructura

5 **Contesten.** *(Answer.)*

14. ¿Cuántos años tienes?
15. ¿Tiene tu familia una casa o un apartamento?
16. ¿Tienen ustedes un perro?

To review **tener**, turn to page 178.

6 **Completen con tener.** *(Complete with* tener.*)*

17–18. —Yo ___ tres hermanos.
—Perdón, Enrique. ¿Cuántos hermanos ___?

7 **Completen.** *(Complete.)*

19. Yo ___ compr__ un regalo para Sarita porque mañana es su cumpleaños.
20. Yo no ___ com__ mucho durante la fiesta.

To review **tener que** and **ir a**, turn to page 181.

8 **Escojan.** *(Choose.)*

21. ¿Dónde está el carro de Jorge? ___ carro está en el garaje.
    a. Mi **b.** Su **c.** Nuestro
22. ¿Cuántos años tiene tu hermana? ___ hermana tiene trece años.
    a. Mi **b.** Nuestra **c.** Tu
23. —¿Ustedes tienen un perro?
    —Sí, y ___ perro es adorable.
    a. su **b.** nuestro **c.** nuestros

To review possessive adjectives, turn to page 183.

Cultura

9 **Contesten.** *(Answer.)*

24. Cuando una persona hispana habla de su familia, ¿de quiénes habla?
25. ¿Quiénes asisten al bebé durante el bautizo y luego forman parte de la familia?

To review this cultural information, turn to page 188.

Assessment

SPANISH Online

The **Glencoe Spanish Web** site (spanish.glencoe.com) offers options that enable you and your students to experience the Spanish-speaking world via the Internet. For each **Capítulo,** there are activities, games, and quizzes. In addition, an *Enrichment* section offers students an opportunity to visit Web sites related to the theme of the chapter.

FOLDABLES™ Study Organizer **Dinah Zike's Study Guides**

Your students may wish to use Foldable 8 to organize, display, and arrange data as they learn about new topics in Spanish. You may wish to encourage them to add information from each chapter as they continue to learn how to discuss many different aspects of their lives in Spanish.

Encourage students to keep this *minibook* foldable in a safe place so they can refer to it and add content as they acquire more knowledge.

Music Connection

Canta con Justo
The song **Mi familia** will be easy for learners of all ability levels. It will help students practice the vocabulary related to family introduced in this chapter. You may wish to have students hear the recorded version of **Mi familia.** It can be found on Track 3 of the **Canta con Justo** music CD. In addition, students can watch Justo perform this song on the **Justo Lamas ¡En vivo!** music video that accompanies **¡Buen viaje!**

Answers to 

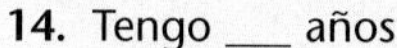

5
14. Tengo ___ años.
15. Mi familia tiene una casa (un apartamento).
16. Sí, (No, no) tenemos un perro.

6
17. tengo
18. tienes

7
19. tengo que comprar
20. voy a comer

8
21. b
22. a
23. b

9
24. Habla de toda su familia—sus abuelos, tíos, primos, etc.
25. Los padrinos asisten al bebé durante el bautizo y luego forman parte de la familia.

¡Hablo como un pro!

This unique page gives students the opportunity to speak freely and say whatever they can, using the vocabulary and structures they have learned in the chapter. The illustration serves to remind students of precisely what they know how to say in Spanish. There are no activities that students do not have the ability to describe or talk about in Spanish. The art not only depicts the vocabulary and content of this chapter, but also reinforces what they learned in previous chapters.

You may wish to use this page in many ways. Some possibilities are to have students do the following:

1. Look at the illustration and identify items by giving the correct Spanish words.
2. Make up sentences about what they see in the illustration.
3. Make up questions about the illustration. They can call on another class member to respond if you do this as a class activity, or you may prefer to allow students to work in small groups. This activity is extremely beneficial because it enables students to actively use interrogative words.
4. Answer questions you ask them about the illustration.
5. Work in pairs and make up a conversation based on the illustration.
6. Look at the illustration and give a complete oral review of what they see.
7. Look at the illustration and write a paragraph (or essay) about it.

You can also use this page as an assessment or testing tool, taking into account individual differences by having students go from simple to quite complicated tasks. The assessment can be either oral or written. You may wish to use the rubrics provided on pages T20–T21 as you give students the following directions.

1. Identify the topic or situation of the illustration.
2. Give the Spanish words for as many items as you can.
3. Think of as many sentences as you can to describe the illustration.
4. Go over your sentences and put them in the best sequencing to give a coherent story based on the illustration.

¡Hablo como un pro!

Tell all you can about this illustration.

Identifying family members

la familia	el/la nieto(a)
los parientes	el/la tío(a)
el padre	el/la sobrino(a)
la madre	el/la primo(a)
el esposo, el marido	el gato
la esposa, la mujer	el perro
el/la hijo(a)	joven
el/la hermano(a)	viejo(a), anciano(a)
el/la abuelo(a)	

Talking about family affairs or events

el cumpleaños	tener
el regalo	cumplir... años
la celebración	invitar

Identifying rooms of the house

la sala
el comedor
la cocina
el cuarto, el dormitorio, la recámara
el cuarto de baño

How well do you know your vocabulary?

- Identify the cognates.
- Use as many of them as you can to write a story.

Talking about a home

la casa	el piso
el apartamento, el departamento	el ascensor
la calle	la escalera
el jardín	privado(a), particular
el garaje	alrededor de
el carro	cerca de
la planta baja	subir

Discussing some home activities

el periódico	la emisión deportiva
la revista	las noticias
el libro	ver la televisión
la película	escribir una carta

VIDEOTUR

Episodio 6

In this video episode, you will join Claudia and Francisco as they celebrate Claudia's cousin's birthday. See page 497 for more information.

Vocabulario

Vocabulary Review

The words and phrases in the **Vocabulario** have been taught for productive use in this chapter. They are summarized here as a resource for both student and teacher. This list also serves as a convenient resource for the **¡Te toca a ti!** activities on pages 194 and 195. There are approximately nine cognates in this vocabulary list. Have students find them.

VIDEO VHS/DVD

The Video Program allows students to see how the chapter vocabulary and structures are used by native speakers within an engaging story line. For maximum reinforcement, show the video episode as a final activity for Chapter 6.

Reaching All Students

For the Younger Students

Mi álbum de fotos If you think it's appropriate, ask students to bring in some family photos and have them talk about their family.

¡OJO! You will notice that the vocabulary list here is not translated. This has been done intentionally, since we feel that by the time students have finished the material in the chapter they should be familiar with the meanings of all the words. If there are several words they still do not know, we recommend that they refer to the **Palabras 1** and **2** sections in the chapter or go to the dictionaries at the end of this book to find the meanings. However, if you prefer that your students have the English translations, please refer to Vocabulary Transparency 6.1, where you will find all these words with their translations.

Planning for Chapter 7

SCOPE AND SEQUENCE, PAGES 200–231

Topics

- Team sports
- Physical activities

Culture

- El Real Madrid versus el Atlético de Madrid
- The World Cup of soccer
- The importance of soccer and baseball in the Spanish-speaking world
- The sport of **jai alai**
- Archeological sites in Honduras, Mexico, and Puerto Rico
- **Vistas de Puerto Rico**

Functions

- How to talk about team sports and other physical activities
- How to tell what one wants to do or prefers to do
- How to discuss what one is able to do
- How to express what interests, bores, or pleases you

Structure

- Stem-changing verbs **e → ie**
- Stem-changing verbs **o → ue**
- **Interesar, aburrir,** and **gustar**

National Standards

- Communication Standard 1.1 pages 200, 204, 205, 208, 209, 211, 212, 213, 214, 215, 216, 217, 219, 226
- Communication Standard 1.2 pages 205, 209, 212, 214, 216, 217, 218, 219, 221, 222, 223, 225, 226, 227
- Communication Standard 1.3 page 227
- Cultures Standard 2.1 pages 218, 220–221, 222, 223, 227
- Cultures Standard 2.2 page 216
- Connections Standard 3.1 pages 224–225
- Comparisons Standard 4.1 page 215

PACING AND PRIORITIES

The chapter content is color coded below to assist you in planning.

■ **required** ■ **recommended** ■ **optional**

Vocabulario *(required)* *Days 1–4*

- ■ Palabras 1
  El fútbol
- ■ Palabras 2
  El béisbol
  El básquetbol, El baloncesto

Estructura *(required)* *Days 5–7*

- ■ Verbos de cambio radical **e → ie** en el presente
- ■ Verbos de cambio radical **o → ue** en el presente
- ■ **Interesar, aburrir** y **gustar**

Conversación *(required)*

- ■ ¿Quieres jugar?

Pronunciación *(recommended)*

- ■ Las consonantes **s, c, z**

Lecturas culturales

- ■ El fútbol *(recommended)*
- ■ Deportes populares *(optional)*
- ■ El «jai alai» o la pelota vasca *(optional)*

Conexiones

- ■ La arqueología *(optional)*

■ **¡Te toca a ti!** *(recommended)*

■ **Assessment** *(recommended)*

■ **¡Hablo como un pro!** *(optional)*

RESOURCE GUIDE

Section	Pages	Section Resources
Vocabulario PALABRAS 1		
El fútbol	202–205	Vocabulary Transparencies 7.2–7.3 Audio CD 5 Audio Activities TE, pages 79–81 Workbook, pages 71–72 Quiz 1, pages 32–33 ExamView® Pro
Vocabulario PALABRAS 2		
El béisbol El básquetbol, El baloncesto	206, 208–209 207, 208–209	Vocabulary Transparencies 7.4–7.5 Audio CD 5 Audio Activities TE, pages 81–84 Workbook, page 73 Quiz 2, pages 34–35 ExamView® Pro
Estructura		
Verbos de cambio radical **e → ie** en el presente Verbos de cambio radical **o → ue** en el presente **Interesar, aburrir** y **gustar**	210–212 213–214 215–217	Audio CD 5 Audio Activities TE, pages 85–88 Workbook, pages 74–78 Quizzes 3–4, pages 36–37 ExamView® Pro
Conversación		
¿Quieres jugar?	218	Audio CD 5 Audio Activities TE, page 88 Interactive CD-ROM
Pronunciación		
Las consonantes **s, c, z**	219	Pronunciation Transparency P 7 Audio CD 5 Audio Activities TE, page 89
Lecturas culturales		
El fútbol Deportes populares El «jai alai» o la pelota vasca	220–221 222 223	Audio CD 5 Audio Activities TE, page 89 Tests pages 102, 105
Conexiones		
La arqueología	224–225	Tests, page 106
¡Te toca a ti!		
	226–227	**¡Viva el mundo hispano!** Video, Episode 7 Video Activities, Chapter 7 Spanish Online Activities spanish.glencoe.com
Assessment		
	228–229	Communication Transparency C 7 Quizzes 1–4, pages 32–37 Performance Assessment, Task 7 Tests, pages 99–112 Situation Cards, Chapter 7 ExamView® Pro **Maratón mental** Videoquiz

Using Your Resources for Chapter 7

Transparencies

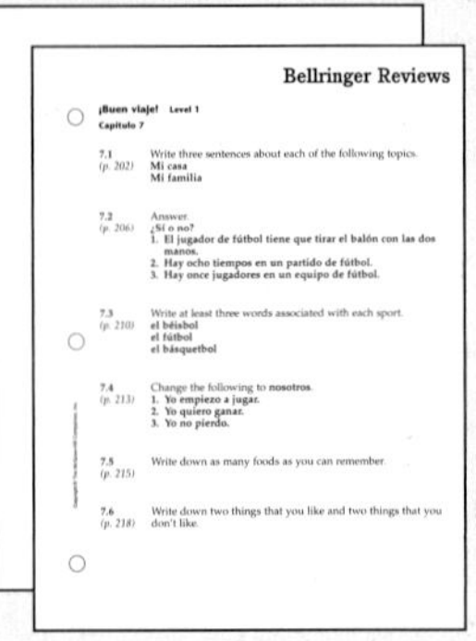

Bellringer 7.1–7.6

Vocabulary 7.1–7.5

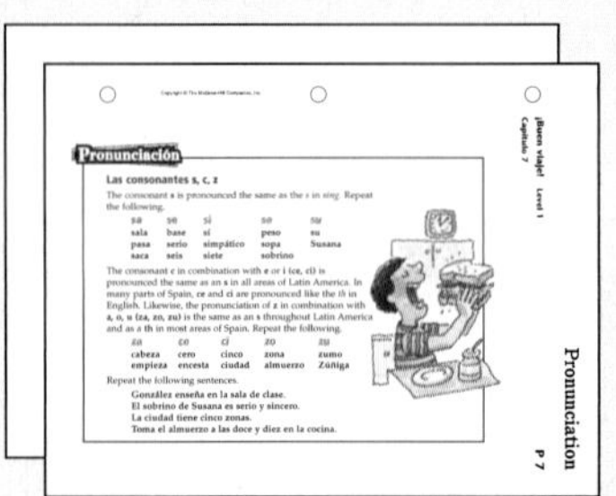

Pronunciation P 7

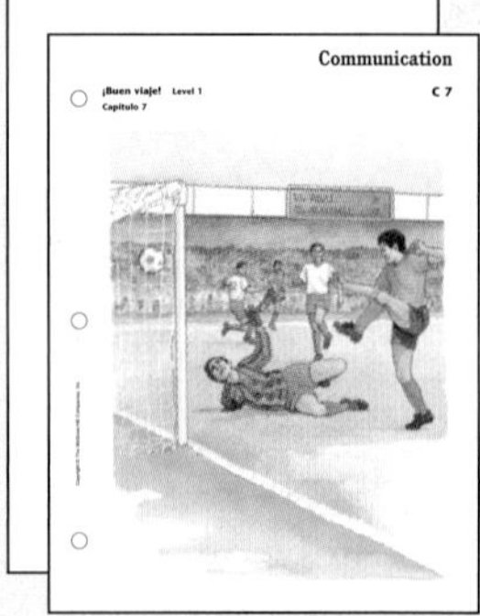

Communication C 7

Workbook

Vocabulary,
pages 71–73

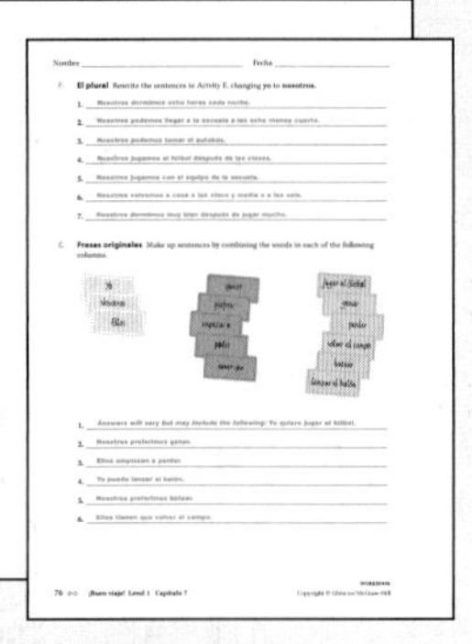

Structure,
pages 74–78

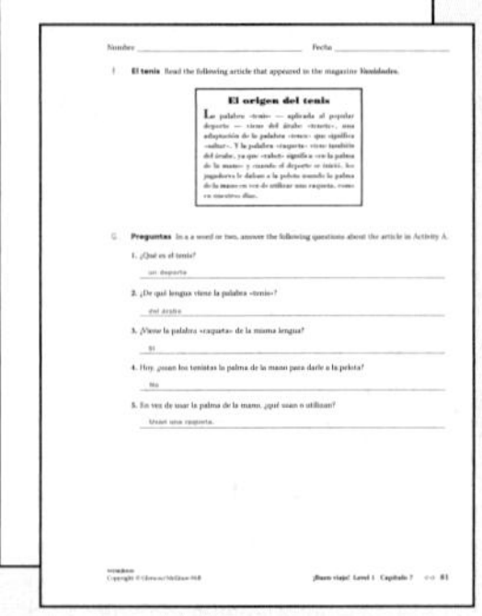

Enrichment,
pages 79–82

Audio Activities

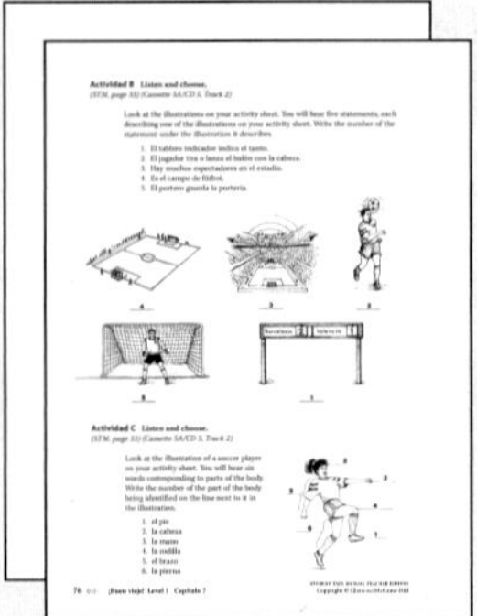

Vocabulary,
pages 79–84

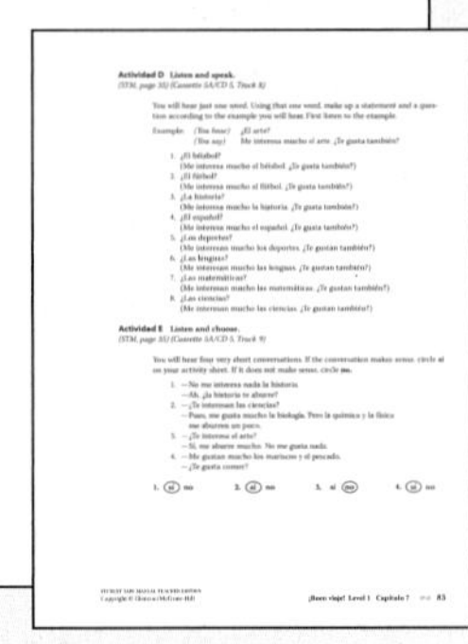

Structure,
pages 85–88

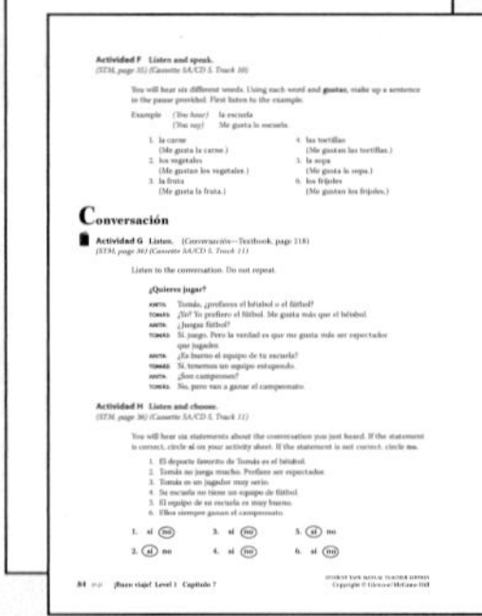

Conversation,
Pronunciation,
pages 88–89

Additional Practice,
pages 90–92

Assessment

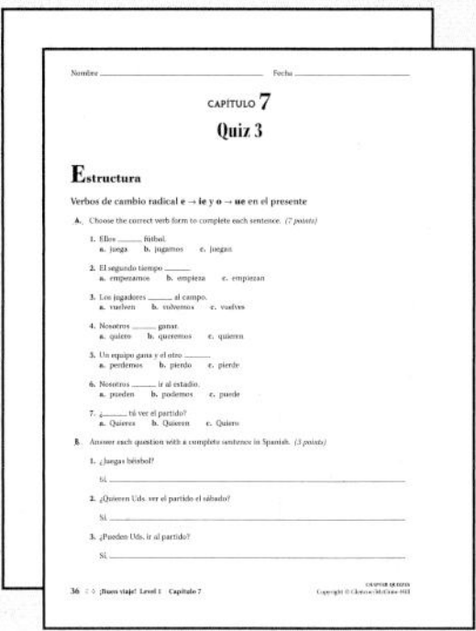

Vocabulary and Structure Quizzes, pages 32–37

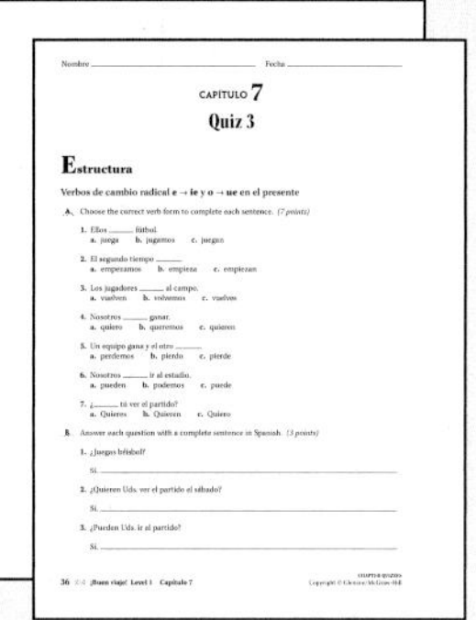

Chapter Tests, pages 99–112

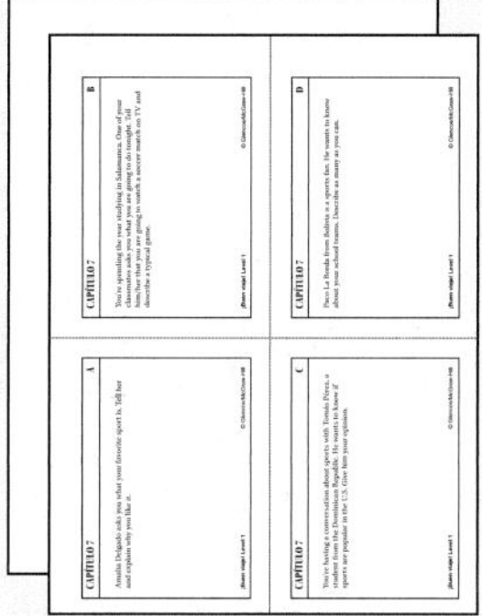

Situation Cards, Chapter 7

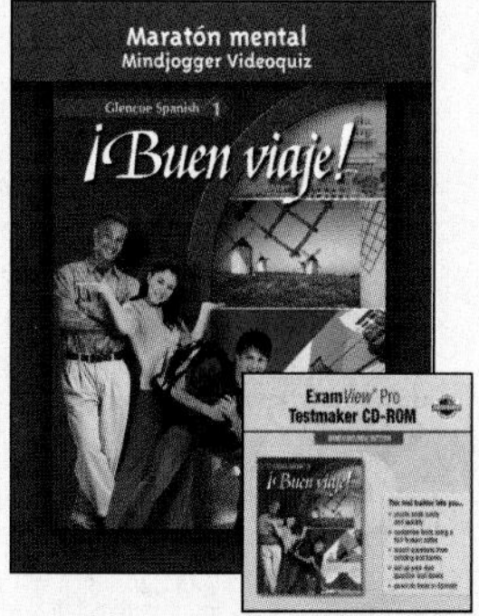

MindJogger Videoquiz, ExamView® Pro, Chapter 7

Timesaving Teacher Tools

TeacherWorks™ is your all-in-one teacher resource center. Personalize lesson plans, access resources from the Teacher Wraparound Edition, connect to the Internet, or make a to-do list. These are only a few of the many features that can assist you in the planning and organizing of your lessons.

Includes:

- A calendar feature
- Access to all program blackline masters
- Standards correlations and more

ExamView® Pro

Test Bank software for Macintosh and Windows makes creating, editing, customizing, and printing tests quick and easy.

Technology Resources

In the Chapter 7 Internet Activity, you will have a chance to learn more about the Spanish-speaking world. Visit spanish.glencoe.com

On the interactive CD-ROM, students can listen to and take part in a recorded version of the conversation in Chapter 7.

¡Viva el mundo hispano! Video and Video Activities, Chapter 7. Available on VHS and DVD.

Help your students prepare for the chapter test by playing the **Maratón mental** Videoquiz game show. Teams will compete against each other to review chapter vocabulary and structure and sharpen listening comprehension skills. Available on VHS and DVD.

¡Buen viaje! is also available on CD or Online.

Preview

In this chapter, students will learn to discuss and describe team sports. To do this they will learn basic vocabulary related to soccer, basketball, and baseball. They will also learn some stem-changing verbs—**empezar, querer, preferir, perder, volver, poder,** and **jugar.** Students will be able to use these verbs to describe team sports.

They will also learn verbs such as **interesar, aburrir,** and **gustar** so they can tell which sports they like. Students will also learn about the popularity of sports in various areas of the Spanish-speaking world.

National Standards

Communication

In Chapter 7 students will communicate in spoken and written Spanish on the following topics:

- describing team sports; namely soccer, basketball, and baseball
- expressing interests, likes, and dislikes

Students will obtain and provide information, express personal preferences and dislikes, and engage in conversations about sports events as they fulfill the objectives listed on this page.

Capítulo 7

Deportes de equipo

Objetivos

In this chapter you will learn to:

- talk about team sports and other physical activities
- tell what you want to, begin to, and prefer to do
- talk about people's activities
- express what interests, bores, or pleases you
- discuss the role of sports in the Hispanic world

Ángel Zarraga *Futbolistas en el llano*

Capítulo 7

Spotlight on Culture

Arte Ángel Zarraga (1886–1946) was a Mexican artist born in Durango. He was influenced by the Academic art which was extremely popular in Europe at the end of the nineteenth century. Academic artists worked from the artistic standards of the **Académie française** or other European Academies, and their styles were either Neoclassicism or Romanticism. Since Latin American revolutions such as the Mexican Revolution were modeled on the French Revolution, some Latin American artists, including Zarraga, became influenced by French culture and its artistic movements. His works include murals and religious subjects.

Fotografía These young men are playing soccer in Retiro Park in Madrid. This park is a very popular gathering spot for both **madrileños** and tourists. Students will learn more about parks in the Spanish-speaking world in **¡Buen viaje! Level 2.**

Vocabulario

PALABRAS 1

1 PREPARATION

Resource Manager

Vocabulary Transparencies 7.2–7.3
Audio Activities TE, pages 79–81
Audio CD 5
Workbook, pages 71–72
Quizzes, pages 32–33
ExamView® Pro

Bellringer Review

Use BRR Transparency 7.1 or write the following on the board.
Write three sentences about each of the following topics.
Mi casa
Mi familia

2 PRESENTATION

Step 1 Use Vocabulary Transparencies 7.2–7.3 for the initial presentation of the new vocabulary.

Step 2 After the oral presentation, as suggested in previous chapters, have students open their books and read the new vocabulary for additional reinforcement.

Step 3 Project Vocabulary Transparency 7.2 again and let students ask one another questions about what they see. For example, they might ask: **¿Cuántas personas hay en el equipo? ¿Qué tiene la muchacha en las manos? ¿Hay muchos espectadores en el estadio o pocos espectadores?**

Vocabulario

PALABRAS 1

El fútbol

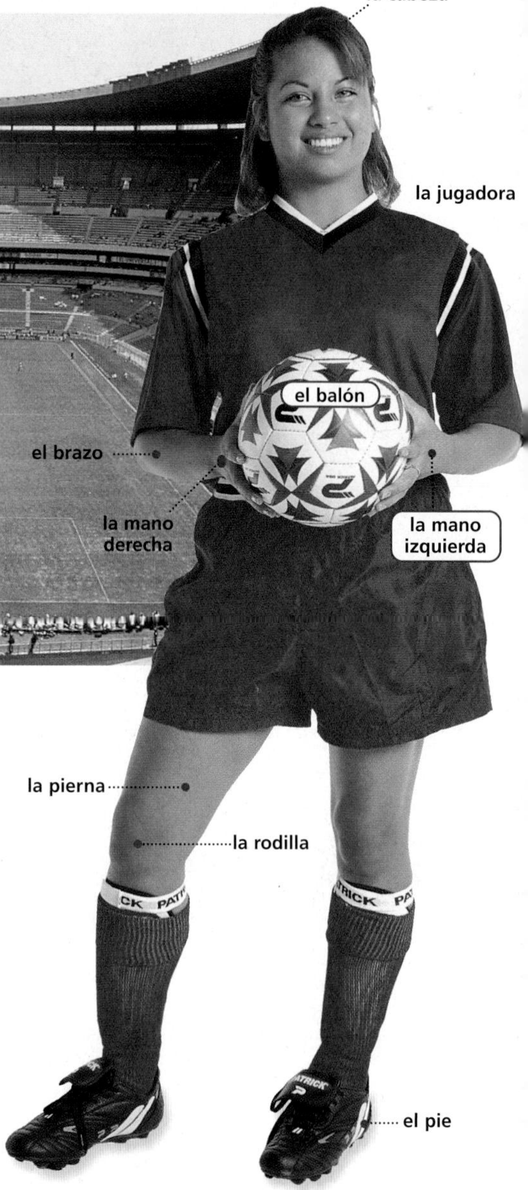

el estadio
el espectador, la espectadora
el campo de fútbol
el portero, la portera
la portería
la cabeza
la jugadora
el balón
el brazo
la mano derecha
la mano izquierda
la pierna
la rodilla
el pie

el equipo

Reaching All Students

Total Physical Response

TPR 1 Teach **rebotar** *(bounce)*, **pelota** *(ball)*, **tirar** *(throw)*, and **atrapar** *(catch)* by using the appropriate gestures as you say each word.
(Student 1), **levántate. Ven acá.**
Toma la pelota. Rebota la pelota cinco veces.
Ahora, tira la pelota. Tira la pelota a ____.
(Student 2), **atrapa la pelota.**
Y ahora, tira la pelota a ____. Gracias.

TPR 2 The following TPR activity can be done with the entire class participating.
Indícame la mano derecha.
Indícame la mano izquierda.
Indícame la rodilla.
Indícame la pierna.
Levanta la mano derecha.
Y ahora levanta el pie derecho.
Levanta el pie izquierdo. Gracias.

Hay un partido hoy.
Hay un partido entre el Real Madrid y el Barcelona.
El Real Madrid juega contra el Barcelona.

Los jugadores juegan (al) fútbol.
Un jugador lanza el balón.
Tira el balón con el pie.
El portero guarda la portería.

El segundo tiempo empieza.
Los dos equipos vuelven al campo.
El tanto queda empatado en cero.

El portero no puede bloquear (parar) el balón.
El balón entra en la portería.
González mete un gol.
Él marca un tanto.

El Real Madrid gana el partido.
El Barcelona pierde.
Pero el Barcelona no pierde siempre.
A veces gana.

Vocabulario

Step 4 Model the sentences under each illustration on page 203. Have students repeat the sentences. As they do, intersperse your presentation with questions such as the following:

¿Qué juegan los jugadores?
¿Qué lanza el jugador?
¿Tira el balón con la mano o con el pie?
¿Quién guarda la portería?

Have students answer with the complete sentence or sometimes have them use just the specific word or expression that responds to the question word.

About the Spanish Language

- The verb **jugar** can be followed by **a**, or the **a** can be eliminated. It is probably safe to say that the **a** is more commonly used in Spain, but it is also heard in areas of Latin America.
- Another commonly used term for *scoreboard* is **el marcador.**
- **El partido** is used to refer to a sports match or game. **La partida** is used for a card game, for example.
- Note the use of the article **el** with **el Real Madrid** and **el Barcelona.** The article **el** is used because **el equipo** is understood. Later in the chapter students will see **la Argentina ante el Perú**, for example, when talking about the **Copa mundial.** The article refers to the country, not the team.

LEVELING

E: Vocabulary

Chapter Projects

¡Nachos! ¡Chorizo! ¡Churros! Have the Spanish Club sell some snacks at sporting events to raise money for a trip to a Spanish-speaking country. Easy snacks would be: **nachos (tortillitas con queso), chorizo, churros,** or **arroz y habichuelas (frijoles).**

3 PRACTICE

¿Qué palabra necesito?

¡OJO! When students are doing the **¿Qué palabra necesito?** activities, accept any answer that makes sense. The purpose of these activities is to have students use the new vocabulary. They are not factual recall activities. Thus, it is not necessary for students to remember specific factual information from the vocabulary presentation when answering. If you wish, have students use the photos on this page as a stimulus, when possible.

Historieta Each time **Historieta** appears, it means that the answers to the activity form a short story. Encourage students to look at the title of the **Historieta,** since it can help them do the activity.

1 and 2 After going over Activities 1 and 2 on pages 204 and 205, call on one or more students to retell the stories in their own words.

Note: Activities 1 and 2 use only the third-person form of the stem-changing verbs so that the students can immediately answer questions and speak without having to change endings. Students will learn how to manipulate the stem-changing verbs in the **Estructura** section of this chapter.

Writing Development

Have students write the answers to Activity 1 in a paragraph to illustrate how the answers to all the items tell a story.

¿Qué palabra necesito?

1 Historieta Un partido de fútbol Contesten. *(Answer.)*

1. ¿Cuántos equipos de fútbol hay en el campo de fútbol?
2. ¿Cuántos jugadores hay en cada equipo?
3. ¿Qué tiempo empieza, el primero o el segundo?
4. ¿Vuelven los jugadores al campo cuando empieza el segundo tiempo?
5. ¿Tiene un jugador el balón?
6. ¿Lanza el balón con el pie o con la mano?
7. ¿Para el balón el portero o entra el balón en la portería?
8. ¿Mete el jugador un gol?
9. ¿Marca un tanto?
10. ¿Queda empatado el tanto?
11. ¿Quién gana, el Real Madrid o el Barcelona?
12. ¿Qué equipo pierde?
13. ¿Siempre pierde?

El estadio Atahualpa, Quito, Ecuador

Answers to ¿Qué palabra necesito?

1. Hay dos equipos de fútbol en el campo de fútbol.
2. Hay once jugadores en cada equipo.
3. El primer (segundo) tiempo empieza.
4. Sí, los jugadores vuelven al campo cuando el segundo tiempo empieza.
5. Sí (No), un jugador (no) tiene el balón.
6. Lanza el balón con el pie.
7. El balón entra en la portería.
8. Sí, el jugador mete un gol.
9. Sí, marca un tanto.
10. No, el tanto no queda empatado.
11. El Real Madrid (El Barcelona) gana.
12. El Barcelona (El Real Madrid) pierde.
13. No, a veces gana.

Vocabulario

2 Historieta El fútbol

Contesten según se indica. *(Answer according to the cues.)*

1. ¿Cuántos jugadores hay en el equipo de fútbol? (once)
2. ¿Cuántos tiempos hay en un partido de fútbol? (dos)
3. ¿Quién guarda la portería? (el portero)
4. ¿Cuándo mete un gol el jugador? (cuando el balón entra en la portería)
5. ¿Qué marca un jugador cuando el balón entra en la portería? (un tanto)
6. En el estadio, ¿qué indica el tablero? (el tanto)
7. ¿Cuándo queda empatado el tanto? (cuando los dos equipos tienen el mismo tanto)

El equipo de Chile, La Copa mundial

3 Un partido de fútbol Work with a classmate. Take turns asking and answering each other's questions about the photograph below.

Learning from Photos

(page 204) Have students look at this photo of the stadium in Quito, Ecuador. It will give them a feel for how the city is surrounded by mountains.

Games are held at the **Estadio Olímpico Atahualpa** from March to December at 10 A.M. on Saturdays and 3 P.M. on Sundays. Atahualpa, for whom the stadium is named, was the last reigning Inca. Pizarro ordered his death in 1533.

(page 205 top) Have students describe the uniform of the Chilean team at **La Copa mundial.** Have them describe anything else they see in the photo, using the vocabulary they learned in **Palabras 1.**

LEVELING

E: Activities 1, 2

A: Activity 3

FUN-FACTS

Los estadios de fútbol The largest sports stadiums in the world are soccer stadiums in Hispanic countries, with capacities in excess of 100,000 spectators. Among the largest stadiums are **el Estadio Azteca** in Mexico City and **el Estadio del Boca Juniors,** nicknamed **la Bombonera** *(The Candy Store),* in Buenos Aires.

Answers to ¿Qué palabra necesito?

2

1. Hay once jugadores en el equipo de fútbol.
2. Hay dos tiempos en un partido de fútbol.
3. El portero guarda la portería.
4. El jugador mete un gol cuando el balón entra en la portería.
5. Un jugador marca un tanto cuando el balón entra en la portería.
6. En el estadio el tablero indica el tanto.
7. El tanto queda empatado cuando los dos equipos tienen el mismo tanto.

3 *Answers will vary, but students should use the vocabulary from* Palabras 1.

Vocabulario

PALABRAS 2

1 PREPARATION

Resource Manager

Vocabulary Transparencies 7.4–7.5
Audio Activities TE, pages 81–84
Audio CD 5
Workbook, page 73
Quizzes, pages 34–35
ExamView® Pro

Bellringer Review

Use BRR Transparency 7.2 or write the following on the board.
Answer.

¿Sí o no?

1. **El jugador de fútbol tiene que tirar el balón con las dos manos.**
2. **Hay ocho tiempos en un partido de fútbol.**
3. **Hay once jugadores en un equipo de fútbol.**

2 PRESENTATION

Step 1 Model the new words and phrases on pages 206 and 207 using Vocabulary Transparencies 7.4–7.5 and Audio CD 5.

Vocabulario

PALABRAS 2

El béisbol

El pícher lanza la pelota.

El cátcher devuelve la pelota.

El bateador batea.
Batea un jonrón.
El jugador corre de una base a otra.

Reaching All Students

Total Physical Response You may wish to bring in some props (glove, bat, baseball, basketball, hoop) to use with these activities.

TPR 1

(Student 1), **ven acá. Tú vas a ser el pícher.**
Ponte el guante. Toma la pelota.
(Student 2), **ven acá. Tú vas a ser el bateador. Toma el bate.**
(Student 1), **tira la pelota a** *(Student 2).*
(Student 2), **pega la pelota.**
La pelota vuela. *(Student 2),* **corre.**
Corre a la primera base. Gracias, *(Student 1)* **y** *(Student 2).* **Siéntense.**

TPR 2

(Student 1) **y** *(Student 2),* **vengan aquí.**
Vamos a jugar al básquetbol.
(Student 1), **toma el balón.**
Dribla con el balón. Dribla cinco veces.
Y ahora, pasa el balón a *(Student 2).*
(Student 2), **dribla y corre con el balón.**
Tira el balón.
No, no encesta. Toma el balón de nuevo.
Dribla con el balón.
Tira el balón y encesta. Gracias, *(Student 1)* **y** *(Student 2).* **Siéntense.**

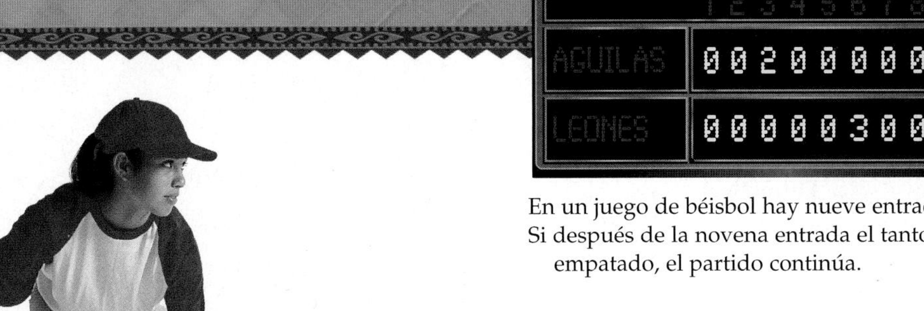

En un juego de béisbol hay nueve entradas. Si después de la novena entrada el tanto queda empatado, el partido continúa.

La jugadora atrapa la pelota. Atrapa la pelota con el guante.

El básquetbol, El baloncesto

Vocabulario

Step 2 Have students repeat each word or expression two or three times.

Step 3 As you present the vocabulary with the overhead transparencies you may wish to ask the following questions:

¿Lleva un guante un jugador de béisbol?

¿Quién lanza la pelota, el pícher o el cátcher?

Si el bateador no batea la pelota, ¿quién devuelve la pelota?

¿De dónde batea el bateador la pelota?

Del platillo, ¿corre a la primera base o a la tercera base?

Cuando el bateador batea, ¿quién atrapa la pelota con frecuencia? ¿El receptor o el jardinero?

About the Spanish Language

- As students will learn later in the chapter, most baseball vocabulary is similar to the English because baseball is a sport that originated in the United States.
- **La pelota** refers to a small ball. **El balón** refers to a larger ball. A very small ball such as a golf ball is **la bola.**
- There is no definite rule as to when to use **el campo** vs. **la cancha.** In Spain, however, **el campo** is heard in many instances where **la cancha** would be preferred in Latin America.

Chapter Projects

Los deportes Have students attend one of their school's athletic events. Then have them discuss it in Spanish. Their discussion should include the name of the sport, who the players are, how many players are on the team, and how good the team is.

3 PRACTICE

¿Qué palabra necesito?

4, 5, and 6 It is recommended that you go over the activities orally in class before assigning them for homework.

Writing Development
After going over Activity 5, have students write a short description of a basketball game.

Learning from Photos
(page 208 top) Many Texans like to weekend in Monterrey, Mexico's third largest city. Monterrey affords many cultural highlights, such as the Alfa Cultural Center and the Baseball Hall of Fame.
(page 208 bottom) This photo was taken in San Juan, Puerto Rico. Note the young women playing basketball. Until rather recently it was not very common to see women participating in sports in Hispanic countries, particularly team sports. This is no longer the case. Women are participating in team sports such as basketball, baseball, and volleyball, as well as tennis and golf.

Learning from Realia
(page 209) Have students look at the ad and tell what this factory manufactures.

LEVELING
E: Activities 4, 6, 7
A: Activity 5

¿Qué palabra necesito?

4 Historieta El béisbol
Escojan. *(Choose.)*

1. Juegan al béisbol en ____ de béisbol.
   a. un campo b. una pelota
   c. una base
2. El pícher ____ la pelota.
   a. lanza b. encesta c. batea
3. El receptor atrapa la pelota en ____.
   a. una portería b. un cesto
   c. un guante
4. El jugador ____ de una base a otra.
   a. tira b. devuelve c. corre
5. En un partido de béisbol hay ____ entradas.
   a. dos b. nueve c. once

Monterrey, México

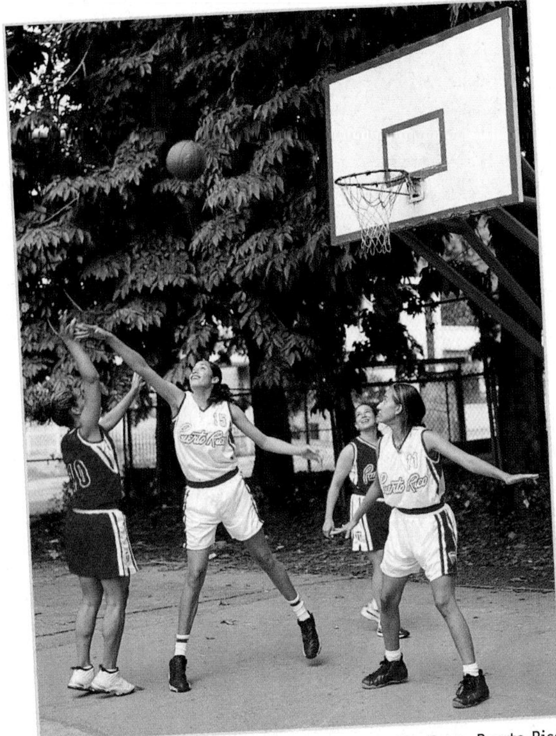

San Juan, Puerto Rico

5 Historieta El baloncesto
Contesten. *(Answer.)*

1. ¿Es el baloncesto un deporte de equipo o un deporte individual?
2. ¿Hay cinco o nueve jugadores en un equipo de baloncesto?
3. Durante un partido de baloncesto, ¿los jugadores driblan con el balón o lanzan el balón con el pie?
4. ¿El jugador tira el balón en el cesto o en la portería?
5. ¿El encestado (canasto) vale dos puntos o seis puntos?

Answers to ¿Qué palabra necesito?

4
1. a
2. a
3. c
4. c
5. b

5
1. El baloncesto es un deporte de equipo.
2. Hay cinco jugadores en un equipo de baloncesto.
3. Durante un partido de baloncesto los jugadores driblan con el balón.
4. El jugador tira el balón en el cesto.
5. El encestado (canasto) vale dos puntos.

6 **¿Qué deporte es?** Escojan. *(Choose.)*

el béisbol

el baloncesto

el fútbol

1. El jugador lanza el balón con el pie.
2. Hay cinco jugadores en el equipo.
3. Hay nueve entradas en el partido.
4. El jugador corre de una base a otra.
5. El portero para o bloquea el balón.
6. El jugador tira el balón y encesta.

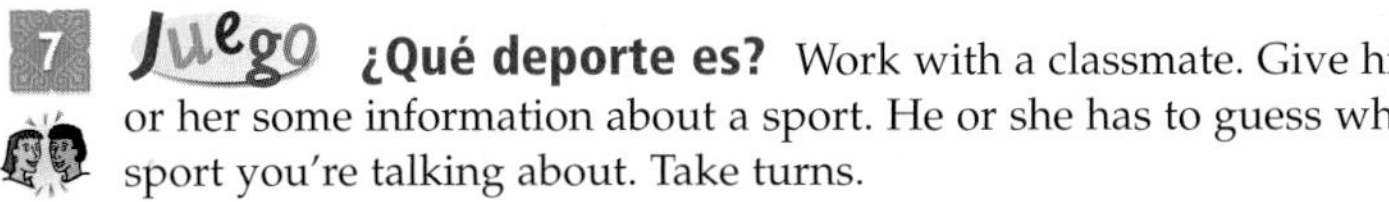

7 *Juego* **¿Qué deporte es?** Work with a classmate. Give him or her some information about a sport. He or she has to guess what sport you're talking about. Take turns.

WWS
FÁBRICA DE UNIFORMES DEPORTIVOS
La casa de las urgencias
27 años de experiencia nos respaldan
Pedidos al interior de la República
y en los Estados Unidos
Fabricante de balones de Futbol, Voli, Basket, Pelotas de Beisball, Gorras, Playeras y todo para el deporte.
UNIFORMES SUBLIMADOS DE EQUIPOS NACIONALES
Y EXTRANJEROS A PRECIOS MUY BAJOS. CONSÚLTANOS
SCHUMANN No. 165-2o PISO, COL, VALLEJO MÉXICO D.F. 07870
55-17-24-25 /57-59-21-71 / 55-17-53-29

Vocabulario

¡OJO! Note that the activities are color-coded. All the activities in the text are communicative. However, the ones with blue titles are guided communication. The red titles indicate that the answers to the activity are more open-ended and can vary more. You may wish to correct students' mistakes more so in the guided activities than in the activities with a red title, which lend themselves to a freer response.

6 Have students do Activity 6 with books open.

7 *Juego* This is a good activity to use when students need a "break" during the class period, or as an opening or closing activity.

Reaching All Students

For the Younger Students

Mi atleta favorito You may wish to have students bring in pictures of their favorite sports figures. Have other students say something about them. Ask the student who brought in the photo or picture why the athlete is his or her favorite player. **¿Por qué es ___ tu jugador(a) favorito(a)?**

Answers to ¿Qué palabra necesito?

6

1. el fútbol
2. el baloncesto
3. el béisbol
4. el béisbol
5. el fútbol
6. el baloncesto

7 *Answers will vary, but students should use vocabulary presented in* Palabras 2. *They may wish to model their descriptions after Activity 6.*

Estructura

Verbos de cambio radical e → ie en el presente

Telling what you want or prefer

1. There are certain groups of verbs in Spanish that have a stem change in the present tense. The verbs **empezar** *(to begin)*, **comenzar** *(to begin)*, **querer** *(to want)*, **perder** *(to lose)*, and **preferir** *(to prefer)* are stem-changing verbs. The **e** of the stem changes to **ie** in all forms except **nosotros** and **vosotros.** The endings are the same as those of regular verbs. Study the following forms.

INFINITIVE	empezar	querer	preferir
yo	empiezo	quiero	prefiero
tú	empiezas	quieres	prefieres
él, ella, Ud.	empieza	quiere	prefiere
nosotros(as)	empezamos	queremos	preferimos
vosotros(as)	*empezáis*	*queréis*	*preferís*
ellos, ellas, Uds.	empiezan	quieren	prefieren

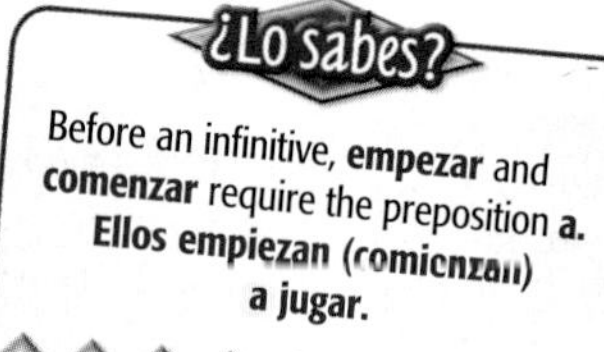

¿Lo sabes?
Before an infinitive, **empezar** and **comenzar** require the preposition **a.**
Ellos empiezan (comienzan) a jugar.

2. The verbs **empezar, comenzar, querer,** and **preferir** are often followed by an infinitive.

Ellos quieren ir al gimnasio.
¿Por qué prefieres jugar al fútbol?

Lima, Perú

Estructura

1 PREPARATION

Resource Manager

Audio Activities TE, pages 85–88
Audio CD 5
Workbook, pages 74–78
Quizzes, pages 36–37
ExamView® Pro

Bellringer Review

Use BRR Transparency 7.3 or write the following on the board.
Write at least three words associated with each sport.
el béisbol
el fútbol
el básquetbol

2 PRESENTATION

Verbos de cambio radical e → ie en el presente

Step 1 Write the verb forms on the board. Have students repeat them aloud.

Step 2 You may wish to start with the **nosotros** form, to show that it is different from the other forms.

Step 3 Use different colored chalk for **nosotros** (and **vosotros**) to emphasize the difference in sound and spelling in comparison to the other forms.

Step 4 Read the information to the students about the use of **a** + infinitive from the **¿Lo sabes?** box on page 210.

Learning from Photos

(page 210) Have students describe what they see in the photo taken in Lima, Peru. Ask them:
¿Son equipos profesionales o equipos de una escuela secundaria? ¿Hay muchos espectadores?

Chapter Projects

Una entrevista Have students interview some of the school athletes who are taking Spanish. They can prepare a broadcast report on the interview. If the interviewee is in the class, the interview can be done "live."

¿Cómo lo digo?

8 Historieta Queremos ganar. Contesten. *(Answer.)*

1. ¿Empiezan ustedes a jugar?
2. ¿Empiezan ustedes a jugar a las tres?
3. ¿Quieren ustedes ganar el partido?
4. ¿Quieren ustedes marcar un tanto?
5. ¿Pierden ustedes a veces o ganan siempre?
6. ¿Prefieren ustedes jugar en el parque o en la calle?

Buenos Aires, Argentina

9 Historieta El partido continúa.
Sigan el modelo. *(Follow the model.)*

el segundo tiempo / empezar →
El segundo tiempo empieza.

1. los jugadores / empezar a jugar
2. los dos equipos / querer ganar
3. ellos / preferir marcar muchos tantos
4. Sánchez / querer meter un gol
5. el portero / querer parar el balón
6. el equipo de Sánchez / no perder

10 Historieta ¿Un(a) aficionado(a) a los deportes?
Contesten personalmente. *(Answer about yourself.)*

1. ¿Prefieres jugar al béisbol o al fútbol?
2. ¿Prefieres jugar con un grupo de amigos o con un equipo formal?
3. ¿Prefieres jugar en el partido o prefieres mirar el partido?
4. ¿Prefieres ser jugador(a) o espectador(a)?
5. ¿Siempre quieres ganar?
6. ¿Pierdes a veces?

Estructura

3 PRACTICE

¿Cómo lo digo?

8, 9, and 10 Each activity on this page tells a story. After going over the activities you can have students retell all the information in their own words.

Note: In Activities 8 and 10, you can ask the questions, or you can have students do them as paired or group activities. One student asks the questions and calls on another to respond. It is preferable to vary this procedure because it is more time-consuming as a paired activity.

LEVELING

E: Activities 9, 10

A: Activities 8, 9, 10

ANSWERS TO ¿Cómo lo digo?

8

1. Sí, (No, no) empezamos a jugar.
2. Sí, (No, no) empezamos a jugar a las tres.
3. Sí, (No, no) queremos ganar el partido.
4. Sí, queremos marcar un tanto.
5. Perdemos a veces. (Ganamos siempre.)
6. Preferimos jugar en el parque (la calle).

9

1. Los jugadores empiezan a jugar.
2. Los dos equipos quieren ganar.
3. Ellos prefieren marcar muchos tantos.
4. Sánchez quiere meter un gol.
5. El portero quiere parar el balón.
6. El equipo de Sánchez no pierde.

10

1. Prefiero jugar al béisbol (fútbol).
2. Prefiero jugar con un grupo de amigos (un equipo formal).
3. Prefiero jugar en el partido (mirar el partido).
4. Prefiero ser jugador(a) (espectador[a]).
5. Sí, siempre quiero ganar. (No, no quiero ganar siempre.)
6. Sí, pierdo a veces. (No, no pierdo.)

3 PRACTICE *(continued)*

11 This activity has students use different forms of the various stem-changing verbs.

12 **Expansion:** In Activity 12, you can also have students describe in their own words everything they see in each illustration.

Reaching All Students

Additional Practice

¿Cuál es tu deporte favorito? Each group chooses a leader who asks the others what their favorite sports are and whether they prefer to play sports, watch them on TV, or go to games. The leader will take notes and report to the class. You can follow up with a class survey, grouping names of students on the board according to their preferences, and then discuss the results.

Class Motivator

¿Sí o no? Divide the class into two teams and play the following *true / false* game.

1. **Es necesario tener un cesto para jugar al voleibol.**
2. **Es necesario tener una red para jugar al voleibol.**
3. **El jugador de básquetbol puede correr con el balón en la mano.**
4. **El jugador de básquetbol tiene que driblar con el balón.**
5. **El balón de voleibol tiene que pasar por encima de la red.**
6. **El voleibol no puede tocar la red.**
7. **Los jugadores de básquetbol llevan guantes.**
8. **Los jugadores de béisbol corren de un canasto a otro.**

LEVELING

E: Activity 12
A: Activities 12, 13
C: Activity 11

11 **Historieta ¿Baloncesto o béisbol?** Completen. *(Complete.)*

Rosita __1__ (querer) jugar al baloncesto. Yo __2__ (querer) jugar al béisbol. Y tú, ¿ __3__ (preferir) jugar al baloncesto o __4__ (preferir) jugar al béisbol? Si tú __5__ (querer) jugar al béisbol, tú y yo __6__ (ganar) y Rosita __7__ (perder). Pero si tú __8__ (querer) jugar al baloncesto, entonces tú y Rosita __9__ (ganar) y yo __10__ (perder).

12 **¿Qué prefieres?** With a partner, look at the illustrations below. They each depict two activities. Find out from your partner which activity he or she prefers to do and which one he or she doesn't want to do. Take turns.

Answers to ¿Cómo lo digo?

11

1. quiere
2. quiero
3. prefieres
4. prefieres
5. quieres
6. ganamos
7. pierde
8. quieres
9. ganan
10. pierdo

12 *Answers will vary but may include:*

—¿Prefieres jugar al béisbol o prefieres mirar el partido de béisbol?
—Prefiero jugar al béisbol. No quiero mirar el partido de béisbol.

Verbos de cambio radical o → ue en el presente

Describing more activities

1. The verbs **volver** *(to return to a place)*, **devolver** *(to return a thing)*, **poder** *(to be able)*, and **dormir** *(to sleep)* are also stem-changing verbs. The **o** of the stem changes to **ue** in all forms except **nosotros** and **vosotros**. The endings are the same as those of regular verbs. Study the following forms.

INFINITIVE	volver	poder	dormir
yo	vuelvo	puedo	duermo
tú	vuelves	puedes	duermes
él, ella, Ud.	vuelve	puede	duerme
nosotros(as)	volvemos	podemos	dormimos
vosotros(as)	*volvéis*	*podéis*	*dormís*
ellos, ellas, Uds.	vuelven	pueden	duermen

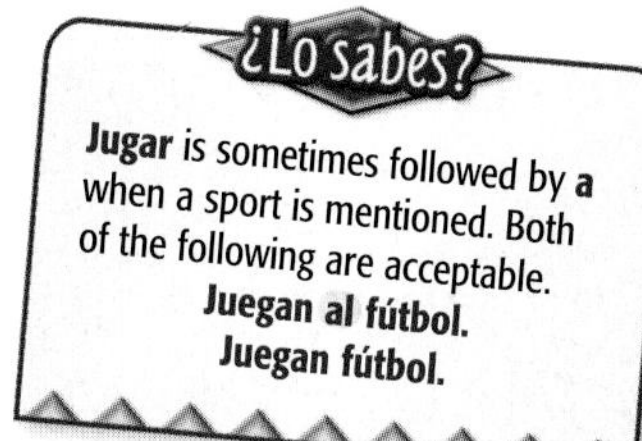

¿Lo sabes?

Jugar is sometimes followed by **a** when a sport is mentioned. Both of the following are acceptable.

Juegan al fútbol.
Juegan fútbol.

2. The **u** in the verb **jugar** changes to **ue** in all forms except **nosotros** and **vosotros**.

jugar **juego, juegas, juega, jugamos,** ***jugáis,*** **juegan**

¿Cómo lo digo?

13 Historieta Un partido de béisbol

Contesten. *(Answer.)*

1. ¿Juegan ustedes al béisbol?
2. ¿Juegan ustedes con unos amigos o con el equipo de la escuela?
3. ¿Vuelven ustedes al campo después de cada entrada?
4. ¿Pueden ustedes continuar el partido si el tanto queda empatado después de la novena entrada?
5. ¿Duermen ustedes bien después de un buen partido de béisbol?

La Liga mexicana

Answers to ¿Cómo lo digo?

 13

1. Sí, (No, no) jugamos al béisbol.
2. Jugamos con unos amigos (con el equipo de la escuela).
3. Sí, volvemos al campo después de cada entrada.
4. Sí, podemos continuar el partido si el tanto queda empatado después de la novena entrada.
5. Sí, (No, no) dormimos bien después de un buen partido de béisbol.

Estructura

1 PREPARATION

Bellringer Review

Use BRR Transparency 7.4 or write the following on the board.

Change the following to **nosotros.**

1. **Yo empiezo a jugar.**
2. **Yo quiero ganar.**
3. **Yo no pierdo.**

2 PRESENTATION

Verbos de cambio radical o → ue en el presente

Step 1 Write the verb forms from page 213 on the board and have students repeat them after you.

Step 2 To reinforce the spellings visually, use different colored chalk when writing the **nosotros** (and **vosotros**) forms on the board.

Step 3 Have students open their books to page 213 and lead them through Items 1 and 2.

3 PRACTICE

¿Cómo lo digo?

13 This activity can be done orally with books closed.

Writing Development

Have students write a paragraph about **un partido de béisbol** after going over Activity 13.

Estructura

3 PRACTICE *(continued)*

14 After students answer the questions in Activity 14, see whether they can make up similar questions using the verbs **querer, preferir,** and **poder.**
Expansion: Ask students to describe the top photo, **Una clase de español en los Estados Unidos,** on page 214. **¿Leen o juegan los alumnos?**
Now, have students talk about their Spanish class. Encourage them to say as much as they can.

15 In this activity, students have to use all the different forms of the various stem-changing verbs.

16 Tell students to be as creative as possible. They can make up some outlandish reasons why they can't do something.

UN POCO MÁS This *InfoGap* Activity will allow students to practice in pairs. The activity should be very manageable for them, since all vocabulary and structures are familiar to them.

Estructura

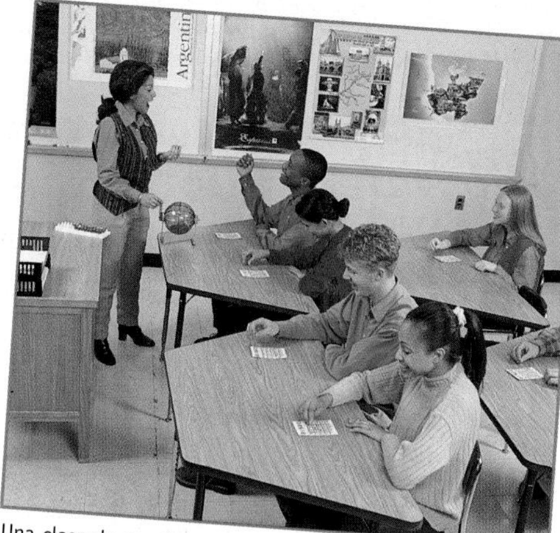

Una clase de español en Estados Unidos

14 Historieta En la clase de español

Contesten. *(Answer.)*

1. ¿Juegas al Bingo en la clase de español?
2. ¿Juegas al Loto en la clase de español?
3. ¿Puedes hablar inglés en la clase de español?
4. ¿Qué lengua puedes o tienes que hablar en la clase de español?
5. ¿Duermes en la clase de español?
6. ¿Devuelve el/la profesor(a) los exámenes pronto?

San Juan, Puerto Rico

15 Historieta Sí, pero ahora no puede.

Completen. *(Complete.)*

Yo __1__ (jugar) mucho al fútbol y Diana __2__ (jugar) mucho también, pero ahora ella no __3__ (poder).

—Diana, ¿por qué no __4__ (poder) jugar ahora?

—No __5__ (poder) porque __6__ (querer) ir a casa.

Sí, Diana __7__ (querer) ir a casa porque ella __8__ (tener) un amigo que __9__ (volver) hoy de Puerto Rico y ella __10__ (querer) estar en casa. Pero mañana todos nosotros __11__ (ir) a jugar. Y el amigo puertorriqueño de Diana __12__ (poder) jugar también. Su amigo __13__ (jugar) muy bien.

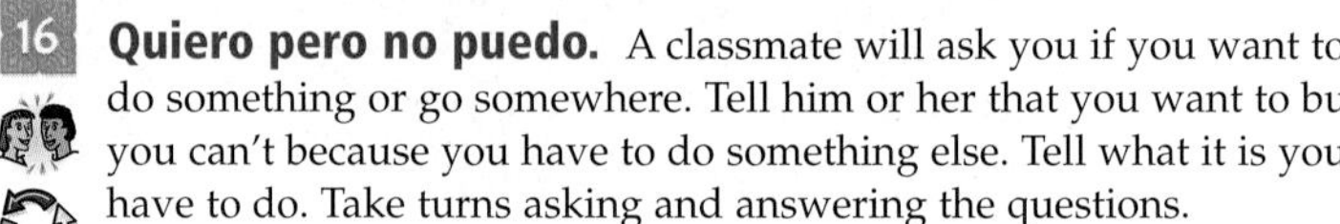

16 Quiero pero no puedo.

A classmate will ask you if you want to do something or go somewhere. Tell him or her that you want to but you can't because you have to do something else. Tell what it is you have to do. Take turns asking and answering the questions.

For more practice using stem-changing verbs, do Activity 7 on page H8 at the end of this book.

Answers to ¿Cómo lo digo?

14

1. Sí, (No, no) juego al Bingo en la clase de español.
2. Sí, (No, no) juego al Loto en la clase de español.
3. Sí, (No, no) puedo hablar inglés en la clase de español.
4. Puedo (Tengo que) hablar español en la clase de español.
5. No, no duermo (Sí, duermo) en la clase de español.
6. Sí (No), el / la profesor(a) (no) devuelve los exámenes pronto.

15

1. juego
2. juega
3. puede
4. puedes
5. puedo
6. quiero
7. quiere
8. tiene
9. vuelve
10. quiere
11. vamos
12. puede
13. juega

16 *Answers will vary. Students will typically begin their question with:* ¿Quieres + *infinitive . . .? Their partner will answer with:* Sí, quiero… pero no puedo porque...

Interesar, aburrir y gustar

Expressing what interests, bores, or pleases you

1. The verbs **interesar** and **aburrir** function the same in Spanish and in English. Study the following examples.

¿Te aburre el arte?	*Does art bore you?*
No, el arte me interesa.	*No, art interests me.*
¿Te aburren los deportes?	*Do sports bore you?*
No, los deportes me interesan.	*No, sports interest me.*

2. The verb **gustar** in Spanish functions the same as **interesar** and **aburrir. Gustar** conveys the meaning *to like,* but its true meaning is *to please.* The Spanish equivalent of *I like baseball* is *Baseball pleases me.* Study the following examples.

   ¿Te gusta el béisbol? Ah, sí, me gusta mucho.
   ¿Te gustan los deportes? Sí, me gustan mucho.

3. The verb **gustar** is often used with an infinitive to tell what you like to do.

   ¿Te gusta jugar al fútbol? Sí, me gusta jugar.
   ¿Te gusta comer? Sí, me gusta comer.

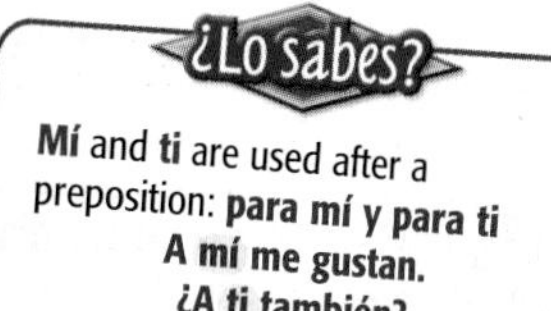

Mí and **ti** are used after a preposition: **para mí y para ti**
A mí me gustan.
¿A ti también?

¿Cómo lo digo?

17 ¿Qué cursos te interesan y qué cursos te aburren?

Contesten. *(Answer.)*

1. ¿Te interesa la historia?
2. ¿Te interesa la geografía?
3. ¿Te interesa la biología?
4. ¿Te interesa la educación física?
5. ¿Te interesan las matemáticas?
6. ¿Te interesan las ciencias?
7. ¿Te interesan las lenguas?

Colegio San José, Estepona, España

Answers to ¿Cómo lo digo?

17

1. Sí, (No, no) me interesa la historia. (No, me aburre la historia.)
2. Sí, (No, no) me interesa la geografía. (No, me aburre la geografía.)
3. Sí, (No, no) me interesa la biología. (No, me aburre la biología.)
4. Sí, (No, no) me interesa la educación física. (No, me aburre la educación física.)
5. Sí, (No, no) me interesan las matemáticas. (No, me aburren las matemáticas.)
6. Sí, (No, no) me interesan las ciencias. (No, me aburren las ciencias.)
7. Sí, (No, no) me interesan las lenguas. (No, me aburren las lenguas.)

Estructura

1 PREPARATION

Bellringer Review

Use BRR Transparency 7.5 or write the following on the board.
Write down as many foods as you can remember.

2 PRESENTATION

Interesar, aburrir y gustar

¡OJO! English-speaking students often have a problem grasping the concept of **gustar.** Introducing **interesar** and **aburrir** in conjunction with **gustar** makes it much easier for students since we do have an exact parallel construction in English.

Step 1 As you go over the explanation and the **Para continuar** activities, have students point to themselves as they say **me** and have them look at a friend as they say **te.**

3 PRACTICE

¿Cómo lo digo?

17 Note that Items 1–4 have singular subjects and Items 5–7 have plural subjects. We have separated them to help students understand the concept.

LEVELING

E: Activities 14, 17
A: Activity 16
C: Activity 15

3 PRACTICE *(continued)*

18 **thru** 23 After going over Activities 18–23 on pages 216 and 217, permit students to make up original sentences with **interesar, aburrir,** and **gustar** using any vocabulary they know.

Recycling

All of these activities recycle vocabulary from the preceding chapters.

LEVELING

E: Activities 18, 19, 20, 21, 23

A: Activities 22, 24

C: Activity 25

18 ¿Te interesa o te aburre? Sigan el modelo. *(Follow the model.)*

la biología →
La biología me interesa. No me aburre.

1. el álgebra
2. la geometría
3. la historia
4. el español
5. la geografía

19 ¿Te interesan o te aburren? Sigan el modelo. *(Follow the model.)*

las películas →
—¿Te interesan las películas o te aburren?
—Las películas me interesan. No me aburren.

1. los partidos de fútbol
2. las películas románticas
3. las emisiones deportivas
4. las noticias

20 Los deportes Contesten. *(Answer.)*

1. ¿Te gusta el fútbol?
2. ¿Te gusta el béisbol?
3. ¿Te gusta el voleibol?
4. ¿Te gusta más el béisbol o el fútbol?
5. ¿Te gusta más el voleibol o el básquetbol?

DEPORTES

FÚTBOL

Los siguientes partidos de FÚTBOL corresponden a la Liga Nacional de Primera División.
Se recomienda consulten fechas por posibles cambios de fechas. / Please check dates for any changes.

• ESTADIO SANTIAGO BERNABÉU
P.º DE LA CASTELLANA, 104.
TEL.: 91 344 00 52. (METRO: SANTIAGO BERNABÉU).

4 Oct.
Real Madrid - Tenerife.

25 Oct.
Real Madrid - Racing.

• ESTADIO VICENTE CALDERÓN
VIRGEN DEL PUERTO, 67.
TEL.: 91 366 47 07. (METRO: PIRÁMIDES Y MARQUÉS DE VADILLO).

18 Oct.
Atlético de Madrid - Tenerife.

21 Los alimentos Contesten. *(Answer.)*

1. ¿Te gusta la ensalada?
2. ¿Te gusta un sándwich de jamón y queso?
3. ¿Te gusta la sopa?
4. ¿Te gusta la carne?
5. ¿Te gustan las tortillas?
6. ¿Te gustan las enchiladas?
7. ¿Te gustan los frijoles?
8. ¿Te gustan los tomates?

ANSWERS TO ¿Cómo lo digo?

18

1. El álgebra me interesa. No me aburre.
2. La geometría me interesa. No me aburre.
3. La historia me interesa. No me aburre.
4. El español me interesa. No me aburre.
5. La geografía me interesa. No me aburre.

19

1. ¿Te interesan los partidos de fútbol o te aburren? Los partidos de fútbol me interesan. No me aburren.
2. ¿Te interesan las películas románticas o te aburren? Las películas románticas me interesan. No me aburren.
3. ¿Te interesan las emisiones deportivas o te aburren? Las emisiones deportivas me interesan. No me aburren.
4. ¿Te interesan las noticias o te aburren? Las noticias me interesan. No me aburren.

20

1. Sí, (No, no) me gusta el fútbol.
2. Sí, (No, no) me gusta el béisbol.
3. Sí, (No, no) me gusta el voleibol.
4. Me gusta más el béisbol (el fútbol).
5. Me gusta más el voleibol (el básquetbol).

21

1. Sí, (No, no) me gusta la ensalada.
2. Sí, (No, no) me gusta un sándwich de jamón y queso.
3. Sí, (No, no) me gusta la sopa.
4. Sí, (No, no) me gusta la carne.
5. Sí, (No, no) me gustan las tortillas.
6. Sí, (No, no) me gustan las enchiladas.
7. Sí, (No, no) me gustan los frijoles.
8. Sí, (No, no) me gustan los tomates.

22 **¿Te gusta la ropa?** Sigan el modelo. *(Follow the model.)*

—¿Te gusta la gorra?
—Sí, a mí me gusta.

23 **¿Qué te gusta hacer?** Contesten. *(Answer.)*

1. ¿Te gusta cantar?
2. ¿Te gusta bailar?
3. ¿Te gusta comer?
4. ¿Te gusta leer?
5. ¿Te gusta más hablar o escuchar?
6. ¿Te gusta más jugar o ser espectador(a)?

24 **¿Qué te interesa?** Work with a classmate. Take turns telling those things that interest you and those that bore you. Decide which interests you have in common.

25 **Gustos** Get together with a classmate. Tell one another some things you like and don't like. Some categories you may want to explore are: **comida, ropa, cursos, deportes, actividades.** Decide whether you and your classmates have any of the same likes and dislikes.

Andas bien. ¡Adelante!

22 After doing Activity 22, quickly review the colors students learned in Chapter 3.

23 Ask students to think of additional verbs of action they have learned. Write these on the board.

24 and 25 Let students select the activity they wish to take part in.
Expansion: After doing Activities 24 and 25, follow up by having each pair of students report to the class those things that interest them, those things that bore them, those things they like, and those they dislike.

¡Adelante!
At this point in the chapter, students have learned all the vocabulary and structure necessary to complete the chapter. The conversation and cultural readings that follow recycle all the material learned up to this point.

Answers to ¿Cómo lo digo?

22

1. ¿Te gusta la camisa?
   Sí, a mí me gusta.
2. ¿Te gustan los tenis?
   Sí, a mí me gustan.
3. ¿Te gusta la falda?
   Sí, a mí me gusta.
4. ¿Te gustan los zapatos?
   Sí, a mí me gustan.
5. ¿Te gusta el pantalón?
   Sí, a mí me gusta.
6. ¿Te gusta la chaqueta?
   Sí, a mí me gusta.

23

1. Sí, (No, no) me gusta cantar.
2. Sí, (No, no) me gusta bailar.
3. Sí, (No, no) me gusta comer.
4. Sí, (No, no) me gusta leer.
5. Me gusta más hablar (escuchar).
6. Me gusta más jugar (ser espectador[a]).

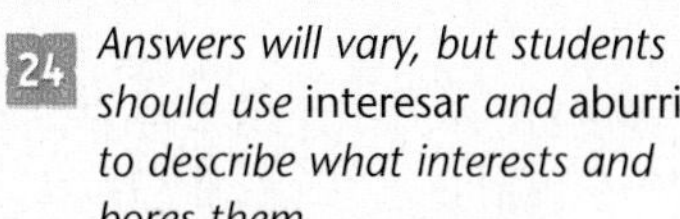
24 *Answers will vary, but students should use* interesar *and* aburrir *to describe what interests and bores them.*

25 *Answers will vary, but students should use* gustar *to describe things they like and don't like.*

1 PREPARATION

Resource Manager

Audio Activities TE, page 88
Audio CD 5

Bellringer Review

Use BRR Transparency 7.6 or write the following on the board.
Write down two things that you like and two things that you don't like.

2 PRESENTATION

Step 1 Have students open their books to page 218. Half the class will take the part of **Anita,** the other half will take the part of **Tomás.** Each half will read in unison.

Step 2 Now, call on one individual to be **Anita** and another to be **Tomás.** Have them read the conversation aloud.

Step 3 You may wish to play the recording on Audio CD 5 for them.

Step 4 Go over the **¿Comprendes?** activity.

Step 5 Call on students to present a similar conversation of their own.

Conversación

¿Quieres jugar?   

Anita Tomás, ¿prefieres el béisbol o el fútbol?
Tomás ¿Yo? Yo prefiero el fútbol. Me gusta más que el béisbol.
Anita ¿Juegas al fútbol?
Tomás Sí, juego. Pero la verdad es que me gusta más ser espectador que jugador.
Anita ¿Es bueno el equipo de tu escuela?
Tomás Sí, tenemos un equipo estupendo.
Anita ¿Son campeones?
Tomás No, pero van a ganar el campeonato.

¿Comprendes?

Contesten. *(Answer.)*

1. ¿Prefiere Tomás el béisbol o el fútbol?
2. ¿Juega mucho al fútbol?
3. ¿Qué prefiere ser?
4. ¿Es bueno el equipo de su escuela?
5. ¿Qué va a ganar el equipo?

Answers to ¿Comprendes?

1. Tomás prefiere el fútbol.
2. No, no juega mucho al fútbol.
3. Prefiere ser espectador.
4. Sí, tiene un equipo estupendo.
5. El equipo va a ganar el campeonato.

LEVELING

E: Conversation

Vamos a hablar más

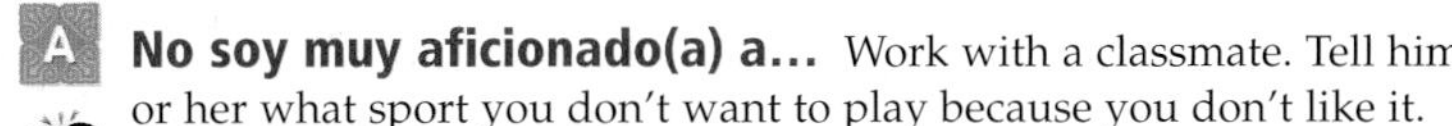

A **No soy muy aficionado(a) a...** Work with a classmate. Tell him or her what sport you don't want to play because you don't like it. Tell what you prefer to play. Then ask your classmate questions to find out what sports he or she likes.

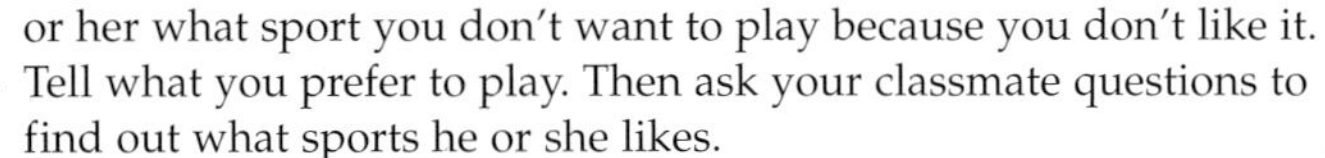

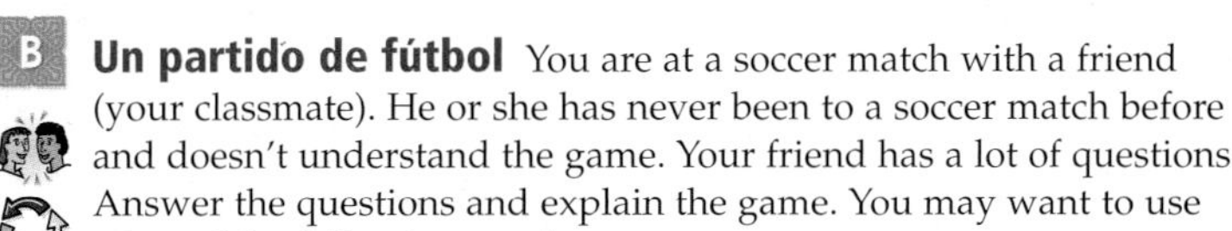

B **Un partido de fútbol** You are at a soccer match with a friend (your classmate). He or she has never been to a soccer match before and doesn't understand the game. Your friend has a lot of questions. Answer the questions and explain the game. You may want to use some of the following words.

Pronunciación

Las consonantes s, c, z

The consonant **s** is pronounced the same as the *s* in *sing*. Repeat the following.

sa	se	si	so	su
sala	**base**	**sí**	**peso**	**su**
pasa	**serio**	**simpático**	**sopa**	**Susana**
saca	**seis**	**siete**	**sobrino**	

The consonant **c** in combination with **e** or **i (ce, ci)** is pronounced the same as an **s** in all areas of Latin America. In many parts of Spain, **ce** and **ci** are pronounced like the *th* in English. Likewise, the pronunciation of **z** in combination with **a, o, u (za, zo, zu)** is the same as an **s** throughout Latin America and as a **th** in most areas of Spain. Repeat the following.

za	ce	ci	zo	zu
cabeza	**cero**	**cinco**	**zona**	**zumo**
empieza	**encesta**	**ciudad**	**almuerzo**	**Zúñiga**

Repeat the following sentences.

González enseña en la sala de clase.
El sobrino de Susana es serio y sincero.
La ciudad tiene cinco zonas.
Toma el almuerzo a las doce y diez en la cocina.

Conversación

3 PRACTICE

Vamos a hablar más

A Have each pair of students report to the class, telling what sport(s) each partner prefers.

B If possible, have several pairs of students present their conversations to the entire class.

Glencoe Technology

CD-ROM

On the CD-ROM, students can watch a dramatization of this conversation. They can then play the role of either one of the characters and record themselves in the conversation.

Pronunciación

Step 1 Have students carefully repeat the consonant sounds after you or Audio CD 5.

Step 2 Be sure students do not make an English *z* sound when pronouncing words with the letter **z**.

Step 3 Have students open their books to page 219. Call on individuals to read the sentences.

Step 4 The words and sentences presented here can also be used for dictation. It is important to review these sounds and their spellings frequently since they are often misspelled.

Answers to Vamos a hablar más

A *Answers will vary. Students should use stem-changing verbs like* querer *and* preferir *and the verb* gustar.

B *Answers will vary, but encourage students to use as many of the words in the colored boxes as possible.*

Chapter Projects

Un reportaje Have students prepare a TV sports broadcast in Spanish. The broadcast can be an audio, video, or "live" broadcast.

Lecturas culturales

Resource Manager

Audio Activities TE, page 89
Audio CD 5

National Standards

Cultures
The reading about soccer and the World Cup and the related activities give students an understanding of the importance of this sport in Hispanic culture.

PRESENTATION

¡OJO! If your students are not interested in sports, you can go over the **Lectura** quickly. If several students in your class play sports, you may wish to do the **Lectura** more thoroughly.

Pre-reading

Give students a brief oral synopsis of the reading in Spanish.

Reading

Step 1 Ask students to open their books to page 220. Call on individuals to read two or three sentences. After each student reads, ask the others follow-up questions. Continue in this manner through the entire reading.

Step 2 Ask five or six questions that review the main points of the reading. The answers to these questions will give a coherent oral summary of the **Lectura.**

Step 3 Call on a more able student to give a summary of the **Lectura** in his or her own words. Call on less able students to answer questions about the oral summary just given. Then have a less able student give an oral summary based on the summary of the more able student.

Lecturas culturales

Reading Strategy

Scanning for specific information Scanning for specific information means reading to find out certain details without concerning yourself with the other information in the passage. Some examples of scanning are looking up words in a dictionary or searching a television listing to find out when certain programs are on. Another example of scanning is reading articles to find out something specific, such as sports results.

El fútbol

La Liga española

Estamos en el estadio Santiago Bernabéu en Madrid. ¡Qué emoción! El Real Madrid juega contra el Atlético de Madrid. Quedan[1] dos minutos en el segundo tiempo. El partido está empatado en cero. ¿Qué va a pasar[2]? Da Silva pasa el balón a Casero. Casero lanza el balón con el pie izquierdo. El balón vuela[3]. El portero quiere parar el balón. ¿Puede o no? No, no puede. El balón entra en la portería. Casero mete un gol y marca un tanto. En los últimos dos minutos del partido, el equipo de Casero y da Silva gana. El Real Madrid derrota[4] al Atlético de Madrid uno a cero. El Real Madrid es triunfante, victorioso. Casero y da Silva son sus héroes.

La Copa mundial

Casero y da Silva son jugadores muy buenos y van a jugar en la Copa mundial. Pero da Silva no va a jugar con el mismo equipo que Casero. ¿Por qué? Porque da Silva no es español. Es de Brasil y en la Copa él va a jugar con el equipo de Brasil. Casero va a jugar con el equipo de España porque es español.

Cada cuatro años las estrellas[5] de cada país forman parte de un equipo nacional. Hay treinta y dos equipos nacionales que juegan en la Copa mundial. Los equipos de los treinta y dos países de todas partes del mundo compiten[6] para ganar la Copa y ser el campeón del mundo.

[1]Quedan *Remain*
[2]pasar *happen*
[3]vuela *flies*
[4]derrota *defeats*
[5]estrellas *stars*
[6]compiten *compete*

El estadio Santiago Bernabéu

FUN-FACTS

La Copa mundial The World Cup matches were played in the United States for the first time ever in 1994. The very first World Cup matches were held in Uruguay in 1930. The Uruguayan national team was the winner. Uruguay and Argentina have each won twice. Three-time winners are Italy and Germany. Brazil has won the cup four times. The World Cup competition takes place every four years.

¿Comprendes?

A Lo mismo Escojan la palabra equivalente. *(Choose the equivalent term.)*

1. la mayoría
2. el vocabulario
3. lanzar
4. el campeón
5. triunfante
6. el jugador
7. parar

a. victorioso
b. tirar
c. el/la que gana
d. la mayor parte
e. no permitir pasar, bloquear
f. las palabras
g. el miembro del equipo

B Lo contrario Escojan la palabra contraria. *(Choose the opposite term.)*

1. el/la jugador(a)
2. últimos
3. izquierdo
4. gana
5. entra

a. primeros
b. derecho
c. el/la espectador(a)
d. pierde
e. sale

C El partido de fútbol

Contesten. *(Answer.)*

1. ¿A qué juegan los dos equipos?
2. ¿Cuántos minutos quedan en el segundo tiempo?
3. ¿Quién pasa el balón?
4. ¿Quién lanza el balón?
5. ¿Cómo lanza el balón?
6. ¿Puede parar el balón el portero?
7. ¿Qué mete Casero?
8. ¿Qué marca?
9. ¿Qué equipo es victorioso?
10. ¿Quiénes son los héroes?

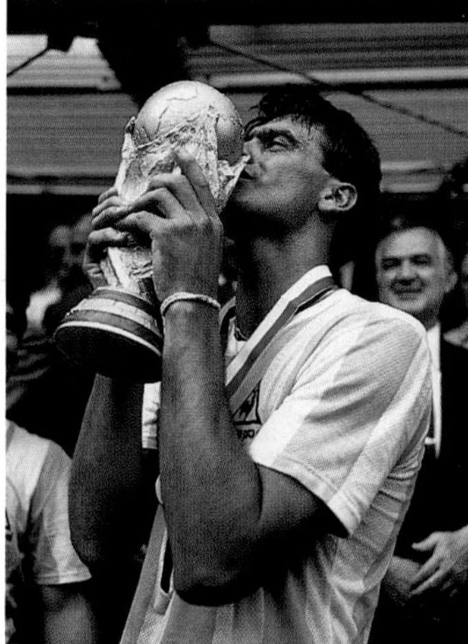

La Copa mundial

D La Copa mundial Sí o no? *(True or false?)*

1. Los equipos juegan en la Copa mundial cada año.
2. Todos los jugadores de un equipo son de la misma nacionalidad.
3. Cada equipo que juega en la Copa representa un país.
4. Los equipos de veintidós naciones juegan en la Copa mundial.
5. Todos los equipos son de Europa.

Lecturas culturales

Step 4 With more able classes, have students write their own summary. This should take approximately seven minutes.

Post-reading

Step 1 Have students form three groups. Have each group write a brief news announcement for a different type of sporting event and present their announcement to the class.

Step 2 Now have students do the **¿Comprendes?** activities on page 221.

¿Comprendes?

A and B You may assign both of these activities before going over them in class.

C Activity C will help students prepare an oral or written summary of the **Lectura.**

D Have more able students give the correct answer to any false statements in this activity.

LEVELING

A: Reading

Answers to ¿Comprendes?

A

1. d
2. f
3. b
4. c
5. a
6. g
7. e

B

1. c
2. a
3. b
4. d
5. e

C

1. Los dos equipos juegan al fútbol.
2. Quedan dos minutos en el segundo tiempo.
3. Da Silva pasa el balón.
4. Casero lanza el balón.
5. Lanza el balón con el pie izquierdo.
6. No, el portero no puede parar el balón.
7. Casero mete un gol.
8. Marca un tanto.
9. El Real Madrid es victorioso.
10. Casero y Da Silva son los héroes.

D

1. No, los equipos no juegan en la Copa mundial cada año.
2. Sí, todos los jugadores de un equipo son de la misma nacionalidad.
3. Sí, cada equipo que juega en la Copa representa un país.
4. No, los equipos de treinta y dos naciones juegan en la Copa mundial.
5. No, no todos los equipos son de Europa.

Lectura opcional 1

National Standards

Cultures
In the reading on this page students learn where soccer and baseball are popular in the Spanish-speaking world. They will demonstrate an understanding of the importance of these two sports in Hispanic culture.

PRESENTATION

Step 1 Have students read the passage quickly as they look at the photos that accompany it. Have students discuss the information they find interesting.

Assessment

You may wish to give students who read this selection the following quiz.
Answer.

1. **¿Dónde es popular el fútbol?**
2. **¿Tiene muchos aficionados?**
3. **¿Cuándo está lleno el estadio?**
4. **¿Dónde es popular el béisbol?**
5. **¿Por qué hay mucha influencia del inglés en el vocabulario del béisbol?**

FUN-FACTS

El básquetbol After soccer, the sport that has reached the highest worldwide popularity is basketball. The professional basketball league in Spain is one of the best in Europe. Many American college players that are not able to play in the NBA (National Basketball Association) in the United States are able to obtain lucrative contracts in European leagues, especially in Italy and Spain. The sport has reached its highest levels in Brazil in South America and in Puerto Rico in the Caribbean.

Lectura opcional 1

Argentina contra Croacia

Deportes populares

El fútbol

El fútbol es un deporte muy popular en todos los países hispanos. Los equipos nacionales tienen millones de aficionados. Cuando el equipo de un país juega contra el equipo de otro país, el estadio está lleno[1] de espectadores.

El béisbol

El béisbol no es un deporte popular en todos los países hispanos. Es popular en sólo algunos. El béisbol tiene o goza de popularidad en Cuba, Puerto Rico, la República Dominicana, Venezuela, Nicaragua, México y Panamá. Como el béisbol es esencialmente un deporte norteamericano, la mayoría del vocabulario del béisbol es inglés: las bases, el pícher, el out, el jonrón.

Muchos jugadores de béisbol de las Grandes Ligas son hispanos. Entre 1919 y hoy más de cien jugadores latinos juegan en la Serie Mundial.

[1]lleno *full*

La Liga mexicana

¿Comprendes?

A ¿Es la verdad o no? Contesten con **sí** o **no.** (*Answer with* sí *or* no.)

1. El fútbol es un deporte popular en todas partes de Latinoamérica.
2. Casi todos los países tienen su equipo nacional de fútbol.
3. Cuando un equipo nacional juega contra otro equipo nacional—un equipo de otro país—hay muy poca gente en el estadio; hay muy pocos espectadores.
4. El béisbol es también un deporte popular en todos los países hispanos.
5. El béisbol es muy popular en los países del Caribe.
6. Muchos beisbolistas famosos de las Grandes Ligas de Estados Unidos son de origen hispano o latino.

B Las nacionalidades Completen. (*Complete.*)

1. Un puertorriqueño es de ____.
2. Un cubano es de ____.
3. Un panameño es de ____ y un nicaragüense es de ____.
4. Un mexicano es de ____ y un dominicano es de la ____.

Answers to ¿Comprendes?

A

1. Sí, el fútbol es un deporte popular en todas partes de Latinoamérica.
2. Sí, casi todos los países tienen su equipo nacional de fútbol.
3. No, cuando un equipo nacional juega contra otro equipo nacional el estadio está lleno de espectadores.
4. No, el béisbol no es un deporte popular en todos los países hispanos.
5. Sí, el béisbol es muy popular en los países del Caribe.
6. Sí, muchos beisbolistas famosos de las Grandes Ligas de Estados Unidos son de origen hispano o latino.

B

1. Puerto Rico
2. Cuba
3. Panamá, Nicaragua
4. México, República Dominicana

Lectura opcional 2

El país vasco, España

Miami, la Florida

El «jai alai» o la pelota vasca

Jai alai es una palabra vasca. El país vasco es una región del norte de España y del sudoeste de Francia. El jai alai tiene otro nombre—la pelota vasca. El jai alai es un juego vasco popular.

Juegan al jai alai o a la pelota vasca en una cancha. Los jugadores son «pelotaris». Llevan un pantalón blanco, una camisa blanca, una faja roja y alpargatas. Tienen una cesta. Usan la cesta para lanzar y recibir la pelota.

En la cancha de jai alai hay tres paredes[1]. El frontón es la pared delantera[2]. «Frontón» es también el nombre de toda la cancha. El jugador lanza la pelota con la cesta contra la pared. Cuando la pelota pega[3] contra el frontón y rebota[4] hacia el jugador, el «pelotari» tiene que devolver la pelota. ¡Y la pelota viaja[5] a unas ciento cincuenta millas por hora!

[1]paredes *walls*
[2]delantera *front*
[3]pega *hits*
[4]rebota *rebounds*
[5]viaja *travels*

faja

cesta

alpargatas

¿Comprendes?

Jai alai Completen. *(Complete.)*

1. El jai alai o la ____ es un juego popular vasco.
2. Los pelotaris son ____ de jai alai.
3. Llevan un pantalón ____, una camisa ____ y una faja ____.
4. Los pelotaris no llevan zapatos cuando juegan. Llevan ____.
5. Los pelotaris usan una ____ para lanzar y recibir la pelota.
6. El ____ es la cancha de jai alai.
7. En una cancha de jai alai hay tres ____.
8. El jugador tiene que ____ la pelota cuando pega contra el frontón.
9. En un juego de jai alai la pelota viaja a unas ____ millas por hora.

Lectura opcional 2

¡OJO! The readings on pages 222–223 are optional. You may skip them completely, have the entire class read them, have only several students read them and report to the class, or assign them for extra credit.

Assessment

You may wish to give the following quiz to students who read this selection.
Answer.

1. **¿Dónde está el país vasco? ¿Cuál es otro nombre del jai alai?**
2. **¿Dónde juegan al jai alai? ¿Qué llevan los jugadores del jai alai?**
3. **¿Qué usan para lanzar la pelota?**
4. **¿Cuántas paredes tiene la cancha?**
5. **¿A cuántas millas por hora viaja la pelota cuando el jugador devuelve la pelota?**

FUN-FACTS

Jai alai This sport is played in Florida and Connecticut. Rather than being called **jai alai** or **pelota vasca,** it is often called **frontón,** the name of the court.

LEVELING

E: Reading 1

A: Reading 2

Answers to ¿Comprendes?

1. pelota vasca
2. jugadores
3. blanco, blanca, roja
4. alpargatas
5. cesta
6. frontón
7. paredes
8. devolver
9. unas ciento cincuenta

Geography Connection

The Basque country has a great deal of beautiful scenery, but it is also a very industrial area. The Basques, **los vascos,** speak a mystery language —**el vasco** in Spanish, **euskera** in Basque. There is a strong separatist movement in the Basque country.

Conexiones

National Standards

Connections
This reading about archeology establishes a connection with another discipline, allowing students to reinforce and further their knowledge of the social sciences through the study of Spanish.

¡OJO! The readings in the **Conexiones** section are optional. They focus on some of the major disciplines taught in schools and universities. The vocabulary is useful for discussing such topics as history, literature, art, economics, business, science, etc. You may choose any of the following ways to do the readings in the **Conexiones** sections.

Independent reading Have students read the selections and do the post-reading activities as homework, which you collect. This option is least intrusive on class time and requires a minimum of teacher involvement.

Homework with in-class follow-up Assign the readings and post-reading activities as homework. Review and discuss the material in class the next day.

Intensive in-class activity This option includes a pre-reading vocabulary presentation, in-class reading and discussion, assignment of the activities for homework, and a discussion of the assignment in class the following day.

LEVELING

A: Reading

Conexiones

Las ciencias sociales

La arqueología

Archeology is a fascinating field. Archeologists travel to every corner of the globe searching for places to excavate and study the ruins of ancient civilizations. There have been interesting archeological discoveries in Latin America where many pre-Columbian civilizations existed long before the arrival of the Spaniards. Let's read about some of these archeological sites. A few famous ones revealed some interesting information about sports and games in pre-Columbian cultures.

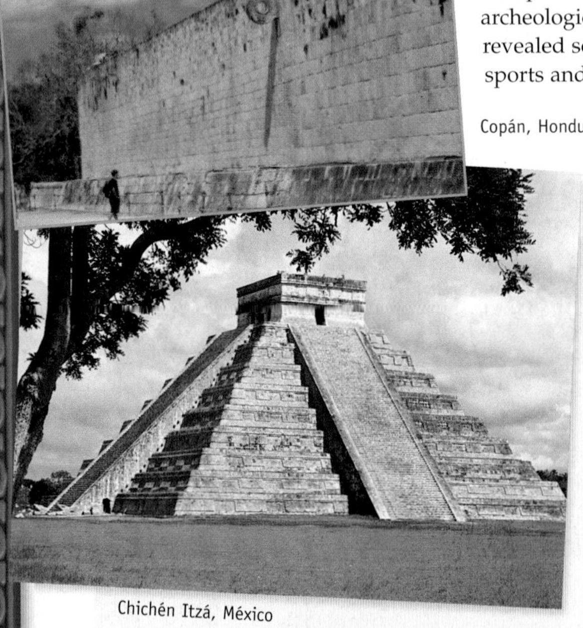

Copán, Honduras

Chichén Itzá, México

La arqueología

La arqueología es el estudio de los monumentos y artefactos de la antigüedad. Los arqueólogos excavan y estudian los objetos antiguos hechos o producidos por seres humanos. En Latinoamérica hay muchos sitios arqueológicos famosos. Algunos tienen canchas de pelota que datan del siglo ocho.

Honduras y México

En Copán en Honduras y en Chichén Itzá en México hay ruinas de varias canchas de pelota. La cancha en Copán data del año 775 después de Cristo. Es interesante notar que los juegos de los mayas de Copán y los juegos de los mayas de Chichén Itzá son bastante similares. Los indios usan una pelota grande de goma[1] y no pueden tocar[2] la pelota con las manos. El juego es una diversión[3] pero en Chichén Itzá tiene también sentido religioso. Después del juego sacrifican a los jugadores que ganan.

[1]goma *rubber* [2]tocar *touch* [3]diversión *amusement*

Learning from Photos

(page 224 top) This is the ball court in Copán, Honduras. It was here that the Mayan athletes played before thousands of spectators. The ball court dates from 775 A.D. and was built upon ruins of two former ball courts. The object of the game seems to have been to bounce the ball up the slanted walls and hit one of the carved, stone goals at the top. The players were not allowed to use their hands, arms, or feet. The ball was large and made of solid rubber. It appears that the game was a combination of football and handball. In the Copán museum there are scenes of the ballplayers in action.

Chichén Itzá, México

Puerto Rico

Recientemente hay una excavación arqueológica cerca de Ponce en Puerto Rico. ¿Y qué descubren? Descubren una cancha de pelota. Y el juego que juegan los indios taínos de Puerto Rico es parecido o similar al juego de los mayas de Centroamérica. El juego de los taínos es el batú. El batú es un juego de diversión pero tiene también sentido religioso. En el juego hay dos bandos o equipos. Juegan con una pelota de goma. Uno de los bandos lanza la pelota al otro bando. El otro bando tiene que devolver la pelota. Y no pueden usar las manos. Tienen que lanzar la pelota con la pierna, la rodilla o el brazo pero no pueden tocar la pelota con la mano. El equipo que deja rodar[4] la pelota por el suelo[5] el mayor número de veces[6] pierde el juego.

[4]deja rodar *lets roll*
[5]suelo *ground*
[6]mayor número de veces *greatest number of times*

For more information about archeological sites in the Spanish-speaking world, go to the Glencoe Spanish Web site: spanish.glencoe.com

Ponce, Puerto Rico

¿Comprendes?

¡A discutir! Discutan. *(Discuss with your classmates.)*
There are many interesting and unbelievable things in this reading selection. This is particularly true when one realizes that the games took place centuries ago and that there is quite a distance between these areas of Central America and Puerto Rico. Discuss some of these interesting facts. You may wish to have your discussion in English.

Conexiones

PRESENTATION

Las ciencias sociales
La arqueología

Step 1 This selection makes students aware that in areas of the Spanish-speaking world there are archeological sites that are as important and impressive as those in Greece, Italy, and Egypt.

Step 2 Have students skim the reading to familiarize themselves with some of this interesting information. It is not necessary that they learn it in depth.

Learning from Photos

(page 225 top) The pyramid pictured here is **el Castillo.** On top of the castle there is a temple dedicated to Kukulcán, or Quetzalcóatl, the famous leader who was turned into a god and incarnated as a plumed serpent.

There are seven ball courts in Chichén Itzá. One is the largest in Mesoamerica. Its two parallel walls are 272 feet long. Historians and archeologists believe that it was the winners who were sacrificed. It was thought to be the ultimate honor.

(page 225 middle) This park in Ponce, Puerto Rico, has many artifacts of the **taíno** Indians.

Answers to ¿Comprendes?

Discussion should focus on the following:

- The courts discovered at the archeological sites indicate that these games were played centuries ago.
- The game the Taíno Indians of Puerto Rico played was very similar to that of the Central American Mayas.
- In the game played by the Mayas of Chichén Itzá, the winners were sacrificed!

Career Connection

La arqueología Many important archeological sites and digs are located in the Spanish-speaking world. Students interested in a career in this area would need a reading knowledge of Spanish for research purposes and good verbal skills to communicate with native speakers in the field.

¡Te toca a ti!

Use what you have learned

Recycling

These activities allow students to use the vocabulary and structure from this chapter in completely open-ended, real-life situations.

PRESENTATION

Encourage students to say as much as possible when they do these activities. Tell them not to be afraid to make mistakes, since the goal of the activities is real-life communication. If someone in the group makes an error, allow the others to politely correct him or her. Let students choose the activities they would like to do.

You may wish to divide students into pairs or groups. Encourage students to elaborate on the basic theme and to be creative. They may use props, pictures, or posters if they wish.

LEVELING

These activities encompass all three levels. All students will be able to do them at a sophistication level commensurate with their ability in Spanish. Some students will be able to speak for several minutes, and others may be able to give just a few sentences. This is to be expected when students are functioning completely on their own generating their own language to the best of their ability.

5 Be sure that within each group there is at least one student who is interested in sports. The other two students should write down their questions.

6 Each sporting event should include the date, time, place, and the names of the two opposing teams.

¡Te toca a ti!

Use what you have learned

HABLAR **1** **Soy muy aficionado(a) a...**

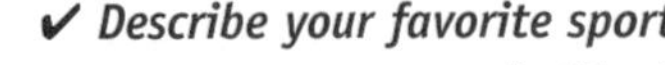

✔ *Describe your favorite sport*

Name a sport you really like. Then give a description of that sport.

HABLAR **2** **Una entrevista con el capitán**

✔ *Ask someone questions about a sports team*

You are to interview the captain (your classmate) of one of the school's sports teams for the local Spanish language television station. Try to find out as much information as possible. Then change roles.

HABLAR **3** **Los deportes**

✔ *Compare the sports you like and don't like*

Get together with a classmate. Take turns describing sports you like and don't like.

HABLAR **4** **Juego** **¡Adivina quién es!**

✔ *Talk about your favorite sports hero*

Think of your favorite sports hero. Tell a classmate something about him or her. Your classmate will ask you three questions about your hero before guessing who it is. Then reverse roles and you guess who your classmate's hero is.

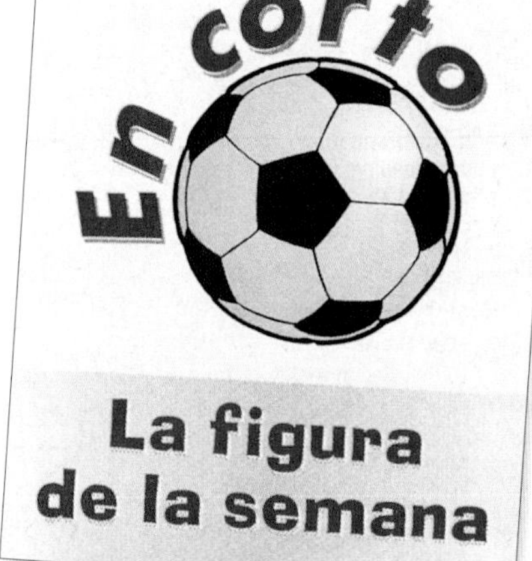

La estrella es...

DON BALON LA REVISTA NÚMERO 1 DEL FÚTBOL

ANSWERS TO ¡Te toca a ti!

1 *Answers will vary. Encourage students to describe a team sport so they can use the chapter vocabulary.*

2 *Answers will vary but should include stem-changing verbs such as* preferir *and* querer, *the verbs* gustar, interesar, *and* aburrir, *and vocabulary related to sports. Students may wish to use the conversation on page 218 as a model.*

3 *Answers will vary but should include the verb* gustar *and the chapter vocabulary related to sports.*

4 *Answers will vary, but students should use the related vocabulary from the chapter. Students may also wish to use the verb* ser *with the descriptive adjectives learned in* Palabras 1, Capítulo 1 *to describe physical characteristics of their hero and where their hero is from.*

Un reportaje

✔ Write a description of a sporting event

Work in groups of three. One of you is the captain of one of the school's teams. The other two are sports reporters for a Spanish newspaper. The two reporters will prepare an interview with the captain about the team's last game. The reporters will edit the information they get from the interview and write their report for tomorrow's paper. The report can be in the present tense.

Horario deportivo

✔ Post a schedule of sporting events

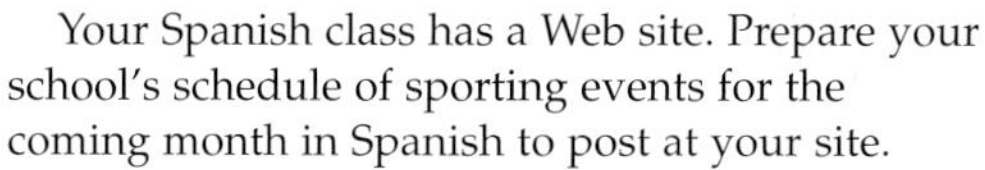

Your Spanish class has a Web site. Prepare your school's schedule of sporting events for the coming month in Spanish to post at your site.

Writing Strategy

Gathering information If your writing project deals with a topic you are not familiar with, you may need to gather information before you begin to write. Some of your best sources are the library, the Internet, and people who know something about the topic. Even if you plan to interview people about the topic, it may be necessary to do some research in the library or on the Internet to acquire enough knowledge to prepare good interview questions.

La Copa mundial

Many of you already know that the World Cup is a soccer championship. Try to give a description of the World Cup as best you can in Spanish. If you are not familiar with it, you will need to do some research. It might be interesting to take what you know or find out about the World Cup and compare it to the World Series in baseball. Gather information about both these championships and write a report.

¡Te toca a ti!

PRACTICE

Writing Development

Have students keep a notebook or portfolio containing their best written work from each chapter. These selected writings can be based on assignments from the Student Textbook and the Workbook. The activities on page 227 are examples of writing assignments that may be included in each student's portfolio. On page 82 in the Workbook, students will begin to develop an organized autobiography **(Mi autobiografía).** These workbook pages may also become a part of their portfolio.

Answers to ¡Te toca a ti!

5 *Answers will vary but should include the sports-related vocabulary from the chapter.*

6 *Answers will vary but should include the sports-related vocabulary from the chapter. Students should include-the date, event(s), team names, times, etc.*

7 *Answers will vary depending on the variety of information sources each student uses.*

Writing Strategy

Gathering Information Have students read the Writing Strategy on page 227. Encourage students to use the Internet as part of their research. Also encourage them to ask native Spanish speakers in their school or community about the World Cup.

Resource Manager

Communication Transparency C 7
Quizzes, pages 32–37
Performance Assessment, Task 7
Tests, pages 99–112
Situation Cards, Chapter 7
ExamView® Pro, Chapter 7
Maratón mental Videoquiz, Chapter 7

Assessment

This is a pre-test for students to take before you administer the chapter test. Note that each section is cross-referenced so students can easily find the material they have to review in case they made errors. You may use Assessment Answers Transparency A 7 to do the assessment in class, or you may assign this assessment for homework. You can correct the assessment yourself, or you may prefer to project the answers on the overhead in class.

Glencoe Technology

MINDJOGGER VHS/DVD

You may wish to help your students prepare for the chapter test by playing the MindJogger game show. Teams will compete against each other to review chapter vocabulary and structure and sharpen listening comprehension skills.

Vocabulario

To review **Palabras 1**, turn to pages 202–203.

1 Escojan. *(Choose.)*

1. El campo de fútbol está en ____.
   a. la portería **b.** el tablero **c.** el estadio
2. Los ____ miran el partido.
   a. porteros **b.** espectadores **c.** jugadores
3. El portero ____ el balón.
   a. bloquea **b.** marca **c.** gana
4. En un partido de fútbol, el jugador tira o lanza el balón con ____.
   a. la mano **b.** el tablero **c.** el pie

To review **Palabras 2**, turn to pages 206–207.

2 Completen. *(Complete.)*

5. En un juego de béisbol, el pícher ____ la pelota.
6. Otro jugador batea y ____ de una base a otra.
7. La jugadora atrapa la pelota con el ____.
8. Hay nueve ____ en un juego de béisbol.
9. En un juego de básquetbol, el jugador ____ con el balón.
10. El jugador de básquetbol marca un tanto cuando ____.

Answers to Assessment

1

1. c
2. b
3. a
4. c

2

5. lanza
6. corre
7. guante
8. entradas
9. dribla
10. encesta

Music Connection

Canta con Justo
The song **El gran campeón** will be easy for learners of all ability levels. It will help students practice vocabulary related to sports introduced in this chapter. You can find this song on Track 1 of the music CD.

Assessment

Estructura

3 Contesten. *(Answer.)*

11. ¿Quieres jugar al fútbol?
12. ¿Quieren ustedes ganar?
13. ¿Prefieres el fútbol o el básquetbol?
14. ¿Qué deporte prefieren ustedes?
15. ¿Puedes ver el partido en la televisión?
16. ¿Pueden ustedes hablar con los jugadores?

To review **stem-changing verbs,** turn to pages 210 and 213.

4 Completen. *(Complete.)*

17–18. Ellos ____ al béisbol y nosotros ____ al fútbol. (jugar)
19. ¿Tú ____ a jugar a qué hora? (empezar)

5 Completen. *(Complete.)*

20–21. Me gust__ mucho los deportes. No me aburr__.
22. ¿Te interes__ más ver una película o una emisión deportiva?

To review **interesar, aburrir,** and **gustar,** turn to page 215.

Cultura

6 ¿Sí o no? *(True or false?)*

23. El estadio Santiago Bernabéu es un equipo de fútbol español.
24. Todos los jugadores del Real Madrid, un equipo español, son españoles.
25. Todos los jugadores de un equipo que juega en la Copa mundial tienen que ser de la misma nacionalidad.

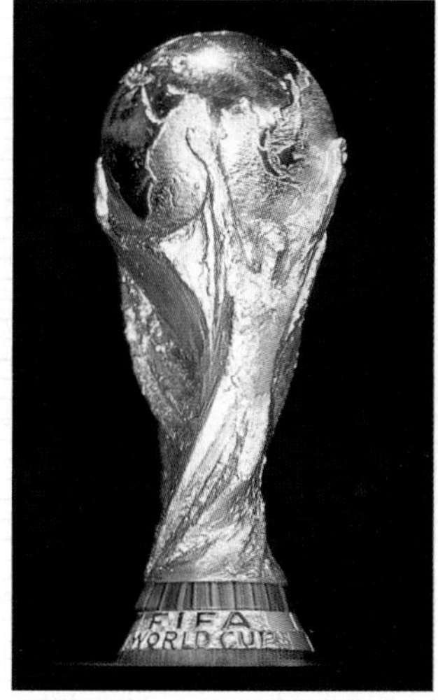

La Copa de la FIFA

To review this cultural information, turn to page 220.

SPANISH Online

The **Glencoe Spanish Web** site (**spanish.glencoe.com**) offers options that enable you and your students to experience the Spanish-speaking world via the Internet. For each **Capítulo,** there are activities, games, and quizzes. In addition, an *Enrichment* section offers students an opportunity to visit Web sites related to the theme of the chapter.

FOLDABLES™ Study Organizer — Dinah Zike's Study Guides

Your students may wish to use Foldable 9 to organize, display, and arrange data as they learn how to talk about how they feel in Spanish. You may wish to encourage them to add information from each chapter as they continue to expand upon their ability to describe situations and emotions.

A *paper file folder organizer* foldable is also ideal for having students add information to different categories over a period of time.

Chapter Projects

Un artículo Have students prepare a short sports column in Spanish for the school newspaper. They could make this a regular feature.

ANSWERS TO 

3

11. Sí, (No, no) quiero jugar al fútbol.
12. Sí, (No, no) queremos ganar.
13. Prefiero el fútbol (el básquetbol).
14. Preferimos ___.
15. Sí, (No, no) puedo ver el partido en la televisión.
16. Sí, (No, no) podemos hablar con los jugadores.

4

17. juegan
18. jugamos
19. empiezas

5

20. gustan
21. aburren
22. interesa

6

23. No
24. No
25. Sí

¡Hablo como un pro!

This unique page gives students the opportunity to speak freely and say whatever they can, using the vocabulary and structures they have learned in the chapter. The illustration serves to remind students of precisely what they know how to say in Spanish. There are no activities that students do not have the ability to describe or talk about in Spanish. The art not only depicts the vocabulary and content of this chapter, but also reinforces what they learned in previous chapters.

You may wish to use this page in many ways. Some possibilities are to have students do the following:

1. Look at the illustration and identify items by giving the correct Spanish words.
2. Make up sentences about what they see in the illustration.
3. Make up questions about the illustration. They can call on another class member to respond if you do this as a class activity, or you may prefer to allow students to work in small groups. This activity is extremely beneficial because it enables students to actively use interrogative words.
4. Answer questions you ask them about the illustration.
5. Work in pairs and make up a conversation based on the illustration.
6. Look at the illustration and give a complete oral review of what they see.
7. Look at the illustration and write a paragraph (or essay) about it.

You can also use this page as an assessment or testing tool, taking into account individual differences by having students go from simple to quite complicated tasks. The assessment can be either oral or written.

¡Hablo como un pro!

Tell all you can about this illustration.

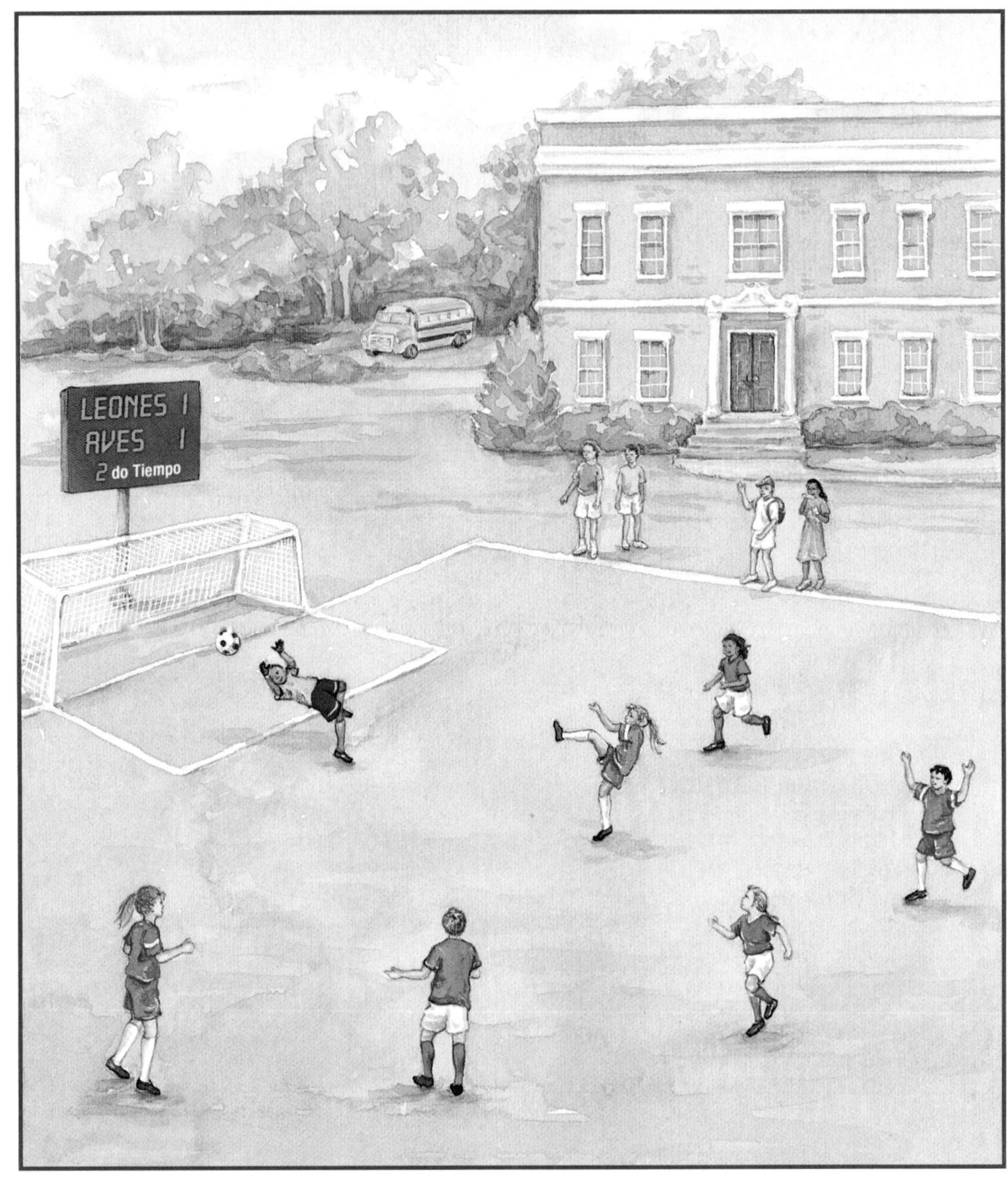

You may wish to use the rubrics provided on pages T20–T21 as you give students the following directions.

1. Identify the topic or situation of the illustration.
2. Give the Spanish words for as many items as you can.
3. Think of as many sentences as you can to describe the illustration.
4. Go over your sentences and put them in the best sequencing to give a coherent story based on the illustration.

Vocabulario

Identifying sports

el fútbol
el béisbol
el básquetbol, el baloncesto

Describing a sports event in general

el estadio
el/la espectador(a)
el campo
la cancha
el partido
el/la jugador(a)
el equipo
el tablero indicador
el tanto
empatado(a)
empezar, comenzar
tirar
lanzar
perder
ganar
entre
contra

Describing a football game

el fútbol
el balón
el tiempo
el/la portero(a)
la portería
jugar
bloquear
parar
marcar un tanto
meter un gol

Describing a baseball game

el béisbol
el/la bateador(a)
el pícher, el lanzador
el cátcher, el receptor
el jardinero
el guante
el platillo
el jonrón
la base
la entrada
la pelota
el bate
batear
correr
atrapar
devolver

Describing a basketball game

el básquetbol, el baloncesto
el cesto, la canasta
driblar
pasar
encestar
meter

How well do you know your vocabulary?

- Choose a sport from the list.
- Ask classmates to give you as many words as they can associated with the sport you chose.

Expressing likes and interests

gustar
interesar
aburrir

Identifying some parts of the body

el pie
la pierna
la rodilla
la mano
el brazo
la cabeza

Other useful expressions

poder
querer
volver
preferir
a veces
siempre
izquierdo(a)
derecho(a)

VIDEOTUR

Episodio 7

In this video episode, you will join Julián and Alberto as they sign up for a new extracurricular activity. See page 498 for more information.

Vocabulario

Vocabulary Review

The words and phrases in the **Vocabulario** have been taught for productive use in this chapter. They are summarized here as a resource for both student and teacher. This list also serves as a convenient resource for the **¡Te toca a ti!** activities on pages 226 and 227. There are approximately fourteen cognates in this vocabulary list. Have students find them.

VIDEO VHS/DVD

The Video Program allows students to see how the chapter vocabulary and structures are used by native speakers within an engaging story line. For maximum reinforcement, show the video episode as a final activity for Chapter 1.

Reaching All Students

For the Younger Students

Tarjetas de colección Many younger students collect baseball and football cards. You may have them bring some to class and talk about their favorite teams and players.

Afiches Have groups of students make posters for a sports day at your school. They should include the date, event(s), team names, times, etc.

Biografías Have students choose their favorite athlete. Have them prepare a short biography about him or her.

¡OJO! You will notice that the vocabulary list here is not translated. This has been done intentionally, since we feel that by the time students have finished the material in the chapter they should be familiar with the meanings of all the words. If there are several words they still do not know, we recommend that they refer to the **Palabras 1** and **2** sections in the chapter or go to the dictionaries at the end of this book to find the meanings. However, if you prefer that your students have the English translations, please refer to Vocabulary Transparency 7.1, where you will find all these words with their translations.

Preview

This section reviews the salient points from Chapters 5–7. In the **Conversación** students will review sports vocabulary, regular **-ir** verbs, and some stem-changing verbs in context. In the **Estructura** sections, they will study the conjugations of regular **-er** and **-ir** verbs, stem-changing verbs, possessive adjectives, and the conjugations of verbs like **interesar, aburrir,** and **gustar.** They will practice these structures as they talk about a Spanish party.

Resource Manager

Workbook: Check-Up 2, pages 83–86
Tests, pages 113–121
Performance Assessment, Tasks 5–7

PRESENTATION

Conversación

Step 1 Have students open their books to page 232 and repeat the conversation after you in unison.

Step 2 Then call on a pair of students to read the first half of the conversation.

Step 3 Intersperse questions from the **¿Comprendes?** section.

Step 4 Do the same with the second half of the conversation.

Learning from Realia

(page 232) This ticket is for a game in Caracas. Tell students **Bs** stands for **bolívares,** the monetary unit of Venezuela.

Conversación

Un partido importante

Julio Alberto, Carlos y yo vamos al Café Miramar. ¿Quieres ir con nosotros?
Alberto No, Julio, no puedo porque quiero ver el partido.
Julio ¿De qué partido hablas?
Alberto Los Osos juegan contra los Tigres y mi equipo favorito son los Osos.
Julio ¿Vas al estadio a ver el partido?
Alberto No. Las entradas (los boletos) cuestan mucho. Voy a ver el partido en la televisión.
Julio ¿A qué hora empieza?
Alberto A las siete y media. ¿Quieres ver el partido también?
Julio Sí. ¿Dónde vives?
Alberto Vivo en la calle Central, número 32.
Julio Bien. ¡Hasta pronto!

¿Comprendes?

Los tres amigos Contesten. *(Answer.)*

1. ¿Adónde quieren ir los dos muchachos?
2. ¿Invitan a Alberto?
3. ¿Puede ir Alberto?
4. ¿Por qué no?
5. ¿Por qué no va al estadio?
6. ¿Dónde va a ver el partido?
7. ¿A qué hora empieza?
8. ¿Van los muchachos a casa de Alberto?

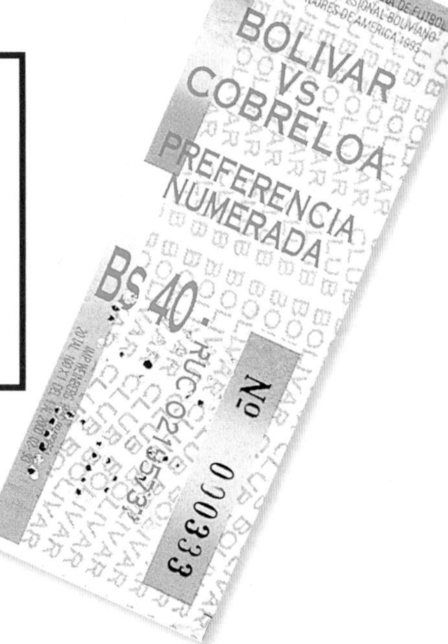

Answers to ¿Comprendes?

1. Los dos muchachos quieren ir al Café Miramar.
2. Sí, invitan a Alberto.
3. No, no puede ir.
4. Quiere ver el partido de su equipo favorito.
5. No va al estadio porque las entradas cuestan mucho.
6. Va a ver el partido en la televisión.
7. Empieza a las siete y media.
8. Sí, los muchachos van a su casa.

Estructura

Verbos en -er, -ir

Review the forms of regular **-er** and **-ir** verbs.

COMER	**como**	**comes**	**come**	**comemos**	***coméis***	**comen**
VIVIR	**vivo**	**vives**	**vive**	**vivimos**	***vivís***	**viven**

Tú y tus amigos

Contesten. *(Answer.)*

1. ¿Qué comes cuando vas a un café?
2. ¿Qué bebes cuando estás en un café?
3. ¿Qué aprenden tú y tus amigos en la escuela?
4. ¿Qué leen ustedes en la clase de inglés?
5. ¿Qué escriben ustedes?
6. ¿Comprenden los alumnos cuando el profesor de español habla?
7. ¿Reciben ustedes notas buenas en todas las asignaturas?

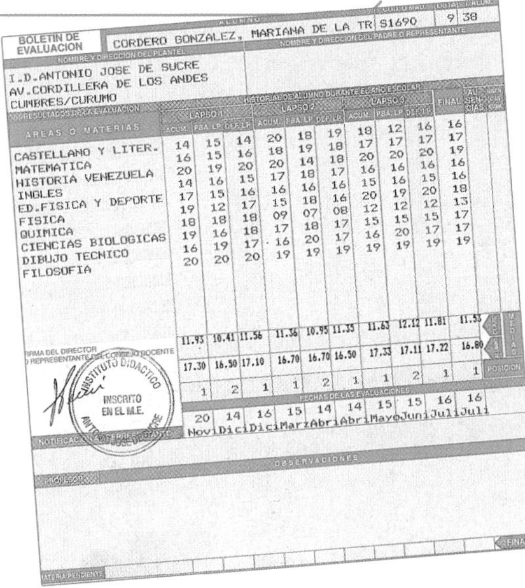

BOLETIN DE EVALUACION

ALUMNO: CORDERO GONZALEZ, MARIANA DE LA TR — S1690 — 9 — 38

NOMBRE Y DIRECCION DEL PLANTEL: I.D.ANTONIO JOSE DE SUCRE, AV.CORDILLERA DE LOS ANDES, CUMBRES/CURUMO

NOMBRE Y DIRECCION DEL PADRE O REPRESENTANTE

RESULTADOS DE LA EVALUACION — HISTORIAL DE ALUMNO DURANTE EL AÑO ESCOLAR

AREAS O MATERIAS	LAPSO 1 ACUM.	LAPSO 1 PBA. LP	LAPSO 1 DEF. LP	LAPSO 2 ACUM.	LAPSO 2 PBA. LP	LAPSO 2 DEF. LP	LAPSO 3 ACUM.	LAPSO 3 PBA. LP	LAPSO 3 DEF. LP	FINAL
CASTELLANO Y LITER.	14	15	14	20	18	19	18	12	16	16
MATEMATICA	16	15	16	18	19	18	17	17	17	17
HISTORIA VENEZUELA	20	19	20	20	14	18	20	20	20	19
INGLES	14	16	15	17	18	17	16	16	16	16
ED.FISICA Y DEPORTE	17	15	16	16	16	16	15	16	15	16
FISICA	19	12	17	15	18	16	20	19	20	18
QUIMICA	18	18	18	09	07	08	12	12	12	13
CIENCIAS BIOLOGICAS	19	16	18	17	18	17	15	15	15	17
DIBUJO TECNICO	16	19	17	16	20	17	16	20	17	17
FILOSOFIA	20	20	20	19	19	19	19	19	19	19
MEDIAS	11.93	10.41	11.56	11.36	10.95	11.35	11.63	12.12	11.81	11.53
	17.30	16.50	17.10	16.70	16.70	16.50	17.33	17.11	17.22	16.80
POSICION	1	2	1	1	2	1	1	2	1	1
FECHAS DE LAS EVALUACIONES	20 Novi	14 Dici	16 Dici	15 Marz	14 Abri	14 Abri	15 Mayo	15 Juni	16 Juli	16 Juli

FIRMA DEL DIRECTOR O REPRESENTANTE DEL CONSEJO DOCENTE

INSTITUTO DIDACTICO — INSCRITO EN EL M.E. — ANTONIO JOSE DE SUCRE

NOTIFICACION AL REPRESENTANTE

OBSERVACIONES

PROFESOR

FINAL

MATERIA PENDIENTE

Verbos de cambio radical

1. Review the forms of stem-changing verbs.

			e → ie			
EMPEZAR	**empiezo**	**empiezas**	**empieza**	**empezamos**	***empezáis***	**empiezan**
PERDER	**pierdo**	**pierdes**	**pierde**	**perdemos**	***perdéis***	**pierden**
			o → ue			
VOLVER	**vuelvo**	**vuelves**	**vuelve**	**volvemos**	***volvéis***	**vuelven**
PODER	**puedo**	**puedes**	**puede**	**podemos**	***podéis***	**pueden**

2. Review the forms of the verb **tener.** Note that this verb also has a change in the stem.

TENER	**tengo**	**tienes**	**tiene**	**tenemos**	***tenéis***	**tienen**

CAPÍTULOS 5-7

PRESENTATION

Verbos en -er, -ir

Step 1 Write the verbs on the board and have students read all forms aloud.

Step 2 Have students give another **-er** and another **-ir** verb and supply the endings.

Step 3 Now have students do Activity 1 orally before assigning it for homework.

PRESENTATION

Verbos de cambio radical

Step 1 Follow the same procedure as outlined above to review these verbs. For additional practice, have students make up original sentences with each of the verbs before doing the activities on page 234.

ANSWERS TO Repaso

1. Como ___ cuando voy a un café.
2. Bebo ___ cuando estoy en un café.
3. Aprendemos muchas cosas en la escuela.
4. Leemos novelas en la clase de inglés.
5. Escribimos composiciones.
6. Sí (No), los alumnos (no) comprenden cuando el profesor de español habla.
7. Sí (No), nosotros (no) recibimos notas buenas en todas las asignaturas.

PRACTICE

2 This activity practices irregular and stem-changing verbs in a sports context.

3 After going over Activity 3, call on a student to summarize the information in his or her own words.

PRESENTATION

Adjetivos posesivos

Step 1 Go over the forms of the possessive adjectives with the students. Ask them questions in Spanish to be sure they know the meaning of each adjective form and in which context it is used—masculine, feminine, singular, or plural.

PRACTICE

4 Have students provide the name of their town and street.
Expansion: After going over Activity 4, have students describe their own home orally.

Learning from Photos

(page 234) Students have already learned that **una colonia** is the word used to refer to the sections of Mexico City. Two very upscale **colonias** that have homes such as the one shown here are Chapultepec and Polanco.

2 **Historieta Un juego de béisbol**
Completen. *(Complete.)*

El juego de béisbol __1__ (empezar) a las tres y media. Habla Teresa: —Hoy yo __2__ (querer) ser la pícher.

La verdad es que Teresa __3__ (ser) una pícher muy buena. Ella __4__ (jugar) muy bien. Nosotros __5__ (tener) un equipo bueno. Todos nosotros __6__ (jugar) bien. Nuestro equipo no __7__ (perder) mucho. Hoy yo __8__ (tener) que jugar muy bien porque nuestro equipo no __9__ (poder) perder. __10__ (Tener) que ganar.

3 **Entrevista** Contesten personalmente.
(Answer about yourself.)

1. ¿Cuántos años tienes?
2. ¿Cuántos hermanos tienes?
3. ¿Cuántos años tienen ellos?
4. ¿Tienen ustedes un perro o un gato?

Adjetivos posesivos

Review the forms of possessive adjectives.

mi, mis	**nuestro, nuestra, nuestros, nuestras**
tu, tus	
su, sus	**su, sus**

4 **Historieta Nuestra casa**
Completen. *(Complete.)*

Vivo en __1__. __2__ casa está en la calle __3__. __4__ padres tienen un carro. Y yo tengo una bicicleta. __5__ carro está en el garaje y __6__ bicicleta está en el garaje también. Nosotros tenemos un perro. __7__ perro está en el jardín. El jardín alrededor de __8__ casa es bonito. Mi hermano y __9__ amigos siempre juegan en el jardín.

Málaga, España

Answers to Repaso

2

1. empieza
2. quiero
3. es
4. juega
5. tenemos
6. jugamos
7. pierde
8. tengo
9. puede
10. Tiene

3

1. Tengo ___ años.
2. Tengo ___ hermanos. (No tengo hermanos.)
3. *Answers will vary.*
4. Sí, tenemos un perro (un gato). (No, no tenemos un perro [un gato].)

4

1. *(name of town)*
2. Mi
3. *(name of street)*
4. Mis
5. Nuestro (Su)
6. mi
7. Nuestro
8. nuestra
9. sus

Verbos como **interesar, aburrir, gustar**

Review the construction for verbs such as **gustar**, **interesar**, and **aburrir**.

¿Te gusta el arte?	**Sí, me gusta el arte.** **El arte me interesa mucho.** **No me aburre nada.**
¿Te gustan los deportes?	**Los deportes, sí, me gustan mucho.** **Los deportes me interesan.** **No me aburren nada.**

5 **Información** Den cuantas respuestas posibles.
(Give as many answers as possible.)

1. ¿Qué te gusta?
2. ¿Qué te interesa?
3. ¿Qué te aburre?

6 **Una fiesta familiar** With a classmate, look at the illustration. Take turns describing the illustration, giving as much detail as you can.

Literary Companion

You may wish to read the adaptation of «Una moneda de oro» by Francisco Monterde. This literary selection is found on pages 472–477.

PRESENTATION

Verbos como **interesar, aburrir, gustar**

Step 1 Have students open their books to page 235 and read the explanation with them.

Step 2 Have students identify the subject of each sentence. Point out to them that if the subject is plural, the verb is plural.

PRACTICE

5 If students have problems doing Activity 5, review some of the activities in Chapter 7, pages 215–217.

6 You can also have the students make up questions about the illustration. Then have them ask their classmates the questions.

Literary Companion

When you finish this review section, if you wish, have students read the adaptation of **«Una moneda de oro»** by Francisco Monterde on pages 472–477.

ANSWERS TO Repaso

5

1. Me gusta(n) ___. (___ me gusta[n].)
2. Me interesa(n) ___. (___ me interesa[n].)
3. Me aburre(n) ___. (___ me aburre[n].)

6 *Answers will vary, but students should use the vocabulary from Chapters 5 and 6.*

People EN ESPAÑOL

Entérate Cono sur

This section was prepared by Time Learning Ventures of Time Incorporated. Its purpose is to give students greater insight, through visual images and fun articles, into the culture and people of the **Cono sur.** You may wish to explain to your students that Argentina, Chile, Paraguay, and Uruguay are the four countries included when we talk about this region.

Have students look at the photographs and read the articles. Encourage the students to talk about what they've seen and read. Let them say anything they can, using the vocabulary they have learned to this point.

Though they are most commonly known for their troubled political and economic history, Argentina, Chile, Paraguay and Uruguay should also be known for their stunning landscapes, environmental importance, and strong cultural traditions. From the waterfalls of Argentina and the mystery of Chile's Easter Island, to the favored dances in Uruguay and Paraguay, these **Cono sur** countries are an endless source of geographic and cultural exploration.

People EN ESPAÑOL

Entérate Cono sur

Monumentos naturales e históricos

Argentina tiene nueve lugares que la UNESCO considera Patrimonio de la Humanidad. Entre ellos se destacan:

Quebrada de Humahuaca

Quebrada de Humahuaca Montañas de intensos colores que el ser humano habita[1] desde hace 10 mil años.

Parque Nacional de Ischigualasto Más conocido como el "Valle de la Luna", es un terreno de formas fantásticas y fósiles de vegetales, dinosaurios y otros animales de hace 180 millones de años.

Cueva[2] de las Manos Cueva de la provincia de Santa Cruz, con más de 800 impresiones de manos y otras pinturas rupestres[3], a la que los científicos calculan unos 9,300 a 13,000 años de antigüedad.

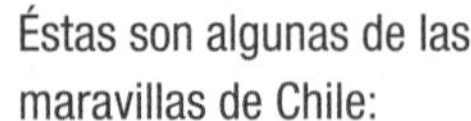
Parque Nacional Los Glaciares En la provincia de Santa Cruz hay 47 glaciares mayores. El más conocido e imponente[4] es el Perito Moreno.

Cataratas[5] del Iguazú Son las cataratas más anchas[6] del mundo, entre Argentina, Paraguay y Brasil.

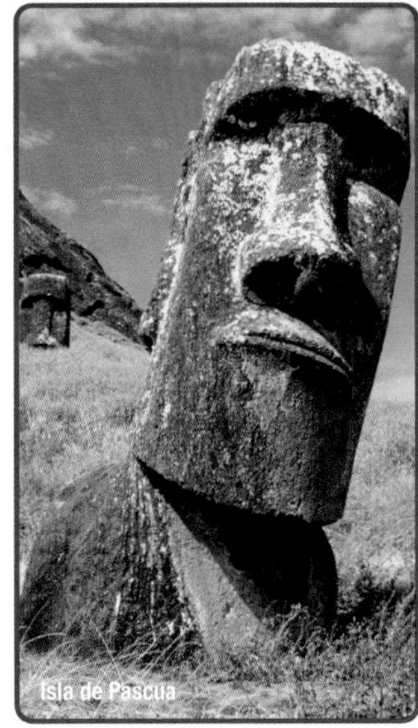
Isla de Pascua

Éstas son algunas de las maravillas de Chile:

Isla de Pascua[7] Isla del Pacífico; aún hoy la cultura de sus antiguos[8] habitantes se considera muy avanzada, especialmente por la arquitectura y los conocimientos[9] de astronomía.

Valparaíso Se la llama Perla del Pacífico. Los chilenos la consideran su capital cultural. Toda ella es un museo, con tranvías y ascensores[10] para ascender por los cerros[11].

Isla de Chiloé Tiene palafitos[12], que son construcciones de madera, y varias iglesias declaradas Patrimonio de la Humanidad.

Colonia del Sacramento

En Uruguay tienes que visitar esta joya de ciudad:

Colonia del Sacramento Es la única ciudad fundada por los portugueses en las costas del Río de la Plata. Todas las tardes, los jóvenes de esta ciudad colonial se reúnen a charlar y a ver las maravillosas puestas de sol[13] sobre el río.

Y si vas por Paraguay, no olvides visitar estos bellos lugares:

Ciudad del Este Es parte del complejo de parques donde se hallan las Cataratas del Iguazú.

Misiones de Jesús de Tavarangue y Santísima Trinidad Estas construcciones se consideran Patrimonio de la Humanidad desde 1993.

[1] habita: *inhabits*
[2] cueva: *cave*
[3] pinturas rupestres: *cave paintings*
[4] imponente: *impressive*
[5] cataratas: *waterfalls*
[6] anchas: *wide*
[7] Isla de Pascua: *Easter Island*
[8] antiguos: *ancient*
[9] conocimientos: *knowledge*
[10] ascensores: *elevators*
[11] cerros: *hills*
[12] palafitos: *stilt houses*
[13] puestas de sol: *sunsets*

LEVELING

E: Activity A
A: Activity B
C: Activity C

el mundo salvaje

Gigantes del reino vegetal en Chile
Los bosques de araucarias se consideran monumentos nacionales en Chile. Algunos de estos árboles tienen 600 a 1,200 años de edad.

Araucarias de Chile

La Patagonia argentina
■ ¿Te imaginas un bosque hecho piedra? El bosque petrificado de Jaramillo mide 10,000 hectáreas y en él se encuentran los árboles petrificados más grandes del mundo.
■ Si tienes que ir a Usuahia, la capital de Tierra del Fuego, vas a estar en la ciudad más austral[1] del planeta.
■ ¿Te interesan las ballenas? Ver jugar a estos gigantes horas y horas con sus crías[2] es un espectáculo[3] que se disfruta[4] desde las playas de Península de Valdés.
■ Al pingüino de magallanes no le preocupa el frío. No hay nadie como este animalito para soportar[5] las bajas temperaturas.

La Patagonia

Piedras semipreciosas del Uruguay
Muchas ágatas y amatistas que adornan joyas[6] y decorados en todo el mundo son uruguayas.

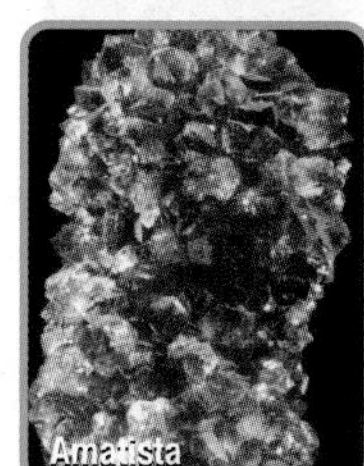
Amatista

[1] austral: *southernmost*
[2] crías: *calves*
[3] espectáculo: *show*
[4] se disfruta: *one enjoys*
[5] soportar: *withstand*
[6] joyas: *jewelry*

SUCESOS

Mariel Davesa vive contra viento y marea[1]. Es campeona nacional de *windsurf* en Estados Unidos.

Eva Perón es un personaje de la política argentina. Es tema de una ópera y Madonna la representa en la película *Evita*.

Un día, **Pablo Neruda** escribe a un amor: "Puedo escribir los versos más tristes esta noche". Hoy grupos de rock como **Maná** y **Los Fabulosos Cadillacs** y cantantes como **Alejandro Sanz** y **Beto Cuevas** rinden tributo[2] en un CD a este famoso poeta chileno.

Beto Cuevas

[1] contra viento y marea: *against all odds*
[2] rinden tributo: *pay tribute*

Empanadas a la Ferro

mi cocina

Candela comparte una sabrosa tradición
A la argentina Candela Ferro, presentadora de "Ocurrió así" (Telemundo), le gusta cocinar para sus amigos. ¿Su receta preferida? ¡Empanadas! Las empanadas son un plato típico del Cono sur. La preparación varía según la región. ¡Anímate a prepararlas!

Ingredientes
Discos
2 tazas de harina de trigo
1/2 taza de manteca[1]
1 huevo pequeño
1 cdta. de pimentón rojo dulce[2]
1/2 cdta. de sal
agua tibia

Relleno
1/2 taza de aceitunas deshuesadas[3]
6 huevos duros en rodajas
1 lb. de carne de res molida
1 cebolla
1 pimiento morrón[4] cortado finito
2 dientes de ajo
1/2 taza de pasas o ciruelas[5]
sal y pimienta al gusto
2 cucharadas de aceite de oliva

Preparación
Masa: Batir el huevo con el pimentón, sal y agua. Mezclar la harina con la manteca y la mezcla de huevo. Formar una bola con la masa y dejarla reposar. Dividir la masa, amasar[6] y hacer los discos.

Relleno: Calentar el aceite en una sartén. Sofreír[7] la cebolla, el ajo y el pimiento. Agregar la carne y sofreírla. Poner los huevos, las aceitunas y las pasas.

Armar las empanadas. Ponerlas al horno, precalentado a 200 grados, hasta que estén doradas, y ¡buen provecho!

[1] manteca: *Arg.: butter*
[2] pimentón rojo dulce: *sweet paprika*
[3] aceitunas deshuesadas: *pitted olives*
[4] pimiento morrón: *canned roasted peppers*
[5] pasas o ciruelas: *raisins or prunes*
[6] amasar: *knead*
[7] sofreír: *sautee*

People EN ESPAÑOL

A Monumentos naturales e históricos ¿Verdadero o falso? Escojan.
1. La isla de Chiloé pertenece a Argentina.
2. La colonia del Sacramento es una ciudad fundada por los portugueses.
3. La ciudad del Este es parte del Patrimonio de la Humanidad desde 1993.

B El mundo salvaje Escojan.
1. Muchas ágatas y amatistas son de ___.
   a. Chile
   b. Paraguay
   c. Uruguay
2. La Tierra del Fuego queda en ___.
   a. Uruguay
   b. Argentina
   c. Chile
3. ___ pueden suportar temperaturas muy bajas. Le gusta mucho el frío.
   a. las araucarias
   b. las ágatas
   c. los pingüinos

C El mundo salvaje Escojan la palabra o palabras.
a. bajo
b. ágatas y amatistas
c. austral
d. gigante
e. el bosque
f. crías
1. lugar donde hay muchos árboles
2. del sur
3. contrario de alto
4. algo o alguien muy grande
5. piedras preciosas
6. bebés de las ballenas

D Sucesos Contesten.
1. ¿Quién escribe "Puedo escribir los versos más tristes esta noche"?
2. ¿De qué país es Eva Perón?
3. ¿Quién es un famoso poeta chileno?

E ¿De qué país son? Contesten.
1. los uruguayos
2. los paraguayos
3. los chilenos
4. los argentinos

Answers

A
1. falso
2. verdadero
3. falso

B
1. c
2. b
3. c

C
1. e
2. c
3. a
4. d
5. b
6. f

D
1. El poeta chileno Pablo Neruda.
2. Ella es de Argentina.
3. Pablo Neruda.

E
1. Uruguay
2. Paraguay
3. Chile
4. Argentina

People en Español

The **Cono sur** has a diverse range of artistic presence and expression. European influence permeates most aspects of Argentine and Chilean culture. In recent years, Paraguayan and Uruguayan artists, musicians, writers, and especially playwrights have been widely recognized for the richness of their work.

People en Español

Isabel Allende

Una vida de cuento

A Isabel Allende la llaman la Scherezada latinoamericana. Como el personaje de *Las mil y una noches*, esta escritora chilena sabe tejer[1] un cuento tras otro y encantar[2] a grandes y chicos. Dos de sus novelas son ya películas: *La casa de los espíritus* y *De amor y de sombra.* ¿Sabes que todos los 8 de enero empieza un nuevo libro? Hoy tiene un estudio muy bien montado[3] en Sausalito, California, pero en sus comienzos, ¡escribía[4] por las noches en la cocina de su casa!

Isabel Allende es una excelente escritora y una gran recicladora[5]. ¡Tiene el poder de convertir a sus familiares y amigos en personajes de novelas! Sus abuelos, por ejemplo, son dos de los personajes de *La casa de los espíritus,* su primera novela. En *Paula,* su hija del mismo nombre es personaje y motivo[6] del libro. ¡Incluso la novela *Afrodita* es el producto de un sueño en el que aparece su amigo Antonio Banderas!

Si todavía no conoces *El Reino del Dragón de Oro,* su libro más reciente, tienes que hacerlo pronto y dejarte encantar.

[1] tejer: *weave*
[2] encantar: *charm*
[3] montado: *equipped*
[4] escribía: *would write*
[5] recicladora: *recycler*
[6] motivo: *inspiration*

Primera novela de Allende, publicada ya en 27 idiomas

238

YA QUE AMARNOS LOS UNOS A LOS OTROS NO RESULTA ¿POR QUÉ NO PROBAMOS AMARNOS LOS OTROS A LOS UNOS?

El mundo según Mafalda (¡y Quino!)

Joaquín Salvador Lavado, conocido como Quino, es el genial creador de Mafalda, personaje de una tira cómica[1], leída[2] y querida en todo el mundo. Los personajes principales de Mafalda son niños, pero Quino dice que siempre se dirige[3] a los adultos. Mafalda es sinónimo de imaginación y visión crítica y cuestionadora de la vida. Sus numerosos premios[4] lo confirman. En 1977, la UNICEF ilustra con Mafalda y sus amigos la Declaración de los Derechos del Niño. ¿Te interesa conocer a Mafalda? Arriba tienes una muestra[5].

[1] tira cómica: *comic strip*
[2] leída: *read*
[3] dirige: *addresses*
[4] premios: *awards*
[5] muestra: *example*

Quino

música

Justo para ti

Justo Lamas

Damas y caballeros... ¡aquí viene Justo! ¡Sí, **Justo Lamas,** el que canta "La bamba", "Magdalena" y "Cielito lindo"! Verlo actuar[1] es asistir[2] a algo más que un concierto. Sus actuaciones[3] derrochan[4] inspiración a la par[5] que permiten aprender español. Ha grabado tres discos compactos: "Justo para ti", "Un día especial" y "Vivir". El cantautor[6] siempre tiene algo importante que comunicar: "Si piensas que la vida a veces te lastima[7], despierta[8], tú puedes, confía[9]..." dice en "No hay camino sin salida".

[1] actuar: *perform*
[2] asistir: *attend*
[3] actuaciones: *performances*
[4] derrochan: *radiate*
[5] a la par: *at the same time*
[6] cantautor: *singer-songwriter*
[7] lastima: *hurts*
[8] despierta: *wake up*
[9] confía: *trust*

¿Argentina o mexicana?

Dorismar

Al decir música argentina, se piensa en tango, rock o folklore. **Dorismar** quiere algo diferente: Canta música grupera[1], ¡y lo hace muy bien! Cuando no está de gira[2] con Los Tucanes de Tijuana o actúa en telenovelas, esta joven argentina prefiere la tranquilidad de su apartamento en Miami.

[1] música grupera: *Mexican regional music*
[2] gira: *tour*

De sur a norte

Desde la década de los setenta, **Alejandro Lerner** canta y vive "todo a pulmón"[1], como se titula[2] una de sus canciones. El legendario Carlos Santana sabe cuánto vale este argentino, y por eso cantan juntos en la gira del famoso guitarrista por Estados Unidos.

Alejandro Lerner

[1] todo a pulmón: *with my best efforts*
[2] titula: *entitled*

Reto[1] de a dos

El tango, baile de argentinos y uruguayos, se impone[2] cada vez más en fiestas y salones de todo el mundo. No es sólo un baile. Es más que un ritmo, ¡es un rito![3] Su influencia llega hasta el lenguaje de todos los días.

Carlos Saura, el director de cine español, muestra en su película "Tango", pasos de bailes espectaculares. La música de la película es de Lalo Schifrin, compositor argentino muy reconocido por su tema de la serie de televisión "Misión imposible".

Escena de "Tango"

Un toque de lunfardo

El tango tiene su propio idioma[4]: el lunfardo. ¿Te interesa saber un poco de lunfardo? Estas son palabras que dicen los jóvenes argentinos y uruguayos.

al divino botón: *inútilmente*[5]
bronca: *enojo*[6]
guita: *dinero*
laburo: *trabajo*
macanudo: *excelente*
morfar: *comer*

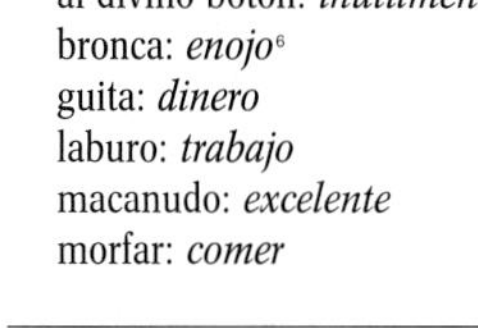
El tango

[1] reto: *challenge*
[2] impone: *gains recognition*
[3] rito: *ritual*
[4] idioma: *language*
[5] inútilmente: *uselessly*
[6] enojo: *anger*

239

A Una vida de cuento Contesten.

1. ¿De qué nacionalidad es Isabel Allende?
2. ¿Qué día empieza ella a escribir un nuevo libro?
3. ¿Dónde vive ella ahora?
4. ¿A quiénes puede ella convertir en personajes de novelas?

B Música ¿Quién es?

1. Ha grabado tres discos compactos.
2. Actúa en telenovelas y prefiere la tranquilidad de su apartamento.
3. Canta con Carlos Santana.

C Reto de a dos Contesten.

1. ¿Qué es el tango?
2. ¿Qué es Carlos Saura?
3. ¿Qué muestra en su película (filme) *Tango*?
4. ¿Qué es el lunfardo?

LEVELING

E: Activity A
A: Activity B
C: Activity C

Answers

A

1. chilena
2. el 8 de enero
3. en Sausalito, California
4. a sus familiares y amigos

B

1. Justo Lamas
2. Dorismar
3. Alejandro Lerner

C

1. el baile de argentinos y uruguayos es también un rito
2. un director de cine español
3. pasos de bailes espectaculares
4. el idioma del tango

Planning for Chapter 8

SCOPE AND SEQUENCE, PAGES 240–271

Topics

- Minor illnesses
- Symptoms of a cold, flu, or fever
- Medical exams
- Parts of the body
- Prescriptions

Culture

- Patricia goes to the doctor with a minor illness
- Differences between pharmacies in the United States and pharmacies in Spanish-speaking countries
- A famous Cuban American doctor: Antonio Gassett
- Information about nutrition in Spanish

Functions

- How to describe symptoms of a minor illness
- How to have a prescription filled at a pharmacy
- How to tell someone where you are from
- How to describe origin and location
- How to describe characteristics or conditions
- How to discuss what happens to you or to someone else

Structure

- **Ser** and **estar**
- **Me, te, nos**

National Standards

- Communication Standard 1.1 pages 240, 244, 245, 248, 249, 250, 251, 252, 253, 254, 255, 256, 259, 266
- Communication Standard 1.2 pages 245, 249, 251, 252, 253, 257, 258, 259, 261, 262, 263, 266, 267
- Communication Standard 1.3 page 267
- Cultures Standard 2.1 pages 258, 260–261, 262
- Cultures Standard 2.2 page 263
- Connections Standard 3.1 page 264
- Connections Standard 3.2 page 266
- Comparisons Standard 4.1 page 250
- Comparisons Standard 4.2 pages 260, 262

PACING AND PRIORITIES

The chapter content is color coded below to assist you in planning.

■ required ■ recommended ■ optional

Vocabulario *(required)* *Days 1–4*

- ■ Palabras 1
  ¿Cómo está?
- ■ Palabras 2
  En la consulta del médico
  En la farmacia

Estructura *(required)* *Days 5–7*

- ■ **Ser** y **estar**
- ■ **Ser** y **estar**
- ■ **Me, te, nos**

Conversación *(required)*

- ■ En la consulta del médico

Pronunciación *(recommended)*

- ■ La consonante **c**

Lecturas culturales

- ■ Una joven nerviosa *(recommended)*
- ■ La farmacia *(optional)*
- ■ Una biografía—El doctor Antonio Gassett *(optional)*

Conexiones

- ■ La nutrición *(optional)*

■ **¡Te toca a ti!** *(recommended)*

■ **Assessment** *(recommended)*

■ **¡Hablo como un pro!** *(optional)*

RESOURCE GUIDE

Section	Pages	Section Resources
Vocabulario PALABRAS 1		
¿Cómo está?	242–245	Vocabulary Transparencies 8.2–8.3 Audio CD 5 Audio Activities TE, pages 93–94 Workbook, pages 87–88 Quiz 1, page 38 ExamView® Pro
Vocabulario PALABRAS 2		
En la consulta del médico En la farmacia	246, 248–249 247, 248–249	Vocabulary Transparencies 8.4–8.5 Audio CD 5 Audio Activities TE, pages 95–96 Workbook, pages 89–90 Quiz 2, page 39 ExamView® Pro
Estructura		
Ser y **estar** **Ser** y **estar** **Me, te, nos**	250–252 253–255 256–257	Audio CD 5 Audio Activities TE, pages 97–100 Workbook, pages 91–93 Quizzes 3–5, pages 40–42 ExamView® Pro
Conversación		
En la consulta del médico	258	Audio CD 5 Audio Activities TE, pages 100–101 Interactive CD-ROM
Pronunciación		
La consonante **c**	259	Pronunciation Transparency P 8 Audio CD 5 Audio Activities TE, page 101
Lecturas culturales		
Una joven nerviosa La farmacia Una biografía—El doctor Antonio Gassett	260–261 262 263	Audio CD 5 Audio Activities TE, page 102 Tests, pages 126, 129
Conexiones		
La nutrición	264–265	Tests, page 130
¡Te toca a ti!		
	266–267	**¡Viva el mundo hispano!** Video, Episode 8 Video Activities, Chapter 8 Spanish Online Activities spanish.glencoe.com
Assessment		
	268–269	Communication Transparency C 8 Quizzes 1–5, pages 38–42 Performance Assessment, Task 8 Tests, pages 123–138 Situation Cards, Chapter 8 ExamView® Pro **Maratón mental** Videoquiz

Using Your Resources for Chapter 8

Transparencies

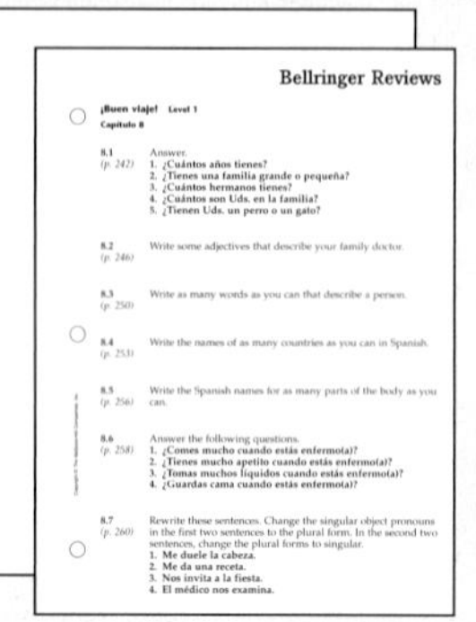
Bellringer 8.1–8.7

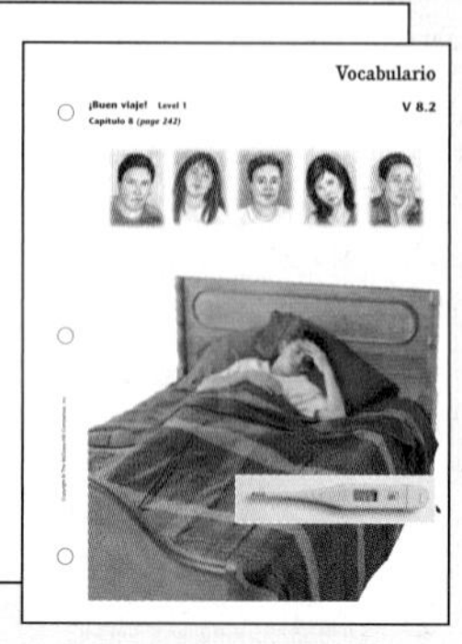
Vocabulary 8.1–8.5

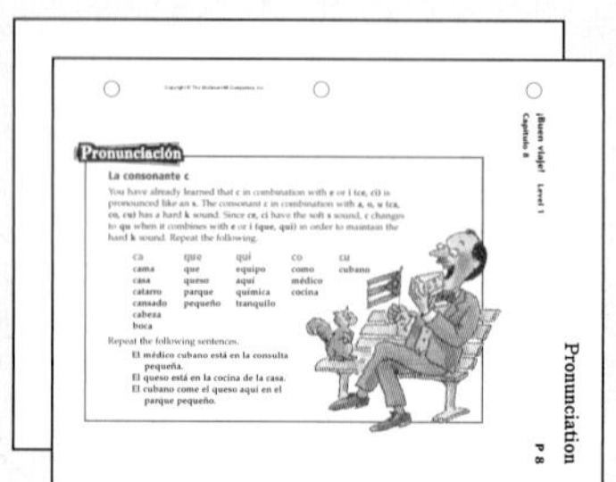
Pronunciation P 8

Communication C 8

Workbook

Vocabulary, pages 87–90

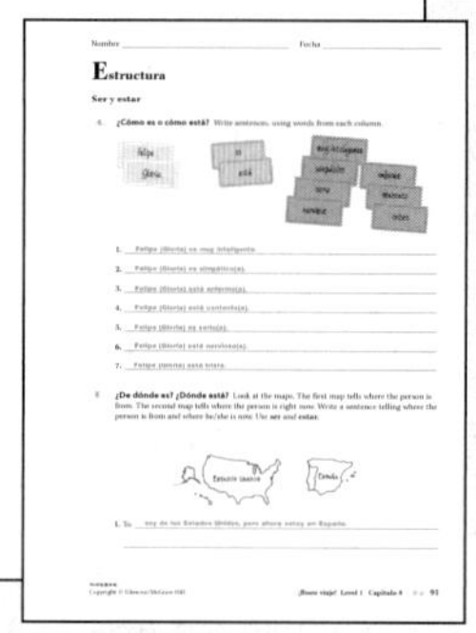
Structure, pages 91–93

Enrichment, pages 94–98

Audio Activities

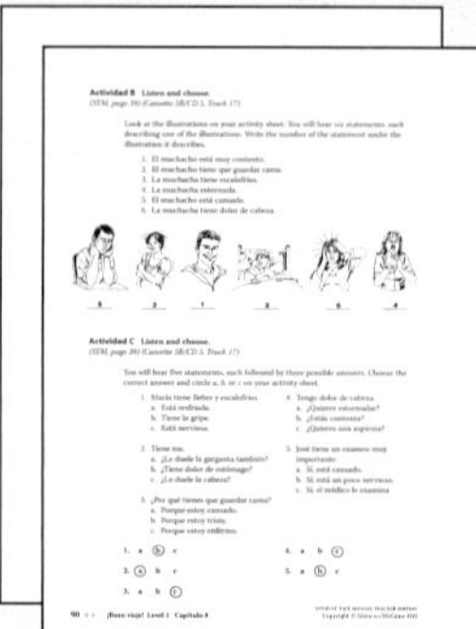
Vocabulary, pages 93–96

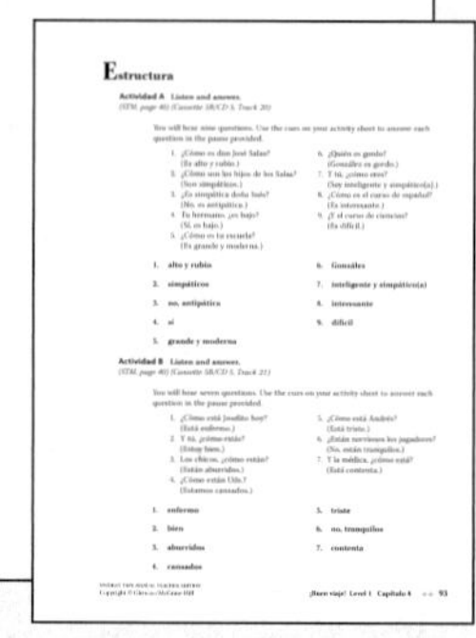
Structure, pages 97–100

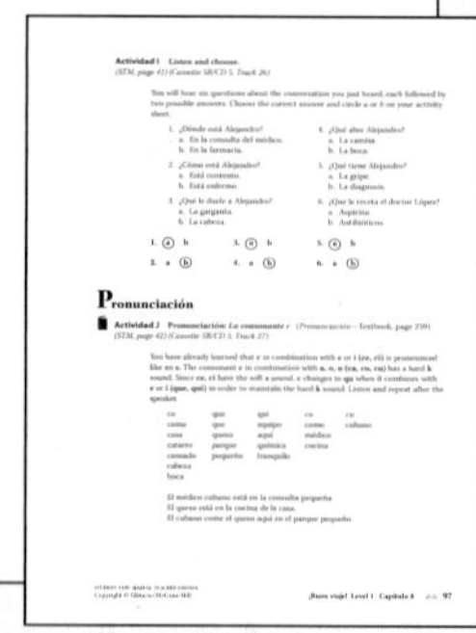
Conversation, Pronunciation, pages 100–101

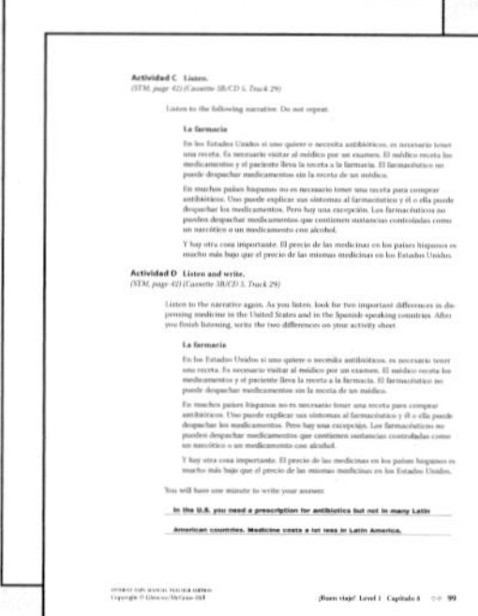
Additional Practice, pages 102–104

Assessment

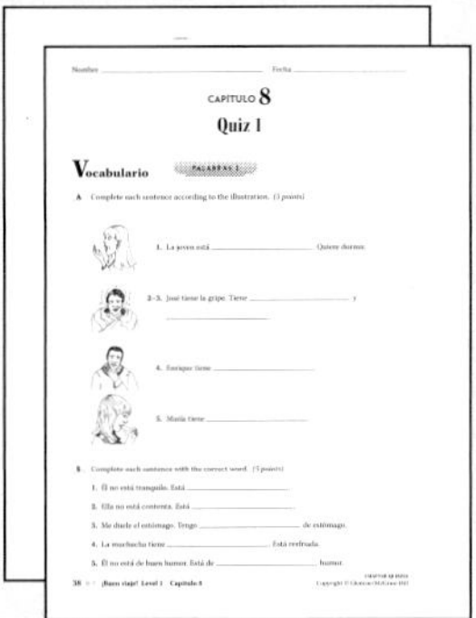

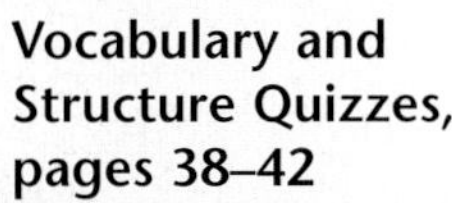

Vocabulary and Structure Quizzes, pages 38–42

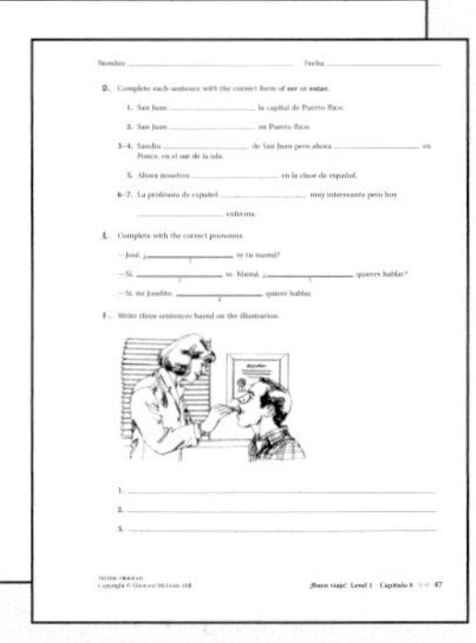

Chapter Tests, pages 123–138

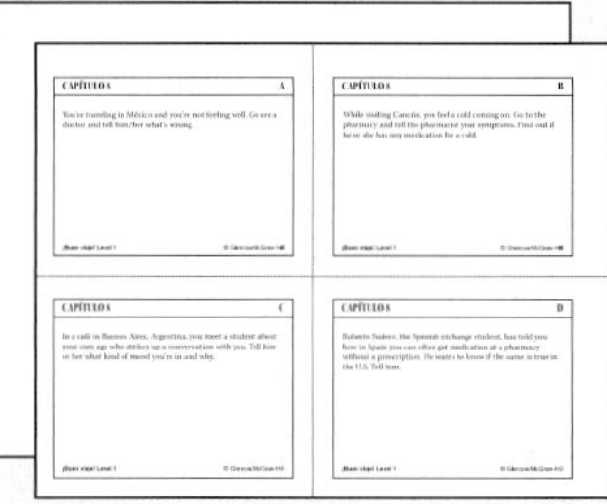

Situation Cards, Chapter 8

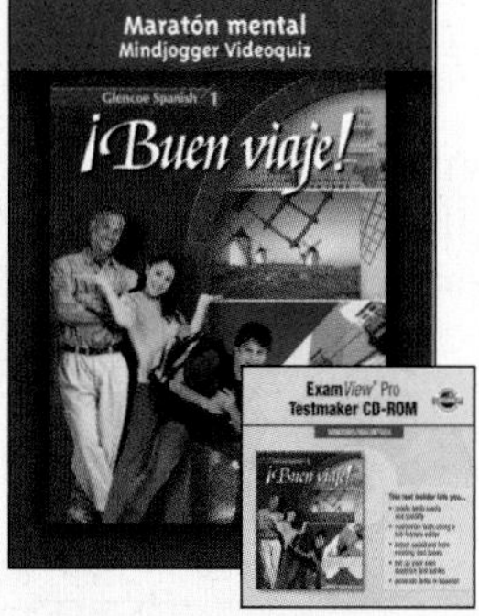

MindJogger Videoquiz, ExamView® Pro, Chapter 8

Timesaving Teacher Tools

TeacherWorks™ is your all-in-one teacher resource center. Personalize lesson plans, access resources from the Teacher Wraparound Edition, connect to the Internet, or make a to-do list. These are only a few of the many features that can assist you in the planning and organizing of your lessons.

Includes:

- A calendar feature
- Access to all program blackline masters
- Standards correlations and more

ExamView® Pro

Test Bank software for Macintosh and Windows makes creating, editing, customizing, and printing tests quick and easy.

Technology Resources

In the Chapter 8 Internet Activity, you will have a chance to learn more about the Spanish-speaking world. Visit spanish.glencoe.com

On the interactive CD-ROM, students can listen to and take part in a recorded version of the conversation in Chapter 8.

¡Viva el mundo hispano! Video and Video Activities, Chapter 8. Available on VHS and DVD.

Help your students prepare for the chapter test by playing the **Maratón mental** Videoquiz game show. Teams will compete against each other to review chapter vocabulary and structure and sharpen listening comprehension skills. Available on VHS and DVD.

¡Buen viaje! is also available on CD or Online.

Preview

In this chapter, students will learn to talk about routine illnesses and describe their symptoms to a doctor. They will use vocabulary associated with medical exams, prescriptions, and minor illnesses such as colds, flu, and headaches. Students will talk about themselves and others using the pronouns **me, te,** and **nos**. They will express characteristics and origin using the verb **ser** and conditions and location using the verb **estar.**

The cultural focus of the chapter is on medical services and health problems in Spanish-speaking countries.

National Standards

Communication

In Chapter 8, students will communicate in spoken and written Spanish on the following topics:

- describing symptoms of minor ailments
- getting a prescription at a pharmacy
- expressing emotions and conditions

Students will obtain and provide information and engage in conversations dealing with health and health services as they fulfill the objectives listed on this page.

Capítulo 8

La salud y el médico

Objetivos

In this chapter you will learn to:

- explain a minor illness to a doctor
- describe some feelings
- have a prescription filled at a pharmacy
- describe characteristics and conditions
- tell where things are and where they're from
- tell where someone or something is now
- tell what happens to you or someone else

Pablo Picasso *Head of a Medical Student*

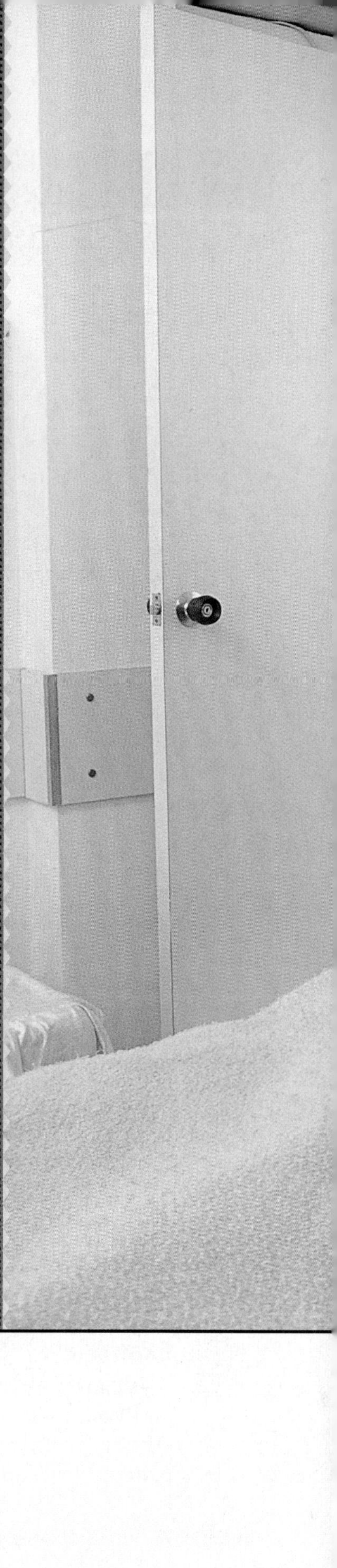

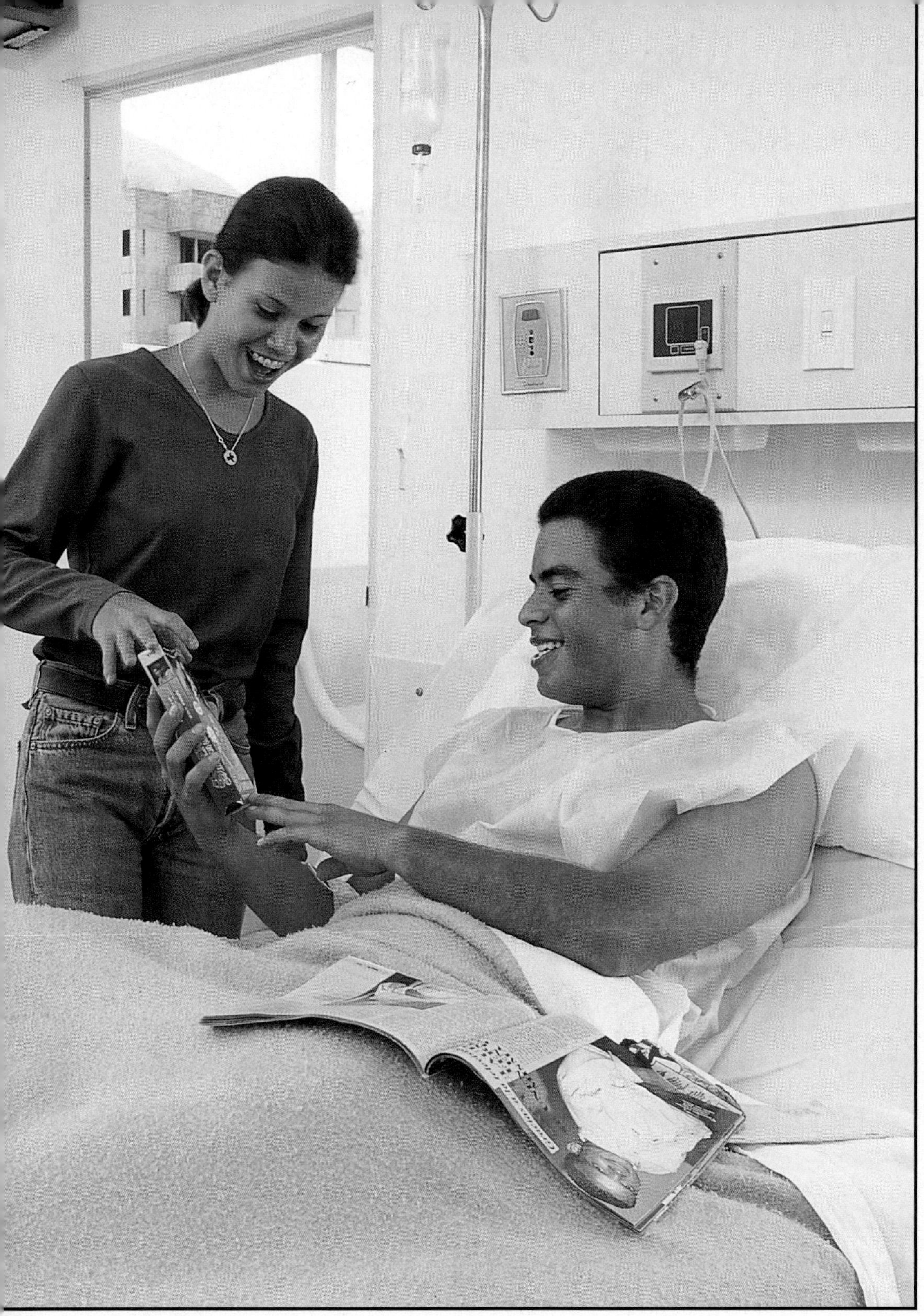

Capítulo 8

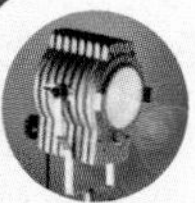

Spotlight on Culture

Arte Pablo Ruiz y Picasso (1881–1973) helped begin the movement of cubism, which broke existing artistic conventions. His work continued to evolve and he had a profound influence on other artistic movements.

Fotografía This photo shows a young lady visiting a friend in a hospital in Caracas, Venezuela. Students may also find it interesting that the patient's room opens directly on the outdoors, rather than on an interior corridor.

Learning from Photos

(pages 240–241) Ask the following questions about the photo after presenting the new vocabulary on pages 242–243:

¿Quién está en cama, Irene o Carlos?
¿A quién visita Irene?
¿Está muy enfermo Carlos?
¿Tiene Carlos una revista?
¿Lee la revista? ¿Por qué no lee la revista? ¿Qué mira?

LEVELING

The activities, conversations, and readings within each chapter are marked according to level of difficulty. **E** indicates easy. **A** indicates average. **C** indicates challenging. Some activities cover a range of difficulty. In some activities, for example, advanced students will be able to produce more extensive responses while students who learn at a different rate may give less detailed responses. The leveling indicators will help you individualize instruction to best meet your students' needs.

Vocabulario

PALABRAS 1

1 PREPARATION

Resource Manager

Vocabulary Transparencies 8.2–8.3
Audio Activities TE, pages 93–94
Audio CD 5
Workbook, pages 87–88
Quizzes, page 38
ExamView® Pro

Bellringer Review

Use BRR Transparency 8.1 or write the following on the board.
Answer.

1. **¿Cuántos años tienes?**
2. **¿Tienes una familia grande o pequeña?**
3. **¿Cuántos hermanos tienes?**
4. **¿Cuántos son Uds. en la familia?**
5. **¿Tienen Uds. un perro o un gato?**

2 PRESENTATION

Step 1 Have students close their books. Present the vocabulary using Vocabulary Transparencies 8.2–8.3.

Step 2 Point to yourself as you teach the words **la garganta, la cabeza, el estómago.**

Step 3 You can easily use gestures to teach the following words and expressions: **enfermo, cansado, contento, triste, nervioso, toser, estornudar, tener escalofríos, tener dolor de garganta, tener dolor de cabeza, tener dolor de estómago.**

Step 4 Have students repeat the words and sentences on pages 242–243. Then have them open their books and read the new vocabulary aloud.

Vocabulario

PALABRAS 1

¿Cómo está?

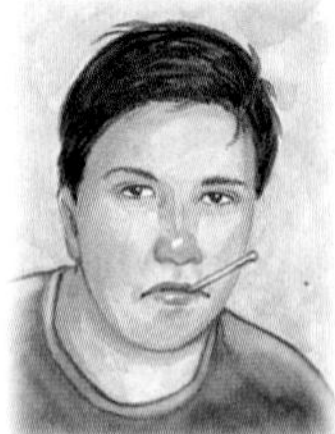
enfermo

cansada

contento

triste

nervioso

El pobre muchacho está enfermo.
Tiene fiebre.
Tiene la gripe.

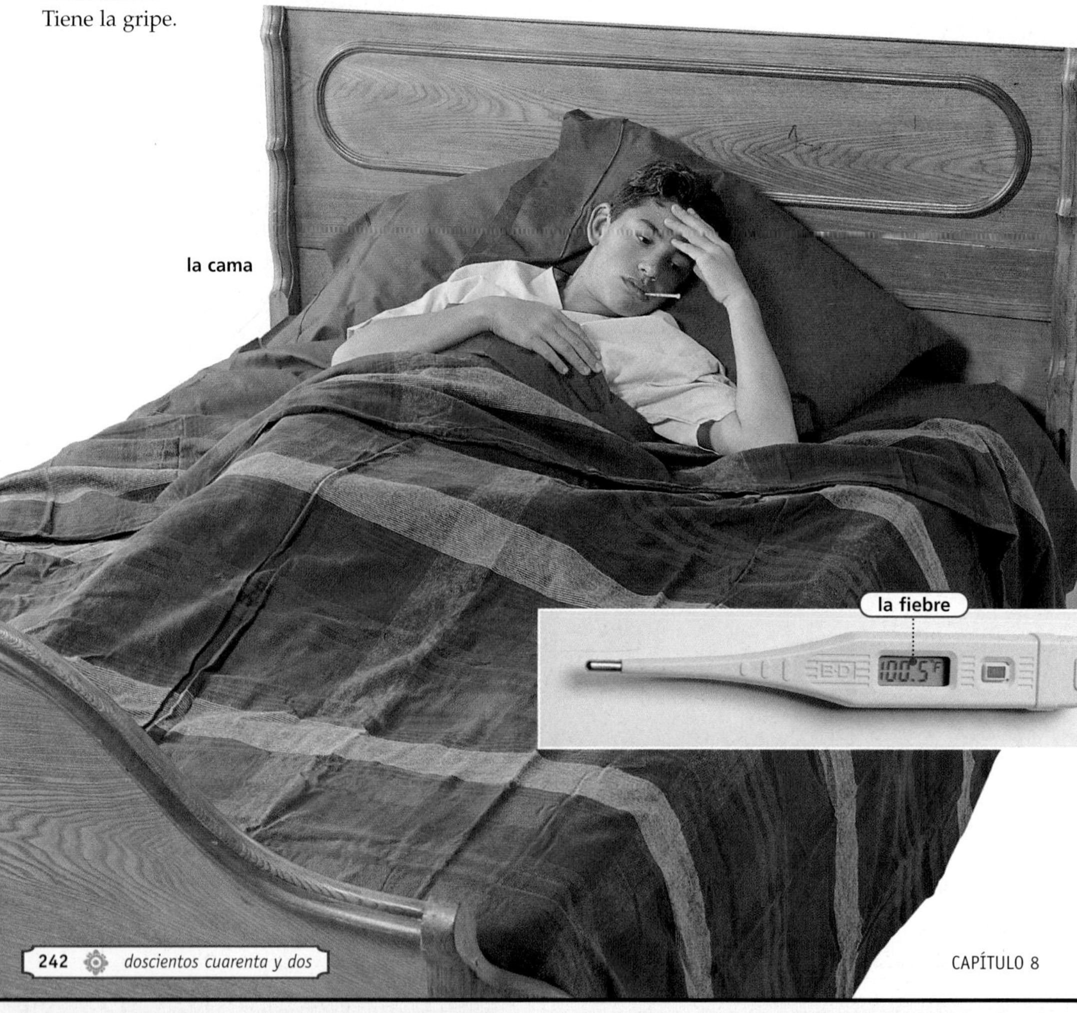

Reaching All Students

Total Physical Response

(Student 1), **ven acá por favor. Imagínate que estás enfermo(a).**
Indícame que estás cansado(a).
Indícame que tienes fiebre.
Indícame que tienes escalofríos.
Indícame que tienes dolor de garganta.
Indícame que tienes dolor de cabeza.
Indícame que tienes dolor de estómago.
Indícame que tienes tos.
Indícame que estás estornudando mucho.
Gracias, *(Student 1).* **Y ahora puedes regresar a tu asiento.**

La muchacha tiene catarro.
Está resfriada.

El muchacho tiene tos.
Tiene dolor de garganta.

La muchacha tiene dolor de cabeza.

El muchacho tiene dolor de estómago.

El enfermo tiene que guardar cama.
Tiene escalofríos porque tiene fiebre.
Él está de mal humor.
No está de buen humor.

Vocabulario

About the Spanish Language

- One can say **Estoy resfriado(a)** or **Tengo un resfriado.**
- In some areas **la fiebre** is **la calentura.**
- Note that no article is used with the expression **guardar cama.** Also, note the difference between **estar en cama** *(to be in bed sick)* and **estar en la cama** *(to be in bed sleeping).*
- You may wish to explain to students that one must be aware of false cognates. A very common way to say *to have a cold* is **estar constipado(a). Constipado** does not mean *constipated* as one would expect; that expression is **estar estreñido(a). Embarazada** is another false cognate. **Embarazada** means *pregnant,* not *embarrassed.*

Vocabulary Expansion

Tourists often experience stomach problems when traveling. If you wish, you may give students the following expressions they may find useful.

Tengo náuseas.
Tengo vómitos.
Tengo diarrea.
Estoy estreñido(a). *(constipated)*
Tengo calambres. *(cramps)*

LEVELING
A: Vocabulary

Class Motivator

Simón dice... After practicing the **Palabras 1** vocabulary, you may wish to play a game of **Simón dice.** Call the first round yourself and have the students act out the following.
Simón dice: Tienes dolor de cabeza.
Simón dice: Tienes dolor de garganta.
Simón dice: Tienes tos.
Simón dice: Tose.
Simón dice: Estornuda.
Simón dice: Tienes escalofríos.

3 PRACTICE

¿Qué palabra necesito?

¡OJO! When students are doing the **¿Qué palabra necesito?** activities, accept any answer that makes sense. The purpose of these activities is to have students use the new vocabulary. They are not factual recall activities. Thus, it is not necessary for students to remember specific factual information from the vocabulary presentation when answering. If you wish, have students use the photos on this page as a stimulus, when possible.

Historieta Each time **Historieta** appears, it means that the answers to the activity form a short story. Encourage students to look at the title of the **Historieta,** since it can help them do the activity.

Writing Development

Have students write the answers to Activities 1 and 2 in a paragraph to illustrate how the answers to all the items tell a story.

Learning from Realia

(page 244) Have students look at the ad and find where it gives the following information.

1. **TOA** is for a cough.
2. **TOA** has a nice flavor.
3. It enables you to stay active.

LEVELING

E: Activities 1, 2, 3

A: Activity 4

C: Activities 4, 5

¿Qué palabra necesito?

1 Historieta El pobre joven está enfermo. Contesten.

1. ¿Está enfermo el pobre muchacho?
2. ¿Tiene la gripe?
3. ¿Tiene tos?
4. ¿Tiene dolor de garganta?
5. ¿Tiene fiebre?
6. ¿Tiene escalofríos?
7. ¿Tiene dolor de cabeza?
8. ¿Está siempre cansado?

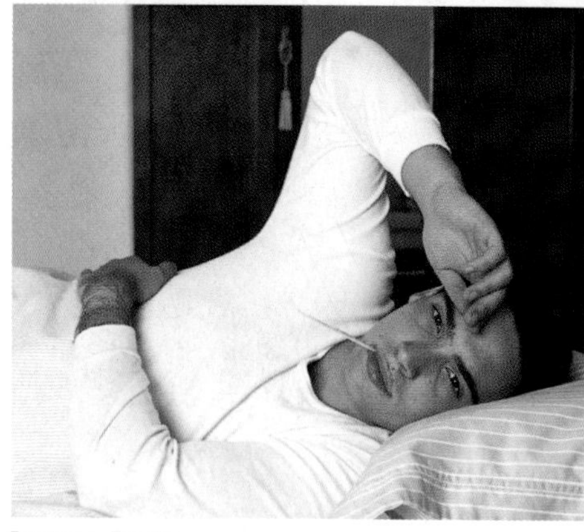

Estepona, España

2 Historieta La pobre muchacha Contesten.

San Miguel de Allende, México

1. ¿Está enferma la muchacha?
2. ¿Tiene tos?
3. ¿Estornuda mucho?
4. ¿Tiene dolor de cabeza?
5. ¿Está resfriada?
6. ¿Está en cama?
7. ¿Tiene que guardar cama?
8. ¿Qué opinión tienes? ¿Qué crees? ¿Está la muchacha de buen humor o de mal humor?

TOA...¡PARA TOA LA TOS!
Toa...
adulto e infantil
Toa
infantil
DEXTROMETORFANO
PSEUDOEFEDRINA
Toa
adulto
DEXTROMETORFANO
PSEUDOEFEDRINA
Toa
infantil
Toa
adulto
TOA tiene un agradable sabor y además te permite seguir activo.
Y para sus niños... ¡TOA INFANTIL!

Answers to ¿Qué palabra necesito?

1

1. Sí, el pobre muchacho está enfermo.
2. Sí, tiene la gripe.
3. Sí, (No, no) tiene tos.
4. Sí, (No, no) tiene dolor de garganta.
5. Sí, (No, no) tiene fiebre.
6. Sí, (No, no) tiene escalofríos.
7. Sí, (No, no) tiene dolor de cabeza.
8. Sí, (No, no) está siempre cansado.

2

1. Sí, la muchacha está enferma.
2. Sí, (No, no) tiene tos.
3. Sí, (No, no) estornuda mucho.
4. Sí, tiene dolor de cabeza.
5. Sí, está resfriada.
6. Sí, está en cama.
7. Sí, tiene que guardar cama.
8. Creo que la muchacha está de mal humor.

3 **¿Cómo está?** Contesten según las fotos.

1. ¿Cómo está el joven?
¿Está triste o contento?

2. Y la joven, ¿cómo está?
¿Está triste o contenta?

3. El señor, ¿está bien o
está enfermo?

4. Y la señora, ¿está nerviosa
o está tranquila?

4 **¿Cómo estás tú?** Contesten personalmente.

1. ¿Cómo estás hoy?
2. Cuando estás enfermo(a), ¿estás de buen humor o estás de mal humor?
3. Cuando tienes dolor de cabeza, ¿estás contento(a) o triste?
4. Cuando tienes catarro, ¿siempre estás cansado(a) o no?
5. Cuando tienes catarro, ¿tienes fiebre y escalofríos?
6. Cuando tienes la gripe, ¿tienes fiebre y escalofríos?
7. ¿Tienes que guardar cama cuando tienes catarro?
8. ¿Tienes que guardar cama cuando tienes fiebre?

5 **¿Qué te pasa?** Work with a classmate. Ask your partner what's the matter—**¿Qué te pasa?** He or she will tell you. Then suggest something he or she can do to feel better. **¿Por qué no... ?** Take turns.

¡OJO! Note that the activities are color-coded. All the activities in the text are communicative. However, the ones with blue titles are guided communication. The red titles indicate that the answers to the activity are more open-ended and can vary more. You may wish to correct students' mistakes more so in the guided activities than in the activities with a red title, which lend themselves to a freer response.

3 **Expansion:** Ask for volunteers to imitate the people in Activity 3. Then have other students give the appropriate description. Have students do the same using the other words and expressions taught on pages 242–243.

4 Activity 4 can be done as an interview or a paired activity.

5 Encourage students to be as creative as possible when doing this activity. They can have a lot of fun with it. Students should use the following model:

—¿Qué te pasa?
—Estoy nervioso(a) porque tengo un examen mañana.
—¿Por qué no vas al cine?

ANSWERS TO ¿Qué palabra necesito?

3

1. Está triste.
2. Está contenta.
3. Está enfermo.
4. Está nerviosa.

4

1. Estoy ___.
2. Cuando estoy enfermo(a), estoy de mal humor.
3. Cuando tengo dolor de cabeza, estoy triste.
4. Cuando tengo catarro, siempre estoy cansado(a).
5. Sí (No), cuando tengo catarro, (no) tengo fiebre y escalofríos.
6. Sí, cuando tengo la gripe, tengo fiebre y escalofríos.
7. Sí, (No, no) tengo que guardar cama cuando tengo catarro.
8. Sí, tengo que guardar cama cuando tengo fiebre.

5 *Answers will vary; however, students should follow the model.*

—¿Qué te pasa?
—*(response)*
—¿Por qué no ___?

Vocabulario

PALABRAS 2

1 PREPARATION

Resource Manager

Vocabulary Transparencies 8.4–8.5
Audio Activities TE, pages 95–96
Audio CD 5
Workbook, pages 89–90
Quizzes, page 39
ExamView® Pro

Bellringer Review

Use BRR Transparency 8.2 or write the following on the board.
Write some adjectives that describe your family doctor.

2 PRESENTATION

Step 1 Have students close their books. Present the new words using Vocabulary Transparencies 8.4–8.5. As you point to each item, have students repeat the corresponding word or expression after you two or three times.

Step 2 Have students keep their books closed. Dramatize the following words or expressions from **Palabras 2: abrir la boca, examinar los ojos, me duele la cabeza, me duele la garganta, me duele el pecho, me duele el estómago.**

Step 3 Ask students to open their books to pages 246–247. Have them read along and repeat the new material after you or Audio CD 5.

Step 4 Make sure that students know the meanings of the cognates listed on page 247.

Vocabulario

PALABRAS 2

En la consulta del médico

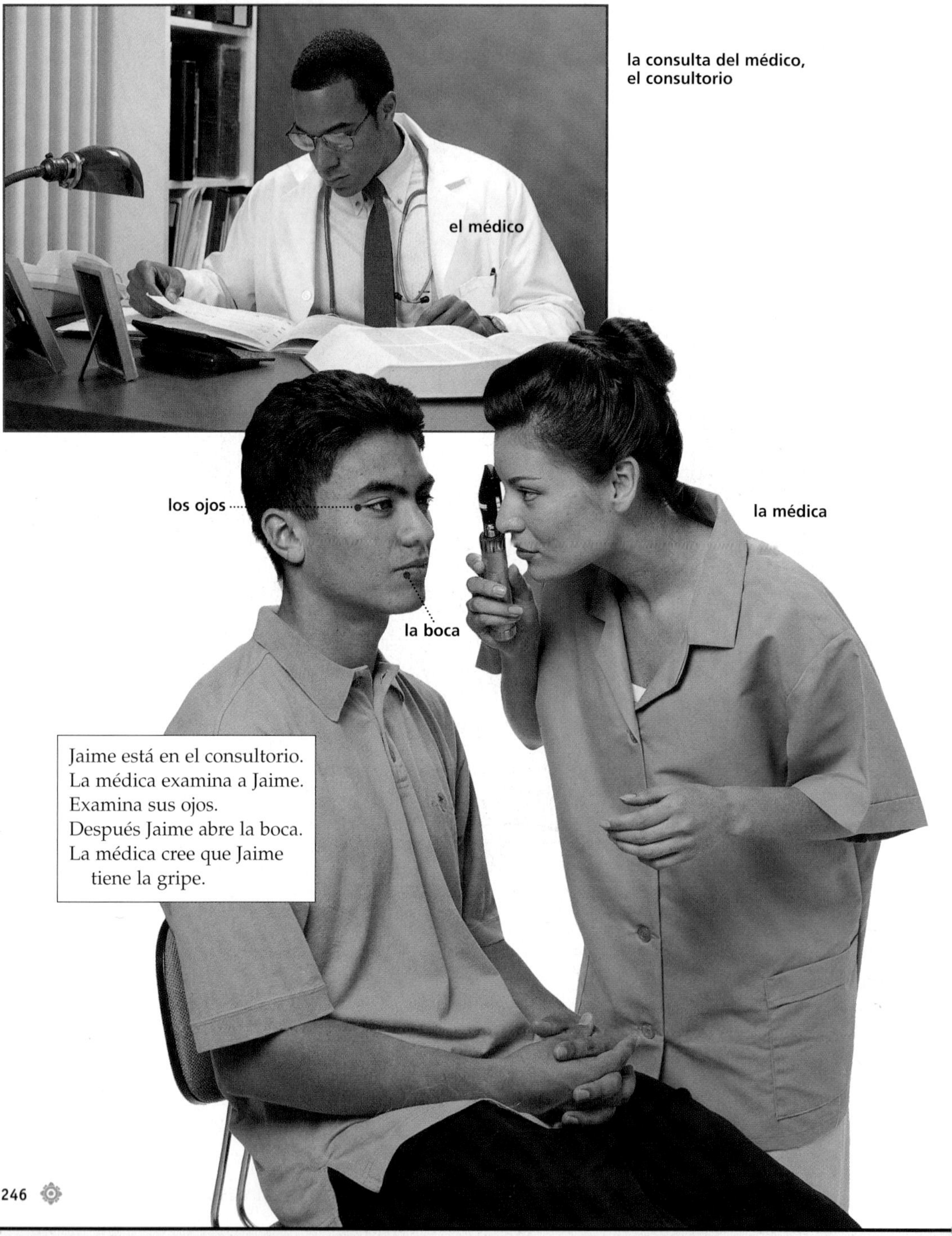

la consulta del médico, el consultorio

el médico

los ojos

la médica

la boca

Jaime está en el consultorio.
La médica examina a Jaime.
Examina sus ojos.
Después Jaime abre la boca.
La médica cree que Jaime tiene la gripe.

246

Reaching All Students

Total Physical Response

(Student 1), ven acá. Tú vas a ser el / la médico(a).
(Student 2), ven acá. Tú vas a ser el / la enfermo(a).
(Student 2), siéntate.
(Student 2), indica al médico que te duele la garganta.
(Student 2), abre la boca.
(Student 1), examina la garganta.
(Student 1), y ahora examina los ojos.
(Student 1), dale una pastilla.
(Student 2), toma la pastilla.

Vocabulario

Me duele la cabeza.

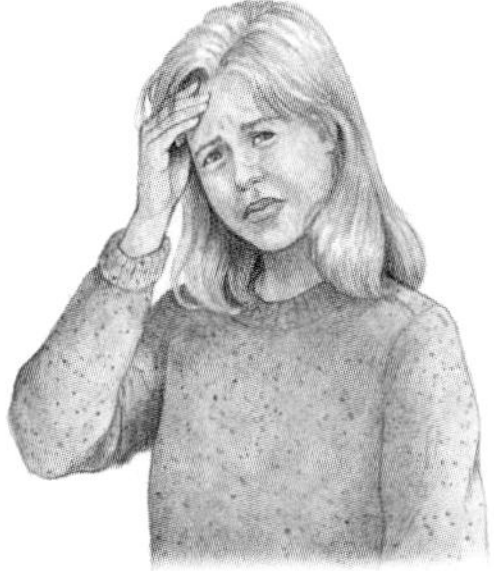

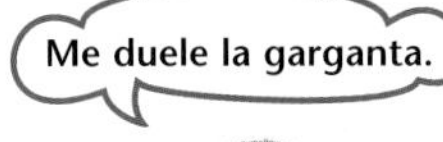

En la farmacia

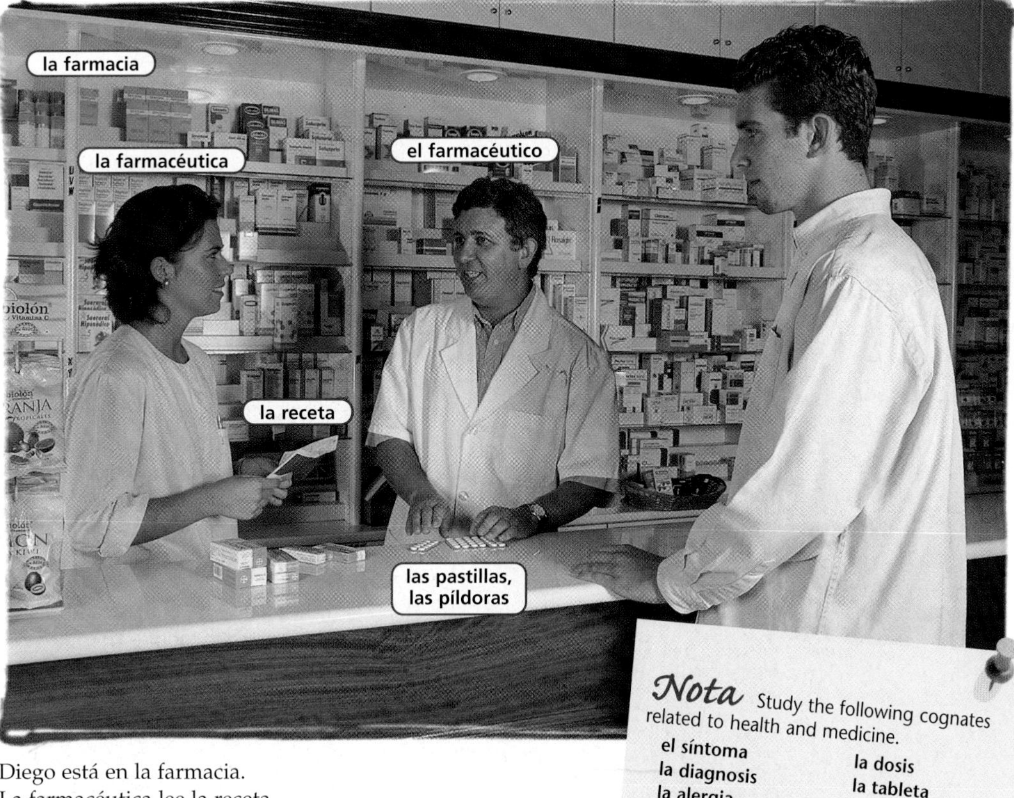

Diego está en la farmacia.
La farmacéutica lee la receta.
Ella vende (despacha) los medicamentos.

Nota Study the following cognates related to health and medicine.

el síntoma	la dosis
la diagnosis	la tableta
la alergia	la aspirina
la inyección	el antibiótico
la medicina	

FUN-FACTS

Médicas Note that the doctor in the blue uniform on page 246 is a woman. In recent years in the United States, more and more women have entered the medical profession. In Spain and Latin America this is not a recent trend. There has always been a large number of female doctors.

Recycling

Review previously learned vocabulary by asking: **¿Dónde te duele?** and point to your arm, foot, finger, and hand.

About the Spanish Language

- Other words that are used often in addition to **las pastillas** and **las píldoras** are: **los comprimidos, las tabletas, las cápsulas.**
- Explain to students that many nouns that end in **-ma** come from Greek, and that they are masculine and take the article **el: el problema, el programa, el síntoma, el drama.**
- Almost all nouns that end in **-osis** are feminine: **la dosis, la diagnosis, la prognosis, la tuberculosis.**

Chapter Projects

Primeros auxilios Obtain a video on first-aid, health, or nutrition in Spanish or English from the health department in your school. Use it as a springboard for discussing health and illnesses with the new vocabulary from this chapter.

3 PRACTICE

¿Qué palabra necesito?

6 Have students act out Activity 6 using as much expression as possible.

7 Go over Activity 7 once with the entire class. Then have students retell the story in their own words.

Learning from Photos

(page 248 middle) Ask the following questions about the boy in the doctor's office in San Miguel de Allende, Mexico. **¿Dónde está el muchacho? ¿Quién examina al muchacho? ¿El médico o la médica? ¿Qué abre el muchacho? ¿Lleva ella una máscara?** *(page 248 bottom)* Have students look at the pharmacist in the photo. Note that she is wearing a type of smock. Wearing a smock, lab coat, or some type of uniform is more common in many professions in Spain and Latin America than in the United States. There are also many female pharmacists in both Spain and Latin America.

Reaching All Students

For the Younger Students Está enfermo(a). Have students draw a picture of someone who isn't feeling too well. Then have them describe their pictures to the class or have them write descriptions of their drawings.

Vocabulario

¿Qué palabra necesito?

6 **¿Qué te pasa?** Preparen una conversación según el modelo.

Me duele la garganta.

—¿Qué te pasa? ¿Tienes dolor de garganta?
—Sí, me duele mucho. ¡Qué enfermo(a) estoy!

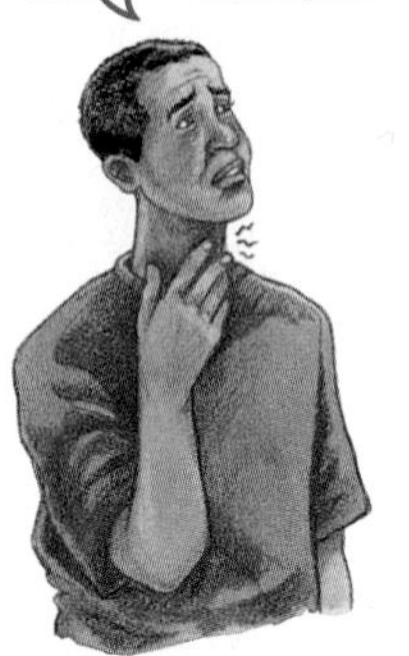

Me duele el estómago.

1.

Me duele la cabeza.

2.

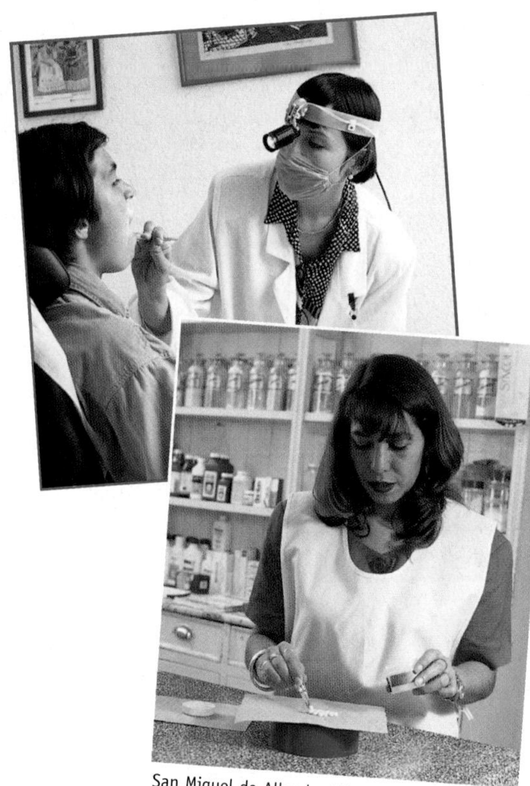

San Miguel de Allende, México

7 **Historieta En el consultorio**
Contesten.

1. ¿Dónde está Alberto? ¿En la consulta de la médica o en el hospital?
2. ¿Quién está enfermo? ¿Alberto o la médica?
3. ¿Quién examina a Alberto? ¿La médica o la farmacéutica?
4. ¿Qué examina la médica? ¿La cabeza o la garganta?
5. ¿Qué tiene que tomar Alberto? ¿Una inyección o una pastilla?
6. ¿Quién receta los antibióticos? ¿La médica o la farmacéutica?
7. ¿Adónde va Alberto con la receta? ¿A la clínica o a la farmacia?
8. ¿Qué despacha la farmacéutica? ¿Los medicamentos o las recetas?

ANSWERS TO ¿Qué palabra necesito?

6

1. —¿Qué te pasa? ¿Tienes dolor de estómago?
   —Sí, me duele mucho. ¡Qué enfermo(a) estoy!
2. —¿Qué te pasa? ¿Tienes dolor de cabeza?
   —Sí, me duele mucho. ¡Qué enfermo(a) estoy!

7

1. Alberto está en la consulta de la médica.
2. Alberto está enfermo.
3. La médica examina a Alberto.
4. La médica examina la garganta.
5. Alberto tiene que tomar una pastilla (una inyección).
6. La médica receta los antibióticos.
7. Alberto va a la farmacia con la receta.
8. La farmacéutica despacha los medicamentos.

8 Historieta Alberto está enfermo, el pobre.
Corrijan las oraciones.

1. Alberto está muy bien.
2. Alberto está en el hospital.
3. Alberto examina a la médica.
4. Alberto abre la boca y la médica examina los ojos.
5. La médica habla con Alberto de sus síntomas.
6. La farmacéutica receta unos antibióticos.
7. Alberto va al consultorio con la receta.
8. La médica despacha los medicamentos.

9 Buenos días, doctor. Look at the illustration. Pretend you're the patient. Tell the doctor how you're feeling.

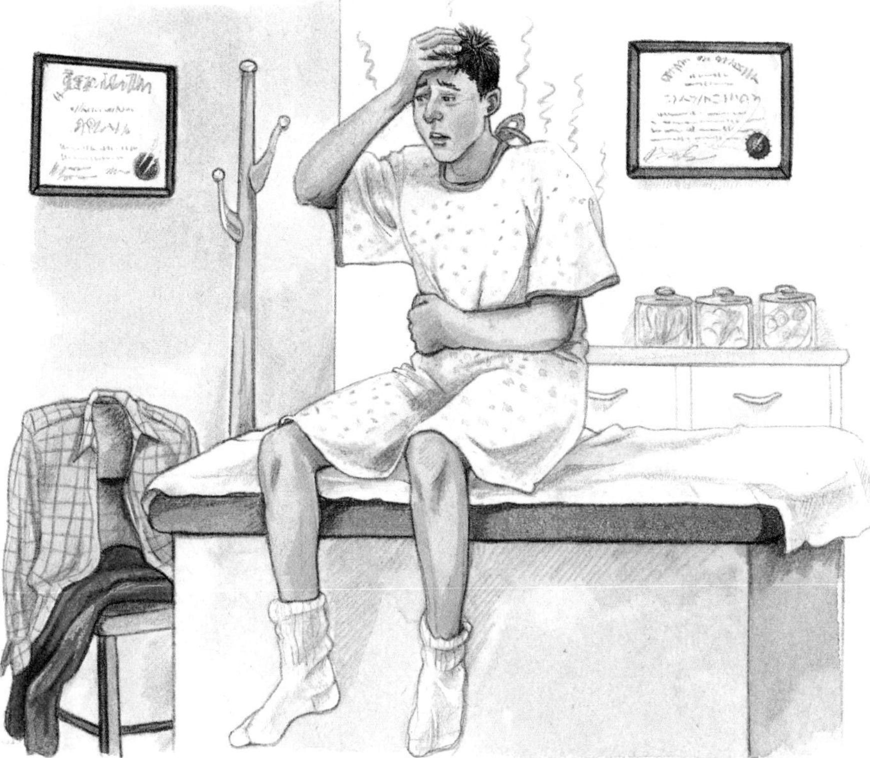

10 En la consulta del médico Work with a classmate. You're sick with a cold or the flu. The doctor (your partner) will ask you questions about your symptoms. Answer the doctor's questions as completely as you can. Then change roles.

Vocabulario

8 Have students do Activity 8 with books open. After you go over it once with the entire class, have students retell the story in their own words.

¡OJO! Activities 9 and 10 encourage students to use the chapter vocabulary and grammar in open-ended situations. It is not necessary to have them do both activities. Choose the one you consider most appropriate.

9 and 10 You may have students present their conversations to the class.

Expansion: In Activity 9 have individual students each come up with a symptom. See how many symptoms the class can think of.

LEVELING

E: Activities 7, 9
A: Activities 6, 8, 9
C: Activity 10

ANSWERS TO ¿Qué palabra necesito?

8

1. Alberto está enfermo.
2. Alberto está en el consultorio (la consulta) de la médica.
3. La médica examina a Alberto.
4. Alberto abre la boca y la médica examina la garganta.
5. Alberto habla con la médica de sus síntomas.
6. La médica receta unos antibióticos.
7. Alberto va a la farmacia con la receta.
8. La farmacéutica despacha los medicamentos.

9 *Answers will vary, but students should use the vocabulary from* Palabras 1 *and* 2. *Answers may include:* Tengo dolor de cabeza, tengo escalofríos, tengo dolor de estómago, *etc.*

10 *Answers will vary. Students will begin with either* Tengo la gripe *or* Estoy resfriado(a).

1 PREPARATION

Resource Manager

Audio Activities TE, pages 97–100
Audio CD 5
Workbook, pages 91–93
Quizzes, pages 40–42
ExamView® Pro

Bellringer Review

Use BRR Transparency 8.3 or write the following on the board.
Write as many words as you can that describe a person.

2 PRESENTATION

Ser y estar

¡OJO! Explain to students that the verb **ser** comes from the Latin verb **esse,** from which the English word *essence* is derived. Therefore, the verb **ser** is used to describe the essence of something, that which is inherent or characteristic.

On the other hand, the verb **estar** is derived from the Latin **stare,** from which the English word *state* is derived. Therefore, **estar** is used to describe a state or a condition.

Step 1 Read Items 1 and 2 aloud.

Step 2 Have students repeat the examples in Items 1 and 2 as you write them on the board.

Ser y estar
Characteristics and conditions

1. In Spanish there are two verbs that mean *to be.* They are **ser** and **estar.** These verbs have very distinct uses. They are not interchangeable. **Ser** is used to express a trait or characteristic that does not change.

   Ella es muy sincera.
   La casa de apartamentos es muy alta.

2. **Estar** is used to express a temporary condition or state.

   Eugenio está enfermo.
   Está cansado y nervioso.

La familia está contenta, San Miguel de Allende

¿Cómo lo digo?

11 Al contrario Sigan el modelo.

Roberto es rubio.

Al contrario. No es rubio.
Roberto es moreno.

1. Teresa es morena.
2. Justo es alto.
3. Héctor es feo.
4. Catalina es muy seria.
5. La clase de biología es aburrida.
6. Los cursos son fáciles.
7. Nuestro equipo de fútbol es malo.
8. Su familia es grande.

Answers to ¿Cómo lo digo?

11

1. Al contrario. No es morena. Teresa es rubia.
2. Al contrario. No es alto. Justo es bajo.
3. Al contrario. No es feo. Héctor es guapo.
4. Al contrario. No es muy seria. Catalina es muy cómica (graciosa).
5. Al contrario. No es aburrida. La clase de biología es interesante.
6. Al contrario. No son fáciles. Los cursos son difíciles.
7. Al contrario. No es malo. Nuestro equipo de fútbol es bueno.
8. Al contrario. No es grande. Mi familia es pequeña.

12 **Tu escuela y tus clases** Contesten.

1. ¿Cómo es tu escuela?
2. ¿Quién en la clase de español es rubio?
3. ¿Quién es moreno?
4. ¿Cuál es un curso interesante?
5. ¿Cuál es una clase aburrida?
6. ¿El equipo de qué deporte es muy bueno?

13 **¿Cómo está o cómo es?** Describan a la persona en cada foto.

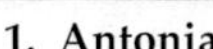

1. Antonia

2. Jorge

3. Beatriz

4. Teresa

5. Susana

14 **¿Cómo eres?** Den una descripción personal.

INFOR-MED

La Medicina cada día avanza más en el desarrollo de nuevas formas de proteger la salud del ser humano. ¡Manténgase informado al respecto!

Estructura

3 PRACTICE

¿Cómo lo digo?

11 You may wish to have students do Activity 11 on page 250 with books open. Students can do this as a paired activity.
Expansion: Have students change the subjects in Activity 11 from singular to plural. This will review the forms of adjectives as well as the forms of the verb **ser.**

12 After going over Activity 12, have students say as much as they can about their school or one of their classes.

13 Note that Activity 13 makes students come up with **ser** or **estar** on their own.

14 See who can come up with the most complete description of himself or herself.

Learning from Realia

(page 251) Have students read the Infor-Med ad and tell what it says in English.

LEVELING

E: Activities 11, 12, 14

A: Activity 13

Answers to ¿Cómo lo digo?

12 *Answers will vary.*

13 *Answers will vary but may include:*

1. Antonia está resfriada (enferma).
2. Jorge está cansado (aburrido).
3. Beatriz está contenta.
4. Teresa está triste (cansada).
5. Susana es inteligente.

14 *Answers will vary. Students can use adjectives that they learned in earlier chapters, including those listed in Chapter 1, page 41, as well as the words and expressions taught in this chapter.*

3 PRACTICE *(continued)*

15 If necessary, have students quickly review the explanation of **ser** and **estar** on page 250 before beginning this activity.
Expansion: Have students retell in their own words as much of the story from Activity 15 as they can.

16 Students will begin their conversations with: **¡Hola! ¿Cómo estás?** You may wish to have students present their descriptions to the class.

UN POCO MÁS This *InfoGap* Activity will allow students to practice in pairs. The activity should be very manageable for them, since all vocabulary and structures are familiar to them.

LEVELING

E: Activity 18
A: Activities 16, 17
C: Activity 15

Estructura

15 Historieta Están enfermos.
Completen con la forma correcta de **ser** o **estar.**

Rubén y Marisol __1__ enfermos. Rubén no tiene energía. __2__ muy cansado. __3__ triste. Y Marisol tiene tos. Su garganta __4__ muy roja. La mamá de Rubén y Marisol __5__ muy nerviosa. Su papá __6__ nervioso también porque sus dos hijos __7__ enfermos. Pero su médico __8__ muy bueno. El doctor Rodríguez __9__ muy inteligente. Su consultorio __10__ muy moderno. El doctor Rodríguez examina a Rubén y a Marisol. El médico habla:

—Ustedes no __11__ muy enfermos. Tienen la gripe. Aquí tienen unos antibióticos. Los antibióticos __12__ muy buenos.

Ahora todos __13__ muy contentos y los padres no __14__ nerviosos. No __15__ nerviosos porque Rubén no __16__ muy enfermo y Marisol no __17__ muy enferma. Dentro de poco, sus hijos van a __18__ muy bien.

16 ¿Por qué? There is usually a reason for everything. Talk to a classmate. He or she will ask you how you're feeling. Answer and explain why you are feeling as you are. Some of the following words may be helpful to you.

*For more practice using words from **Palabras 1** and **ser** and **estar**, do Activity 8 on page H9 at the end of this book.*

ANSWERS TO ¿Cómo lo digo?

15

1. están
2. Está
3. Está
4. está
5. está
6. está
7. están
8. es
9. es
10. es
11. están
12. son
13. están
14. están
15. están
16. está
17. está
18. estar

16 *Answers will vary. Encourage students to use as many words as possible from the colored boxes.*

17 **Virtudes y defectos** Work in small groups. Make a list of characteristics and personality traits. Divide them into two groups—**características positivas (virtudes)** and **características negativas (defectos).** Then have some fun. Make up a description of a person with many virtues. Make up another description of a person with many defects or faults. Be as creative as possible.

Ser y estar
Origin and location

1. The verb **ser** is used to express where someone or something is from.

   La muchacha es de Cuba.
   El café es de Colombia.

2. **Estar** is used to express where someone or something is located.

   Los alumnos están en la escuela.
   Los libros están en el salón de clase.

San Andrés, Colombia

¿Cómo lo digo?

18 **¿De dónde es?** Contesten según el modelo.

¿Es cubano el muchacho?
Sí, creo que es de Cuba.

1. ¿Es colombiana la muchacha?
2. ¿Es guatemalteco el muchacho?
3. ¿Es puertorriqueña la joven?
4. ¿Es española la profesora?
5. ¿Es peruano el médico?
6. ¿Son venezolanos los amigos?
7. ¿Son chilenas las amigas?
8. ¿Son costarricenses los jugadores?

Answers to ¿Cómo lo digo?

17 *Answers will vary. Students can use adjectives that they learned in earlier chapters, including those listed in Chapter 1, page 41, as well as the words and expressions taught in this chapter.*

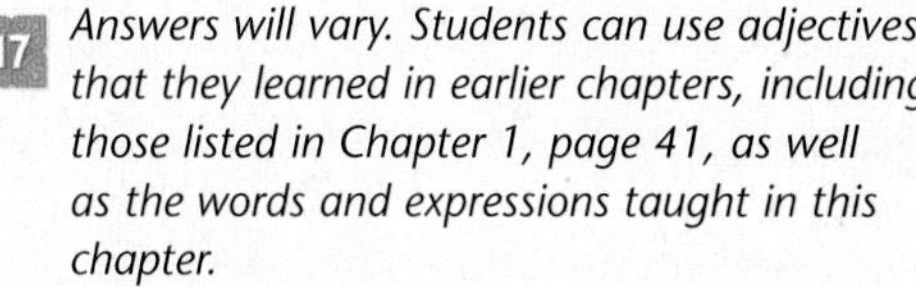

18

1. Sí, creo que es de Colombia.
2. Sí, creo que es de Guatemala.
3. Sí, creo que es de Puerto Rico.
4. Sí, creo que es de España.
5. Sí, creo que es del Perú.
6. Sí, creo que son de Venezuela.
7. Sí, creo que son de Chile.
8. Sí, creo que son de Costa Rica.

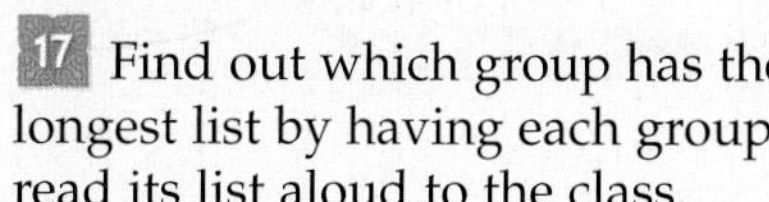

Estructura

17 Find out which group has the longest list by having each group read its list aloud to the class.

1 PREPARATION

Bellringer Review

Use BRR Transparency 8.4 or write the following on the board.
Write the names of as many countries as you can in Spanish.

2 PRESENTATION

Ser y estar

¡OJO! You may wish to emphasize that **estar** is used with both permanent and temporary locations. For example: **Madrid está en España. Los alumnos de la señora Rivera están en Madrid ahora.**

Step 1 Read Items 1 and 2 with the students and have them read the model sentences aloud.

3 PRACTICE

¿Cómo lo digo?

18 Have students do Activity 18 orally as a paired activity. Be sure they know the meaning of **creo.** Say **Sí, creo que es de Cuba** as you nod your head and give an expression of belief but not absolute certainty. Say the model sentences with the appropriate intonation to indicate the naturalness of the exchange.

3 PRACTICE *(continued)*

Writing Development

Have students write out Activity 19 as a short letter.

20 The purpose of this activity is to contrast the uses of **ser** and **estar** and hopefully make it easy for students to understand the difference between origin and location. **Note:** You may have to supply some additional countries to enable students to respond to these questions. You may also ask students to name the countries that they wrote down for the Bellringer Review activity on page 253.

Learning from Photos

(page 254) Caracas is a modern, fast-paced city with many high-rise buildings such as those seen in the photo. Home to more than four million people, Caracas is often referred to as the Miami of South America.

Estructura

19 **Historieta Una carta a un amigo**

Completen la carta.

Caracas, Venezuela

Hola David,

¿Qué tal? ¿Cómo ___1___? Yo ___2___ muy bien. Yo ___3___ Alejandro Salas. ___4___ de Venezuela. Mi casa ___5___ en Caracas, la capital. ___6___ en la calle Rómulo Gallegos. Nuestro apartamento ___7___ moderno. Y ___8___ bastante grande. ___9___ en el quinto piso del edificio. El edificio ___10___ muy alto. Tiene muchos pisos. Me gusta nuestro apartamento.

David, ¿cómo ___11___ tu casa? ¿___12___ muy grande y moderna? Y tu familia, ¿___13___ grande o pequeña?

20 **¿De dónde es y dónde está ahora?** Contesten.

1. Bernardo es de México pero ahora está en Venezuela.
   ¿De dónde es Bernardo?
   ¿Dónde está ahora?
   ¿De dónde es y dónde está?
2. Linda es de Estados Unidos pero ahora está en Colombia.
   ¿De dónde es Linda?
   ¿Dónde está ahora?
   ¿De dónde es y dónde está?
3. La señora Martín es de Cuba pero ahora está en Puerto Rico.
   ¿De dónde es la señora Martín?
   ¿Dónde está ella ahora?
   ¿De dónde es y dónde está?

ANSWERS TO ¿Cómo lo digo?

19

1. estás
2. estoy
3. soy
4. Soy
5. está
6. Está
7. es
8. es
9. Está
10. es
11. es
12. Es
13. es

20

1. Bernardo es de México.
   Ahora está en Venezuela.
   Es de México y ahora está en Venezuela.
2. Linda es de Estados Unidos.
   Ahora está en Colombia.
   Es de Estados Unidos y ahora está en Colombia.
3. La señora Martín es de Cuba.
   Ahora está en Puerto Rico.
   Es de Cuba y ahora está en Puerto Rico.

21 **Entrevista** Contesten personalmente.

1. ¿Estás en la escuela ahora?
2. ¿Dónde está la escuela?
3. ¿En qué clase estás?
4. ¿En qué piso está la sala de clase?
5. ¿Está el/la profesor(a) en la clase también?
6. ¿De dónde es él/ella?
7. ¿Y de dónde eres tú?
8. ¿Cómo estás hoy?
9. Y el/la profesor(a), ¿cómo está?
10. ¿Y cómo es?

22 **Historieta Un amigo, Ángel**
Completen con **ser** o **estar.**

West New York, New Jersey

Ángel __1__ un amigo muy bueno. __2__ muy atlético y __3__ muy inteligente. Además __4__ sincero y simpático. Casi siempre __5__ de buen humor. Pero hoy no. Al contrario, __6__ de mal humor. __7__ muy cansado y tiene dolor de cabeza. __8__ enfermo. Tiene la gripe. __9__ en casa. __10__ en cama.

La casa de Ángel __11__ en la calle 60. La calle 60 __12__ en West New York. West New York no __13__ en Nueva York. __14__ en Nueva Jersey. Pero la familia de Ángel no __15__ de West New York. Sus padres __16__ de Cuba y sus abuelos __17__ de España. Ellos __18__ de Galicia, una región en el noroeste de España. Galicia __19__ en la costa del Atlántico y del mar Cantábrico. Ángel tiene una familia internacional.

Pero ahora todos __20__ en West New York y __21__ contentos. Muchas familias en West New York __22__ de ascendencia cubana. El apartamento de la familia de Ángel __23__ muy bonito. __24__ en el tercer piso y tiene una vista magnífica de la ciudad de Nueva York.

Estructura

21 **and** **22** You may have two students come to the front of the class and present Activity 21 as an interview. This activity incorporates all uses of **ser** and **estar** as does Activity 22.

FUN-FACTS

Activity 22 gives the students a great deal of cultural information. Many people from Galicia in northwestern Spain migrated to the United States and areas of Latin America, particularly the Caribbean.

When many Cubans left Cuba for political reasons in the early 1960s, a number went to Miami, Florida, and to West New York, Union City, and Weehawken, New Jersey, on the palisades overlooking New York City. Many businesses became Cuban-owned and operated. Although there are still many people of Cuban descent in these communities, they have been joined by others from Central and South America and the Dominican Republic.

LEVELING

E: Activities 20, 21
A: Activities 20, 21
C: Activities 19, 22

ANSWERS TO ¿Cómo lo digo?

21

1. Sí, (No, no) estoy en la escuela ahora.
2. La escuela está en ___.
3. Estoy en la clase de ___.
4. La sala de clase está en el ___ piso.
5. Sí, el / la profesor(a) está en la clase también.
6. Él / Ella es de ___.
7. Yo soy de ___.
8. Estoy ___.
9. El / La profesor(a) está ___.
10. Es ___.

22

1. es
2. Es
3. es
4. es
5. está
6. está
7. Está
8. Está
9. Está
10. Está
11. está
12. está
13. está
14. Está
15. es
16. son
17. son
18. son
19. está
20. están
21. están
22. son
23. es
24. Está

1 PREPARATION

Bellringer Review

Use BRR Transparency 8.5 or write the following on the board.
Write the Spanish names for as many parts of the body as you can.

2 PRESENTATION

Me, te, nos

¡OJO! Only the pronouns **me, te,** and **nos** are presented in this chapter. At this point students do not have to distinguish between direct and indirect objects. The pronouns **lo, la, los, las** are presented in Chapter 9 and **le, les** in Chapter 10.

The pronouns **me, te, nos** are presented first because they are less complicated than the third person pronouns. They are both direct and indirect objects. They are the only pronouns that are absolutely necessary for communication. For example, if asked a question with **te,** it is necessary to answer with **me.** When speaking in the third person, one could answer with a noun instead of a pronoun: **¿Invitaste a Juan? Sí, invité a Juan.**

Step 1 Have students point to themselves as they say **me** and point to or look at a friend as they say **te.**

Step 2 Have students read the model sentences aloud. You can call on an individual to read them or have the entire class read them in unison.

Me, te, nos

Telling what happens to whom

Me, te, and **nos** are object pronouns. Note that the pronoun is placed right before the verb.

¿Te ve el médico?
Sí, el médico me ve. Me examina.
¿Te da una receta?
Sí, me da una receta.
Cuando tenemos la gripe, el médico nos receta antibióticos.

¿Cómo lo digo?

23 Historieta En el consultorio

Contesten.

1. ¿Estás enfermo(a)?
2. ¿Vas a la consulta del médico?
3. ¿Te ve el médico?
4. ¿Te examina?
5. ¿Te habla el médico?
6. ¿Te da una diagnosis?
7. ¿Te receta unas pastillas?
8. ¿Te despacha los medicamentos la farmacéutica?

24 Una invitación Completen.

—Aquí tienes una carta.
¿Quién __1__ escribe?
—Carlos __2__ escribe.
—¿Ah, sí?
—Sí, __3__ invita a una fiesta.
—¿ __4__ invita a una fiesta?
—Sí, Carlos siempre __5__ invita cuando tiene una fiesta.

Los Integrantes de la Promoción XXVIII
de
Institutos Educacionales Asociados
Tienen el gusto de invitarle a la fiesta que ofrecen
con motivo de su Graduación,
el Miércoles 30 de Julio
Recepción:
Hotel Tamanaco
Salón "Naiguatá"
Hora: 8:30 p.m.
Traje formal.
1 Persona.
Indispensable la presentacion de esta tarjeta.

Answers to ¿Cómo lo digo?

23

1. Sí, (No, no) estoy enfermo(a).
2. Sí, (No, no) voy a la consulta del médico.
3. Sí, (No, no) me ve el médico.
4. Sí, (No, no) me examina.
5. Sí, (No, no) me habla el médico.
6. Sí, (No, no) me da una diagnosis.
7. Sí, (No, no) me receta unas pastillas.
8. Sí (No), la farmacéutica (no) me despacha los medicamentos.

24

1. te
2. me
3. me
4. Te
5. me

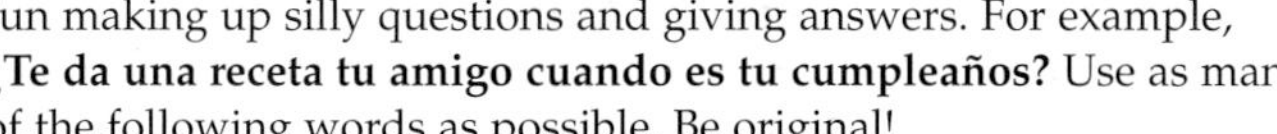

25 **Preguntas y más preguntas** Work with a partner. Have some fun making up silly questions and giving answers. For example, **¿Te da una receta tu amigo cuando es tu cumpleaños?** Use as many of the following words as possible. Be original!

Facultad de Farmacia, Universidad de Madrid

Answers to ¿Cómo lo digo?

25 *Answers will vary. Encourage students to use as many words as possible from the colored boxes.*

3 PRACTICE

¿Cómo lo digo?

24 Call on two students to present Activity 24 on page 256 as a miniconversation.

25 You may wish to do this activity with the entire class. As students give silly statements, the laughter of the other class members indicates comprehension. You can call on another student to correct the silly statement and say something that makes sense.

Learning from Photos

(page 257) The University of Madrid has an excellent School of Pharmacy. You may wish to point out to students that the term *school* in Spanish is **la facultad** when referring to a school at a university.

¡Adelante!
At this point in the chapter, students have learned all the vocabulary and structure necessary to complete the chapter. The conversation and cultural readings that follow recycle all the material learned up to this point.

LEVELING

E: Activity 23
A: Activities 23, 25
C: Activities 24, 25

Conversación

1 PREPARATION

Resource Manager

Audio Activities TE, pages 100–101
Audio CD 5

Bellringer Review

Use BRR Transparency 8.6 or write the following on the board.
Answer the following questions.

1. **¿Comes mucho cuando estás enfermo(a)?**
2. **¿Tienes mucho apetito cuando estás enfermo(a)?**
3. **¿Tomas muchos líquidos cuando estás enfermo(a)?**
4. **¿Guardas cama cuando estás enfermo(a)?**

2 PRESENTATION

Step 1 Tell students they will hear a conversation between Alejandro and a doctor. Have students close their books and listen as you read the conversation or play Audio CD 5.

Step 2 Have students keep their books closed as you reread the conversation to them, stopping after every three sentences to ask simple comprehension questions.

Step 3 Have students open their books and read the conversation aloud.

Step 4 Have them dramatize the conversation.

Step 5 Have a student summarize the visit to the doctor in his or her own words.

Expansion: Have students present other versions of the conversation. The student playing the patient should give different symptoms. The "doctor" will have to change his or her responses accordingly.

Conversación

En la consulta del médico

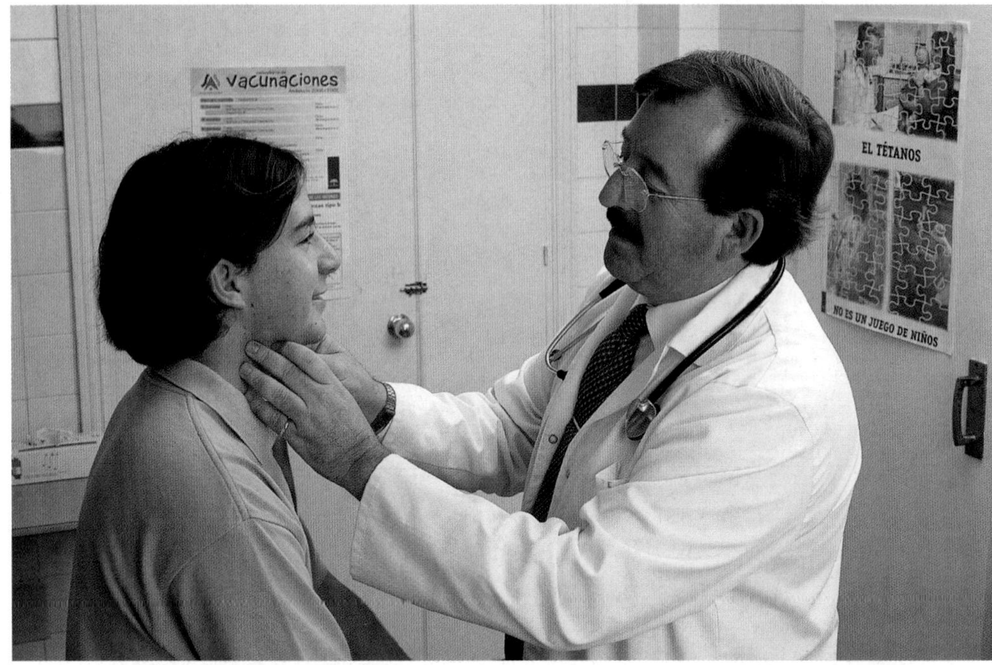

Alejandro Buenos días, doctor López.
Doctor Buenos días, Alejandro. ¿Qué te pasa? ¿Qué tienes?
Alejandro Doctor López, ¡qué enfermo estoy!
Doctor ¿Me puedes explicar tus síntomas?
Alejandro Pues, tengo fiebre. Y tengo escalofríos.
Doctor ¿Te duele la garganta?
Alejandro ¿La garganta? Me duele todo— la garganta, la cabeza.
Doctor Bien, Alejandro. ¿Puedes abrir la boca? *(Después de mirar)* Ya veo. Tienes la garganta muy roja.
Alejandro ¿Qué tengo, doctor?
Doctor No es nada serio. Tienes la gripe. Te voy a recetar unos antibióticos. Dentro de dos días vas a estar muy bien.

¿Comprendes?

Contesten.

1. ¿Dónde está Alejandro?
2. ¿Con quién habla?
3. ¿Cómo está Alejandro?
4. ¿Qué tiene?
5. ¿Tiene dolor de garganta?
6. ¿Tiene dolor de cabeza?
7. ¿Abre la boca Alejandro?
8. ¿Qué examina el médico?
9. ¿Cómo está la garganta?
10. ¿Qué cree el médico que Alejandro tiene?

Answers to ¿Comprendes?

1. Alejandro está en la consulta (el consultorio) del médico.
2. Habla con el médico (doctor).
3. Alejandro está enfermo.
4. Tiene fiebre y escalofríos.
5. Sí, tiene dolor de garganta.
6. Sí, tiene dolor de cabeza.
7. Sí, Alejandro abre la boca.
8. El médico examina la garganta de Alejandro.
9. La garganta está muy roja.
10. El médico cree que Alejandro tiene la gripe.

Vamos a hablar más

 **¿Debes o no debes ser médico(a)?** Work with a classmate. Interview one another and decide who would be a good doctor. Make a list of questions for your interview. One question you may want to ask is: **¿Tienes mucha o poca paciencia?**

B Juego **¿Quién es?** Play a guessing game with a classmate. Give some features and characteristics of someone in the class. Then tell how the person appears to be today. Your partner will guess who it is you are talking about. Then your partner will describe someone and it will be your turn to guess.

ALUMNO 1: **Es morena y alta. Está contenta hoy.**
ALUMNO 2: **¡Es Alicia!**
ALUMNO 1: **Sí, es ella.**

Pronunciación

La consonante c

You have already learned that **c** in combination with **e** or **i (ce, ci)** is pronounced like an **s.** The consonant **c** in combination with **a, o, u (ca, co, cu)** has a hard **k** sound. Since **ce, ci** have the soft **s** sound, **c** changes to **qu** when it combines with **e** or **i (que, qui)** in order to maintain the hard **k** sound. Repeat the following.

ca	que	qui	co	cu
cama	**que**	**equipo**	**como**	**cubano**
casa	**queso**	**aquí**	**médico**	
catarro	**parque**	**química**	**cocina**	
cansado	**pequeño**	**tranquilo**		
cabeza				
boca				

Repeat the following sentences.

El médico cubano está en la consulta pequeña.
El queso está en la cocina de la casa.
El cubano come el queso aquí en el parque pequeño.

Conversación

3 PRACTICE

Vamos a hablar más

B **Juego** This game makes a good end-of-class activity. It also recycles descriptive adjectives from Chapters 1 and 2.

Pronunciación

Step 1 Remind students that the **c** sound is somewhat softer in Spanish than it is in English. Have them imitate your pronunciation or that of the speaker on Audio CD 5.

Step 2 You may also use these words and sentences for a dictation.

Step 3 To see if students are grasping this spelling concept, you may wish to dictate the following words, which they do not know.

queda	**quiste**
cate	**quita**
coco	**quema**
quiosco	**coloca**
culebra	**loco**

LEVELING

E: Conversation

Glencoe Technology

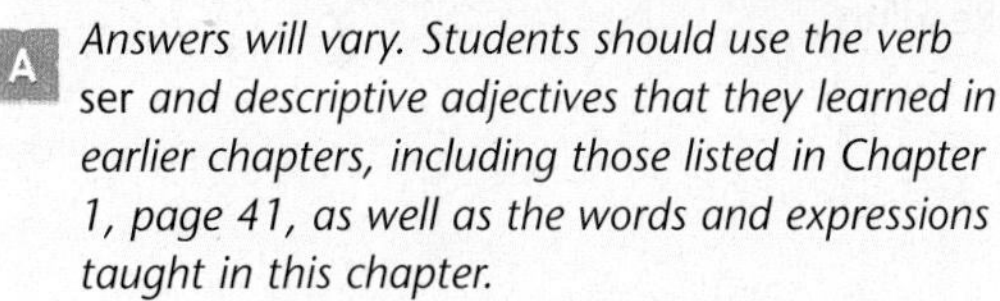

CD-ROM

On the CD-ROM, students can watch a dramatization of this conversation. They can then play the role of either one of the characters and record themselves in the conversation.

Answers to Vamos a hablar más

A *Answers will vary. Students should use the verb* ser *and descriptive adjectives that they learned in earlier chapters, including those listed in Chapter 1, page 41, as well as the words and expressions taught in this chapter.*

B *Answers will vary, but students should follow the model given.*

Lecturas culturales

Resource Manager

Audio Activities TE, page 102
Audio CD 5

Bellringer Review

Use BRR Transparency 8.7 or write the following on the board.
Rewrite these sentences. Change the singular object pronouns in the first two sentences to the plural form. In the second two sentences, change the plural forms to singular.

1. **Me duele la cabeza.**
2. **Me da una receta.**
3. **Nos invita a la fiesta.**
4. **El médico nos examina.**

National Standards

Cultures

The reading about a visit to the doctor on pages 260–261 and the related activities give students an understanding of daily life in the Spanish-speaking world.

Comparisons

Have students look at the prescription on page 260. It is from the **Clínica Nuestra Señora de América. Clínica** has a different meaning from the English word *clinic.* A **clínica** is often a private hospital owned by either one or several doctors.

Lecturas culturales

Reading Strategy

Visualizing As you are reading, try to visualize (or make a mental picture of) exactly what it is you are reading. Allow your mind to freely develop an image. This will help you to remember what you read. It may also help you identify with the subject you are reading about.

Una joven nerviosa 

La pobre Patricia está muy enferma hoy. No tiene energía. Está cansada. Tiene dolor de garganta y tiene tos. Está de muy mal humor porque mañana tiene que jugar en un partido importante de fútbol. No quiere perder[1] el partido pero no puede jugar si está tan enferma y débil[2]. Pues, no hay más remedio para Patricia. Tiene que ir a ver al médico. Llega al consultorio.

[1]perder *to miss*
[2]débil *weak*

Málaga, España

Tegretol® 400 mg
Carbamazepina
Liberación Controlada
Grageas
7 702635 185291

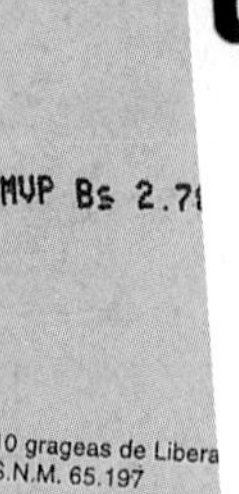

NOVARTIS
PMVP Bs 2.7
10 grageas de Libera
S.N.M. 65.197
CLINICA NUESTRA SEÑORA DE AMERICA
NO VALIDO PARA FACTURA

LEVELING
E: Reading

PRESENTATION

Pre-reading

Step 1 Have students scan the passage to look for cognates.

Step 2 Give students a brief synopsis of the **Lectura** in Spanish. Ask a few questions based on it.

En el consultorio Patricia habla con el médico. Explica que tiene un partido importante que no quiere perder. El médico examina a Patricia. Ella abre la boca y el médico examina la garganta. Sí, está un poco roja pero no es nada serio. Su condición no es grave.

Habla Patricia:

—Doctor, no puedo guardar cama. Tengo que jugar fútbol mañana.

—Patricia, estás muy nerviosa. Tienes que estar tranquila. No hay problema. Aquí tienes una receta. Vas a tomar una pastilla tres veces al día—una pastilla con cada comida. Mañana vas a estar mucho mejor[3] y no vas a perder tu partido. Y, ¡buena suerte[4]!

[3]mucho mejor *much better*
[4]buena suerte *good luck*

Madrid, España

¿Comprendes?

Pobre Patricia

Contesten.

1. ¿Quién está enferma?
2. ¿Cuáles son sus síntomas?
3. ¿Está de buen humor o de mal humor?
4. ¿Por qué está nerviosa?
5. ¿Cuál es el único remedio para Patricia?
6. ¿Con quién habla Patricia en el consultorio?
7. ¿Qué examina el médico?
8. ¿Cómo está la garganta?
9. ¿Cómo es su condición?
10. ¿Tiene que guardar cama Patricia?
11. ¿Qué tiene que tomar?
12. ¿Cuándo tiene que tomar las pastillas?
13. ¿Cómo va a estar mañana?

Lecturas culturales

Reading

Call on a student to read three or four sentences. Ask several questions to check comprehension before calling on the next student to read. Continue in this way until the selection has been completed.

Post-reading

Assign the reading selection and the **¿Comprendes?** activity on page 261 as homework. Go over the homework the next day in class.

Learning from Photos

(page 261) Ask the following questions about the photo:

¿Es una clínica o una farmacia?

¿Lleva uniforme los farmacéuticos?

¿De qué color es?

Answers to ¿Comprendes?

1. Patricia está enferma.
2. No tiene energía. Está cansada. Tiene dolor de garganta y tiene tos.
3. Está de muy mal humor.
4. Está nerviosa porque mañana tiene que jugar en un partido importante de fútbol y no puede jugar si está tan enferma y débil.
5. Tiene que ir a ver al médico.
6. Patricia habla con el médico en el consultorio.
7. El médico examina la garganta.
8. Está un poco roja pero no es nada serio.
9. Su condición no es grave.
10. No, no tiene que guardar cama.
11. Tiene que tomar las pastillas que receta el médico.
12. Tiene que tomar las pastillas tres veces al día—una pastilla con cada comida.
13. Mañana va a estar mucho mejor.

Lectura opcional 1

National Standards

Cultures

The reading about pharmacies and the related activities on this page give students an understanding of medical services in the Spanish-speaking world.

Comparisons

In this selection students learn that, unlike pharmacists in the United States, Spanish and Latin American pharmacists can dispense many medicines without a prescription. Pharmacists will also listen to a patient's symptoms and recommend a medicine.

¡OJO! This reading is optional. You may skip it completely, have the entire class read it, have only several students read it and report to the class, or assign it for extra credit.

PRESENTATION

Step 1 After the students read the selection, ask them to state the main difference between pharmacies in the United States and those in many Hispanic countries.

Step 2 You may wish to use the **¿Comprendes?** questions as an informal quiz to find out how well the students understood the reading.

Learning from Photos

(page 262) This photo is of a traditional pharmacy sometimes called **una apoteca** or **una botica.** The person who works there is called **un apotecario** or **un boticario.** These traditional pharmacies sell only medical products. Some newer pharmacies, however, now sell cosmetics, too.

Lectura opcional 1

La farmacia

En Estados Unidos si uno quiere o necesita antibióticos, es necesario tener una receta. Es necesario visitar al médico para un examen. El médico receta los medicamentos y el paciente lleva la receta a la farmacia. El farmacéutico no puede despachar medicamentos sin la receta de un médico.

En muchos países hispanos no es necesario tener una receta para comprar antibióticos. Uno puede explicar sus síntomas al farmacéutico y él o ella puede despachar los medicamentos. Pero hay una excepción. Los farmacéuticos no pueden despachar medicamentos que contienen sustancias controladas como un narcótico o un medicamento con alcohol.

Y hay otra cosa importante. El precio[1] de las medicinas en los países hispanos es mucho más bajo que el precio de las mismas medicinas en Estados Unidos.

[1]precio *price*

Buenos Aires, Argentina

¿Comprendes?

¿Sí o no? Digan que sí o que no.

1. El farmacéutico en Estados Unidos no puede despachar medicamentos si el cliente no tiene una receta de su médico.
2. En Latinoamérica el médico despacha los medicamentos.
3. En Latinoamérica es necesario ir a una clínica por los antibióticos.
4. El farmacéutico en Latinoamérica puede despachar antibióticos sin una receta del médico.
5. El farmacéutico en Latinoamérica no puede vender medicamentos que contienen o llevan una droga o alcohol sin una receta.
6. Los medicamentos cuestan más en los países hispanos que en Estados Unidos.

Answers to ¿Comprendes?

1. Sí
2. No
3. No
4. Sí
5. Sí
6. No

LEVELING

E: Reading 1

C: Reading 2

Lectura opcional 2

La Habana, Cuba

Una biografía—El doctor Antonio Gassett

El doctor Antonio Gassett es de La Habana, Cuba. Recibe su bachillerato en ciencias en la Universidad de Belén, en Cuba. Más tarde estudia en la Facultad de Medicina de la Universidad de La Habana. Poco después, sale de[1] Cuba por motivos políticos. Va a Boston donde trabaja de técnico de laboratorio en la Fundación de Retina de Boston.

Le interesa mucho el trabajo con los ojos y decide estudiar oftalmología. Estudia en Harvard y en la Universidad de la Florida.

Hoy el doctor Gassett es una persona famosa. Descubre un método para tratar la córnea. Con el tratamiento del doctor Gassett muchas personas ciegas—que no pueden ver—recobran la vista[2]. El doctor recibe muchos premios[3] por sus investigaciones y descubrimientos[4].

[1]sale de *he leaves*
[2]recobran la vista *regain sight*
[3]premios *prizes, awards*
[4]descubrimientos *discoveries*

A Estudio de palabras Contesten.

1. The word **investigar** is a cognate of *investigate.* What does *to investigate* mean? In Spanish, **investigar** can mean both *to investigate* and *to do research.* Related words are: **las investigaciones, el investigador.** Use these words in a sentence.
2. In the reading, find a word related to each of the following: **tratar, descubrir.**

B Palabras sinónimas Busquen una expresión equivalente.

1. obtiene su bachillerato
2. por razones políticas
3. le fascina el trabajo
4. es una persona célebre, renombrada

Answers to ¿Comprendes?

A

1. In English, *to investigate something* means *to observe or study something closely* or *to conduct an official inquiry. Answers will vary.*
2. el tratamiento, descubrimientos

B

1. recibe su bachillerato
2. por motivos políticos
3. le interesa mucho el trabajo
4. es una persona famosa

Lectura opcional 2

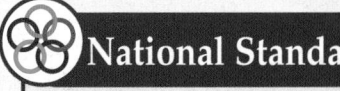

National Standards

Cultures
In this selection, students learn about an important contribution to medicine made by a Cuban American.

¡OJO! This reading is optional. You may skip it completely, have the entire class read it, have only several students read it and report to the class, or assign it for extra credit.

PRESENTATION

Step 1 Have students read the selection silently. Ask them to give a one-sentence summary in Spanish of what Dr. Gassett's contribution to medicine is.

Step 2 Now have them quickly do the **¿Comprendes?** activities.

Learning from Photos

(page 263) Havana, the capital of Cuba, is noted for its beautiful colonial architecture, examples of which can be seen in this photo.

Conexiones

National Standards

Connections
This reading about nutrition establishes a connection with another discipline, allowing students to reinforce and further their knowledge of the natural sciences through the study of Spanish.

¡OJO! The readings in the **Conexiones** section are optional. They focus on some of the major disciplines taught in schools and universities. The vocabulary is useful for discussing such topics as history, literature, art, economics, business, science, etc. You may choose any of the following ways to do the readings in the **Conexiones** sections.

Independent reading Have students read the selections and do the post-reading activities as homework, which you collect. This option is least intrusive on class time and requires a minimum of teacher involvement.

Homework with in-class follow-up Assign the readings and post-reading activities as homework. Review and discuss the material in class the next day.

Intensive in-class activity This option includes a pre-reading vocabulary presentation, in-class reading and discussion, assignment of the activities for homework, and a discussion of the assignment in class the following day.

Conexiones

Las ciencias naturales

La nutrición

Good nutrition is very important. What we eat can determine if we will enjoy good health or have poor health. For this reason, it is most important to have a balanced diet and avoid the temptation to eat "junk food."

Read the following information about nutrition in Spanish. Before reading this selection, however, look at the following groups of related words. Often if you know the meaning of one word you can guess the meaning of several other words related to it.

varía, la variedad, la variación
activo, la actividad
los adolescentes, la adolescencia
proveen, la provisión, el proveedor
el consumo, consumir, el consumidor
elevar, la elevación, elevado

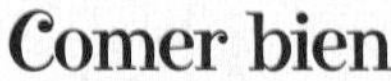

Comer bien

Es muy importante comer bien para mantener la salud. Cada día debemos[1] comer una variedad de vegetales, frutas, granos y cereales y carnes o pescado.

Calorías

El número de calorías que necesita o requiere una persona depende de su metabolismo, de su tamaño y de su nivel[2] de actividad física. Los adolescentes necesitan más calorías que los ancianos o viejos. Requieren más calorías porque son muy activos y están creciendo[3]. Una persona anciana de tamaño pequeño con un nivel bajo de actividad física requiere menos calorías.

[1]debemos *we should* [2]nivel *level* [3]creciendo *growing*

Class Motivator

La nutrición Those students who are interested in nutrition may prepare a food chart with the following heads.

Alimentos altos en calorías
Alimentos bajos en calorías
Grasas
Carbohidratos
Vitamina A
Vitamina B
Vitamina C
Vitamina D
Vitamina E

Under each heading they can put photos or drawings labeled in Spanish of appropriate foods that they have already learned to identify.

Proteínas

Las proteínas son especialmente importantes durante los períodos de crecimiento. Los adolescentes, por ejemplo, deben comer comestibles o alimentos ricos[4] en proteínas porque están creciendo.

Carbohidratos

Los carbohidratos son alimentos como los espaguetis, las papas y el arroz. Los carbohidratos proveen mucha energía.

Grasas

Las grasas o lípidos son otra fuente[5] importante de energía. Algunas carnes contienen mucha grasa. Pero es necesario controlar el consumo de lípidos o grasa porque en muchos individuos elevan el nivel de colesterol.

Vitaminas

Las vitaminas son indispensables para el funcionamiento del organismo o cuerpo. ¿Cuáles son algunas fuentes de las vitaminas que necesita el cuerpo humano?

VITAMINA	FUENTE
A	vegetales, leche, algunas frutas
B	carne, huevos, leche, cereales, vegetales verdes
C	frutas cítricas, tomates, lechuga
D	leche, huevos, pescado
E	aceites[6], vegetales, huevos, cereales

[4]ricos *rich* [5]fuente *source* [6]aceites *oils*

Estepona, España

¿Comprendes?

La nutrición Contesten.

1. ¿Qué debemos comer cada día?
2. ¿De qué depende el número de calorías que requiere una persona?
3. ¿Quiénes requieren más calorías? ¿Por qué?
4. ¿Por qué necesitan los adolescentes alimentos ricos en proteínas?
5. ¿Qué proveen los carbohidratos?
6. ¿Por qué es necesario controlar el consumo de grasas o lípidos?

Conexiones

PRESENTATION

Las ciencias naturales
La nutrición

Recycling

You may wish to have all students read this selection, since many students are interested in good eating habits. This reading reviews and reinforces the names for many foods.

Reaching All Students

Additional Practice
Have students write out a balanced menu for **el desayuno, el almuerzo,** and **la cena** for one day. They should use the information they learned in the **Conexiones** reading when planning their meals.

LEVELING

A: Reading

Answers to ¿Comprendes?

1. Cada día debemos comer una variedad de vegetales, frutas, granos y cereales y carnes o pescado.
2. El número de calorías que requiere una persona depende de su metabolismo, de su tamaño y de su nivel de actividad física.
3. Los adolescentes requieren más calorías porque son muy activos y están creciendo.
4. Los adolescentes deben comer alimentos ricos en proteínas porque están creciendo.
5. Los carbohidratos proveen mucha energía.
6. Es necesario controlar el consumo de grasas o lípidos porque en muchos individuos elevan el nivel de colesterol.

Use what you have learned

Recycling

These activities allow students to use the vocabulary and structure from this chapter in completely open-ended, real-life situations.

PRESENTATION

Encourage students to say as much as possible when they do these activities. Tell them not to be afraid to make mistakes, since the goal of the activities is real-life communication. If someone in the group makes an error, allow the others to politely correct him or her. Let students choose the activities they would like to do.

You may wish to divide students into pairs or groups. Encourage students to elaborate on the basic theme and to be creative. They may use props, pictures, or posters if they wish.

PRACTICE

1 You may also wish to have one student act out the symptoms for the entire class as the other student describes them.

2 Have students write out a prescription on a piece of paper to use in the activity.

3 You may wish to have some groups present to the entire class.

LEVELING

These activities encompass all three levels. All students will be able to do them at a sophistication level commensurate with their ability in Spanish. Some students will be able to speak for several minutes, and others may be able to give just a few sentences. This is to be expected when students are functioning completely on their own generating their own language to the best of their ability.

Use what you have learned

HABLAR 1

Todos están enfermos.

✔ *Describe cold symptoms and minor ailments*

Work with a classmate. Choose one of the people in the illustrations. Describe him or her. Your partner will guess which person you're talking about and say what's the matter with the person. Take turns.

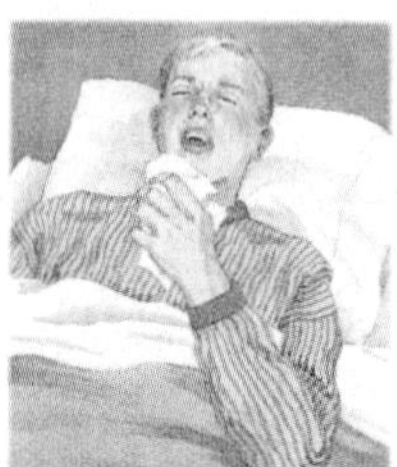

Paco

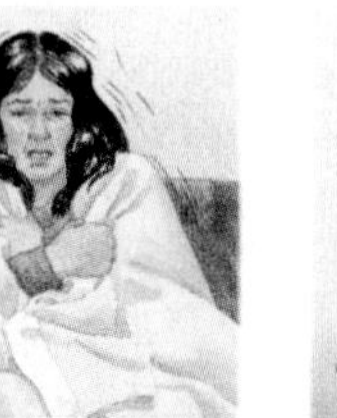

Gloria

Ana

David

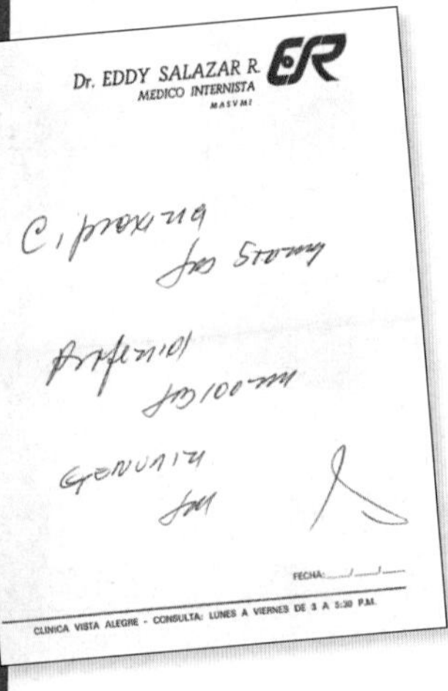

HABLAR 2

Una receta

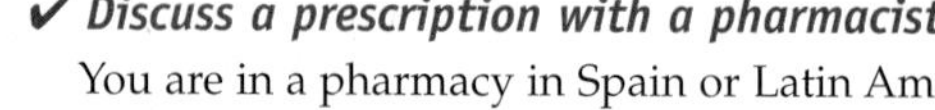

✔ *Discuss a prescription with a pharmacist*

You are in a pharmacy in Spain or Latin America. Your classmate will be the pharmacist. Make up a conversation about your prescription. Explain why and how you have to take the medicine.

HABLAR 3

¿Qué te pasa? ¿Qué tienes?

✔ *Explain an illness to a doctor*

With a partner, prepare a skit about a nervous person in a doctor's office. If you want, prepare the skit based on the story about **Una joven nerviosa.** Your skit can be about Patricia and her doctor.

HABLAR 4

Juego ¡Qué enfermo(a) estoy!

✔ *Talk about how you are feeling*

Work with a partner. Make gestures to indicate how you're feeling today. Your partner will ask you why you feel that way. Tell him or her. Be as creative and humorous as possible.

Answers to ¡Te toca a ti!

1 *Answers will vary. Be sure that students describe all four individuals. Answers may include:*

El joven estornuda. Está en cama.
El joven tiene escalofríos. Está en cama.
El joven tiene tos.
El joven toma pastillas.

2 *Answers will vary. Students should discuss their symptoms and the proposed treatment, including prescription information such as how often to take the medicine.*

3 *Answers will vary, but students can use the conversation on page 258 as a model.*

4 *Answers will vary but should include health-related vocabulary from the chapter.*

¡Te toca a ti!

ESCRIBIR

5 ¡Por favor!

✔ *Write a note describing a minor illness*

You're supposed to take a Spanish test today but you're not feeling well. Write a note to your Spanish teacher explaining why you can't take the test, and mention some symptoms you have.

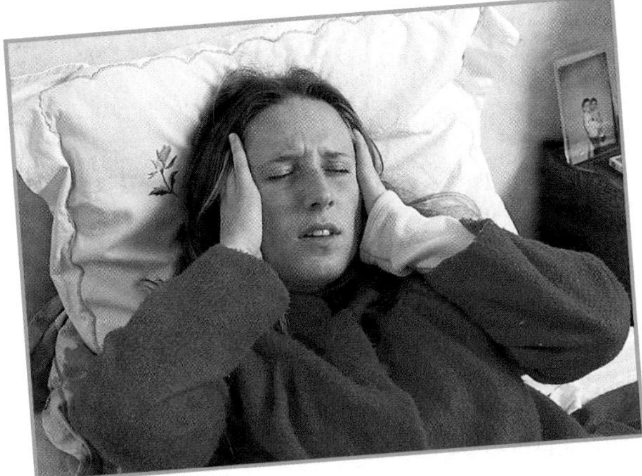

SPANISH Online

For more information about medical services in the Spanish-speaking world, go to the Glencoe Spanish Web site: spanish.glencoe.com

Writing Development

Have students keep a notebook or portfolio containing their best written work from each chapter. These selected writings can be based on assignments from the Student Textbook and the Workbook. The activities on page 267 are examples of writing assignments that may be included in each student's portfolio. On page 98 in the Workbook, students will begin to develop an organized autobiography **(Mi autobiografía).** These workbook pages may also become a part of their portfolio.

National Standards

Communities

The writing assignment in Activity 6 encourages students to use the language beyond the school setting.

ESCRIBIR

6 El servicio en la comunidad

Your Spanish Club has a community service requirement. You have decided to work in the emergency room **(la sala de emergencia)** at your local hospital. You serve as a translator or interpreter for patients who speak only Spanish. Write a flyer for your Spanish Club. Tell about your experience with one or more patients. Give your feelings about the work you do and try to encourage other club members to volunteer their services, too.

Writing Strategy

Writing a personal essay In writing a personal essay, a writer has several options: to tell a story, describe something, or encourage someone to think a certain way or to do something. Whatever its purpose, a personal essay allows a writer to express a viewpoint about a subject he or she has experienced. Your essay will be much livelier if you allow your enthusiasm to be obvious; do so by choosing interesting details and vivid words to relay your message.

Answers to ¡Te toca a ti!

5 *Answers will vary. Students might use phrases such as:*

No puedo tomar el examen hoy. Estoy en cama. Tengo fiebre y escalofríos. Creo que tengo la gripe.

6 *Answers will vary. Students should use health-related vocabulary from the chapter,* ser *and* estar, *and structures from previously learned chapters such as* gustar *and* interesar.

Writing Strategy

Writing a personal essay

Have students read the Writing Strategy on page 267. Then have them refer to the **Vocabulario** on page 271 as they jot down ideas for their essay.

Resource Manager

Communication Transparency C 8
Quizzes, pages 38–42
Performance Assessment, Task 8
Tests, pages 123–138
Situation Cards, Chapter 8
ExamView® Pro, Chapter 8
Maratón mental Videoquiz, Chapter 8

Assessment

This is a pre-test for students to take before you administer the chapter test. Note that each section is cross-referenced so students can easily find the material they have to review in case they made errors. You may use Assessment Answers Transparency A 8 to do the assessment in class, or you may assign this assessment for homework. You can correct the assessment yourself, or you may prefer to project the answers on the overhead in class.

Glencoe Technology

MINDJOGGER VHS/DVD

You may wish to help your students prepare for the chapter test by playing the MindJogger game show. Teams will compete against each other to review chapter vocabulary and structure and sharpen listening comprehension skills.

Vocabulario

To review **Palabras 1**, turn to pages 242–243.

1 Escojan.

1. Roberto está enfermo.
   - **a.** No está bien.
   - **b.** Está contento.
   - **c.** Está nervioso.
2. Ella tiene fiebre.
   - **a.** No tiene síntomas.
   - **b.** Y tiene escalofríos.
   - **c.** Está tranquila.
3. El muchacho tiene catarro.
   - **a.** Está nervioso.
   - **b.** Está resfriado.
   - **c.** Tiene dolor de estómago.
4. ¿Por qué tiene que guardar cama?
   - **a.** Porque no está de buen humor.
   - **b.** Tiene tos.
   - **c.** Tiene la gripe y tiene fiebre.

2 Identifiquen.

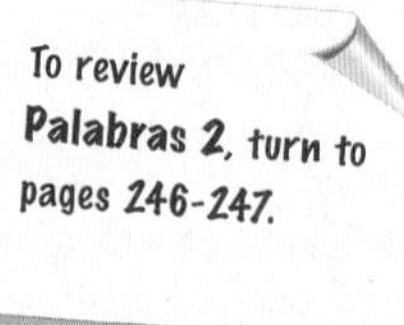
To review **Palabras 2**, turn to pages 246–247.

Answers to Assessment

1

1. a
2. b
3. b
4. c

2

5. el ojo/los ojos
6. la boca
7. la garganta
8. el estómago

3 **Expresen de otra manera.**

9. Tengo dolor de cabeza.

Estructura

4 **Completen con ser o estar.**

10. Él ____ rubio.
11. Alicia ____ enferma.
12. El curso de historia ____ muy interesante.
13. Él ____ de mal humor porque ____ cansado.
14. ¿Dónde ____ la sala de consulta del médico?
15. Madrid ____ en España.
16. El amigo de Teresa ____ de Cuba.
17. Ahora (él) ____ en Nueva York.

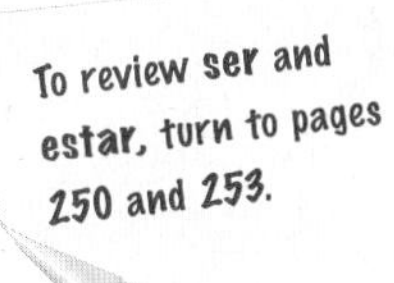
To review **ser** and **estar**, turn to pages 250 and 253.

5 **Completen.**

18–19. —Cuando tienes la gripe, ¿el médico ____ da una receta?
—Sí, ____ da una receta para unos antibióticos.

20. Sí, cuando tenemos la gripe, el médico siempre ____ receta antibióticos.

To review object pronouns, turn to page 256.

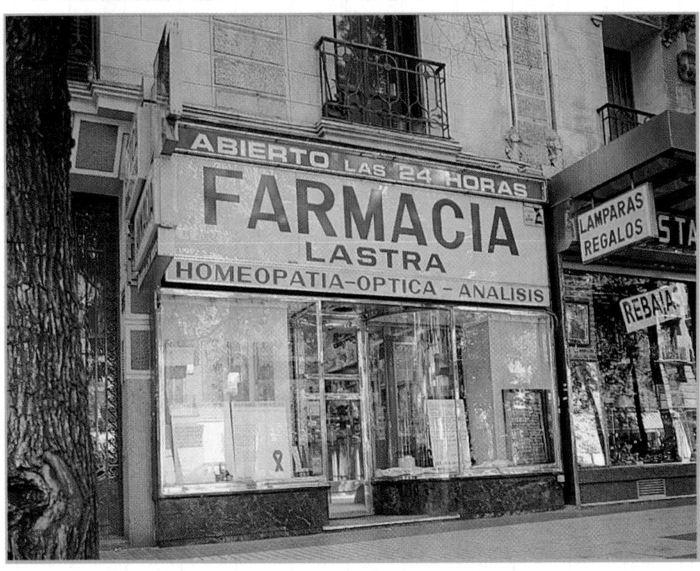

Madrid, España

Assessment

SPANISH Online

The **Glencoe Spanish Web** site (**spanish.glencoe.com**) offers options that enable you and your students to experience the Spanish-speaking world via the Internet. For each **Capítulo,** there are activties, games, and quizzes. In addition, an *Enrichment* section offers students an opportunity to visit Web sites related to the theme of the chapter.

FOLDABLES™ Study Organizer **Dinah Zike's Study Guides**

Your students may wish to use Foldable 4 to organize, display, and arrange data as they expand their Spanish vocabulary. You may wish to encourage them to add information from each chapter as they continue to learn new words related to the different topics they will be studying.

A *vocabulary book* foldable is an ideal reference, especially as students begin to make word associations and write simple passages in Spanish.

Note: You may wish to have students store their foldables in a plastic bag in their notebooks.

Answers to Assessment

 3

9. Me duele la cabeza.

 4

10. es
11. está
12. es
13. está, está
14. está
15. está
16. es
17. está

5

18. te
19. me
20. nos

¡Hablo como un pro!

This unique page gives students the opportunity to speak freely and say whatever they can, using the vocabulary and structures they have learned in the chapter. The illustration serves to remind students of precisely what they know how to say in Spanish. There are no activities that students do not have the ability to describe or talk about in Spanish. The art not only depicts the vocabulary and content of this chapter, but also reinforces what they learned in previous chapters.

You may wish to use this page in many ways. Some possibilities are to have students do the following:

1. Look at the illustration and identify items by giving the correct Spanish words.
2. Make up sentences about what they see in the illustration.
3. Make up questions about the illustration. They can call on another class member to respond if you do this as a class activity, or you may prefer to allow students to work in small groups. This activity is extremely beneficial because it enables students to actively use interrogative words.
4. Answer questions you ask them about the illustration.
5. Work in pairs and make up a conversation based on the illustration.
6. Look at the illustration and give a complete oral review of what they see.
7. Look at the illustration and write a paragraph (or essay) about it.

You can also use this page as an assessment or testing tool, taking into account individual differences by having students go from simple to quite complicated tasks. The assessment can be either oral or written.

¡Hablo como un pro!

Tell all you can about this illustration.

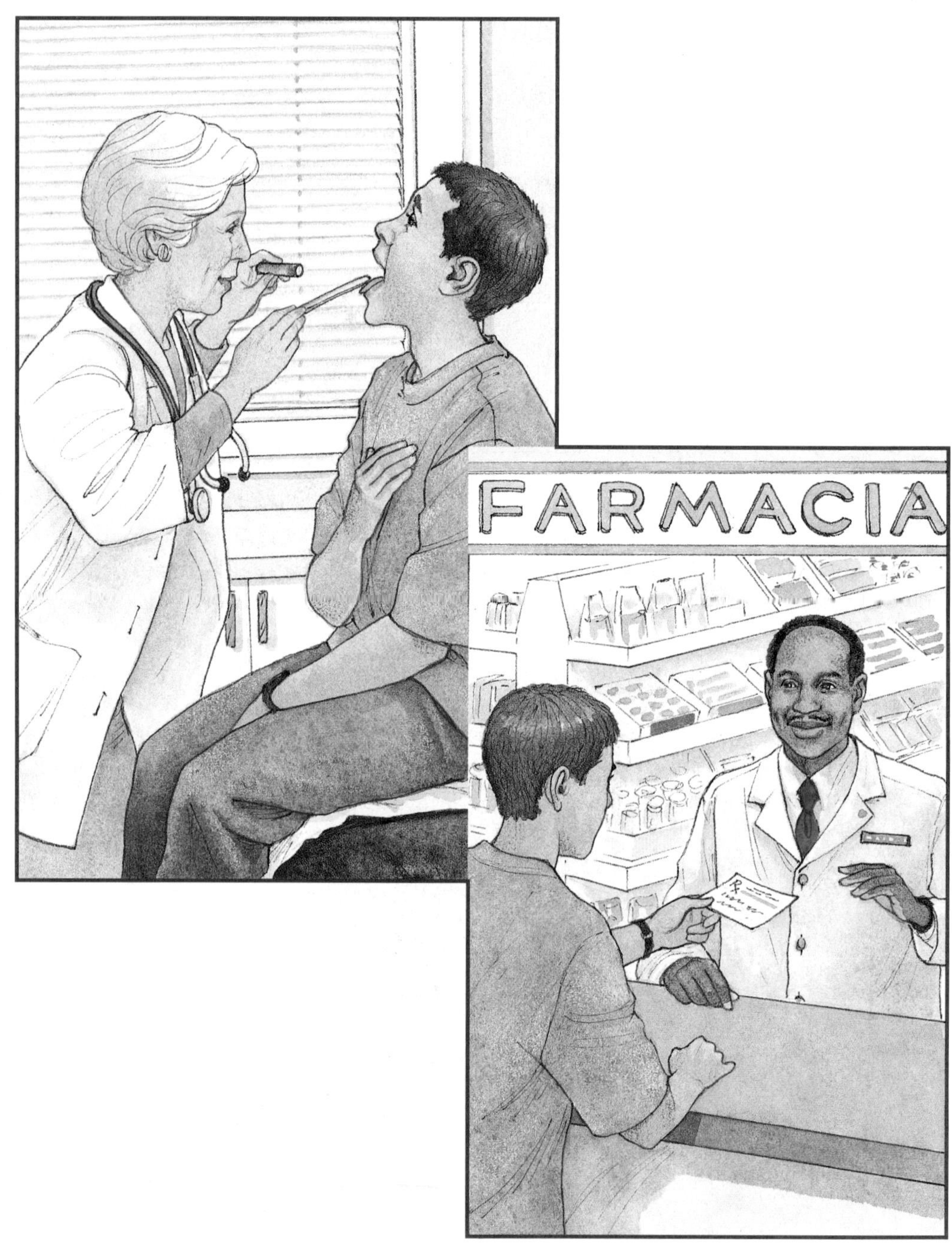

You may wish to use the rubrics provided on pages T20–T21 as you give students the following directions.

1. Identify the topic or situation of the illustration.
2. Give the Spanish words for as many items as you can.
3. Think of as many sentences as you can to describe the illustration.
4. Go over your sentences and put them in the best sequencing to give a coherent story based on the illustration.

Vocabulario

Describing minor health problems

la salud	el dolor
la fiebre	enfermo(a)
los escalofríos	cansado(a)
la gripe	estornudar
el catarro	estar resfriado(a)
la tos	toser
la energía	

Speaking with the doctor

¿Qué te pasa?	Me duele...
la consulta, el consultorio	Tengo dolor de...
el/la médico(a)	creer
el hospital	examinar
el síntoma	abrir la boca
la diagnosis	guardar cama
la alergia	recetar
la inyección	

Describing some emotions

contento(a)	nervioso(a)
triste	tranquilo(a)
de buen humor, de mal humor	

Identifying more parts of the body

la garganta	la boca
los ojos	el estómago

Speaking with a pharmacist

la farmacia
el/la farmacéutico(a)
la receta
el medicamento, la medicina
la aspirina
el antibiótico
la pastilla, la píldora, la tableta
la dosis
despachar, vender

How well do you know your vocabulary?

- Find as many cognates as you can in the list.
- Use five cognates to write several sentences.

VIDEOTUR

Episodio 8

In this video episode, you will learn another facet of Alberto's personality. See page 499 for more information.

Vocabulario

Vocabulary Review

The words and phrases in the **Vocabulario** have been taught for productive use in this chapter. They are summarized here as a resource for both student and teacher. This list also serves as a convenient resource for the **¡Te toca a ti!** activities on pages 266 and 267. There are approximately fifteen cognates in this vocabulary list. Have students find them.

VIDEO VHS/DVD

The Video Program allows students to see how the chapter vocabulary and structures are used by native speakers within an engaging story line. For maximum reinforcement, show the video episode as a final activity for Chapter 8.

Career Connection

Hablo español Because the Hispanic population in the United States is continually growing, Spanish is a very useful tool for communication in all the medical professions. Ask students to think of several positions in the health care field where knowledge of Spanish would be useful or essential. If possible, invite a bilingual health care professional to speak to your class on this topic.

¡OJO! You will notice that the vocabulary list here is not translated. This has been done intentionally, since we feel that by the time students have finished the material in the chapter they should be familiar with the meanings of all the words. If there are several words they still do not know, we recommend that they refer to the **Palabras 1** and **2** sections in the chapter or go to the dictionaries at the end of this book to find the meanings. However, if you prefer that your students have the English translations, please refer to Vocabulary Transparency 8.1, where you will find all these words with their translations.

Planning for Chapter 9

SCOPE AND SEQUENCE, PAGES 272–303

Topics

- Summer and winter weather
- Summer and winter sports and leisure activities

Culture

- World-class beaches and resorts in the Spanish-speaking world
- Opposite seasons in the northern and southern hemispheres
- Snowboarding in Chile
- Weather and climate in the Spanish speaking world

Functions

- How to describe summer and winter weather
- How to talk about summer and winter sports such as swimming, tennis, and skiing
- How to relate actions and events that took place in the past
- How to refer to persons and things already mentioned

Structure

- **-ar** verbs in the preterite
- Direct object pronouns—**lo, la, los, las**
- **Ir** and **ser** in the preterite

National Standards

- Communication Standard 1.1 pages 272, 276, 277, 280, 281, 283, 284, 285, 286, 287, 288, 291, 298
- Communication Standard 1.2 pages 277, 281, 285, 289, 290, 291, 293, 294, 295, 297, 298
- Communication Standard 1.3 page 299
- Cultures Standard 2.1 pages 290, 292–293, 294, 299
- Cultures Standard 2.2 pages 285, 292, 295
- Connections Standard 3.1 pages 296–297
- Comparisons Standard 4.1 page 282
- Comparisons Standard 4.2 pages 294, 295
- Communities Standard 5.2 page 303

PACING AND PRIORITIES

The chapter content is color coded below to assist you in planning.

■ required ■ recommended ■ optional

Vocabulario *(required)* *Days 1–4*

- ■ Palabras 1
  - El balneario
  - La natación
  - El tenis
- ■ Palabras 2
  - El invierno
  - El tiempo en el invierno
  - La estación de esquí

Estructura *(required)* *Days 5–7*

- ■ Pretérito de los verbos en **-ar**
- ■ Pronombres—**lo, la, los, las**
- ■ **Ir** y **ser** en el pretérito

Conversación *(required)*

- ■ ¡A la playa!

Pronunciación *(recommended)*

- ■ La consonante **g**

Lecturas culturales

- ■ Paraísos del mundo hispano *(recommended)*
- ■ Estaciones inversas *(optional)*
- ■ El «snowboarding» *(optional)*

Conexiones

- ■ El clima *(optional)*

■ **¡Te toca a ti!** *(recommended)*

■ **Assessment** *(recommended)*

■ **¡Hablo como un pro!** *(optional)*

RESOURCE GUIDE

SECTION	PAGES	SECTION RESOURCES
Vocabulario PALABRAS 1		
El balneario La natación El tenis	274, 276–277 275, 276–277 275, 276–277	Vocabulary Transparencies 9.2–9.3 Audio CD 6 Audio Activities TE, pages 105–107 Workbook, pages 99–103 Quiz 1, pages 43–44 ExamView® Pro
Vocabulario PALABRAS 2		
El invierno El tiempo en el invierno La estación de esquí	278, 280–281 278, 280–281 279, 280–281	Vocabulary Transparencies 9.4–9.5 Audio CD 6 Audio Activities TE, pages 107–109 Workbook, pages 103–104 Quiz 2, pages 45–46 ExamView® Pro
Estructura		
Pretérito de los verbos en **-ar** Pronombres—**lo, la, los, las** **Ir** y **ser** en el pretérito	282–285 286–288 288–289	Audio CD 6 Audio Activities TE, pages 109–111 Workbook, pages 105–110 Quizzes 3–5, pages 47–49 ExamView® Pro
Conversación		
¡A la playa!	290	Audio CD 6 Audio Activities TE, pages 111–112 Interactive CD-ROM
Pronunciación		
La consonante **g**	291	Pronunciation Transparency P 9 Audio CD 6 Audio Activities TE, page 112
Lecturas culturales		
Paraísos del mundo hispano Estaciones inversas El «snowboarding»	292–293 294 295	Audio CD 6 Audio Activities TE, pages 112–113 Tests, pages 142, 145
Conexiones		
El clima	296–297	Tests, page 147
¡Te toca a ti!		
	298–299	**¡Viva el mundo hispano!** Video, Episode 9 Video Activities, Chapter 9 Spanish Online Activities spanish.glencoe.com
Assessment		
	300–301	Communication Transparency C 9 Quizzes 1–5, pages 43–49 Performance Assessment, Task 9 Tests, pages 139–154 Situation Cards, Chapter 9 ExamView® Pro **Maratón mental** Videoquiz

Using Your Resources for Chapter 9

Transparencies

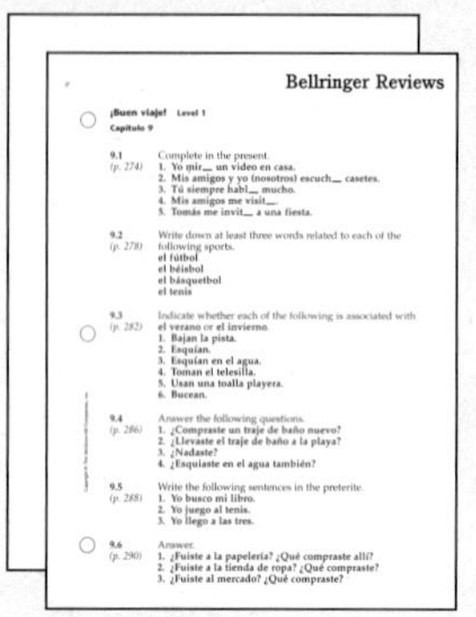
Bellringer 9.1–9.6

Vocabulary 9.1–9.5

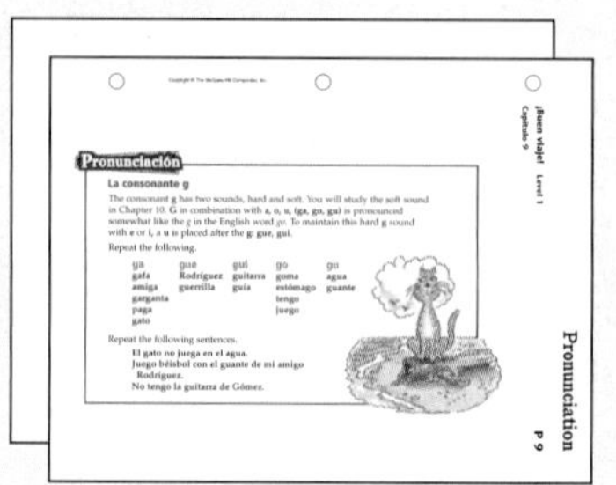
Pronunciation P 9

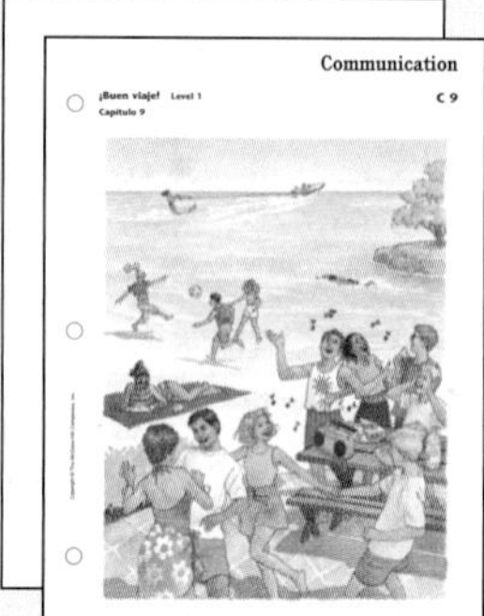
Communication C 9

Workbook

Vocabulary, pages 99–104

Structure, pages 105–110

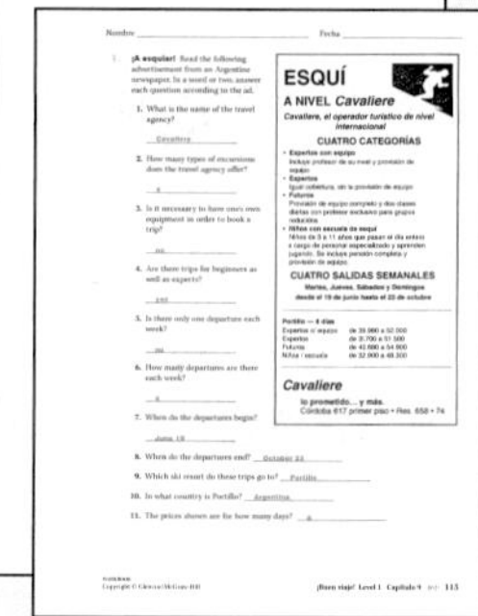
Enrichment, pages 111–116

Audio Activities

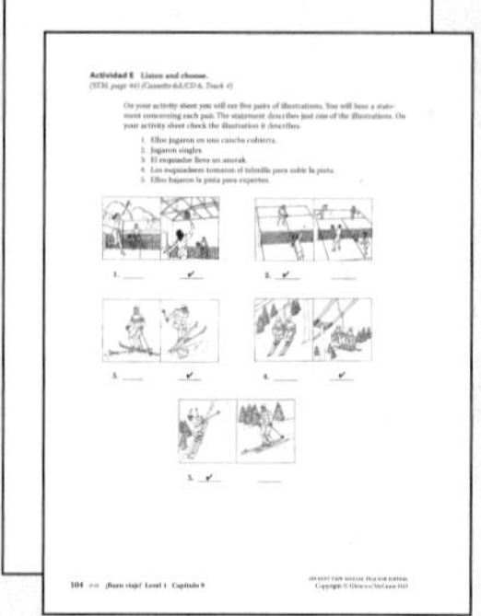
Vocabulary, pages 105–109

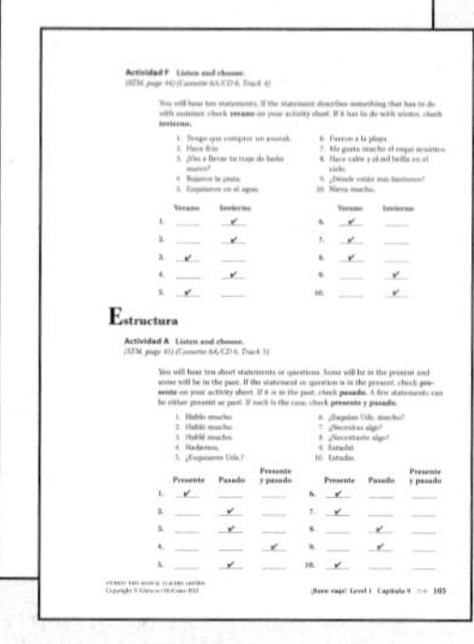
Structure, pages 109–111

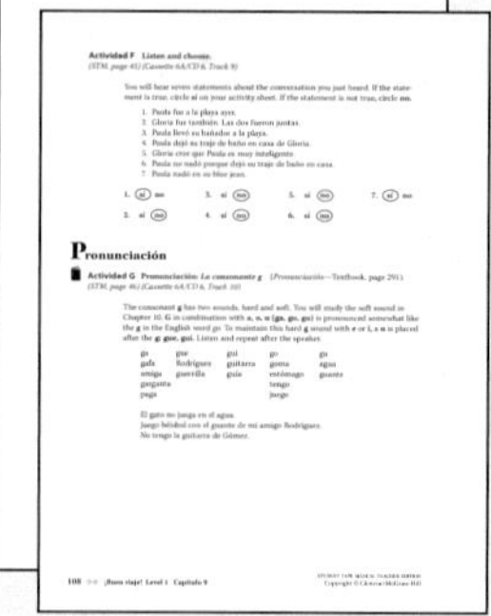
Conversation, Pronunciation, pages 111–112

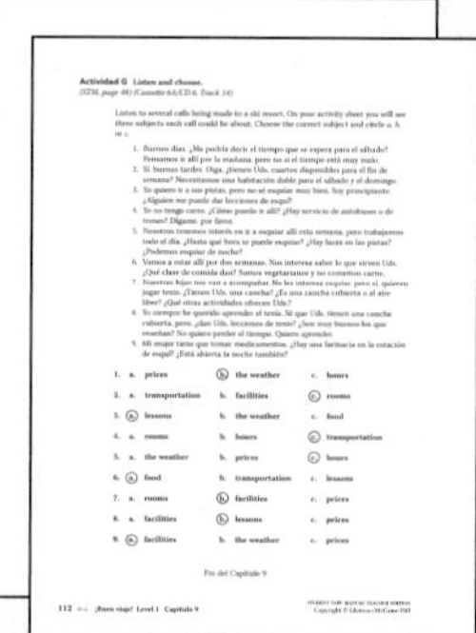
Additional Practice, pages 113–116

Assessment

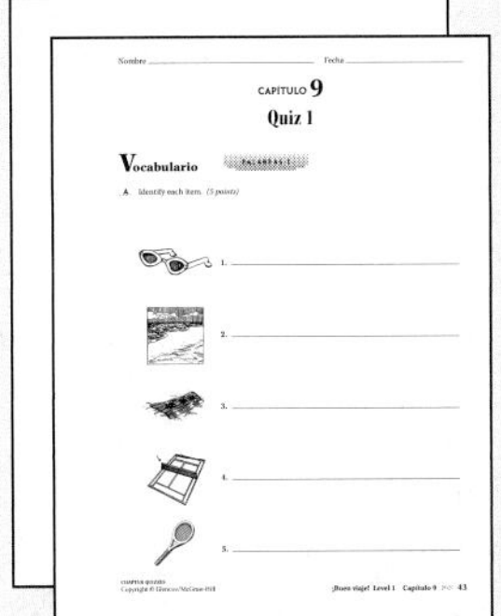
Vocabulary and Structure Quizzes, pages 43–49

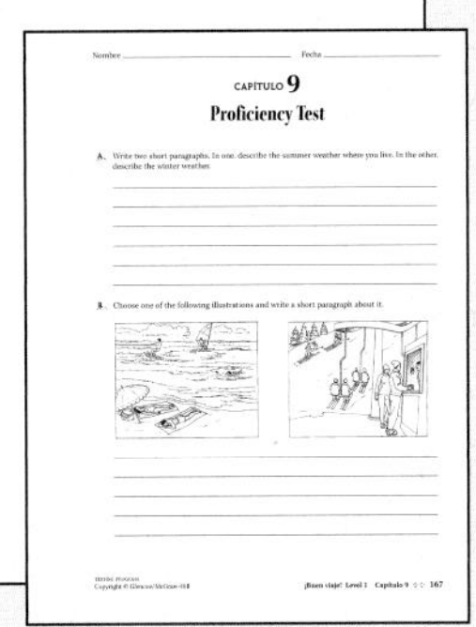
Chapter Tests, pages 139–154

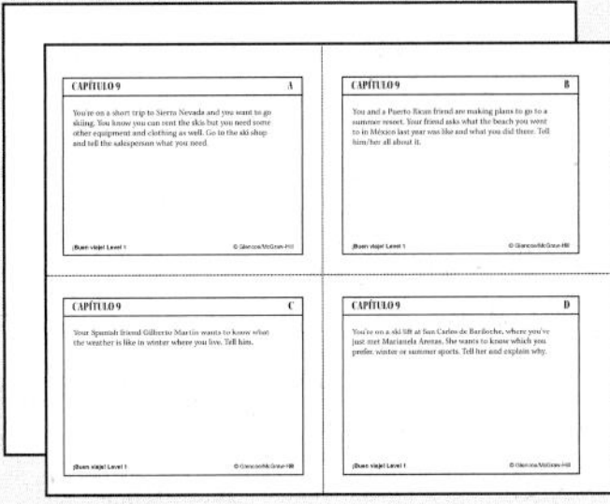
Situation Cards, Chapter 9

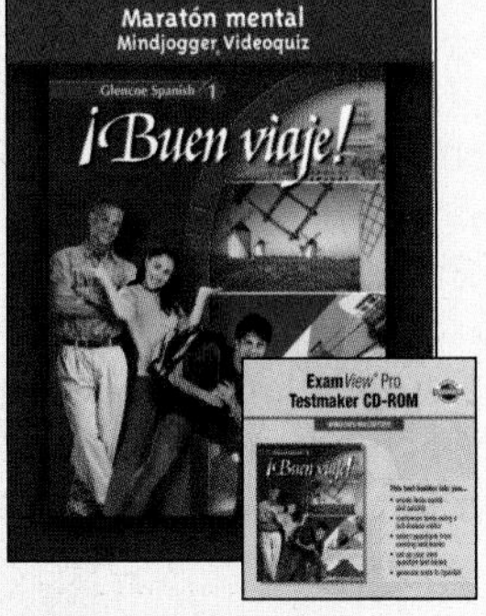

MindJogger Videoquiz, ExamView® Pro, Chapter 9

Timesaving Teacher Tools

TeacherWorks™ is your all-in-one teacher resource center. Personalize lesson plans, access resources from the Teacher Wraparound Edition, connect to the Internet, or make a to-do list. These are only a few of the many features that can assist you in the planning and organizing of your lessons.

Includes:

- A calendar feature
- Access to all program blackline masters
- Standards correlations and more

ExamView® Pro

Test Bank software for Macintosh and Windows makes creating, editing, customizing, and printing tests quick and easy.

Technology Resources

In the Chapter 9 Internet Activity, you will have a chance to learn more about the Spanish-speaking world. Visit spanish.glencoe.com

On the interactive CD-ROM, students can listen to and take part in a recorded version of the conversation in Chapter 9.

¡Viva el mundo hispano! Video and Video Activities, Chapter 9. Available on VHS and DVD.

Help your students prepare for the chapter test by playing the **Maratón mental** Videoquiz game show. Teams will compete against each other to review chapter vocabulary and structure and sharpen listening comprehension skills. Available on VHS and DVD.

¡Buen viaje! is also available on CD or Online.

Capítulo 9

Preview

In this chapter, students will learn to describe summer and winter weather and talk about summer and winter activities. To do this they will learn to use vocabulary associated with the beach, as well as with skiing. Students will also learn to narrate in the past. In order to do this they will learn the preterite of **-ar** verbs. Students will also learn about the many wonderful summer and winter resorts in the Spanish-speaking world.

National Standards

Communication

In Chapter 9, students will communicate in spoken and written Spanish on the following topics:

- summer weather and summer activities
- winter weather and winter activities

Students will also learn to narrate past events. They will obtain and provide information and engage in conversations about beach and ski resorts, water sports, tennis, and skiing as they fulfill the chapter objectives listed on this page.

LEVELING

The activities, conversations, and readings within each chapter are marked according to level of difficulty. **E** indicates easy. **A** indicates average. **C** indicates challenging. Some activities cover a range of difficulty. In some activities, for example, advanced students will be able to produce more extensive responses while students who learn at a different rate may give less detailed responses. The leveling indicators will help you individualize instruction to best meet your students' needs.

Capítulo 9

El verano y el invierno

Objetivos

In this chapter you will learn to:

- describe summer and winter weather
- talk about summer activities and sports
- talk about winter sports
- discuss past actions and events
- refer to people and things already mentioned
- talk about resorts in the Hispanic world

Daniel Hernández *A Breath of Fresh Air*

Capítulo 9

Spotlight on Culture

Arte Daniel Hernández (1856–1932), a Peruvian painter, is considered to be a master of painting. The museum that bears his name, **el Museo Regional Daniel Hernández,** is located in Huancavelica, Perú and contains fossils, historical artifacts, and works by Hernández and other famous Peruvian artists.

Fotografía The beach resort shown here is Benidorm, between Valencia and Alicante on the **Costa Blanca.** Benidorm has two white, crescent-shaped beaches. Like many of the other resorts on the **Costa Blanca,** it has become somewhat overdeveloped.

Learning from Photos

(pages 272–273) Ask the following questions about the photo after presenting the vocabulary on pages 274–275:

¿Es grande o pequeña la playa?
¿Hay mucha gente en la playa?
¿Hay mucha gente en el mar?
¿Son grandes las olas?
¿Qué tiempo hace?

Vocabulario

PALABRAS 1

1 PREPARATION

Resource Manager

Vocabulary Transparencies 9.2–9.3
Audio Activities TE, pages 105–107
Audio CD 6
Workbook, pages 99–103
Quizzes, pages 43–44
ExamView® Pro

Bellringer Review

Use BRR Transparency 9.1 or write the following on the board.
Complete in the present.

1. **Yo mir__ un video en casa.**
2. **Mis amigos y yo (nosotros) escuch__ casetes.**
3. **Tú siempre habl__ mucho.**
4. **Mis amigos me visit__.**
5. **Tomás me invit__ a una fiesta.**

2 PRESENTATION

Step 1 You may wish to present the vocabulary initially with books closed as students focus their attention on Vocabulary Transparencies 9.2–9.3. Point to each item and have the class repeat the word in unison. Ask questions such as: **¿Es una plancha de vela? ¿Es una plancha de vela o una toalla playera? ¿Qué es?**

Vocabulario

PALABRAS 1

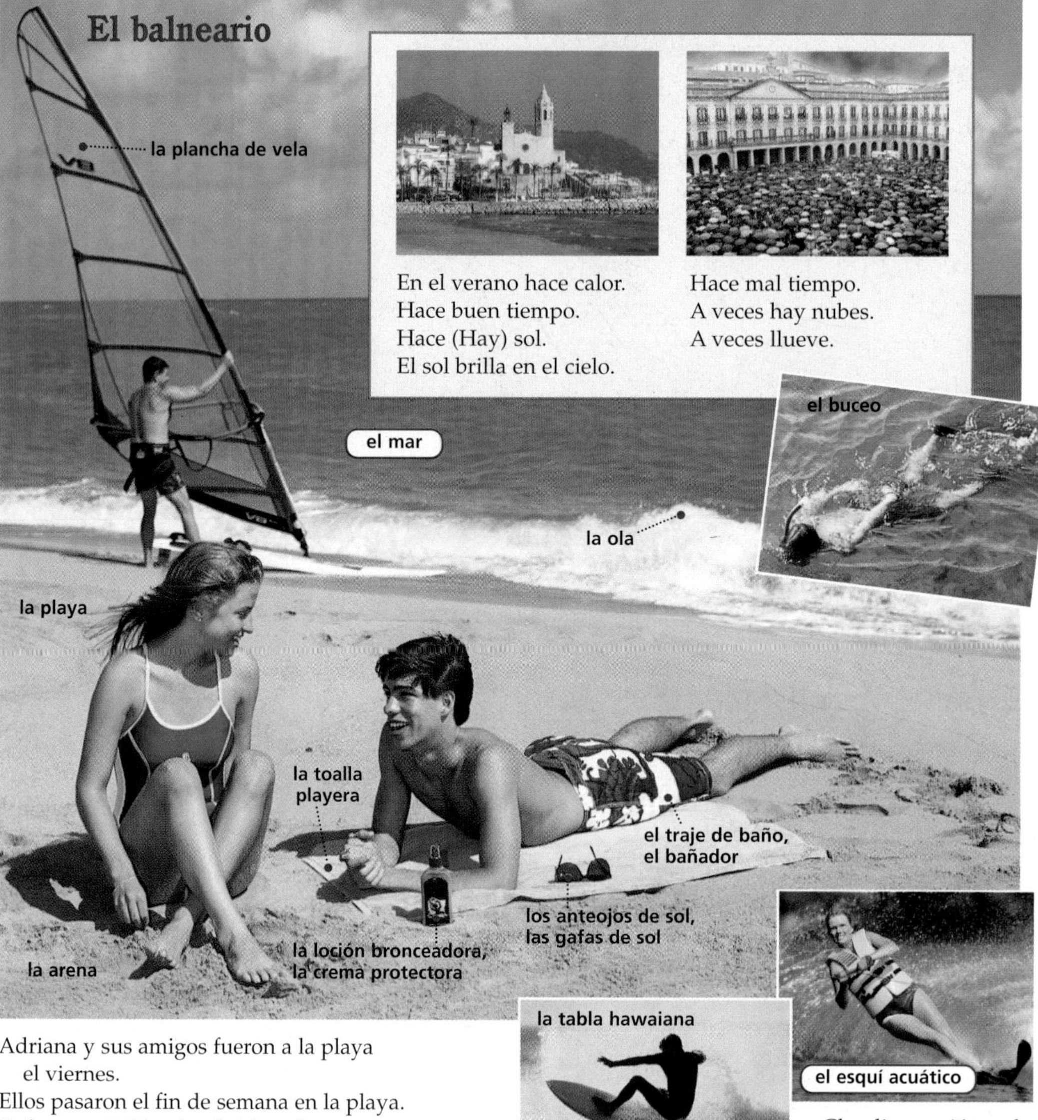

Adriana y sus amigos fueron a la playa el viernes.
Ellos pasaron el fin de semana en la playa.
Pedro practicó la plancha de vela.
Diego buceó.
Carlos tomó el sol.

Alejandro practicó el surfing.

Claudia esquió en el agua.

Reaching All Students

Total Physical Response You may wish to bring in the following props to use in this activity: tube of sunscreen, tennis ball, tennis racquet. Demonstrate the following verbs using the appropriate gestures: **abre, ponte, tapa, rebota, golpea.**

(Student 1), **ven acá. Aquí tienes un tubo de crema bronceadora.**
(Student 1), **abre el tubo.**
Ponte la crema protectora en el brazo, en la pierna y en la cara.
Y ahora, tapa el tubo.
Pon el tubo en tu mochila.
Ahora, estás en la playa.
Pon la toalla playera en la arena.
Siéntate. Toma el sol.
Ahora, levántate.
Ve al agua, al mar. Nada.
Gracias, *(Student 1).* **Siéntate, por favor.**

(Student 2), **ven acá.**
Toma la pelota. Rebota la pelota.
Rebota la pelota una vez más.
Toma la raqueta.
Golpea la pelota con la raqueta.
Siéntate, por favor. Gracias, *(Student 2).*

La natación

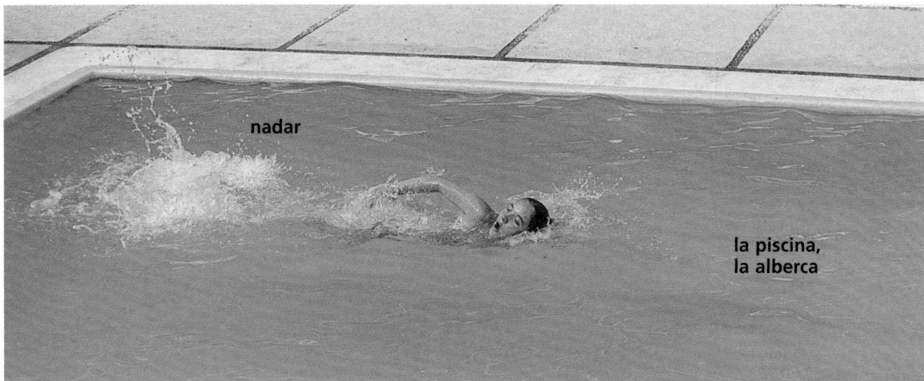

Sandra fue a la piscina.
Ella nadó en la piscina.

El tenis

Los amigos jugaron (al) tenis.
Jugaron tenis en una cancha al aire libre.
No jugaron en una cancha cubierta.

Jugaron singles, no dobles.
Un jugador golpeó la pelota.
La pelota pasó por encima de la red.

Vocabulario

Step 2 When presenting the sentences, break them into logical parts as in the following example: **Adriana y sus amigos fueron a la playa. Fueron a la playa el viernes.** Intersperse your presentation with questions building from simple to more complex. For example: **¿Fueron los amigos a la playa? ¿Quiénes fueron a la playa? ¿Fueron a la playa el lunes? ¿Cuándo fueron a la playa?**

Step 3 Note that the preterite verbs are presented in the third person so students can use them immediately in answering questions without having to change the endings.

Step 4 You can also use gestures or have students dramatize the following expressions: **usar la loción bronceadora, tomar el sol, esquiar en el agua, nadar, jugar (al) tenis.**

Step 5 After the oral presentation of the vocabulary, have students open their books and read the material for additional reinforcement.

About the Spanish Language

La piscina is the most commonly used word for *swimming pool.* **La alberca** is used in Mexico. You will also hear **la pila** which more frequently means *basin* or *trough.*

LEVELING

A: Vocabulary

Vocabulary Expansion

You may wish to teach some additional vocabulary related to the beach.

el malecón	*road that parallels the beach*
la silla playera	*beach chair*
la sombrilla	*umbrella*
correr las olas	*to body surf*
alquilar (rentar) un barco	*to rent a boat*
pescar (ir de pesca)	*to go fishing*

3 PRACTICE

¿Qué palabra necesito?

¡OJO! When students are doing the **¿Qué palabra necesito?** activities, accept any answer that makes sense. The purpose of these activities is to have students use the new vocabulary. They are not factual recall activities. Thus, it is not necessary for students to remember specific factual information from the vocabulary presentation when answering. If you wish, have students use the photos on this page as a stimulus, when possible.

1 Activity 1 can be done first with books closed for oral practice. You may then do it again with books open for reinforcement.

2 Activity 2 should be done with books open.

3 **Expansion:** Ask students if they can think of additional items Claudia may have bought. **¿Qué más compró Claudia en la tienda?**

Geography Connection

San Juan, Puerto Rico, has some beautiful beaches. Many people think the beaches are on the Caribbean, but they are not. San Juan is actually on the northeastern coast of Puerto Rico on the Atlantic Ocean. There are more beaches on the northern or Atlantic coast.

¿Qué palabra necesito?

1 Historieta ¡A la playa!

Contesten con **sí.**

1. ¿Fue Isabel a la playa?
2. ¿Pasó el fin de semana allí?
3. ¿Nadó en el mar?
4. ¿Esquió en el agua?
5. ¿Buceó?
6. ¿Tomó el sol?
7. ¿Usó una crema protectora?

San Juan, Puerto Rico

Acapulco, México

2 Historieta El tiempo

Completen.

En el verano __1__ calor. Hay __2__. El sol brilla en el __3__. Pero no hace buen tiempo siempre. A veces hay __4__. Cuando hay __5__, el cielo está nublado. No me gusta cuando __6__ cuando estoy en la playa.

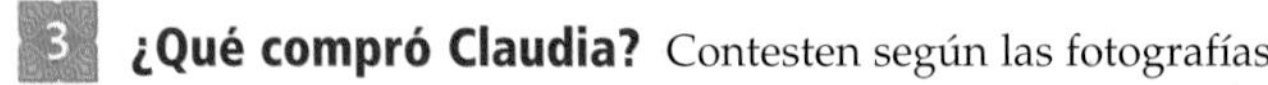

3 ¿Qué compró Claudia? Contesten según las fotografías.

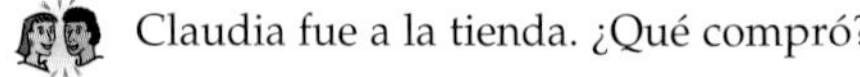

Claudia fue a la tienda. ¿Qué compró?

1. 

2. 

3. 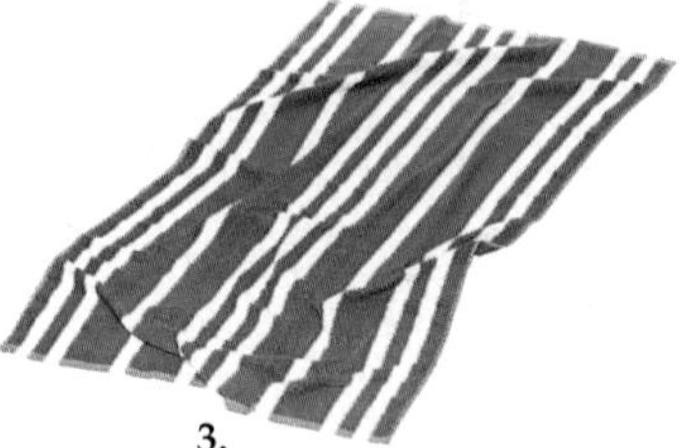

4. 

ANSWERS TO ¿Qué palabra necesito?

1

1. Sí, Isabel fue a la playa.
2. Sí, pasó el fin de semana allí.
3. Sí, nadó en el mar.
4. Sí, esquió en el agua.
5. Sí, buceó.
6. Sí, tomó el sol.
7. Sí, usó una crema protectora.

2

1. hace
2. sol
3. cielo
4. nubes
5. nubes
6. llueve

3

1. los anteojos (las gafas) de sol
2. el bañador (traje de baño)
3. la toalla playera
4. la crema protectora (loción bronceadora)

Cancún, México

4 Historieta El balneario

Completen.

1. Un balneario tiene ____.
2. El Mediterráneo es un ____ y el Caribe es un ____.
3. En un mar o en un océano hay ____.
4. En la playa la gente ____ y ____ el sol.
5. ____ da protección contra el sol.
6. Una persona lleva ____ y ____ cuando va a la playa.
7. Me gusta mucho ir a la playa en el ____ cuando hace ____ y hay mucho ____.
8. Si uno no vive cerca de la costa y no puede ir a la playa, puede nadar en ____.

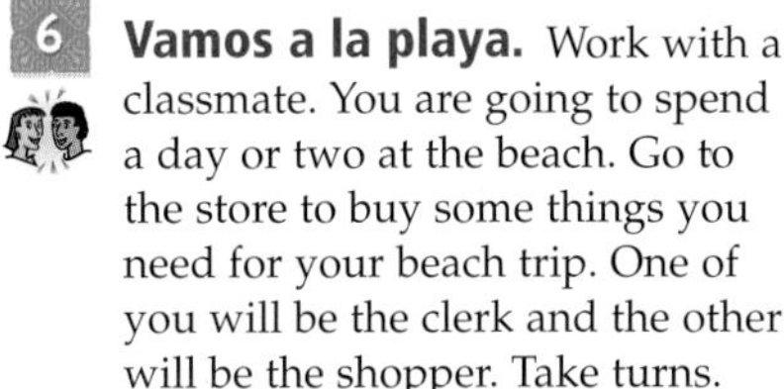

5 Historieta Un juego de tenis

Contesten.

1. ¿Dónde jugaron los tenistas al tenis?
2. ¿Jugaron singles o dobles?
3. ¿Cuántas personas hay en la cancha cuando juegan dobles?
4. ¿Golpearon los tenistas la pelota?
5. ¿La pelota tiene que pasar por encima de la red?

Estepona, España

6 Vamos a la playa. Work with a classmate. You are going to spend a day or two at the beach. Go to the store to buy some things you need for your beach trip. One of you will be the clerk and the other will be the shopper. Take turns.

7 ¿Dónde vamos a jugar tenis? Call some friends (your classmates) to try to arrange a game of doubles. Decide where you're going to play, when, and with whom.

SPANISH Online

For more information about the popularity of tennis in the Spanish-speaking world, go to the Glencoe Spanish Web site: spanish.glencoe.com

Vocabulario

4 Do Activity 4 first with books open.

5 Activity 5 can be done first with books open for oral practice. You can do it again with books closed for additional reinforcement.

¡OJO! Note that the activities are color-coded. All the activities in the text are communicative. However, the ones with blue titles are guided communication. The red titles indicate that the answers to the activity are more open-ended and can vary more. You may wish to correct students' mistakes more so in the guided activities than in the activities with a red title, which lend themselves to a freer response.

6 Each student should make a list of the items before beginning the paired activity. Ask several pairs to present to the class.

7 Role-play this activity with a more able student first.

Learning from Photos

(page 277 left) This resort in Cancún is one of the most popular tourist destinations in Mexico. Development started here in 1974. The resort was carved out of the jungle. The hotel area is on a 22-kilometer barrier reef off the Yucatán peninsula in the Caribbean. Cancún is also close to the fabulous Mayan ruins of Chichén Itzá, Tulum, and Cobá. The thatched roof cabanas you see in the photo originated in pre-Hispanic days. They are called **palapas.** People sit under them for protection from the sun.

Answers to ¿Qué palabra necesito?

4

1. una playa
2. mar, mar
3. olas
4. nada, toma
5. La loción bronceadora (crema protectora)
6. un traje de baño (bañador), anteojos (gafas) de sol, (una toalla playera)
7. verano, calor, sol
8. una piscina (alberca)

5

1. Los tenistas jugaron al tenis en una cancha al aire libre.
2. Jugaron dobles.
3. Hay cuatro personas en la cancha cuando juegan dobles.
4. Sí, los tenistas golpearon la pelota.
5. Sí, la pelota tiene que pasar por encima de la red.

6 *Answers will vary.*

7 *Answers will vary.*

LEVELING

E: Activities 1, 3

A: Activities 2, 4, 5, 6

C: Activity 7

1 PREPARATION

Resource Manager

Vocabulary Transparencies 9.4–9.5
Audio Activities TE, pages 107–109
Audio CD 6
Workbook, pages 103–104
Quizzes, pages 45–46
ExamView® Pro

Bellringer Review

Use BRR Transparency 9.2 or write the following on the board.
Write down at least three words related to each of the following sports.
el fútbol
el béisbol
el básquetbol
el tenis

2 PRESENTATION

Step 1 Have students close their books. Have them focus their attention on Vocabulary Transparencies 9.4–9.5. Point to each item and have the class repeat the word two or three times in unison. Ask questions such as: **¿Es una esquiadora? ¿Lleva un anorak, guantes y botas? ¿Qué lleva?**

Step 2 When presenting the sentences, break them into logical parts as in the following example: **En el invierno hace frío. Hace frío. Nieva,** etc. Intersperse with questions building from simple to more complex: **¿Hace frío en el invierno? ¿Cuando hace calor, en el invierno o en el verano? ¿Nieva o llueve en el invierno? ¿Cuándo nieva?**

Vocabulario

PALABRAS 2

El invierno

la esquiadora
el esquí
los guantes
el anorak
el bastón
la bota

El tiempo en el invierno

En el invierno hace frío.
Nieva.
Hay mucha nieve.
La temperatura baja a cinco grados bajo cero.

Reaching All Students

Total Physical Response

(Student 1), levántate y ven acá, por favor.
Siéntate.
Vamos a hacer gestos.
Ponte las botas.
Ponte los esquís.
Y ahora levántate.
Ponte el anorak.
Ponte las gafas.
Toma el bastón.
Pon el bastón en la mano derecha.
Toma el otro bastón.
Pon este bastón en la mano izquierda.
Y ahora, esquía.
Gracias, *(Student 1)*. Ahora puedes regresar a tu asiento.
Siéntate, por favor.

La estación de esquí

Los esquiadores compraron los boletos en la ventanilla.

Ellos tomaron el telesilla para subir la montaña.

Bajaron la pista.
Esquiaron muy bien.
Bajaron la pista para expertos, no la pista para principiantes.

Nota You are familiar with the following expressions to talk about things that happen in the present. Look also at time expressions you use to talk about things that happened in the past.

EL PRESENTE	EL PASADO
hoy	ayer
esta noche	anoche
esta tarde	ayer por la tarde
esta mañana	ayer por la mañana
este año	el año pasado
esta semana	la semana pasada

Vocabulario

Step 3 After the oral presentation of the vocabulary, have students open their books and read the material for additional reinforcement.

About the Spanish Language

- An airplane or train ticket is called **un billete** in Spain and **un boleto** throughout Latin America. **El ticket** or any of its variations—**el tique, el tiqué, el tiquete**—is commonly used in Spain and throughout Latin America to refer to any small ticket like an admission ticket.
- **La boletería** is used throughout Latin America. It is not used in Spain.
- **El telesilla** is masculine because it is a compound noun.

Vocabulary Expansion

You may wish to present some words related to ice skating.

el hielo	*ice*
el patinaje	*skating*
los patines	*skates*
patinar	*to skate*
la pista de patinaje, el patinadero	*skating rink*

Chapter Projects

Un folleto Have students work in groups to prepare a brochure in Spanish about a winter resort, its features, and the weather. Have them include ads in the brochure for winter sports equipment and clothes.

Reaching All Students

Total Physical Response Teach the expression **ponte en fila** by putting several students in a line. Also demonstrate **debajo del brazo** and **empieza a esquiar.**

(Student 1), **levántate y ven acá, por favor.**
Ponte en fila. Espera el telesquí.
Siéntate en el telesquí.
Pon los bastones debajo del brazo izquierdo.
Adiós. Ahora estás en la parte superior de la montaña.
Bájate del telesquí.
Pon un bastón en la mano izquierda y otro en la mano derecha.
Empieza a esquiar.
Baja la pista.
Gracias, *(Student 1).* **Ahora puedes volver a tu asiento.**

3 PRACTICE

¿Qué palabra necesito?

¡OJO! It is recommended that you go over the **¿Qué palabra necesito?** activities before assigning them for homework.

8 Quickly review the weather expressions taught on pages 274 and 278 before doing Activity 8. Students should be able to give at least five or six weather expressions.

Writing Development

Students can write Activities 8 and 9 in paragraph form.

Learning from Photos

(page 280 top) Villarrica, in the Chilean lake region which borders Argentina, is one of Chile's most famous resorts. In addition to skiing in the winter, people swim in the Andean waters of Lake Villarrica in the summer.

¿Qué palabra necesito?

8 **¿Qué tiempo hace?** Describan el tiempo en la foto.

Villarrica, Chile

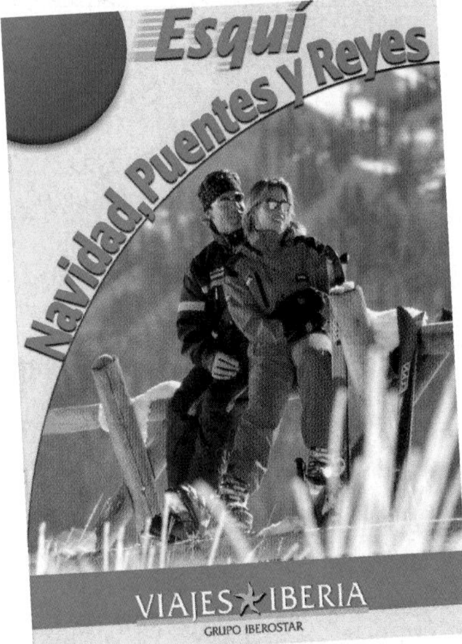

9 **Historieta En una estación de esquí**
Contesten según se indica.

1. ¿Cuándo son populares las estaciones de esquí? (en el invierno)
2. ¿Qué tipo de pistas hay en una estación de esquí? (para expertos y para principiantes)
3. ¿Dónde compraron los esquiadores los tickets para el telesquí? (en la ventanilla)
4. ¿Qué tomaron los esquiadores para subir la montaña? (el telesilla)
5. ¿Qué bajaron los esquiadores? (la pista)

10 **Me gusta esquiar.** Completen.

En el __1__ hace frío. A veces nieva. Cuando hay mucha __2__ me gusta ir a una __3__ de esquí. Llevo mis __4__, mis botas y los __5__ y voy a las montañas. Tomo el __6__ para subir la montaña. No soy un esquiador muy bueno. Siempre bajo una __7__ para principiantes.

Answers to ¿Qué palabra necesito?

8 *Answers will vary but may include:*
Es el invierno. Hace frío. Hay mucha nieve. Hace sol. El sol brilla en el cielo.

9

1. Las estaciones de esquí son populares en el invierno.
2. En una estación de esquí hay pistas para expertos y pistas para principiantes.
3. Los esquiadores compraron los tickets para el telesquí en la ventanilla.
4. Los esquiadores tomaron el telesilla para subir la montaña.
5. Los esquiadores bajaron la pista.

10

1. invierno
2. nieve
3. estación
4. guantes
5. esquís
6. telesilla
7. pista

11 **¡A esquiar!** You're at a ski resort in Chile and have to rent **(alquilar)** some equipment for a day on the slopes. Tell the clerk (your partner) what you need. Find out whether he or she has what you need and how much it all costs.

12 **En una estación de esquí** Have a conversation with a classmate. Tell as much as you can about what people do at a ski resort. Find out which one of you knows more about skiing. If skiing is a sport that is new to you, tell whether you think it would interest you.

13 **¿A qué ciudad?** With a classmate, look at the following weather map that appeared in a Spanish newspaper. You are in Madrid and want to take a side trip. Since you both have definite preferences regarding weather, use the map to help you make a decision. After you choose a city to go to, tell what you are going to do there.

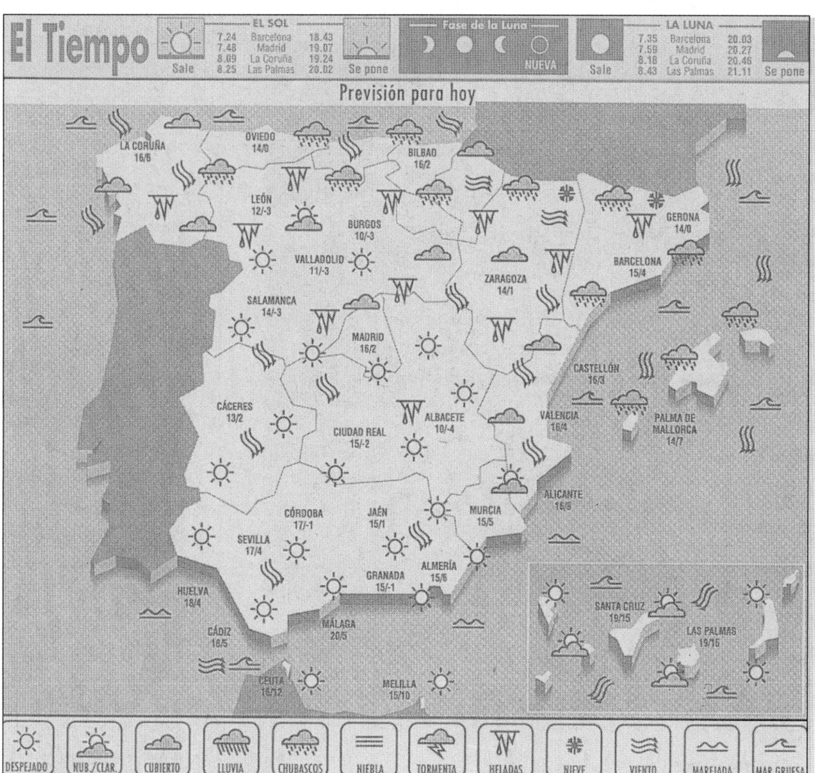

ANSWERS TO ¿Qué palabra necesito?

11 and **12** *Answers will vary; however, students should use the vocabulary from* Palabras 2.

13 *Answers will vary; however, the students' choice of city and plans should correspond to the weather conditions shown on the map.*

LEVELING

E: Activities 8, 9, 11
A: Activities 9, 11, 13
C: Activities 10, 12

¡OJO! Activities 11, 12, and 13 encourage students to use the chapter vocabulary and structures in open-ended situations. It is not necessary to have them do all the activities. Allow students to select the activity or activities they wish to do.

11 You may want to do Activity 11 only with students who are interested in skiing. Determine how much each item will cost in dollars before students begin this activity.

12 **Expansion:** Have one partner try to convince the other that skiing is interesting. Have him or her give as many reasons as possible.

13 Before doing Activity 13, review the meaning of the icons at the bottom of the weather map.

11 **and** **13** You may wish to ask one of the groups doing Activity 11 or Activity 13 to volunteer to present the conversation to the entire class.

Learning from Realia

(page 281) This weather map is from the newspaper ***El ABC*** in Madrid. You may wish to play the following *true / false* game.

1. **Hay sol en Málaga.**
2. **Llueve en Córdoba.**
3. **Llueve en Bilbao.**
4. **Está nublado (Hay nubes) al norte de Madrid.**
5. **Palma de Mallorca está en una isla.**
6. **Alicante está en una isla también.**
7. **Ceuta está en el norte de África.**

Estructura

1 PREPARATION

Resource Manager

Audio Activities TE, pages 109–111
Audio CD 6
Workbook, pages 105–110
Quizzes, pages 47–49
ExamView® Pro

Bellringer Review

Use BRR Transparency 9.3 or write the following on the board.
Indicate whether each of the following is associated with **el verano** or **el invierno.**

1. **Bajan la pista.**
2. **Esquían.**
3. **Esquían en el agua.**
4. **Toman el telesilla.**
5. **Usan una toalla playera.**
6. **Bucean.**

2 PRESENTATION

Pretérito de los verbos en -ar

Step 1 Have students open their books to page 282. Read Item 1 aloud. Then have the class repeat the two model sentences after you.

Step 2 Write the verbs **hablar, tomar,** and **nadar** on the board. Have the class repeat each form after you. After you write the forms for one verb on the board, you may wish to have students provide the forms for the other verbs. For example, under **hablar,** write **hablé.** Underline the ending. Rather than give the endings for **tomar** and/or **nadar,** ask: If it's **hablé** for **hablar,** what's the form for **tomar? Nadar?** Have students repeat all forms.

Step 3 For Item 3, have students look at the examples and point out the spelling changes.

Estructura

Pretérito de los verbos en -ar
Describing past actions

1. You use the preterite to express actions that began and ended at a definite time in the past.

 Ayer María pasó el día en la playa.
 Yo, no. Pasé el día en la escuela.

2. The preterite of regular **-ar** verbs is formed by dropping the infinitive ending **-ar** and adding the appropriate endings to the stem. Study the following forms.

INFINITIVE	hablar	tomar	nadar	ENDINGS
STEM	habl-	tom-	nad-	
yo	hablé	tomé	nadé	-é
tú	hablaste	tomaste	nadaste	-aste
él, ella, Ud.	habló	tomó	nadó	-ó
nosotros(as)	hablamos	tomamos	nadamos	-amos
vosotros(as)	*hablasteis*	*tomasteis*	*nadasteis*	*-asteis*
ellos, ellas, Uds.	hablaron	tomaron	nadaron	-aron

3. Note that verbs that end in **-car, -gar,** and **-zar** have a spelling change in the **yo** form.

¿Marcaste un tanto?	**Sí, marqué un tanto.**
¿Llegaste a tiempo?	**Sí, llegué a tiempo.**
¿Jugaste (al) baloncesto?	**Sí, jugué (al) baloncesto.**
¿Empezaste a jugar?	**Sí, empecé a jugar.**

DEPORTES
* Basquet
* VoleyFutbol
* Handball
* Raquetball
* Pelota a mano
* Gimnasia deportiva

LEVELING
E: Activities 14, 15
A: Activity 16
C: Activity 17

¿Cómo lo digo?

14 Historieta Una tarde en la playa

Contesten.

1. Ayer, ¿pasó Rubén la tarde en la playa?
2. ¿Tomó él mucho sol?
3. ¿Usó crema protectora?
4. ¿Nadó en el mar?
5. ¿Buceó?
6. ¿Esquió en el agua?

San Juan, Puerto Rico

15 Historieta Un partido de tenis

Contesten según se indica.

1. ¿Qué compraron los amigos? (una raqueta)
2. ¿A qué jugaron los jóvenes? (tenis)
3. ¿Jugaron en una cancha cubierta? (no, al aire libre)
4. ¿Golpearon la pelota? (sí)
5. ¿Jugaron singles o dobles? (dobles)
6. ¿Quiénes marcaron el primer tanto? (Alicia y José)
7. ¿Quiénes ganaron el partido? (ellos)

MERIDIANO TELEVISIÓN

MAÑANA
06:00 Golf Boomme Valley Classic 2 Ronda
07:30 Formula 1 Gran Premio de Luxemburgo (En Vivo)
10:00 Máxima Velocidad
11:00 Mundo Marcial
11:30 Basket Nacional: Cocodrilos vs Tanqueros (En Vivo)
TARDE
01:30 Formula 1 Gran Premio de Luxemburgo
04:00 Fútbol Nacional: Caracas F.C. vs Minerven (En Vivo)
06:00 Supergolazo
06:30 Revista Semanal
NOCHE
07:00 Tenis Copa Davis USA vs Italia
09:00 Retrospectiva de Golf
09:30 Revista Semanal
10:00 Tercer Tiempo
10:30 Noticiero Meridiano
11:30 Wheelies

NOTA: Esta programación puede estar sujeta a cambios por motivos de fuerza mayor.

16 Historieta En casa

Contesten personalmente.

1. Anoche, ¿a qué hora llegaste a casa?
2. ¿Preparaste la comida?
3. ¿Estudiaste?
4. ¿Miraste la televisión?
5. ¿Escuchaste CDs?
6. ¿Hablaste por teléfono?
7. ¿Con quién hablaste?

17 Historieta Yo llegué al estadio.

Cambien **nosotros** a **yo.**

Ayer nosotros llegamos al estadio y empezamos a jugar fútbol. Jugamos muy bien. No tocamos el balón con las manos. Lo lanzamos con el pie o con la cabeza. Marcamos tres tantos.

Estructura

Teaching Tip

While going over Item 3 of the structure explanation, you may wish to review the following sound/spelling correspondences:
ca, que, qui, co cu
ga, gue, gui, go, gu
za, ce, ci, zo, zu
These explain the spelling of **jugó, jugué, buscó, busqué, empezó, empecé.**

3 PRACTICE

¿Cómo lo digo?

¡OJO! The activities on pages 283 and 284 build from easy to more complex. Some deal with one subject pronoun only. Activity 20 on page 284 combines all subjects.

14, 15, and 16 It is suggested you go over these activities orally with books closed. Do these activities a second time with books open. **Expansion:** You can have students retell the story in each activity in their own words.

Writing Development
Students can also write Activities 14, 15, and 16 in paragraph form.

ANSWERS TO ¿Cómo lo digo?

14

1. Sí, ayer Rubén pasó la tarde en la playa.
2. Sí, (No, no) tomó mucho sol.
3. Sí, (No, no) usó crema protectora.
4. Sí, (No, no) nadó en el mar.
5. Sí, (No, no) buceó.
6. Sí, (No, no) esquió en el agua.

15

1. Los amigos compraron una raqueta.
2. Los jóvenes jugaron al tenis.
3. No, jugaron al aire libre.
4. Sí, golpearon la pelota.
5. Jugaron dobles.
6. Alicia y José marcaron el primer tanto.
7. Ellos ganaron el partido.

16

1. Anoche llegué a casa a las ___.
2. Sí, (No, no) preparé la comida.
3. Sí, (No, no) estudié.
4. Sí, (No, no) miré la televisión.
5. Sí, (No, no) escuché CDs.
6. Sí, (No, no) hablé por teléfono.
7. Hablé con ___. (No hablé por teléfono.)

17

Ayer yo llegué al estadio y empecé a jugar fútbol. Jugué muy bien. No toqué el balón con las manos. Lo lancé con el pie y con la cabeza. Marqué tres tantos.

Estructura

3 PRACTICE *(continued)*

18 Have pairs of students present Activity 18 as a miniconversation, using as much expression as possible.

20 Have students retell the story in Activity 20 in their own words.

LEVELING

E: Activities 18, 19, 21

A: Activity 21

C: Activities 20, 22

Chapter Projects

Mis vacaciones

Have students share their family's vacation experiences by bringing in photos and vacation memorabilia. You may wish to group students according to their vacation destinations—mountains, beach, city, camping, etc.—and have each group tell as much as they can about their vacations there.

18 El baloncesto

Formen preguntas según el modelo.

—¿Jugó Pablo?
—A ver, Pablo, ¿jugaste?

1. ¿Jugó Pablo al baloncesto?
2. ¿Dribló con el balón?
3. ¿Pasó el balón a un amigo?
4. ¿Tiró el balón?
5. ¿Encestó?
6. ¿Marcó un tanto?

19 Historieta Una fiesta

Sigan el modelo.

hablar →
Mis amigos y yo hablamos durante la fiesta.

1. bailar
2. cantar
3. tomar un refresco
4. tomar fotos
5. escuchar música

Valdesquí, España

20 Historieta En una estación de esquí

Completen.

El fin de semana pasado José, algunos amigos y yo __1__ (esquiar). __2__ (Llegar) a la estación de esquí el viernes por la noche. Luego nosotros __3__ (pasar) dos días en las pistas.

José __4__ (comprar) un pase para el telesquí. Todos nosotros __5__ (tomar) el telesquí para subir la montaña. Pero todos nosotros __6__ (bajar) una pista diferente. José __7__ (bajar) la pista para expertos porque él esquía muy bien. Pero yo, no. Yo __8__ (tomar) la pista para principiantes. Y yo __9__ (bajar) con mucho cuidado.

Answers to ¿Cómo lo digo?

18

1. A ver, Pablo, ¿jugaste al baloncesto?
2. A ver, Pablo, ¿driblaste con el balón?
3. A ver, Pablo, ¿pasaste el balón a un amigo?
4. A ver, Pablo, ¿tiraste el balón?
5. A ver, Pablo, ¿encestaste?
6. A ver, Pablo, ¿marcaste un tanto?

19

1. Mis amigos y yo bailamos durante la fiesta.
2. Mis amigos y yo cantamos durante la fiesta.
3. Mis amigos y yo tomamos un refresco durante la fiesta.
4. Mis amigos y yo tomamos fotos durante la fiesta.
5. Mis amigos y yo escuchamos música durante la fiesta.

20

1. esquiamos
2. Llegamos
3. pasamos
4. compró
5. tomamos
6. bajamos
7. bajó
8. tomé
9. bajé

21 **Pasaron el fin de semana en la playa.** Look at the illustration. Work with a classmate, asking and answering questions about what these friends did at the beach in Acapulco.

22 **Pasé un día en una estación de esquí.** You went on a skiing trip in the Sierra Nevada, Granada, Spain. You had a great time. Call your friend (a classmate) to tell him or her about your trip. Your friend has never been skiing so he or she will have a few questions for you.

*For more practice using words from **Palabras 1** and **2** and the preterite, do Activity 9 on page H10 at the end of this book.*

Answers to ¿Cómo lo digo?

21 *Answers will vary; however, students should use the vocabulary from* Palabras 1. *Answers should be expressed in the preterite. Answers may include:*

—¿Pasaron el día en la playa?
—Sí, pasaron el día en la playa.
—¿Nadaron?
—Sí, nadaron y tomaron el sol.

22 *Answers will vary. Answers should be expressed using the preterite.*

Estructura

21 and 22 These activities encourage students to use the chapter vocabulary and structures in open-ended situations. It is not necessary to have them do all the activities. Choose the ones you consider most appropriate. We have provided visuals with these activities to aid students to speak in the past using the preterite of **-ar** verbs only. It is important that we not give students activities that would force them to use unknown preterite forms or the imperfect.

21 Before students do this activity, you may want them to quickly review the vocabulary presented on pages 274 and 275. Now have students look at the illustration and ask one another questions about it.

22 In addition to using the postcard as a stimulus, students can quickly review Activity 20 on page 284 for some ideas regarding what to say.

UN POCO MÁS This *InfoGap* activity will allow students to practice in pairs. The activity should be very manageable for them, since all vocabulary and structures are familiar to them.

FUN-FACTS

Many people are surprised to learn that there are so many ski resorts in different areas of Spain. There are major ski resorts in the Pyrenees, in the Sierra Nevada near Granada, and just north of Madrid in the Sierra de Guadarrama and Sierra de Gredos.

Estructura

1 PREPARATION

Bellringer Review

Use BRR Transparency 9.4 or write the following on the board.
Answer the following questions.
1. **¿Compraste un traje de baño nuevo?**
2. **¿Llevaste el traje de baño a la playa?**
3. **¿Nadaste?**
4. **¿Esquiaste en el agua también?**

2 PRESENTATION

Pronombres—lo, la, los, las

Step 1 Write several of the model sentences from Item 1 on the board. Draw a box around the direct object (noun). Now circle the direct object pronoun. Then draw a line from the box to the circle. This visual technique helps many students grasp the concept that one word replaces the other.

Step 2 Have students open their books to page 286. Instead of providing or having students read the information in Item 2, you may wish to have students come up with the answers: Does **lo** replace a masculine or feminine noun? What pronoun replaces a feminine noun?

Pronombres—lo, la, los, las
Referring to items already mentioned

1. The following sentences each have a direct object. The direct object is the word in the sentence that receives the action of the verb. The direct object can be either a noun or a pronoun.

Ella compró el bañador.	**Ella lo compró.**
Compró los anteojos de sol.	**Los compró en la misma tienda.**
¿Compró loción bronceadora?	**Sí, la compró.**
¿Compró las toallas en la misma tienda?	**No, no las compró en la misma tienda.**
¿Invitaste a Juan a la fiesta?	**Sí, lo invité.**
¿Invitaste a Elena?	**Sí, la invité.**

2. Note that **lo, los, la,** and **las** are direct object pronouns. They must agree with the noun they replace. They can replace either a person or a thing. The direct object pronoun comes right before the verb.

Ella compró el regalo.	**Ella lo compró.**
Invitó a Juan.	**Lo invitó.**
No miré la fotografía.	**No la miré.**
No miré a Julia.	**No la miré.**

¿Cómo lo digo?

23 ¿Dónde está? Sigan el modelo.

¿El bañador?

Aquí lo tienes.

1. ¿El traje de baño?
2. ¿El tubo de crema?
3. ¿La pelota?
4. ¿La crema protectora?
5. ¿Los anteojos de sol?
6. ¿Los boletos?
7. ¿Los esquís acuáticos?
8. ¿Las toallas playeras?
9. ¿Las raquetas?
10. ¿Las tablas hawaianas?

ANSWERS TO ¿Cómo lo digo?

23

1. Aquí lo tienes.
2. Aquí lo tienes.
3. Aquí la tienes.
4. Aquí la tienes.
5. Aquí los tienes.
6. Aquí los tienes.
7. Aquí los tienes.
8. Aquí las tienes.
9. Aquí las tienes.
10. Aquí las tienes.

24

1. —¿Cuándo compraste la toalla playera?
—La compré ayer.
—¿Dónde la compraste?
—La compré en ___.
—¿Cuánto te costó?
—Me costó ___.

2. —¿Cuándo compraste los anteojos de sol?
—Los compré ayer.
—¿Dónde los compraste?
—Los compré en ___.
—¿Cuánto te costaron?
—Me costaron ___.

3. —¿Cuándo compraste la mochila?
—La compré ayer.
—¿Dónde la compraste?
—La compré en ___.
—¿Cuánto te costó?
—Me costó ___.

24 De compras Sigan el modelo.

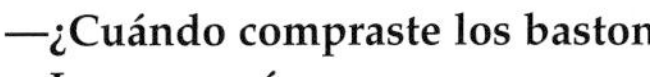

—¿Cuándo compraste los bastones?
—Los compré ayer.
—¿Dónde los compraste?
—Los compré en la tienda Padín.
—¿Cuánto te costaron?
—Me costaron ciento cinco pesos.

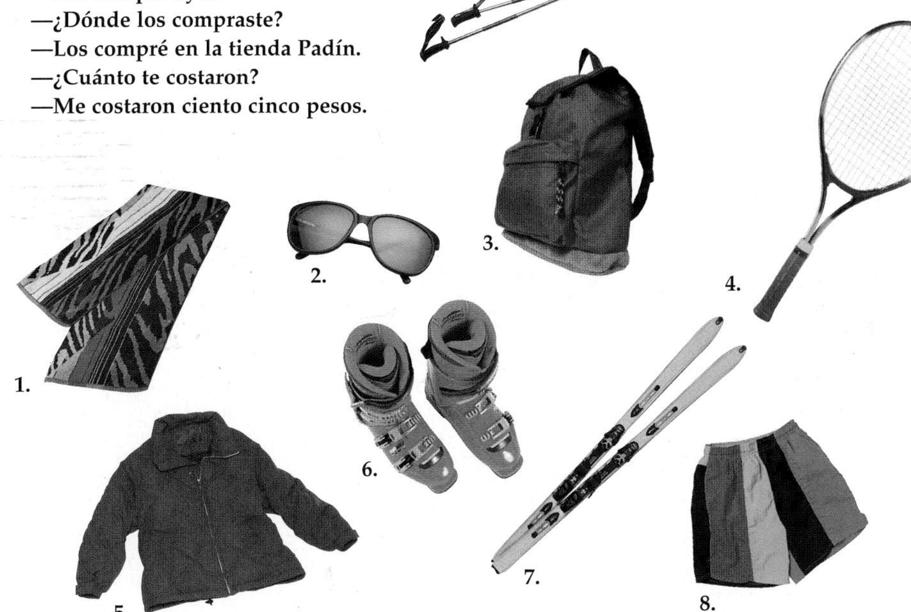

25 Historieta Un regalo que le gustó
Completen.

Yo compré un regalo para Teresa. __1__ compré en la tienda de departamentos Corte Inglés. Compré unos anteojos de sol. A Teresa le gustaron mucho. Ella __2__ llevó el otro día cuando fue a la piscina. Ella tiene algunas fotografías con sus anteojos de sol. Su amigo Miguel __3__ tomó.

Madrid, España

Estructura

3 PRACTICE

¿Cómo lo digo?

23 Have students do Activity 23 as a paired activity as shown in the model.
Expansion: Have students hold up additional items they know. For example, **¿El lápiz? ¿El cuaderno? ¿El libro?**

24 Have students present each part of Activity 24 as a miniconversation between two people. Have students make up a price for each item in Activity 24.

25 Have students retell the story in Activity 25 in their own words.

Learning from Photos

(page 287) Have students take turns describing the photo. This will review vocabulary taught in Chapter 3.

Answers to ¿Cómo lo digo?

4. —¿Cuándo compraste la raqueta?
—La compré ayer.
—¿Dónde la compraste?
—La compré en ___.
—¿Cuánto te costó?
—Me costó ___.
5. —¿Cuándo compraste el anorak?
—Lo compré ayer.
—¿Dónde lo compraste?
—Lo compré en ___.
—¿Cuánto te costó?
—Me costó ___.
6. —¿Cuándo compraste las botas?
—Las compré ayer.
—¿Dónde las compraste?
—Las compré en ___.
—¿Cuánto te costaron?
—Me costaron ___.
7. —¿Cuándo compraste los esquís?
—Los compré ayer.
—¿Dónde los compraste?
—Los compré en ___.
—¿Cuánto te costaron?
—Me costaron ___.
8. —¿Cuándo compraste el traje de baño (bañador)?
—Lo compré ayer.
—¿Dónde lo compraste?
—Lo compré en ___.
—¿Cuánto te costó?
—Me costó ___.

25

1. Lo
2. los
3. las

1 PREPARATION

Bellringer Review

Use BRR Transparency 9.5 or write the following on the board.

Write the following sentences in the preterite.

1. **Yo busco mi libro.**
2. **Yo juego al tenis.**
3. **Yo llego a las tres.**

2 PRESENTATION

Ir y ser en el pretérito

Step 1 Ask students to open their books to page 288. As you go over the explanation, tell students that the meaning of the sentences makes it clear whether it is the verb **ser** or **ir.**

Step 2 Have students repeat the verb forms on page 288 in unison.

Step 3 In Item 2, call on a student to read the model sentences or have the entire class repeat them.

LEVELING

A: Activities 23, 25

C: Activity 24

26 Historieta Una fiesta Contesten.

1. ¿Invitaste a Juan a la fiesta?
2. ¿Invitaste a Alejandra?
3. ¿Compraste los refrescos?
4. ¿Preparaste la ensalada?
5. ¿Tomó Pepe las fotografías de la fiesta?

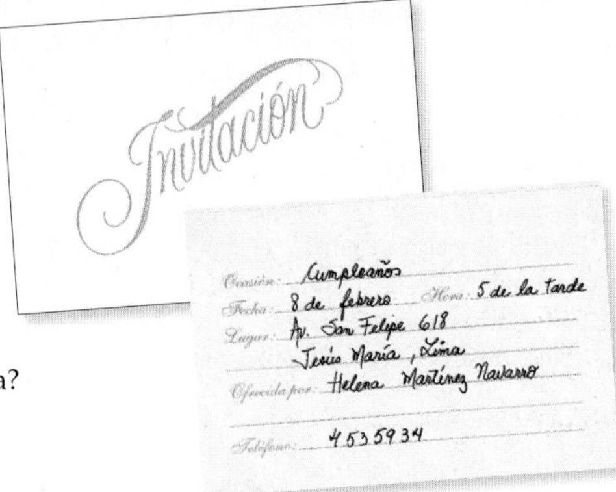

Ir y ser en el pretérito
Describing past actions

1. The verbs **ir** and **ser** are irregular in the preterite tense. Note that they have identical forms.

INFINITIVE	ir	ser
yo	fui	fui
tú	fuiste	fuiste
él, ella, Ud.	fue	fue
nosotros(as)	fuimos	fuimos
vosotros(as)	*fuisteis*	*fuisteis*
ellos, ellas, Uds.	fueron	fueron

2. The context in which each verb is used in the sentence will clarify the meaning. The verb **ser** is not used very often in the preterite.

El Sr. Martínez fue profesor de español.
Él fue a España.
Mi abuela fue médica.
Mi abuela fue al consultorio de la médica.

Answers to ¿Cómo lo digo?

1. Sí, (No, no) lo invité a la fiesta.
2. Sí, (No, no) la invité.
3. Sí, (No, no) los compré.
4. Sí, (No, no) la preparé.
5. Sí (No), Pepe (no) las tomó.

Chapter Projects

Agencia de viaje Have students go to a travel agency to get some brochures on winter and summer resorts in the Spanish-speaking world. They can present the material to the class in Spanish or prepare a bulletin board display.

¿Cómo lo digo?

27 **¿Y tú?** Contesten personalmente.

1. Ayer, ¿fuiste a la escuela?
2. ¿Fuiste a la playa?
3. ¿Fuiste a la piscina?
4. ¿Fuiste al campo de fútbol?
5. ¿Fuiste a la cancha de tenis?
6. ¿Fuiste a las montañas?
7. ¿Fuiste a casa?
8. ¿Fuiste a la tienda?

28 **¿Quién fue y cómo?** Contesten personalmente.

1. ¿Fuiste a la escuela ayer?
2. ¿Fue tu amigo también?
3. ¿Fueron juntos?
4. ¿Fueron en carro?
5. ¿Fue también la hermana de tu amigo?
6. ¿Fue ella en carro o a pie?

29 **Anteayer** Work with a classmate. Ask whether he or she went to one of the places below the day before yesterday **(anteayer)**. Your partner will respond. Take turns asking and answering the questions.

1.

2.

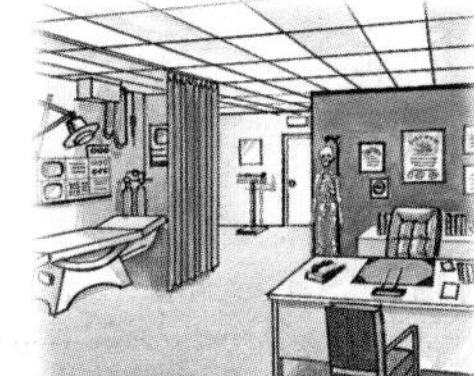
3.

4.

5.

3 PRACTICE

¿Cómo lo digo?

27 **and** **28** Students very often confuse **fui** and **fue.** For this reason, Activity 27 gives practice using **fui.** After you finish Activity 28, call on several students to retell the story in their own words. This will assist in evaluating whether they understand the difference between **fui** and **fue.** Activity 28 starts with **fui** and then uses **fue** and **fueron.**

29 Make sure students can identify each place illustrated: **la playa, la cancha de tenis, el consultorio del médico, la tienda de ropa, el restaurante.**
Expansion: After students finish Activity 29, have them look at each illustration and say as much as they can about it.

¡Adelante!

At this point in the chapter, students have learned all the vocabulary and structure necessary to complete the chapter. The conversation and cultural readings that follow recycle all the material learned up to this point.

Answers to ¿Cómo lo digo?

27

1. Sí (No), ayer (no) fui a la escuela.
2. Sí, (No, no) fui a la playa.
3. Sí, (No, no) fui a la piscina.
4. Sí, (No, no) fui al campo de fútbol.
5. Sí, (No, no) fui a la cancha de tenis.
6. Sí, (No, no) fui a las montañas.
7. Sí, (No, no) fui a casa.
8. Sí, (No, no) fui a la tienda.

28

1. Sí, (No, no) fui a la escuela ayer.
2. Sí (No), mi amigo (no) fue.
3. Sí, (No, no) fuimos juntos.
4. Sí, (No, no) fuimos en carro.
5. Sí (No), la hermana de mi amigo (no) fue.
6. Ella fue en carro (a pie).

29 *Answers should follow this model:*

1. —___, ¿fuiste a la playa anteayer?
—Sí, (No, no) fui a la playa anteayer.

Conversación

1 PREPARATION

Resource Manager

Audio Activities TE, pages 111–112
Audio CD 6

Bellringer Review

Use BRR Transparency 9.6 or write the following on the board.
Answer.

1. **¿Fuiste a la papelería? ¿Qué compraste allí?**
2. **¿Fuiste a la tienda de ropa? ¿Qué compraste?**
3. **¿Fuiste al mercado? ¿Qué compraste?**

2 PRESENTATION

Step 1 Have students close their books. Read the conversation to them or play Audio CD 6.

Step 2 Have the class repeat the conversation once or twice in unison.

Step 3 Call on pairs to read the conversation. Encourage them to be as animated as possible.

Step 4 Change the names of the characters to boys' names. Have pairs act out the conversation for the class allowing them to make any changes that make sense.

Step 5 After presenting the conversation, go over the **¿Comprendes?** activity. If students can answer the questions with relative ease, move on. Students should not be expected to memorize the conversation.

LEVELING

E: Conversation

A: Conversation

Conversación

¡A la playa!

Gloria ¿Adónde fuiste ayer?
Paula Pues, fui a la playa. Y no puedes imaginar lo que me pasó.
Gloria ¿Qué te pasó?
Paula Llegué a la playa sin mi traje de baño.
Gloria ¿Sin tu traje de baño?
Paula Sí, ¡sin mi traje de baño! Lo dejé en casa.
Gloria ¡Fuiste a la playa y dejaste tu traje de baño en casa! ¡Muy inteligente, Paula!
Paula Ah, pero lo pasé muy bien. Fui a nadar.
Gloria ¿Nadaste? ¿Sin traje de baño?
Paula Querer es poder. Fui al agua en mi blue jean.

¿Comprendes?

Contesten.

1. ¿Adónde fue Paula ayer?
2. ¿Llegó a la playa con su traje de baño?
3. ¿Dónde dejó su traje de baño?
4. Pero, ¿lo pasó bien en la playa?
5. ¿Nadó?
6. ¿Qué llevó cuando fue al agua?

Answers to ¿Comprendes?

1. Paula fue a la playa ayer.
2. No, no llegó a la playa con su traje de baño.
3. Dejó su traje de baño en casa.
4. Sí, lo pasó bien en la playa.
5. Sí, nadó.
6. Llevó su blue jean cuando fue al agua.

Vamos a hablar más

A **¿Qué tiempo hace?** Work with a classmate. One of you lives in tropical San Juan, Puerto Rico. The other lives in Buffalo, New York. Describe the winter weather where you live.

B **Fuimos de vacaciones.** Work with a classmate. Take turns telling one another what you did last summer. You may wish to use the following words.

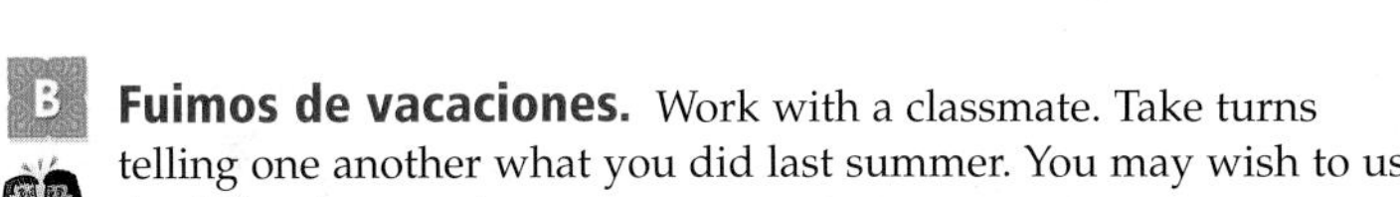

Pronunciación

La consonante g

The consonant **g** has two sounds, hard and soft. You will study the soft sound in Chapter 10. **G** in combination with **a, o, u, (ga, go, gu)** is pronounced somewhat like the *g* in the English word *go*. To maintain this hard **g** sound with **e** or **i,** a **u** is placed after the **g: gue, gui.**

Repeat the following.

ga	gue	gui	go	gu
gafa	**Rodríguez**	**guitarra**	**goma**	**agua**
amiga	**guerrilla**	**guía**	**estómago**	**guante**
garganta			**tengo**	
paga			**juego**	
gato				

Repeat the following sentences.

El gato no juega en el agua.
Juego béisbol con el guante de mi amigo Rodríguez.
No tengo la guitarra de Gómez.

Answers to Vamos a hablar más

A *Answers will vary; however, students should use the appropriate weather expressions taught on pages 274 and 278.*

B *Answers will vary; however, all answers should be expressed in the preterite. Encourage students to use as many words as possible from the colored boxes.*

Reaching All Students

Additional Practice

A escuchar Give students the following directions in order to practice auditory discrimination: Listen to the following. If I am talking about the present, raise one hand. If I am talking about the past, raise both hands.

Habló. Miró. Esquío. Miro.
Nadó. Compro. Pagó.

3 PRACTICE

Vamos a hablar más

¡OJO! Although we want students to speak freely in these cooperative and communicative activities, students must take into account what they can realistically say based on their knowledge of the language. Since they now know the preterite of **-ar** verbs, students can discuss past events that call for **-ar** verbs. We have been careful not to give activities that would be impossible for students to do, such as discussing a past event that would necessitate the use of **-er** or **-ir** verbs, irregular verbs, or the imperfect. These activities incorporate all previously learned material but do not frustrate students by leading them into errors that are beyond their control.

Pronunciación

Step 1 Have students carefully repeat **ga, gue, gui, go, gu** after you or Audio CD 6.
Note: English speakers tend to make the **g** sound too hard when speaking Spanish. As students repeat **ga, gue, gui, go, gu,** indicate to them that the sound is produced very softly toward the back of the throat.

Step 2 Now have students repeat the words after you.

Step 3 Use Pronunciation Transparency P 9 to model the first sentence: **El gato no juega en el agua.**

Step 4 Have students open their books to page 291. Call on individuals to read the sentences carefully.

Step 5 All model sentences on page 291 can be used for dictation.

Lecturas culturales

Resource Manager

Audio Activities TE, pages 112–113
Audio CD 6

National Standards

Cultures
The reading about beach resorts in the Spanish-speaking world and the related activities allow students to find out more about famous tourist destinations in Spain and Latin America.

PRESENTATION

Pre-reading

Have students scan the **Lectura** for cognates.

Reading

Step 1 Have the class read the selection once silently.

Step 2 Now call on individuals to read about four sentences each.

Step 3 Ask comprehension questions based on each series of four sentences. For example, **¿En qué países hay playas fantásticas?**

Step 4 Do the Reading Strategy on page 292.

Post-reading

Step 1 If possible, bring in photos, slides, or videos of some popular beach resorts in Spain or Latin America. You may obtain videos from local travel agencies or the library. Additional information is available on the Internet.

Step 2 Have students read the **Lectura** at home and write the answers to the **¿Comprendes?** activities.

Lecturas culturales

Paraísos del mundo hispano

¿Viajar[1] por el mundo hispano y no pasar unos días en un balneario? ¡Qué lástima[2]! En los países de habla española hay playas fantásticas. España, Puerto Rico, Cuba, México, Uruguay—todos son países famosos por sus playas.

En el verano cuando hace calor y un sol bonito brilla en el cielo, ¡qué estupendo es pasar un día en la playa! Y en lugares (sitios) como México, Puerto Rico y Venezuela, el verano es eterno. Podemos ir a la playa durante todos los meses del año.

Muchas personas toman sus vacaciones en una playa donde pueden disfrutar de[3] su tiempo libre. En la playa nadan o toman el sol. Vuelven a casa muy tostaditos o bronceados. Pero, ¡cuidado! Es necesario usar una crema protectora porque el sol es muy fuerte[4] en las playas tropicales.

[1]Viajar *To travel*
[2]lástima *pity*
[3]disfrutar de *enjoy*
[4]fuerte *strong*

Reading Strategy

Summarizing When reading an informative passage, we try to remember what we read. Summarizing helps us to do this. The easiest way to summarize is to begin to read for the general sense and take notes on what you are reading. It is best to write a summarizing statement for each paragraph and then one for the entire passage.

Marbella, España

Cancún, México

LEVELING
E: Reading

Chapter Projects

Un viaje ideal Have groups plan the ideal four-week vacation trip through a region of their choice in Spain or Latin America.

La playa de Varadero, Cuba

Playa de Guajataca, Puerto Rico

Pocitos, Uruguay

¿Comprendes?

A La palabra, por favor.
Den la palabra apropiada.

1. un lugar que tiene playas donde la gente puede nadar
2. una cosa triste y desagradable
3. maravillosas, estupendas
4. célebres
5. lindo, hermoso
6. de y para siempre
7. regresan a casa

B En la playa Contesten.

1. ¿Qué hay en los países de habla española?
2. ¿Cuándo es estupendo pasar un día en la playa?
3. ¿Cómo disfruta de su tiempo la gente que va a la playa?
4. ¿Cómo es el sol en las playas tropicales?

Lecturas culturales

Learning from Photos

(page 293 left) This area in Varadero, Cuba, was the playground of the wealthy prior to the takeover by Castro. It is a beautiful beach and is frequented today by many Canadians and Europeans.

¿Comprendes?

A and B Allow students to refer to the reading for the answers, or you may use these activities as a testing device for factual recall.

Answers to ¿Comprendes?

A

1. un balneario
2. una lástima
3. fantásticas
4. famosos
5. bonito
6. eterno
7. vuelven a casa

B

1. Hay playas fantásticas en los países de habla española.
2. En el verano cuando hace calor y un sol bonito brilla en el cielo, es estupendo pasar un día en la playa.
3. Nadan o toman el sol.
4. El sol es muy fuerte en las playas tropicales.

Lectura opcional 1

National Standards

Cultures
The reading about winter resorts and the related activities on this page make students aware of the fact that the seasons are reversed in the northern and southern hemispheres.

Comparisons
This reading allows students to compare their activities with activities that their counterparts might engage in in South America.

¡OJO! This reading is optional. You may skip it completely, have the entire class read it, have only several students read it and report to the class, or assign it for extra credit.

Geography Connection

The **Costa del Sol** runs along the Mediterranean from the Cabo de Gata beyond Almería all the way to the tip of Tarifa beyond Gibraltar. The most popular resort area is located between Málaga and Estepona. Although many parts of this region are very beautiful, there is great concern that it has been overdeveloped.

Have students locate Málaga and the **Costa del Sol** on the map of Spain on page xxx or use Map Transparency M 2.

Lectura opcional 1

Estaciones inversas

Es el mes de julio. En España es el verano y la gente va a la playa a nadar. Y en la Argentina y Chile la gente va a las montañas a esquiar. ¿Cómo es que esquían en julio? Pues, el mes de julio es invierno. En el hemisferio sur las estaciones son inversas de las estaciones del hemisferio norte.

Sitges, España

Los Andes, Chile

¿Comprendes?

A ¿A esquiar o a nadar? Contesten.

1. ¿Qué mes es?
2. ¿Qué estación es en España?
3. ¿Adónde va la gente?
4. ¿Qué estación es en Argentina y Chile?
5. ¿Adónde va la gente?
6. En julio, ¿dónde nada la gente?
7. En julio, ¿dónde esquía la gente?

B ¿Qué estación es? Explica por qué es invierno en julio en Chile y Argentina.

Answers to ¿Comprendes?

A

1. Es el mes de julio.
2. Es el verano.
3. La gente va a la playa.
4. Es el invierno.
5. La gente va a las montañas a esquiar.
6. En julio, la gente nada en el hemisferio norte.
7. En julio, la gente esquía en el hemisferio sur.

B

Es invierno en julio en Chile y la Argentina porque en el hemisferio sur las estaciones son inversas de las estaciones del hemisferio norte.

Lectura opcional 2

«Snowboarding» en Chile

El «snowboarding»

¿Qué es el «snowboarding» o «el surf de nieve»? Es un deporte como el surfing—pero no sobre el agua. Practican el «snowboarding» sobre la nieve. Hay dos tipos o modalidades de surf de nieve—las carreras[1] y las exhibiciones.

Para practicar el «snowboarding», necesitas una tabla, un casco[2], guantes y rodilleras[3].

Sobre el «snowboard»—que es un tipo de tabla—el aficionado[4] hace unas piruetas y movimientos difíciles. Hay competencias de «snowboarding» en los Juegos Olímpicos.

[1]carreras *races*
[2]casco *helmet*
[3]rodilleras *kneepads*
[4]aficionado *fan*

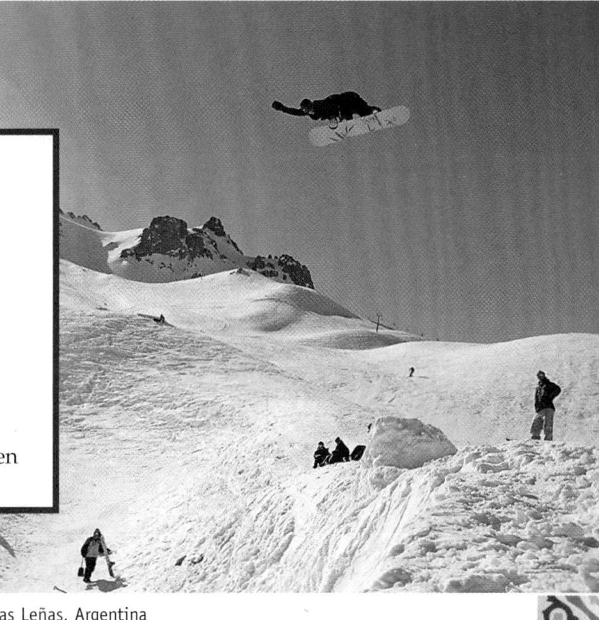
Las Leñas, Argentina

¿Comprendes?

¿Sí o no? Digan que sí o que no.

1. El «snowboarding» es como el surfing sobre el agua, pero los aficionados lo practican en la nieve.
2. Hay solamente un tipo de surf de nieve.
3. El «snowboard» es un tipo de tabla, similar a una tabla hawaiana.
4. El aficionado de «snowboarding» hace unas piruetas en el aire.
5. Hay competencias de .«snowboarding» en la Copa mundial.

Lectura opcional 2

¡OJO! This reading is optional. You may skip it completely, have the entire class read it, have only several students read it and report to the class, or assign it for extra credit.

PRESENTATION

Step 1 Find out if any of your students prefer snowboarding to skiing: **¿Prefieres el snowboarding o el esquí?** If any student indicates a preference for snowboarding, you may wish to ask this student to describe his or her experience, using the vocabulary learned in this chapter.

Step 2 Quickly go over the **¿Comprendes?** activities.

LEVELING

E: Reading 1
A: Reading 2

Answers to ¿Comprendes?

1. Sí
2. No
3. Sí
4. Sí
5. No

Conexiones

National Standards

Connections
This reading about climate and weather in the Spanish-speaking world establishes a connection with another discipline, allowing students to reinforce and further their knowledge of the social sciences through the study of Spanish.

¡OJO! The readings in the **Conexiones** section are optional. They focus on some of the major disciplines taught in schools and universities. The vocabulary is useful for discussing such topics as history, literature, art, economics, business, science, etc. You may choose any of the following ways to do the readings in the **Conexiones** sections.

Independent reading Have students read the selections and do the post-reading activities as homework, which you collect. This option is least intrusive on class time and requires a minimum of teacher involvement.

Homework with in-class follow-up Assign the readings and post-reading activities as homework. Review and discuss the material in class the next day.

Intensive in-class activity This option includes a pre-reading vocabulary presentation, in-class reading and discussion, assignment of the activities for homework, and a discussion of the assignment in class the following day.

Conexiones

Las ciencias sociales

El clima

We often talk about the weather, especially when on vacation. When planning a vacation trip, it's a good idea to take into account the climate of the area we are going to visit. When we talk about weather or climate, we must remember, however, that there is a difference between the two. Weather is the condition of the atmosphere for a short period of time. Climate is the term used for the weather that prevails in a region over a long period of time. Let's read about weather and climate throughout the vast area of the Spanish-speaking world.

El Parque Nacional de los Glaciares, Argentina

El clima y el tiempo

El clima y el tiempo son dos cosas muy diferentes. El tiempo es la condición de la atmósfera durante un período breve o corto. El tiempo puede cambiar[1] frecuentemente. Puede cambiar varias veces en un solo día.

El clima es el término que usamos para el tiempo que prevalece[2] en una zona por un período largo. El clima es el tiempo que hace cada año en el mismo lugar.

Zonas climáticas

En el mundo de habla española hay muchas zonas climáticas. Mucha gente cree que toda la América Latina tiene un clima tropical, pero es erróneo. El clima de Latinoamérica varía de una región a otra.

[1]cambiar *change*
[2]prevalece *prevails*

La vegetación tropical, Costa Rica

El río Santiago Cayapas, Ecuador

El Amazonas

Toda la zona o cuenca amazónica es una región tropical. Hace mucho calor y llueve mucho durante todo el año.

Los Andes

En los Andes, aún en las regiones cerca de la línea ecuatorial, el clima no es tropical. En las zonas montañosas el clima depende de la elevación. En los picos andinos, por ejemplo, hace frío.

Clima templado

Algunas partes de Argentina, Uruguay y Chile tienen un clima templado. España también tiene un clima templado. En una región de clima templado hay cuatro estaciones: el verano, el otoño, el invierno y la primavera. Y el tiempo cambia con cada estación. ¡Y una cosa importante! Las estaciones en la América del Sur son inversas de las de la América del Norte.

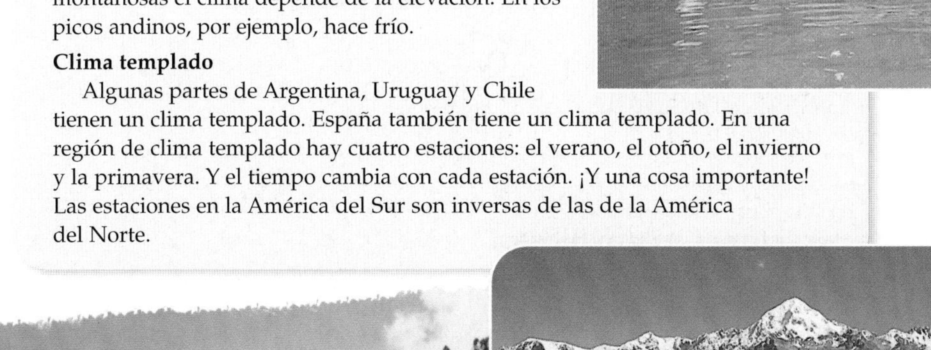

Los picos andinos cerca de Cuzco, Perú

Una aldea en las montañas, Ecuador

¿Comprendes?

¿Sabes? Contesten en inglés.

1. What's the difference between weather and climate?
2. What is an erroneous idea that many people have about Latin America?
3. How can it be cold in some areas that are actually on the equator?
4. What is a characteristic of a tropical area?
5. What is a characteristic of a region with a temperate climate?

Answers to ¿Comprendes?

1. Weather is the condition of the atmosphere during a short period of time. It can change frequently. Climate is the weather prevailing in a region over a long period of time. It's the weather that a given place has every year.
2. Many people think all of Latin America has a tropical climate.
3. In mountainous areas the climate depends on the elevation.
4. It's hot all year, and it rains a lot.
5. It has four seasons, and the weather changes with each season.

Conexiones

Las ciencias sociales

El clima

PRESENTATION

Step 1 As students read about these climate zones, have them locate each area being discussed on the map of South America on page xxxi, or on Map Transparency M 3.

Step 2 Have students read the introduction in English on page 296. They should then proceed to the main reading.

¡Te toca a ti!

Use what you have learned

Recycling

These activities allow students to use the vocabulary and structure from this chapter in completely open-ended, real-life situations.

PRESENTATION

Encourage students to say as much as possible when they do these activities. Tell them not to be afraid to make mistakes, since the goal of the activities is real-life communication. If someone in the group makes an error, allow the others to politely correct him or her. Let students choose the activities they would like to do.

You may wish to divide students into pairs or groups. Encourage students to elaborate on the basic theme and to be creative. They may use props, pictures, or posters if they wish.

Writing Development

Have students keep a notebook or portfolio containing their best written work from each chapter. These selected writings can be based on assignments from the Student Textbook and the Workbook. The activities on page 299 are examples of writing assignments that may be included in each student's portfolio. On page 116 in the Workbook, students will begin to develop an organized autobiography **(Mi autobiografía).** These workbook pages may also become a part of their portfolio.

¡Te toca a ti!

Use what you have learned

HABLAR 1

¿El mar o la montaña?

✔ *Talk about summer or winter vacations*

Work with a classmate. Tell him or her where you like to go on vacation. Tell what you do there and some of the reasons why you enjoy it so much. Take turns.

HABLAR 2

¡Unas vacaciones maravillosas!

✔ *Talk about different vacation activities*

Work with a classmate. Pretend you each have a million dollars. Take turns describing your millionaire's dream vacation.

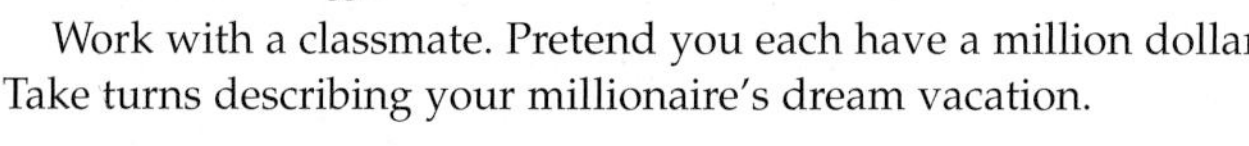

HABLAR 3

El esquí

✔ *Talk about skiing*

You are at a café near the slopes of Bariloche in Argentina. You meet an Argentine skier (your partner). Find out as much as you can about each other's skiing habits and abilities.

San Carlos de Bariloche, Argentina

Answers to ¡Te toca a ti!

1 and 2 *Answers will vary; however, encourage students to make maximum use of the words and expressions they have learned thus far.*

3 *Answers will vary, but students should use the ski-related vocabulary learned in this chapter.*

ESCRIBIR 4

Una tarjeta postal

✔ *Write about a summer or winter vacation destination*

Look at these postcards. Choose one. Pretend you spent a week there. Write the postcard to a friend.

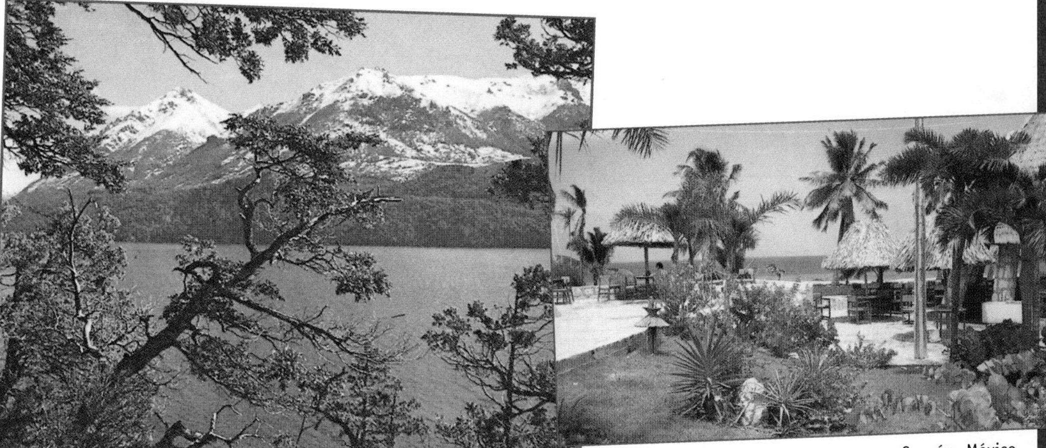

Bariloche, Argentina

Cancún, México

ESCRIBIR 5

Irene y José Luis durante un día de julio

It's a typical July day. But Irene is in Santiago de Chile and José Luis is in Santiago de Compostela in Spain. The days are quite different in these two places. Write a comparison between a July day in Santiago de Chile and in Santiago de Compostela. Explain why the days are so different.

Because of the type of weather, Irene's activities on this day are probably different from those of José Luis. Explain what each one is doing. Are they wearing the same clothing or not?

Not everything is different, however. What are Irene and José Luis both doing on this July day in two different places in spite of the different weather?

Writing Strategy

Comparing and contrasting
Before you begin to write a comparison of people, places, or things, you must be aware of how they are alike and different. When you compare, you are emphasizing similarities; when you contrast, you are emphasizing differences. Making a diagram or a list of similarities and differences is a good way to organize your details before you begin to write.

¡Te toca a ti!

Writing Strategy

Comparing and contrasting
Have students read the Writing Strategy on page 299. Then have students make a list of similarities and differences between a July day in Santiago de Chile and in Santiago de Compostela, Spain. Have students refer to the maps of Spain and South America in their textbook on pages xxx and xxxi, or you may wish to project Map Transparencies M 2 and M 3. As students develop the last paragraph, remind them that much of their daily routine could be the same as those of the students they are describing.

Geography Connection

Bariloche is in the heart of the Argentine lake area on the southern end of Lago Nahuel Huapi. It resembles a European ski village with chaletlike houses made of wood and stone.

Bariloche is a ski resort in the winter. The snow festival is held every August. Fishing is great from mid-November to mid-March. In the summer, Bariloche is popular with campers, swimmers, and anglers.

Answers to ¡Te toca a ti!

4 *Answers will vary. Accept any answers that describe the location shown on the postcard. Answers should include use of the preterite tense.*

5 *Answers will vary, but students will indicate that in July it's summer in Spain and winter in Chile. Answers should include activities typically associated with each season.*

Leveling

These activities encompass all three levels. All students will be able to do them at a sophistication level commensurate with their ability in Spanish. Some students will be able to speak for several minutes, and others may be able to give just a few sentences. This is to be expected when students are functioning completely on their own generating their own language to the best of their ability.

Resource Manager

Communication Transparency C 9
Quizzes, pages 43–49
Performance Assessment, Task 9
Tests, pages 139–154
Situation Cards, Chapter 9
ExamView® Pro, Chapter 9
Maratón mental Videoquiz, Chapter 9

Assessment

This is a pre-test for students to take before you administer the chapter test. Note that each section is cross-referenced so students can easily find the material they have to review in case they made errors. You may use Assessment Answers Transparency A 9 to do the assessment in class, or you may assign this assessment for homework. You can correct the assessment yourself, or you may prefer to project the answers on the overhead in class.

Glencoe Technology

MINDJOGGER VHS/DVD

You may wish to help your students prepare for the chapter test by playing the MindJogger game show. Teams will compete against each other to review chapter vocabulary and structure and sharpen listening comprehension skills.

Vocabulario

To review **Palabras 1**, turn to pages 274–275.

1 Identifiquen.

3.

4.

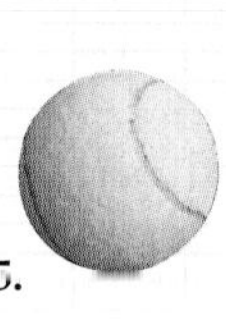
5.

2 Contesten.

6. ¿Qué tiempo hace en el verano?

To review **Palabras 2**, turn to pages 278–279.

3 Completen.

7. La esquiadora lleva un ____ cuando hace frío y nieva mucho.
8. Para esquiar es necesario tener (uno necesita) ____ y bastones.
9. Los esquiadores tomaron el ____ para subir la montaña.
10. Los esquiadores que no esquían bien bajan la ____ para principiantes.

Answers to Assessment

1

1. la loción bronceadora (crema protectora)
2. las gafas (los anteojos) de sol
3. el esquí acuático
4. la raqueta
5. la pelota

2

6. En el verano hace calor. Hace buen tiempo. Hace sol.

3

7. anorak
8. guantes / botas
9. telesilla (telesquí)
10. pista

Assessment

Estructura

4 Completen con el pretérito.

11. Él ____ en el mar. (nadar)
12. Sus amigos ____ en la piscina. (nadar)
13. Y tú, ¿____ en el agua? (esquiar)
14. No. Yo ____ el sol. (tomar)
15. Nosotros ____ toda la tarde en la playa. (pasar)
16. Y ustedes, ¿____ a la playa también? (ir)

To review the preterite, turn to pages 282 and 288.

5 Escriban en el pretérito.

17. Juego al fútbol.
18. Sí, empiezo a jugar.

6 Escriban con un pronombre.

To review direct object pronouns, turn to page 286.

19. No tengo *mis anteojos de sol.*
20. Compré *la loción bronceadora* en la farmacia.
21. Tomás tomó *las fotografías.* Yo, no.
22. Invitamos *a José* a ir a la playa.
23. Ella compró *el bañador* en El Corte Inglés.

Cultura

To review this cultural information, turn to page 292.

7 ¿Sí o no?

24. Un balneario es una estación de esquí.
25. Muchos países de habla española tienen playas fabulosas.

SPANISH Online

The **Glencoe Spanish Web** site (spanish.glencoe.com) offers options that enable you and your students to experience the Spanish-speaking world via the Internet. For each **Capítulo,** there are activities, games, and quizzes. In addition, an *Enrichment* section offers students an opportunity to visit Web sites related to the theme of the chapter.

FOLDABLES™ Study Organizer — Dinah Zike's Study Guides

Your students may wish to use Foldable 2 to organize, display, and arrange data as they develop communication skills in Spanish. You may wish to encourage them to add information from each chapter as they continue to expand their vocabulary in Spanish.

A *forward-backward book* foldable is also ideal in helping students visually connect words to the objects they represent.

Music Connection

Canta con Justo The song **El verano es lo mejor** will be easy for learners of all ability levels. It will help students practice the preterite tense and the weather expressions introduced in this chapter. You may wish to have students hear the recorded version of **El verano es lo mejor.** It can be found on Track 2 of the **Canta con Justo** music CD. In addition, students can watch Justo perform this song on the **Justo Lamas ¡En vivo!** music video that accompanies **¡Buen viaje!** On the DVD of this music video, as an additional feature, students can perform karaoke to any of Justo's songs.

ANSWERS TO Assessment

4

11. nadó
12. nadaron
13. esquiaste
14. tomé
15. pasamos
16. fueron

5

17. Jugué al fútbol.
18. Sí, empecé a jugar.

6

19. No los tengo.
20. La compré en la farmacia.
21. Tomás las tomó. Yo, no.
22. Lo invitamos a ir a la playa.
23. Ella lo compró en El Corte Inglés.

7

24. No
25. Sí

¡Hablo como un pro!

This unique page gives students the opportunity to speak freely and say whatever they can, using the vocabulary and structures they have learned in the chapter. The illustration serves to remind students of precisely what they know how to say in Spanish. There are no activities that students do not have the ability to describe or talk about in Spanish. The art not only depicts the vocabulary and content of this chapter, but also reinforces what they learned in previous chapters.

You may wish to use this page in many ways. Some possibilities are to have students do the following:

1. Look at the illustration and identify items by giving the correct Spanish words.
2. Make up sentences about what they see in the illustration.
3. Make up questions about the illustration. They can call on another class member to respond if you do this as a class activity, or you may prefer to allow students to work in small groups. This activity is extremely beneficial because it enables students to actively use interrogative words.
4. Answer questions you ask them about the illustration.
5. Work in pairs and make up a conversation based on the illustration.
6. Look at the illustration and give a complete oral review of what they see.
7. Look at the illustration and write a paragraph (or essay) about it.

You can also use this page as an assessment or testing tool, taking into account individual differences by having students go from simple to quite complicated tasks. The assessment can be either oral or written. You may wish to use the rubrics provided on pages T20–T21 as you give students the following directions.

1. Identify the topic or situation of the illustration.
2. Give the Spanish words for as many items as you can.
3. Think of as many sentences as you can to describe the illustration.
4. Go over your sentences and put them in the best sequencing to give a coherent story based on the illustration.

¡Hablo como un pro!

Tell all you can about this illustration.

Vocabulario

Describing the beach

el balneario	la arena	el mar
la playa	la ola	la piscina, la alberca

Describing summer weather

el verano	el cielo	Hace buen (mal) tiempo.
la nube	Hace (Hay) sol.	Llueve.
estar nublado	Hace calor.	El sol brilla.

Identifying beach gear

el traje de baño, el bañador	los anteojos (las gafas) de sol	el esquí acuático
la loción bronceadora, la crema protectora	la toalla playera	la plancha de vela
		la tabla hawaiana

Describing summer and beach activities

la natación	nadar	esquiar en el agua	pasar el fin de semana
el buceo	tomar el sol	bucear	practicar el surfing

Describing a tennis game

el tenis	el/la tenista	la red	jugar (al) tenis
la cancha de tenis (al aire libre, cubierta)	la raqueta	singles	golpear la pelota
	la pelota	dobles	

Describing a ski resort

la estación de esquí	el ticket, el boleto	la pista	el/la principiante
la ventanilla, la boletería	el/la esquiador(a)	el telesquí, el telesilla	
	la montaña	el/la experto(a)	

Identifying ski gear

el esquí	el bastón	el guante
la bota	el anorak	

Describing winter activities

esquiar	tomar (subir en) el telesilla	bajar la pista

Describing winter weather

el invierno	el grado	Hace frío.
la nieve	bajo cero	Nieva.
la temperatura		

Other useful expressions

ayer	por encima de

How well do you know your vocabulary?

- Choose one season—**el verano, el invierno**—from the list.
- Have a classmate make up sentences that tell about that season.

VIDEOTUR

Episodio 9

In this video episode, you will join Claudia and Alberto in a ski shop. See page 500 for more information

¡OJO! You will notice that the vocabulary list here is not translated. This has been done intentionally, since we feel that by the time students have finished the material in the chapter they should be familiar with the meanings of all the words. If there are several words they still do not know, we recommend that they refer to the **Palabras 1** and **2** sections in the chapter or go to the dictionaries at the end of this book to find the meanings. However, if you prefer that your students have the English translations, please refer to Vocabulary Transparency 9.1, where you will find all these words with their translations.

Vocabulario

Vocabulary Review

The words and phrases in the **Vocabulario** have been taught for productive use in this chapter. They are summarized here as a resource for both student and teacher. This list also serves as a convenient resource for the **¡Te toca a ti!** activities on pages 298 and 299. There are approximately sixteen cognates in this vocabulary list. Have students find them.

VIDEO VHS/DVD

The Video Program allows students to see how the chapter vocabulary and structures are used by native speakers within an engaging story line. For maximum reinforcement, show the video episode as a final activity for Chapter 9.

Critical Thinking Activity

Decision making, evaluating consequences

Write the following on the board or on an overhead transparency.

1. **Maripaz va a la playa. Pero ella sabe que cada vez que va a la playa, no vuelve bronceada. Vuelve quemada. Es un problema para ella. Por consiguiente, ella debe comprar una crema protectora muy fuerte. Ella tiene 1.000 pesos. Quiere comprar un par de anteojos de sol que son fabulosos. Pero si ella compra los anteojos, no va a tener bastante dinero para comprar la crema protectora. ¿Qué debe ella hacer?**
2. **La tentación sale victoriosa. Maripaz compró los anteojos de sol y ella no va a cambiar sus planes. Va a ir a la playa. ¿Cuáles pueden ser las consecuencias de su decisión?**
3. **¿Qué otras alternativas tiene Maripaz?**

Planning for Chapter 10

SCOPE AND SEQUENCE, PAGES 304–333

Topics

- Attending cultural events
- Teen dating customs

Culture

- Verónica talks about teen dating customs in the Spanish-speaking world compared to dating customs in the United States
- El Teatro Nacional, San José, Costa Rica
- La zarzuela
- Palacio de Bellas Artes
- The Ballet Folklórico de México
- Music of the Spanish-speaking world

Functions

- How to talk about going to cultural events and purchasing a ticket
- How to discuss movies, plays, and museums
- How to express cultural preferences
- How to relate actions or events that took place in the past
- How to tell for whom something is done

Structure

- **-er** and **-ir** verbs in the preterite
- Indirect object pronouns **le, les**

National Standards

- Communication Standard 1.1 pages 304, 308, 309, 312, 313, 315, 316, 317, 318, 328
- Communication Standard 1.2 pages 309, 312, 313, 316, 319, 320, 321, 323, 324, 325, 327, 328
- Communication Standard 1.3 pages 309, 321, 327, 329
- Cultures Standard 2.1 pages 322–323, 324–325
- Cultures Standard 2.2 pages 309, 311, 324, 325
- Connections Standard 3.1 pages 326–327
- Connections Standard 3.2 page 324
- Comparisons Standard 4.2 pages 313, 322–323
- Communities Standard 5.1 pages 321, 327, 329
- Communities Standard 5.2 page 321

PACING AND PRIORITIES

The chapter content is color coded below to assist you in planning.

■ required ■ recommended ■ optional

Vocabulario *(required)* *Days 1–4*
- ■ Palabras 1
  - Al cine
  - En el cine
- ■ Palabras 2
  - En el museo
  - En el teatro

Estructura *(required)* *Days 5–7*
- ■ Pretérito de los verbos en **-er** e **-ir**
- ■ Complementos **le, les**

Conversación *(required)*
- ■ ¿Saliste?

Pronunciación *(recommended)*
- ■ Las consonantes **j, g**

Lecturas culturales
- ■ Dating *(recommended)*
- ■ La zarzuela *(optional)*
- ■ El baile *(optional)*

Conexiones
- ■ La música *(optional)*

■ **¡Te toca a ti!** *(recommended)*

■ **Assessment** *(recommended)*

■ **¡Hablo como un pro!** *(optional)*

RESOURCE GUIDE

SECTION	PAGES	SECTION RESOURCES
Vocabulario PALABRAS 1		
Al cine En el cine	306, 308–309 306–309	Vocabulary Transparencies 10.2–10.3 Audio CD 6 Audio Activities TE, pages 117–120 Workbook, pages 117–118 Quiz 1, page 50 ExamView® Pro
Vocabulario PALABRAS 2		
En el museo En el teatro	310, 312–313 310–313	Vocabulary Transparencies 10.4–10.5 Audio CD 6 Audio Activities TE, pages 121–122 Workbook, pages 118–120 Quiz 2, pages 51–52 ExamView® Pro
Estructura		
Pretérito de los verbos en **-er** e **-ir** Complementos **le, les**	314–316 317–319	Audio CD 6 Audio Activities TE, pages 123–125 Workbook, pages 121–124 Quizzes 3–4, pages 53–54 ExamView® Pro
Conversación		
¿Saliste?	320	Audio CD 6 Audio Activities TE, page 126 Interactive CD-ROM
Pronunciación		
Las consonantes **j, g**	321	Pronunciation Transparency P 10 Audio CD 6 Audio Activities TE, page 127
Lecturas culturales		
Dating La zarzuela El baile	322–323 324 325	Audio CD 6 Audio Activities TE, page 127 Tests, pages 159, 163
Conexiones		
La música	326–327	Tests, page 164
¡Te toca a ti!		
	328–329	**¡Viva el mundo hispano!** Video, Episode 10 Video Activities, Chapter 10 Spanish Online Activities spanish.glencoe.com
Assessment		
	330–331	Communication Transparency C 10 Quizzes 1–4, pages 50–54 Performance Assessment, Task 10 Tests, pages 155–168 Situation Cards, Chapter 10 ExamView® Pro **Maratón mental** Videoquiz

Using Your Resources for Chapter 10

Transparencies

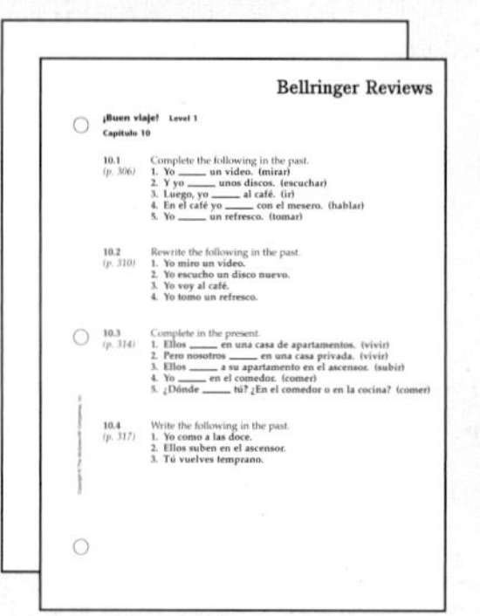

Bellringer 10.1–10.4

Vocabulary 10.1–10.5

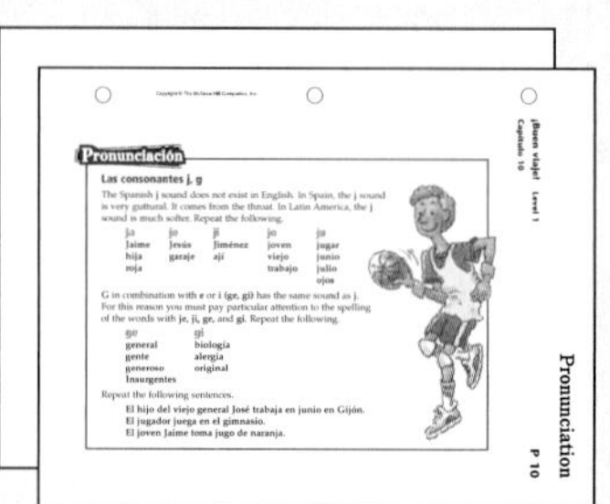

Pronunciation P 10

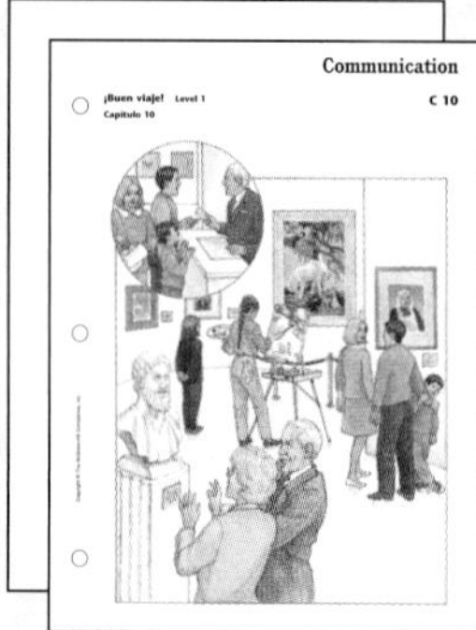

Communication C 10

Workbook

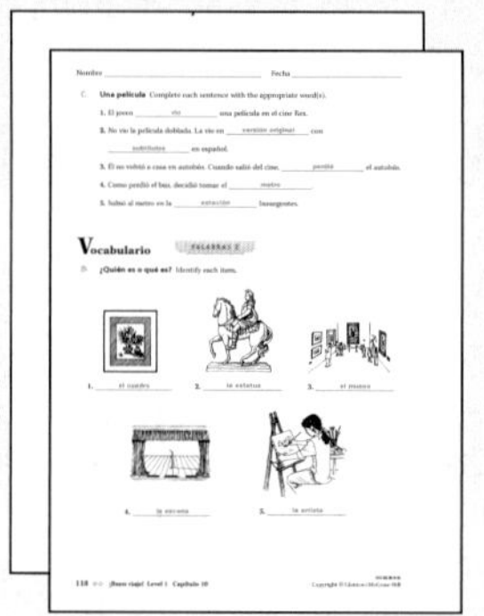

Vocabulary, pages 117–120

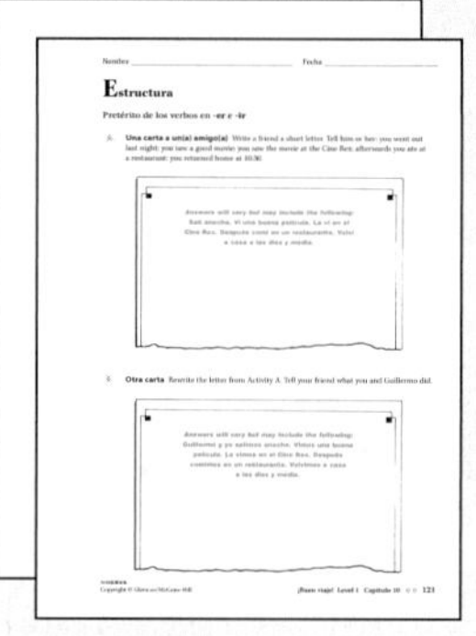

Structure, pages 121–124

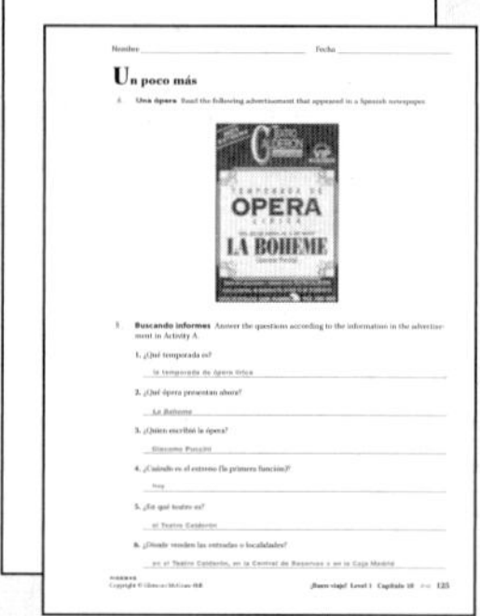

Enrichment, pages 125–128

Audio Activities

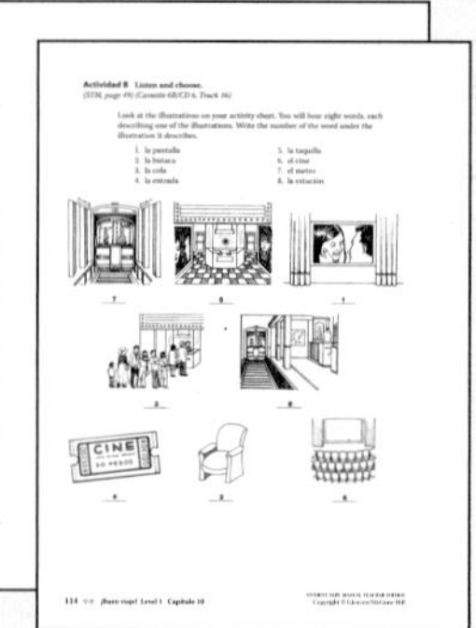

Vocabulary, pages 117–122

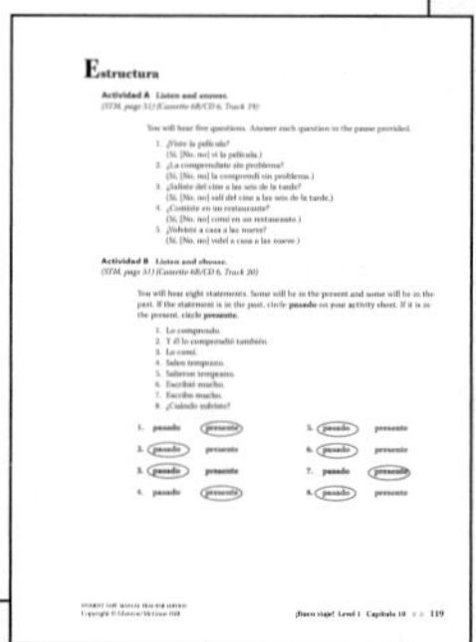

Structure, pages 123–125

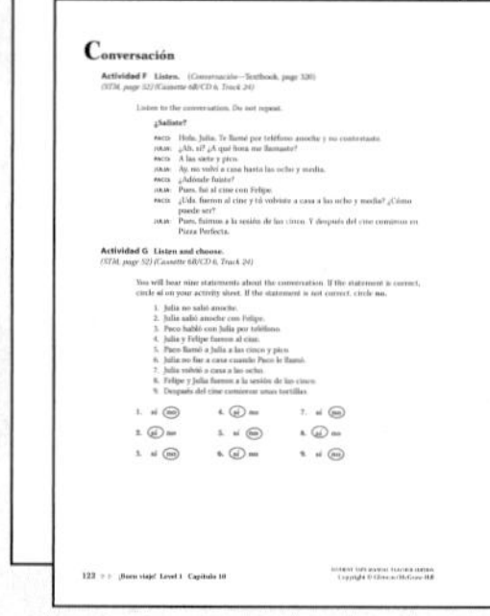

Conversation, Pronunciation, pages 126–127

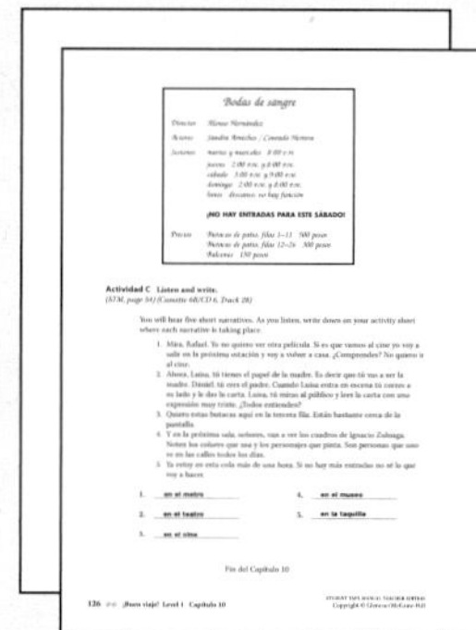

Additional Practice, pages 128–130

Assessment

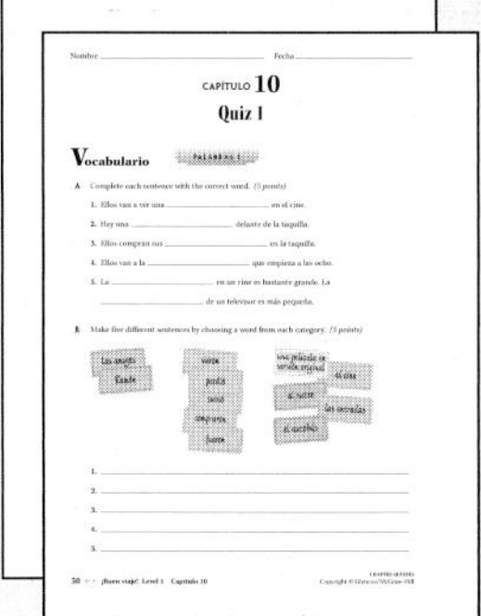

Vocabulary and Structure Quizzes, pages 50–54

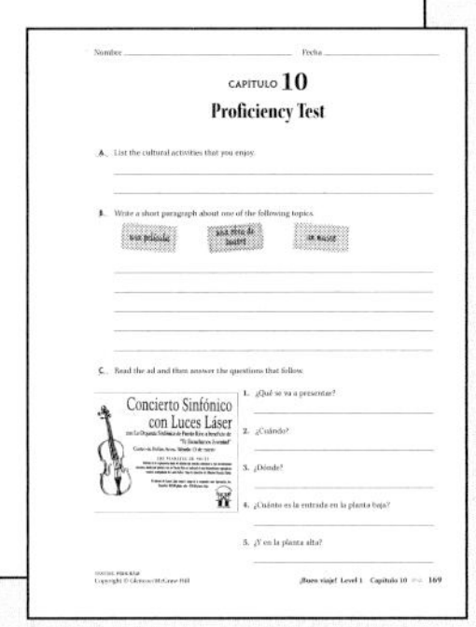

Chapter Tests, pages 155–168

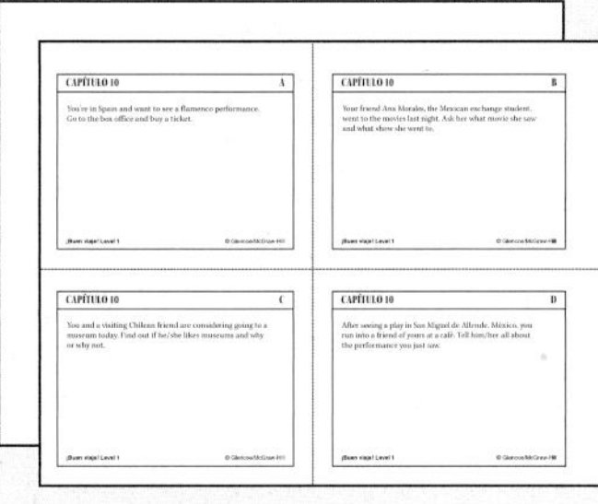

Situation Cards, Chapter 10

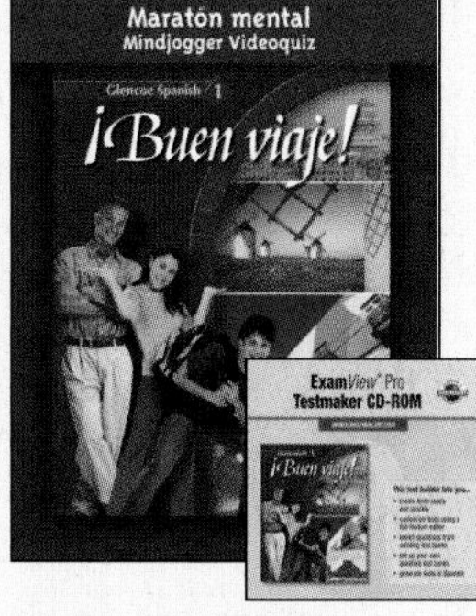

MindJogger Videoquiz, ExamView® Pro, Chapter 10

Timesaving Teacher Tools

TeacherWorks™ is your all-in-one teacher resource center. Personalize lesson plans, access resources from the Teacher Wraparound Edition, connect to the Internet, or make a to-do list. These are only a few of the many features that can assist you in the planning and organizing of your lessons.

Includes:

- A calendar feature
- Access to all program blackline masters
- Standards correlations and more

ExamView® Pro

Test Bank software for Macintosh and Windows makes creating, editing, customizing, and printing tests quick and easy.

Technology Resources

In the Chapter 10 Internet Activity, you will have a chance to learn more about the Spanish-speaking world. Visit spanish.glencoe.com

On the interactive CD-ROM, students can listen to and take part in a recorded version of the conversation in Chapter 10.

¡Viva el mundo hispano! Video and Video Activities, Chapter 10. Available on VHS and DVD.

Help your students prepare for the chapter test by playing the **Maratón mental** Videoquiz game show. Teams will compete against each other to review chapter vocabulary and structure and sharpen listening comprehension skills. Available on VHS and DVD.

¡Buen viaje! is also available on CD or Online.

Capítulo 10

Preview

In this chapter, students will learn to discuss several types of cultural activities. To do this they will learn basic vocabulary associated with movies, museums, and the theater. They will also continue to express themselves in the past by learning the preterite of **-er** and **-ir** verbs. The cultural focus of the chapter will be dating customs and cultural events in the Spanish-speaking world.

National Standards

Communication

In Chapter 10, students will communicate in spoken and written Spanish on the following topics:

- going to the movies
- visiting a museum
- attending a theater performance

Students will obtain and provide information about these topics and engage in conversations about their personal exposure to cultural events. They will also continue learning to express themselves in the past tense.

LEVELING

The activities, conversations, and readings within each chapter are marked according to level of difficulty. **E** indicates easy. **A** indicates average. **C** indicates challenging. Some activities cover a range of difficulty. In some activities, for example, advanced students will be able to produce more extensive responses while students who learn at a different rate may give less detailed responses. The leveling indicators will help you individualize instruction to best meet your students' needs.

Capítulo 10

Diversiones culturales

Objetivos

In this chapter you will learn to:

- **discuss movies, museums, and theater**
- **discuss cultural events**
- **relate more past actions or events**
- **tell for whom something is done**
- **discuss some dating customs in the United States and compare them with those in Spanish-speaking countries**
- **talk about cultural activities that are popular in the Spanish-speaking world**

Rufino Tamayo *Músicos*

Capítulo 10

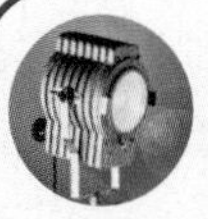

Spotlight on Culture

Arte Rufino Tamayo (1899–1991) was a Mexican painter who considered the value of a work of art to come only from its physical qualities. He shared with many of his national contemporaries an interest in pre-Colombian heritage. Many of his forms took an angular, almost cubist form, but his works had a greater affinity with surrealism.

Fotografía This photo shows the Prado Museum in Madrid. The building was originally commissioned by Carlos III in 1785 to house a natural history museum. When the Prado was completed in 1819, however, it became an art museum to exhibit the vast collection of the Spanish royalty. Painting represents one of Spain's greatest contributions to world cultures. The Prado collection includes the works of three great masters: Francisco de Goya, Diego Velázquez, and El Greco, as well as other masterpieces by Flemish and Italian artists. The room we see in this photo contains works by El Greco.

Vocabulario

PALABRAS 1

1 PREPARATION

Resource Manager

Vocabulary Transparencies 10.2–10.3
Audio Activities TE, pages 117–120
Audio CD 6
Workbook, pages 117–118
Quizzes, page 50
ExamView® Pro

Bellringer Review

Use BRR Transparency 10.1 or write the following on the board.
Complete the following in the past.

1. **Yo ___ un video. (mirar)**
2. **Y yo ___ unos discos. (escuchar)**
3. **Luego, yo ___ al café. (ir)**
4. **En el café yo ___ con el mesero. (hablar)**
5. **Yo ___ un refresco. (tomar)**

2 PRESENTATION

Step 1 Using Vocabulary Transparencies 10.2–10.3, play the **Palabras 1** presentation on Audio CD 6. Point to the appropriate illustration as you play the CD.

Step 2 Have students repeat each word or expression after you two or three times as you point to the corresponding item on the transparency.

Step 3 Now call on individual students to point to the corresponding illustration on the transparency as you say the word or expression.

Vocabulario

PALABRAS 1

Al cine

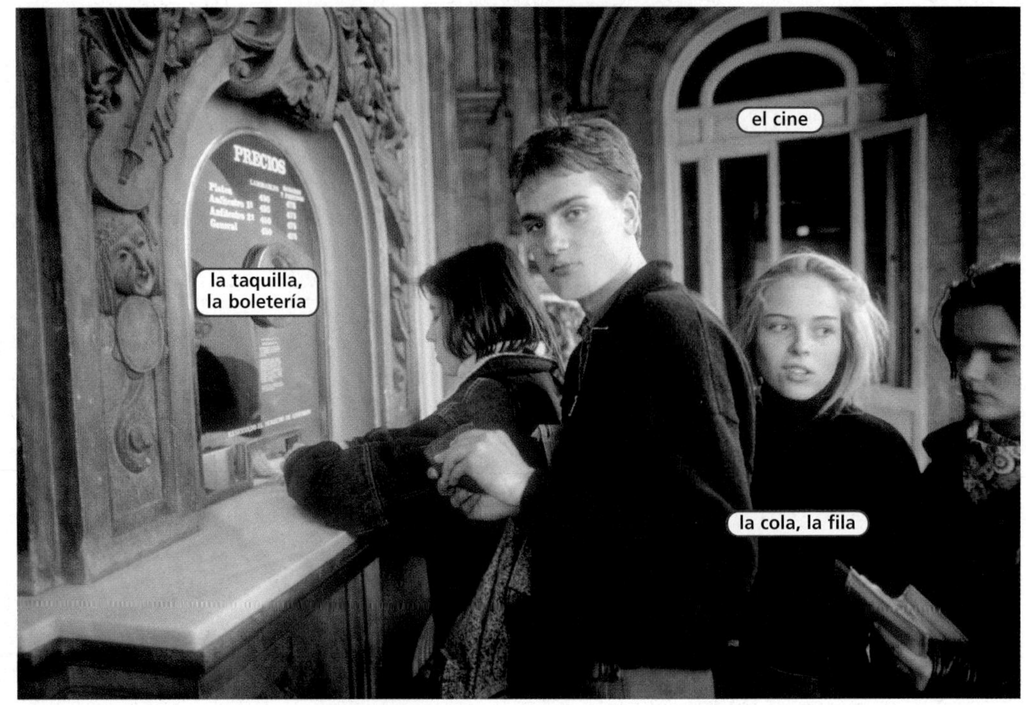

Hay una cola delante de la taquilla.
Los amigos van a ver una película (un film).
Compran sus entradas (boletos).
Van a la sesión de las cuatro de la tarde.

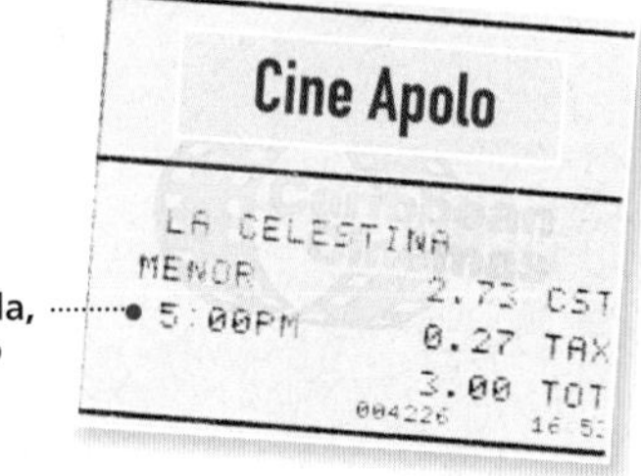

la entrada, el boleto

El joven vio una película.
Vio una película americana.
No la vio en versión original (en inglés).
La vio doblada al español.
Si la película no está doblada, lleva subtítulos.

Reaching All Students

Total Physical Response

(Student 1), **levántate, por favor.**
Ven acá. Imagínate que quieres ir al cine.
Ve por el autobús. Allí está.
¡Corre! ¡Anda rápido! Vas a perder el bus.
¡Ay! Perdiste el bus. Pero no hay problema.
Ve a la estación de metro.
Baja al metro. Espera.
Aquí viene el metro. Sube.
El metro llega a la estación que quieres. Baja del metro.
Sube la escalera.
Allí está el cine. Ve a la taquilla.
Ponte en fila.
Indica a la taquillera que quieres una entrada.
Gracias, *(Student 1).* **Y ahora toma tu asiento.**

Luego salió del cine.
¡Ay! Perdió el autobús (la guagua, el camión).

Como perdió el autobús, el joven fue a la estación de metro.
Subió al metro en la estación Insurgentes.
Volvió a casa en el metro.

Nota The verb **salir** has several uses. Note the following meanings the verb can convey.

Diego salió anoche.
Diego went out last night.
Diego left last night.

Diego salió con Sandra.
Diego went out with (dated) Sandra.

Todo salió muy bien.
Everything turned out fine.

Vocabulario

¡OJO! Note that only the third-person singular forms of the preterite of **-er** and **-ir** verbs are used in the vocabulary presentation so that students can immediately answer questions and use the new vocabulary without having to make ending changes.

FUN-FACTS

Insurgentes is one of the main subway stations in Mexico City. Mexico City's subway system is one of the world's best, as well as one of the safest and cheapest. The stations are immaculate and brightly lit. The trains are French-designed and, like the famous Paris **métro,** they run very quietly on rubber tires. The Mexico City subway transports more than five million passengers daily.

Vocabulary Expansion

You may wish to give students the following additional vocabulary.

una película policíaca
una película documental
una película de amor (romántica)
una película de ciencia ficción
una película de aventuras (de acción)
una película de vaqueros (del oeste)

LEVELING

A: Vocabulary

About the Spanish Language

- The ticket to a movie or theater is often referred to as **la entrada** rather than **el boleto** or **el billete. La localidad** is used for both a ticket or a seat in a theater.
- **La taquilla** is the most common word for a movie or theater ticket window. **La boletería** is used in Latin America, **la taquilla** in Spain. In some areas you also hear **la ventanilla.**
- The word **la fila** or **la cola** can be used for a line of people. **La cola** is heard more in Latin America, **la fila** in Spain.
- In addition to **la película** and **el film,** you will often hear and see **el filme.**
- In addition to **el autobús,** the shortened form **el bus** is more and more frequently heard. In the Caribbean area the word for *bus* is **la guagua;** in Mexico, it is **el camión.** Other regional terms for *bus* are **el ómnibus, el micro, la góndola,** and **el colectivo.** (In many areas **colectivo** means *public taxi;* in Argentina, however, it means *bus*).

3 PRACTICE

¿Qué palabra necesito?

¡OJO! When students are doing the **¿Qué palabra necesito?** activities, accept any answer that makes sense. The purpose of these activities is to have students use the new vocabulary. They are not factual recall activities. Thus, it is not necessary for students to remember specific factual information from the vocabulary presentation when answering. If you wish, have students use the photos on this page as a stimulus, when possible.

Historieta Each time **Historieta** appears, it means that the answers to the activity form a short story. Encourage students to look at the title of the **Historieta,** since it can help them do the activity.

1 and 2 After going over Activities 1 and 2, have students retell the stories in their own words. It is recommended that you go over all the activities once in class before assigning them for homework.

Writing Development
Have students write the answers to Activities 1 and 2 in a paragraph to illustrate how all of the items tell a story.

Learning from Realia
(page 308) Ask the following: What does **diez viajes** mean? What words tell you not to fold the ticket? Is it okay to throw the ticket away after entering the subway? Can you guess what **sencillo** means?

¿Qué palabra necesito?

1 Historieta Al cine Contesten.

1. ¿Fue Eduardo al cine?
2. ¿Compró su entrada en la taquilla?
3. ¿Fue a la sesión de las ocho de la tarde?
4. ¿Tomó una butaca en una fila cerca de la pantalla?
5. ¿Vio la película en versión original o doblada?
6. ¿A qué hora salió del cine?
7. ¿Perdió el autobús?
8. ¿Volvió a casa en el metro?

Málaga, España

2 Historieta En la taquilla
Escojan.

1. La gente hace cola delante de ____.
   a. la pantalla **b.** la fila **c.** la taquilla
2. Compran ____ en la taquilla.
   a. butacas **b.** películas **c.** entradas
3. En el cine presentan o dan ____ americana.
   a. una entrada **b.** una película **c.** una novela
4. No es la versión original de la película. Está ____ al español.
   a. entrada **b.** doblada **c.** en fila
5. Los clientes entran en el cine y toman ____.
   a. una pantalla **b.** una entrada **c.** una butaca
6. Proyectan la película en ____.
   a. la pantalla **b.** la butaca **c.** la taquilla

Una taquilla, España

Answers to ¿Qué palabra necesito?

1

1. Sí, Eduardo fue al cine.
2. Sí, compró su entrada en la taquilla.
3. Sí, (No, no) fue a la sesión de las ocho de la tarde.
4. Sí, (No, no) tomó una butaca en una fila cerca de la pantalla.
5. Vio la película doblada (en versión original).
6. Salió del cine a las ___.
7. Sí, (No, no) perdió el autobús.
8. Sí, (No, no) volvió a casa en el metro.

2

1. c
2. c
3. b
4. b
5. c
6. a

3 Lo mismo Den un sinónimo.

1. la película
2. el autobús
3. la boletería
4. la entrada

4 Vamos al cine. Work with a classmate. Pretend you and your partner are making plans to go out tonight to a Spanish-language movie. Discuss your plans together.

La estación de metro en la Puerta del Sol, Madrid

5 Una encuesta Work in groups of four. Conduct a survey. Find out the answers to the following:

- ¿Eres muy aficionado(a) al cine o no?
- ¿Cuántas películas ves en una semana?
- ¿Ves las películas en el cine o las alquilas (rentas) en una tienda de videos?

Compile the information and report the results of your survey to the class.

Vocabulario

3 If necessary, have students refer to pages 306 and 307 to find the answers.

¡OJO! Note that the activities are color-coded. All the activities in the text are communicative. However, the ones with blue titles are guided communication. The red titles indicate that the answers to the activity are more open-ended and can vary more. You may wish to correct students' mistakes more so in the guided activities than in the activities with a red title, which lend themselves to a freer response.

5 Each group should appoint a leader to gather the information and report to the class. You may want to write these three questions on the board and have a student tally the results for the entire class.

About the Spanish Language

The subway entrance is called **la boca del metro.**

LEVELING

E: Activities 1, 2, 3, 5

A: Activities 2, 3, 4, 5

Answers to ¿Qué palabra necesito?

3

1. el film
2. la guagua (el camión)
3. la taquilla
4. el boleto

4 *Answers will vary. Students should mention the name of the movie, what time it's playing, and how they will get to the movie.*

5 *Answers will vary, but students should use the vocabulary from pages 306–307.*

Reaching All Students

Additional Practice You may wish to ask students:

1. **¿Donde hay una cola?**
2. **¿Qué venden o despachan en la taquilla?**
3. **¿Dónde venden (despachan) las entradas?**
4. **¿Dónde proyectan la película en el cine?**

Vocabulario
PALABRAS 2

1 PREPARATION

Resource Manager

Vocabulary Transparencies 10.4–10.5
Audio Activities TE, pages 121–122
Audio CD 6
Workbook, pages 118–120
Quizzes, pages 51–52
ExamView® Pro

Bellringer Review

Use BRR Transparency 10.2 or write the following on the board.
Rewrite the following in the past.

1. **Yo miro un video.**
2. **Yo escucho un disco nuevo.**
3. **Yo voy al café.**
4. **Yo tomo un refresco.**

¡OJO! In **Palabras 1** the preterite of **-er** and **-ir** verbs is presented in the **-ió** form. In **Palabras 2** the preterite of these verbs is presented in the **-ió** and **-ieron** forms. This enables you to ask questions that students can answer without having to manipulate the verb endings. The other forms will be taught immediately afterwards in the **Estructura** section of this chapter.

2 PRESENTATION

Step 1 Have students close their books. Show Vocabulary Transparencies 10.4–10.5. Point to each item and have students repeat the corresponding word or expression after you two or three times.

Step 2 Ask questions of individual students such as the following: **¿Es el actor o la actriz? ¿Es el telón o la escena? ¿Quién es? ¿Qué es?**

Vocabulario
PALABRAS 2

En el museo

Los turistas fueron al museo.
Vieron una exposición de arte.

En el teatro

El autor escribió la obra.
Escribió una obra teatral.
García Lorca escribió la obra *Bodas de Sangre.*

Reaching All Students

Total Physical Response
(Student 1), **levántate y ven acá, por favor.**
Vas a hacer algunos gestos. ¿De acuerdo?
Muy bien, eres escultor(a). Haz una estatua.
Eres artista. Pinta un cuadro.
Eres actor (actriz). Entra en escena. Dile algo al público, a los espectadores.
Eres director(a) de orquesta. Dirige a la orquesta.
Ahora, eres espectador(a) al concierto.
Escucha la música de la orquesta.
Gracias, *(Student 1).* **Siéntate.**

Los actores dieron una representación de *Bodas de Sangre.*
Los actores entraron en escena.
El público vio el espectáculo.
Les gustó mucho (el espectáculo).
Todos aplaudieron. Los actores recibieron aplausos.

Después de la función, el público salió del teatro.

Vocabulario

Step 3 Have students open their books to page 310. Reinforce the new vocabulary by reading the words and sentences on pages 310–311 or play Audio CD 6.

Step 4 Point out to students that the man in the photo on page 310 is **García Lorca.**

National Standards

Cultures

In this chapter students will learn about the famous author García Lorca. García Lorca was born in 1898 in Granada. He was assassinated by anti-Republican rebels at the beginning of the Spanish Civil War in 1936. An extremely talented writer, he is considered by many to be a "brilliantly endowed child of the muses." García Lorca was a poet, dramatist, artist, and musician. More has now been written about García Lorca than about any other Spanish writer with the exception of Cervantes. He is also the most translated Spanish author of all time. His plays fill theaters all over the world.

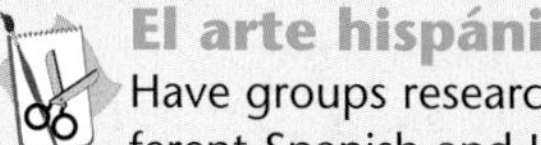

Chapter Projects

El arte hispánico

Have groups research different Spanish and Latin American painters and / or sculptors. Each group can put on an art show using prints of the artists' most famous works.

3 PRACTICE

¿Qué palabra necesito?

6 Students should answer in complete sentences. For example, **Los turistas fueron al museo.**

7 Ask students to add any additional information as they do Activity 7. For example, for Item 1 they might say, **Hay muchos espectadores en el teatro.**

Art Connection

Give students the following information: **Fernando Botero es un artista muy conocido. Nació en Medellín, Colombia, en 1932. En su obra combina lo mágico con lo real. Transforma retratos de grandes artistas e imágenes de las familias de la burguesía de Latinoamérica en cuadros y esculturas. Sus figuras son siempre grandes (gordas).**

¿Qué palabra necesito?

6 Historieta En el museo

Contesten según se indica.

1. ¿Adónde fueron los turistas? (al museo)
2. ¿Qué vieron? (una exposición de arte)
3. ¿Vieron unos cuadros de Botero, el artista colombiano? (sí)
4. ¿Qué más vieron de Botero? (unas estatuas en bronce)
5. ¿Les gustó la obra de Botero? (sí, mucho)

7 ¿Qué es? Identifiquen.

1.

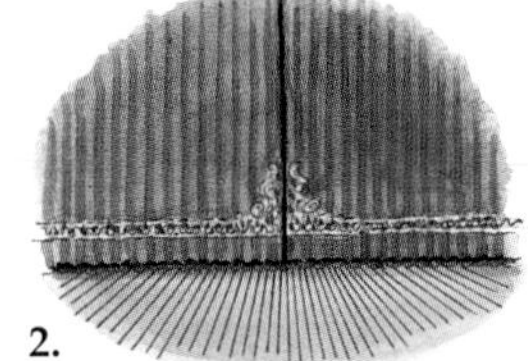
2.

3.

4.

5.

6.

7.

8.

9.

Answers to ¿Qué palabra necesito?

6

1. Los turistas fueron al museo.
2. Vieron una exposición de arte.
3. Sí, vieron unos cuadros de Botero, el artista colombiano.
4. Vieron unas estatuas en bronce.
5. Sí, la obra de Botero les gustó mucho.

7

1. Es el teatro.
2. Es el telón.
3. Es la escena.
4. Es la taquilla (boletería).
5. Es el escenario.
6. Son los actores.
7. Es el museo.
8. Es una estatua.
9. Es un cuadro.

8 Historieta Una noche en Buenos Aires

Contesten según se indica.

1. ¿Quiénes salieron anoche? (Susana y sus amigos)
2. ¿Adónde fueron? (al Teatro Colón)
3. ¿Qué vieron? (una obra de García Lorca)
4. ¿Quién escribió la obra? (García Lorca)
5. ¿Le gustó la representación al público? (sí, mucho)
6. ¿Quiénes recibieron aplausos? (los actores)
7. ¿A qué hora salieron del teatro Susana y sus amigos? (a eso de las diez y media)
8. ¿Cómo volvieron a casa? (en taxi)

El Teatro Colón, Buenos Aires

9 La palabra, por favor.

Escojan.

1. El ____ escribió la obra.
   a. actor **b.** autor **c.** artista
2. Cuando empieza el espectáculo, levantan ____.
   a. la pantalla **b.** el telón **c.** el escenario
3. El ____ es magnífico y muy bonito. Es una obra de arte.
   a. autor **b.** público **c.** escenario
4. Los ____ actuaron muy bien.
   a. autores **b.** actores **c.** escenarios
5. Al público le gustó mucho la representación y todos ____.
   a. aplaudieron **b.** salieron
   c. entraron en escena

10 Me gusta ir al museo.

Work with a classmate. One of you likes to go to museums and the other one finds them boring but really likes the theater. Discuss the reasons for your preferences.

El interior del Teatro Colón, Buenos Aires

Answers to ¿Qué palabra necesito?

8

1. Susana y sus amigos salieron anoche.
2. Fueron al teatro Colón.
3. Vieron una obra de García Lorca.
4. García Lorca escribió la obra.
5. Sí, al público le gustó mucho la representación.
6. Los actores recibieron aplausos.
7. Susana y sus amigos salieron del teatro a eso de la diez y media.
8. Volvieron a casa en taxi.

9

1. b
2. b
3. c
4. b
5. a

 **10** *Answers will vary; however, students may use expressions such as* me gusta *and* me aburre *in their answers.*

10 Encourage students to use expressions such as **Me gusta ir a...** and **Me aburre porque...**

National Standards

Comparisons

Have students look at the photo of the interior of the **Teatro Colón.** In Spain and Latin America the dress code is still quite formal for many cultural functions.

Learning from Photos

(page 313) **El Teatro Colón** is one of the world's leading opera houses. It hosts concerts and ballets from other countries, but it also has its own ballet troupe, opera company, and symphony orchestra. The theater covers almost an entire city block.

Chapter Projects

El museo Visit a local museum so that students can see different styles of art and, hopefully, some work by Hispanic artists.

LEVELING

E: Activities 7, 8, 9

A: Activities 6, 8, 9, 10

1 PREPARATION

Resource Manager

Audio Activities TE, pages 123–125
Audio CD 6
Workbook, pages 121–124
Quizzes, pages 53–54
ExamView® Pro

Bellringer Review

Use BRR Transparency 10.3 or write the following on the board.
Complete in the present.

1. **Ellos ___ en una casa de apartamentos. (vivir)**
2. **Pero nosotros ___ en una casa privada. (vivir)**
3. **Ellos ___ a su apartamento en el ascensor. (subir)**
4. **Yo ___ en el comedor. (comer)**
5. **¿Dónde ___ tú? ¿En el comedor o en la cocina? (comer)**

2 PRESENTATION

Pretérito de los verbos en -er e -ir

Step 1 Write the verbs from Item 1 on the board. Underline the endings and have students repeat each form after you.

Step 2 After you have written a form for **comer**—for example, **yo comí**—you may wish to have students give you the forms for **volver, vivir,** and **subir.**

Step 3 Point out to students that the preterite endings for the **-er** and **-ir** verbs are exactly the same.

Step 4 Have students open their books to page 314. Go over the forms of **dar** and **ver** in Item 2 with them.

Step 5 Have students read aloud the model sentences in Item 3.

Pretérito de los verbos en -er e -ir

Telling what people did

1. You have already learned the preterite forms of regular **-ar** verbs. Study the preterite forms of regular **-er** and **-ir** verbs. Note that they also form the preterite by dropping the infinitive ending and adding the appropriate endings to the stem. The preterite endings of regular **-er** and **-ir** verbs are the same.

INFINITIVE	comer	volver	vivir	subir	ENDINGS
STEM	com-	volv-	viv-	sub-	
yo	comí	volví	viví	subí	-í
tú	comiste	volviste	viviste	subiste	-iste
él, ella, Ud.	comió	volvió	vivió	subió	-ió
nosotros(as)	comimos	volvimos	vivimos	subimos	-imos
vosotros(as)	*comisteis*	*volvisteis*	*vivisteis*	*subisteis*	*-isteis*
ellos, ellas, Uds.	comieron	volvieron	vivieron	subieron	-ieron

2. The preterite forms of the verbs **dar** and **ver** are the same as those of regular **-er** and **-ir** verbs.

INFINITIVE	dar	ver
yo	di	vi
tú	diste	viste
él, ella, Ud.	dio	vio
nosotros(as)	dimos	vimos
vosotros(as)	*disteis*	*visteis*
ellos, ellas, Uds.	dieron	vieron

3. Remember that the preterite is used to tell about an event that happened at a specific time in the past.

Ellos salieron anoche.
Ayer no comí en casa. Comí en el restaurante.
¿Viste una película la semana pasada?

ANSWERS TO ¿Cómo lo digo?

11

1. Sí, Carlos dio una fiesta.
2. Sí, (No, no) dio la fiesta para celebrar el cumpleaños de Teresa.
3. Sí (No), Carlos (no) escribió las invitaciones.
4. Sí (No), los amigos de Teresa (no) recibieron las invitaciones.
5. Sí (No), Teresa (no) vio a todos sus amigos en la fiesta.
6. Sí, (No, no) le dieron regalos a Teresa.
7. Sí (No), Teresa (no) recibió muchos regalos.
8. Sí (No), durante la fiesta todos (no) comieron.
9. Salieron de la fiesta a (eso de) las ___.
10. Sí, (No, no) volvieron a casa muy tarde.

¿Cómo lo digo?

11 Historieta Una fiesta fabulosa

Contesten.

1. ¿Dio Carlos una fiesta?
2. ¿Dio la fiesta para celebrar el cumpleaños de Teresa?
3. ¿Escribió Carlos las invitaciones?
4. ¿Recibieron las invitaciones los amigos de Teresa?
5. ¿Vio Teresa a todos sus amigos en la fiesta?
6. ¿Le dieron regalos a Teresa?
7. ¿Recibió Teresa muchos regalos?
8. Durante la fiesta, ¿comieron todos?
9. ¿A qué hora salieron de la fiesta?
10. ¿Volvieron a casa muy tarde?

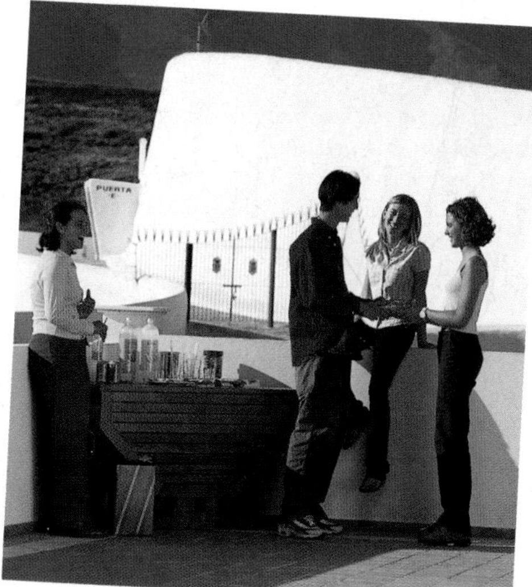

Málaga, España

12 En la escuela Contesten personalmente.

1. ¿A qué hora saliste de casa esta mañana?
2. ¿Perdiste el bus escolar o no?
3. ¿Aprendiste algo nuevo en la clase de español?
4. ¿Escribiste una composición en la clase de inglés?
5. ¿Comprendiste la nueva ecuación en la clase de álgebra?
6. ¿Viste un video en la clase de español?
7. ¿A qué hora saliste de la escuela?
8. ¿A qué hora volviste a casa?

El Teatro Ayacucho, Caracas, Venezuela

13 Al cine

Sigan el modelo.

ir al cine →
—¿Fuiste al cine?
—Sí, fui al cine.

1. ver una película en versión original
2. comprender la película en versión original
3. aplaudir
4. perder el autobús
5. volver a casa un poco tarde

3 PRACTICE

¿Cómo lo digo?

¡OJO! Note that the activities on pages 315–316 build from simple to more complex. Activity 11 reintroduces the third-person forms presented in the **Vocabulario.** Activity 12 enables students to hear the **tú** form as they respond with the **yo** form. Activity 13 makes them use both **tú** and **yo.** Activities 14 and 15, on page 316, together make them use all forms.

11 This activity recycles vocabulary from earlier chapters as it practices the preterite.

12 Activity 12 can be done as an interview. Have several students report back to the class after they have finished their interview.

13 Activity 13 can be done as a paired activity.

LEVELING

E: Activities 11, 12
A: Activity 12
C: Activity 13

Answers to ¿Cómo lo digo?

12

1. Salí de casa a (eso de) las ___ esta mañana.
2. Sí, (No, no) perdí el bus escolar.
3. Sí, (No, no) aprendí algo (nada) nuevo en la clase de español.
4. Sí, (No, no) escribí una composición en la clase de inglés.
5. Sí, (No, no) comprendí la nueva ecuación en la clase de álgebra.
6. Sí, (No, no) vi un video en la clase de español.
7. Salí de la escuela a (eso de) las ___.
8. Volví a casa a (eso de) las ___.

13

1. —¿Viste una película en versión original?
   —Sí, vi una película en versión original.
2. —¿Comprendiste la película en versión original?
   —Sí, comprendí la película en versión original.
3. —¿Aplaudiste?
   —Sí, aplaudí.
4. —¿Perdiste el autobús?
   —Sí, perdí el autobús.
5. —¿Volviste a casa un poco tarde?
   —Sí, volví a casa un poco tarde.

3 PRACTICE *(continued)*

Writing Development

After going over Activity 14 in class, have students write the information in their own words in paragraph form.

15 Have students present Activity 15 as a miniconversation. Ask several pairs to present the conversation to the entire class.

¡OJO! Activity 16 encourages students to use the chapter vocabulary and structures in open-ended situations. However, since students do not yet know the preterite of irregular verbs, be sure that they use the verbs in the colored boxes when doing Activity 16. This will deter them from trying to use unknown forms.

16 Each student in the group should take turns asking someone else a question, using one of the words provided.

UN POCO MÁS This *InfoGap* Activity will allow students to practice in pairs. The activity should be very manageable for them, since all vocabulary and structures are familiar to them.

LEVELING

E: Activities 14, 16

A: Activities 15, 16, 17

14 Historieta Al cine y al restaurante

Contesten.

1. ¿Salieron tú y tus amigos anoche?
2. ¿Vieron una película?
3. ¿Qué vieron?
4. ¿A qué hora salieron del cine?
5. ¿Fueron a un restaurante?
6. ¿Qué comiste?
7. Y tus amigos, ¿qué comieron?
8. ¿A qué hora volviste a casa?

Caracas, Venezuela

15 Historieta En la clase de español

Completen.

—Ayer en la clase de español, ¿ __1__ (aprender) tú una palabra nueva?

—¿Una? __2__ (Aprender) muchas.

—¿Les __3__ (dar) un examen el profesor?

—Sí, nos __4__ (dar) un examen.

—¿ __5__ (Salir) ustedes bien en el examen?

—Pues, yo __6__ (salir) bien pero otros no __7__ (salir) muy bien.

—Entonces tú __8__ (recibir) una nota buena, ¿no?

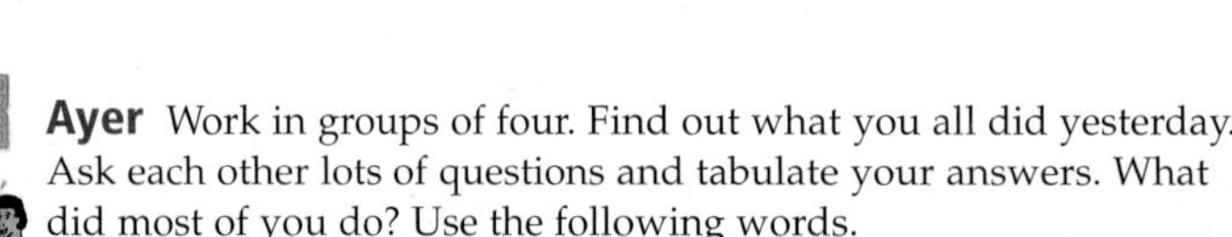

16 Ayer

Work in groups of four. Find out what you all did yesterday. Ask each other lots of questions and tabulate your answers. What did most of you do? Use the following words.

UN POCO MÁS *For more practice using words from **Palabras 1** and **2** and the preterite, do Activity 10 on page H11 at the end of this book.*

ANSWERS TO ¿Cómo lo digo?

14

1. Sí, mis amigos y yo salimos anoche.
2. Sí, vimos una película.
3. Vimos ___.
4. Salimos del cine a (eso de) las ___.
5. Sí, fuimos a un restaurante.
6. Comí ___.
7. Mis amigos comieron ___.
8. Volví a casa a (eso de) las ___.

15

1. aprendiste
2. Aprendí
3. dio
4. dio
5. Salieron
6. salí
7. salieron
8. recibiste

16 *Answers will vary; however, students should use the verbs from the colored boxes in the preterite.*

Complementos le, les

Telling what you do for others

1. You have already learned the direct object pronouns **lo, la, los,** and **las.** Now you will learn the indirect object pronouns **le** and **les.** Observe the difference between a direct object and an indirect object in the following sentences.

    Juan lanzó la pelota. **Juan le lanzó la pelota a Carmen.**

    In the preceding sentences, **la pelota** is the direct object because it is the direct receiver of the action of the verb **lanzó** *(threw)*. **Carmen** is the indirect object because it indicates "to whom" the ball was thrown.

2. The indirect object pronoun **le** is both masculine and feminine. **Les** is used for both the feminine and masculine plural. **Le** and **les** are often used along with a noun phrase—**a Juan, a sus amigos.**

    María le dio un regalo a Juan.
    María les dio un regalo a sus amigos.

    Juan le dio un regalo a María.
    Juan les dio un regalo a sus amigas.

3. Since **le** and **les** can refer to more than one person, they are often clarified as follows:

Le hablé	**a él.** **a ella.** **a Ud.**	**Les hablé**	**a ellos.** **a ellas.** **a Uds.**

¿Cómo lo digo?

17 **¿Qué o a quién?** Indiquen el complemento directo y el indirecto.

1. Carlos recibió la carta.
2. Les vendimos la casa a ellos.
3. Vimos a Isabel ayer.
4. Le hablamos a Tomás.
5. ¿Quién tiene el periódico? Tomás lo tiene.
6. El profesor nos explicó la lección.
7. Ella le dio los apuntes a su profesor.
8. Ellos vieron la película en el cine.

Madrid, España

Answers to ¿Cómo lo digo?

17

1. la carta: complemento directo
2. Les, a ellos: complemento indirecto; la casa: complemento directo
3. Isabel: complemento directo
4. Le, a Tomás: complemento indirecto
5. el periódico, lo: complementos directos
6. nos: complemento indirecto; la lección: complemento directo
7. le, a su profesor: complemento indirecto; los apuntes: complemento directo
8. la película: complemento directo

Estructura

1 PREPARATION

Bellringer Review

Use BRR Transparency 10.4 or write the following on the board.
Write the following in the past.
1. **Yo como a las doce.**
2. **Ellos suben en el ascensor.**
3. **Tu vuelves temprano.**

2 PRESENTATION

Complementos le, les

Step 1 Write the sentences in Item 1 on the board. The arrows will help students understand the concept of direct vs. indirect objects. As students look at these sentences, tell them that Juan doesn't throw Carmen. He throws the ball. To whom does he throw the ball? To Carmen. The ball is the direct object because it receives the action of the verb directly. Carmen is the indirect object because she receives the action of the verb indirectly.

Step 2 Now have students open their books to page 317. Lead them through Items 1–3.

Step 3 As you write the sentences from Item 2 on the board, circle **le** and circle **a Juan.** Then draw arrows back and forth to indicate that they are the same person. This visual explanation helps many students.

Note: Be sure that students learn that **le** and **les** are both masculine and feminine.

3 PRACTICE

¿Cómo lo digo?

17 Activity 17 is a diagnostic tool to determine if students understand the concept of direct and indirect objects.

3 PRACTICE *(continued)*

¡OJO! It is recommended that you not wait for every student to use these pronouns perfectly. If certain students find the concept difficult, they can still function by answering with nouns. **¿Hablaste a Juan? Sí, hablé a Juan.** Direct and indirect objects will be reintroduced throughout this textbook series.

18, 19, and 21 Do Activities 18, 19, and 21 on pages 318–319 orally with books closed. Then have students open their books and read these activities for additional reinforcement. When books are open, you can either ask the questions and have students answer or have students do the activities in pairs.

20 Have students present Activity 20 as a miniconversation.

Chapter Projects

El video Show a Spanish movie and discuss it with students in class.

18 Historieta Pobre Eugenio

Contesten según la foto.

1. ¿Qué le duele?
2. ¿Qué más le duele?
3. ¿Quién le examina la garganta?
4. ¿Quién le da la diagnosis?
5. ¿Qué le da la médica?
6. ¿Quién le da los medicamentos?

19 Sí que le hablé. Contesten.

1. ¿Le hablaste a Rafael?
2. ¿Le hablaste por teléfono?
3. ¿Le diste las noticias?
4. ¿Y él les dio las noticias a sus padres?
5. ¿Les escribió a sus padres?
6. ¿Les escribió en inglés o en español?

20 Historieta Tiene que tener la dirección.

Completen.

—¿__1__ hablaste a Juan ayer?

—Sí, __2__ hablé por teléfono y __3__ hablé a Sandra también. __4__ hablé a los dos.

—¿__5__ diste la dirección de Maricarmen?

—No, porque Adriana __6__ dio la dirección. Y __7__ dio su número de teléfono también.

SPANISH Online

For more information about El Prado and other museums in the Spanish-speaking world, go to the Glencoe Spanish Web site: spanish.glencoe.com

El Museo del Prado, Madrid

ANSWERS TO ¿Cómo lo digo?

18

1. Le duele la garganta.
2. *Answers will vary.*
3. La médica le examina la garganta.
4. La médica le da la diagnosis.
5. La médica le da una receta.
6. El farmacéutico le da los medicamentos.

19

1. Sí, le hablé a Rafael.
2. Sí, le hablé por teléfono.
3. Sí, (No, no) le di las noticias.
4. Sí (No), él (no) les dio las noticias a sus padres.
5. Sí, (No, no) les escribió a sus padres.
6. Les escribió en inglés (español).

20

1. Le
2. le
3. le
4. Les
5. Les
6. les
7. les

21 Historieta Juan es aficionado al arte.

Contesten.

1. ¿A Juan le interesa el arte?
2. ¿Le gusta ir a los museos?
3. ¿Le encantan las exposiciones de arte?
4. ¿Le gusta mucho la obra de Velázquez?
5. ¿Le gustan también los cuadros de Goya?
6. A sus amigos, ¿les interesa también el arte?
7. ¿Les gustan las obras de los muralistas mexicanos?

La fragua de Vulcano de Diego Velázquez

22 Regalos para todos

Work in pairs. Tell what each of the following people is like. Then tell what you buy or give to each one as a gift.

mi mamá
mi hermano
mi profesor(a) de español
mi papá
mis abuelos
mi amigo(a)

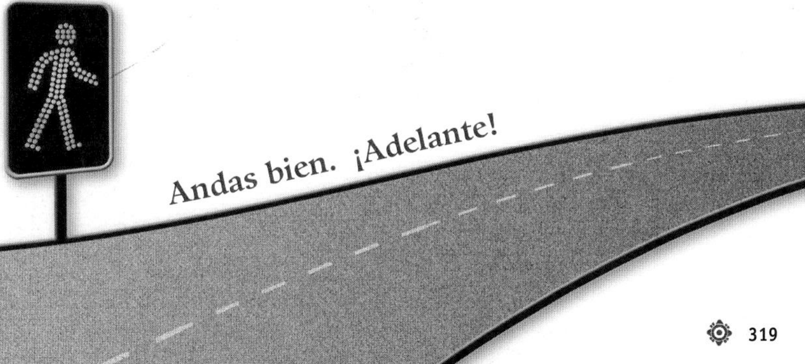

21 Expansion: Show the Fine Art transparency of this painting by Velázquez. You may wish to have students read the background information provided in the Transparency Binder and have them do the related activities. For further enrichment, you may also wish to show the Fine Art transparency of ***Familia de Carlos IV*** by Francisco de Goya.

22 Students should use **gustar** when telling what each person likes. They will use either **comprar** or **dar** when telling what they buy or give as a gift.

Learning from Photos

(page 319) In 1629 Velázquez was sent on a trip to Italy to buy some works of art for the Royal collection. On this trip he went to Venice, Rome, and Naples, where he met Ribera, the Spanish painter. While in Italy he studied the Italian painters and worked to improve his ability to convey space. He painted ***La fragua de Vulcano*** during his stay.

For additional information on other paintings by Velázquez, see page 191 in the student textbook.

¡Adelante!

At this point in the chapter, students have learned all the vocabulary and structure necessary to complete the chapter. The conversation and cultural readings that follow recycle all the material learned up to this point.

LEVELING

E: Activities 18, 19
A: Activities 21, 22
C: Activity 20

Answers to ¿Cómo lo digo?

21

1. Sí, a Juan le interesa el arte.
2. Sí, le gusta ir a los museos.
3. Sí, le encantan las exposiciones de arte.
4. Sí, (No, no) le gusta mucho la obra de Velázquez.
5. Sí, (No, no) le gustan los cuadros de Goya.
6. Sí (No), a sus amigos (no) les interesa el arte.
7. Sí, (No, no) les gustan las obras de los muralistas mexicanos.

22 *Answers will vary but may follow this model:*

Mi papá trabaja en una oficina. Es gerente. A él le gusta la ropa formal.
Le doy una corbata. (Le compro una corbata).

Conversación

1 PREPARATION

Resource Manager

Audio Activities TE, page 126
Audio CD 6

2 PRESENTATION

Step 1 Have students listen to Audio CD 6 with books closed.

Step 2 Ask students to tell you in one or two sentences what the conversation is about. This can be done in either Spanish or English.

Step 3 Have students open their books. Give them two or three minutes to read the conversation silently.

Step 4 Call on one student to read aloud the part of **Paco** and another the part of **Julia.**

Step 5 Then go over the **¿Comprendes?** questions that follow.

Step 6 Call on a student to retell the conversation in narrative form.

Note: If students can answer the **¿Comprendes?** questions with relative ease, move on. Students should not be expected to memorize the conversation.

Conversación

¿Saliste?

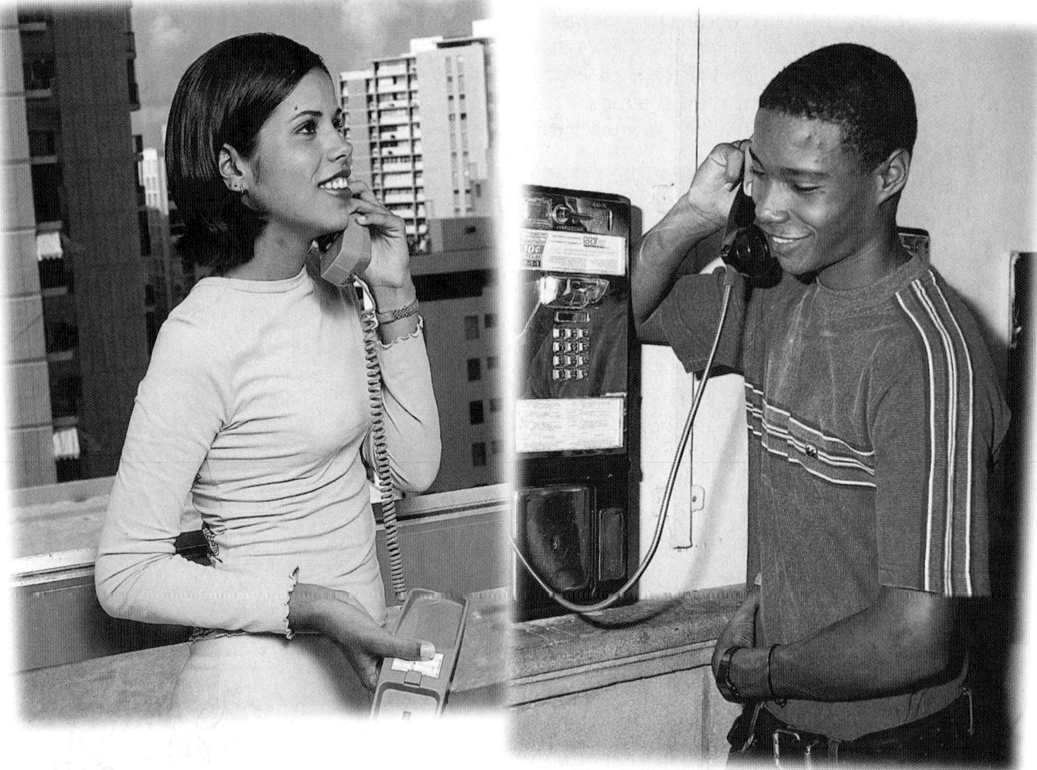

Paco Hola, Julia. Te llamé por teléfono anoche y no contestaste.
Julia ¿Ah, sí? ¿A qué hora me llamaste?
Paco A las siete y pico.
Julia Ay, no volví a casa hasta las ocho y media.
Paco ¿Adónde fuiste?
Julia Pues, fui al cine con Felipe.
Paco ¿Ustedes fueron al cine y tú volviste a casa a las ocho y media? ¿Cómo puede ser?
Julia Pues, fuimos a la sesión de las cinco. Y después del cine comimos en Pizza Perfecta.

¿Comprendes?

Contesten.

1. ¿A quién telefoneó Paco anoche?
2. ¿Ella contestó?
3. ¿A qué hora la llamó Paco?
4. ¿A qué hora volvió Julia a casa?
5. ¿Adónde fue?
6. ¿Con quién fue?
7. ¿A qué sesión fueron?
8. ¿Dónde comieron?

Answers to ¿Comprendes?

1. Paco le telefoneó a Julia anoche.
2. No, ella no contestó.
3. Paco la llamó a las siete y pico.
4. Julia no volvió a casa hasta las ocho y media.
5. Fue al cine.
6. Fue con Felipe.
7. Fueron a la sesión de las cinco.
8. Comieron en Pizza Perfecta.

Glencoe Technology

CD-ROM

On the CD-ROM, students can watch a dramatization of this conversation. They can then play the role of either one of the characters and record themselves in the conversation.

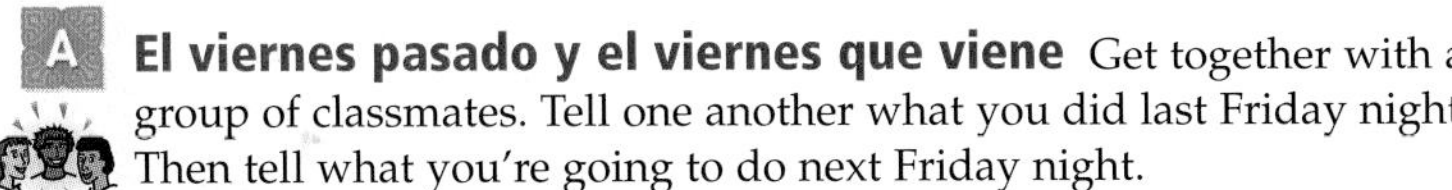

Vamos a hablar más

A **El viernes pasado y el viernes que viene** Get together with a group of classmates. Tell one another what you did last Friday night. Then tell what you're going to do next Friday night.

B **Un viaje escolar** The Spanish Club is going on a field trip. It's just in the planning stages. You may go to a museum that's showing the works of an Hispanic artist, a Spanish-language movie, a play in Spanish, or a Mexican or Spanish restaurant. Your Spanish teacher wants some input from you. With your classmates, discuss where you want to go and why.

C **¿Por qué volviste tan tarde?** You got home really late last night. One of your parents (your partner) wants to know why. He or she will ask a lot of questions. You'd better have some good answers!

Pronunciación

Las consonantes j, g

The Spanish **j** sound does not exist in English. In Spain, the **j** sound is very guttural. It comes from the throat. In Latin America, the **j** sound is much softer. Repeat the following.

ja	je	ji	jo	ju
Jaime	**Jesús**	**Jiménez**	**joven**	**jugar**
hija	**garaje**	**ají**	**viejo**	**junio**
roja			**trabajo**	**julio**
			ojos	

G in combination with **e** or **i (ge, gi)** has the same sound as **j**. For this reason you must pay particular attention to the spelling of the words with **je, ji, ge,** and **gi.** Repeat the following.

ge	gi
general	**biología**
gente	**alergia**
generoso	**original**
Insurgentes	

Repeat the following sentences.

El hijo del viejo general José trabaja en junio en Gijón.
El jugador juega en el gimnasio.
El joven Jaime toma jugo de naranja.

Answers to Vamos a hablar más

A *Answers will vary; however, students should use the preterite as well as* ir a + *infinitive in their answers.*

B *Answers will vary but should include vocabulary learned on pages 306–307 and 310–311. Each student in the group should have the opportunity to answer.*

C *Answers will vary, but students should use the preterite tense in their conversations.*

Reaching All Students

Additional Practice Have students work in pairs to make up a brief telephone conversation about any topic that interests them. Have several pairs present their conversations to the class. Students should use the conversation on page 320 as a model.

3 PRACTICE

Vamos a hablar más

A Activity A contrasts past and future events.

National Standards

Communities
By organizing a field trip to one of the locales suggested in Activity B, you will give your students the opportunity to use their Spanish beyond the school setting.

Pronunciación

¡OJO! This is another sound that is radically different in Spain and Latin America. The sound of the letter **j** is very guttural in Spain. It is similar to the German **ach.** In Latin America, however, it is a very soft sound. In many countries it is barely audible. Since the **g** and **j** can present spelling problems, it is recommended that you have students commit to memory the spelling of these words.

Step 1 Have students carefully repeat the sounds **ja, je, ji, jo, ju; ge, gi** after you or Audio CD 6.

Step 2 Now have them repeat the words and sentences.

Step 3 Have students open their books to page 321. Call on individuals to read the sentences carefully.

Step 4 You may use these sentences for dictation.

LEVELING

E: Conversation

Lecturas culturales

Resource Manager

Audio Activities TE, page 127
Audio CD 6

National Standards

Cultures
The reading about teen dating habits in the Spanish-speaking world and the related activities allow students to gain an understanding of cultural practices in the Spanish-speaking world.

Comparisons
The reading on this page allows students to make comparisons between dating customs and some other teenage activites in the Spanish-speaking world and in the United States.

PRESENTATION

¡OJO! It is extremely difficult to generalize about current dating customs in the Spanish-speaking world. The general statements in this **Lectura** hold true, but there are some differences that must be taken into account. The more cosmopolitan an urban area is, the more students tend to pair off and date on their own. In rural areas, however, doing things in groups is still more common.

Pre-reading

Step 1 Have students briefly discuss dating customs in the United States.

Step 2 Tell them that they are going to read about dating customs in the Spanish-speaking world. Explain that dating customs are changing, but ask them to look for some differences between their dating customs and those of their Spanish-speaking counterparts. Also have them look for similarities.

Lecturas culturales

Reading Strategy

Recognizing text organization Before you read a passage, try to figure out how the text is organized. If you can follow the organization of a text, you will understand the main ideas more quickly and be able to look for certain ideas and information more easily.

Dating

Algunas diferencias culturales son muy interesantes. Y las diferencias culturales pueden tener una influencia en la lengua que hablamos. Por ejemplo, *dating, boyfriend* y *girlfriend* son palabras que usamos mucho en inglés, ¿no? Y son palabras que no tienen equivalente en español. ¿Cómo es posible? Pues, vamos a hablar con Verónica. Ella es de Perú.

—Verónica, ¿saliste anoche?

—Sí, salí con un grupo de amigos de la escuela.

—¿Adónde fueron?

—Fuimos al cine. Vimos una película muy buena. Fue una película americana. La vimos en versión original con subtítulos en español.

—Verónica, ¿no sales a veces sola con un muchacho, con un amigo de la escuela?

—Pues, no mucho. Generalmente salimos en grupo. Pero es algo que está cambiando[1]. Está cambiando poco a poco[2]. Hoy en día una pareja[3] joven puede salir a solas. Podemos ir a un café, por ejemplo, a tomar un refresco. A veces vamos al cine o sólo damos un paseo[4] por el parque. Pero, para nosotros, es algo bastante nuevo.

[1]cambiando *changing*
[2]poco a poco *little by little*
[3]pareja *couple*
[4]damos un paseo *take a walk*

Buenos Aires, Argentina

Teatro Colón, Lima, Perú

FUN-FACTS

Explain to students that **un novio** or **una novia** implies a more serious relationship than our concept of *boyfriend* or *girlfriend*. **Novio(a)** can also mean *fiancé* or *newlywed*.

LEVELING
E: Reading

Marbella, España

¿Comprendes?

A ***Dating*** Contesten.

1. ¿En qué lengua usamos las palabras *dating, boyfriend* y *girlfriend?*
2. ¿Tienen equivalente en español?
3. ¿Hay mucho *dating* entre los jóvenes de Latinoamérica y España?
4. ¿Ahora empiezan a salir en parejas?
5. Por lo general, ¿cómo salen?
6. ¿Con quién salió Verónica?
7. ¿Adónde fueron?
8. ¿Qué vieron?

B **Aquí** Contesten personalmente.

1. Donde tú vives, ¿salen los jóvenes con más frecuencia en grupos o en parejas?
2. Y tú, ¿sales a veces con sólo un(a) muchacho(a)?
3. ¿Adónde van?
4. ¿Pueden salir durante la semana?
5. ¿Qué noche salen?
6. ¿A qué hora tienes que estar en casa?

Lecturas culturales

Reading

Step 1 Have students open their books to page 322 and read the selection silently and quickly.

Step 2 Call on an individual to read approximately half a paragraph. Then stop and ask pertinent comprehension questions.

Post-reading

After going over the **Lectura** in class, assign it for homework. Also assign the **¿Comprendes?** activities on page 323. Go over them in class the next day.

¿Comprendes?

A Allow students to refer to the reading to find the answers, or you may use this activity as a testing device for factual recall.

B Depending on the class, this topic may lead to a lively discussion involving all of your students.

Answers to ¿Comprendes?

A

1. En inglés.
2. No, no tienen equivalente en español.
3. No, no hay mucho dating entre los jóvenes de Latinoamérica y España.
4. Sí, ahora empiezan a salir en parejas.
5. Por lo general, salen en grupo.
6. Salió con un grupo de amigos de la escuela.
7. Fueron al cine.
8. Vieron una película americana.

B

1. Los jóvenes salen en grupos (en parejas).
2. Sí, salgo a veces con sólo un(a) muchacho(a). (No, no salgo con sólo un[a] muchacho[a].)
3. Vamos al cine (al partido de ___, a la casa de mis amigos, etc.).
4. Sí, (No, no) podemos salir durante la semana.
5. Salimos el viernes o el sábado.
6. Tengo que estar en casa a las ___.

Lectura opcional 1

National Standards

Cultures
The reading about Spanish operetta, **la zarzuela,** and the related activity on this page give students an appreciation of one of the significant art forms of the Spanish-speaking world.

¡OJO! This reading is optional. You may skip it completely, have the entire class read it, have only several students read it and report to the class, or assign it for extra credit.

PRESENTATION

Step 1 Have students read the paragraph silently.

Step 2 Do the **¿Comprendes?** activity. This activity provides a quick and informal assessment of how well students understood this reading.

Learning from Realia

(page 324) **El Teatro de la Zarzuela** is popular with both Spaniards and tourists. Because of the light nature of a **zarzuela,** it can be enjoyed even by those who have a limited knowledge of Spanish. Ask students the following questions about the ticket: **¿Cuánto costó la entrada? ¿A qué hora es el espectáculo? ¿Qué número es la butaca?**

Lectura opcional 1

La zarzuela

Hay un género teatral exclusivamente español. Es la zarzuela. La zarzuela es una obra dramática muy ligera. No es profunda. Generalmente tiene un argumento[1] gracioso.

La zarzuela es un tipo de opereta. A veces, durante la presentación, los actores hablan y a veces cantan.

[1]argumento *plot*

Una zarzuela, Madrid, España

El Chaleco Blanco
Teatro de La Zarzuela
La Gran Vía

¿Comprendes?

La zarzuela Digan que sí o que no.

1. La zarzuela es una novela española.
2. La zarzuela es un tipo de obra teatral.
3. En una zarzuela los actores no hablan, sólo bailan.
4. Una zarzuela es un tipo de opereta.
5. Los actores en una zarzuela hablan y cantan.
6. El tema o argumento de una zarzuela es siempre serio y profundo.

Answers to ¿Comprendes?

1. No
2. Sí
3. No
4. Sí
5. Sí
6. No

Lectura opcional 2

El Palacio de Bellas Artes, México

El baile

El Ballet Folklórico de México goza de fama mundial. El espectáculo que presenta el Ballet Folklórico todos los domingos y miércoles en el Palacio de Bellas Artes es uno de los shows más populares de la Ciudad de México. La compañía baila una variedad de danzas regionales de México. A veces la coreografía del Ballet Folklórico de México es muy graciosa y divertida.

Hay también el Ballet Folklórico Nacional de México. Esta compañía presenta un programa auténtico y clásico de danzas mexicanas regionales en el Teatro de la Ciudad.

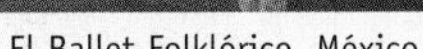
El Ballet Folklórico, México

¿Comprendes?

Una comparación Expliquen la diferencia entre el Ballet Folklórico de México y el Ballet Folklórico Nacional de México.

Lectura opcional 2

National Standards

Cultures
The reading about the **Ballet Folklórico de México** and the related activity on this page familiarize students with a world-famous ballet company from Mexico and give them an appreciation of an important Mexican art form.

¡OJO! This reading is optional. You may skip it completely, have the entire class read it, have only several students read it and report to the class, or assign it for extra credit.

Learning from Photos

(page 325 top) The **Palacio de Bellas Artes** was constructed as an opera house between 1904 and 1934. Construction on it was halted during the Mexican Revolution (1910–1917). Today the **Palacio** is a handsome theater which houses the **Ballet Folklórico de México** and hosts other Mexican and international artists. The building is renowned for its architecture. It was designed by the Italian architect Adamo Boari. It also contains an impressive collection of paintings by Mexican artists including Rufino Tamayo and the famous muralists Rivera, Orozco, and Siqueiros.

LEVELING
E: Readings 1, 2

Answers to ¿Comprendes?

Answers may include the following:

El Ballet Folklórico de México baila una variedad de danzas regionales de México en el Palacio de Bellas Artes. El Ballet Folklórico Nacional de México presenta un programa auténtico y clásico de danzas mexicanas regionales en el Teatro de la Ciudad.

Conexiones

National Standards

Connections
This reading about music in the Spanish-speaking world establishes a connection with another discipline, allowing students to reinforce and deepen their knowledge of world music through the study of Spanish.

¡OJO! The readings in the **Conexiones** section are optional. They focus on some of the major disciplines taught in schools and universities. The vocabulary is useful for discussing such topics as history, literature, art, economics, business, science, etc. Please refer to page 296 for presentation suggestions for the readings in the **Conexiones** sections.

PRESENTATION

Las bellas artes
La música

Step 1 Most students will be familiar with these musical terms in English. Model the terms in Spanish and have students repeat after you.

Step 2 Ask students to scan the readings on pages 326 and 327 and make a list of words they do not know. Explain the meaning of these words as a whole-class activity.

Step 3 It is suggested that you play some recordings of the types of Spanish music discussed in this section. Ask a music teacher to help you assemble some selections from the Music Department's library.

Conexiones

Las bellas artes

La música

Music does not attempt to reproduce what we see in the world in such a tangible way as do painting and literature. Music is, and has been, however, an integral part of the daily lives of people in even the most primitive cultures.

First let's take a look at the many cognates that exist in the language of music. Then let's read some general information about music. Finally, let's take a look at some special music of the Hispanic world.

In addition, many names of musical instruments are cognates: **el piano, el órgano, el violín, la viola, la guitarra, la trompeta, el clarinete, el saxofón, la flauta, el trombón.**

Música y músicos

Instrumentos musicales

Clasificamos los instrumentos musicales en cuatro grupos. Son los instrumentos de cuerda, los instrumentos de viento, los instrumentos de metal y los instrumentos de percusión. Dividimos la orquesta en secciones de cuerda, viento, metal y percusión.

Una orquesta y una banda

¿Cuál es la diferencia entre una orquesta y una banda? En una banda no hay instrumentos de cuerda. No hay violines ni violas, por ejemplo.

Glencoe Technology

Audio Program
Audio CD 1 of the Audio Program features a variety of songs from the Spanish-speaking world that you might like to play for your students. The lyrics to these songs are in the Audio Activities Teacher Edition, pages v–vi.

Cuzco, Perú

La ópera

La ópera es una obra teatral. Pero en una ópera los actores no hablan. Cantan al acompañamiento de una orquesta.

La música popular

Además de[1] la música clásica hay muchas variaciones de música popular. De influencia afroamericana hay jazz y «blues». Hay «reggae» de Jamaica.

De las islas hispanohablantes de las Antillas hay salsa y merengue. Hay una relación íntima entre el canto (la canción) y la danza (el baile) en la música latinoamericana. Por ejemplo, en la lengua quechua del área andina, una sola palabra—taqui—significa «canción y baile».

Ejemplos de la música típica de Latinoamérica

Un instrumento muy popular entre los indios andinos es la flauta. El yaraví es una canción muy popular. En quechua esta palabra significa «lamento». Es una canción triste. A veces cantan un yaraví pero a veces sólo lo tocan con la flauta sin cantar.

Un instrumento popular de los indígenas de Guatemala es la marimba. Hay orquestas de marimba que van de un pueblo a otro para tocar en las fiestas locales.

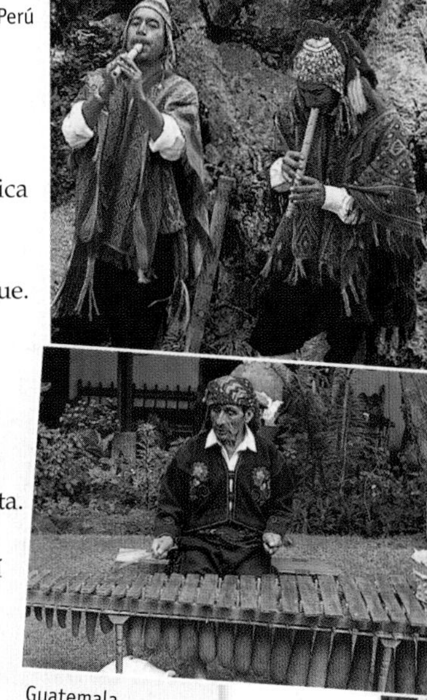

Guatemala

La banda mariachi es un pequeño grupo de músicos ambulantes. Tocan guitarras, violines y trompetas. La música mariachi tiene su origen en Guadalajara, México, en el estado de Jalisco.

La salsa, el merengue y el mambo de Cuba, Puerto Rico y la República Dominicana son canciones y bailes.

El cante jondo es una canción triste y espontánea de los gitanos[2] andaluces. Es apasionada y emocional como lo es también el baile flamenco.

México

[1]Además de *In addition to* [2]gitanos *gypsies*

¿Comprendes?

A ¿Cuáles son? Identifiquen.

1. algunos instrumentos de cuerda
2. algunos instrumentos de viento
3. algunos instrumentos de metal

B Distintos tipos de música Expliquen la diferencia entre una orquesta y una banda.

C ¿Sabes? Contesten.

1. ¿Qué es una ópera?
2. ¿Cuáles son algunos tipos de música popular?
3. ¿Entre qué hay una relación íntima en la música latinoamericana?

Murcia, España

Conexiones

National Standards

Communities

If you have any Hispanic students in your class, ask if they know any dances from their countries that they could perform for the class or any musical groups who might put on a performance. You could also ask them to bring in recordings from home to share with the class.

Learning from Photos

(page 327 top right) The Indians from Cuzco, Perú, are playing **una flauta.** There are several different types of flutes. Some are made from wood and others are ceramic. Note that the flute being played here is a single tube. The **zampoña** has several tubes and is played somewhat like a harmonica but has a very different sound.
(page 327 top right) The Indian from Guatemala is playing a typical **marimba.**
(page 327 left) The Mexican group is a **mariachi** band.
(page 327 bottom right) The guitarists and singers from Spain are called **tunos. Los tunos** form **una tuna** or **una estudiantina,** which is a musical group traditionally made up of university students. These groups go to various locales in the community, stopping to sing and play at each location. In Spain they go from restaurant to restaurant or **mesón** to **mesón.** When they finish their performance they pass around a tambourine, and their audience makes a donation. The **tunos** are popular only in Spain and in one town in Mexico, Guanajuato.

Answers to ¿Comprendes?

A

1. el violín, la viola, la guitarra
2. el clarinete, el saxófono, la flauta
3. la trompeta, el trombón

B

En una banda no hay instrumentos de cuerda.

C

1. Es una obra teatral pero los actores no hablan. Cantan al acompañamiento de una orquesta.
2. Unos tipos de música popular son: jazz, blues, reggae, salsa y merengue.
3. Hay una relación íntima en la música latinoamericana entre el canto (la canción) y la danza (el baile).

LEVELING

A: Reading
C: Reading

¡Te toca a ti!

Use what you have learned

Recycling

These activities allow students to use the vocabulary and structure from this chapter in completely open-ended, real-life situations.

PRESENTATION

Encourage students to say as much as possible when they do these activities. Tell them not to be afraid to make mistakes, since the goal of the activities is real-life communication. If someone in the group makes an error, allow the others to politely correct him or her. Let students choose the activities they would like to do.

You may wish to divide students into pairs or groups. Encourage students to elaborate on the basic theme and to be creative. They may use props, pictures, or posters if they wish.

Writing Development

Have students keep a notebook or portfolio containing their best written work from each chapter. These selected writings can be based on assignments from the Student Textbook and the Workbook. The activities on page 329 are examples of writing assignments that may be included in each student's portfolio. On page 128 in the Workbook, students will begin to develop an organized autobiography **(Mi autobiografía)**. These workbook pages may also become a part of their portfolio.

¡Te toca a ti!

Use what you have learned

HABLAR

Diversiones

✔ *Discuss movies, plays, and museums*

Work with a classmate. Pretend you're on vacation in Cancún, México. You meet a Mexican teenager (your partner) who's interested in what you do for fun in your free time **(cuando tienes tiempo libre).** Tell him or her about your leisure activities. Then your partner will tell you what he or she does.

HABLAR

Una visita al museo

✔ *Ask and answer questions about a museum visit*

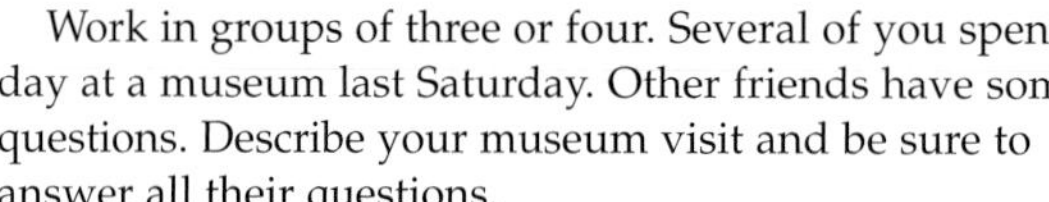

Work in groups of three or four. Several of you spent the day at a museum last Saturday. Other friends have some questions. Describe your museum visit and be sure to answer all their questions.

ESCRIBIR

Información, por favor.

✔ *Write for information about cultural events*

You're going to spend a month in the Spanish-speaking city of your choice. Write a letter or an e-mail to the tourist office **(la oficina de turismo)** asking for information about cultural events during your stay. Be sure to mention your age, what kind of cultural activities you like, and the dates of your stay.

ANSWERS TO ¡Te toca a ti!

1 *Answers will vary. In addition to the leisure activities presented in this chapter, students might mention activities they learned to talk about in earlier chapters, such as listening to music, watching TV, going out to eat, playing sports, etc.*

2 *Answers will vary. Students should use the preterite tense and the museum-related vocabulary presented in this chapter.*

3 *Answers will vary. Students should use the vocabulary presented in this chapter and leisure-time activities they learned to talk about in earlier chapters, such as going out to eat or to the movies. Students should use* tener, gustar, *and* interesar *to describe their interests.*

¡Te toca a ti!

4 Un anuncio

✔ *Make a poster for a play*

Prepare a poster in Spanish for your school play. Give all the necessary information to advertise **el espectáculo.**

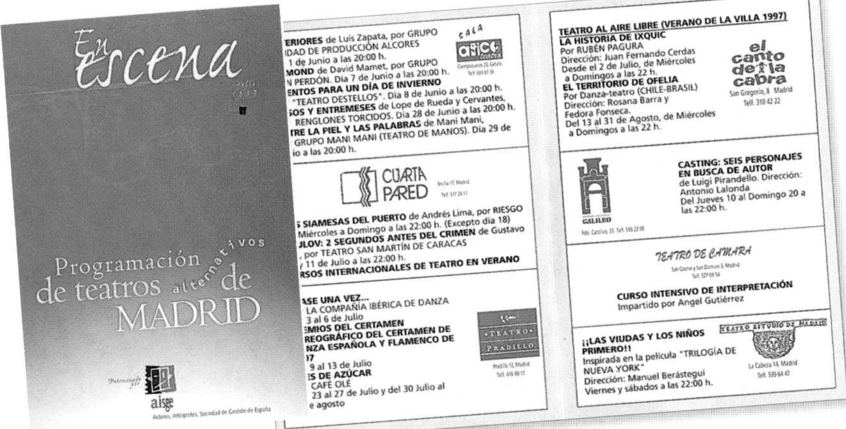

Writing Strategy

Persuasive writing Persuasive writing is writing that encourages a reader to do something or to accept an idea. Newspaper and magazine advertisements, as well as certain articles, are examples of persuasive writing. As you write, present a logical argument to encourage others to follow your line of thinking. Your writing should contain sufficient evidence to persuade readers to "buy into" what you are presenting. Explain how your evidence supports your argument; end by restating your argument.

5 Un reportaje

Your local newspaper has asked you to write an article to attract Spanish-speaking readers to a cultural event taking place in your hometown. You can write about a real or fictitious event. You have seen the event and you really liked it. Tell why as you try to convince or persuade your readers to go see it.

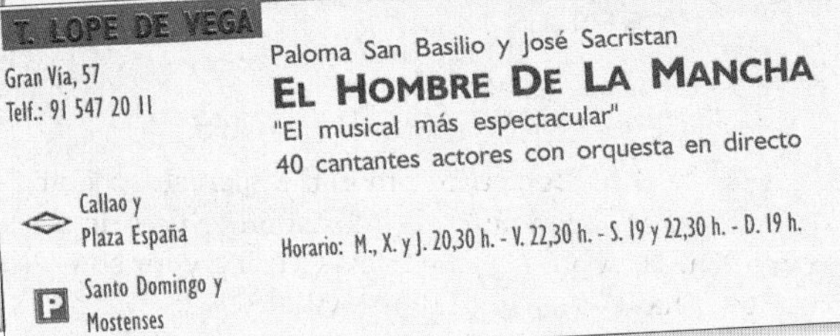

PRACTICE

4 Your class should ask students who are performing in the school play and the Theatre Department for information for the posters. Display the best ones.

Writing Strategy

Persuasive writing Have students read the Writing Strategy on page 329. Before students begin to write their articles, they should make a list of reasons why readers should see the event. Even though *Man of La Mancha* is in English, you may want to play a song from the musical.

Leveling

These activities encompass all three levels. All students will be able to do them at a sophistication level commensurate with their ability in Spanish. Some students will be able to speak for several minutes, and others may be able to give just a few sentences. This is to be expected when students are functioning completely on their own generating their own language to the best of their ability.

ANSWERS TO ¡Te toca a ti!

4 *Posters should include the following information:*

¿Qué es? ¿Cuándo? ¿Dónde es? ¿Cuánto cuestan los boletos?

5 *Answers will vary. Students should use the preterite tense to describe the event. Students may use* gustar *and* interesar *to describe how much they enjoyed it.*

Chapter Projects

Visita al cine Organize a field trip to a local movie theater to see a Spanish film. If all of the Spanish classes at your school plan to go, you may be able to have the theater order the film of your choice for a special screening.

Resource Manager

Communication Transparency C 10
Quizzes, pages 50–54
Performance Assessment, Task 10
Tests, pages 155–168
Situation Cards, Chapter 10
ExamView® Pro, Chapter 10
Maratón mental Videoquiz, Chapter 10

Assessment

This is a pre-test for students to take before you administer the chapter test. Note that each section is cross-referenced so students can easily find the material they have to review in case they made errors. You may use Assessment Answers Transparency A 10 to do the assessment in class, or you may assign this assessment for homework. You can correct the assessment yourself, or you may prefer to project the answers on the overhead in class.

Glencoe Technology

MINDJOGGER VHS/DVD

You may wish to help your students prepare for the chapter test by playing the MindJogger game show. Teams will compete against each other to review chapter vocabulary and structure and sharpen listening comprehension skills.

Vocabulario

To review **Palabras 1**, turn to pages 306–307.

1 Completen.

1. Si mucha gente quiere ver la película, hay una ____ delante de la taquilla.
2. Un boleto para ir al cine es una ____.
3. Hay una ____ a las cuatro y otra a las siete de la tarde.
4. No, la película no está ____, pero no hay problema porque lleva subtítulos.
5. Él perdió el autobús y tomó el ____. El ____ es un tren subterráneo.

2 Identifiquen.

To review **Palabras 2**, turn to pages 310–311.

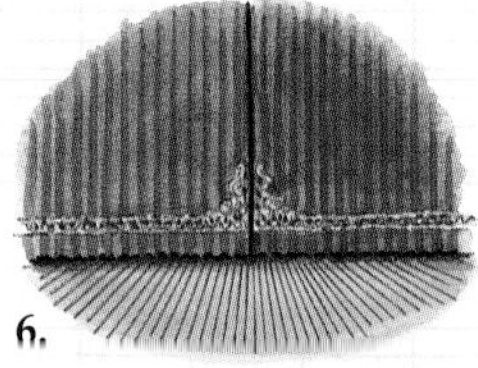
6.

7.

8.

9.

10.

Answers to Assessment

1

1. fila (cola)
2. entrada
3. sesión
4. doblada
5. metro, metro

2

6. el telón
7. los actores
8. el cuadro
9. la estatua
10. el artista

Assessment

Estructura

3 Escojan.

11. Yo ____ una hamburguesa con papas fritas.
a. comió **b.** comí **c.** comimos

12. Ellos ____ del cine.
a. volvimos **b.** volvió **c.** volvieron

13. ¿Cuándo ____ (tú) en Bogotá?
a. vivió **b.** viviste **c.** volvisteis

14. Los actores ____ muchos aplausos.
a. recibieron **b.** recibió **c.** recibiste

15. Él lo ____ en la escuela.
a. vi **b.** vieron **c.** vio

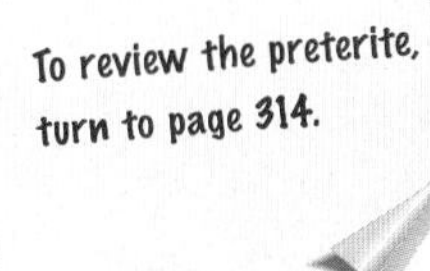
To review the preterite, turn to page 314.

4 Completen con un pronombre.

16. María ____ dio un regalo a su amigo Felipe.
17. Ella ____ devolvió el balón a la otra jugadora.
18. A los amigos ____ gustó mucho la película.

To review **le** and **les**, turn to page 317.

Cultura

5 Contesten.

19. ¿Cuáles son dos palabras inglesas que no tienen equivalente en español?
20. Por lo general, ¿cómo salen los jóvenes en los países hispanos?

To review this cultural information, turn to page 322.

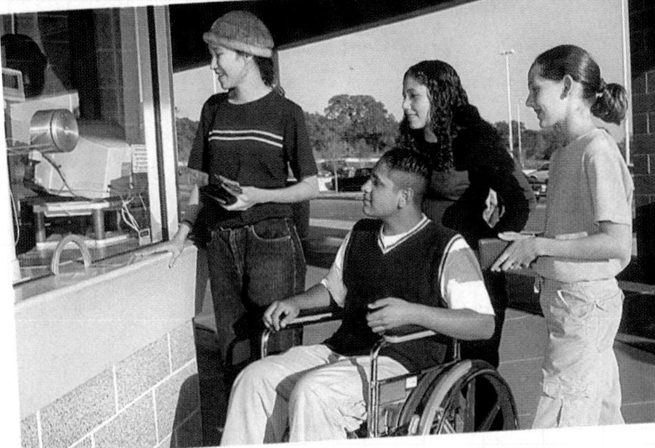

Los amigos salen juntos.

SPANISH Online

The **Glencoe Spanish Web** site (**spanish.glencoe.com**) offers options that enable you and your students to experience the Spanish-speaking world via the Internet. For each **Capítulo,** there are activities, games, and quizzes. In addition, an *Enrichment* section offers students an opportunity to visit Web sites related to the theme of the chapter.

FOLDABLES™ Study Organizer — Dinah Zike's Study Guides

Your students may wish to use Foldable 12 to organize, display, and arrange data as they learn to describe cultural events. You may wish to encourage them to add information from each chapter as they continue to watch movies in Spanish.

A *project board with tabs* foldable is also ideal for having students illustrate and describe scenes from other events that they will be learning about.

Answers to Assessment

3

11. b
12. c
13. b
14. a
15. c

4

16. le
17. le
18. les

5

19. Dos palabras que no tienen equivalente en español son *dating* y *boyfriend (girlfriend).*
20. Por lo general, los jóvenes salen en grupo en los países hispanos.

¡Hablo como un pro!

This unique page gives students the opportunity to speak freely and say whatever they can, using the vocabulary and structures they have learned in the chapter. The illustration serves to remind students of precisely what they know how to say in Spanish. There are no activities that students do not have the ability to describe or talk about in Spanish. The art not only depicts the vocabulary and content of this chapter, but also reinforces what they learned in previous chapters.

You may wish to use this page in many ways. Some possibilities are to have students do the following:

1. Look at the illustration and identify items by giving the correct Spanish words.
2. Make up sentences about what they see in the illustration.
3. Make up questions about the illustration. They can call on another class member to respond if you do this as a class activity, or you may prefer to allow students to work in small groups. This activity is extremely beneficial because it enables students to actively use interrogative words.
4. Answer questions you ask them about the illustration.
5. Work in pairs and make up a conversation based on the illustration.
6. Look at the illustration and give a complete oral review of what they see.
7. Look at the illustration and write a paragraph (or essay) about it.

You can also use this page as an assessment or testing tool, taking into account individual differences by having students go from simple to quite complicated tasks. The assessment can be either oral or written. You may wish to use the rubrics provided on pages T20–T21 as you give students the following directions.

1. Identify the topic or situation of the illustration.
2. Give the Spanish words for as many items as you can.
3. Think of as many sentences as you can to describe the illustration.
4. Go over your sentences and put them in the best sequencing to give a coherent story based on the illustration.

¡Hablo como un pro!

Tell all you can about this illustration.

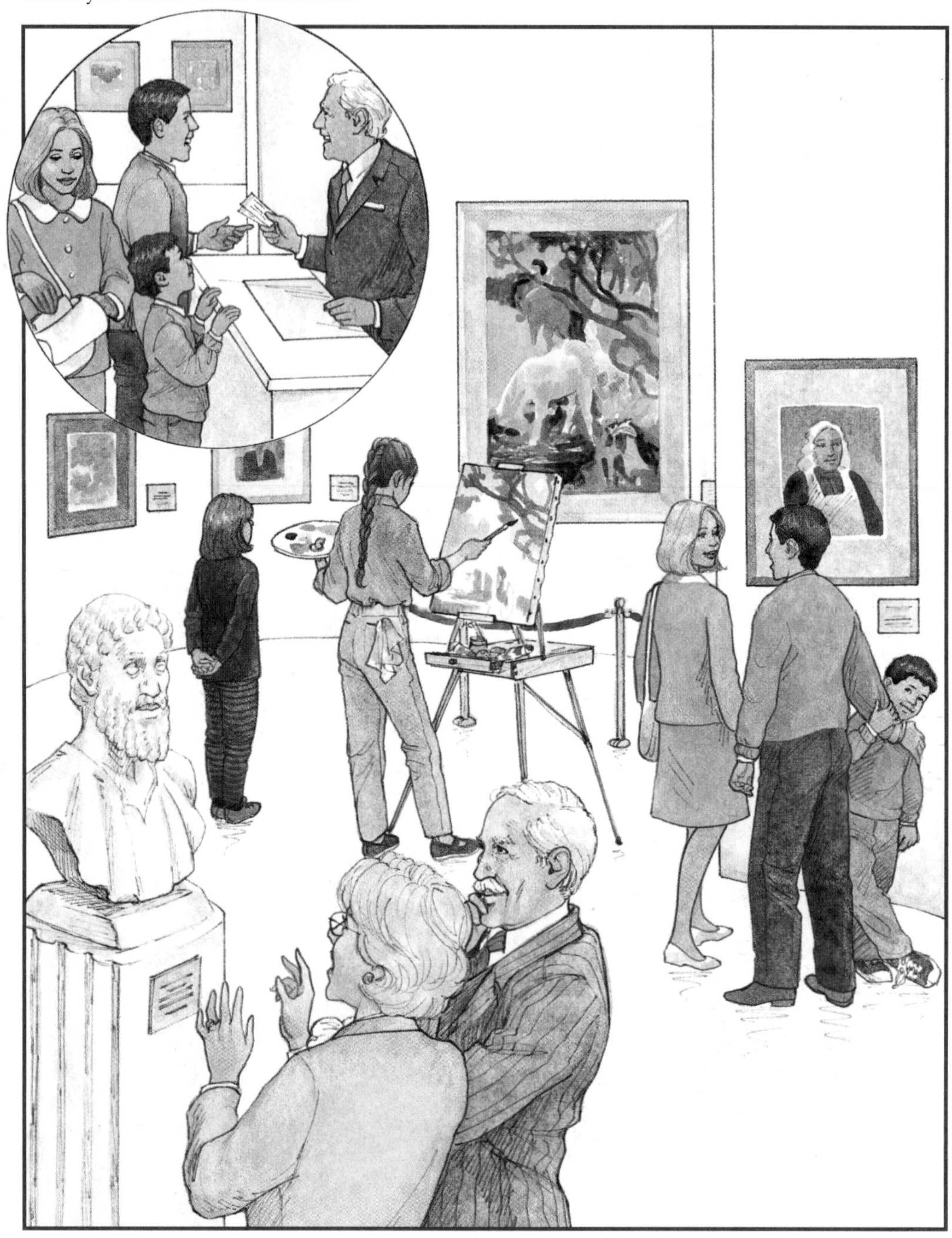

Vocabulario

Discussing a movie theater

el cine
la taquilla, la boletería
la entrada, el boleto
la sesión
la cola
la butaca
la fila
la pantalla
la película, el film
en versión original
con subtítulos
doblado(a)

Describing a museum visit

el museo
la exposición
el mural
el cuadro
la estatua
el/la artista
el/la escultor(a)

Describing a play

el teatro
la escena
el escenario
el telón
el actor
la actriz
la representación
la obra teatral
el público

Describing cultural events and activities

una diversión cultural
ver una película (un espectáculo)
dar una representación
entrar en escena
aplaudir
salir del teatro

Discussing transportation

perder el autobús (la guagua, el camión)
la estación de metro

Other useful expressions

el/la joven
delante de
luego

How well do you know your vocabulary?

- Choose the name of a cultural event or an artistic profession.
- Have a classmate tell you his or her favorite in the category you chose.

VIDEOTUR

Episodio 10

In this video episode, you will join Vicky and Alejandra as they discuss the meaning of "culture." See page 501 for more information.

Vocabulario

Vocabulary Review

The words and phrases in the **Vocabulario** have been taught for productive use in this chapter. They are summarized here as a resource for both student and teacher. This list also serves as a convenient resource for the **¡Te toca a ti!** activities on pages 328 and 329. There are approximately fifteen cognates in this vocabulary list. Have students find them.

VIDEO VHS/DVD

The Video Program allows students to see how the chapter vocabulary and structures are used by native speakers within an engaging story line. For maximum reinforcement, show the video episode as a final activity for Chapter 10.

Reaching All Students

For the Younger Students Ask the music teacher to come in and teach some of the songs from the Audio Program (Audio CD 1) to your students. If your students are musically inclined, you may wish to ask them if they would like to perform a Spanish song in the school concert.

¡OJO! You will notice that the vocabulary list here is not translated. This has been done intentionally, since we feel that by the time students have finished the material in the chapter they should be familiar with the meanings of all the words. If there are several words they still do not know, we recommend that they refer to the **Palabras 1** and **2** sections in the chapter or go to the dictionaries at the end of this book to find the meanings. However, if you prefer that your students have the English translations, please refer to Vocabulary Transparency 10.1, where you will find all these words with their translations.

Planning for Chapter 11

SCOPE AND SEQUENCE, PAGES 334–363

Topics

- ❖ Air travel
- ❖ Travel-related activities

Culture

- ❖ The importance of air travel in Latin America
- ❖ The Andes Mountains
- ❖ The Amazon River
- ❖ Comparing the flight time from New York to Madrid versus the flight time from Caracas to Buenos Aires
- ❖ The Nazca lines of Peru
- ❖ Everyday finances in the Spanish-speaking world
- ❖ **Vistas de España**

Functions

- ❖ How to check in for a flight
- ❖ How to talk about services on board the plane
- ❖ How to talk about the plane crew
- ❖ How to get through the airport after deplaning
- ❖ How to tell what you and others are presently doing
- ❖ How to tell what you and others know

Structure

- ❖ **Hacer, poner, traer, salir** in the present
- ❖ The present progressive
- ❖ **Saber** and **conocer** in the present

National Standards

- ❖ Communication Standard 1.1 pages 334, 338, 339, 342, 343, 345, 346, 347, 349, 351, 358
- ❖ Communication Standard 1.2 pages 339, 342, 343, 346, 349, 350, 351, 353, 354, 355, 357, 358
- ❖ Communication Standard 1.3 pages 351, 359
- ❖ Cultures Standard 2.1 page 350
- ❖ Cultures Standard 2.2 pages 343, 352–353, 355, 356
- ❖ Connections Standard 3.1 pages 356–357
- ❖ Comparisons Standard 4.2 page 354
- ❖ Communities Standard 5.1 page 358
- ❖ Communities Standard 5.2 page 363

PACING AND PRIORITIES

The chapter content is color coded below to assist you in planning.

■ **required** ■ **recommended** ■ **optional**

Vocabulario *(required)* *Days 1–4*

- ■ Palabras 1
  - Antes del vuelo
- ■ Palabras 2
  - Después del vuelo
  - El vuelo
  - La tripulación

Estructura *(required)* *Days 5–7*

- ■ **Hacer, poner, traer, salir** en el presente
- ■ El presente progresivo
- ■ **Saber** y **conocer** en el presente

Conversación *(required)*

- ■ Está saliendo nuestro vuelo.

Pronunciación *(recommended)*

- ■ La consonante **r**

Lecturas culturales

- ■ El avión el la América del Sur *(recommended)*
- ■ Distancias y tiempo de vuelo *(optional)*
- ■ Las líneas de Nazca *(optional)*

Conexiones

- ■ Las finanzas *(optional)*

■ **¡Te toca a ti!** *(recommended)*

■ **Assessment** *(recommended)*

■ **¡Hablo como un pro!** *(optional)*

RESOURCE GUIDE

Section	Pages	Section Resources
Vocabulario PALABRAS 1		
Antes del vuelo	336–339	Vocabulary Transparencies 11.2–11.3 Audio CD 7 Audio Activities TE, pages 131–133 Workbook, pages 129–130 Quiz 1, page 55 ExamView® Pro
Vocabulario PALABRAS 2		
Después del vuelo El vuelo La tripulación	340, 342–343 341, 342–343 341, 342–343	Vocabulary Transparencies 11.4–11.5 Audio CD 7 Audio Activities TE, pages 133–135 Workbook, pages 131–132 Quiz 2, page 56 ExamView® Pro
Estructura		
Hacer, poner, traer, salir en el presente El presente progresivo **Saber** y **conocer** en el presente	344–346 347–348 348–349	Audio CD 7 Audio Activities TE, pages 135–137 Workbook, pages 133–137 Quizzes 3–5, pages 57–59 ExamView® Pro
Conversación		
Está saliendo nuestro vuelo.	350	Audio CD 7 Audio Activities TE, page 138 Interactive CD-ROM
Pronunciación		
La consonante **r**	351	Pronunciation Transparency P 11 Audio CD 7 Audio Activities TE, page 139
Lecturas culturales		
El avión en la América del Sur Distancias y tiempo de vuelo Las líneas de Nazca	352–353 354 355	Audio CD 7 Audio Activities TE, page 139 Tests, pages 172, 176
Conexiones		
Las finanzas	356–357	Tests, page 177
¡Te toca a ti!		
	358–359	**¡Viva el mundo hispano!** Video, Episode 11 Video Activities, Chapter 11 Spanish Online Activities spanish.glencoe.com
Assessment		
	360–361	Communication Transparency C 11 Quizzes 1–5, pages 55–59 Performance Assessment, Task 11 Tests, pages 169–184 Situation Cards, Chapter 11 ExamView® Pro **Maratón mental** Videoquiz

Using Your Resources for Chapter 11

Transparencies

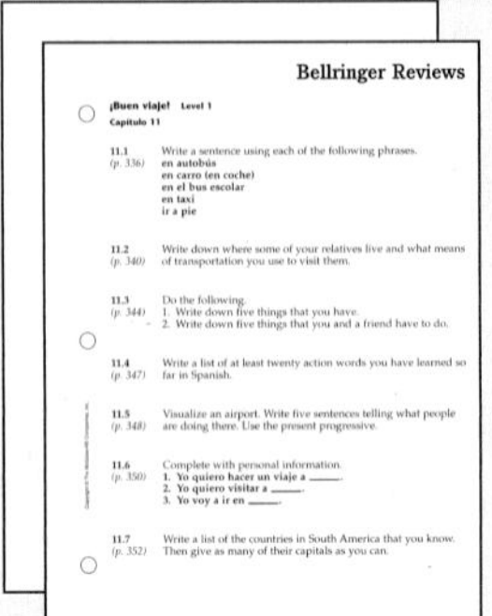
Bellringer 11.1–11.7

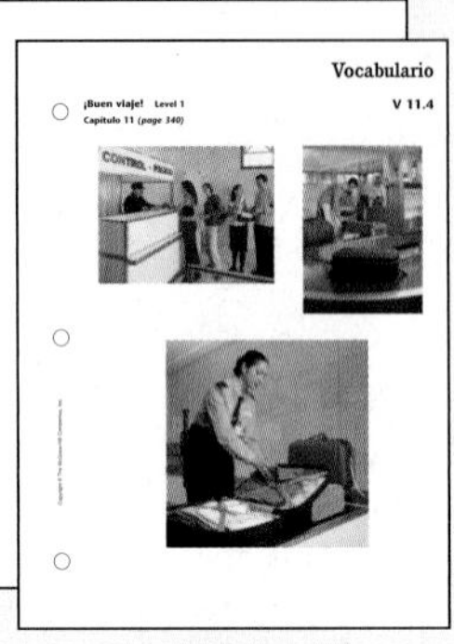
Vocabulary 11.1–11.5

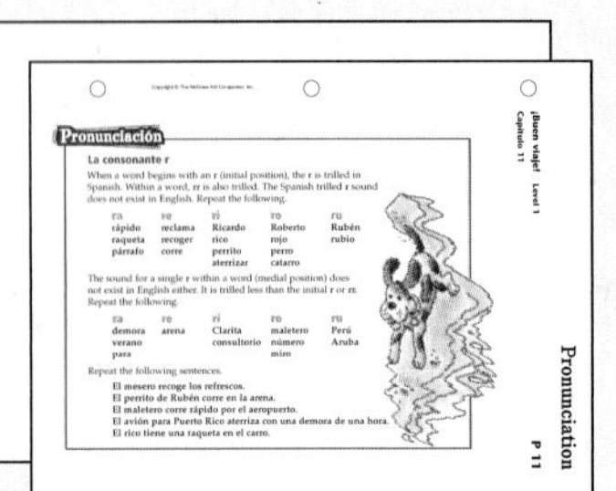
Pronunciation P 11

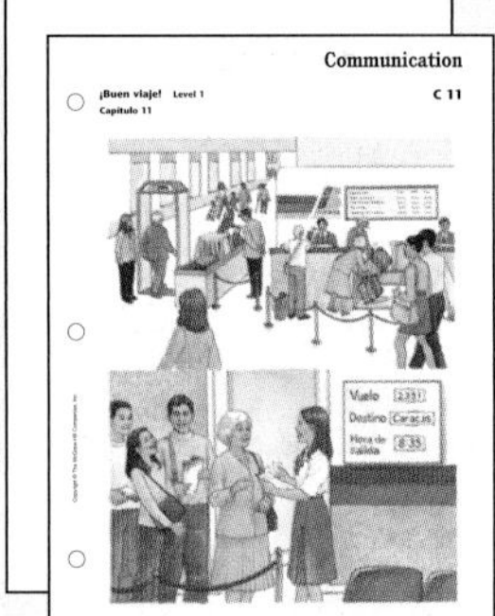
Communication C 11

Workbook

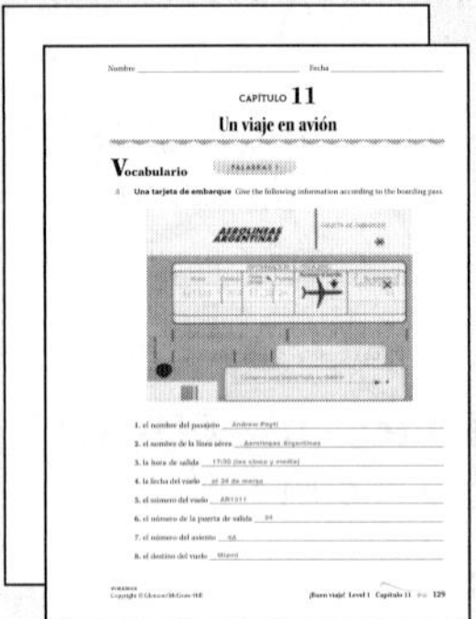
Vocabulary, pages 129–132

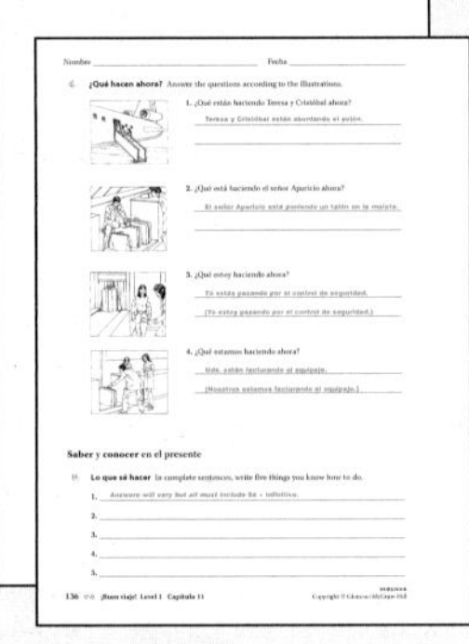
Structure, pages 133–137

Enrichment, pages 138–142

Audio Activities

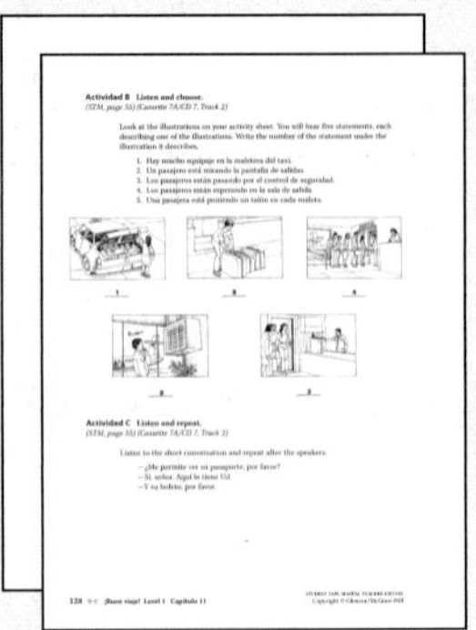
Vocabulary, pages 131–135

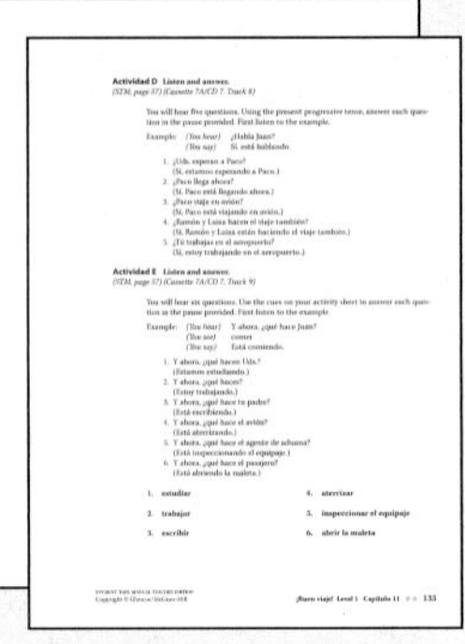
Structure, pages 135–137

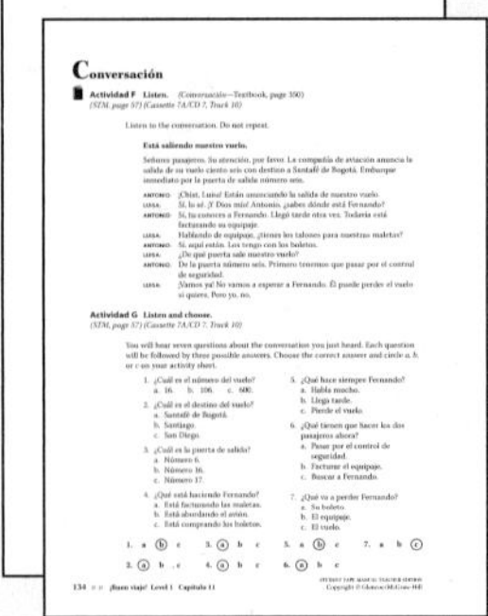
Conversation, Pronunciation, pages 138–139

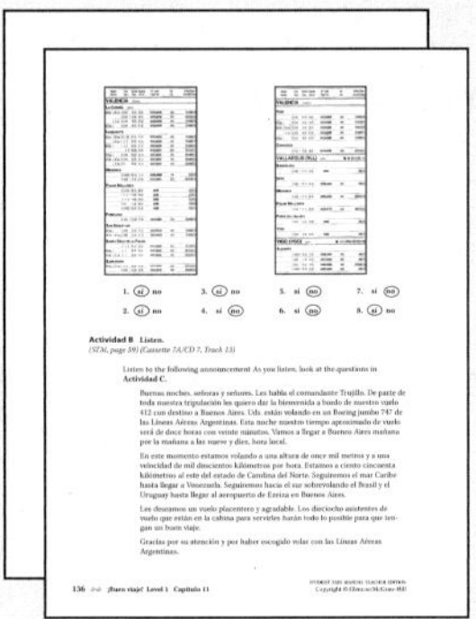
Additional Practice, pages 140–142

Assessment

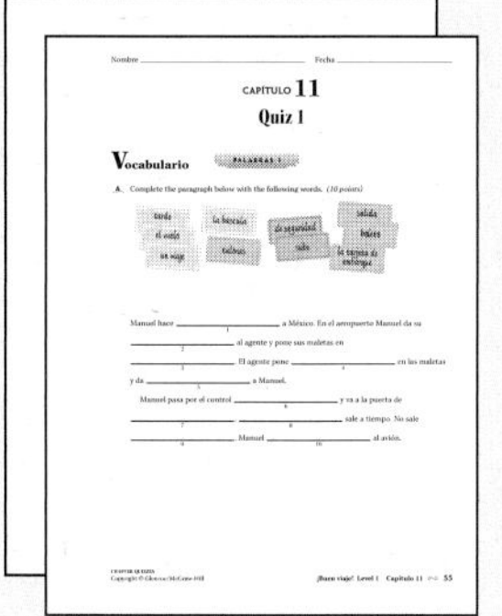

Vocabulary and Structure Quizzes pages 55–59

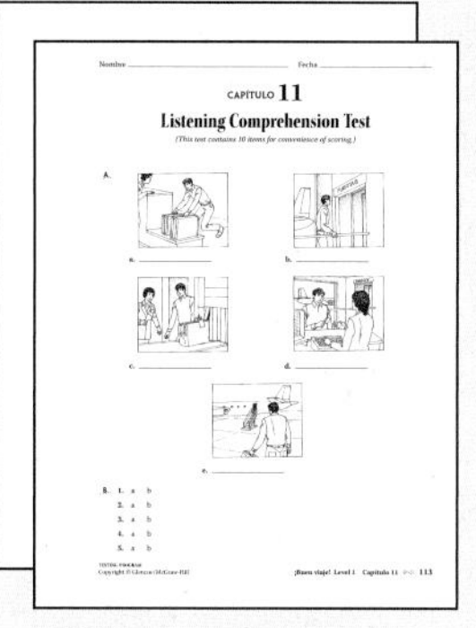

Chapter Tests, pages 169–184

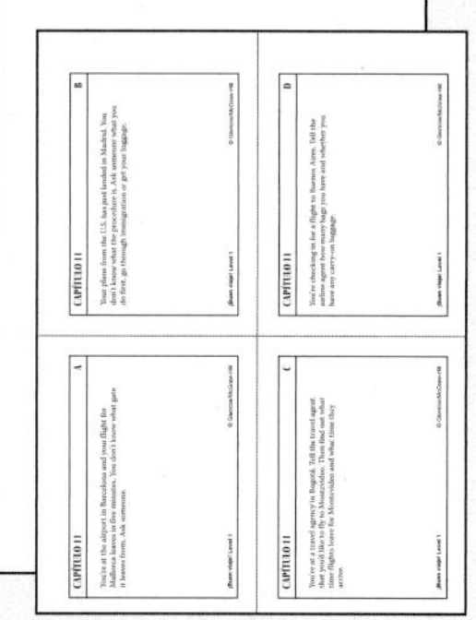

Situation Cards, Chapter 11

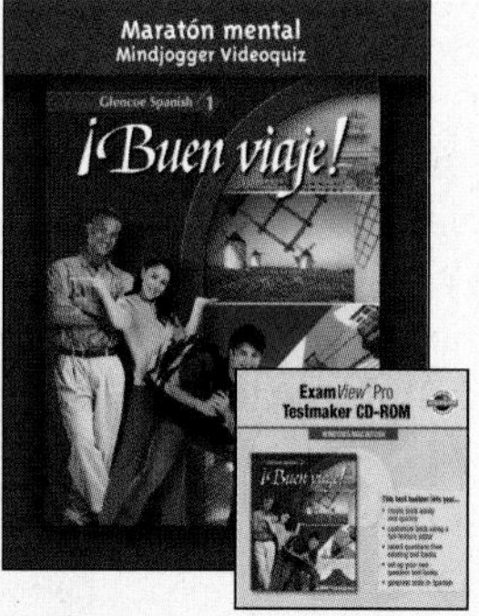

MindJogger Videoquiz, ExamView® Pro, Chapter 11

Timesaving Teacher Tools

TeacherWorks™ is your all-in-one teacher resource center. Personalize lesson plans, access resources from the Teacher Wraparound Edition, connect to the Internet, or make a to-do list. These are only a few of the many features that can assist you in the planning and organizing of your lessons.

Includes:

- A calendar feature
- Access to all program blackline masters
- Standards correlations and more

ExamView® Pro

Test Bank software for Macintosh and Windows makes creating, editing, customizing, and printing tests quick and easy.

Technology Resources

In the Chapter 11 Internet Activity, you will have a chance to learn more about the Spanish-speaking world. Visit spanish.glencoe.com

On the interactive CD-ROM, students can listen to and take part in a recorded version of the conversation in Chapter 11.

¡Viva el mundo hispano! Video and Video Activities, Chapter 11. Available on VHS and DVD.

Help your students prepare for the chapter test by playing the **Maratón mental** Videoquiz game show. Teams will compete against each other to review chapter vocabulary and structure and sharpen listening comprehension skills. Available on VHS and DVD.

¡Buen viaje! is also available on CD or Online.

Capítulo 11

Preview

In this chapter, students will learn the vocabulary associated with air travel and airports. (Vocabulary for on board the plane is presented in **¡Buen viaje! Level 2**). In order to describe their travels, students will learn the present tense of verbs with a **g** in the **yo** form, as well as the present progressive.

Students will also learn about the importance of air travel in South America because of its geographical characteristics.

National Standards

Communication

In Chapter 11 students will communicate in Spanish on the following topics:

- checking in at the airport
- going through security and finding their departure gate
- going through customs and passport control
- claiming their bags

Students will obtain and provide information about taking a flight and about procedures at an airport. They will learn to engage in conversations with various types of airline employees.

Capítulo 11

Un viaje en avión

Objetivos

In this chapter you will learn to:

- check in for a flight
- talk about some services on board the plane
- get through the airport after deplaning
- tell what you or others are currently doing
- tell what you know and whom you know
- discuss the importance of air travel in South America

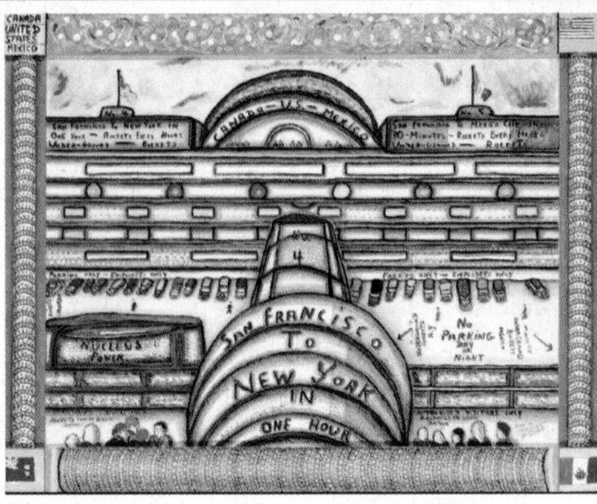

Alexander Aramburo Maldonado *San Francisco to New York in one hour*

Capítulo 11

Arte Alexander Arambuco Maldonado (1901–1969) emigrated to the U.S. from Mexico at age ten. He worked as a riveter, professional boxer and factory worker in San Francisco. He began to paint when he retired at age sixty. His paintings express a vision of technological progress and hope for the future.

Fotografía The airport shown here serves San Salvador, the capital of El Salvador. **TACA,** owned by several Central American countries, is a major international carrier, serving many destinations throughout the area.

LEVELING

The activities, conversations, and readings within each chapter are marked according to level of difficulty. **E** indicates easy. **A** indicates average. **C** indicates challenging. Some activities cover a range of difficulty. In some activities, for example, advanced students will be able to produce more extensive responses while students who learn at a different rate may give less detailed responses. The leveling indicators will help you individualize instruction to best meet your students' needs.

Vocabulario

PALABRAS 1

1 PREPARATION

Resource Manager

Vocabulary Transparencies 11.2–11.3
Audio Activities TE, pages 131–133
Audio CD 7
Workbook, pages 129–130
Quizzes, page 55
ExamView® Pro

Bellringer Review

Use BRR Transparency 11.1 or write the following on the board.
Write a sentence using each of the following phrases.
en autobús
en carro (en coche)
en el bus escolar
en taxi
ir a pie

2 PRESENTATION

Step 1 Have students close their books. Using Vocabulary Transparencies 11.2–11.3, introduce the words on pages 336–337. Have students repeat after you or Audio CD 7 as you point to the illustrations.

Step 2 Ask questions such as **¿Es la maletera? ¿Qué es? ¿Es la maletera del taxi?**

Step 3 When presenting the contextualized sentences, you may wish to ask questions that progress from simple to more complex. For example: **¿Hace Clarita un viaje? ¿Quién hace un viaje? ¿Hace un viaje a España o a la América del Sur? ¿Adónde hace un viaje?**

Vocabulario

PALABRAS 1

Antes del vuelo

La agente revisa el pasaporte y el boleto.

Reaching All Students

Total Physical Response If students don't already know the meaning of **llámalo, se para,** and **busca,** teach these expressions by using the appropriate gestures as you say each expression.

(Student 1), **ven acá. Imagínate que vas a hacer un viaje. Tienes que ir al aeropuerto.**
Aquí viene un taxi. Llámalo. El taxi se para.
Pon tu maleta en la maletera.
Sube al taxi y siéntate. Llegas al aeropuerto.
Págale al taxista. Dale el dinero.
Abre la puerta. Baja (Bájate) del taxi.
Toma tu maleta. Entra en el aeropuerto.
Busca el mostrador de la línea aérea.
Ve al mostrador de la línea aérea.
Pon tu maleta en la báscula.
Gracias, *(Student 1).* **Siéntate.**

Los pasajeros están pasando por el control de seguridad.

Clarita hace un viaje en avión.
Hace un viaje a la América del Sur.
Toma un vuelo a Lima.
Clarita está facturando su equipaje.
Pone sus maletas en la báscula.
El agente pone un talón en cada maleta.

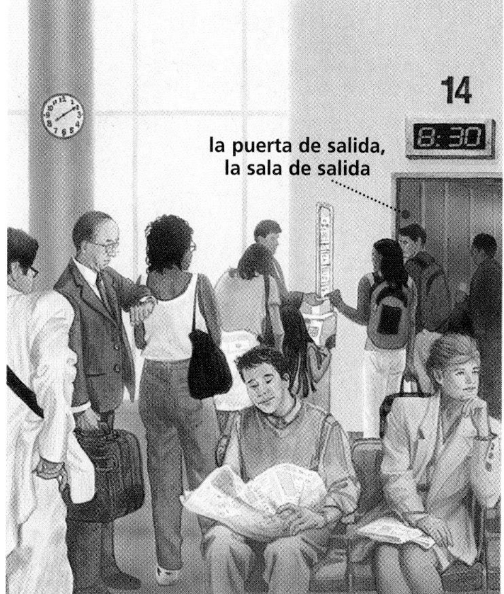

Los pasajeros están esperando en la puerta de salida.
El avión sale de la puerta número catorce.
El vuelo sale a tiempo.
No sale tarde. No sale con una demora.

About the Spanish Language

You may wish to give students the following additional vocabulary and information concerning the words they have learned.

- **La tarjeta de embarque** is universally understood, as is **el pase de abordar.** Students will also hear **el pasabordo.**
- Explain to students that they are going to see and hear the words **el asiento** and **la plaza.** They both mean *seat,* but **asiento** is more the "physical" seat. One will often hear: **Quiero una plaza en la sección de no fumar.**
- The older type of arrival and departure board is **el tablero.** The more modern airports have a TV screen, **la pantalla.**
- **El billete** is used in Spain for *ticket,* **el boleto** throughout Latin America.
- **La maletera** and **el maletero** are heard with equal frequency for *the trunk of a car.* **El baúl** is also used in certain areas.
- **El talón** is the baggage tag that is used for checked baggage. The personal identification tag is **una etiqueta.**
- The large scale shown in the illustration (page 337) is **una báscula. Básculas** have a flat surface and are usually used for heavier weights. **Una balanza** is a scale with weights on one end or the hanging scale used for produce.
- **Facturar** means to check luggage through to a destination. **Depositar** means to check something for safe-keeping, as in a checkroom.
- In Spanish there is no direct equivalent of *to check in.* What is heard is **Señores pasajeros, favor de presentarse en el mostrador.**

Reaching All Students

Cooperative Learning Divide the class into three or four groups, depending on the class size. Each member of each group contributes two activities that could take place at an airport. Each group writes down all its activities and then pantomimes them in front of the class. Members of the other teams guess and say what they are doing in Spanish.

LEVELING

E: Vocabulary

3 PRACTICE

¿Qué palabra necesito?

¡OJO! When students are doing the **¿Qué palabra necesito?** activities, accept any answer that makes sense. The purpose of these activities is to have students use the new vocabulary. They are not factual recall activities. Thus, it is not necessary for students to remember specific factual information from the vocabulary presentation when answering. If you wish, have students use the photos on this page as a stimulus, when possible.

Historieta Each time **Historieta** appears, it means that the answers to the activity form a short story. Encourage students to look at the title of the **Historieta,** since it can help them do the activity.

Writing Development
Have students write the answers to Activity 1 in one paragraph to illustrate how the answers to all the items tell a story.

3 Have students refer to the boarding pass in Activity 2 as they do Activity 3.

Learning from Realia
(page 338) On the boarding pass, the code **C** under **Clase** is for business class. Different carriers have different names for the categories. **Iberia** calls their business class **Clase preferente.**

¿Qué palabra necesito?

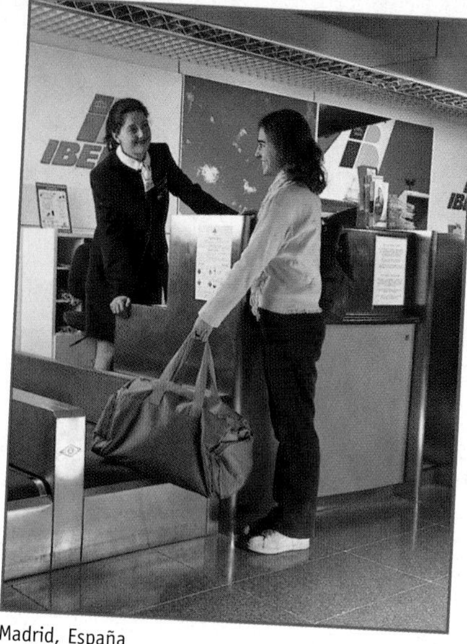
Madrid, España

1 Historieta En el aeropuerto
Contesten.

1. ¿Hace Lupe un viaje a la América del Sur?
2. ¿Está en el aeropuerto?
3. ¿Está hablando con la agente de la línea aérea?
4. ¿Dónde pone sus maletas?
5. ¿Está facturando su equipaje a Bogotá?
6. ¿Pone la agente un talón en cada maleta?
7. ¿Revisa la agente su boleto?
8. ¿Tiene Lupe su tarjeta de embarque?
9. ¿De qué puerta va a salir su vuelo?

2 La tarjeta de embarque
Den la información siguiente.

IBERIA TARJETA DE EMBARQUE

INFORMACION AL PASAJERO

Vuelo	Destin	Hora Limite	Puerta	Clase	Su asiento
IB3127	MAD	12:45	15	C	8A

DÍAZ/ROBERTO
LIS/22APR C 047
Conserve esta tarjeta hasta su destino

1. el nombre de la línea aérea
2. el número del vuelo
3. el destino del vuelo
4. la hora de embarque
5. la fecha del vuelo, el día que sale

3 ¿Dónde está su asiento? Completen según la tarjeta de embarque.

1. ¿Cuál es la letra del asiento que tiene el pasajero?
2. ¿En qué fila está el asiento?
3. ¿De qué puerta sale el avión?
4. ¿Tiene que conservar el pasajero la tarjeta durante el vuelo?
5. ¿Está su asiento en la sección de fumar o de no fumar?

Answers to ¿Qué palabra necesito?

1

1. Sí, Lupe hace un viaje a la América del Sur.
2. Sí, está en el aeropuerto.
3. Sí, está hablando con la agente de la línea aérea.
4. Pone sus maletas en la báscula.
5. Sí, está facturando su equipaje a Bogotá.
6. Sí, la agente pone un talón en cada maleta.
7. Sí, la agente revisa su boleto.
8. Sí, Lupe tiene su tarjeta de embarque.
9. Su vuelo va a salir de la puerta número ___.

2

1. Iberia
2. (IB)3127
3. Madrid
4. 12:45
5. 22 de abril

3

1. La letra del asiento es A.
2. El asiento está en la fila 8.
3. El avión sale de la puerta 15.
4. Sí, el pasajero tiene que conservar la tarjeta durante el vuelo.
5. Su asiento está en la sección de no fumar.

4 Historieta Antes de la salida Escojan.

1. ____ indica el asiento que tiene el pasajero a bordo del avión.
   a. El talón **b.** La tarjeta de embarque **c.** El boleto
2. Bogotá es ____ del vuelo.
   a. el número **b.** la ciudad **c.** el destino
3. Inspeccionan el equipaje de mano de los pasajeros en ____.
   a. el mostrador de la línea aérea **b.** el control de seguridad
   c. la puerta de salida
4. El vuelo para Bogotá sale ____ número cinco.
   a. del mostrador **b.** del control **c.** de la puerta
5. Los pasajeros están ____ por el control de seguridad.
   a. saliendo **b.** facturando **c.** pasando

5 En el aeropuerto

Work with a classmate. You're checking in at the airport for your flight to Quito, Ecuador. Have a conversation with the airline agent (your partner) at the ticket counter.

6 Un vuelo

Work with a classmate. Look at the following photograph. You are a passenger on this flight. Tell as much as you can about your experience at the airport.

UN POCO MÁS *For more practice using words from **Palabras 1**, do Activity 11 on page H12 at the end of this book.*

4 You may wish to have more able students make up a sentence using the incorrect choices from Activity 4.

¡OJO! Note that the activities are color-coded. All the activities in the text are communicative. However, the ones with blue titles are guided communication. The red titles indicate that the answers to the activity are more open-ended and can vary more. You may wish to correct students' mistakes more so in the guided activities than in the activities with a red title, which lend themselves to a freer response.

5 Students can refer to the photo on page 336 to get themselves started.

6 The most logical way to do this activity would be to have students use the preterite.

UN POCO MÁS This *InfoGap* Activity will allow students to practice in pairs. The activity should be very manageable for them, since all vocabulary and structures are familiar to them.

ANSWERS TO ¿Qué palabra necesito?

4

1. b
2. c
3. b
4. c
5. c

5 *Answers will vary, but students should include related vocabulary from* Palabras 1.

6 *Answers will vary. Students should use the preterite tense and the related vocabulary from* Palabras 1.

LEVELING

E: Activities 1, 2, 3, 6

A: Activities 2, 3, 4, 5, 6

C: Activity 5

1 PREPARATION

Resource Manager

Vocabulary Transparencies 11.4–11.5
Audio Activities TE, pages 133–135
Audio CD 7
Workbook, pages 131–132
Quizzes, page 56
ExamView® Pro

Bellringer Review

Use BRR Transparency 11.2 or write the following on the board.
Write down where some of your relatives live and what means of transportation you use to visit them.

2 PRESENTATION

Step 1 Have students look at Vocabulary Transparencies 11.4–11.5 as they repeat each word or expression after you or Audio CD 7.

Step 2 As you present the new vocabulary, you may intersperse comprehension questions. For example: **¿Los pasajeros tienen que pasar por el control de pasaportes? ¿Los pasajeros necesitan pasaporte cuando llegan de un país extranjero? ¿Qué abre la agente de aduana? ¿Qué inspecciona?**

Vocabulario

PALABRAS 2

Después del vuelo

Cuando los pasajeros desembarcan, tienen que pasar por el control de pasaportes.
Tienen que pasar por el control de pasaportes cuando llegan de un país extranjero.

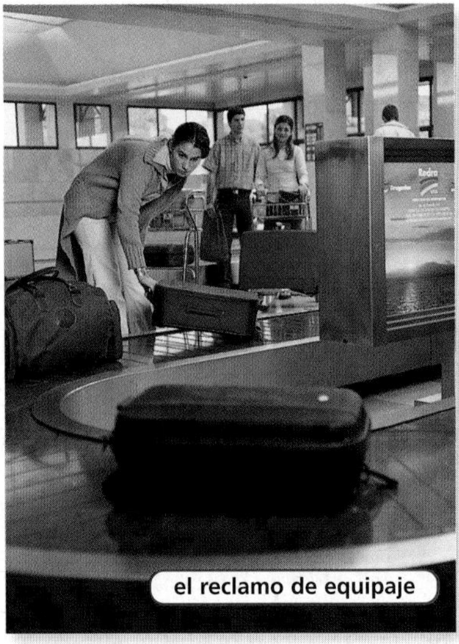

Los pasajeros están reclamando (recogiendo) sus maletas.

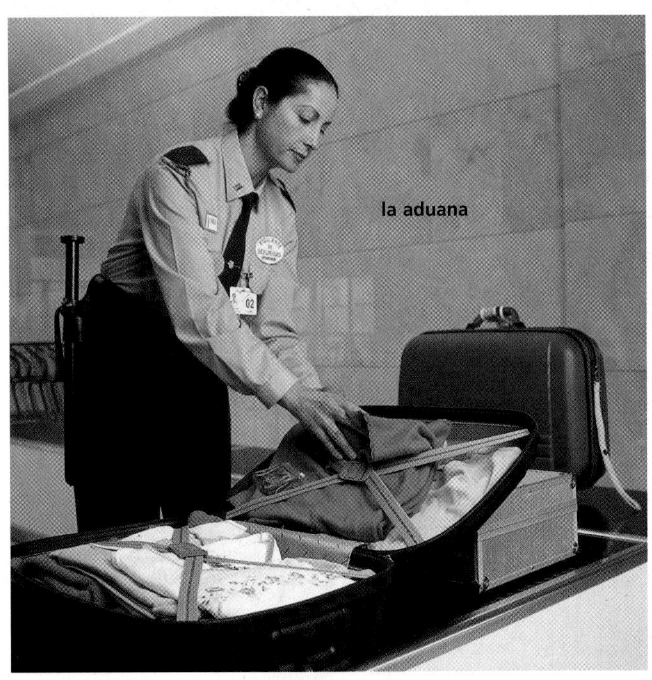

La agente de aduana está abriendo las maletas.
Está inspeccionando el equipaje.
Quiere saber lo que está en las maletas.

Reaching All Students

Total Physical Response
(Student 1), ven acá, por favor.
Tu vuelo está llegando. Vas a desembarcar.
Toma tu equipaje de mano.
Dile «adiós» a la asistente de vuelo.
Sal o baja del avión.
Aquí estás en el control de pasaportes.
Pasa por el control de pasaportes.
Dale tu pasaporte al agente.
Tienes que reclamar tu equipaje. Está llegando. Tienes dos maletas.
Aquí llega una de tus maletas. Toma tu maleta.
Aquí viene la otra. Tómala.
Ahora estás en la aduana.
Abre tu maleta para la agente de aduana.
Gracias, *(Student 1).* Siéntate.

El vuelo

Un avión está despegando.

Otro avión está aterrizando.

La tripulación

La tripulación trabaja a bordo del avión. Los asistentes de vuelo les dan la bienvenida a los pasajeros.

Vocabulary Expansion

You may wish to teach students the following:

El avión sale para Madrid.
Es un vuelo con destino a Madrid.
El avión llega (viene) de Madrid.
Es un vuelo procedente de Madrid.

Fun Facts

In recent years, customs formalities have become less complicated in many countries (but not all). In many cases, tourists with nothing to declare can follow a green arrow and pass through customs without having to open their suitcases.

Many Spanish and Latin American airlines are nationalized, that is, owned by the government. However, there is presently a move toward privatization of some national industries, including the airline industry.

About the Spanish Language

Other ways to express **el / la asistente de vuelo** are **el sobrecargo, el / la aeromozo(a). La asistente** can also be **la asistenta. La azafata** is used in Spain for a female flight attendant. The original meaning of **azafata** was *a queen's lady-in-waiting.*

Chapter Projects

Pasaporte hispano Have each student create his or her Spanish passport. Have students fill out forms in Spanish with their name, address, nationality, birth date, metric weight, etc. Students could use a real photo or draw a picture of themselves. Covers can be made of construction paper.

3 PRACTICE

¿Qué palabra necesito?

7 After going over Activity 7, have students retell the story in their own words.

8 After going over Activity 8, have students correct the false statements.

Learning from Realia

(page 342) Ask students the following question about the brochure: **¿Cuál es el nombre del aeropuerto de Madrid?**

Chapter Projects

Visita al aeropuerto If your students have had little opportunity to travel, you may want to plan a field trip to a nearby airport. This is a wonderful enrichment experience for some students. As you tour the airport, have them use as much of their Spanish vocabulary as possible.

¿Qué palabra necesito?

7 Historieta La llegada

Contesten.

1. Cuando el avión aterriza, ¿abordan o desembarcan los pasajeros?
2. ¿Tienen que pasar por el control de pasaportes cuando llegan a un país extranjero?
3. ¿Van los pasajeros al reclamo de equipaje?
4. ¿Reclaman su equipaje?
5. ¿Tienen que pasar por la aduana?
6. ¿Abre las maletas el agente?

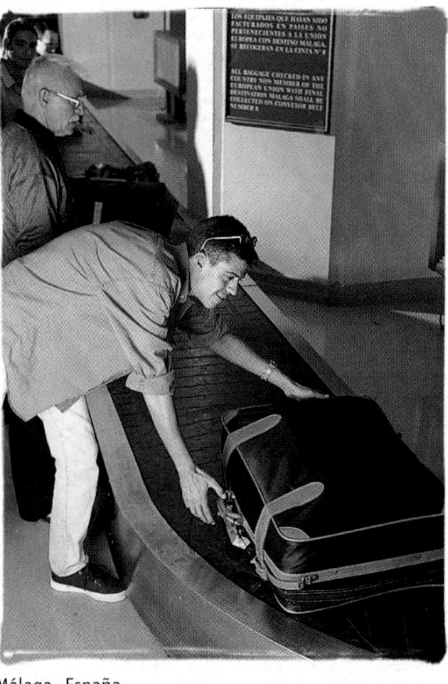

Málaga, España

8 ¿Sí o no? Digan que sí o que no.

1. El avión aterriza cuando sale.
2. El avión despega cuando llega a su destino.
3. Un vuelo internacional es un vuelo que va a un país extranjero.
4. Los agentes de la línea aérea que trabajan en el mostrador en el aeropuerto son miembros de la tripulación.
5. La tripulación consiste en los empleados que trabajan a bordo del avión.

9 Pareo Busquen una palabra relacionada.

1. asistir	a. la llegada
2. controlar	b. la salida
3. reclamar	c. el asistente, la asistente
4. inspeccionar	d. el despegue
5. despegar	e. el aterrizaje
6. aterrizar	f. el control
7. salir	g. la inspección
8. llegar	h. el reclamo
9. embarcar	i. el vuelo
10. volar	j. el embarque

Answers to ¿Qué palabra necesito?

7

1. Cuando el avión aterriza, los pasajeros desembarcan.
2. Sí, tienen que pasar por el control de pasaportes cuando llegan a un país extranjero.
3. Sí, los pasajeros van al reclamo de equipaje.
4. Sí, reclaman su equipaje.
5. Sí, tienen que pasar por la aduana.
6. Sí, el agente abre las maletas.

8

1. No
2. No
3. Sí
4. No
5. Sí

9

1. c
2. f
3. h
4. g
5. d
6. e
7. b
8. a
9. j
10. i

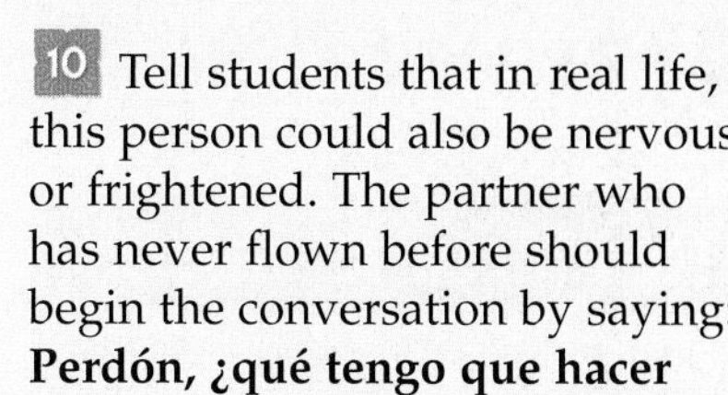

10 **¿Qué tenemos que hacer?** You're on a flight to Caracas. The person seated next to you (your partner) has never flown before. He or she is confused as to what you have to do when you get off the plane. Be as helpful as possible in answering his or her questions.

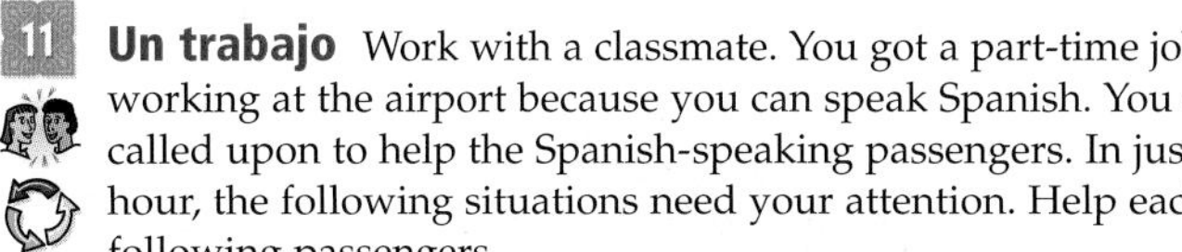

11 **Un trabajo** Work with a classmate. You got a part-time job working at the airport because you can speak Spanish. You are called upon to help the Spanish-speaking passengers. In just one hour, the following situations need your attention. Help each of the following passengers.

- A person is leaving on flight 125 for Chicago. He doesn't know if it's leaving on time. Help him out.
- Another passenger is confused. He doesn't know his flight number to New York. Let him know what it is. Be extra helpful and let him know what time his flight leaves.
- Another passenger is in a real hurry. She's changing **(cambiar)** flights and wants to know what gate to go to for her flight to Los Angeles. Tell her.
- A young woman missed her flight and has to change her ticket. Go with her to the airline counter and explain to her what the agent says she has to do.

Lan Chile
Nombre del Pasajero
RUIZ/CARMEN
Vuelo Nº
LA961
Desde
LPB
Hacia
SCL
Clase
Y
Fecha
26JAN
Hora de Salida
1245
Hora de Embarque
1145
Puerta
P
Asiento
9A
Maletas
2
Peso
18

12 **Una tarjeta de embarque** This is a boarding card for a flight you are about to take. Tell a classmate (your partner) all you can about your flight based on the information on the card.

Punta Arenas, Chile

10 Tell students that in real life, this person could also be nervous or frightened. The partner who has never flown before should begin the conversation by saying: **Perdón, ¿qué tengo que hacer cuando desembarco del avión (cuando llegamos al aeropuerto)?**

11 Students should take turns being the part-time worker and the passenger in distress. The student playing the passenger should explain briefly what the problem is in each case, according to the information provided on page 343.

12 Students may need some help figuring out the codes on the **Lan Chile** boarding pass. See the Learning from Realia box below for the necessary information. Remind students that "18" refers to kilos, not pounds.
Expansion: Have students figure out how much the two bags weigh in pounds (1 kilo = 2.2 lbs.).

Learning from Realia

(page 343) Tell students that **Lan Chile** is the national airline of Chile.

It will probably be necessary to explain some of the codes on this boarding pass, or you may wish to have students guess.

LPB **La Paz, Bolivia**
SCL **Santiago de Chile**
LA **Lan Chile**

The code **Y** under **clase** indicates coach or economy class.

Answers to ¿Qué palabra necesito?

10 *Answers will vary. Students should use the vocabulary from* Palabras 1 *and* Palabras 2.

11 *Answers will vary. Students should use the vocabulary from* Palabras 1 *and* Palabras 2, *as well as forms and expressions learned in previous chapters.*

12 *Answers will vary but may include:*

El avión sale de La Paz y va a Santiago.
El número del vuelo es LA961.
El avión sale de La Paz el 26 de enero a las 12:45 de la tarde.
La hora de embarque es a las 11:45.
El avión sale de la puerta P.
Mi asiento es 9A.
Tengo dos maletas. Pesan 18 kilos.

LEVELING

E: Activities 7, 10, 12
A: Activities 8, 10, 11, 12
C: Activities 9, 11

Estructura

1 PREPARATION

Resource Manager

Audio Activities TE, pages 135–137
Audio CD 7
Workbook, pages 133–137
Quizzes, pages 57–59
ExamView® Pro

Bellringer Review

Use BRR Transparency 11.3 or write the following on the board.

Do the following.

1. Write down five things that you have.
2. Write down five things that you and a friend have to do.

2 PRESENTATION

Hacer, poner, traer, salir en el presente

Step 1 Have students open their books to page 344. You may wish to say the infinitives from Item 1 aloud.

Step 2 Then point to yourself as you say **hago, pongo, traigo, salgo.**

Step 3 Write the **yo** forms on the board and ask students what they have in common.

Step 4 Have students repeat the **yo** forms.

Step 5 Write the other forms on the board and indicate to students that they are the same as any regular **-er** or **-ir** verb they have already learned. These endings actually serve as a review of **-er** and **-ir** verbs.

Estructura

Hacer, poner, traer, salir en el presente
Telling what people do

1. The verbs **hacer** *(to do, to make)*, **poner, traer** *(to bring)*, and **salir** have an irregular **yo** form. The **yo** form has a **g.** All other forms are the same as those of a regular **-er** or **-ir** verb.

INFINITIVE	hacer	poner	traer	salir
yo	hago	pongo	traigo	salgo
tú	haces	pones	traes	sales
él, ella, Ud.	hace	pone	trae	sale
nosotros(as)	hacemos	ponemos	traemos	salimos
vosotros(as)	*hacéis*	*ponéis*	*traéis*	*salís*
ellos, ellas, Uds.	hacen	ponen	traen	salen

¿Te acuerdas?
The verb **tener** also has a **g** in the **yo** form: **tengo**

2. The verb **venir** *(to come)* also has an irregular **yo** form. Note that in addition it has a stem change **e → ie** in all forms except **nosotros** and **vosotros.**

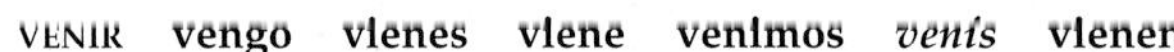

VENIR **vengo vienes viene venimos** ***venís*** **vienen**

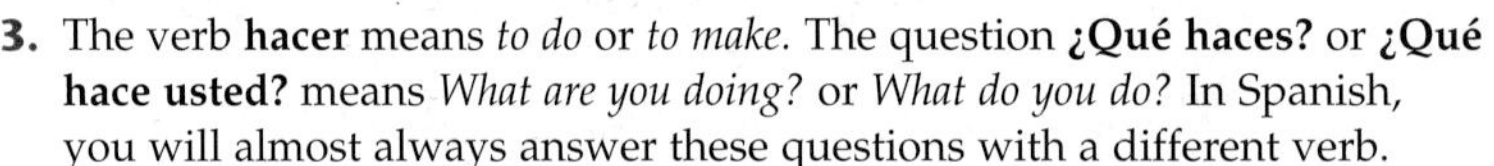

3. The verb **hacer** means *to do* or *to make.* The question **¿Qué haces?** or **¿Qué hace usted?** means *What are you doing?* or *What do you do?* In Spanish, you will almost always answer these questions with a different verb.

¿Qué haces? Trabajo en el aeropuerto.

4. The verb **hacer** is used in many idiomatic expressions. An idiomatic expression is one that does not translate directly from one language to another. The expression **hacer un viaje** *(to take a trip)* is an idiomatic expression because in Spanish the verb **hacer** is used, whereas in English we use the verb *to take.* Another idiomatic expression is **hacer la maleta** which means *to pack a suitcase.*

"Transportación Terrestre Aeropuerto",
S.A. de C.V.
R.F.C. TTA - 880304 - 4R9
Alameda de León 1-G Tel. 4-43-50 Oaxaca,Oax.
Nº 15368 CLIENTE
Incluído Seguro del Viajero
Viaje Especial N$ 90.00
Nombre
Domicilio
ZONA 2 Fecha

LEVELING

E: Activity 13

A: Activity 14

¿Cómo lo digo?

13 **Historieta Un viaje en avión** Contesten.

1. ¿Haces un viaje?
2. ¿Haces un viaje a Europa?
3. ¿Haces un viaje a España?
4. ¿Sales para el aeropuerto?
5. ¿Sales en coche o en taxi?
6. ¿Traes equipaje?
7. ¿Pones el equipaje en la maletera del taxi?
8. En el aeropuerto, ¿pones el equipaje en la báscula?
9. ¿En qué vuelo sales?
10. ¿Sales de la puerta de salida número ocho?

Hoyo de Manzanares, Madrid, España

14 **Historieta Al aeropuerto** Sigan el modelo.

Ellos hacen un viaje...

Ellos hacen un viaje y nosotros también hacemos un viaje.

1. Ellos salen para el aeropuerto.
2. Ellos salen en taxi.
3. Ellos traen mucho equipaje.
4. Ellos ponen las maletas en la maletera.
5. Ellos salen a las seis.
6. Ellos vienen solos.

Estructura

Step 6 For Item 2, have students repeat the forms of the verb **venir.** Point out that it has a **g** in the **yo** form; it also has a stem change, the same as **querer** or **preferir.**

Step 7 Now lead students through Items 3 and 4.

3 PRACTICE

¿Cómo lo digo?

13 Activity 13 focuses on the **yo** form to give students practice using the **g** form.

14 This activity reviews the first and third person plural forms that students already know.

Learning from Photos

(page 345) Hoyo de Manzanares is a residential area that takes its name from the Manzanares River that flows through Madrid.

Answers to ¿Cómo lo digo?

13

1. Sí, hago un viaje.
2. Sí, hago un viaje a Europa.
3. Sí, hago un viaje a España.
4. Sí, salgo para el aeropuerto.
5. Salgo en coche (taxi).
6. Sí, traigo equipaje.
7. Sí, (No, no) pongo el equipaje en la maletera del taxi.
8. Sí, en el aeropuerto pongo el equipaje en la báscula.
9. Salgo en el vuelo número ___.
10. Sí, (No, no) salgo de la puerta de salida número ocho.

14

1. Ellos salen para el aeropuerto y nosotros también salimos para el aeropuerto.
2. Ellos salen en taxi y nosotros también salimos en taxi.
3. Ellos traen mucho equipaje y nosotros también traemos mucho equipaje.
4. Ellos ponen las maletas en la maletera y nosotros también ponemos las maletas en la maletera.
5. Ellos salen a las seis y nosotros también salimos a las seis.
6. Ellos vienen solos y nosotros también venimos solos.

3 PRACTICE *(continued)*

15 Activity 15 has students use all forms.
Expansion: Have students retell the story from Activity 15 in their own words.

Recycling

Activity 16 allows students to use vocabulary from many of the preceding chapters. Activity 17 reviews the weather expressions from Chapter 9.

16 This activity gives students practice asking questions with **hacer** and answering with another verb. Tell students that while it is sometimes possible to answer with **hacer,** they will most often use another verb.
Expansion: Have students make a list of each location mentioned and write down one activity they do at that location. Have students exchange their lists and compare.

17 One student will begin by asking the partner: **¿Qué haces cuando...?**

Learning from Realia

(page 347) **Iberia** is the major Spanish airline. Explain to students that its name comes from the name of the peninsula where Spain is located: **España está en la península ibérica. Dos países forman la península ibérica. Son España y Portugal.** Explain that **los iberos** were the original inhabitants of Spain.

LEVELING

E: Activity 18
A: Activities 16, 17
C: Activity 15

15 Historieta Un viaje a Marbella

Completen.

Yo __1__ (hacer) un viaje a Marbella. Marbella __2__ (estar) en la Costa del Sol en el sur de España. Mi amiga Sandra __3__ (hacer) el viaje también. Nosotros __4__ (hacer) el viaje en avión hasta Málaga y luego __5__ (ir) a tomar el autobús a Marbella.

—¡Ay, ay, Sandra! Pero tú __6__ (traer) mucho equipaje.

—No, yo no __7__ (traer) mucho. __8__ (Tener) sólo dos maletas. Tú exageras. Tú también __9__ (venir) con mucho equipaje.

—¡Oye! ¿A qué hora __10__ (salir) nuestro vuelo?

—No __11__ (salir) hasta las seis y media. Nosotros __12__ (tener) mucho tiempo.

Marbella, España

16 ¿Adónde vas y qué haces?

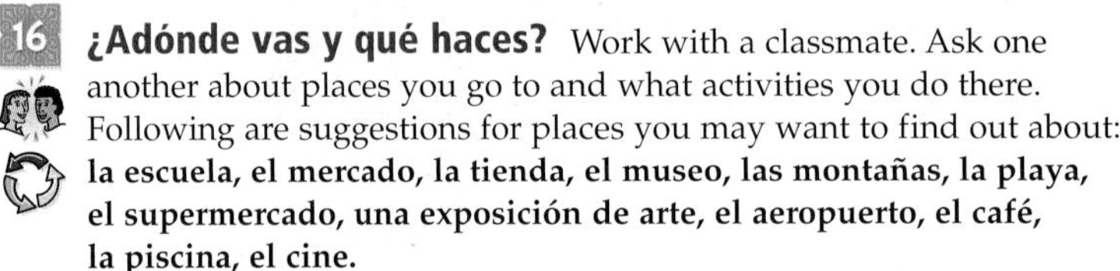

Work with a classmate. Ask one another about places you go to and what activities you do there. Following are suggestions for places you may want to find out about: **la escuela, el mercado, la tienda, el museo, las montañas, la playa, el supermercado, una exposición de arte, el aeropuerto, el café, la piscina, el cine.**

17 ¿Qué haces cuando... ?

Work with a classmate. Find out what he or she does under the following weather conditions. Take turns asking and answering questions.

Geography Connection

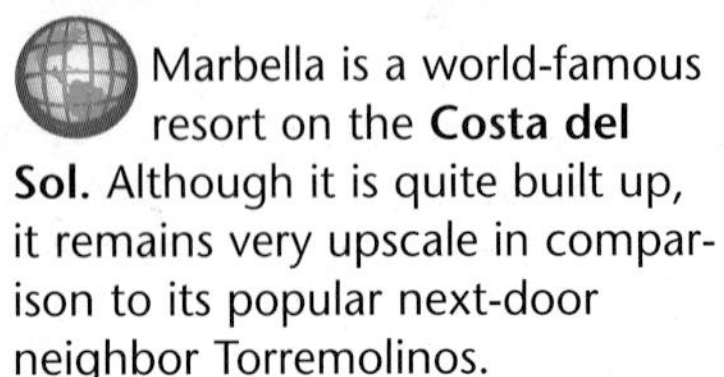

Marbella is a world-famous resort on the **Costa del Sol.** Although it is quite built up, it remains very upscale in comparison to its popular next-door neighbor Torremolinos.

Answers to ¿Cómo lo digo?

15

1. hago
2. está
3. hace
4. hacemos
5. vamos
6. traes
7. traigo
8. Tengo
9. vienes
10. sale
11. sale
12. tenemos

16 *Answers will vary; however, students will ask in the* tú *form, and their partners will answer in the* yo *form.*

17 *Answers will vary. Students should use* hacer *to form questions. Responses will include activities that correlate to each type of weather.*

El presente progresivo
Describing an action in progress

1. The present progressive is used in Spanish to express an action that is presently going on—an action in progress. The present progressive is formed by using the present tense of the verb **estar** and the present participle—*speaking, doing.* To form the present participle of most verbs in Spanish you drop the ending of the infinitive and add **-ando** to the stem of **-ar** verbs and **-iendo** to the stem of **-er** and **-ir** verbs. Study the following forms of the present participle.

INFINITIVE	hablar	llegar	comer	hacer	salir
STEM	habl-	lleg-	com-	hac-	sal-
PARTICIPLE	hablando	llegando	comiendo	haciendo	saliendo

2. Note that the verbs **leer** and **traer** have a **y** in the present participle.

   leyendo **trayendo**

3. Study the following examples of the present progressive.

   ¿Qué está haciendo Isabel?
   Ahora está esperando el avión.
   Ella está mirando y leyendo su tarjeta de embarque.
   Y yo estoy buscando mi boleto.

¿Cómo lo digo?

Historieta En el aeropuerto

Contesten según se indica.

1. ¿Adónde están llegando los pasajeros? (al aeropuerto)
2. ¿Cómo están llegando? (en taxi)
3. ¿Adónde están viajando? (a Europa)
4. ¿Cómo están haciendo el viaje? (en avión)
5. ¿Dónde están facturando el equipaje? (en el mostrador de la línea aérea)
6. ¿Qué está mirando el agente? (los boletos y los pasaportes)
7. ¿De qué puerta están saliendo los pasajeros para Madrid? (número siete)
8. ¿Qué están abordando? (el avión)

• Tarjeta Iberia Plus Platino
IBERIA plus
La Tarjeta Iberia Plus Platino es el mayor reconocimiento de Iberia a su confianza. Una distinción exclusiva al acumular 7.000 Puntos Aéreos Básicos[1] en un año[2] para que disfrute de servicios de prestigio que le llevarán a lo más alto: crédito personal de hasta 1.500 puntos, servicio especial de limusina**, máxima franquicia de equipaje, etc.
** En aquellos aeropuertos donde exista este servicio, en utilización de puntos, para vuelos intercontinentales, en Gran Clase o Business Class.
[1] Puntos Aéreos Básicos son aquellos publicados en tablas sin tener en cuenta las promociones y ofertas.
Para titulares residentes fuera de España:
Tarjeta Iberia Plus Platino 6.500 Puntos Aéreos Básicos
[2] Periodo comprendido entre el 1 de abril del año en curso al 31 de marzo del siguiente año.
IBERIA plus

Answers to ¿Cómo lo digo?

1. Los pasajeros están llegando al aeropuerto.
2. Están llegando en taxi.
3. Están viajando a Europa.
4. Están haciendo el viaje en avión.
5. Están facturando el equipaje en el mostrador de la línea aérea.
6. El agente está mirando los boletos y los pasaportes.
7. Los pasajeros para Madrid están saliendo de la puerta número siete.
8. Están abordando el avión.

Estructura

1 PREPARATION

Bellringer Review

Use BRR Transparency 11.4 or write the following on the board.
Write a list of at least twenty action words you have learned so far in Spanish.

2 PRESENTATION

El presente progresivo

Step 1 Have students open their books to page 347 and lead them through Item 1.

Step 2 Give students other **-ar, -er,** and **-ir** verbs they know and have them give the present participle after they have seen how it is formed.

Step 3 Now lead students through Items 2 and 3.

Step 4 Have students take out their Bellringer Review paper (see above). Ask each student to choose a verb from the list and put it in the present progressive tense. For example: **Estoy bailando.**

3 PRACTICE

¿Cómo lo digo?

18 Have students retell the story from Activity 18 in their own words.

3 PRACTICE *(continued)*

19 Have students repeat Activity 19, this time adding a word or expression. For example: **Estoy viajando a España.**

1 PREPARATION

Bellringer Review

Use BRR Transparency 11.5 or write the following on the board.
Visualize an airport. Write five sentences telling what people are doing there. Use the present progressive.

2 PRESENTATION

Saber y conocer en el presente

¡OJO! These verb forms should be easy for students since only the **yo** form is new. Students will, however, need constant reinforcement with **yo sé.**

Step 1 Have students repeat **sé** and **conozco** as they point to themselves. Explain to them that once again they are going to learn two verbs that are irregular in the **yo** form only.

Step 2 Have students open their books to page 348 and repeat all forms of the verbs in Item 1. You may also wish to write the forms on the board.

Step 3 Lead students through Items 2 and 3 concerning the specific uses of these verbs. Have students read all the model sentences aloud.

19 **¿Qué estás haciendo?** Formen oraciones según el modelo.

Estoy viajando.
No estoy viajando. viajar

Saber y conocer en el presente

Telling what and whom you know

1. The verbs **saber** and **conocer** both mean *to know.* Note that like many Spanish verbs they have an irregular **yo** form in the present tense. All other forms are regular.

INFINITIVE	saber	conocer
yo	sé	conozco
tú	sabes	conoces
él, ella, Ud.	sabe	conoce
nosotros(as)	sabemos	conocemos
vosotros(as)	*sabéis*	*conocéis*
ellos, ellas, Uds.	saben	conocen

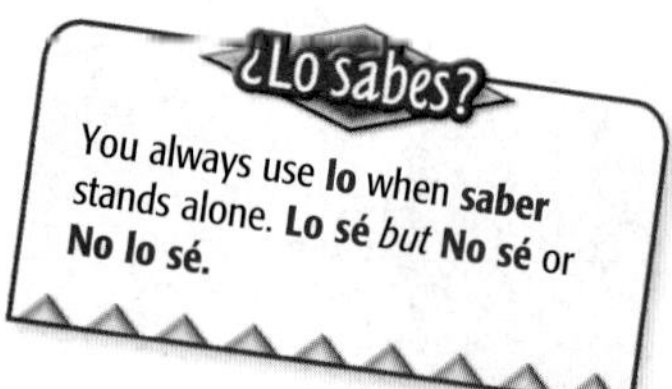

¿Lo sabes?
You always use **lo** when **saber** stands alone. **Lo sé** *but* **No sé** or **No lo sé.**

2. The verb **saber** means *to know a fact* or *to have information about something.* It also means *to know how to do something.*

Yo sé el número de nuestro vuelo.
Pero no sabemos a qué hora sale.
Yo sé esquiar y jugar tenis.

3. The verb **conocer** means *to know* in the sense of *to be acquainted with.* It is used to talk about people and complex or abstract concepts rather than simple facts.

Yo conozco a Luis.
Teodoro conoce muy bien la literatura mexicana.

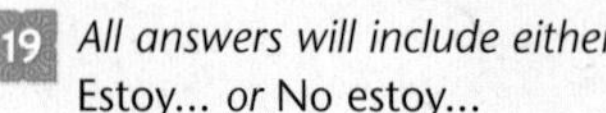

ANSWERS TO ¿Cómo lo digo?

19 *All answers will include either* Estoy... *or* No estoy...

1. comiendo
2. hablando
3. estudiando
4. bailando
5. escribiendo
6. aprendiendo
7. trabajando
8. haciendo un viaje
9. leyendo
10. saliendo para España

LEVELING

E: Activities 19, 20
A: Activity 22
C: Activities 21, 22

¿Cómo lo digo?

20 **Mi vuelo** Contesten.

1. ¿Sabes el número de tu vuelo?
2. ¿Sabes a qué hora sale?
3. ¿Sabes de qué puerta va a salir?
4. ¿Sabes la hora de tu llegada a Cancún?
5. ¿Conoces al comandante del vuelo?
6. ¿Conoces a mucha gente en Cancún?

21 **Historieta Adela Del Olmo**
Completen con **saber** o **conocer.**

PEPITA Sandra, ¿ __1__ tú a Adela Del Olmo?
SANDRA Claro que __2__ a Adela. Ella y yo somos muy buenas amigas.
PEPITA ¿ __3__ tú que ella va a Panamá?
SANDRA ¿Ella va a Panamá? No, yo no __4__ nada de su viaje. ¿Cuándo va a salir?
PEPITA Pues, ella no __5__ exactamente qué día va a salir. Pero __6__ que va a salir en junio. Ella va a hacer su reservación mañana. Yo __7__ que ella quiere tomar un vuelo directo.
SANDRA ¿Adela __8__ Panamá?
PEPITA Creo que sí. Pero yo no __9__ definitivamente. Pero yo __10__ que ella __11__ a mucha gente en Panamá.
SANDRA ¿Cómo es que ella __12__ a mucha gente allí?
PEPITA Pues, tú __13__ que ella tiene parientes en Panamá, ¿no?
SANDRA Ay, sí, es verdad. Yo __14__ que tiene familia en Panamá porque yo __15__ a su tía Lola. Y __16__ que ella es de Panamá.

La bahía de Panamá

22 **Juego** **Lo/La conozco muy bien.** Work with a classmate. Think of someone in the class whom you know quite well. Tell your partner some things you know about this person. Don't say who it is. Your partner will guess. Take turns.

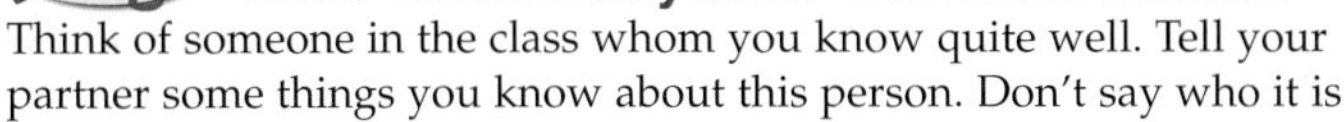

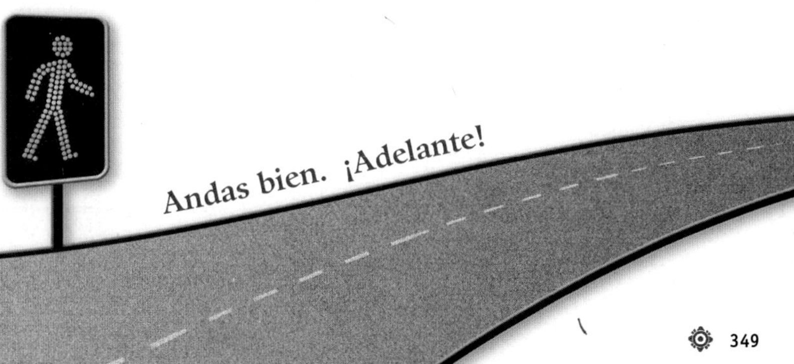

Answers to ¿Cómo lo digo?

20

1. Sí, sé el número de mi vuelo.
2. Sí, sé a qué hora sale.
3. Sí, sé de qué puerta va a salir.
4. Sí, sé la hora de mi llegada a Cancún.
5. Sí, (No, no) conozco al comandante del vuelo.
6. Sí, (No, no) conozco a mucha gente en Cancún.

21

1. conoces
2. conozco
3. Sabes
4. sé
5. sabe
6. sabe
7. sé
8. conoce
9. sé
10. sé
11. conoce
12. conoce
13. sabes
14. sé
15. conozco
16. sé

22 *Answers will vary. Students should use the vocabulary from previous chapters in their descriptions.*

3 PRACTICE

¿Cómo lo digo?

20 Activity 20 focuses on the **yo** forms of **saber** and **concocer.**

21 Since all the other forms of **saber** and **conocer** are the same as those of regular verbs, Activity 21 makes students use all forms of these two verbs.

22 **Juego** This is a good activity to use as a warm-up at the beginning of the class period.

¡Adelante!
At this point in the chapter, students have learned all the vocabulary and structure necessary to complete the chapter. The conversation and cultural readings that follow recycle all the material learned up to this point.

Learning from Photos

(page 349) Panama City is a very interesting city on the Bay of Panama on the Pacific Ocean. The original settlement, **Panamá Vieja,** was burned and sacked by the pirate Henry Morgan. There are still some ruins there. As this photo indicates, Panama City is also a city of modern high-rises: offices, banks, condominiums. The **Casco Viejo** of Panama City still maintains a colonial flavor with narrow streets of low white houses with iron balconies.

1 PREPARATION

Resource Manager

Audio Activities TE, page 138
Audio CD 7

Bellringer Review

Use BRR Transparency 11.6 or write the following on the board.
Complete with personal information.

1. **Yo quiero hacer un viaje a ___.**
2. **Yo quiero visitar a ___.**
3. **Yo voy a ir en ___.**

2 PRESENTATION

Step 1 Tell students they are going to hear a conversation between a couple who are about to take a plane trip. They are at the airport.

Step 2 Ask students to open their books to page 350 and follow along as you read the conversation aloud or have them listen to Audio CD 7.

Step 3 Have several pairs of students role-play the conversation with their books open. Let students make any changes that make sense.

Step 4 Extend the activity by having students make up their own dialogues based on the conversation at the airport.

Step 5 After presenting the conversation, go over the **¿Comprendes?** activity. If students can answer the questions with relative ease, move on. Students should not be expected to memorize the conversation.

LEVELING

A: Conversation

Conversación

Está saliendo nuestro vuelo.   

Señores pasajeros. Su atención, por favor. La compañía de aviación anuncia la salida de su vuelo ciento seis con destino a Santafé de Bogotá. Embarque inmediato por la puerta de salida número seis.

Antonio ¡Chist, Luisa! Están anunciando la salida de nuestro vuelo.
Luisa Sí, lo sé. ¡Y Dios mío! Antonio, ¿sabes dónde está Fernando?
Antonio Sí, tú conoces a Fernando. Llegó tarde otra vez. Todavía está facturando su equipaje.
Luisa Hablando de equipaje, ¿tienes los talones para nuestras maletas?
Antonio Sí, aquí están. Los tengo con los boletos.
Luisa ¿De qué puerta sale nuestro vuelo?
Antonio De la puerta número seis. Primero tenemos que pasar por el control de seguridad.
Luisa ¡Vamos ya! No vamos a esperar a Fernando. Él puede perder el vuelo si quiere. Pero yo, no.

¿Comprendes?

Contesten.

1. ¿Está Fernando con Antonio y Luisa?
2. ¿Sabe Antonio dónde está Fernando?
3. ¿Qué está haciendo Fernando?
4. ¿Siempre llega tarde?
5. ¿Qué va a perder?

Answers to ¿Comprendes?

1. No, Fernando no está con Antonio y Luisa.
2. Sí, Antonio sabe donde está Fernando.
3. Fernando está facturando su equipaje.
4. Sí, siempre llega tarde.
5. Va a perder el vuelo.

Vamos a hablar más

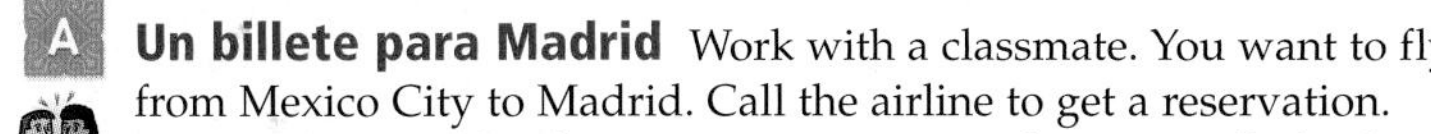

A **Un billete para Madrid** Work with a classmate. You want to fly from Mexico City to Madrid. Call the airline to get a reservation. Your partner will be the reservation agent. Before you call, think about all the information you will need to give or get from the agent: date of departure, departure time, arrival time in Madrid, flight number, price.

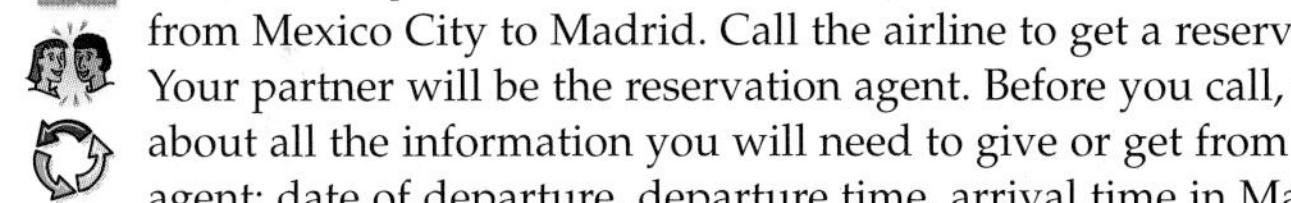

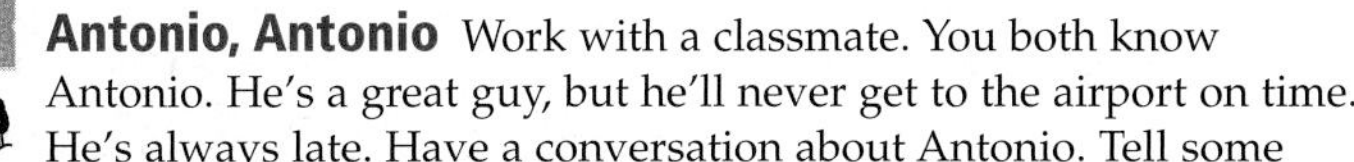

B **Antonio, Antonio** Work with a classmate. You both know Antonio. He's a great guy, but he'll never get to the airport on time. He's always late. Have a conversation about Antonio. Tell some things you know about him that always make him late.

Pronunciación

La consonante r

When a word begins with an **r** (initial position), the **r** is trilled in Spanish. Within a word, **rr** is also trilled. The Spanish trilled **r** sound does not exist in English. Repeat the following.

ra	re	ri	ro	ru
rápido	**reclama**	**Ricardo**	**Roberto**	**Rubén**
raqueta	**recoger**	**rico**	**rojo**	**rubio**
párrafo	**corre**	**perrito**	**perro**	
		aterrizar	**catarro**	

The sound for a single **r** within a word (medial position) does not exist in English either. It is trilled less than the initial **r** or **rr**. Repeat the following.

ra	re	ri	ro	ru
demora	**arena**	**Clarita**	**maletero**	**Perú**
verano		**consultorio**	**número**	**Aruba**
para			**miro**	

Repeat the following sentences.

El mesero recoge los refrescos.
El perrito de Rubén corre en la arena.
El maletero corre rápido por el aeropuerto.
El avión para Puerto Rico aterriza con una demora de una hora.
El rico tiene una raqueta en el carro.

Conversación

3 PRACTICE

Vamos a hablar más

A Before beginning this activity, students should make a list in Spanish of the information they will need to give the airline agent (their partner).

B Use the conversation on page 350 as a model for this activity.

Pronunciación

¡OJO! The following information may help students pronounce the **r** sound correctly. Remember that this is an extremely difficult sound for Americans to make. Do not frustrate a student who cannot pronounce perfectly. Many (or most) people do not, and a mild accent can be readily understood. Any native speaker will understand **"el caro"** as **el carro** even if the **r**'s are mispronounced.

Step 1 The Spanish **r** sound does not exist in English. A single **r** in medial position is pronounced like a soft **t** in English. The tongue hits the upper part of the mouth in a position similar to when we say "a lot of" *(a lotta)* very quickly in English.

Step 2 Have students play a game trying to trill the initial **r** or the **rr.** Let them exaggerate as much as they wish, and they may get it right.

Step 3 Have students repeat the sounds and words after you or Audio CD 7. Have them imitate very carefully.

Step 4 Have students open their books to page 351. Call on individuals to read the sentences carefully.

Step 5 All model sentences on page 351 can be used for dictation.

Answers to Vamos a hablar más

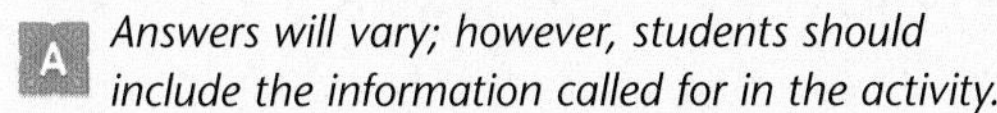

A *Answers will vary; however, students should include the information called for in the activity.*

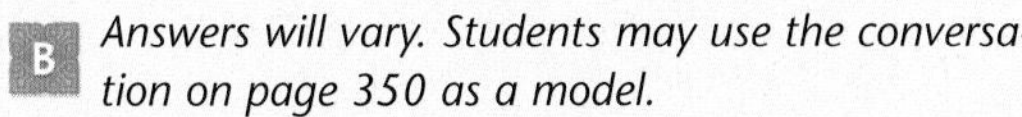

B *Answers will vary. Students may use the conversation on page 350 as a model.*

Fun Facts

Spaniards and other citizens of the European Union no longer need a passport to travel to nations within the EU. Each country in the European Union does require, however, that its citizens carry a national identification card. In Spain it is called the **Cédula de Identidad.** This ID card can be used for travel within the EU.

Lecturas culturales

Resource Manager

Audio Activities TE, page 139
Audio CD 7

Bellringer Review

Use BRR Transparency 11.7 or write the following on the board.
Write a list of the countries in South America that you know. Then give as many of their capitals as you can.

National Standards

Cultures
The reading about airline travel in South America on page 352 and the related activities on page 353 allow students to demonstrate an understanding of the importance of this mode of transportation on this continent.

PRESENTATION

Pre-reading

Step 1 Ask which members of the class have traveled by air. Did they take a domestic or international flight? What are some of the differences between domestic and international air travel? What were the good points about their trip? The bad points?

Step 2 Have students open their books to page 352. Do the Reading Strategy activity on this page. Then have students study the photos. Have them try to imagine what it is like to fly over the landscape they see in these photos.

Reading

Present the reading in two or three segments. Call on an individual to read three sentences. Then ask comprehension questions. For

Lecturas culturales

El avión en la América del Sur

El avión es un medio de transporte muy importante en la América del Sur. ¿Por qué? Pues, vamos a mirar un mapa del continente sudamericano. Van a ver que es un continente inmenso. Por consiguiente[1], toma mucho tiempo viajar de una ciudad a otra, sobre todo por tierra.

En la mayoría de los casos es imposible viajar de un lugar a otro por tierra. ¿Por qué? Porque es imposible cruzar[2] los picos de los Andes o la selva (jungla) tropical del río Amazonas. Por eso, a todas horas del día y de la noche, los aviones de muchas líneas aéreas están sobrevolando[3] el continente. Hay vuelos nacionales que enlazan[4] una ciudad con otra en el mismo país. Y hay vuelos internacionales que enlazan un país con otro.

[1]Por consiguiente *Consequently*
[2]cruzar *to cross*
[3]sobrevolando *flying over*
[4]enlazan *connect*

Reading Strategy

Identifying the main idea When reading, it is important to identify the main idea the author is expressing. Each paragraph usually discusses a different idea. The main idea is often found in the first or second sentence of a paragraph. Go through the reading quickly to find the main idea in each paragraph. Do not read every word. Once you know the main idea of the passage, go back and read it again more carefully.

El río Amazonas

Los Andes, Chile

LEVELING
A: Reading

La selva amazónica cerca de Iquitos, Perú

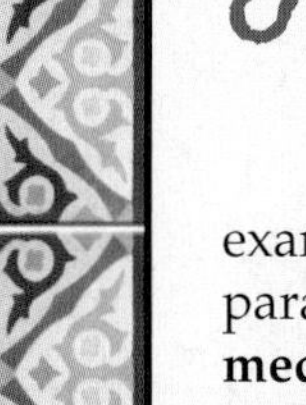

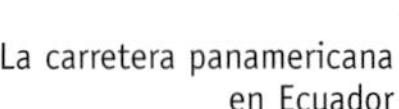

La carretera panamericana en Ecuador

¿Comprendes?

A ¿Sí o no? Digan que sí o que no.

1. El continente sudamericano es muy pequeño.
2. El tren es un medio de transporte importante en la América del Sur.
3. En muchas partes de la América del Sur, es difícil viajar por tierra.
4. Los picos andinos son muy altos.
5. Las selvas tropicales están en los picos andinos.

B Análisis Contesten.

1. ¿Por qué es el avión un medio de transporte importante en la América del Sur?
2. ¿Por qué es imposible viajar por tierra de una ciudad a otra en muchas partes de la América del Sur?
3. ¿Cuál es la diferencia entre un vuelo nacional y un vuelo internacional?
4. ¿Cuál es la idea principal de esta lectura?

Lecturas culturales

example, questions for the first paragraph may be: **¿Cuál es un medio de transporte importante en la América del Sur? ¿Cómo es el continente sudamericano? ¿Toma mucho tiempo viajar de una ciudad a otra? ¿Por qué?**

Post-reading

Have students explain in their own words why air travel is so important in South America.

¿Comprendes?

A and B Allow students to refer to the reading to look up the answers, or you may use these activities for informal assessment.

Geography Connection

The Amazon is the longest river in South America. It flows through Brazil and has many tributaries in Colombia, Ecuador, and Peru. Other important rivers of South America are **el Magdalena** (Colombia), **el Orinoco** (Venezuela), **el Paraná** (Uruguay, Paraguay, and Argentina).

Have students locate these rivers on the map of South America on page xxxi or on Map Transparency M 3.

Answers to ¿Comprendes?

A

1. No
2. No
3. Sí
4. Sí
5. No

B

1. El avión es un medio de transporte importante en la América del Sur porque el continente es inmenso.
2. Es imposible viajar por tierra en muchas partes de la América del Sur porque es imposible cruzar los picos de los Andes o las junglas de la selva tropical del río Amazonas.
3. Los vuelos nacionales enlazan una ciudad con otra en el mismo país. Los vuelos internacionales enlazan un país con otro.
4. El avión es muy importante como medio de transporte en la América del Sur.

Lectura opcional 1

National Standards

Comparisons

This reading about travel time to various locales and the related activity on this page allow students to appreciate the immensity of the Spanish-speaking world.

¡OJO! Many people find the information about distances in this **Lectura** unbelievable. Even if you do not read this selection in depth, you may wish to have students scan it to get the basic idea.

¿Comprendes?

Have students refresh their knowledge about the locations mentioned by looking at the maps on pages xxii–xxiii, xxx, and xxxi. You may also wish to project Map Transparencies M 1, M 2, and M 3.

Learning from Photos

(page 354 left) **El aeropuerto internacional de Simón Bolívar** serves Caracas. It is located on the coast in the suburb of Maiquetía.

Lectura opcional 1

El aeropuerto JFK en Nueva York

Distancias y tiempo de vuelo

Nueva York a Madrid

Los vuelos entre Estados Unidos y Europa son muy largos, ¿no? El Atlántico es un océano grande. Para cruzar el océano Atlántico toma mucho tiempo. Pero los vuelos dentro de la América del Sur pueden ser muy largos también. Vamos a hacer algunas comparaciones.

Susana Rogers está abordando un jet en el aeropuerto internacional de John F. Kennedy en Nueva York. Va a ir a Madrid. Es un vuelo sin escala[1] y después de unas siete horas, el avión va a aterrizar en el aeropuerto de Barajas en Madrid.

El aeropuerto en Caracas, Venezuela

Caracas a Buenos Aires

A la misma hora que Susana está abordando el vuelo para Madrid, José Dávila está saliendo de Caracas, Venezuela. Él va a Buenos Aires, Argentina. Su vuelo es también un vuelo sin escala. ¿Sabe usted cuánto tiempo va a tomar? José va a llegar a Ezeiza, el aeropuerto de Buenos Aires, después de un vuelo de unas siete horas. Como ven ustedes, hay muy poca diferencia entre el vuelo que cruza el océano de Nueva York a Madrid y el vuelo de Caracas a Buenos Aires.

[1]sin escala *nonstop*

A Buenos Aires
todos los días
Dinar
Dinar
Líneas Aéreas
Excelente Servicio
Unica línea aérea de cabotaje con exclusivo Menú a la carta
a Trelew 60 Km.
Tel: 45-1845
a Buenos Aires 12 Km.

¿Comprendes?

¿Lo sabes? Busquen la siguiente información.

1. el nombre de un océano
2. el nombre de un país
3. el nombre de una ciudad norteamericana
4. el nombre de una ciudad sudamericana
5. la duración del vuelo entre Nueva York y Madrid
6. la duración del vuelo entre Caracas y Buenos Aires

Answers to ¿Comprendes?

1. el Atlántico
2. los Estados Unidos (Venezuela, Argentina)
3. Nueva York
4. Caracas (Buenos Aires)
5. unas siete horas
6. unas siete horas

LEVELING

E: Reading 1

C: Reading 2

Lectura opcional 2

Las líneas de Nazca

Un vuelo muy interesante es el vuelo en una avioneta de un solo motor sobre las figuras o líneas de Nazca. ¿Qué son las figuras de Nazca? En el desierto entre Nazca y Palpa en el Perú, hay toda una serie de figuras o dibujos misteriosos en la arena. Hay figuras de aves[1], peces[2] y otros animales. Hay también figuras geométricas—rectángulos, triángulos y líneas paralelas.

El origen de las figuras de Nazca es un misterio. No sabemos de dónde vienen. Pero sabemos que tienen unos tres o cuatro mil años de edad. Y son tan[3] grandes y cubren[4] un área tan grande que para ver las figuras bien es necesario tomar un avión. La avioneta para Nazca sale todos los días de Jorge Chávez, el aeropuerto internacional de Lima.

[1]aves *birds* [2]peces *fish* [3]tan *so* [4]cubren *cover*

¿Comprendes?

Nazca Contesten.

1. ¿Sobre qué vuela la avioneta?
2. ¿Cuántos motores tiene la avioneta?
3. ¿Dónde están las figuras o líneas de Nazca?
4. ¿Están en un desierto las figuras?
5. ¿Es un misterio el origen de las figuras o sabemos de dónde vienen?
6. ¿Qué tipo de figuras o líneas hay?
7. ¿Cuántos años tienen?
8. ¿Cubren un área muy grande las líneas?
9. ¿De dónde salen los aviones para ver las líneas?

Answers to ¿Comprendes?

1. La avioneta vuela sobre las figuras o líneas de Nazca.
2. La avioneta tiene sólo un motor.
3. Las figuras o líneas de Nazca están entre Nazca y Palpa en el Perú.
4. Sí, las figuras están en un desierto.
5. Es un misterio el origen de las figuras.
6. Hay figuras de aves, peces y otros animales. Hay también figuras geométricas.
7. Tienen unos tres o cuatro mil años.
8. Sí, las líneas cubren un área muy grande.
9. Los aviones salen de Jorge Chávez, el aeropuerto internacional de Lima.

Lectura opcional 2

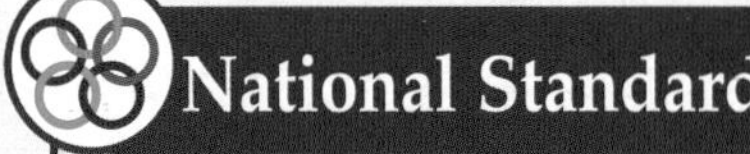

National Standards

Cultures

The reading about the Nazca lines in Peru and the related activity on this page allow students to learn about one of the unsolved prehistoric mysteries in the Spanish-speaking world.

¡OJO! The readings on pages 354–355 are optional. You may skip them completely, have the entire class read them, have only several students read them and report to the class, or assign either of them for extra credit.

Teaching Tips

Use the questions in **¿Comprendes?** to judge how well students understood the reading.

Learning from Photos

(page 355) The Pan American Highway goes right through the area where the Nazca lines are located, but it is impossible to see them from the road. The purpose of the lines is unknown, but they have caused a great deal of speculation. Some say they may have served as a calendar.

Unfortunately the Nazca lines suffered some damage in 1998 because of the flooding caused by El Niño.

Conexiones

National Standards

Connections
This reading about finances establishes a connection with another discipline, allowing students to reinforce and further their knowledge of mathematics through the study of Spanish.

¡OJO! The readings in the **Conexiones** section are optional. They focus on some of the major disciplines taught in schools and universities. The vocabulary is useful for discussing such topics as history, literature, art, economics, business, science, etc. You may choose any of the following ways to do the readings in the **Conexiones** sections.

Independent reading Have students read the selections and do the post-reading activities as homework, which you collect. This option is least intrusive on class time and requires a minimum of teacher involvement.

Homework with in-class follow-up Assign the readings and post-reading activities as homework. Review and discuss the material in class the next day.

Intensive in-class activity This option includes a pre-reading vocabulary presentation, in-class reading and discussion, assignment of the activities for homework, and a discussion of the assignment in class the following day.

Conexiones

Las matemáticas

Las finanzas

When we travel we have to take into account how much the trip will cost. A wise traveler has some idea of an affordable travel budget. Can the budget afford a luxury hotel or is it better to stay in an inexpensive hostel? Some travel ads, like this one below, suggest that people can travel now and pay later. Before making a decision, one must consider the financial impact. When are the payments due? What is the interest rate?

Here is some important information about everyday finances that may come in handy when traveling to a Spanish-speaking country.

la tarjeta de crédito

el cheque de viajero

el dinero en efectivo

Vocabulary Expansion

el presupuesto	*budget*	**pagar a plazos**	*to pay off (in installments)*
los gastos	*expenses*	**un pronto, un pie**	*down payment*
la factura	*bill*	**una mensualidad**	*monthly payment*
una tarjeta de crédito	*credit card*	**la tasa de interés**	*interest rate*
(el dinero) en efectivo	*cash*		
cambiar dinero	*to change money*		
el tipo de cambio	*exchange rate*		

Las finanzas

Si vamos a hacer un viaje, es necesario saber cuánto va a costar. Es una buena idea preparar un presupuesto[1]. El presupuesto nos permite saber cuánto dinero tenemos y cuánto podemos gastar[2]. El presupuesto tiene que incluir los siguientes gastos[3]:

precio del vuelo
transporte local
hotel
comidas y refrescos
entradas
—museos, teatros

Cuando viajamos, podemos pagar nuestras cuentas o facturas con una tarjeta de crédito, cheques de viajero o (dinero) en efectivo.

En un país extranjero no vamos a pagar con dólares. Vamos a usar la moneda nacional—pesos o soles, por ejemplo. Tenemos que cambiar dinero. En México es necesario cambiar dólares en pesos. Antes de cambiar dinero, es importante saber el tipo de cambio[4].

Si decidimos pagar a plazos[5], es necesario pagar un pronto[6] (un pie, un enganche). Luego hay que hacer un pago cada mes—una mensualidad. Antes de decidir pagar algo a plazos, es necesario saber la tasa de interés[7] que tenemos que pagar. Todos debemos ser consumidores inteligentes porque la tasa de interés puede ser muy alta.

[1]presupuesto *budget*
[2]gastar *to spend*
[3]gastos *expenses*
[4]tipo de cambio *exchange rate*
[5]pagar a plazos *to pay in installments*
[6]pronto *down payment*
[7]tasa de interés *interest rate*

Guanajuato, México

¿Comprendes?

La palabra, por favor. Completen.

1. El ____ nos indica cuánto dinero tenemos y cuánto podemos gastar en varias categorías.
2. El dinero que tenemos que pagar es un ____.
3. Los ____ no pueden exceder la cantidad de dinero que tenemos.
4. Podemos pagar nuestras ____ con una tarjeta de crédito, ____ o ____.
5. En un país ____, no vamos a pagar con dólares.
6. En México tenemos que ____ dólares en pesos mexicanos. En España tenemos que ____ dólares en euros.
7. Antes de cambiar dinero es necesario saber el ____.
8. Si uno decide comprar algo a plazos, es necesario pagar un ____ al principio.
9. Un pago mensual es una ____.
10. Si vamos a comprar algo a plazos, es siempre necesario saber la ____ que puede ser bastante alta.

Conexiones

PRESENTATION

Las matemáticas
Las finanzas

Step 1 This reading contains some very useful vocabulary for students interested in fields such as retailing, accounting, etc. The Vocabulary Expansion box on page 356 contains some high-frequency financial terms that appear in the reading. You may want to go over them before beginning the reading.

Step 2 Have students read the introduction in English on page 356.

Step 3 Have students read the selection on page 357 and do the **¿Comprendes?** activity that follows.

Assessment

You may wish to give the following quiz to students who have done the **Conexiones** section. Answer.

1. **¿Qué debemos preparar antes de hacer un viaje?**
2. **¿Qué nos permite saber el presupuesto?**
3. **¿Cuáles son algunos gastos que tenemos cuando viajamos?**
4. **¿Cómo podemos pagar nuestras cuentas o facturas?**
5. **¿Por qué tenemos que cambiar dinero?**
6. **Si vamos a pagar a plazos, ¿qué es necesario pagar enseguida?**
7. **¿Qué tenemos que saber antes de decidir pagar algo a plazos?**

Answers to ¿Comprendes?

1. presupuesto
2. gasto
3. gastos
4. cuentas (facturas), cheques de viajero, (dinero) en efectivo
5. extranjero
6. cambiar, cambiar
7. tipo de cambio
8. pronto (pie, enganche)
9. mensualidad
10. tasa de interés

LEVELING

A: Reading

Use what you have learned

Recycling

These activities allow students to use the vocabulary and structure from this chapter in completely open-ended, real-life situations.

PRESENTATION

Encourage students to say as much as possible when they do these activities. Tell them not to be afraid to make mistakes, since the goal of the activities is real-life communication. If someone in the group makes an error, allow the others to politely correct him or her. Let students choose the activities they would like to do.

You may wish to divide students into pairs or groups. Encourage students to elaborate on the basic theme and to be creative. They may use props, pictures, or posters if they wish.

PRACTICE

1 Encourage students to be creative regarding their destinations!

2 This activity can be done individually, or students may prefer to plan their trip with a partner. Have students tell the class about their trip.

¡Te toca a ti!

Use what you have learned

1 ¿Adónde vas?

✔ *Talk about a plane trip*

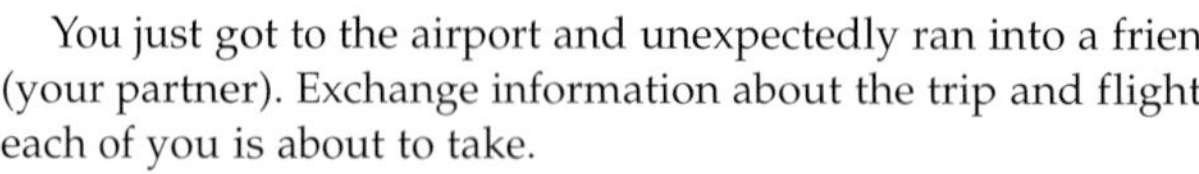

You just got to the airport and unexpectedly ran into a friend (your partner). Exchange information about the trip and flight each of you is about to take.

2 ¿Vas a hacer un viaje?

✔ *Plan a plane trip to a Spanish-speaking destination*

Go to a travel agency in your community. Get some travel brochures and plan a plane trip. Tell all about your trip.

For more information about travel agencies and tours in the Spanish-speaking world, go to the Glencoe Spanish Web site: spanish.glencoe.com

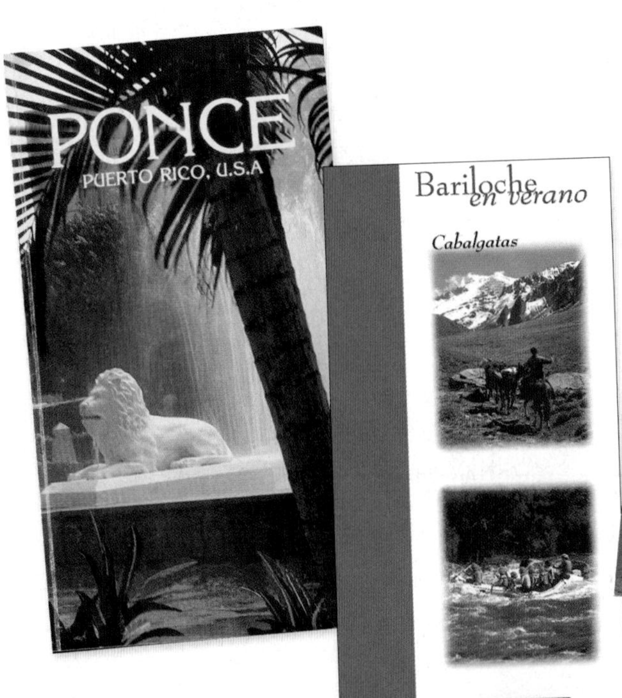

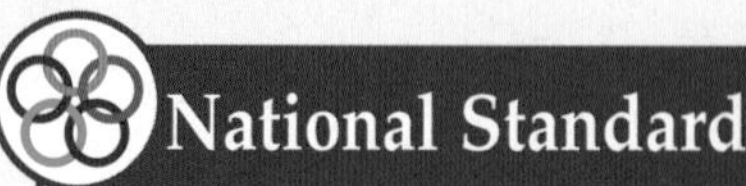

National Standards

Communities

Students who do Activity 2 will find out more about the Spanish-speaking world by using resources in their community.

Answers to ¡Te toca a ti!

1 *Answers will vary; however, students should give as many details about their flight as possible using the vocabulary from this chapter.*

2 *Answers will vary; however, students should use the vocabulary presented in this chapter to describe their trip.*

ESCRIBIR

3 Un viaje en avión

✔ ***Write about airport activities and services aboard the plane***

You have a Venezuelan pen pal who is going to visit you this winter. This will be his or her first flight. Write your pen pal a letter and explain all the things he or she is going to experience before, during, and after the flight.

4 Un concurso

In order to win an all-expense-paid trip to the Spanish-speaking country of your choice, you have to write an essay in Spanish and send it to the company sponsoring the trip. Read the following essay questions and then write your answers. You really want to go, so be sure to plan your answers carefully and check your work.

¿A qué país quiere usted viajar?
¿Cómo quiere usted viajar?
¿Por qué quiere usted ir allí?
¿Qué quiere usted hacer allí?
¿Qué quiere aprender?

Writing Strategy

Answering an essay question
When writing an answer to an essay question, first read the question carefully to look for clues to determine how your answer should be structured. Then begin by restating the essay question in a single statement in your introduction. Next, support the statement in the body of the answer with facts, details, and reasons. Finally, close with a conclusion that summarizes your answer.

ANSWERS TO ¡Te toca a ti!

3 *Answers will vary. Students should use the vocabulary and forms presented in this chapter.*

4 *Answers will vary depending on the students' destinations and their reasons for wanting to go there.*

¡Te toca a ti!

Writing Development

Have students keep a notebook or portfolio containing their best written work from each chapter. These selected writings can be based on assignments from the Student Textbook and the Workbook. The two activities on page 359 are examples of writing assignments that may be included in each student's portfolio. On page 142 in the Workbook, students will begin to develop an organized autobiography **(Mi autobiografía).** These workbook pages may also become a part of their portfolio.

3 In addition to describing what the pen pal is going to do at the airport, students may want to include the name of the city where the pen pal will land and what the weather is like there.

Writing Strategy

Answering an essay question Have students read the Writing Strategy on page 359. Encourage students to first make an outline that includes the elements mentioned in the Writing Strategy. The illustration on page 359 suggests one reason for wanting to go to a Spanish-speaking country. However, students should be encouraged to give other reasons if they wish.

Leveling

These activities encompass all three levels. All students will be able to do them at a sophistication level commensurate with their ability in Spanish. Some students will be able to speak for several minutes, and others may be able to give just a few sentences. This is to be expected when students are functioning completely on their own generating their own language to the best of their ability.

Resource Manager

Communication Transparency C 11
Quizzes, pages 55–59
Performance Assessment, Task 11
Tests, pages 169–184
Situation Cards, Chapter 11
ExamView® Pro, Chapter 11
Maratón mental Videoquiz, Chapter 11

Assessment

This is a pre-test for students to take before you administer the chapter test. Note that each section is cross-referenced so students can easily find the material they have to review in case they made errors. You may use Assessment Answers Transparency A 11 to do the assessment in class, or you may assign this assessment for homework. You can correct the assessment yourself, or you may prefer to project the answers on the overhead in class.

Glencoe Technology

MINDJOGGER VHS/DVD

You may wish to help your students prepare for the chapter test by playing the MindJogger game show. Teams will compete against each other to review chapter vocabulary and structure and sharpen listening comprehension skills.

Vocabulario

1 Identifiquen.

To review **Palabras 1**, turn to pages 336–337.

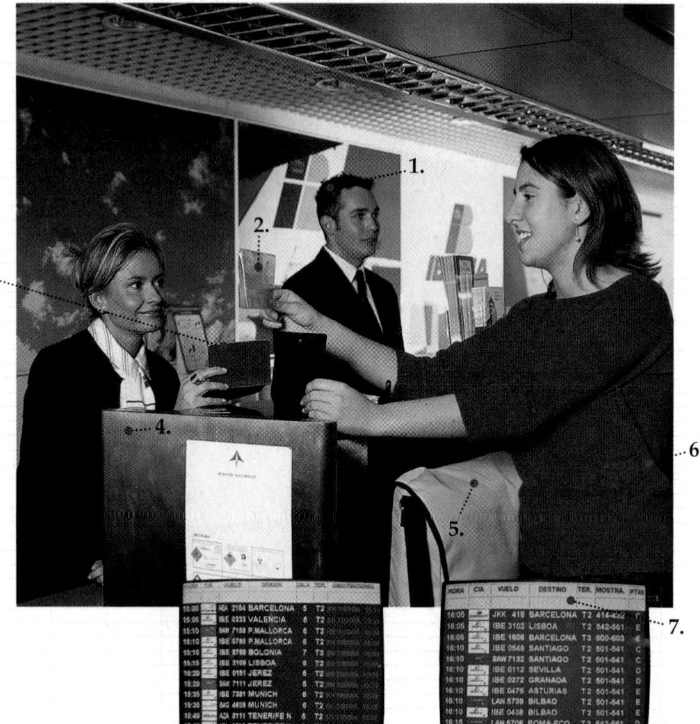

2 ¿Sí o no?

To review **Palabras 2**, turn to pages 340–341.

8. Cuándo los pasajeros desembarcan de un vuelo, tienen que pasar por el control de seguridad.
9. Después de un vuelo, los pasajeros reclaman su equipaje.
10. A veces un(a) agente de aduana inspecciona el equipaje de los pasajeros cuando desembarcan de un vuelo internacional (cuando llegan de un país extranjero).

Music Connection

Canta con Justo

The song **Viajando por Latinoamérica** will be easy for learners of all ability levels. It will help students practice vocabulary related to travel introduced in this chapter. You may wish to have students hear the recorded version of **Viajando por Latinoamérica.** It can be found on Track 6 of the **Canta con Justo** music CD. In addition, students can watch Justo perform this song on the **Justo Lamas ¡En vivo!** music video that accompanies **¡Buen viaje!** On the DVD of this music video, students can perform karaoke to any of Justo's songs.

Answers to

1

1. el agente
2. el billete (el boleto)
3. el pasaporte
4. el mostrador
5. el equipaje
6. la pasajera
7. la pantalla de salidas y llegadas

2

8. No
9. Sí
10. Sí

Estructura

3 Contesten.

11. Cuando haces un viaje, ¿pones tu ropa en una maleta o en una mochila?
12. ¿Traes mucho equipaje cuando haces un viaje largo?
13. ¿Vienen ustedes a la fiesta de Marta?
14. ¿Sale el vuelo para Madrid del aeropuerto internacional?

To review **hacer, poner, traer, salir,** turn to page 344.

4 Escriban según el modelo.

El avión aterriza ahora. →
El avión está aterrizando ahora.

15. Ellas hacen sus maletas ahora.
16. Su vuelo llega ahora.
17. No como nada.
18. ¿Qué lees?

To review the present progressive, turn to page 347.

5 Completen con **saber** o **conocer.**

19. Yo no ____ a qué hora sale nuestro vuelo.
20. Ellos ____ muchas ciudades de España.
21. Yo ____ al amigo de Maricarmen. Es un tipo muy simpático.
22. ¿Tú ____ dónde vive (él)?

To review **saber** and **conocer,** turn to page 348.

Cultura

6 ¿Sí o no?

23. El continente sudamericano es bastante pequeño.
24. Es imposible cruzar los picos altos de los Andes por tierra.
25. Hay muchas selvas tropicales en los picos andinos donde hace mucho frío.

To review this cultural information, turn to page 352.

Assessment

SPANISH Online

The **Glencoe Spanish Web** site (spanish.glencoe.com) offers options that enable you and your students to experience the Spanish-speaking world via the Internet. For each **Capítulo,** there are activties, games, and quizzes. In addition, an *Enrichment* section offers students an opportunity to visit Web sites related to the theme of the chapter.

Career Connection

Because of the popularity of international travel (for business and pleasure) to and from the Spanish-speaking world, Spanish is an important communication tool. Have students make a list of at least four professions in the travel industry for which Spanish would be useful or necessary. Have students try to arrange interviews with some people in these professions.

FOLDABLES™ Study Organizer **Dinah Zike's Study Guides**

Your students may wish to use Foldable 10 to organize, display, and arrange data as they learn to describe many situations in Spanish. You may wish to encourage them to draw a picture from each chapter as they continue to gather facts and make observations about all the different topics they will be studying.

An *envelope fold* is also ideal for collecting and reviewing information students have learned about particular subjects.

Answers to Assessment

3

11. Cuando hago un viaje, pongo mi ropa en una maleta.
12. Sí, (No, no) traigo mucho equipaje cuando hago un viaje largo.
13. Sí, (No, no) venimos a la fiesta de Marta.
14. Sí (No), el vuelo para Madrid (no) sale del aeropuerto internacional.

4

15. Ellas están haciendo sus maletas ahora.
16. Su vuelo está llegando ahora.
17. No estoy comiendo nada.
18. ¿Qué estás leyendo?

5

19. sé
20. conocen
21. conozco
22. sabes

6

23. No
24. Sí
25. No

¡Hablo como un pro!

This unique page gives students the opportunity to speak freely and say whatever they can, using the vocabulary and structures they have learned in the chapter. The illustration serves to remind students of precisely what they know how to say in Spanish. There are no activities that students do not have the ability to describe or talk about in Spanish. The art not only depicts the vocabulary and content of this chapter, but also reinforces what they learned in previous chapters.

You may wish to use this page in many ways. Some possibilities are to have students do the following:

1. Look at the illustration and identify items by giving the correct Spanish words.
2. Make up sentences about what they see in the illustration.
3. Make up questions about the illustration. They can call on another class member to respond if you do this as a class activity, or you may prefer to allow students to work in small groups. This activity is extremely beneficial because it enables students to actively use interrogative words.
4. Answer questions you ask them about the illustration.
5. Work in pairs and make up a conversation based on the illustration.
6. Look at the illustration and give a complete oral review of what they see.
7. Look at the illustration and write a paragraph (or essay) about it.

You can also use this page as an assessment or testing tool, taking into account individual differences by having students go from simple to quite complicated tasks. The assessment can be either oral or written. You may wish to use the rubrics provided on pages T20–T21 as you give students the following directions.

1. Identify the topic or situation of the illustration.
2. Give the Spanish words for as many items as you can.
3. Think of as many sentences as you can to describe the illustration.
4. Go over your sentences and put them in the best sequencing to give a coherent story based on the illustration.

¡Hablo como un pro!

Tell all you can about this illustration.

Vocabulario

Getting around an airport—Departure

el aeropuerto
el taxi
la línea aérea
el avión
el mostrador
el/la agente
el billete, el boleto
el pasaporte
la pantalla de salidas y llegadas
la tarjeta de embarque
el número del asiento
el número del vuelo
el destino
la puerta de salida, la sala de salida
la sección de no fumar
la báscula
el talón
la maleta
el/la maletero(a)
el/la pasajero(a)
el equipaje (de mano)
el control de seguridad

Getting around an airport—Arrival

el control de pasaportes
la aduana
el reclamo de equipaje

Identifying airline personnel

el/la agente
la tripulación
el/la comandante, el/la piloto
el/la copiloto
el asistente de vuelo
la asistente de vuelo

How well do you know your vocabulary?

- Choose a word from the list.
- Have a classmate give a related word: **el viaje, viajar.**

Describing airport activities

hacer un viaje
dar la bienvenida
salir a tiempo
  tarde
  con una demora
revisar el boleto
pasar por el control de seguridad
tomar un vuelo
facturar el equipaje
abrir las maletas
inspeccionar
abordar
desembarcar
despegar
aterrizar
reclamar (recoger) el equipaje

VIDEOTUR

Episodio 11

In this video episode, you will join Julián and Francisco as they discuss Julián's travel plans. See page 502 for more information.

Other useful expressions

el país
extranjero(a)
permitir
venir
poner
saber
conocer

¡OJO! You will notice that the vocabulary list here is not translated. This has been done intentionally, since we feel that by the time students have finished the material in the chapter they should be familiar with the meanings of all the words. If there are several words they still do not know, we recommend that they refer to the **Palabras 1** and **2** sections in the chapter or go to the dictionaries at the end of this book to find the meanings. However, if you prefer that your students have the English translations, please refer to Vocabulary Transparency 11.1, where you will find all these words with their translations.

Vocabulario

Vocabulary Review

The words and phrases in the **Vocabulario** have been taught for productive use in this chapter. They are summarized here as a resource for both student and teacher. This list also serves as a convenient resource for the **¡Te toca a ti!** activities on pages 358 and 359. There are approximately twelve cognates in this vocabulary list. Have students find them.

VIDEO VHS/DVD

The Video Program allows students to see how the chapter vocabulary and structures are used by native speakers within an engaging story line. For maximum reinforcement, show the video episode as a final activity for Chapter 11.

Reaching All Students

For the Younger Students

Mi tarjeta de embarque Have students draw a boarding pass for the destination of their choice similar to the one on page 338 or page 343. Have them fill it in with the appropriate information and then have them tell all about it.

La pantalla de salidas y llegadas Have students draw an airport departure and arrival screen similar to the one on page 336. Now have them work in pairs and ask each other questions about the information on it.

Preview

This section reviews the salient points from Chapters 8–11. In the **Conversación** students will review health vocabulary, verbs with an irregular **yo** form, and the preterite in context. In the **Estructura** section, they will study the uses of **ser** vs. **estar,** the conjugations of irregular verbs, and the formation of the preterite. They will practice these structures as they talk about skiing, sports, and other leisure activities.

Resource Manager

Workbook: Check-Up 3, pages 143–148
Tests, pages 185–193
Performance Assessment, Tasks 8–11

PRESENTATION

Conversación

Step 1 Have students open their books to page 364. Ask two students to read the conversation aloud using as much expression as possible.

Step 2 Go over the questions in the **¿Comprendes?** section.

Learning from Realia

(page 364) Ask students to figure out what services are offered by this clinic in Granada.

Repaso

Conversación

El pobre Juanito

Anita Juanito fue a Navacerrada a esquiar.

Antonio Ah, sí. ¿Qué tal lo pasó?

Anita Muy bien. Pasó un fin de semana estupendo. Pero, ¿sabes dónde está ahora?

Antonio No sé. No tengo idea.

Anita Pues, está en la consulta del médico.

Antonio ¿Qué tiene? ¿Qué le pasó?

Anita No sé. Le duele mucho el estómago y no sabe si tiene fiebre.

Antonio Pues, tú conoces a Juanito. Siempre está haciendo cosas que no debe hacer. ¿Qué comió?

¿Comprendes?

El pobre Juanito Contesten.

1. ¿Adónde fue Juanito?
2. ¿Por qué fue a Navacerrada?
3. ¿Qué tal fue el fin de semana?
4. ¿Dónde está Juanito ahora?
5. ¿Por qué? ¿Qué tiene?
6. ¿Qué está haciendo siempre Juanito?
7. ¿Comió algo malo Juanito?

CLINICA MEDICA ARABIAL

HOMEOPATIA — OXIGENOTERAPIA
— HOMOTOXICOLOGIA
— HOMEOSINIATRIA
TERAPIAS BIOLOGICAS — MESOTERAPIA
— ACUPUNTURA
— NEURALTERAPIA
— MEDICINA ESTETICA
— FITOTERAPIA

C/. Arabial, 118 - 1.º D
Teléfono 42 1...
GRANADA

RECUERDE:

«PORQUE HAY OTROS CAMINOS PARA SU CURACION, NO DEJE DE CONSULTARNOS CUALQUIERA QUE SEA SU PROBLEMA».

CLINICA MEDICA ARABIAL

SE RUEGA PEDIR CITA AL TELEFONO 42 13 57

Answers to ¿Comprendes?

1. Juanito fue a Navacerrada.
2. Fue a Navacerrada a esquiar.
3. Pasó un fin de semana estupendo.
4. Juanito está en la consulta del médico.
5. Le duele mucho el estómago.
6. Siempre está haciendo cosas que no debe hacer.
7. No sabemos si Juanito comió algo malo.

Estructura

Ser y estar

1. The verbs **ser** and **estar** both mean *to be*. **Ser** is used to tell where someone or something is from. It is also used to describe an inherent trait or characteristic.

   Roberto es de Los Ángeles.
   Roberto es inteligente y guapo.

2. **Estar** is used to tell where someone or something is located. It is also used to describe a temporary condition or state.

   Ahora Roberto está en Madrid.
   Madrid está en España.
   Roberto está muy contento en Madrid.

3. **Estar** is used with a present participle to form the progressive tense.

   Estamos estudiando y aprendiendo mucho.

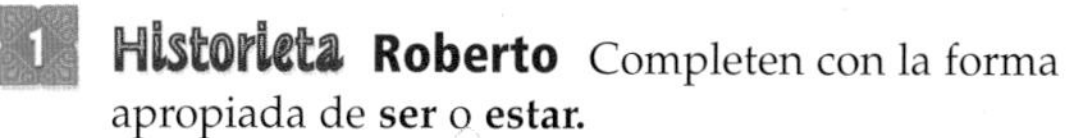

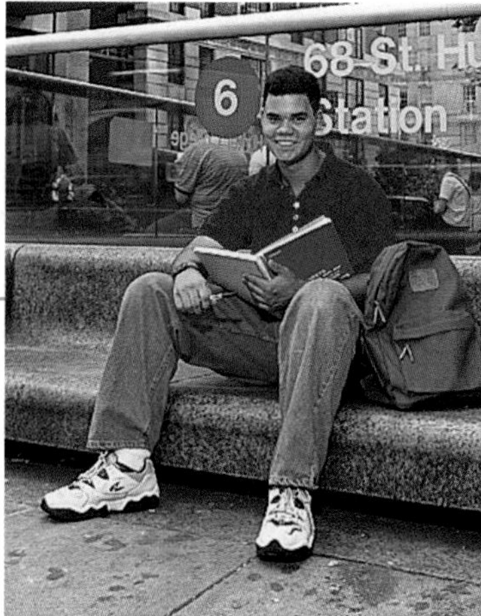

Nueva York

1 **Historieta Roberto** Completen con la forma apropiada de **ser** o **estar**.

Roberto __1__ de Caracas. Él __2__ muy simpático. __3__ muy gracioso también. Ahora él __4__ en Nueva York. __5__ estudiando en la universidad. Roberto __6__ muy contento en Nueva York.

Nueva York __7__ en el noreste de Estados Unidos. Nueva York __8__ muy grande. __9__ muy interesante también. A Roberto le gusta mucho.

Hoy Roberto __10__ de mal humor. No __11__ muy contento. La nota que recibió en un curso no __12__ muy buena y Roberto __13__ muy inteligente.

Verbos irregulares en el presente

The following verbs all have an irregular **yo** form in the present tense. All other forms are regular.

HACER	**yo hago**	TRAER	**yo traigo**	SABER	**yo sé**
PONER	**yo pongo**	SALIR	**yo salgo**	CONOCER	**yo conozco**

PRESENTATION

Ser y estar

Step 1 For review purposes, reverse the usual procedure and have students read the Spanish sentences and explain why either **ser** or **estar** is used.

Step 2 Write **ser** and **estar** on the board and list their uses under the appropriate infinitive as students explain the rules.

PRACTICE

1 After going over Activity 1, have a student tell all about Roberto in his or her own words.

PRESENTATION

Verbos irregulares en el presente

Have students give all the forms of some of these verbs. Emphasize that all other forms are regular. Only **yo** is irregular.

ANSWERS TO Repaso

1

1. es
2. es
3. Es
4. está
5. Está
6. está
7. está
8. es
9. Es
10. está
11. está
12. es
13. es

PRACTICE

2 Activity 2 can be done as a paired activity.

PRESENTATION

Los pronombres de complemento

Step 1 Have students open their books to page 366. Read Items 1–3 with them.

Step 2 When going over Item 2, you may write the sentences on the board. Put a box around the direct object (noun) and draw an arrow from the noun to the pronoun as you box in the pronoun.

PRACTICE

3 This is a point that students find quite difficult. It will be reinforced many times. If students have problems doing Activity 3, review some of the activities in the **Estructura** section of Chapters 9 and 10.

Literary Companion

When you finish this review section, if you wish, have students read the adaptation of **«La camisa de Margarita»** by Ricardo Palma on pages 478–483.

2 **Entrevista** Contesten personalmente.

1. ¿Haces un viaje a Madrid?
2. ¿A qué hora sales para el aeropuerto?
3. ¿Pones las maletas en la maletera del carro?
4. ¿Traes mucho equipaje?
5. ¿Sabes a qué hora sale tu vuelo?
6. ¿Sabes el número del vuelo?
7. ¿Conoces Madrid?
8. ¿Sabes hablar español?

Los pronombres de complemento

1. The object pronouns **me, te,** and **nos** can function as either direct or indirect object pronouns. Note that the object pronouns in Spanish precede the conjugated verb.

   ¿Te vio Juan? **Sí, Juan me vio y me dio el libro.**

2. **Lo, los, la,** and **las** function as direct object pronouns only. They can replace persons or things.

Pablo compró el boleto.	**Pablo lo compró.**
Pablo compró los boletos.	**Pablo los compró.**
Elena compró la raqueta.	**Elena la compró.**
Elena compró las raquetas.	**Elena las compró.**
Yo vi a los muchachos.	**Yo los vi.**

3. **Le** and **les** function as indirect object pronouns only.

   Yo le escribí una carta (a él, a ella, a usted).
   Yo les escribí una carta (a ellos, a ellas, a ustedes).

Chacaltaya, una estación de esquí en Bolivia

 **¡A esquiar!** Cambien los sustantivos a pronombres.

1. Llevo *los esquís* a la cancha.
2. También llevo *las botas.*
3. Compro *el boleto* en la taquilla.
4. Veo a *mi hermana* en el telesquí.
5. Doy *el boleto* a mi hermana.
6. Ella da *los esquís* a los muchachos.

Literary Companion

You may wish to read the adaptation of «La camisa de Margarita» by Ricardo Palma. You will find this literary selection on pages 478–483.

Answers to Repaso

1. Sí, hago un viaje a Madrid.
2. Salgo para el aeropuerto a las ___.
3. Sí, (No, no) pongo las maletas en la maletera del carro.
4. Sí, (No, no) traigo mucho equipaje.
5. Sí, (No, no) sé a qué hora sale mi vuelo.
6. Sí, (No, no) sé el número del vuelo.
7. Sí, (No, no) conozco Madrid.
8. Sí, (No, no) sé hablar español.

1. Los llevo a la cancha.
2. También las llevo.
3. Lo compro en la taquilla.
4. La veo en el telesquí.
5. Lo doy a mi hermana.
6. Ella los da a los muchachos. (Los da a los muchachos.)

El pretérito

1. The preterite is used to express an event that started and ended in the past. Review the forms of the preterite of regular verbs.

INFINITIVE	mirar	comer	vivir
yo	miré	comí	viví
tú	miraste	comiste	viviste
él, ella, Ud.	miró	comió	vivió
nosotros(as)	miramos	comimos	vivimos
vosotros(as)	*mirasteis*	*comisteis*	*vivisteis*
ellos, ellas, Uds.	miraron	comieron	vivieron

2. The forms of **ir** and **ser** in the preterite are identical. The meaning is made clear by the context of the sentence.

fui **fuiste** **fue** **fuimos** ***fuisteis*** **fueron**

4 **¿Qué hicieron todos?** Contesten.

1. ¿Fuiste al museo ayer?
   ¿Viste una exposición de arte?
   ¿Tomaste un refresco en la cafetería del museo?
2. ¿Salieron ustedes anoche?
   ¿Fueron al cine?
   ¿Tomaron el metro?
3. ¿Esquió Roberto?
   ¿Subió la pista en el telesilla?
   ¿Bajó la pista para expertos?
4. ¿Pasaron tus amigos el fin de semana en la playa?
   ¿Te escribieron una tarjeta postal?
   ¿Nadaron y tomaron el sol en la playa?

5 **Deportes** The Latin American exchange student (your partner) at your school asks you what sports you played last year. Tell him or her and say which one you liked most and why. Then ask the exchange student the same questions.

6 **Diversiones** Work with a classmate. Discuss what you each do when you have free time. Do you like to do the same activities?

PRESENTATION

El pretérito

Step 1 Have students open their books to page 367. Write the verb forms from the chart on the board. Underline the endings.

Step 2 Have the class repeat all forms of the same verb. Then have them read across—all the **yo** forms, all the **tú** forms, etc.

PRACTICE

4 The preterite will be reintroduced frequently. If students have problems doing Activity 4, review some of the activities in the **Estructura** section of Chapters 9 and 10.

5 **and** **6** Allow students to select the activity they want to do.

Answers to Repaso

4

1. Sí, (No, no) fui al museo ayer.
   Sí, (No, no) vi una exposición de arte. Sí, (No, no) tomé un refresco en la cafetería del museo.
2. Sí, (No, no) salimos anoche.
   Sí, (No, no) fuimos al cine.
   Sí, (No, no) tomamos el metro.
3. Sí (No), Roberto (no) esquió.
   Sí, (No, no) subió la pista en el telesilla.
   Sí, (No, no) bajó la pista para expertos.
4. Sí (No), mis amigos (no) pasaron el fin de semana en la playa.
   Sí, (No, no) me escribieron una tarjeta postal.
   Sí, nadaron y tomaron el sol en la playa.

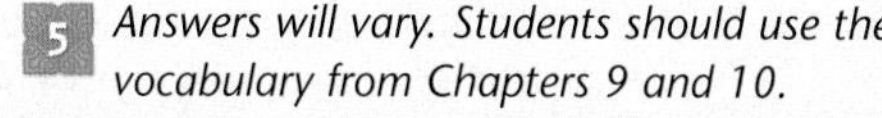

5 *Answers will vary. Students should use the vocabulary from Chapters 9 and 10.*

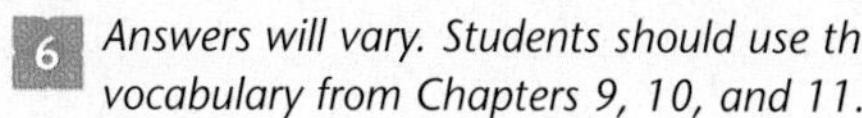

6 *Answers will vary. Students should use the vocabulary from Chapters 9, 10, and 11.*

People EN ESPAÑOL

Entérate Región andina

This section was prepared by Time Learning Ventures of Time Incorporated. Its purpose is to give students greater insight, through visual images and fun articles, into the culture and people of the **Región andina.** You may wish to explain to your students that Peru, Bolivia, and Ecuador are the three countries included when we talk about this region.

Have students look at the photographs and read the articles. Encourage the students to talk about what they've seen and read. Let them say anything they can, using the vocabulary they have learned to this point.

In addition to their spectacular beauty and formidable volcanic mountain ranges, Peru, Bolivia, and Ecuador are also known for the richness of their indigenous cultures. During Spanish rule of this region, many of the indigenous groups incorporated colonial traditions into their own—the result is a fascinating cultural kaleidoscope including music, artisan crafts, religious practices, and cuisine.

People EN ESPAÑOL Entérate Región andina

Una expedición a los países andinos

Bolivia es un país sudamericano. ¿De dónde o de qué origen es el nombre Bolivia? Antes de[1] llegar los conquistadores españoles, ¿qué país es el centro de la civilización de los famosos incas? Y, ¿de qué origen es el nombre de otro país de los Andes, Ecuador? ¿Cómo contestas?

- **"Bolivia" es del nombre del gran héroe y libertador latinoamericano, Simón Bolívar. Es la contestación correcta.**
- **Perú es el centro de la civilización incaica—de los incas. Una vez más, una respuesta correcta.**
- **Ecuador recibe su nombre de la línea del ecuador, de la línea ecuatorial que divide el mundo en dos hemisferios: el hemisferio norte y el hemisferio sur.**

Hay otros datos de la región andina que son muy interesantes. La UNESCO de las Naciones Unidas declara los siguientes sitios Patrimonio Mundial de la Humanidad.

Entérate Perú

Machu Picchu Las famosas ruinas de los incas están en un pico estrecho[2] de los majestuosos Andes. En Machu Picchu hay torres de vigilancia, acueductos, casas, observatorios y un reloj solar[3]. El reloj solar marca las estaciones del año. En quechua, la lengua de los incas, Machu Picchu significa "montaña vieja". En la época en que llegan los españoles, los incas no tienen una forma escrita[4] de su lengua. Interpretan mensajes[5] y números con cuerdas de muchos colores con nudos[6].

Muchos aspectos de la historia de Machu Picchu son un misterio. Pero algo está muy claro; en la época en que construyen los incas la fabulosa ciudad no tienen cemento, no tienen ruedas y no tienen caballos ni bestias de carga ni carritos.

Cuzco Por mucho tiempo Cuzco es la capital de los incas y es el centro de un sistema de caminos que une Sudamérica. Cuando llega Francisco Pizarra a Cuzco y conquista la ciudad, los españoles transforman los templos y palacios de los incas en iglesias y magníficas casas.

Arequipa Arequipa es "la Ciudad Blanca." Es una ciudad blanca porque construyen las casas y los otros edificios de una piedra volcánica que hay en Arequipa. La piedra tiene un color blanco brillante.

Machu Picchu

[1]antes de: *before*
[2]estrecho: *narrow*
[3]reloj solar: *solar clock*
[4]escrita: *written*
[5]mensajes: *messages*
[6]cuerdas... con nudos: *cords... with knots*

Entérate Bolivia

Potosí Durante una parte de la época colonial Potosí es la ciudad más grande de las Américas a causa de la explotación de plata[1] en la región. Hoy Potosí es la ciudad más alta[2] del mundo.

Sucre La ciudad colonial de Sucre es muy importante porque es en Sucre donde acuñan monedas[3] de plata. Los españoles envían[4] las monedas a España. El dinero que envían a España tiene mucha importancia en la economía de España y Europa en el siglo XVII.

[1]plata: *silver*
[2]más alta: *highest*
[3]acuñan monedas: *they mint coins*
[4]envían: *send*

Potosí

Answers

A

1. famosas ruinas de los incas
2. las estaciones del año
3. el idioma de los incas
4. montaña vieja
5. Sí.
6. de una piedra volcánica

B

1. F
2. V
3. V

C

1. V
2. F
3. V
4. F
5. V

Las Islas Galápagos

Entérate Ecuador

Parque Nacional Sangay En el parque hay tres volcanes. El parque lleva el nombre de uno de los volcanes—el volcán Sangay. De todos los volcanes del mundo el Sangay es activo durante más tiempo que cualquier otro[1]. Varias comunidades indígenas viven en el parque que está en la lista de Patrimonios en Peligro[2]. ¿Por qué está en peligro? A causa de la construcción de una carretera moderna y la caza[3] ilegal.

Quito Cerca del volcán Pichincha, la bella ciudad de Quito tiene iglesias coloniales decoradas de pan de oro[4]. El barrio antiguo de la ciudad con sus calles estrechas de piedra y casas con balcones y patios refleja la influencia española.

Las Islas Galápagos Galápagos son las tortugas[5] gigantes que habitan el archipiélago de las Galápagos a unos mil kilómetros de la costa ecuatoriana. En el pasado naturalistas como Charles Darwin estudian las especies de flora y fauna del archipiélago. Algunas son únicas en el mundo.

[1]cualquier otro: *any other*
[2]peligro: *danger*
[3]caza: *hunting*
[4]pan de oro: *gold leaf*
[5]tortugas: *turtles*

Calendario de fiestas

Carnaval, Oruro, Bolivia, febrero
Declarado Obra Maestra por la UNESCO el carnaval de Oruro, Bolivia, es una fiesta muy alegre. Hay danzantes en las calles que llevan trajes y máscaras vistosas[1] de muchos colores.

Carnaval, Oruro, Bolivia

Pachamama Raymi, todo el país, Perú, 1° de agosto
Pachamama es la diosa de la Tierra de los indígenas peruanos. El 1° de agosto marca el comienzo del año andino y los indígenas hacen tributo[2] a su diosa con una ceremonia de ofrenda[3] que llaman[4] "Pago de la Tierra".

Tradiciones ancestrales, Amazonia, Ecuador
En la comunidad indichuris y la comunidad de los quechuas—poblaciones indígenas—habitan shamanes que practican sus tradiciones ancestrales. A veces dejan a los visitantes participar en los rituales.

[1]vistosas: *colorful*
[2]hacen tributo: *pay tribute*
[3]ofrenda: *offering*
[4]llaman: *they call*

música

El sonido andino

En todo el mundo goza de cierta popularidad la música andina. Pero hay muchos que no son familiares con los instrumentos musicales de los Andes. Unos son de origen puro andino y datan de miles de años. Otros son de origen europeo pero adaptados a los distintos ritmos y tonos andinos. ¡A tocar la zampoña!

La zampoña

La zampoña Es un instrumento de tubos de caña de tamaños diferentes. La nota musical varía según el tamaño del tubo.

La quena Es un instrumento de viento. Es de caña, madera[1] o hueso[2]. El tamaño del instrumento varía de una región a otra.

El charango Es como la guitarra, pero el instrumento es más pequeño que la guitarra y tiene catorce cuerdas[3].

El charango

[1]madera: *wood*
[2]hueso: *bone*
[3]cuerdas: *strings*

369

People EN ESPAÑOL

A Entérate Perú Contesten.
1. ¿Qué hay en Machu Picchu?
2. ¿Qué marca el reloj solar?
3. ¿Qué es el quechua?
4. ¿Qué significa Machu Picchu en quechua?
5. Cuando llegan los españoles a Perú, ¿tienen los incas un sistema de escritura?
6. ¿De qué construyen las casas y otros edificios en Arequipa?

B Entérate Bolivia
¿Verdadero o falso?
1. Hoy Potosí es la ciudad más grande de las Américas.
2. Hoy Potosí es la ciudad más alto del mundo.
3. Durante la época colonial, es en Sucre donde hacer o acuñar monedas de plata.

C Entérate Ecuador
¿Verdadero o falso?
1. En el parque nacional Sangay hay tres volcanes.
2. El volcán Sangay no es activo.
3. Quito es una ciudad que tiene mucha influencia colonial.
4. Los galápagos son pingüinos.
5. Las islas Galápagos son una parte de Ecuador.

D El sonido andino Completen.
1. ____ es un instrumento andino que es similar a la guitarra.
2. Los instrumentos andinos datan de ____.
3. La quena es un instrumento de ____.
4. ____ es más pequeño que una guitarra pero tiene catorce cuerdos.

E Calendario de fiestas
Contesten.
1. ¿Qué hay en las calles de Oruro durante el Carnaval?
2. ¿Qué llevan?
3. ¿Quién es Pachamama?
4. ¿Qué día marca el comienzo del año andino?
5. ¿A quién hacen tributo las indígenas el 1° de agosto?
6. ¿Qué practican los shamanes?

Answers

D
1. El charango
2. miles de años
3. viento
4. El charango

E
1. danzantes
2. máscaras de muchos colores
3. la diosa de la Tierra
4. el 1° de agosto
5. a su diosa Pachamama
6. tradiciones ancestrales

LEVELING
E: Activity A
A: Activities B–D
C: Activity E

As descendants of ancient Andean empires, Ecuadorians, Bolivians, and Peruvians bear a proud cultural heritage: their ancestors were among the most powerful precolonial civilizations in the Americas. Today, despite centuries of colonial efforts to wipe out the indigenous groups, many of those groups still exist, as do their complex languages and traditions.

A ¿Te apetecen papas fritas coloreadas? Contesten.
1. ¿Dónde cultiva la gente papas nativas?
2. ¿Comes papas nativas?
3. ¿De qué colores son las papas nativas?
4. ¿Tienen las papas nativas una variedad de textura?
5. ¿Es de Irlanda la papa?
6. ¿De dónde es la papa?

B ¡La gente! Corrijan.
1. Los curanderos curan con aspirina.
2. Una selva tropical tiene pocas plantas.
3. La Paz, Lima y Quito son pueblos pequeños.

C El mundo salvaje Contesten.
1. ¿Hay miles de especies de qué en la cordillera de los Andes?
2. ¿Para qué sirve la llama?
3. ¿De qué origen son las Islas Galápagos?

micocina

Ceviche

Ingredientes

2 libras de pescado y mariscos mixtos, incluyendo un pescado de carne firme, almejas[1], camarones[2]

1 cebolla grande en rebanadas[3] finas

$\frac{1}{2}$ taza de perejil[4] picado

chiles serranos al gusto

jugo[5] de limón para cubrir

Preparación

Combinar todos los ingredientes y refrigerar durante dos horas. El resultado es un platillo delicioso. Delicioso para una fiesta.

[1]almejas: *clams*
[2]camarones: *shrimp*
[3]rebanadas: *slices*
[4]perejil: *parsley*
[5]jugo: *juice*

Ceviche

Gente andina

¿Te apetecen papas fritas coloreadas?

En las montañas de Perú y Bolivia, la gente cultiva papas nativas, pero no son las mismas papas que comes tú. Son de varios colores. Son rojas, azules, amarillas y blancas. Además de ser coloreadas, tienen mucha variedad de textura, sabor y olor. Los pueblos indígenas llevan miles de años cultivando miles de variedades de papas. Hay hasta cientos de variedades en una sola parcela de cultivo.

Muchas papas están adaptadas a florecer[1] en las regiones muy altas de los Andes. Mucha gente cree[2] que la papa es de Irlanda. Pero no es verdad. La papa es un producto de las Américas, gracias a las comunidades indígenas. Hoy la papa es uno de los alimentos[3] básicos del mundo entero.

[1]florecer: *bloom* [2]cree: *believe* [3]alimentos: *foods*

¡La gente!

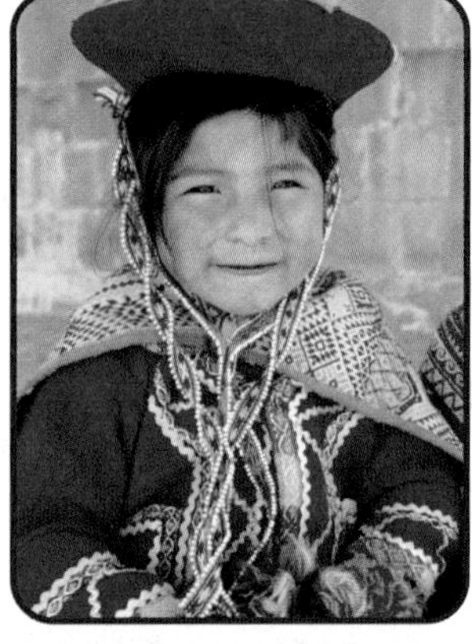

Si viajas[1] por los Andes vas a ver a gente de muchas etnias y culturas. Tienes que tratar[2] de asistir a unos ritos ancestrales de curanderos[3] y shamanes. Los curanderos curan a sus pacientes con hierbas medicinales.

Si vas a la selva tropical[4] es posible ver de lejos[5] a comunidades indígenas que no tienen contacto con otras personas. Ellos viven como sus antepasados o ancestros desde hace ya cientos de años.

¿Vas a comprar artesanía? ¿Por qué no visitas un mercado indígena de colores y olores[6] exóticos? Si tienes hambre cuando estás en el mercado, puedes[7] comer algo en uno de los puestos de comida[8]. Si estás en una de las ciudades como La Paz, Lima o Quito, puedes comer en un restaurante elegante o ir de compras en una tienda bonita.

[1]viajas: *you travel*
[2]tratar: *try*
[3]curanderos: *healers*
[4]selva tropical: *rainforest*
[5]de lejos: *from a distance*
[6]olores: *smells*
[7]puedes: *you can*
[8]puestos de comida: *food stands*

Answers

A
1. en las montañas de Perú y Bolivia
2. No
3. varios colores; son rojas, azules, amarillas y blancas
4. Sí
5. No
6. Es de las Américas.

B
1. Los curanderos curan con hierbas medicinales.
2. Una selva tropical tiene muchas plantas.
3. La Paz, Lima y Quito son ciudades.

C
1. orquídeas
2. un medio de transporte importante
3. de origen volcánico

el mundo salvaje

Entérate de detalles interesantes

El Salar de Uyuni

Lugares sorprendentes

■ **El Salar de Uyuni** es el fondo de un mar desaparecido en Bolivia. Aquí hay hoteles construidos de bloques de sal.

■ **La línea ecuatorial** pasa por Ecuador. Así, puedes estar de pie en dos hemisferios al mismo tiempo—con un pie en el hemisferio sur y el otro en el hemisferio norte.

■ **El lago Titicaca** en Bolivia es el lago navegable más alto del mundo.

■ **Las Islas Galápagos** son de origen volcánico y tienen una intensa actividad sísmica y volcánica con varias erupciones al año.

Orquídeas

Flora fascinante

■ En la región amazónica de Ecuador, hay un sinnúmero de **plantas,** muchas de ellas desconocidas[1].

■ En muchas partes de la cordillera de los Andes hay miles de especies de **orquídeas**.

■ Muchas **especies de árboles** en la región amazónica están en peligro[2] de extinción. A causa de la deforestación bosques[3] enteros de miles de años de edad ya no existen.

Fauna fenomenal

■ ¿Cuál es el animal más típico de los Andes? Es **la llama,** el amigo de toda la población andina. La llama es un medio de transporte importante.

■ El clima del altiplano de Bolivia no permite sobrevivir[4] muchas especies de aves. Pero aquí viven miles de **flamencos rosados**[5].

■ Según los científicos, hay más de 4,200 especies de **mariposas**[6] en Perú. Pero hasta ahora sólo 3,700 especies son conocidas.

Flamencos

[1]desconocidas: *unknown*
[2]peligro: *danger*
[3]bosques: *forests*
[4]permite sobrevivir: *enable to survive*
[5]flamencos rosados: *pink flamingos*
[6]mariposas: *butterflies*

SUCESOS

Mario Vargas Llosa

■ El escritor peruano **Mario Vargas Llosa** es considerado uno de los grandes novelistas latinoamericanos por sus obras como *La ciudad de los perros.* Él pasa mucho tiempo en París pero aquí está en su Perú natal donde escribe su autógrafo para una de sus aficionados.

■ ¿Qué es **un sombrero de jipijapa?** La traducción en inglés es "Panama hat," pero no es de Panamá. ¡Es de Ecuador!

■ El conductor **Miguel Harth-Bedoya** es de Perú. Va a Nueva York donde estudia en la famosa Juilliard School of Music. Ahora es el director musical de una orquesta sinfónica norteamericana.

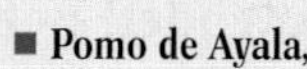
Miguel Harth-Bedoya

■ **Pomo de Ayala,** de madre indígena y padre español, capta perfectamente el cultivo de papas en los Andes. ¿Toma una fotografía? No, de ninguna manera. Él pinta una escena del cultivo de papas en el año 1580. Pomo de Ayala es un conocido cronista peruano (1534–1615).

371

People EN ESPAÑOL

D El mundo salvaje
¿Verdadero o falso?

1. La línea ecuatorial divide el hemisferio en dos.
2. El lago Titicaca está en Ecuador.
3. El lago Titicaca es el lago navegable más alto del mundo.
4. No hay erupciones volcánicas en las islas Galápagos.
5. Hay muchas especies de orquídeas en la región amazónica de Ecuador.
6. La deforestación es un problema muy serio en la región amazónica.
7. La llama es el amigo de toda la gente que vive en los Andes. Este animal es un medio de transporte importante.
8. Los flamencos son flores.

E Sucesos ¿Qué o quién es?

1. Pasa mucho tiempo en París y es uno de los grandes novelistas.
2. Es conductor peruano y es director musical de una orquesta sinfónica.
3. Es un sombrero ecuatoriano cuyo nombre en inglés es "Panama hat".

F ¿De qué país son? Contesten.

1. los bolivianos
2. los peruanos
3. los ecuatorianos

LEVELING

E: Activity B
A: Activities D–F
C: Activities A, C

Answers

D

1. V
2. F
3. V
4. F
5. F
6. V
7. V
8. F

E

1. Mario Vargas Llosa
2. Miguel Harth-Bedoya
3. un sombrero jipijapa

F

1. Bolivia
2. Perú
3. Ecuador

Planning for Chapter 12

SCOPE AND SEQUENCE, PAGES 372–401

Topics

- Daily routines
- Grooming habits
- Camping

Culture

- Iván Orama describes a backpacking trip in northern Spain
- Picos de Europa, Spain
- El Parque Nacional de Covadonga, Spain
- San Sebastián
- **El Camino de Santiago** in Northern Spain
- The Cathedral in Santiago de Compostela
- Ecology in the Spanish-speaking world

Functions

- How to describe personal grooming habits
- How to talk about your daily routine
- How to describe a backpacking trip
- How to tell about things you do for yourself
- How to discuss what others do for themselves

Structure

- Reflexive verbs
- Stem-changing reflexive verbs

National Standards

- Communication Standard 1.1 pages 372, 376, 377, 380, 381, 383, 384, 385, 386, 387, 389, 396
- Communication Standard 1.2 pages 377, 380, 381, 385, 387, 388, 389, 391, 393, 395, 396, 397
- Communication Standard 1.3 page 397
- Cultures Standard 2.1 pages 388, 390–391
- Cultures Standard 2.2 pages 392–393, 397
- Connections Standard 3.1 page 394
- Communities Standard 5.2 page 401

PACING AND PRIORITIES

The chapter content is color coded below to assist you in planning.

■ required ■ recommended ■ optional

Vocabulario *(required)* *Days 1–4*

- ■ Palabras 1
  La rutina
- ■ Palabras 2
  Una gira
  ¿Qué ponen o llevan en la mochila?

Estructura *(required)* *Days 5–7*

- ■ Verbos reflexivos
- ■ Verbos reflexivos de cambio radical

Conversación *(required)*

- ■ ¿A qué hora te despertaste?

Pronunciación *(recommended)*

- ■ La **h,** la **y,** la **ll**

Lecturas culturales

- ■ Del norte de España *(recommended)*
- ■ El Camino de Santiago *(optional)*

Conexiones

- ■ La ecología *(optional)*

■ **¡Te toca a ti!** *(recommended)*

■ **Assessment** *(recommended)*

■ **¡Hablo como un pro!** *(optional)*

RESOURCE GUIDE

Section	Pages	Section Resources
Vocabulario PALABRAS 1		
La rutina	374–377	Vocabulary Transparencies 12.2–12.3 Audio CD 7 Audio Activities TE, pages 143–145 Workbook, pages 149–150 Quiz 1, pages 60–61 ExamView® Pro
Vocabulario PALABRAS 2		
Una gira ¿Qué ponen o llevan en la mochila?	378, 380–381 379, 380–381	Vocabulary Transparencies 12.4–12.5 Audio CD 7 Audio Activities TE, pages 146–147 Workbook, pages 151–152 Quiz 2, page 62 ExamView® Pro
Estructura		
Verbos reflexivos Verbos reflexivos de cambio radical	382–385 386–387	Audio CD 7 Audio Activities TE, pages 147–148 Workbook, pages 153–155 Quizzes 3–4, pages 63–64 ExamView® Pro
Conversación		
¿A qué hora te despertaste?	388	Audio CD 7 Audio Activities TE, page 149 Interactive CD-ROM
Pronunciación		
La **h,** la **y**, la **ll**	389	Pronunciation Transparency P 12 Audio CD 7 Audio Activities TE, page 150
Lecturas culturales		
Del norte de España El Camino de Santiago	390–391 392–393	Audio CD 7 Audio Activities TE, page 151 Tests, pages 197, 200
Conexiones		
La ecología	394–395	Tests, page 201
¡Te toca a ti!		
	396–397	**¡Viva el mundo hispano!** Video, Episode 12 Video Activities, Chapter 12 Spanish Online Activities spanish.glencoe.com
Assessment		
	398–399	Communication Transparency C 12 Quizzes 1–4, pages 60–64 Performance Assessment, Task 12 Tests, pages 195–206 Situation Cards, Chapter 12 ExamView® Pro **Maratón mental** Videoquiz

Using Your Resources for Chapter 12

Transparencies

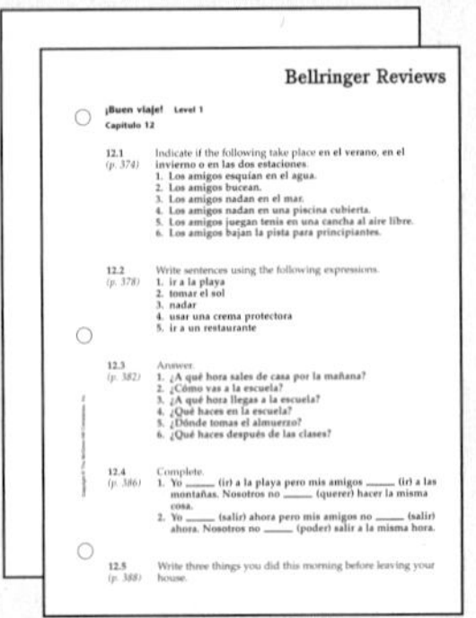

Bellringer 12.1–12.5

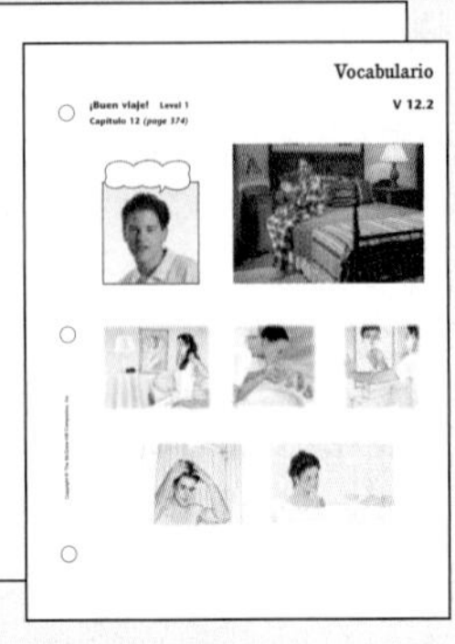

Vocabulary 12.1–12.5

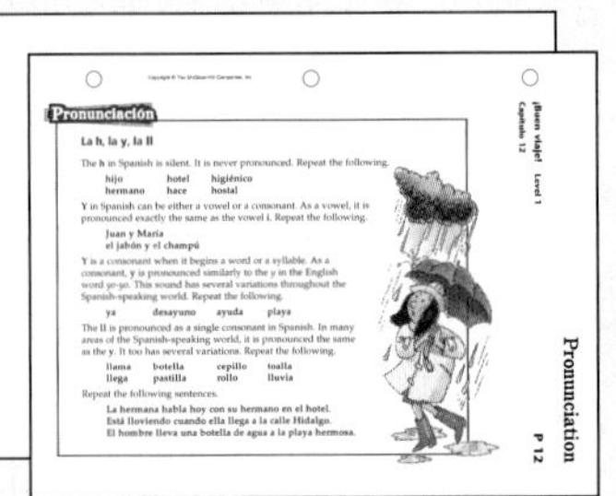

Pronunciation P 12

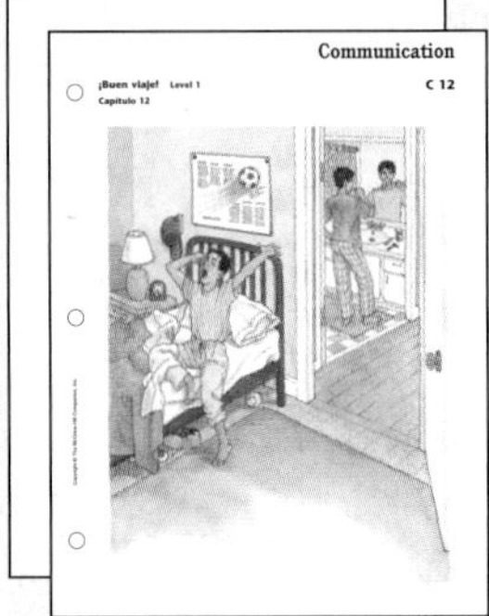

Communication C 12

Workbook

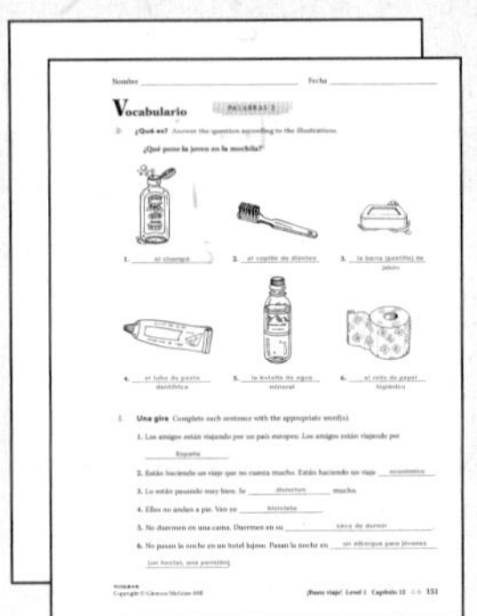

Vocabulary, pages 149–152

Structure, pages 153–155

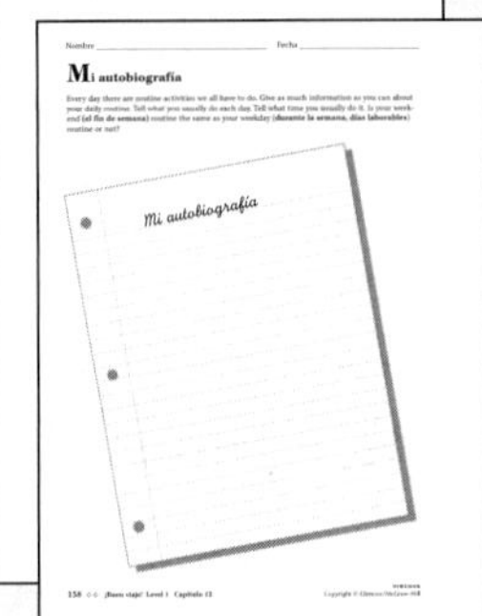

Enrichment, pages 156–158

Audio Activities

Vocabulary, pages 143–147

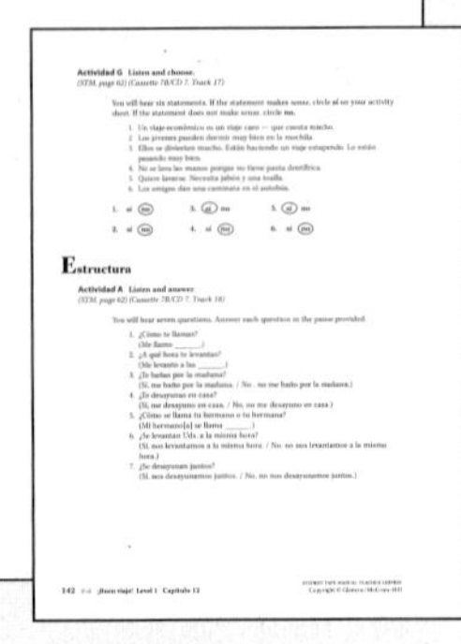

Structure, pages 147–148

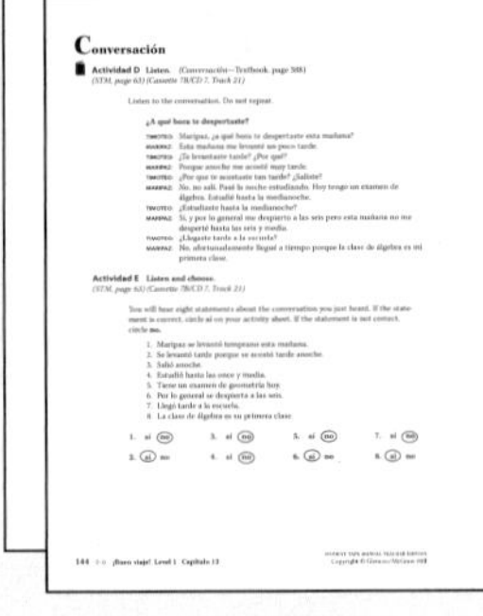

Conversation, Pronunciation, pages 149–150

Additional Practice, pages 151–152

Assessment

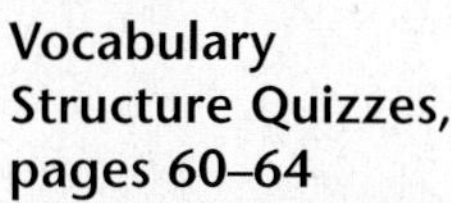

Vocabulary Structure Quizzes, pages 60–64

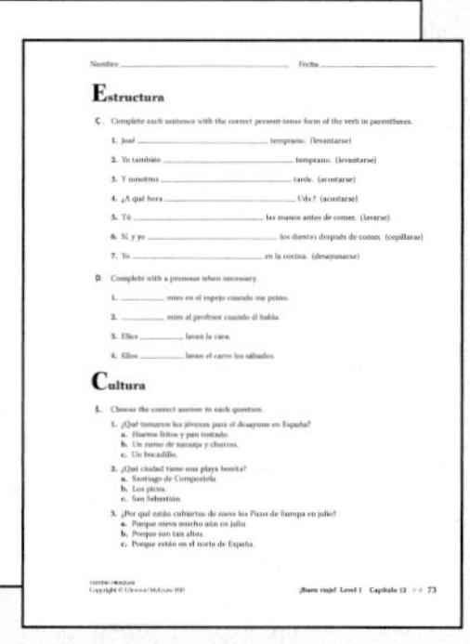

Chapter Tests, pages 195–206

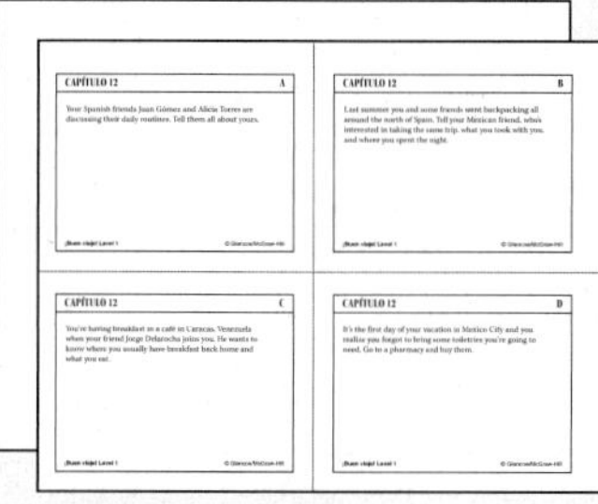

Situation Cards, Chapter 12

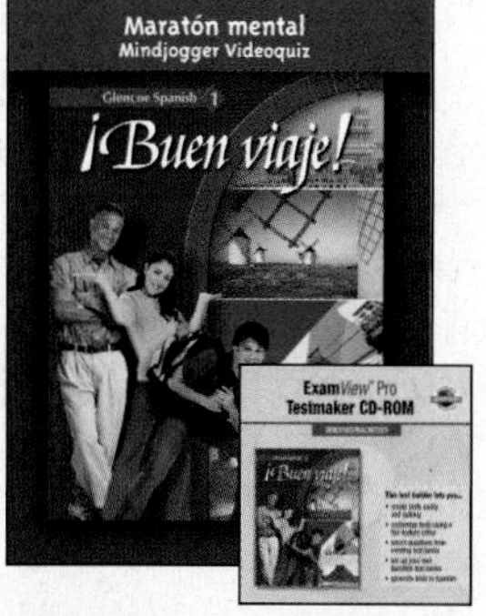

MindJogger Videoquiz, ExamView® Pro, Chapter 12

Timesaving Teacher Tools

TeacherWorks™ is your all-in-one teacher resource center. Personalize lesson plans, access resources from the Teacher Wraparound Edition, connect to the Internet, or make a to-do list. These are only a few of the many features that can assist you in the planning and organizing of your lessons.

Includes:

- A calendar feature
- Access to all program blackline masters
- Standards correlations and more

ExamView® Pro

Test Bank software for Macintosh and Windows makes creating, editing, customizing, and printing tests quick and easy.

Technology Resources

In the Chapter 12 Internet Activity, you will have a chance to learn more about the Spanish-speaking world. Visit spanish.glencoe.com

On the interactive CD-ROM, students can listen to and take part in a recorded version of the conversation in Chapter 12.

¡Viva el mundo hispano! Video and Video Activities, Chapter 12. Available on VHS and DVD.

Help your students prepare for the chapter test by playing the **Maratón mental** Videoquiz game show. Teams will compete against each other to review chapter vocabulary and structure and sharpen listening comprehension skills. Available on VHS and DVD.

¡Buen viaje! is also available on CD or Online.

Capítulo 12

Preview

In this chapter, students will learn to discuss their daily routine with particular emphasis on hygiene. To do this they will learn reflexive verbs. The cultural focus is on the routine of the many young cyclists and backpackers who today follow the **Camino de Santiago** in Spain.

National Standards

Communication

In Chapter 12 students will communicate in spoken and written Spanish on the following topics:

- daily routines
- taking care of oneself
- enjoying a good backpacking trip

Students will obtain and provide information about these topics and engage in conversations about everyday habits, including daily hygiene, as they fulfill the chapter objectives listed on this page.

Capítulo 12

Una gira

Objetivos

In this chapter you will learn to:

- **describe your personal grooming habits**
- **talk about your daily routine**
- **tell some things you do for yourself**
- **talk about a backpacking trip**

Susana González-Pagliere *Southern Lake*

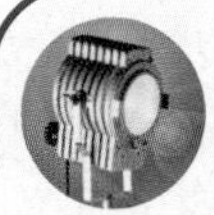

Spotlight on Culture

Fotografía This photo was taken in the small town of Punta la Reina in Navarra. Queen Urraca had this bridge constructed in the eleventh century for the use of pilgrims on their way to Santiago de Compostela.

LEVELING

The activities, conversations, and readings within each chapter are marked according to level of difficulty. **E** indicates easy. **A** indicates average. **C** indicates challenging. Some activities cover a range of difficulty. In some activities, for example, advanced students will be able to produce more extensive responses while students who learn at a different rate may give less detailed responses. The leveling indicators will help you individualize instruction to best meet your students' needs.

Vocabulario

PALABRAS 1

1 PREPARATION

Resource Manager

Vocabulary Transparencies 12.2–12.3
Audio Activities TE, pages 143–145
Audio CD 7
Workbook, pages 149–150
Quizzes, pages 60–61
ExamView® Pro

Bellringer Review

Use BRR Transparency 12.1 or write the following on the board.
Indicate if the following take place **en el verano, en el invierno o en las dos estaciones.**

1. **Los amigos esquían en el agua.**
2. **Los amigos bucean.**
3. **Los amigos nadan en el mar.**
4. **Los amigos nadan en una piscina cubierta.**
5. **Los amigos juegan tenis en una cancha al aire libre.**
6. **Los amigos bajan la pista para principiantes.**

2 PRESENTATION

Step 1 Have students close their books. Model the new words using Vocabulary Transparencies 12.2–12.3. Point to each illustration and have the class repeat the corresponding word or expression after you or Audio CD 7.

Step 2 Now have students open their books and repeat the procedure as they read.

Step 3 Act out the new words: **despertarse, levantarse, afeitarse, peinarse, lavarse, cepillarse, ponerse la ropa, sentarse.**

Vocabulario

PALABRAS 1

La rutina

Hola. Yo me llamo José.
¿Y tú? ¿Cómo te llamas?

El muchacho se llama José.

José se acuesta.
Se acuesta a las once de la noche.
Él se duerme enseguida.

La muchacha se despierta temprano.
Se levanta enseguida.

El muchacho se lava la cara.

El muchacho se afeita.
Se afeita con la navaja.

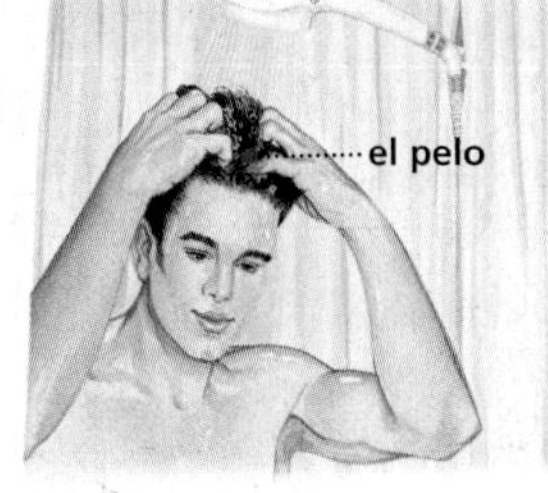

El muchacho toma una ducha.
El muchacho se lava el pelo.

La muchacha se baña.

Reaching All Students

Total Physical Response You may use a chair for a bed. Bring in a mirror and an alarm clock, or make a buzzing sound when you say **despertador.**

(Student 1), **ven acá, por favor.**
Son las siete de la mañana. Estás durmiendo.
Oyes el despertador. Te despiertas.
Te levantas. Vas al cuarto de baño.
Te lavas.
Te miras en el espejo.
Te cepillas los dientes.
Te peinas. Te pones la ropa.
Sales para la escuela.
Gracias, *(Student 1).* **Y ahora puedes regresar a tu asiento.**

El muchacho se cepilla (se lava) los dientes.

La muchacha se maquilla.
Se pone el maquillaje.

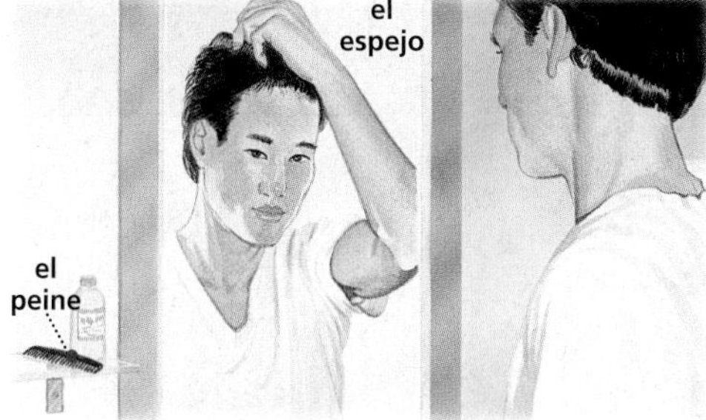

El muchacho se peina.
Se mira en el espejo cuando se peina.

Ella se pone la ropa.

La muchacha se sienta a la mesa.
Toma el desayuno.
Se desayuna.

Vocabulario

Step 4 As you present the new vocabulary, ask questions such as the following: **¿La muchacha se despierta por la mañana o por la noche? Entonces, ¿ella se levanta o se acuesta? ¿Ella se levanta o se acuesta a las diez de la noche? ¿El muchacho se lava la cara o las manos? ¿Se cepilla los dientes?**

Step 5 Call out the following verbs and have students pantomime each one: **despertarse, levantarse, lavarse, cepillarse los dientes, afeitarse.**

Vocabulary Expansion

You may wish to teach students the following additional words so they can describe a typical breakfast in the United States: **huevos (fritos, revueltos, pasados por agua), tocino, jamón, salchicha, panqueques con jarabe** *(syrup).*

About the Spanish Language

- The word for *pajamas* is **pijamas.**
- **Dientes** are *teeth* and **muelas** are *molars.* Both are often used as generic terms for *teeth.* A *toothache* is a **dolor de muelas.** You may wish to ask students what **diente** and **muela** mean in English. You may also ask them to identify the **dientes caninos** and the **incisivos.**
- The first meal of the day is breakfast, *to break a fast.* The same concept applies to the Spanish word. Ask students what the word for *a fast* would be in Spanish **(ayuno).** You will hear both **desayunar** and **desayunarse** when referring to breakfast.

Fun Facts

The girl in the photo is eating a breakfast that is typical of the United States and one that is becoming more common in many Hispanic countries. However, the usual breakfast in Spain and Latin America continues to be **café con leche** (with a great deal of **leche**), toast, and maybe juice or fruit. At mid-morning, people eat a sandwich or snack to tide themselves over until the midday meal.

LEVELING

E: Vocabulary

3 PRACTICE

¿Qué palabra necesito?

¡OJO! When students are doing the **¿Qué palabra necesito?** activities, accept any answer that makes sense. The purpose of these activities is to have students use the new vocabulary. They are not factual recall activities. Thus, it is not necessary for students to remember specific factual information from the vocabulary presentation when answering. If you wish, have students use the photos on this page as a stimulus, when possible.

Historieta Each time **Historieta** appears, it means that the answers to the activity form a short story. Encourage students to look at the title of the **Historieta,** since it can help them do the activity.

1 After going over Activity 1, have students retell the story in their own words.

2 Have students look at each photograph or illustration on page 376 and describe it in their own words.

Writing Development

Have students write the answers to Activity 1 in a paragraph to illustrate how the answers to all the items tell a story.

¿Qué palabra necesito?

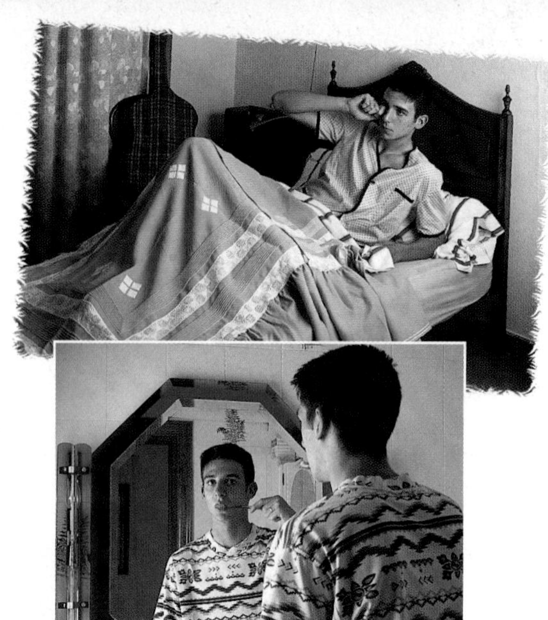

1 Historieta Un día en la vida de...

Contesten según se indica.

1. ¿Cómo se llama el joven? (Paco)
2. ¿A qué hora se despierta? (a las seis y media)
3. ¿Cuándo se levanta? (enseguida)
4. ¿Adónde va? (al cuarto de baño)
5. ¿Qué hace? (se lava la cara y se cepilla los dientes)
6. Luego, ¿adónde va? (a la cocina)
7. ¿Se sienta a la mesa? (sí)
8. ¿Qué toma? (el desayuno)

2 ¿Qué hace el muchacho o la muchacha? Describan.

1.

2.

3.

4.

5.

6.

Answers to ¿Qué palabra necesito?

1

1. El joven se llama Paco.
2. Se despierta a las seis y media.
3. Se levanta enseguida.
4. Va al cuarto de baño.
5. Se lava la cara y se cepilla los dientes.
6. Luego va a la cocina.
7. Sí, se sienta a la mesa.
8. Toma el desayuno.

2

1. El muchacho se levanta.
2. La muchacha se acuesta.
3. La muchacha se peina.
4. El muchacho se lava el pelo.
5. La muchacha (se) desayuna (toma el desayuno).
6. El muchacho se afeita.

3 Historieta Las actividades de Sarita

Completen.

Sarita __1__ por la mañana. Ella __2__ la cara y las manos. Ella __3__ los dientes. Ella __4__ el pelo. Ella __5__ la ropa—un blue jean y una camiseta. Ella __6__ en la cocina. Ella __7__ a la mesa.

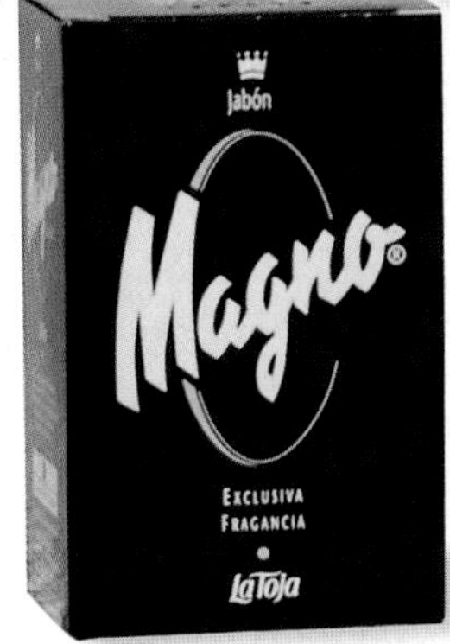

Málaga, España

4 Entrevista

Contesten personalmente.

1. ¿Cómo te llamas?
2. ¿A qué hora tomas el desayuno?
3. ¿Tomas el desayuno en la cocina o en el comedor?
4. ¿Te gusta tomar un desayuno grande?
5. ¿Qué comes en el desayuno?
6. ¿Te gustan los cereales?

5 La rutina

Work with a classmate. Each of you will choose one family member and tell each other about that person's daily activities.

*For more practice using words from **Palabras 1**, do Activity 12 on page H13 at the end of this book.*

Vocabulario

3 After students do Activity 3, have them retell the story in their own words.

4 Activity 4 can be done in pairs as an interview. Encourage students to ask additional, related questions. For example: **¿Qué pones en el cereal? ¿Fruta, leche o azúcar?**

Expansion: See how many food items students can identify in the photo.

¡OJO! Note that the activities are color-coded. All the activities in the text are communicative. However, the ones with blue titles are guided communication. The red titles indicate that the answers to the activity are more open-ended and can vary more. You may wish to correct students' mistakes more so in the guided activities than in the activities with a red title, which lend themselves to a freer response.

5 The partner should take notes. At the end of the description he or she should refer to the notes and repeat what was said.

Learning from Realia

(page 377) **Magno** is a well-known Spanish soap made on the small island of La Toja in Galicia.

Answers to ¿Qué palabra necesito?

3

1. se levanta (se despierta)
2. se lava
3. se cepilla
4. se peina (se cepilla, se lava)
5. se pone
6. se desayuna (se sienta)
7. se sienta (se desayuna)

4

1. Me llamo ___.
2. Tomo el desayuno a (eso de) las ___.
3. Tomo el desayuno en la cocina (el comedor).
4. Sí, (No, no) me gusta tomar un desayuno grande.
5. Como ___ y ___ en el desayuno.
6. Sí, (No, no) me gustan los cereales.

5 *Answers will vary. Students should use the words in the colored boxes and the verbs they learned in* Palabras 1.

LEVELING

E: Activities 1, 2

A: Activities 3, 4, 5

1 PREPARATION

Resource Manager

Vocabulary Transparencies 12.4–12.5
Audio Activities TE, pages 146–147
Audio CD 7
Workbook, pages 151–152
Quizzes, page 62
ExamView® Pro

Bellringer Review

Use BRR Transparency 12.2 or write the following on the board.
Write sentences using the following expressions.

1. **ir a la playa**
2. **tomar el sol**
3. **nadar**
4. **usar una crema protectora**
5. **ir a un restaurante**

2 PRESENTATION

Step 1 Have students close their books. Present the vocabulary using Vocabulary Transparencies 12.4–12.5. Have students repeat after you or Audio CD 7.

Step 2 As you present the vocabulary you may wish to ask the following questions:

¿Por dónde están viajando los amigos?
¿Quiénes están viajando?
¿Qué tipo de viaje están haciendo?
¿Está costando mucho dinero el viaje?
¿Cómo están pasando el viaje?
¿Se divierten mucho?
¿Duermen en el saco de dormir?
¿Duermen en su cuarto o al aire libre?

Una gira

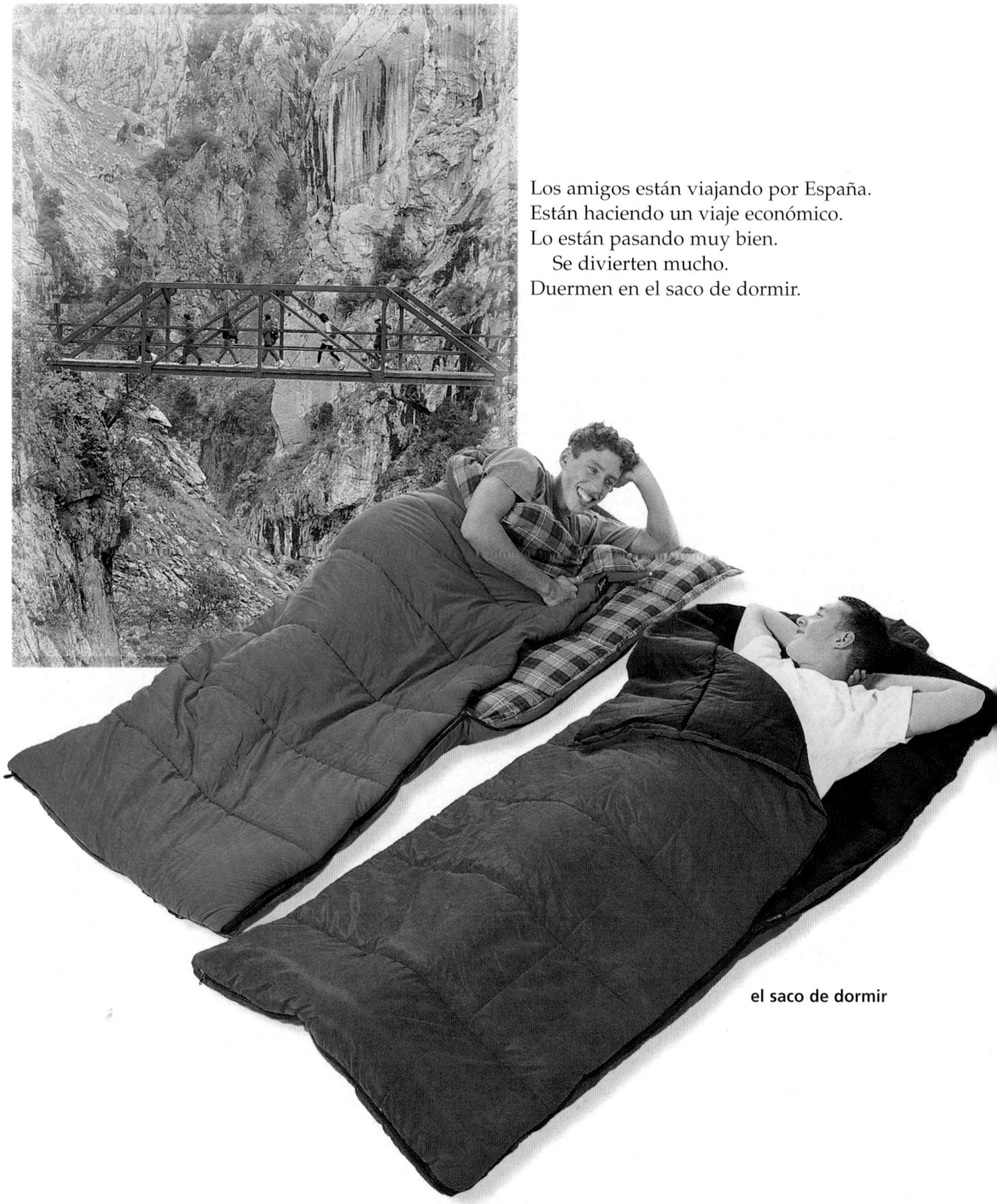

Los amigos están viajando por España.
Están haciendo un viaje económico.
Lo están pasando muy bien.
Se divierten mucho.
Duermen en el saco de dormir.

el saco de dormir

Class Motivator

¿Qué llevas en la mochila? Put items like those on page 379 in a bag or knapsack. You may want to include additional items, such as an alarm clock, a plastic safety razor, shaving cream, makeup, a comb, and a hand mirror. Now pass the knapsack around the room and have each student pull out an item and identify it. Divide the class and make this a contest to see which side can name the most items.

Vocabulario

¿Qué ponen o llevan en la mochila?

Los amigos dan una caminata.
Algunos van a pie.
Y otros van en bicicleta.

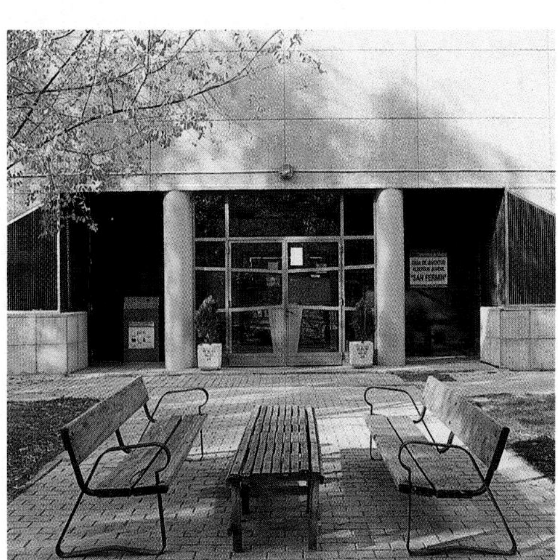

Pasan la noche en un albergue para jóvenes.
Y a veces pasan la noche en un hostal o en una pensión.

Step 3 After you have presented all the vocabulary, have students open their books and read the words and sentences for additional reinforcement.

About the Spanish Language

- In addition to **el cepillo de dientes** you will also see and hear **el cepillo para los dientes.**
- **Un rollo de papel higiénico** is the most commonly used term. You will also hear **papel de baño** particularly among Spanish-speaking groups in the United States.
- **Una pastilla de jabón** is used in Spain.

Vocabulary Expansion

You may wish to give students a few extra words that have to do with personal hygiene:

el desodorante *deodorant*
cortarse las uñas *trim your nails*
echarse perfume *apply perfume*
la colonia *cologne*

Chapter Projects

La buena higiene Have students prepare a booklet on good hygiene. Have them make a list of do's and don't's **(rutinas positivas / rutinas negativas).** For example, under **rutinas positivas** they might say **cepillarse los dientes antes de acostarse.** Under **rutinas negativas** they might say **acostarse a la medianoche.** Finally, students can compile a master list of good and bad habits of hygiene to display on a school bulletin board.

3 PRACTICE

¿Qué palabra necesito?

6 Activity 6 can be done as a game. Using a stopwatch, see who can identify the most items in the least amount of time.

Writing Development

After going over Activity 7, have students write the story in their own words in paragraph form.

¿Qué palabra necesito?

6 ¿Qué pierde Pepe de la mochila? Identifiquen.

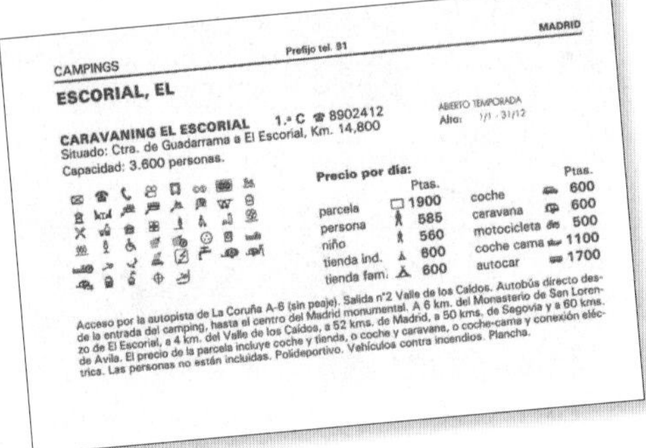

MADRID

Prefijo tel. 91

CAMPINGS

ESCORIAL, EL

CARAVANING EL ESCORIAL 1.ª C ☎ 8902412

Situado: Ctra. de Guadarrama a El Escorial, Km. 14,800

Capacidad: 3.600 personas.

ABIERTO TEMPORADA

Alta: 1/1 - 31/12

Precio por día:

	Ptas.		Ptas.
parcela	1900	coche	600
persona	585	caravana	600
niño	560	motocicleta	500
tienda ind.	800	coche cama	1100
tienda fam.	600	autocar	1700

Acceso por la autopista de La Coruña A-6 (sin peaje). Salida nº2 Valle de los Caídos. Autobús directo desde la entrada del camping, hasta el centro del Madrid monumental. A 6 km. del Monasterio de San Lorenzo de El Escorial, a 4 km. del Valle de los Caídos, a 52 kms. de Madrid, a 50 kms. de Segovia y a 60 kms. de Avila. El precio de la parcela incluye coche y tienda, o coche y caravana, o coche-cama y conexión eléctrica. Las personas no están incluidas. Polideportivo. Vehículos contra incendios. Plancha.

7 Historieta Una gira Contesten.

1. ¿Hacen los jóvenes un viaje de lujo o un viaje económico?
2. ¿Por dónde están viajando?
3. ¿En qué llevan sus cosas?
4. ¿Cuáles son algunas cosas que ponen en la mochila?
5. ¿Cómo van de un lugar (sitio) a otro?
6. ¿En qué duermen a veces?
7. ¿Dónde pasan la noche de vez en cuando (a veces)?
8. ¿Se divierten?

ANSWERS TO ¿Qué palabra necesito?

6

Pepe pierde un cepillo, un rollo de papel higiénico, una navaja, un tubo de pasta dentífrica, una pastilla de jabón, un peine, un cepillo de dientes, crema de afeitar.

7

1. Los jóvenes hacen un viaje económico (un viaje de lujo).
2. Están viajando por España *(or any country of student's choice).*
3. Llevan sus cosas en una mochila.
4. Algunas cosas que ponen en la mochila son: una botella de agua mineral, un tubo de pasta dentífrica, un cepillo de dientes, una barra (pastilla) de jabón, un rollo de papel higiénico y un cepillo.
5. Van de un lugar a otro en bicicleta (a pie, en tren, por avión).
6. A veces duermen en un saco de dormir.
7. De vez en cuando (A veces) pasan la noche en un albergue para jóvenes (en un hostal, una pensión).
8. Sí, se divierten mucho.

Vocabulario

8 **Historieta En el cuarto de baño** Completen.

1. El muchacho va a tomar una ducha. Necesita ____.
2. La muchacha quiere peinarse pero, ¿dónde está ____?
3. El muchacho va a afeitarse. Necesita ____.
4. Juanito quiere lavarse los dientes. ¿Dónde está ____?
5. No hay pasta dentífrica. Tengo que comprar otro ____.
6. No hay más jabón. Tengo que comprar otra ____.
7. Siempre uso ____ para lavarme el pelo.

9 **En la farmacia** You're a clerk in a drugstore. A classmate is a Spanish-speaking customer who wants to buy the following toiletries. Have a conversation.

9 As a preliminary step for this activity, quickly decide as a class approximately how many **euros (pesos)** each item will cost. Put the items and prices on the board so students can refer to them during the activity. You can have groups present their conversations to the class.

Reaching All Students

Additional Practice Write the following list on the board: **el pelo, las manos, los ojos, la cara, los dientes.** Have students write down all the toiletries and verbs from this chapter that they associate with each word. For example, **el pelo: lavarse, peinarse, cepillarse, el peine, el champú.**

LEVELING

E: Activity 6
A: Activities 7, 8
C: Activities 8, 9

Answers to ¿Qué palabra necesito?

8

1. una barra (pastilla) de jabón, champú
2. su peine
3. una navaja y crema de afeitar
4. su cepillo de dientes (pasta dentífrica)
5. tubo
6. barra (pastilla)
7. champú

9 *Answers will vary; however, students should begin their conversation with the customary greetings, followed by* Quiero (Necesito) comprar...

1 PREPARATION

Resource Manager

Audio Activities TE, pages 147–148
Audio CD 7
Workbook, pages 153–155
Quizzes, pages 63–64
ExamView® Pro

Bellringer Review

Use BRR Transparency 12.3 or write the following on the board.
Answer.

1. **¿A qué hora sales de casa por la mañana?**
2. **¿Cómo vas a la escuela?**
3. **¿A qué hora llegas a la escuela?**
4. **¿Qué haces en la escuela?**
5. **¿Dónde tomas el almuerzo?**
6. **¿Qué haces después de las clases?**

2 PRESENTATION

Verbos reflexivos

Step 1 Have students open their books to page 382 and look at the illustrations.

Step 2 Ask students in which illustrations someone is doing something to himself (herself) and in which illustrations the person is doing something to someone (something) else.

Step 3 Ask what additional word is used when the person is doing something to himself or herself **(se).**

Step 4 Explain to them that **se** is a reflexive pronoun and refers to the subject.

Step 5 Then read the explanation that follows in Item 1 on page 382.

Verbos reflexivos
Telling what people do for themselves

1. Compare the following pairs of sentences.

Mariana baña al perro.

Mariana se baña.

Mariana cepilla al perro.

Mariana se cepilla.

In the sentences above the illustrations, Mariana performs the action. The dog receives the action. In the sentences below the drawings, Mariana both performs and receives the action of the verb. For this reason, the pronoun **se** must be used. **Se** refers back to Mariana in these sentences and is called a "reflexive pronoun." It indicates that the action of the verb is reflected back to the subject.

2. Study the forms of a reflexive verb.

INFINITIVE	lavarse	levantarse
yo	me lavo	me levanto
tú	te lavas	te levantas
él, ella, Ud.	se lava	se levanta
nosotros(as)	nos lavamos	nos levantamos
vosotros(as)	*os laváis*	*os levantáis*
ellos, ellas, Uds.	se lavan	se levantan

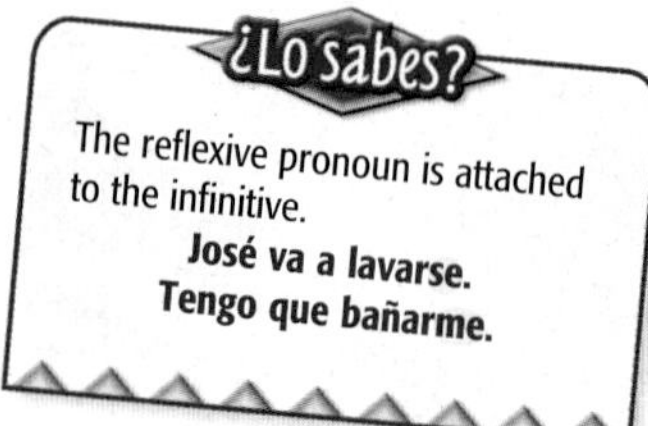

¿Lo sabes?

The reflexive pronoun is attached to the infinitive.

José va a lavarse.
Tengo que bañarme.

3. In the negative form, **no** is placed before the reflexive pronoun.

¿No te lavas las manos?
La familia Martínez no se desayuna en el comedor.

FUN-FACTS

The word for *German shepherd* is **pastor alemán.** For the names of other breeds, see Vocabulary Expansion on page 180.

LEVELING

E: Activity 10
A: Activity 11
C: Activity 11

4. In Spanish when you refer to parts of the body and articles of clothing, you often use the definite article, not the possessive adjective.

Él se lava la cara.
Me lavo los dientes.
Me pongo la camisa.

¿Cómo lo digo?

10 Historieta Teresa Contesten.

1. ¿A qué hora se levanta Teresa?
2. ¿Se baña por la mañana o por la noche?
3. ¿Se desayuna en casa?
4. ¿Se lava los dientes después del desayuno?
5. ¿Se pone una chaqueta si sale cuando hace frío?

11 El aseo Contesten personalmente.

1. ¿A qué hora te levantas? ¿Y a qué hora te levantaste esta mañana?
2. ¿Te bañas por la mañana o tomas una ducha? Y esta mañana, ¿te bañaste o tomaste una ducha?
3. ¿Te cepillas los dientes con frecuencia? ¿Cuántas veces te cepillaste los dientes hoy?
4. ¿Te desayunas en casa o en la escuela? Y esta mañana, ¿dónde te desayunaste?
5. ¿Te afeitas o no? Y hoy, ¿te afeitaste?
6. ¿Te peinas con frecuencia? ¿Te miras en el espejo cuando te peinas? ¿Cuántas veces te peinaste hoy?

Answers to ¿Cómo lo digo?

10

1. Teresa se levanta a las ___.
2. Se baña por la mañana (por la noche).
3. Sí, (No, no) se desayuna en casa.
4. Sí, (No, no) se lava los dientes después del desayuno.
5. Sí, se pone una chaqueta si sale cuando hace frío.

11

1. Me levanto a ___. Esta mañana me levanté ___.
2. Me baño (Tomo una ducha) ___. Esta mañana me bañé (tomé una ducha).
3. Sí, (No, no) me cepillo ___. Me cepillé ___.
4. Me desayuno en casa (en la escuela). Esta mañana me desayuné en casa (en la escuela).
5. Sí, (No, no) me afeito. Sí, (No, no) me afeité hoy.
6. Sí, (No, no) me peino ___. Sí, (No, no) me miro ___ me peino. Hoy me peiné ___.

Estructura

Step 6 Call on students to read the model sentences for each illustration or have the class read them in unison.

Step 7 Write the verbs **lavarse** and **levantarse** on the board. After you say **me lavo,** have students supply **me levanto.** Do the same with each subject.

Step 8 Read Items 3 and 4 and have the class read the model sentences aloud.

Step 9 You may wish to give additional examples of verbs that can be both reflexive and nonreflexive.

Yo me lavo.	**Lavo mi carro.**
Él se acuesta.	**Él acuesta al bebé.**
Nos peinamos.	**Peinamos al gato.**

About the Spanish Language

You may wish to explain the following to students:
Ellos se lavan la cara.
Ellos se ponen la chaqueta.
La cara and **la chaqueta** are in the singular because each person has only one face or one jacket. In English the plural forms are used because of the plural subject.

You may also wish to point out to students that the possessive adjectives are not used in Spanish in these reflexive constructions as they are in English.

3 PRACTICE

¿Cómo lo digo?

10 You can do Activity 10 with books closed and then with books open. Have students describe in their own words what Teresa does.

11 Activity 11 reinforces the use of the reflexive with both the present and the preterite.

3 PRACTICE *(continued)*

12 Remind students to use the definite article when referring to parts of the body, as in the model.

13 Have students volunteer additional items. For example: **Ellos salen a las ocho. Ellos se acuestan a las diez.**

LEVELING

E: Activities 12, 14, 15, 17

A: Activities 13, 14, 15, 16, 17

12 **¿Qué hace?** Sigan el modelo.

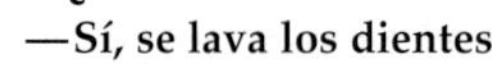

—¿Se lava los dientes?
—Sí, se lava los dientes.

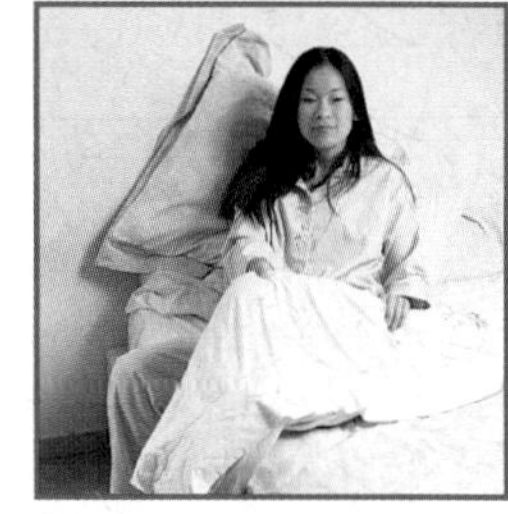

1. 2. 3.

4. 5. 6.

13 **¿Y ustedes?** Sigan el modelo.

Ellos se levantan a las siete.
Nos levantamos a las siete también.

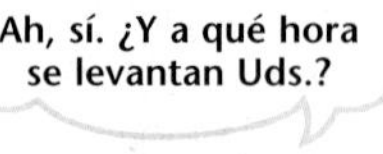

Ah, sí. ¿Y a qué hora se levantan Uds.?

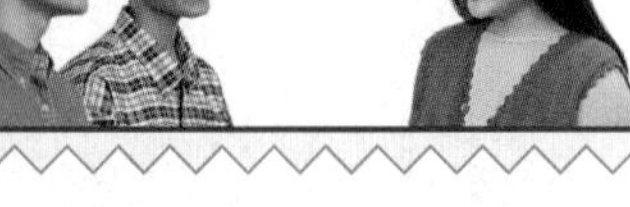

1. Ellos se levantan a las seis y media.
2. Ellos se bañan a las siete menos cuarto.
3. Ellos se desayunan a las siete y media.

ANSWERS TO ¿Cómo lo digo?

12

1. ¿Se afeita? Sí, se afeita.
2. ¿Se sienta? Sí, se sienta.
3. ¿Se lava la cara? Sí, se lava la cara.
4. ¿Se maquilla? (¿Se pone el maquillaje?) Sí, se maquilla (se pone el maquillaje).
5. ¿Se despierta? Sí, se despierta.
6. ¿Se acuesta? Sí, se acuesta.

13 *Answers will begin with:*

Ah, sí. ¿Y a qué hora...

1. ... se levantan Uds.?
   —Nos levantamos a las seis y media también.
2. ... se bañan Uds.?
   —Nos bañamos a las siete menos cuarto también.
3. ... se desayunan Uds.?
   —Nos desayunamos a las siete y media también.

14 **Nombres** Contesten.

1. ¿Cómo te llamas?
2. Y tu hermano(a), ¿cómo se llama?
3. ¿Cómo se llama tu profesor(a) de español?
4. ¿Y cómo se llaman tus abuelos?
5. Una vez más, ¿cómo te llamas?

15 **¿Qué hacen todos?** Completen según las fotos.

1. Yo
   Él
   Tú
   Usted

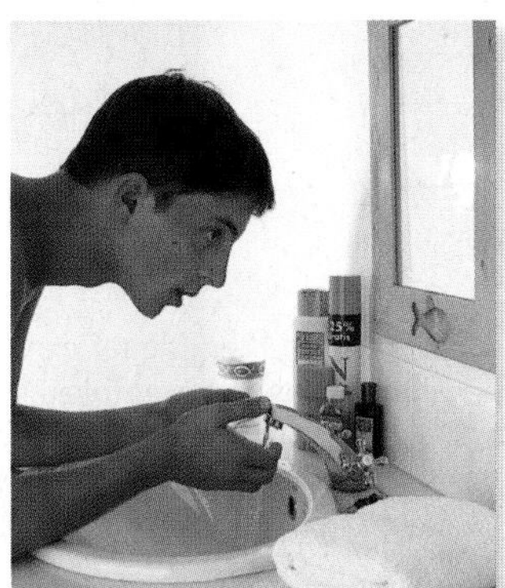

2. Nosotros
   Ellos
   Ustedes
   Él y yo

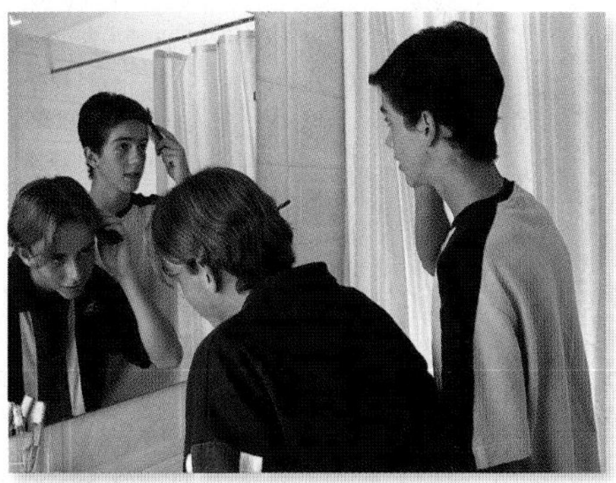

16 **Me desayuno y luego...** Work in groups of three or four. Tell the order of your daily activities from morning to night. Do you all do everything in the same order? Does anyone do things really differently? What's the most common routine? What's the weirdest routine?

17 *Juego* **Me pongo...** Describe some clothing you're putting on. A classmate will guess where you are going or what you are going to do.

Estructura

14 When doing Activity 14, you may wish to go around the room and ask each student **¿Cómo te llamas?** The more times they hear **Me llamo ___,** the better, since students often put **es** after **me llamo.** Up to this point students have identified themselves by using **soy** to avoid this problem.

Reaching All Students

Additional Practice Read this conversation to the class and then ask the questions that follow.

—¿A qué hora te levantas, Carlos?
—¿Quieres saber a qué hora me levanto o a qué hora me despierto?
—¿A qué hora te levantas?
—Me levanto a las siete.
—¿Y a qué hora sales de la casa?
—Salgo a las siete y media. Me lavo, me cepillo los dientes, me afeito y tomo el desayuno en media hora.
—¿Y te pones la ropa también?
—Claro que me pongo la ropa.

Now ask the following questions:

1. **¿Cómo se llama el muchacho?**
2. **¿A qué hora se levanta?**
3. **¿Se cepilla los dientes?**
4. **¿Se afeita?**
5. **¿A qué hora sale de casa?**
6. **¿Se pone la ropa también?**

Answers to ¿Cómo lo digo?

14

1. Me llamo ___.
2. Mi hermano(a) se llama ___. (No tengo un[a] hermano[a]).
3. Mi profesor(a) de español se llama ___.
4. Mis abuelos se llaman ___.
5. Me llamo ___.

15

1. Yo me lavo la cara.
   Él se lava la cara.
   Tú te lavas la cara.
   Ud. se lava la cara.
2. Nosotros nos peinamos.
   Ellos se peinan.
   Uds. se peinan.
   Él y yo nos peinamos.

16 *Answers will vary. Students should come up with at least a dozen activities that they do from morning to night.*

17 *Answers will vary but may include:*

—Me pongo una corbata.
—¿Vas al teatro?
—Me pongo un traje de baño.
—¿Vas a la playa? ¿Vas a nadar?

1 PREPARATION

Bellringer Review

Use BRR Transparency 12.4 or write the following on the board.

Complete.

1. **Yo ___ (ir) a la playa pero mis amigos ___ (ir) a las montañas. Nosotros no ___ (querer) hacer la misma cosa.**
2. **Yo ___ (salir) ahora pero mis amigos no ___ (salir) ahora. Nosotros no ___ (poder) salir a la misma hora.**

2 PRESENTATION

Verbos reflexivos de cambio radical

¡OJO! There is actually no new concept here since students are already familiar with the stem-changing verbs and the reflexive pronouns.

Step 1 Model the forms in the chart on page 386. Have students repeat after you.

Step 2 Quickly go over the examples in Item 2.

3 PRACTICE

¿Cómo lo digo?

18 You may wish to have students do this activity in pairs.

Verbos reflexivos de cambio radical
Telling what people do for themselves

1. The reflexive verbs **acostarse (o → ue)** and **(divertirse e → ie)** are stem-changing verbs. Study the following forms.

INFINITIVE	acostarse	divertirse
yo	me acuesto	me divierto
tú	te acuestas	te diviertes
él, ella, Ud.	se acuesta	se divierte
nosotros(as)	nos acostamos	nos divertimos
vosotros(as)	*os acostáis*	*os divertís*
ellos, ellas, Uds.	se acuestan	se divierten

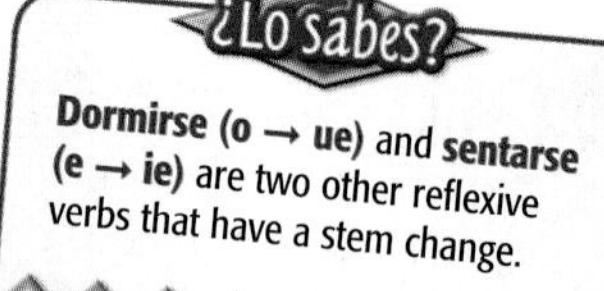

¿Lo sabes?

Dormirse (o → ue) and **sentarse (e → ie)** are two other reflexive verbs that have a stem change.

2. Many verbs in Spanish can be used with a reflexive pronoun. Often the reflexive pronoun gives a different meaning to the verb. Study the following examples.

María pone la blusa en la mochila. *Mary puts the blouse in the backpack.*
María se pone la blusa. *Mary puts on her blouse.*

María duerme ocho horas. *Mary sleeps eight hours.*
María se duerme enseguida. *Mary falls asleep immediately.*

María llama a Carlos. *Mary calls Carlos.*
Ella se llama María. *She calls herself Mary. (Her name is Mary.)*

María divierte a sus amigos. *Mary amuses her friends.*
María se divierte. *Mary amuses herself. (Mary has a good time.)*

¿Cómo lo digo?

18 ¿Cómo lo haces tú?

Contesten personalmente.

1. ¿Duermes en una cama o en un saco de dormir?
2. Cuando te acuestas, ¿te duermes enseguida?
3. Y cuando te despiertas, ¿te levantas enseguida?
4. ¿Te sientas a la mesa para tomar el desayuno?
5. ¿Te diviertes en la escuela?

Cataluña, España

Answers to ¿Cómo lo digo?

18

1. Duermo en una cama (un saco de dormir).
2. Sí (No), cuando me acuesto (no) me duermo enseguida.
3. Sí (No), cuando me despierto (no) me levanto enseguida.
4. Sí, (No, no) me siento a la mesa para tomar el desayuno.
5. Sí, (No, no) me divierto en la escuela.

19 **Historieta Duermo ocho horas.** Completen.

Cuando yo __1__ (acostarse), yo __2__ (dormirse) enseguida. Cada noche yo __3__ (dormir) ocho horas. Yo __4__ (acostarse) a las once y __5__ (levantarse) a las siete de la mañana. Cuando yo __6__ (despertarse), __7__ (levantarse) enseguida. Pero cuando mi hermana __8__ (despertarse), ella no __9__ (levantarse) enseguida. Y mi hermano, cuando él __10__ (acostarse), no __11__ (dormirse) enseguida. Él pasa horas escuchando música en la cama. Así él __12__ (dormir) solamente unas seis horas.

20 **¿Lo está pasando bien? ¿Se divierte?** Choose an illustration below and describe it. A classmate will tell which one you're describing and let you know whether he or she thinks the people are having fun. Take turns.

1. 2. 3. 4.

21 **Juego** **¿Qué tengo?** You have something you have to use every day for part of your daily routine. Tell a classmate what it is. He or she will then guess what you do with it.

—Tengo una navaja.
—Ah, te afeitas.

19 This activity gives students practice using the **yo** and **él** forms of the stem-changing reflexive verbs.

20 Partners should take turns describing each illustration.

21 **Juego** This is a good activity to use at the beginning or end of the class period.
Expansion: To expand this activity, have students think of items they know from earlier chapters. For example: **Tengo unos discos compactos. Tengo un pasaporte,** etc. Have the class choose sides and make this a contest to see which side can think of the most items.

¡Adelante!
At this point in the chapter, students have learned all the vocabulary and structure necessary to complete the chapter. The conversation and cultural readings that follow recycle all the material learned up to this point.

LEVELING
A: Activities 18, 20, 21
C: Activity 19

ANSWERS TO ¿Cómo lo digo?

19

1. me acuesto
2. me duermo
3. duermo
4. me acuesto
5. me levanto
6. me despierto
7. me levanto
8. se despierta
9. se levanta
10. se acuesta
11. se duerme
12. duerme

20 *Answers will vary. Students will use vocabulary learned in previous chapters—going to the beach, watching television, taking a test at school—to describe the illustrations. Students should also use* divertirse *to describe the people.*

21 *Answers will vary. Students should follow the model.*

Conversación

1 PREPARATION

Resource Manager

Audio Activities TE, page 149
Audio CD 7

Bellringer Review

Use BRR Transparency 12.5 or write the following on the board.
Write three things you did this morning before leaving your house.

2 PRESENTATION

Step 1 Have students open their books and scan the conversation.

Step 2 Have them close their books. Read the conversation to them aloud or have them listen to Audio CD 7.

Step 3 Call on two students to read the conversation aloud.

Step 4 After each third of the conversation, ask some comprehension questions from the **¿Comprendes?** section.

Step 5 Have students who like to perform read the entire conversation aloud to the class using as much expression as possible.

Step 6 After presenting the conversation, go over the **¿Comprendes?** activity. If students can answer the questions with relative ease, move on. Students should not be expected to memorize the conversation.

Conversación

¿A qué hora te despertaste?

Timoteo Maripaz, ¿a qué hora te despertaste esta mañana?
Maripaz Esta mañana me levanté un poco tarde.
Timoteo ¿Te levantaste tarde? ¿Por qué?
Maripaz Porque anoche me acosté muy tarde.
Timoteo ¿Por qué te acostaste tan tarde? ¿Saliste?
Maripaz No, no salí. Pasé la noche estudiando. Hoy tengo un examen de álgebra. Estudié hasta la medianoche.
Timoteo ¿Estudiaste hasta la medianoche?
Maripaz Sí, y por lo general me despierto a las seis pero esta mañana no me desperté hasta las seis y media.
Timoteo ¿Llegaste tarde a la escuela?
Maripaz No, afortunadamente llegué a tiempo porque la clase de álgebra es mi primera clase.

¿Comprendes?

Contesten.

1. Esta mañana, ¿se levantó tarde o temprano Maripaz?
2. ¿Por qué se levantó tarde?
3. ¿Salió ella anoche?
4. ¿Cómo pasó la noche?
5. ¿Hasta qué hora estudió?
6. Por lo general, ¿a qué hora se despierta ella?
7. ¿A qué hora se despertó esta mañana?
8. ¿Llegó tarde a la escuela?
9. ¿Cuál es la primera clase de Maripaz?

Answers to ¿Comprendes?

1. Esta mañana Maripaz se levantó un poco tarde.
2. Se levantó tarde porque anoche se acostó muy tarde.
3. No, ella no salió anoche.
4. Pasó la noche estudiando.
5. Estudió hasta la medianoche.
6. Por lo general se despierta a las seis.
7. Esta mañana no se despertó hasta las seis y media.
8. No, no llegó tarde a la escuela; llegó a tiempo.
9. La primera clase de Maripaz es la clase de álgebra.

Vamos a hablar más

A **Me acosté muy tarde.** You got to bed really late last night and you're feeling tired. Tell a classmate why. Then he or she will ask you some questions about what you're doing today and how things are.

B **Vamos a dar una caminata.** You're planning to backpack through a Spanish-speaking country. Work with a classmate. Decide what country you want to go to. Then decide what you are going to take with you, how long you'll be away, how much money you'll need, and how you plan to get around.

Pronunciación

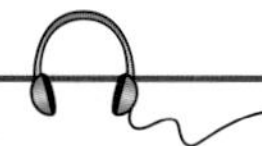

La h, la y, la ll

The **h** in Spanish is silent. It is never pronounced. Repeat the following.

hijo **hotel** **higiénico**
hermano **hace** **hostal**

Y in Spanish can be either a vowel or a consonant. As a vowel, it is pronounced exactly the same as the vowel **i.** Repeat the following.

Juan y María
el jabón y el champú

Y is a consonant when it begins a word or a syllable. As a consonant, **y** is pronounced similarly to the *y* in the English word *yo-yo*. This sound has several variations throughout the Spanish-speaking world. Repeat the following.

ya **desayuno** **ayuda** **playa**

The **ll** is pronounced as a single consonant in Spanish. In many areas of the Spanish-speaking world, it is pronounced the same as the **y**. It too has several variations. Repeat the following.

llama **botella** **cepillo** **toalla**
llega **pastilla** **rollo** **lluvia**

Repeat the following sentences.

La hermana habla hoy con su hermano en el hotel.
Está lloviendo cuando ella llega a la calle Hidalgo.
El hombre lleva una botella de agua a la playa hermosa.

Answers to **Vamos a hablar más**

A *Answers will vary. Students can use the conversation on page 388 as a model for this activity.*

B *Answers will vary. Students should use the vocabulary from* Palabras 1 *and* 2 *and travel-related vocabulary learned in previous chapters.*

Glencoe Technology

CD-ROM

On the CD-ROM, students can watch a dramatization of this conversation. They can then play the role of either one of the characters and record themselves in the conversation.

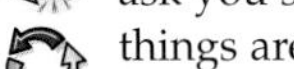

Conversación

3 PRACTICE

Vamos a hablar más

Recycling

Activities A and B allow students to use a great deal of material from earlier chapters.

Pronunciación

¡OJO! In all areas of the Spanish-speaking world the **h** is silent. There are no exceptions. The **ll** and **y** have several variations. In most areas they are pronounced somewhat like the *y* in the English word *yoyo* or in the German word **ja.** In Argentina and Uruguay they are pronounced somewhat like the *j* in *Joe.* In Spain you will also hear a **j** sound, similar to the *y* sound Americans make when they pronounce quickly *Did ya . . . .*

Tell students that it is not unusual for Spanish speakers to misspell words with **y** and **ll.** Since the two letters sound the same, they often mix them up. They will also omit the **h** in words that should have it. Students may find it reassuring that others sometimes have spelling problems too.

Step 1 Have students very carefully repeat the sounds and words after you or Audio CD 7.

Step 2 Ask students to open their books to page 389. Call on individuals to read the sentences.

Step 3 All model sentences on this page can be used for dictation.

LEVELING

E: Conversation

Lecturas culturales

Resource Manager

Audio Activities TE, page 151
Audio CD 7

National Standards

Cultures
The reading on page 390 and the related activities on page 391 allow students to learn about a very popular hiking or biking trip through northern Spain that follows the old **Camino de Santiago.**

PRESENTATION

Pre-reading

Step 1 Students should open their books to page 390.

Step 2 Have them skim the passage as recommended in the Reading Strategy.

Step 3 Have students go to the map of Spain on page xxx or project Map Transparency M 2. Indicate the area of Spain described in this reading. Point out San Sebastián and Santiago de Compostela.

Reading

As you go over each paragraph using any of the suggestions given throughout the textbook, you can call on a student to summarize the paragraph in his or her own words.

Post-reading

Have students do the **¿Comprendes?** activities on page 391.

LEVELING

E: Reading

Lecturas culturales

Del norte de España

Reading Strategy

Skimming There are several ways to read an article or a passage—each one with its own purpose. Skimming means reading quickly in order to find out the general idea of a passage. To skim means to read without paying careful attention to small details, noting only information about the main theme or topic. Sometimes a reader will skim a passage only to decide whether it's interesting enough to then read it in detail.

¡Hola! Me llamo Iván Orama. Soy de San Juan, Puerto Rico. Pero ahora no estoy en Puerto Rico. Estoy en España donde un grupo de amigos de nuestro colegio estamos pasando el verano. Es una experiencia fabulosa. Nos divertimos mucho. ¿Me permites describir un día típico?

Esta mañana nos despertamos temprano. Todos nos levantamos enseguida. Con la mochila en la espalda[1] salimos de la pensión. Fuimos a una cafetería donde nos desayunamos. Yo tomé un jugo de china o, como lo llaman aquí en España, un zumo de naranja. Marta comió churros, una cosa típica española. Y los otros, no sé lo que comieron.

Cuando salimos del café, fuimos en nuestras bicicletas en dirección a Santiago de Compostela. Estamos siguiendo[2] más o menos el Camino[3] de Santiago.

[1]en la espalda *on our backs*
[2]siguiendo *following*
[3]Camino *Way, Route*

El lago Enol en el Parque Nacional de Covadonga, España

Learning from Photos

(page 390 bottom) In the **Parque Nacional de la Sierra de Covadonga** in Asturias, there are two alpine lakes with cold, crystal-clear water. They are Lake Enol, seen here, and Lake Ercina. At a higher elevation there is a lookout called **el Mirador de la reina** from which one gets a view all the way to the ocean.
(page 391) The sophisticated city of San Sebastián arcs around the lovely beach La Concha, seen in the photo on this page. It is called La Concha because it has almost the exact same shape as a scallop shell. In the middle of the entrance to the Bay of Biscay there is a tiny island, **Isla de Santa Clara.** This island protects the city from the storms that come from the Bay of Biscay. La Concha is one of the calmest beaches on the northern coast of Spain.

El otro día pasamos un día estupendo en San Sebastián. Nos sentamos en la playa y nos bañamos en el mar Cantábrico. Te aseguro[4] que el agua del Cantábrico está mucho más fría que el agua del Caribe en nuestro Puerto Rico.

El lunes dimos una caminata por los Picos de Europa. Fue increíble. Los picos son tan altos que aún[5] en julio están cubiertos de nieve.

No sabemos cuándo vamos a llegar a Santiago. Pero lo estamos pasando muy bien. Nos divertimos mucho.

[4]Te aseguro *I assure you*
[5]aún *even*

San Sebastián, España

¿Comprendes?

A Un día con los amigos Contesten.

1. ¿Cómo se llama el muchacho?
2. ¿De dónde es?
3. ¿Dónde está ahora?
4. ¿Con quiénes está?
5. ¿Qué están haciendo?
6. ¿Cuándo se levantaron esta mañana?
7. ¿Adónde fueron cuando salieron de la pensión?
8. ¿Qué comió Marta en el desayuno?

B Más sobre la caminata Escojan.

1. Cuando salieron del café, fueron ____.
   a. al albergue juvenil
   b. a San Sebastián
   c. hacia Santiago de Compostela
2. Pasaron el otro día ____.
   a. en la playa
   b. en el Camino de Santiago
   c. en el Cantábrico
3. Hay una playa bonita en ____.
   a. Santiago de Compostela
   b. los Picos de Europa
   c. San Sebastián
4. El agua del mar está fría en ____.
   a. el mar Cantábrico
   b. el mar Caribe
   c. los Picos de Europa
5. Los Picos de Europa están cubiertos de nieve porque ____.
   a. están cerca del mar Cantábrico
   b. son muy altos y allí hace mucho frío
   c. son increíbles

C La ruta Dibujen un mapa de la ruta de los jóvenes.

Lecturas culturales

¿Comprendes?

A and **B** These activities may be used as testing devices to see how well students understood the **Lectura.**

C Have students trace the map of Spain on page xxx or use it as a model to draw an outline map of Spain for them. You may also wish to use Map Transparency M 2 for this activity.

History Connection

For centuries San Sebastián was a place of little importance. In 1845, however, Isabel II went to San Sebastián seeking relief from a skin ailment in the icy waters of the Atlantic. Much of the aristocracy followed her to San Sebastián, and in very little time the city became a favorite spot of the wealthy. To this day the city attracts an upscale group of Spanish summer vacationers who prefer the cooler weather and cultural events of San Sebastián to the hotter, sunnier beaches of the South.

Answers to

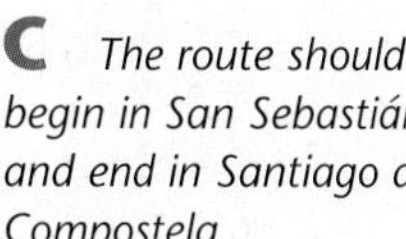

A

1. El muchacho se llama Iván Orama.
2. Es de San Juan, Puerto Rico.
3. Ahora está en España.
4. Está con un grupo de amigos de su colegio.
5. Están pasando el verano en España.
6. Esta mañana se levantaron temprano.
7. Fueron a una cafetería cuando salieron de la pensión.
8. Marta comió churros.

B

1. c
2. a
3. c
4. a
5. b

C *The route should begin in San Sebastián and end in Santiago de Compostela.*

Lectura opcional

National Standards

Cultures

This reading about **el Camino de Santiago** in northern Spain allows students to learn about one of the historic pilgrimages that took place during the Middle Ages.

¡OJO! This reading is optional. You may skip it completely, have the entire class read it, have only several students read it and report to the class, or assign it for extra credit.

PRESENTATION

Step 1 Have students look at the photos on these two pages as they read about these places in the **Lectura.**

Step 2 Have students discuss the information they find interesting.

Learning from Photos

(page 392 right) This cathedral was built to be an impressive edifice. Have students try to imagine pilgrims some five centuries ago walking across Spain for thirty long days and finally arriving at the foot of this magnificent cathedral. Its size alone inspires awe.

Lectura opcional

El Camino de Santiago

Durante la Edad Media[1] hay tres peregrinaciones[2] famosas—la peregrinación a Jerusalén en Israel, la peregrinación a Roma y la peregrinación a Santiago de Compostela.

Santiago de Compostela está en Galicia, una región pintoresca en el noroeste de España. Galicia se parece más a[3] Irlanda que al resto de España. Llueve mucho en Galicia y todo es muy verde.

El Camino de Santiago es el camino que tomaron los peregrinos de la Edad Media. El camino empieza en los Pirineos, en el pueblo de Roncesvalles y termina en Santiago. Atraviesa o cruza todo el norte de España. ¿Por qué quieren ir a Santiago los peregrinos? Porque creen que allí está enterrado[4] el apóstol Santiago.

[1]Edad Media *Middle Ages*
[2]peregrinaciones *pilgrimages*
[3]se parece más a *looks more like*
[4]enterrado *buried*

Galicia, España

La catedral en Santiago de Compostela

Los peregrinos viajan a pie (caminan) de un pueblo a otro. Cada día cubren un trecho[5] (tramo) fijo. Al final de cada trecho hay un hostal donde los peregrinos pueden pasar la noche. En el siglo XI hay hostales que pueden alojar[6] a unos mil peregrinos.

Una vez más el Camino de Santiago es muy popular. Hoy día muchos turistas toman la misma ruta. Pero no van a pie. Van en carro. Y muchos jóvenes van en bicicleta.

[5]trecho *stretch*
[6]alojar *lodge, accommodate*

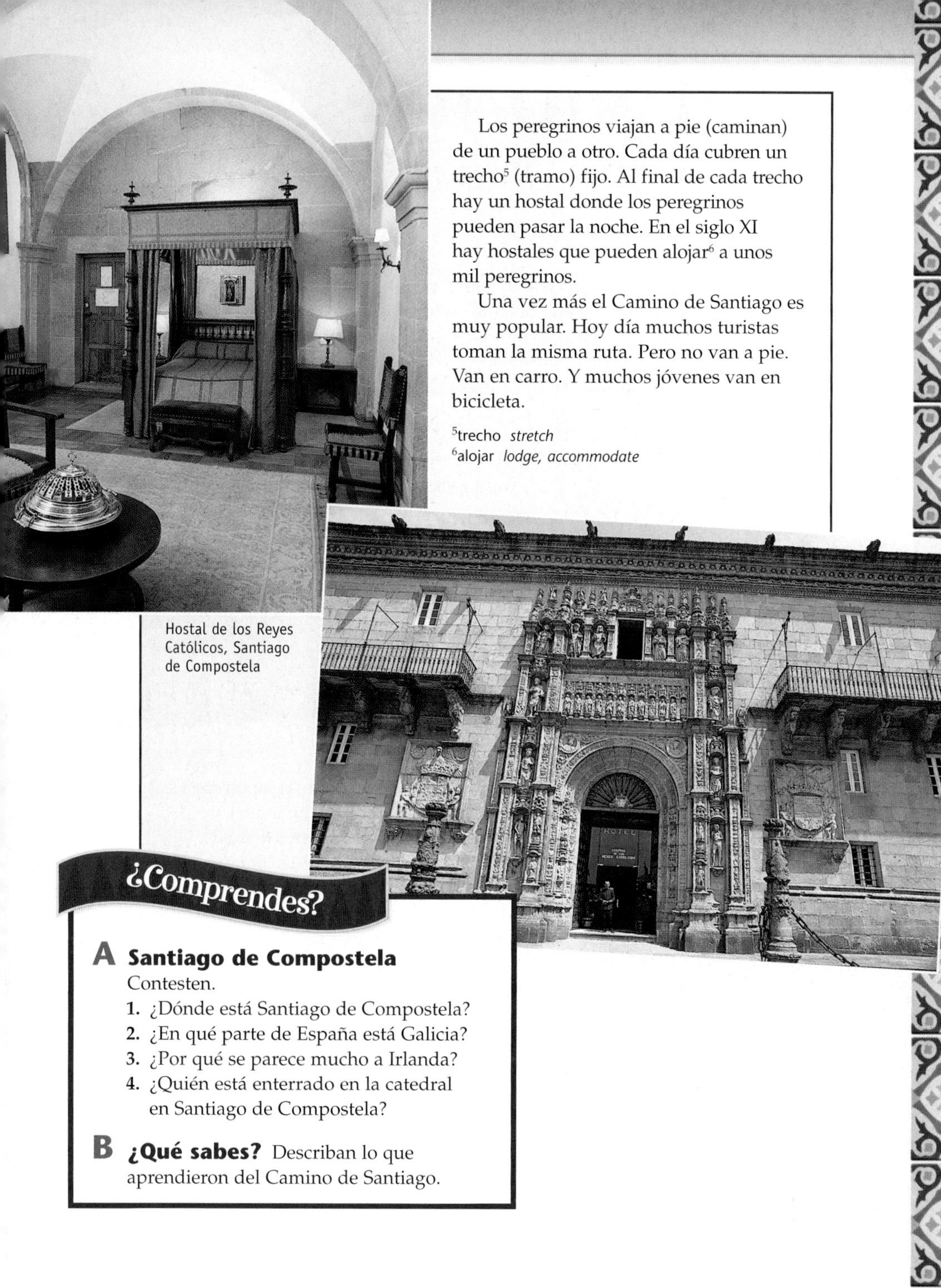

Hostal de los Reyes Católicos, Santiago de Compostela

¿Comprendes?

A Santiago de Compostela
Contesten.

1. ¿Dónde está Santiago de Compostela?
2. ¿En qué parte de España está Galicia?
3. ¿Por qué se parece mucho a Irlanda?
4. ¿Quién está enterrado en la catedral en Santiago de Compostela?

B ¿Qué sabes? Describan lo que aprendieron del Camino de Santiago.

Learning from Photos

(page 393) Another magnificent structure on the same square as the cathedral is the **Hostal de los Reyes Católicos.** It was constructed by Fernando and Isabel in 1499 in gratitude to Santiago for having expelled the Moors. It is the oldest hotel in the world, receiving guests for five centuries. It was a hospital for those who fell ill on the road during their pilgrimage. It remained a hospital until 1953 when it was converted into a luxurious **parador.** It is one of the most beautiful and famous of all the Spanish **paradores.** Students will learn more about these **paradores** in **¡Buen viaje! Level 2.**

¿Comprendes?

A You may use this activity to assess how well your students understood the reading.

B Have each student say one thing about the reading.

LEVELING

A: Reading

Answers to ¿Comprendes?

A *Answers will vary but may include:*

1. Santiago de Compostela está en Galicia.
2. Está en el noroeste de España.
3. Se parece mucho a Irlanda porque llueve mucho en Galicia y todo es muy verde.
4. El apóstol Santiago está enterrado allí.

B *Answers will vary; however, the description should be brief, rather than detailed.*

Conexiones

National Standards

Connections
This reading about ecology establishes a connection with another discipline, allowing students to reinforce and further their knowledge of the natural sciences through the study of Spanish.

¡OJO! The readings in the **Conexiones** section are optional. They focus on some of the major disciplines taught in schools and universities. The vocabulary is useful for discussing such topics as history, literature, art, economics, business, science, etc. You may choose any of the following ways to do the readings in the **Conexiones** sections.

Independent reading Have students read the selections and do the post-reading activities as homework, which you collect. This option is least intrusive on class time and requires a minimum of teacher involvement.

Homework with in-class follow-up Assign the readings and post-reading activities as homework. Review and discuss the material in class the next day.

Intensive in-class activity This option includes a pre-reading vocabulary presentation, in-class reading and discussion, assignment of the activities for homework, and a discussion of the assignment in class the following day.

Conexiones

Las ciencias naturales

La ecología

Ecology is a subject of great interest to young people around the world. No one wants to wake up each morning and breathe polluted air. No one wants to hike along a river bank that is loaded with debris or swim in a contaminated ocean. As people travel around the world, they are appalled by the destruction they see done to the environment. We are all aware that urgent and dramatic steps must be taken to avert future ecological disasters.

Santiago, Chile

La ecología

El término «ecología» significa el equilibrio entre los seres vivientes—los seres humanos—y la naturaleza[1]. Hoy en día hay grandes problemas ecológicos en casi todas partes del mundo.

Caracas, Venezuela

La contaminación del aire

La contaminación del medio ambiente[2] es el problema número uno. La contaminación de todos los tipos es la plaga de nuestros tiempos.

El aire que respiramos[3] está contaminado. Está contaminado principalmente por las emisiones de gases que escapan de los automóviles y camiones. Está contaminado también por el humo[4] que emiten las chimeneas de las fábricas[5] que queman[6] sustancias químicas.

[1]naturaleza *nature*
[2]medio ambiente *environment*
[3]respiramos *we breathe*
[4]humo *smoke*
[5]fábricas *factories*
[6]queman *burn*

Vocabulary Expansion

You may wish to give students a few extra words and phrases:

el aumento de la temperatura global	*global warming*
la lluvia ácida	*acid rain*
la erosión	*erosion*
la energía solar	*solar energy*
la extinción	*extinction*
los fluoro-carburos	*fluorocarbons*
la conservación	*conservation*

Learning from Photos

(pages 394–395) For each photo, have students choose one sentence from the reading that best describes that photo. For example, for Santiago they might say: **La contaminación del medio ambiente es el problema número uno.**

El agua

Nuestras aguas están contaminadas también. Buques petroleros derraman[7] cantidades de petróleo cada año en nuestros mares y océanos. En las zonas industriales las fábricas echan los desechos[8] industriales en los ríos. Muchos de los desechos son tóxicos. Los ríos contaminados son portadores[9] de enfermedades serias.

El reciclaje

Hoy en día hay grandes campañas de reciclaje. El reciclaje consiste en recoger los desechos—papel, vidrio[10], metal—para transformar y poder utilizar estos productos de nuevo (una vez más).

[7]Buques petroleros derraman *Oil tankers spill*
[8]desechos *wastes*
[9]portadores *carriers*
[10]vidrio *glass*

Río de la Plata, Buenos Aires

A En español, por favor. Busquen las palabras equivalentes en español.

1. ecology
2. ecological problems
3. air pollution
4. toxic wastes
5. recycling

B Para discutir Contesten.

1. ¿Está contaminado el aire donde ustedes viven?
2. ¿Hay mucha industria donde viven?
3. ¿Hay muchas fábricas?
4. ¿Hay muchos automóviles y camiones?
5. ¿Escapan gases de los automóviles?
6. ¿Hay campañas de reciclaje donde viven?

For more information about environmental issues in the Spanish-speaking world, go to the Glencoe Spanish Web site: spanish.glencoe.com

Conexiones

PRESENTATION

Las ciencias naturales
La ecología

¡OJO! Even if you do not have students read this selection in depth, you may have them skim it since the information is of interest to many. It will also expose students to some current ecological terms that are useful for them to know, if only for receptive purposes.

Step 1 Have students read the introduction in English on page 394.

Step 2 Have students scan each reading section for cognates. Then have them do the reading again, this time for comprehension.

¿Comprendes?

A This activity encourages students to look for cognates as they read.

B This activity is designed to encourage students to think about ecological conditions in their immediate community.

Reaching All Students

For the Younger Students Have students identify an ecological problem at your school or in your community. Have them make a poster in Spanish identifying the problem and offering some solutions to it. Hang the posters up in the classroom or around the school. You might consider doing this for Earth Day.

LEVELING

A: Reading

ANSWERS TO ¿Comprendes?

A

1. la ecología
2. problemas ecológicos
3. la contaminación del aire
4. los desechos tóxicos
5. el reciclaje

B *Answers will vary but may include:*

1. Sí (No), el aire donde vivimos (no) está contaminado.
2. Sí, (No, no) hay mucha industria donde vivimos.
3. Sí, (No, no) hay muchas fábricas.
4. Sí, (No, no) hay muchos automóviles y camiones.
5. Sí, escapan gases de los automóviles.
6. Sí, (No, no) hay campañas de reciclaje donde vivimos.

¡Te toca a ti!

Use what you have learned

Recycling

These activities allow students to use the vocabulary and structure from this chapter in completely open-ended, real-life situations.

PRESENTATION

Encourage students to say as much as possible when they do these activities. Tell them not to be afraid to make mistakes, since the goal of the activities is real-life communication. If someone in the group makes an error, allow the others to politely correct him or her. Let students choose the activities they would like to do.

You may wish to divide students into pairs or groups. Encourage students to elaborate on the basic theme and to be creative. They may use props, pictures, or posters if they wish.

Writing Development

Have students keep a notebook or portfolio containing their best written work from each chapter. These selected writings can be based on assignments from the Student Textbook and the Workbook. Activities 4 and 5 on page 397 are examples of writing assignments that may be included in each student's portfolio. On page 158 in the Workbook, students will begin to develop an organized autobiography **(Mi autobiografía).** These workbook pages may also become a part of their portfolio.

¡Te toca a ti!

Use what you have learned

HABLAR **1**

Mi familia

✔ ***Compare your family's routine to someone else's***

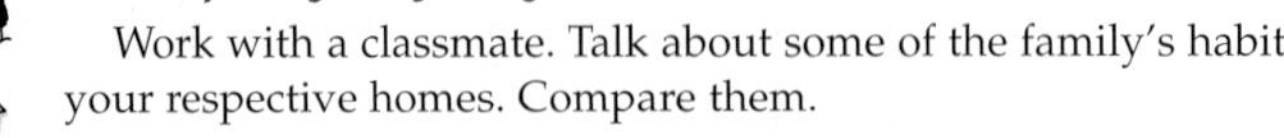

Work with a classmate. Talk about some of the family's habits in your respective homes. Compare them.

HABLAR **2**

Una gira

✔ ***Talk about a backpacking trip***

Work with a classmate. The two of you plan to backpack around Spain next summer. Discuss all the things you plan or want to do.

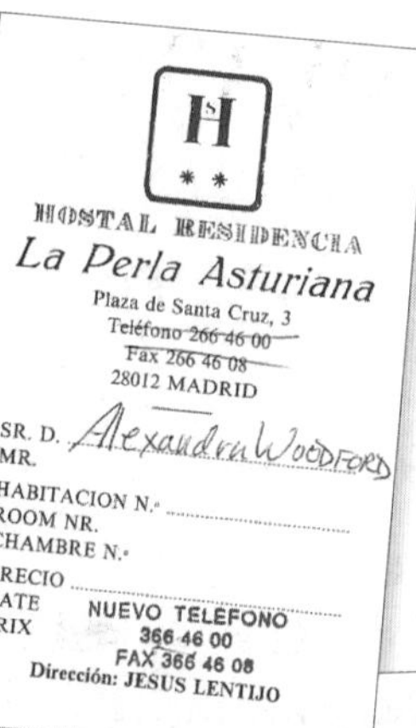

H
HOSTAL RESIDENCIA
La Perla Asturiana
Plaza de Santa Cruz, 3
Teléfono 266 46 00
Fax 266 46 08
28012 MADRID
SR. D. MR. Alexandra Woodford
HABITACION N.º ROOM NR. CHAMBRE N.º
PRECIO RATE PRIX
NUEVO TELEFONO 366 46 00
FAX 366 46 08
Dirección: JESUS LENTIJO
Hostal Goya
Barrio de Santa Cruz
Habitación Chambre n.º 30
Mateos Gago, 31 - 41004 SEVILLA - Teléfono 421 11 70 - Fax 456 29 88

ANSWERS TO ¡Te toca a ti!

1 *Answers will vary. Students should use reflexive verbs to talk about their family's routines.*

2 *Answers will vary. Students should use reflexive verbs and travel-related vocabulary from this and previous chapters.*

3 Hay una diferencia.

✔ *Talk about your weekday and weekend routines*

Most people like a change of pace on the weekend. Talk with a classmate about things that students do or don't do during the week. Your partner will say how that differs on the weekend and why. Take turns.

Durante la semana los alumnos se despiertan muy temprano.

Durante los fines de semana los alumnos se despiertan más tarde.

4 Un día típico

✔ *Write about your daily routine*

Your Colombian pen pal is curious about your daily routine. Send him or her an e-mail describing all the activities you do on a typical day from the time you wake up to the time you go to bed.

5 Un trabajo de verano

You are working abroad this summer. You are going to help take care of two small children in Seville, Spain. The children's mother gives you many instructions about the children's routine and activities. Since you probably will not remember all she is telling you, you jot down notes. Take your notes and organize them to describe each child's day. Then write down your responsibilities—what it is you have to do.

Writing Strategy

Taking notes Taking notes gives you a written record of important information you may need for later use. When taking notes, write down key words and phrases as you continue to focus on what the speaker is still saying. When the speaker has finished, go back over your notes as soon as possible, highlighting the most important points and adding details to make them as complete as possible. If necessary, rewrite your notes, organizing them so they will be of utmost use to you.

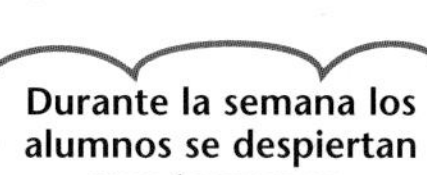

¡Te toca a ti!

PRACTICE

3 Students can also tell each other how their own routine changes on the weekend. For example: **Durante la semana me levanto a las seis pero los sábados me levanto a las nueve.**

4 If students have done Activity 16, page 385, they will be well prepared to write this e-mail.

Writing Strategy

Taking notes Have students read the Writing Strategy on page 397. You may wish to have them work in pairs to do this pre-writing activity. Students can take turns playing the role of the mother as the other takes notes. Encourage them to be as creative as possible when outlining the children's routine. Students may want to arbitrarily assign Spanish names to the two children.

Leveling

These activities encompass all three levels. All students will be able to do them at a sophistication level commensurate with their ability in Spanish. Some students will be able to speak for several minutes, and others may be able to give just a few sentences. This is to be expected when students are functioning completely on their own generating their own language to the best of their ability.

Answers to ¡Te toca a ti!

3 *Answers will vary. Students will typically answer by giving a description of a normal school day or a weekend day using reflexive verbs.*

4 *Answers will vary. Students will use reflexive verbs.*

5 *Answers will vary. Students should use the verbs from this chapter reflexively and nonreflexively.*

Resource Manager

Communication Transparency C 12
Quizzes, pages 60–64
Performance Assessment, Task 12
Tests, pages 195–206
Situation Cards, Chapter 12
ExamView® Pro, Chapter 12
Maratón mental Videoquiz, Chapter 12

Assessment

This is a pre-test for students to take before you administer the chapter test. Note that each section is cross-referenced so students can easily find the material they have to review in case they made errors. You may use Assessment Answers Transparency A 12 to do the assessment in class, or you may assign this assessment for homework. You can correct the assessment yourself, or you may prefer to project the answers on the overhead in class.

Glencoe Technology

MINDJOGGER VHS/DVD

You may wish to help your students prepare for the chapter test by playing the MindJogger game show. Teams will compete against each other to review chapter vocabulary and structure and sharpen listening comprehension skills.

Vocabulario

To review **Palabras 1**, turn to pages 374–375.

1 Pareen.

a. 
b. 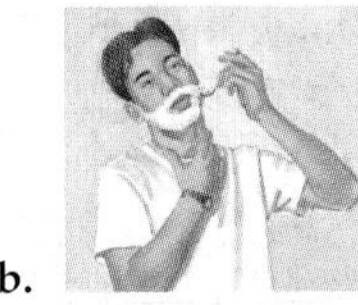
c. 
d. 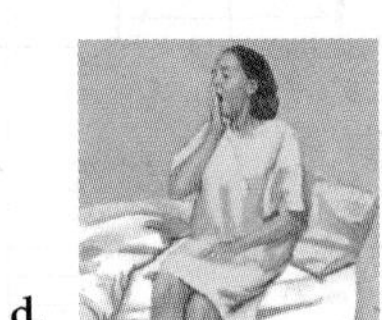

1. ____ Se afeita.
2. ____ Se acuesta.
3. ____ Se peina.
4. ____ Se levanta.

2 Identifiquen.

To review **Palabras 2**, turn to pages 378–379.

3 Completen.

8. Lo están pasando muy bien. ____ mucho.
9. No duermen en una cama. Duermen en un ____.
10. Un ____ es un tipo de hotel económico donde un cuarto no cuesta mucho.

4 Identifiquen.

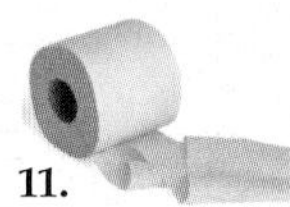
11.

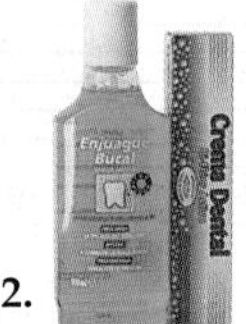

12.

13.

Answers to Assessment

1
1. b
2. d
3. a
4. c

2
5. el pan tostado
6. (un vaso de) jugo de naranja
7. el cereal

3
8. Se divierten
9. saco de dormir
10. albergue (hostal)

4
11. un rollo de papel higiénico
12. (un tubo de) pasta (crema) dentífrica
13. una barra (una pastilla) de jabón

Estructura

5 Completen en el presente.

14–15. Cuando yo ____, ____ la cara enseguida. (levantarse, lavarse)
16. ¿A qué hora ____ ustedes? (acostarse)
17. ¿Tu hermano ____? (afeitarse)
18. Nosotros ____ mucho. (divertirse)
19–20. Cuando tú ____, ¿____ enseguida? (acostarse, dormirse)

To review reflexive verbs, turn to pages 382 and 386.

6 Completen cuando necesario.

21. Yo ____ pongo mi chaqueta en la maleta porque ____ pongo la chaqueta cuando hace frío.
22. Ella ____ duerme enseguida y luego ____ duerme ocho horas sin problema.

Cultura

7 Den la(s) palabra(s).

23. *orange juice* en España y Puerto Rico
24. una cosa típica que comen los españoles en el desayuno
25. el mar que baña las costas de Puerto Rico

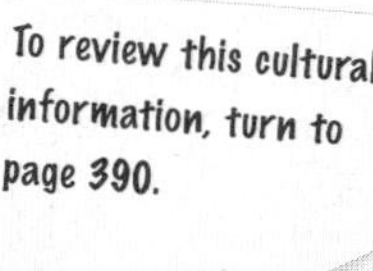
To review this cultural information, turn to page 390.

San Juan, Puerto Rico

Assessment

SPANISH Online

The **Glencoe Spanish Web** site (spanish.glencoe.com) offers options that enable you and your students to experience the Spanish-speaking world via the Internet. For each **Capítulo,** there are activities, games, and quizzes. In addition, an *Enrichment* section offers students an opportunity to visit Web sites related to the theme of the chapter.

FOLDABLES™ Study Organizer **Dinah Zike's Study Guides**

Your students may wish to use Foldable 6 to organize, display, and arrange data as they develop communication skills in Spanish. You may wish to encourage them to add information from each chapter as they continue to expand their ability to describe, explain, and discuss all the different topics they are studying.

A *miniature matchbook* foldable is ideal in helping students to give more complex descriptions about topics they have studied in Spanish.

Answers to Assessment

5

14. me levanto
15. me lavo
16. se acuestan
17. se afeita
18. nos divertimos
19. te acuestas
20. te duermes

6

21. —, me
22. se, —

7

23. zumo de naranja, jugo de china
24. churros
25. el mar Caribe

¡Hablo como un pro!

This unique page gives students the opportunity to speak freely and say whatever they can, using the vocabulary and structures they have learned in the chapter. The illustration serves to remind students of precisely what they know how to say in Spanish. There are no activities that students do not have the ability to describe or talk about in Spanish. The art not only depicts the vocabulary and content of this chapter, but also reinforces what they learned in previous chapters.

You may wish to use this page in many ways. Some possibilities are to have students do the following.

1. Look at the illustration and identify items by giving the correct Spanish words.
2. Make up sentences about what they see in the illustration.
3. Make up questions about the illustration. They can call on another class member to respond if you do this as a class activity, or you may prefer to allow students to work in small groups. This activity is extremely beneficial because it enables students to actively use interrogative words.
4. Answer questions you ask them about the illustration.
5. Work in pairs and make up a conversation based on the illustration.
6. Look at the illustration and give a complete oral review of what they see.
7. Look at the illustration and write a paragraph (or essay) about it.

You can also use this page as an assessment or testing tool, taking into account individual differences by having students go from simple to quite complicated tasks. The assessment can be either oral or written.

¡Hablo como un pro!

Tell all you can about this illustration.

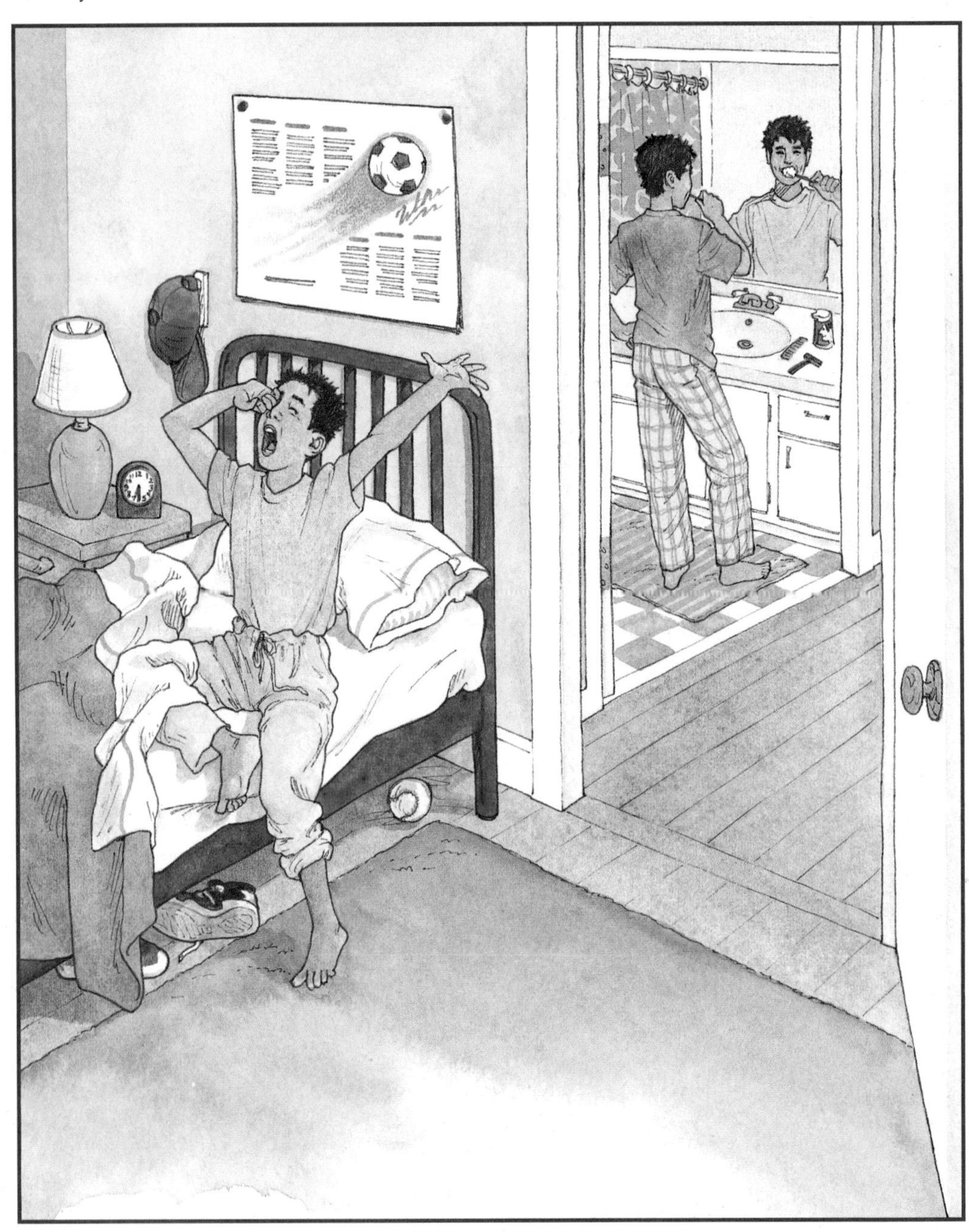

You may wish to use the rubrics provided on pages T20–T21 as you give students the following directions.

1. Identify the topic or situation of the illustration.
2. Give the Spanish words for as many items as you can.
3. Think of as many sentences as you can to describe the illustration.
4. Go over your sentences and put them in the best sequencing to give a coherent story based on the illustration.

Vocabulario

Stating daily activities

la rutina
despertarse(ie)
levantarse
lavarse
bañarse
tomar una ducha
afeitarse
ponerse la ropa
mirarse
maquillarse
cepillarse
peinarse
sentarse(ie)
desayunarse
acostarse(ue)
dormirse(ue)
llamarse
divertirse(ie)

Identifying articles for grooming and hygiene

la navaja
la crema de afeitar
el cepillo
el peine
el cepillo de dientes
el espejo
el maquillaje
una barra (una pastilla) de jabón
un tubo de pasta (crema) dentífrica
un rollo de papel higiénico
el champú

How well do you know your vocabulary?

- Choose an expression from the list that describes something you do as part of your daily routine.
- Ask a classmate to give words related to that particular daily activity.

Identifying more parts of the body

la cara
los dientes
el pelo

Identifying more breakfast foods

una botella de agua mineral
un vaso de jugo de naranja
el cereal
el pan tostado

Episodio 12

In this video episode, you will join Claudia and Alejandra on a hike. See page 503 for more information.

Describing backpacking

una gira
la mochila
el saco de dormir
el albergue para jóvenes
el hostal
la pensión
dar una caminata
ir en bicicleta

Other useful expressions

el lugar
de vez en cuando

Vocabulario

Vocabulary Review

The words and phrases in the **Vocabulario** have been taught for productive use in this chapter. They are summarized here as a resource for both student and teacher. This list also serves as a convenient resource for the **¡Te toca a ti!** activities on pages 396 and 397. There are approximately five cognates in this vocabulary list. Have students find them.

The Video Program allows students to see how the chapter vocabulary and structures are used by native speakers within an engaging story line. For maximum reinforcement, show the video episode as a final activity for Chapter 12.

¡OJO! You will notice that the vocabulary list here is not translated. This has been done intentionally, since we feel that by the time students have finished the material in the chapter they should be familiar with the meanings of all the words. If there are several words they still do not know, we recommend that they refer to the **Palabras 1** and **2** sections in the chapter or go to the dictionaries at the end of this book to find the meanings. However, if you prefer that your students have the English translations, please refer to Vocabulary Transparency 12.1, where you will find all these words with their translations.

Planning for Chapter 13

SCOPE AND SEQUENCE, PAGES 402–431

Topics

- ❖ Train travel
- ❖ Travel-related activities

Culture

- ❖ José Luis and Maripaz take the AVE train to Seville
- ❖ Taking the train from Cuzco to Machu Picchu
- ❖ La Plaza de Armas, Cuzco
- ❖ Machu Picchu
- ❖ The 24-hour clock and the metric system

Functions

- ❖ How to use words and expressions related to train travel
- ❖ How to describe various types of trains and train services
- ❖ How to tell what people say
- ❖ How to talk about events or activities that took place at a definite time in the past

Structure

- ❖ **Hacer, querer,** and **venir** in the preterite
- ❖ Irregular verbs in the preterite
- ❖ **Decir** in the present and in the preterite

National Standards

- ❖ Communication Standard 1.1 pages 406, 407, 410, 412, 413, 415, 416, 417, 426
- ❖ Communication Standard 1.2 pages 407, 411, 413, 418, 419, 421, 423, 425, 426, 427
- ❖ Communication Standard 1.3 pages 411, 427
- ❖ Cultures Standard 2.1 pages 418, 419
- ❖ Cultures Standard 2.2 pages 407, 420–421, 422–423
- ❖ Connections Standard 3.1 pages 424–425
- ❖ Comparisons Standard 4.2 pages 424–425
- ❖ Communities Standard 5.1 page 407

PACING AND PRIORITIES

The chapter content is color coded below to assist you in planning.

■ required ■ recommended ■ optional

Vocabulario *(required)* *Days 1–4*

- ■ Palabras 1
  En la estación de ferrocarril
- ■ Palabras 2
  En el tren

Estructura *(required)* *Days 5–7*

- ■ **Hacer, querer** y **venir** en el pretérito
- ■ Verbos irregulares en el pretérito
- ■ **Decir** en el presente y en el pretérito

Conversación *(required)*

- ■ En la ventanilla

Pronunciación *(recommended)*

- ■ Las consonantes **ñ, ch**

Lecturas culturales

- ■ En el AVE *(recommended)*
- ■ De Cuzco a Machu Picchu *(optional)*

Conexiones

- ■ Conversiones aritméticas *(optional)*

■ **¡Te toca a ti!** *(recommended)*

■ **Assessment** *(recommended)*

■ **¡Hablo como un pro!** *(optional)*

RESOURCE GUIDE

Section	Pages	Section Resources
Vocabulario PALABRAS 1		
En la estación de ferrocarril	404–407	Vocabulary Transparencies 13.2–13.3 Audio CD 8 Audio Activities TE, pages 153–156 Workbook, pages 159–160 Quiz 1, page 65 ExamView® Pro
Vocabulario PALABRAS 2		
En el tren	408–411	Vocabulary Transparencies 13.4–13.5 Audio CD 8 Audio Activities TE, pages 157–158 Workbook, pages 161–162 Quiz 2, page 66 ExamView® Pro
Estructura		
Hacer, querer y **venir** en el pretérito Verbos irregulares en el pretérito **Decir** en el presente y en el pretérito	412–413 414–416 416–417	Audio CD 8 Audio Activities TE, pages 159–161 Workbook, pages 163–166 Quizzes 3–5, pages 67–69 ExamView® Pro
Conversación		
En la ventanilla	418	Audio CD 8 Audio Activities TE, pages 161–162 Interactive CD-ROM
Pronunciación		
Las consonantes **ñ, ch**	419	Pronunciation Transparency P 13 Audio CD 8 Audio Activities TE, page 162
Lecturas culturales		
En el AVE De Cuzco a Machu Picchu	420–421 422–423	Audio CD 8 Audio Activities TE, page 163 Tests, pages 209, 211–212
Conexiones		
Conversiones aritméticas	424–425	Tests, page 213
¡Te toca a ti!		
	426–427	**¡Viva el mundo hispano!** Video, Episode 13 Video Activities, Chapter 13 Spanish Online Activities spanish.glencoe.com
Assessment		
	428–429	Communication Transparency C 13 Quizzes 1–5, pages 65–69 Performance Assessment, Task 13 Tests, pages 207–220 Situation Cards, Chapter 13 ExamView® Pro **Maratón mental** Videoquiz

Using Your Resources for Chapter 13

Transparencies

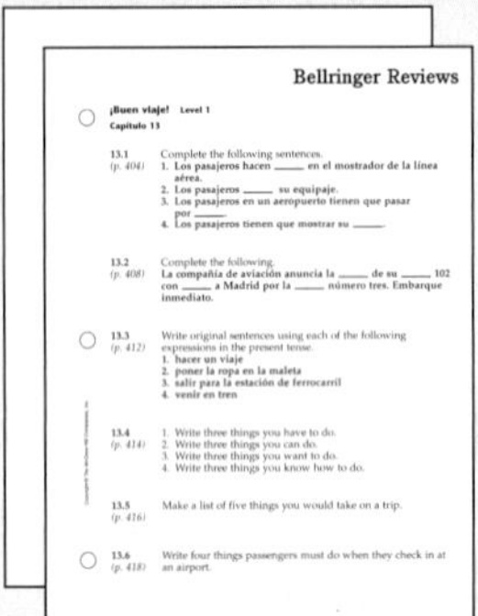
Bellringer 13.1–13.6

Vocabulary 13.1–13.5

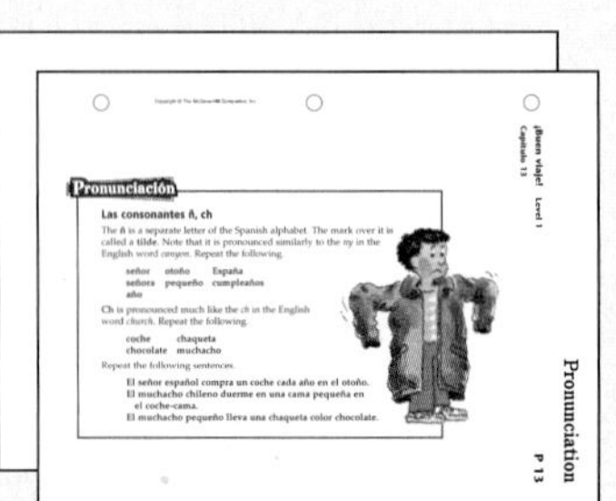
Pronunciation P 13

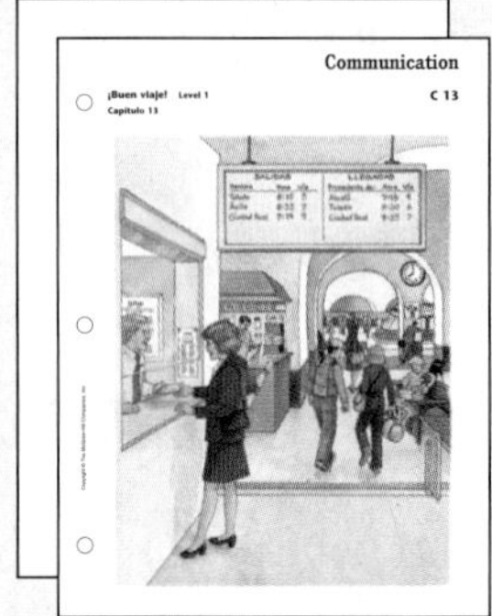
Communication C 13

Workbook

Vocabulary, pages 159–162

Structure, pages 163–166

Enrichment, pages 167–170

Audio Activities

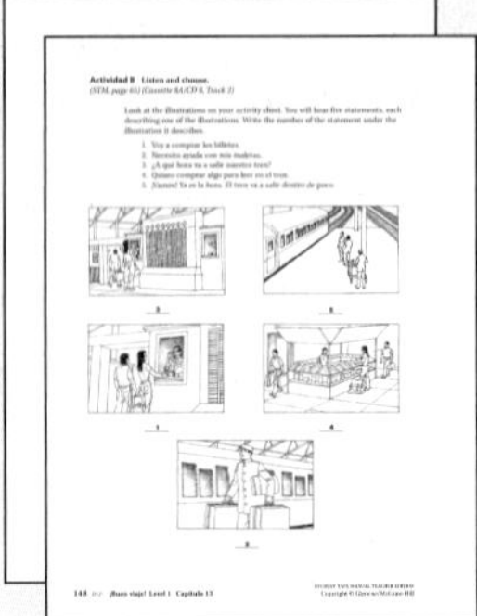
Vocabulary, pages 153–158

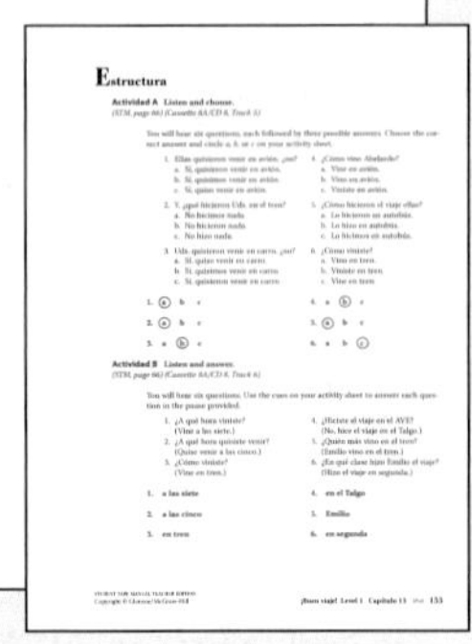
Structure, pages 159–161

Conversation, Pronunciation, pages 161–162

Additional Practice, pages 163–164

Assessment

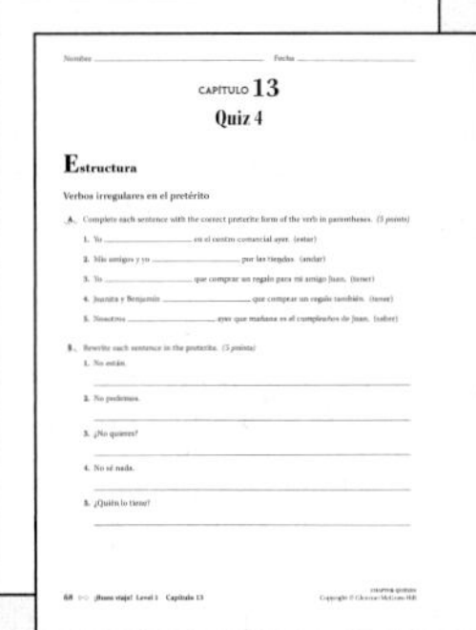

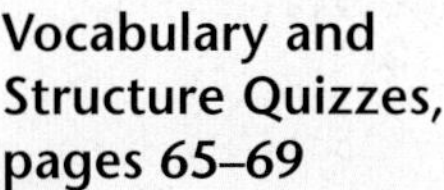

Vocabulary and Structure Quizzes, pages 65–69

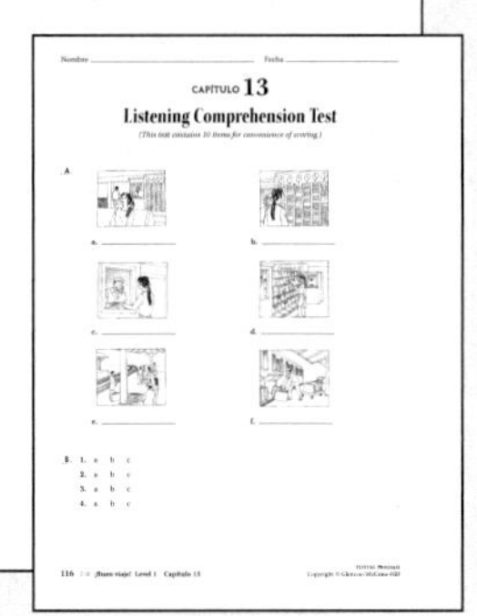

Chapter Tests, pages 207–220

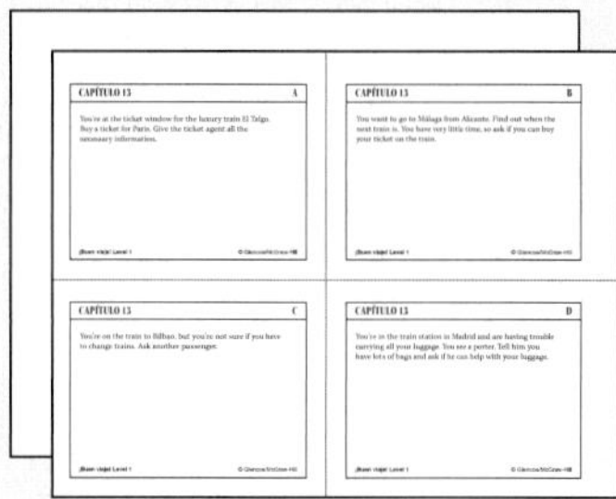

Situation Cards, Chapter 13

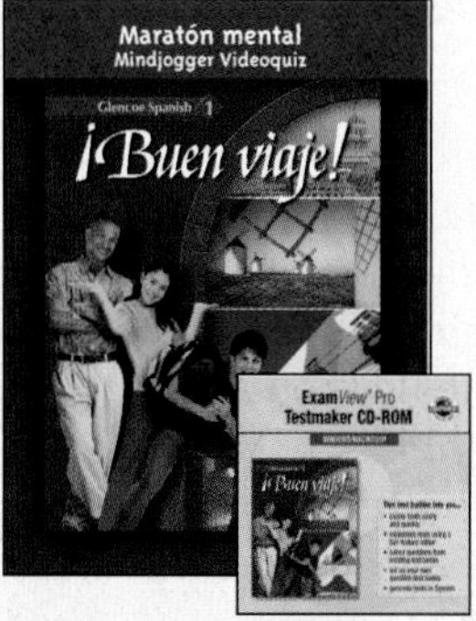

MindJogger Videoquiz, ExamView® Pro, Chapter 13

Timesaving Teacher Tools

TeacherWorks™ is your all-in-one teacher resource center. Personalize lesson plans, access resources from the Teacher Wraparound Edition, connect to the Internet, or make a to-do list. These are only a few of the many features that can assist you in the planning and organizing of your lessons.

Includes:

- A calendar feature
- Access to all program blackline masters
- Standards correlations and more

ExamView® Pro

Test Bank software for Macintosh and Windows makes creating, editing, customizing, and printing tests quick and easy.

Technology Resources

In the Chapter 13 Internet Activity, you will have a chance to learn more about the Spanish-speaking world. Visit spanish.glencoe.com

On the interactive CD-ROM, students can listen to and take part in a recorded version of the conversation in Chapter 13.

¡Viva el mundo hispano! Video and Video Activities, Chapter 13. Available on VHS and DVD.

Help your students prepare for the chapter test by playing the **Maratón mental** Videoquiz game show. Teams will compete against each other to review chapter vocabulary and structure and sharpen listening comprehension skills. Available on VHS and DVD.

¡Buen viaje! is also available on CD or Online.

Capítulo 13

Preview

In this chapter, students will learn to talk about a train trip. In order to do this they will learn vocabulary related to the train station and train travel. They will also continue to learn how to talk about past events by learning the preterite forms of some irregular verbs. The cultural focus of the chapter is on train travel in Spain and Latin America.

National Standards

Communication

In Chapter 13 students will communicate in spoken and written Spanish on the following topics:

- purchasing a train ticket and consulting a timetable
- getting through a train station
- traveling on board a train

Students will obtain and provide information about these topics and learn to engage in conversations with a ticket agent, train conductor, and fellow passengers as they fulfill the chapter objectives listed on this page.

Capítulo 13

Un viaje en tren

Objetivos

In this chapter you will learn to:

- use expressions related to train travel
- purchase a train ticket and request information about arrival, departure, etc.
- talk about more past events or activities
- tell what people say
- discuss an interesting train trip in Spain and in Peru

Casimiro Castro *Álbum del ferrocarril mexicano*

Capítulo 13

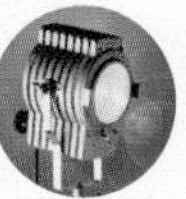

Spotlight on Culture

Arte Casimiro Castro (1826–1889) is considered a master 19th century Mexican illustrator, lithographer, and water color painter. He was known for nationalistic themes—with a particular interest in Mexico City—portrayed in many of his works.

Fotografía This photo was taken at the Estació de Sants in Barcelona. Note that the name of the station is in **catalán.** There are two other train stations in Barcelona.

Learning from Photos

(pages 402–403) You may wish to ask the following questions about the photo after presenting the new vocabulary on pages 404–405:

¿Dónde están los jóvenes?
¿Qué está mirando la muchacha?
¿El muchacho tiene un plano de qué ciudad?
¿Cuántos trenes ves en la foto?

LEVELING

The activities, conversations, and readings within each chapter are marked according to level of difficulty. **E** indicates easy. **A** indicates average. **C** indicates challenging. Some activities cover a range of difficulty. In some activities, for example, advanced students will be able to produce more extensive responses while students who learn at a different rate may give less detailed responses. The leveling indicators will help you individualize instruction to best meet your students' needs.

PALABRAS 1

1 PREPARATION

Resource Manager

Vocabulary Transparencies 13.2–13.3
Audio Activities TE, pages 153–156
Audio CD 8
Workbook, pages 159–160
Quizzes, page 65
ExamView® Pro

Bellringer Review

Use BRR Transparency 13.1 or write the following on the board.
Complete the following sentences.

1. **Los pasajeros hacen ___ en el mostrador de la línea aérea.**
2. **Los pasajeros ___ su equipaje.**
3. **Los pasajeros en un aeropuerto tienen que pasar por ___.**
4. **Los pasajeros tienen que mostrar su ___.**

2 PRESENTATION

Step 1 Have students close their books. Present the vocabulary using Vocabulary Transparencies 13.2–13.3.

Step 2 Now have students open their books and repeat the new words and sentences after you or Audio CD 8.

Step 3 Have students act out the short dialogue on page 404.

Step 4 As you present the new vocabulary, intersperse it with questions such as the following:

¿La muchacha compra un billete de primera o segunda clase?
¿Compra un billete sencillo o de ida y vuelta?
¿Subió al tren o bajó del tren la señora?

Vocabulario

PALABRAS 1

En la estación de ferrocarril

el tablero de llegadas
el tablero de salidas
el quiosco
la sala de espera
el horario
Un billete para Madrid, por favor.
¿En primera o en segunda?
En segunda—de ida y vuelta.
la ventanilla
el billete de ida y vuelta
el billete sencillo

Reaching All Students

Total Physical Response A piece of paper with the word **maleta** written on it can represent a suitcase.

(Student 1), **levántate y ven acá, por favor.**
Vas a hacer algunos gestos. Aquí tienes una maleta.
Toma la maleta. Mira la maleta.
Abre la maleta. Pon la ropa en la maleta.
Cierra la maleta.
Ve al teléfono. Llama un taxi.
Toma la maleta y ve a la calle.
Espera el taxi.
El taxi llega. Pon la maleta en la maletera del taxi. Abre la puerta del taxi.
Sube al taxi. Siéntate.
Gracias, *(Student 1).* **Y ahora puedes volver a tu asiento.**

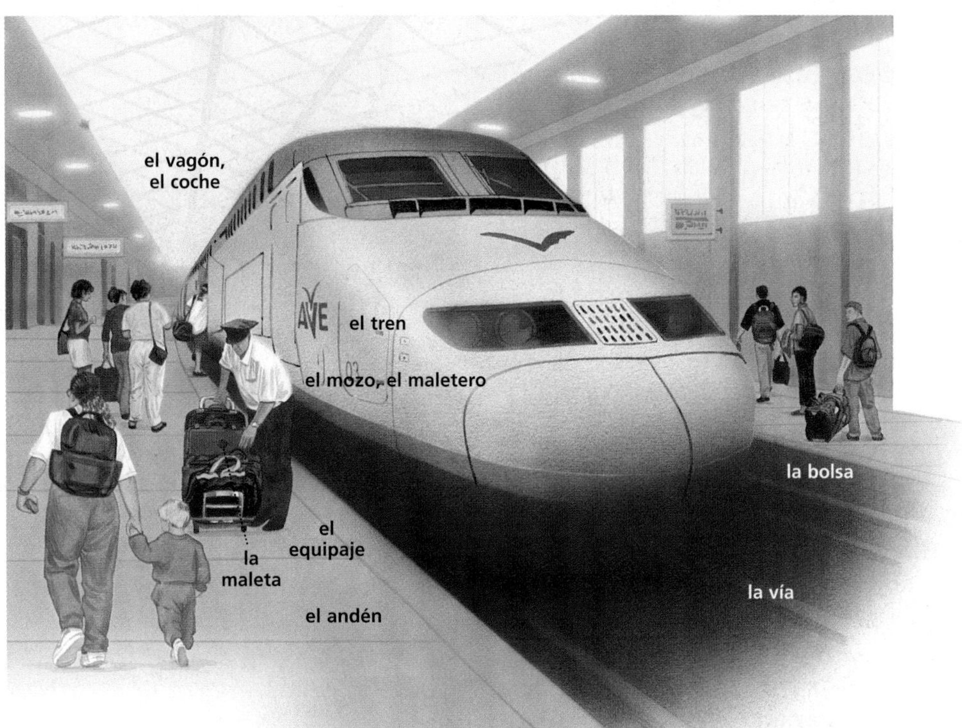

La señora hizo un viaje.
Hizo el viaje en tren.
Tomó el tren porque no quiso ir en carro.
Subió al tren.

El mozo vino con el equipaje.
El mozo puso el equipaje en el tren.
Los mozos ayudaron a los pasajeros con su equipaje.

El tren salió del andén número dos.
Algunos amigos estuvieron en el andén.

¿Tiene el mozo bolsas y maletas?
¿Qué tiene el mozo?
¿Dónde puso el equipaje?

Have students answer with complete sentences or sometimes just have them use the specific word or phrase that responds to the question word.

About the Spanish Language

- The word **el billete** is used in Spain. **El boleto** is used in Latin America. The expression *to buy a ticket* is **sacar un billete** in Spain and **comprar un boleto** in Latin America.
- **El tablero** is the word used for an arrival or departure board. In some stations there is a modern type of TV screen that is called either **la pantalla** or **el monitor.**

Assessment

As an informal assessment, you may wish to show Vocabulary Transparencies 13.2–13.3 again and let students identify items at random. Then have students make up questions about what they see on the transparencies. You may answer the questions yourself or have them call on other students to answer.

Chapter Projects

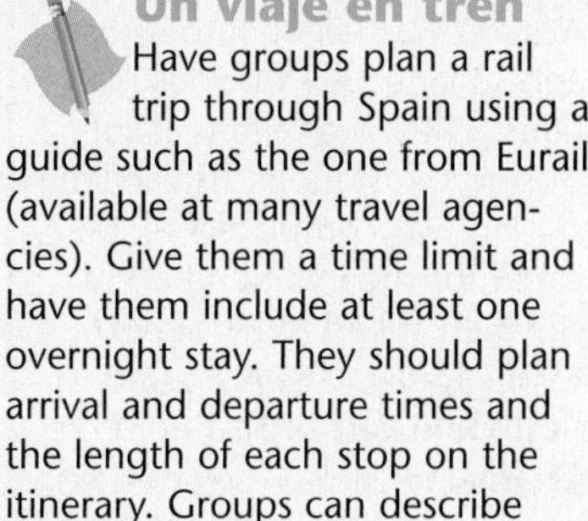

Un viaje en tren Have groups plan a rail trip through Spain using a guide such as the one from Eurail (available at many travel agencies). Give them a time limit and have them include at least one overnight stay. They should plan arrival and departure times and the length of each stop on the itinerary. Groups can describe their trips to the class.

LEVELING

A: Vocabulary

Reaching All Students

Total Physical Response Have your desk be **la ventanilla.** One student can be **el agente** and another student can be **el pasajero.** Numbers on the board can represent **los andenes.** A piece of paper with the word **boleto** or **billete** can be the ticket.

(Student 1), **levántate y ven acá.**
Ésta es la estación de ferrocarril.
Estamos en la sala de espera.
Ve a la ventanilla.
Compra un boleto.
Págale al agente.
Toma tu boleto. Mira el boleto.
Pon el boleto en tu bolsillo.
Busca el andén número dos.
Ve al andén. Espera el tren.
Aquí viene el tren. Sube al tren.
Gracias, *(Student 1).* **Regresa a tu asiento.**

Vocabulario

3 PRACTICE

¿Qué palabra necesito?

¡OJO! When students are doing the **¿Qué palabra necesito?** activities, accept any answer that makes sense. The purpose of these activities is to have students use the new vocabulary. They are not factual recall activities. Thus, it is not necessary for students to remember specific factual information from the vocabulary presentation when answering. If you wish, have students use the photos on this page as a stimulus, when possible.

Historieta Each time **Historieta** appears, it means that the answers to the activity form a short story. Encourage students to look at the title of the **Historieta,** since it can help them do the activity.

1 Have students retell the story from Activity 1 in their own words.

2 After completing Activity 2, have students ask questions using the other answer choices from this activity.

Learning from Photos

(page 406) Until recently, **Atocha** was falling into disuse and serving very few destinations. There was even talk of closing the station. Instead, the station was completely renovated for the inauguration of the high speed AVE train in 1992. Today it serves points south and east of Madrid. The **Chamartín** station serves trains heading to the north and to Barcelona. The **Norte** station is primarily for local trains serving the western suburbs.

Vocabulario

¿Qué palabra necesito?

1 Historieta En la estación de ferrocarril

Contesten según se indica.

1. ¿Cómo vino la señora a la estación? (en taxi)
2. ¿Dónde puso sus maletas? (en la maletera del taxi)
3. En la estación, ¿adónde fue? (a la ventanilla)
4. ¿Qué compró? (un billete)
5. ¿Qué tipo de billete compró? (de ida y vuelta)
6. ¿En qué clase? (segunda)
7. ¿Dónde puso su billete? (en su bolsa)
8. ¿Qué consultó? (el horario)
9. ¿Adónde fue? (al andén)
10. ¿De qué andén salió el tren? (del número dos)
11. ¿Por qué hizo la señora el viaje en tren? (no quiso ir en coche)

Atocha, una estación de ferrocarril en Madrid

En la estación de Atocha

2 Historieta Antes de abordar el tren

Escojan.

1. ¿Dónde espera la gente el tren?
   a. en la ventanilla **b.** en la sala de espera **c.** en el quiosco
2. ¿Dónde venden o despachan los billetes?
   a. en la ventanilla **b.** en el equipaje **c.** en el quiosco
3. ¿Qué venden en el quiosco?
   a. boletos **b.** maletas **c.** periódicos y revistas
4. ¿Qué consulta el pasajero para verificar la hora de salida del tren?
   a. la llegada **b.** la vía **c.** el horario
5. ¿Quién ayuda a los pasajeros con el equipaje?
   a. el mozo **b.** el tablero **c.** el andén
6. ¿De dónde sale el tren?
   a. de la ventanilla **b.** del andén **c.** del tablero

ANSWERS TO ¿Qué palabra necesito?

1

1. La señora vino a la estación en taxi.
2. Puso sus maletas en la maletera del taxi.
3. En la estación fue a la ventanilla.
4. Compró un billete.
5. Compró un billete de ida y vuelta.
6. Compró un billete en segunda.
7. Puso su billete en su bolsa.
8. Consultó el horario.
9. Fue al andén.
10. El tren salió del andén número dos.
11. La señora hizo el viaje en tren porque no quiso ir en coche.

2

1. b
2. a
3. c
4. c
5. a
6. b

3 Historieta El billete del tren Contesten.

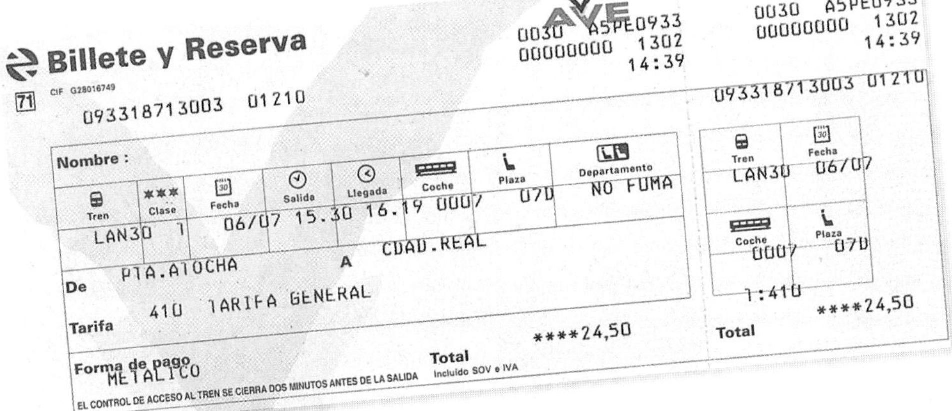

1. ¿De qué estación sale el tren?
2. ¿Adónde va el tren?
3. ¿Cuál es la fecha del billete?
4. ¿A qué hora sale el tren?
5. ¿Está el asiento en la sección de fumar o de no fumar?
6. ¿Qué clase de billete es?
7. ¿Con qué pagó el/la pasajero(a)?

4 RENFE (Red Nacional de Ferrocarriles Españoles)

You're in Spain and you want to visit one of the cities on the map. A classmate will be the ticket agent. Get yourself a ticket and ask the agent any questions you have about your train trip.

ANSWERS TO ¿Qué palabra necesito?

3

1. El tren sale de la estación de Atocha.
2. El tren va a Ciudad Real.
3. La fecha del billete es 06/07.
4. El tren sale a las 15:30.
5. El asiento está en la sección de no fumar.
6. Es un billete de primera clase.
7. El / La pasajero(a) pagó en metálico.

4 *Answers will vary. Students may use the conversation on page 404 as a model.*

Learning from Realia

(page 407) Have students look at the train ticket. Ask them to guess what the word **metálico** under **Forma de pago** means. What do we say in English instead of **metálico?** *(cash)*

¡OJO! Note that the activities are color-coded. All the activities in the text are communicative. However, the ones with blue titles are guided communication. The red titles indicate that the answers to the activity are more open-ended and can vary more. You may wish to correct students' mistakes more so in the guided activities than in the activities with a red title, which lend themselves to a freer response.

4 You may wish to have some students present their skits to the class.

LEVELING

E: Activities 1, 2, 3

A: Activities 2, 3, 4

Vocabulario

PALABRAS 2

1 PREPARATION

Resource Manager

Vocabulary Transparencies 13.4–13.5
Audio Activities TE, pages 157–158
Audio CD 8
Workbook, pages 161–162
Quizzes, page 66
ExamView® Pro

Bellringer Review

Use BRR Transparency 13.2 or write the following on the board.
Complete the following.
La compañía de aviación anuncia la ___ de su ___ 102 con ___ a Madrid. Pasajeros deben abordar por la ___ número tres. Embarque inmediato.

2 PRESENTATION

Step 1 Have students close their books. Present the vocabulary, using Vocabulary Transparencies 13.4–13.5. Have students repeat each word or expression two or three times after you or Audio CD 8.

Step 2 Ask the following questions as you present the vocabulary: **¿Los jóvenes están en el tren o están en la ventanilla? ¿Qué tiene que ver el revisor? ¿Hay muchos o pocos asientos libres en el coche? ¿Los pasajeros toman asiento o se sientan en el pasillo? ¿Qué hacen los pasajeros en el coche-cama? ¿En el coche-comedor? ¿El tren sale a tiempo o sale tarde? ¿Sale con retraso? ¿Dónde bajan los pasajeros?**

Vocabulario

PALABRAS 2

En el tren

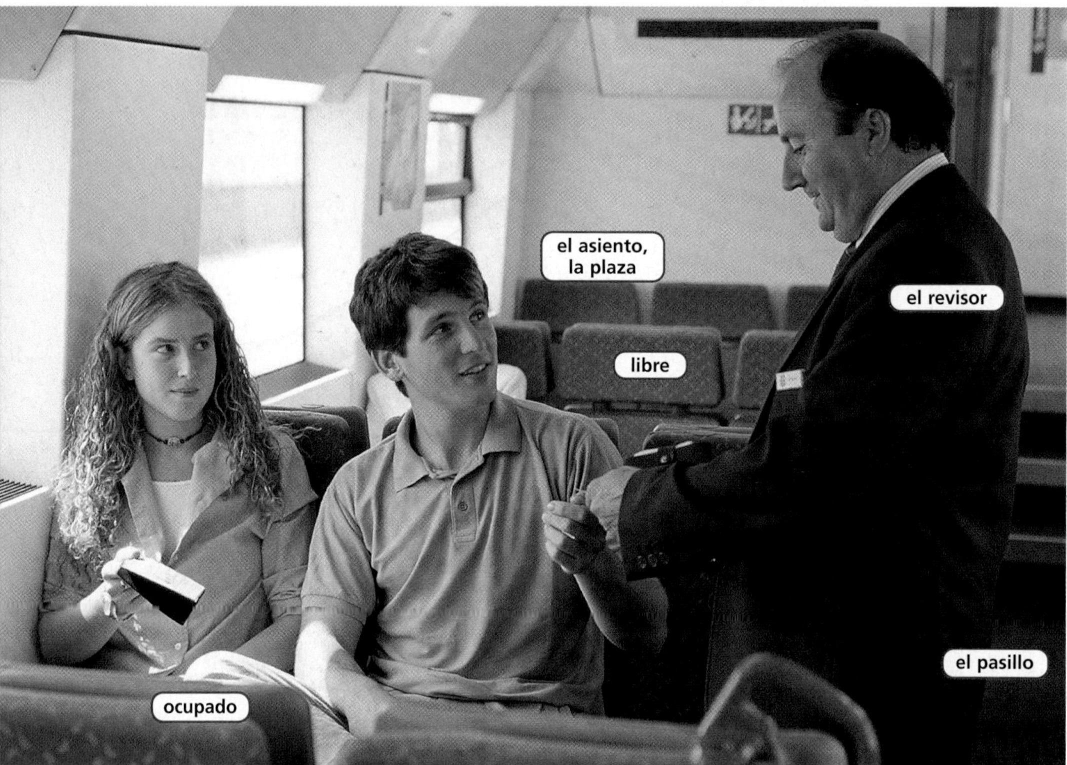

Reaching All Students

Total Physical Response Set up an area in the front of the classroom as **el tren** and place three chairs together. Tell students that those chairs are seats in the train. Then call on one student to act as **el / la pasajero(a).**

(Student 1), **levántate y ven acá, por favor.**
Sube al tren. Busca tu asiento.
Pon tu maleta en el asiento. Abre la maleta.
Saca un libro de la maleta.
Cierra la maleta.
Pon la maleta en el compartimiento.
Siéntate. Toma tu asiento.
Abre tu libro. Lee el libro.
Gracias, *(Student 1).* **Y ahora puedes volver a tu asiento.**

MADRID Puerta de Atocha CADIZ	LLANO	
NUMERO DE TREN	9220	41 (1)
DIAS DE CIRCULACION	LMXJVSD	LMXJVSD
MADRID Puerta de Atocha	10:05	16:05
CIUDAD REAL	11:06	17:06
PUERTOLLANO	11:23	17:23
CORDOBA	12:12	18:11
SEVILLA Santa Justa	13:19	19:26
JEREZ DE LA FRONTERA	14:16	20:23
EL PUERTO DE STA. MARIA	14:27	20:36
SAN FERNANDO DE CADIZ	14:41	20:50
CADIZ	14:55	21:05

El tren salió a tiempo.
No salió tarde.
No salió con retraso (con una demora).

Los pasajeros van a bajar en la próxima parada (estación).
Van a transbordar en la próxima parada.

bajar(se) del tren

transbordar

About the Spanish Language

Note that we have used the expression **bajar del tren,** which is grammatically correct. In many areas of Latin America one will hear **bajarse del tren.** In contemporary novels, **bajar** and **bajarse** are sometimes used in the same work.

SPANISH Online

The **Glencoe Spanish Web** site (**spanish.glencoe.com**) offers options that enable you and your students to experience the Spanish-speaking world via the Internet. For each **Capítulo,** there are activities, games, and quizzes. In addition, an *Enrichment* section offers students an opportunity to visit Web sites related to the theme of the chapter.

Chapter Projects

Una ciudad Have the groups select one city from the itinerary they wrote in the **Un viaje en tren** project, and have them find out some information about it. They can do a brief report for a presentation to the class.

Vocabulario

3 PRACTICE

¿Qué palabra necesito?

5, 6, and 7 After going over these activities, students can summarize all the information in their own words.

FUN-FACTS

Students have already learned about the importance of air travel in South America in Chapter 11. Train travel in South America can be very interesting, but in many areas it is not convenient (and in some cases it is nonexistent). In addition to long distances, there are often mechanical delays, flooding during the rainy season, and rugged terrain, all of which can make travel slow and tedious. The railway service is fairly good in Argentina and Chile. Most of Chile's 5,200 miles of track run north to south.

LEVELING

E: Activities 5, 6
A: Activities 7, 9
C: Activities 7, 8, 9

¿Qué palabra necesito?

5 Historieta En el tren

Contesten.

1. Cuando llegó el tren a la estación, ¿subieron los pasajeros a bordo?
2. ¿El tren salió tarde?
3. ¿Con cuántos minutos de demora salió?
4. ¿Vino el revisor?
5. ¿Revisó él los boletos?

Santiago, Chile

Madrid, España

6 Historieta El tren

Contesten según la foto.

1. ¿Tiene el tren compartimientos?
2. ¿Tiene el coche o vagón un pasillo?
3. ¿Cuántos asientos hay a cada lado del pasillo?
4. ¿Hay asientos libres o están todos ocupados?
5. ¿Está completo el tren?
6. ¿Hay pasajeros de pie en el pasillo?

7 Historieta Un viaje en tren Completen.

1. Entre Granada y Málaga el tren local hace muchas ____.
2. No hay un tren directo a Benidorm. Es necesario cambiar de tren. Los pasajeros tienen que ____.
3. Los pasajeros que van a Benidorm tienen que ____ en la próxima ____ o ____.
4. ¿Cómo lo sabes? El ____ nos informó que nuestro tren no es directo.

ANSWERS TO ¿Qué palabra necesito?

5

1. Sí, cuando el tren llegó a la estación, los pasajeros subieron a bordo.
2. Sí (No), el tren (no) salió tarde.
3. Salió con una demora de ___ minutos.
4. Sí, el revisor vino.
5. Sí, él revisó los boletos.

6

1. No, el tren no tiene compartimientos.
2. Sí, el coche (vagón) tiene un pasillo central.
3. Hay tres asientos a cada lado del pasillo.
4. Hay asientos libres.
5. No, el tren no está completo.
6. No, no hay pasajeros de pie en el pasillo.

7

1. paradas
2. transbordar
3. transbordar, parada, estación
4. revisor

8 **¿Qué tienes que hacer?**
Work with a classmate. You are spending a month in Madrid and your Spanish hosts are taking you to San Sebastián. You're trying to pack your bags and their child (your partner) has a lot of questions. Answer his or her questions and try to be patient. The child has never taken a train trip before.

¿Dónde nos sentamos en el tren?
Nos sentamos en un compartimiento.

Madrid

San Sebastián

9 **De Santiago a Puerto Montt** You're planning a trip from Santiago de Chile to Puerto Montt. A classmate will be your travel agent. Get as much information as you can about the trip from Santiago to Puerto Montt. It gets rather cold and windy there and it rains a lot. You may want to find out if there are frequent delays. The following are some words and expressions you may want to use with the travel agent: **la demora, la tarifa, reservar, el número de paradas, el horario, el boleto de ida y vuelta, primera (segunda) clase.**

*For more practice using words from **Palabras 2**, do Activity 13 on page H14 at the end of this book.*

Answers to ¿Qué palabra necesito?

8 *Answers will vary. Students should use the vocabulary from* Palabras 1 *and* 2.

9 *Answers will vary. Students should use as many words as possible from the list given.*

Learning from Photos

(page 411 left) This view of Madrid is looking up the **Gran Vía** from Cibeles. The **Gran Vía** is a very busy street with hotels, night clubs, clothing stores, jewelry stores, bookstores, and **cafeterías.**

8 and 9 These activities encourage students to use the chapter vocabulary and structures in open-ended situations. It is not necessary to have them do all the activities. Choose the ones you consider most appropriate.

8 Before students begin this activity, have them make a list of questions they will ask. You may wish to have students present their conversations to the class.

9 Have students working on Activity 9 locate Puerto Montt on the map of South America on page xxxi or on Map Transparency M 3.

Geography Connection

You may either have students look up some information on Puerto Montt on the Internet or give them the following information.

Puerto Montt is a city of some 120,000 inhabitants, many of German descent. A large number of its small houses are unpainted, and one can see the Germanic influence in the architecture. In bakery shop windows there are still signs in Spanish and German—**Pasteles** and **Kuchen.**

Puerto Montt is the northernmost town in Chilean Patagonia. The weather can be very harsh with strong winds and a great deal of rain. The train trip to Puerto Montt from Santiago takes twenty hours.

Un poco más: This *InfoGap* Activity will allow students to practice in pairs. The activity should be very manageable for them, since all vocabulary and structures are familiar to them.

1 PREPARATION

Resource Manager

Audio Activities TE, pages 159–161
Audio CD 8
Workbook, pages 163–166
Quizzes, pages 67–69
ExamView® Pro

Bellringer Review

Use BRR Transparency 13.3 or write the following on the board.
Write original sentences using each of the following expressions in the present tense.
1. **hacer un viaje**
2. **poner la ropa en la maleta**
3. **salir para la estación de ferrocarril**
4. **venir en tren**

2 PRESENTATION

Hacer, querer y venir en el pretérito

Step 1 Have students open their books to page 412. Read Items 1 and 2 to the class.

Step 2 Have the class repeat the verb forms aloud.

Step 3 Call on an individual to read the model sentences.

Step 4 Point out to students that all these irregular verbs have the ending **e** in the **yo** form.

Note: Many of the verbs students will be learning in this chapter are not used very frequently in the preterite. For this reason, it is recommended that you do not spend a great deal of time on this topic. The most important verbs are **venir, hacer,** and **poner.**

Hacer, querer y venir en el pretérito
Relating more past actions

1. The verbs **hacer, querer,** and **venir** are irregular in the preterite. Note that they all have an **i** in the stem and the endings for the **yo, él, ella,** and **usted** forms are different from the endings of regular verbs.

INFINITIVE	hacer	querer	venir
yo	hice	quise	vine
tú	hiciste	quisiste	viniste
él, ella, Ud.	hizo	quiso	vino
nosotros(as)	hicimos	quisimos	vinimos
vosotros(as)	*hicisteis*	*quisisteis*	*vinisteis*
ellos, ellas, Uds.	hicieron	quisieron	vinieron

2. The verb **querer** has several special meanings in the preterite.

Quise ayudar. *I tried to help.*
No quise ir en carro. *I refused to go by car.*

SPANISH Online
For more information about travel in Peru and other areas of the Spanish-speaking world, go to the Glencoe Spanish Web site:
spanish.glencoe.com

¿Cómo lo digo?

Historieta ¿Cómo viniste?
Contesten.

1. ¿Viniste a la estación en taxi?
2. ¿Viniste en un taxi público o privado?
3. ¿Hiciste el viaje en tren?
4. ¿Hiciste el viaje en el tren local?
5. ¿Lo hiciste en tren porque no quisiste ir en carro?

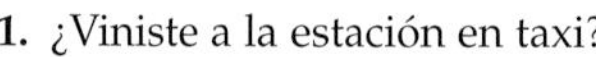

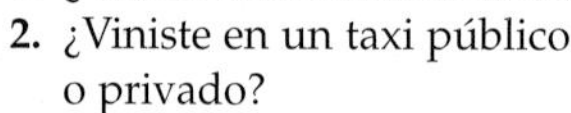

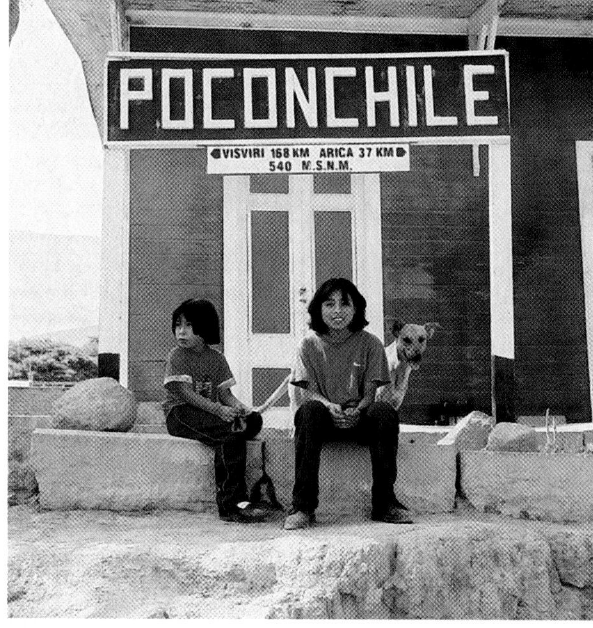

Poconchile, Chile

Answers to ¿Cómo lo digo?

1. Sí, vine a la estación en taxi.
2. Vine en un taxi público.
3. Sí, hice el viaje en tren.
4. Sí, (No, no) hice el viaje en el tren local.
5. Sí, lo hice en tren porque no quise ir en coche. (No, no lo hice en tren porque quise ir en coche.)

LEVELING

E: Activities 10, 12, 13
A: Activities 12, 13
C: Activity 11

11 **No quisieron.** Completen.

1. —Ellos no __1__ (querer) hacer el viaje.
   —¿No lo __2__ (querer) hacer?
   —No, de ninguna manera.
   —Pues, ¿qué pasó entonces? ¿Lo __3__ (hacer) o no lo __4__ (hacer)?
   —No lo __5__ (hacer).
2. —¿Por qué no __6__ (venir) ustedes esta mañana?
   —Nosotros no __7__ (venir) porque no __8__ (hacer) las reservaciones.
3. —Carlos no __9__ (querer) hacer la cama.
   —Entonces, ¿quién la __10__ (hacer)?
   —Pues, la __11__ (hacer) yo.
   —¡Qué absurdo! ¿Tú la __12__ (hacer) porque él no la __13__ (querer) hacer?

12 **¡Rebelde!** A friend of yours (your classmate) is in trouble with his or her parents because he or she didn't help to get ready for their trip. Find out what your friend didn't do and why. Use the model as a guide.

¿Hiciste la maleta?
No.
¿Por qué no hiciste la maleta?
No hice la maleta porque no quise.

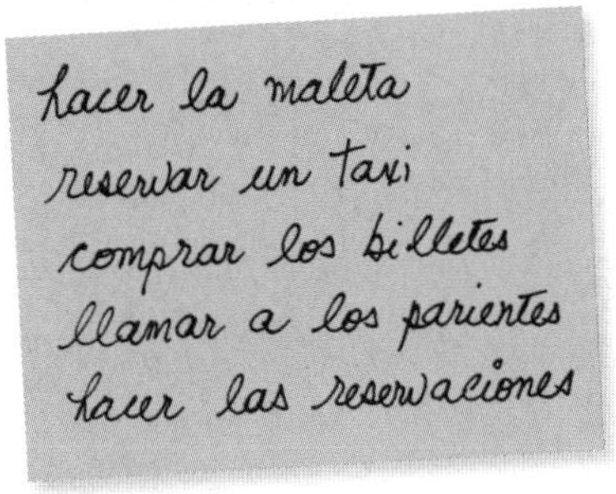

hacer la maleta
reservar un taxi
comprar los billetes
llamar a los parientes
hacer las reservaciones

13 **¿Qué hiciste durante el fin de semana?** With a classmate, take turns asking each other what you and other friends did over the weekend.

3 PRACTICE

¿Cómo lo digo?

10 Activity 10 on page 412 practices the **tú** and **yo** forms.

11 Have students present Activity 11 as a series of miniconversations.

12 Ask for volunteers to roleplay the model dialogue. Have them do one or two examples from the handwritten list on the right before students work on their own in pairs.
Expansion: Encourage students to come up with their own list of things they were supposed to do.

13 This is a good warm-up activity to begin the class period. Students might begin by saying: **¿Qué hiciste durante el fin de semana?** or **¿Qué hicieron ustedes durante el fin de semana?**

Answers to ¿Cómo lo digo?

11

1. quisieron
2. quisieron
3. hicieron
4. hicieron
5. hicieron
6. vinieron
7. vinimos
8. hicimos
9. quiso
10. hizo
11. hice
12. hiciste
13. quiso

12 *Answers will vary, but students should follow the model.*

13 *Answers will vary, but students should use the preterite tense.*

1 PREPARATION

Bellringer Review

Use BRR Transparency 13.4 or write the following on the board.

1. Write three things you have to do.
2. Write three things you can do.
3. Write three things you want to do.
4. Write three things you know how to do.

2 PRESENTATION

Verbos irregulares en el pretérito

Step 1 Have students open their books to page 414. Read Items 1 and 2 to the class.

Step 2 Have the class repeat the verb forms from the chart.

Step 3 Call on an individual to read the model sentences in Item 2.

Art Connection

Show the Fine Art Transparency from the Transparency Binder of ***Vista de Toledo*** by El Greco. You may wish to have students read the background information accompanying this transparency and do the related activities.

Expansion: Have students look at a photo of Toledo today. Ask them if they see a resemblance between today's photo and El Greco's painting done about four centuries ago. For further enrichment, you may also wish to show the Fine Art Transparency ***El actor*** by Pablo Picasso.

Verbos irregulares en el pretérito
Describing more past actions

1. The verbs **estar, andar,** and **tener** are irregular in the preterite. They all have a **u** in the stem. Study the following forms.

INFINITIVE	estar	andar	tener
yo	estuve	anduve	tuve
tú	estuviste	anduviste	tuviste
él, ella, Ud.	estuvo	anduvo	tuvo
nosotros(as)	estuvimos	anduvimos	tuvimos
vosotros(as)	*estuvisteis*	*anduvisteis*	*tuvisteis*
ellos, ellas, Uds.	estuvieron	anduvieron	tuvieron

2. The verb **andar** means *to go,* but not to a specific place. The verb **ir** is used with a specific place.

Fueron a Toledo.
They went to Toledo.

Anduvieron por las plazas pintorescas de Toledo.
They wandered through (walked around) the picturesque squares of Toledo.

Vista de Toledo de El Greco

About the Spanish Language

In Spain the verb **andar** means *to walk.* **Caminar** is used in Latin America. **Ir a pie** means *to go on foot,* and **dar un paseo** or **pasear(se)** means *to take a walk.*

LEVELING

E: Activity 14

3. The verbs **poder, poner,** and **saber** are also irregular in the preterite. Like the verbs **estar, andar,** and **tener,** they all have a **u** in the stem. Study the following forms.

INFINITIVE	poder	poner	saber
yo	pude	puse	supe
tú	pudiste	pusiste	supiste
él, ella, Ud.	pudo	puso	supo
nosotros(as)	pudimos	pusimos	supimos
vosotros(as)	*pudisteis*	*pusisteis*	*supisteis*
ellos, ellas, Uds.	pudieron	pusieron	supieron

4. Like **querer,** the verbs **poder** and **saber** have special meanings in the preterite.

Pude parar.	*(After trying hard) I managed to stop.*
No pude parar.	*(I tried but) I couldn't stop.*
Yo lo supe ayer.	*I found it out (learned it) yesterday.*

¿Cómo lo digo?

14 Historieta ¿Dónde está mi tarjeta de identidad estudiantil?

Contesten según se indica.

1. ¿Estuviste ayer en la estación de ferrocarril? (sí)
2. ¿Tuviste que tomar el tren a Toledo? (sí)
3. ¿Pudiste comprar un billete de precio reducido? (no)
4. ¿Tuviste que presentar tu tarjeta de identidad estudiantil? (sí)
5. ¿Dónde la pusiste? (no sé)
6. ¿La perdiste? (sí, creo)
7. ¿Cuándo supiste que la perdiste? (cuando llegué a la estación)

Toledo, España

Estructura

Step 4 Have the class repeat the verb forms from the chart in Item 3.

Step 5 Point out to students that all these irregular verbs have a **u** in the stem.

Step 6 Call on an individual to read the model sentences from Item 4.

3 PRACTICE

¿Cómo lo digo?

14 Allow students to refer to the verb charts on these two pages as they do the activity.

Writing Development

Have students write a note telling someone what happened in Activity 14.

History Connection

Toledo is one of the most magnificent cities in Spain. The rock on which it stands was inhabited in prehistoric times. The Romans came in 192 B.C. and built a large fort where the **Alcázar** now stands. Toledo was inhabited by the Iberians, Romans, Visigoths, and the Moors, who arrived early in the eighth century.

Alfonso VI, aided by El Cid, took Toledo from the Moors in 1085. During the Renaissance, Toledo was a center of humanism. However, it began to decline in the sixteenth century. The expulsion of the Jews in 1492 had severe economic consequences, and the decision in 1561 to move the court to Madrid led to Toledo's political decline. The years El Greco spent in Toledo (1572 until his death in 1614) were the years of Toledo's decline.

Answers to ¿Cómo lo digo?

14

1. Sí, ayer estuve en la estación de ferrocarril.
2. Sí, tuve que tomar el tren a Toledo.
3. No, no pude comprar un billete de precio reducido.
4. Sí, tuve que presentar mi tarjeta de identidad estudiantil.
5. No sé dónde la puse.
6. Sí, creo que la perdí.
7. Supe que la perdí cuando llegué a la estación.

3 PRACTICE *(continued)*

 For additional practice, have students retell the story in their own words.

1 PREPARATION

Bellringer Review

Use BRR Transparency 13.5 or write the following on the board.
Make a list of five things you would take on a trip.

2 PRESENTATION

Decir en el presente y en el pretérito

Step 1 Have students open their books to page 416 and repeat the forms of the verb **decir** after you.

Step 2 Write the forms of the verb on the board. Underline the stem for each form.

Step 3 Now do the activities on page 417.

Learning from Realia

(page 416) The **quetzal** is the monetary unit of Guatemala. The **quetzal** is a multicolored bird, and it is the national symbol of Guatemala.

Ask students: **¿Cuántos quetzales hay en la página 416?**

15 Historieta En el mercado

Completen.

El otro día yo __1__ (estar) en el mercado de Chichicastenango, en Guatemala. Ramón __2__ (estar) allí también. Nosotros __3__ (andar) por el mercado pero no __4__ (poder) comprar nada. No es que no __5__ (querer) comprar nada, es que no __6__ (poder) porque __7__ (ir) al mercado sin un quetzal.

Chichicastenango, Guatemala

Decir en el presente y en el pretérito

Telling what people say

1. The verb **decir** *(to say)* is irregular in the present and preterite tenses. Study the following forms.

	Presente	Pretérito
yo	digo	dije
tú	dices	dijiste
él, ella, Ud.	dice	dijo
nosotros(as)	decimos	dijimos
vosotros(as)	*decís*	*dijisteis*
ellos, ellas, Uds.	dicen	dijeron

Answers to ¿Cómo lo digo?

1. estuve
2. estuvo
3. anduvimos
4. pudimos
5. quisimos
6. pudimos
7. fuimos

¿Cómo lo digo?

16 **¿Qué dices?** Sigan el modelo.

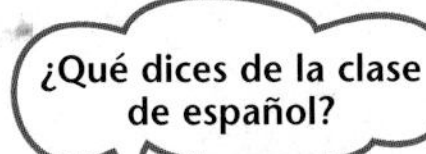

¿Qué dices de la clase de español?

Pues, yo digo que es fantástica. Estoy aprendiendo mucho.

1. ¿Qué dices de la clase de matemáticas?
2. ¿Qué dices de la clase de inglés?
3. ¿Qué dices de la clase de biología?
4. ¿Qué dices de la clase de educación física?
5. ¿Qué dices de la clase de historia?

17 **¿Qué dicen todos?** Completen con la forma apropiada del presente de **decir.**

Yo __1__ que quiero ir en tren pero Elena me __2__ que prefiere tomar el avión. Ella y Tomás también __3__ que no hay mucha diferencia entre la tarifa del avión y la tarifa del tren.

—¿Qué __4__ tú?

—Yo __5__ que es mejor ir en tren.

—Bien. Tú y yo __6__ la misma cosa. Estamos de acuerdo.

18 **¿Qué dijeron todos?** Contesten.

1. ¿Dijiste tú que quieres ir?
2. ¿Dijeron ustedes que es mejor ir en tren?
3. ¿Dije yo que sí?
4. ¿Dijo Elena que ella tiene los boletos?
5. ¿Dijimos la misma cosa?

Andas bien. ¡Adelante!

Answers to ¿Cómo lo digo?

16 *Answers will follow the model.*

17
1. digo
2. dice
3. dicen
4. dices
5. digo
6. decimos

18
1. Sí, (No, no) dije que quiero ir.
2. Sí, (No, no) dijimos que es mejor ir en tren.
3. Sí, (No, no) dijiste que sí.
4. Sí (No), Elena (no) dijo que ella tiene los boletos.
5. Sí, (No, no) dijimos (dijeron) la misma cosa.

Estructura

3 PRACTICE

¿Cómo lo digo?

16 Have students do Activity 16 as a miniconversation, working in pairs.

Expansion: Have students think of additional topics to talk about, such as their school teams and clubs. For example:

—¿Qué dices del equipo de fútbol?

—Pues, yo digo que es fantástico porque está ganando.

17 This activity uses all forms of **decir** in the present.

18 This activity uses all forms of **decir** in the preterite.

¡Adelante!

At this point in the chapter, students have learned all the vocabulary and structure necessary to complete the chapter. The conversation and cultural readings that follow recycle all the material learned up to this point.

LEVELING

A: Activities 16, 17

C: Activities 15, 18

Conversación

1 PREPARATION

Resource Manager

Audio Activities TE, pages 161–162
Audio CD 8

Bellringer Review

Use BRR Transparency 13.6 or write the following on the board.
Write four things passengers must do when they check in at an airport.

2 PRESENTATION

Step 1 Have students close their books. Read the conversation to them or play Audio CD 8.

Step 2 Have the class repeat each line after you once.

Step 3 Call on two students to read the conversation with as much expression as possible.

Step 4 After completing the conversation, have students summarize it in their own words.

Step 5 After presenting the conversation, go over the **¿Comprendes?** activity. If students can answer the questions with relative ease, move on. Students should not be expected to memorize the conversation.

Learning from Photos

(page 418) The photo on this page was taken at the Toledo train station, which has beautiful mosaics and tilework.

Conversación

En la ventanilla   

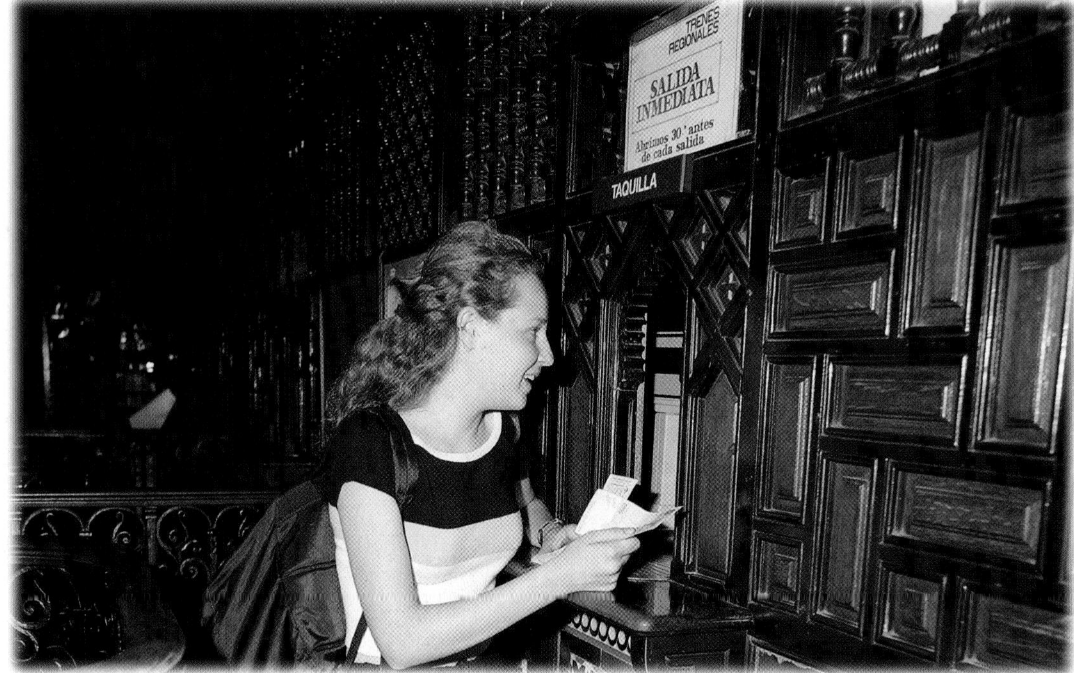

Pasajera Un billete para Madrid, por favor.
Agente ¿Sencillo o de ida y vuelta?
Pasajera Sencillo, por favor.
Agente ¿Para cuándo, señorita?
Pasajera Para hoy.
Agente ¿En qué clase, primera o segunda?
Pasajera En segunda. ¿Tiene usted una tarifa reducida para estudiantes?
Agente Sí. ¿Tiene usted su tarjeta de identidad estudiantil?
Pasajera Sí, aquí la tiene usted.
Agente Con el descuento son veintidós euros.
Pasajera ¿A qué hora sale el próximo tren?
Agente Sale a las veinte y diez del andén número ocho.
Pasajera Gracias.

¿Comprendes?

Contesten.

1. ¿Dónde está la señorita?
2. ¿Adónde va?
3. ¿Qué tipo de billete quiere?
4. ¿Para cuándo lo quiere?
5. ¿En qué clase quiere viajar?
6. ¿Es alumna la señorita?
7. ¿Hay una tarifa reducida para estudiantes?
8. ¿Qué tiene la señorita?
9. ¿Cuánto cuesta el billete con el descuento estudiantil?
10. ¿A qué hora sale el tren?
11. ¿De qué andén sale?

Answers to ¿Comprendes?

1. La señorita está en la ventanilla.
2. Va a Madrid.
3. Quiere un billete sencillo.
4. Lo quiere para hoy.
5. Quiere viajar en segunda (clase).
6. Sí, la señorita es alumna.
7. Sí, hay una tarifa reducida para estudiantes.
8. La señorita tiene su tarjeta de identidad estudiantil.
9. Con el descuento estudiantil el billete cuesta tres mil pesetas.
10. El tren sale a las veinte y diez.
11. Sale del andén número ocho.

Vamos a hablar más

A **El horario** Look at the train schedule. With a classmate, ask and answer as many questions as you can about it.

B **Vamos a Barcelona.** You and a classmate are spending a semester in Spain. You will be going to Barcelona for a couple of days. One of you is going to fly and the other is going to take the train. Compare your trips: time, cost, and what you have to do the day of departure.

TIPO DE TREN	REGIONAL	REGIONAL	REGIONAL	REGIONAL	REGIONAL	REGIONA
PRESTACIONES	2.ª	2.ª	2.ª	2.ª	2.ª	2.ª
ORIGEN		■	■	MADRID CH. 9.25	■	■
MADRID-ATOCHA		7.20	8.25	9.39	10.55	12.25
VILLAVERDE BAJO		7.28	8.33	|	11.03	12.33
LOS ANGELES		7.30	8.35	|	11.05	12.35
SAN CRISTOBAL DE LOS ANGELES		7.33	8.38	|	11.08	12.38
GETAFE-INDUSTRIAL		7.36	8.41	|	11.11	12.41
PINTO		7.41	8.46	|	11.16	12.46
VALDEMORO		7.47	8.52	|	11.22	12.52
CIEMPOZUELOS		7.52	8.57	|	11.27	12.57
ARANJUEZ	■ 6.20	8.03	9.08	|	11.38	13.08
CASTILLEJO-AÑOVER	|	8.13	9.18	10.11	11.53	13.18
VILLAMEJOR	|	|	|	|	|	|
ALGODOR	6.37	8.22	|	|	12.02	13.27
TOLEDO-INDUSTRIAL	|	8.29	|	|	12.09	|
TOLEDO	6.50	8.36	9.44	10.40	12.16	13.39
DESTINO	■	■	■	■	■	■
OBSERVACIONES	L M X J V S – (1)	Diario (2)	L M X J V – – (4)	– – – – – S D (3)	Diario	Diario

OBSERVACIONES:
(1) No circula 25-VII y 15-VIII.
(2) Efectua parada en Santa Catalina (7.26).
(3) Circula 25-VII y 15-VIII.
(4) No circula 25-VII y 15-VIII. Diario hasta Aranjuez.
(5) Efectua parada en Santa Catalina (14.31).

(L) Lunes
(M) Martes
(X) Miércoles
(J) Jueves
(V) Viernes
(S) Sábado
(D) Domingo

Pronunciación

La consonante ñ y la combinación ch

The **ñ** is a separate letter of the Spanish alphabet. The mark over it is called a **tilde**. Note that it is pronounced similarly to the *ny* in the English word *canyon*. Repeat the following.

señor	**otoño**	**España**
señora	**pequeño**	**cumpleaños**
año		

Ch is pronounced much like the *ch* in the English word *church*. Repeat the following.

coche	**chaqueta**
chocolate	**muchacho**

Repeat the following sentences.

El señor español compra un coche cada año en el otoño.
El muchacho chileno duerme en una cama pequeña en el coche-cama.
El muchacho pequeño lleva una chaqueta color chocolate.

Conversación

3 PRACTICE

Vamos a hablar más

A Give students a few minutes to study the train schedule before they begin the activity.

B Students should write down their answers and then compare notes with their partners.

Glencoe Technology

CD-ROM

On the CD-ROM, students can watch a dramatization of this conversation. They can then play the role of either one of the characters and record themselves in the conversation.

Pronunciación

Step 1 Most students have no particular problem with these sounds. Have them pronounce each word carefully after you or Audio CD 8.

Step 2 Have students open their books to page 419. Call on individuals to read the words and sentences.

Step 3 All model sentences on page 419 can be used for dictation.

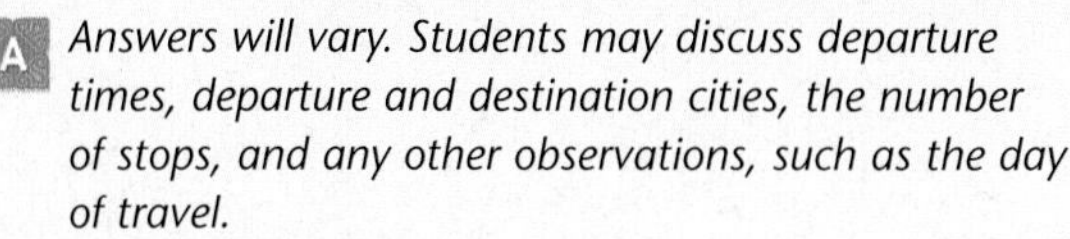

Answers to Vamos a hablar más

A *Answers will vary. Students may discuss departure times, departure and destination cities, the number of stops, and any other observations, such as the day of travel.*

B *Answers will vary, but students should include the time of departure, the cost of the trip, and a brief description of what they have to do the day they leave.*

LEVELING

E: Conversation

Lecturas culturales

Resource Manager

Audio Activities TE, page 163
Audio CD 8

National Standards

Cultures
The reading about the AVE train in Spain and the related activities on page 421 allow students to demonstrate an understanding of the importance of train travel in Spain.

PRESENTATION

Pre-reading

Step 1 Have students open their books to page 420 and read the information in the Reading Strategy.

Step 2 Tell them that the illustration at the bottom of the page is of **un ave.**

Step 3 Then have them scan the **Lectura** and the photos to look for the connection between the bird and the train.

Step 4 Have students locate Madrid and Sevilla on the map of Spain on page xxx or use Map Transparency M 2.

Reading

Step 1 Call on a student to read three or four sentences aloud.

Step 2 Intersperse the oral reading with comprehension questions from **¿Comprendes?** Activity A, page 421.

Post-reading

Step 1 Assign the reading and the **¿Comprendes?** activities on page 421 for homework.

Step 2 Have a student summarize the reading selection in his or her own words.

Lecturas culturales

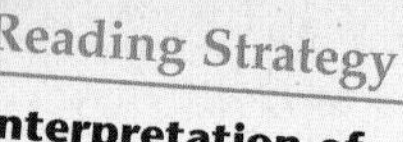

Reading Strategy

Interpretation of images Reading passages sometimes use images as a symbol to create an impression. Many times these images are animals. If you are able to identify an image, it is helpful to stop for a moment and think about the qualities and characteristics of the particular symbol the author is using in his or her imagery. Then when you have finished reading, go back and think about how the image and the topic of the reading are alike.

En el AVE

José Luis y su hermana, Maripaz, pasan dos días en Sevilla. Vinieron a visitar a sus abuelos. El viaje que hicieron de Madrid, donde viven, fue fantástico. Tomaron el tren y llegaron a Sevilla en sólo dos horas y quince minutos. Salieron de Atocha en Madrid a las 17:00 y bajaron del tren en Sevilla a las 19:15. ¿Es posible recorrer el trayecto[1] Madrid–Sevilla en dos horas quince minutos? Es una distancia de 538 kilómetros. ¡Es increíble!

[1]recorrer el trayecto *cover the route*

A bordo del AVE

Plaza de España, Sevilla

Sí, es increíble, pero es verdad. El tren español de alta velocidad es uno de los trenes más rápidos del mundo. Viaja a 250 kilómetros por hora. El tren se llama el AVE. ¿Por qué el AVE? Porque el tren vuela como un ave o pájaro.

José Luis y Maripaz tomaron el AVE. Según ellos, el viaje fue fantástico. ¿Por qué? Primero la velocidad. Pero el tren es también muy cómodo[2]. Lleva ocho coches en tres clases. Los pasajeros pueden escuchar música estereofónica o mirar tres canales de video. El tren también dispone de[3] teléfono por si acaso[4] un pasajero quiere o necesita hacer una llamada telefónica.

[2]cómodo *comfortable*
[3]dispone de *has available*
[4]por si acaso *in case*

Torre del Oro, Sevilla

¿Comprendes?

A Una visita a los abuelos
Contesten.

1. ¿Quiénes hicieron un viaje de Madrid a Sevilla?
2. ¿Quiénes vinieron a Sevilla, José Luis y su hermana o sus abuelos?
3. ¿Cómo hicieron el viaje?
4. ¿Qué tal fue el viaje?
5. ¿Cuánto tiempo tardó el viaje?
6. ¿A qué hora salieron de Madrid?
7. ¿A qué hora llegaron a Sevilla?

B Información Busquen la información.

1. uno de los trenes más rápidos del mundo
2. el nombre del tren
3. el número de coches que lleva el tren
4. el número de clases que tiene
5. algunas comodidades que el tren ofrece a los pasajeros

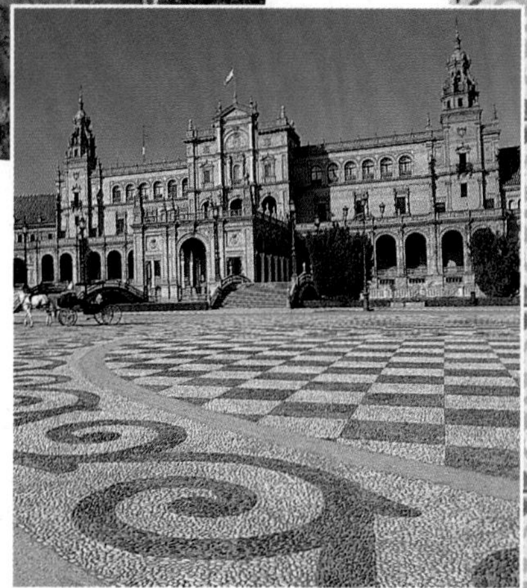

Plaza de España, Sevilla

Lecturas culturales

History Connection

The grandiose structure on the **Plaza de España** was designed by the architect Aníbal González. It was Spain's pavillion at the 1929 Hispanic-American Exhibition Fair. There are four bridges over the ornamental lake. One of the bridges is seen here. Each bridge represents one of the medieval kingdoms of the Iberian peninsula.

For information about the **Torre del Oro**, see History Connection, Chapter 4, page 117.

¿Comprendes?

A Allow students to refer to the reading to look up the answers, or you may use this activity as a testing device for factual recall.

B Have individual students read the appropriate phrase or sentence aloud. Make sure all students find the information in the **Lectura.**

LEVELING

E: Reading

Answers to ¿Comprendes?

A

1. José Luis y su hermana, Maripaz, hicieron un viaje de Madrid a Sevilla.
2. José Luis y su hermana vinieron a Sevilla.
3. Hicieron el viaje en el tren.
4. El viaje fue fantástico.
5. El viaje tardó dos horas quince minutos.
6. Salieron de Madrid a las 17:00.
7. Llegaron a Sevilla a las 19:15.

B

1. el tren español de alta velocidad
2. el AVE
3. ocho
4. tres
5. música estereofónica, tres canales de video, teléfono

Lectura opcional

National Standards

Cultures

This reading about Machu Picchu in Peru and the related activities on page 423 allow students to develop an appreciation for one of the unique archeological sites in the Spanish-speaking world.

¡OJO! This reading is optional. You may skip it completely, have the entire class read it, have only several students read it and report to the class, or assign it for extra credit.

PRESENTATION

Step 1 Have students locate Cuzco on the map of South America on page xxxi or use Map Transparency M 3.

Step 2 Have students read the passage quickly as they look at the photos that accompany it. The photos will increase their comprehension because students will be able to visualize what they are reading about.

Step 3 Have students discuss the information that they find interesting.

Lectura opcional

De Cuzco a Machu Picchu

Un viaje muy interesante en tren es el viaje de Cuzco a Machu Picchu en el Perú. Cada día a las siete de la mañana, un tren de vía estrecha[1] sale de la estación de San Pedro en Cuzco y llega a Machu Picchu a las diez y media. Cuzco está a unos 3.500 metros sobre el nivel del mar. El tren tiene que bajar a 2.300 metros para llegar a Machu Picchu. Tiene que bajar 1.200 metros y en el viaje de regreso tiene que subir 1.200 metros.

Pero, ¿quiénes toman el tren para ir a Machu Picchu? Es un tren que lleva a muchos turistas que quieren ir a ver las famosas ruinas de los incas. Machu Picchu es una ciudad entera, totalmente aislada[2] en un pico andino al borde de[3] un cañón. Un dato histórico increíble es que los españoles no

[1]de vía estrecha *narrow gauge*
[2]aislada *isolated*
[3]al borde de *on the edge of*

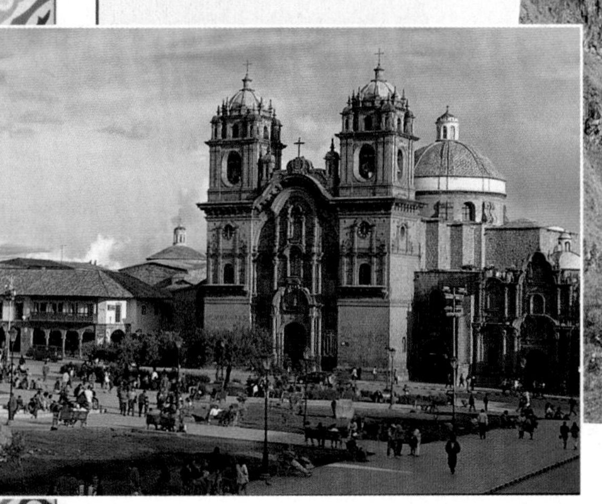

La Plaza de Armas, Cuzco

El valle del Urubamba, Perú

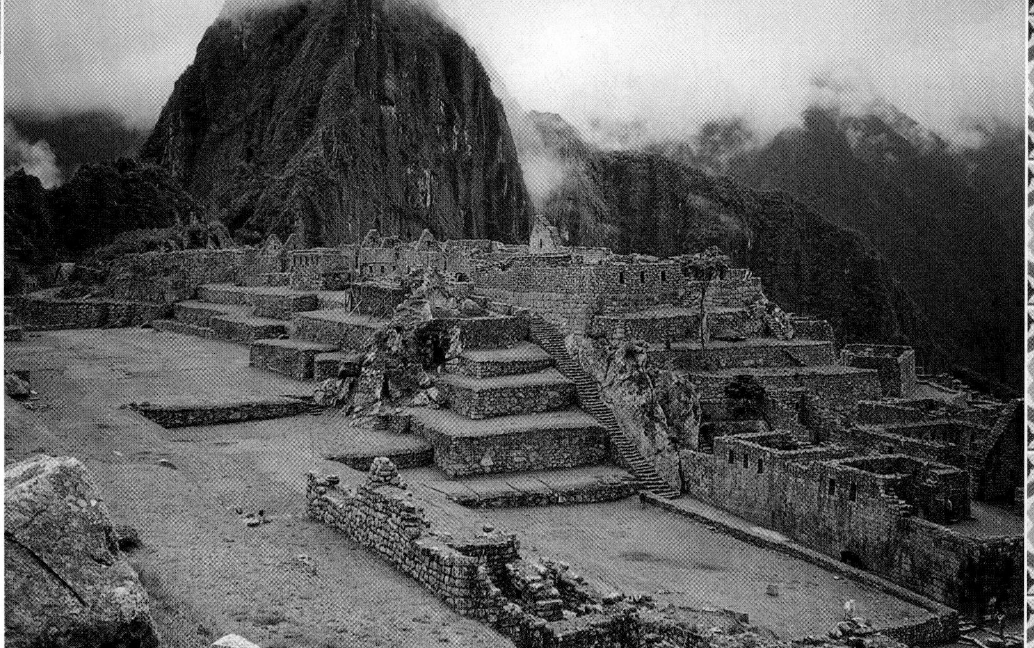

Machu Picchu

descubrieron a Machu Picchu durante su conquista de Perú. Los historiadores creen que Machu Picchu fue el último refugio de los nobles incas al escaparse[4] de los españoles.

Machu Picchu fue descubierto por Hiram Bingham, el explorador y senador de Estados Unidos, en 1911. ¿Cómo llegó Bingham a Machu Picchu en 1911? ¡A pie! Y aún hoy hay sólo dos maneras de ir a Machu Picchu—a pie o en el tren que sale a las siete y media de Cuzco.

[4]al escaparse *upon escaping*

¿Comprendes?

¿Sí o no? Digan que sí o que no.

1. Machu Picchu está a una altura más elevada que Cuzco.
2. El tren que va de Machu Picchu a Cuzco tiene que subir 1.200 metros.
3. El viaje de Cuzco a Machu Picchu toma tres horas y media.
4. Hay muy pocos turistas en el tren a Machu Picchu.
5. En Machu Picchu hay ruinas famosas de los incas.
6. Machu Picchu fue una ciudad de los incas.
7. Los españoles descubrieron la ciudad de Machu Picchu durante su conquista de Perú.
8. Hiram Bingham fue un senador de Estados Unidos.
9. Él también fue a Machu Picchu en tren.

Learning from Photos

(page 422 top) This photo, taken through a stone portal or doorway, gives us a beautiful view of one of the many terraces at Machu Picchu. Many of the original stone buildings have been reconstructed. However, since the original roofs were made of thatch, they have not been rebuilt.
(page 422 middle) This is the train that takes tourists from Cuzco to Machu Picchu.
(page 422 bottom right) This valley is referred to as the "Sacred Valley of the Incas." The name "Inca" originally applied to the royal family only. Today it is used to describe the people as a whole.
(page 422 bottom left) Cuzco is a city of 200,000 people. Its population is a blend of Indian, **mestizo,** and Spanish cultures. In the days of the Incas, the **Plaza de Armas** was called **Huacaypata.** This square was lined with the sumptuous palaces of dead and mummified Incas and with the imperial residences of the living Incas. Today, the palaces have been replaced by Spanish mansions. The first floors of these mansions are occupied by small stores and restaurants.

LEVELING

A: Reading

Answers to ¿Comprendes?

1. No
2. Sí
3. Sí
4. No
5. Sí
6. Sí
7. No
8. Sí
9. No

Assessment

As an informal assessment, you may wish to use the **¿Comprendes?** activity to see how well students understood the reading selection.

Conexiones

National Standards

Connections
This reading about the 24-hour clock and the metric system establishes a connection with another discipline, allowing students to reinforce and further their knowledge of mathematics through the study of Spanish.

Comparisons
This reading allows students to compare the English system of measurement with the metric system, which is used in most of the Spanish-speaking world.

¡OJO! The readings in the **Conexiones** section are optional. They focus on some of the major disciplines taught in schools and universities. The vocabulary is useful for discussing such topics as history, literature, art, economics, business, science, etc. You may choose any of the following ways to do the readings in the **Conexiones** sections.

Independent reading Have students read the selections and do the post-reading activities as homework, which you collect. This option is least intrusive on class time and requires a minimum of teacher involvement.

Homework with in-class follow-up Assign the readings and post-reading activities as homework. Review and discuss the material in class the next day.

Intensive in-class activity This option includes a pre-reading vocabulary presentation, in-class reading and discussion, assignment of the activities for homework, and a discussion of the assignment in class the following day.

Conexiones

Las matemáticas

Conversiones aritméticas

When traveling through many of the Spanish-speaking countries, you will need to make some mathematical conversions. For example, train as well as plane schedules and hours for formal events, radio, and television are given using the twenty-four-hour clock. The metric system rather than the English system is used for weights and measures. Let's take a look at some of the conversions that must be made.

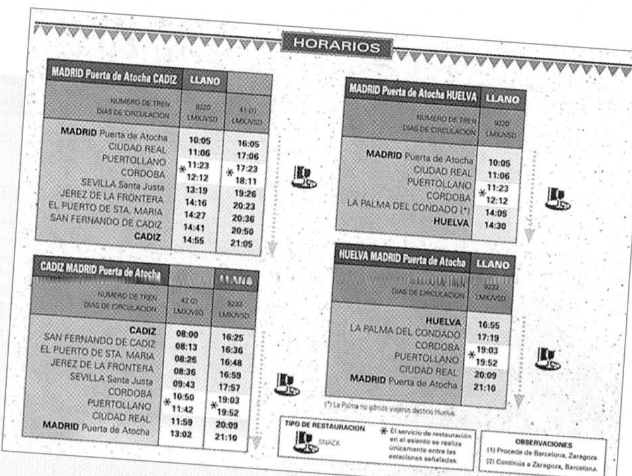

HORARIOS

MADRID Puerta de Atocha CADIZ	LLANO	
NUMERO DE TREN / DIAS DE CIRCULACION	9220 LMXJVSD	41 (1) LMXJVSD
MADRID Puerta de Atocha	10:05	16:05
CIUDAD REAL	11:06	17:06
PUERTOLLANO	* 11:23	* 17:23
CORDOBA	12:12	18:11
SEVILLA Santa Justa	13:19	19:26
JEREZ DE LA FRONTERA	14:16	20:23
EL PUERTO DE STA. MARIA	14:27	20:36
SAN FERNANDO DE CADIZ	14:41	20:50
CADIZ	14:55	21:05

CADIZ MADRID Puerta de Atocha		LLANO
NUMERO DE TREN / DIAS DE CIRCULACION	42 (2) LMXJVSD	9233 LMXJVSD
CADIZ	08:00	16:25
SAN FERNANDO DE CADIZ	08:13	16:36
EL PUERTO DE STA. MARIA	08:26	16:48
JEREZ DE LA FRONTERA	08:36	16:59
SEVILLA Santa Justa	09:43	17:57
CORDOBA	* 10:50	* 19:03
PUERTOLLANO	11:42	19:52
CIUDAD REAL	11:59	20:09
MADRID Puerta de Atocha	13:02	21:10

MADRID Puerta de Atocha HUELVA	LLANO
NUMERO DE TREN / DIAS DE CIRCULACION	9220 LMXJVSD
MADRID Puerta de Atocha	10:05
CIUDAD REAL	11:06
PUERTOLLANO	* 11:23
CORDOBA	12:12
LA PALMA DEL CONDADO (*)	14:05
HUELVA	14:30

HUELVA MADRID Puerta de Atocha	LLANO
NUMERO DE TREN / DIAS DE CIRCULACION	9233 LMXJVSD
HUELVA	16:55
LA PALMA DEL CONDADO	17:19
CORDOBA	* 19:03
PUERTOLLANO	19:52
CIUDAD REAL	20:09
MADRID Puerta de Atocha	21:10

(*) La Palma no admite viajeros destino Huelva.

TIPO DE RESTAURACION: SNACK

* El servicio de restauración en el asiento se realiza únicamente entre las estaciones señaladas.

OBSERVACIONES
(1) Procede de Barcelona, Zaragoza.
(2) Continúa a Zaragoza, Barcelona.

La hora

Cuando lees el horario para el tren o un anuncio para un programa cultural, dan la hora usando las 24 horas. La una (1:00) es la una de la mañana y las doce (12:00) es el mediodía. Las trece (13:00), una hora después del mediodía, es la una de la tarde y las veinticuatro horas (00:00) es la medianoche.

Nuestros amigos José Luis y Maripaz salieron de Madrid a las 17:00 y llegaron a Sevilla a las 19:15. Es decir que salieron de Madrid a las 5:00 de la tarde y llegaron a las 7:15 de la tarde.

El sistema métrico—pesos y medidas[1]

Pesos

Las medidas tradicionales para peso en los Estados Unidos son la onza, la libra y la tonelada. En el sistema métrico decimal, las medidas para peso están basadas en el kilogramo, o kilo.

[1]pesos y medidas *weights and measures*

About the Spanish Language

Terms from the English system—**el pie, la yarda, el galón**—are seldom heard in Spanish.

Hay mil gramos en un kilo. El kilo es igual a 2,2 libras. Una libra estadounidense es un poco menos de medio kilo.

Líquidos

Las medidas para líquidos en Estados Unidos son la pinta, el cuarto y el galón. En el sistema métrico es el litro. Un litro contiene un poco más que un cuarto.

Distancia y altura

Para medir la distancia y la altura en Estados Unidos usamos la pulgada, el pie, la yarda y la milla. El sistema métrico usa el metro. El metro es un poco más que una yarda. Un kilómetro (mil metros) es 0,621 millas—un poco más que media milla.

¿Comprendes?

A La hora Read the schedule on page 424 and give the arrival and departure times of the trains using our system of telling time.

B El sistema métrico Contesten según las fotografías.

1. ¿Cuánto cuesta un litro de gasolina?
2. ¿Cuál es el límite de velocidad?
3. ¿Cuánto cuesta un litro de leche?
4. ¿Cuánto cuesta un kilo de carne?

Conexiones

PRESENTATION

Las matemáticas
Conversiones aritméticas

¡OJO! The material in this section will probably be of more interest to students who like math and science. However, it is useful information for all students because when traveling through most areas of the Spanish-speaking world, one has to use the metric system.

Step 1 Have students read the introduction in English on page 424.

Step 2 Now have them read the selection quickly. Students should already be familiar with the metric terms used in the reading.

Step 3 Explain to students some basic strategies to use when reading unfamiliar material. They should learn to: (1) recognize cognates and (2) derive meaning from context.

Step 4 Now do the **¿Comprendes?** activities.

LEVELING

A: Reading

Answers to ¿Comprendes?

A *Answers will vary. Students will have to convert from 24-hour clock times to our system of telling time.*

B

1. Un litro de gasolina super cuesta ,089 euros.
2. El límite de velocidad es de 60 kilómetros por hora.
3. Un litro de leche cuesta 0,79 euros.
4. Un kilo de carne cuesta 7,95 euros.

¡Te toca a ti!

Use what you have learned

These activities allow students to use the vocabulary and structure from this chapter in completely open-ended, real-life situations.

PRESENTATION

Encourage students to say as much as possible when they do these activities. Tell them not to be afraid to make mistakes, since the goal of the activities is real-life communication. If someone in the group makes an error, allow the others to politely correct him or her. Let students choose the activities they would like to do.

You may wish to divide students into pairs or groups. Encourage students to elaborate on the basic theme and to be creative. They may use props, pictures, or posters if they wish.

PRACTICE

1 You may wish to assign one type of travel to each group.

Writing Development

Have students keep a notebook or portfolio containing their best written work from each chapter. These selected writings can be based on assignments from the Student Textbook and the Workbook. Activities 4 and 5 on page 427 are examples of writing assignments that may be included in each student's portfolio. On page 170 in the Workbook, students will begin to develop an organized autobiography **(Mi autobiografía).** These workbook pages may also become a part of their portfolio.

¡Te toca a ti!

Use what you have learned

HABLAR **1**

El tren, el bus o el avión

✔ *Discuss train, bus, and plane travel*

Work in groups of three or four. Discuss the advantages **(las ventajas)** and the disadvantages **(las desventajas)** of bus, train, and air travel. In your discussion, include such things as speed, price, location of stations, and anything else you consider important.

HABLAR **2**

Y ahora, ¿qué hacemos?

✔ *Discuss what to do if you miss your train*

You and a classmate are on a bus on the way to the Atocha station in Madrid. There's an awful traffic jam **(un tapón, un atasco).** You know you are going to miss your train. Discuss your predicament with one another and figure out what you can do.

La estación de ferrocarril, Málaga

ANSWERS TO ¡Te toca a ti!

1 *Answers will vary. Students should use train vocabulary from this chapter and air travel vocabulary from Chapter 11.*

2 *Answers will vary. Students should use travel vocabulary from this chapter to discuss alternative options such as buying a ticket for a later train.*

¡Te toca a ti!

HABLAR

3 **En la estación de ferrocarril**

✔ Talk about activities at a train station

With a classmate look at the photograph and talk about it.

ESCRIBIR

4 **¡Una experiencia!**

✔ Write about an interesting train trip in Spain

You took the AVE from Madrid to Sevilla. Write home and tell all about it.

ESCRIBIR

5 **Un viaje excelente**

Write about a trip you took to a place you love. The place can be real or imaginary. Describe how and where you went and when. Then describe what the weather is like in that place and what clothing you need there. Continue writing about what you saw and how you got to each place you visited. In your description of the place, try to make your readers understand what it is about the place that you think is so great.

Writing Strategy

Writing a descriptive paragraph Your overall goal in writing a descriptive paragraph is to enable the reader to visualize your scene. To achieve this you must select and organize details that create an impression. Using a greater number of specific nouns and vivid adjectives will make your writing livelier.

Writing Strategy

Writing a descriptive paragraph Have students read the Writing Strategy on page 427. Your students may enjoy writing about a trip to Machu Picchu or one of the other beautiful tourist destinations in the Spanish-speaking world. To help stimulate your students' "creative juices," have them find a photo in the textbook of a place they'd like to visit. Ask them to look at the photo for inspiration as they do Activity 5 on page 427.

Leveling

These activities encompass all three levels. All students will be able to do them at a sophistication level commensurate with their ability in Spanish. Some students will be able to speak for several minutes, and others may be able to give just a few sentences. This is to be expected when students are functioning completely on their own generating their own language to the best of their ability.

ANSWERS TO ¡Te toca a ti!

3 *Answers will vary. Students should discuss all activities associated with train travel.*

4 *Answers will vary. Students should use the preterite tense to describe their train trip.*

5 *Answers will vary. Students should use the preterite tense to describe their train trip.*

Resource Manager

Communication Transparency C 13
Quizzes, pages 65–69
Performance Assessment, Task 13
Tests, pages 207–220
Situation Cards, Chapter 13
ExamView® Pro, Chapter 13
Maratón mental Videoquiz, Chapter 13

Assessment

This is a pre-test for students to take before you administer the chapter test. Note that each section is cross-referenced so students can easily find the material they have to review in case they made errors. You may use Assessment Answers Transparency A 13 to do the assessment in class, or you may assign this assessment for homework. You can correct the assessment yourself, or you may prefer to project the answers on the overhead in class.

Glencoe Technology

MINDJOGGER VHS/DVD

You may wish to help your students prepare for the chapter test by playing the MindJogger game show. Teams will compete against each other to review chapter vocabulary and structure and sharpen listening comprehension skills.

Assessment

Vocabulario

1 Completen.

To review **Palabras 1**, turn to pages 404–405.

1. Elena va de Madrid a Córdoba y va a volver a Madrid. Quiere un billete ____.
2. Los pasajeros esperan el tren en el andén o en la ____.
3. El ____ de llegadas indica a qué hora llegan los trenes a la estación.
4. Venden periódicos y revistas en el ____ en la estación de ferrocarril.
5. Un tren tiene varios vagones o ____.

2 ¿Sí o no?

To review **Palabras 2**, turn to pages 408–409.

6. El revisor trabaja en la estación de ferrocarril.
7. Una litera es un tipo de cama donde puede dormir un pasajero en un tren.
8. El tren que salió a tiempo salió con una demora.
9. Los pasajeros que van de Cuzco a Machu Picchu bajan del tren en Cuzco.

ANSWERS TO 

1

1. de ida y vuelta
2. sala de espera
3. tablero
4. quiosco
5. coches

2

6. No
7. Sí
8. No
9. No

Estructura

3 Escriban en el pretérito.

10. Los turistas andan por la plaza principal.
11. Él hace la cama por la mañana.
12. Lo pongo en la maleta.
13. ¿Quién lo sabe?
14. No estamos en la capital.

To review the preterite, turn to pages 412, 414, and 415.

4 Completen con decir.

15–16. Yo lo ____ ahora y lo ____ ayer.
17–18. Ellos lo ____ ahora y lo ____ ayer.

To review **decir**, turn to page 416.

Cultura

5 Contesten.

19. ¿Qué es el AVE?
20. ¿A qué ciudad de Andalucía fueron José Luis y su hermana?

To review this cultural information, turn to page 420.

Assessment

FOLDABLES™ Study Organizer **Dinah Zike's Study Guides**

Your students may wish to use Foldable 11 to organize, display, and arrange data as they learn to use the preterite tense in Spanish. You may wish to encourage them to add pairs of sentences as they continue to expand their understanding of how to use the past and present tenses.

Large sentence strips are also ideal for having students compare and contrast other grammatical structures that they will learn.

Answers to Assessment

 **3**

10. Los turistas anduvieron por la plaza principal.
11. Él hizo la cama en la mañana.
12. Lo puse en la maleta.
13. ¿Quién lo supo?
14. No estuvimos en la capital.

4

15. digo
16. dije
17. dicen
18. dijeron

 **5**

19. El AVE es un tren español de alta velocidad.
20. José Luis y su hermana fueron a Sevilla.

¡Hablo como un pro!

This unique page gives students the opportunity to speak freely and say whatever they can, using the vocabulary and structures they have learned in the chapter. The illustration serves to remind students of precisely what they know how to say in Spanish. There are no activities that students do not have the ability to describe or talk about in Spanish. The art not only depicts the vocabulary and content of this chapter, but also reinforces what they learned in previous chapters.

You may wish to use this page in many ways. Some possibilities are to have students do the following:

1. Look at the illustration and identify items by giving the correct Spanish words.
2. Make up sentences about what they see in the illustration.
3. Make up questions about the illustration. They can call on another class member to respond if you do this as a class activity, or you may prefer to allow students to work in small groups. This activity is extremely beneficial because it enables students to actively use interrogative words.
4. Answer questions you ask them about the illustration.
5. Work in pairs and make up a conversation based on the illustration.
6. Look at the illustration and give a complete oral review of what they see.
7. Look at the illustration and write a paragraph (or essay) about it.

You can also use this page as an assessment or testing tool, taking into account individual differences by having students go from simple to quite complicated tasks. The assessment can be either oral or written.

¡Hablo como un pro!

Tell all you can about this illustration.

SALIDAS
Destino Hora Vía
Toledo 8:10 5
Ávila 8:55 7
Ciudad Real 9:14 4
LLEGADAS
Procedente de: Hora Vía
Alcalá 7:45 4
Toledo 8:30 6
Ciudad Real 9:25 7
ERIÓDICOS
Vía 5

You may wish to use the rubrics provided on pages T20–T21 as you give students the following directions.

1. Identify the topic or situation of the illustration.
2. Give the Spanish words for as many items as you can.
3. Think of as many sentences as you can to describe the illustration.
4. Go over your sentences and put them in the best sequencing to give a coherent story based on the illustration

Vocabulario

How well do you know your vocabulary?

- Choose five words from the vocabulary list.
- Use the words in original sentences to tell a story.

Getting around a train station

la estación de ferrocarril
la ventanilla
el billete, el boleto sencillo
de ida y vuelta
la sala de espera
el mozo, el maletero
el equipaje
la maleta
la bolsa
el tablero de llegadas, de salidas
el horario
el quiosco
el tren
el andén
la vía
en segunda (clase)
en primera (clase)

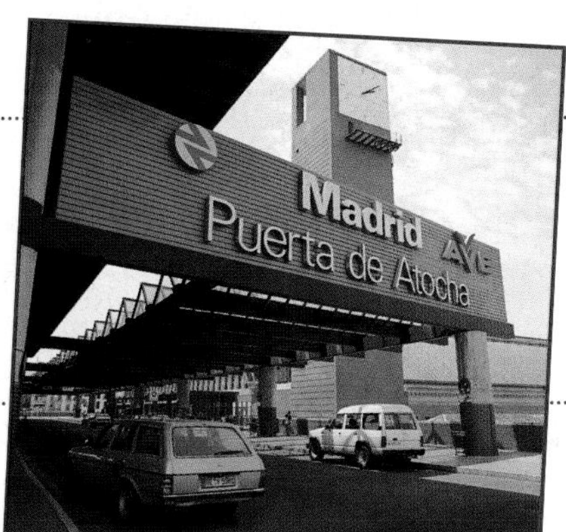

Describing activities at a train station

bajar(se) del tren
subir al tren
transbordar
salir a tiempo
con retraso, con una demora

On board the train

el coche, el vagón
el pasillo
el compartimiento
el asiento, la plaza
libre
ocupado(a)
reservado(a)
completo(a)
el coche-cama
el coche-comedor, el coche-cafetería
la litera
el revisor
la parada
en la próxima parada

VIDEOTUR

Episodio 13

In this video episode, you will join Claudiá and Francisco in an unusual train experience. See page 504 for more information.

Vocabulario

Vocabulary Review

The words and phrases in the **Vocabulario** have been taught for productive use in this chapter. They are summarized here as a resource for both student and teacher. This list also serves as a convenient resource for the **¡Te toca a ti!** activities on pages 426 and 427. There are approximately four cognates in this vocabulary list. Have students find them.

VIDEO VHS/DVD

The Video Program allows students to see how the chapter vocabulary and structures are used by native speakers within an engaging story line. For maximum reinforcement, show the video episode as a final activity for Chapter 13.

¡OJO! You will notice that the vocabulary list here is not translated. This has been done intentionally, since we feel that by the time students have finished the material in the chapter they should be familiar with the meanings of all the words. If there are several words they still do not know, we recommend that they refer to the **Palabras 1** and **2** sections in the chapter or go to the dictionaries at the end of this book to find the meanings. However, if you prefer that your students have the English translations, please refer to Vocabulary Transparency 13.1, where you will find all these words with their translations.

Planning for Chapter 14

SCOPE AND SEQUENCE, PAGES 432–459

Topics

- Restaurants
- Foods and eating utensils

Culture

- Typical cuisine from Mexico
- Typical cuisine from Spain
- Typical foods from the Caribbean
- Regional vocabulary in the Spanish-speaking world
- **Vistas del Ecuador**

Functions

- How to order food or beverage at a restaurant
- How to identify eating utensils and dishes
- How to make a reservation at a restaurant
- How to explain how you like certain foods prepared
- How to talk about present and past events and activities

Structure

- Stem-changing verbs in the present
- Stem-changing verbs in the preterite

National Standards

- Communication Standard 1.1 pages 436, 437, 440, 441, 442, 443, 454
- Communication Standard 1.2 pages 437, 441, 443, 445, 446, 447, 449, 450, 451, 453, 454, 455
- Communication Standard 1.3 pages 444, 447, 455
- Cultures Standard 2.1 page 446
- Cultures Standard 2.2 pages 448–449, 450, 451, 452
- Connections Standard 3.1 pages 452–453
- Comparisons Standard 4.1 page 452
- Communities Standard 5.2 pages 440, 459

PACING AND PRIORITIES

The chapter content is color coded below to assist you in planning.

■ required ■ recommended ■ optional

Vocabulario *(required)* *Days 1–4*

- ■ Palabras 1
  En el restaurante
- ■ Palabras 2
  Más alimentos o comestibles

Estructura *(required)* *Days 5–7*

- ■ Verbos con el cambio **e → i** en el presente
- ■ Verbos con el cambio **e → i, o → u** en el pretérito

Conversación *(required)*

- ■ En el restaurante

Pronunciación *(recommended)*

- ■ La consonante **x**

Lecturas culturales

- ■ La comida mexicana *(recommended)*
- ■ La comida española *(optional)*
- ■ La comida del Caribe *(optional)*

Conexiones

- ■ El lenguaje *(optional)*

■ **¡Te toca a ti!** *(recommended)*

■ **Assessment** *(recommended)*

■ **¡Hablo como un pro!** *(optional)*

RESOURCE GUIDE

SECTION	PAGES	SECTION RESOURCES
Vocabulario PALABRAS 1		
En el restaurante	434–437	Vocabulary Transparencies 14.2–14.3 Audio CD 8 Audio Activities TE, pages 165–167 Workbook, pages 171–172 Quiz 1, page 70 ExamView® Pro
Vocabulario PALABRAS 2		
Más alimentos o comestibles	438–441	Vocabulary Transparencies 14.4–14.5 Audio CD 8 Audio Activities TE, pages 167–170 Workbook, pages 173–174 Quiz 2, pages 71–72 ExamView® Pro
Estructura		
Verbos con el cambio e → i en el presente Verbos con el cambio **e → i, o → u** en el pretérito	442–443 444–445	Audio CD 8 Audio Activities TE, pages 170–171 Workbook, pages 175–176 Quizzes 3–4, pages 73–74 ExamView® Pro
Conversación		
En el restaurante	446	Audio CD 8 Audio Activities TE, page 172 Interactive CD-ROM
Pronunciación		
La consonante **x**	447	Pronunciation Transparency P 14 Audio CD 8 Audio Activities TE, page 173
Lecturas culturales		
La comida mexicana La comida española La comida del Caribe	448–449 450 451	Audio CD 8 Audio Activities TE, page 173 Tests, pages 223, 226
Conexiones		
El lenguaje	452–453	Tests, page 227
¡Te toca a ti!		
	454–455	**¡Viva el mundo hispano!** Video, Episode 14 Video Activities, Chapter 14 Spanish Online Activities spanish.glencoe.com
Assessment		
	456–457	Communication Transparency C 14 Quizzes 1–4, pages 70–74 Performance Assessment, Task 14 Tests, pages 221–232 Situation Cards, Chapter 14 ExamView® Pro **Maratón mental** Videoquiz

Using Your Resources for Chapter 14

Transparencies

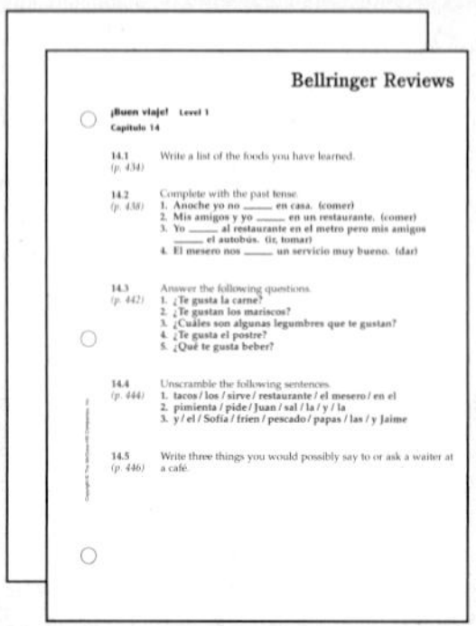
Bellringer Reviews

Bellringer 14.1–14.5

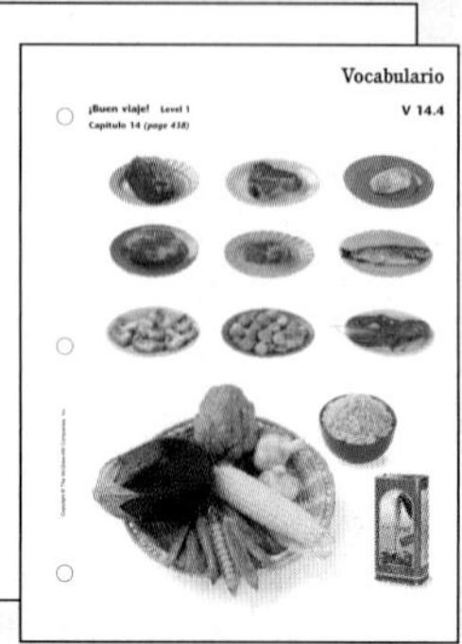
Vocabulario
V 14.4

Vocabulary 14.1–14.5

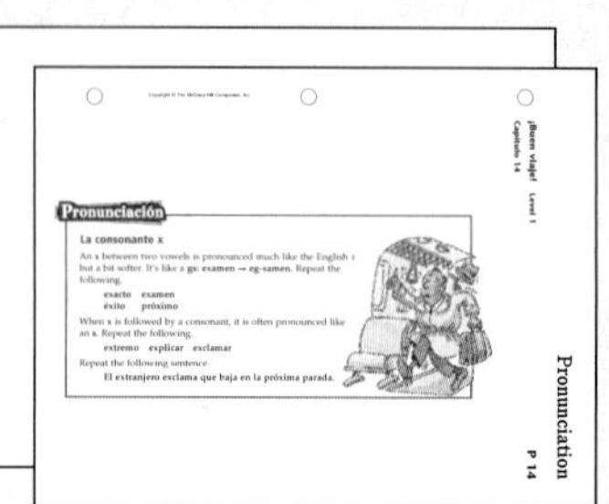
Pronunciación

Pronunciation P 14

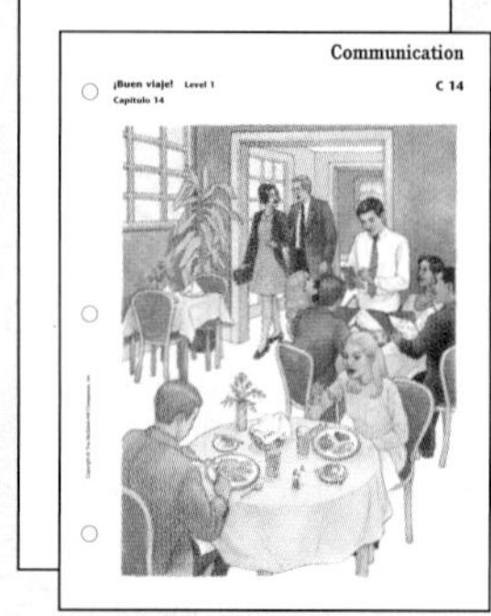
Communication
C 14

Communication C 14

Workbook

CAPÍTULO 14
En el restaurante

Vocabulary, pages 171–174

Estructura

Structure, pages 175–176

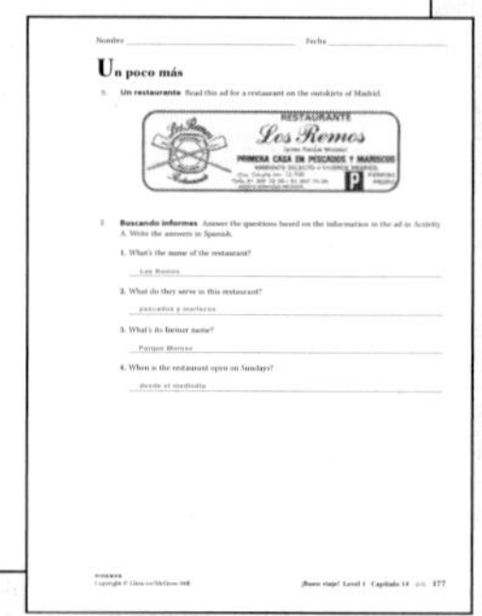
Un poco más

Enrichment, pages 177–180

Audio Activities

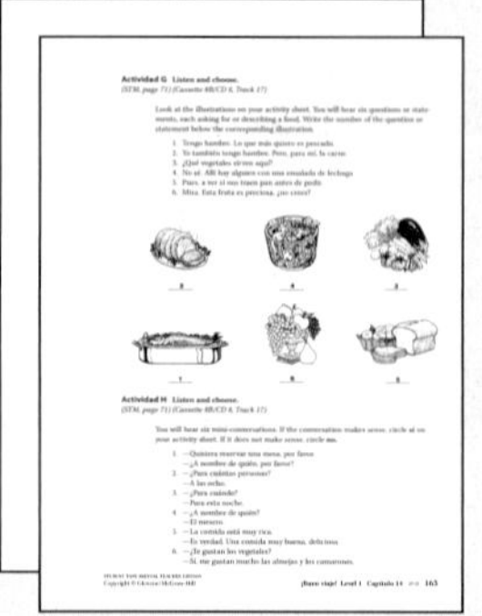
Vocabulary, pages 165–170

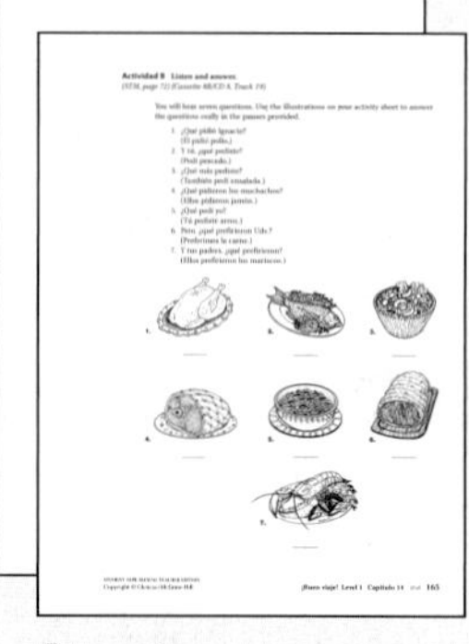
Structure, pages 170–171

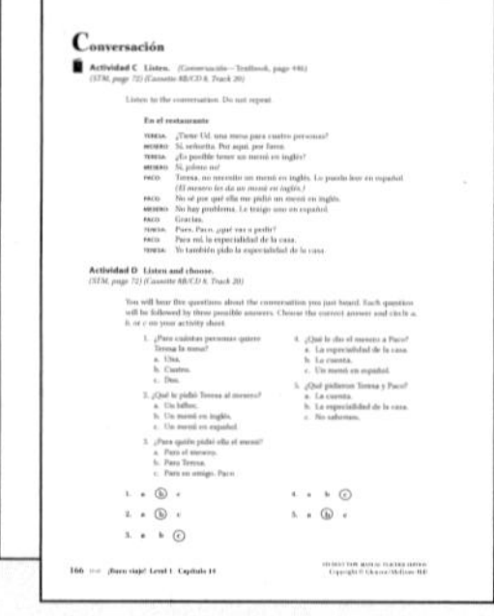
Conversación

Conversation, Pronunciation, pages 172–173

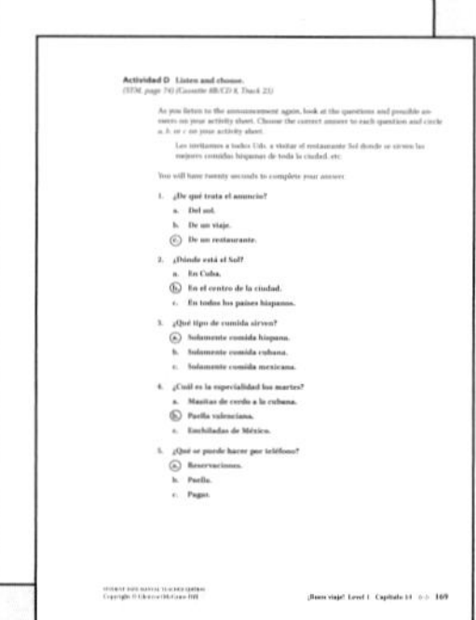
Additional Practice, pages 173–175

Assessment

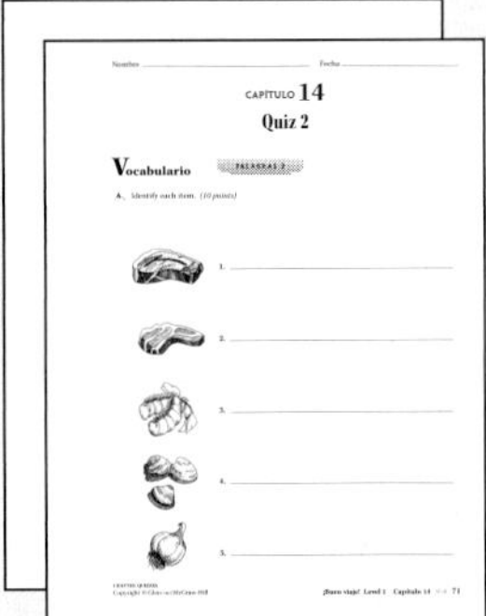

Vocabulary and Structure Quizzes, pages 70–74

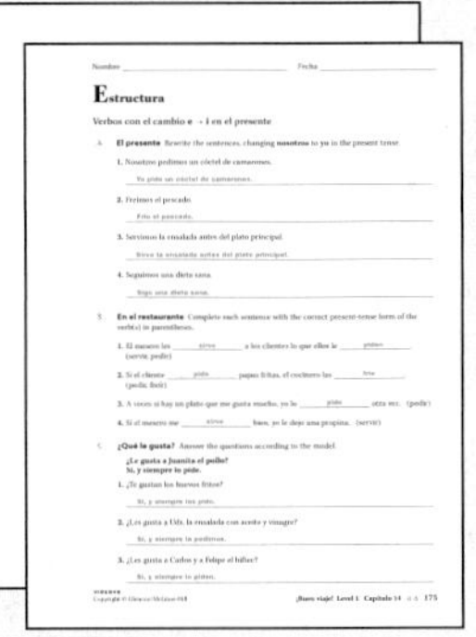

Chapter Tests, pages 221–232

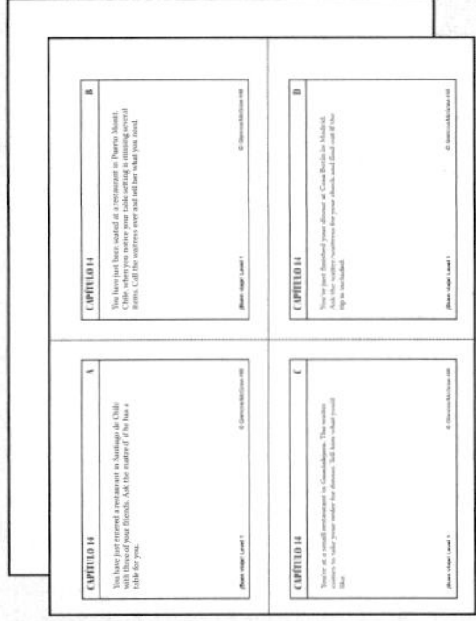

Situation Cards, Chapter 14

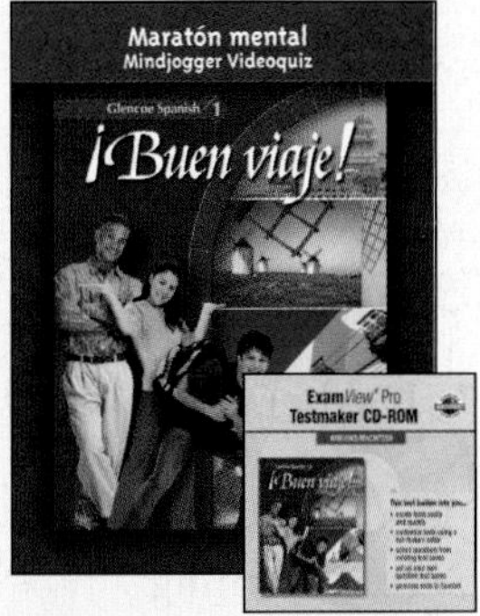

MindJogger Videoquiz, ExamView® Pro, Chapter 14

Timesaving Teacher Tools

TeacherWorks™ is your all-in-one teacher resource center. Personalize lesson plans, access resources from the Teacher Wraparound Edition, connect to the Internet, or make a to-do list. These are only a few of the many features that can assist you in the planning and organizing of your lessons.

Includes:

- A calendar feature
- Access to all program blackline masters
- Standards correlations and more

ExamView® Pro

Test Bank software for Macintosh and Windows makes creating, editing, customizing, and printing tests quick and easy.

Technology Resources

In the Chapter 14 Internet Activity, you will have a chance to learn more about the Spanish-speaking world. Visit spanish.glencoe.com

On the interactive CD-ROM, students can listen to and take part in a recorded version of the conversation in Chapter 14.

¡Viva el mundo hispano! Video and Video Activities, Chapter 14. Available on VHS and DVD.

Help your students prepare for the chapter test by playing the **Maratón mental** Videoquiz game show. Teams will compete against each other to review chapter vocabulary and structure and sharpen listening comprehension skills. Available on VHS and DVD.

¡Buen viaje! is also available on CD or Online.

Preview

In this chapter, students will learn how to order food in a restaurant. To do this, they will learn expressions needed to speak with a server, vocabulary associated with utensils, and additional items of food. They will continue to narrate in the present and past by learning the present and preterite of stem-changing verbs they can use at a restaurant—**pedir, servir, repetir.** The cultural focus of the chapter is on some typical cuisines of the Spanish-speaking world.

National Standards

Communication

In Chapter 14 students will learn to communicate in spoken and written Spanish on the following topics:

- ordering a meal
- describing a restaurant experience
- discussing cuisines of the Spanish-speaking world

Students will obtain and provide information about these topics and engage in conversations that would typically take place at a restaurant as they fulfill the chapter objectives listed on this page.

Capítulo 14

En el restaurante

Objetivos

In this chapter you will learn to:

- order food or a beverage at a restaurant
- identify eating utensils and dishes
- identify more foods
- make a reservation at a restaurant
- talk about present and past events
- describe some cuisines of the Hispanic world

Hernán Miranda *Interiores con mesa*

Capítulo 14

Spotlight on Culture

Arte Hernán Miranda (1960) is a self-taught, contemporary Paraguayan artist. From 1993 until 1997, he was Professor of Art at the Escuela Nacional de Bellas Artes in Asunción. His recent works focus primarily on the objects of daily life such as utensils, fruit, and dishware.

Fotografía The restaurant shown on this page is in Lima.

Learning from Photos

(pages 432–433) Ask the following questions about the photo after presenting the new vocabulary in this chapter:

¿Está poniendo la mesa el mesero?

Identifica todo lo que ves en la mesa.

¿Cuántas personas hay en la familia que está en el restaurante?

¿Cómo está vestido el papá? ¿Qué lleva?

¿Qué leen la mamá y el papá?

LEVELING

The activities, conversations, and readings within each chapter are marked according to level of difficulty. **E** indicates easy. **A** indicates average. **C** indicates challenging. Some activities cover a range of difficulty. In some activities, for example, advanced students will be able to produce more extensive responses while students who learn at a different rate may give less detailed responses. The leveling indicators will help you individualize instruction to best meet your students' needs.

Vocabulario

PALABRAS 1

1 PREPARATION

Resource Manager

Vocabulary Transparencies 14.2–14.3
Audio Activities TE, pages 165–167
Audio CD 8
Workbook, pages 171–172
Quizzes, page 70
ExamView® Pro

Bellringer Review

Use BRR Transparency 14.1 or write the following on the board.
Write a list of the foods you have learned.

2 PRESENTATION

Step 1 Have students close their books. Show Vocabulary Transparencies 14.2–14.3. Point to individual items and have students repeat each word or expression two or three times after you or Audio CD 8.

Step 2 Intersperse the presentation with simple questions that enable students to use the new words. For example: **¿Tienes hambre? ¿Quieres comer? ¿Tienes sed? ¿Qué pone el mesero? ¿Usas la taza para beber o para cortar la carne?** Have students answer with complete sentences or sometimes have them answer with a word or an expression.

Step 3 After presenting the vocabulary orally, have students open their books and read the new vocabulary aloud. You can have the class read in chorus or call on individuals to read. Intersperse with questions such as those outlined above.

Vocabulario

PALABRAS 1

En el restaurante

El mesero pone la mesa.

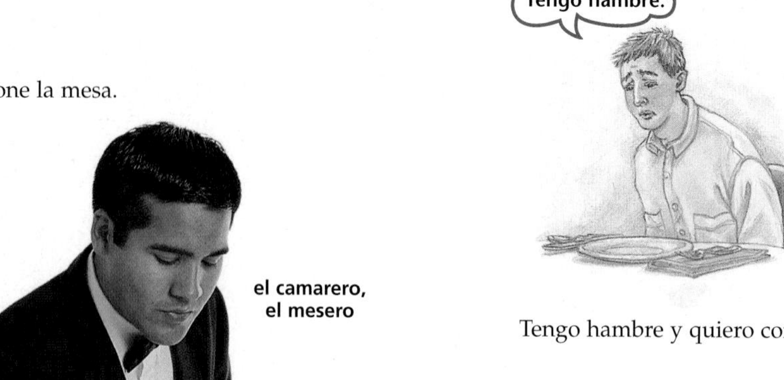

Tengo hambre y quiero comer.

Tengo sed y quiero beber algo.

Reaching All Students

Total Physical Response Teach the following words by using the appropriate gestures as you say each expression: **cubre, dobla, a la derecha, a la izquierda, deja.**

(Student 1), **ven acá, por favor.**
Vas a poner la mesa.
Cubre la mesa con un mantel.
Dobla las servilletas. Pon un plato en la mesa.
Pon la cucharita y el cuchillo a la derecha.
Pon el tenedor a la izquierda. Gracias.

(Student 2), **ven acá, por favor.**
Vas a hacer unos gestos.
Toma el menú. Abre el menú.
Lee el menú. Cierra el menú.
Corta la carne con el cuchillo. Come.
Bebe. Deja una propina para el mesero.
Gracias, *(Student 2).* **Regresa a tu asiento.**

La señorita pide el menú.

El cocinero fríe las papas.
Está friendo las papas.

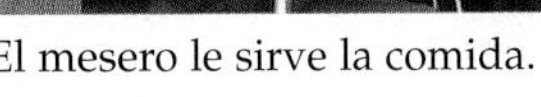

El mesero le sirve la comida.

La señorita pide la cuenta.
El servicio no está incluido.
Ella deja una propina.

FUN-FACTS

In Spain and in many countries of Latin America, a saltshaker is put on the table but not a pepper shaker or pepper mill. If you want pepper you have to ask for it. The only exceptions would be in some international restaurants and hotels.

Reaching All Students

Additional Practice You may have students make up a brief conversation using the words **hambre** and **sed.** For example:
¿Sabes? Tengo hambre.
¿Ah sí? ¿Qué quieres comer?
Pues, creo que voy a pedir ___.

For the Younger Students You may wish to bring in silverware and have students set a table as they learn to identify each item.

LEVELING
A: Vocabulary

About the Spanish Language

- The word **mesero** is used in Latin America. **Camarero** is used in Spain.
- The word **el menú** is universally understood. Other words frequently used for **menú** are **la minuta** and **la carta.**
- We have presented the words **sal** and **pimienta** but not **el salero** and **el pimentero,** since these words are hardly ever used. One would say: **Sal, por favor.**

3 PRACTICE

¿Qué palabra necesito?

¡OJO! When students are doing the **¿Qué palabra necesito?** activities, accept any answer that makes sense. The purpose of these activities is to have students use the new vocabulary. They are not factual recall activities. Thus, it is not necessary for students to remember specific factual information from the vocabulary presentation when answering. If you wish, have students use the photos on this page as a stimulus, when possible.

Historieta Each time **Historieta** appears, it means that the answers to the activity form a short story. Encourage students to look at the title of the **Historieta,** since it can help them do the activity.

1 Have students work with a partner.

Expansion: Ask students to volunteer additional items. For example: **Para tomar una limonada, una sopa,** etc.

2 After going over Activity 2, have students retell the story in their own words.

¿Qué palabra necesito?

1 ¿Qué necesitas? Contesten según el modelo.

¿Para tomar leche? ⟶
Para tomar leche necesito un vaso.

1. ¿Para tomar agua?
2. ¿Para tomar café?
3. ¿Para comer la ensalada?
4. ¿Para comer el postre?
5. ¿Para cortar la carne?

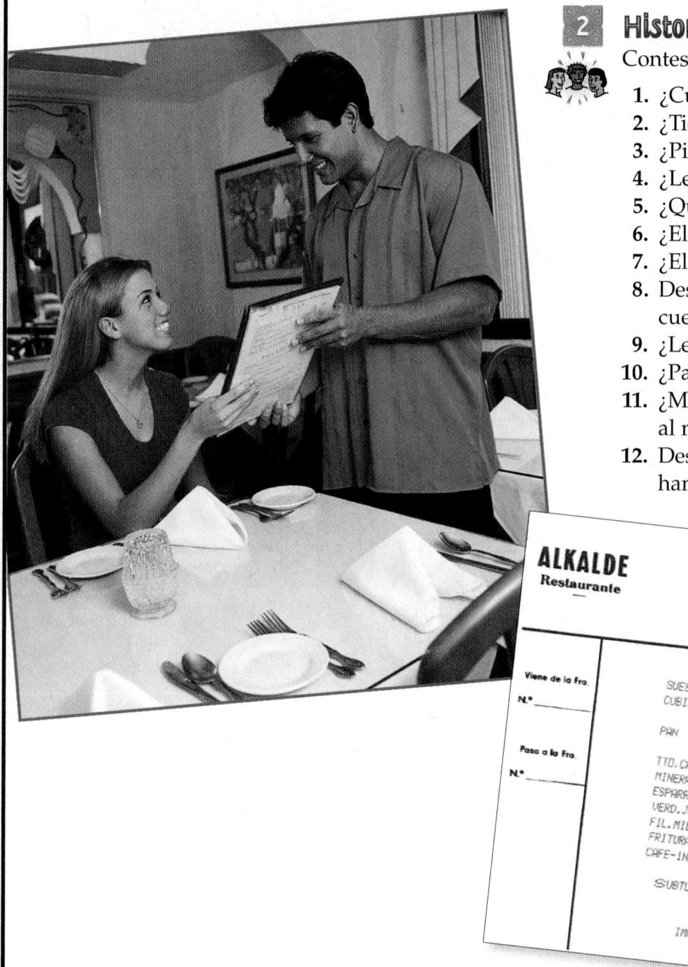

2 Historieta En el restaurante

Contesten.

1. ¿Cuántas personas hay en la mesa?
2. ¿Tiene hambre María?
3. ¿Pide María el menú?
4. ¿Le trae el menú el mesero?
5. ¿Qué pide María?
6. ¿El mesero le sirve?
7. ¿El mesero le sirve bien?
8. Después de la comida, ¿le pide la cuenta al mesero?
9. ¿Le trae la cuenta el mesero?
10. ¿Paga con su tarjeta de crédito María?
11. ¿María le da (deja) una propina al mesero?
12. Después de la comida, ¿tiene hambre María?

ANSWERS TO ¿Qué palabra necesito?

1. Para tomar agua necesito un vaso.
2. Para tomar café necesito una taza.
3. Para comer la ensalada necesito un tenedor.
4. Para comer el postre necesito una cucharita (un tenedor).
5. Para cortar la carne necesito un cuchillo.

2

1. Hay una persona en la mesa.
2. Sí, María tiene hambre.
3. Sí, María pide el menú.
4. Sí, el mesero le trae el menú.
5. María pide ___.
6. Sí, el mesero le sirve.
7. Sí, el mesero le sirve bien.
8. Sí, le pide la cuenta al mesero después de la comida.
9. Sí, el mesero le trae la cuenta.
10. Sí (No), María (no) paga con su tarjeta de crédito.
11. Sí, María le da (deja) una propina al mesero.
12. No, María no tiene hambre después de la comida.

3 Palabras relacionadas Pareen las palabras relacionadas.

1. la mesa	a. el servicio
2. la cocina	b. la bebida
3. servir	c. el cocinero
4. freír	d. la comida
5. comer	e. el mesero
6. beber	f. frito

Alcalá de Henares, España

4 Historieta El mesero pone la mesa. Completen.

1. Para comer, los clientes necesitan ____, ____, ____ y ____.
2. Dos condimentos son la ____ y la ____.
3. El mesero cubre la mesa con ____.
4. En la mesa el mesero pone una ____ para cada cliente.
5. El niño pide un ____ de leche y sus padres piden una ____ de café.
6. Ellos tienen ____ y piden una botella de agua mineral.

5 En el restaurante Look at the advertisement for a restaurant in Santiago de Chile. Tell as much as you can about the restaurant based on the information in the advertisement. A classmate will tell whether he or she wants to go to the restaurant and why.

Aquí está Coco
El sabor de los mejores pescados y mariscos del Pacífico Sur, preparados como usted quiera, en un ambiente agradable e informal.

Vocabulario

3 This activity helps students learn to identify word families.

¡OJO! Note that the activities are color-coded. All the activities in the text are communicative. However, the ones with blue titles are guided communication. The red titles indicate that the answers to the activity are more open-ended and can vary more. You may wish to correct students' mistakes more so in the guided activities than in the activities with a red title, which lend themselves to a freer response.

5 Students should base their descriptions on both the descriptive paragraph and the two photos in this ad. Explain to the class that the phrase **e informal** is not a spelling error. After students have done **Palabras 2,** pages 438–439, see how many seafood items they can identify in this ad.

Learning from Realia

(page 436) The name of the restaurant on the check is **Alkalde.** It is a Basque restaurant. The Basques are considered to be some of the best cooks in Spain.
(page 437) There is something in this ad that indicates that the restaurant must be in South America. What is it? **(del Pacífico Sur)**

Answers to ¿Qué palabra necesito?

1. e
2. c
3. a
4. f
5. d
6. b

1. un plato, un tenedor, un cuchillo, una cucharita (una cuchara)
2. sal, pimienta
3. un mantel
4. servilleta
5. vaso, taza
6. sed

5 *Answers will vary; however, students should mention the type of dishes served* (pescados y mariscos) *and whether the restaurant is formal or informal.*

LEVELING

E: Activities 1, 2, 3
A: Activities 1, 2, 4, 5

Vocabulario

PALABRAS 2

1 PREPARATION

Resource Manager

Vocabulary Transparencies 14.4–14.5
Audio Activities TE, pages 167–170
Audio CD 8
Workbook, pages 173–174
Quizzes, pages 71–72
ExamView® Pro

Bellringer Review

Use BRR Transparency 14.2 or write the following on the board.
Complete with the past tense.

1. **Anoche yo no ___ en casa. (comer)**
2. **Mis amigos y yo ___ en un restaurante. (comer)**
3. **Yo ___ al restaurante en el metro pero mis amigos ___ el autobús. (ir, tomar)**
4. **El mesero nos ___ un servicio muy bueno. (dar)**

Vocabulario

PALABRAS 2

Más alimentos o comestibles

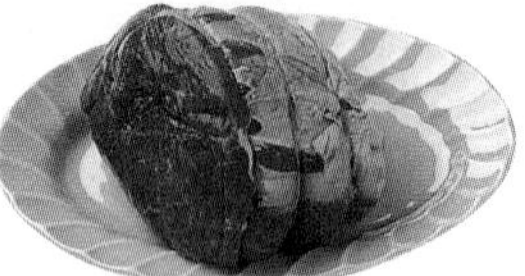
la carne

la carne de res, el biftec

la ternera

el cerdo

el cordero

el pescado

los mariscos

los camarones

las almejas

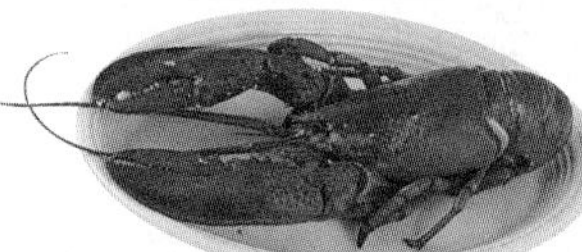
la langosta

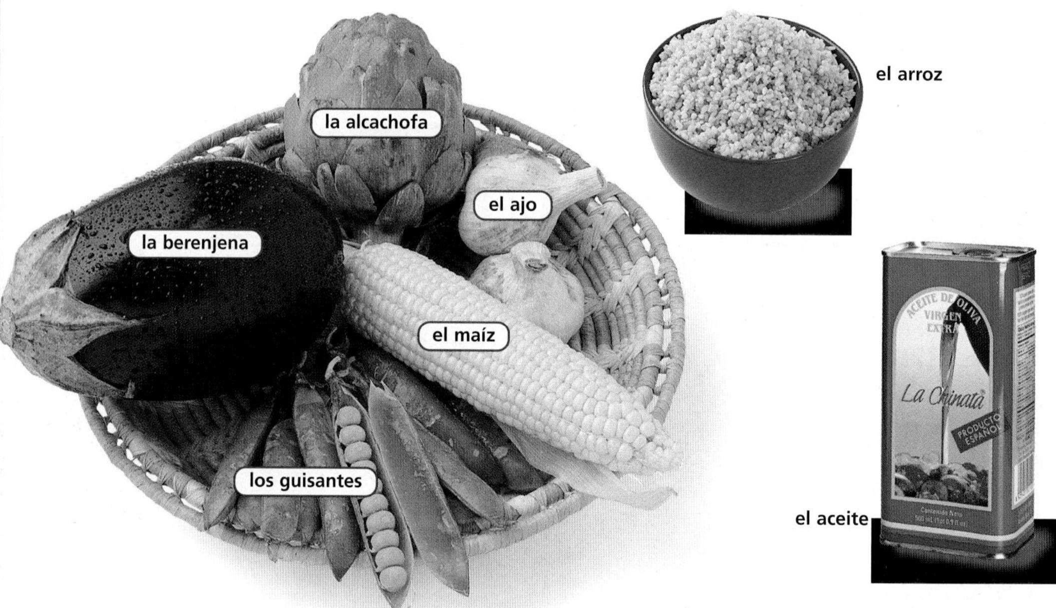

Reaching All Students

Total Physical Response

(Student 1), **levántate y ven acá, por favor.**
Estamos en el restaurante Mendoza.
Siéntate, *(Student 1).*
Toma el menú. Ábrelo. Lee el menú.
Llama al mesero.
(Student 2), **ven acá. Tú vas a ser el mesero.**
(Student 1), **pídele al mesero lo que quieres comer.**
(Student 2), **escribe lo que pide.**
Ve a la cocina. Vuelve con la comida.
Sirve la comida. Pon los platos en la mesa.
(Student 1), **come.**

Ah, tenemos un problema. Pediste la carne bien hecha y el mesero te sirvió la carne casi cruda. Llama al mesero.
(Student 2), **ve a la mesa.**
(Student 1), **dale el plato.**
Pide la cuenta. Mira la cuenta.
Saca el dinero de tu bolsillo o de tu cartera.
Paga. Levántate.
Sal del restaurante.
Gracias, *(Student 1).* **Ahora puedes volver a tu asiento.**
Y tú también, *(Student 2).* **Gracias.**

La joven pidió un biftec.
El mesero sirvió el biftec.
La comida está rica, deliciosa.

¡Diga!
Quisiera reservar una mesa, por favor.
Sí, señor. ¿Para cuándo?
Para esta noche a las nueve y media.
¿Cuántas personas?
Cuatro.
¿A nombre de quién, por favor?
A nombre de Julio Amaral.
Conforme, señor.

Vocabulario

2 PRESENTATION

Step 1 Have students close their books. Then model the new vocabulary on pages 438–439 using Vocabulary Transparencies 14.4–14.5. Have students repeat each word or expression two or three times after you or Audio CD 8.

Step 2 Clarify any cuts of meat that are not evident. For example, students may not know **carne de res** *(beef)*, **ternera** *(veal)*, **cerdo** *(pork)*, **cordero** *(lamb)*.

Step 3 Have students read the dialogue on page 439 aloud. You may want to have several students perform the telephone conversation for the class.

Vocabulary Expansion

You may wish to introduce the following expressions:

bien hecho(a), cocido(a)	*well-done*
a término medio	*medium*
casi crudo, no muy cocido(a)	*rare*

A waiter will frequently ask:
¿Qué les apetece? *(What would you like to order?)*

About the Spanish Language

- Explain the difference between **La comida está buena** and **La comida es buena. (La comida está buena significa que la comida está deliciosa, que tiene buen sabor. La comida es buena significa que es buena para la salud—contiene vitaminas, etc.)**
- In addition to **el maíz,** you will also hear **el elote** (Mexico) and **el choclo** (South America).
- In addition to **la alcachofa,** you will also hear **la cotufa.**
- There are several ways to say *shrimp.* The differences in names reflect type and size. In addition to **el camarón** you will hear **la gamba** (usually small shrimp in Spain), **el langostino** (large, but not a lobster), and **la quisquilla.**
- There are many ways to say *steak* in Spanish. **Biftec** and **bistec** are commonly used for steak. You will also hear **filete** and **entrecot. Filete,** however, can be a filet of any type of meat or fish. **El entrecot** is meat only. The word **lomo** refers to any cut from the loin area. **Lomo de carne de res** is similar to a sirloin steak. **Solomillo** or **lomo fino** is similar to a tenderloin or filet mignon. In many areas of Latin America **el churrasco** is a grilled steak.

3 PRACTICE

¿Qué palabra necesito?

¡OJO! It is recommended that you go over all the activities in class before assigning them for homework.

6 After doing Activity 6, go back to page 438 and ask students whether they like the other food items on that page.

7 After doing Activity 7, have one or two students retell the story in their own words.

Learning from Photos

(page 440) Have students describe what they see in these photos in their own words.

¿Qué palabra necesito?

6 ¿Te gusta(n) o no te gusta(n)? Contesten según los dibujos.

1.

2.

3.

4.

5.

6.

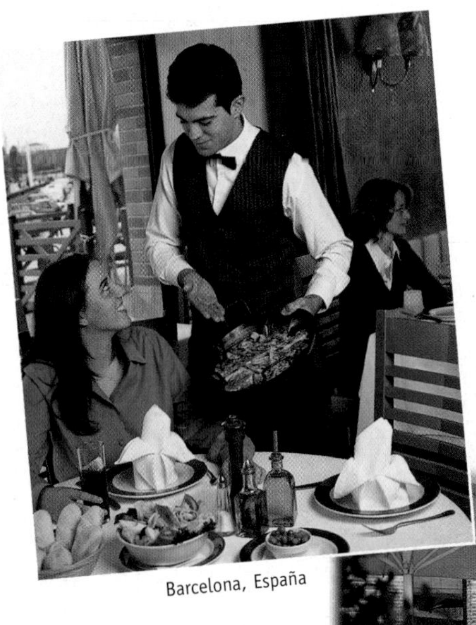
Barcelona, España

7 Historieta Cenó en el restaurante.
Contesten.

1. ¿Fue Victoria al restaurante anoche?
2. ¿Quién le sirvió?
3. ¿Pidió Victoria un biftec?
4. ¿Pidió también una ensalada?
5. ¿Le sirvió el mesero una ensalada de lechuga y tomate?
6. ¿Le sirvió una comida deliciosa o una comida mala?

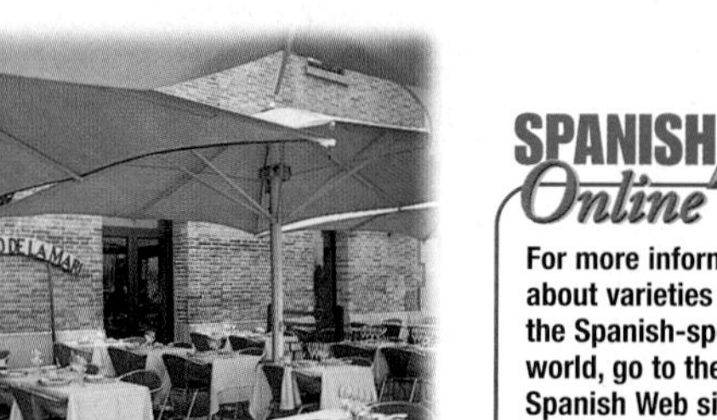

SPANISH Online
For more information about varieties of food in the Spanish-speaking world, go to the Glencoe Spanish Web site: spanish.glencoe.com

Answers to ¿Qué palabra necesito?

1. (No) Me gusta el biftec.
2. (No) Me gusta el pescado.
3. (No) Me gustan los camarones (las gambas).
4. (No) Me gustan los guisantes.
5. (No) Me gusta el maíz.
6. (No) Me gustan las almejas.

1. Sí, Victoria fue al restaurante anoche.
2. El mesero le sirvió.
3. Sí (No), Victoria (no) pidió un biftec.
4. Sí, (No, no) pidió una ensalada.
5. Sí (No), el mesero (no) le sirvió una ensalada de lechuga y tomate.
6. Le sirvió una comida deliciosa (mala).

8 **¿Qué te gusta?** Contesten personalmente.

1. ¿Te gusta la ensalada?
2. ¿Te gusta la ensalada con aceite y vinagre?
3. ¿Te gusta el biftec?
4. ¿Te gusta el sándwich de jamón y queso? ¿Te gusta más con pan tostado?
5. ¿Te gusta la tortilla de queso?
6. ¿Te gustan los huevos con jamón?

9 **Una reservación** You call a restaurant in Buenos Aires. The headwaiter (a classmate) answers. Make a reservation for yourself and a group of friends.

10 **¿Qué recomienda usted?** Here's a menu from a very famous restaurant in Madrid. In fact, it's the oldest restaurant in the city, dating from 1725. There are many items on the menu that you will be able to recognize. A classmate will be the server. Ask what he or she recommends and then order.

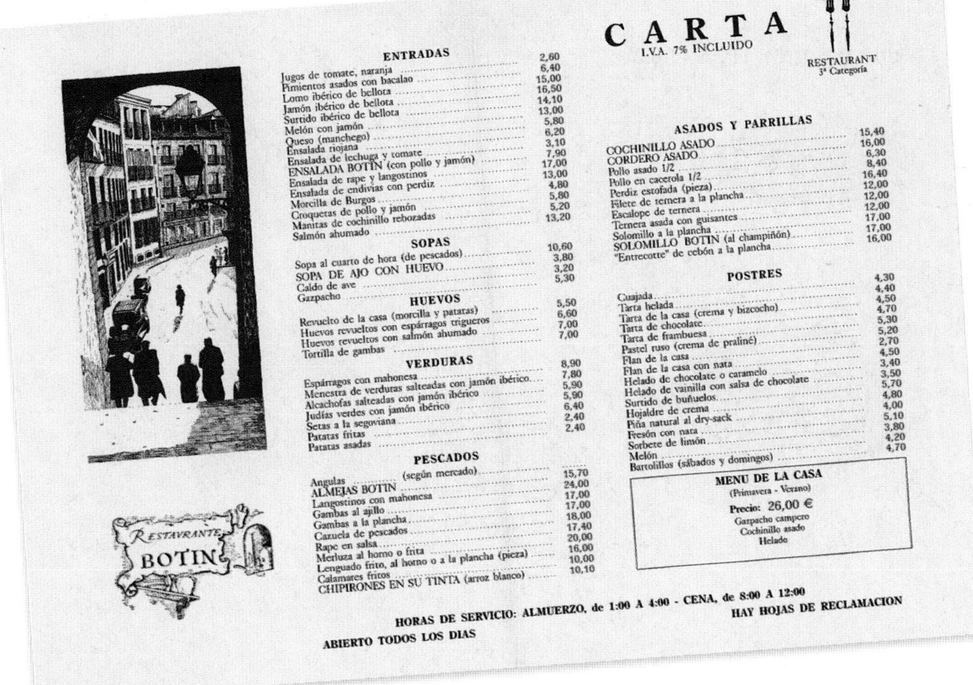

CARTA
I.V.A. 7% INCLUIDO
RESTAURANT
3ª Categoría

ENTRADAS
Jugos de tomate, naranja
Pimientos asados con bacalao
Lomo ibérico de bellota
Jamón ibérico de bellota
Surtido ibérico de bellota
Melón con jamón
Queso (manchego)
Ensalada riojana
Ensalada de lechuga y tomate
ENSALADA BOTIN (con pollo y jamón)
Ensalada de rape y langostinos
Ensalada de endivias con perdiz
Morcilla de Burgos
Croquetas de pollo y jamón
Manitas de cochinillo rebozadas
Salmón ahumado

2,60 · 6,40 · 15,00 · 16,50 · 14,10 · 13,00 · 5,80 · 6,20 · 3,10 · 7,90 · 17,00 · 13,00 · 4,80 · 5,80 · 5,20 · 13,20

SOPAS
Sopa al cuarto de hora (de pescados)
SOPA DE AJO CON HUEVO
Caldo de ave
Gazpacho

10,60 · 3,80 · 3,20 · 5,30

HUEVOS
Revuelto de la casa (morcilla y patatas)
Huevos revueltos con espárragos trigueros
Huevos revueltos con salmón ahumado
Tortilla de gambas

5,50 · 6,60 · 7,00 · 7,00

VERDURAS
Espárragos con mahonesa
Menestra de verduras salteadas con jamón ibérico
Alcachofas salteadas con jamón ibérico
Judías verdes con jamón ibérico
Setas a la segoviana
Patatas fritas
Patatas asadas

8,90 · 7,80 · 5,90 · 5,90 · 6,40 · 2,40 · 2,40

PESCADOS
(según mercado)
Angulas
ALMEJAS BOTIN
Langostinos con mahonesa
Gambas al ajillo
Gambas a la plancha
Cazuela de pescados
Rape en salsa
Merluza al horno o frita
Lenguado frito, al horno o a la plancha (pieza)
Calamares fritos
CHIPIRONES EN SU TINTA (arroz blanco)

15,70 · 24,00 · 17,00 · 17,00 · 18,00 · 17,40 · 20,00 · 16,00 · 10,00 · 10,10

ASADOS Y PARRILLAS
COCHINILLO ASADO
CORDERO ASADO
Pollo asado 1/2
Pollo en cacerola 1/2
Perdiz estofada (pieza)
Filete de ternera a la plancha
Escalope de ternera
Ternera asada con guisantes
Solomillo a la plancha
SOLOMILLO BOTIN (al champiñón)
"Entrecotte" de cebón a la plancha

15,40 · 16,00 · 6,30 · 8,40 · 16,40 · 12,00 · 12,00 · 12,00 · 17,00 · 17,00 · 16,00

POSTRES
Cuajada
Tarta helada
Tarta de la casa (crema y bizcocho)
Tarta de chocolate
Tarta de frambuesa
Pastel ruso (crema de praliné)
Flan de la casa
Flan de la casa con nata
Helado de chocolate o caramelo
Helado de vainilla con salsa de chocolate
Surtido de buñuelos
Hojaldre de crema
Piña natural al dry-sack
Fresón con nata
Sorbete de limón
Melón
Bartolillos (sábados y domingos)

4,30 · 4,40 · 4,50 · 4,70 · 5,30 · 5,20 · 2,70 · 4,50 · 3,40 · 3,50 · 5,70 · 4,80 · 4,00 · 5,10 · 3,80 · 4,20 · 4,70

MENU DE LA CASA
(Primavera - Verano)
Precio: 26,00 €
Gazpacho campero
Cochinillo asado
Helado

HORAS DE SERVICIO: ALMUERZO, de 1:00 A 4:00 - CENA, de 8:00 A 12:00
ABIERTO TODOS LOS DIAS
HAY HOJAS DE RECLAMACION

Vocabulario

8 Students can do this activity in pairs.

Expansion: You may wish to have students expand Activity 8 into a miniconversation:

—¿Te gusta la ensalada?
—Sí, mucho. ¿Y a ti te gusta?
—Sí, me gusta. (No, no me gusta.)

9 Students should use the dialogue on page 439 as a model.

10 The famous **Casa de Botín** restaurant specializes in **cordero asado** and **cochinillo asado. Cochinillo** is called **lechón** in Latin America. You may also wish to point out that the word **carta** is used here, rather than **menú.**

Chapter Projects

Visita a un restaurante hispano Plan a class outing to an inexpensive restaurant that serves food from a Spanish-speaking country. If possible, distribute the restaurant's menu in advance so students can think about what they will order. You may also have them use the menus to practice ordering in Spanish.

LEVELING

E: Activities 6, 7, 8
A: Activities 7, 9, 10
C: Activity 10

Answers to ¿Qué palabra necesito?

8

1. Sí, (No, no) me gusta la ensalada.
2. Sí, (No, no) me gusta la ensalada con aceite y vinagre.
3. Sí, (No, no) me gusta el biftec.
4. Sí, (No, no) me gusta el sándwich de jamón y queso. Sí, (No, no) me gusta más con pan tostado.
5. Sí, (No, no) me gusta la tortilla de queso.
6. Sí, (No, no) me gustan los huevos con jamón.

9 *Answers will vary. Students should use the conversation on page 439 as a model.*

10 *Answers will vary. Students should use* recomendar *and the foods listed on the menu.*

Estructura

1 PREPARATION

Resource Manager

Audio Activities TE, pages 170–171
Audio CD 8
Workbook, pages 175–176
Quizzes, pages 73–74
ExamView® Pro

Bellringer Review

Use BRR Transparency 14.3 or write the following on the board.
Answer the following questions.

1. **¿Te gusta la carne?**
2. **¿Te gustan los mariscos?**
3. **¿Cuáles son algunas legumbres que te gustan?**
4. **¿Te gusta el postre?**
5. **¿Qué te gusta beber?**

2 PRESENTATION

Verbos con el cambio e → i en el presente

Step 1 Have students open their books to page 442. Write the verb forms on the board. Underline the stem and have students repeat each form after you.
Note: Oral practice with these verbs is important, because if students pronounce them correctly, they will be inclined to spell them correctly.

Step 2 When going over the verb **seguir,** review with students the following sound/spelling correspondence: **ga, gue, gui, go, gu.**

Estructura

Verbos con el cambio e → i en el presente
Describing more present activities

1. The verbs **pedir, servir, repetir, freír, seguir** *(to follow),* and **vestirse** *(to get dressed)* are stem-changing verbs. The **e** of the infinitive stem changes to **i** in all forms of the present tense except the **nosotros** and **vosotros** forms. Study the following forms. Note the spelling of **seguir.**

INFINITIVE	pedir	servir	seguir	vestirse
yo	pido	sirvo	sigo	me visto
tú	pides	sirves	sigues	te vistes
él, ella, Ud.	pide	sirve	sigue	se viste
nosotros(as)	pedimos	servimos	seguimos	nos vestimos
vosotros(as)	*pedís*	*servís*	*seguís*	*os vestís*
ellos, ellas, Uds.	piden	sirven	siguen	se visten

¿Cómo lo digo?

11 Lo que yo pido Digan si piden lo siguente o no.

1.

2.

3.

4.

5.

6.

Answers to ¿Cómo lo digo?

11

1. Sí, (No, no) pido una langosta.
2. Sí, (No, no) pido queso.
3. Sí, (No, no) pido papas.
4. Sí, (No, no) pido un pollo.
5. Sí, (No, no) pido una botella de agua mineral.
6. Sí, (No, no) pido una ensalada.

LEVELING

E: Activities 11, 14
A: Activities 11, 12, 13, 15

12 Lo que pedimos en el restaurante

Sigan el modelo.

A Juan le gusta el pescado.
¿Qué pide él?

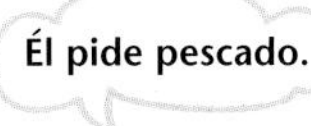

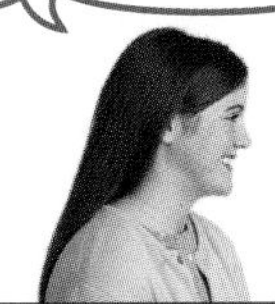

1. A Teresa le gustan los mariscos. ¿Qué pide ella?
2. A Carlos le gusta el biftec. ¿Qué pide él?
3. A mis amigos les gustan las legumbres. ¿Qué piden ellos?
4. A mis padres les gusta mucho la ensalada. ¿Qué piden ellos?
5. Nos gusta el postre. ¿Qué pedimos?
6. Nos gustan las tortillas. ¿Qué pedimos?
7. ¿Qué pides cuando tienes sed?
8. ¿Qué pides cuando tienes hambre?

13 Historieta Vamos al restaurante. Completen.

Cuando mi amiga y yo __1__ (ir) al restaurante, nosotros __2__ (pedir) casi siempre una hamburguesa. Yo la __3__ (pedir) con lechuga y tomate y ella la __4__ (pedir) con queso. A mi amiga le __5__ (gustar) mucho las papas fritas. Ella __6__ (decir) que le __7__ (gustar) más cuando el cocinero las __8__ (freír) en aceite de oliva.

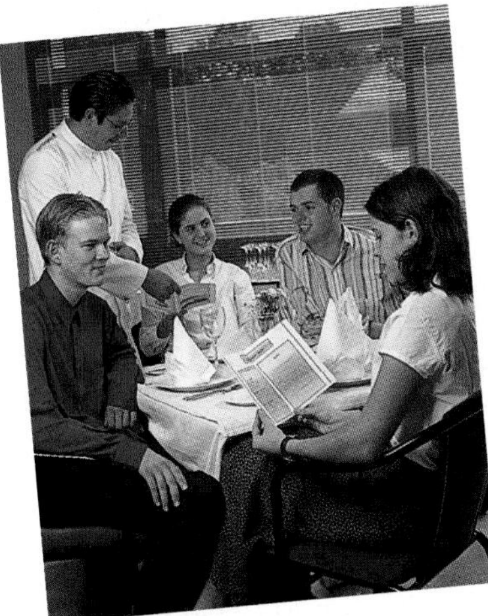

Marbella, España

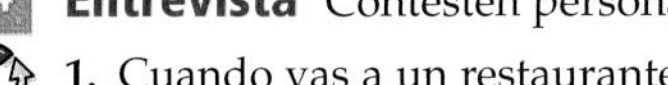

14 Entrevista Contesten personalmente.

1. Cuando vas a un restaurante, ¿qué pides?
2. ¿Pides papas? Si no pides papas, ¿pides arroz?
3. ¿Qué más pides con la carne y las papas o el arroz?
4. ¿Quién te sirve en el restaurante?
5. Si te sirve bien, ¿qué le dejas?

15 ¿Por qué no pides... ?

You're in a restaurant with a friend (a classmate). You are hungry and thirsty, but you don't know what to order. Your friend will suggest something. Then you decide.

UN POCO MÁS *For more practice using words from **Palabras 2** and the verb **pedir**, do Activity 14 on page H15 at the end of this book.*

3 PRACTICE

¿Cómo lo digo?

11 Students will answer using the **yo** form.

12 Activity 12 reviews the use of **gustar** as it practices stem-changing verbs.

13 After going over Activity 13, students can summarize the information in their own words.

14 Activity 14 may be done in pairs.

15 In this activity, the first student can begin by asking: **¿Te gusta(n)... ?** or **¿Por qué no pides... ?**

UN POCO MÁS This *InfoGap* Activity will allow students to practice in pairs. The activity should be very manageable for them, since all vocabulary and structures are familiar to them.

Answers to ¿Cómo lo digo?

12

1. Ella pide mariscos.
2. Él pide biftec.
3. Ellos piden legumbres.
4. Ellos piden ensalada.
5. Pedimos postre.
6. Pedimos tortillas.
7. Cuando tengo sed pido ___.
8. Cuando tengo hambre pido ___.

13

1. vamos
2. pedimos
3. pido
4. pide
5. gustan
6. dice
7. gustan
8. fríe

14

1. Cuando voy a un restaurante, pido ___.
2. Sí, (No, no) pido papas. Sí, si no pido papas, pido arroz. (No, si no pido papas, no pido arroz.)
3. Pido ___.
4. El mesero me sirve en el restaurante.
5. Si me sirve bien le dejo una propina.

15 *Answers will vary. Students should use the phrase* ¿Por qué no pides... ? *to make their suggestions.*

Estructura

1 PREPARATION

Bellringer Review

Use BRR Transparency 14.4 or write the following on the board.
Unscramble the following sentences.
1. **tacos / los / sirve / restaurante / el mesero / en el**
2. **pimienta / pide / Juan / sal / la / y / la**
3. **y / el / Sofía / fríen / pescado / papas / las / y Jaime**

2 PRESENTATION

Verbos con el cambio e → i, o → u en el pretérito

Step 1 Have students repeat the verb forms shown in the charts on page 444, paying particular attention to the stem changes and correct pronunciation.

3 PRACTICE

¿Cómo lo digo?

16 The items in Activity 16 describe an unfortunate experience in a restaurant.
Expansion: After going over Activity 16, have students make up original stories about a horrible experience in a restaurant. This can be done as a narrative.
Note: This is a good preparatory activity for Activity 18, page 445. In that activity students converse with the restaurant manager about a problem with their meal and the service.

Verbos con el cambio e → i, o → u en el pretérito

Describing more activities in the past

1. The verbs **pedir, repetir, freír, servir,** and **vestirse** have a stem change in the preterite. The **e** of the infinitive stem changes to **i** in the **él** and **ellos** forms.

INFINITIVE	pedir	repetir	vestirse
yo	pedí	repetí	me vestí
tú	pediste	repetiste	te vestiste
él, ella, Ud.	pidió	repitió	se vistió
nosotros(as)	pedimos	repetimos	nos vestimos
vosotros(as)	*pedisteis*	*repetisteis*	*os vestisteis*
ellos, ellas, Uds.	pidieron	repitieron	se vistieron

2. The verbs **preferir, divertirse,** and **dormir** also have a stem change in the preterite. The **e** in **preferir** and **divertirse** changes to **i** and the **o** in **dormir** changes to **u** in the **él** and **ellos** forms.

INFINITIVE	preferir	divertirse	dormir
yo	preferí	me divertí	dormí
tú	preferiste	te divertiste	dormiste
él, ella, Ud.	prefirió	se divirtió	durmió
nosotros(as)	preferimos	nos divertimos	dormimos
vosotros(as)	*preferisteis*	*os divertisteis*	*dormisteis*
ellos, ellas, Uds.	prefirieron	se divirtieron	durmieron

¿Cómo lo digo?

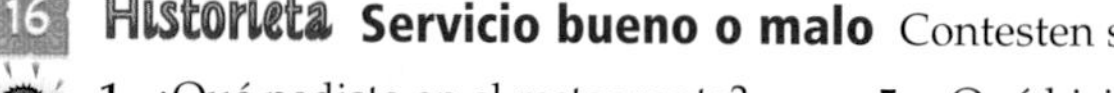

16 Historieta Servicio bueno o malo Contesten según se indica.

1. ¿Qué pediste en el restaurante? (una ensalada)
2. ¿Cómo la pediste? (sin aceite y vinagre)
3. ¿Cuántas veces repetiste «sin aceite y vinagre»? (dos veces)
4. Y, ¿cómo sirvió el mesero la ensalada? (con aceite y vinagre)
5. ¿Qué hiciste? (pedí otra ensalada)
6. ¿Qué pidió tu amigo? (puré de papas)
7. ¿Y qué pasó? (el cocinero frió las papas)
8. ¿Qué sirvió el mesero? (papas fritas)
9. ¿Pidieron ustedes una bebida? (sí)
10. ¿Qué pidieron para beber? (una limonada)
11. ¿Qué sirvió el mesero? (un té)
12. ¿Le dieron ustedes una propina al mesero? (no)

Answers to ¿Cómo lo digo?

16

1. Pedí una ensalada en el restaurante.
2. La pedí sin aceite y vinagre.
3. Repetí «sin aceite y vinagre» dos veces.
4. El mesero sirvió la ensalada con aceite y vinagre.
5. Pedí otra ensalada.
6. Mi amigo pidió puré de papas.
7. El cocinero frió las papas.
8. El mesero sirvió papas fritas.
9. Sí, pedimos una bebida.
10. Pedimos una limonada.
11. El mesero sirvió un té.
12. No, no le dimos una propina al mesero.

17 Historieta Preparando la comida

Completen con el pretérito.

Anoche mi hermano y yo __1__ (preparar) la comida para la familia. Yo __2__ (freír) el pescado. Mi hermano __3__ (freír) las papas. Mamá __4__ (poner) la mesa. Y papá __5__ (servir) la comida. Todos nosotros __6__ (comer) muy bien. A todos nos __7__ (gustar) mucho el pescado. Mi hermano y mi papá __8__ (repetir) el pescado. Luego yo __9__ (servir) el postre, un sorbete. Después de la comida mi hermano tomó una siesta. Él __10__ (dormir) media hora. Yo no __11__ (dormir). No me gusta dormir inmediatamente después de comer.

Valparaíso, Chile

18 Lo siento mucho. You're in a restaurant and you're fed up with the waiter. He hasn't done a thing right. Call over the manager (a classmate) and tell him or her all that happened. He or she will apologize and say something to try to make you happy.

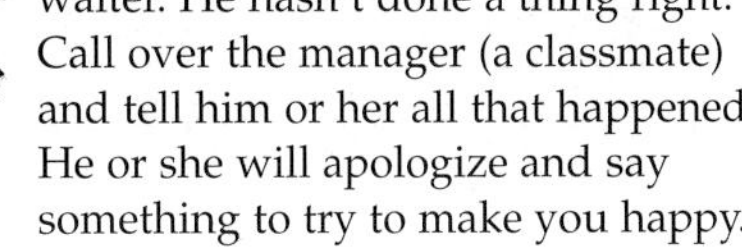

Answers to ¿Cómo lo digo?

17

1. preparamos
2. freí
3. frió
4. puso
5. sirvió
6. comimos
7. gustó
8. repitieron
9. serví
10. durmió
11. dormí

18 *Answers will vary. Students should use the illustration as a prompt for ideas. Students may also want to use the sentences from Activity 16 on page 444 as a model.*

17 After doing Activity 17, have several students retell the story in their own words.

Learning from Photos

(page 445) Have students describe the family members and their activities in this photo.

18 Have students examine the illustration accompanying Activity 18 carefully. There are quite a few things that have gone wrong!

Before students begin to work on their conversations, you may wish to ask them to describe the people in the illustration and to have them say what's wrong. See who can come up with the longest list.

¡Adelante!

At this point in the chapter, students have learned all the vocabulary and structure necessary to complete the chapter. The conversation and cultural readings that follow recycle all the material learned up to this point.

LEVELING

A: Activities 16, 18

C: Activity 17

1 PREPARATION

Resource Manager

Audio Activities TE, page 172
Audio CD 8

Bellringer Review

Use BRR Transparency 14.5 or write the following on the board.
Write three things you would possibly say to or ask a waiter at a café.

2 PRESENTATION

Step 1 Have students close their books. Then read the conversation to them or play Audio CD 8.

Step 2 After introducing the conversation, you may wish to set up a café in the classroom and have groups of students perform the conversation for the class.

Step 3 Have students summarize the conversation in their own words.

Step 4 After presenting the conversation, go over the **¿Comprendes?** activity. If students can answer the questions with relative ease, move on. Students should not be expected to memorize the conversation.

LEVELING

E: Conversation

Conversación

En el restaurante

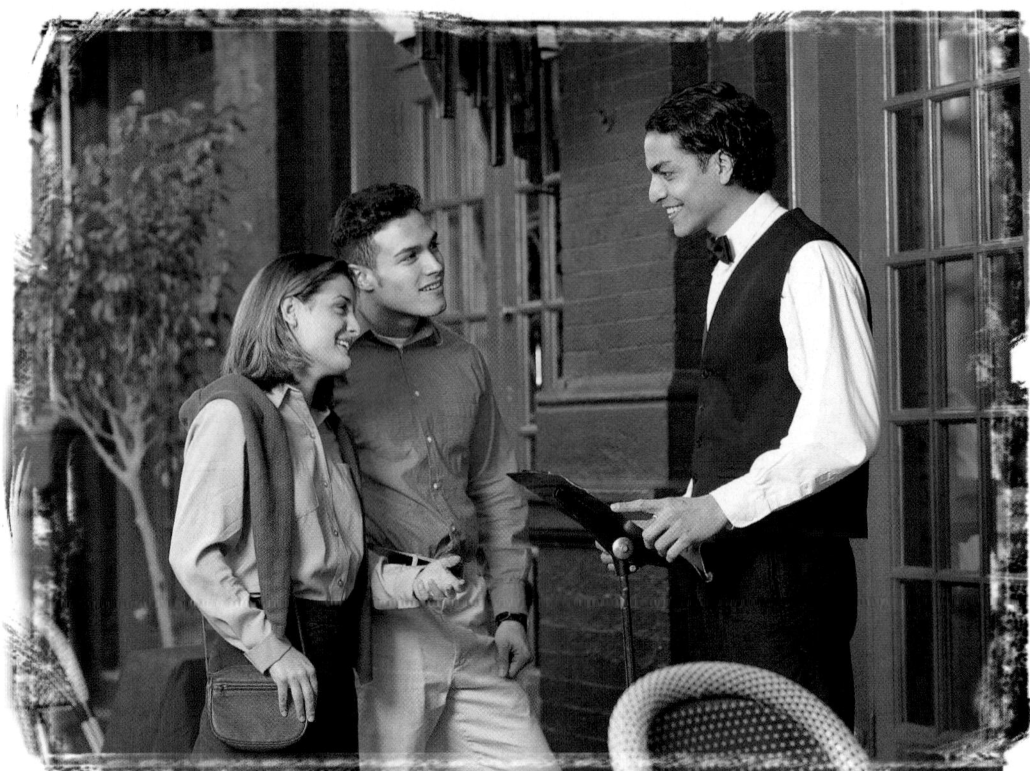

Teresa ¿Tiene usted una mesa para dos personas?
Mesero Sí, señorita. Por aquí, por favor.
Teresa ¿Es posible tener un menú en inglés?
Mesero Sí, ¡cómo no!
Paco Teresa, no necesito un menú en inglés. Lo puedo leer en español.
(El mesero les da un menú en inglés.)
Paco No sé por qué ella me pidió un menú en inglés.
Mesero No hay problema. Le traigo uno en español.
Paco Gracias.
Teresa Pues, Paco, ¿qué vas a pedir?
Paco Para mí, la especialidad de la casa.
Teresa Yo también pido la especialidad de la casa.

¿Comprendes?

Completen.

1. ¿Para cuántas personas quiere la mesa Teresa?
2. ¿Tiene el mesero una mesa libre?
3. ¿Qué tipo de menú pide Teresa?
4. ¿Necesita un menú en inglés Paco?
5. ¿Sabe él por qué ella le pidió un menú en inglés?
6. ¿Qué va a pedir Paco?
7. Y Teresa, ¿qué pide ella?

Answers to ¿Comprendes?

1. Teresa quiere la mesa para dos personas.
2. Sí, el mesero tiene una mesa libre.
3. Teresa pide un menú en inglés.
4. No, Paco no necesita un menú en inglés.
5. No, no sabe por qué ella le pidió un menú en inglés.
6. Paco va a pedir la especialidad de la casa.
7. Ella también pide la especialidad de la casa.

Vamos a hablar más

A **Fuimos al restaurante.** You and your parents went to a restaurant last night. A classmate will ask you questions about your experience. Answer him or her.

B **Preferencias** Work with a classmate and discuss whether you prefer to eat at home or in a restaurant. Give reasons for your preferences.

Pronunciación

La consonante x

An **x** between two vowels is pronounced much like the English *x* but a bit softer. It's like a **gs: examen → eg-samen.** Repeat the following.

exacto **examen**
éxito **próximo**

When **x** is followed by a consonant, it is often pronounced like an **s.** Repeat the following.

extremo **explicar** **exclamar**

Repeat the following sentence.

El extranjero exclama que baja en la próxima parada.

Conversación

3 PRACTICE

Vamos a hablar más

A Students can base their answers on any outing to a restaurant with their parents. They may wish to use the conversation on page 446 as a model.

B Students should use the verb **preferir** for this exchange.

Glencoe Technology

CD-ROM

On the CD-ROM, students can watch a dramatization of this conversation. They can then play the role of either one of the characters and record themselves in the conversation.

Pronunciación

¡OJO! Whenever **x** is followed by a consonant in Spanish, it is pronounced as **s.** There are no exceptions to this rule.

However, there is a variation in the pronunciation of **x** between two vowels. In some geographic areas the **x** in the word **exacto,** for example, is pronounced like **s (esacto)** and in others it is **gs (eg-sacto).**

Step 1 Have students repeat the words after you or Audio CD 8. Have them imitate very carefully.

Step 2 Have students open their books to page 447. Call on individuals to read the words and sentences carefully.

Step 3 The model sentence on page 447 can be used for dictation.

Answers to Vamos a hablar más

A *Answers will vary, but students may use the conversation on page 446 as a model.*

B *Answers will vary; however, students will typically begin the conversation by asking:* ¿Prefieres comer en casa o en el restaurante?

Learning from Realia

(page 447) Have students take a look at the ad to see how much of the vocabulary they already know. Ask if they can guess what **a domicilio** means *(home delivery).* The expression for *take out* is **para llevar.**

Lecturas culturales

Resource Manager

Audio Activities TE, page 173
Audio CD 8

National Standards

Cultures
The reading about Mexican cuisine on page 448 and the related activity on page 449 familiarize students with typical Mexican food and dishes.

PRESENTATION

Pre-reading

Step 1 Have students open their books and do the Reading Strategy activity on page 448. Then ask them what they think the reading is about.

Step 2 Have students tell some things they already know about Mexican food.

Reading

Step 1 Now have students open their books. Call on individuals to read.

Step 2 Intersperse oral reading with some comprehension questions. Then continue reading.

Post-reading

Step 1 Have students tell what they see on the plate at the bottom of the page.

Step 2 Go over the **¿Comprendes?** activity on page 449 orally. Then assign it for homework. Go over the activity again the following day.

Lecturas culturales

Reading Strategy

Thinking while reading
Good readers always think while reading. They think about what the passage might be about after reading the title and looking at the visuals. They predict, create visual images, compare, and check for understanding; they continually think while the author is explaining.

La comida mexicana

Es muy difícil decir lo que es la comida hispana porque la comida varía mucho de una región hispana a otra.

Aquí en Estados Unidos la comida mexicana es muy popular. Hay muchos restaurantes mexicanos. Algunos sirven comida típicamente mexicana y otros sirven variaciones que vienen del suroeste de Estados Unidos donde vive mucha gente de ascendencia mexicana.

La base de muchos platos mexicanos es la tortilla. La tortilla es un tipo de panqueque. Puede ser de harina[1] de maíz o de trigo[2]. Con las tortillas, los mexicanos preparan tostadas, tacos, enchiladas, etc. Rellenan[3] las tortillas de pollo, carne de res o frijoles y queso.

[1]harina *flour*
[2]trigo *wheat*
[3]Rellenan *They fill*

San Miguel de Allende, México

Learning from Photos

(page 448 right) Ask the following questions about the photo:
¿Dónde está la señora? ¿Está en la cocina o en el comedor?
¿Qué está haciendo ella? ¿Tortillas o arroz?
¿De qué son las tortillas? ¿De papas o de maíz?

Chapter Projects

La cocina hispana Prepare a dish from one of the Spanish-speaking countries or have students prepare some Hispanic foods and bring them to class. A number of typical dishes are described in this chapter. Students can go to the library to find recipes for these dishes.

El cultivo del maíz
de Diego Rivera

SECRETARIA DE EDUCACION, CULTURA
Y RECREACION
MUSEO CASA
"DIEGO RIVERA"
GUANAJUATO, GTO.
COOPERACION N$ 5.00

¿Comprendes?

La comida mexicana Contesten.

1. ¿Varía mucho la cocina hispana de una región a otra?
2. ¿Dónde es popular la comida mexicana?
3. ¿De dónde vienen muchas variaciones de la cocina mexicana?
4. ¿Qué sirve de base para muchos platos mexicanos?
5. ¿Qué es una tortilla? ¿De qué puede ser?
6. ¿De qué rellenan las tortillas?

Lecturas culturales

¿Comprendes?

Allow students to refer to the story to look up the answers, or you may use this activity as a testing device for factual recall.

Art Connection

Throughout his life, Diego Rivera was vitally interested in the suffering of Mexico's poor. Ask students if they can figure out why he would do a painting depicting someone cultivating corn. (Corn is extremely important to Mexico because it is the sustenance for Mexico's poor. Corn is for Mexico what potatoes, bread, or rice are to people in other parts of the world.)

Expansion: Show the Fine Art Transparency of ***El cultivo del maíz*** by Diego Rivera. You may wish to have students read the background information accompanying this transparency and do the related activities. For further enrichment, you may also wish to show the Fine Art Transparency ***Dos niños comiendo melón y uvas,*** by Bartolomé Esteban Murillo.

LEVELING

E: Reading

Answers to ¿Comprendes?

1. Sí, la comida hispana varía mucho de una región a otra.
2. La comida mexicana es popular aquí en los Estados Unidos.
3. Vienen del suroeste de los Estados Unidos.
4. La tortilla sirve de base para muchos platos mexicanos.
5. Una tortilla es un tipo de panqueque. Puede ser de harina de maíz o de harina de trigo.
6. Rellenan las tortillas de pollo, carne de res o frijoles y queso.

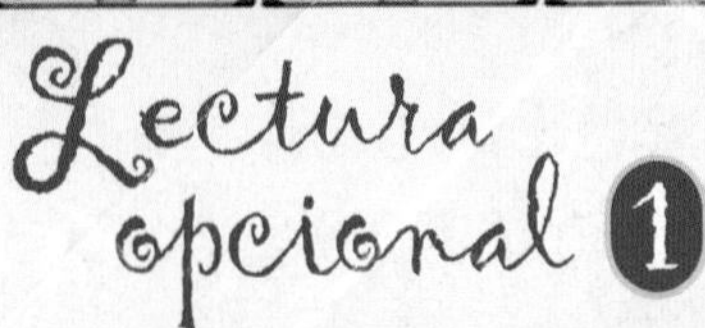

National Standards

Cultures
This reading about Spanish cuisine and the related activity on this page familiarize students with some typical foods from Spain.

¡OJO! This reading is optional. You may skip it completely, have the entire class read it, have only several students read it and report to the class, or assign it for extra credit.

PRESENTATION

Step 1 Have students read the passage quickly as they look at the photos that accompany it. The photos will increase comprehension because students can visualize what they are reading about.

Step 2 Have students discuss the information they find interesting.

Learning from Photos

(page 450) Have students look at the three photos on this page to see how many items they can identify.

LEVELING
E: Readings 1, 2

Lectura opcional 1

Málaga, España

La comida española

En España, como en México, hay tortillas también. Pero hay una gran diferencia entre una tortilla mexicana y una tortilla española. La tortilla española no es de maíz. El cocinero español prepara la tortilla con huevos. La tortilla española, que es muy típica, lleva patatas (papas) y cebollas[1].

La cocina española es muy buena y muy variada. Como España es un país que tiene mucha costa, muchos platos españoles llevan marisco y pescado. Y los cocineros preparan muchos platos con aceite de oliva.

[1]cebollas *onions*

Málaga, España

¿Comprendes?

La cocina española Contesten.

1. ¿Cuál es la diferencia entre una tortilla española y una tortilla mexicana?
2. ¿Qué lleva la típica tortilla española?
3. ¿Por qué llevan marisco y pescado muchos platos españoles?
4. ¿Qué usan muchos cocineros españoles para preparar una comida?

Answers to ¿Comprendes?

1. La tortilla española no es de maíz. El cocinero español la prepara con huevos.
2. Lleva patatas y cebollas.
3. Muchos platos españoles llevan marisco y pescado porque España es un país que tiene mucha costa.
4. Usan aceite de oliva para preparar una comida.

Lectura opcional 2

La comida del Caribe

Humacao, Puerto Rico

En el Caribe, en Puerto Rico, Cuba y la República Dominicana, la gente come muchos mariscos y pescado. Es natural porque Puerto Rico, Cuba y la República Dominicana son islas. Pero la carne favorita de la región es el puerco o el lechón[1]. No hay nada más delicioso que un buen lechón asado[2]. Sirven el lechón con arroz, frijoles (habichuelas) y tostones. Para hacer tostones el cocinero corta en rebanadas[3] un plátano, una banana grande, verde y dura. Luego fríe las rebanadas en manteca[4].

[1]lechón *suckling pig*
[2]asado *roast*
[3]rebanadas *slices*
[4]manteca *lard*

¿Comprendes?

¿Lo sabes? Busquen la información.

1. algunos países de la región del Caribe
2. por qué come la gente muchos mariscos y pescado en la región del Caribe
3. una carne favorita de los puertorriqueños, cubanos y dominicanos
4. lo que sirven con el lechón asado
5. lo que son tostones

Lectura opcional 2

National Standards

Cultures
This reading about Caribbean cuisine and the related activity familiarize students with some typical foods from the Spanish-speaking countries of the Caribbean.

¡OJO! This reading is optional. You may skip it completely, have the entire class read it, have only several students read it and report to the class, or assign it for extra credit.

PRESENTATION

Step 1 Have students read the selection to themselves.

Step 2 Now have students do the **¿Comprendes?** activity on page 451.

Learning from Photos

(page 451 bottom) Have students look at the meal in the photo. Point out to them that the dish in the foreground contains **arroz, tostones,** and **habichuelas rosadas.** Tell them that red beans are favored in Puerto Rico and black beans are favored in Cuba.

Answers to ¿Comprendes?

1. Puerto Rico, Cuba y la República Dominicana
2. porque son islas
3. el puerco o el lechón
4. arroz, frijoles (habichuelas) y tostones
5. rebanadas de plátano fritas en manteca

Geography Connection

Humacao is on the western coast of Puerto Rico. The well-known resort and condominium complex **Palmas del Mar** is in Humacao.

Conexiones

National Standards

Connections
This reading about linguistic differences in the Spanish-speaking world establishes a connection with another discipline, allowing students to reinforce and further their knowledge of the humanities through the study of Spanish.

Comparisons
This reading on regional differences in pronunciation and vocabulary in Spanish and the related activities, which illustrate the same concepts in English, give students a better understanding of the nature of language.

¡OJO! The readings in the **Conexiones** section are optional. They focus on some of the major disciplines taught in schools and universities. The vocabulary is useful for discussing such topics as history, literature, art, economics, business, science, etc. You may choose any of the following ways to do the readings in the **Conexiones** sections.

Independent reading Have students read the selections and do the post-reading activities as homework, which you collect. This option is least intrusive on class time and requires a minimum of teacher involvement.

Homework with in-class follow-up Assign the readings and post-reading activities as homework. Review and discuss the material in class the next day.

Intensive in-class activity This option includes a pre-reading vocabulary presentation, in-class reading and discussion, assignment of the activities for homework, and a discussion of the assignment in class the following day.

Conexiones

Las humanidades

El lenguaje

As we already know, Spanish is a language that is spoken in many areas of the world. In spite of the fact that the Spanish-speaking world covers a large area of the globe, it is possible to understand a speaker of Spanish regardless of where he or she is from. Although there are regional differences, these differences do not cause serious comprehension problems.

However, pronunciation does change from area to area. For example, people from San Juan, Puerto Rico; Buenos Aires, Argentina; and Madrid, Spain have pronunciations that are quite different from one another. However, the same is true of English. People from New York, Memphis, and London also have a distinct pronunciation, but they can all understand one another.

The use of certain words also changes from one area to another. This is particularly true in the case of words for foods. Let's look at some regional differences with regard to vocabulary.

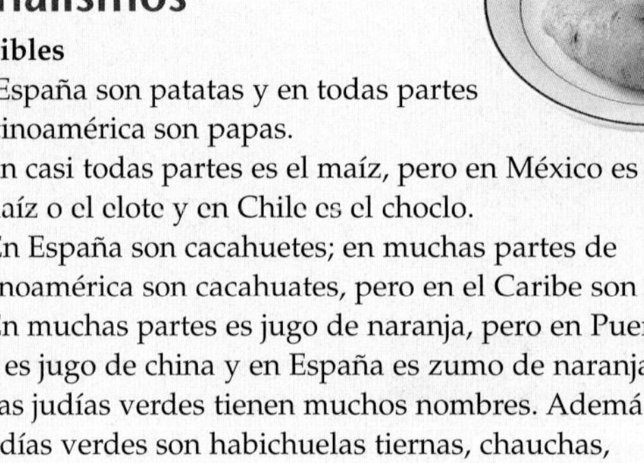

Regionalismos

Comestibles

En España son patatas y en todas partes de Latinoamérica son papas.

En casi todas partes es el maíz, pero en México es el maíz o el elote y en Chile es el choclo.

En España son cacahuetes; en muchas partes de Latinoamérica son cacahuates, pero en el Caribe son maní.

En muchas partes es jugo de naranja, pero en Puerto Rico es jugo de china y en España es zumo de naranja.

Las judías verdes tienen muchos nombres. Además de judías verdes son habichuelas tiernas, chauchas, vainitas, ejotes y porotos.

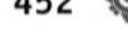

The **Glencoe Spanish Web** site (**spanish.glencoe.com**) offers options that enable you and your students to experience the Spanish-speaking world via the Internet. For each **Capítulo,** there are activities, games, and quizzes. In addition, an *Enrichment* section offers students an opportunity to visit Web sites related to the theme of the chapter.

Cosas que no son comestibles

Tomamos el autobús en España, el camión en México y la guagua en el Caribe y en las Islas Canarias.

En España todos duermen en el dormitorio o en la habitación. En México duermen en la recámara y en muchas partes en el cuarto o en el cuarto de dormir.

En España sacas un billete en la ventanilla y en Latinoamérica compras un boleto en la ventanilla o en la boletería.

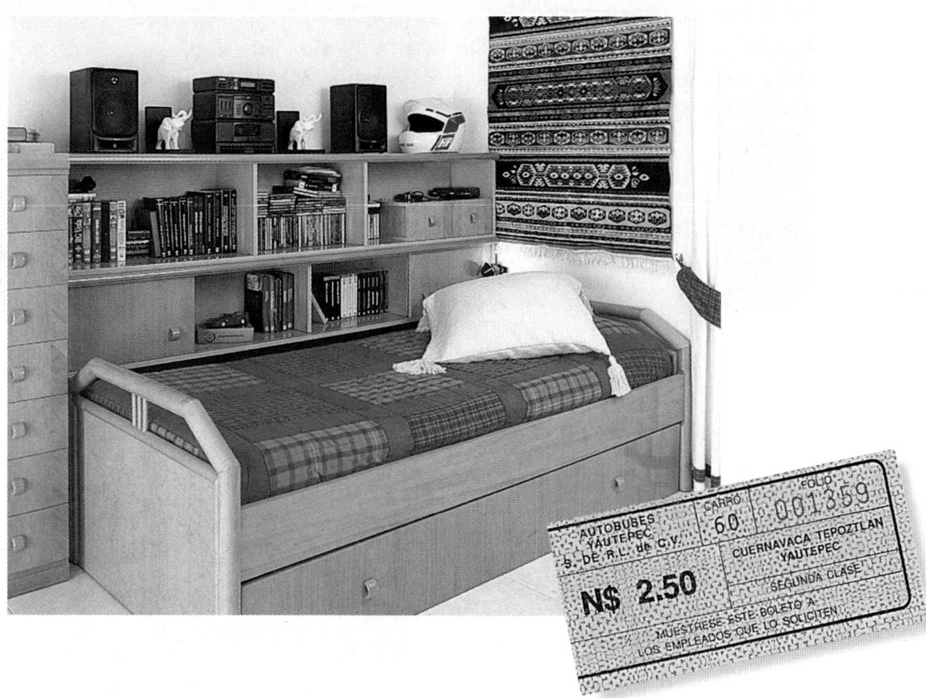

¿Comprendes?

A Hispanohablantes If any of your classmates are heritage speakers of Spanish, ask them to compare the way they say things. Have them share this information with you.

B El inglés There are variations in the use of English words. Discuss the following terms and where they might be heard.

1. bag, sack
2. soda, pop
3. elevator, lift
4. line, queue
5. pram, baby carriage
6. truck, lorry
7. traffic circle, rotary, roundabout
8. subway, underground

Conexiones

PRESENTATION

Las humanidades
El lenguaje

Step 1 Have students read the introduction in English on page 452.

Step 2 You may wish to have students skim this section for general interest.

Step 3 For a more in-depth treatment, have students identify each item of food pictured on page 452. Then have them give the additional regional names for each item. Now do the same with regard to the nonfood items in the photos on page 453.

¿Comprendes?

B Ask students whether they know of additional examples in English. They might mention: purse / pocketbook.

Reaching All Students

For the Heritage Speakers Have heritage speakers make a list of at least twenty common items of food and clothing. Then have each student compare his or her list with those of the other heritage speakers in the class. Finally, have them make a list of the items that have different names.

Answers to ¿Comprendes?

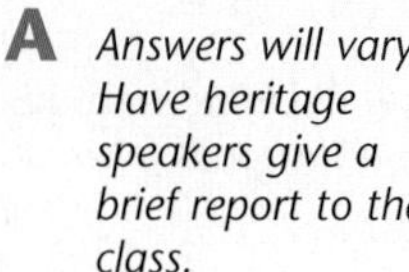

A *Answers will vary. Have heritage speakers give a brief report to the class.*

B *Answers will include the following:*

1. bag: U.S.
   sack: UK and parts of U.S.
2. soda: East and West Coasts, South
   pop: Midwest
3. elevator: U.S.; lift: UK
4. line: U.S.; queue: UK
5. pram: UK; baby carriage: U.S.
6. truck: U.S.
   lorry: UK
7. traffic circle: U.S.
   rotary: New England states, Canada
   roundabout: UK
8. subway: U.S.
   underground: UK

¡Te toca a ti!

Use what you have learned

Recycling

These activities allow students to use the vocabulary and structure from this chapter in completely open-ended, real-life situations.

PRESENTATION

Encourage students to say as much as possible when they do these activities. Tell them not to be afraid to make mistakes, since the goal of the activities is real-life communication. If someone in the group makes an error, allow the others to politely correct him or her. Let students choose the activities they would like to do.

You may wish to divide students into pairs or groups. Encourage students to elaborate on the basic theme and to be creative. They may use props, pictures, or posters if they wish.

PRACTICE

2 This activity is an excellent follow-up to the readings in Chapter 14, pages 448–451.

3 This is a good activity to use when students need a "break" during the class period or as an opening or closing activity.

¡Te toca a ti!

Use what you have learned

HABLAR

1 Vamos a un restaurante

✔ ***Order food and beverages at a restaurant***

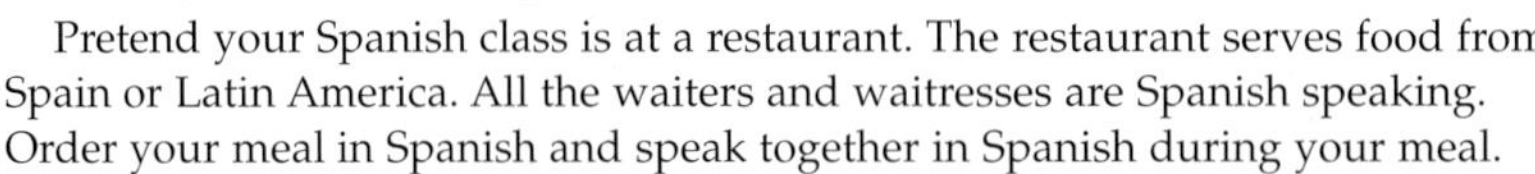

Pretend your Spanish class is at a restaurant. The restaurant serves food from Spain or Latin America. All the waiters and waitresses are Spanish speaking. Order your meal in Spanish and speak together in Spanish during your meal.

HABLAR

2 Una comida hispana

✔ ***Describe a meal from some area of the Spanish-speaking world***

Work with a classmate. You have learned about some Hispanic cuisines. Talk about a meal or dish that you want to try **(probar).**

HABLAR

3 La comida

✔ ***Talk about categories of food***

Mention a food category, such as meat, seafood, fruit, vegetable. Your partner will give the name of a food that belongs in that category. Take several turns each. Try to use as much as possible of the food vocabulary you've learned.

Answers to ¡Te toca a ti!

1 *Answers will vary. Students should order foods presented in this chapter. After ordering, students may discuss regional differences in foods, the restaurant, or any other topic.*

2 *Answers will vary. Students might use the names of foods and dishes from the readings on pages 448–451.*

3 *Answers will vary. Students should use the foods presented in this chapter and the foods presented in Chapter 5.*

4 *Answers will vary. The selections for each meal should be logical.*

5 *Answers will vary. The illustration on page 455 gives clues as to what students could say in their letter.*

¡Te toca a ti!

4 El menú

✔ *Plan a menu*

Write out the menu for several meals in Spanish. You can plan meals for **el desayuno, el almuerzo,** and **la cena.**

35º Aniversario

La Estancia

ASADOR CRIOLLO

Lechón al Asador	$ 14,00
Chivito «La Estancia»	$ 16,00
Asado al Asador	$ 11,00

COCINA

Costilla de Cerdo con puré de manzana	$ 10,00
Costilla de Cerdo a la Riojana	$ 12,00
Lomo a la Pimienta con papas a la crema	$ 16,00
Lomo al Champignon	$ 17,00
Milanesa de Lomo	$ 6,50
Milanesa de Lomo a la Napolitana	$ 9,50
Milanesa de Pollo	$ 6,00
Milanesa de Pollo a la Napolitana	$ 9,00
Suprema de Pollo «La Estancia»	$ 10,50
Suprema de Pollo a la Maryland	$ 10,00
1/2 Pollo deshuesado a la Parrilla	$ 10,00

BIFES

Bife de costilla con Lomo con guarnición de papas fritas	$ 8,50
Bife de Chorizo	$ 7,50
Bife especial «La Estancia»	$ 12,50
Bife de Lomo especial «La Estancia».	$ 15,00
Costillas de Cerdo	$ 8,00
Chorizos (c/u)	$ 2,50
Salchicha Criolla (c/u)	$ 3,00
Morcillas (c/u)	$ 2,50
Matambrito Tiernizado	$ 10,00
Bife Aniversario con Lomo	$ 17,00
Mollejas porción	$ 11,00
Longaniza (c/u)	$ 4,00
Riñones porción	$ 5,00
Chinchulines de Ternera porción	$ 5,00
Chinchulines de Cordero porción	$ 9,00
Ubre porción	$ 4,50

Writing Strategy

Writing a letter of complaint When you write a letter of complaint, you must clearly identify the problem and suggest solutions; you should use a businesslike tone. You might be angry when you write a letter of complaint. But to be effective, you must control your emotions since your goal is to get the problem corrected. Your tone of voice is reflected in writing as much as it is in speech; your results will be better if you address the situation calmly and reasonably.In addition, it is important that the letter be addressed to the person who has the most authority.

5 ¡Qué desastre!

Pretend you went to a restaurant where you had a very bad experience. The waiter didn't serve you what you ordered nor the way you ordered it. Write a letter to the management complaining about the food and the service.

Writing Development

Have students keep a notebook or portfolio containing their best written work from each chapter. These selected writings can be based on assignments from the Student Textbook and the Workbook. The activities on page 455 are examples of writing assignments that may be included in each student's portfolio. On page 180 in the Workbook, students will begin to develop an organized autobiography **(Mi autobiografía).** These workbook pages may also become a part of their portfolio.

4 Students can use the food items taught in Chapter 5, as well as those taught in this chapter. Encourage students to list only those foods that they know how to say in Spanish.

Writing Strategy

Writing a letter of complaint Have students do the Writing Strategy activity on page 455. Based on the strategy, ask students which statement in the Critical Thinking Activity below would be most effective when writing a letter of complaint.

LEVELING

These activities encompass all three levels. All students will be able to do them at a sophistication level commensurate with their ability in Spanish. Some students will be able to speak for several minutes, and others may be able to give just a few sentences. This is to be expected when students are functioning completely on their own generating their own language to the best of their ability.

Critical Thinking Activity

Drawing conclusions Ask students which statement would be most effective when writing a letter of complaint.

1. **Tuvimos que esperar cinco minutos para la mesa y no pudimos leer el menú en español.**
2. **Nos gustó la comida, pero hay un problema con el servicio.**
3. **¡Su restaurante es horrible!**

Assessment

Resource Manager

Communication Transparency C 14
Quizzes, pages 70–74
Performance Assessment, Task 14
Tests, pages 221–232
Situation Cards, Chapter 14
ExamView® Pro, Chapter 14
Maratón mental Videoquiz, Chapter 14

Assessment

This is a pre-test for students to take before you administer the chapter test. Note that each section is cross-referenced so students can easily find the material they have to review in case they made errors. You may use Assessment Answers Transparency A 14 to do the assessment in class, or you may assign this assessment for homework. You can correct the assessment yourself, or you may prefer to project the answers on the overhead in class.

Glencoe Technology

MINDJOGGER VHS/DVD

You may wish to help your students prepare for the chapter test by playing the MindJogger game show. Teams will compete against each other to review chapter vocabulary and structure and sharpen listening comprehension skills.

Assessment

Vocabulario

1 Identifiquen.

To review **Palabras 1**, turn to pages 434–435.

2 Identifiquen.

6.

7.

8.

To review **Palabras 2**, turn to pages 438–439.

9.

10.

3 **¿Sí o no?** Indiquen si la persona contesta bien.

11. —¿Para cuándo quiere usted la reservación?
—Para cuatro.
12. —¿A nombre de quién, por favor?
—Conforme, señor Pereda.

Answers to 

1

1. el mantel
2. el plato
3. el cuchillo
4. la taza
5. la servilleta

2

6. el aceite
7. el arroz
8. la carne
9. el pescado
10. los camarones

3

11. No
12. No

Estructura

4 Completen con el presente.

13. El mesero les ____ a los clientes en el restaurante. (servir)
14. Yo siempre ____ la misma cosa, un biftec. (pedir)
15. Ellas ____ elegantemente para ir al restaurante. (vestirse)
16. Nosotros no lo ____. (repetir)
17. El cocinero ____ las papas. (freír)

To review the present of stem-changing verbs, turn to page 442.

5 Sigan el modelo.

Él lo pidió. →
Y yo lo pedí, también.

18. Ellos se divirtieron.
    Y yo ____, también.
19. Yo dormí bien.
    Y él ____ bien, también.
20. Tú lo repetiste.
    Y nosotros lo ____, también.
21. Ellos lo prefirieron.
    Y su amigo lo ____, también.
22. Nos vestimos.
    Y ellos ____, también.

To review the preterite of stem-changing verbs, turn to page 444.

Cultura

6 Contesten.

23. ¿Cuál es la base de muchas comidas mexicanas?
24. ¿Qué es una tortilla mexicana?
25. ¿De qué rellenan las tortillas para hacer tacos y enchiladas?

To review this cultural information, turn to page 448.

Assessment

FOLDABLES™ Study Organizer **Dinah Zike's Study Guides**

Your students may wish to use Foldable 13 to organize, display, and arrange data as they review the vocabulary, verbs, and verb forms they know in Spanish. You may wish to encourage them to add information from each chapter as they continue to expand their vocabulary.

A *sentence strip holder* foldable is also ideal as students continue their study of Spanish and learn more and more words.

ANSWERS TO 

 **4**

13. sirve
14. pido
15. se visten
16. repetimos
17. fríe

 **5**

18. me divertí
19. durmió
20. repetimos
21. prefirió
22. se vistieron

6

23. La base de muchas comidas mexicanas es la tortilla.
24. Una tortilla mexicana es un tipo de panqueque.
25. Rellenan las tortillas de pollo, carne de res o frijoles y queso.

¡Hablo como un pro!

This unique page gives students the opportunity to speak freely and say whatever they can, using the vocabulary and structures they have learned in the chapter. The illustration serves to remind students of precisely what they know how to say in Spanish. There are no activities that students do not have the ability to describe or talk about in Spanish. The art not only depicts the vocabulary and content of this chapter, but also reinforces what they learned in previous chapters.

You may wish to use this page in many ways. Some possibilities are to have students do the following:

1. Look at the illustration and identify items by giving the correct Spanish words.
2. Make up sentences about what they see in the illustration.
3. Make up questions about the illustration. They can call on another class member to respond if you do this as a class activity, or you may prefer to allow students to work in small groups. This activity is extremely beneficial because it enables students to actively use interrogative words.
4. Answer questions you ask them about the illustration.
5. Work in pairs and make up a conversation based on the illustration.
6. Look at the illustration and give a complete oral review of what they see.
7. Look at the illustration and write a paragraph (or essay) about it.

You can also use this page as an assessment or testing tool, taking into account individual differences by having students go from simple to quite complicated tasks. The assessment can be either oral or written.

¡Hablo como un pro!

Tell all you can about this illustration.

You may wish to use the rubrics provided on pages T20–T21 as you give students the following directions.

1. Identify the topic or situation of the illustration.
2. Give the Spanish words for as many items as you can.
3. Think of as many sentences as you can to describe the illustration.
4. Go over your sentences and put them in the best sequencing to give a coherent story based on the illustration.

Getting along at a restaurant

el restaurante
la mesa
el/la mesero(a), el/la camarero(a)
el/la cocinero(a)
el menú
la cuenta
la tarjeta de crédito
la propina
el dinero

Identifying a place setting

el vaso
la taza
el platillo
el plato
el tenedor
el cuchillo
la cucharita
la cuchara
el mantel
la servilleta

How well do you know your vocabulary?

- Choose a food category from the list, for example, **la carne.**
- Have classmates choose the names of foods that belong to that category.

Describing some restaurant activities

poner la mesa
pedir
servir
freír
repetir
reservar
tener hambre
tener sed

Identifying more foods

la carne
la carne de res, el biftec
la ternera
el cerdo
el cordero
el pescado
los mariscos
los camarones
las almejas
la langosta
el ajo
la berenjena
la alcachofa
el arroz
el maíz
la sal
la pimienta
el aceite
el vinagre

Describing food

rico(a), delicioso(a)

VIDEOTUR

Episodio 14

In this video episode, you will join Vicky and Alberto as they help out at his father's restaurant. See page 505 for more information.

Vocabulary Review

The words and phrases in the **Vocabulario** have been taught for productive use in this chapter. They are summarized here as a resource for both student and teacher. This list also serves as a convenient resource for the **¡Te toca a ti!** activities on pages 454 and 455. There are approximately eight cognates in this vocabulary list. Have students find them.

VIDEO VHS/DVD

The Video Program allows students to see how the chapter vocabulary and structures are used by native speakers within an engaging story line. For maximum reinforcement, show the video episode as a final activity for Chapter 14.

¡OJO! You will notice that the vocabulary list here is not translated. This has been done intentionally, since we feel that by the time students have finished the material in the chapter they should be familiar with the meanings of all the words. If there are several words they still do not know, we recommend that they refer to the **Palabras 1** and **2** sections in the chapter or go to the dictionaries at the end of this book to find the meanings. However, if you prefer that your students have the English translations, please refer to Vocabulary Transparency 14.1, where you will find all these words with their translations.

Preview

This section reviews the salient points from Chapters 12–14. In the **Conversación** students will review train travel vocabulary, reflexive verbs, and irregular verbs in the preterite in context. In the **Estructura** section, they will study the conjugations of irregular verbs and stem-changing verbs in the preterite. They will also review reflexive verbs in the present tense. They will practice these structures as they talk about their daily routines and what they eat every day.

Resource Manager

Workbook: Check-Up 4, pages 181–184
Tests, pages 233–241
Performance Assessment, Tasks 12–14

PRESENTATION

Conversación

Step 1 Have students open their books to page 460. Call on two students to read the conversation aloud.

Step 2 Ask the questions from the **¿Comprendes?** section.

Learning from Realia

(page 460) Have students look for the information that tells them this ticket is for a sleeper **(Billete Coches-cama)**. Where does it indicate for how many people the compartment is? **(Doble familiar)**.

RENFE means **la Red Nacional de Ferrocarriles Españoles.**

Conversación

El viaje en tren

Alberto ¿Te gustó el viaje que hiciste en tren?
María Sí, bastante. Dormí bien en la litera.
Alberto ¿Te desayunaste en el tren?
María No, porque llegamos a Madrid a las seis y media.
Alberto Y, ¿a qué hora salieron de San Sebastián?
María Salimos de San Sebastián a las veinte cuarenta.

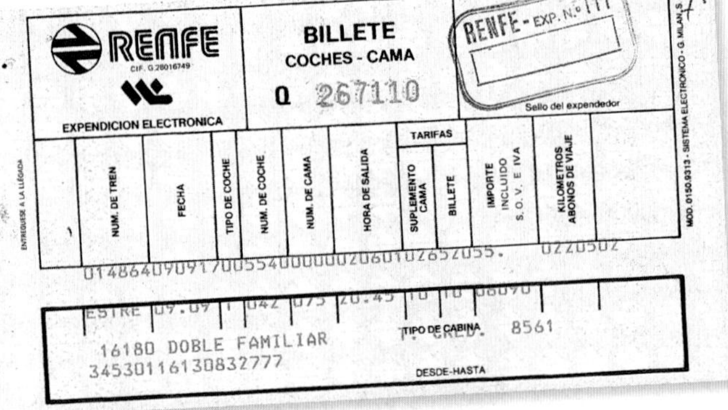

¿Comprendes?

Los pasajeros Contesten.

1. ¿A María le gustó el viaje que hizo en tren?
2. ¿Cómo durmió en la litera?
3. ¿Se desayunó en el tren?
4. ¿A qué hora llegaron a Madrid?
5. ¿A qué hora salieron de San Sebastián?

Answers to ¿Comprendes?

1. Sí, a María le gustó el viaje bastante.
2. Durmió bien en la litera.
3. No se desayunó en el tren.
4. Llegaron a Madrid a las seis y media.
5. Salieron de San Sebastián a las veinte cuarenta.

Estructura

Verbos irregulares en el pretérito

1. Review the preterite forms of the following irregular verbs.

HACER	**hice**	**hiciste**	**hizo**	**hicimos**	*hicisteis*	**hicieron**
QUERER	**quise**	**quisiste**	**quiso**	**quisimos**	*quisisteis*	**quisieron**
VENIR	**vine**	**viniste**	**vino**	**vinimos**	*vinisteis*	**vinieron**
ANDAR	**anduve**	**anduviste**	**anduvo**	**anduvimos**	*anduvisteis*	**anduvieron**
ESTAR	**estuve**	**estuviste**	**estuvo**	**estuvimos**	*estuvisteis*	**estuvieron**
TENER	**tuve**	**tuviste**	**tuvo**	**tuvimos**	*tuvisteis*	**tuvieron**
PODER	**pude**	**pudiste**	**pudo**	**pudimos**	*pudisteis*	**pudieron**
PONER	**puse**	**pusiste**	**puso**	**pusimos**	*pusisteis*	**pusieron**
SABER	**supe**	**supiste**	**supo**	**supimos**	*supisteis*	**supieron**

1 Historieta En la estación de ferrocarril

Completen con el pretérito.

El otro día yo __1__ (tener) que ir a Toledo. Carlos __2__ (ir) también. Nosotros __3__ (estar) en la estación de ferrocarril. Carlos __4__ (hacer) cola en la ventanilla. Él me __5__ (dar) mi billete y yo lo __6__ (poner) en mi bolsa. Nosotros __7__ (estar) en el andén. Cuando __8__ (venir) el tren, yo no __9__ (poder) hallar mi billete. No sé dónde lo __10__ (poner). No sé dónde está.

Verbos de cambio radical

1. Some verbs have a stem change in both the present and preterite tenses. Verbs like **pedir (i, i)** change the **e** to **i** in both the present and preterite.

PRESENT	**pido**	**pides**	**pide**	**pedimos**	*pedís*	**piden**
PRETERITE	**pedí**	**pediste**	**pidió**	**pedimos**	*pedisteis*	**pidieron**

PRESENTATION

Verbos irregulares en el pretérito

Step 1 Have students open their books to page 461. Ask them to look at these verbs. You may also have them repeat the verbs aloud. Many of these verbs, however, are not frequently used in the preterite.

PRACTICE

1 After students do Activity 1, you may wish to have them retell the story in their own words.

PRESENTATION

Verbos de cambio radical

Step 1 Go over Items 1–3 on pages 461–462 with the students. Have them carefully repeat the verbs after you.

Step 2 Explain to students that if they pronounce these verbs correctly, they will have no trouble spelling them.

ANSWERS TO Repaso

1. tuve
2. fue
3. estuvimos
4. hizo
5. dio
6. puse
7. estuvimos
8. vino
9. pude
10. puse

PRACTICE

2 and **3** If students have problems doing Activities 2 and 3, review some of the activities in the **Estructura** section of Chapters 13 and 14.

4 After going over Activity 4, have students retell the story in their own words.

2. Verbs like **preferir (ie, i)** change the **e** to **ie** in the present; they change **e** to **i** in the preterite.

PRESENT	**prefiero**	**prefieres**	**prefiere**	**preferimos**	*preferís*	**prefieren**
PRETERITE	**preferí**	**preferiste**	**prefirió**	**preferimos**	*preferisteis*	**prefirieron**

3. Verbs like **dormir (ue, u)** change the **o** to **ue** in the present; they change **o** to **u** in the preterite.

PRESENT	**duermo**	**duermes**	**duerme**	**dormimos**	*dormís*	**duermen**
PRETERITE	**dormí**	**dormiste**	**durmió**	**dormimos**	*dormisteis*	**durmieron**

2 Información Completen con el presente.

1. Yo te ___ el café y tú me ___ el postre. Nosotros nos ___. (servir)
2. Tú lo ___ y yo lo ___. Nosotros dos lo ___. (preferir)
3. Ellos lo ___ y yo lo ___. Todos nosotros lo ___. (repetir)
4. Él ___ enseguida y yo ___ enseguida. Todos ___ enseguida. (dormirse)

3 Información Completen con el pretérito.

1. Yo pedí un biftec y usted ___ un biftec también.
2. Yo freí el biftec y usted también lo ___.
3. Nosotros les servimos a todos los clientes y ustedes también les ___ a todos.
4. Seguimos trabajando en el comedor hasta las once y ustedes también ___ trabajando hasta las once.

4 Historieta En un restaurante mexicano

Contesten.

1. ¿Quién pidió tacos, tú o tu amigo(a)?
2. ¿Quién pidió enchiladas?
3. ¿Sirvieron las enchiladas con mucho queso?
4. ¿Pediste arroz y frijoles también?
5. ¿Frió el cocinero los frijoles?
6. ¿Sirvió el mesero la ensalada con la comida?
7. Después de comer, ¿dormiste?
8. Y tu amigo(a), ¿durmió él/ella también?

Comida mexicana en el restaurante «La Fonda», San Miguel de Allende

ANSWERS TO Repaso

2

1. sirvo, sirves, servimos
2. prefieres, prefiero, preferimos
3. repiten, repito, repetimos
4. se duerme, me duermo, nos dormimos

3

1. pidió
2. frió
3. sirvieron
4. siguieron

4

1. Yo pedí (Mi amigo pidió) tacos.
2. Yo pedí (Mi amigo pidió) enchiladas.
3. Sí, (No, no) sirvieron las enchiladas con mucho queso.
4. Sí, (No, no) pedí arroz y frijoles.
5. Sí (No), el cocinero (no) frió los frijoles.
6. Sí (No), el mesero (no) sirvió la ensalada con la comida.
7. Sí, (No, no) dormí.
8. Sí (No), mi amigo (no) durmió.

Verbos reflexivos

The subject of a reflexive verb both performs and receives the action of the verb. Each subject has its corresponding reflexive pronoun.

INFINITIVE	levantarse	acostarse
yo	me levanto	me acuesto
tú	te levantas	te acuestas
él, ella, Ud.	se levanta	se acuesta
nosotros(as)	nos levantamos	nos acostamos
vosotros(as)	*os levantáis*	*os acostáis*
ellos, ellas, Uds.	se levantan	se acuestan

5 ¿Y tú?
Contesten personalmente.

1. ¿A qué hora te acuestas?
2. ¿Te duermes enseguida?
3. Y, ¿a qué hora te despiertas?
4. ¿Te levantas enseguida?
5. ¿Cuántas horas duermes?

6 ¿Y ellos? Escriban las respuestas de Actividad 5, cambiando **yo** a **mis hermanos.**

7 Un día típico Work with a classmate. Compare a typical day in your life with a typical day in your partner's life.

8 Comidas Work with a classmate. Ask your partner about the meals he or she ate yesterday. Which meals did he or she eat, at what time, and what foods? Your partner will answer and tell you what he or she liked and didn't like to eat. Take turns.

Tapas, Estepona, España

Literary Companion

You may wish to read the adaptation of *El Quijote* by Miguel de Cervantes Saavedra. You will find this literary selection on pages 484–489.

PRESENTATION

Verbos reflexivos

Step 1 Have students read the reflexive verb forms aloud.

PRACTICE

5 and 6 If students have problems doing Activities 5 and 6, review some of the activities in the **Estructura** section of Chapter 12.

7 and 8 These activities contrast the use of the present (Activity 7) and the preterite (Activity 8).

Learning from Photos

(page 463) **Tapas** are delicious little dishes that are eaten before lunch and before dinner. They are most often enjoyed at a **taberna** or café. Some people, especially tourists and students, will make an inexpensive meal out of **tapas.**

Literary Companion

When you finish this chapter, if you wish, have students read the adaptation of ***El Quijote*** by Miguel de Cervantes Saavedra on pages 484–489.

Answers to 

5

1. Me acuesto a las ___.
2. Sí, (No, no) me duermo enseguida.
3. Me despierto a las ___.
4. Sí, (No, no) me levanto enseguida.
5. Duermo ___ horas.

6

1. Mis hermanos se acuestan a las ___.
2. Sí, (No, no) se duermen enseguida.
3. Se despiertan a las ___.
4. Sí, (No, no) se levantan enseguida.
5. Duermen ___ horas.

7 *Answers will vary. Students will use reflexive verbs.*

8 *Answers will vary. Students will use the preterite and the food vocabulary from Chapter 14.*

Entérate España

This section was prepared by Time Learning Ventures of Time Incorporated. Its purpose is to give students greater insight, through visual images and fun articles, into the culture and people of Spain. You may wish to ask your students if they are already familiar with any of Spain's unique regions and provinces.

Have students look at the photographs and read the articles. Encourage the students to talk about what they've seen and read. Let them say anything they can, using the vocabulary they have learned to this point.

Geographically and culturally, Spain is a fascinatingly rich country. From tiny, Moorish villages to bustling, cosmopolitan metropolises, Spain's diversity makes it an endless source of study. Likewise, Spanish history is an important gateway for learning about colonialism and post-colonialism in the Americas, as well as understanding current political divisions in Western Europe.

A Trovadores de hoy
¿Verdadero o falso?

1. La Tuna es una comida.
2. La Tuna tiene sus comienzos hace nueve siglos.
3. Los trovadores universitarios cantan para ganar dinero.

B Trovadores de hoy.
Contesten.
¿Qué es la Tuna?

C Hemingway y Obras maestras de la historia Escojan.

1. Alcalá de Henares es el lugar de nacimiento de ___.
   a. Cervantes
   b. Hemingway
   c. El Greco

People en Español Entérate España

Trovadores de hoy

Si te encuentras con un grupo de chicos que llevan traje[1] medieval, medias[2] y capa[3] negra con lazos[4] de colores, no son actores de una obra[5] de Shakespeare. Son universitarios que forman parte de grupos musicales que se llaman La Tuna. La Tuna, en sus comienzos ya hace siete siglos, es un grupo de trovadores universitarios que probablemente cantan para ganar el dinero que necesitan para pagar el viaje de vuelta a casa cuando llegan las vacaciones. Algunas cosas no cambian nunca.

[1]traje: *clothes, suit*
[2]medias: *stockings*
[3]capa: *cape*
[4]lazos: *ribbons*
[5]obra: *work*

¡A comer como Hemingway!

¿Sabes que en el corazón del viejo Madrid, se encuentra el restaurante más antiguo del mundo, que una vez fue el sitio favorito de Ernest Hemingway? Entérate de la historia de Casa Botín:

- *El Libro Guinness de los Records* proclama a Casa Botín, fundado en 1725, el restaurante más antiguo del mundo. Además, afirma que un adolescente con el nombre de Goya trabajó allí como lavaplatos[1].
- Al principio, Casa Botín sirve de posada donde los comerciantes terminan su viaje, cenan y duermen.
- Ernest Hemingway lo nombra en su libro *The Sun Also Rises.*
- Tiene cuatro plantas[2].
- La especialidad es el cochinillo asado[3].
- A eso de la medianoche, La Tuna normalmente llega para tocar y bailar.

[1]lavaplatos: *dishwasher*
[2]plantas: *floors*
[3]cochinillo asado: *roast suckling pig*

Ernest Hemingway

Obras maestras[1] de la historia

España es el país del mundo que más ciudades tiene con el título "Ciudades Patrimonio de la Humanidad," una distinción de la UNESCO. Son 11 las ciudades españolas que no tienen precio[2]. Hacemos un breve recorrido[3] por algunas de ellas:

Alcalá de Henares: Lugar de nacimiento de Cervantes.
Ávila: Una ciudad completamente amurallada[4].
Córdoba: Cuenta con más de 2,000 años de historia.
Salamanca: Sinónimo de universidad con sus catedrales y palacios.
Santiago de Compostela: Miles de peregrinos[5] viajaron aquí a través del Camino de Santiago.
Segovia: Una calle principal pasa por debajo de un acueducto[6] romano.
Toledo: El Greco pintó aquí.

[1]obras maestras: *masterpieces*
[2]no tienen precio: *priceless*
[3]breve recorrido: *short journey*
[4]amurallada: *walled*
[5]peregrinos: *pilgrims*
[6]acueducto: *aquaduct*

Answers

A

1. falso
2. falso
3. verdadero

B

La Tuna es un grupo musical de universitarios. Cantan para ganar dinero.

C

1. a
2. c
3. b
4. b

Un éxito[1] a pedir de boca[2]

Teresa Barrenechea encuentra la receta[3] de su fama: una pizca[4] de sabor y bastante nostalgia

De joven en Bilbao, Teresa Barrenechea se cuela[5] en las sociedades gastronómicas privadas donde solamente los socios[6] se reúnen a cocinar. Cada vez que la descubren, la mandan a casa. Sin embargo, Barrenechea es hoy una de los jefes de cocina más respetados de España y Estados Unidos. En su restaurante en Manhattan, dice que "la gente ahora sabe que las enchiladas no son españolas." ¿Y qué ocurre cuando Barrenechea regresa a Bilbao? La dejan entrar en los clubes de cocina.

[1]éxito: *success*
[2]a pedir de boca: *just right, exactly as one wishes*
[3]receta: *recipe*
[4]pizca: *pinch of*
[5]se cuela: *slips into*
[6]socios: *members*

Calendario de fiestas

Marzo: Valencia
Las Fallas son monumentos satíricos, hechos con materiales combustibles como el cartón[1] y la madera[2]. Se montan[3] unas 300 en las plazas de la ciudad. En la noche del 19 de marzo, festividad de San José, se queman[4].

Abril: Sevilla
Se construye una "ciudad" de casetas[5] adornadas con farolillos[6] de papel para celebrar la Feria de Abril. Mucha gente llega en carrozas tiradas por caballos[7], se visten en trajes tradicionales y bailan las sevillanas, un baile tradicional.

Octubre: Zaragoza
El día 12 de ocubre, para celebrar las Fiestas del Pilar, miles de zaragozanos recorren las calles en un desfile[8]—llamado la ofrenda de flores[9]—en el que llevan todo tipo de flores a la catedral. A la vez, bailan la jota, un típico baile folklórico.

[1]cartón: *cardboard*
[2]madera: *wood*
[3]se montan: *are set up*
[4]se queman: *they're burned*
[5]casetas: *tents*
[6]farolillos: *little lanterns*
[7]carrozas tiradas por caballos: *horse-drawn carriages*
[8]desfile: *parade*
[9]ofrenda de flores: *flower offering*

micocina

El plato más típico de la cocina española, sin ninguna duda, es la paella. Se originó como el plato tradicional de la provincia de Valencia, tomando su nombre de la sartén[1] ancha con dos asas[2]—llamada "paellera"—en la que se prepara. Actualmente, aparte de[3] la paella valenciana, existen muchas clases de paella, como la paella marinera que se hace con mariscos. Cada cocinero añade ingredientes distintos, como las aceitunas[4], los guisantes, el pimiento[5] y las gambas[6]. Sin embargo, hay quien dice que la paella valenciana es la más auténtica. He aquí los ingredientes del sabroso plato tradicional.

Paella valenciana
Ingredientes *(para 6 personas)*
- 1 pollo
- 200 gramos de judías verdes
- 200 gramos de judías blancas
- 400 gramos de arroz
- 100 gramos de tomate
- 1 diente de ajo
- 1½ litros de agua
- sal y pimenta
- azafrán[7]
- aceite de oliva
- 24 caracoles[8]

[1]sartén: *pan*
[2]asas: *handles*
[3]aparte de: *aside from*
[4]aceitunas: *olives*
[5]pimiento: *pepper*
[6]gambas: *shrimp*
[7]azafrán: *saffron*
[8]caracoles: *snails*

Paella marinera

465

People en Español

2. *The Sun Also Rises* es ___.
   a. una canción de La Tuna
   b. el nombre de una calle en Segovia
   c. una novela de Ernest Hemingway

3. Córdoba cuenta con más de ___ años de historia.
   a. tres mil
   b. dos mil
   c. siete mil

4. ¿Qué es Casa Botín?
   a. una especialidad de la casa
   b. un restaurante muy antiguo
   c. la casa de Goya

D Hemingway y Obras maestros de la historia Identifiquen.
1. un autor español
2. un autor norteamericano
3. dos artistas españoles
4. ciudad que tiene un acueducto romano
5. ciudad rodeada de murallas

E Un éxito a pedir de boca Contesten.
1. ¿De dónde es Teresa Barrenechea?
2. ¿Qué es ella hoy?
3. ¿Dónde está su restaurante?

F Calendario de fiestas ¿Verdadero o falso?
1. Las Fallas son monumentos de materiales combustibles.
2. La Feria de Abril tiene lugar en Valencia.
3. Durante las fiestas en Sevilla la gente lleva trajes tradicionales y bailan las sevillanas, un baile tradicional.
4. El día 12 de octubre la gente construye una ciudad de casetas o casas muy pequeñas en la ciudad de Zaragoza.
5. Para celebra las Fiestas del Pilar la gente desfile por las calles de Zaragoza. Llevan flores a la catedral.

ANSWERS

D
1. Cervantes
2. Hemingway
3. Goya y El Greco
4. Segovia
5. Ávila

E
1. Bilbao, España
2. una de los jefes de cocina más respetados
3. en Nueva York

F
1. V
2. F
3. V
4. F
5. V

LEVELING

E: Activity A
A: Activities B, C, D, F
C: Activity E

People EN ESPAÑOL

Contemporary Spanish pop culture represents a wide range of geographic, ethnic, and artistic influences. The Spanish film industry for example, has become internationally recognized and celebrated for cutting-edge, unique cinematic techniques. Current Spanish music encompasses a vast range of styles from traditional **flamenco** to **bakalao**—Spain's unique interpretation of *techno.*

Anthony Hopkins y Antonio Banderas

Un festival de película[1]

Cada año durante los últimos días del mes de septiembre, la ciudad de San Sebastián recibe una dosis de "glamour." Se celebra el Festival Internacional de Cine. Cuando empieza el festival, el público espera ansioso la llegada de las estrellas. Actores, actrices y directores famosos asisten para ver las proyecciones de las películas del momento. Más de una docena[2] de filmes de distintas nacionalidades compiten por el máximo premio, la Concha de Oro[3]. Además, hay ruedas de prensa[4] y retrospectivas. Y... las palomitas de maíz[5].

[1]de película: *awesome, incredible, fantastic*
[2]docena: *dozen*
[3]Concha de Oro: *Golden Shell*
[4]ruedas de prensa: *press conferences*
[5]palomitas de maíz: *popcorn*

Banderas

Cruz

Almodóvar

Bardem

Antonio Banderas, actor: Ha actuado en más de 69 filmes en español e inglés, entre ellos *Evita* y *Spy Kids.* Hizo su debut en Broadway en un musical.

Penélope Cruz, actriz: Actuó en una película española ganadora[1] del Óscar. Trasciende las fronteras[2] de España, ya que es una estrella de Hollywood.

Pedro Almodóvar, cineasta[3]: Una de sus películas en español ganó el Óscar a la mejor película extranjera[4]. Otra ganó el Óscar al mejor guión[5] original.

Javier Bardem, actor: Es muy conocido en España y América Latina. Fue candidato al Óscar al mejor actor protagonista.

[1]ganadora: *winner*
[2]trasciende las fronteras: *transcends the borders*
[3]cineasta: *filmmaker*
[4]extranjera: *foreign*
[5]guión: *script*

466

Un museo de sueño[1]

He aquí unas obras maestras de unos pintores españoles. ¿Adivinas[2] el nombre del artista que pintó cada cuadro[3]?

[1]de sueño: *a dream*
[2]adivinas: *can you guess*
[3]cuadro: *painting*

1

2

3

4

Respuestas:
1. Joan Miró
2. El Greco (Domenikos Theotocopoulos)
3. Francisco de Goya
4. Pablo Picasso

música

Lo mejor del año

Jarabe de Palo

¿Quién escribe cartas a su perro reflexionando acerca de la vida y detesta la palabra "hit?" Pau Donés, vocalista de **Jarabe de Palo.** Es un cantautor[1] español con un mensaje sencillo[2]: canta lo que vive y vive lo que canta. Dice, "Es importante cantarle a la gente que aún quiere crear un mundo mejor."

Paco de Lucia

Cuando toca la guitarra **Paco de Lucía,** quizá el más popular de los guitarristas flamencos, el público suele[3] dar palmas[4], gritar "¡Óle!" e incluso bailar. Nació en Cádiz, y en su niñez está rodeado[5] del cante y del baile flamencos. Ha intervenido[6] en algunas películas, entre ellas *Carmen* de Carlos Saura. Se venden sus discos mundialmente.

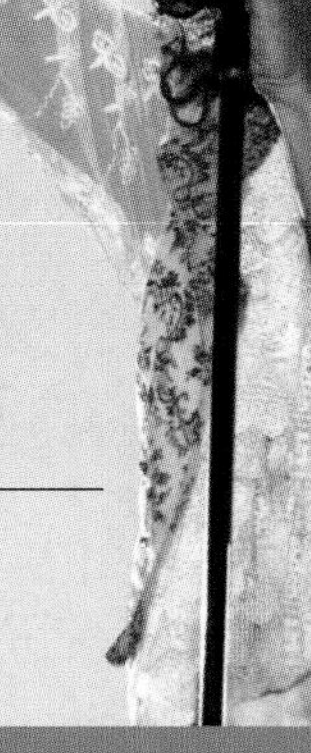
Rosario Flores ha logrado un Grammy como el "Mejor Álbum de Cantante Pop."

Con su disco *Muchas flores,* **Rosario Flores,** ha logrado[7] un Grammy como el "Mejor Álbum de Cantante Pop." Además, fue protagonista de la película española del cineasta Almodóvar que ganó el Óscar al mejor guión. Dice, "Crecí en una familia llena de amor, alegría, comida, flores, gente, guitarras, baile y cante."

[1]cantautor: *singer/songwriter*
[2]mensaje sencillo: *simple message*
[3]suele: *usually*
[4]dar palmas: *claps*
[5]rodeado: *surrounded*
[6]intervenido: *appeared*
[7]logrado: *captured*

Atletas que destacan

Sánchez Vicario

Arantxa Sánchez Vicario La mejor tenista española de todos los tiempos, nació en Barcelona. Fue la primera jugadora de España en ganar el Abierto de Estados Unidos de América. Tiene tres títulos más de Grand Slam en singles.

Beckham

David Beckham Cuando el centrocampista[1] inglés se unió al Real Madrid, pasó a ser uno de sus jugadores más famosos. Dice el futbolista[2], "Formar parte del Real Madrid es un sueño hecho realidad[3]."

García

Sergio García Llamado "El Niño," es el mejor jugador de golf español, siguiendo los pasos[4] de Seve Ballesteros y José María Olazábal. Empezó a jugar a los 3 años. Se hizo profesional en 1999, batiendo[5] el record del jugador más joven en disputar[6] un PGA (terminó en segundo lugar; Tiger Woods ganó).

[1]centrocampista: *midfielder*
[2]futbolista: *soccer player*
[3]sueño hecho realidad: *a dream come true*
[4]siguiendo los pasos: *following in the footsteps*
[5]batiendo: *breaking*
[6]disputar: *playing in*

SUCESOS

100,000 personas se comieron la paella más grande del mundo en España.

El ingenioso hidalgo Don Quijote de la Mancha, de Miguel de Cervantes, fue elegido como el mejor libro de ficción de todos los tiempos, en un sondeo[1] realizado entre los autores más prestigiosos del mundo.

El escritor **José Jiménez Lozano** recibió de manos del Rey **Don Juan Carlos de España** el Premio Cervantes, considerado como el Nóbel de la literatura en castellano. La ceremonia tuvo lugar en Alcalá de Henares.

[1]sondeo: *opinion poll*

467

People EN ESPAÑOL

A En el set ¿Quién es?

1. Una de sus películas ganó el Oscar al mejor guión original.
2. Hizo su debut en Broadway en un musical.
3. Es una estrella de Hollywood.

B Música Busquen.

1. el más popular de los guitarristas flamencas
2. lo que grita la gente mientras cantan o bailan flamenco
3. película en que Paco de Lucia tomó parte
4. una cantante pop
5. un famoso cineasta español

C Atletas que destacan Contesten.

1. ¿Quién es la mejor tenista española de todos los tiempos?
2. ¿Dónde nació ella?
3. ¿Qué deporte juega David Beckham?
4. ¿De qué nacionalidad es él?
5. ¿Con qué equipo juega?
6. ¿Quién tiene el nombre de "El Niño"?
7. ¿Qué deporte juega?

LEVELING

E: Activity A
A: Activity B
C: Activity C

Answers

A

1. Pedro Almodóvar
2. Antonio Banderas
3. Penélope Cruz

B

1. Paco de Lucia
2. Olé
3. Carmen
4. Rosario Flores
5. Almodóvar

C

1. Arantxa Sánchez Vicario
2. en Barcelona
3. fútbol
4. es inglés
5. el Real Madrid
6. Sergio García
7. el golf

Preview

All literary selections are optional. You may wish to skip them or present them very thoroughly. In some cases you may have students read the selection quickly just to get a general idea of the selection.

LEVELING

A: Literary Selections

Literary Companion

These literary selections develop reading and cultural skills and introduce students to Hispanic literature.

Biblioteca, Universidad de México

¡OJO! The exposure to literature early in one's study of another language should be a pleasant experience. As students read these selections, it is not necessary for them to understand every word. Explain to them that they should try to enjoy the experience of reading literature in a new language. As they read they should look for the following:

- who the main characters are
- what they are like
- what they are doing—the plot
- what happens to them—the outcome of the story

Learning from Photos

(pages 468–469) This photo shows the **Biblioteca Central** of the **Universidad Nacional de México.** It is the most spectacular building on the campus. The beautiful mosaics depicting different periods of Mexican history and scientific achievements were done by Juan O'Gorman.

Versos sencillos

National Standards

Cultures
Students experience, discuss, and analyze the poem from ***Versos sencillos*** by José Martí.

¡OJO! This literary selection is optional. You may wish to present it after students have completed Chapters 1–4, as they will have acquired the vocabulary and structures necessary to read the selection by this point.

You may present the piece thoroughly as a class activity or you may have some or all students read it on their own. If you present it as a class activity, some options are:

- Students read silently.
- Students read after you in unison.
- Call on individuals to read aloud.

With any of the above procedures, intersperse some comprehension questions. Call on a student or students to give a brief synopsis in Spanish.

Note: The following teaching suggestions are for a thorough presentation of ***Versos sencillos.***

Teaching Vocabulary

¡OJO! Students merely need to be familiar with the vocabulary to help them understand the story. This vocabulary does not have to be a part of their active, productive vocabulary. All high-frequency words will be reintroduced in **¡Buen viaje! Levels 2** and **3** as new vocabulary.

Step 1 Present the new vocabulary on page 470 using the teaching suggestions given in the regular chapters in this textbook.

Step 2 Quickly go over the activity with the class.

Literatura 1

Versos sencillos José Martí

Vocabulario

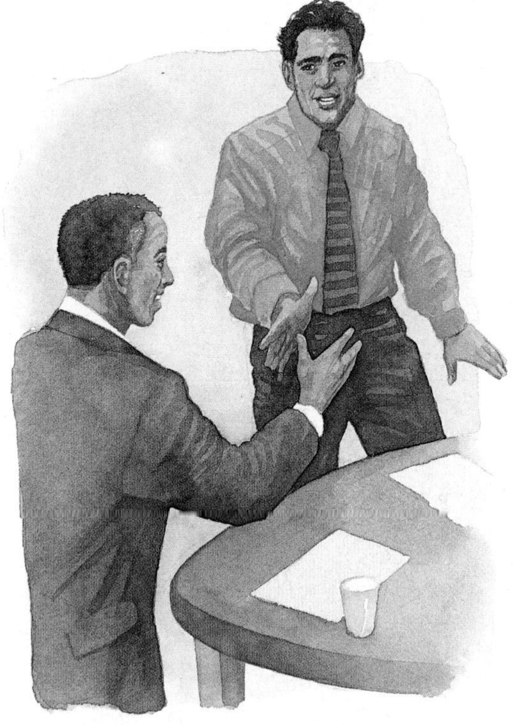

El señor da la mano.

Actividad

¿Sí o no? Digan que sí o que no.

1. Una rosa es una flor bonita.
2. El corazón es un órgano vital.
3. Damos la mano a un amigo.

Answers to Actividad

1. Sí
2. Sí
3. Sí

La Habana, Cuba

INTRODUCCIÓN José Martí (1853–1895) es cubano. Es un hombre muy famoso. Es poeta y es también un héroe. Durante toda la vida Martí lucha[1] por la independencia de Cuba.

Estudia en Madrid y en Zaragoza en España. José Martí admira mucho a la España artística y humana. Pero ataca la España política porque su país, Cuba, en aquel entonces[2] es una colonia de España.

Martí pasa mucho tiempo en varias repúblicas hispanoamericanas—México, Guatemala, Venezuela y Honduras. «De América soy hijo»—proclama Martí. Pasa también unos catorce años en Estados Unidos. Publica *Versos sencillos* en Nueva York en 1891.

Versos sencillos es una colección de poemas (poesías).

[1]lucha *fights*
[2]en aquel entonces *at that time*

Versos sencillos

Cultivo una rosa blanca,
en julio como en enero
para el amigo sincero
que me da su mano franca.

Y para el cruel que me arranca°
el corazón con que vivo,
cardo ni ortiga° cultivo
cultivo la rosa blanca.

arranca *pulls out*
cardo ni ortiga *thistle nor nettle*

¿Comprendes?

En inglés, por favor. Contesten.
1. Is the theme of this short poem gardening, friendship, or roses?
2. What two types of people does the poet speak about?
3. In your own words, explain how the poet tells us that he treats all people equally.
4. How does the poet express "all the time"?

Literatura 1

Discussing Literature

Introducción

Step 1 You may go over the **Introducción** with the students or you may decide to omit it and just have them read the poem.

Step 2 You can ask the following questions about the **Introducción:**
¿De qué nacionalidad es José Martí?
¿Qué es José Martí?
¿Martí lucha por la independencia de qué país? ¿Dónde estudia?
¿A qué España admira Martí? ¿A qué España ataca Martí?
Durante la vida de Martí, ¿qué es Cuba?

Versos sencillos

Step 1 Have students close their books. Explain the meaning of **cardo** and **ortiga** to them.

Step 2 Read the poem to the class. Use as much expression as you can. Hold out your hand as you say: **me da su mano franca.** Gesture pulling out your heart as you say: **me arranca el corazón.** Smile as you say: **cultivo la rosa blanca.**

Step 3 Have students open their books to page 471. Have them read the poem once in unison. Give them a couple of minutes to read the poem silently and then call on an individual to read aloud.

Step 4 You can ask the following: **¿Qué cultiva el autor? ¿Cuándo cultiva la rosa blanca? ¿Para quién cultiva una rosa blanca? Para una persona cruel, ¿cultiva un cardo o una ortiga? ¿Qué cultiva para una persona cruel?**

Step 5 Go over the **¿Comprendes?** activity and have students answer in English.

ANSWERS TO ¿Comprendes?

1. friendship
2. a sincere friend, a cruel person
3. *Answers will vary. Students should give their interpretation of the poet growing a white rose for both sincere friends and cruel people.*
4. He says, "in July as in January."

Class Motivator

Using Audio CD 1, play the song ***Guantanamera.*** Have students sing the words in the poem on page 471 to the melody. Explain to students that, although Pete Seeger composed the melody, the words to the song ***Guantanamera*** were taken from ***Versos sencillos.***

«Una moneda de oro»

National Standards

Cultures
Students experience, discuss, and analyze the adaptation of the story *«Una moneda de oro»* by Francisco Monterde.

¡OJO! This literary selection is optional. You may wish to present it after students have completed Chapters 5–7, as they will have acquired the vocabulary and structures necessary to read the selection by this point.

You may present the piece thoroughly as a class activity or you may have some or all students read it on their own. If you present it as a class activity, you may wish to vary presentation procedures from section to section. Some options are:

- Students read silently.
- Students read after you in unison.
- Call on individuals to read aloud.
- When dialogue appears in the story, call on students to take parts.

With any of the above procedures, intersperse some comprehension questions. Call on a student or students to give a brief synopsis of a section in Spanish.

Note: The following teaching suggestions are for a thorough presentation of ***«Una moneda de oro».***

Teaching Vocabulary

¡OJO! Students merely need to be familiar with the vocabulary to help them understand the story. This vocabulary does not have to be a part of their active, productive vocabulary. All high-frequency words will be reintroduced in **¡Buen viaje! Levels 2** and **3** as new vocabulary.

Step 1 Have students open their books to page 472. Have them repeat the new vocabulary words and sentences after you.

Literatura 2

«Una moneda de oro» Francisco Monterde

Vocabulario

Es temprano por la noche (8:30).
Hay una moneda en el suelo.

La moneda refleja la luz de la luna.
Un señor halla la moneda.

La señora enciende la luz.

Ella cose el bolsillo porque tiene un agujero.

La señora cuelga el chaleco en la silla.

Actividades

A and **B** Quickly go over these activities orally to be sure that students will understand the words in the reading.

El señor esconde la moneda.
Mete la moneda debajo del mantel.

El señor levanta el mantel.
Debajo del mantel hay dinero.
El señor está muy alegre.

Es la Navidad.
El señor recoge el juguete.
La niña está dormida.

Actividades

A **¿Sabes la palabra?** Escojan.

1. El ___ de diciembre es la Navidad.
   a. veinticinco **b.** veinticuatro
2. Los niños reciben ___ para la Navidad.
   a. sillas **b.** juguetes
3. Ella tiene que coser el bolsillo porque tiene ___.
   a. un agujero **b.** una moneda
4. El señor no pierde la moneda. ___ la moneda.
   a. Busca **b.** Halla
5. La señora cuelga ___ en la silla.
   a. el chaleco **b.** el mantel
6. El señor mete la moneda debajo del mantel. Él ___ la moneda.
   a. recoge **b.** esconde
7. En la mano hay cinco ___.
   a. monedas **b.** dedos

B **La moneda** Contesten.

1. ¿Dónde está el señor? (en el parque)
2. ¿Qué parte del día es? (la noche)
3. ¿Qué halla el señor? (una moneda)
4. ¿Recoge la moneda? (sí)
5. ¿De qué es la moneda? (de oro)
6. ¿Qué refleja la moneda? (la luna)

Answers to Actividad

A

1. a
2. b
3. a
4. b
5. a
6. b
7. b

B

1. El señor está en el parque.
2. Es la noche.
3. El señor halla una moneda.
4. Sí, recoge la moneda.
5. La moneda es de oro.
6. La moneda refleja la luna.

Literatura 2

Discussing Literature

Introducción

You may go over the **Introducción** with the students or you may decide to omit it and just have them read the story.

«Una moneda de oro»

Step 1 Before reading this selection you may wish to give students the following introduction in English to set the scene and help them understand the story: "We are going to read a story about an underprivileged family in Mexico. A certain holiday is coming up. Just before the holiday something exciting happens to the father."

Step 2 If you are presenting the story as a class activity, you can use many gestures or expressions to help students with comprehension. Examples:

Section 1 Pick up a coin. Look at it with an amazed, excited face. Caress the coin.

Section 2 If you have a pocket, put the coin in it. Take it out and check your pocket for a hole. Shake your head "no" and put the coin back. Indicate that you are doubtful. Look at the coin again and cheer up.

INTRODUCCIÓN Francisco Monterde es de México. Nace en 1894. Es poeta, dramaturgo y novelista. Es también cuentista. Publica una colección de cuentos[1] en 1943. Sus cuentos presentan un estudio serio de la historia de México.

Aquí tenemos el cuento «Una moneda de oro». Es un cuento sencillo[2] y tierno[3]. El autor habla de una pobre familia mexicana del campo.

[1] cuentos *stories* [2] sencillo *simple* [3] tierno *tender*

«Una moneda de oro»

Es una Navidad alegre para el pobre. El pobre es Andrés. No tiene dinero y no tiene trabajo desde el otoño.

Es temprano por la noche. Andrés pasa por el parque. En el suelo ve una moneda que refleja la luz de la luna. —¿Es una moneda de oro?—pregunta Andrés. —Pesa° mucho. ¡Imposible! No puede ser una moneda de oro. Es sólo una medalla.

Andrés sale del parque y examina la moneda. No, no es una medalla. Es realmente una moneda de oro. Andrés acaricia° la moneda. ¡Es muy agradable su contacto!

Pesa *It weighs*

acaricia *caresses*

Con la moneda entre los dedos, mete la mano derecha en el bolsillo de su pantalón. No, no puede meter la moneda en el bolsillo. Tiene miedo° de perder la moneda. Examina el bolsillo. No, no tiene agujeros. No hay problema. Puede meter la moneda en el bolsillo. No va a perder la moneda.

Andrés va a casa a pie. Anda rápido. La moneda de oro salta° en el bolsillo. El pobre Andrés está muy contento.

Luego tiene una duda. ¿Es falsa la moneda? Andrés tiene una idea. Va a entrar en una tienda. Va a comprar algo. Y va a pagar con la moneda. Si el dependiente acepta la moneda, es buena, ¿no? Y si no acepta la moneda, ¿qué? Andrés reflexiona. No, no va a ir a la tienda. Prefiere ir a casa con la moneda. Su mujer va a estar muy contenta.

Tiene miedo *He is afraid*

salta *jumps around*

Su casa es una casa humilde. Tiene sólo dos piezas o cuartos. Cuando llega a casa, su mujer no está. No está porque cada día tiene que ir a entregar° la ropa que cose para ganar unos pesos.

Andrés enciende una luz. Pone la moneda en la mesa. En unos momentos oye° a su mujer y a su hija. Ellas vuelven a casa. Esconde la moneda debajo del mantel.

La niña entra. Andrés toma la niña en sus brazos. Luego llega su mujer. Tiene una expresión triste y melancólica. —¿Tienes trabajo?—pregunta ella. —Hoy no puedo comprar pan. No me pagan cuando entrego la costura°.

Andrés no contesta. Levanta el mantel. Su mujer ve la moneda. Toma la moneda en las manos. —¿Quién te da la moneda?

—Nadie°—Andrés habla con su mujer. Explica como halla la moneda en el parque.

La niña toma la moneda y empieza a jugar con la moneda. Andrés tiene miedo. No quiere perder la moneda. Puede irse por° un agujero.

Andrés toma la moneda y pone la moneda en uno de los bolsillos de su chaleco. —¿Qué compramos con la moneda?—pregunta Andrés.

—No compramos nada. Tenemos que pagar mucho—suspira su mujer. Debemos° mucho.

—Es verdad—contesta Andrés. —Pero hoy es Nochebuena°. Tenemos que celebrar.

—No—contesta su mujer. —Primero tenemos que pagar el dinero que debemos.

entregar *return, deliver*

oye *he hears*

costura *sewing*

Nadie *No one*

irse por *slip through*

Debemos *We owe*

Nochebuena *Christmas Eve*

Una casa humilde, México

Section 3 Put the coin on a table. Cover it with anything that can be a tablecloth. Tell the class you are now **la niña.** Take the coin, play with it, and drop it.

Now be Andrés again. Anxiously retrieve the coin and put it in your jacket pocket. Take the jacket off and hang it over the chair.

Literatura 2

Discussing Literature

Section 4 Look all over for the coin. Search all the clothing you have on. Show your empty hands. Be **la niña.** Sit on a chair. Wake up. Stretch your arms and make a noise with the coin under the table.

¿Comprendes?

Note: Each of the four **¿Comprendes?** activities corresponds to a different section of the reading. Activity A corresponds to Section 1, B to Section 2, C to Section 3, and D to Section 4. As you finish each section of the story you can go over the corresponding activity.

Andrés está un poco malhumorado. Se quita° el chaleco y el saco. Cuelga el chaleco y el saco en la silla.

—Bueno, Andrés. Si quieres, puedes ir a comprar algo. Pero tenemos que guardar lo demás°.

Andrés acepta. Se pone° el chaleco y el saco y sale de casa.

Se quita *He takes off*

guardar lo demás *keep the rest*

Se pone *He puts on*

En la calle Andrés ve a su amigo Pedro.

—¿Adónde vas? ¿Quieres ir a tomar algo?

Andrés acepta. Los amigos pasan un rato en un café pequeño. Beben y hablan. Y luego Andrés sale. Va a la tienda. Sólo va a comprar comida para esta noche. Y un juguete para la niña.

Andrés compra primero los alimentos. El paquete está listo°. Andrés busca la moneda. Busca en el chaleco. No está. Busca en el saco. No está. Busca en su pantalón. La moneda no está en ninguno de sus bolsillos. El pobre Andrés está lleno de terror. Tiene que salir de la tienda sin la comida.

Una vez más está en la calle. Vuelve a casa. Llega a la puerta. No quiere entrar. Pero tiene que entrar. Entra y ve a la niña dormida con la cabeza entre los brazos sobre la mesa. Su mujer está cosiendo a su lado.

—La moneda...

—¿Qué?

—No tengo la moneda.

—¿Cómo?

La niña sobresalta°. Abre los ojos. Baja los brazos y bajo la mesa Andrés y su mujer oyen el retintín° de la moneda de oro.

¡Qué contentos están Andrés y su mujer! Recogen la moneda que la niña había escamoteado° del chaleco cuando estaba colgado en la silla.

listo *ready*

sobresalta *jumps up*

retintín *jingle*

había escamoteado *had secretly taken out*

¿Comprendes?

A Comprensión Contesten.

1. ¿Quién es el pobre?
2. ¿Por qué no tiene dinero?
3. ¿Por dónde pasa Andrés?
4. ¿Qué ve en el suelo?
5. ¿Es una moneda de oro o es una medalla?

B Andrés y la moneda Escojan.

1. ¿Por qué no debe Andrés meter la moneda en el bolsillo de su pantalón?
   a. Porque el bolsillo tiene un agujero.
   b. Porque puede perder la moneda.

Answers to ¿Comprendes?

A

1. El pobre es Andrés.
2. No tiene dinero porque no tiene trabajo desde el otoño.
3. Andrés pasa por el parque.
4. Ve una moneda en el suelo.
5. Es una moneda de oro.

2. Cuando Andrés examina el bolsillo, ¿qué decide?
   a. Puede meter la moneda en el bolsillo porque no tiene agujero.
   b. Va a perder la moneda.
   c. La moneda de oro es sólo una medalla.
3. ¿Cómo va Andrés a casa?
   a. Salta.
   b. A pie y rápido.
   c. Con miedo.
4. ¿Qué duda tiene Andrés?
   a. Si tiene que comprar algo.
   b. Si la moneda es falsa o no.
   c. Si su pantalón tiene un agujero.
5. Si compra algo en una tienda, ¿por qué quiere pagar con la moneda?
   a. Si el dependiente acepta la moneda, no es falsa.
   b. Porque la moneda es falsa y Andrés no quiere la moneda.
   c. Porque no tiene dinero.
6. ¿Qué decide Andrés?
   a. Decide que la moneda es falsa.
   b. Decide que no necesita nada.
   c. Decide que no va a la tienda. Prefiere ir a casa.

Una vista del campo, México

C **¿Sí o no?** Digan que sí o que no.

1. La casa de Andrés es muy humilde.
2. La casa tiene cuatro piezas.
3. Cuando llega Andrés, su mujer cose.
4. Su mujer cose para ganar dinero.
5. Su mujer y su hija vuelven a casa.
6. Andrés toma a su mujer en sus brazos.
7. Su mujer está muy contenta.
8. Hoy ella compra pan.
9. Cuando Andrés levanta el mantel, su mujer ve la moneda.
10. La niña empieza a jugar con la moneda.
11. Andrés quiere comprar algo para celebrar la Navidad.
12. Su mujer quiere comprar mucho.
13. Por fin Andrés puede ir a la tienda a comprar algo.

La Navidad, México

D **Andrés sale.** Contesten.

1. ¿A quién ve Andrés en la calle?
2. ¿Adónde van los dos?
3. Luego, ¿adónde va Andrés?
4. ¿Qué va a comprar?
5. ¿Qué busca Andrés?
6. ¿Qué no puede hallar?
7. ¿Qué ve cuando entra en la casa?
8. ¿Dónde está la moneda?

Answers to ¿Comprendes?

B

1. b
2. a
3. b
4. b
5. a
6. c

C

1. Sí
2. No
3. No
4. Sí
5. Sí
6. No
7. No
8. No
9. Sí
10. Sí
11. Sí
12. No
13. Sí

D

1. Andrés ve a su amigo Pedro.
2. Los dos van a un café pequeño.
3. Andrés va a la tienda.
4. Va a comprar comida para la noche y un juguete para la niña.
5. Andrés busca la moneda.
6. No puede hallar la moneda.
7. Ve a la familia.
8. La moneda está bajo la mesa.

«La camisa de Margarita»

National Standards

Cultures
Students experience, discuss, and analyze the adaptation of the story *«La camisa de Margarita»* by Ricardo Palma.

¡OJO! This literary selection is optional. You may wish to present it after students have completed Chapters 8–11, as they will have acquired the vocabulary and structures necessary to read the selection by this point.

You may present the piece thoroughly as a class activity or you may have some or all students read it on their own. If you present it as a class activity, you may wish to vary presentation procedures from section to section. Some options are:

- Students read silently.
- Students read after you in unison.
- Call on individuals to read aloud.
- When dialogue appears in the story, call on students to take parts.

With any of the above procedures, intersperse some comprehension questions. Call on a student or students to give a brief synopsis of a section in Spanish.

Note: The following teaching suggestions are for a thorough presentation of *«La camisa de Margarita»*.

Teaching Vocabulary

¡OJO! Students merely need to be familiar with the vocabulary to help them understand the story. This vocabulary does not have to be a part of their active, productive vocabulary. All high-frequency words will be reintroduced in **¡Buen viaje! Levels 2** and **3** as new vocabulary.

Step 1 Have students open their books to page 478. Have them repeat the new vocabulary words and sentences after you.

Literatura 3

«La camisa de Margarita» Ricardo Palma

Vocabulario

Es un galán.
Es un señor muy elegante.
Es soltero. No tiene esposa.
No está casado.

Los jóvenes están enamorados.
El joven le echa flores a la señorita.
La joven le flecha el corazón al joven.
Los jóvenes tienen una sonrisita.

una cadena de diamantes (brillantes)

El sacerdote habla con los recién casados.
Están en la iglesia.

Nota In this story you will come across the following words that describe money used in Peru in the eighteenth century. From the context of the reading you will be able to tell which were of little value and which were of great value. It is not necessary for you to learn these words: **un ochavo, un real, un maravedí, un duro, un morlaco.**

el suegro el padre del marido o de la mujer
el sacerdote un padre (religioso) católico
el pobretón un muchacho pobre que no tiene dinero
el chisme la historieta, un rumor
los muebles la silla, la mesa, la cama, etc., son muebles
altivo arrogante
con mucha plata que tiene mucho dinero, rico

Actividades

A Los jóvenes Contesten según los dibujos.

1. ¿Es un tipo galán el joven?
2. ¿Es un poco altivo?
3. ¿Es soltero?
4. ¿Tiene esposa?
5. ¿Está enamorado el joven?
6. ¿Qué le echa a la señorita?
7. ¿Qué tiene en la cara?
8. ¿Tiene la señorita una cadena de diamantes en el cuello?

B El galán Expresen de otra manera.

1. Él no tiene mujer. No está casado.
2. Es un señor elegante.
3. Es un tipo muy arrogante.
4. No es un joven que tiene mucho dinero.
5. No sé si es verdad. Es un rumor.

Actividades

A and B Quickly go over these activities orally to be sure that students will understand the words in the reading.

Answers to Actividad

A

1. Sí, el joven es un tipo galán.
2. Sí, es un poco altivo.
3. Sí, es soltero.
4. No, no tiene esposa.
5. Sí, el joven está enamorado.
6. Le echa flores a la señorita.
7. Tiene una sonrisita.
8. No, la señorita no tiene una cadena de diamantes en el cuello.

B

1. Él es soltero.
2. Es un galán.
3. Es muy altivo.
4. Es un pobretón.
5. Es un chisme.

Literatura 3

Discussing Literature

Introducción

You may go over the **Introducción** with the class or you may decide to omit it and just have them read the story.

«La camisa de Margarita»

Step 1 Tell students they are going to read a story that takes place in colonial days, the 1600s, in Lima, Peru. The families involved are quite wealthy, but there is a discussion about a wedding dress. You'll find out why.

Step 2 You may wish to have students take a few minutes to read each section silently before going over it orally in class.

Step 3 Since this reading is rather long you may wish to go over only certain sections orally and have students read the other sections silently.

Step 4 Call on a more able student to give a synopsis of each section. This helps less able students understand the selection.

Step 5 Here are some additional hints to help you teach the various sections of the reading:

Section 1

A. Tell students **un colector** is a tax collector.
B. El Callao is the port for Lima, Peru.
C. Ask students if they know what **arrogante** means. If they don't, put on an arrogant air.

Section 2

A. Ask what they think the symbolism is behind the expression **le flecha el corazón.**

INTRODUCCIÓN Ricardo Palma es uno de los hombres más famosos de letras peruanas de todos los tiempos. Él da origen a un nuevo género literario—la tradición. La tradición es una anécdota histórica.

Ricardo Palma publica sus *Tradiciones peruanas* en diez tomos de 1872 a 1910. Las tradiciones presentan la historia de Perú desde la época precolombina hasta la guerra con Chile (1879–1883). Las tradiciones más interesantes y más famosas son las tradiciones que describen la época colonial. «La camisa de Margarita» es un ejemplo de una tradición de la época colonial.

«La camisa de Margarita»

Cuando las señoras viejas de Lima quieren describir algo que cuesta mucho, ¿qué dicen? Dicen: —¡Qué! Si esto es más caro que la camisa de Margarita Pareja.

Margarita Pareja es por los años 1765 la hija mimada° de don Raimundo Pareja, un colector importante del Callao. La muchacha es una de estas limeñitas que es tan bella que puede cautivar° al mismo diablo°. Tiene unos ojos negros cargados° de dinamita que hacen explosión sobre el alma° de los galanes limeños.

Llega de España un arrogante joven llamado don Luis de Alcázar. Don Luis tiene en Lima un tío aragonés, don Honorato. Don Honorato es solterón y es muy rico. Si el tío es rico, no lo es el joven. No tiene ni un centavo.

mimada *spoiled*
cautivar *captivate, charm*
diablo *devil*
cargados *charged*
alma *soul*

En la procesión de Santa Rosa, Alcázar conoce a la linda Margarita. La muchacha le flecha el corazón. El joven le echa flores. Ella no le contesta ni sí ni no. Pero con sonrisitas y otras armas del arsenal femenino le da a entender al joven que es plato muy de su gusto.

Los enamorados olvidan° que existe la aritmética. Don Luis no considera su presente condición económica un obstáculo. Va al padre de Margarita y le pide su mano°. Al padre de Margarita, don Raimundo, no le gusta nada la petición del joven arrogante. Le dice que Margarita es demasiado joven para tomar marido.

olvidan *forget*
le pide su mano *asks for her hand*

Pero la edad de su hija no es la verdadera razón. Don Raimundo no quiere ser suegro de un pobretón. Les dice la verdad a algunos de sus amigos. Uno de ellos va con el chisme al tío aragonés. El tío, que es un tipo muy altivo, se pone° furioso.

—¡Cómo! ¡Desairar° a mi sobrino! No hay más gallardo en todo Lima. Ese don Raimundo va a ver…

se pone *becomes*
Desairar *To snub*

3

Y la pobre Margarita se pone muy enferma. Pierde peso° y tiene ataques nerviosos. Sufre mucho. Su padre se alarma y llama a varios médicos y curanderos. Todos declaran que la única medicina que va a salvar a la joven no se vende en la farmacia. El padre tiene que permitir a la muchacha casarse° con el varón de su gusto.

Don Raimundo va a la casa de don Honorato. Le dice: —Usted tiene que permitir a su sobrino casarse con mi hija. Porque si no, la muchacha va a morir.

—No puede ser—contesta de la manera más desagradable el tío. —Mi sobrino es un pobretón. Lo que usted debe buscar para su hija es un hombre con mucha plata.

El diálogo entre los dos es muy borrascoso°.

—Pero, tío, no es cristiano matar° a quien no tiene la culpa°—dice don Luis.

peso *weight*
casarse *to marry*
borrascoso *stormy*
matar *kill*
culpa *blame*

Iglesia de San Francisco, Lima, Perú

B. Explain: **Los enamorados olvidan que existe la aritmética. → Los jóvenes olvidan o no quieren aceptar que es necesario tener dinero para vivir.**

C. Tell students Margarita's father makes up an excuse. Ask them what the excuse is.

D. Have students explain in English how don Honorato, don Luis' uncle, finds out what's going on.

Section 3

A. Explain: **El varón es una persona de sexo masculino.**

B. **morir → no va a vivir**

Literatura 3

Section 4

A. Have students take a look at the sidenotes before reading.

B. Explain that **la puesta** refers to what she is wearing.

—¿Tú quieres casarte con esa joven?

—Sí, de todo corazón, tío y señor.

—Pues bien, muchacho. Si tú quieres, consiento. Pero con una condición. Don Raimundo me tiene que jurar° que no va a regalar un ochavo a su hija. Y no le va a dejar un real en la herencia—. Aquí empieza otra disputa.

—Pero, hombre, mi hija tiene veinte mil duros de dote°.

—Renunciamos a la dote. La niña va a venir a casa de su marido con nada más que la ropa que lleva o tiene puesta°.

—Entonces me permite regalar a mi hija los muebles° y el ajuar (vestido) de novia.

—Ni un alfiler°.

—Usted no es razonable, don Honorato. Mi hija necesita llevar una camisa para reemplazar la puesta.

—Bien, usted le puede regalar la camisa de novia y se acaba°.

Al día siguiente don Raimundo y don Honorato van a la Iglesia de San Francisco a oír misa°. En el momento que el sacerdote eleva la Hostia, dice el padre de Margarita: —Juro no dar a mi hija más que la camisa de novia.

Y don Raimundo cumple con° su promesa. Ni en la vida ni en la muerte le da después a su hija un maravedí.

Los encajes° de Flandes que adornan la camisa de la novia cuestan dos mil setecientos duros. El cordoncillo que ajusta al cuello es una cadena de brillantes que tienen un valor de treinta mil morlacos.

Los recién casados hacen creer al tío aragonés que la camisa no vale° nada. Porque don Honorato es tan testarudo°, que a saber el valor real de la camisa, le hace al sobrino divorciarse.

Ahora sabemos por qué es muy merecida° la fama que tiene la camisa nupcial de Margarita Pareja.

jurar *to swear*

dote *dowry*

tiene puesta *has on*

muebles *furniture*

alfiler *pin*

se acaba *that's it*

oír misa *to hear mass*

cumple con *fulfills*

encajes *lace*

vale *is worth*

testarudo *hard-headed*

merecida *deserved*

Palacio arzobispal, Lima

Answers to ¿Comprendes?

A

1. Las señoras viejas de Lima lo dicen.
2. Margarita es la hija mimada de don Raimundo Pareja.
3. Margarita es tan bella que puede cautivar al mismo diablo.
4. Un arrogante joven llamado don Luis de Alcázar llega al Perú.
5. Viene de España.
6. Es sobrino de don Honorato.
7. El tío es solterón y muy rico.
8. El sobrino no tiene ni un centavo.

Literatura 3

¿Comprendes?

Note: Each of the four **¿Comprendes?** activities corresponds to a different section of the reading. Activity A corresponds to Section 1, B to Section 2, C to Section 3, and D to Section 4. As you finish each section of the story, you can go over the corresponding activity.

¿Comprendes?

A Margarita Pareja Contesten.

1. ¿Quiénes dicen: —¡Qué! ¡Si esto es más caro que la camisa de Margarita Pareja?
2. ¿Quién es Margarita Pareja?
3. ¿Cómo es Margarita?
4. ¿Quién llega a Perú?
5. ¿De dónde viene?
6. ¿Quién es?
7. ¿Cómo es el tío?
8. ¿Cómo es el sobrino?

B Don Luis Completen.

1. Don Luis conoce a Margarita en ____.
2. Margarita le ____. Y don Luis le ____.
3. Don Luis no considera su condición económica ____.
4. Don Luis va al padre de Margarita y ____.
5. Al padre no le gusta nada ____.
6. No le gusta la petición porque ____.
7. Cuando el tío sabe lo que dice don Raimundo, él se pone ____.

Palacio arzobispal, Lima

C En español, por favor.
Contesten en español.

1. What happens to Margarita?
2. What medicine does she need?
3. Why does the young man's uncle say his nephew cannot marry Margarita?
4. Under what condition does the uncle consent?

D En tus propias palabras
In your own words in English, explain the ending of this story. What does Margarita's father do?

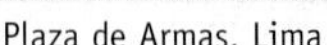

Plaza de Armas, Lima

Learning from Photos

(page 483) The Palace of the Archbishop and the other beautiful buildings in Lima pictured here were all constructed during the colonial period.

Answers to ¿Comprendes?

B

1. la procesión de Santa Rosa
2. flecha el corazón, echa flores
3. un obstáculo
4. le pide su mano
5. la petición del joven arrogante
6. no quiere ser suegro de un pobretón
7. furioso

C

1. Margarita se pone muy enferma.
2. La única medicina que necesita es casarse.
3. El tío del joven dice que su sobrino no puede casarse con Margarita porque es un pobretón.
4. Con la condición de que don Raimundo jure que no va a regalar un ochavo a su hija y no le va a dejar un real en la herencia.

D *Answers will vary. Students should explain how Margarita's father is true to both his daughter and his promise to don Luis' uncle.*

El Quijote

National Standards

Cultures
Students experience, discuss, and analyze an adapted excerpt from the novel ***El Quijote*** by Miguel de Cervantes Saavedra.

¡OJO! This literary selection is optional. You may wish to present it after students have completed Chapters 12–14, as they will have acquired the vocabulary and structures necessary to read the selection by this point.

You may present the piece thoroughly as a class activity or you may have some or all students read it on their own. If you present it as a class activity, you may wish to vary presentation procedures from section to section. Some options are:

- Students read silently.
- Students read after you in unison.
- Call on individuals to read aloud.
- When dialogue appears in the story, call on students to take parts.

With any of the above procedures, intersperse some comprehension questions. Call on a student or students to give a brief synopsis of a section in Spanish.

Note: The following teaching suggestions are for a thorough presentation of *El Quijote.*

Teaching Vocabulary

¡OJO! Students merely need to be familiar with the vocabulary to help them understand the story. This vocabulary does not have to be a part of their active, productive vocabulary. All high-frequency words will be reintroduced in **¡Buen viaje! Levels 2** and **3** as new vocabulary.

Step 1 Have students open their books to page 484. Have them repeat the new vocabulary words after you.

El Quijote Miguel de Cervantes Saavedra

Vocabulario

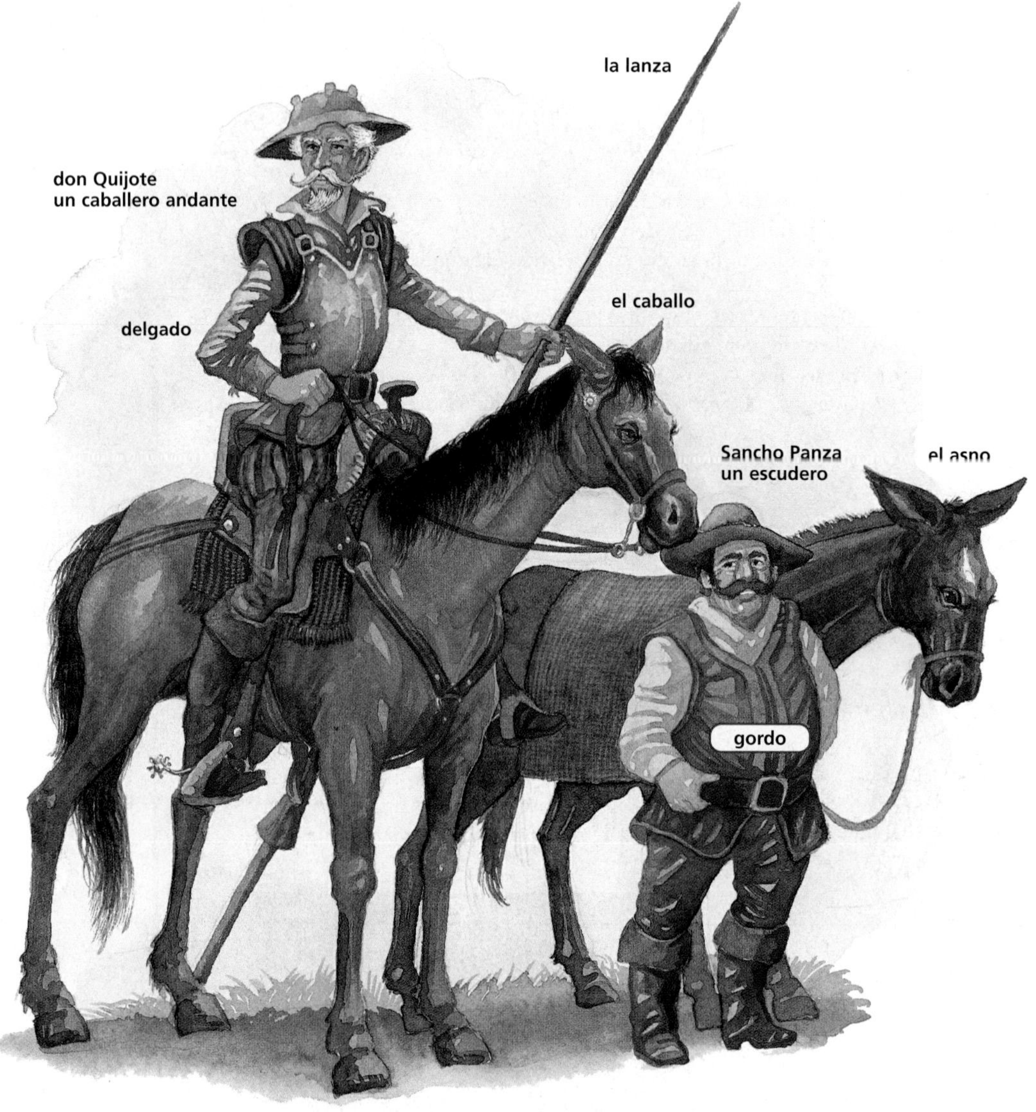

un(a) vecino(a) una persona que vive cerca, en la misma calle, por ejemplo
sabio(a) inteligente, astuto(a)
espantoso horrible, terrible
a toda prisa muy rápido
de nuevo otra vez
socorrer ayudar, dar auxilio o ayuda
no les hizo caso no les prestó atención

Actividades

A **Don Quijote y Sancho Panza** Contesten.

1. ¿Es don Quijote delgado o gordo?
2. ¿Quién es gordo?
3. ¿Quién es un caballero andante?
4. ¿Quién es su escudero?
5. ¿Quién tiene una lanza?
6. ¿Quién tiene un caballo?
7. Y Sancho Panza, ¿qué tiene él?
8. ¿Tiene aspas un molino de viento?

B **¿Cómo son?** Describan a don Quijote y a Sancho Panza.

C **¿Cómo se dice?** Expresen de otra manera.

1. Ellos viven en *una región rural.*
2. Fue una aventura *horrible.*
3. Él salió *rápido.*
4. No le *prestó atención* a su vecino.
5. Él es un señor *inteligente y astuto.*
6. Él lo hizo *otra vez.*
7. Trató pero no pudo *ayudar* a su vecino.

Step 2 Quickly go over the activities on page 485 orally to ascertain that the students can recognize the vocabulary for receptive purposes.

Actividades

B **Expansion:** If any of your students are artistic, ask them to draw a picture of don Quijote and/or Sancho Panza. Have them describe their picture either orally or in written form.

FUN-FACTS

It is claimed that after the Bible, **El Quijote** is the most widely read book in the world.

Reaching All Students

Cooperative Learning
Una representación You may have students work in groups and prepare a play entitled **Don Quijote y los molinos de viento.** This windmill episode lends itself to some very funny skits. Students can present their play to the entire class, other Spanish classes, or to the Spanish Club.

Answers to Actividad

A

1. Don Quijote es delgado.
2. Sancho Panza es gordo.
3. Don Quijote es un caballero andante.
4. Sancho Panza es su escudero.
5. Don Quijote tiene una lanza.
6. Don Quijote tiene un caballo.
7. Sancho Panza tiene un asno.
8. Sí, un molino de viento tiene aspas.

B *Answers will vary, but may include:*

Don Quijote es alto y delgado.
Sancho Panza es bajo y gordo.

C

1. el campo
2. espantoso
3. a toda prisa
4. hizo caso
5. sabio
6. de nuevo
7. socorrer

Literatura 4

Discussing Literature

Introducción

You may go over the **Introducción** with the class or you may decide to omit it and just have them read the story.

El Quijote

Step 1 Tell students that this reading is an excerpt from the novel written in the early 1600s. The novel was written as a parody to poke fun at the idealistic adventure novels of the time.

Step 2 You may wish to have students take a few minutes to read each section silently before going over it orally in class.

Step 3 Since this reading is rather long you may wish to go over only certain sections orally and just have students read the others silently.

Step 4 Call on a more able student to give a synopsis of each section. This helps less able students understand the selection.

Step 5 Here are some additional hints to help you teach the various sections of the reading:

Section 1 Ask students what **la categoría de don Quijote** might refer to. Give students the opportunity to make comparisons between don Quijote's lifestyle and present-day idealists.

Section 2

A. Have students discuss the difference between idealistic and realistic points of view.

B. Tell students that **Vuestra Merced** is a form of address to show respect for someone in a position of power or authority.

INTRODUCCIÓN La obra más famosa de todas las letras hispanas es la novela *El ingenioso hidalgo don Quijote de la Mancha* de Miguel de Cervantes Saavedra.

Los dos personajes principales de la novela son don Quijote y Sancho Panza. Don Quijote, un hombre alto y delgado, es un caballero andante. Es un idealista que quiere conquistar todos los males[1] del mundo. Su escudero, Sancho Panza, es un hombre bajo y gordo. Él es un realista puro. Siempre trata de desviar[2] a don Quijote de sus ilusiones y aventuras.

[1]males *evils*

[2]trata de desviar *tries to dissuade*

El Quijote

1

Un día, don Quijote salió de su pueblo en la región de la Mancha. Un idealista sin par°, don Quijote salió en busca de aventuras para conquistar los males del mundo. Es el trabajo de un verdadero caballero andante. Pero después de unos pocos días, don Quijote volvió a casa porque hizo su primera expedición sin escudero. No hay caballero andante sin escudero—sobre todo un caballero andante de la categoría de don Quijote.

Cuando volvió a su pueblo, empezó a buscar un escudero. Por fin encontró a un vecino, Sancho Panza, un hombre bajo y gordo. Salió por segunda vez, esta vez acompañado de su escudero. Don Quijote montó a su caballo, Rocinante, y Sancho lo siguió° montado en su asno.

sin par *without equal*

siguió *followed*

2

Los dos hicieron muchas expediciones por la región de la Mancha. El idealista don Quijote hizo muchas cosas que no quiso hacer el realista Sancho Panza. Más de una vez Sancho le dijo: —Pero, don Quijote, noble caballero y fiel compañero. Vuestra Merced° está loco. ¿Por qué no dejamos° con estas tonterías°? ¿Por qué no volvemos a casa? Yo quiero comer. Y quiero dormir en mi cama.

Don Quijote no les hizo mucho caso a los consejos° de Sancho. Uno de los episodios más famosos de nuestro estimado caballero es el episodio de los molinos de viento.

Vuestra Merced *Your Highness*

no dejamos con *put an end to*

tonterías *foolish things*

consejos *advice*

3

Del buen suceso que el valeroso don Quijote tuvo en la espantable y jamás imaginada aventura de los molinos de viento.

En esto descubrieron treinta o cuarenta molinos de viento que hay en aquel campo; y así como° don Quijote los vio, dijo a su escudero: —¡Sancho! ¡Mira! ¿Tú ves lo que veo yo?

—No, Vuestra Merced. No veo nada.

—Amigo Sancho, ¿no ves allí unos treinta o más gigantes que vienen hacia nosotros a hacer batalla?

—¿Qué gigantes?

—Aquellos que allí ves, de los brazos largos.

—Don Quijote. No son gigantes. Son simples molinos de viento. Y lo que en ellos parecen° brazos son aspas.

—Bien parece, Sancho, que tú no sabes nada de aventuras. Ellos son gigantes. Y si tienes miedo…

—¡Don Quijote! ¿Adónde va Vuestra Merced?

así como *as soon as*

parecen *appear to be*

Molinos de viento, La Mancha, España

Section 3 Ask students what they think the symbolism is behind don Quijote seeing the **molinos de viento** as **gigantes que vienen a hacer batalla.**

Literatura 4

Section 4

As you present this reading there are many opportunities to use gestures to assist students with comprehension. Some examples are:

- **Don Quijote los atacó.** (Attack two chairs.)
- **Puso su lanza en el aspa.** (Put a long ruler or pointer through the space in the back of a chair.)
- **Vino un viento fuerte.** (Make a howling sound.)
- **El viento movió el aspa.** (Move your hand in a circular motion.)

Reaching All Students

For the Younger Students

Some students may enjoy drawing don Quijote attacking the windmills. Using their drawing, they can describe the episode in their own words, either orally or in writing.

Class Motivator

¡Vamos a cantar! After reading this passage, you may wish to play some songs from the show *Man of La Mancha.*

4

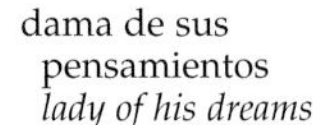

¿Adónde fue don Quijote? Él fue a hacer batalla con los terribles gigantes. Gigantes como éstos no deben ni pueden existir en el mundo. En nombre de Dulcinea, la dama de sus pensamientos°, don Quijote los atacó. Puso su lanza en el aspa de uno de los molinos. En el mismo instante vino un viento fuerte. El viento movió el aspa. El viento la revolvió con tanta furia que hizo pedazos° de la lanza de don Quijote y levantó a don Quijote en el aire.

A toda prisa el pobre Sancho fue a socorrer a su caballero andante. Lo encontró° en el suelo muy mal herido°.

—Don Quijote, no le dije a Vuestra Merced que no vio gigantes. Vio simples molinos de viento. No puedo comprender por qué los atacó.

—Sancho, tú no sabes lo que dices. Son cosas de guerra° que tú no comprendes. Tú sabes que tengo un enemigo. Mi enemigo es el horrible pero sabio monstruo Frestón. Te dije las cosas malas que él hace. Y ahora convirtió a los gigantes en molinos de viento.

—Yo no sé lo que hizo vuestro enemigo, Frestón. Pero yo sé lo que le hizo el molino de viento.

Sancho levantó a don Quijote del suelo. Don Quijote subió de nuevo sobre Rocinante. Habló más de la pasada aventura pero Sancho no le hizo caso. Siguieron el camino hacia Puerto Lápice en busca de otras jamás imaginadas aventuras.

dama de sus pensamientos *lady of his dreams*

pedazos *pieces*

encontró *found*

herido *wounded*

guerra *war*

Plaza de España, Madrid

¿Comprendes?

A Don Quijote y Sancho Panza Escojan.

1. Don Quijote es ____.
   - **a.** un realista
   - **b.** un idealista
   - **c.** un escudero
2. Don Quijote salió de su pueblo ____.
   - **a.** en busca de la Mancha
   - **b.** en busca de un escudero
   - **c.** en busca de aventuras
3. Don Quijote volvió a casa para ____.
   - **a.** comenzar su primera expedición
   - **b.** buscar un escudero
   - **c.** ver a Dulcinea
4. Sancho Panza es ____.
   - **a.** un caballero andante también
   - **b.** un idealista sin par
   - **c.** un vecino de don Quijote
5. Sancho Panza tiene ____.
   - **a.** un asno
   - **b.** un caballo
   - **c.** una lanza

B ¿Sí o no? Digan que sí o que no.

1. Don Quijote y Sancho Panza hicieron sólo dos expediciones.
2. Sancho le dice a don Quijote que está loco.
3. Don Quijote siempre quiere volver a casa.
4. Un episodio famoso del *Quijote* es el episodio de los molinos de viento.

C Los molinos de viento Completen.

1. Don Quijote ve unos treinta o cuarenta ____.
2. Sancho no ve ____.
3. Según don Quijote, los ____ quieren hacer ____.
4. Según don Quijote, los ____ que ve tienen ____ largos.
5. Según Sancho, no son gigantes. Don Quijote ve unos ____ y no tienen brazos. Tienen ____.

D La batalla Contesten.

1. ¿Contra quiénes fue don Quijote a hacer batalla?
2. ¿En dónde puso su lanza?
3. ¿Qué hizo mover al aspa?
4. ¿Revolvió rápidamente el aspa?
5. ¿Adónde levantó a don Quijote?
6. ¿Dónde encontró Sancho a don Quijote?
7. ¿Quién convirtió a los gigantes en molinos de viento?
8. Cuando Sancho levantó a don Quijote del suelo, ¿volvieron a casa?
9. Después de este episodio, ¿admite don Quijote que los gigantes son molinos de viento?

¿Comprendes?

Note: Each of the four **¿Comprendes?** activities corresponds to a different section of the reading. Activity A corresponds to Section 1, B to Section 2, C to Section 3, and D to Section 4. As you finish each section of the story you can go over the corresponding activity.

Answers to ¿Comprendes?

A

1. b
2. c
3. b
4. c
5. a

B

1. No
2. Sí
3. No
4. Sí

C

1. gigantes
2. nada
3. gigantes, batalla
4. gigantes, brazos
5. molinos de viento, aspas

D

1. Don Quijote fue a hacer batalla con los terribles gigantes.
2. Puso su lanza en el aspa de uno de los molinos.
3. Un viento fuerte hizo mover al aspa.
4. Sí, el aspa revolvió rápidamente.
5. Levantó a don Quijote en el aire.
6. Sancho encontró a don Quijote en el suelo.
7. El sabio monstruo Frestón convirtió a los gigantes en molinos de viento.
8. No, no volvieron a casa.
9. No, don Quijote no admite que los gigantes son molinos de viento.

Video Companion

Using video in the classroom

The use of video in the classroom can be a wonderful asset to the World Languages teacher and a most beneficial learning tool for the language student. Video enables students to experience whatever it is they are learning in their textbook in a real-life setting. With each lesson, they are able to take a vicarious field trip. They see people interacting at home, at school, at the market, etc., in an authentic milieu. Students sitting in a classroom can see real people going about their real life in real places. They may experience the target culture in many countries. The cultural benefits are limitless.

Developing listening and viewing skills

In addition to its tremendous cultural value, video, when properly used, gives students much needed practice in developing good listening and viewing skills. Video allows students to look for numerous clues that are evident in a tone of voice, facial expressions, and gestures. Through video students can see and hear the diversity of the target culture and, as discerning viewers and listeners, compare and contrast the Spanish-speaking cultures to each other and to their own culture. Video introduces a dimension into classroom instruction that no other medium—teachers, overhead, text, audio CDs—can provide.

Reinforcing learned language

Video that is properly developed for classroom use has speakers reincorporate the language students have learned in a given lesson. In keeping with reality, however, speakers introduce some new words, expressions, and structures because students functioning in a real-life situation would not know every word native speakers use with them in a live conversation. The lively and interactive nature of video allows students to use their listening and viewing skills to comprehend new language in addition to seeing and hearing the language they have learned come to life.

Getting the most out of video

The intrinsic benefit of video is often lost when students are allowed to read the scripted material before viewing. In many cases, students will have come to understand language used by the speakers in the video by means of reading comprehension, thus negating the inherent benefits of video as a tool to develop listening and viewing skills. Because today's students are so accustomed to the medium of video as a tool for entertainment and learning, a well-written and well-produced video program will help them develop real-life language skills and confidence in those skills in an enjoyable way.

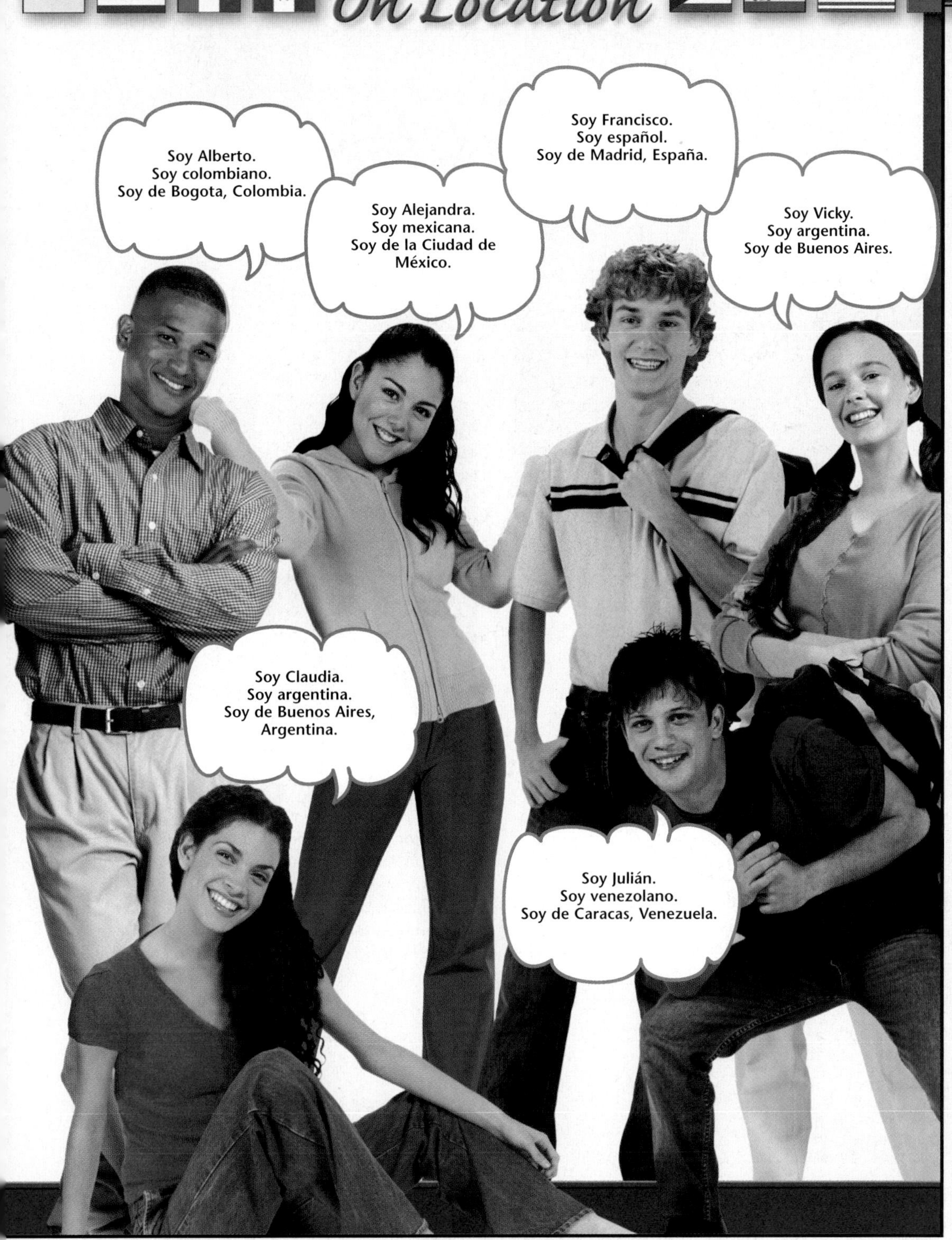
Soy Alberto.
Soy colombiano.
Soy de Bogota, Colombia.
Soy Alejandra.
Soy mexicana.
Soy de la Ciudad de México.
Soy Francisco.
Soy español.
Soy de Madrid, España.
Soy Vicky.
Soy argentina.
Soy de Buenos Aires.
Soy Claudia.
Soy argentina.
Soy de Buenos Aires, Argentina.
Soy Julián.
Soy venezolano.
Soy de Caracas, Venezuela.

Video Synopsis

In this first episode, we meet the six main characters of the video series as they run into each other in downtown Buenos Aires, Argentina. We learn that Alberto is from Colombia, Alejandra is from Mexico, Francisco is from Spain, Vicky is from Argentina, Claudia is from Argentina, and Julián is from Venezuela. As they introduce themselves and ask for directions, they discover that they are all students at the same international school. Finally, the bus comes, and they all run to catch it.

VIDEOTUR

¡Viva el mundo hispano!

Episodio 1

Julián y Francisco en Buenos Aires

Alberto y Claudia en El Caminito

Antes de mirar

Make an educated guess!

In the photos you see several of our new Spanish friends—Francisco and Julián and Alberto and Claudia. One of them is from Spain. What clue is there in one of the photos to let you know that he or she is from there?

Después de mirar

Expansión In the video you have just taken a tour of Argentina, Mexico, and Spain. What similarities did you notice among the three countries? What differences did you see? Choose a place in one of the countries that you would like to visit. Do some research to find out more about that place. Why do you find it interesting?

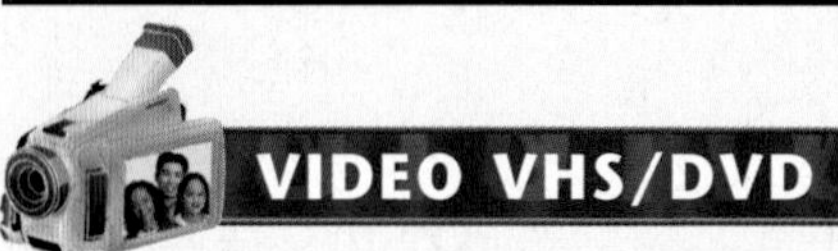

The two photos above show highlights from the Chapter 1 video episode. Discuss the photos with your students before viewing the episode.

VIDEOTUR

¡Viva el mundo hispano!

Episodio 2

Alberto y Claudia en la escuela

Alberto en la clase
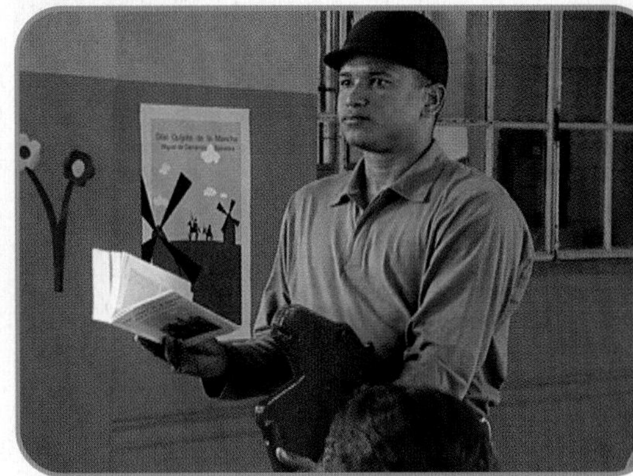

Antes de mirar

Can you spot the following?

1. un muchacho
2. una alumna
3. una clase
4. un libro
5. una escuela

Después de mirar

Expansión *El Quijote* by Miguel de Cervantes de Saavedra is one of the most famous novels of all times. Do some research to find out about this author. When did he live? What jobs did he have? Did anything unusual happen to him during his lifetime? You may also want to research more about the story of don Quijote. It has been retold in other forms. Can you find out what musical was based on the story of don Quijote? Are you familiar with any of the music from this musical? What is one of the important themes of this story?

VIDEOTUR

Video Synopsis

This episode begins with Claudia and Alberto running into each other in the school hallway. Claudia teases Alberto that his clothing is inappropriate for school: he is wearing horseback riding breeches, boots, a polo shirt, and a riding hat. In the next scene, Claudia and Alberto are in class and the teacher—who is very theatrical—decides to have Alberto read the part of don Quijote. Although he is embarrassed and hesitant at first, Alberto gets into the part and does a very dramatic interpretation.

VIDEO VHS/DVD

The two photos above show highlights from the Chapter 2 video episode. Discuss the photos with your students before viewing the episode.

VIDEOTUR

Video Synopsis

This episode begins with Julián trying to get the attention of an attractive salesclerk in an outdoor market. Vicky arrives and drags Julián off to look at clothing. She tells him that he needs an updated look. Julián then tries on a series of increasingly silly outfits which Vicky insists will make him look "cool." Finally, Julián sneaks off to put back on his own clothes and then teases Vicky about changing her clothing choices.

VIDEOTUR

¡Viva el mundo hispano!

Episodio 3

El mercado al aire libre

Julián con un "look" nuevo

Antes de mirar

Make an educated guess!

1. What do you think would be sold in the market you see in the first photograph?
2. In the second photograph, does Julián look as though he is having a good time?
3. What do you think Vicky might be saying to Julián?

Después de mirar

Expansión After you view the video about weavers in Peru, do some research on some of the patterns the weavers use. Choose a pattern and duplicate it either by drawing it or creating it from colored construction paper.

VIDEO VHS/DVD

The two photos above show highlights from the Chapter 3 video episode. Discuss the photos with your students before viewing the episode.

VIDEOTUR

¡Viva el mundo hispano!

Episodio 4

La clase de matemáticas

Francisco y Vicky después de las clases

Antes de mirar

Can you see the following? If so, give an adjective to describe each.

1. una pizarra
2. unos alumnos
3. una sala de clase
4. un profesor
5. una mochila

Después de mirar

Expansión When you first met Francisco in the video, you may remember that he was wearing a shirt that said **Danza flamenco Madrid.** Flamenco is one of the traditional forms of music from Spain. Do some research to find more information about flamenco music.

Video Synopsis

This episode begins with an unseen male putting together a series of secret admirer gifts. Next we see Vicky arrive late to math class, where Francisco is waiting for her to notice a rose on her desk. As Vicky reads the note attached to the rose, she becomes increasingly pleased and confused. After class, with Francisco at her side, Vicky wonders aloud about who her secret admirer might be. Not realizing that the admirer is Francisco, Vicky makes a comment that inadvertantly hurts his feelings.

VIDEO VHS/DVD

The two photos above show highlights from the Chapter 4 video episode. Discuss the photos with your students before viewing the episode.

VIDEOTUR

Video Synopsis

In this episode, we see Julián running through a park, reading a magazine aloud to himself, and drinking a can of juice. He runs past Alejandra, who is seated at a café nearby. Alejandra calls out to Julián to join her. Julián sits down at the table and begins to tell Alejandra how he is going to be healthier. When the waiter takes their order, Julián worries about the purity of the water, chastises Alejandra for ordering cake, and orders the vegetarian meal for himself. When the food arrives, Julián decides that Alejandra's cake looks a lot better than his vegetarian platter and switches their plates when Alejandra isn't looking.

VIDEOTUR

¡Viva el mundo hispano!

Episodio 5

Julián en el parque

Alejandra saluda a Julián

Antes de mirar

Invent the following.

1. el nombre de la revista que Julián lee
2. el nombre del café
3. lo que Alejandra toma
4. lo que Julián toma

Después de mirar

Expansión As you can imagine from what you saw in the video, café life is an important part of Spanish culture. Do you have any cafés near where you live? If you do, do you and your friends go there often? If not, do you think you might enjoy them based on what you viewed in the video?

VIDEO VHS/DVD

The two photos above show highlights from the Chapter 5 video episode. Discuss the photos with your students before viewing the episode.

VIDEOTUR

¡Viva el mundo hispano!

Episodio 6

Francisco y Claudia en la estancia

Dentro de la casa de la tía de Claudia

Antes de mirar

Can you see the following? If so, describe each.

1. una casa
2. unos amigos
3. una madre
4. una fiesta
5. una mochila

Después de mirar

Expansión In the video you visited San Lorenzo de Escorial and saw a festival called **La Romería.** Do some research on the Internet about the monastery at **El Escorial** or about **La Romería.** Write a travel guide for someone who might visit these places.

Video Synopsis

This episode begins with Francisco and Claudia standing outside a very elegant house at an estancia. The house belongs to Claudia's aunt who is throwing a birthday party for her daughter. As Francisco and Claudia help prepare for the party, Claudia's aunt brags continuously about her daughter and Claudia becomes increasingly annoyed. Meanwhile, Francisco starts to become interested in Claudia's cousin. When the party begins and Claudia's cousin arrives, we learn that she is a very spoiled little girl.

VIDEO VHS/DVD

The two photos above show highlights from the Chapter 6 video episode. Discuss the photos with your students before viewing the episode.

VIDEOTUR

Video Synopsis

In the first scene of this episode, we see Julián reading an announcement for a team tryout. When the next scene begins, Julián is wearing a soccer uniform and practicing with a soccer ball. Alberto arrives wearing a diffent uniform because the tryouts are in fact for a **pato** team. Julián explains that he doesn't know how to ride a horse and Alberto tries to teach him some basic skills. At the very moment that Julián expresses concern that he won't make the team, the famous **pato** player, Javier Montes, arrives. He encourages both Julián and Alberto to try out for the **pato** team and he invites them to a professional game that evening.

VIDEOTUR

¡Viva el mundo hispano!

Episodio 7

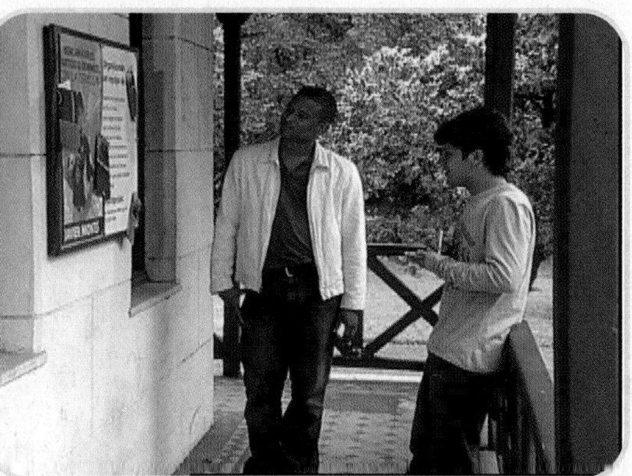

Alberto y Julián afuera de la escuela

Alberto habla con Julián.

Antes de mirar

Answer the questions.

1. ¿Dónde están los amigos?
2. ¿Quién lee?
3. ¿Quién escribe?

Después de mirar

Expansión In the video you hear about a game called **pato.** From what you learned does it remind you of any other sport you are familiar with? Do some research on the Internet to find out the countries it is played in, what the rules of the game are, and who some of its most famous players are. Discuss with a friend the skills you need to participate and whether or not you think this is a sport you would enjoy.

The two photos above show highlights from the Chapter 7 video episode. Discuss the photos with your students before viewing the episode.

VIDEOTUR

¡Viva el mundo hispano!

Episodio 8

Vicky llama al «médico».

Alberto tiene una condición muy grave.

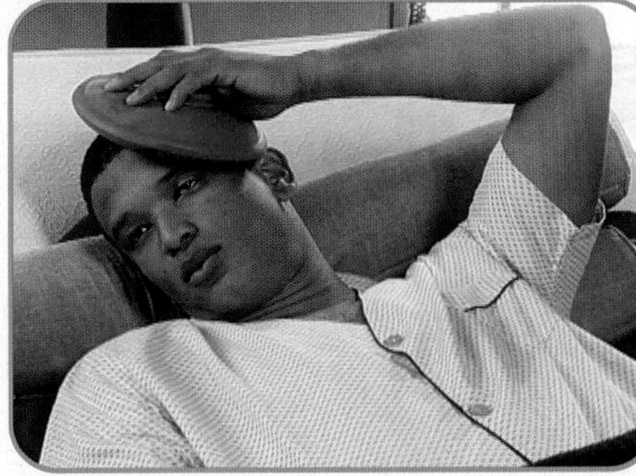

Antes de mirar

Answer the questions.

1. ¿Dónde está Alberto?
2. ¿Cómo está Alberto?
3. ¿Quién llega para ayudar?
4. ¿Qué le duele a Alberto?
5. ¿Qué piensas? ¿Está muy enfermo Alberto o no?

Después de mirar

Expansión In the video you travel to the rainforest in Costa Rica. Do some research on Costa Rica to find out more about the jungle and the conservation of the rainforest there. Why do you think Costa Rica is so important for scientists and conservationists like Luis Poveda?

VIDEOTUR

Video Synopsis

When this episode begins, Alberto is lying on a couch and is ill. Vicky arrives and tells Alberto to hurry because the movie they have planned to see is about to start. Alberto tells Vicky that he is too sick to go. Vicky suspects that Alberto isn't as sick as he appears, so she enlists the help of a friend to play the part of a doctor. When Vicky's friend arrives, he confirms Alberto's worst fears by telling him that his condition is very grave. The "doctor" then suggests a very strange, unpleasant remedy for Alberto's illness and suddenly, Alberto undergoes a miraculous recovery.

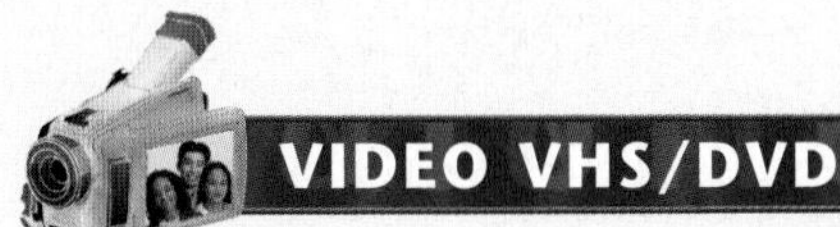

VIDEO VHS/DVD

The two photos above show highlights from the Chapter 8 video episode. Discuss the photos with your students before viewing the episode.

VIDEOTUR

Video Synopsis

In this episode we see Alberto and Claudia walking past a shop window. They enter and Claudia is very excited as she begins to try on ski clothing. Claudia asks Alberto if he skis and Alberto, not wanting to admit that he hasn't, begins an outrageous story about all his ski escapades and the fancy equipment he owns. Just as a crowd gathers to hear all that Alberto has to say about his expertise, Claudia exposes Alberto's lie.

VIDEOTUR

¡Viva el mundo hispano!

Episodio 9

Alberto y Claudia van de compras.

Ellos miran el escaparate de la tienda.

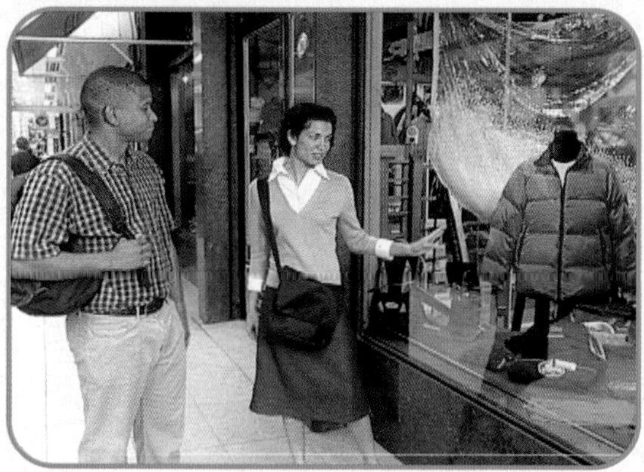

Antes de mirar

Answer the questions.

1. ¿Dónde están Alberto y Claudia?
2. ¿Qué tipo de tienda es?
3. ¿Qué hay en el escaparate?
4. ¿Es ropa para el invierno y para el verano?
5. ¿Para qué pueden usar este tipo de ropa?

Después de mirar

Expansión You are going on a short vacation. Do some research on the Internet to find out more about beaches to visit in Puerto Rico. Choose a beach you like. Discuss how you will get there and what you will do there. Tell what you might eat on this vacation to Puerto Rico.

VIDEO VHS/DVD

The two photos above show highlights from the Chapter 9 video episode. Discuss the photos with your students before viewing the episode.

Videotur

¡Viva el mundo hispano!

Episodio 10

Alejandra y Vicky en la Plaza de San Telmo

Vicky y Alejandra hablan mientras escuchan una orquesta típica.

Antes de mirar

Can you spot the following?

1. un artista
2. una orquesta
3. unas pinturas
4. un museo

Después de mirar

Expansión In the video you see a very colorful event known as the **charreada.** Carmen mentions in the video that **Un charro no se hace. Un charro se nace.** What do you think this means? Why do you think she says this? Do some research on the Internet to find out more about this very popular cultural event in Mexico.

Videotur

Video Synopsis

This episode shows Alejandra and Vicky in a crowded plaza. They are making a short video segment for a school project. As they start to film various musicians, artists, and street performers, they get into a discussion about what constitutes art and culture. Alejandra has more traditional tastes, while Vicky has a more contemporary point of view. As they continue walking through the plaza, filming all the activities, Vicky asks Alejandra a series of questions which she hopes will challenge her friend's more conservative ideas.

The two photos above show highlights from the Chapter 10 video episode. Discuss the photos with your students before viewing the episode.

VIDEOTUR

Video Synopsis

In this episode, Julián proudly tells Francisco that for his vacation to Caracas, he's just bought a cheap airline ticket from a discount Web site. Francisco warns Julián that things that seem too good to be true, usually are. The next scene begins a long dream sequence in which everything that could go wrong with Julián's trip, does. When Julián awakes from his dream, he realizes that Francisco is probably right and he immediately makes a phone call to cancel his tickets.

VIDEOTUR

¡Viva el mundo hispano!

Episodio 11

Julián y Francisco hablan de algo importante.

Francisco y Julián llegan al aeropuerto.

Antes de mirar

Let's invent!

Make up a conversation that Julián and Francisco might be having. Take clues from the photographs to finish the dialogue.

Julián: Francisco, voy de vacación.

Francisco: ¿Ah, sí? ¿Adónde vas?

Después de mirar

Expansión In the video you see a form of art that is famous in Venezuela. Do some research on the Internet to find other forms of art that are typical of Venezuela. **El arte murano** originated in Italy. What are the origins of the other art forms you found out about?

VIDEO VHS/DVD

The two photos above show highlights from the Chapter 11 video episode. Discuss the photos with your students before viewing the episode.

VIDEOTUR

¡Viva el mundo hispano!

Episodio 12

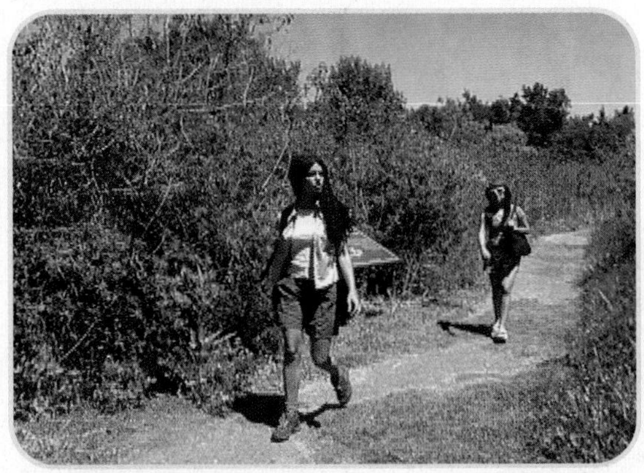
Claudia y Alejandra en camino

Alejandra y Claudia descansan un poco.

Antes de mirar

Let's invent!

1. ¿Dónde están las amigas?
2. ¿Qué llevan?
3. ¿Qué tiempo hace?
4. ¿A quién llama Alejandra?
5. ¿Se divierten Alejandra y Claudia?

Después de mirar

Expansión In the video you see the Inca trail. Do some research on the Internet to find out more about the Incas. We already know that they built the beautiful **pueblo** of Macchu Picchu. What else did they build or invent?

VIDEOTUR

Video Synopsis

In this episode, Claudia and Alejandra are going on a 10 kilometer hike. Claudia makes it clear that she wants to complete the hike to prove to the boys that girls can do anything they set their minds to. Alejandra seems more interested in the cute boys they run into while beginning their hike. After walking only 3 kilometers, the girls see two hikers with food and realize that they are both hungry and tired. Alejandra uses her cell phone to order a picnic lunch, which is subsequently delivered to them in the park.

VIDEO VHS/DVD

The two photos above show highlights from the Chapter 12 video episode. Discuss the photos with your students before viewing the episode.

VIDEOTUR

Video Synopsis

This episode begins with Francisco reading a book while waiting at a train station quai. Meanwhile, Claudia is at a kiosk buying chocolates made to look like gold coins. When Claudia approaches Francisco on the bench, he barely notices her and she takes his book to see why he is so engrossed. As she begins reading where Francisco left off, we see the enactment of the story about a mysterious, very elegant, international female spy. When the enactment of the spy story ends, Francisco wonders aloud about what the female spy had in her briefcase and as a joke, Claudia gives him her chocolate coins.

VIDEOTUR

¡Viva el mundo hispano!

Episodio 13

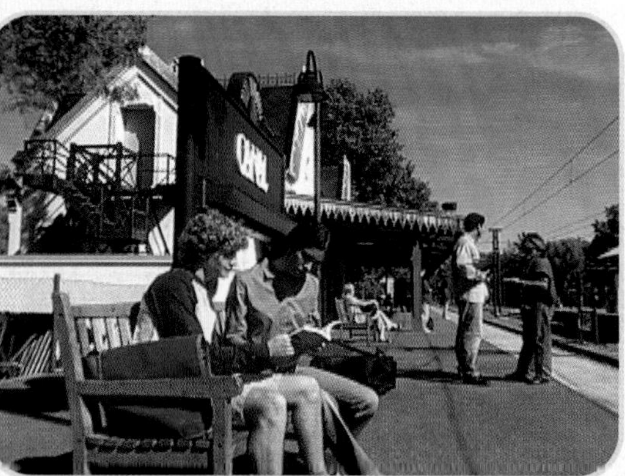

Francisco y Claudia leen un libro.

«Una mujer misteriosa» en la estación de ferrocarril

Antes de mirar

Let's invent!

1. ¿Dónde están Francisco y Claudia?
2. ¿Qué tipo de libro leen?
3. ¿Hacen un viaje?
4. ¿Adónde van?
5. ¿Quién es el otro señor con «la mujer misteriosa»?

Después de mirar

Expansión As you can see from the video, train travel is very popular in some Spanish-speaking countries. Do you think it is as popular where you live? What is your favorite means of transportation for long trips? Why? Survey your friends to find out their preferred means of travel. Share your results with the class.

VIDEO VHS/DVD

The two photos above show highlights from the Chapter 13 video episode. Discuss the photos with your students before viewing the episode.

VIDEOTUR

¡Viva el mundo hispano!

Episodio 14

Alberto en el restaurante de su tío

Vicky y Alberto con cara de sorpresa
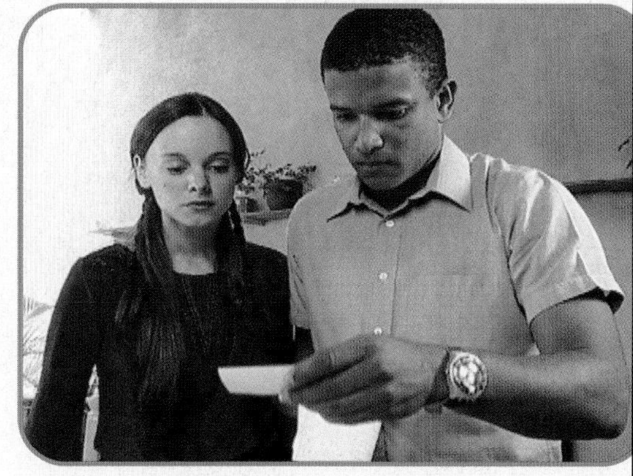

Antes de mirar

Can you spot the following?

1. un camarero
2. un cliente
3. las papas
4. una propina
5. un vaso de agua

Después de mirar

Expansión Are there many Hispanic restaurants in your community? Are they representative of a variety of different Spanish-speaking countries? Which ones are they? Do you have a favorite? Look at the menus of the different restaurants in your community or do research on the Internet to find some menus of Hispanic restaurants in this country. Are the foods very different? If any of the Hispanic restaurants in your community are run by a family, speak with one of the family members about the history of their business. Try to do this in Spanish if possible.

VIDEOTUR

Video Synopsis

As this episode begins, we see Alberto working in a restaurant kitchen. Vicky arrives and reminds him that they are supposed to study together. Alberto explains that his uncle has had to leave the restaurant and left him in charge. Just at that moment, an important food critic calls to arrange a visit to the restaurant. Alberto panics but Vicky assures him that they can handle the situation. When two people simultaneously arrive at the resaurant, Alberto and Vicky make an incorrect assumption about which person is the critic. As a result, they offend the critic and only discover their mistake once the critic has left the restaurant.

VIDEO VHS/DVD

The two photos above show highlights from the Chapter 14 video episode. Discuss the photos with your students before viewing the episode.

Handbook

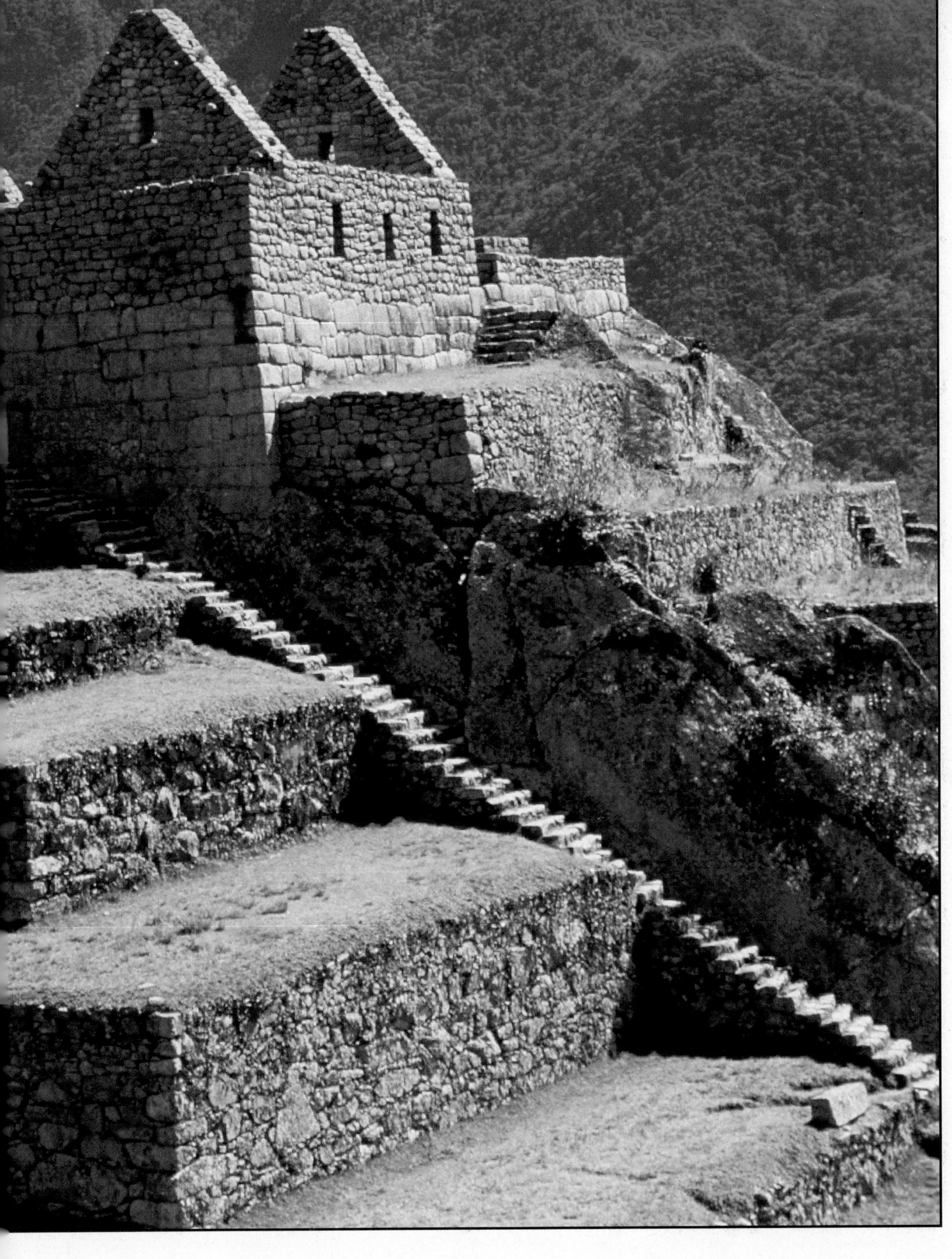

InfoGap

Activity 1

CAPÍTULO 1, Palabras 1, pages 14–15

Alumno A Ask your partner the following questions. Correct answers are in parentheses.

1. ¿Cómo es Antonio, rubio o moreno? *(Antonio es moreno.)*
2. ¿Cómo es Fernando, gracioso o serio? *(Fernando es gracioso.)*
3. ¿Cómo es María, alta o baja? *(María es baja.)*
4. ¿Cómo es Ricardo, ambicioso o perezoso? *(Ricardo es perezoso.)*
5. ¿Cómo es Elena, cómica o seria? *(Elena es seria.)*
6. ¿Cómo es Ana, alta o baja? *(Ana es alta.)*

Alumno A Now answer your partner's questions based on the pictures below.

Alberto

Isabel

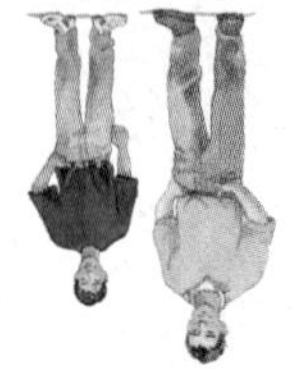

Alejandro / Eduardo

Sara

Cristina

Alumno B Answer your partner's questions based on the pictures below.

Ana / María

Ricardo

Elena

Fernando

Antonio

Alumno B Ask your partner the following questions. Correct answers are in parentheses.

1. ¿Cómo es Alejandro, alto o bajo? *(Alejandro es alto.)*
2. ¿Cómo es Isabel, ambiciosa o perezosa? *(Isabel es perezosa.)*
3. ¿Cómo es Sara, graciosa o seria? *(Sara es graciosa.)*
4. ¿Cómo es Cristina, rubia o morena? *(Cristina es rubia.)*
5. ¿Cómo es Eduardo, alto o bajo? *(Eduardo es bajo.)*
6. ¿Cómo es Alberto, ambicioso o perezoso? *(Alberto es ambicioso.)*

Activity 2

CAPÍTULO 2, Estructura, pages 58–59

Alumno A Ask your partner **¿Qué hora es?** Correct answers are in parentheses.

1. ¿Qué hora es? *(Son las dos.)*
2. ¿Qué hora es? *(Son las tres y cinco.)*
3. ¿Qué hora es? *(Son las cuatro y veinticinco.)*
4. ¿Qué hora es? *(Son las cinco menos veinte.)*
5. ¿Qué hora es? *(Son las seis y media.)*
6. ¿Qué hora es? *(Es la una.)*
7. ¿Qué hora es? *(Son las siete menos cuarto.)*
8. ¿Qué hora es? *(Es la una y diez.)*

Alumno A Answer your partner's questions based on the pictures below.

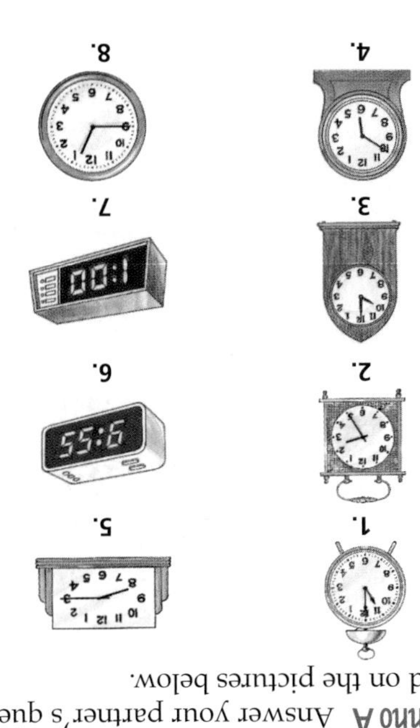

Alumno B Answer your partner's questions based on the pictures below.

1.

2.

3.

4.

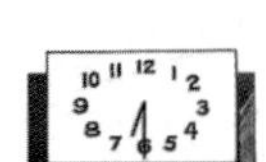

5.

6.

7.

8.

Alumno B Ask your partner **¿Qué hora es?** Correct answers are in parentheses.

1. ¿Qué hora es? *(Son las once.)*
2. ¿Qué hora es? *(Son las dos y veinticinco.)*
3. ¿Qué hora es? *(Son las diez.)*
4. ¿Qué hora es? *(Son las seis menos diez.)*
5. ¿Qué hora es? *(Son las ocho y cuarto.)*
6. ¿Qué hora es? *(Son las diez menos cinco.)*
7. ¿Qué hora es? *(Es la una.)*
8. ¿Qué hora es? *(Es la una menos cuarto.)*

InfoGap

Activity 3

CAPÍTULO 3, Palabras 1, 2, Estructura, pages 76–77, 80–81, 84

Alumno A Ask your partner the following questions. Correct answers are in parentheses.

1. ¿Buscas una gorra? *(Sí, busco una gorra.)*
2. ¿Necesitas un disquete? *(No, no necesito un disquete.)*
3. ¿Buscas un bolígrafo? *(No, no busco un bolígrafo.)*
4. ¿Compras una camisa? *(Sí, compro una camisa.)*
5. ¿Llevas un traje? *(No, no llevo un traje.)*
6. ¿Necesitas una mochila? *(Sí, necesito una mochila.)*
7. ¿Compras una falda? *(No, no compro una falda.)*
8. ¿Buscas pantalones? *(Sí, busco pantalones.)*

Alumno A Answer your partner's questions based on the pictures below.

Alumno B Answer your partner's questions based on the pictures below.

Alumno B Ask your partner the following questions. Correct answers are in parentheses.

1. ¿Buscas una falda? *(Sí, busco una falda.)*
2. ¿Necesitas una calculadora? *(Sí, necesito una calculadora.)*
3. ¿Llevas un traje? *(No, no llevo un traje.)*
4. ¿Buscas una mochila? *(No, no busco una mochila.)*
5. ¿Compras un bolígrafo? *(Sí, compro un bolígrafo.)*
6. ¿Buscas un libro? *(No, no busco un libro.)*
7. ¿Necesitas un par de tenis? *(Sí, necesito un par de tenis.)*
8. ¿Compras una camisa? *(No, no compro una camisa.)*

Activity 4

CAPÍTULO 4, Palabras 1, pages 104–105

Alumno A Ask your partner the following questions. Correct answers are in parentheses.

1. ¿Cómo llegan a la escuela Antonio y Ernesto? *(Antonio y Ernesto llegan a pie.)*
2. ¿Cómo llegan a la escuela Alicia y Pepe? *(Alicia y Pepe llegan en el bus escolar.)*
3. ¿Cómo llegan a la escuela José y Sara? *(José y Sara llegan en carro/coche.)*
4. ¿Cómo llegan a la escuela Anita y Paco? *(Anita y Paco llegan a pie.)*
5. ¿Cómo llegan a la escuela Conchita y Beatriz? *(Conchita y Beatriz llegan en carro/coche.)*

Alumno A Answer your partner's questions based on the pictures below.

Lupe
Rodolfo

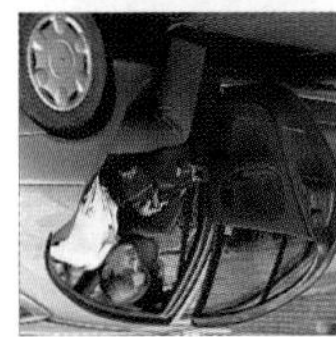

Juan
Elena
Marisol
Vicente

Pedro
Silvia
Ana
Pablo

Alumno B Answer your partner's questions based on the pictures below.

José
Conchita
Sara
Beatriz

Antonio
Anita
Ernesto
Paco

Alicia
Pepe

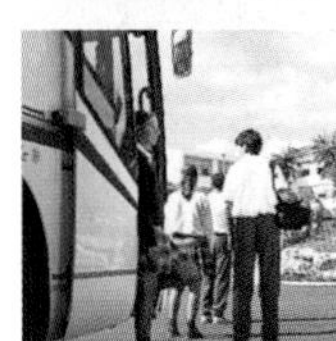

Alumno B Ask your partner the following questions. Correct answers are in parentheses.

1. ¿Cómo llegan a la escuela Lupe y Rodolfo? *(Lupe y Rodolfo llegan en carro/coche.)*
2. ¿Cómo llegan a la escuela Silvia y Pedro? *(Silvia y Pedro llegan en el bus escolar.)*
3. ¿Cómo llegan a la escuela Elena y Marisol? *(Elena y Marisol llegan a pie.)*
4. ¿Cómo llegan a la escuela Ana y Pablo? *(Ana y Pablo llegan en el bus escolar.)*
5. ¿Cómo llegan a la escuela Vicente y Juan? *(Vicente y Juan llegan a pie.)*

Activity 5

CAPÍTULO 5, Palabras 1, 2, Estructura, pages 142–143, 146–147, 150

Alumno A Ask your partner the following questions. Correct answers are in parentheses.

1. ¿Comes pan dulce? *(Sí, como pan dulce.)*
2. ¿Comes pollo? *(No, no como pollo.)*
3. ¿Comes sopa? *(Sí, como sopa.)*
4. ¿Comes pescado? *(No, no como pescado.)*
5. ¿Comes un bocadillo? *(Sí, como un bocadillo.)*
6. ¿Comes mariscos? *(Sí, como mariscos.)*
7. ¿Comes queso? *(No, no como queso.)*
8. ¿Comes jamón? *(Sí, como jamón.)*

Alumno A Answer your partner's questions based on the pictures below.

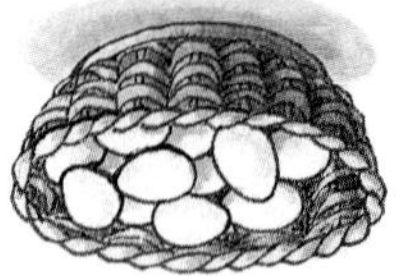

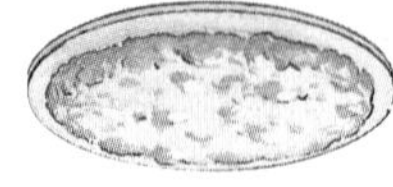

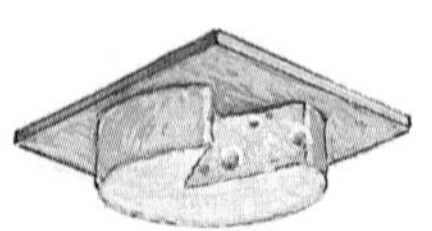

Alumno B Answer your partner's questions based on the pictures below.

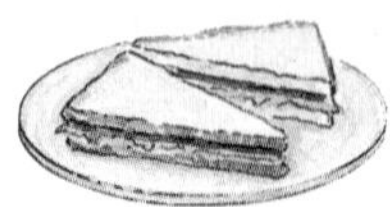

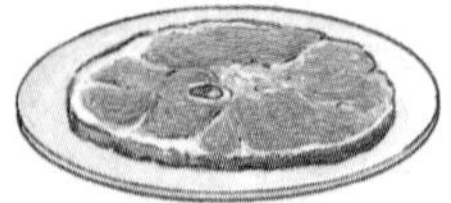

Alumno B Ask your partner the following questions. Correct answers are in parentheses.

1. ¿Comes sopa? *(No, no como sopa.)*
2. ¿Comes pollo? *(Sí, como pollo.)*
3. ¿Comes pescado? *(Sí, como pescado.)*
4. ¿Comes huevos? *(Sí, como huevos.)*
5. ¿Comes un bocadillo? *(No, no como un bocadillo.)*
6. ¿Comes una tortilla? *(Sí, como una tortilla.)*
7. ¿Comes queso? *(Sí, como queso.)*
8. ¿Comes mariscos? *(No, no como mariscos.)*

Activity 6

CAPÍTULO 6, Estructura, page 178

Alumno A Ask your partner the following questions. Correct answers are in parentheses.

1. ¿Cuántos años tiene Armando?
   (Armando tiene catorce años.)
2. ¿Cuántos años tienen Paco y José?
   (Paco y José tienen diecisiete años.)
3. ¿Cuántos años tienes tú?
   (Yo tengo _____ años.)
4. ¿Cuántos años tiene el profesor de ciencias? *(El profesor de ciencias tiene treinta y seis años.)*
5. ¿Cuántos años tienen Susana y Gabriela?
   (Susana y Gabriela tienen veintidós años.)
6. ¿Cuántos años tiene Pepe?
   (Pepe tiene ocho años.)

Alumno A Use the chart below to answer your partner's questions. Reminder: **tú** is you.

Sofía	15 años
Los abuelos	75 años
Pedro y Alicia	16
Tú	?
Teresa	9 años
Juan y Norma	13 años

Alumno B Ask your partner the following questions. Correct answers are in parentheses.

1. ¿Cuántos años tiene Sofía?
   (Sofía tiene quince años.)
2. ¿Cuántos años tienen los abuelos?
   (Los abuelos tienen setenta y cinco años.)
3. ¿Cuántos años tienen Pedro y Alicia?
   (Pedro y Alicia tienen dieciséis años.)
4. ¿Cuántos años tienes tú?
   (Yo tengo _____ años.)
5. ¿Cuántos años tiene Teresa?
   (Teresa tiene nueve años.)
6. ¿Cuántos años tienen Juan y Norma?
   (Juan y Norma tienen trece años.)

Alumno B Use the chart below to answer your partner's questions. Reminder: **tú** is you.

Armando	14 años
Paco y José	17 años
Tú	?
El profesor de ciencias	36 años
Susana y Gabriela	22 años
Pepe	8 años

Activity 7

CAPÍTULO 7, Estructura, pages 210 and 213

Alumno A Ask your partner the following questions. Correct answers are in parentheses.

1. ¿Qué juega Antonio? *(Antonio juega al baloncesto.)*
2. ¿Qué quiere el portero? *(El portero quiere bloquear el balón.)*
3. ¿Qué prefieren Luisa y Carlos? *(Luisa y Carlos prefieren el fútbol.)*
4. ¿Prefieres ser espectador(a) o jugador(a)? *(Yo prefiero ser _____.)*
5. ¿Qué devuelve el cátcher? *(El cátcher devuelve la pelota.)*

Alumno A Use the chart below to answer your partner's questions. Reminder: **tú** is you.

Tomás y Sara	el fútbol
Marco	ser espectador
Los jugadores	marcar muchos tantos
Tú	?
Marta	el béisbol

Alumno B Use the chart below to answer your partner's questions. Reminder: **tú** is you.

Antonio	el baloncesto
El portero	bloquear el balón
Luisa y Carlos	el fútbol
Tú	?
El cátcher	la pelota

Alumno B Ask your partner the following questions. Correct answers are in parentheses.

1. ¿Qué juega Marta? *(Marta juega al béisbol.)*
2. ¿Prefieres ser espectador(a) o jugador(a)? *(Yo prefiero ser _____.)*
3. ¿Qué quieren los jugadores? *(Los jugadores quieren marcar muchos tantos.)*
4. ¿Qué prefiere Marco? *(Marco prefiere ser espectador.)*
5. ¿Qué juegan Tomás y Sara? *(Tomás y Sara juegan al fútbol.)*

Activity 8

CAPÍTULO 8, Palabras 1, Estructura, pages 242–243, 250

Alumno A Ask your partner the following questions. Correct answers are in parentheses.

1. ¿Cómo está Sara, triste o contenta? *(Sara está triste.)*
2. ¿Cómo es Fernando, ambicioso o perezoso? *(Fernando es ambicioso.)*
3. ¿Cómo está Paco, contento o enfermo? *(Paco está enfermo.)*
4. ¿Cómo está Elena, de buen humor o de mal humor? *(Elena está de buen humor.)*
5. ¿Cómo es Isabel, ambiciosa o perezosa? *(Isabel es perezosa.)*

Alumno A Answer your partner's questions based on the pictures below.

Alberto

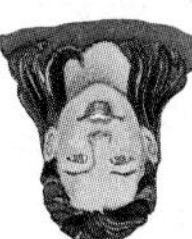
Silvia

Beatriz

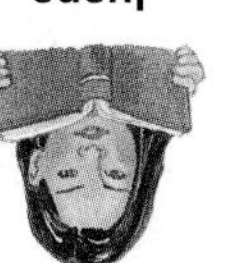
Juana

Ernesto

Alumno B Answer your partner's questions based on the pictures below.

Isabel

Fernando

Elena

Sara

Paco

Alumno B Ask your partner the following questions. Correct answers are in parentheses.

1. ¿Cómo es Silvia, rubia o morena? *(Silvia es morena.)*
2. ¿Cómo está Ernesto, contento o nervioso? *(Ernesto está nervioso.)*
3. ¿Cómo está Beatriz, contenta o cansada? *(Beatriz está cansada.)*
4. ¿Cómo es Alberto, gracioso o serio? *(Alberto es serio.)*
5. ¿Cómo es Juana, ambiciosa o perezosa? *(Juana es ambiciosa.)*

Activity 9

CAPÍTULO 9, Palabras 1, 2, Estructura, pages 274–275, 278–279, 282

Alumno A Ask your partner the following questions. Correct answers are in parentheses.

1. ¿Qué jugaron Roberto y Ernesto? *(Roberto y Ernesto jugaron tenis.)*
2. ¿Jugaron singles o dobles? *(Jugaron singles.)*
3. ¿Quién buceó? *(Juan buceó.)*
4. ¿Quién esquió en el agua? *(Claudia esquió en el agua.)*
5. ¿Nadó Sandra o practicó el surfing? *(Sandra nadó.)*
6. ¿Los jóvenes pasaron el día en la playa o en la estación de esquí? *(Los jóvenes pasaron el día en la playa.)*

Alumno A Answer your partner's questions based on the pictures below.

Susana / Manuel

María / Patricio / Teresa / Armando

Tomás / Alicia

Alumno B Answer your partner's questions based on the pictures below.

Claudia

Juan

Roberto / Ernesto

Sandra

Alumno B Ask your partner the following questions. Correct answers are in parentheses.

1. ¿Patricio y Teresa tomaron el telesilla o compraron boletos? *(Patricio y Teresa tomaron el telesilla.)*
2. ¿Qué compró Susana en la ventanilla? *(Susana compró boletos en la ventanilla.)*
3. ¿Quiénes bajaron la pista? *(Tomás y Alicia bajaron la pista.)*
4. ¿Esquiaron en el agua o en la nieve? *(Esquiaron en la nieve.)*
5. ¿Tomó el telesilla Armando? *(Sí, Armando tomó el telesilla.)*
6. ¿Los jóvenes pasaron el día en la playa o en la estación de esquí? *(Los jóvenes pasaron el día en la estación de esquí.)*

Activity 10

CAPÍTULO 10, Palabras 1, 2, Estructura, pages 306–307, 310–311, 314

Alumno A Ask your partner the following questions. Correct answers are in parentheses.

1. ¿Adónde fueron los turistas? *(Los turistas fueron al museo.)*
2. ¿Qué vieron los turistas? *(Los turistas vieron una exposición de arte.)*
3. ¿Qué miraron los niños? *(Los niños miraron un mural.)*

Alumno A Answer your partner's questions based on the picture below.

Alumno B Answer your partner's questions based on the picture below.

Alumno B Ask your partner the following questions. Correct answers are in parentheses.

1. ¿Adónde fue el joven? *(El joven fue al cine.)*
2. ¿Qué vio el joven? *(El joven vio una película.)*
3. ¿Lleva subtítulos la película? *(No, la película no lleva subtítulos.)*

InfoGap

Activity 11

CAPÍTULO 11, Palabras 1, pages 336–337

Alumno A Ask your partner the following questions about his or her airplane ticket. Correct answers are in parentheses.

1. ¿Cuál es el nombre el la línea aérea? *(Lan Chile)*
2. ¿Cuál es el número del vuelo? *(doscientos)*
3. ¿Cuál es el destino del vuelo? *(Santiago)*
4. ¿Cuál es la fecha del vuelo? *(el veintiocho de julio)*
5. ¿Cuántas maletas tiene el/la pasajero(a)? *(dos)*
6. ¿Cuál es la hora de salida? *(las diez y media)*

Alumno A Answer your partner's questions based on your plane ticket below.

Mexicana			
Vuelo	Destino	Puerta	Clase
4	Guadalajara	8	C
Fecha	Hora de salida	Asiento	
13 abril	06:30	28A	
Maletas	Peso	Nombre del pasajero	
2	18	____________	

Alumno B Answer your partner's questions based on your plane ticket below.

Lan Chile			
Vuelo	Destino	Puerta	Clase
200	Santiago	15	C
Fecha	Hora de salida	Asiento	
28 julio	10:30	48B	
Maletas	Peso	Nombre del pasajero	
2	20	____________	

Alumno B Ask your partner the following questions about his or her airplane ticket. Correct answers are in parentheses.

1. ¿Cuál es el nombre el la línea aérea? *(Mexicana)*
2. ¿Cuál es el número del vuelo? *(cuatro)*
3. ¿De qué puerta sale el vuelo? *(ocho)*
4. ¿Cuál es la fecha del vuelo? *(el trece de abril)*
5. ¿Cuál es el destino del vuelo? *(Guadalajara)*
6. ¿Cuál es la hora de salida? *(las seis y media)*

Activity 12

CAPÍTULO 12, Palabras 1, pages 374–375

Alumno A Ask your partner the following questions. Correct answers are in parentheses.

1. ¿Quién se lava la cara? *(Francisco se lava la cara.)*
2. ¿Se baña un muchacho o una muchacha? *(Una muchacha se baña.)*
3. ¿Quién se despierta? *(Paco se despierta.)*
4. ¿Se afeita un muchacho o una muchacha? *(Un muchacho se afeita.)*
5. ¿Quién se sienta? *(Graciela se sienta.)*

Alumno A Answer your partner's questions based on the pictures below.

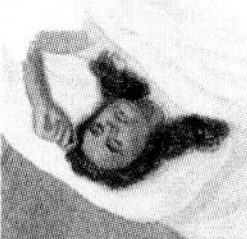

Faviola

Gabriela

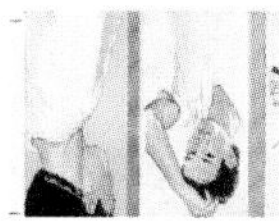

Pepe

Juana

Irene

Alumno B Answer your partner's questions based on the pictures below.

Graciela

Felipe

Paco

Adela

Francisco

Alumno B Ask your partner the following questions. Correct answers are in parentheses.

1. ¿Quién se cepilla los dientes? *(Gabriela se cepilla los dientes.)*
2. ¿Quién se peina? *(Pepe se peina.)*
3. ¿Se duerme un muchacho o una muchacha? *(Una muchacha se duerme.)*
4. ¿Quién se maquilla? *(Irene se maquilla.)*
5. ¿Se pone la ropa un muchacho o una muchacha? *(Una muchacha se pone la ropa.)*

InfoGap

Activity 13

CAPÍTULO 13, Palabras 2, pages 408–409

Alumno A Ask your partner the following questions. Correct answers are in parentheses.

1. ¿Quién es el revisor? *(El señor Martínez es el revisor.)*
2. ¿El revisor está en el coche-cama o en el pasillo? *(El revisor está en el pasillo.)*
3. ¿Están Pablo y Ramona en el coche-comedor o en sus asientos? *(Están en sus asientos.)*
4. ¿Luis y Antonia van a bajar o van a subir? *(Luis y Antonia van a bajar.)*

Alumno A Answer your partner's questions based on the pictures below.

Alberto

Señor Rivas

Susana y Pedro

Alumno B Answer your partner's questions based on the pictures below.

Ramona Pablo Señor Martínez

Luis y Antonia

Alumno B Ask your partner the following questions. Correct answers are in parentheses.

1. ¿Dónde comen Susana y Pedro? *(Susana y Pedro comen en el coche-comedor/ coche-cafetería.)*
2. ¿Alberto sube al tren o baja del tren? *(Alberto baja del tren.)*
3. ¿El señor Rivas compra un billete o transborda? *(El señor Rivas transborda.)*
4. ¿El señor Rivas va a subir al tren o va a la sala de espera? *(El señor Rivas va a subir al tren.)*

Activity 14

CAPÍTULO 14, Palabras 2, Estructura, pages 438–439, 442

Alumno A Ask your partner the following questions. Correct answers are in parentheses.

1. ¿Quién pide el pescado?
   (Juanita pide el pescado.)
2. ¿Qué piden Marta y Teresa?
   (Marta y Teresa piden la langosta.)
3. ¿Quién pide una ensalada?
   (José pide una ensalada.)
4. ¿Qué piden los muchachos?
   (Los muchachos piden pollo.)

Alumno A Answer your partner's questions based on the pictures below.

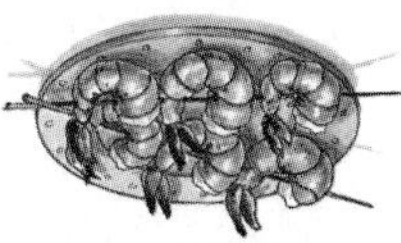
Norma

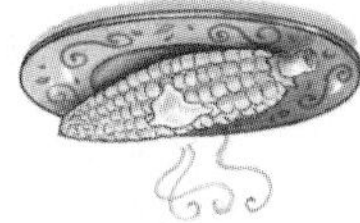
Los turistas

Antonio

Paco y Mercedes

Alumno B Answer your partner's questions based on the pictures below.

Marta y Teresa

José

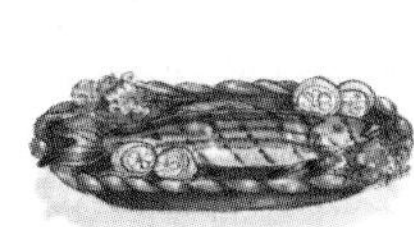
Juanita

Los muchachos

Alumno B Ask your partner the following questions. Correct answers are in parentheses.

1. ¿Quién pide las almejas?
   (Antonio pide las almejas.)
2. ¿Qué piden Paco y Mercedes?
   (Paco y Mercedes piden la carne.)
3. ¿Qué piden los turistas?
   (Los turistas piden el maíz.)
4. ¿Quién pide los camarones?
   (Norma pide los camarones.)

Study Tips

For students and parents/guardians

This guide is designed to help you as students achieve success as you embark on the adventure of learning another language and to enable your parents or guardians to help you in this exciting journey. There are many ways to learn new information. You may find some of these suggestions more useful than others, depending upon which style of learning works best for you. Before you begin, it is important to understand how we acquire language.

Receptive Skills

Each day of your life you receive a great deal of information through the use of language. In order to get this information, it is necessary to understand the language being used. It is necessary to understand the language in two different ways. First you must be able to understand what people are saying when they speak to you. This is referred to as oral or listening comprehension. Oral comprehension or listening comprehension is the ability to understand the spoken language.

You must also be able to understand what you read. This is referred to as reading comprehension. Reading comprehension is the ability to understand the written language.

Listening comprehension and reading comprehension are called the *receptive skills.* They are receptive skills because as you listen to what someone else says or read what someone else has written you receive information without having to produce any language yourself.

It is usually very easy to understand your native language. It is a bit more problematic to understand a second language that is new to you. As a beginner, you are still learning the sounds of the new language, and you recognize only a few words. Throughout **¡Buen viaje!** we will give you hints or suggestions to help you understand when people are speaking to you in Spanish or when you are reading in Spanish.

Hints for Listening Comprehension

When you are listening to a person speaking Spanish, don't try to understand every word. It is not necessary to understand everything to get the idea of what someone is saying. Listen for the general message. If some details escape you, it doesn't matter. Also, never try to translate what people are saying in Spanish into English. It takes a great deal of experience and expertise to be a translator. Trying to translate will hinder your ability to understand.

Hints for Reading Comprehension Just as you will not always understand every word you hear in a conversation, you will not necessarily understand every word you encounter in a reading selection, either. In **¡Buen viaje!,** we have used only words you know or can easily figure out in the reading selections. This will make reading comprehension much easier for you. However, if at some time you wish to read a newspaper or magazine article in Spanish, you will most certainly come across some unfamiliar words. Do not stop reading. Continue to read to get the "gist" of the selection. Try to guess the meanings of words you do not know.

Productive Skills

There are two productive skills in language. These two skills are speaking and writing. They are called productive skills because it is you who has to produce the language when you say or write something. When you speak or write, you have control over the language and which words you use. If you don't know how to say something, you don't have to say it. With the receptive skills, on the other hand, someone else produces the language that you listen to or read, and you have no control over the words they use.

There's no doubt that you can easily speak your native language. You can write, too, even though you may sometimes make errors in spelling or punctuation. In Spanish, there's not a lot you can say or write as a beginner. You can only talk or write about those topics you have learned in Spanish class.

Hints for Speaking Try to be as accurate as possible when speaking. Try not to make mistakes. However, if you do, it's not the end of the world. Spanish speakers will understand you. You're not expected to speak a language perfectly after a limited time. You have probably spoken with people from other countries who do not speak English perfectly, but you can understand them. Remember:

- Keep talking! Don't become inhibited for fear of making a mistake.
- Say what you know how to say. Don't try to branch out in the early stages and attempt to talk about topics or situations you have not yet learned in Spanish.

Hints for Writing There are many activities throughout each chapter of **¡Buen viaje!** that will help you to speak and write in Spanish. When you have to write something on your own, however, without the guidance or assistance of an activity in your book, be sure to choose a topic for which you know the vocabulary in Spanish. Never attempt to write about a topic you have not yet studied in Spanish. Write down the topic you are going to write about. Then think of the words you know that are related to the topic. Be sure to include some action words (verbs) that you will need.

From your list of words, write as many sentences as you can. Read them and organize them into a logical order. Fill in any gaps. Then proof your paragraph(s) to see if you made any errors. Correct any that you find.

When writing on your own, be careful not to rely heavily, if at all, on a bilingual dictionary. It's not that bilingual dictionaries are bad, but when you look up a word you will very often find that there are several translations for the same word. As a beginning language student, you do not know which translation to choose; the chances are great that you will pick the wrong one.

As a final hint, never prepare your paragraph(s) in English and attempt to translate word for word. Always write from scratch in Spanish.

Capítulo 1

Vocabulario

PALABRAS 1 y 2 *(pages 14–21)*

1. Repeat each new word in the **Palabras** section as many times as possible. The more you use a word, the more apt you are to remember it and keep it as part of your active vocabulary.
2. Read the words as you look at the illustrations.
3. If you're the type of learner who has to write something down in order to remember it, copy each word once or twice.
4. Do these activities diligently. They provide you with the opportunity to use your new words many times.
5. This may sound strange, but it's a good idea to read these activities aloud at home or when using the CD-ROM.
6. When doing the vocabulary activities by yourself or for homework, try to do each item orally before writing the answer.
7. After doing any activity that says **Historieta,** read all the answers aloud. Each time you do this, you will be telling a story in Spanish. It's an excellent way to keep using the material you are learning.

Classroom Suggestion Listen to what your classmates say when they respond in class. Do not tune them out. Paying attention to them allows you additional opportunities to hear your new words. The more you hear them, the more likely you are to learn them.

Study Tips

Estructura

Los adjetivos y los artículos *(pages 22–24)*
Pay particular attention to the final sound of many of the nouns and adjectives that you are learning. Remember that the vowel **o** is associated with masculine and the vowel **a** is associated with feminine.

El verbo ser *(pages 25–27)*

1. **Ser** is the first verb you are learning in Spanish. Throughout your study of Spanish, you will continue to learn many more verbs. The form of a verb in Spanish changes according to the subject. At this point you know three verb forms:

soy	when talking about yourself
eres	when talking to someone
él/ella es	when talking about someone

Get off to a good start! Learn these three simple forms and remember them.

2. As you do the more open-ended activities, don't try to use words you don't know in Spanish. For example, you may want to talk about someone who is very outgoing, but you don't know a Spanish equivalent for *outgoing.* Give the message using what you do know. For example, you can say: **Juan no es tímido.** You can also say: **¿Es tímida María? No, no. María no es tímida.** Using **no** with a word you know enables you to convey the meaning you wish even though you do not know the precise word.

Classroom Suggestion Listen to your classmates as they respond to the structure activities. Remember, the more you hear a form, the more readily you will be able to use it.

3. After doing any activity that says **Historieta,** read all the answers aloud. Each time you do this, you will be telling a story in Spanish. It's an excellent way to keep using the material you are learning.

Lectura cultural

El Quijote *(pages 30–31)*

1. Always read the Reading Strategy at the beginning of the **Lectura cultural.** Practice these strategies and try applying them to other selections you read in Spanish. The Reading Strategy on page 30 talks about cognates and how they help you guess the meanings of words you do not know. For example, you read: **El Quijote es una novela muy famosa.** Even if you had never seen the word **famosa,** you could guess its meaning because it is a cognate of the English word *famous.*
2. Let's take a look at another way to guess meaning. You read: **El Quijote es una novela famosa, muy conocida.** You don't know the meaning of **conocida.** However, when you come across a word or expression followed by a comma and then another word (in apposition), the word in apposition almost always clarifies the previous word and has the same or similar meaning. Which of the following do you think **conocida** means? *Talented, creative? Famous, well-known? Good, interesting?*

   Hopefully you chose *famous, well-known.* Think about how and why you arrived at this correct answer.

Hints for Writing As you complete your first chapter in Spanish, you are able to write a description of a person. At this point, you cannot tell what the person does because you don't have the necessary vocabulary. So avoid this. However, you are able to tell what he or she is like. Write down the words you know in order to write your description. Do not think of words in English. Try to think only of the words you know in Spanish. Begin to write your description. Remember what you learned about **o, a.** Be sure to use the **o** ending when describing a boy and the **a** ending as you describe a girl.

Vocabulario *(page 40)*
As you complete the chapter, look at the reference vocabulary list. If there are several words you don't remember, go back to the **Palabras 1** and **Palabras 2** sections and review. If there are only one or two, you can choose to look them up in the dictionaries beginning on page H34 at the end of this book.

Capítulo 2

Get off to a good start! Do your Spanish homework diligently and study for a short period of time each day. Do not skip some days and then try to cram. It doesn't work when studying a foreign language.

In each lesson of **¡Buen viaje!** you will learn a very manageable amount of new material. Since Spanish is a romance language, much of the new material will involve word endings. Study each small set of new endings on a daily basis, and you'll have no problem. Don't wait until you have lots of them and try to cram them in all at once.

Vocabulario

PALABRAS 1 y 2 *(pages 44–51)*

1. In Chapter 1 you learned that adjectives describing something masculine end in **o** and those describing something feminine end in **a**. In Chapter 2, you have seven new words that reinforce the same concept. They are **cuánto, pequeño, poco, mucho, aburrido, duro, mismo.**

Es una clase aburrida.
Es un curso aburrido.

Hint for Pronouncing New Words Imitate the pronunciation of your teacher, the CDs, or the CD-ROM to the best of your ability. Try to acquire the best pronunciation possible. However, don't be worried if you have a slight American accent.

There are three levels of pronunciation.

- **Near-native** Try to pronounce like a native. Strive for a near-native pronunciation.
- **Accented but comprehensible** Many people have an accent when they speak a foreign language. You can tell they are not native speakers, but in spite of their accent, you can understand them. If you have such an accent, don't be concerned.
- **Very accented and incomprehensible** Some people have such a strong accent that it's impossible to understand what they're saying. If you have such a strong accent, it will be necessary to repeat and imitate more carefully.

Always remember to listen carefully, repeating as accurately as possible, and you'll succeed in acquiring acceptable pronunciation.

Hint for Speaking Listen to your teacher pronounce new words or phrases and then repeat them several times. Once you know how to pronounce the words, read the words in your book. If you try to read a word in Spanish before ever hearing it, you will probably mispronounce it. Always try to listen, repeat, and then read.

2. The vocabulary in **Palabras 2** should be very easy to recognize and learn because many words are cognates. A cognate is a word that looks alike in both English and Spanish and has the same meaning in both languages. In the early lessons of **¡Buen viaje!** we have used many cognates to help you acquire a substantial vocabulary quickly and easily. However, be careful with the pronunciation of cognates. Even though they look alike and mean the same thing in both languages, they can be pronounced very differently.

Study Tips

Estructura

Sustantivos, artículos y adjetivos en el plural *(pages 52–53)*

When studying a new grammar or structure point try to simplify the rule to make it easy for you to remember. When it comes to adjectives, remember:

adjectives that end in **o** have four forms:

-o, -os, -a, -as

adjectives that end in **e** and most adjectives that end in a consonant have two forms:

-e, -es consonant, **-es**

Presente de ser en el plural *(pages 54–57)*

1. In this lesson, you learn two new verb forms:
   - **somos** when talking about yourself and someone else
   - **son** when talking about or to two or more people
2. Go over all forms of the verb **ser** until you feel confident that you know them.
3. Do each activity aloud and then write the answers.

Lectura cultural

El español en Estados Unidos *(pages 62–63)*

1. Read the Reading Strategy at the beginning of the **Lectura cultural.** Look at the title of the reading on page 62. It lets you know immediately the general topic you'll be reading about.
2. Read the two subtitles or heads in the passage. They give you a more specific idea of what you'll be reading. Without having read the reading selection, you now have some understanding of what the reading is about. This will make comprehension much easier.
3. After looking at the title and subtitles, you may very quickly skim the reading. Rather than trying to remember all the information, look at the comprehension questions that follow it. Then go back to the reading and look for the specific factual information called for.

Capítulo 3

Vocabulario

PALABRAS 1 y 2 *(pages 76–83)*

1. Look at each photo or illustration carefully.
2. Read each isolated word or sentence aloud.
3. When learning another language it is sometimes necessary to guess. In doing so, you may come up with the right answer. For example, suppose you're not quite sure what **compra** means. If someone goes to a store, looks for something he or she needs, finds out how much it costs and then pays for it, you could possibly figure out that **compra** means *buys.*
4. It is strongly recommended that you not translate the vocabulary into English.
5. It is very important to know your question or interrogative words. Activity 4 on page 79 and Activity 8 on page 82 will help you do this. The answer in parenthesis in Activity 8 on page 82 tells you the meaning of the question word in the sentence.

QUESTION	ANSWER
Qué	a thing
Quién	a person
Dónde	location
Cuándo	time

6. After you have practiced your new words in the **Palabras 1** and **2** sections, cover up the words. Look at the photo or illustration and see how much you can say about it.

Hint for Speaking Whenever possible, read all the answers aloud to any activity labeled **Historieta.** Every time you do, you'll be telling a story on your own with the guidance of the activity in the text. This is an easy and useful way to get yourself speaking lots of Spanish.

Estructura

Presente de los verbos en -ar en el singular *(pages 84–86)*

1. As you already know, the verb ending indicates who performs the action of the verb.
   - **-o** yourself
   - **-as** to a friend
   - **-a** about someone
2. The verb endings will be presented to you in very manageable segments. You now know three endings for an **-ar** verb. They are:
   - **-o**
   - **-as**
   - **-a**

   Be sure to learn these three simple endings and how to use them. Learning just three is very easy. You will continue to learn more endings. Do not wait until you have lots of endings. Learn them step by step and you will have no problem.

Hint Note that the structure activities in your book build from easy to more complex. For example, in Activity 14 on page 85 you use only **-a.** In Activity 15, you hear **-as** and respond always with **-o.** Activity 18 on page 86 makes you use and manipulate all three endings.

3. Do all the activities aloud before writing the answers.
4. Read all the answers to any activity labeled **Historieta** as a story.

Conversación *(page 88)*

This conversation should be very easy for you. You have already learned all the Spanish used in the conversation. When practicing this conversation with a classmate, feel free to make as many changes as you want, as long as they make sense. For example you can change **camisa** to another article of clothing you know.

Lectura cultural

Un alumno madrileño *(pages 90–91)*

1. Look at the photos on pages 90 and 91. Based on these photos, what do you think the reading is about?
   - schools and students
   - shopping for clothing
   - planning a meal
2. Skim the reading selection and look for the important information such as:
   - Who's the story about?
   - Where does he live and go to school?
   - What does he wear to school?
3. Factual recall is an important reading skill. First, find the facts in the reading and then commit them to memory. Activity B on page 91 tells you what factual information to look for.

Vocabulario *(page 100)*

As you complete the chapter, look at the reference vocabulary list. If there are several words you don't remember, go back to the **Palabras 1** and **Palabras 2** sections and review. If there are only one or two, you can choose to look them up in the dictionaries beginning on page H34 at the end of this book.

Capítulo 

Vocabulario

PALABRAS 1 y 2 *(pages 104–111)*

1. Notice how one sentence can clarify the meaning of another.

   Los alumnos llegan a la escuela a eso de las ocho menos cuarto.

   No llegan a las ocho menos cuarto en punto.

   Llegan a las ocho menos veinte o a las ocho menos diez.

2. Notice how the way in which a word is used in several sentences helps to clarify meaning.
   Los alumnos llegan a la escuela.
   ¿A qué hora llegan?
   Llegan a las ocho menos cuarto.
   Algunos alumnos van a la escuela a pie.
   Otros alumnos van en carro.

Which word do you think means *arrive?* Which one means *go?*

Hint If you're the type of learner who has to write something before you can remember, copy the words in the **Palabras** section once or twice. Use the following learning sequence: listen, repeat, read, write.

3. Activity 1 on page 106 once again helps you to respond correctly to the question or interrogative words.

4. After you have learned the new words in **Palabras 2,** look at each illustration, cover up the sentences, and say as much as you can about the illustration. If you can describe the illustration, you know your vocabulary. If you cannot describe it, you have to study some more.

Hint Read or say aloud all the answers to the **Historieta** activities to give you practice telling coherent stories in Spanish.

Estructura

Presente de los verbos en -ar en el plural
(pages 112–115)

1. You will now learn two more verb endings. Be sure to remember them and how to use them.

-amos	when talking about yourself and someone else
-an	when talking about two or more people
	when talking to two or more people

2. It's always a good idea to review something you already know that's related to something new that you are learning.

-o	when talking about yourself
-a	when talking about one person
-amos	when talking about yourself and someone
-an	when talking about more than one person

Hint Be diligent in doing your Spanish homework. Work for at least a brief period of time each day. This enables you to learn everything in small doses. Do not let things pile up.

Presente de los verbos ir, dar, estar
(pages 116–117)

1. We always try to group material together to make it as easy as possible for you to learn. With these three new verbs you have to learn only one new form—when talking about yourself.
   voy doy estoy
2. All other forms are the same as a regular **-ar** verb. You are therefore reviewing the same endings.
3. Recall—What is the **yo** form of the irregular verb **ser? Soy, ¿no?** Notice the similarity.
   soy voy doy estoy

Conversación *(page 120)*

1. Pay careful attention when you listen to the conversation on the CD-ROM or when other students are repeating it in class. The more you hear spoken Spanish, the easier it will be for you to understand.
2. In this conversation there are two very common expressions. **Oye** is used to get a friend's attention. **Pues** has no specific meaning, but it is frequently used before answering a question.

Lectura cultural

Escuelas del mundo hispano *(pages 122–123)*

As you read this selection, concentrate on some differences between schools in the United States and in the Spanish-speaking world.

Capítulo 5

Vocabulario
PALABRAS 1 y 2 *(pages 142–149)*

1. It can be fun to study with a classmate. You can do the following.
   - Ask one another questions in Spanish about the illustrations.
   - Have a contest. See who can give more Spanish words describing the illustrations in a three-minute period.
   - Tell your friend which of the items you would order if you were at a café.
2. When doing the activities that follow each **Palabras** section, read aloud all the answers to each **Historieta** activity. By doing this you will be telling a story in Spanish. Always remember, the more you practice speaking Spanish, the better you'll be able to communicate.
3. In class, pay attention to the responses of the other students in class. Don't turn them off. The more you hear the new words used, the easier it will be for you to remember them.

Estructura
Presente de los verbos en -er e -ir
(pages 150–153)

1. Note the similarities in **-er, -ir** verb endings and those of the **-ar** verbs. The vowel **-a** is **-e** in most forms of the **-er** and **-ir** verbs.
2. Pay particular attention to the **nosotros** form, since it is the only one that is different.

   comemos **vivimos**
   aprendemos **escribimos**

Hint The more you practice speaking Spanish, the better. When doing your homework, go over all the activities aloud. Don't just do your Spanish homework silently.

Conversación *(page 154)*

1. Listen carefully to the conversation. You can listen to your teacher or use the CD-ROM. Listen more than once. Each time you'll pick up some more information.
2. Read the conversation several times aloud.
3. Try to answer the questions that follow without looking up the answers in the conversation.

Lectura cultural
En un café en Madrid *(pages 156–157)*

1. Based on the Reading Strategy, guess the meaning of the words **inmediatamente** and **cenan.**
2. Read the selection fast to get the general idea.
3. Read it a second time to get more details.
4. Making comparisons while reading is an important reading comprehension skill. In this reading, you learned about a cultural difference that's quite interesting. What is it? You may want to share this information with family or friends who don't know any Spanish.

¡Te toca a ti! *(pages 162–163)*

In Activity 6 on page 163, you're going to write about a restaurant in Spanish.

1. Make a mental picture of the restaurant.
2. Write words you know in Spanish to describe a restaurant and restaurant activities.
3. List items that people may order.
4. Put these words into sentences. Your first paragraph will describe the restaurant. Your second paragraph will tell what your "characters" order. To finish your article, tell who paid for the meal.

Capítulo 

Vocabulario
PALABRAS 1 y 2 *(pages 170–177)*

1. In **Palabras 1,** remember to listen to the words and repeat them orally before reading them.

Hint If you're the type of learner who has to write something in order to remember it, copy the words in the **Palabras** section once or twice. Use the following learning sequence: listen, repeat, read, write.

2. After you have learned the new words in **Palabras 2,** look at each illustration, cover up the sentences, and say as much as you can about the illustration. If you can describe the illustration, you know your vocabulary. If you cannot describe it, you have to study some more.

Hint Read or say aloud all the answers to the **Historieta** activities to give you practice in telling coherent stories in Spanish.

Estructura

Presente de tener *(pages 178–180)*

1. Familiarize yourself with the forms of **tener** as you read the verb chart.
2. Do the activities that follow the explanation diligently. They give you the practice you need to learn and retain the verb forms. To help you, they build from easy to more difficult.
3. Do the activities orally and in writing.
4. After doing all the activities, reread the grammar explanation. See if you can give the forms of the verb **tener** on your own without reading them.

Tener que, Ir a *(pages 181–182)*

Review Once again, review all the verbs you know so that you will be able to use the correct infinitive form.

-AR	-ER	-IR	IRREGULAR
necesitar	**leer**	**escribir**	**ser**
buscar	**comer**	**recibir**	**tener**
mirar	**beber**	**vivir**	**ir**
comprar	**vender**	**subir**	**dar**
pagar	**comprender**	**cumplir**	**estar**
usar, calzar	**aprender**		**ver**
llevar			
hablar			
trabajar			
llegar			

-AR *(cont'd)*
estudiar
enseñar
mirar
escuchar
prestar
tomar
sacar
bailar
cantar
preparar
desear
invitar

Conversación *(page 186)*

1. This conversation should be very easy for you. You have already learned all the Spanish that is used in the conversation. When practicing this conversation with a classmate, feel free to make as many changes as you want, as long as they make sense.
2. In this conversation, you hear Tadeo ask **¿Verdad? ¿Verdad?** is used a great deal by speakers to get confirmation of what they said.
3. **Hombre** is often used as a "flavor" word when speaking to a male rather than using his name.

Lectura cultural

La familia hispana *(pages 188–189)*

1. As you read each paragraph, draw a mental picture of what you're reading. To help you draw your mental picture, look at the photographs, too.

¡Te toca a ti! *(pages 194–195)*

In Activity 5 on page 195, you are going to write about your house or a house of your dreams.

1. Picture the house.
2. In Spanish, think of or write a list of words you can use to identify parts of the house.
3. Think about or write a list of words you know in Spanish to describe a house or rooms of a house.

4. Organize your story. Divide the house into parts, such as living area, sleeping area, first floor, second floor. You may even want to make a drawing of your house. Write a few sentences about each area.
5. Put the sentences in a logical order.
6. Add a few sentences to describe the area around your house.

Vocabulario *(page 198)*
As you complete the chapter, look at the reference vocabulary list. If there are several words you don't remember, go back to the **Palabras 1** and **Palabras 2** sections and review. If there are only one or two, you can choose to look them up in the dictionaries beginning on page H34 at the end of this book.

Capítulo  7

Vocabulario
PALABRAS 1 y 2 *(pages 202–209)*
1. Look at each photo or illustration carefully.
2. Read the labels. What does each word refer to?
3. The words are then used in a meaningful context in a complete sentence. Repeat the sentence aloud as you look at the illustration.
4. To help you learn vocabulary, work with a friend or classmate. Have a contest. See who can say the most about each illustration or photo.
5. To review the vocabulary and see how much of it you know, cover the words and sentences and say as much as you can about each photo or illustration.
6. Do the activities that follow both orally and in writing.

Estructura
Verbos de cambio radical *(pages 210–214)*
1. Always simplify a grammatical rule to bare essentials to be able to hold onto it.
   a. These verbs take the same endings as any regular verb belonging to that conjugation.
   b. The stem change **ie** or **ue** takes place in all forms except **nosotros** (and **vosotros**).

Interesar, aburrir, gustar *(pages 215–217)*
1. Note that **mí** and **ti** are used after prepositions. All other forms are the same as the subject: **para él, ella, usted, ellos, ellas, ustedes, nosotros(as)**

Conversación *(page 218)*
1. Intonation is the melody of a language. Intonation is produced by the rise and fall of the voice. Each language has its own intonation patterns. English intonation is very different from Spanish intonation. Pay special attention to the rise and fall of the speakers' voices as you listen to the conversations on the CD or CD-ROM.
2. Try to imitate the speakers' intonation as accurately as possible. If you do, you'll sound much more like a heritage Spanish speaker. Don't be inhibited. Pretend you are acting while you imitate the intonation.

Lectura cultural
El fútbol *(pages 220–221)*
1. Scan the reading. Get a general idea of what the **Liga española** is and what the **Copa mundial** is.
2. Read the passage a second time and look for the answer to the following question. Why can't the team members of **el Real Madrid** de Casero and da Silva play together on the same team during the **Copa mundial?**

Vocabulario *(page 230)*
Look at each word and see if you can use it in a short sentence.

Study Tips

Capítulo 8

Vocabulario

PALABRAS 1 y 2 *(pages 242–249)*

1. Whenever you have a chance to review previously learned material, do so. As you do **Palabras 1,** think of all the parts of the body you have learned in Spanish.
2. After studying the vocabulary, cover up the print and say as much about each photo or illustration as you can.

Estructura

Ser y estar *(pages 250–255)*

1. Keep the grammatical rule simple.
   Remember:

Characteristic	**ser**
Condition	**estar**
Place of origin	**ser**
Location, permanent or temporary	**estar**

2. As you do the practice activities, very quickly say why you used **ser** or **estar.** This will help you remember the rule.

Lectura cultural

Una joven nerviosa *(pages 260–261)*

1. As you read this selection, visualize Patricia's appearance and demeanor.
2. As you read, look for the following information.
   - ❖ What's wrong with Patricia
   - ❖ Why she's upset
   - ❖ What the doctor does
   - ❖ What the doctor tells Patricia

Capítulo 9

Vocabulario

PALABRAS 1 y 2 *(pages 274–281)*

1. For **Palabras 1,** after going over the new vocabulary, review immediately. Sit back for a moment and say aloud or to yourself five words or expressions associated with the beach.
2. Pretend you are on the beach. Think of three things you would like to do while on the beach. Start your sentences with **Quiero...**
3. After completing each activity on pages 276 and 277, read all the answers aloud or silently. You're not only reading a story with words you know; you're also having another opportunity to use your new words.
4. In **Palabras 2,** when learning the winter weather expressions, review the summer expressions on pages 274 and 275.
5. As you do the activities on pages 280 and 281, work with a classmate. Take turns asking and answering the questions orally. Then write your answers individually. Correct each other's work.

Estructura

Pretérito de los verbos en -ar *(pages 282–285)*

1. So far, all the verb endings you have learned are for the present tense. Be sure you are very familiar with these present tense endings that you have already learned because you are now about to learn a new set of endings.
2. The endings in this lesson are used with regular **-ar** verbs to express a past action. Compare present and past tense endings.

	PRESENT	PAST
yo	**-o**	**-é**
tú	**-as**	**-aste**
él, ella, Ud.	**-a**	**-ó**
nosotros	**-amos**	**-amos**
vosotros	***-áis***	***-asteis***
ellos, ellas, Uds.	**-an**	**-aron**

3. Go over all the practice activities very diligently. Do each activity aloud. Then write the answers. Then read your written answers. If you find any errors, correct them.
4. The more you practice using the endings, the easier it will be to remember them.
5. After doing the practice activities, see if you can give the correct verb ending for each subject without looking them up.

Pronombres lo, la, los, las *(pages 286–288)*
A direct object pronoun answers the question *whom* or *what.*

Whom did you see?	I saw my friend.
What did you buy?	I bought a gift.

Conversación *(page 290)*

1. As you listen to or read the conversation find out Paula's predicament and what she did about it.
2. Try to answer the questions without looking up the answers.

Lectura cultural

Paraísos del mundo hispano *(pages 292–293)*
Look at the photographs as you read this selection. They will help you visualize what you are reading about.

Capítulo 10

Vocabulario

PALABRAS 1 y 2 *(pages 306–313)*

1. Remember to listen to the words and repeat them orally before reading them.
2. After you have gone over the new vocabulary, see how many words you remember. Think of seven words about a movie. Think of five words about a play.
3. Go over each activity orally before you write the answers.

Estructura

Pretérito de los verbos en -er e -ir
(pages 314–316)

1. Remember that the verb ending in Spanish indicates not only who performed the action of the verb but also when he or she preformed the action. The tense of a verb indicates when the action was performed.
2. In this lesson you are learning the endings for the past tense (preterite) of **-er** and **-ir** verbs.
3. **Review** Contrast the endings for the past tense of **-ar** verbs and **-er, -ir** verbs.

-AR	-ER, -IR
-é	**-í**
-aste	**-iste**
-ó	**-ió**
-amos	**-imos**
-asteis	***-isteis***
-aron	**-ieron**

4. Do all the activities that follow the grammatical explanation diligently. We suggest you first do the activities aloud, even by yourself, and then write the answers. Practice using the verb endings is very important. The more practice you get, the better.
5. It is important to keep the verb endings straight without mixing up one group with another.

Complementos le, les *(pages 317–319)*
Here's an easy way to tell the difference between a direct object and an indirect object. A direct object answers the question *whom* or *what.*

What did Juan throw?	The ball.
Whom did Juan see?	His friend.

An indirect object answers the question to (for) whom or to (for) what.

Lectura cultural

Dating *(pages 322–323)*

1. When reading, it helps to understand the passage when you have some idea of the information you are looking for. First, read the title. It tells you what the reading selection is about.
2. As you read, look for the following.
   - Differences, if any, in dating customs in Latin America and the United States
   - How dating customs are changing in Spain and Latin America

Study Tips

Capítulo 11

Vocabulario

PALABRAS 1 y 2 *(pages 336–343)*

1. Repeat each new word in the **Palabras** sections several times. Look at the photo or illustration as you pronounce the word.
2. Some of you may remember information more easily after writing it down. Try copying each vocabulary word once or twice.
3. You may want to do the activities aloud with a friend as a paired activity. Then, individually write the answers and check each other's work.
4. Listen carefully to what your classmates say when they respond in class. The more you hear people use the new words, the more likely you are to remember them.

Estructura

Hacer, poner, traer, salir en el presente
(pages 344–346)

1. Review the present tense of a regular **-er** and **-ir** verb.

COMER	VIVIR
como	**vivo**
comes	**vives**
come	**vive**
comemos	**vivimos**
coméis	***vivís***
comen	**viven**

2. Remember, the verbs **hacer, traer, poner,** and **salir** have the same endings as a regular verb except in the **yo** form. Concentrate on the **yo** form.
   hago pongo traigo salgo
3. Two other **g** verbs are **tener** and **venir.**
   hago pongo traigo salgo
   tengo vengo

Saber y conocer en el presente
(pages 348–349)

1. Simplify the grammatical rule: just remember that **saber** means to know something simple, and **conocer** means to know or be familiar with something complex.
2. When doing these activities, pay particular attention to the object of each verb to determine the use of **saber** or **conocer.**

Conversación *(page 350)*
Note that **chist** is used in some areas of the Spanish-speaking world to have someone be quiet. It's like *shh* in English.

Lectura cultural

El avión en la América del Sur
(pages 352–353)
To identify the main idea of this reading selection, look for the following information: two reasons why air travel is so important in South America.

Capítulo 12

Vocabulario

PALABRAS 1 y 2 *(pages 374–381)*

1. After learning the new vocabulary, cover up the print and tell what you see in each illustration.

Hint If you are the type of learner who has to write something to remember it, write the new words on a separate sheet of paper.

Estructura

Verbos reflexivos *(pages 382–385)*

1. Remember that if a person is doing something to or for himself or herself, the verb in Spanish is a reflexive verb, and you must use the additional pronoun.
2. You have already learned all the verb endings that are used in these activities. The only new concept is the use of the reflexive pronoun. Pay particular attention to this pronoun as you do these activities.

Verbos reflexivos de cambio radical
(pages 386–387)

Review These reflexive verbs have the same stem change as verbs you have already learned.

e → ie	**empezar, comenzar, querer, perder, preferir**
o → ue	**volver, devolver, poder**

Lectura cultural

Del norte de España *(pages 390–391)*

1. Go to the map of Spain on page xxx. Look at the area of northern Spain from the Pyrenees to the city of Santiago de Compostela to familiarize yourself with the area you'll be reading about.
2. To review the past tense of verbs you have already learned, look for all the preterite forms in this reading. There are quite a few of them.

Capítulo 13

Vocabulario

PALABRAS 1 y 2 *(pages 404–411)*

1. Listen to the new words in **Palabras 1** and repeat them orally before reading them.
2. After learning the new words, match the following opposites.

la llegada	**bajar de**
de ida y vuelta	**ocupado**
subir a	**la salida**
libre	**tarde**
a tiempo	**sencillo**

3. Read the answers aloud to all the **Historieta** activities.

Estructura

El pretérito de los verbos irregulares
(pages 412–416)

Note that these irregular verbs have the same endings in the preterite as regular verbs except in the **yo** and **él, ella, usted** forms.

	Regular	Irregular
yo	**-í**	**-e**
él, ella, Ud.	**-ió**	**-o**

Lectura cultural

En el AVE *(pages 420–421)*

1. Before reading this selection, look at the photo of the bird—**el ave, el pájaro.** What's the association of the bird with the train?
2. Scan the reading selection to get just the general idea.
3. Read the selection again and look for some more precise details about a trip on the **AVE.**

Capítulo 14

Vocabulario

PALABRAS 1 y 2 *(pages 434–441)*

1. Do some review as you learn this new vocabulary. Think of all the foods you have learned in Spanish. You may wish to refer back to Chapter 5.

Hint If you're the type of learner who has to write something before you can remember it, write the new words several times.

2. Activity 8 on page 441 reviews the use of **gustar.** You may review **interesar** and **gustar** on page 215.

Estructura

Verbos con el cambio e → i *(pages 442–443)*

1. You have already come across this type of stem change in the irregular verb **decir.**
   digo, dices, dice, decimos, *decís*, dicen
2. As with other stem-changing verbs you have learned so far **(e → ie, o → ue),** these verbs take the same endings as any other verb that belongs to that conjugation.

Hint If you pronounce these verbs correctly, you will never have trouble spelling them. Remember **i** is pronounced like *ee* in English *see* and **e** is pronounced like the *a* in *ate.*

Lectura cultural

La comida mexicana *(pages 448–449)*

If you have ever been to a Mexican restaurant, think about what you ate there. It will help you visualize what you are reading about.

REGULAR VERBS			
INFINITIVO	**hablar** *to speak*	**comer** *to eat*	**vivir** *to live*
PRESENTE	hablo hablas habla hablamos *habláis* hablan	como comes come comemos *coméis* comen	vivo vives vive vivimos *vivís* viven
PRETÉRITO	hablé hablaste habló hablamos *hablasteis* hablaron	comí comiste comió comimos *comisteis* comieron	viví viviste vivió vivimos *vivisteis* vivieron

STEM-CHANGING VERBS (-**ar** and -**er** verbs)				
INFINITIVO	**empezar (e → ie)**[1] *to begin*	**almorzar (o → ue)**[2] *to eat lunch*	**perder (e → ie)**[3] *to lose*	**volver (o → ue)** *to return*
PRESENTE	empiezo empiezas empieza empezamos *empezáis* empiezan	almuerzo almuerzas almuerza almorzamos *almorzáis* almuerzan	pierdo pierdes pierde perdemos *perdéis* pierden	vuelvo vuelves vuelve volvemos *volvéis* vuelven

[1] ***Comenzar, sentar,*** *and* ***pensar*** *are similar.*
[2] ***Acostar, costar,*** *and* ***jugar (ue → ue)*** *are similar.*
[3] ***Defender*** *and* ***entender*** *are similar.*

STEM-CHANGING VERBS (-ir verbs)			
INFINITIVO	**preferir (e → ie, i)** *to prefer*	**dormir (o → ue, u)**[1] *to sleep*	**pedir (e → i, i)**[2] *to ask for*
PRESENTE	prefiero prefieres prefiere preferimos *preferís* prefieren	duermo duermes duerme dormimos *dormís* duermen	pido pides pide pedimos *pedís* piden
PRETÉRITO	preferí preferiste prefirió preferimos *preferisteis* prefirieron	dormí dormiste durmió dormimos *dormisteis* durmieron	pedí pediste pidió pedimos *pedisteis* pidieron

IRREGULAR VERBS				
INFINITIVO	**andar** *to walk*	**dar** *to give*	**decir** *to tell, to say*	**estar** *to be*
PRESENTE	*(regular)*	doy das da damos *dais* dan	digo dices dice decimos *decís* dicen	estoy estás está estamos *estáis* están
PRETÉRITO	anduve anduviste anduvo anduvimos *anduvisteis* anduvieron	di diste dio dimos *disteis* dieron	dije dijiste dijo dijimos *dijisteis* dijeron	estuve estuviste estuvo estuvimos *estuvisteis* estuvieron

[1] ***Morir*** *is similar.*
[2] ***Repetir*** *and* ***servir*** *are similar.*

IRREGULAR VERBS

INFINITIVO	**hacer** *to do*	**ir** *to go*	**poder** *to be able*	**poner** *to put*
PRESENTE	hago haces hace hacemos *hacéis* hacen	voy vas va vamos *vais* van	puedo puedes puede podemos *podéis* pueden	pongo pones pone ponemos *ponéis* ponen
PRETÉRITO	hice hiciste hizo hicimos *hicisteis* hicieron	fui fuiste fue fuimos *fuisteis* fueron	pude pudiste pudo pudimos *pudisteis* pudieron	puse pusiste puso pusimos *pusisteis* pusieron

INFINITIVO	**querer** *to want*	**saber** *to know*	**salir** *to leave*	**ser** *to be*
PRESENTE	quiero quieres quiere queremos *queréis* quieren	sé sabes sabe sabemos *sabéis* saben	salgo sales sale salimos *salís* salen	soy eres es somos *sois* son
PRETÉRITO	quise quisiste quiso quisimos *quisisteis* quisieron	supe supiste supo supimos *supisteis* supieron	*(regular)*	fui fuiste fue fuimos *fuisteis* fueron

IRREGULAR VERBS

INFINITIVO	tener *to have*	traer *to bring*	venir *to come*	ver *to see*
PRESENTE	tengo tienes tiene tenemos *tenéis* tienen	traigo traes trae traemos *traéis* traen	vengo vienes viene venimos *venís* vienen	veo ves ve vemos *veis* ven
PRETÉRITO	tuve tuviste tuvo tuvimos *tuvisteis* tuvieron	traje trajiste trajo trajimos *trajisteis* trajeron	vine viniste vino vinimos *vinisteis* vinieron	vi viste vio vimos *visteis* vieron

VERBS WITH A SPELLING CHANGE IN THE PRETERITE (-car, -gar, -zar)

INFINITIVO	practicar[1] *to practice*	llegar[2] *to arrive*	comenzar[3] *to begin*
PRETÉRITO	practiqué practicaste practicó practicamos *practicasteis* practicaron	llegué llegaste llegó llegamos *llegasteis* llegaron	comencé comenzaste comenzó comenzamos *comenzasteis* comenzaron

[1] ***Buscar*** *and* ***sacar*** *are similar.*
[2] ***Jugar*** *and* ***pagar*** *are similar.*
[3] ***Empezar*** *and* ***almorzar*** *are similar.*

Spanish-English Dictionary

This Spanish-English Dictionary contains all productive and receptive vocabulary from the text. The numbers following each productive entry indicate the chapter and vocabulary section in which the word is introduced. For example, ***3.2*** *means that the word was taught in* ***Capítulo 3, Palabras 2.*** *BV refers to the preliminary* ***Bienvenidos*** *lessons. If there is no number following an entry, this means that the word or expression is there for receptive purposes only.*

a at; to
a bordo de aboard, on board, 11.2
a eso de at about (time), 4.1
a fines de at the end of
a la española Spanish style
a pie on foot, 4.1
a plazos in installments
a solas alone
a tiempo on time, 11.1
a veces sometimes, 7.1
a ver let's see
abordar to get on, board
abril April, BV
abrir to open, 8.2
abstracto(a) abstract
la **abuela** grandmother, 6.1
el **abuelo** grandfather, 6.1
los **abuelos** grandparents, 6.1
abundante plentiful
aburrido(a) boring, 2.1
aburrir to bore
la **academia** academy, school
acariciar to caress
el **acceso** access
el **aceite** oil, 14.2
aceptar to accept
el **acompañamiento** accompaniment
acompañar to accompany
acordarse (ue) to remember
acostarse (ue) to go to bed, 12.1
el **acrílico** acrylic
la **actividad** activity
activo(a) active
el **actor** actor, 10.2
la **actriz** actress, 10.2
la **acuarela** watercolor
acuático(a): el esquí acuático water-skiing, 9.1
acuerdo: de acuerdo OK, all right
adaptar to adapt
además moreover; besides
¡Adiós! Good-bye! BV
adivinar to guess
admirar to admire
admitir to admit
la **adolescencia** adolescence
el/la **adolescente** adolescent, teenager
¿adónde? where?, 1.1
adorable adorable
adorar to adore
adornar to adorn
la **aduana** customs, 11.2
aérea: la línea aérea airlines
el **aeropuerto** airport, 11.1
afeitarse to shave, 12.1
la crema de afeitar shaving cream, 12.1
aficionado(a) a fond of, 10.1
el/la **aficionado(a)** fan (sports)
afortunadamente fortunately
africano(a) African
afroamericano(a) African-American
el/la **agente** agent, 11.1
el/la agente de aduana customs agent, 11.2
agosto August, BV
agradable pleasant
el **agua** *(f.)* water, 9.1
el agua mineral mineral water, 12.2
esquiar en el agua to water-ski, 9.1
el **agujero** hole
ahora now, 4.2
el **aire** air
al aire libre outdoor *(adj.)*
el **ají** chili pepper
el **ajo** garlic, 14.2
el **ajuar de novia** trousseau
ajustar to adjust
al to the
al aire libre outdoor *(adj.)*
al contrario on the contrary
al principio at the beginning
alarmarse to be alarmed
la **alberca** swimming pool, 9.1
el **albergue para jóvenes (juvenil)** youth hostel, 12.2
el **álbum** album
la **alcachofa** artichoke, 14.2
el **alcohol** alcohol
alegre happy
el **alemán** German, 2.2
la **alergia** allergy, 8.2
el **álgebra** algebra, 2.2
algo something, 5.2
¿Algo más? Anything else?, 5.2
algunos(as) some, 4.1
el **alimento** food, 14.2
allí there
almacenar to store
la **almeja** clam, 14.2
almorzar (ue) to eat lunch
el **almuerzo** lunch, 5.2
tomar el almuerzo to have, eat lunch
la **alpargata** sandal
alquilar to rent
alrededor de around, 6.2
los **alrededores** outskirts
altivo arrogant, haughty
alto(a) tall, 1.1; high, 4.2
en voz alta aloud
la nota alta high grade, 4.2

la **altura** height
el/la **alumno(a)** student, 1.1
amarillo(a) yellow, 3.2
amazónico(a) Amazonian
ambicioso(a) hardworking, 1.1
ambulante itinerant
la **América Central** Central America
la **América del Norte** North America
la **América del Sur** South America
americano(a) American, 1.1
el/la **amigo(a)** friend, 1.1
el **análisis** analysis
analítico(a) analytical
analizar to analyze
anaranjado(a) orange, 3.2
anciano(a) old, 6.1
el/la **anciano(a)** old person
andaluz(a) Andalusian
andante: el caballero andante knight errant
andar to walk, to go to
el **andén** railway platform, 13.1
andino(a) Andean
la **anécdota** anecdote
el **animal** animal
anoche last night, 9.2
el **anorak** parka, 9.2
la **Antártida** Antarctic
anteayer the day before yesterday
los **anteojos de sol** sunglasses, 9.1
antes de before, 5.1
el **antibiótico** antibiotic, 8.2
la **antigüedad** antiquity
antiguo(a) old, ancient
anunciar to announce
el **anuncio** announcement
el **año** year, BV
cumplir... años to be . . . years old
el año pasado last year, 9.2
este año this year, 9.2
tener... años to be . . . years old, 6.1
el **apartamento** apartment, 6.2
la casa de apartamentos apartment house, 6.2
apasionado(a) passionate
la **apertura: la apertura de clases** beginning of the school year
aplaudir to applaud, 10.2
el **aplauso** applause, 10.2
recibir aplausos to receive applause, 10.2
aplicar to apply
el **apóstol** apostle
aprender to learn, 5.1
el **apunte: tomar apuntes** to take notes, 4.2
aquel that
en aquel entonces at that time
aquí here
Aquí tiene (tienes, tienen)... Here is (are) ...
por aquí right this way
aragonés(a) from Aragon (Spain)
el **árbol** tree
el **arco** arc
el **área** *(f.)* area
la **arena** sand, 9.1
argentino(a) Argentinian, 2.1
el **argumento** plot
la **aritmética** arithmetic, 2.2
el **arma** *(f.)* weapon
la **arqueología** archeology
arqueológico(a) archeological
el/la **arqueólogo(a)** archeologist
arrancar to pull out
arrogante arrogant
el **arroyo** stream, brook
el **arroz** rice, 5.2
el **arsenal** arsenal
el **arte** *(f.)* art, 2.2
las bellas artes fine arts
el **artefacto** artifact
el/la **artista** artist, 10.2
artístico(a) artistic
la **ascendencia** background
el **ascensor** elevator, 6.2
así so, 12
el **asiento** seat, 11.1
el número del asiento seat number, 11.1
la **asignatura** subject, discipline, 2.2
el/la **asistente de vuelo** flight attendant, 11.2
asistir to attend
el **asno** donkey
el **aspa** *(f.)* sail (of a windmill)
la **aspirina** aspirin, 8.2
astuto(a) astute
atacar to attack
el **ataque** attack
la **atención: prestar atención** to pay attention, 4.2
aterrizar to land, 11.2
atlético(a) athletic
la **atmósfera** atmosphere
atrapar to catch, 7.2
atrás behind, in the rear
atravesar (ie) to cross
el **atún** tuna, 5.2
aún even
austral former Argentine unit of currency
auténtico(a) authentic
el **autobús** bus, 10.1
perder el autobús (la guagua, el camión) to miss the bus, 10.1
el/la **autor(a)** author, 10.2
el **autorretrato** self-portrait
el **ave** *(f.)* bird
la **aventura** adventure
la **aviación** aviation
el **avión** airplane, 11.1
la **avioneta** small airplane
ayer yesterday, 9.2
ayer por la mañana yesterday morning, 9.2
ayer por la tarde yesterday afternoon, 9.2
ayudar to help, 13.1
azul blue, 3.2

B

el **bachillerato** bachelor's degree
la **bacteria** bacteria
la **bahía** bay
bailar to dance, 4.2
el **baile** dance

bajar to lower; to go down, 9.2; to get off, 13.2
bajar(se) del tren to get off the train, 13.2
bajo: bajo cero below zero, 9.2
bajo(a) short, 1.1; low, 4.2
la nota baja low grade, 4.2
la planta baja ground floor, 6.2
el **balneario** beach resort, 9.1
el **balón** ball, 7.1
tirar el balón to throw (kick) the ball, 7.2
el **baloncesto** basketball, 7.2
la **banana** banana
la **banda** music band
el **bando** team
el **bañador** bathing suit 9.1
bañarse to take a bath, 12.1
el **baño** bathroom, 6.2; bath
el cuarto de baño bathroom, 6.2
el traje de baño bathing suit, 9.1
barato(a) cheap, inexpensive, 3.2
la **barra: la barra de jabón** bar of soap, 12.2
basado(a) based (on)
basar to base
basarse to be based
la **báscula** scales, 11.1
la **base** base, 7.2; basis
básico(a) basic
el **básquetbol** basketball, 7.2
la cancha de básquetbol basketball court, 7.2
bastante enough, rather, quite, 1.1
el **bastón** ski pole, 9.2
la **batalla** battle
el **bate** bat, 7.2
el/la **bateador(a)** batter, 7.2
batear to hit (sports), 7.2
el **batú** Taíno Indian game
el **bautizo** baptism
el/la **bebé** baby
beber to drink, 5.1
la **bebida** beverage, drink
el **béisbol** baseball, 7.2
el campo de béisbol baseball field, 7.2
el juego de béisbol baseball game, 7.2
el/la jugador(a) de béisbol baseball player, 7.2
el/la **beisbolista** baseball player
bello(a) beautiful, pretty, 1.1
las bellas artes fine arts
la **berenjena** eggplant, 14.2
la **bicicleta** bicycle
ir en bicicleta to go by bike, 12.2
bien fine, well, BV
muy bien very well, BV
la **bienvenida: dar la bienvenida** to welcome, 11.2
el **biftec** steak, 14.2
bilingüe bilingual
el **billete** ticket, 11.1
el billete de ida y vuelta round-trip ticket, 13.1
el billete sencillo one-way ticket, 13.1
la **biografía** biography
la **biología** biology, 2.2
biológico(a) biological
el/la **biólogo(a)** biologist
blanco(a) white, 3.2
el **bloc** writing pad, 3.1
bloquear to stop, block, 7.1
el **blue jean** jeans, 3.2
la **blusa** blouse, 3.2
la **boca** mouth, 8.2
el **bocadillo** sandwich, 5.1
la **boletería** ticket window, 9.2
el **boleto** ticket, 9.2
el **bolígrafo** ballpoint pen, 3.1
la **bolsa** bag, 5.2; pocketbook, 13.1
el **bolsillo** pocket
bonito(a) pretty, 1.1
la **bota** boot, 9.2
el **bote** can, 5.2
la **botella: la botella de agua mineral** bottle of mineral water, 12.2
el **brazo** arm, 7.1
breve brief
brillante bright
brillar to shine, 9.1
el **bronce** bronze, 10.2
bronceado(a) tan
bronceador(a): la loción bronceadora suntan lotion, 9.1
bucear to dive; to swim underwater, 9.1
el **buceo** diving, underwater swimming, 9.1
buen good
estar de buen humor to be in a good mood, 8.1
Hace buen tiempo. The weather is nice., 9.1
bueno(a) good, 1.2
Buenas noches. Good evening., BV
Buenas tardes. Good afternoon., BV
Buenos días. Hello, Good morning., BV
sacar una nota buena to get a good grade, 4.2
el **bus** bus, 4.1
el bus escolar school bus, 4.1
busca: en busca de in search of
buscar to look for, 3.1
la **butaca** seat (theater), 10.1

C

el **caballero** knight
el caballero andante knight errant
el **caballete** easel
la **cabeza** head, 7.1
el **cacahuete (cacahuate)** peanut
cada each, every, 1.2
la **cadena** chain (necklace)
el **café** coffee, BV; café, 5.1
el café al aire libre outdoor café
el café con leche coffee with milk, 5.1
el café solo black coffee, 5.1

la **cafetería** cafeteria
la **caja** cash register, 3.1
los **calcetines** socks, 3.2
la **calculadora** calculator, 3.1
calcular to calculate
el **cálculo** calculus, 2.2
la **calle** street, 6.2
el **calor: Hace calor.** It's hot., 9.1
la **caloría** calorie
calzar to take, wear (shoe size), 3.2
la **cama** bed, 8.1
guardar la cama to stay in bed, 8.1
hacer la cama to make the bed
el/la **camarero(a)** waiter, waitress, 5.1
el **camarón** shrimp, 14.2
cambiar to change; exchange
cambiar de tren to change trains (transfer), 13.2
caminar to walk
la **caminata: dar una caminata** to take a hike, 12.2
el **camino** trail, path
el **camión** bus (Mex.), 10.1
la **camisa** shirt, 3.2
la **camiseta** T-shirt, undershirt, 3.2
la **campaña** campaign
el/la **campeón(a)** champion
el **campeonato** championship
el **campo** country; field
el campo de béisbol baseball field, 7.2
el campo de fútbol soccer field, 7.1
la casa de campo country home
el **canal** channel (TV)
la **canasta** basket, 7.2
el **canasto** basket, 7.2
la **cancha** court, 7.2
la cancha cubierta enclosed court, 9.1
la cancha de básquetbol basketball court, 7.2
la cancha de tenis tennis court, 9.1
la **canción** song
cansado(a) tired, 8.1
cantar to sing, 4.2
el **cante jondo** traditional flamenco singing
la **cantidad** amount
el **canto** singing
el **cañón** canyon
la **capital** capital
el/la **capitán** captain
el **capítulo** chapter
la **cara** face, 12.1
el **carbohidrato** carbohydrate
cardinal: los puntos cardinales cardinal points
el **cardo** thistle
el **Caribe** Caribbean
el mar Caribe Caribbean Sea
la **carne** meat, 5.2
la carne de res beef, 14.2
caro(a) expensive, 3.2
la **carpeta** folder, 3.1
el **carro** car, 4.1
en carro by car, 4.1
la **carta** letter, 6.2
la **casa** home, house, 6.2
en casa at home
la casa de apartamentos (departamentos) apartment house, 6.2
la casa de campo country home
la casa privada (particular) private house, 6.2
casado(a): estar casado(a) to be married
casi almost, practically
el **caso** case
el **catarro** cold (illness), 8.1
tener catarro to have a cold, 8.1
el/la **cátcher** catcher, 7.2
la **catedral** cathedral
la **categoría** category
católico(a) Catholic
catorce fourteen, BV
el **CD** compact disc (CD), 4.2
la **celebración** celebration
celebrar to celebrate
célebre famous
la **célula** cell
celular cellular
la **cena** dinner, 5.2
cenar to have dinner
el **centavo** penny
central central
el **centro** center
cepillarse to brush one's hair, 12.1
cepillarse los dientes to brush one's teeth, 12.1
el **cepillo** brush, 12.2
el cepillo de dientes toothbrush, 12.2
cerca de near, 6.2
el **cerdo** pig (pork), 14.2
el **cereal** cereal, 5.2
cero zero, BV
la **cesta** basket (jai alai)
el **cesto** basket, 7.2
el **chaleco** vest
el **chalet** chalet
el **champú** shampoo, 12.2
¡Chao! Good-bye!, BV
la **chaqueta** jacket, 3.2
la **chaucha** string beans
el **cheque de viajero** traveler's check
chileno(a) Chilean
la **chimenea** chimney
la **china** orange (fruit)
el **chisme** piece of gossip
¡chist! shh!
el **choclo** corn
el **chocolate: de chocolate** chocolate *(adj.)*, 5.1
el **churro** (type of) doughnut
el **cielo** sky, 9.1
las **ciencias** science, 2.2
las ciencias naturales natural sciences
las ciencias sociales social sciences, 2.2
científico(a) scientific
el/la **científico(a)** scientist
cien(to) one hundred, 3.2
cinco five, BV
cincuenta fifty, 2.2

el **cine** movie theater, 10.1
el **círculo** circle
la **ciudad** city
el **clarinete** clarinet
¡claro! certainly!, of course!
la **clase** class (school) 2.1; class (ticket). 13.1
la apertura de clases beginning of the school year
la sala de clase classroom, 4.1
el salón de clase classroom, 4.1
primera clase first-class, 13.1
segunda clase second-class, 13.1
clásico(a) classic
clasificar to classify
el/la **cliente** customer, 5.1
el **clima** climate
climático(a) climatic
la **clínica** clinic
el **club** club, 4.2
el Club de español Spanish Club, 4.2
el **coche** car, 4.1; train car, 13.2
en coche by car, 4.1
el **coche-cafetería** cafeteria (dining) car, 13.2
el **coche-cama** sleeping car, 13.2
el **coche-comedor** dining car, 13.2
la **cocina** kitchen, 6.2
el/la **cocinero(a)** cook, 14.1
la **coincidencia** coincidence
la **cola** line (queue), 10.1
hacer cola to stand in line, 10.1
la **colección** collection
el **colector** collector
el **colegio** school, 1.1
el **colesterol** cholesterol
colgar (ue) to hang
colocar to put, place
colombiano(a) Colombian, 1.1
la **colonia** suburb, colony
el **color** color, 3.2
de color marrón brown, 3.2
¿De qué color es? What color is it?, 3.2

el/la **comandante** captain, 11.2
el **comedor** dining room, 6.2
comenzar (ie) to begin
comer to eat, 5.1
el **comestible** food, 14.2
cómico(a) funny, 1.1
la **comida** food, meal, 5.2
como like; as; since, 1.2
¿cómo? how?, what?, 1.1
¿Cómo está... ? How is. . . ?, 8.1
¡Cómo no! Of course!
la **comodidad** comfort
compacto(a): el disco compacto compact disc, CD, 4.2
el/la **compañero(a)** friend, 1.2
la **compañía** company
la **comparación** comparison
comparar to compare
la **competencia** competition
la **competición** competition, contest
competir (i, i) to compete
completo(a) full (train), 13.2
la **composición** composition
la **compra: ir de compras** to go shopping, to shop, 5.2
comprar to buy, 3.1
comprender to understand, 5.1
la **computadora** computer
con with
con mucha plata rich
¿con quién? with whom?
con retraso with a delay, 13.2
con una demora with a delay, 11.1
el **concierto** concert
el **conde** count
la **condición** condition
el **condimento** seasoning
el **condominio** condominium
conectar to connect
la **conferencia** lecture
Conforme. Agreed., Fine., 14.2
congelado(a): los productos congelados frozen food, 5.2

el **conjunto** set, collection
conocer to know, to be familiar with, 11.1
la **conquista** conquest
conquistar to conquer
consentir (ie, i) to allow, tolerate
conservar to save
considerar to consider
consistir (en) to consist of
la **consulta: la consulta del médico** doctor's office, 8.2
consultar to consult, 13.1
el **consultorio** medical office, 8.2
el/la **consumidor(a)** consumer
consumir to consume
el **consumo** consumption
el **contacto** touch
la **contaminación** pollution
contaminado(a) polluted
contaminar to pollute
contener to contain
contento(a) happy, 8.1
contestar to answer
el **continente** continent
continuar to continue, 7.2
contra against, 7.1
el **control** inspection, 11.1
el control de pasaportes passport inspection, 11.1
el control de seguridad security check, 11.1
controlar to control
conversar to talk, speak
convertir (ie, i) to convert, transform
la **copa: la Copa mundial** World Cup
copiar to copy
el/la **copiloto** copilot, 11.2
el **corazón** heart
la **corbata** tie, 3.2
el **cordero** lamb, 14.2
el **cordoncillo** piping (embroidery)
la **coreografía** choreography
la **córnea** cornea
el **coro** choir, chorus
el **correo: el correo electrónico** e-mail, electronic mail

correr to run, 7.2
cortar to cut
la **cortesía** courtesy, BV
corto(a) short, 3.2
el pantalón corto shorts, 3.2
la **cosa** thing
coser to sew
la **costa** coast
costar (ue) to cost, 3.1
costarricense Costa Rican
la **costumbre** custom
la **costura** sewing
crear to create
el **crecimiento** growth
crédito: la tarjeta de crédito credit card, 14.1
creer to believe, 8.2; to think so
la **crema: la crema de afeitar** shaving cream, 12.1
la crema dentífrica toothpaste, 12.2
la crema protectora sunblock, 9.1
criollo(a) Creole
cristiano(a) Christian
cruzar to cross
el **cuaderno** notebook, 3.1
el **cuadro** painting, 10.2
¿cuál? which?, what?, BV
¿Cuál es la fecha de hoy? What is today's date?, BV
¿cuáles? which ones?, what?
cuando when, 4.2
¿cuándo? when?, 4.1
¿cuánto? how much?, 3.1
¿A cuánto está(n)... ? How much is (are) . . . ?, 5.2
¿Cuánto cuesta(n)... ? How much do(es) . . . cost?, 3.1
¿Cuánto es? How much does it cost?, 3.1
¿cuántos(as)? how many?, 2.1
cuarenta forty, 2.2
el **cuarto** room, bedroom 6.2; quarter
el cuarto de baño bathroom, 6.2
el cuarto de dormir bedroom
menos cuarto a quarter to (the hour)
y cuarto a quarter past (the hour)
cuarto(a) fourth, 6.2
cuatro four, BV
cuatrocientos(as) four hundred, 3.2
cubano(a) Cuban
cubanoamericano(a) Cuban-American
cubrir to cover
la **cuchara** tablespoon, 14.1
la **cucharita** teaspoon, 14.1
el **cuchillo** knife, 14.1
el **cuello** neck
la **cuenca** basin
la **cuenta** bill, check, 5.1
el/la **cuentista** short-story writer
el **cuento** story
la **cuerda** string (instrument)
el **cuerpo** body
¡cuidado! careful!
con mucho cuidado very carefully
cultivar to cultivate
el **cumpleaños** birthday, 6.1
cumplir: cumplir... años to be . . . years old, 6.1
el/la **curandero(a)** folk healer
el **curso** course, class, 2.1
el curso obligatorio required course
el curso opcional elective course

D

la **dama** lady-in-waiting, woman
la **danza** dance
dar to give, 4.2
dar a entender to imply that
dar auxilio to help
dar énfasis to emphasize
dar la mano to shake hands
dar un examen to give a test, 4.2
dar una fiesta to give (throw) a party, 4.2
dar una representación to put on a performance, 10.2
datar to date
los **datos** data, information
de of, from, for, BV
de... a... from (time) to (time), 2.2
de joven as a young person
De nada. You're welcome., BV
de ninguna manera by no means, 1.1
de vez en cuando sometimes
debajo (de) under, below
deber must; should; to owe
decidir to decide
décimo(a) tenth, 6.2
decir to say, 13
¡Diga! Hello! (answering the telephone—Spain), 14.2
declarar to declare
el **dedo** finger
el **defecto** fault, flaw
definitivamente once and for all
dejar to leave (something), 14.1; to let, allow
del of the, from the
delante de in front of, 10.1
delantero(a) front
delgado(a) thin
delicioso(a) delicious
demás other, rest
demasiado too much
la **demora: con una demora** with a delay, 11.1
dentífrico(a): la pasta (crema) dentífrica toothpaste, 12.2
dentro de within
dentro de poco soon
el **departamento** apartment, 6.2
la casa de departamentos apartment house, 6.2
depender (de) to depend (on)

el/la **dependiente(a)** employee, 3.1
el **deporte** sport, 7.1
el deporte de equipo team sport
el deporte individual individual sport
deportivo(a) (related to) sports, 6.2
la emisión deportiva sports program (TV), 6.2
derecho(a) right, 7.1
derrotar to defeat
desagradable unpleasant
desamparado(a): los niños desamparados homeless children
desayunarse to eat breakfast, 12.1
el **desayuno** breakfast, 5.2
tomar el desayuno to eat breakfast, 12.1
el/la **descendiente** descendant
describir to describe
descubrir to discover
el **descuento** discount
desde since
desear to want, wish, 3.2
¿Qué desea usted? May I help you? (in a store), 3.2
los **desechos** waste
desembarcar to disembark, 11.2
el **desierto** desert
despachar to sell, 8.2
despegar to take off (airplane), 11.2
despertarse (ie) to wake up, 12.1
después (de) after, 5.1; later
el **destino** destination, 11.1
con destino a to
devolver (ue) to return (something), 7.2
el **día** day, BV
Buenos días. Good morning., BV
hoy (en) día nowadays, these days
¿Qué día es (hoy)? What day is it (today)?, BV
la **diagnosis** diagnosis, 8.2
el **diálogo** dialogue
el **diamante** diamond
dibujar to draw
el **dibujo** drawing
diciembre December, BV
diecinueve nineteen, BV
dieciocho eighteen, BV
dieciséis sixteen, B
diecisiete seventeen, BV
el **diente: cepillarse los dientes** to brush one's teeth, 12.1
el cepillo de dientes toothbrush, 12.2
diez ten
la **diferencia** difference
diferente different
difícil difficult, 2.1
¡Diga! Hello! (telephone), 14.2
diminuto(a) tiny, minute
la **dinamita** dynamite
el **dinero** money, 14.1
el dinero en efectivo cash
¡Dios mío! Gosh!
la **dirección** address; direction
en dirección a toward
directo(a) direct
el/la **director(a)** director, principal
la **disciplina** subject area (school), 2.2
el **disco: el disco compacto** compact disc, CD, 4.2
discutir to discuss
el/la **diseñador(a)** designer
el **diseño** design
disfrutar to enjoy
la **disputa** quarrel, argument
el **disquete** diskette, 3.1
la **distancia** distance
la **diversión** amusement
divertido(a) fun, amusing
divertirse (ie, i) to enjoy oneself, 12.2
dividir to divide
la **división** division
divorciarse to get divorced
doblado(a) dubbed, 10.1
dobles doubles, 9.1
doce twelve, BV
la **docena** dozen
el/la **doctor(a)** doctor
el **dólar** dollar
doler (ue) to hurt, 8.2
Me duele(n)... My . . . hurt(s) me, 8.2
el **dolor** pain, ache, 8.1
el dolor de cabeza headache, 8.1
el dolor de estómago stomachache, 8.1
el dolor de garganta sore throat, 8.1
Tengo dolor de... I have a pain in my . . . , 8.2
doméstico(a) domestic
la economía doméstica home economics, 2.2
el **domingo** Sunday, BV
dominicano(a) Dominican, 2.1
la República Dominicana Dominican Republic
don courteous way of addressing a male
donde where, 1.2
¿dónde? where?, 1.2
dormido(a) asleep
dormir (ue, u) to sleep
el saco de dormir sleeping bag, 12.2
dormirse (ue, u) to fall asleep, 12.1
el **dormitorio** bedroom, 6.2
dos two, BV
doscientos(as) two hundred, 3.2
la **dosis** dose, 8.2
el/la **dramaturgo(a)** playwright
driblar to dribble, 7.2
la **droga** drug
la **ducha** shower, 12.1
tomar una ducha to take a shower, 12.1
la **duda** doubt
dulce: el pan dulce sweet roll, 5.1
la **duración** duration
durante during
duro(a) hard, difficult, 2.1
el **DVD** digital video disc (DVD), 4.2

E

echar to throw
echar (tomar) una siesta to take a nap
echarle flores to pay someone a compliment
la **ecología** ecology
ecológico(a) ecological
la **economía** economics; economy
la economía doméstica home economics, 2.2
económico(a) economical, 12.2
la **ecuación** equation
ecuatoriano(a) Ecuadorean, 2.1
la **edad** age
el **edificio** building
la **educación** education
la educación física physical education, 2.2
efectivo: en efectivo in cash
el **ejemplo: por ejemplo** for example
el **ejote** string beans
el the *(m. sing.)*, 1.1
él he, 1.1
electrónico(a) electronic
el correo electrónico e-mail, electronic mail
la **elevación** elevation
elevado(a) elevated
elevar to elevate
ella she, 1.1
ellos(as) they, 2.1
el **elote** corn (Mex.)
embarcar to board, 11.2
embarque: la tarjeta de embarque boarding pass, 11.1
la puerta de embarque departure gate
la **emisión** program (TV), 6.2; emission
la emisión deportiva sports program, 6.2
emitir to emit
la **emoción** emotion
emocional emotional
empatado(a) tied (score), 7.1
El tanto queda empatado. The score is tied., 7.1
empezar (ie) to begin, 7.1
el/la **empleado(a)** employee, 3.1
en in; on
en aquel entonces at that time
en punto on the dot, sharp, 4.1
el/la **enamorado(a)** sweetheart, lover
encantador(a) charming
encantar to delight
encender (ie) to light
encestar to put in (make) a basket, 7.2
encima: por encima de above, 9.1
encontrar (ue) to find
el/la **enemigo(a)** enemy
la **energía** energy
enero January, BV
el **énfasis: dar énfasis** to emphasize
enfatizar to emphasize
la **enfermedad** illness
enfermo(a) sick, 8.1
el/la **enfermo(a)** sick person, 8.1
el **enganche** down payment
enlatado(a) canned
la **ensalada** salad, 5.1
enseguida right away, immediately, 5.1
enseñar to teach, 4.1
entero(a) entire, whole
enterrar (ie) to bury
el **entierro** burial
entonces then
en aquel entonces at that time
la **entrada** inning, 7.2; admission ticket, 10.1
entrar to enter, 4.1
entrar en escena to come (go) on stage, 10.2
entre between, 7.1
entregar to deliver
la **entrevista** interview
enviar to send
envuelto(a) wrapped
el **episodio** episode
la **época** period of time, epoch
el **equilibrio** equilibrium
el **equipaje** baggage, luggage, 11.1
el equipaje de mano carry-on luggage, 11.1
el **equipo** team, 7.1; equipment
el deporte de equipo team sport, 7.2
erróneo(a) wrong, erroneous
la **escala** stopover
la **escalera** stairway, 6.2
los **escalofríos** chills, 8.1
escamotear to secretly take
escapar to escape
la **escena** scene
entrar en escena to come (go) on stage, 10.2
el **escenario** scenery, set (theater), 10.2
escoger to choose
escolar (related to) school, 2.1
el bus escolar school bus, 4.1
el horario escolar school schedule
los materiales escolares school supplies, 3.1
la vida escolar school life
esconder to hide
escribir to write, 5.1
escuchar to listen (to), 4.2
el **escudero** squire, knight's attendant
la **escuela** school, 1.1
la escuela intermedia middle school
la escuela primaria elementary school
la escuela secundaria high school, 1.1
la escuela superior high school
el/la **escultor(a)** sculptor, 10.2
la **escultura** sculpture
esencialmente essentially

eso: a eso de at about (time), 4.1
el **espagueti** spaghetti
espantoso frightful
España Spain
español(a) Spanish *(adj.)*
el **español** Spanish, 2.2
la **espátula** palette knife, spatula
especial special
la **especialidad** specialty
especialmente especially
el **espectáculo** show, 10.2
ver un espectáculo to see a show, 10.2
el/la **espectador(a)** spectator, 7.1
el **espejo** mirror, 12.1
espera: la sala de espera waiting room, 13.1
esperar to wait (for), 11.1
espontáneo(a) spontaneous
la **esposa** wife, spouse, 6.1
el **esposo** husband, spouse, 6.1
el **esquí** skiing, 9.2; ski
el esquí acuático waterskiing, 9.1
el/la **esquiador(a)** skier, 9.2
esquiar to ski, 9.2
esquiar en el agua to water-ski, 9.1
la **estación** season, BV; resort; station, 10.1
la estación de esquí ski resort, 9.2
la estación de ferrocarril train station, 13.1
la estación de metro subway station, 10.1
el **estadio** stadium, 7.1
el **estado** state
Estados Unidos United States
estadounidense from the United States
estar to be, 4.1
estar resfriado(a) to have a cold, 8.1
la **estatua** statue, 10.2
el **este** east
estereofónico(a) stereo
el **estilo** style
estimado(a) esteemed
el **estómago** stomach, 8.1

estornudar to sneeze, 8.1
la **estrategia** strategy
la **estrella** star
la **estructura** structure
el/la **estudiante** student
estudiantil (relating to) student
estudiar to study, 4.1
el **estudio** study
estupendo(a) stupendous
eterno(a) eternal
étnico(a) ethnic
Europa Europe
exactamente exactly
exagerar to exaggerate
el **examen** test, exam, 4.2
examinar to examine, 8.2
la **excavación** excavation
excavar to dig, excavate
exceder to exceed
excelente excellent
la **excepción** exception
exclamar to exclaim
exclusivamente exclusively
la **exhibición** exhibition
existir to exist
el **éxito** success
la **expedición** expedition
la **experiencia** experience
el/la **experto(a)** expert, 9.2
explicar to explain, 4.2
el/la **explorador(a)** explorer
la **explosión** explosion
la **exposición (de arte)** (art) exhibition, 10.2
la **expresión: el modo de expresión** means of expression
extranjero(a) foreign
el país extranjero foreign country, 11.2
el/la **extranjero(a)** foreigner
extraordinario(a) extraordinary

la **fábrica** factory
fabuloso(a) fabulous
fácil easy, 2.1

la **factura** invoice
facturar el equipaje to check luggage, 11.1
la **Facultad** school (of a university)
la **faja** sash
la **falda** skirt, 3.2
la **fama** fame
la **familia** family, 6.1
familiar (related to the) family
famoso(a) famous, 1.2
fantástico(a) fantastic, 1.2
el/la **farmacéutico(a)** pharmacist, 8.2
la **farmacia** pharmacy, 8.2
fascinar to fascinate
febrero February, BV
la **fecha** date, BV
¿Cuál es la fecha de hoy? What is today's date?, BV
feo(a) ugly, 1.1
la **fiebre** fever, 8.1
tener fiebre to have a fever, 8.1
fiel faithful
la **fiesta** party
dar una fiesta to give (throw) a party, 4.2
la **figura** figure
figurativo(a) figurative
fijo(a) fixed
la **fila** line (queue); row (of seats), 10.1
el **film** film, 10.1
el **fin** end
el fin de semana weekend, BV
a fines de at the end of
el **final: al final (de)** at the end (of)
las **finanzas** finances
la **física** physics, 2.1
físico(a): la educación física physical education, 2.2
flaco(a) thin, 1.2
la **flauta** flute
flechar to become enamored of (to fall for)
la **flor** flower
formar to make up, to form

la **foto** photo
la **fotografía** photograph
el **francés** French, 2.2
franco(a) frank, candid, sincere
la **frase** phrase, sentence
frecuentemente frequently
freír (i, i) to fry, 14.1
fresco(a) fresh
el **frijol** bean, 5.2
el **frío: Hace frío.** It's cold., 9.2
frito(a) fried, 5.1
las papas fritas French fries, 5.1
el **frontón** wall (of a jai alai court)
la **fruta** fruit, 5.2
la **fuente** source
fuerte strong
fumar: la sección de (no) fumar (no) smoking area, 11.1
la **función** performance, 10.2
el **funcionamiento** functioning
la **fundación** foundation
fundar to found, establish
la **furia** fury
furioso(a) furious
el **fútbol** soccer, 7.1
el campo de fútbol soccer field, 7.1
el **futuro** future

G

las **gafas de sol** sunglasses, 9.1
el **galán** beau, heartthrob
gallardo(a) gallant, fine-looking
el **galón** gallon
ganar to win, 7.1; to earn
la **ganga** bargain
el **garaje** garage, 6.2
la **garganta** throat, 8.1
el **gas** gas
gastar to spend
el/la **gato(a)** cat, 6.1
general: en general generally
por lo general in general
generalmente usually, generally
el **género** genre
generoso(a) generous, 1.2
la **gente** people
la **geografía** geography, 2.2
la **geometría** geometry, 2.2
geométrico(a) geometric
el **gigante** giant
el **gimnasio** gymnasium
la **gira** tour, 12.2
el **gol: meter un gol** to score a goal, 7.1
el **golfo** gulf
golpear to hit, 9.2
la **goma: la goma de borrar** eraser, 3.1
gordo(a) fat, 1.2
la **gorra** cap, hat, 3.2
gozar to enjoy
Gracias Thank you., BV
gracioso(a) funny, 1.1
el **grado** degree (temperature), 9.2
la **gramática** grammar
el **gramo** gram
gran, grande big, large, great
las Grandes Ligas Major Leagues
el **grano** grain
la **grasa** fat
grave serious, grave
la **gripe** flu, 8.1
gris gray, 3.2
el **grupo** group
la **guagua** bus (P.R., Cuba), 10.1
el **guante** glove, 7.2
guapo(a) handsome, 1.1
guardar to guard, 7.1; to keep
guardar cama to stay in bed, 8.1
guatemalteco(a) Guatemalan
la **guerra** war
la **guerrilla** guerrilla
el/la **guía** tour guide
el **guisante** pea, 5.2
la **guitarra** guitar
gustar to like, to be pleasing
el **gusto** pleasure
Mucho gusto. Nice to meet you.

H

la **habichuela** bean, 5.2
la habichuela tierna string bean
la **habitación** bedroom
el/la **habitante** inhabitant
habla: los países de habla española Spanish-speaking countries
hablar to speak, talk, 3.1
hace: Hace buen tiempo. The weather is nice., 9.1
Hace calor. It's hot., 9.1
Hace frío. It's cold., 9.2
Hace mal tiempo. The weather is bad., 9.1
Hace sol. It's sunny., 9.1
hacer to do, to make
hacer caso to pay attention
hacer la cama to make the bed
hacer la maleta to pack one's suitcase
hacer un viaje to take a trip, 11.1
hacia toward
hallar to find
hambre: tener hambre to be hungry, 14.1
la **hamburguesa** hamburger, 5.1
hasta until, BV
¡Hasta luego! See you later!, BV
¡Hasta mañana! See you tomorrow!, BV
¡Hasta pronto! See you soon!, BV
hay there is, there are, BV
hay que one must
Hay sol. It's sunny., 9.1
No hay de qué. You're welcome., BV

hecho(a) made
helado(a): el té helado iced tea, 5.1
el **helado** ice cream, 5.1
el helado de chocolate chocolate ice cream, 5.1
el helado de vainilla vanilla ice cream, 5.1
el **hemisferio norte** northern hemisphere
el **hemisferio sur** southern hemisphere
la **herencia** inheritance
la **hermana** sister, 6.1
el **hermano** brother, 6.1
hermoso(a) beautiful, pretty, 1.1
el/la **héroe** hero
higiénico(a): el papel higiénico toilet paper, 12.2
la **hija** daughter, 6.1
el **hijo** son, 6.1
los **hijos** children, 6.1
hispano(a) Hispanic
hispanoamericano(a) Spanish-American
hispanohablante Spanish-speaking
el/la **hispanohablante** Spanish speaker
la **historia** history, 2.2; story
el/la **historiador(a)** historian
histórico(a) historical
la **historieta** little story
la **hoja: la hoja de papel** sheet of paper, 3.1
¡Hola! Hello!, BV
el **hombre** man
¡hombre! good heavens!, you bet!
honesto(a) honest, 1.2
el **honor** honor
la **hora** hour; time
la hora de salida departure hour
¿A qué hora? At what time?, 2.2
¿Qué hora es? What time is it?, 2.2
el **horario** schedule, 13.1
el horario escolar school schedule
horrible horrible
el **hospital** hospital
el **hostal** inexpensive hotel, 12.2
la **Hostia** Host (religious)
el **hotel** hotel
hoy today, BV
hoy (en) día nowadays, these days
el **huarache** sandal
el **huevo** egg, 5.2
humano(a): el ser humano human being
humilde humble
el **humor** mood, 8.1
estar de buen humor to be in a good mood, 8.1
estar de mal humor to be in a bad mood, 8.1
el **huso horario** time zone

I

ida: de ida y vuelta round-trip (ticket), 13.1
la **idea** idea
ideal ideal, 1.2
el/la **idealista** idealist
la **iglesia** church
igual equal
la **ilusión** illusion
imaginado(a) imagined, dreamed of
imaginar to imagine
importante important
imposible impossible
la **impresora** printer
el/la **inca** Inca
incluido(a): ¿Está incluido el servicio? Is the tip included?, 5.1
incluir to include, 5.1
increíble incredible
la **independencia** independence
el **indicador: el tablero indicador** scoreboard, 7.1
indicar to indicate, 11.1
indígena native, indigenous
el/la **indígena** native person
indio(a) Indian
indispensable indispensable
individual individual
el deporte individual individual sport
el **individuo** individual
industrial industrial
la **influencia** influence
la **información** information
informar to inform, 13.2
la **informática** computer science, 2.2
el **inglés** English, 2.2
inmediatamente immediately
inmediato(a) immediate
inmenso(a) immense
inspeccionar to inspect, 11.1
el **instante** instant
la **instrucción** instruction
el **instrumento** instrument
el instrumento musical musical instrument
íntegro(a) integral
inteligente intelligent, 2.1
el **interés** interest
interesante interesting, 2.1
interesar to interest
intermedio(a): la escuela intermedia middle school
internacional international
la **interpretación** interpretation
íntimo(a) intimate
inverso(a) reverse
la **investigación** investigation
el/la **investigador(a)** researcher
el **invierno** winter, BV
la **invitación** invitation
invitar to invite, 6.1
la **inyección** injection, 8.2
ir to go, 4.1
ir a + infinitive to be going to (do something)
ir a pie to go on foot, to walk 4.1
ir de compras to go shopping, 5.2
ir en bicicleta to go by bicycle, 12.2
ir en carro (coche) to go by car, 4.1
ir en tren to go by train

la **isla** island
italiano(a) Italian
izquierdo(a) left, 7.1

el **jabón** soap, 12.2
la barra (pastilla) de jabón bar of soap, 12.2
jamás never
el **jamón** ham, 5.1
el **jardín** garden, 6.2
el/la **jardinero(a)** outfielder, 7.2
el **jet** jet
el **jonrón** home run, 7.2
joven young, 6.1
de joven as a young person
el/la **joven** youth, young person, 10.1
la **judía: la judía verde** green bean, 5.2
el **juego** game
el juego de béisbol baseball game, 7.2
el juego de tenis tennis game, 9.1
los Juegos Olímpicos Olympic Games
el **jueves** Thursday, BV
el/la **jugador(a)** player, 7.1
el/la jugador(a) de béisbol baseball player, 7.2
jugar (ue) to play, 7.1
jugar (al) béisbol (fútbol, baloncesto, etc.) to play baseball (soccer, basketball, etc.), 7.1
el **jugo** juice
el jugo de naranja orange juice, 12.1
el **juguete** toy
julio July, BV
la **jungla** jungle
junio June, BV
junto(a) together
juvenil: el albergue juvenil youth hostel, 12.2

K

el **kilo** kilogram, 5.2
el **kilómetro** kilometer

la the *(f. sing.)*, 1.1; it, her *(pron.)*
el **laboratorio** laboratory
el **lado** side
el **lago** lake
el **lamento** lament
la **lana** wool
la **langosta** lobster, 14.2
la **lanza** lance
el/la **lanzador(a)** pitcher, 7.2
lanzar to throw, 7.1
el **lápiz** pencil, 3.1
largo(a) long, 3.2
las them *(f. pl.) (pron.)*
la **lata** can, 5.2
lateral side *(adj.)*, 13.2
el **latín** Latin, 2.2
latino(a) Latin *(adj.)*
Latinoamérica Latin America, 1.1
latinoamericano(a) Latin American
lavarse to wash oneself, 12.1
lavarse los dientes to brush one's teeth, 12.1
le to him, to her; to you *(formal) (pron.)*
la **lección** lesson, 4.2
la **leche** milk
el café con leche coffee with milk, 5.1
el **lechón** suckling pig
la **lechuga** lettuce, 5.2
la **lectura** reading
leer to read, 5.1
la **legumbre** vegetable, 14
la **lengua** language, 2.2
el **lenguaje** language
les to them; to you *(formal pl.) (pron.)*

la **letra** letter (of alphabet)
levantar to lift
levantarse to get up, 12.1
el/la **libertador(a)** liberator
la **libra** pound
libre free, 5.1
al aire libre outdoor *(adj.)*
el **libro** book, 3.1
el **liceo** high school
el **lienzo** canvas (painting)
la **liga** league
las Grandes Ligas Major Leagues
ligero(a) light (cheerful)
limeño(a) from Lima (Peru)
la **limonada** lemonade, BV
lindo(a) pretty, 1.1
la **línea** line
la línea aérea airline
la línea ecuatorial equator
la línea paralela parallel line
la línea telefónica telephone line
el **lípido** lipid, fat
líquido(a) liquid
listo(a) ready
la **litera** berth, 13.2
literal literal
literario(a) literary
la **literatura** literature, 2.1
el **litro** liter
llamado(a) called
llamar to call
llamarse to be named, to call oneself, 12.1
la **llegada** arrival, 11.1
llegar to arrive, 4.1
lleno(a) full
llevar to carry, 3.1; to wear, 3.2; to bring, 6.1; to bear; to have (subtitles, ingredients, etc.)
llover (ue) to rain
Llueve. It's raining., 9.1
la **lluvia** rain
lo it; him *(m. sing.) (pron.)*
lo que what, that which

local local, 13.2
la **loción: la loción bronceadora** suntan lotion, 9.1
loco(a) insane
los them *(m. pl.) (pron.)*
el **loto** lotto
luchar to fight
luego later; then, BV
¡Hasta luego! See you later!, BV
el **lugar** place
lujo: de lujo deluxe
lujoso(a) luxurious
la **luna** moon
el **lunes** Monday, BV
la **luz** light

M

la **madre** mother, 6.1
madrileño(a) native of Madrid
la **madrina** godmother
el/la **maestro(a)** teacher; master
magnífico(a) magnificent
el **maíz** corn, 14.2
mal bad, 14.2
estar de mal humor to be in a bad mood, 8.1
Hace mal tiempo. The weather's bad., 9.1
la **maleta** suitcase, 11.1
la **maletera** trunk (of a car), 13.1
el/la **maletero(a)** porter, 11.1
malhumorado(a) bad-tempered
malo(a) bad, 2.1
sacar una nota mala to get a bad grade, 4.2
la **mamá** mom
la **manera** way, manner, 1.1
de ninguna manera by no means, 1.1
el **maní** peanut
la **mano** hand, 7.1
dar la mano to shake hands
el **mantel** tablecloth, 14.1
mantener to maintain
la **manzana** apple, 5.2
mañana tomorrow, BV
¡Hasta mañana! See you tomorrow!, BV
la **mañana** morning
de la mañana A.M. (time), 2.2
por la mañana in the morning
el **mapa** map
el **maquillaje** makeup, 12.1
poner el maquillaje to put one's makeup on, 12.1
maquillarse to put one's makeup on, 12.1
el **mar** sea, 9.1
el mar Caribe Caribbean Sea
maravilloso(a) marvelous
el **marcador** marker, 3.1
marcar: marcar un tanto to score a point, 7.1
el **marido** husband, 6.1
los **mariscos** shellfish, 5.2
marrón: de color marrón brown, 3.2
el **martes** Tuesday, BV
marzo March, BV
más more, 2.2
más o menos more or less
más tarde later
la **masa** mass
las **matemáticas** mathematics, 2.1
la **materia** matter, subject
el **material: los materiales escolares** school supplies, 3.1
el **matrimonio** marriage
el/la **maya** Maya
mayo May, BV
mayor greater
la mayor parte the greater part, the most
la **mayoría** majority
me me *(pron.)*
la **medalla** medal
media: y media half-past (time), 2.2
la **medianoche** midnight, 2.2
el **medicamento** medicine (drugs), 8.2
la **medicina** medicine (discipline), 8.2
el/la **médico(a)** doctor, 8.2
la **medida** measurement
el **medio** medium, means
el medio de transporte means of transportation
medio(a) half, 5.2
media hora half an hour
el **mediodía** noon
medir (i, i) to measure
melancólico(a) melancholic
menos less, fewer
menos cuarto a quarter to (the hour)
la **mensualidad** monthly installment
el **menú** menu, 5.1
el **mercado** market, 5.2
el **merengue** merengue
la **merienda** snack, 4.2
tomar una merienda to have a snack, 4.2
la **mermelada** marmalade
el **mes** month, BV
la **mesa** table, 5.1; plateau
la **mesera** waitress, 5.1
el **mesero** waiter, 5.1
el/la **mestizo(a)** mestizo
el **metabolismo** metabolism
el **metal: instrumentos de metal** brass (instruments in orchestra)
meter to put, place, 7.1
meter un gol to score a goal, 7.1
el **método** method
el **metro** subway, 10.1; meter
mexicano(a) Mexican, 1.1
mexicanoamericano(a) Mexican-American
la **mezcla** mixture
mi my
mí (to) me *(pron.)*
el **microbio** microbe
microscópico(a) microscopic
el **microscopio** microscope

el **miedo** fear
tener miedo to be afraid
el **miembro** member, 4.2
mientras while
el **miércoles** Wednesday, BV
mil (one) thousand, 3.2
la **milla** mile
el **millón** million
el **minuto** minute
mirar to look at, watch, 3.1
¡Mira! Look!
mirarse to look at oneself, 12.1
mismo(a) same, 2.1; itself
el **misterio** mystery
misterioso(a) mysterious
mixto(a) co-ed (school)
la **mochila** backpack, 3.1; knapsack, 12.2
la **modalidad** mode, type
el/la **modelo** model
el **módem** modem
moderno(a) modern
el **modo** manner, way
el modo de expresión means of expression
el **molino de viento** windmill
el **momento** moment
la **moneda** coin, currency
el **monitor** monitor
monocelular single-celled
el **monstruo** monster
la **montaña** mountain, 9.2
montañoso(a) mountainous
montar (caballo) to mount, get on (horse)
el **monumento** monument
moreno(a) dark, brunette, 1.1
morir (ue, u) to die
el **mostrador** counter, 11.1
el **motivo** reason, motive; theme
el **motor** motor
mover (ue) to move
el **movimiento** movement
el **mozo** porter, 13.1
la **muchacha** girl, 1.1
el **muchacho** boy, 1.1
mucho(a) a lot; many, 2.1
Mucho gusto. Nice to meet you.
los **muebles** furniture
la **muerte** death
la **mujer** wife, 6.1
la **multiplicación** multiplication
multiplicar to multiply
mundial worldwide, (related to the) world
la Copa mundial World Cup
la Serie mundial World Series
el **mundo** world
todo el mundo everyone
el **mural** mural, 10.2
el/la **muralista** muralist, 10
el **museo** museum, 10.2
la **música** music, 2.2
el/la **músico(a)** musician
muy very, BV
muy bien very well, BV

N

nacer to be born
nacido(a) born
nacional national
la **nacionalidad** nationality, 1.2
¿de qué nacionalidad? what nationality?
nada nothing, 5.2
De nada. You're welcome., BV
Nada más. Nothing else., 5.2
Por nada. You're welcome., BV
nadar to swim, 9.1
nadie no one
la **naranja** orange, 5.2
el **narcótico** narcotic
la **natación** swimming, 9.1
natural: los recursos naturales natural resources, 2.1
las ciencias naturales natural sciences
la **navaja** razor, 12.1
navegar to navigate
navegar por la red to surf the Net
la **Navidad** Christmas
necesario(a) necessary
necesitar to need, 3.1
negro(a) black, 3.2
nervioso(a) nervous, 8.1
nevar (ie) to snow, 9.2
la **nieta** granddaughter, 6.1
el **nieto** grandson, 6.1
la **nieve** snow, 9.2
ninguno(a) not any, none
de ninguna manera by no means, 1.1
el/la **niño(a)** child
los niños desamparados homeless children
el **nivel** level
no no, BV
No hay de qué. You're welcome., BV
no hay más remedio there's no other alternative
noble noble
la **noche** night, evening
Buenas noches. Good night., BV
de la noche P.M. (time), 2.2
esta noche tonight, 9.2
por la noche in the evening, at night
la **Nochebuena** Christmas Eve
el **nombre** name
¿a nombre de quién? in whose name?, 14.2
el **noroeste** northwest
el **norte** north
norteamericano(a) North American
nos (to) us *(pl. pron.)*
nosotros(as) we, 2.2
la **nota** grade, 4.2
la nota buena (alta) good (high) grade, 4.2
la nota mala (baja) bad (low) grade, 4.2
sacar una nota buena (mala) to get a good (bad) grade, 4.2

notable notable
notar to note
las **noticias** news, 6.2
novecientos(as) nine hundred, 3.2
la **novela** novel
el/la **novelista** novelist
noveno(a) ninth, 6.2
noventa ninety, 2.2
noviembre November, BV
el/la **novio(a)** boyfriend/girlfriend; fiancé(e)
la **nube** cloud, 9.1
Hay nubes. It's cloudy., 9.1
nublado(a) cloudy, 9.1
nuestro(a) our
nueve nine, BV
nuevo(a) new
de nuevo again
el **número** number, 1.2; size (shoes), 3.2
el número del asiento seat number, 11.1
el número del vuelo flight number, 11.1
nupcial nuptial, wedding
la **nutrición** nutrition

el **objeto** object
obligatorio(a): el curso obligatorio required course
la **obra** work
la obra de arte work of art
la obra dramática play
la obra teatral play, 10.2
la **observación** observation
el/la **observador(a)** observer
observar to observe
el **obstáculo** obstacle
obtener to obtain
el **océano** ocean
ochenta eighty, 2.2
ocho eight, BV
ochocientos(as) eight hundred, 3.2
octavo(a) eighth, 6.2
octubre October, BV
ocupado(a) occupied, taken, 5.1
el **oeste** west
oficial official
ofrecer to offer
la **oftalmología** ophthalmology
oír to hear
el **ojo** eye, 8.2
la **ola** wave, 9.1
el **óleo** oil
la **oliva: el aceite de oliva** olive oil
once eleven, BV
la **onza** ounce
opcional: el curso opcional elective course
la **ópera** opera
el/la **operador(a)** operator
la **opereta** operetta
opinar to think
oralmente orally
la **orden** order (restaurant), 5.1
el **ordenador** computer
el **orfanato** orphanage
el **organismo** organism
el **órgano** organ
el **origen** origin
original: en versión original in its original (language) version, 10.1
el **oro** gold
la **orquesta** orchestra
la orquesta sinfónica symphonic orchestra
la **ortiga** nettle
oscuro(a) dark
otavaleño(a) of or from Otavalo, Ecuador
el **otoño** autumn, BV
otro(a) other, another
¡oye! listen!

la **paciencia** patience
el/la **paciente** patient
el **padre** father, 6.1
el padre (religioso) father (religious)
los **padres** parents, 6.1
el **padrino** godfather
los **padrinos** godparents
pagar to pay, 3.1
la **página** page
la página Web Web page
el **pago** payment
el pago mensual monthly payment
el **país** country, 11.2
el país extranjero foreign country
el **paisaje** landscape
el **pájaro** bird
la **palabra** word
el **pan: el pan dulce** sweet roll, 5.1
el pan tostado toast, 5.2
panameño(a) Panamanian, 2.1
el **panqueque** pancake
la **pantalla** screen, 10.1
la pantalla de salidas y llegadas arrival and departure screen, 11.1
el **pantalón** pants, trousers, 3.2
el pantalón corto shorts, 3.2
la **papa** potato, 5.1
las papas fritas French fries, 5.1
el **papá** dad
el **papel** paper, 3.1
la hoja de papel sheet of paper, 3.1
el papel higiénico toilet paper, 12.2
la **papelería** stationery store, 3.1
el **paquete** package, 5.2
el **par: el par de tenis** pair of tennis shoes, 3.2
para for
¿para cuándo? for when?, 14.2
la **parada** stop, 13.2
el **paraíso** paradise
parar to stop, to block, 7.1
parecerse to look like
parecido(a) similar
la **pared** wall
la **pareja** couple

el/la **pariente** relative, 6.1
el **parque** park
el **párrafo** paragraph
la **parte** part
la mayor parte the greatest part, the most
por todas partes everywhere
particular private, 6.2
la casa particular private house, 6.2
particularmente especially
el **partido** game, 7.1
pasado(a) past; last
el (año) pasado last (year)
el/la **pasajero(a)** passenger, 11.1
el **pasaporte** passport, 11.1
pasar to pass, 7.2; to spend; to happen
Lo están pasando muy bien. They're having a good time., 12.2
pasar por to go through, 11.1
¿Qué te pasa? What's the matter (with you)?, 8.1
el **pase** pass (permission)
el **pasillo** aisle, 13.2
la **pasta (crema) dentífrica** toothpaste, 12.2
la **pastilla** pill, 8.2
la pastilla de jabón bar of soap, 12.2
la **patata** potato
pedir (i, i) to ask for, 14.1
peinarse to comb one's hair, 12.1
el **peine** comb, 12.1
la **película** film, movie, 6.2
ver una película to see a film, 10.1
pelirrojo(a) redheaded, 1.1
el **pelo** hair, 12.1
la **pelota** ball, 7.2
la pelota vasca jai alai
el/la **pelotari** jai alai player
la **península** peninsula
el **pensamiento** thought
pensar (ie) to think
la **pensión** boarding house, 12.2
pequeño(a) small, 2.1
la **percusión** percussion
perder (ie) to lose, 7.1; to miss, 10.2
perder el autobús (la guagua, el camión) to miss the bus, 10.2
Perdón. Excuse me.
el/la **peregrino(a)** pilgrim
perezoso(a) lazy, 1.1
el **periódico** newspaper, 6.2
el **período** period
permitir to permit, 11.1
pero but
el **perrito** puppy
el **perro** dog, 6.1
la **persona** person, 1.2
el **personaje** character
peruano(a) Peruvian
pesar to weigh
el **pescado** fish, 5.2
la **peseta** former monetary unit of Spain
el **peso** peso (monetary unit of several Latin American countries), BV; weight
la **petición** petition
el **petróleo** petroleum, oil
petrolero(a) oil
el **piano** piano
el/la **pícher** pitcher, 7.2
el **pico** peak, mountain
y pico just after (time)
el **pie** foot, 7.1; down payment
a pie on foot, 4.1
de pie standing
la **pierna** leg, 7.1
la **pieza** room
la **píldora** pill, 8.2
el/la **piloto** pilot, 11.2
la **pimienta** pepper, 14.1
el **pincel** brush, paintbrush
la **pinta** pint
pintar to paint
el/la **pintor(a)** painter
pintoresco(a) picturesque
la **pintura** painting
la **pirueta** pirouette, maneuver
la **piscina** swimming pool, 9.1
el **piso** floor, 6.2; apartment
la **pista** (ski) slope, 9.2
la **pizarra** chalkboard, 4.2
el **pizarrón** chalkboard, 4.2
la **pizza** pizza, BV
la **plaga** plague, menace
la **plancha de vela** sailboard, 9.1
practicar la plancha de vela to go windsurfing, 9.1
planear to plan
la **planta** floor, 6.2; plant
la planta baja ground floor, 6.2
la **plata** money (income)
el **plátano** banana, plantain, 5.2
el **platillo** base, 7.2; saucer, 14.1
el **plato** plate, dish, 14.1
la **playa** beach, 9.1
playera: la toalla playera beach towel, 9.1
la **plaza** plaza, square; seat, 13.2
la **pluma** pen, 3.1
la **población** population, people
pobre poor
el/la **pobre** the poor boy (girl)
le **pobretón** poor man
poco(a) little, few, 2.1
un poco (de) a little
poder (ue) to be able, 7.1
el **poema** poem
la **poesía** poetry
el **poeta** poet
político(a) political
el **pollo** chicken, 5.2
el **poncho** poncho, shawl, wrap
poner to put, 11.1
poner la mesa to set the table, 14.1
ponerse to put on, 12.1
ponerse el maquillaje to put on makeup, 12.1
ponerse la ropa to dress oneself, to put on clothes, 12.1
popular popular, 2.1
la **popularidad** popularity

por for
por aquí over here
por ciento percent
por ejemplo for example
por eso therefore, for this reason, that's why
por favor please, BV
por fin finally
por hora per hour
por la noche in the evening
por lo general in general
Por nada. You're welcome., BV
¿por qué? why?
por tierra overland
el **poroto** string bean
porque because
la **portería** goal line, 7.1
el/la **portero(a)** goalkeeper, goalie, 7.1
la **posibilidad** possibility
posible possible
el **postre** dessert, 5.1
practicar to practice
practicar el surfing (la plancha de vela, etc.) to go surfing (windsurfing, etc.), 9.1
el **precio** price
precolombino(a) pre-Columbian
preferir (ie, i) to prefer
la **pregunta** question
preguntar to ask (a question)
el **premio: el Premio Nóbel** Nobel Prize
preparar to prepare
la **presentación** presentation
presentar to present; to show (movie)
prestar: prestar atención to pay attention, 4.2
prevalecer to prevail
primario(a): la escuela primaria elementary school
la **primavera** spring, BV
primero(a) first, BV
en primera (clase) first-class, 13.1
el/la **primo(a)** cousin, 6.1
la **princesa** princess
principalmente mainly
el/la **principiante** beginner, 9.2
prisa: a toda prisa as fast as possible
privado(a) private
la casa privada private house, 6.2
el **problema** problem
procesar to process
la **procesión** procession
proclamar to proclaim
producido(a) produced
el **producto** product, 5.2
los productos congelados frozen food, 5.2
el/la **profesor(a)** teacher, professor, 2.1
profundo(a) deep
el **programa** program
la **promesa** promise
pronto: ¡Hasta pronto! See you soon!, BV
la **propina** tip, 14.1
la **protección** protection
protector(a): la crema protectora sunblock, 9.1
la **proteína** protein
el **protoplasma** protoplasm
el/la **proveedor(a)** provider
proveer to provide
la **provisión** provision
próximo(a) next, 13.2
en la próxima parada at the next stop, 13.2
proyectar to project, 10.1
publicar to publish
público(a) public
el **público** audience, 10.2
el **pueblo** town
el **puerco** pork
la **puerta** door; gate, 11.1
la puerta de salida departure gate, 11.1
puertorriqueño(a) Puerto Rican
pues well
la **pulgada** inch
el **punto: en punto** on the dot, sharp, 4.1
los puntos cardinales cardinal points
el **puré de papas** mashed potatoes
puro(a) pure

Q

qué what; how, BV
¡Qué absurdo! How absurd!
¡Qué enfermo(a) estoy! I'm so sick!
¿Qué tal? How are you?, BV
¿Qué te pasa? What's the matter (with you)?, 8.2
quechua Quechuan
quedar to remain, 7.1
querer (ie) to want, wish
el **queso** cheese, 5.1
el **quetzal** quetzal (currency of Guatemala)
¿quién? who?, 1.1
¿quiénes? who? (pl.), 2.1
la **química** chemistry, 2.2
químico(a) chemical
quince fifteen, BV
la **quinceañera** fifteen-year old (girl)
quinientos(as) five hundred, 3.2
quinto(a) fifth, 6.2
el **quiosco** newsstand, 13.1
Quisiera... I would like . . . , 14.2
quitarse to take off

R

rápido quickly
la **raqueta** racket (sports), 9.1
el **rato** while
el **ratón** mouse
la **razón** reason
razonable reasonable
real royal

realista realistic
el/la **realista** realist
realmente really
rebotar to rebound
la **recámara** bedroom, 6.2
el/la **receptor(a)** catcher, 7.2
la **receta** prescription, 8.2
recetar to prescribe, 8.2
recibir to receive, 5.1
el **reciclaje** recycling
recién recently
recientemente recently
reclamar to claim (luggage), 11.2
el **reclamo de equipaje** baggage claim, 11.2
recoger to pick up
recoger el equipaje to claim one's luggage, 11.2
el **rectángulo** rectangle
el **recurso: los recursos naturales** natural resources
la **red** net, 9.1
navegar por la red to surf the Net
reducido(a) reduced (price)
reemplazar to replace
reflejar to reflect
el **reflejo** reflection
reflexionar to reflect
el **refresco** drink, beverage, 5.1
el **refugio** refuge
regalar to give
el **regalo** gift, 6.1
la **región** region
regional regional
el **regionalismo** regionalism
regresar to return
regreso: el viaje de regreso return trip, trip back
regular regular, average, 2.2
la **reina** queen
la **relación** relation
relacionado(a) related
relativamente relatively
religioso(a) religious
rellenar to fill
el **remedio** solution
renombrado(a) well-known
rentar to rent
renunciar to renounce, give up
repetir (i, i) to repeat; to take seconds (meal)
el **reportaje** report
la **representación** performance (theater), 10.2
dar una representación to put on a performance, 10.2
representar to represent
la **República Dominicana** Dominican Republic
requerir (ie, i) to require
la **reservación** reservation
reservado(a) reserved, 13.2
reservar to reserve, 14.2
resfriado(a): estar resfriado(a) to have a cold, 8.1
el/la **residente** resident
resolver (ue) to solve
la **respuesta** answer
restar to subtract
el **restaurante** restaurant, 14.1
el **resto** rest, remainder
la **retina** retina
el **retintín** jingle
el **retraso: con retraso** with a delay, late, 13.2
el **retrato** portrait
revisar to inspect, 11.1
revisar el boleto to check the ticket, 11.1
el/la **revisor(a)** (train) conductor, 13.2
la **revista** magazine, 6.2
revolver (ue) to turn around
el **rey** king
rico(a) rich; delicious, 14.2
el/la **rico(a)** rich person
el **río** river
rodar (ue) to roll
la **rodilla** knee, 7.1
rojo(a) red, 3.2
el **rollo de papel higiénico** roll of toilet paper, 12.2
romántico(a) romantic
la **ropa** clothing, 3.2
la tienda de ropa clothing store, 3.2
la **rosa** rose
rosado(a) pink, 3.2
rubio(a) blond, 1.1
la **ruina** ruin
el **rumor** rumor
rural rural
la **ruta** route
la **rutina** routine, 12.1

S

el **sábado** Saturday, BV
saber to know (how), 11.2
sabio(a) wise
sabroso(a) delicious
sacar to get, 4.2
sacar un billete to buy a ticket
sacar una nota buena (mala) to get a good (bad) grade, 4.2
el **sacerdote** priest
el **saco** jacket
el saco de dormir sleeping bag, 12.2
sacrificar to sacrifice
la **sal** salt, 14.1
la **sala** room; living room, 6.2
la sala de clase classroom, 4.1
la sala de espera waiting room, 13.1
la sala de salida departure area, 11.1
la **salida** departure, 11.1
la hora de salida departure hour, 13.1
la pantalla de llegadas y salidas arrival and departure screen, 11.1
la sala de salida departure area, 11.1
salir to leave, 10.1; to go out; to turn out
salir a tiempo to leave on time, 11.1
salir bien (en un examen) to do well (on an exam)
salir tarde to leave late, 11.1

el **salón: el salón de clase** classroom, 4.1
saltar to jump
la **salud** health
el **saludo** greeting, BV
salvar to save
el **sándwich** sandwich, BV
la **sangre** blood
el **santo** saint
el **saxofono** saxophone
la **sección de (no) fumar** (no) smoking section, 11.1
secundario(a): la escuela secundaria high school, 1.1
sed: tener sed to be thirsty, 14.1
seguir (i, i) to follow, 14
según according to
segundo(a) second, 6.2
  el segundo tiempo second half (soccer), 7.1
  en segunda (clase) second-class, 13.1
la **seguridad: el control de seguridad** security (airport), 11.1
seis six, BV
seiscientos(as) six hundred, 3.2
la **selección** selection
seleccionar to select
la **selva** jungle
la **semana** week, BV
  el fin de semana weekend, BV
  el fin de semana pasado last weekend
  la semana pasada last week, 9.2
el/la **senador(a)** senator
sencillo(a): el billete sencillo one-way ticket, 13.1
sentarse (ie) to sit down, 12.1
el **sentido** meaning, significance
el **señor** sir, Mr., gentleman, BV
la **señora** Ms., Mrs., madam, BV
la **señorita** Miss, Ms., BV
septiembre September, BV
séptimo(a) seventh, 6.2
ser to be
el **ser: el ser humano** human being
  el ser viviente living creature, being
la **serie: la Serie mundial** World Series
serio(a) serious, 1.1
el **servicio** service, tip, 5.1
  ¿Está incluido el servicio? Is the tip included?, 5.1
la **servilleta** napkin, 14.1
servir (i, i) to serve, 14.1
sesenta sixty, 2.2
la **sesión** show (movies), 10.1
setecientos(as) seven hundred, 3.2
setenta seventy, 2.2
sexto(a) sixth, 6.2
el **show** show
si if
sí yes
siempre always, 7.1
  de siempre y para siempre eternally, forever
la **sierra** sierra, mountain range
siete seven, BV
el **siglo** century
el **significado** meaning
significar to mean
siguiente following
la **silla** chair
similar similar
simpático(a) nice, 1.2
simple simple
sin without
  sin escala nonstop
sincero(a) sincere, 1.2
singles singles, 9.1
el **síntoma** symptom, 8.2
el **sistema métrico** metric system
el **sitio** place
sobre on top of; over; on, about
  sobre todo especially
sobresaltar to jump up
la **sobrina** niece, 6.1
el **sobrino** nephew, 6.1
social: las ciencias sociales social sciences
la **sociedad** society
la **sociología** sociology
socorrer to help
el **sol** Peruvian coin; sun, 9.1
  Hace (Hay) sol. It's sunny., 9.1
  tomar el sol to sunbathe, 9.1
solamente only
soler (ue) to be accustomed to, tend to
solo(a) alone
  a solas alone
  el café solo black coffee, 5.1
sólo only
soltero(a) single, bachelor
la **solución** solution
el **sombrero** hat
la **sonrisita** little smile
la **sopa** soup, 5.1
el **sorbete** sherbet, sorbet, 14
el/la **sordo(a)** deaf
su his, her, their, your
subir to go up, 6.2; to board, to get on
  subir al tren to get on, to board the train, 13.1
el **subtítulo** subtitle, 10.1
  con subtítulos with subtitles, 10.1
el **suburbio** suburb
suceso: el buen suceso great event
sudamericano(a) South American
el **sudoeste** southwest
el **suegro** father-in-law
el **suelo** ground
el **sueño** dream
sufrir to suffer
sumar to add
superior: la escuela superior high school
el **supermercado** supermarket, 5.2
el **sur** south

el **surf de nieve** snowboarding
el **surfing** surfing, 9.1
practicar el surfing to surf, 9.1
el **suroeste** southwest
el **surtido** assortment
sus their, your *(pl.),* 6.1
suspirar to sigh
la **sustancia: la sustancia controlada** controlled substance

T

el **T-shirt** T-shirt, 3.2
la **tabla: la tabla hawaiana** surfboard, 9.1
el **tablero** board, 7.1
el tablero de llegadas arrival board, 13.1
el tablero de salidas departure board, 13.1
el tablero indicador scoreboard, 7.1
la **tableta** pill, 8.2
taíno(a) Taino
tal: ¿Qué tal? How are you?, BV
la **talla** size, 3.2
el **talón** luggage claim ticket, 11.1
el **tamal** tamale, BV
el **tamaño** size, 3.2
también also
tan so
el **tango** tango
el **tanto** point, 7.1
marcar un tanto to score a point
tanto(a) so much
la **taquilla** box office, 10.1
tardar to take time
tarda el viaje the trip takes (+ time)
tarde late
la **tarde** afternoon
Buenas tardes. Good afternoon., BV
esta tarde this afternoon, 9.2
por la tarde in the afternoon
la **tarifa** fare, rate
la **tarjeta** card, 11.1
la tarjeta de crédito credit card, 14.1
la tarjeta de embarque boarding pass, 11.1
la tarjeta de identidad estudiantil student I.D. card
el **taxi** taxi, 11.1
la **taza** cup, 14.1
te you *(fam. pron.)*
el **té** tea, 5.1
el té helado iced tea, 5.1
teatral theatrical, 10.2
el **teatro** theater, 10.2
salir del teatro to leave the theater, 10.2
el **teclado** keyboard
el/la **técnico(a)** technician
la **tecnología** technology
telefonear to telephone
telefónico(a) (related to the) telephone
la línea telefónica telephone line
el **teléfono** telephone
hablar por teléfono to talk on the phone
el **telesilla** chairlift, 9.2
el **telesquí** ski lift, 9.2
la **televisión** television, 6.2
el **telón** curtain (stage), 10.2
el **tema** theme, subject
la **temperatura** temperature, 9.2
templado(a) temperate
temprano early, 12.1
el **tenedor** fork, 14.1
tener (ie) to have, 6.1
tener... años to be . . . years old, 6.1
tener hambre to be hungry, 14.1
tener miedo to be afraid
tener que to have to
tener sed to be thirsty, 14.1
el **tenis** tennis, 9.1
los **tenis** tennis shoes, 3.2
el par de tenis pair of tennis shoes, 3.2
el/la **tenista** tennis player
tercer(o)(a) third, 6.2
la **terminal** terminal
terminar to end
el **término** term
la **ternera** veal, 14.2
la **terraza** terrace (sidewalk café)
terrible terrible
el **terror** terror, fear
la **tía** aunt, 6.1
el **ticket** ticket, 9.2
el **tiempo** time; weather, 9.1; half (game)
a tiempo on time, 11.1
el segundo tiempo second half (game), 7.1
la **tienda** store, 3.2
la tienda de departamentos department store
la tienda de ropa clothing store, 3.2
la tienda de videos video store
tierno(a) tender
la **tierra: por tierra** by land, overland
el **tilde** accent
tímido(a) timid, shy, 1.2
el **tío** uncle, 6.1
los tíos aunt(s) and uncle(s), 6.1
típicamente typically
típico(a) typical
el **tipo** type
tirar to kick, 7.1
tirar el balón to kick (throw) the ball, 7.2
la **toalla playera** beach towel, 9.1
tocar to touch; to play (music)
todavía yet, still
todo: todo el mundo everyone
todos(as) everybody, 2.2; everything, all
por todas partes everywhere

tomar to take, 4.1
tomar agua (leche, café) to drink water (milk, coffee)
tomar apuntes to take notes, 4.2
tomar el bus (escolar) to take the (school) bus, 4.1
tomar el desayuno to eat breakfast, 12.1
tomar el sol to sunbathe, 9.1
tomar fotos to take photos
tomar un jugo to drink some juice
tomar un refresco to have (drink) a beverage
tomar un vuelo to take a flight, 11.1
tomar una ducha to take a shower, 12.1
tomar una merienda to have a snack, 4.2
el **tomate** tomato
el **tomo** volume
la **tonelada** ton
tonto(a) foolish
la **tortilla** tortilla, 5.1
la **tos** cough, 8.1
tener tos to have a cough, 8.1
toser to cough, 8.1
la **tostada** toast
tostadito(a) sunburned, tanned
tostado(a): el pan tostado toast, 5.2
el **tostón** fried plantain slice
totalmente totally, completely
tóxico(a) toxic
trabajar to work, 3.2
el **trabajo** work
la **tradición** tradition
tradicional traditionally
traer to bring, 14.1
el **tráfico** traffic
el **traje** suit, 3.2
el traje de baño bathing suit, 9.1
el traje de gala evening gown, dress
el **tramo** stretch
tranquilo(a) peaceful; calm; quiet
transbordar to transfer, 13.2
transformar to transform
transmitir to send, to transmit
el **transporte** transportation
el **tratamiento** treatment
tratar to treat; to try
trece thirteen, BV
treinta thirty, BV
treinta y uno thirty-one, 2.2
el **tren** train, 13.2
el tren directo nonstop train, 13.2
el tren local local train, 13.2
tres three, BV
trescientos(as) three hundred, 3.2
el **triángulo** triangle
la **tripulación** crew, 11.2
triste sad, 8.1
triunfante triumphant
el **trombón** trombone
la **trompeta** trumpet
tropical tropical
tu your *(sing. fam.)*
tú you *(sing. fam.)*
el **tubo: el tubo de pasta (crema) dentífrica** tube of toothpaste, 12.2
el/la **turista** tourist, 10.2

Ud., usted you *(sing. form.)*, 3.2
Uds., ustedes you *(pl.)*, 2.2
último(a) last
un a, 1.1
la **una** one o'clock, 2.2
único(a) only
la **unidad** unit
el **uniforme** uniform
la **universidad** university
universitario(a) (related to) university
uno(a) one, a, BV
unos(as) some
urbano(a) urban
usar to wear (size), 3.2; to use
utilizar to use

la **vacación** vacation
el **vagón** train car, 13.1
vainilla: de vainilla vanilla *(adj.)*, 5.1
la **vainita** string bean
¡vale! OK!
valer to be worth
valeroso(a) brave
el **valor real** true value
vamos a let's go
la **variación** variation
variado(a) varied
variar to vary, change
la **variedad** variety
varios(as) various
el **varón** male
vasco(a) Basque
la pelota vasca jai alai
el **vaso** (drinking) glass, 12.1
el/la **vecino(a)** neighbor
el **vegetal** vegetable, 5.2
el/la **vegetariano(a)** vegetarian
veinte twenty, BV
veinticinco twenty-five, BV
veinticuatro twenty-four, BV
veintidós twenty-two, BV
veintinueve twenty-nine, BV
veintiocho twenty-eight, BV
veintiséis twenty-six, BV
veintisiete twenty-seven, BV
veintitrés twenty-three, BV
veintiuno twenty-one, BV
la **velocidad** speed
vender to sell, 5.2
venezolano(a) Venezuelan

venir to come, 11.1
el viernes (sábado, etc.) que viene next Friday (Saturday, etc.)
la **ventanilla** ticket window, 9.2
ver to see; to watch, 5.1
el **verano** summer, BV
¡verdad! that's right (true)!
verdadero(a) true
verde green, 3.2
la judía verde green bean, 5.2
verificar to verify, 13.1
la **versión: en versión original** in (its) original version, 10.1
el **vestido** dress
vestirse (i, i) to get dressed
la **vez** time
a veces at times, sometimes, 7.1
de vez en cuando now and then
una vez más one more time, again
la **vía** track, 13.1
viajar to travel
viajar en avión to travel by air, 11.1
el **viaje** trip
el viaje de regreso return trip
hacer un viaje to take a trip, 11.1
victorioso(a) victorious
la **vida** life
la vida escolar school life
el **video** video
viejo(a) old, 6.1
el/la **viejo(a)** old person
el **viento** wind
el **viernes** Friday, BV
el **vinagre** vinegar
la **viola** viola
el **violín** violin, 2.1
visible visible
visitar to visit
vital vital
la **vitamina** vitamin
viviente: el ser viviente living creature, being
vivir to live, 5.2
vivo(a) living, alive
la **vocal** vowel
volar (ue) to fly
el **voleibol** volleyball
volver (ue) to return, 7.1
volver a casa to return home, 10.2
la **voz** voice
en voz alta aloud
el **vuelo** flight, 11.1
el número del vuelo flight number, 11.1
tomar un vuelo to take a flight, 11.1
el vuelo nacional domestic flight

Y

y and, BV
y cuarto a quarter past (the hour)
y media half past (the hour)
y pico just after (the hour)
ya already; now
la **yarda** yard
yo I, 1.1
el **yogur** yogurt

Z

la **zanahoria** carrot, 5.2
la **zapatería** shoe store
el **zapato** shoe, 3.2
la **zona** zone, area, neighborhood
el **zumo de naranja** orange juice

English-Spanish Dictionary

The English-Spanish Dictionary contains all productive and receptive vocabulary from the text. The numbers following each productive entry indicate the chapter and vocabulary section in which the word is introduced. For example, **3.2** *means that the word was taught in* **Capítulo 3, Palabras 2.** *BV refers to the preliminary* **Bienvenidos** *lessons. If there is no number following an entry, this means that the word or expression is there for receptive purposes only.*

a un(a)
able: to be able poder (ue), 7.1
aboard a bordo de, 11.2
about (time) a eso de, 4.1
above por encima de
abstract abstracto(a)
academy la academia
to **accept** aceptar
access el acceso
to **accompany** acompañar
according to según
ache doler
My . . . aches Me duele… , 8.2
acrylic el acrílico
activity la actividad
actor el actor, 10.2
actress la actriz, 10.2
to **adapt** adaptar
to **add** sumar
to **adjust** ajustar
to **admire** admirar
admission ticket la entrada, 10.1
to **admit** admitir
adorable adorable
to **adore** adorar
to **adorn** adornar
adventure la aventura
African africano(a)
after después de, 5.1; **(time)** y
It's ten after one. Es la una y diez.
afternoon la tarde
Good afternoon. Buenas tardes., BV
in the afternoon por la tarde
this afternoon esta tarde, 9.2
against contra, 7.1
agent el/la agente, 11.1
customs agent el/la agente de aduana, 11.1
agreed conforme, 14.2
air el aire
open-air (outdoor) café (market) el café (mercado) al aire libre
airline la línea aérea
airplane el avión, 11.1
by plane en avión, 11.1
airport el aeropuerto, 11.1
aisle el pasillo, 13.2
a lot muchos(as), 2.1; mucho, 3.2
alarmed: to be alarmed alarmarse
album el álbum
algebra el álgebra, 2.2
alive vivo(a)
all todos(as)
All right. De acuerdo.
allergy la alergia, 8.2
to **allow** dejar; consentir (ie, i)
almost casi
alone solo(a)
aloud en voz alta
also también, 1.2
always siempre, 7.1
A.M. de la mañana
American americano(a)
amusement la diversión
analysis el análisis
analytical analítico(a)
to **analyze** analizar
ancient antiguo(a)
and y, BV
Andean andino(a)
anecdote la anécdota
animal el animal
another otro(a)
answer la respuesta
to **answer** contestar
Antarctic la Antártida
antibiotic el antibiótico, 8.2
antiquity la antigüedad
Anything else? ¿Algo más?, 5.2
apartment el apartamento, el piso, el departamento, 6.2
apartment house la casa de apartamentos (apartamentos), 6.2
to **applaud** aplaudir, 10.2
applause el aplauso, 10.2
apple la manzana, 5.2
to **apply** aplicar
April abril, BV
Aragon: from Aragon (Spain) aragonés(a)
arc el arco
archeological arqueológico(a)
archeologist el/la arqueólogo(a)
archeology la arqueología
area el área *(f.)*, la zona
Argentinian argentino(a), 2.1
argument la disputa
arithmetic la aritmética, 2.2
arm el brazo, 7.1
around alrededor de, 6.2; **(time)** a eso de, 4.1
arrival la llegada, 11.1
arrival and departure screen la pantalla de salidas y llegadas, 11.1
arrival board el tablero de llegadas, 13.1
to **arrive** llegar, 4.1

arrogant altivo, arrogante
arsenal el arsenal
art el arte, *(f.)* 2.2
artichoke la alcachofa, 14.2
artifact el artefacto
artist el/la artista, 10.2
artistic artístico(a)
as como
to **ask (a question)** preguntar
to **ask for** pedir (i, i), 14.1
asleep dormido(a)
aspirin la aspirina, 8.2
assortment el surtido
astute astuto(a)
at a, en
at about (time) a eso de, 4.1
at home en casa, 6.2
at night por la noche
at that time en aquel entonces
at the end of a fines de
at what time? ¿a qué hora?, 10.1
athletic atlético
attack el ataque
to **attack** atacar
to **attend** asistir
attention: to pay attention prestar atención, 4.2
audience el público, 10.2
August agosto, BV
aunt la tía, 6.1
aunt(s) and uncle(s) los tíos, 6.1
Australia la Australia
author el/la autor(a), 10.2
autumn el otoño, BV
average regular, 2.2

B

baby el/la bebé
back to school la apertura de clases
background la ascendencia
backpack la mochila, 3.1
bacteria la bacteria
bad malo(a), 2.1
to be in a bad (good) mood estar de mal (buen) humor, 8.1
bag la bolsa, 5.2
baggage el equipaje, 11.1
baggage claim el reclamo de equipaje, 11.2
carry-on baggage el equipaje de mano, 11.1
ball (basketball, soccer) el balón, 7.1; **(tennis, baseball)** la pelota , 7.2
to throw (kick) the ball tirar el balón, 7.2
ballpoint pen el bolígrafo, 3.1
banana el plátano, 5.2
baptism el bautizo
bar: bar of soap la barra de jabón, la pastilla de jabón, 12.2
bargain la ganga
base (baseball) la base, 7.2
baseball el béisbol, 7.2
baseball field el campo de béisbol, 7.2
baseball game el juego de béisbol, 7.2
baseball player el/la jugador(a) de béisbol, 7.2; el/la beisbolista
basic básico(a)
basket (basketball) el cesto, la canasta, 7.2
to make a basket encestar, meter el balón en el cesto, 7.2
basketball el básquetbol, el baloncesto, 7.2
basketball court la cancha de básquetbol, 7.2
Basque vasco(a)
bat el bate, 7.2
bathing suit el traje de baño, el bañador, 9.1
bathroom el baño, el cuarto de baño, 6.2
batter el/la bateador(a), 7.2
battle la batalla
bay la bahía
to **be** ser, 1.1; estar, 4.1
to be able poder (ue), 7.1
to be accustomed to soler (ue)
to be afraid tener miedo
to be born nacer
to be going to ir a
to be hungry tener hambre, 14.1
to be included estar incluido, 14.1
to be named (called) llamarse, 12.1
to be pleasing gustar
to be thirsty tener sed, 14.1
to be tied (score) quedar empatado, 7.1
to be worth valer, 7.2
to be . . . years old tener... años, 6.2; cumplir... años
beach la playa, 9.1
beach resort el balneario, 9.1
beach towel la toalla playera, 9.1
bean el frijol, la habichuela, 5.2
green bean la judía verde, 5.2
to **bear (name)** llevar (el nombre)
beau el galán
beautiful hermoso(a), bello(a), 1.1
because porque
bed la cama, 8.1
to make the bed hacer la cama
to stay in bed guardar cama, 8.1
bedroom la recámara, el dormitorio, el cuarto (de dormir), 6.2
beef la carne de res, 14.2
before antes de, 5.1
to **begin** comenzar (ie); empezar (ie), 7.1
beginner el/la principiante, 9.2
beginning: beginning of school la apertura de clases

behind atrás
being: human being el ser humano
living being el ser viviente
to **believe** creer, 8.2
below debajo (de); bajo
below zero bajo cero, 9.2
berth la litera, 13.2
between entre, 7.1
beverage el refresco, 5.1
bicycle la bicicleta
to go by bicycle ir en bicicleta, 13.2
big grande, 2.1
bilingual bilingüe
bill la cuenta, 5.1
biography la biografía
biological biológico(a)
biologist el/la biólogo(a)
biology la biología, 2.1
birthday el cumpleaños, 6.1
black negro(a), 3.2
black coffee el café solo, 5.1
to **block** bloquear, parar, 7.1
blond rubio(a), 1.1
blood la sangre
blouse la blusa, 3.2
blue azul, 3.2
blue jeans el blue jean, 3.2
board: arrival board el tablero de llegadas, 13.1;
departure board el tablero de salidas, 13.1
to **board** embarcar, 11.2; abordar; **(the train)** subir al tren, 13.1
boarding el embarque
boarding house la pensión, 12.2
boarding pass la tarjeta de embarque, 11.1
book el libro, 3.1
boot la bota, 9.2
to **bore** aburrir
boring aburrido(a), 2.1
born nacido(a)
bottle la botella, 12.2
boy el muchacho, 1.1
boyfriend/girlfriend el/la novio(a)
brave valeroso(a)
bread el pan, 5.1
breakfast el desayuno, 5.2
to eat breakfast desayunarse, tomar el desayuno, 12.1
bright brillante
to **bring** llevar, 6.1; traer, 14.1
broadcast la emisión, 6.2
sports broadcast la emisión deportiva, 6.2
bronze el bronce, 10.2
brook el arroyo
brother el hermano, 6.1
brown de color marrón, 3.2
brunette moreno(a), 1.1
brush el cepillo, 12.2
to **brush one's hair** cepillarse, 12.1
to **brush one's teeth** cepillarse (lavarse) los dientes, 12.1
building el edificio
bus el bus, 4.1; el autobús (la guagua [P.R., Cuba], el camión [Mex.]), 10.1
school bus el bus escolar, 4.1
to miss the bus perder el autobús (la guagua, el camión), 10.1
but pero
to **buy** comprar, 3.1
by (plane, car, bus, etc.) en (avión, carro, autobús, etc.)

C

cafe el café, BV
cafeteria la cafetería
to **calculate** calcular
calculator la calculadora, 3.1
calculus el cálculo, 2.2
called llamado(a)
can el bote, la lata, 5.2
candid franco(a)
canned enlatado(a)
cap la gorra, 3.2
capital la capital
captain el/la capitán; el/la comandante, 11.2
car el carro, el coche, 4.1
by car en carro, en coche, 4.1
cafeteria car el coche-cafetería, 13.2
dining car el coche-comedor, 13.2
sleeping car el coche-cama, 13.2
train car el coche, el vagón, 13.2
card la tarjeta, 11.1
credit card la tarjeta de crédito, 14.1
cardinal: cardinal points los puntos cardinales
careful! ¡cuidado!
carefully: very carefully con mucho cuidado
to **caress** acariciar
Caribbean el Caribe
carrot la zanahoria, 5.2
to **carry** llevar, 3.1
carry-on luggage el equipaje de mano, 11.1
case el caso
cash register la caja, 3.1
cat el/la gato(a), 6.1
to **catch** atrapar, 7.2
catcher el/la receptor(a), el/la cátcher, 7.2
Catholic católico(a)
to **celebrate** celebrar
celebration la celebración
cell la célula
cellular celular
center el centro
central central, 13.2
Central America la América Central
century el siglo
cereal el cereal, 5.2
certainly! ¡claro!
chain (necklace) la cadena
chair la silla
chairlift el telesilla, 9.2
chalet el chalet

chalkboard la pizarra, el pizarrón, 4.2
champion el/la campeón(a)
championship el campeonato
to **change** cambiar
to change trains (transfer) cambiar de tren, transbordar, 13.2
chapter el capítulo
character el personaje
charming encantador(a)
cheap barato(a), 3.2
check la cuenta, 5.1
to **check luggage** facturar el equipaje, 11.1
to **check one's ticket** revisar el boleto, 11.1
cheese el queso, 5.1
chemical químico(a)
chemistry la química, 2.2
chicken el pollo, 5.2
child el/la niño(a)
children los niños, 6.1
homeless children los niños desamparados
Chilean chileno(a)
chills: to have chills tener escalofríos, 8.1
chocolate chocolate, 5.1
chocolate ice cream el helado de chocolate, 5.1
choir el coro
to **choose** escoger
chorus el coro
Christian cristiano(a)
Christmas la Navidad
Christmas Eve la Nochebuena
church la iglesia
circle el círculo
city la ciudad
to **claim (luggage)** reclamar (el equipaje), 11.2
clam la almeja, 14.2
class la clase, el curso, 2.1
first class primera clase, en primera, 13.1
second class segunda clase, en segunda, 13.1
to **classify** clasificar
classroom la sala de clase, el salón de clase, 4.1
clinic la clínica
cloth el lienzo
clothing la ropa, 3.2
clothing store la tienda de ropa, 3.2
cloud la nube, 9.1
cloudy: to be cloudy estar nublado, 9.1
It's cloudy. Hay nubes., 9.1
club el club, 4.2
Spanish Club el Club de español, 4.2
coast la costa
co-ed mixto(a)
coffee el café, BV
black coffee, el café solo, 5.1
coffee with milk el café con leche, 5.1
cognate la palabra afina
coin la moneda
coincidence la coincidencia
cold (illness) el catarro, 8.1
to have a cold tener catarro, estar resfriado(a), 8.1
cold: It's cold. Hace frío., 9.2
collection la colección, el conjunto
collector el colector
Colombian colombiano(a), 1.1
colonial colonial
colony la colonia
color el color, 3.2
What color is . . . ? ¿De qué color es… ?, 3.2
comb el peine, 12.2
to **comb one's hair** peinarse, 12.1
to **come** venir
to come (go) on stage entrar en escena, 10.2
compact disk el disco compacto, 4.2
to **compare** comparar
to **compete** competir (i, i)
competition la competición
complete completo(a), 13.2
compliment: to pay someone compliments echarle flores
composition la composición
computer el ordenador, la computadora
computer science la informática, 2.2
concert el concierto
condominium el condominio
conductor (train) el/la revisor(a), 13.2
confirmed bachelor el solterón
to **connect** conectar
to **conquer** conquistar
to **conserve** conservar, 11.1
to **consider** considerar
to **consist of** consistir (en)
to **consult** consultar
consultation la consulta, 8.2
contest la competición
continent el continente
to **continue** continuar, 7.2
to **convert** convertir (ie, i)
cook el/la cocinero(a), 14.1
copilot el/la copiloto, 11.2
to **copy** copiar
corn el maíz, 14.2
to **cost** costar (ue), 3.1
How much does . . . cost? ¿Cuánto cuesta(n)… ?, 3.1
Costa Rican costarricense
cough la tos, 8.1
to have a cough tener tos, 8.1
to **cough** tener tos, 8.1
counter el mostrador, 11.1
country el país, 11.2
foreign country el país extranjero, 11.2
course el curso, 2.1
elective course el curso opcional
required course el curso obligatorio

court la cancha, 2.1
basketball court la cancha de básquetbol, 7.2
indoor court la cancha cubierta, 9.1
outdoor court la cancha al aire libre, 9.1
tennis court la cancha de tenis, 9.1
courtesy la cortesía, BV
cousin el/la primo(a), 6.1
to **cover** cubrir
to **create** crear
credit card la tarjeta de crédito, 14.1
Creole el/la criollo(a)
crew la tripulación, 11.2
Cuban cubano(a)
Cuban American cubanoamericano(a)
to **cultivate** cultivar
cultural cultural
cup la taza, 14.1
World Cup la Copa mundial
curtain (stage) el telón, 10.2
custom la costumbre
customer el/la cliente, 5.1
customs la aduana, 11.2
to **cut** cortar, 14.1

D

dad el papá
to **dance** bailar, 4.2
dark (haired) moreno(a), 1.1
data los datos
date la fecha, BV
What is today's date? ¿Cuál es la fecha de hoy?, BV
to **date** datar
daughter la hija, 6.1
day el día, BV
day before yesterday anteayer
deaf person el/la sordo(a)
death la muerte
December diciembre, BV
to **decide** decidir
to **declare** declarar
to **defeat** derrotar
degree (temperature) el grado, 9.2
delay: with a delay con una demora, 11.1; con retraso, 13.2
delicious delicioso(a), rico, 14.2; sabroso(a)
to **delight** encantar
to **deliver** entregar
deluxe de lujo
departure la salida, 11.1
arrival and departure screen la pantalla de llegadas y salidas, 11.1
departure board el tablero de salidas, 13.1
departure gate la puerta de salida, la sala de salida, 11.1
departure hour la hora de salida
descendant el/la descendiente
design el diseño
designer el/la diseñador(a)
dessert el postre, 5.1
destination el destino, 11.1
diagnosis la diagnosis, 8.2
dialogue el diálogo
diamond el diamante
to **die** morir (ue, u)
difference la diferencia
different diferente
difficult duro(a), difícil, 2.1
to **dig** excavar
dining car el coche-comedor, el coche-cafetería, 13.2
dining room el comedor, 6.2
dinner la cena, 5.2
to have dinner cenar
direct directo(a), 11
director el/la director(a)
discipline la asignatura, la disciplina, 2.1
to **discover** descubrir
to **discuss** discutir
to **disembark** desembarcar, 11.2
dish el plato, 14.1
disk: compact disk el disco compacto, 4.2
diskette el disquete, 3.1
to **dive** bucear, 9.1
to **divide** dividir
diving el buceo, 9.1
divorced: to get divorced divorciarse
doctor el/la médico(a), 8.2
doctor's office la consulta del médico, el consultorio, 8.2
to **do** hacer, 11
to do well (on an exam) salir bien (en un examen)
dog el perro, 6.1
domestic doméstico(a), 2.1
Dominican dominicano(a), 2.1
Dominican Republic la República Dominicana
donkey el asno
door la puerta
dose la dosis, 8.2
dot: on the dot en punto, 4.1
doubles dobles, 9.1
doubt la duda
doughnut (a type of) el churro
dozen la docena
drawing el dibujo
dream el sueño
dreamed of imaginado(a)
dress el vestido
to **dribble (basketball)** driblar, 7.2
drink (beverage) el refresco, 5.1; la bebida
to **drink** beber, 5.1
to drink water (milk, coffee) tomar agua (leche, café), 14.1
druggist el/la farmacéutico(a), 8.2
drugstore la farmacia, 8.2
dubbed doblado(a), 10.1
during durante
DVD el DVD, 4.2

E

e-mail el correo electrónico
each cada, 1.2
early temprano, 12.1
to **earn** ganar
easel el caballete
east el este
easy fácil, 2.1
to **eat** comer, 5.1
to eat breakfast desayunarse, tomar el desayuno, 12.1
economical económico(a), 12.2
economics: home economics la economía doméstica, 2.1
economy la economía
Ecuadorean ecuatoriano(a), 2.1
education: physical education la educación física, 2.2
egg el huevo, 5.2
eggplant la berenjena, 14.2
eight ocho, BV
eight hundred ochocientos(as), 3.2
eighteen dieciocho, BV
eighth octavo(a), 6.2
eighty ochenta, 2.1
electronic mail (e-mail) el correo electrónico
elegant elegante
element el elemento
elevator el ascensor, 6.2
eleven once, BV
else: Anything else? ¿Algo más?, 5.2
No, nothing else. No, nada más, 5.2
emotion la emoción
emphasis el énfasis
to **emphasize** dar énfasis, enfatizar
employee el/la empleado(a), el/la dependiente(a), 3.1
enamored: to become enamored of (to fall for) flechar
enchilada la enchilada, BV
end el fin, BV
at the end of a fines de
enemy el/la enemigo(a)
energy la energía, 8
English el inglés, 2.2
to **enjoy** gozar
to enjoy oneself divertirse (ie, i), 12.2
enough bastante, 1.1
to **enter** entrar, 4.1
entire entero(a)
episode el episodio
epoch la época
equation la ecuación
equipment el equipo, 7.1
to **erase** borrar, 3.1
eraser la goma de borrar, 3.1
errant: knight errant el caballero andante
especially especialmente, particularmente, sobre todo
essentially esencialmente
to **establish** fundar
esteemed estimado(a)
ethnic étnico(a)
Europe Europa
evening la noche
evening gown el traje de gala
Good evening. Buenas noches., BV
in the evening por la noche
everyone todos, 2.2; todo el mundo
everything todos(as)
exactly exactamente, 11
to **exaggerate** exagerar, 11
exam el examen, 4.2
to **examine** examinar, 8.2
example: for example por ejemplo
to **excavate** excavar
excavation la excavación
excellent excelente
Excuse (me). Perdón.
exhibition (art) la exposición (de arte), 10.1
to **exist** existir
expedition la expedición
expensive caro(a), 3.2
expert el/la experto(a), 9.2
to **explain** explicar, 4.2
explosion la explosión
expression la expresión
means of expression el modo de expresión
extraordinary extraordinario(a)
extreme extremo(a)
eye el ojo

F

face la cara, 12.1
faithful fiel
to **fall asleep** dormirse (ue, u), 12.1
false falso(a)
fame la fama
family la familia, 6.1
family (related to) familiar
famous famoso(a), 1.2
fan (sports) el/la aficionado(a)
fantastic fantástico(a), 1.2
fare la tarifa
fast rápido(a)
as fast as possible a toda prisa
fat gordo(a), 1.2
father el padre, 6.1
father-in-law el suegro
favorite favorito(a)
fear el miedo, el terror
February febrero, BV
fever la fiebre, 8.1
to have a fever tener fiebre, 8.1
few pocos(as), 2.1
a few unos(as)
fiancé(e) el/la novio(a)

comemos

field el campo
baseball field el campo de béisbol, 7.2
soccer field el campo de fútbol, 7.1
fifteen quince, BV
fifteen-year-old (girl) la quinceañera
fifth quinto(a), 6.2
fifty cincuenta, 2.1
to **fight** luchar
figurative figurativo(a)
film la película, 6.2; el film, 10.1
finally por fin
to **find** hallar; encontrar (ue)
fine bien, BV; Conforme., 14.2
fine-looking gallardo(a)
finger el dedo
first primero(a), BV
fish el pescado, 5.2
five cinco, BV
five hundred quinientos(as) 3.2
flight el vuelo, 11.1
flight attendant el/la asistente de vuelo, 11.2
flight number el número del vuelo, 11.1
floor la planta, el piso, 6.2
ground floor la planta baja, 6.2
flower la flor
flu la gripe, 8.1
to **fly** volar (ue)
folder la carpeta, 3.1
folk healer el/la curandero(a)
to **follow** seguir (i, i)
following siguiente
fond of aficionado(a)
food la comida, 5.2; el alimento, el comestible, 14.2
foolish tonto(a)
foot el pie, 7.1
on foot a pie, 4.1
for por, para
for example por ejemplo
foreign extranjero(a), 11.2
fork el tenedor, 14.1
to **form** formar
forty cuarenta, 2.1
to **found** fundar
four cuatro, BV
four hundred cuatrocientos(as), 3.2
fourteen catorce, BV
fourth cuarto(a), 6.2
frank franco(a)
free libre, 5.1
French el francés, 2.2
French fries las papas fritas, 5.1
fresh fresco(a)
Friday el viernes, BV
fried frito(a), 5.1
friend el/la amigo(a), el/la compañero(a), 1.1
frightful espantoso
from de, BV
front: in front of delante de, 10.1
frozen congelado(a), helado(a), 5.1
frozen foods los productos congelados, 5.2
fruit la fruta, 5.2
to **fry** freír (i, i), 14.1
full (train, bus, etc.) completo(a)
funny cómico(a); gracioso(a), 1.1
furious furioso(a)
furniture los muebles
fury la furia
future el futuro

G

gallant gallardo(a)
game el partido, 7.1; el juego, 7.2
baseball game el juego de béisbol, 7.2
garage el garaje, 6.2
garden el jardín, 6.2
garlic el ajo, 14.2
gate: departure gate la puerta de salida, 11.1
generally generalmente
generous generoso(a), 1.2
gentleman el señor, BV
geography la geografía, 2.2
geometry la geometría, 2.2
German el alemán, 2.1
to **get a good (bad) grade** sacar una nota buena (mala), 4.2
to **get dressed** vestirse (i, i); ponerse la ropa, 12.1
to **get off (bus, train, etc.)** bajar(se) (del bus, tren, etc.), 13.2
to **get on** abordar; subir, 13.1
to **get on (horse)** montar (caballo)
to **get on board (bus, train, etc.)** subir (al bus, tren, etc.), 13.1
to **get up** levantarse, 12.1
giant el gigante
gift el regalo, 6.1
girl la muchacha, 1.1
to **give** dar, 4.2; **(gift)** regalar
to give (throw) a party dar una fiesta, 4.2
to **give up** renunciar
glass (drinking) el vaso, 12.1
glove el guante, 7.2
to **go** ir, 4.1
to go by bicycle ir en bicicleta, 12.2
to go by car ir en coche
to **go back** volver (ue)
to **go down** bajar
to **go home** volver a casa
to **go shopping** ir de compras, 5.2
to **go through** pasar por, 11.1
to **go to bed** acostarse (ue), 12.1
to **go up** subir, 6.2
to **go (walk) around** andar
goal el gol, 7.1; la portería, 7.1
to score a goal meter un gol, 7.1
goalie el/la portero(a), 7.1
goalkeeper el/la portero(a), 7.1
godfather el padrino
godmother la madrina
godparents los padrinos

gold el oro
good bueno(a); buen
Good afternoon. Buenas tardes., BV
Good evening. Buenas noches., BV
Good morning. Buenos días., BV
good-bye! ¡adiós!, ¡chao!, BV
good-looking guapo(a), bonito(a), lindo(a), 1.1
Gosh! ¡Dios mío!, 11
gossip: piece of gossip el chisme
grade la nota, 4.2
grammar la gramática
grandchildren los nietos, 6.1
granddaughter la nieta, 6.1
grandfather el abuelo, 6.1
grandmother la abuela, 6.1
grandparents los abuelos, 6.1
grandson el nieto, 6.1
gray gris, 3.2
great gran(de)
great event el buen suceso
greater mayor
green verde, 3.2
green bean la judía verde, 5.2
greeting el saludo, BV
ground el suelo
group el grupo
to **guard** guardar, 7.1
Guatemalan guatemalteco(a)
to **guess** adivinar
guitar la guitarra
gulf el golfo
gymnasium el gimnasio

hair el pelo, 12.1
half medio(a), 5.2
half an hour media hora, 14
second half el segundo tiempo, 7.1
ham el jamón, 5.1
hamburger la hamburguesa, 5.1
hand la mano, 7.1
to shake hands dar la mano
handsome guapo(a), 1.1
to **hang** colgar (ue)
to **happen** pasar
What happened (to you)? ¿Qué te pasó?
happy contento(a), 8.1
hard duro(a), 2.1
hardworking ambicioso(a), 1.1
hat el sombrero, la gorra, 3.2
to **have** tener (ie), 6.1
to have chills tener escalofríos, 8.1
to have a cold tener catarro, estar resfriado(a), 8.1
to have a drink (snack) tomar un refresco (una merienda), 4.2
to have a fever tener fiebre, 8.1
to have a headache tener dolor de cabeza, 8.1
to have a sore throat tener dolor de garganta, 8.1
to have a stomachache tener dolor de estómago, 8.1
to have to tener que
They're having a good time. Lo están pasando muy bien., 12.2
he él, 1.1
head la cabeza, 7.1
headache el dolor de cabeza, 8.1
health la salud, 8.1
to **hear** oír
heart el corazón
heartthrob el galán
Hello! ¡Hola!, BV; **(answering the telephone—Spain)** ¡Diga!, 14.2
to **help** ayudar, 13.1
her su, 6.1; la *(pron.)*
here aquí
Here is (are)... Aquí tiene...
heritage la ascendencia
hero el héroe
Hi! ¡Hola!, BV
to **hide** esconder
high alto(a), 1.1
high school el colegio, la escuela secundaria, la escuela superior, 1.1
hike: to take a hike dar una caminata, 12.2
him lo
his su, 6.1
historical histórico(a)
history la historia, 2.1
to **hit (tennis)** golpear, 9.1; **(baseball)** batear, 7.2
hole el agujero
home la casa, 6.2
at home en casa
country home la casa de campo
home economics la economía doméstica, 2.2
home plate (baseball) el platillo, 7.2
home run el jonrón, 7.2
homeless desamparado(a)
homeless children los niños desamparados
honest honesto(a), 1.2
honor el honor
horrible horrible
hospital el hospital, 8.2
hot: It's hot. Hace calor., 9.1
hotel (inexpensive) el hostal, 12.2
hour la hora
per hour por hora
house la casa, 6.2
apartment house la casa de apartamentos (departamentos), 6.2
private house la casa privada (particular), 6.2
how? ¿cómo?, 1.1
How absurd! ¡Qué absurdo!
How are you? ¿Qué tal?, BV; ¿Cómo estás?, 8.1

How many? ¿Cuántos(as)?, 2.1
How much? ¿Cuánto?, 3.1
How much does it cost? ¿Cuánto es?, ¿Cuánto cuesta?, 3.1
How old is (are) . . . ? ¿Cuántos años tiene(n)... ?, 6.1
human humano(a)
human being el ser humano
humble humilde
hungry: to be hungry tener hambre, 14.1
to **hurt** doler (ue), 8.2
My . . . hurt(s) me. Me duele(n)..., 8.2
husband el marido, el esposo, 6.1

I yo, 1.2
ice cream el helado, 5.1
chocolate (vanilla) ice cream el helado de chocolate (de vainilla),
5.1
iced tea el té helado, 5.1
idea la idea
ideal ideal, 1.2
idealist el/la idealista
if si
illusion la ilusión
imagined imaginado(a)
immediately enseguida, inmediatamente, 5.1
immense inmenso(a)
to **imply that** dar a entender
important importante
impossible imposible
in en
in front of delante de
Inca el/la inca
to **include** incluir, 5.1
included incluido(a), 5.1
Is the tip included? ¿Está incluido el servicio?, 5.1
incredible increíble
independence la independencia
Indian indio(a)
to **indicate** indicar, 11.1
indicator el indicador, 7.1
indigenous indígena
individual individual, 7.2
individual sport el deporte individual, 7.2
inexpensive barato(a), 3.2
influence la influencia
to **inform** informar, 13.2
information la información
inhabitant el/la habitante
inheritance la herencia
injection la inyección, 8.2
inning la entrada, 7.2
insane loco(a)
to **inspect** inspeccionar, 11.2
to inspect (check) the ticket revisar el boleto, 11.1
inspection: passport inspection el control de pasaportes, 11.2
inspection: security inspection el control de seguridad, 11.1
instant el instante
instruction la instrucción
instrument el instrumento
integral íntegro(a)
intelligent inteligente, 2.1
interest el interés
to **interest** interesar
interesting interesante, 2.1
intermediate intermedio(a)
international internacional
interpretation la interpretación
interview la entrevista, 4.1
invitation la invitación
to **invite** invitar (a), 6.1
island la isla
it la *(f.)*; lo *(m.)*
Italian italiano(a)

jacket la chaqueta, el saco, 3.2
jai alai la pelota vasca
January enero, BV
jingle el retintín
July julio, BV
to **jump** saltar
to jump up sobresaltar
June junio, BV

keyboard el teclado
to **kick** tirar (con el pie), 7.1
to kick the ball tirar el balón, 7.2
kilogram el kilo, 5.2
king el rey
kitchen la cocina, 6.2
knapsack la mochila, 3.1
knee la rodilla, 7.1
knife el cuchillo, 14.1
knight el caballero
knight errant el caballero andante
knight's attendant el escudero
to **know** saber, 11.2; conocer, 11.1
to know how saber, 11.2

laboratory el laboratorio, 2.1
lady la dama
lady-in-waiting la dama
lake el lago
lamb el cordero, 14.2
lance la lanza
to **land** aterrizar, 11.2
landscape el paisaje
language la lengua, 2.2
large grande
last último(a)
last night anoche, 9.2
last week la semana pasada, 9.2
last weekend el fin de semana pasado
last year el año pasado, 9.2
late tarde; con una demora, 11.1; con retraso, 13.2

later luego, BV
See you later! ¡Hasta luego!, BV
Latin el latín, 2.2
Latin latino(a)
Latin America Latinoamérica
Latin American latinoamericano(a)
lazy perezoso(a), 1.1
league la liga
Major Leagues las Grandes Ligas
to **learn** aprender, 5.1
to **leave** salir
to leave late salir tarde, 11.1
to leave on time salir a tiempo, 11.1
to leave something behind dejar, 14.1
lecture la conferencia
left izquierdo(a), 7.1
leg la pierna, 7.1
lemonade la limonada, BV
to **lend** prestar, 4.2
lesson la lección, 4.2
to **let** dejar; permitir, 11.1
let's see a ver
Will you please let me see your passport? Me permite ver su pasaporte, por favor?, 11.1
letter la carta, 6.2; **(of the alphabet)** la letra, 11.1
lettuce la lechuga, 5.2
liberator el/la libertador(a)
life la vida
school life la vida escolar
to **lift** levantar
light la luz
to **light** encender (ie)
like el gusto
to **like** gustar
Lima: from Lima (Peru) limeño(a)
line (of people) la cola, la fila, 10.1
linen el lienzo
to **listen (to)** escuchar, 4.2
listen! ¡oye!, 1.1
literal literal
literary literario(a)
literature la literatura, 2.1
little: a little poco(a)
live vivo(a)
to **live** vivir, 5.2
living viviente
living creature el ser viviente
living room la sala, 6.2
lobster la langosta, 14.2
local local, 13.2
long largo(a), 3.2
Look! ¡Mira!
to **look at** mirar, 3.1
to **look at oneself** mirarse, 12.1
to **look for** buscar, 3.1
to **lose** perder (ie), 7.1
lotion: suntan lotion la loción bronceadora, 9.1
lotto el loto
lover el/la enamorado(a)
low bajo(a), 4.2
to **lower** bajar
luggage el equipaje, 11.1
carry-on luggage el equipaje de mano, 11.1
luggage claim ticket el talón, 11.1
lunch el almuerzo, 5.2
to have lunch almorzar (ue)
luxurious lujoso(a)

M

ma'am la señora, BV
made hecho(a)
Madrid (native of) madrileño(a)
magazine la revista, 6.2
magnificent magnífico(a)
mail el correo
e-mail (electronic mail) el correo electrónico
main principal
mainly principalmente
Major Leagues las Grandes Ligas
majority la mayor parte, la mayoría
to **make** hacer
to make a basket (basketball) encestar, 7.2
to make the bed hacer la cama, 13
makeup el maquillaje, 12.1
to put one's makeup on maquillarse, ponerse el maquillaje, 12.1
male el varón
man el hombre, el señor
manner la manera, el modo
many muchos(as), 2.1
map el mapa
March marzo, BV
marker el marcador, 3.1
market el mercado, 5.2
marmalade la mermelada, 5.2
marriage el matrimonio
married: to be married estar casado(a)
marvelous maravilloso(a)
mass la masa
master el/la maestro(a)
material el material, 3.1
mathematics las matemáticas, 2.2
matter: What's the matter (with you)? ¿Qué te pasa?
May mayo, BV
Maya el/la maya
me mí, 5.1; me, 8
meal la comida, 5.2
meaning el significado, el sentido
means el medio, el modo
by no means de ninguna manera, 1.1
means of expression el modo de expresión
meat la carne, 5.2
medal la medalla
medical office la consulta del médico, el consultorio, 8.2
medicine (drug) el medicamento, 8.2; **(discipline, field),** la medicina, 8.2

medium el medio
melancholic melancólico(a)
member el miembro, 4.2
menu el menú, 5.1
mestizo el/la mestizo(a)
Mexican mexicano(a), 1.1
Mexican American mexicanoamericano(a)
microbe el microbio, 2.1
microscope el microscopio, 2.1
microscopic microscópico(a)
middle: middle school la escuela intermedia
midnight la medianoche
mile la milla
milk la leche
million el millón
mineral water el agua mineral, 12.2
minute el minuto
mirror el espejo, 12.1
Miss señorita, BV
to **miss the bus** perder el autobús (la guagua, el camión), 10.1
mixed mixto(a)
mixture la mezcla
model el modelo
modem el módem
modern moderno(a)
mom la mamá
moment el momento
Monday el lunes, BV
money el dinero, 14.1
monitor el monitor
monster el monstruo
month el mes, BV
monument el monumento
mood el humor, 8.1
  to be in a bad mood estar de mal humor, 8.1
  to be in a good mood estar de buen humor, 8.1
moon la luna
more más
moreover además
morning la mañana
  Good morning. Buenos días., BV
  in the morning por la mañana
  this morning esta mañana
mother la madre, 6.1
motive el motivo
to **mount (horse)** montar (caballo)
mountain la montaña
mountain range la sierra
mouse el ratón
to **move** mover (ue)
movie la película, 6.2; el film, 10.1
movie theater el cine, 10.1
Mr. el señor, BV
Mrs. la señora, BV
Ms. la señorita, la señora, BV
much mucho, 3.2
multiplication la multiplicación
to **multiply** multiplicar
mural el mural, 10.2
muralist el/la muralista
museum el museo, 10.1
music la música, 2.2
my mi, 6.1

name el nombre
  My name is . . . Me llamo… , 12.1
napkin la servilleta, 14.1
national nacional
nationality la nacionalidad, 1.2
  what nationality? ¿de qué nacionalidad?
native indígena
natural: natural resources los recursos naturales
  natural sciences las ciencias naturales
near cerca de, 6.2
necessary necesario(a)
neck el cuello
necktie la corbata, 3.2
to **need** necesitar, 3.1
neighbor el/la vecino(a)
nephew el sobrino, 6.1
nervous nervioso(a), 8.1
net la red
  to go over the net pasar por encima de la red, 9.1
  to surf the Net navegar por la red
nettle la ortiga
never jamás, nunca
new nuevo(a)
news las noticias, 6.2
newspaper el periódico, 6.2
newsstand el quiosco, 13.1
next próximo(a), 13.2
nice simpático(a), 1.2
  Nice to meet you. Mucho gusto.
niece la sobrina, 6.1
night la noche
  at night por la noche
  Good night. Buenas noches., BV
  last night anoche, 9.2
nine nueve, BV
nine hundred novecientos(as), 3.2
nineteen diecinueve, BV
ninety noventa, 2.1
ninth noveno(a), 6.2
no no, BV
  by no means de ninguna manera, 1.1
  no one nadie
noble noble
nobody nadie
none ninguno(a), 1.1
noon el mediodía
north el norte
North America la América del Norte
North American norteamericano(a)
northwest noroeste, 8
no-smoking section la sección de no fumar, 11.1
not at all de ninguna manera
notable notable
note: to take notes tomar apuntes, 4.2
to **note** apuntar
notebook el cuaderno, el bloc, 3.1

nothing nada, 5.2
Nothing else. Nada más., 5.2
novel la novela
novelist el/la novelista
November noviembre, BV
now ahora, 4.2
now and then de vez en cuando
nowadays hoy día
number el número, 1.2
flight number el número del vuelo, 11.1
seat number el número del asiento, 11.1
nuptial nupcial

O

object el objeto
obligatory obligatorio(a), 2.1
observation la observación
to **observe** observar
observer el/la bservador(a)
obstacle el obstáculo
occupied (taken) ocupado(a), 5.1
ocean el océano
o'clock: It's (two) o'clock. Son las (dos).
October octubre, BV
of de, BV
of course! ¡claro!
official oficial
oil el aceite, 14.2
OK! ¡vale!
old anciano(a), antiguo(a), viejo(a), 6.1
olive: olive oil el aceite de oliva
on en
on board a bordo de, 11.2
on the contrary al contrario
on the dot en punto, 4.1
on time a tiempo, 11.1
on top of encima de; sobre, 9.1
once and for all definitivamente, 11
one uno, BV
one hundred cien(to), 2.1
one thousand mil, 3.2
one-way: one-way ticket el billete sencillo, 13.1
only sólo, solamente
to **open** abrir, 8.2
to open one's suitcases abrir las maletas, 11.2
opening: opening of school la apertura de clases
opera la ópera, 2.1
operator el/la operador(a)
opinion: What's your opinion? ¿Qué opinas?
optional opcional
orally oralmente
orange (color) anaranjado(a), 3.2
orange (fruit) la naranja, 5.2
orange juice el jugo de naranja, 12.1
order la orden, 5.1
organism el organismo
origin el origen
original: in its original language version en versión original, 10.1
orphanage el orfanato
Otavalo (of or from) otavaleño(a)
other otro(a), 2.2
our nuestro(a)
outdoor al aire libre
outfielder el/la jardinero(a), 7.2
outskirts los alrededores
over por encima de
to **owe** deber

P

to **pack one's suitcase** hacer la maleta, 11.2
package el paquete, 5.2
page la página
Web page la página Web
pain el dolor, 8.1
I have a pain in . . . Tengo dolor de... , 8.2
to **paint** pintar
painter el/la pintor(a)
painting el cuadro, la pintura, 2.1
pair el par, 3.2
pair of tennis shoes el par de tenis, 3.2
Panamanian panameño(a), 2.1
pants el pantalón, 3.2
paper el papel, 3.1
sheet of paper la hoja de papel, 3.1
parents los padres, 6.1
park el parque
parka el anorak, 9.2
part la parte
party la fiesta, 4.2
to give (throw) a party dar una fiesta, 4.2
pass (permission) el pase
to **pass** pasar, 7.2
passenger el/la pasajero(a), 11.1
passport el pasaporte, 11.1
passport inspection el control de pasaportes, 11.2
past pasado(a)
patient el/la enfermo(a), 8.1
to **pay** pagar, 3.1
to pay attention prestar atención, 4.2; hacer caso
pea el guisante, 5.2
peaceful tranquilo(a)
pen la pluma; **(ballpoint)** el bolígrafo, 3.1
pencil el lápiz, 3.1
peninsula la península
penny el centavo
people la gente
pepper la pimienta, 14.1
percent por ciento
performance la función, la representación, 10.2
to put on a performance dar una representación, 10.2
to **permit** permitir, 11.1
person la persona, 1.2
Peruvian peruano(a)
peso el peso, BV

petition la petición
pharmacist el/la farmacéutico(a), 8.2
pharmacy la farmacia, 8.2
photo la foto
photograph la fotografía
phrase la frase
physical education la educación física, 2.2
physics la física, 2.2
piano el piano
to **pick up** recoger
to pick up (claim) the luggage recoger el equipaje, 11.2
picture el cuadro, 10.2
pig (pork) el cerdo, 14.2
pill la pastilla, la píldora, la tableta, 8.2
pilot el/la piloto, 11.2
pink rosado(a), 3.2
piping (embroidery) el cordoncillo
pitcher el/la lanzador(a), el/la pícher, 7.2
pizza la pizza, BV
place el lugar, el sitio
to **place** colocar, meter, 7.1
to place one's suitcase poner la maleta, 11.2
plane el avión, 11.1
plate el plato, 14.1
home plate el platillo, 7.2
plateau la mesa
platform (railroad) el andén, 13.1
play la obra teatral, 10.2
to **play** jugar (ue), 7.1
player el/la jugador(a), 7.1
baseball player el/la jugador(a) de béisbol, 7.2
playwright el/la dramaturgo(a)
plaza la plaza
pleasant agradable
please por favor, BV
P.M. de la tarde, de la noche
pocket el bolsillo
pocketbook la bolsa, 13.1
poem el poema
poet el poeta
poetry la poesía
point (score) el tanto, el punto, 7.1
cardinal points los puntos cardinales
to score a point marcar un tanto, 7.1
pole: ski pole el bastón, 9.2
political político(a)
poncho el poncho
pool la alberca, la piscina, 9.1
poor pobre
poor boy (girl) el/la pobre
popular popular, 2.1
popularity la popularidad
pork el cerdo, 14.2
porter el/la maletero(a), el mozo, 13.1
portrait el retrato
possibility la posibilidad
possible posible
potato la papa, 5.1
mashed potatoes el puré de papas
to **practice** practicar
pre-Columbian precolombino(a)
to **prefer** preferir (ie, i)
to **prepare** preparar, 4.2
to **prescribe** recetar, 8.2
prescription la receta, 8.2
to **present** presentar
pretty hermoso(a), lindo(a), bonito(a), bello(a), 1.1
price el precio
priest el sacerdote
primary primario(a)
princess la princesa
principal principal
printer la impresora
private particular, privado(a), 6.2
private house la casa particular (privada), 6.2
prize el premio
Nobel Prize el Premio Nóbel
problem el problema
to **process** procesar
procession la procesión
to **proclaim** proclamar
produced producido(a)
product el producto, 2.1
professor el/la profesor(a), 2.1
program (TV) la emisión, 6.2
sports program la emisión deportiva, 6.2
to **project** proyectar, 10.1
promise la promesa
protoplasm el protoplasma
public público(a)
to **publish** publicar
Puerto Rican puertorriqueño(a)
to **pull out** arrancar
puppy el perrito
purchase la compra, 3.1
pure puro(a)
to **put** poner, 11.1
to put on a performance dar una representación, 10.2
to put on clothes ponerse la ropa, 12.1
to put on makeup ponerse el maquillaje, maquillarse, 12.1

quarrel la disputa
quarter: a quarter to menos cuarto
a quarter past y cuarto
queen la reina
question la pregunta
to ask a question preguntar
quetzal el quetzal
quickly rápido
quite bastante, 1.1

racquet la raqueta, 9.1
railroad el ferrocarril
railroad station la estación de ferrocarril, 13.1

railroad track la vía, 13.1
railway platform el andén, 13.1
to **rain: It's raining.** Llueve., 9.1
rate la tarifa
rather bastante, 1.1
razor la navaja, 12.1
to **read** leer, 5.1
reading la lectura
ready listo(a)
realist el/la realista
realistic realista
really realmente
rear (in the) atrás
reasonable razonable
to **rebound** rebotar
to **receive** recibir, 5.1
to receive a good (bad) grade recibir una nota buena (mala), 4.2
recently recientemente
rectangle el rectángulo
red rojo(a), 3.2
redheaded pelirrojo(a), 1.1
reduced reducido(a)
to **reflect** reflexionar, reflejar
reflection el reflejo
refreshment el refresco, 5.1
region la región
regular regular, 2.2
relative el/la pariente, 6.1
religious religioso(a)
to **remain** quedar, 7.1
to **remember** acordarse (ue) de, 3.2
to **renounce** renunciar
to **rent** alquilar, rentar, 10.1
to **repeat** repetir (i, i)
to **replace** reemplazar
report el reportaje
to **represent** representar
republic la república
Dominican Republic la República Dominicana
to **request** pedir (i, i), 14.1
required: required course el curso obligatorio, 2.1
reservation la reservación
to **reserve** reservar, 14.2
reserved reservado(a), 13.2
resident el/la residente
resort: seaside resort el balneario, 9.1
resource el recurso
natural resources los recursos naturales
rest lo demás
restaurant el restaurante, 14.1
to **return** volver (ue), 7.1; **(something)** devolver (ue), 7.2
rice el arroz, 5.2
rich rico(a); con mucha plata
right derecho(a), 7.1
right away enseguida, 5.1
river el río
to **roll** rodar
roll (bread) el pan dulce, 5.1
roll of toilet paper el rollo de papel higiénico, 12.2
romantic romántico(a)
room la sala, el salón, el cuarto, la pieza, 4.1
bathroom el cuarto de baño, 6.2
classroom la sala (el salón) de clase, 4.1
dining room el comedor, 6.2
living room la sala, 6.2
waiting room la sala de espera, 13.1
rose la rosa
round-trip ticket el billete de ida y vuelta, 13.1
routine la rutina, 12.1
row (of seats) la fila, 10.1
royal real
rubber la goma, 3.1
ruin la ruina
rumor el rumor
to **run** correr, 7.2
rural rural

S

to **sacrifice** sacrificar
sad triste
sail (of a mill) el aspa
sailboard la plancha de vela, 9.1
saint el santo
salad la ensalada, 5.1
salesperson el/la dependiente(a), el/la empleado(a), 3.1
salt la sal, 14.1
same mismo(a), 2.1
sand la arena, 9.1
sandal el huarache, la alpargata
sandwich el bocadillo, 5.1, el sándwich, BV
sash la faja
Saturday el sábado, BV
saucer el platillo, 14.1
to **save** salvar
to **say** decir
scale la báscula, 11.1
scene la escena
schedule el horario, 13.1
school schedule el horario escolar
school la escuela, el colegio, 1.1
elementary school la escuela primaria
high school el colegio, la escuela secundaria, la escuela superior
middle school la escuela intermedia
school (pertaining to) escolar
school bus el bus escolar, 4.1
school life la vida escolar, 4.1
school schedule el horario escolar
school supplies los materiales escolares, 3.1
science la ciencia, 2.2
natural sciences las ciencias naturales
social sciences las ciencias sociales
scientific científico(a)
scientist el/la científico(a)
score el tanto, 7.1
to **score: to score a goal** meter un gol, 7.1
to score a point marcar un tanto, 7.1

scoreboard el tablero indicador, 7.1
screen la pantalla, 10.1
sculptor el/la escultor(a), 10.2
sculpture la escultura
sea el mar, 9.1
  Caribbean Sea el mar Caribe
search: in search of en busca de
season la estación, BV
seasoning el condimento, 14.1
seat (theater) la butaca, 10.1; **(airplane, train, etc.)** el asiento, 11.1; la plaza, 13.2
  seat number el número del asiento, 11.1
second segundo(a), 6.2
  second half el segundo tiempo, 7.1
secondary secundario(a), 1.1
secret secreto(a)
security: security control el control de seguridad, 11.1
to **see** ver, 5.1
  See you later! ¡Hasta luego!, BV
  See you soon! ¡Hasta mañana!, BV
  See you tomorrow! ¡Hasta mañana!, BV
  to see a film ver una película, 10.2
to **select** seleccionar
selection la selección
to **sell** vender, 5.2; despachar, 8.2
to **send** transmitir, enviar
sentence la frase
September septiembre, BV
series la serie
  World Series la Serie mundial
serious serio(a), 1.1
to **serve** servir (i, i), 14.1
service (tip) el servicio, 5.1
set (theater) el escenario, 10.2
to **set the table** poner la mesa, 14.1
seven siete, BV
seven hundred setecientos(as), 3.2
seventeen diecisiete, BV
seventh séptimo(a), 6.2
seventy setenta, 2.1
several varios(as)
to **sew** coser
sewing la costura
to **shake hands** dar la mano
shampoo el champú, 12.2
sharp en punto, 4.1
to **shave** afeitarse, 12.1
shaving cream la crema de afeitar, 12.1
shawl el poncho
she ella, 1.1
sheet: sheet of paper la hoja de papel, 3.1
shellfish el marisco, 5.2
sherbet el sorbete
to **shine** brillar, 9.1
shirt la camisa, 3.2
shoe el zapato, 3.2
shoe size el número, 3.2
shoe store la zapatería
to **shop** ir de compras, 5.2
short (person) bajo(a), 1.1; **(length)** corto(a), 3.2
  short story la historieta
shorts el pantalón corto, 3.2
shot (injection) la inyección, 8.2
show la sesión, 10.1; el espectáculo, 10.2
  to see a show ver un espectáculo, 10.2
shower: to take a shower tomar una ducha, 12.1
shrimp el camarón, 14.2
shy tímido(a), 1.2
sick enfermo(a), 8.1
sick person el/la enfermo(a), 8.1
side el lado; *(adj.)* lateral, 13.2
sierra la sierra
to **sigh** suspirar
similar parecido(a), similar
simple sencillo(a); simple
since como; desde, 1.2
sincere sincero(a), 1.2
to **sing** cantar, 4.2
single soltero(a)
single-celled monocelular
singles (tennis) singles, 9.1
sir el señor, BV
sister la hermana, 6.1
to **sit down** sentarse (ie), 12.1
six seis, BV
six hundred seiscientos(as), 3.2
sixteen dieciséis, BV
sixth sexto(a), 6.2
sixty sesenta, 2.1
size (clothes) el tamaño, la talla; **(shoes)** el número, 3.2
  What size do you take? ¿Qué talla (número) usa usted?, ¿Qué número usa (calza) usted?, 3.2
ski el esquí, 9.2
  water-ski el esquí acuático, 9.1
to **ski** esquiar, 9.1
ski lift el telesquí, 9.2
ski pole el bastón, 9.2
ski resort la estación de esquí, 9.2
ski slope la pista, 9.2
skier el/la esquiador(a), 9.2
skiing el esquí, 9.2
skirt la falda, 3.2
sky el cielo, 9.1
to **sleep** dormir (ue, u)
sleeping bag el saco de dormir, 12.2
sleeping car el coche-cama, 13.2
small pequeño(a), 2.1
smile: little smile la sonrisita
smoking (no-smoking) section la sección de (no) fumar, 13.1
snack la merienda, 4.2
  to have (eat) a snack tomar una merienda, 4.2
sneakers los tenis, 3.2
to **sneeze** estornudar, 8.1
snow la nieve, 9.2
to **snow** nevar (ie), 9.2

so tan
so much tanto(a)
soap el jabón, 12.2
bar of soap la barra (la pastilla) de jabón, 12.2
soccer el fútbol, 2.1
soccer field el campo de fútbol, 7.1
social sciences las ciencias sociales
society la sociedad
sociology la sociología
socks los calcetines, 3.2
solution la solución
to **solve** resolver (ue)
some algunos(as), 4.1
something algo, 5.2
sometimes a veces, 7.1
son el hijo, 6.1
soon pronto, BV; dentro de poco
See you soon! ¡Hasta pronto!, BV
sorbet el sorbete
sore throat el dolor de garganta, 8.1
soup la sopa, 5.1
south el sur
South America la América del Sur
South American sudamericano(a)
southwest el sudoeste
Spain España
Spanish español(a)
Spanish American hispanoamericano(a)
Spanish (language) el español, 2.2
Spanish-speaking hispanohablante
Spanish speaker el/la hispanohablante
to **speak** hablar, 3.1
special especial
specialty la especialidad
spectator el/la espectador(a), 7.1
to **spend: to spend the weekend** pasar el fin de semana, 9.1
spoon (tablespoon) la cuchara, 14.1; **(teaspoon)** la cucharita, 14.1
sport el deporte, 7.2
individual sport el deporte individual
team sport el deporte de equipo
sports (related to) deportivo(a), 6.2
sports program (TV) la emisión deportiva, 6.2
spouse el/la esposo(a), 6.1
spring la primavera, BV
square la plaza
squire el escudero
stadium el estadio, 7.1
stage el escenario, la escena, 10.2
to come (go) on stage entrar en escena, 10.2
stairway la escalera, 6.2
standing de pie
star la estrella
state el estado
station la estación, 13.1
subway station la estación de metro, 10.1
train station la estación de ferrocarril, 13.1
stationery: stationery store la papelería, 3.1
statue la estatua, 2.1
to **stay in bed** guardar cama, 8.1
steak el biftec, 5.2
stomach el estómago, 8.1
stomachache el dolor de estómago, 8.1
stop la parada, 13.1
to **stop** parar, bloquear, 7.1
store la tienda, 3.2
clothing store la tienda de ropa, 3.2
department store la tienda de departamentos
stationery store la papelería, 3.1
to **store** almacenar
story: little story la historieta
strategy la estrategia
stream el arroyo
street la calle, 6.2
strong fuerte
structure la estructura
student el/la alumno(a), 1.1; el/la estudiante
student I.D. card la tarjeta de identidad estudiantil
study el estudio
to **study** estudiar, 4.1
stupendous estupendo(a)
style el estilo
subject la asignatura, la disciplina, 2.2
subtitle el subtítulo, 10.1
The movie has subtitles. El film lleva subtítulos., 10.1
to **subtract** restar
suburb el suburbio, la colonia
subway el metro, 10.1
subway station la estación de metro, 10.1
such tal
suckling pig el lechón, 14.2
to **suffer** sufrir
suit el traje, 3.2
bathing suit el traje de baño, el bañador, 9.1
suitcase la maleta, 11.1
to pack one's suitcase hacer la maleta, 11.2
summer el verano, BV
sun el sol, 9.1
to **sunbathe** tomar el sol, 9.1
sunblock la crema protectora, 9.1
Sunday el domingo, BV
sunglasses los anteojos de sol, las gafas de sol, 9.1
sunny: It's sunny. Hace (Hay) sol., 9.1
suntan lotion la crema protectora, la loción bronceadora, 9.1
superior superior
supermarket el supermercado, 5.2
supplies: school supplies los materiales escolares, 3.1
to **surf** practicar la tabla hawaiana, 9.1
to surf the Net navegar por la red

surfboard la tabla hawaiana, 9.1
surfing el surfing, 9.1
sweet roll el pan dulce, 5.1
sweetheart el/la enamorado(a)
to **swim** nadar, 9.1
swimming la natación, 9.1
underwater swimming el buceo, 9.1
swimming pool la alberca, la piscina, 9.1
swimsuit el bañador, el traje de baño, 9.1
symptom el síntoma, 8.2

T-shirt el T-shirt, la camiseta, 3.2
table la mesa, 5.1
to set the table poner la mesa, 14.1
tablecloth el mantel, 14.1
tablespoon la cuchara, 14.1
tablet la tableta, 8.2
taco el taco, BV
Taino taíno(a)
to **take** tomar, 4.1
to take a bath bañarse, 12.1
to take a flight tomar un vuelo, 11.1
to take a hike dar una caminata, 12.2
to take a nap echar (tomar) una siesta
to take a shower tomar una ducha, 12.1
to take a trip hacer un viaje, 11.2
to take notes tomar apuntes, 4.2
to take off (airplane) despegar, 11.2
to take photos tomar fotos
to take (clothing size) usar, 3.2
to take (shoe size) calzar, 3.2
to take time tardar
taken ocupado(a), 5.1
to **talk** hablar, conversar, 3.1
tall alto(a), 1.1
tamale el tamal, BV
taxi el taxi, 10.2
tea el té, 5.1
iced tea el té helado, 5.1
to **teach** enseñar, 4.1
teacher el/la maestro(a), el/la profesor(a), 2.1
team el equipo, 7.1
team sport el deporte de equipo, 7.2
teaspoon la cucharita, 14.1
technology la tecnología
teeth los dientes, 12.2
telephone el teléfono
to speak on the telephone hablar por teléfono
telephone (related to) telefónico(a)
television la televisión, 6.2
to **tell** decir
temperature la temperatura, 9.2
ten diez, BV
to **tend to** soler (ue)
tender tierno(a)
tennis el tenis, 2.1
tennis court la cancha de tenis, 9.1
tennis game el juego de tenis, 9.1
tennis player el/la tenista, 9.1
tennis shoes los tenis, 3.2
pair of tennis shoes el par de tenis, 3.2
tenth décimo(a), 6.2
term el término
terminal la terminal
terrace la terraza
terrible terrible
terror el terror
test el examen, 4.2
to give a test dar un examen, 4.2
thank you gracias, BV
that aquel; eso, 4.1
at that time en aquel entonces
that's right (true)! ¡verdad!
the el, la, 1.1
theater el teatro, 10.2
theatrical teatral, 10.2
their sus, 6.1
them las *(f. pl.)*; los *(m. pl.)*
theme el tema
then luego, BV; entonces, 2.1
there allí
there is/are hay, BV
they ellos(as), 2.1
thin flaco(a), 1.2; delgado(a)
thing la cosa
to **think** pensar (ie), opinar
to think so creer
third tercer(o), 6.2
thirsty: to be thirsty tener sed, 14.1
thirteen trece, BV
thirty treinta, BV
thirty-one treinta y uno, 2.1
this este (esta)
thistle el cardo
thought el pensamiento
thousand mil, 3.2
three tres, BV
three hundred trescientos(as), 3.2
throat la garganta, 8.1
to have a sore throat tener dolor de garganta, 8.1
to **throw** lanzar, 7.1; tirar, 7.2
Thursday el jueves, BV
ticket el boleto, la entrada, 7.2; el ticket, 9.2; el billete, 11.1
one-way ticket el billete sencillo, 13.1
round-trip ticket el billete de ida y vuelta, 13.1
ticket window la ventanilla, la boletería, 9.2; la taquilla, 10.1
tie la corbata, 3.2
tied (score) empatado(a), 7.1
The score is tied. El tanto queda empatado., 7.1

time el tiempo; la vez; la hora

at times a veces

at what time? ¿a qué hora?

on time a tiempo

one more time une vez más, 12

timid tímido(a), 1.2

tiny diminuto(a)

tip el servicio, 5.1; la propina, 14.1

Is the tip included? ¿Está incluido el servicio?

to leave a tip dejar una propina, 14.1

tired cansado(a), 8.1

to a; con destino a, 11.1

toast el pan tostado, 5.2

toasted tostado(a), 5.2

today hoy, BV

together junto(a), 5.1

toilet paper el papel higiénico, 12.2

to **tolerate** consentir (ie, i)

tomato el tomate, 5.2

tomorrow mañana, BV

See you tomorrow! ¡Hasta mañana!, BV

tonight esta noche, 9.2

too también, 1.2

too much demasiado

tooth el diente, 12.1

toothbrush el cepillo de dientes, 12.2

toothpaste la pasta (crema) dentífrica, 12.2

tube of toothpaste el tubo de pasta dentífrica, 12.1

tortilla la tortilla, 5.1

to **touch** tocar

touch el contacto

tour la gira, 12.2

tourist el/la turista

toward hacia

towel: beach towel la toalla playera, 9.1

town el pueblo

toy el juguete

track la vía, 13.1

tradition la tradición

traffic el tráfico

trail (ski) la pista, 9.2

train el tren, 13.1

local train el tren local, 13.2

nonstop train el tren directo, 13.2

train car el coche, el vagón, 13.1

train station la estación de ferrocarril, 13.1

to **transfer** transbordar, 13.2

to **transmit** transmitir

to **travel** viajar

to travel by air viajar en avión, 11.1

tree el árbol

triangle el triángulo

trip el viaje, 11.1

to take a trip hacer un viaje, 11.1

triumphant triunfante

trousers el pantalón, 3.2

trousseau el ajuar de novia

true verdadero(a)

true value el valor real

trunk (of a car) el/la maletero(a), 11.1

truth la verdad

to **try** tratar

tube el tubo, 12.2

Tuesday el martes, BV

tuna el atún, 5.2

to **turn around** revolver (ue)

twelve doce, BV

twenty veinte, BV

twenty-one veintiuno, BV

two dos, BV

two hundred doscientos(as), 3.2

type el tipo

typical típico(a)

ugly feo(a), 1.1

uncle el tío, 6.1

aunt(s) and uncle(s) los tíos, 6.1

under bajo, debajo (de)

undershirt la camiseta, 3.2

to **understand** comprender, 5.1

uniform el uniforme

unit la unidad

United States Estados Unidos

university la universidad

university (related to) universitario(a)

until hasta, BV

urban urbano(a)

us nos

to **use** usar, 3.2

usually generalmente

vacation la vacación

vanilla *(adj.)* de vainilla, 5.1

vanilla ice cream el helado de vainilla, 5.1

various varios(as)

to **vary** variar

veal la ternera, 14.2

vegetable el vegetal, 5.2; la legumbre

vegetarian el/la vegetariano(a)

Venezuelan venezolano(a)

version: in (its) original version en versión original, 10.1

very muy, BV

very well muy bien, BV

vest el chaleco

victorious victorioso(a)

video el video, 4.2

video store la tienda de videos, 10.1

view la vista, BV

vinegar el vinagre, 14.2

violin el violín, 2.1

visible visible

vital vital

voice la voz

volleyball el voleibol, 2.1

volume (book) el tomo

vowel la vocal

to **wait (for)** esperar, 11.1
waiter el camarero, el mesero, 5.1
waiting room la sala de espera, 13.1
waitress la camarera, la mesera, 5.1
to **wake up** despertarse, 12.1
to **walk (around, through)** andar
wall la pared; **(of a jai alai court)** el frontón
to **want** querer (ie), desear, 3.2
war la guerra
to **wash oneself** lavarse, 12.1
to wash one's face (hands, etc.) lavarse la cara (las manos, etc.), 12.1
to **watch** mirar, ver, 3.1
water el agua *(f.)*, 9.1
watercolor la acuarela
waterskiing el esquí acuático, 9.1
to go waterskiing esquiar en el agua, 9.1
wave la ola, 9.1
way la manera, el modo, 1.1
we nosotros(as), 2.1
weapon el arma *(f.)*
to **wear** llevar, usar; **(shoe size)** calzar, 3.2
weather el tiempo, 9.1
The weather is bad. Hace mal tiempo., 9.1
The weather is nice. Hace buen tiempo., 9.1
Wednesday el miércoles, BV
week la semana, BV
last week la semana pasada, 9.2
weekend el fin de semana, BV
last weekend el fin de semana pasado
to **weigh** pesar
to **welcome** dar la bienvenida, 11.2
well bien; pues, BV
very well muy bien, BV
west el oeste
what? ¿qué?, ¿cuál?, ¿cuáles?, ¿cómo?, 1.1
What is he (she, it) like? ¿Cómo es?, 1.1
What is it? ¿Qué es?, 1.1
What is today's date? ¿Cuál es la fecha de hoy?, BV
What time is it? ¿Qué hora es?
when cuando
for when ¿para cuándo?, 14.2
when? ¿cuándo?
where donde, adonde, 1.2
where? ¿dónde?, ¿adonde?
Where is he (she, it) from? ¿De dónde es?, 1.1
which? ¿cuál?, ¿cuáles?, BV
while el rato
while mientras
white blanco(a), 3.2
who? ¿quién?, 1.1; quiénes, 2.1
Who is it (he, she)? ¿Quién es?, 1.1
whole entero(a)
why? ¿por qué?
wife la esposa, la mujer, 6.1
to **win** ganar, 7.1
windmill el molino de viento
to **windsurf** practicar la plancha de vela, 9.1
winter el invierno, BV
wise sabio(a)
to **wish** querer (ie), desear, 3.2
with con
within dentro de
woman la dama
wool la lana
word la palabra
work el trabajo; la obra
work of art la obra de arte
to **work** trabajar, 3.2
world el mundo
world (related to) mundial
World Cup la Copa mundial
World Series la Serie mundial
worldwide mundial
wrap el poncho
to **wrap** envolver (ue)
to **write** escribir, 5.1
writing pad el bloc, 3.1

year el año, BV
last year el año pasado, 9.2
this year este año, 9.2
to be . . . years old tener… años, cumplir… años, 6.1
yellow amarillo(a), 3.2
yesterday ayer, 9.2
the day before yesterday anteayer
yesterday afternoon ayer por la tarde, 9.2
yesterday morning ayer por la mañana, 9.2
yogurt el yogur, 5.2
you tú *(sing. fam.)*, Ud. *(sing. form.)*; Uds. *(pl.)*; te *(fam. pron.)*, le *(pron.)*
You're welcome. De nada., No hay de qué., BV
young joven, 6.1
as a young person de joven
young person el/la joven, 8.1
your tu(s), su(s)
youth hostel el albergue para jóvenes (juvenil), 12.2

zero cero, BV
zone la zona

Index

Index

Credits

Glencoe would like to acknowledge the artists and agencies who participated in illustrating this program: Matthew Pippin represented by Beranbaum Artist's Representative; Meg Aubrey represented by Cornell & McCarthy; Eureka Cartography; Glencoe; Higgins Bond represented by Anita Grien Representing Artists; Viviana Diaz represented by Irmeli Holmberg; Carlos Lacamara; Beverly Lazor-Behr; Joe LeMonnier; Karen Maizel; Betty Maxey; Rebecca Merrilees; Lyle Miller; Stephen Moore; Ortelius Design, Inc.; David Broad, Susan Jaekel, Jane McCreary and DJ Simison represented by Remen-Willis Design Group; Ed Sauk; Don Stewart; Carol Strebel; Studio InkLink; Diana Thewlis; Ann Barrow and Kathleen O'Malley represented by Christina A. Tugeau; Joe Veno represented by Gwen Walters; Qin-Zhong Yu.

Photo Credits

Cover (t to b)Jeremy Horner/CORBIS, John Hicks/CORBIS, Bo Zaunders/CORBIS, Dallas and John Heaton/CORBIS, (students)Ed McDonald; **iv** (t)Ken Karp, (bl)Suzanne Murphy-Larronde/DDB Stock Photo, (bc)Robert Ginn/PhotoEdit, (br)Antonio Azcona West; **v–vi** Curt Fischer; **vii** (l)Michelle Chaplow, (r)Timothy Fuller, (others)Curt Fischer; **ix** (tl bl)Michelle Chaplow, (tr)Luis Delgado, (br)Morgan Cain & Associates; **x** (t)Andrew Payti, (bl)Larry Hamill, (br)Luis Delgado; **xi** Curt Fischer; **xii** (tl tr)Timothy Fuller, (b)Michelle Chaplow, (l)Suzanne Murphy-Larronde/DDB Stock Photo; **viii** Curt Fischer; **xiv** (l)Suzanne Murphy-Larronde/DDB Stock Photo, (r)Robert Fried/Robert Fried Photography; **xv** (l)Michelle Chaplow, (r)Andrew Payti; **xvi** (tl)Michelle Chaplow, (tr)Luis Delgado, (b)Luis Delgado; **xvii** (l)Luis Delgado, (r)Robert Fried/Stock Boston; **xviii** (l)Timothy Fuller, (r)Curt Fischer; **xxi** (l)Andrew Payti, (cr)Randy Faris/CORBIS, (br)Andrew Payti; **xxxiv** (t)Timothy Fuller, (c)Mark Smestad, (b)Curt Fischer; **xxxv** (t)Timothy Fuller, (b)Ed McDonald; **xxxviii** Newberry Library/SuperStock; **1** Timothy Fuller; **2** (t)Ken Karp, (b)Luis Delgado; **3** (tl tc)Michelle Chaplow, (tr)Ken Karp, (bl)Luis Delgado, (br)Timothy Fuller; **4** Luis Delgado; **5** (tl tr)Michelle Chaplow, (b)Robert Frerck/Odyssey/Chicago; **6** Ann Summa; **7** CORBIS; **9** (t)Ken Karp, (c)Chad Ehlers/Stone, (b)David Young-Wolfe/PhotoEdit; **10** CORBIS; **11** Luis Delgado; **12** Boys Climbing a Tree, 1792. Francisco de Goya y Lucientes. Oil on canvas, 141 X 111cm. Museo del Prado, Madrid.; **12–13** Luis Delgado; **14** (l)Curt Fischer, (r)Timothy Fuller; **16** (tr)Timothy Fuller, (bl)Michelle Chaplow, (br)Tom & Therisa Stack/Tom Stack & Associates; **17** (tl)Ken Karp, (tr)Mark Smestad, (others)Aaron Haupt; **18 19 20** Curt Fischer; **21** (t)Ed McDonald, (b)Randy Faris/CORBIS; **22** Curt Fischer; **23** (t)Richard Glover/CORBIS, (b)Macduff Everton/Stone; **24** (tl)Aaron Haupt, (tr)Luis Delgado, (b)Timothy Fuller; **25** (t)Laura Sifferlin, (b)Eye Ubiquitous/CORBIS; **26** (t)Ken Karp, (b)Robert Frerck/DDB Stock Photo; **27** (l)Timothy Fuller, (r)Robert Fried/Tom Stack & Associates, (b)Curt Fischer; **28** (inset)Ed McDonald, (bkgd)Bob Krist/eStock; **29** Tim Fuller; **30** Robert Frerck/Woodfin Camp & Associates; **31** (t)CORBIS, (b)Musee, St. Denis-Seine/1999 Estate of Pablo Picasso/Artists Rights Society (ARS), New York; **32** (t)Luis Delgado, (bl)Norman Tomalin/Bruce Coleman, Inc.; **33** (t)Norman Tomalin/Bruce Coleman, Inc., (b)Organization of American States; **34** (l)Ludovic Maisant/CORBIS, (r)CORBIS; **35** (tl)Curt Fischer, (tr)Andrew Payti, (br)CORBIS; **36** (t)Luis Delgado, (b)Mark Smestad; **39** Robert Frerck/Woodfin Camp & Associates; **41** (t)Timothy Fuller, (b)Curt Fischer; **42** Zurbaran Galeria, Buenos Aires, Argentina/SuperStock; **42–43** Michelle Chaplow; **44** Luis Delgado; **45** (tl tr)Aaron Haupt, (bl)Curt Fischer, (br)Michelle Chaplow; **46** (t)Luis Delgado, (b)Curt Fischer; **47** (t)Ken Karp, **47** (b)Larry Hamill; **48–50** Curt Fischer; **51** Robert Frerck/Odyssey/Chicago; **53** (t)Luis Rosendo/Getty Images, (others)Laura Sifferlin; **55** (l)Doug Martin, (r)John Evans; **56** (t)Larry Hamill, (b)Ken Karp; **57** Ken Karp; **60** (t)Robert Fried, (b)Laura Sifferlin; **61** Sven Martson/The Image Works; **62** Curt Fischer; **63** (l)Luis Delgado, (r)CORBIS; **64** (t)CORBIS, (b)James Ranklev/Stone; **65** (t)Robert Frerck/Odyssey/Chicago; (c)Nicolas Sapieha/Art Resource; **66** (tl)David Young-Wolfe/PhotoEdit, (tc)Chuck Savage/The Stock Market, (tr)Robert Fried/Tom Stack & Associates, (cl)Suzanne Murphy-Larronde/DDB Stock Photo, (c)H. Huntly Hersch/DDB Stock Photo, (cr)Antonio Azcona West, (b)Robert Ginn/PhotoEdit; **67** The Museum of Modern Art, New York. Photograph ©1996 the Museum of Modern Art, New York. National Palace, Patio Corido, Mexico; **68** Timothy Fuller; **69** Andrew Payti; **71** Lindsay Hebberd/CORBIS; **73** Ken Karp; **74** Albright-Knox Art Gallery/CORBIS; **74–75** Robert Frerck/Odyssey/Chicago; **76** Curt Fischer; **77** Timothy Fuller; **78** Luis Delgado; **79** Michelle Chaplow; **80** (c)Luis Delgado, (clockwise from top) (1)file photo, (2–3)John Evans, (4)Esbin-Anderson/The Image Works, (5)Anthony Azcona, (6)Timothy Fuller, (7)Anthony Azcona, (8–10)file photo, (11)Barb Stimpert; **81** (tl)Ken Karp, (tr)Luis Delgado, (cl)Esbin-Anderson/The Image Works, (cr)Curt Fischer, (b)Esbin-Anderson/The Image Works; **82** (c)Antonio Azcona, (b)Luis Delgado, (others)Luis Delgado; **83** (5)Siede Preis/Photodisc, (bl)Ken Karp, (br)Michelle Chaplow, (others)Luis Delgado; **84** file photo; **85** Ken Karp; **85** Luis Delgado; **86** Andrew Payti; **87** (5)Luis Delgado, (others) Andrew Payti; **88** Timothy Fuller; **89** Ken Karp; **90** (l)PhotoDisc, (r)Michelle Chaplow; **91** (t)Michelle Chaplow, (b)CORBIS; **92** (tl)Oliver Benn/Stone, (tc)Robert Fried/Robert Fried Photography, (tr)Stephanie Maze/Woodfin Camp & Associates, (cl cr)Loren McIntyre/Woodfin Camp & Associates, (b)Curt Fischer; **93** Courtesy Oscar de la Renta; **94** Esbin-Anderson/The Image Works; **95** Jeff Greenberg/eStock Photo; **96** (t)Matt Meadows, (b)Michelle Chaplow; **98** Curt Fischer; **99** Joe Viesti/The Viesti Collection; **101** Curt Fischer; **102** Schalkwijk/Art Resource, NY; **102–103** Pablo Corral Vega/CORBIS; **104** (t)Photodisc, (tr)Michelle Chaplow, (c)Michelle Chaplow, (b)Michelle Chaplow, (bkgd)Lori Shetler; **105** (t)Ann Summa, (b)Timothy Fuller; **106** Michelle Chaplow; **107** (t)Andrew Payti, (b)Doug Bryant/DDB Stock Photo; **108** Michelle Chaplow; **109** (t)Tom & Teresa Stack/Tom Stack & Associates, (b)Anthony Azcona; **110** (t)Michelle Chaplow, (b)Ann Summa; **111** (t)Aaron Haupt, (b)Philadelphia Museum of Art, A.E. Gallatin Collection; **112** Aaron Haupt; **113** (t)Michelle Chaplow, (b)Antonio Azcona; **114** (t)Ken Karp, (b)Andrew Payti; **116** Mark Smestad; **117** (t)Michelle Chaplow, (b)Dallas & John Heaton/Westlight; **118** Robin Sachs/PhotoEdit; **119** Curt Fischer; **120** Ken Karp; **122** (t)Luis Delgado, (b)Luis Rosendo/FPG; **123** Luis Rosendo/FPG; **124** (t)Mark C. Burnett/Stock Boston, (b)Joe Viesti/Viesti Associates; **125** (t)UPI/Corbis-Bettmann, (b c)Andrew Payti; **126** (l)Luis Delgado, (r)Andrew Payti; **127** Luis Delgado; **128** (t)Michelle Chaplow, (b)Doug Bryant/DDB Stock Photography; **129** Michelle Chaplow; **131** Mark Smestad; **133** (t)Mark Smestad, (b)Luis Delgado; **134** Morgan Cain & Associates; **135** Michelle Chaplow; **136** (tl)Randy Faris/CORBIS, (tc)CORBIS, (tr)CORBIS, (cl)Newscom136, (cr)Bettmann/CORBIS, (b)Reuters; **137** (tl)Newscom, (tc)Richard Cummins/CORBIS, (tr)Anita Calero, (c)AP Photo/Jose Luis Magana, (bl)Sunset Boulevard/CORBIS, (bc)Newscom; **138** (l)STX/The Grosby Group, (tr)Robert Mora/Newscom, (cr br)Newscom; **139** (tl)Getty Images/Newscom, (tr)Time Life Pictures/Getty Images, (cl)Eniac Martinez, (bl)Newscom, (bc)Kevin Winter/Getty Images, (br)Camilo Salas/Reforma-Edred via Newscom; **140** (c)Kactus Foto, Santiago, Chile/SuperStock; **140–141** Telegraph Color Library/FPG; **142** (t)Doug Bryant/DDB Stock Photo, (l r)Ken Karp; **144** Morgan Cain & Associates; **145** Michelle Chaplow; **146** (t)Robert Frerck/Odyssey, (l)Michelle Chaplow, (r)Curt Fischer; **147** (t)Timothy Fuller, (c)Andrew Payti, (bl)Aaron Haupt, (br)Doug Bryant/DDB Stock Photo; **148–149** Andrew Payti; **151** Luis Delgado; **152** Morgan Cain & Associates; **154 156–157** Michelle Chaplow; **158** (t)Curt Fischer, (b)Peter Menzel; **159** Andrew Payti; **160** Michelle Chaplow; **161** Curt Fischer; **162** Andrew Payti; **163** (l b)Andrew Payti, (r)Michelle Chaplow; **164** (9)David Buffington/Photodisc, (10)Andrew Payti, (11)C. Squared Studios/Photodisc, (12)Marshall Gordon/Cole Group/Photodisc; **165** Antonio Azcona West; **168** Schalkwijk/Art Resource, NY; **169** Robert Frerck/Woodfin Camp & Associates; **171** Ann Summa/Getty Images; **172** (t)Ken Karp, (b)Luis Delgado; **173** (t)Larry Hamill, (b)Ken Karp; **175** (inset t tr)Anthony Azcona, (tl)John Evans, (br)Mark Smestad; **176** Michelle Chaplow; **177** (t)Robert Fried/Robert Fried Photography, (c)Andrew Payti, (b)Robert Fried/Robert Fried Photography; **178** Tony Freeman/PhotoEdit; **179** (tl tc tr)Ed McDonald, (b)Luis Delgado; **180** (t)Anthony Azcona, (b)Curt Fischer; **181** Matt Meadows; **182** Michelle Chaplow; **183** Andrew Payti; **184** (t 2 3)Curt Fischer, (1 4)Anthony Azcona; **185** Andrew Payti; **186** Timothy Fuller; **188** Michelle Chaplow; **189** Antonio Gaudi y Cornet; **190** Ann Summa; **191** Prado Museum/Art Resource, NY;

Credits

192 (t)Jacques & Natasha Gilman Collection/Museo Diego Rivera, Mexico City, **192** (b)Pablo Corral V/CORBIS; **193** (t)Anthony Azcona, (c)The Museum of Modern Art, NY, (b)House of El Grecco, Toledo, Spain; **195** (t)Matt Meadows, (b)Andrew Payti; **198** Ken Karp; **200** Christie's Images/SuperStock; **200–201** Luis Delgado; **202** (l)David Cannon/Allsport, (r)Curt Fischer; **204** David Leah/Allsport; **205** (t)Clive Brunskill/International Stock, (b)Doug Bryant/DDB Stock Photography; **206** (t)Macduff Everton/CORBIS, (l)Curt Fischer; **207** (tl)Curt Fischer, (tr)Image Club Graphics, (cl bl)Aaron Haupt, (cr)Getty Images, (br)Curt Fischer; **208** (t)David Leah/Allsport Mexico, (b)Luis Delgado; **209** Getty Images; **210–211** Luis Delgado; **213** Martin Venegas/Allsport Mexico; **214** (t)Ken Karp, (b)David R. Frazier/Photo Researchers; **215** Michelle Chaplow; **216** Andrew Payti; **217** Curt Fischer; **218** Michelle Chaplow; **220** (t)Paul Marriott/Empics Ltd., (b)CORBIS; **221** Allsport/Getty Images; **222** (t)Doug Persinger/Allsport, (b)David Leah/Allsport Mexico; **223** (l)Tom & Therisa Stack/Tom Stack & Associates, (r)Antonio Azcona; **224** (t)Andrew Payti, (b)Rich Brommer; **225** (t)Rich Brommer, (b)Robert Fried/Robert Fried Photography; **228** Luis Delgado; **229** Simon Bruty/Allsport; **231** Curt Fischer; **232** Luis Delgado; **234** Andrew Payti; **236** (tl)Sergio Pitamitz/CORBIS, (tr)diego Lezama Orezzoli/CORBIS, (b)Art Wolfe/Getty Images; **237** (tl)Galen Rowell/CORBIS, (tr)Erik Rank/FoodPix, (cl)Galen Rowell/CORBIS, (c)Jose Manuel Calvete/CORBIS, (cr)Zuma Press/Newscom, (b)Reuters/Newscom; **238** (t)Ed Kashi/CORBIS, (b)Manuel Zambrara/CORBIS; **239** (t)Courtesy Justo Lamas, (cl)Juan Carlos Algarin, (cr)Newscom , (bl)Telemundo, (br)Dennis Degnan/CORBIS,; **240** Digital Image, the Museum of Modern Art/Licensed by SCALA/Art Resource, NY; **240–241** Timothy Fuller; **242** Curt Fischer; **243** (cr)Ann Summa, (others)Curt Fischer; **244** (t)Michelle Chaplow, (b)Timothy Fuller; **246** (t)Ken Karp, (bl)Aaron Haupt, (br)Curt Fischer, (others)Curt Fischer; **247** Michelle Chaplow; **248** Timothy Fuller; **250** (t)Timothy Fuller, (b)Ken Karp; **251** Aaron Haupt; **253** (t)Andrew Payti, (b)Ken Karp; **254** Robert Fried/Robert Fried Photography; **255** Ken Karp; **257–258** Michelle Chaplow; **260** Andrew Payti; **261** Antonio Azcona; **262** Luis Delgado; **263** (t)Siegfried Tauqueuer/Estock, (b)Courtesy Dr. Antonio Gassett; **264** Curt Fischer; **265** (c)Andrew Payti, (b)Curt Fischer; **267** (t)Timothy Fuller, (b)Andrew Payti; **268** Timothy Fuller; **269** Luis Delgado; **271** Curt Fischer; **272** Whitford & Hughes, London, UK/Bridgeman Art Library, UK; **272–273** Superstock; **274** (tl c)Andrew Payti, (tr)Reuters NewMedia Inc./CORBIS, (bl)CORBIS, (br)Getty Images, (bkgd)Luis Delgado; **275** Timothy Fuller; **276** (t)Luis Delgado, (c)CORBIS, (1 2 3)C. Squared Studios/Photodisc, (4)Doug Bryant/DDB Stock Photo; **277** (t)Digital Vision, (b)Michelle Chaplow; **278** (tr l)Curt Fischer, (br)Buddy Mays/CORBIS; **280** John Curtis/DDB Stock Photo; **283** Luis Delgado; **284** (t)Michelle Chaplow, (b)J.L.G. Grande/Tourist Office of Spain; **286** Ken Karp; **287** (t1 5)Aaron Haupt, (2)Timothy Fuller, (3)Ryan McVay/Photodisc, (4)Curt Fischer, (6)Alaska Stock Images, (7)Thomas Veneklasen, (8)C. Squared Studios/Photodisc, (b)Luis Delgado; **290** (bkgd)Zbigniew Bzdak/The Image Works, (inset) Laura Sifferlin; **292** (l)PhotoDisc, (r)Andrew Payti; **293** (tl)Donald Nausbaum/Getty Images, (tr)Andrew Payti, (b)Andrew Payti; **294** (t)Andrew Payti, (b)Buddy Mays/ImageState; **295** Jeff Curtes/CORBIS; **296** (l)Derke/O'Hara/Stone, (r)Andrew Payti; **297** (t)Harold Castro/FPG, (bl)Andrew Payti, (br)Mireille Vautier/Woodfin Camp & Associates; **298** Marco Corsetti/FPG; **300** (1)Doug Bryant/DDB Stock Photo, (2)C. Squared Studios/Photodisc, (4)Jeff Curtes/CORBIS, (5)Jack Hollingsworth/Stock Photo; **301** Andrew Payti; **303** Superstock; **304** (c)Christie's Images/CORBIS; **304–305** Dave G. Houser/CORBIS; **306** Markow Tatiana/CORBIS SYGMA; **308** (t)Michelle Chaplow, (b)Antonio Azcona; **309** Dallas & John Heaton/Westlight; **310** Culver Pictures; **311** Owen Franken/CORBIS; **313** (t)Andrew Payti, (b)Robert Frerck/Odyssey/Chicago; **315** (t)Michelle Chaplow, (b)Robert Fried/Robert Fried Photography; **316** file photo; **317** Andrew Payti; **318** (t)Aaron Haupt, (b)Juan de Villanueva; **319** Prado Museum, Madrid; **320** Luis Delgado; **322** (l)Luis Delgado, (r)Andrew Payti; **323** Michelle Chaplow; **324** Luis Delgado; **325** (t)Gene Dekovic, (bl)Jorge Contreras Chacel/International Stock, (br)Robert Frerck/Odyssey/Chicago; **327** (l)Suzanne Murphy-Larronde/DDB Stock Photo, (tr)Ulrike Welsch, (c)Doug Bryant/DDB Stock Photo, (br)Robert Frerck/Odyssey/Chicago; **328** Matt Meadows; **331** Bob Daemmrich/The Image Works; **333** Andrew Payti; **334** Smithsonian American Art Museum, Washington, DC/ArtResource, NY; **335** Thomas D. Mayes, Jr.; **336 337 338** Michelle Chaplow; **339** Andrew Payti; **340** Michelle Chaplow; **341** (t)Andrew Payti, (c)Ismael Jordá/Airliners.net, (b)Michelle Chaplow; **342** Michelle Chaplow; **343** Andrew Payti; **345** Michelle Chaplow; **346** Andrew Payti; **348** (t)Curt Fischer, (b)Thomas Veneklasen; **349** Andrew Payti; **350** (l)Robert Fried, (r)Aaron Haupt; **352** (l)D. Rivademar/Odyssey/Chicago, (r)Jacques Jangouz/Stone; **353** (l)Jay Dickman/CORBIS, (r)Boyd Norton/The Image Works; **354** (t)Reuters NewMedia Inc./CORBIS, (c)Luis Delgado, (b)Andrew Payti; **355** Andrew Payti; **356** (l)Larry Hamill, (r)Curt Fischer; **357** Doug Bryant/DDB Stock Photo; **360** Michelle Chaplow; **361** Andrew Payti; **363–364** Michelle Chaplow; **365** Ken Karp; **366** Photoworks/P. Lang/DDB Stock Photo; **368** (t)CORBIS, (b)Tiziana and Gianni Baldizzone/CORBIS; **369** (tl)Hubert Stadler/CORBIS, (tr)AFP/CORBIS, (bl)Reuters/Newscom, (br)Craig Lovell/CORBIS; **370** (t)AP Photo/Martin Mejia, (bl)Philip Salaverry/FoodPix, (br)Wolfgang Kaehler/CORBIS; **371** (tl tr)AP Photo/Peter McFarren, (cl)Galen Rowell/CORBIS, (cr)Owen Franken/CORBIS, (bl)Tui De Roy/Minden Pictures, (br)Steve Labadessa; **372** Kactus Foto/SuperStock; **372–373** Adam Woolfitt/CORBIS; **374 375** Curt Fischer; **376** Michelle Chaplow; **377** (l)Morgan Cain & Associates, (r)Andrew Payti; **378** (t)Guido Cozzi/Atlantide/Bruce Coleman, Inc., (b)Curt Fischer; **379** (l to r, t to b)Antonio Azcona, (tl)Curt Fischer, (bl)Luis Delgado, (br)Michelle Chaplow, (2 6 7)Andrew Payti, (3–5)Curt Fischer; **381** Curt Fischer; **383** Michelle Chaplow; **384** (t)Timothy Fuller, (b)Ken Karp, (1 4–6)Timothy Fuller, (2 3) Aaron Haupt; **385** Michelle Chaplow; **386 388** Luis Delgado; **390** (l)Robert Frerck/Odyssey/Chicago, (r)Luis Delgado; **391** Robert Fried/Robert Fried Photography; **392** (bl)Robert Frerck/Woodfin Camp and Associates, (br)Massimo Borchi/Atlantide/Bruce Coleman, Inc.; **392** K. Gillham/Photo 20-20; **393** Robert Frerck/Odyssey/Chicago; **394** (l)Luis Delgado, (r)Reuters NewMedia Inc./CORBIS; **395** (t)Bernard P. Wolfe/Photo Researchers, (b)Andrew Payti; **397** Ken Karp; **398** (t)Curt Fischer, (bl)Curt Fischer, (bc)Andrew Payti, (br)Andrew Payti; **399** CORBIS; **401** Curt Fischer; **402** The Stapleton Collection/The Bridgeman Art Library; **402–403** Luis Delgado; **404** (t b)Michelle Chaplow, (inset)Luis Delgado; **405** Andrew Payti; **406** Luis Delgado; **408** (t)Michelle Chaplow, (b)Doug Bryant/DDB Stock Photo; **409** (tr)Andrew Payti, (cr)Photodisc, (bl)Doug Bryant/DDB Stock Photo; **410** (t)Luis Delgado, (b)Michelle Chaplow; **411** (l)CORBIS, (tr)Ken Karp, (br)Robert Fried/Robert Fried Photography; **412** Andrew Payti; **413** Ken Karp; **414** House of El Greco, Toledo Spain; **415** Yoichiro Miyazaki/FPG; **416** Robert Fried/Robert Fried Photography; **417** Ken Karp; **418 420** Luis Delgado; **421** (t b)Robert Fried/Robert Fried Photography, (c)Telegraph Color Library/FPG; **422** (t br)Robert Fried/Robert Fried Photography, (c)Robert Fried/Stock Boston, (bl)Robert Frerck/Odyssey/Chicago; **423** Andrew Payti; **425** (t)Curt Fischer, (b)Michelle Chaplow, (others)Luis Delgado; **426** Morgan Cain & Associates; **427** file photo; **428** Andrew Payti; **429** Robert Fried/Robert Fried Photography; **431** Luis Delgado; **432** Kactus Foto/SuperStock; **432–433** Luis Delgado; **434** Curt Fischer; **435** (t)Andrew Payti, (cl c cr)Doug Bryant/DDB Stock Photo, (bl)Doug Bryant/DDB Stock Photo, (br)Aaron Haupt; **436** (t)Ed McDonald, (b)Luis Delgado; **437** Luis Delgado; **438** Curt Fischer; **439** (t bl)Timothy Fuller, (br)Curt Fischer; **440** Michelle Chaplow; **443** (t)Ken Karp, (b)Morgan Cain & Associates; **445–446** Ken Karp; **448** (l)Curt Fischer, (r)Timothy Fuller; **449** National Palace, Mexico City; **450** (l)Curt Fischer, (tr)Michelle Chaplow, (br)Andrew Payti; **451** (t)Robert Fried/Robert Fried Photography, (b)Laura Sifferlin; **452** (bl)Andrew Payti, (others)Curt Fischer; **453** Michelle Chaplow; **454** Timothy Fuller; **456** Curt Fischer; **459** (t)Timothy Fuller, (b)Curt Fischer; **460** Luis Delgado; **462** Timothy Fuller; **463** Michelle Chaplow/Andalucia Slide Library; **464** (t)Sandy Perez, (c)Bettmann/CORBIS, (l to r)Franz-Marc Frei/CORBIS, (1)Jon Bradley/Getty Images, (2)Jon Bradley/Getty Images, (3)Eric & David Hosking/CORBIS, (4)Sheldan Collins/CORBIS; **465** (t)Frank Veronsky, (bl)AP Photo/Cristina Quicler, (br)Royalty Free/CORBIS; **466** (tl)Pablo Sanchez/Newscom, (tcl)Rufus F. Folkks/CORBIS, (cl)Fred Prouser/Newscom, (bl)David Cruz/Newscom, (bc)Sergio Perez/Newscom, (1)Visual Arts Library/Art Resource, (2 3)Archivo Icongrafico/CORBIS,